The
Bowker
Annual

45th Edition **2000**

The Bowker Annual

Library and Book Trade Almanac™

Editor Dave Bogart

Consultant Julia C. Blixrud

CBowker®

Published by R. R. Bowker,
a division of Reed Elsevier Inc.
Copyright © 2000 by Reed Elsevier Inc.
All rights reserved
Printed and bound in the United States of America
Bowker® is a registered trademark of Reed Elsevier Inc.
The Bowker Annual Library and Book Trade Almanac™ is a trademark of Reed
Elsevier Properties Inc., used under license.

International Standard Book Number 0–8352–4324–9
International Standard Serial Number 0068–0540
Library of Congress Catalog Card Number 55–12434

ISBN 0 - 8352 - 4324 - 9

9 780835 243247

Contents

Part 2
Legislation, Funding, and Grants

Part 3
Library/Information Science
Education, Placement, and Salaries

Part 4
Research and Statistics

Book Trade Research and Statistics

Part 5
Reference Information

Bibliographies

Ready Reference

Distinguished Books

Part 6
Directory of Organizations

Preface

Welcome to the 45th edition of the *Bowker Annual*. Like its predecessors, it presents a combination of informed analysis and practical information of interest to the library, information, and book trade worlds.

The impact of the Information Age is felt more strongly year by year. It is challenging the way we think about the dissemination of knowledge and about intellectual freedom and intellectual property. As one of our contributing authors puts it, "Information is the oxygen of the new economy."

This year's Special Reports look at the major trends:

- The growing phenomenon of electronic journals is examined by Edward Valauskas, chief editor of *First Monday,* a peer-reviewed scholarly Internet journal.

- Action in Congress on an important aspect of intellectual property law is detailed in "The Database Protection Debate in the United States" by Jonathan Band and Makoto Kono.

- Copyright law in general is constantly evolving as we publish, research, teach, and learn in new ways in the digital era. Laura N. Gasaway, law librarian and professor of law at the University of North Carolina, appropriately titles her report "Change—The Only Certainty in Copyright."

- Results of the KALIPER study, a major multinational assessment of library and information science education, are presented by Karen Pettigrew and Joan Durrance.

- The increasingly important and complex relationship between publishing houses and library consortia is examined in "Consortia, Networks, and Publishing in 1999" by Angee Baker of SOLINET and Tom Sanville of OhioLINK.

Also in Part 1, federal agencies, federal libraries, and national and international library and publishing organizations tell how they are meeting the technical and intellectual challenges of the new millennium.

Part 2 includes detailed examinations of the past year's legislation affecting libraries and publishing, plus reports from two major funding and grant-making agencies.

Part 3 contains professional information for librarians: guides to scholarship and employment sources, a look at trends in placements and salaries, and the roster of 1999's major scholarship and award winners.

Research and statistics on libraries and publishing make up Part 4, including reports on current research projects, library acquisition expenditures, book output and price data, and examinations of national and international trends in the publishing trade.

Basic reference information is found in Part 5: how to obtain an ISBN, ISSN, or SAN; who won the year's top literary prizes; and lists of bestsellers, notable books, and recommended resources for children and young adults.

Part 6 includes an expanded Directory of Library and Related Organizations at the state, national, and international levels, a calendar of information industry events, and detailed indexes.

The *Bowker Annual* represents the efforts of many people, and our thanks go to all those who contributed articles, assembled reports, supplied statistics, and responded to our requests for information. Special thanks are due Consultant Editor Julia C. Blixrud and consultant Catherine Barr.

We believe you will find this a valuable and frequently used resource, and—as always—we welcome your comments and suggestions for future editions.

Dave Bogart
Editor

Part 1
Reports from the Field

Federal Agency and Federal Library Reports

National Technical Information Service

Technology Administration
U.S. Department of Commerce, Springfield, VA 22161
800-553-NTIS (6847) or 703-605-6000
World Wide Web http://www.ntis.gov

Linda Davis
Marketing Communications

The National Technical Information Service (NTIS), a unique government organization located on the outskirts of Washington, D.C., serves as the nation's largest central source and primary disseminator of scientific, technical, engineering, and business information produced or sponsored by U.S. and international government sources. NTIS is a federal agency within the Technology Administration of the U.S. Department of Commerce.

For more than 50 years, the NTIS mission has been to operate a central point of access within the U.S. government for scientific and technical information useful to American industry and government—information to improve the efficiency and effectiveness of the U.S. research and development enterprise, increase productivity and innovation in the United States, and increase U.S. competitiveness in the world market. NTIS is directed by statute to

- Collect technical information from both international and domestic sources
- Classify, maintain, and disseminate that information in the forms and formats most useful to NTIS customers
- Develop electronic and other new methods and media for information dissemination
- Provide information processing services to other federal agencies
- Charge fees for its products and services that are reasonable and that permit NTIS to recover its costs

The NTIS collection of approximately 3 million titles contains products available in various formats. Such information includes reports describing research conducted or sponsored by federal agencies and their contractors, statistical and business information, U.S. military publications, multimedia training programs, computer software and electronic databases developed by federal agencies, and technical reports prepared by research organizations worldwide.

Approximately 100,000 new titles are added and indexed annually. NTIS maintains a permanent repository of its information products.

Customers learn of the availability of NTIS information products through a variety of ways, including the NTIS Web site, NTIS publications that index and abstract newly accessioned material, ongoing subscriptions for all reports that meet a customer's preestablished selection criteria, press releases and other media announcements, and searches of the NTIS Database.

U.S. Government Contributors

More than 200 U.S. government agencies contribute to the NTIS collection. Contributors include the National Aeronautics and Space Administration, the Environmental Protection Agency, the National Institute of Standards and Technology, the National Institutes of Health, and the Departments of Agriculture, Commerce, Defense, Energy, Health and Human Services, Interior, Labor, Treasury, Veterans Affairs, Housing and Urban Development, Education, and Transportation.

With the passage of the American Technology Preeminence Act (ATPA) of 1991 (P.L. 102-245), all federal agencies are required to submit their federally funded unclassified scientific, technical, and engineering information products to NTIS within 15 days of the date the product is made publicly available. The primary purposes of ATPA are to help U.S. industries accelerate the development of new processes and products and help the United States maintain a leading economically competitive position worldwide. Under ATPA, information products include technical reports, articles, papers, and books; regulations, standards, and specifications; charts, maps, and graphs; software, data collection, datafiles, and data compilations software; audio and video products; technology application assessments; training packages; and other federally owned or originated technologies. Since the passage of ATPA, NTIS's wealth of information has increased dramatically, and NTIS is able to provide customers with timely access to a more diverse and practical range of information.

Worldwide Source Contributors

NTIS is a leading U.S. government agency in international technical and business information exchange. It actively acquires and distributes valuable information produced by a large number of international government departments and other organizations.

NTIS continues to negotiate agreements to improve the coverage of reports from major industrialized countries, as well as from newly industrialized countries producing advanced technologies. NTIS focuses its acquisition efforts on topics of major interest to NTIS customers.

Online International Trade and Business Bookstore

In 1997 NTIS opened the online International Trade and Business Bookstore (http://tradecenter.ntis.gov), operated by NTIS on behalf of the Department of Commerce. This site brings together the world's most comprehensive collection of business and international trade information from U.S. government and non-profit organizations. The International Trade and Business Bookstore site helps users locate international bestsellers and industry trading standards, and also provides links to other trade-related sites. The Web site is fully implemented with secure online ordering.

National Audiovisual Center

The National Audiovisual Center (NAC) at NTIS consolidates the U.S. government's collection of audiovisual and multimedia training and educational programs. These federally sponsored or produced materials are thus available to state and local governments, businesses, schools, universities, and private individuals.

NAC's collection includes approximately 9,000 active titles covering 600 subject areas from more than 200 federal agencies. Included in the collection are language training materials, occupational safety and health training materials, fire service and law enforcement training materials, drug education programs for schools and industry, fine arts programs, and documentaries chronicling American history.

Award-winning World War II films from many of Hollywood's most celebrated directors are included in the NAC collection. John Ford's *December 7th* is one example. Another important film, *The Negro Soldier*, directed by Frank Capra and Stuart Heisler, highlights the contributions and sacrifices made by black Americans in the nation's armed conflicts from 1776 to 1944.

NAC has videos on such current topics of concern as ergonomics, security, workplace safety, and AIDS and other sexually transmitted diseases (STDs). For example, *Ergonomic Programs that Work* shows how to improve work conditions in various situations, and *Computer Security* helps computer users protect themselves and their organizations. *Emergency Response to Terrorism* helps police and EMS personnel better serve the public. *Like Any Other Employee: HIV/AIDS in the Workplace* covers appropriate health and safety precautions, laws, and insurance issues, and *1998 Guidelines for Treatment of STDs* helps doctors and clinicians provide better service. NAC also has courses on running a business and how industry should deal with hazardous materials. NAC's language programs cover everything from French and Spanish to English as a second language and hard-to-find African language courses.

NAC's staff is dedicated to helping customers find the multimedia program suitable for their needs. Call 703-605-6000 for assistance, or visit the NAC Web site (http://www.ntis.gov/nac) for the latest news about the center and its wide array of products.

Federal Computer Products Center

The Federal Computer Products Center was established at NTIS to provide access to information in electronic formats. The current inventory of computer products obtained since 1990 includes more than 1,200 titles from hundreds of U.S. government agencies. Products include datafiles and software on diskette, CD-ROM, and magnetic tape, covering such topics as banking, business, the environment, health care, health statistics, science, and technology. Most of the center's products are developed or sponsored by the federal government; NTIS does, however, also announce and distribute products developed by state governments and, in a few cases, by private sector organizations. Examples of some of the center's titles include *Stream Corridor Restoration, Showcase Europe, EPA Water Testing Methods, FDA's Food Code*, and the *NOAA Dive Manual*.

Full descriptions of the software and data available from NTIS appear on the center's Web site at http://www.ntis.gov/fcpc.

FedWorld

Since 1992 NTIS FedWorld Information Technologies has served as the online locator service for a comprehensive inventory of information disseminated by the federal government. FedWorld assists federal agencies and the public in electronically locating federal government information—information housed within the NTIS repository as well as information that FedWorld makes accessible through an electronic gateway to other government agencies. FedWorld currently serves tens of thousands of customers daily.

FedWorld maximizes the potential of the Internet and the World Wide Web by offering multiple distribution channels for government agencies to disseminate information. The modes of access, the variety of documents available, and the technological expertise at FedWorld are expanding with technology. FedWorld offers the user a comprehensive central access point for searching, locating, ordering, and acquiring government and business information.

NTIS FedWorld offers simple, global access to government and business information in an efficient and cost-effective manner. To connect to FedWorld via the World Wide Web, open http://www.fedworld.gov. For Internet file transfer protocol services, connect to ftp.fedworld.gov. To connect to FedWorld by modem, set modem parity to none, data bits to 8, and stop bit to 1; set terminal emulation to ANSI; set duplex to full; then set your communication software to dial FedWorld at 703-321-FEDW (3339).

For more details on FedWorld, call 703-605-6585.

NTIS on the World Wide Web

The NTIS Web site (http://www.ntis.gov) continues to be enhanced to help customers quickly locate, identify, and order information they need. The site lists nearly 400,000 items, including government manuals, handbooks, computer software, electronic databases/datafiles, multimedia/training programs, CD-ROMs, and other information products added to the NTIS collection within the last ten years. The NTIS Web site is a powerful access tool for researching and pricing NTIS products. Recently, NTIS implemented direct and secure ordering via the World Wide Web. A product that can be ordered from NTIS via the Web features an order button on its Web page. The traditional telephone and fax services for ordering are also still an option. Products orderable via the Web for shipment to customers outside the United States, Canada, and Mexico are now the same price as those products ordered for domestic shipment. (International customers who choose to fax, mail, or phone their orders will not qualify for this special "ordered via the Web" price.) However, the handling fee for international orders placed via the Web is not reduced.

The NTIS Web site provides several search options for locating products in its vast collection. Visitors to the site can use the Search by Keyword feature to query nearly half a million product listings across all collections. For those who prefer a more structured search, the site also provides an advanced search option. This feature can be used to specify a collection and to provide more control over how the search results are presented.

The NTIS Web site offers a number of subject-specific collections for such fields of interest as business, the environment, Army manuals and publications, health and safety, industry standards, science and technology, databases, computer products, and audiovisuals. The What's New section focuses on the latest information on the site, including recent product announcements, the NTIS exhibit/trade show schedule, and news about other NTIS-managed Web sites such as the International Trade and Business Bookstore. A Help section assists users in navigating the site and in locating the government information needed. This section provides a guided tour, frequently asked questions, and a site map.

Specialized Online Subscriptions

Those wishing to expand their access to subject-specific resources through use of the Internet are likely to benefit from the NTIS online options highlighted below. Online subscriptions offer quick, convenient online access to the most current information available.

Government Research Center

The GOV.Research_Center (GRC) is a collection of well-known government-sponsored research databases available on the World Wide Web via online subscription. The following databases made available at GRC by NTIS and the National Information Services Corporation (NISC) are searchable at the site utilizing NISC's powerful search engine Biblioline: the NTIS Database, Federal Research in Progress, NIOSHTIC, Energy Science and Technology, Nuclear Science Abstracts, AgroBase, and AGRICOLA. Databases are added regularly.

NTIS and NISC are constantly improving the content and features of GRC. Online ordering allows a user to order documents directly from the NTIS Database by using a credit card or NTIS deposit account. Cross-database searching allows a user to search all databases within a subscription plan with only one search query. Day-pass access to GRC for a nominal fee allows a user to access the database for a limited amount of time. NTIS anticipates day-pass access to additional GRC databases in the future.

Visit GRC at http://grc.ntis.gov for more information and to sign up for a free online trial, or call 703-605-6541.

World News Connection

World News Connection (WNC) is an NTIS online news service accessible via the World Wide Web. WNC was developed to help individuals obtain information they could not find elsewhere, particularly in English. WNC provides English-language translations of time-sensitive news and information from thousands of non-U.S. media. Particularly effective in its coverage of local media, WNC enables users to identify what is really happening in a specific country or region. Compiled from speeches, television and radio broadcasts, newspaper articles, periodicals, and books, the information focuses on socioeconomic, political, scientific, technical, and environmental issues and events.

The information in WNC is provided to NTIS by the Foreign Broadcast Information Service (FBIS), a U.S. government agency. For more than 50 years, analysts from FBIS's domestic and overseas bureaus have monitored timely and pertinent open-source material, including "gray literature." Uniquely, WNC allows subscribers to take advantage of the intelligence-gathering experience of FBIS.

WNC is updated every business day. Generally, new information is available within 48 to 72 hours of original publication or broadcast.

Subscribers can conduct unlimited interactive searches and can set up automated searches known as profiles. When a profile is created, a search is run against WNC's latest news feed to identify articles relevant to a subscriber's topic of interest. Once the search is completed, the results are automatically sent to the subscriber's e-mail address.

For WNC pricing and subscription information, visit http://wnc.fedworld.gov.

U.S. Export Administration Regulations

The U.S. Export Administration Regulations (EAR) provides exporters with the latest rules controlling the export of U.S. dual-use commodities, technology, and software. Step by step, EAR explains when an export license is necessary and when it is not, how to obtain an export license, policy changes as they are issued, new restrictions on exports to certain countries and certain types of items, and where to obtain further help.

This information is now available through NTIS in three convenient formats:

- Online—Offers access to new and revised regulations within 48 hours of publication in the *Federal Register*; this Web-based service also features full-search capability and provides access to the Prohibited Parties database for screening an export order prior to shipment
- CD-ROM—Features full-search and bookmark capability to locate specific data (thus eliminating time-consuming manual maintenance) and allows

user to print and download parts of EAR as needed (CD-ROM pricing includes four quarterly update issues)

• Looseleaf—Includes EAR Base Manual plus three bulletin updates

For additional information, access EAR's Web site at http://bxa.fedworld.gov.

Davis-Bacon Wage Determination Database

Updated weekly, the Davis-Bacon Wage Determination database contains wage determinations made by the U.S. Department of Labor under the mandate of the Davis-Bacon Act and related legislation. The department determines prevailing wage rates for construction-related occupations in most counties in the United States. All federal government construction contracts and most contracts for federally assisted construction over $2,000 must contain Davis-Bacon wage determinations.

A variety of access plans are available; for additional information, access http://davisbacon.fedworld.gov.

Service Contract Wage Determination Database

Updated weekly, the Service Contract Wage Determination database contains unsigned copies of the latest wage determinations made by the U.S. Department of Labor. These wage determinations, issued in response to specific notices filed, set the minimum wage on federally funded service contracts. Although not official determinations for specific solicitations or contracts, this information does provide an excellent source for those interested in an advanced approximation of what minimum rates may be specified by the Wage and Hour Division. These data also form a convenient and accurate basis for comparing rates by occupation and geography. The database is updated each Tuesday with all wage changes effective on the preceding Thursday.

A variety of access plans are available; for additional information, access http://servicecontract.fedworld.gov.

Additional Reference Tools

NTIS Alerts

More than 1,000 new titles are added to the NTIS collection every week. NTIS Alerts were developed in response to requests from customers to search and tap into this newly obtained information. NTIS prepares search criteria that are run against all new studies and R&D reports in 16 subject areas. An NTIS Alert provides a twice-monthly information briefing service covering a wide range of technology topics. An NTIS Alert provides numerous benefits:

• Efficient, economical, and timely access to the latest U.S. government technical studies
• Concise, easy-to-read summaries
• Information not readily available from any other source

- Contributions from more than 100 countries
- Subheadings within each copy, designed to identify essential information quickly

For more information, call the NTIS Subscriptions Department at 703-605-6060, or access the Web site at http://www.ntis.gov/alerts.htm.

NTIS E-Alerts

NTIS E-Alerts provide subscribers with convenient online access to the same information as the printed NTIS Alerts. Each week subscribers receive summaries via e-mail of new titles in their choice of as many as 37 subject areas.

For more information, access the Web site at http://www.ntis.gov/alerts.htm.

SRIM

Selected Research in Microfiche (SRIM) is an inexpensive, tailored information service that delivers "full-text" microfiche copies of technical reports. Customers choose from Standard SRIM Service, selecting one or more of the 380 existing subject areas, or Custom SRIM Service, which creates a new subject area based on a customer's profile. Custom SRIM requires a one-time fee to cover the cost of setting up a profile; except for this fee, the cost of Custom SRIM is the same as that for Standard SRIM. Through this ongoing subscription service, customers receive microfiche copies of new reports in their field of interest as NTIS obtains the reports.

For more information on SRIM, access the NTIS Web site at http://www. ntis.gov/srim.htm. Call the NTIS Subscriptions Department at 800-363-2068 or 703-605-6060 to place an order for a SRIM subscription or to receive a free copy of the *Selected Research in Microfiche Guide*, NTISPR271LOS.

NTIS Catalogs

Many of NTIS's most popular catalogs can be viewed, downloaded, or ordered at the NTIS Web site (http://www.ntis.gov/catalogs.htm). Catalogs include the following:

- *NTIS Catalog of Products* (NTISPR827LOS)
- *Catalog of Educational Multimedia Products* (NTISPR1047LOS)
- *Catalog of Multimedia and Training Products* (NTISPR1001LOS)
- *Video Training for Law Enforcement Agencies* (NTISPR1000LOS)
- *Search Guide for the NTIS Database* (PB96-153606)

To receive a free catalog by mail, call the NTIS Sales Desk at 800-553-NTIS (6847) or 703-605-6000 or fax a request to 703-605-6900. Please quote the appropriate NTISPR number.

Databases Available from NTIS

NTIS offers several valuable research oriented database products. To learn more about accessing the databases, visit NTIS Web site (http://www.ntis.gov) or contact the NTIS Office of Product Management at 703-605-6515.

NTIS Database

The NTIS Database (listing information products acquired by NTIS since 1964) offers unparalleled bibliographic coverage of U.S. government-sponsored and worldwide government-sponsored research. It represents hundreds of billions of research dollars and covers a range of important topics, including agriculture, biotechnology, business, communication, energy, engineering, the environment, health and safety, medicine, research and development, science, space, technology, and transportation. The complete NTIS Database provides access to more than 2 million records.

Each year NTIS adds approximately 100,000 new entries to the NTIS Database (most entries include abstracts). Entries describe technical reports, datafiles, multimedia/training programs, and software. These titles are often unique to NTIS and generally are difficult to locate from any other source. If a user is looking for information about state-of-the-art technology or about practical and applied research, or wants to learn more about available government-sponsored software, the NTIS Database is the answer.

Free 30-day trials are available through the GOV.Research_Center (http://grc.ntis.gov), NTIS's online search service. The database can be leased directly from NTIS, and it can also be accessed through the following commercial vendors:

Cambridge Scientific Abstracts	800-843-7751
Canada Institute for Scientific and Technical Information	800-668-1222
DATA-STAR	800-221-7754
DIALOG	800-334-2564
EBSCO	800-653-2726
Manning & Napier	800-278-5356
NERAC	860-872-7000
NISC/NTIS	800-363-2068
Ovid Technologies	800-950-2035
Questel-Orbit	800-456-7248
SilverPlatter Information	800-343-0064
STN International/CAS	800-848-6533

To lease the NTIS Database directly from NTIS, contact the Office of Product Management at 703-605-6515.

FEDRIP

As the U.S. government's central technical and scientific information service, NTIS is responsible for providing access to summaries of current and ongoing projects via the Federal Research in Progress (FEDRIP) database. FEDRIP provides advance information about the more than 150,000 research projects currently under way. The U.S. government funds billions of dollars on R&D and engineering programs annually. The ongoing research announced in FEDRIP is an important component of the technology transfer process in the United States.

FEDRIP focuses on such topics as health, physical sciences, agriculture, engineering, and life sciences. Users search FEDRIP to avoid research duplication, to locate sources of support, to identify leads in the literature, to stimulate ideas for planning, to identify gaps in areas of investigation, and to locate individuals with expertise.

AGRICOLA

As one of the most comprehensive sources of U.S. agricultural and life sciences information, the Agricultural Online Access database AGRICOLA contains bibliographic records for documents acquired by the National Agricultural Library (NAL) of the U.S. Department of Agriculture. The complete database dates from 1970 and contains more than 3.3 million citations to journal articles, monographs, theses, patents, software, audiovisual materials, and technical reports related to agriculture. AGRICOLA serves as the document locator and bibliographic control system for the NAL collection. The extensive file provides comprehensive coverage of newly acquired worldwide publications in agriculture and related fields. AGRICOLA covers the field of agriculture in the broadest sense. Subjects include agricultural economics, agricultural education, agricultural products, animal science, aquaculture, biotechnology, botany, cytology, energy, engineering, feed science, fertilizers, fibers and textiles, food and nutrition, forestry, horticulture, human ecology, human nutrition, hydrology, hydroponics, microbiology, natural resources, pesticides, physiology, plant sciences, public health, rural sociology, soil sciences, veterinary medicine, and water quality.

AGRIS

The international information system for the Agricultural Science and Technology (AGRIS) database is a cooperative system (in which more than 100 national and multinational centers take part) for collecting and disseminating information on the world's agricultural literature. References to U.S. publications covered in AGRICOLA are not included in AGRIS, and a large number of citations in AGRIS are not found in any other database. References to nonconventional literature (that is, documents not commercially available) indicate where a copy can be obtained. Anyone needing information pertaining to agriculture should use AGRIS to find citations to government documents, technical reports, and nonconventional literature from developed and developing countries around the world.

NIOSH Certified Equipment List

The National Institute for Occupational Safety and Health (NIOSH) Certified Equipment List contains comprehensive certification information on self-contained breathing apparatuses, gas masks, supplied-air respirators, particulate respirators, chemical cartridges, and powered purifiers. The database is useful to such audiences as manufacturers, labor organizations, industrial hygienists, safety professionals, and emergency response personnel.

Energy Science and Technology Database

The Energy Science and Technology database (EDB) is a multidisciplinary file containing worldwide references to basic and applied scientific and technical research literature. The information is collected for use by government managers, researchers at the national laboratories, and other research efforts sponsored by the U.S. Department of Energy, and the results of this research are available to the public. Abstracts are included for records from 1976 to the present. EDB also contains the Nuclear Science Abstracts, a comprehensive index of the international nuclear science and technology literature for the period 1948–1976. Included are scientific and technical reports of the U.S. Atomic Energy Commission, the U.S. Energy Research and Development Administration and its contractors, other agencies, universities, and industrial and research organizations. The entire Energy Science and Technology database contains more than 3 million bibliographic records.

Immediately Dangerous to Life or Health Concentrations Database

The NIOSH Documentation for the Immediately Dangerous to Life or Health Concentrations (IDLHs) database contains air concentration values used by NIOSH as respirator selection criteria. This compilation is the rationale and source of information used by NIOSH during the original determination of 387 IDLH categories and their subsequent review and revision in 1994. Toxicologists, persons concerned with the use of respirators, industrial hygienists, persons concerned with indoor air quality, and emergency response personnel will find this product beneficial. This database will enable users to compare NIOSH limits to other limits and it is an important resource for those concerned with acute chemical exposures.

NIOSH Manual of Analytical Methods

The NIOSH Manual of Analytical Methods (NMAM) database is a compilation of methods for sampling and analyzing contaminants in workplace air and in the bodily fluids of workers who are occupationally exposed to that air. These highly sensitive and flexible methods have been developed to detect the lowest concentrations as well as those concentrations exceeding safe levels of exposure, as regulated by the Occupational Safety and Health Administration (OSHA) and recommended by NIOSH. The Threshold Values and Biological Exposure Indices of the American Conference of Governmental Industrial Hygienists are also cited.

NIOSH Pocket Guide to Chemical Hazards

Intended as a quick and convenient source of general industrial hygiene information for workers, employers, and occupational health professionals, the NIOSH Pocket Guide to Chemical Hazards (NPG) presents key information and data in abbreviated tabular form for chemicals or substance groupings (for example, cyanides, fluorides, manganese compounds) that are found in the work environment. The industrial hygiene information found in NPG should help users recognize and control occupational chemical hazards. The information in NPG includes chemical structures or formulas, identification codes, synonyms, exposure limits, chemical and physical properties, incompatibilities and reactivities, measurement methods, recommended respirator selections, signs and symptoms of exposure, and procedures for emergency treatment. Industrial hygienists, industrial hygiene technicians, safety professionals, occupational health physicians and nurses, and hazardous-material managers will find that the database can be a versatile and indispensable tool in their work.

NIOSHTIC

NIOSHTIC is a bibliographic database of literature in the field of occupational safety and health developed by NIOSH. About 160 current, English-language technical journals provide approximately 35 percent of the additions to NIOSHTIC annually. Retrospective information, some of which is from the 19th century, is also acquired and entered. NIOSH examines all aspects of adverse effects experienced by workers; thus much of the information contained in NIOSHTIC has been selected from sources that do not have a primary occupational safety and health orientation. NIOSHTIC is a beneficial resource for anyone needing information on the subject of occupational safety and health. NIOSHTIC subject coverage includes the behavioral sciences; biochemistry, physiology, and metabolism; biological hazards; chemistry; control technology; education and training; epidemiological studies of diseases/disorders; ergonomics; hazardous waste; health physics; occupational medicine; pathology and histology; safety; and toxicology.

Registry of Toxic Effects of Chemical Substances

The Registry of Toxic Effects of Chemical Substances (RTECS) is a database of toxicological information compiled, maintained, and updated by NIOSH. The program is mandated by the Occupational Safety and Health Act of 1970. The original edition, known as the "Toxic Substances List," was published in 1971 and included toxicological data for approximately 5,000 chemicals. Since that time, the list has continuously grown and been updated, and its name changed to the current title. RTECS now contains more than 133,000 chemicals as NIOSH strives to fulfill the mandate to list "all known toxic substances . . . and the concentrations at which . . . toxicity is known to occur." RTECS is a compendium of data extracted from the open scientific literature, recorded in the format developed by the RTECS staff and arranged in alphabetical order by prime chemical name. No attempt has been made to evaluate the studies cited in RTECS; the user has the responsibility to make such assessments.

NTIS Customer Service

New improved processes and automated systems keep NTIS in the customer service forefront. Electronic document storage is fully integrated with NTIS's order-taking process, which allows NTIS to provide rapid reproduction for the most recent additions to the NTIS document collection. Most orders are filled and delivered anywhere in the United States in five to seven business days. Rush service is available for an additional fee.

NTIS successfully prepared all systems for the Y2K rollover and avoided potential computer failures. Critical systems include document input and output systems, customer records, and ordering systems; all systems are operating and interacting accurately, with no disruptions for customers.

Key NTIS Contacts

Order by Phone

Sales Desk 8:00 A.M.–6:00 P.M. Eastern time, Monday–Friday	800-553-NTIS (6847) or 703-605-6000
Subscriptions 8:30 A.M.–5:00 P.M. Eastern time, Monday–Friday	800-363-2068 or 703-605-6060
TDD (hearing impaired only): 8:30 A.M.–5:00 P.M. Eastern time, Monday–Friday	703-487-4639

Order by Fax

24 hours a day, seven days a week	703-605-6900
To verify receipt of fax, call 7:00 A.M.–5:00 P.M. Eastern time, Monday–Friday	703-605-6090

Order by Mail

National Technical Information Service
5285 Port Royal Road
Springfield, VA 22161

RUSH Service (available for an additional fee)   800-553-NTIS (6847)
                                                        or (703) 605-6000

Note: If requesting RUSH Service, please do not mail your order.

Order Via World Wide Web

Direct and secure online ordering   http://www.ntis.gov

Order Via E-Mail

24 hours a day, seven days a week   orders@ntis.fedworld.gov

NTIS understands the concerns customers may have about Internet security when placing an order via the Internet. Customers can register their credit cards at NTIS, thus avoiding the need to send an account number with each e-mail order. To register, call 703-605-6070, between 7:00 A.M. and 5:00 P.M. Eastern time, Monday through Friday. NTIS will automatically charge the credit card when an e-mail order is processed.

[For discussion of the proposal to reorganize NTIS, read NTIS Closure and Transfer at http://www.nclis.gov/ or visit http://ntis.webjump.com/.—*Ed.*]

National Archives and Records Administration

700 Pennsylvania Ave. N.W., Washington, DC 20408
202-501-5400
World Wide Web http://www.nara.gov

Marion H. Vecchiarelli
Policy and Planning Staff

The National Archives and Records Administration (NARA), an independent federal agency, ensures for the citizen, the public servant, the president, Congress, and the courts ready access to essential evidence that documents the rights of American citizens, the actions of federal officials, and the national experience.

NARA is singular among the world's archives as a unified federal institution that accessions and preserves materials from all three branches of government. NARA assists federal agencies in documenting their activities, administering records management programs, scheduling records, and retiring noncurrent records to federal records centers. The agency also manages the presidential libraries; assists the National Historical Publications and Records Commission in its grant program for state and local records and documentary publications of the papers of prominent Americans; publishes the laws, regulations, presidential documents, and other official notices of the federal government; and oversees classification and declassification policy in the federal government through the Information Security Oversight Office. NARA constituents include the federal government, a history-minded public, the media, the archival community, and a broad spectrum of professional associations and researchers in such fields as history, political science, law, library and information services, and genealogy.

The size and breadth of NARA's holdings are staggering. Together, NARA's facilities hold approximately 21.5 million cubic feet of original textual materials—more than 4 billion pieces of paper from the executive, legislative, and judicial branches of the federal government. Its multimedia collections include nearly 300,000 reels of motion picture films; more than 5 million maps, charts, and architectural drawings; 200,000 sound and video recordings; 15 million aerial photographs; 10 million still pictures and posters; and about 100,000 files of electronic records.

Strategic Directions

NARA's strategic priorities are laid out in *Ready Access to Essential Evidence: The Strategic Plan of the National Archives and Records Administration, 1997–2007*. Success for the agency as envisioned in the plan will mean reaching four strategic goals:

- Essential evidence will be created, identified, appropriately scheduled, and managed for as long as needed.
- Essential evidence will be easy to access regardless of where it is or where users are for as long as needed.

- All records will be preserved in appropriate space for use as long as needed.
- NARA's capabilities for making changes necessary to realize its vision will continuously expand.

The plan lays out strategies for reaching these goals, sets milestone targets for accomplishment through the next ten years, and identifies measurements for gauging progress. The targets and measurements are further delineated in NARA's Annual Performance Plans.

During fiscal year (FY) 2000 NARA will be updating its Strategic Plan as required by the Government Performance and Results Act. Suggestions for updates may be sent electronically to Vision@arch2.nara.gov or by mail to VISION, 8601 Adelphi Rd., Room 4100, College Park, MD 20740-6001. The Strategic Plan and NARA's Annual Performance Plans and Reports are available on the NARA Web site at http://www.nara.gov/nara/vision or by calling the Policy and Planning Staff at 301-713-7360, ext. 232.

Records and Access

Internet

NARA's Web site provides the most widely available means of electronic access to information about NARA, including directions on how to contact the agency and do research at its facilities; descriptions of its holdings in an online catalog; digital copies of selected archival documents; electronic mailboxes for customer questions, comments, and complaints; an automated index to the John F. Kennedy assassination records collection; electronic versions of *Federal Register* publications; online exhibits; and classroom resources for students and teachers. NARA is continually expanding the kinds and amount of information available on its Web site and evaluating and redesigning the site to make it easier to use.

Electronic Access Project

As a result of the Electronic Access Project, funded through the support of Sen. Bob Kerrey (D-Neb.), anyone, anywhere with a computer connected to the Internet can search descriptions of NARA's nationwide holdings and view digital copies of some of its most popular documents. This is a significant piece of NARA's electronic access strategy as outlined in its strategic plan. The centerpiece of the project is the Archival Research Catalog (ARC)—an online card catalog of all NARA holdings nationwide—which will allow the public, for the first time, to use computers to search descriptions of NARA's vast holdings, including those in regional archives and presidential libraries. Moreover, anyone can perform these searches through the Internet rather than having to travel to a NARA facility. This effort began with the creation of a prototype catalog, the NARA Archival Information Locator (NAIL). In 1999 NARA completed a two-year project to digitize 124,000 high-interest documents and made them available online through NAIL. Completion of the development of ARC is expected in November 2000. Although the prototype catalog contains more than 400,000 descriptions and 124,000 digital images, it represents only a limited portion of NARA's vast holdings. It is available at http://www.nara.gov/nara/nail.html.

Archives Library Information Center

The Archives Library Information Center (ALIC) provides access to information on ready reference, American history and government, archival administration, information management, and government documents. ALIC is physically located in two traditional libraries in the National Archives Building and the National Archives at College Park. In addition, customers can visit ALIC on the Internet at http://www.nara.gov/nara/naralibrary/refmenu.html where they will find "Reference at Your Desk" Internet links, staff-compiled bibliographies and publications, an online library catalog, and more.

Government Documents

Publications of the U.S. Government (Record Group 287) is a collection of selected publications of U.S. Government agencies, arranged by the classification system ("SuDoc System") devised by the Office of the Superintendent of Documents, Government Printing Office (GPO). These publications are also available to researchers at many of the 1,400 congressionally designated depository libraries throughout the United States.

The core of the collection is a library created in 1895 by GPO's Public Documents Division. By 1972, when NARA acquired the library, it included official publications dating from the early years of the federal government and selected publications produced for and by federal government agencies. The collection has been augmented since 1972 with accessions of multiyear blocks of U.S. Government publications, selected by the Office of the Superintendent of Documents as a byproduct of its monthly cataloging activity. The collection is estimated at 34,000 cubic feet. Only about one-half to two-thirds of all U.S. Government publications are represented in this collection.

Fax-on-Demand

Fax-on-Demand is NARA's interactive fax retrieval system in which digital copies of documents are stored on the hard drive of a computer. Customers can request faxed copies of available documents at any time (24 hours a day, 365 days a year) by calling 301-713-6905 from a fax machine with a handset. Except for those customers who are making long-distance calls to Fax-on-Demand, there are no other charges for using this service.

Currently available documents include brochures regarding NARA internships, NARA and federal government employment, and the semiannual Modern Archives Institute; published General Information Leaflets; other fact sheets about various NARA holdings, programs, and facilities, especially those located in Washington, D.C., College Park and Suitland, Maryland, and St. Louis (National Personnel Records Center); instructions, forms, and vendor lists for ordering copies of records; and finding aids for some textual, audiovisual, and micrographic records.

Publications

Agency publications, including facsimiles of certain documents, finding aids to records, and *Prologue*, a scholarly journal published quarterly, are available from the National Archives Shop (NWCDS), NARA, 700 Pennsylvania Ave. N.W., Washington, DC 20408-0001 (telephone 800-234-8861 or 202-501-5235, fax 202-501-7170). Many publications are also available on the Internet at http://www.nara.gov/publications/.

Federal Register

The *Federal Register* is the daily newspaper of the federal government and includes proposed and final regulations, agency notices, and presidential legal documents. The *Federal Register* is published by the Office of the Federal Register and printed and distributed by the Government Printing Office (GPO). The two agencies also cooperate to produce the annual revisions of the *Code of Federal Regulations* (*CFR*). Free access to the full text of the electronic version of the *Federal Register* and the *CFR* is available through GPO's electronic delivery system (http://www.access.gpo.gov). In addition to these publications, the full texts of other *Federal Register* publications are available at the same Internet address, including the *Weekly Compilation of Presidential Documents*, *Public Papers of the President*, slip laws, *U.S. Statutes at Large*, and *United States Government Manual*. All of these publications are maintained at all federal depository libraries. Public Law Electronic Notification Service (PENS) is a free subscription e-mail service available for notification of recently enacted public laws. Publication information concerning laws, regulations, and presidential documents and services is available from the Office of the Federal Register (telephone 202-523-5227). Information is also available via the Internet at http://www.nara.gov/fedreg/.

Customer Service

Customers

Few archives serve as many customers as NARA. In FY 1999 more than 286,000 research visits were made to NARA facilities nationwide, including presidential libraries. At the same time, customers made approximately 819,000 requests by mail and by phone. The National Personnel Records Center in St. Louis answered approximately 1.5 million requests for information from military and civilian government service records. In addition to providing research and reference services, NARA provided informative exhibits for almost 1 million people in the National Archives Rotunda in Washington, D.C., and 1.5 million more visited the presidential library museums. NARA also served the executive agencies of the federal government, the courts, and Congress by providing records storage, reference service, training, advice, and guidance on many issues relating to records management. The *Customer Service Plan* and *Customer Service Report*, available free in research rooms nationwide and on NARA's Web site at http://www.nara.gov/nara/vision/convers.html list the many types of customers served and describe standards and accomplishments in customer service.

Customer Opinion

Among the specific strategies published in NARA's strategic plan is an explicit commitment to expanding the opportunities of its customers to inform NARA about information and services that they need. In support of that strategy, NARA continues to survey, hold focus groups, and meet with customers to evaluate and improve services. NARA joined Vice President Al Gore's initiative to engage federal workers in two-way conversations with the American public on how to improve government service, and it established a Web page as a gateway to information about the agency: "Conversations with America" (http://www.nara.gov/nara/vision/convers.html) and an e-mail box (comments@nara.gov) for feedback from customers about what is most important to them and what NARA might do to meet their needs.

Grants

The National Historical Publications and Records Commission is the grant-making affiliate of NARA. The Archivist of the United States chairs the commission and makes grants on its recommendation. The commission's other 14 members represent the president of the United States (two appointees), the federal judiciary, the U.S. Senate and House of Representatives, the Departments of State and Defense, the Librarian of Congress, the American Association for State and Local History, the American Historical Association, the Association for Documentary Editing, the National Association of Government Archives and Records Administrators, the Organization of American Historians, and the Society of American Archivists.

The commission carries out a statutory mission to ensure understanding of the nation's past by promoting nationwide the identification, preservation, and dissemination of essential historical documentation. These grants help state and local archives, universities, historical societies, and other nonprofit organizations solve preservation problems dealing with electronic records, improve training and techniques, strengthen archival programs, preserve and process records collections, and provide access to them through the publication of finding aids and documentary editions of the papers of the Founding Era and other themes and historical figures in American history. The commission works in partnership with a national network of state Historical Records Advisory Boards.

Administration

NARA employs approximately 2,700 people, of whom about 2,200 are full-time permanent staff members. NARA's budget for FY 1999 was $230.7 million, with $8 million to support the National Historical Publications and Records Commission.

National Center for Education Statistics
Library Statistics Program

U.S. Department of Education
Office of Educational Research and Improvement
1990 K St. N.W., Washington, DC 20006

Adrienne Chute
Elementary/Secondary and Libraries Studies Division

Libraries represent an educational resource available to the public regardless of age, socioeconomic status, or educational background. In an effort to collect and disseminate more complete statistical information about this aspect of the educational spectrum, the National Center for Education Statistics (NCES)* initiated a formal library statistics program in 1989 that now includes surveys on academic libraries, public libraries, school library media centers, state library agencies, and library cooperatives. The Library Statistics Program is administered and funded by NCES, under the leadership of Jeffrey Owings, Acting Director of the Elementary/Secondary and Libraries Studies Division. The National Commission on Libraries and Information Science (NCLIS) and the U.S. Bureau of the Census work cooperatively with NCES in implementing the Library Statistics Program.

The five library surveys provide the only current, comprehensive, national data on the status of libraries. They are used by federal, state, and local officials, professional associations, and local practitioners for planning, evaluation, and making policy and drawing samples for special surveys. These data are also available to researchers and educators to analyze the state of the art of librarianship and to improve its practice.

The Library Statistics Program is pleased to announce the availability of a greatly enhanced Web site. To use this tool, please visit http://nces.ed.gov/surveys/libraries. With the assistance of Sierra, Inc., NCES has developed a home page for the Library Statistics Program with links to a calendar of events and links to a sub-page for each of the library surveys. Each of the library survey sub-pages links to the survey publications and data products, the survey questionnaire, the survey definitions, the survey methodology, and the survey manual (if available). There are also links for each of the library surveys to staff contacts and to other related Web sites.

Public Libraries

Descriptive statistics for nearly 9,000 public libraries are collected and disseminated annually through a voluntary census, the Public Libraries Survey. The sur-

Note: Jeffrey Williams and Elaine Kroe of NCES contributed to this article.

*The mandate of the National Center for Education Statistics to collect library statistics is included in the Improving America's Schools Act of 1994 (P.L. 103-382) under Title IV, the National Education Statistics Act of 1994.

vey is conducted by NCES through the Federal-State Cooperative System (FSCS) for Public Library Data. In 1999 FSCS completed its 11th data collection.

The Public Libraries Survey collects data on staffing; type of legal basis; type of geographic boundary; type of administrative structure; interlibrary relationship; type and number of service outlets; operating income and expenditures; size of collection; service measures such as reference transactions, interlibrary loans, circulation, public service hours, library visits, circulation of children's materials, and children's program attendance; and other data items. More recently, a number of technology-oriented data items have been added to the Public Libraries survey. These are

- Does the public library have access to the Internet?
- Is the Internet used by library staff only, patrons through a staff intermediary, or patrons either directly or through a staff intermediary?
- Number of Internet terminals
- Number of users of electronic resources in a typical week
- Web address of the outlet
- Does the library provide access to electronic services?
- Number of library materials in electronic format
- Operating expenditures for library materials in electronic format
- Operating expenditures for electronic access

In general, both unit response and response to specific items in the Public Libraries Survey are very high.

The 50 states and the District of Columbia participate in data collection. Beginning in 1993 the following outlying areas joined the FSCS for Public Library data: Guam, Commonwealth of the Northern Mariana Islands, Republic of Palau, Puerto Rico, and the U.S. Virgin Islands. For the collection of fiscal year (FY) 1997 data, the respondents were the nearly 9,000 public libraries, identified by state library agencies in the 50 states and the District of Columbia plus the Commonwealth of the Northern Mariana Islands.

Data files on diskette that contain FY 1996 data on about 9,000 responding libraries and identifying information about their outlets were made available in 1999 on diskette and on our Web site. The FY 1996 data were also aggregated to state and national levels in an E.D. Tabs, an NCES publication designed to present major findings with minimal statistical analyses.

The following are highlights from E.D. TABS Public Libraries in the United States: FY 1996, released in February 1999; the full report is available on the Library Statistics Program Web site.

Number of Public Libraries and Their Service Outlets and Legal Basis

- There were 8,946 public libraries (administrative entities) in the 50 states and the District of Columbia in 1996.
- Eleven percent of the public libraries served nearly 71 percent of the population of legally served areas in the United States. Each of these public libraries had a legal service area population of 50,000 or more.

- A total of 1,480 public libraries (over 16 percent) had one or more branch library outlets, with a total of 7,124. The total number of central library outlets was 8,923. The total number of stationary outlets (central library outlets and branch library outlets) was 16,047. Nine percent of public libraries had one or more bookmobile outlets, with a total of 966 bookmobiles.

- Nearly 54 percent of public libraries were part of a municipal government; nearly 12 percent were part of a county/parish; nearly 6 percent had multi-jurisdictional legal basis under an intergovernmental agreement; almost 11 percent were non-profit association or agency libraries; over 3 percent were part of a school district; and 8 percent were separate government units known as library districts. Over 1 percent were combinations of academic/public libraries or school/public libraries. About 6 percent reported their legal basis as "other."

- Over 80 percent of public libraries had a single direct-service outlet (an outlet that provides service directly to the public). Just under 20 percent had more than one direct-service outlet.

- Nearly 70 percent of public libraries were a member of a system, federation, or cooperative service, while over 28 percent were not. Over 2 percent served as the headquarters of a system, federation, or cooperative service.

Operating Income and Expenditures

- Over 78 percent of public libraries' total operating income of about $5.9 billion came from local sources, over 12 percent from the state, 1 percent from federal sources, and close to 9 percent from other sources, such as gifts and donations, service fees, and fines.

- Nationwide total per capita* operating income for public libraries was $23.37. Of that, $18.26 was from local sources, $2.84 from state sources, $0.23 from federal sources, and $2.03 from other sources.

- Per capita operating income from local sources was under $3 for close to 12 percent of public libraries, $3 to $14.99 for over 48 percent, and $15 to $29.99 for over 27 percent of public libraries. Per capita income from local sources was $30 or more for nearly 13 percent of libraries.

- Total operating expenditures for public libraries were over $5.5 billion in 1996. Of this, over 64 percent was expended for paid staff and over 15 percent for the library collection. The average U.S. per capita operating expenditure for public libraries was $21.98. The highest average per capita operating expenditure in the 50 states was $38.19 and the lowest was $9.42.

- Close to 38 percent of public libraries had operating expenditures of less than $50,000 in 1995; over 38 percent expended between $50,000 and $399,999; and close to 24 percent expended $400,000 or more.

---

*Per capita figures are based on the total unduplicated population of legal service areas in the states, not on the total population of the states.

Staffing and Collections

- Public libraries had a total of 117,812 paid full-time-equivalent (FTE) staff. Of these, over 23 percent were librarians with the ALA-MLS, and nearly 10 percent were librarians by title but did not have the ALA-MLS. Close to 67 percent reported their staff as "other."
- Nationwide, public libraries had over 711 million books and serial volumes in their collections or 2.8 volumes per capita. By state, the number of volumes per capita ranged from 1.5 to 5.2.
- Nationwide, public libraries had collections of over 25 million audio materials and 13 million video materials.

Services

- Total nationwide circulation of public library materials was over 1.6 billion or 6.5 per capita. Highest statewide circulation per capita in the 50 states was 12.4 and the lowest was 2.8.
- Nationwide, over 10.5 million library materials were loaned by public libraries to other libraries.
- Total nationwide reference transactions in public libraries were over 284 million or 1.1 per capita.
- Total nationwide library visits to public libraries were over 1 billion or 4 per capita.

FY 1997 FSCS data were collected in August 1998. Preliminary files were released on the Library Statistics Program Web site in 1999, under FSCS's early release policy, with final release scheduled for spring 2000. FY 1998 data were collected in September 1999, with final release scheduled for late fall 2000. The FY 1999 data will be collected in July 2000, with final release scheduled for 2001.

As one way of addressing timely release of data, the Public Libraries Survey has an early release policy. In the period between data collection and final data release, preliminary data provided by states are merged and released periodically over the Internet as received by NCES. These are preliminary data subject to revision until replaced by a final fully edited data file.

The FSCS for Public Library Data is an example of the synergy that can result from combing federal/state cooperation with state-of-the-art technology. FSCS was the first national NCES data collection in which the respondents supplied the data electronically. The data can also be edited and tabulated electronically at the state and national levels through NCES-developed software. All 11 FSCS data collections have been collected electronically. In addition, 26 states and one outlying area submitted their data via the Internet in 1999.

In 1992 NCES developed the first comprehensive public library universe file (PLUS) and merged it with existing software into a revised software package called DECPLUS. DECPLUS has also been used to collect identifying information on all known public libraries and their service outlets. This resource has been available for use in drawing samples for special surveys on such topics as literacy, access for the disabled, library construction, and the like. In 1998 NCES introduced WINPLUS, a Windows-based data collection software that is expected to be more user friendly than DECPLUS but also retains its key features.

NCES, in future years, hopes to make available Web-based data collection, Web-based mapping applications, a cost-adjustment calculator, Web-based custom data analysis and table generators, and a Web-based means of drawing samples for libraries of various sizes.

Efforts to improve FSCS data quality are ongoing. For example, beginning with FY 1992 data, most items with response rates below 100 percent include imputations for nonresponse. In prior years the data were based on responding libraries only. NCES has also sponsored a series of six studies on the Public Libraries Survey on coverage, definitions, structure and organization, finance data, and staffing data. These studies were conducted by the Governments Division, Bureau of the Census. In 1999 Census was to complete its sixth and final study, a working paper on data collection processes and technology. Over the years the clarity of FSCS definitions, software, and tables has been significantly improved.

At the state level and in the outlying areas, FSCS is administered by data coordinators, appointed by each state or outlying area's chief officer of the state library agency. FSCS is a working network. State data coordinators collect the requested data from public libraries and submit these data to NCES. NCES aggregates the data to provide state and national totals. An annual training conference is provided for the state data coordinators and a steering committee that represents them is active in development of the Public Libraries Survey and its data-entry software. Technical assistance to states is provided by phone and in person by state data coordinators, by NCES staff, by the Bureau of the Census, and by the National Commission on Libraries and Information Science (NCLIS). NCES also works cooperatively with NCLIS; the U.S. Department of Commerce's Bureau of the Census; the Institute for Museum and Library Services' Office of Library Programs; the Chief Officers of State Library Agencies (COSLA); the American Library Association (ALA); the U.S. Department of Education's National Institute on Postsecondary Education, Libraries, and Lifelong Learning (PLLI); and the National Library of Education. Westat, Inc. works under contract to NCES to support cooperative activities of the NCES Library Statistics Cooperative Program. Sierra Systems works under contract to NCES to support the Library Statistics Program's Web site.

Other Completed Public Library Data Projects

The Library Statistics Program is pleased to announce the availability of the Public Library Locator tool on the Library Statistics Program Web site. This tool, released in 2000, enables users to locate data about a library or a public library service outlet in instances where they know some but not all the identifying information about the library. For example, if you know the city the library is in but not the library's name, you will still be able to locate the library and obtain most of the FSCS data about it, including identifying information, organizational characteristics, services, staffing, size of collection, income, and expenditures.

To use this tool, please visit http://nces.ed.gov/surveys/libraries/liblocator/ default.asp.

In 1998 NCES and PLLI published *How Does Your Library Compare?* by Keri Bassman of the U.S. Department of Education. This Statistics in Brief (available on the Library Statistics Program Web site) categorized the almost 9,000 public libraries in the FY 1995 public libraries data set into peer groups based on size of population of the legal service area and total operating expenditures to control for variability in library size. Once libraries were assigned to peer groups based on these two variables, comparisons of service performance were made. Service performance was defined in terms of five input variables (public library service hours per year, total librarians, total ALA-MLS librarians, total number of subscriptions, and total number of books and serials) and seven output variables (library visits per capita, children's program attendance, circulation of children's materials, interlibrary loans received per 1,000 population, interlibrary loans provided, total per capita reference transactions, and total per capita circulation).

Building on Keri Bassman's work, and with the assistance of Sierra Systems, Inc., the Library Statistics Program has also released a Web-based peer comparison tool on its Web site. Using this tool a user first selects a data year (FY 1996 Final Data, FY 1997 Preliminary Data, or FY 1998 Preliminary Data), and a library of interest (for example, his or her own library). Next, the user can search for a peer group by selecting key characteristics to define it (total operating expenditures, circulation per capita, and so forth). Finally, the user can view customized reports of the comparison between the library of interest and its peers based on the variety of characteristics he or she selects. These reports include bar charts, pie charts, rankings, data reports, and address/telephone reports. One can also view reports on the FSCS data on individual public libraries. This tool also features a tutorial, and a basic and advanced search feature. To use this tool, please visit http://nces.ed.gov/surveys/libraries/publicpeer.

American Institutes for Research has completed a project to develop two indices of inflation for public libraries, an input cost index and a cost of services index. NCES published a report of the project in 1999. The report presents and compares two approaches to measuring inflation for public libraries. One approach is based on a fixed market basket of the prices of library inputs, which yields a public library input cost index. The other approach is based on an econometric model of library services and costs, which yields a public library cost-of-services index. Inflation rates derived from the cost-of-services model show lower average annual rates of inflation than those derived using the fixed-market-basket approach.

Public library questions have also been included as parts of other NCES surveys. For example, in 1996 questions about frequency of use and the purposes for which households use public libraries were included on an expanded household screener for the NCES National Household Education Survey. More than 55,000 households nationwide were surveyed in such a way as to provide state- and national-level estimates on library items. A Statistics in Brief reporting the survey results was published in 1997. A CD-ROM and User's Manual was made available in July 1997.

The following are highlights from *Statistics in Brief: Use of Public Library Services by Households in the United States: 1996*, released in July 1997. The full report is available on the Library Statistics Program Web site.

Public Library Use in the Past Month and Year

- About 44 percent of U.S. households included individuals who had used public library services in the month prior to the interview, and 65 percent of households had used public library services in the past year (including the past month). About one-third of households (35 percent) reported that no household members had used library services in the past year.

- When the entire past year is taken into account, households with children under 18 showed substantially higher rates of use than households without children (82 percent versus 54 percent).

Ways of Using Public Library Services

- The most common way of using public library services in the past month was to go to a library to borrow or drop off books or tapes (36 percent).

- Eighteen percent of households reported visiting a library for other purposes, such as a lecture or story hour or to use library equipment (the second most common form of use).

- About 14 percent of households had called a library for information during the past month.

- Only very small percentages of households reported using a computer to link to a library (4 percent), having materials mailed or delivered to their homes (2 percent), or visiting a bookmobile (2 percent).

Purposes for Using Public Library Services

- The highest percentage of households reported library use for enjoyment or hobbies, including borrowing books and tapes or attending activities (32 percent).

- Two other purposes for using public libraries that were commonly acknowledged by household respondents were getting information for personal use (such as information on consumer or health issues, investments, and so on; 20 percent), and using library services or materials for a school or class assignment (19 percent).

- Fewer household respondents said that household members had used public library services for the purposes of keeping up to date at a job (8 percent), getting information to help find a job (5 percent), attending a program for children (4 percent), or working with a tutor or taking a class to learn to read (1 percent).

Other Planned Public Library Data Projects

NCES has also fostered the use and analysis of FSCS data. A Data Use Subcommittee of the FSCS Steering Committee has been addressing the analysis, dissemination, and use of FSCS data. Several analytical projects, recommended by this committee, are under way.

In 2000 Westat, Inc. will complete a trend analysis report for FY 1992–FY 1996 on 24 key variables from the Public Libraries Survey. As part of this project, FY 1992–1994 Public Libraries Survey data are being imputed for nonresponse and will be released on the Library Statistics Program Web site in spring 2000 (FY 1995–FY1996 have already been imputed).

NCES is developing a public library geographic mapping tool to be available on the Internet in 2000. This tool, being developed by Westat, Inc., will enable public libraries to identify and map census demographic data within their service boundaries or around their service outlets. For example, a library will be able to identify and map areas with poverty, elderly persons, new Americans, and so forth within its service boundaries so that service delivery can be planned with this awareness. Libraries will also be able to compare their statistics on services with the surrounding demography and present the results in the form of maps.

The project links census demographic data with Public Libraries Survey data through geographic-mapping software. Westat digitized the boundaries of the almost 9,000 public library legal service area jurisdictions. These will be matched to Census Tiger files and to Public Libraries Survey data files. A technical report will describe the methods of geocoding, public library mapping, and options for keeping the project up to date. Some consideration is being given to including parts of this tool in the public library locator in the future.

A fast-response survey on the topic of public library programming for adults, including adults at risk, is under way. The questionnaire covers programming for adult literacy instruction, family literacy, workplace literacy, adults with physical disabilities, the limited-English-speaking, homeless adults, homebound adults, the elderly, adult prisoners, and parents. The survey also asks about programming for finding and using information on the Internet. An advisory group was convened in spring 1999 to make recommendations concerning the project. The questionnaire is entering its second pretest and is expected to be fielded in spring 2000, with results available in late fall 2000. Westat, Inc., is conducting the survey. NCES, PLLI, and the National Library of Education are supporting and/or working on this project.

Additional information on Public Libraries data may be obtained from Adrienne Chute, Elementary/Secondary and Libraries Studies Division, National Center for Education Statistics, 1990 K St. N.W., Room 55, Washington, DC 20006 (202-219-1772, e-mail adrienne_chute@ed.gov).

Academic Libraries

The Academic Libraries Survey (ALS) provides descriptive statistics on about 3,500 academic libraries in the 50 states, the District of Columbia, and the outlying areas of the United States. NCES surveyed academic libraries on a three-year cycle between 1966 and 1988. Since 1988, ALS has been a component of the Integrated Postsecondary Education Data System (IPEDS) and is on a two-year cycle. In aggregate, these data provide an overview of the status of academic libraries nationally and by state.

The survey collects data on the libraries in the entire universe of accredited higher education institutions and on the libraries in nonaccredited institutions with a program of four years or more. A small subset of the ALS questions is included in the IPEDS consolidated form for institutions with less than four-year programs.

For a number of years, NCES has used IDEALS, a software package for states to use in submitting ALS data to NCES. IDEALS was used by 45 states in the collection of 1998 data. Beginning with the collection of FY 2000 data in fall 2000, the ALS is changing to a Web-based data-collection system.

ALS has a working group composed of representatives of the academic library community. Its mission is to improve data quality and the timeliness of data collection, processing, and release. This network of academic library professionals works closely with state IPEDS coordinators (representatives from each state who work with NCES to coordinate the collection of IPEDS data from postsecondary institutions in each of their states). NCES also works cooperatively with ALA, NCLIS, the Association of Research Libraries, the Association of College and Research Libraries, and numerous academic libraries in the collection of ALS data.

ALS collects data on total library operating expenditures, full-time-equivalent (FTE) library staff, service outlets, total volumes held at the end of the academic year, circulation, interlibrary loans, public service hours, gate count, reference transactions per typical week, and online services. Beginning in 1996 the libraries were also asked whether they offered the following electronic services: an electronic catalog that includes the library's holdings, electronic full-text periodicals, Internet access, library reference services by e-mail, and electronic document delivery to patron's account-address.

The first release of ALS 1996 data was in November 1997 over the Internet. The following are highlights from the *E.D. TABS Academic Libraries: 1996*, released in January 2000.

Services

- In 1996, 3,408 of the 3,792 institutions of higher education in the United States reported that they had their own academic library.

- In fiscal year 1996, general collection circulation transactions in the nation's academic libraries at institutions of higher education totaled 186.5 million. Reserve collection circulation transactions totaled 44.2 million. For general and reference circulation transactions taken together, the median circulation was 15.0 per full-time-equivalent (FTE) student*. The median total circulation ranged from 8.4 per FTE in less than four-year institutions to 28.0 in doctorate-granting institutions.

- In 1996 academic libraries provided a total of about 9.4 million interlibrary loans to other libraries (both higher education and other types of libraries) and received about 7.5 million loans.

---

*FTE enrollment is calculated by adding one-third of part-time enrollment to full-time enrollment. Enrollment data are from the 1995–96 IPEDS Fall Enrollment Survey.

- Overall, the largest percentage of academic libraries (44 percent) reported having 60–79 hours of service per typical week. However, 40 percent provided 80 or more public service hours per typical week. The percent of institutions providing 80 or more public service hours ranged from 7 percent in less than four-year institutions to 77 percent in doctorate-granting institutions.
- Taken together, academic libraries reported a gate count of about 16.5 million visitors per typical week (about 1.6 visits per total FTE enrollment).
- About 1.9 million reference transactions were reported in a typical week.
- Over the fiscal year 1996, about 407,000 presentations to groups serving about 7.3 million were reported.

Collections

- Taken together, the nation's 3,408 academic libraries at institutions of higher education held a total of 806.7 million volumes (books, bound serials, and government documents), representing about 449.2 million unduplicated titles at the end of FY 1996.
- The median number of volumes held per FTE student was 58.2 volumes. Median volumes held ranged from 19.0 per FTE in less than four-year institutions to 111.2 in doctorate-granting institutions.
- Of the total volumes held at the end of the year, 44 percent (352.1 million) were held at the 125 institutions categorized under the 1994 Carnegie classification as Research I or Research II institutions. About 55 percent of the volumes were at those institutions classified as either Research or Doctoral in the Carnegie classification.
- In FY 1996, the median number of volumes added to collections per FTE student was 1.5. The median number added ranged from 0.6 per FTE in less than four-year institutions to 2.8 in doctorate-granting institutions.

Staff

- There was a total of 95,580 FTE staff working in academic libraries in 1996. Of these about 27,268 (29 percent) were librarians or other professional staff; 40,022 (42 percent) were other paid staff; 291 (less than 0.5 percent) were contributed services staff; and 27,998 (29 percent) were student assistants.
- Excluding student assistants, the institutional median number of academic library FTE staff per 1,000 FTE students was 5.8. The median ranged from 3.6 in less than four-year institutions to 9.5 in doctorate-granting institutions.

Expenditures

- In 1996 total operating expenditures for libraries at the 3,408 institutions of higher education totaled $4.3 billion. The three largest individual expenditure items for all academic libraries were salaries and wages, $2.15 billion (50 percent); current serial subscription expenditures, $780.8

million (18 percent); and books and bound serials, $472.6 million (11.0 percent).

- The libraries of the 538 doctorate-granting institutions (16 percent of the total institutions) accounted for $2.714 billion, or 63 percent of the total operating expenditure dollars at all college and university libraries.
- In 1996 the median total operating expenditure per FTE student was $310.22 and the median for information resource expenditures was $90.07.
- The median percentage of total institutional Education & General (E&G) expenditures for academic libraries was 2.8 percent in 1994. In 1990 the median was 3.0 percent (*Academic Library Survey: 1990*, unpublished tabulation).

Electronic Services

- In FY 1996, 80 percent of institutions with an academic library had access from within the library to an electronic catalog of the library's holdings, 81 percent had Internet access within the library, and 40 percent had library reference service by e-mail.

The Academic Libraries Survey released a FY 1998 data file that was edited, but not imputed for nonresponding libraries, in early 2000, with an E.D. TABS and an imputed data file to follow.

A descriptive report of changes in academic libraries between 1990 and 1994, *The Status of Academic Libraries in the United States: Results from the 1994 Academic Library Survey with Historical Comparisons,* was released in September 1998. A technical report assessing the coverage of academic libraries through the ALS was published in September 1999.

Several questions about the role of academic libraries in distance education were included as part of another survey sponsored by the U.S. Department of Education's National Institute on Postsecondary Education Libraries and Lifelong Learning. The Survey on Distance Education Courses Offered by Higher Education Institutions was conducted in fall 1995 under NCES's Postsecondary Education Quick Information System (PEQIS). The following is a highlight from the resulting *Statistical Analysis Report: Distance Education in Higher Education Institutions,* released October 1997.

Access to library resources varied depending on the type of library resource. Access to an electronic link with the institution's library was available for some or all courses at 56 percent of the institutions, and cooperative agreements for students to use other libraries were available at 62 percent of institutions. Institution library staff were assigned to assist distance education students at 45 percent of the institutions, while library deposit collections were available at remote sites at 39 percent of institutions.

Additional information on academic library statistics may be obtained from Jeffrey Williams, Elementary/Secondary and Libraries Studies Division, National Center for Education Statistics, 1990 K St. N.W., Room 2, Washington, DC 20006 (202-219-1362, e-mail Jeffrey_Williams@ed.gov).

School Library Media Centers

National surveys of school library media centers in elementary and secondary schools in the United States were conducted in 1958, 1962, 1974, 1978, 1985–1986, and school year 1993–1994. NCES plans to continue school library data collection. Surveys are planned for once every five years, with data currently being collected for school year 1999–2000.

NCES, with the assistance of the U.S. Bureau of the Census, conducted the School Library Media Centers Survey as part of the 1994 Schools and Staffing Survey (SASS). The sample of schools surveyed consisted of 5,000 public schools, 2,500 private schools, and the 176 Bureau of Indian Affairs (BIA) schools in the United States. This subsample was drawn from a sample of approximately 13,000 schools in the SASS. The survey consisted of two questionnaires. Data from the school library media specialist questionnaire provided a nationwide profile of the school library media specialist work force. Data from the school library media center questionnaire provided a national picture of school library staffing, collections, expenditures, technology, and services. This effort was used to assess the status of school library media centers nationwide, and to assess the federal role in their support. Data from 1993–1994 were compared with historical data from previous surveys. The report on this survey, *School Library Media Centers 1993–1994*, was released in August 1998.

The following are highlights from the Executive Summary of this report.

- Library media centers are now almost universally available. In 1993–1994, 96 percent of all public schools and 80 percent of all private schools had library media centers. This compares with 50 percent of the public schools in 1950, and 44 percent of private schools in 1962.
- Out of 164,650 school library staff, 44 percent were state-certified library media specialists, 20 percent were other non-certified professional librarians, and 36 percent were other staff.
- Library media centers spent about $828 million in 1992–1993, including federal gifts and grants but not including salaries and wages. For public schools, after adjusting for differences between the two surveys, expenditures were $676 million (in 1993 dollars) in 1985 and $738 million in 1992–1993. Private school expenditures were $61 million (in 1993 dollars) in 1985 and $89 million in 1993.
- School libraries had 879 million book volumes in their collections at the end of the 1992–1993 school year, or a mean of 28.0 books per student. They also had 2.6 million serial subscriptions, 13.3 million tape and disk video materials, 42.5 million other audiovisual materials, 5.4 million microcomputer software items, and 314,000 CD-ROMs. For public schools, the mean number of books per pupil was 5.3 in 1958 and 17.8 in 1993.
- Two-thirds (67 percent) of schools with library media centers had at least one microcomputer that was supervised by library media center staff. Among those centers with staff-supervised computers, the mean number of computers was 8.9. Other equipment and services found at library media centers included a telephone (57 percent), one or more CD-ROMs for such

uses as periodical indices and encyclopedias (41 percent), an automated circulation system (32 percent), a computer with modem (31 percent), database searching with CD-ROM (28 percent), one or more video laser disks (27 percent), an automated catalog (21 percent), a connection to the Internet (11 percent), and online database searching (9 percent).

- The total number of students using library media centers per week was 42.5 million in 1985 and 32.5 million in 1993–1994 in public schools, and 5.3 million in 1985 and 3.4 million in 1993–1994 in private schools. Over the same time period, total enrollment in public schools increased from 39.4 million to 43.5 million. The mean weekly circulation per pupil per school was 1.3 in 1993–1994 in public schools, and 0.9 in 1985 and 1.2 in 1993–1994 in private schools.

- About two-thirds (65 percent) of school head librarians were regular full-time employees at the schools in which they were surveyed, while 19 percent provided library services at more than one school, and 16 percent were employed part time.

- About half (52 percent) of school head librarians reported they earned a master's degree as their highest degree, while another 8 percent reported training beyond the master's level, either as an education specialist (7 percent) or with a doctorate or first-professional degree (1 percent).

- Head librarians generally expressed positive attitudes toward their schools, the library media centers, and their own personal roles. For example, 96 percent said students believed the library media center was a desirable place to be, 95 percent said their jobs as librarians had more advantages than disadvantages, and 89 percent said the school administration's behavior toward the library media center was supportive and encouraging.

- The median base salary of school head librarians was $30,536 during the 1993–1994 academic year, and their median annual earnings from all sources was $32,000.

- In 1993 public school districts employed 51,000 full-time-equivalent (FTE) school librarians, while another 800 FTE positions were either vacant or temporarily filled by a substitute. About 150 FTE positions were abolished or withdrawn because a suitable candidate could not be found, and 450 FTE positions were lost through layoffs at the end of the last school year.

The Bureau of the Census also completed a technical report for NCES, *Evaluation of Definitions and Analysis of Comparative Data for the School Library Statistics Program*, released in September 1998.

NCES has included some library-oriented questions on the parent and the teacher instruments of its new Early Childhood Longitudinal Study. Some of the data from this study will be released in 2000. For additional information, visit the Web site http://nces.ed.gov/ecls.

Additional information on school library media center statistics may be obtained from Jeffrey Williams, Elementary/Secondary and Libraries Studies

Division, National Center for Education Statistics, 1990 K St. N.W., Room 2
Washington, DC 20006 (202-219-1362).

Surveys on Children, Young Adults

In spring 1994, under the sponsorship of the U.S. Department of Education's
Library Programs Office, NCES conducted two fast-response surveys—one on
public library services and resources for children and another on public library
services and resources for young adults. These surveys updated similar surveys
from 1989 and 1988, respectively. The two surveys collected data directly from
two different representative samples of public libraries.

The Survey on Library Services and Resources for Children in Public
Libraries included questions regarding the availability of specialized staff and
resources for children and the adults who live and work with them, use of available services, prevalence of cooperative activities between public libraries and
other organizations serving children, and barriers to providing increased library
services for children.

The Survey on Library Services and Resources for Young Adults in Public
Libraries obtained information on services for young adults, use of available services, cooperation between libraries and other organizations, ways in which
libraries interact with schools, and factors perceived as barriers to increasing
young adult services and their use. The data from the two surveys were consolidated into one report.

The following are highlights from the report *Services and Resources for
Children and Young Adults in Public Libraries (1995)*.

- Sixty percent of the 18 million people entering public libraries during a
typical week in fall 1993 were youth—children and young adults.
- The percentage of libraries with children's and young adult librarians has
not changed since the late 1980s. Thirty-nine percent of libraries employ a
children's librarian, 11 percent have a young adult librarian, and 24 percent have a youth services specialist on staff.
- Librarians report that ethnic diversity of children and young adult patrons
has increased in over 40 percent of U.S. public libraries over the last five
years. Seventy-six percent of public libraries currently have children's
materials and 64 percent have young adult materials in languages other
than English.
- Although computer technologies are among the most heavily used children's and young adult resources in public libraries, they are also among
the most scarce. Only 30 percent of public libraries reported the availability of personal computers for use by children and young adults. However,
75 percent of libraries having this resource report moderate to heavy use
by children, and 71 percent report moderate to heavy use by young adults.
- Less than half of all public libraries (40 percent) offer group programs for
infants and toddlers. These programs are more prevalent now than in
1988, when only 29 percent of libraries offered group programs for

infants to two-year-olds. Eighty-six percent of libraries offer group programs, such as story times, booktalks, puppetry, and crafts, for preschool and kindergarten-age children; 79 percent of libraries offer group programs for school-age children.

- Seventy-six percent of public libraries report working with schools; 66 percent work with preschools and 56 percent with day care centers.
- While almost all libraries provide reference assistance, only about 1 in 7 libraries offer homework assistance programs for children or young adults. However, fairly large percentages of libraries with homework assistance programs report moderate to heavy use by children and young adults. Sixty-four percent report moderate to heavy use by children, and 58 percent report moderate to heavy use by young adults.
- Librarians report that insufficient library staff is a leading barrier to increasing services and resources for both children and young adults. Sixty-five percent of librarians consider this a moderate or major barrier to increasing services for children, and 58 percent consider lack of staff a barrier to increasing services for young adults.

Additional information on these surveys may be obtained from Edith McArthur, National Center for Education Statistics, 1990 K St. N.W., Washington, DC 20006 (202-219-1442).

Federal Libraries and Information Centers

Federal agencies, according to a FY 1994 count, operate over 2,500 libraries and information centers that comprise a highly diverse and decentralized information services network. The libraries range in collection size from the largest library in the world (the Library of Congress) to some of the smallest in the country. They range in function from highly specialized agency service to national public service.

The Federal Libraries and Information Centers Survey was designed to obtain data on the mission and function, administrative and managerial components (e.g., staff size and expenditures), information resources (e.g., collection size), and services of federal libraries and information centers. The Federal Library Survey has been a cooperative effort between NCES and the staff of the Federal Library and Information Center Committee (FLICC) of the Library of Congress. The survey established a nationwide profile of federal libraries and information centers and made available the first national data on federal libraries since 1978. Currently there are no funds budgeted to continue this survey.

The survey was pretested in 1993 and 1994 and the full-scale survey conducted in 1995. Four data products resulted from this survey: an E.D. TABS with the FY 1994 data (released July 1996), the survey database (released 1996), a directory of federal libraries and information centers (released August 1997), and a *Statistical Analysis Report: The Status of Federal Libraries and Information Centers in the United States: Results from the 1994 Federal Libraries and*

Information Centers Survey (released February 1998). One highlight from this report is:

> About 40 percent of responding federal libraries and information centers reported the general public among their users, and about 53 percent reported having services available to the general public.

The Bureau of the Census also completed a technical report on "Coverage Evaluation of the 1994 Federal Libraries and Information Centers Survey," released in August 1998.

Additional information on the Federal Libraries and Information Centers Survey may be obtained from Jeffrey Williams, Elementary/Secondary and Libraries Studies Division, National Center for Education Statistics, 1990 K St. N.W., Room 2, Washington, DC 20006 (202-219-1362, e-mail Jeffrey_Williams @ed.gov).

State Library Agencies

The State Library Agencies (STLA) Survey collects and disseminates information about the state library agencies in the 50 states and the District of Columbia. A state library agency is the official unit of state government charged with statewide library development and the administration of federal funds under the Library Services and Technology Act (LSTA). Increasingly, state library agencies (STLAs) have received broader legislative mandates affecting libraries of all types and are often involved in the development and operation of electronic information networks. STLAs' administrative and developmental responsibilities affect the operation of thousands of public, academic, school, and special libraries in the nation. STLAs provide important reference and information services to state government and sometimes also provide service to the general public. STLAs often administer the state library and special operations such as state archives, libraries for the blind and physically handicapped, and Centers for the Book.

The State Library Agencies Survey began in 1994 as a cooperative effort between NCES, the Chief Officers of State Library Agencies (COSLA), and NCLIS. The survey collects data on 518 items, covering the following areas: direct library services; library development services; resources assigned to allied operations, such as archive and records management; organizational and governance structure within which the agency operates; electronic networking; staffing; collections; and expenditures. These data are edited electronically, and to date have not been imputed for nonresponding libraries. Beginning with FY 1999 data, however, national totals will be imputed for nonresponding states. Another change is that, beginning with FY 1999 data, the STLA has become a Web-based data collection system. The most recent data available are for FY 1998. Two FY 1998 data products were released on the Internet through the NCES Web site: an E.D. TABS, with 28 tables for the 50 states and the District of Columbia (also available in print), and the survey data base, including the universe file.

The following are highlights from *E.D. TABS State Library Agencies, Fiscal Year 1998*, released in February 2000.

Governance

- Nearly all state agencies (48 states and the District of Columbia) are located in the executive branch of government. Of these, over 65 percent are part of a larger agency, the most common being the state department of education. In two states, Arizona and Michigan, the agency is located in the legislative branch.

Allied and Other Special Operations

- A total of 15 state library agencies reported having one or more operations. Allied operations most frequently linked with a state library are the state archives (10 states) and the state records management service (10 states).
- Seventeen state agencies contract with libraries in their states to serve as resource or reference/information service centers. Eighteen state agencies operate a State Center for the Book*.

Electronic Services and Information

- All state library agencies plan or monitor electronic network development, 45 states and the District of Columbia operate such networks, and 44 states and the District of Columbia develop network content†.
- Thirty-four state library agencies were applicants to the Universal Service (E-rate discount) Program established by the Federal Communications Commission (FCC) under the Telecommunications Act of 1996 (P.L. 104-104)‡.
- All state library agencies facilitate library access to the Internet in one or more of the following ways: training or consulting library staff in the use of the Internet; providing a subsidy for Internet participation; providing equipment to access the Internet; providing access to directories, databases, or online catalogs; and managing gopher/Web sites, file servers, bulletin boards, or listservs.
- Forty-four state library agencies provide or facilitate library access to online databases through subscription, lease, license, consortial membership, or agreement.
- Almost all state library agencies facilitate or subsidize electronic access to the holdings of other libraries in their state, most frequently through

---

* The State Center for the Book is part of the Center for the Book program sponsored by the Library of Congress which promotes books, reading, and literacy, and is hosted or funded by the state.
† Network content refers to database development. Database development activities may include the creation of new databases or the conversion of existing databases into electronic format. Includes bibliographic databases as well as full text or data files.
‡ Under this program, FCC promotes affordable access to the Internet and the availability of Internet services to the public, with special attention given to schools and libraries.

Online Computer Library Center (OCLC) participation (42 states and the District of Columbia). Over half provide access via a Web-based union catalog (30 states) or Telnet gateway (27 states).

- Forty-six state library agencies have Internet terminals available for public use, ranging in number from two to five (15 states), five to nine (13 states), ten to 19 (eight states), 20 to 29 (seven states), and 30 or more (three states). Michigan reported the largest number of public-use Internet terminals (41).

Library Development Service

Services to Public Libraries

- Every state library agency provides the following types of services to public libraries: administration of Library Services and Technology Act (LSTA) grants; collection of library statistics; and library planning, evaluation, and research. Nearly every state library agency provides consulting services and continuing education programs.
- Services to public libraries provided by at least three-quarters of state agencies include administration of state aid, interlibrary loan referral services, library legislation preparation or review, literacy program support, reference referral services, state standards or guidelines, summer reading program support, union list development, and review of technology plans for the Universal Service (E-rate discount) Program.
- Over three-fifths of state agencies provide Online Computer Library Center (OCLC) Group Access Capability (GAC) to public libraries and statewide public relations or library promotion campaigns.
- Less common services to public libraries include accreditation of libraries, certification of librarians, cooperative purchasing of library materials, preservation/conservation services, and retrospective conversion of bibliographic records.

Services to Academic Libraries

- At least two-thirds of state library agencies report the following services to the academic library sector: administration of LSTA grants, continuing education, interlibrary loan referral services, and reference referral services.
- Less common services to academic libraries provided by state agencies include cooperative purchasing of library materials, literacy program support, preservation/conservation, retrospective conversion, and state standards or guidelines. No state library agency accredits academic libraries; only Washington state certifies academic librarians.

Services to School Library Media Centers

- At least two-thirds of state library agencies provide the following services to school library media centers (LMCs): administration of LSTA grants, continuing education, interlibrary loan referral services, and reference referral services. Services to LMCs provided by at least half of all state agencies include consulting services and union list development.

- Less common services to LMCs include administration of state aid, cooperative purchasing of library materials, retrospective conversion, and Universal Service Program review. No state library agency accredits LMCs or certifies LMC librarians.

Services to Special Libraries

- Over two-thirds of state agencies serve special libraries* through administration of LSTA grants, consulting services, continuing education, interlibrary loan referral, reference referral, and union list development.
- Less common services to special libraries include administration of state aid, cooperative purchasing of library materials, and summer reading program support. Only Nebraska accredits special libraries and only Indiana and Washington state certify librarians of special libraries.

Services to Systems

- At least three-fifths of state agencies serve library systems† through administration of LSTA grants, consulting services, continuing education, library legislation preparation or review, and library planning, evaluation, and research.
- Accreditation of systems is provided by only six states and certification of librarians by only five states.

Service Outlets

- State library agencies reported a total of 152 service outlets—72 main or central outlets, 71 other outlets (excluding bookmobiles), and nine bookmobiles.

Collections

- The number of books and serial volumes held by state library agencies totaled 22.0 million, with New York accounting for the largest collection (2.4 million). Five state agencies had book and serial volumes of over one million. In other states, these collections ranged from 500,000 to one million (11 states); 200,000 to 499,999 (12 states); 100,000 to 199,999 (eight states); 50,000 to 99,999 (seven states); and 50,000 or less (six states). The state library agency in Maryland does not maintain a collection, and

---

* A library in a business firm, professional association, government agency, or other organized group; a library that is maintained by a parent organization to serve a specialized clientele; or an independent library that may provide materials or services, or both, to the public, a segment of the public, or to other libraries. Scope of collections and services are limited to the subject interests of the host or parent institution. Includes libraries in state institutions.
† A system is a group of autonomous libraries joined together by formal or informal agreements to perform various services cooperatively such as resource sharing, communications, etc. Includes multitype library systems and public library systems. Excludes multiple outlets under the same administration.

the District of Columbia does not maintain a collection in its function as a state library agency.

- The number of serial subscriptions held by state library agencies totaled over 82,000, with New York holding the largest number (over 12,100). Ten state agencies reported serial subscriptions of over 2,000. In other states, these collections ranged from 1,000 to 1,999 (seven states), 500 to 999 (16 states), 100 to 499 (13 states), and under 100 (2 states).

Staff

- The total number of budgeted full-time-equivalent (FTE) positions in state library agencies was 3,766. Librarians with ALA-MLS degrees accounted for 1,206 of these positions, or 32.0 percent of total FTE positions. Rhode Island reported the largest percentage (57.1) of ALA-MLS librarians, and Utah reported the lowest (16.3 percent).

Income

- State library agencies reported a total income of $886.2 million in FY 1998 (81.3 percent came from state sources, 16.7 percent from federal sources, and 2.0 percent from other sources).
- Of state library agency income received from state sources, over $509 million (70.7 percent) was designated for state aid to libraries. In 11 states, over 75 percent of income from state sources was set aside for state aid. Georgia had the largest percentage of state library agency income set aside for state aid (97.3 percent). Six states (Hawaii, Iowa, New Hampshire, South Dakota, Vermont, and Wyoming) and the District of Columbia targeted no state funds for aid to libraries; instead, 95 to 100 percent of their state funds were set aside for state library agency operations.*

Expenditures

- State library agencies reported total expenditures of $863.5 million. The largest percentage (84 percent) came from state funds, followed by federal funds (14.4 percent) and other funds (1.6 percent).
- In five states, over 90 percent of total expenditures were from state sources. These states were Georgia (94.0 percent), Massachusetts (93.4 percent), Maryland (90.4 percent), New York (92.3 percent), and West Virginia (90.7 percent). The District of Columbia had the lowest percentage of expenditures from state sources (36.7 percent), followed by Wyoming (52.2 percent).
- Almost 70 percent of total state library expenditures were for aid to libraries, with the largest percentages expended on individual public

*The District of Columbia Public Library functions as a state library agency and is eligible for federal LSTA (Library Services and Technology Act) funds in this capacity. The state library agency in Hawaii is associated with the Hawaii State Public Library System and operates all public libraries within its jurisdiction. The state funds for aid to libraries for these two agencies are reported on the NCES Public Libraries Survey, rather than on the STLA survey, because of the unique situation of these two state agencies, and in order to eliminate duplicative reporting of these data.

libraries (55.2 percent) and public library systems (15.9 percent). Most aid-to-libraries expenditures (88 percent) were from state sources, and 11.8 percent were from federal sources.

- Library Services and Technology Act (LSTA) expenditures accounted for 84.1 percent of total federal expenditures. The largest percentage of LSTA expenditures was distributed as grants to libraries (57.3 percent). Funds expended directly by the state library agencies on statewide services accounted for 40.5 percent of LSTA expenditures.

- Fourteen state library agencies reported expenditures for allied operations. These expenditures totaled over $23.1 million and represented 2.7 percent of total expenditures by state library agencies. Of states reporting allied operations expenditures, Virginia reported the highest expenditure ($3.8 million) and Kansas the lowest ($110,000).*

- Twenty-seven state library agencies reported a total of almost $19.0 million in grants and contracts expenditures to assist public libraries with state education reform initiatives or the National Education Goals. The area of lifelong learning accounted for the largest proportion of such expenditures (43.4 percent), followed by the areas of adult literacy (29.8 percent) and readiness for school (26.9 percent). Such expenditures were focused exclusively on readiness for school projects in five states (Louisiana, Nebraska, Oregon, Tennessee, and Utah); on adult school projects in three states (New Hampshire, New Jersey, and Oklahoma); and on lifelong learning in two states (Colorado and Massachusetts).

An evaluation study of the state library survey was released in fall 1999.

Additional information on the state library agency survey may be obtained from Elaine Kroe, Elementary/Secondary and Libraries Studies Division, National Center for Education Statistics, 1990 K St. N.W., Washington, DC 20006 (202-219-1361), e-mail pkroe@inet.ed.gov.

Survey of Library Cooperatives

The Library Cooperatives Survey is a new survey of over 400 library cooperatives. A FY 1997 E.D. TABS and a data file (including a universe file) are expected to be released in 2000. It is expected that this survey will be conducted every five years. A planning committee was formed and met annually to work on definitions, a universe file, and survey design.

The survey defines a library cooperative (network, system, consortium) as "an organization that has a formal arrangement whereby library and information services are supported for the mutual benefit of participating libraries." It must meet all of the following criteria: Participants/members are primarily libraries; the organization is a U.S. not-for-profit entity which has its own budget and its own paid staff; the organization serves multiple institutions (e.g., libraries, school districts) that are not under the organization's administrative control; and

*Although Alaska reported allied operations, the expenditures are not from the state library agency budget.

the scope of the organization's activities includes support of library and information services by performing such functions as resource sharing, training, planning, and advocacy.

The survey includes 55 data items and covers the following areas: Type of organization; geographic area served; whether the general public is directly served; cooperative membership; operating income; operating expenditures; capital expenditures; and cooperative services such as reference, interlibrary loan, training, consulting, Internet access, electronic services, statistics, preservation, union lists, public relations, cooperative purchasing, delivery, advocacy, and outreach programming.

Additional information on the Survey of Library Cooperatives may be obtained from Christina Dunn, National Library of Education, Federal Building No. 6, Room 101, 400 Maryland Ave. S.W., Washington, DC 20202 (202-401-6563, e-mail christina_dunn@ed.gov).

Plans for Crosscutting Activities

The Library Statistics Program also sponsors activities that cut across all types of libraries. For example, NCES sponsors the attendance of librarians from all sectors at NCES training opportunities, such as the semiannual Cooperative System Fellows Program.

In 2000 NCES, with the assistance of Sierra, Inc., is continuing to enhance its Web site. Additional publications are being made available in PDF format for ease in downloading. In addition, a library locator is being developed for the Academic Libraries Survey. NCES is also developing Web-based peer analysis tools for the Academic Libraries Survey and the State Library Agencies Survey. Customer feedback mechanisms will be essential to improving the quality of these products over time and will be built into the tools.

In the future NCES also hopes to work with constituent groups from all the surveys in planning an expanded library statistics cooperative. The goal is to facilitate work on crosscutting issues, without interfering with the ability of existing constituent groups to continue their work on individual surveys. Ideas include expanding participation to add local practitioners, experts from allied professions such as publishing and technology, more data users, and possibly the media. One advantage of an expanded cooperative will be the opportunity to address crosscutting policy issues, identify and address data gaps, and encourage participation by diverse groups and all levels of government.

The two projects described below—a Web-based definitions tool and a new product, "The Digest of Libraries"—will lay the groundwork needed to plan the expanded library statistics cooperative.

In support of an expanded library statistics cooperative, American Institutes for Research in 1999 completed a printed matrix of the content and comparability of NCES's library surveys. In 2000, with the assistance of Agee Indexing Services, the Library Statistics Program is developing a Web-based definitions tool for the six library surveys. By topic, the customer will be able to search for data elements and definitions across surveys. There will be links to the use of definitions in questionnaires, and in publications and data products produced by the Library Statistics Program. This is expected to be a powerful tool in enhancing the Library Statistics Program's capacity to present crosscutting comparisons of library data on key policy issues. This activity is a first step in assessing the potential for a more integrated approach to the library surveys. There will be opportunities to eliminate unnecessary duplication and increase consistency of definitions.

The other initiative in support of an expanded library statistics cooperative is the development of a "Digest of Libraries" planned for release in late 2000. The Digest of Libraries will use the most recently available data to present chapters on topics including library services and library users, services to children, income and expenditures, staffing, collections, and technology. The chapters will include an overview, new tables comparing data across surveys, and some graphics. In addition the digest will contain separate chapters for each library survey, in which key issues will be discussed and tables and graphics presented.

Dissemination of Library Statistics, Cooperative Program Reports, and Data

Under its six library surveys, NCES regularly publishes E.D. TABS, which consist of tables, usually presenting state and national totals, a survey description, and data highlights. NCES also publishes separate, more in-depth studies analyzing library data. Many of these publications are available in printed format and through the Library Statistics Program Web site. Edited raw data from the library surveys are also made available on the Web site. Please visit http://nces.ed.gov/surveys/libraries.

Publications

Public Libraries in Forty-Four States and the District of Columbia: 1988; An NCES Working Paper (November 1989). o.p.

Services and Resources for Children in Public Libraries, 1988–89 (March 1990). NCES number 90-098. o.p.

E.D. TABS: Academic Libraries: 1988 (September 1990). NCES number 90374. o.p.

E.D. TABS: Public Libraries in Fifty States and the District of Columbia: 1989 (April 1991). NCES number 91-343. o.p.

E.D. TABS: Public Libraries in the U.S.: 1990 (June 1992). NCES number 92-028. o.p.

E.D. TABS: Academic Libraries: 1990 (December 1992). Government Printing Office No., 065-000-00549-2. o.p.

Survey Report: School Library Media Centers in the United States: 1990–91 (November 1994). NCES number 94326. Government Printing Office, No. 065-000-00715-1. o.p.

E.D. TABS: Public Libraries in the United States: 1991 (April 1993). NCES number 93-297. Government Printing Office, No. 065-000-00561-1. o.p.

E.D. TABS: Public Libraries in the United States: 1992 (August 1994). NCES number 94-030. Government Printing Office, No. 065-000-00670-7. o.p.

E.D. TABS: Academic Libraries: 1992 (November 1994). NCES number 95031. Government Printing Office, No. 065-000-00717-7. $3.75

Data Comparability and Public Policy: New Interest in Public Library Data; papers presented at Meetings of the American Statistical Association. Working Paper No. 94-07. National Center for Education Statistics, November 1994. NCES number 9407.

Report on Coverage Evaluation of the Public Library Statistics Program (June 1994). NCES number 94430. Prepared for the National Center for Education Statistics by the Governments Division, Bureau of the Census. Government Printing Office, No. 065-00-00662-6. o.p.

Finance Data in the Public Library Statistics Program: Definitions, Internal Consistency, and Comparisons to Secondary Sources (1995). NCES number 95209. Prepared for NCES by the Governments Division, Bureau of the Census. Government Printing Office, No 065-000-00794-9. o.p.

Report on Evaluation of Definitions Used in the Public Library Statistics Program (1995). Prepared for the National Center for Education Statistics by the Governments Division, Bureau of the Census. NCES number 95-430. Government Printing Office, No. 065-000-00736-3. o.p.

Staffing Data in the Public Library Statistics Program: Definitions, Internal Consistency, and Comparisons to Secondary Sources (1995). NCES number 95-186. Prepared for NCES by the Governments Division, Bureau of the Census. Government Printing Office, No. 065-000-00795-9. o.p.

Statistical Analysis Report: Services and Resources for Children and Young Adults in Public Libraries (August 1995). Prepared for NCES by Westat, Inc. Government Printing Office, No. 065-000-00797-5. $9.

E.D. TABS: Public Libraries in the United States: 1993 (September 1995). Government Printing Office, No. 065-000-00800-9. $8.

Public Library Structure and Organization in the United States. NCES No. 96-229 (March 1996).

E.D. TABS: State Library Agencies, Fiscal Year 1994 (June 1996). NCES number 96121. Government Printing Office No. 065-000-00878-5.

E.D. TABS: Federal Libraries and Information Centers in the United States: 1994 (July 1996). NCES number 96247.

Statistics in Brief: Use of Public Library Services by Households in the United States: 1996 (March 1997). NCES number 97-446. Government Printing Office.

E.D. TABS: Public Libraries in the United States: FY 1994 (May 1997). NCES number 97-418. Government Printing Office No. 065-000-00998-6.

The Status of Academic Libraries in the United States; Results from the 1990 and 1992 Academic Library Surveys (June 1997). NCES number 97413. Prepared for NCES by American Institutes for Research.

E.D. TABS: State Library Agencies Fiscal Year 1995 (August 1997). NCES number 97434. Government Printing Office, No. 065-000-01051-8.

Technical Report: Directory of Federal Libraries and Information Centers: 1994 (August 1997). NCES number 97507. Government Printing Office.

Statistical Analysis Report: Distance Education in Higher Education Institutions (October 1997). NCES number 98062. Prepared for NCES by Westat, Inc. Government Printing Office.

Statistical Analysis Report: The Status of Federal Libraries and Information Centers in the United States: Results from the 1994 Federal Libraries and Information Centers Survey (February 1988). NCES number 98296. Government Printing Office.

E.D. TABS: Academic Libraries: 1994 (March 1998). Government Printing Office.

E.D. TABS: State Library Agencies: FY 1996 (June 1998). NCES number 98258. Government Printing Office.

Technical Report: Coverage Evaluation of the 1994 Federal Libraries and Information Centers Survey (August 1998). NCES number 98269. Government Printing Office.

E.D. TABS: Public Libraries in the United States: FY 1995 (August 1998). NCES number 98-301. Government Printing Office.

School Library Media Centers 1993–1994 (August 1998). NCES number 98282. Government Printing Office.

Statistics in Brief: How Does Your Public Library Compare? Service Performance of Peer Groups (September 1998). NCES number 98-310. Government Printing Office.

Status of Academic Libraries in the United States; Results from the 1994 Academic Library Survey with Historical Comparisons (September 1998). NCES number 98311. Government Printing Office.

Technical Report: Evaluation of Definitions and Analysis of Comparative Data for the School Library Statistics Program (September 1998). NCES number 98267. Government Printing Office.

E.D. TABS: Public Libraries in the United States: FY 1996 (February 1999). NCES number 1999-306. Government Printing Office, No. 065-000-01233-2. o.p.

E.D. TABS: State Library Agencies: FY 1997 (March 1999). NCES number 1999-304.

Statistical Analysis Report: Measuring Inflation in Public Libraries: A Comparison of Two Approaches, the Input Cost Index and the Cost of Services Index (April 1999). NCES number 1999-326. Government Printing Office, No. 065-000-01235-9. $8.50.

Technical Report: Evaluation of the NCES State Library Agencies Survey; An Examination of Duplication and Definitions in the Fiscal Section of the State Library Agencies Survey (September 1999). NCES number 1999-312. Prepared for NCES by Laura Riley Aneckstein, Bureau of the Census. Government Printing Office.

E.D. TABS: Academic Libraries: 1996 (January 2000). NCES number 2000-326. Government Printing Office.

E.D. TABS: State Library Agencies Fiscal Year 1998 (January 2000). NCES Number 2000-318. Government Printing Office.

Data Files Released on Computer Diskette and/or Over the Internet

Public Libraries in Forty-Four States and the District of Columbia: 1988 (March 1990).) NCES number 90-387.

Public Libraries in Fifty States and the District of Columbia: 1989 (May 1990). NCES number 91-358.

Academic Libraries: 1988 (October 1990).

Public Libraries Data, 1990 (July 1992). NCES number 92-046.

Academic Libraries: 1990 (February 1993). NCES number 92-046.

Public Libraries Data FY 1991 (November 1993). NCES number 93-294. Government Printing Office.

Public Libraries Data FY 1992 (September 1994). NCES number 94-028. Government Printing Office, No. 065-000-00675-8. o.p.

Academic Libraries: 1992 (November 1994). NCES number 94-032. Available through the NEDRC.

Public Libraries Data FY 1993 (July 1995). NCES number 95-120. Government Printing Office, No. 065-000-00790-8. o.p.

State Library Agencies Data, FY 1994 on Disk (May 1996). NCES number 96-856.

Federal Library and Information Centers Survey, Fiscal Year 1994 (April 1997). NCES number 96-249.

Public Libraries Data FY 1994 (June 1997). NCES number 97-125. Government Printing Office, No. 065-000-01043-7. o.p.

National Household Education Survey; 1991, 1993, 1995, and 1996 Surveys Data Files and Electronic Codebook (July 1997).

State Library Agencies Data, FY 1995 on Disk (September 1997). NCES number 97-520.

Public Libraries Data, FY 1995 (June 1998). NCES number 98-262. Government Printing Office, No. 065-000-01152-2.

Academic Libraries Survey: FY 1994 (August 1998). NCES number 98-270.

State Library Agencies Data FY 1996 on Disk (August 1998). NCES number 98-263.

State Library Agency Survey: FY 1997 (March 1999). NCES number 1999-305.

Public Libraries Data FY 1996 (July 1999). NCES number 1999-307.

Ordering

To order one free copy of recent NCES reports, contact the Education Publications Center (ED Pubs), P.O. Box 1398, Jessup, MD 20794-1398; Tel. (toll-free) 877-4-ED-PUBS (877-433-7827), TTY/TDD (toll-free) 877-576-7734, fax 303-470-1244, e-mail EdPubs@inet.ed.gov, World Wide Web www.ed.gov/ pubs/edpubs.html.

For more than one copy of a publication, or if ED Pubs supplies have been exhausted, more recent publications can be purchased from the Government Printing Office (GPO), Superintendent of Documents. Write to: New Orders, Superintendent of Documents, GPO, Box 371954, Pittsburgh, PA 15250-7954 or call the GPO order desk at 202-512-1800. Credit card orders can be placed by fax at 202-512-2250.

Both current and out-of-print publications and data files may be available on the NCES Library Statistics Program Web site (http://nces.ed.gov/surveys/ libraries). The NCES publication number can be used to locate these products on the Web site. These items may also be available through one of the 1,400 Federal Deposit Libraries throughout the United States. The GPO number can be used to locate these products.

National Education Data Resource Center

An information service called the National Education Data Resource Center (NEDRC) is available. The NEDRC helps customers obtain NCES reports and data files through the Internet or the Government Printing Office (GPO). The NEDRC also responds to requests for special tabulations on library and other NCES studies and surveys. These services are free of charge. Contact the NEDRC at 1900 N. Beauregard St., Suite 200, Alexandria, VA 22311-1722; Tel. 703-845-3151, fax 703-820-7465, e-mail nedrc@pcci.com.

Library of Congress

Washington, DC 20540
202-707-5000, World Wide Web http://www.loc.gov

Audrey Fischer
Public Affairs Specialist

The Library of Congress was established in 1800 to serve the research needs of the U.S. Congress. For nearly two centuries the library has grown both in the size of its collections (now totaling nearly 119 million items) and in its mission. As the largest library in the world and the oldest federal cultural institution in the nation, the Library of Congress serves not only Congress but also government agencies, libraries around the world, and scholars and citizens in the United States and abroad. At the forefront of technology, the library now serves patrons on-site in its 21 reading rooms and at remote locations through its highly acclaimed World Wide Web site.

In fiscal year (FY) 1999 (October 1, 1998–September 30, 1999) the library operated with an appropriated budget of $364 million, a 3.8 percent increase above FY 1998, plus authority to spend an additional $28 million in copyright receipts and cataloging data sales.

Approved in October 1998, the Legislative Branch Appropriations Act of 1999 provided the American Folklife Center with permanent authorization and six new trustees for its board of directors. During FY 1999 the center continued its mandate to "preserve and present American folklife" through a number of out-reach programs, including the addition of three online collections.

In May 1999 Congress appropriated $10 million for an "Open World" Russian Leadership Program to bring emerging political leaders from the Russian Federation to the United States to observe the workings of democratic institutions. Administered by the Library of Congress, the program brought more than 2,100 Russian political, civic, business, and intellectual leaders from 83 of 89 regions to the United States between July and September. Hosted by more than 50 members of Congress and 800 American families in 400 communities, the Russian guests visited 46 states and the District of Columbia. Program cochairs were Librarian of Congress James H. Billington and Russian academician Dmitri Sergeevich Likhachev, who died on the last day of the program.

Bicentennial

The library's Bicentennial Program Office continued to coordinate the effort to celebrate the library's 200th birthday in 2000 with commemorative coins and a stamp, exhibitions, publications, symposia, bicentennial-related activities at libraries nationwide, and several projects, such as Favorite Poem, Local Lega-cies, and Gifts to the Nation.

The first bicentennial symposium, "Frontiers of the Mind in the 21st Centu-ry," was held in June 1999. Poet Laureate Consultant in Poetry Robert Pinsky will present to the library the first 50 audio and video segments from a nation-wide Favorite Poem project as part of the April 2000 bicentennial symposium

"Poetry in America: Reading, Performance, and Publication in the 19th and 20th Centuries."

The cornerstone bicentennial project of 1999, Local Legacies, involved members of Congress and their constituents in an effort to document the cultural and historical traditions in their communities for the library's Archive of Folk Culture. Citizens from all 50 states are participating in this grassroots effort to preserve the folk traditions and local histories of our country at the end of the century and millennium. Selections from Local Legacies will be digitized in 2000 and made available on the library's Web site.

The Gifts to the Nation project seeks to enrich the library's collections during its bicentennial year with materials identified as historically significant. A $1 million contribution from Gene and Jerry Jones to reconstitute Thomas Jefferson's library, which he sold to the Library of Congress in 1815, and $1 million from the Doris Duke Charitable Foundation for the Martha Graham archives are among the notable contributions to this effort.

Legislative Support to Congress

Serving Congress is the library's highest priority. During FY 1999 the Congressional Research Service (CRS) delivered more than 545,000 research responses to members and committees of Congress. CRS provided information to Congress on matters ranging from agriculture to taxation and trade, from China to Kosovo, from space and technology to welfare and related issues. CRS also addressed a range of defense issues, among them budget priorities, medical care costs, military intelligence and law enforcement, base closings, acquisition reform, budget process procedures, the cost to the United States of the Kosovo military operation, and long-term defense policy.

On the domestic front, CRS assisted Congress as it considered matters relating to agriculture, education, banking and finance, proposed election campaign finance reforms, impeachment, proposed managed health care reforms, space and technology, Social Security, taxation, trade, welfare, children, and families. CRS continued to prepare expert testimony for Congress on topics related to the Y2K computer problem.

CRS planned and produced a three-day workshop on oversight for congressional staff that resulted in an updated congressional oversight manual, a video for broadcast on the congressional cable network, and a committee print of the proceedings.

The Law Library answered nearly 4,400 in-person reference requests from congressional users. Law Library research staff produced 975 written reports for Congress, including comprehensive multinational studies on such issues as human rights, health care, and crime.

The Copyright Office provided policy advice and technical assistance to Congress on such important copyright-related issues as database protection, extension of the satellite compulsory license, technical corrections in the Digital Millennium Copyright Act (enacted in August 1999), and exemptions for certain educational activities taking place through digital technologies as outlined in a congressionally mandated report on "Copyright and Digital Distance Education."

The office also responded to numerous congressional inquiries about domestic and international copyright law and registration and recordation of works of authorship.

Improved Service Through Technology

The library continued to improve its cataloging, copyright, research, management, and information delivery systems through the development and use of technology in 1999 with notable achievements in a number of areas.

Integrated Library System

As of October 1, 1999, the library had successfully implemented all modules of the Integrated Library System, including cataloging and circulation modules, the online public access catalog (OPAC) in the reading rooms and on the World Wide Web, and the acquisitions and serials check-in modules. The new system will improve automation support for bibliographic control and inventory management activities at the library through the use of a shared bibliographic database that integrates all major Library Services functional areas (such as acquisitions, cataloging, serials management, circulation, inventory control, and reference) while improving bibliographic control and inventory management. The effort involved more than 500 library staff serving on 80 implementation teams. Approximately 12 million bibliographic records, 4 million authority records, as well as some 30,000 vendor records, 54,000 order records, and nearly 26,000 patron records were converted from legacy systems to the ILS production database.

Legislative Information System

The focus of development for the shared Legislative Information System (LIS) during FY 1999 was creation of a Y2K-compliant system for the exchange of data among the House, the Senate, and the Library of Congress. With the transition to the new system in December, LIS became the central point for locating legislative information.

Legislative Alert

To speed legislative analyses to Congress, CRS developed weekly electronic mail delivery of reports, issue briefs, and electronic materials relating to issues likely to receive action each week in the House and the Senate. With links to the most recent products on the CRS Web site, these weekly summaries of legislative issues make information and analysis readily available to members and staff to support legislative deliberations.

Electronic Briefing Books

CRS continued to develop one of its newest products, the electronic briefing book, by adding books for banking and finance, taxation, and the Y2K computer problem.

Internet Resources

The library continued to provide more information to Congress and the nation with a growing amount of information through its Internet-based systems. The library's Web site was repeatedly cited for excellence in 1999 and was included on many "best of" lists, including those of *PC Magazine*, Netscape Net Guide, and the *Scout Report*.

Throughout FY 1999 an average of nearly 80 million transactions were recorded on the library's public electronic systems each month, a 30 percent increase over FY 1998 usage. Use of the American Memory historical collections increased by more than 60 percent, from an average of 9.3 million transactions during FY 1998 to 15 million per month in FY 1999. The publicly accessible legislative information system known as THOMAS continued to be an enormously popular resource, with more than 10 million systems transactions logged on average each month.

Global Legal Information Network

The Global Legal Information Network (GLIN) is a cooperative international network in which member nations contribute the full text of statutes and regulations to a database hosted by the Law Library of Congress. Twelve member countries currently participate via the Internet. In addition, the Law Library contributed information about another 24 nations. In 1999 GLIN transactions totaled 264,000, including searches, inputting, and updating files. A milestone was reached in March with production of a new GLIN file that allows GLIN members to enter legal writings into the database and link them to summaries of laws already included in the GLIN database.

National Digital Library Program

At year's end, approximately 2.5 million Library of Congress items and 85,000 items from collaborating institutions were available online or in digital files. Approximately 2.5 million items from the library's collections and other repositories were put into production as part of a national collaborative effort.

During FY 1999 another 18 new multimedia historical collections were added to the American Memory Web site, bringing the total to 68. Eight existing collections were expanded with additional items, and four new library exhibitions were mounted on the library's Web site.

FY 1999 was the third and final year to award Library/Ameritech grants to other archives and institutions to digitize historically significant American history collections; a total of $615,965 went to 12 recipients. Since the program's inception, 33 award-winning institutions have received support to digitize their historical collections and make them available through the library's Web site.

In FY 1999 the National Digital Library Program held its third American Memory Fellows Institute, welcoming 50 K–12 teachers and school media specialists from 20 states to the library's existing network of master educators, extending the National Digital Library's educational outreach program into 30 states since 1996.

During FY 1999 the National Digital Library Visitors' Center hosted more than 500 programs for more than 7,800 visitors. Center staff also answered 5,074 electronic mail requests for information.

Copyright Office Electronic Registration, Recordation, and Deposit System

Developed in collaboration with the Defense Advanced Research Projects Agency and Corporation for National Research Initiatives, the Copyright Office Electronic Registration, Recordation, and Deposit System (CORDS) will help the Copyright Office streamline its internal registration, recordation, and deposit processes, as well as provide copies of new copyrighted works in digital form for its National Digital Library repository. During 1999 the Copyright Office continued to develop, test, and enhance CORDS for the digital registration and deposit of copyrighted works via the Internet, using the latest advances in networking and computer technology. The major emphasis of CORDS testing and implementation during FY 1999 was focused on successful establishment of system-to-system communications for CORDS electronic copyright registration and deposit with the office's largest copyright remitter, Bell & Howell Information and Learning (previously known as UMI), for electronic receipt and processing of claims for digital dissertations.

Geographic Information Systems

The Geography and Map Division (G&M) continued to work closely with the National Digital Library to digitize cartographic materials for electronic access. In cooperation with the Congressional Research Service and the Congressional Relations Office, G&M produced customized maps and geographic information for members of Congress. Working with the National Digital Library, G&M digitized cartographic materials for electronic access throughout the nation. With help from private-sector partners, G&M continued to expand the collection of large-format images available through the Internet. A new collection, Mapping the National Parks, was introduced in June, and an evolving collection of Places in the News/Contemporary Maps was inaugurated in April 1999. By the end of FY 1999, 2,428 maps (8,120 images) were made available to the world through the Map Collections home page, which now averages more than 410,000 computer transactions each month.

Technologies for the Disabled

The National Library Service for the Blind and Physically Handicapped (NLS/BPH) distributed more than 22 million items to some 765,000 readers in 1999. Braille readers can now access more than 2,700 Web-Braille digital braille book files created by the library; access requires a computer or electronic note-taker and a refreshable braille display (which is an electronic device that raises or lowers an array of pins to create a line of braille characters) or a braille embosser. Work also continued on digital talking-book standards under the auspices of the National Information Standards Organization. Expected to be completed in one year, this digital standard will be used by NLS to develop its new talking book.

Copyright

The Copyright Office received 619,022 claims and made 594,501 registrations in FY 1999. The office responded to nearly 427,000 requests from the public for copyright information, of which more than 10,000 were received electronically. Selected as one of the nation's top Web sites by *PC/Novice/Smart Computing* magazine, the Copyright Office Web site played an increasingly important role in the dissemination of information to the copyright community and the general public. The Web site logged more than 5.6 million hits during the year, nearly a threefold increase over the previous year.

Collections

During FY 1999 the library's collections grew to nearly 119 million items, an increase of approximately 3.5 million items over FY 1998 totals. This figure includes 27.5 million books and other print materials, 53 million manuscripts, 12.5 million microforms, 4.5 million maps, and 13.4 million visual materials (photographs, posters, moving images, prints, and drawings). At year's end the total arrearage stood at 19.8 million items, a decrease of 50 percent from the 39.7 million-item arrearage at the time of the initial census in September 1989.

Linked to the library's arrearage reduction effort is the development of secondary storage sites to house processed materials and to provide for collection growth through the first part of the 21st century. In March 1999 the library and the Architect of the Capitol (AOC) recommended the firm of Tobey & Davis to the David and Lucile Packard Foundation to be the prime architect to design a National Audio-Visual Conservation Center in Culpeper, Virginia.

The library also continued to work closely with AOC and its contractors to ensure that the first storage module at Fort Meade, Maryland, meets the necessary environmental requirements to house and preserve the transferred collections and that materials handling will be as efficient as possible. AOC has advised the library that construction of Module One will be completed and the building ready for occupancy late in 2000. The module will house 2.2 million items of paper-based material, primarily books, shelved by size in containers.

Important new acquisitions came to the library through the copyright deposit system, through other federal agencies, or through gift, exchange, or purchase. Notable acquisitions during FY 1999 included the following:

- More than 600,000 items of Supreme Court Justices Harry Blackmun and Ruth Bader Ginsberg
- Papers and documents in the Marian Carson Collection relating to the early history of the United States
- A multimedia collection of ballet choreographer Bronislava Nijinska
- The "Carte de Canada et des Etats Unis de l'Amerique" (1778), the first map to recognize the independence of the United States
- A Persian Manuscript Celestial Globe (circa 1650)
- The first American Haggadah (New York City, 1837)
- More than 330 issues of the post-Revolutionary newspaper *Claypoole's Daily Advertiser* (1791–1793)

- About 40,000 works by more than 3,000 artists in the J. Arthur Wood, Jr., collection of cartoons and caricature
- The Victor Hammer Archives, containing the works of one of the great handpress printers, printmakers, and type designers of the 20th century
- *Politica* by Aristotle (Cologne, 1492), the earliest version of Aristotle's work to become available in the West

Publications

During FY 1999 the Publishing Office produced more than 25 books, calendars, and other products describing the library's collections, as well as a catalog of the library's selected publications, titled *Celebrating Books*. Major publications in FY 1999 produced by the library or in cooperation with outside publishers included *Sigmund Freud: Conflict and Culture* (Alfred A. Knopf), *The Declaration of Independence: The Evolution of the Text* (University Press of New England), and *Gathering History: The Marian S. Carson Collection of Americana*. *Language of the Land: The Library of Congress Book of Literary Maps* received much media attention and was the subject of feature articles in newspapers across the country.

The award-winning book *Eyes of the Nation* was also released as a multimedia CD-ROM and DVD-ROM by Southpeak Interactive and the History Channel. *Eyes of the Nation* won second place in the American Association of Museums CD-ROM design competition, was named by *Family Life* magazine as one of the top ten family multimedia products, and was the topic of a feature article in the *New York Times*. Publications that garnered overall design excellence awards from Washington Book Publishers were *Freud: Conflict and Culture*, *Gathering History: The Marian S. Carson Collection of Americana*, *Oliphant's Anthem: Pat Oliphant at the Library of Congress*, and *Performing Arts: Motion Pictures*.

The bimonthly *Civilization* magazine, which is published under a licensing agreement with the library, completed its fifth year of publication with more than 250,000 paid subscribers, who are also Library of Congress Associates.

Exhibitions and Literary Events

During FY 1999 the library presented six new exhibitions. Items rotated into the library's permanent exhibition *American Treasures of the Library of Congress* included the Nicolay copy of the Gettysburg Address, Lincoln's 1861 inaugural address, and Thomas Jefferson's rough draft of the Declaration of Independence. The year's two major exhibitions, *Sigmund Freud: Conflict and Culture* (October 15, 1998–January 16, 1999) and *Charles and Ray Eames: A Legacy of Invention* (May 20, 1999–September 4, 1999), were scheduled to visit Germany, Denmark, London, Vienna, Brazil, New York, Los Angeles, and Chicago. The Bicentennial theme of "Libraries, Creativity, Liberty" was reflected in the first two bicentennial exhibitions, *John Bull and Uncle Sam: Four Centuries of British-American Relations* (November 16, 1999–March 6, 2000), featuring materials from the Library of Congress and British Library, and *Eames*. Four new exhibitions, including *Freud* and *Eames,* were added to the library's Web site.

The library piloted a Web broadcasting program starting with Poet Laureate Robert Pinsky's lecture that opened the 1998–1999 poetry season on October 8, 1998. The pilot program explored the practicality of a regular library cybercast during the year of the library's bicentennial.

In April Pinsky was appointed to serve an unprecedented third term as Poet Laureate Consultant in Poetry during the library's bicentennial year. In addition, the following special consultants were appointed to assist with bicentennial poetry programs: former Poet Laureate Rita Dove, Louise Glück, and W. S. Merwin.

The following 25 films were named to the National Film Registry in 1999, bringing the total to 275:

Civilization (1916)

Do the Right Thing (1989)

The Docks of New York (1928)

Duck Amuck (1953)

The Emperor Jones (1933)

Gunga Din (1939)

In the Land of the Head-Hunters (1914), alternately titled
    In the Land of the War Canoes

Jazz on a Summer's Day (1959)

King: A Filmed Record . . . Montgomery to Memphis (1970)

The Kiss (1896)

Kiss Me Deadly (1955)

Lambchops (1929)

Laura (1944)

Master Hands (1936)

My Man Godfrey (1936)

Night of the Living Dead (1968)

The Plow That Broke the Plains (1936)

Raiders of the Lost Ark (1981)

Roman Holiday (1953)

The Shop Around the Corner (1940)

A Streetcar Named Desire (1951)

The Ten Commandments (1956)

Trance and Dance in Bali (1938–1939)

The Wild Bunch (1969)

Woman of the Year (1942)

Security

Securing the library's facilities, staff, collections, and computer resources continued to be a high priority. On October 21, 1998, President Clinton signed an omnibus emergency spending bill that included $17 million for security of library buildings. These funds were part of a $106.8 million package to improve physical security of the Capitol Hill complex.

During the year the library installed X-ray machines in the James Madison, Thomas Jefferson, and John Adams main lobbies, where visitors were screened electronically beginning in May. The library also awarded a single contract for security guards to support certain functions, expanded police presence by adding new posts and patrols, and gained congressional approval of plans to make major physical security improvements (including consolidating the two police command centers, integrating and upgrading intrusion-detection systems, and installing improved access controls, such as vehicle barriers, curb walls, perimeter bollards, and secure police shelters).

In coordination with the Office of the Inspector General, an external auditing firm was contracted to do a random sampling of the collections in the Prints and Photographs Division, the first step in a major undertaking to establish baselines of the library's inventory so that follow-up inspections can measure the extent of theft and mutilation.

The Collection Security Oversight Committee (CSOC) created four standing subcommittees (Policy and Standards, Operations, Security Awareness, and Resources), which have implemented actions outlined in the library's security plan.

The library continued to implement a comprehensive computer security plan to safeguard its valuable electronic resources, and a Y2K plan to ensure that its computer systems would function properly at the turn of the century. As a result of testing, modifying, or replacing systems as necessary, all of the library's mission-critical systems were certified Y2K-compliant at year's end.

Preservation

The library during FY 1999 took action to improve the preservation of its vast and diverse collections by

- Completing the mass deacidification treatment of 75,000 volumes, using the Bookkeeper limited-production contract
- Binding 183,202 paperback volumes and labeling 156,004 hardcover volumes
- Introducing a "conservation fellow" volunteer program, in which five volunteers rehoused 15,101 items
- Identifying and evaluating an improved, commercially available motion picture container
- Developing a new time-saving, accelerated-aging test that will more efficiently predict the longevity of paper products
- Coordinating the preservation microfilming of 1.6 million pages of historically significant U.S. newspapers, adding more than 6,000 titles to the national union list of newspapers, and microfilming 3.3 million papers from the library's collections
- Completing housing for 162,242 technical reports in the Publication Board Collection in the Science, Technology, and Business Division

- Inspecting and processing 364 positive reels and 175 negative reels of microfilm acquired from Moscow's Library of Foreign Literature and Russian State Library, from Lithuania, and from military archives in Hungary, Poland, and Romania
- Identifying laser-marking equipment that can be used to place library property information safely on CDs, audiotapes, and videotapes

Restoration and Renovation

During FY 1999 the library completed a number of moves and actions as part of the multiyear plan to outfit and occupy the remaining renovated spaces of the Thomas Jefferson and John Adams buildings. Major accomplishments include relocating Contracts and Logistics Services from the Landover Annex to the John Adams building, completing the Thomas Jefferson Building and Rare Book roof replacement project, as well as work in the Jefferson Visitors Center, the Concert Office, and the Coolidge Green Room.

Human Resources

The library employs 4,194 permanent staff members. Congress approved two reprogramming actions during FY 1999 totaling $720,000 to accelerate the library's HR 21 initiative to compete successfully for highly qualified staff, retain high performers, reward excellence and innovation, train and manage staff to achieve library missions, and make personnel administration responsive, efficient, and effective. A Strategic Planning Group and a Hiring Improvement Group recommended a new human resources program and a timetable for implementing new systems, programs, and procedures. The library also issued a Human Resources Strategic Plan to guide the transformation effort and ensure that human resources activities clearly align with the agency mission.

In its second year of operation, the Library of Congress Internal University (LCIU) coordinated more than 380 classes for staff, including more than 150 computer training sessions. LCIU also coordinated the quarterly Leadership Lecture Series, a forum for managers and staff to learn from top corporate officers, government officials, and leadership scholars about effective leadership practices and techniques. The library signed an agreement with the labor organizations to establish a pilot mentoring program for library employees.

The library also supported special internship programs, including the Soros Foundation-Library of Congress Intern Program, which hosted 12 librarians and information specialists from Central and Eastern Europe and Central Asia, and the Hispanic Association of Colleges and Universities National Internship Program. The library continued its long-standing relationship with the Catholic University of America School of Library and Information Science by coordinating the effort to offer several graduate-level courses to library staff members.

Additional Sources of Information

Library of Congress telephone numbers for public information:

Main switchboard (with menu)	202-707-5000
Reading room hours and locations	202-707-6400
General reference	202-707-5522
	202-707-4210 TTY
Visitor information	202-707-8000
	202-707-6200 TTY
Exhibition hours	202-707-4604
Research advice	202-707-6500
Copyright information	202-707-3000
Copyright hotline (to order forms)	202-707-9100
Bicentennial Program Office	800-707-7145
Sales shop	202-707-0204

Center for the Book

John Y. Cole
Director, The Center for the Book
Library of Congress, Washington, DC 20540
World Wide Web http://lcweb.loc.gov/loc/cfbook

Since 1977, when it was established by Librarian of Congress Daniel J. Boorstin, the Center for the Book has used the prestige and the resources of the Library of Congress to stimulate public interest in books, reading, and libraries and to encourage the study of books and the printed word. With its network of 37 affiliated state centers and more than 75 national and civic organizations, it is one of the Library of Congress's most dynamic and visible educational outreach programs.

The center is a successful public-private partnership. The Library of Congress supports its four full-time positions, but the center's projects, events, and publications are funded primarily through contributions from individuals, corporations, foundations, and other government organizations.

Highlights of 1999

- The addition of two new states—Utah and Massachusetts—to the center's national network of state affiliates
- The presentation of the Boorstin Center for the Book Awards to the Virginia and Missouri state centers
- The continued use and expansion of the center's Web site, http://lcweb. loc.gov/loc/cfbook/
- The sponsorship of national family literacy workshops in Austin, Texas, and Baton Rouge, Louisiana, as part of the Viburnum Foundation/Center for the Book family literacy project
- Continued support of the Poet Laureate's "Favorite Poem" project through sponsorship of readings in Chicago, St. Louis, and Los Angeles
- Sponsorship of more than 30 programs and events, at the Library of Congress and throughout the country, that promoted books, reading, and libraries
- Sponsorship of the publication of five books: *The Declaration of Independence: The Evolution of the Text*, rev. ed., by Julian P. Boyd, ed. by Gerald W. Gawalt; *Language of the Land: The Library of Congress Book of Literary Maps*, ed. by Martha Hopkins and Michael Buscher; *A Library Head Start to Literacy: The Resource Notebook for the Library-Museum-Head Start Partnership*, by Virginia Mathews and Susan Roman; *Thomas Jefferson and the Education of a Citizen*, ed. by James Gilreath; and *Historical Fiction: A Celebration of the Achievements of Herman Wouk*, ed. by Barbara Paulson (all Washington, D.C.: Library of Congress, 1999).

Themes

The Center for the Book establishes national reading-promotion themes to stimulate interest and support for reading and literacy projects that benefit all age groups. Used by state centers, national organizational partners, and hundreds of schools and libraries across the nation, each theme reminds Americans of the importance of books, reading, and libraries in today's world. A special project was devised to celebrate the Library of Congress's forthcoming bicentennial and to conclude "Building a Nation of Readers," the Center for the Book's reading-promotion theme through the year 2000. Libraries, schools, educational and civic organizations, and other groups were invited to describe their reading-promotion projects for posting on the Center for the Book's Web site.

Reading-Promotion Partners

The center's partnership program includes more than 75 civic, educational, and governmental organizations that work with the center to promote books, reading, libraries, and literacy. On March 22, 1999, representatives of many of these organizations gathered at the Library of Congress to share information about their current projects and discuss potential cooperative arrangements. New reading-promotion partners during 1999 included the Academy of American Poets, the Antiquarian Booksellers Association of America, the Children's Creative Writing Campaign, First Book, the National Center for Learning Disabilities, the National Children's Book and Literacy Alliance, the National Endowment for the Arts, and the National Geographic Society.

State Centers

When James H. Billington became Librarian of Congress in 1987, the Center for the Book had ten affiliated state centers; at the end of 1998 there were 37. The newest centers, Utah and Massachusetts, are located at the Salt Lake City Public Library and the University of Massachusetts at Amherst, respectively.

Each state center works with the Library of Congress to promote books, reading, and libraries as well as the state's own literary and intellectual heritage. Each center also develops and funds its own operations and projects, using Library of Congress reading-promotion themes when appropriate and occasionally hosting Library of Congress-sponsored events and traveling exhibits. When its application is approved, a state center is granted affiliate status for three years. Renewals are for three-year periods.

On May 3, 1999, representatives from the state centers participated in an idea-sharing session at the Library of Congress. In his remarks, the center's director noted that three state centers (Tennessee, Maine, and, most recently, Montana) were now "hosted" by state humanities councils. He also reminded state centers that their affiliations with the Library of Congress must be renewed every three years and that 16 state centers needed to submit renewal applications by the end of 1999. He also stressed the growing importance of the center's Web site, which had expanded dramatically during the year and become a heavily used resource for the book and reading communities.

The highlight of the meeting was the presentation of the 1999 Boorstin Center for the Book Awards to the Virginia and Missouri Centers for the Book. Each of these annual awards includes a cash prize of $5,000. The National Award, won by Virginia, recognizes the contribution that a state center has made to the Center for the Book's overall national program and objectives. The State Award, won by Missouri, recognizes a specific project. In this instance, two achievements were noted: Missouri's annual celebration of the book, a statewide event that attracts much public attention, and the Missouri authors' database, which was created by the Missouri Center for the Book.

Projects

This was the Center for the Book's second year of administering the Viburnum Foundation's program for supporting family literacy projects in rural public libraries. During the year, the foundation awarded 40 grants to small rural libraries in seven states. In August 1999 the Center for the Book sponsored regional workshops in Austin, Texas, and Baton Rouge, Louisiana, that provided training for representatives from the libraries that received the grants.

"Letters About Literature," a student essay contest sponsored with the Weekly Reader Corporation and King's College in Wilkes-Barre, Pennsylvania, concluded another record-breaking year. More than 20,000 students wrote letters to their favorite authors, and 26 state centers honored statewide winners.

The center's annual "River of Words" project, an environmental art and poetry contest for young people, culminated May 8 at the Library of Congress with an awards ceremony and display of winning artworks. The moderator was former Poet Laureate Robert Hass. The project is cosponsored with the International Rivers Network.

The Center for the Book continued to be the Library of Congress's liaison for the Favorite Poem project developed for the forthcoming Library of Congress bicentennial. Headed by Poet Laureate Robert Pinsky, the project records people from all walks of life reciting their favorite poems for the library's Archive of Recorded Poetry and Literature. The center sponsored Favorite Poem readings in St. Louis, Los Angeles, and Chicago, the latter in cooperation with the Poetry Society of America. The center also continued work as the liaison with the American Library Association for another bicentennial project, "Beyond Words: Celebrating America's Libraries," a national photography contest that features photographs of people of all ages using libraries.

Outreach

The center's Web site continued to expand in coverage and use during 1999. Established and maintained by program officer Maurvene D. Williams, the Web site describes Center for the Book projects and book-related events across the country. It also provides information about organizations that promote books, reading, and libraries. Most organizational entries are linked to that organization's Web site or to a general descriptive entry about the organization. In 1999 approximately 25,000 transactions were accessed on the center's Web site each month.

The Center for the Book's "Read More About It" project with CBS Television came to an end in 1999. For two decades, these 30-second messages from the Library of Congress, which directed viewers to suggested books in their local libraries and bookstores, were telecast in conjunction with CBS programs. More than 400 lists were prepared and telecast. New "Read More About It" lists were prepared, however, for 18 digitized collections on the National Digital Library's Web site and for several Library of Congress exhibitions.

During the year, C-SPAN televised many of the presentations sponsored by the Center for the Book for viewing as part of its "Booknotes" and "Book TV" programs.

Five issues of the newsletter *Center for the Book News* were produced in 1999, along with two editions of the state center *Handbook*. The Library of Congress issued 28 press releases about center activities, and a two-page "News from the Center for the Book" appeared in each issue of the library's *Information Bulletin*. Center for the Book Director John Y. Cole made 26 presentations during visits to 16 states. As chair of the Section on Reading of the International Federation of Library Associations and Institutions (IFLA), he presented one paper and chaired several meetings in Bangkok, Thailand, at the 1999 IFLA annual conference.

Events

Sponsorship of events, symposia, and lectures—at the Library of Congress and elsewhere—is an important Center for the Book activity. Through such special events, the center brings diverse audiences together on behalf of books and reading and publicizes its activities nationally and locally. Examples of events in 1999 at the Library of Congress include nine talks by current authors in the center's "Books & Beyond" lecture series; a program sponsored with Oxford University Press and the American Council of Learned Societies to discuss biography and celebrate the publication of the 24-volume *American National Biography*; a symposium about literary publishing, "Bridging Art and Commerce," sponsored with the National Endowment for the Arts; with the Children's Book Council, a program inaugurating "Young People's Poetry Week"; and a public "Preservation Awareness Day," cosponsored with the Library of Congress's Preservation Directorate.

Information about the dozens of events sponsored by the state centers, often in cooperation with the national center, can be found in the Library of Congress *Information Bulletin*.

Federal Library and Information Center Committee

Library of Congress, Washington, DC 20540
202-707-4800
World Wide Web http://lcweb.loc.gov/flicc

Susan M. Tarr
Executive Director

Highlights of the Year

During fiscal year (FY) 1999 the Federal Library and Information Center Committee (FLICC) continued to carry out its mission "to foster excellence in federal library and information services through interagency cooperation and to provide guidance and direction for FEDLINK."

FLICC's annual information policy forum, "Copyright, Electronic Works, and Federal Libraries: Maintaining Equilibrium," focused on how authors, publishers, readers, libraries, and the government are working to redistribute rights and obligations between authors and readers and restore balance to the copyright arena. FLICC also held its annual FLICC Symposium on the Information Professional, this year focusing on the current context for federal outsourcing.

FLICC working groups achieved a broad agenda in FY 1999: the first annual FLICC Awards to recognize the innovative ways federal libraries, librarians, and library technicians fulfill the information demands of government, business, scholarly communities, and the American public; a Web-based handbook of federal librarianship; new educational initiatives in the areas of cartographic and serials cataloging; surveys to members on fees, technical processing, and information technology; knowledge, skills, and abilities statements for federal cataloging librarians; increased federal library participation in the Library of Congress (LC) bicentennial; and expanded access to resources through distance learning and the FLICC Web site.

FLICC also collaborated with LC's General Counsel on a series of meetings between federal agency general counsels and their librarian counterparts. These general counsel forums grew out of the recognition that federal attorneys and librarians face many of the same questions in applying copyright, privacy, the Freedom of Information Act, and other laws to their agencies' activities in the electronic age—with regard both to using information within the agency and to publishing the agency's own information. These meetings have already fostered a closer relationship between agency attorneys and librarians and helped them develop contacts with their counterparts at other agencies.

In addition to supporting the membership projects, FLICC staff identified and implemented a series of customer service initiatives, made substantial improvements to the efficiency of the Federal Library and Information Network (FEDLINK) program, improved members' use of OCLC, negotiated additional and substantial discounts for FEDLINK members, and investigated options to replace the FEDLINK financial system. Staff also sponsored 34 seminars and workshops for 1,343 participants and conducted 105 OCLC, Internet, and related training classes for 1,099 students.

FEDLINK continued to enhance its fiscal operations while providing its members with $50.8 million in transfer-pay services and $67.5 million in direct-pay services, saving federal agencies more than $14 million in vendor volume discounts and approximately $6.6 million more in cost avoidance.

During FY 1999 FEDLINK staff resolved all critical Y2K issues for systems throughout FLICC and automated the billing upload to LC's central financial system to reduce members' interagency agreement (IAG) billing turnaround time. FEDLINK staff also collaborated with the library's central accounting unit to eliminate redundant data entry associated with processing member refunds. Continued success with FEDLINK's document imaging and archiving system streamlined member and vendor billing inquiries and improved records management. Moreover, FEDLINK's continuing financial management efforts ensured that FEDLINK successfully passed the library's financial audit of FY 1998 transactions performed by Clifton Gunderson, LLP.

FLICC managers worked throughout FY 1999 to improve project planning, implementation, and staff participation through effective use of facilitative leadership (FL) techniques and leadership development programs fostered by the library.

Quarterly Membership Meetings

In addition to regular FLICC Working Group updates and reports from FLICC/FEDLINK staff, each FLICC Quarterly Meeting included a special focus on a new or developing trend in federal libraries: the first FLICC Quarterly Membership Meeting featured a report on the Depository Library Council by Fred Wood of the National Library of Medicine and a presentation and tour of the library's Scholarly Program by its director, Prosser Gifford; the second meeting included a demonstration and discussion of OCLC's pilot Cooperative Online Resource Catalog (CORC) project by Terry Noreault, Vice President of the OCLC Office of Research; the third meeting hosted Stephen Griffin, Program Director, Special Projects, National Science Foundation (NSF), who discussed "The Digital Libraries Initiative at the Division of Information and Intelligence Systems" at NSF; and the fourth meeting featured Jay Liebowitz, Robert W. Deutsch Distinguished Professor of Information Systems, University of Maryland–Baltimore County, who addressed the role of federal libraries in knowledge management.

Working Groups

Ad Hoc Bicentennial LC Working Group

In honor of LC's upcoming bicentennial celebration, a FLICC working group formed in FY 1998 to develop programs for the entire federal library community to participate in the celebration and derive expanded promotion of their efforts beyond the bicentennial year. By participating in the library's bicentennial activities, federal libraries and information centers will increase recognition of their programs and link federal libraries to the Library of Congress under the larger campaign to publicize the "Nation's Collections." In FY 1999 the working group began working with an outside contractor to create a poster, bookmark, and promotional tool kit for federal libraries to use in their local celebrations. The working group developed a slogan, celebration guidelines, and a chronology of federal libraries, and began gathering additional materials for an online federal library almanac. In collaboration with the FLICC Preservation and Binding Working Group, members explored opportunities to create a national registry of historical materials in need of preservation and digitization. By the end of FY 1999 the working group had completed the majority of its planned bicentennial tool kit materials and initiated the production and distribution phase of its efforts in time for the bicentennial year.

Awards Working Group

To honor the many innovative ways federal libraries, librarians, and library technicians fulfill the information demands of government, business, research, scholarly communities, and the American public, the Awards Working Group administered a series of national awards for federal librarianship. The three awards are:

- Federal Library/Information Center of the Year—to commend a library or information center's outstanding, innovative, and sustained achievements during the fiscal year in fulfilling its organization's mission, fostering innovation in its services, and meeting the needs of its users
- Federal Librarian of the Year—to honor professional achievements during the fiscal year in the advancement of library and information sciences, the promotion and development of services in support of the agency's mission, and demonstrated professionalism as described in the Special Library Association's "Competencies for Special Librarians in the 21st Century"
- Federal Library Technician of the Year—to recognize the achievements of a federal library technician during the fiscal year for service excellence in support of the library or information center's mission, exceptional technical competency, and flexibility in adapting work methods and dealing with change

In this first year of the program, the Awards Working Group reviewed 19 nominations in the three award categories. Eight entries were selected as finalists for the FLICC Executive Board to review and determine the 1998 winners. At the annual FLICC Forum on Federal Information Policies in March 1999 FLICC announced the winners of the first annual awards:

- Federal Library and/or Information Center of the Year (tie)—National Institutes of Health Library and the Defense Technical Information Center
- Federal Librarian of the Year—Joan Buntzen, Librarian of the Navy
- Federal Library Technician of the Year—Connie Clarkston, David Grant Medical Library, Travis Air Force Base

The individual award winners each received a certificate and an engraved crystal award in the shape of a book to honor their contributions to the field of federal library and information service, and the institutional winners each received a framed, hand-painted certificate. The working group then reviewed the program criteria in the summer of 1999 and initiated promotion efforts for the second annual awards program.

Budget and Finance Working Group

The FLICC Budget and Finance Working Group developed the FY 2000 FEDLINK budget and fee structure in January 1999. When approved unanimously by the FLICC membership in June 1999, the final budget for FY 2000 kept membership fees for transfer-pay customers at FY 1998 levels: 7.75 percent on accounts up to $300,000 and 7 percent on amounts exceeding $300,000. Direct-pay fees also remained at FY 1998 levels.

Education Working Group

During fiscal year 1999 the FLICC Education Working Group developed or supported 34 programs for 1,343 participants in the areas of technology development, copyright issues, technician training, cataloging and classification, and appropriations law. In addition, the FLICC Orientations to National Libraries and Information Centers series and brown-bag luncheon discussions continued throughout the year.

In November 1998 the working group sponsored "Contracting Out: Making It Your Job," with speakers including Sybil Bullock, Director, Redstone Scientific Information Center, U.S. Army Missile Command; Barbara Wrinkle, Director, U.S. Air Force Libraries and Information Systems; Dorothy Fisher Weed, Librarian, Department of Labor; Omar Akchurin, Project Manager, SANAD Support Technologies; and Doria Grimes, Chief, Library Contracts, National Oceanic and Atmospheric Administration (NOAA). Seventy-five federal librarians attended this program to discuss the current context for federal outsourcing of information and library services.

During the winter months FLICC continued its commitment to continuing education for librarians and library technicians by hosting satellite downlinks to two popular teleconferences, "Soaring to . . . Excellence" and "Periodical Database," both sponsored by the College of DuPage (Glen Ellyn, Illinois).

Following the success of previous programs, the working group held the third annual Federal Library Technicians Institute. This week-long institute again focused on orienting library technicians to the full array of library functions in the federal context. Federal and academic librarians joined FLICC professionals to discuss various areas of librarianship, including acquisitions, cataloging, reference, and automation.

The newest FLICC institute, Financial Management Institute for Federal Librarians, reviewed accounting and budgeting principles, federal appropriations law, non-federal funds and fund raising, interpretation and presentation of financial information, cost analysis, and vendor price analysis. Participants gained skills in making financial decisions, budgeting, and accounting for library resources in a federal environment.

The working group also began developing an online handbook of federal librarianship to serve as a resource tool for librarians new to the federal community and as a quick reference guide for established federal librarians.

Information Technology Working Group

In FY 1999 the Information Technology Working Group promoted its new Web-based survey titled "The FLICC Information Technology Assessment for Federal Libraries and Information Centers." This tool helps federal librarians examine how information technology is being used in their organization and glean information about other libraries' equipment and programs. The results of this informative questionnaire, accessible through the FLICC/FEDLINK Web site, allow federal librarians to assess the level of automation in their libraries by comparing their agency's use of technology with other agencies' library profiles.

The working group also cosponsored, with the OCLC Institute, a two-day seminar, "Technology in a Time of Rapid Change," to help libraries explore and quantify current technology trends and their impact on federal libraries. Participants gained a foundation to guide their agencies with improved strategic technology planning.

Nominating Working Group

The FLICC Nominating Working Group oversaw the 1999 election process for FLICC rotating members, FLICC Executive Board members and the FEDLINK Advisory Council (FAC). Librarians representing a variety of federal agencies agreed to place their names in nomination for these positions.

Personnel Working Group

The Personnel Working Group continued its efforts in developing sample knowledge, skills, and abilities (KSAs) statements to help hiring officials specify appropriate quality-ranking factors on vacancy announcements for federal librarian positions. These KSAs are to be used as a guide; they are not associated with specific grade levels nor are they intended to be used for classifying 1410 positions. During FY 1999 the working group formalized KSAs for cataloging librarians and posted them on the FLICC Web site.

The working group also contacted the Office of Personnel Management (OPM) regarding improved recruitment for the 1410 librarian series, requesting that OPM eliminate references to a defunct test previously administered by OPM from the current qualifications standard. Their continued correspondence with OPM also has begun to focus on current qualification requirements for library positions.

Preservation and Binding Working Group

The Preservation and Binding Working Group reorganized and reformed in FY 1999, naming new cochairs late in the year. The goals of the revitalized working group are to identify preservation priorities for federal libraries and information centers, discover alternative sources of funding to support these preservation efforts, and create and disseminate preservation information and resources in an electronic format through the FLICC Web site.

The working group explored the current Government Printing Office (GPO) binding contract and made strides toward developing a standard federal conservation/preservation contract. Through the FLICC/FEDLINK Web site, the working group also promoted the "Disaster Preparedness Workbook for U.S. Navy Libraries and Archives," written by Robert Schnare of the U.S. Naval War College Library.

Publications and Education Office

Publications

In FY 1999 FLICC supported an ambitious publications schedule, producing 11 issues of a completely redesigned *FEDLINK Technical Notes* and two issues of the *FLICC Quarterly Newsletter*.

FLICC also published expanded and enhanced materials to support the FEDLINK program, including the 75-page FY 2000 *FEDLINK Registration Booklet*, six FEDLINK Information Alerts, and the 1999 FLICC Awards brochure. FLICC also produced the minutes of the four FY 1999 FLICC Quarterly Meetings and bimonthly FLICC Executive Board meetings and all FLICC Education Program promotional and support materials, including the FLICC Forum announcement, attendee and speaker badges, press advisories, speeches and speaker remarks, and collateral materials. In addition, FLICC produced 24 FLICC Meeting Announcements to promote FLICC Education Programs; FEDLINK membership, vendor, and OCLC users' meetings; and education institutes, along with badges, programs, certificates of completion, and other supporting materials.

FLICC and FEDLINK staff worked diligently throughout 1999 to continue to expand and update the FLICC/FEDLINK Web site. The site contains a variety of information resources, member information, links to vendors and other members, listings of membership and minutes of various FLICC working groups and governing bodies, access to account data online, award program information, event calendars, and an online training registration system that is updated nightly. FLICC staff converted all publications, newsletters, announcements, alerts, member materials, and working group resources into HTML format, uploading current materials within days of their being printed. Through collaboration with the FEDLINK Network Operations staff, the FLICC Web site continues to expand and offer resources, including OCLC Usage Analysis Reports, pricing data for the FEDLINK Books Procurement Program, and many new documents, including the FY 2000 budget materials, serials procurement materials, and training resources.

Education

In conjunction with the Education Working Group, FLICC offered a total of 34 seminars, workshops, and lunchtime discussions to 1,343 members of the federal library and information center community. Multiday institutes covered serials cooperative cataloging, technology planning, library technician training, metadata, federal financial management, cataloging cartographic materials, and managing interlibrary loan; one-day sessions offered hands-on and theoretical knowledge on serials procurement, managing Web access, periodical databases, implementation of the library's Integrated Library System, and contracting out. The "FLICC Orientations to National Libraries and Information Centers Series," composed of tours of other federal libraries and information centers, continued in FY 1999 with visits to and presentations at the Government Printing Office, the National Oceanic and Atmospheric Administration, the Supreme Court, the U.S. Department of the Interior, and the U.S. Department of State. FLICC also was a host to two general counsel forums, and to the College of DuPage's "Soaring to . . . Excellence," a multi-session satellite downlink program on library science issues for librarians and library technicians, as well as DuPage's "Periodical Database" satellite presentation.

FLICC also provided organizational, promotional, and logistical support for FEDLINK meetings and events including the FEDLINK fall and spring Membership Meetings, two FEDLINK OCLC Users Group meetings, a series of vendor briefings, and a program on "How to Use FEDLINK in Fiscal Year 2000."

FLICC continued to improve its multimedia distance-learning initiative through significant upgrades to equipment (camera, lighting, sound system), software, and video quality. Using these upgraded resources, FLICC produced high-quality, edited educational programs (including title pages, subtitles, voice-overs, and rolling credits, etc.), and through its arrangement with the National Library of Education, made these videos available for interlibrary loan to federal libraries throughout the country and around the world. Planning and testing in FY 1999 moved FLICC's distance-learning initiatives toward a Web-based presentation with the acquisition of Real Media Producer software and equipment.

FEDLINK

In FY 1999 the Federal Library and Information Network (FEDLINK) gave federal agencies cost-effective access to an array of automated information retrieval services for online research, cataloging, and interlibrary loan. FEDLINK members also procured publications, technical processing services, serials, electronic journals, CD-ROMs, books, and document delivery via LC/FEDLINK contracts with major vendors.

The FEDLINK Advisory Council (FAC) met monthly during FY 1999 (except in November, May, and August), holding its first all-electronic meeting in June. During the year, FAC approved the FY 2000 FEDLINK budget and worked with staff to create a White Paper for agency contracting officers on the value and efficiency of using FEDLINK services.

FEDLINK's semiannual Membership Meetings both focused on electronic collection development. The fall meeting featured guest speaker Joyce L. Ogburn (Assistant University Librarian for Information Resources and Systems, Old Dominion University Library, Norfolk, Virginia), who addressed integrating electronic materials into library operations from the librarian's perspective, and Marcia Talley (FEDLINK's OCLC Users Council Delegate), who reported on the October OCLC meeting titled "Digital Libraries: Looking at the Future of the Information Industry." The FEDLINK spring Membership Meeting featured Gil Baldwin (GPO), Janice Beattie (NOAA), and Martin Smith (Smithsonian Institution), who discussed "controlling access to digital resources." FEDLINK staff also presented a description of OCLC's pilot Cooperative Online Resource Catalog (CORC) project, which explores technology to share cataloging of electronic resources.

FEDLINK/OCLC Network Activity

The fall and spring OCLC Users Group Meetings highlighted OCLC advancements in the use of Web and Windows technologies. At the fall meeting, FEDLINK staff outlined both OCLC and FEDLINK plans to implement and train users on a redeployed FirstSearch system that takes advantage of Java scripts and allows libraries to customize library resources to suit user needs and optimize local budgetary requirements. FEDLINK members also heard reviews of OCLC's new simplified cataloging system for use via the Web, designed for use by small libraries or libraries with large copy-cataloging operations. The spring meeting featured presentations that outlined OCLC's Cataloging MicroEnhancer and its other Windows-based packages, which were recently enhanced to automate more complex cataloging functions. All of these packages reached a critical mass of functionality during FY 1999, making them optimum choices for the majority of the federal libraries already contributing to OCLC's WorldCat database.

FEDLINK also promoted increased use of OCLC's and FEDLINK's electronic choices for gathering information via the Web, e-mail, and electronic listservs about products and prices, ordering products, and asking questions. Although about one-third of such information is still made available in printed newsletters and product literature, the majority of OCLC's and FEDLINK's information about OCLC systems, services, and prices is now distributed first or only via electronic means.

Through FEDLINK's efforts, several federal libraries began participating in OCLC's pilot CORC project, agreeing to develop and test this online system for streamlining the collection and cataloging Web resources. The Smithsonian Institution and the National Wetlands Research Center joined the pilot project early in the process, followed by a group of earth sciences libraries organized by the FEDLINK office, including the Environmental Protection Agency, Department of the Interior, Geological Survey, NASA Goddard, NOAA, and the Naval Research Laboratory. Ann Parham, the Army Librarian, then worked with FEDLINK to organize a second group that includes the National Defense University (NDU), the Center for Army Lessons Learned (CALL), an Army Training and Doctrine Command (TRADOC) library at Fort Leavenworth, the Pentagon, the U.S. Military Academy (West Point), the Army War College, and three Army Corps of Engineers libraries (Headquarters, Cold Regions, and Waterways Experiment Station). The Air University and the National Labor Relations Board also began work in the CORC system in early 1999.

Beyond the routine support and administration of OCLC services for FEDLINK members, FEDLINK Network Operations also cross-trained three staff members from FEDLINK Fiscal Operations (FFO), in consecutive 120-day details to a paraprofessional-level position to support OCLC administration. These details benefitted FNO beyond the administrative assistance they provided—they enhanced FNO staff's understanding of fiscal processes and FFO staff's understanding of network operations. This improved communication between units met goals previously established cooperatively by staff and management.

Training Program

The 1999 FEDLINK training program included specialized training classes and customized workshops for FEDLINK members around the globe. OCLC's introduction of its new FirstSearch service provided reason and opportunity to conduct 20 targeted training sessions for members converting to this upgraded retrieval service. Staff held ten of these FirstSearch sessions on site in member libraries and hosted two special sessions at the American Library Association (ALA) conference for Air Force and Army librarians. FNO met other important training needs by tailoring special workshops to specific members; for example, a class on basic acquisition of library materials and an advanced acquisitions class developed for the Military Librarians Workshop in Alexandria, Virginia, in November. Additionally, FNO staff held two workshops on information service licensing for Air Force librarians at the ALA Annual Conference in New Orleans in June. To assist members with integrating their research and library acquisitions/collection development on the Web, FNO staff presented sessions at the second annual cooperative workshop with MINITEX in April.

Overall, FEDLINK conducted 105 OCLC, Internet, and related classes for 1,099 students. Of the 105 classes held, 55 were at field sites. Staff held training sessions in Alabama, Arizona, California, Florida, Illinois, Oklahoma, Texas, and Washington. FEDLINK offered members access to its contract training programs through the OCLC Pacific Network (Vandenberg Air Force Base [AFB], and Travis AFB, both in California) and the Bibliographical Center for Research (Cannon AFB, New Mexico; Malmstrom AFB, Montana; Peterson AFB, Colorado; Warren AFB, Wyoming; and Edwards AFB, California). Federal librarians also continued to have access to training through FEDLINK agreements to four OCLC regional library networks: CAPCON, PALINET, SOLINET, and the Michigan Library Network.

Procurement Program

FEDLINK successfully recompeted its FY 2000 basic ordering agreements (BOAs) for serials subscription services by May and presented these service updates in the same month. BOAs were issued to American Overseas Book Company, Blackwell, EBSCO, and Faxon. FEDLINK subsequently competed 300 serials accounts in FY 1999 for FY 2000 service.

In 1999 FEDLINK took the initiative to research the commercial information retrieval/electronic publications products and services available to its members. The objective of the project was to gain better discounts and more comprehensive offerings for FEDLINK members. In anticipation of beginning the contract renewal process, staff had discussions with AMIGOS, the Bibliographical Center for Research (BCR), INCOLSA, OHIONET, and SOLINET regarding vendors' products and services and the level of discounts offered to those networks and FEDLINK. FEDLINK distributed renewal information to all the service providers, requesting that they review their product offerings and discounts. FEDLINK's top ten database vendors also met with FEDLINK and Contract and Logistics staff to discuss their mergers and acquisitions, new consortial arrangements, additional products/services, revised pricing, and licensing terms.

FEDLINK also collected information from FLICC Executive Board and FEDLINK Advisory Council members regarding their negotiations with commercial vendors for services outside the scope of the FEDLINK program. In addition, staff compared products/services available through FEDLINK with those available via the General Services Administration (GSA) schedules. FEDLINK used the results of this in-depth research as background and briefing information when negotiating with LEXIS-NEXIS, West Group, Information Handling Service, Chemical Abstracts, Gale Research Group, Congressional Quarterly, Dialog (including DataStar and Profound), and Bell & Howell/UMI.

Staff explored a variety of issues with these information retrieval/electronic publications vendors:

- Mergers—Because there have been many consolidations among vendors' organizations, FEDLINK staff led discussions to clarify current and future expectations and ensure the smooth transfer of outstanding invoices and other services.
- One-stop shopping—Staff inquired whether vendors planned to offer all their products and services to FEDLINK members.
- FEDLINK discounts—Staff explored what programmatic changes would encourage vendors to increase their discounts to the FEDLINK program.
- Licenses—Staff reviewed individual vendor licenses to see if any terms and conditions could be problematic for FEDLINK members and/or could delay procurements.
- Community building—Staff stressed the agency viewpoint that vendors are also FEDLINK "customers."

As a result of these discussions, FEDLINK vendors are offering a variety of new discounts and other savings. FEDLINK also worked with a number of vendors to implement a pilot plan to streamline end-of-year billing disputes. Some vendors also agreed to offer additional products and services to FEDLINK members, and others consolidated their offerings into single accounts to streamline billing functions. Throughout the annual contract renewal process FEDLINK staff emphasized with vendors that FEDLINK was a procurement consortium and that FEDLINK contract officers are willing and able to negotiate special arrangements for any FEDLINK members.

During FY 1999 FEDLINK focused on LC's purchasing agreements and staff met with representatives of interested Library units to negotiate library enterprise-wide access to LEXIS-NEXIS and free trial offers from the Bureau of National Affairs (BNA) and Bell & Howell UMI/ProQuest.

Expanding its consortial purchasing efforts, FEDLINK worked closely with Wright-Patterson Technical Libraries to negotiate consortial pricing with Dialog. Currently, Dialog is offering special consortial pricing for Wright-Patterson Technical Libraries: Wright-Patterson, Phillips, Rome, and Tyndall Technical Libraries.

FEDLINK staff also completed site visits to the District of Columbia Corporation Counsel, the Agency for International Development Office of the General Counsel, and the International Trade Office. FEDLINK also assisted the Health Care Finance Administration with cost proposal review of an online vendor's proposal.

To improve contracts/account management, FEDLINK arranged separate agreements for network training contracts in FY 2000. During the fiscal year FEDLINK members will use their FEDLINK training accounts solely for FED-LINK or FLICC events and they will set up separate accounts with other networks (for example, CAPCON) whose training services they plan to use.

Fiscal Operations

During FY 1999 FEDLINK processed 8,675 member service transaction requests for current and prior years, representing $50.8 million in current-year transfer pay, $2.9 million in prior-year transfer pay, $67.5 million in current-year direct pay, and virtually zero in prior-year direct-pay service dollars, saving members more than $14 million in vendor volume discounts and approximately $6.6 million more in cost avoidance. Staff issued 54,087 invoices for payment of current and prior-year orders, earned $12,800 in discounts in excess of interest penalties for late payment of FEDLINK vendor invoices, completed FY 1994 member service dollar refunds to close out obligations for expired appropriations and refund members' remaining account balances, and successfully passed the Library of Congress financial audit of FY 1998 transactions performed by Clifton Gunderson, LLP.

FEDLINK implemented several initiatives to collaborate with members to enhance the effectiveness and efficiency of customer service operations, resolved critical Y2K issues for its financial system, and revised plans to replace the current financial system through the library's planned procurement for financial management software in 2004. Staff also found innovative ways to improve the efficiency of FEDLINK's financial processes and ensured that administrative expenditures and obligations did not exceed program fee projections.

Vendor Services

Total FEDLINK vendor service dollars for FY 1999 alone comprised $50.8 million for transfer-pay customers and $67.5 million for direct-pay customers. Electronic information retrieval services represented $13.5 million and $55.0 million spent, respectively, by transfer-pay and direct-pay customers. Within this service category, online services comprised the largest procurement for transfer-pay and direct-pay customers, representing $13.1 million and $54.4 million, respectively. Publication acquisition services represented $30.7 million and

$12.4 million, respectively, for transfer-pay and direct-pay customers. Within this service category, serials subscription services comprised the largest procurement for transfer-pay and direct-pay customers, representing $23.8 million and $12.3 million, respectively. Library support services represented $6.6 million and $65,000, respectively, for transfer-pay and direct-pay customers. Within this service category, bibliographic utilities constituted the largest procurement area, representing $5.3 million and $65,000 for transfer-pay and direct-pay customers, respectively.

Accounts Receivable and Member Services

FEDLINK processed FY 1999 registrations from federal libraries, information centers, and other federal offices that resulted in 662 signed FY 1999 interagency agreements (IAGs). In addition, FEDLINK processed 2,320 IAG amendments (1,063 for FY 1999 and 1,257 for prior-year adjustments) for agencies that added, adjusted, or ended service funding. These IAGs and IAG amendments represented 8,675 individual service requests to begin, move, convert, or cancel service from FEDLINK vendors. FEDLINK executed service requests by generating 8,375 delivery orders that LC/Contracts and Logistics issued to vendors. For FY 1999 alone FEDLINK processed $50.8 million in service dollars for 2,470 transfer-pay accounts and $67.5 million in service dollars for 177 direct-pay accounts. Included in the above member service transactions were 621 member requests to move prior-year (no-year and multiyear) funds across fiscal year boundaries. These no-year and multiyear service request transactions represented an additional contracting volume of $5.3 million comprising 1,018 delivery orders.

The FEDLINK Fiscal Hotline responded to a variety of member questions, ranging from routine queries about IAGs, delivery orders, and account balances to complicated questions regarding FEDLINK policies and operating procedures. In addition, the FLICC Web site and e-mail contacts continued to offer FEDLINK members and vendors 24-hour access to fiscal operations. Staff continued to schedule appointments with FEDLINK member agencies and FEDLINK vendors to discuss complicated account problems, and senior staff concentrated on resolving complex current and prior-year situations. The FEDLINK online financial service system, ALIX-FS, maintained current and prior-year transfer-pay accounts in FY 1999 and continued to provide members early access to their monthly balance information throughout the fiscal year. FEDLINK prepared monthly mailings that alerted individual members to unsigned IAG amendments, deficit accounts, rejected invoices, and delinquent accounts.

Transfer-Pay Accounts-Payable Services

For transfer-pay users, FEDLINK issued 54,087 invoices for payment during FY 1999 for both current and prior-year orders. Staff efficiently processed vendor invoices and earned $12,800 in discounts in excess of interest payment penalties levied for the late payment of invoices to FEDLINK vendors. FEDLINK continued to maintain open accounts for three prior years to pay publications service invoices ("bill laters" and "back orders") for members using books and serials services. Staff issued 90,036 statements to members (23,047 for the current year and 66,989 for prior years) and continued to generate current fiscal year statements for electronic information retrieval service accounts on the 30th or the last working day of each month, and publications and acquisitions account statements on the 15th of each month. FEDLINK issued final FY 1994 statements in support of closing obligations for expired FY 1994 appropriations. FEDLINK Fiscal Operations (FFO) issued quarterly statements for prior fiscal years and supported the reconciliation of FY 1995 FEDLINK vendor services accounts.

Financial Management

FEDLINK successfully passed the Library of Congress Financial Audit of FY 1998 Transactions. During the same time period, FEDLINK also passed a formal review of its management and internal controls policies and procedures by the library's Inspector General. FEDLINK then completed a limited review of its automated financial system for the library's 1999 financial audit. FFO invested significant time and effort to support these audits including:

* Financial systems briefings
* Documented review and analysis of financial system
* Testing and verification of account balances in the central and subsidiary financial system
* Financial statement preparation support
* Security briefings and reviews
* Research and documented responses to follow-up audit questions and findings

In response to customer service research in FY 1998, FEDLINK implemented several of the initiatives identified by members to enhance the efficacy and efficiency of fiscal operations. Specifically, fiscal managers collaborated with members to develop policies to improve member management of OCLC deficits and reduce the risk of anti-deficiencies. FEDLINK also secured a 30-day extension for year-end deadlines for adding funds to member accounts. Other initiatives included the following:

* Reducing the turnaround time for MIPR signatures, IAG bills, invoice rejection notices, and money-move requests
* Establishing closer working relationships with members and vendors in the areas of customer communication and account management
* Expanding resources and account information access on the FLICC Web site
* Streamlining the acquisition of FEDLINK vendor services through credit card and online e-business procurement

Financial Management Systems

By the end of FY 1999 FEDLINK's financial system and the library's central accounting system were "Y2K ready," denoting that Y2K changes had been made to operating software although functional elements were subject to further testing. During the fiscal year, the FEDLINK systems team resolved all critical Y2K issues for systems throughout FLICC/FEDLINK. Efforts included converting the financial management system from a Banyan Vines network operating system to a Windows NT network operating system; modifying integrated software tables, forms, and reports to accommodate four-character years; and updating Web file management and uploads.

In FY 1999 FEDLINK researched private sector financial management system capabilities to develop requirements for a new automated financial system to replace FEDLINK's current financial system. The research indicated that private sector systems should be part of the choice set for the next-generation FEDLINK system. As part of these research and review efforts, FEDLINK revised and streamlined a request for proposal for private sector and Treasury-approved system providers, determined proposal evaluation strategies, and assembled an evaluation team. Because submitted proposals exceeded FLICC's predetermined cost target for acquiring a new financial management system, FEDLINK revised its strategy to become part of the library's planned financial procurement scheduled for FY 2004 in support of all congressional agencies.

FEDLINK also automated its billing upload program, which significantly reduced members' IAG billing turnaround time, and collaborated with the library's central accounting unit to eliminate redundant data entry associated with processing member refunds. Continued success with FEDLINK's document imaging and archiving system streamlined member and vendor billing inquiries and improved records management. Future efforts include extending the use of this system to other units within FEDLINK's Accounts Receivable and Contracts areas.

Budget and Revenue

During FY 1999 FEDLINK earned only 90 percent of its target FY 1999 operating budget in fee revenue from signed IAGs. Since FEDLINK canceled its request for proposal for a replacement financial system, administrative expenditures and obligations did not exceed program fee projections. As FY 1999 ended, FEDLINK fee revenue was approximately 9 percent below FY 1998 levels for the same time period.

Approximately half of the 9 percent drop in fee revenue is attributed to the FY 1999 budget reduction in fees for transfer-pay service accounts. The other half of the 9 percent drop in fee revenue is attributed to a fall of approximately 5 percent in transfer-pay service dollar volume below FY 1998 levels.

National Agricultural Library

U.S. Department of Agriculture, NAL Bldg., 10301 Baltimore Ave.,
Beltsville, MD 20705-2351
E-mail agref@nal.usda.gov
World Wide Web http://www.nal.usda.gov

Brian Norris
Public Affairs Officer

The National Agricultural Library (NAL) is the primary agricultural information resource for the nation and is the largest agricultural library in the world, with a collection of more than 3.3 million items. Established in 1862 under legislation signed by Abraham Lincoln, NAL is part of the Agricultural Research Service (ARS) of the U.S. Department of Agriculture (USDA). The NAL collection includes books and journals, audiovisuals, reports, theses, software, laser discs, and artifacts. The library receives more than 25,000 serial titles annually.

In addition to being a national library, NAL is the departmental library for USDA, serving thousands of USDA employees around the world. NAL is a keystone of USDA's scientific and research activities.

As the nation's chief resource and service for agricultural information, NAL has a mission to increase the availability and use of current, accurate agricultural information for researchers, educators, policy makers, farmers, consumers, and the public at large. NAL also serves a growing international clientele.

The NAL staff numbers about 190 librarians, computer specialists, administrators, information specialists, and clerical personnel. A number of volunteers, ranging from college students to retired persons, work on various programs at the library. NAL also has an active visiting scholar program that allows scientists, researchers, professors, and students from universities worldwide to work on projects of joint interest.

NAL works closely with land-grant university libraries on programs to improve access to and maintenance of the nation's agricultural knowledge.

AGRICOLA (AGRICultural OnLine Access) is NAL's bibliographic database, providing quick access to the NAL collection. AGRICOLA contains more than 3 million citations of agricultural literature and is available on the Internet at http://www.nal.usda.gov/ag98.

The library maintains specialized information centers in areas of particular interest to the agricultural community. These centers provide a wide variety of customized services, ranging from responding to reference requests and developing reference publications to coordinating outreach activities and setting up dissemination networks. Subjects covered by the information centers include alternative farming systems, animal welfare, food and nutrition, rural information (including rural health), technology transfer, and water quality.

Highlights of the Year

Building Renovation Nears Completion

At the end of 1999 the renovation of the National Agricultural Library was nearing completion, with the Grand Reopening of NAL's public areas scheduled for

April 12, 2000. NAL began the renovation in 1998 because of a severe shortage of storage space for the NAL collection, a need for even more customer-friendly user areas, and a desire to "meet the new millennium with the most modern facilities possible." NAL is planning several events for the reopening ceremony, including a series of agriculture-related symposia and a special reception for invited guests.

NAL Expands USDA History Collection Web Site

During 1999 NAL continued to improve access to the USDA History Collection, one of the best single sources of information on the history of American agriculture. The third year of this project, which is considered a model of interagency cooperation, led to improved organization and access to materials within the collection and also allowed NAL to begin to preserve some of its brittle and deteriorating documents. Consisting of more than 800,000 pages (onion skins, mimeographs, news clippings, and original correspondence), 5,000 photographs, 8,000 books and journals, and numerous audiovisual items, this collection is described by researchers as a unique historical resource.

During the year, NAL

- Provided access to more than 50 on-site researchers and filled 205 requests for copies of individual documents, films, or photographs
- Fielded more than 475 inquiries through Web access that previously required extensive staff research and response
- Increased access by processing segments of the collection and adding item descriptions to the USDA History Collection Web site
- Preserved information contained in 900 items by creating preservation photocopies
- Completed conservation treatment for ten items
- Added comprehensive, subject-oriented presentations to the Web site on such topics as Henry Agard Wallace, Secretary of Agriculture, 1933–1940; Clinton P. Anderson, Secretary of Agriculture, 1945–1948; Charles F. Brannan, Assistant Secretary of Agriculture, 1944–1948, and Secretary of Agriculture, 1948–1953; Ezra Taft Benson, Secretary of Agriculture, 1953–1961; Orville L. Freeman, Secretary of Agriculture, 1961–1969; Paul H. Appleby, Assistant to the Secretary of Agriculture, 1933–1940, and Undersecretary of Agriculture, 1940–1944; Mordecai Ezekiel, Assistant Chief Economist for the Federal Farm Board, 1930–1933, and Economic Adviser to the Secretary of Agriculture, 1933–1939; Rexford G. Tugwell, Assistant Secretary of Agriculture, 1933–1934, and Undersecretary of Agriculture, 1934–1936; images and full text of selected documents; references and bibliographies; and links to such other resources as subject experts, associations, and other manuscript or library collections
- Provided demonstrations and instructional workshops on use of the Web site and collection to USDA staff and administrators
- Received additional funding to continue to provide access and preserve this valuable resource

NAL Developing Screwworm Eradication CD-ROM

The successful eradication of the New World screwworm is a model of the power of agricultural research and interagency cooperation and is one of America's greatest agricultural achievements. NAL's Screwworm Eradication Collection project, initiated in 1997, continued during 1999 to document the events and people who made this story such a success. NAL built the collections and continued to improve access through collection survey, preservation reformatting, and creation of a Web site at http://www.nal.usda.gov/speccoll/screwworm/.

A newly hired project manager surveyed the collections to date and identified key documents, oral histories, and films that illustrate the history of the program that made eradication possible. This story is told in a multimedia CD-ROM distributed during the first quarter of 2000. The CD-ROM sampler highlights the contents of the collections being developed at NAL, where researchers can access materials. The sampler will also demonstrate NAL's ability to vastly improve access to rare historic materials through electronic products.

Significant 1999 acquisitions included original materials from the collection of Edward F. Knipling, one of the key researchers who led the effort to develop methods to eradicate this dangerous economic pest. The collection, which measures approximately 100 linear feet, includes correspondence, bibliographies, oral histories, films, public-awareness ads, and landmark publications.

NAL is committed to the continued development of this collection and plans an improved Web site, an oral history of Dr. Knipling, and an exhibit with accompanying brochures.

Dietary Supplements Database Released

NAL and the Office of Dietary Supplements (ODS), National Institutes of Health (NIH), launched a new Internet site (http://odp.od.nih.gov/ods/databases/ibids.html) to help researchers and the general public find information on dietary supplements. The site is called IBIDS (International Bibliographic Information on Dietary Supplements), and was opened for use at a press conference at the National Press Club on January 6, 1999. The IBIDS database now contains more than 350,000 citations published from 1986 to the present from a core database built around AGRICOLA, AGRIS International, and MEDLINE.

NAL and NIH's Office of Dietary Supplements assessed the need for information on dietary supplements. Survey results from 102 respondents from major health, nutrition, medical, and botanical organizations in the United States revealed a high degree of agreement among responding organizations that there is a need for additional sources of information about dietary supplements. The greatest need was expressed for resources that summarize scientific information for both consumers and professionals on safety, efficacy, and the role of dietary supplements in disease outcomes and prevention. The methods of providing information that were ranked most highly were Web-based and phone-accessed information, followed by written information available by mail. An outline of various methods of providing information services and considerations related to these methods was also presented to ODS.

Food Safety Research Information Office Established

As a result of the Agricultural Research, Extension, and Education Reauthorization Act of 1998, the Food Safety Research Information Office (FSRIO) was established at NAL in March 1999. The office will provide to the research community and the general public information on publicly funded—and, to the extent possible, privately funded—food safety research initiatives. Following studies to define stakeholder needs and identify existing resources related to food safety research, NAL presented a prototype Web site to the ARS Administrator's Council in September 1999. The site contains information about FSRIO, links to specific food safety research databases, program and planning documents, links to other food safety-related sites, and the section "What's New." Plans for fiscal year (FY) 2000 are to hire the head of the office, officially launch the Web site, and create a new FSRIO database.

New Document Delivery Fee Schedule Proposed

NAL is charged with recovering the costs of providing interlibrary loan and document delivery services. After an extensive in-house review, the library determined that increased fees for photographic reproduction and an additional fee for material loans were necessary to continue to provide cost-effective service. NAL also analyzed user fees charged by other scientific and academic libraries during this time and used that information to propose a revision to the current document delivery fee schedule. Revised fees will not be applied to USDA patrons, federal entities, nor cooperators or institutions with which NAL has quid pro quo agreements. A proposed rule for the revised fee schedule was published for comment in the *Federal Register* on August 16, 1999. The library has put forward the final rule for this change in fees and expected the rule to be published in the *Federal Register* in the winter of 1999–2000, with implementation of the new fees to be effective in the spring of 2000.

Support Continues for Egyptian National Agricultural Library

During the year NAL's Document Delivery Services Branch worked closely with a consultant from the Association of Research Libraries (ARL) in providing information toward the design of a curriculum for document delivery librarians at the Egyptian National Agricultural Library (ENAL). The ARL consultant reviewed NAL's services and processes and developed an understanding of document delivery needs unique to the agricultural research community. This was in preparation for providing a week of instruction at ENAL. The effort proved very successful in establishing standards and policies, identifying tools, and introducing the application of new technologies to the ENAL document delivery service. One of the results of this cooperative effort is a letter of agreement between NAL and ENAL in which NAL is a primary document supplier of U.S. imprinted materials.

NAL Participates in USDA Millennium Council

During the year NAL staff served on the USDA Millennium Council, participating in a wide variety of activities celebrating accomplishments of the past and looking to the future. NAL contributed to the following events:

- NAL's Special Collections provided research support for events surrounding the naming of NAL's new Henry A. Wallace Conference Room, the week-long USDA celebration honoring George Washington Carver, and the USDA Secretary's Hall of Heroes. In addition to providing information resources, NAL was a primary source of historic photographs and exhibit materials.
- For the National Agricultural Library's contribution to George Washington Carver Week, NAL's Special Collections created an exhibit based on the Carver personnel records borrowed from the National Archives and Records Administration. The exhibit also highlighted Carver's relationship with Henry A. Wallace as well as publications written by Carver located in NAL.

NAL Expands National Microfilm Archive

During 1999 the Document Delivery Services Branch (DDSB) began Phase Two of NAL's project to establish a national microfilm archive for significant national, state, and local agricultural literature. In January the library obtained microfilm master negatives of the Land Grant Agricultural Publications Microfilming Project of the 1970s and early 1980s from Bell & Howell, and in April NAL contracted with Imagemax (formerly the Spaulding Company) to obtain the remaining microfilm master negatives from this project. The library has also received and processed the microfilm master negatives from Phase One of the current USAIN/NEH microfilming initiative from Auburn University, the University of Wisconsin–Madison, and Penn State University throughout the year.

Receipt of the microfilm from Bell & Howell and from Phase One of the USAIN/NEH project expanded the archive by approximately 1,150 reels of microfilm master negatives, and the microfilm from Imagemax will add approximately 1,900 more reels. The next step in the expansion of the archive will be the addition of the microfilm master negatives from Phase Two of the USAIN/NEH microfilming initiative in 2000. The archive is housed in preservation-quality storage at Iron Mountain National Underground Storage in Boyers, Pennsylvania.

New Contract Provides Additional Staffing Options

In September 1999 NAL implemented a five-year contract with MSTI of Fairfax, Virginia, an 8A company, to provide project-based services in a variety of labor categories, including librarian and computer programming services. This contract allows NAL to request specific projects or support from the contractor as they are needed while reducing the administrative efforts needed to put each project in place. Implementation of this contract provides a valuable tool that can be used to meet a variety of needs: short-term staffing for special projects, interim staffing during long-term absences of federal staff, special skills required for a particular project or initiative, consistent level of staffing in traditionally high-turnover clerical and service positions, or an extra level of service for which in-house resources are not available.

By creating additional options for staffing, the MSTI contract gives NAL more administrative flexibility and allows for the right type of personnel to be chosen for a specific need, whether for a full-time federal employee or short-term contract staff. This contract is already being used to support projects in all three divisions of the library. By partnering with an 8A company on this contract, NAL supports USDA's mandate to encourage small and minority-owned businesses while also providing additional flexibility in meeting its own staffing needs.

Electronic Document Delivery Grows

During the year electronic receipt of document delivery requests continued to grow, although somewhat more slowly than in previous years. Electronic requests accounted for 69 percent of all requests received this year and for 84 percent of all document delivery (non-on-site use) requests. Electronic delivery of materials rose significantly this year, up 24 percent from 1998. Forty-three percent of all materials NAL delivered in 1999 were delivered electronically.

CALS Transitions to Current Contents

In 1998, as part of the ARS Information Technology Management Initiative, an ARS-wide Research Information Needs Action Team was established to determine the information needs of ARS's research community. Based on the results of a survey directed toward ARS researchers, this team recommended that the present Current Awareness Literature Service (CALS) expand its services and reduce costs by using *Current Contents*. In 1999 CALS began offering to the ARS community Web-based access to Current Contents Connect and mediated access to *Current Contents* through the more traditional CALS service. This transition resulted in a doubling of the CALS customer base while simultaneously reducing the cost of the service.

AgNIC Fully Under Way

The Agriculture Network Information Center (AgNIC), found at http://www.agnic.org, began its first year working with an elected executive board. During the annual meeting held at NAL, 18 alliance members formed task forces to develop membership, funding opportunities, Web design, statistics standards, and a technical-requirements document for a new technical infrastructure. The prototype for a truly distributed system is in development. Over the year subject coverage expanded from six to 23 topics. NAL created a permanent position for the AgNIC coordinator, who will continue to work on expanding membership and subject coverage of the center.

Technology Updated

FY 1999 witnessed numerous advancements in the area of information technology at NAL. A new e-mail solution, based on Microsoft Exchange and Outlook 98, was implemented, as was worldwide e-mail access via a standard Web browser. Remote access to NAL's computing resources was enhanced with the establishment of dial-up access to NAL's LAN file and print server and the implementation of a toll-free access number for staff. The renovation of the first floor presented an opportunity to expand the NAL network backbone to include high-speed networking technology with Gigabit Ethernet capability.

In addition to significantly upgrading established systems, several new servers were procured and brought online in support of various initiatives. The Rural Information Center Database was migrated to an NT server, and the Electronic Media Center public NT server was established. A prototype agricultural database classification system was developed and brought online in support of the Agriculture Network Information Center. This system will migrate to an NT server in FY 2000. Unix development and production servers were purchased for the Food Safety and Research Information Center and will be set up in FY 2000.

Computer Security Enhanced

As in many other organizations, computer security has become a major concern at NAL. In FY 1998 NAL contracted for a thorough on site assessment of its security posture. Areas of specific concern included NAL's network infrastructure, server and desktop security, existing security policies and procedures, and proposed future directions to correct vulnerabilities and limit security risks. In FY 1999 NAL began putting into practice many of the resulting recommendations including the appointment of a security coordinator, the procurement of a firewall, and an executive briefing for staff to heighten security awareness. Implementation of the firewall is expected in FY 2000.

Dietary Guidelines for 2000

NAL performed literature searches to assist members of the Dietary Guidelines Advisory Committee who reviewed the 1995 edition of *Nutrition and Your Health: Dietary Guidelines for Americans*. NAL searches included uses of the Dietary Guidelines and the Food Guide Pyramid; whole grains and disease; folate and caloric intake; dairy products and fractures; food safety; and sugar substitutes and body weight. These revised guidelines, expected to be released in 2000, form the basis of federal nutrition policy and assist consumers in making food choices for a healthful diet.

Support to Food Supply Working Group

Since September 1998 NAL has been performing literature searches in support of the Food Supply Working Group (FSWG) for the Year 2000 conversion. Four different search strategies were used, including business journals, newspapers, and world reports; international trade and industry journals; Canadian newspapers; and ABI Inform, providing information related to economic factors.

Child Care Nutrition Web Site Established

NAL established the Child Care Nutrition Resource System (CCNRS) prototype Web site in September 1999 to assist day care providers who participate in the Child and Adult Care Food Program (CACFP). Recipes, resources, and information on serving safe and nutritious meals to children in day care settings are featured on this site.

AWIC Speaks at International Meetings

On June 21 the chief of NAL's Animal Welfare Information Center (AWIC) presented a paper about the AWIC program to approximately 150 participants at the ten-year anniversary of the ZEBET program. ZEBET (Zentralstelle zur Erfassung und Bewertung von Ersatz und Erganzungsmethoden zum Tierversuch) is an agency within the German federal government responsible for the development of a database on validated alternative testing methodologies for research animals. The anniversary symposium was held in Berlin June 20–21. Participants included researchers, organizations, and information providers from Europe and the United States.

Another AWIC staffer attended the Third World Congress on Alternative and Animal Use in the Life Sciences. The congress was held August 29–September 2 in Bologna, Italy. The AWIC staffer was an invited member of a panel on the topic of resources for finding alternative methodologies.

The staffer also gave a presentation on World Wide Web sources on alternative methods and participated in discussions of potential collaborations on the development of an alternatives thesaurus, developing a central information reference point, and to participate on the planning committee for the Fourth World Congress, to be held in Boston in 2002.

AWIC Workshops Helpful

To help researchers, educators, attending veterinarians, facility managers, and others meet the information requirements of the 1985 amendments to the Animal Welfare Act, AWIC continues to provide workshops at NAL on the topic of searching for alternatives to using animals in research. The workshop "Meeting the Information Requirements of the Animal Welfare Act" includes a history of animal-protective legislation in the United States, the concept of alternatives, the concepts and mechanics of database searching, hands-on experience in database searching, and a discussion of participants' results. In 1999 about 65 people attended three workshops. There has been an increased interest by outside organizations to have an abbreviated version of the workshop conducted at facilities. During the year 11 shortened versions of the workshop were conducted at other locations.

As a result of the need for those regulated under the Animal Welfare Act to have access to the AWIC workshop "Meeting the Information Requirements of the Animal Welfare Act," AWIC staff continues to develop materials for the online tutorial. AWIC is receiving financial and other resource support for the project from the Johns Hopkins Center for Alternatives to Animal Testing, the Office for the Protection from Research Risks at the National Institutes of Health (NIH), the Veterans Administration, and the American Association for Laboratory Animal Science. The project was to be completed early in FY 2000.

In 1988 USDA, NAL, and the NIH Office for the Protection from Research Risks (OPRR) were directed by Congress to provide information on environmental enrichment for nonhuman primates. Because it has been several years since the first joint publication on the topic was published, there has been a dramatic increase in information published on the topic. Therefore, it was decided to update the older publication. AWIC received $5,000 from OPRR for this project. The document *Environmental Enrichment for Nonhuman Primates Resource Guide, January 1992–February 1999* (AWIC Resource Series No. 5) is much expanded and includes U.S. laws and regulations, organizations and Web sites, primate centers and animal colonies, relevant listservs, product suppliers, audio-visuals, journals and newsletters, and an updated bibliography on the topic.

In 1999 AWIC responded to more than 1,900 reference requests, and distributed more than 23,400 publications.

GAO Requests NAL Help

AWIC was contacted by staff from the U.S. General Accounting Office (GAO), which was involved in a project to evaluate the alternatives for use of animals in research for Department of Defense Protocols. GAO contracted with AWIC to do an alternatives search for 24 protocols. The results were to be evaluated by a set of outside experts and reported to GAO. The report *DOD Animal Research: Controls on Animal Use Are Generally Effective, but Improvements Are Needed* resulted from the project. The role of AWIC in providing "alternative searches" is referenced a number of times (pages 8, 17, 24, and 27) in the text, scope, and methodologies.

NAL Serves on Animal Care Committee

At the request of USDA's Animal and Plant Health Inspection Service, staff from AWIC served on the development committee to write a policy document on environmental enrichment strategies for nonhuman primates. Other AWIC staff contributed to the editing of the document. The policy was published for public comment in the *Federal Register* (Vol. 64, No. 135, July 15, 1999/ Proposed Rules; pp. 38,145–50) as the *Final Report on Environmental Enhancement to Promote the Psychological Well-Being of Nonhuman Primates*. After review of the 31,000 comments, there will be revisions to the original. When published in final form, it will be used by licensed or registered facilities that use nonhuman primates.

NAL Publications Translated into Spanish

Publications from AWIC were translated into Spanish through a cooperative program with the staff at the Universidad Autonoma de Nuevo Leon in Mexico. The publications included *Selected Databases for Biomedical, Pharmaceutical, Veterinary, and Animal Science Resources* and *Selected Web Sites for Biomedical, Pharmaceutical, Veterinary, and Animal Science Resources*. The selected Web sites publication has been coded into HTML and is currently available on the AWIC Web site. The coding of the selected database document was nearing completion at the end of 1999, and it was to be up on the AWIC site early in 2000.

A translation of the second edition of *Essentials for Animal Research: A Primer for Research Personnel* by B. T. Bennett, M. J. Brown, and J. C. Schofield is in process and should be received by AWIC in 2000.

Desire for Water Quality Information Is High

NAL's Water Quality Information Center (WQIC) continued to manage the popular Internet mailing list Enviro-News, which provides timely environmental news to about 500 subscribers. Subscribers receive notices of upcoming conferences and seminars, requests for proposals, calls for papers, announcements of funding and employment opportunities, and information about new Web services.

WQIC's Pfiesteria Web page was listed as one of five federal sources of information about Pfiesteria in the Environmental Protection Agency publication *What You Should Know About Pfiesteria piscicida*.

NAL's Cataloging Branch and Water Quality Information Center began collaborating on a project to ensure that freely available online publications covering water and agriculture are identified and added to AGRICOLA. The goal is to make it easier for people to access these publications, which are scattered across many different Web sites. More than 250 publications have been added thus far.

WQIC hosted a session on "Observations on Managing an Internet Mailing List: The Enviro-News Experience" at the Agricultural Communicators in Education/National Extension Technology Conference held in Knoxville, Tennessee, in June. Staff from the Water Quality Information Center presented the paper "Electronic Sources of Water Resources Information from the National Agricultural Library" at the American Society of Agricultural Engineers (ASAE) Annual International Meeting in Toronto in July. The paper is available in the conference proceedings on CD-ROM and in hard copy.

Developed by WQIC several years ago and updated continually, the electronic publication "Water Resources Discussion Lists" was cited as a "comprehensive list of water-related listservers" in an article on water and the Internet that appeared in the journal *Water International* (Vol. 24, No. 2).

Responding to emerging and high-interest issues, WQIC created bibliographies on aging dams, citizen participation and water quality, drought and water allocation, phytoremediation, risk assessment and communication, and source water protection.

RIC Web Sites Recognized

The Web site of NAL's Rural Information Center (RIC) received a Links2Go Key Resource Award in the rural development area, one of 19 Web sites to be so honored. In addition, the Web site of the Rural Information Center Health Service, maintained by RIC, was "accepted into the Healthlinkstory, one of the most comprehensive online directories available specifically for the use of health care professionals." The RICHS Web site was also chosen as HMS Beagle's "Web Pick of the Day." (HMS Beagle is a fee-based scientific "Webzine" with daily biological and medical articles, reports, newsgroups, and Web sites and links.)

Interagency Agreement Leads to Resource Guide

An interagency agreement between RIC and the U.S. Forest Service resulted in RIC preparing an Arizona resource guide comprised of local, state, and federal resources for economic and community development, tourism, historic preservation, environmental and natural resources, and land stewardship. The resource guide was provided to Forest Service staff at the six national forests in Arizona.

NAL Supports Small Farms

NAL's Alternative Farming Systems Information Center (AFSIC) and the Sustainable Agriculture Network (SAN) participated in USDA's Small Farms Initiative through attendance, participation, and/or exhibits at several conferences. AFSIC worked closely with the American Farmland Trust (AFT) and the Natural Resource Conservation Service (NRCS). At the National Small Farm Conference in St. Louis and the National Small Farm Trade Show and Conference in Columbia, Missouri, AFSIC worked and jointly exhibited with the Agricultural Research Service, NAL's parent agency.

The revised and greatly expanded edition of *Sustainable Agriculture: Definitions and Terms* (SRB 99-02) was published with small-scale farmers in mind and was widely circulated at the conferences listed above. It is available in print, and electronically at http://www.nal.usda.gov/afsic/AFSIC_pubs/srb9902.htm. SAN published "Tip Sheets for Small Farms," available at http://www.sare.org/san/htdocs/pubs/. AFSIC staff also participated in meetings related to the ARS Organic Farming Initiative, working with the Organic Farming Research Foundation (OFRF) on issues affecting small farms.

SAN, with offices located within AFSIC, published the following in 1999, all of which are available in hard copy and electronically at http://www.sare.org/san/htdocs/pubs/: *How to Conduct Research on Your Farm or Ranch, Diversify Crops to Boost Profits and Stewardship, Marketing Strategies for Farmers and Ranchers*, and *Tip Sheets for Small Farms*.

SAN is the outreach and information arm of the USDA's Sustainable Agriculture Research and Education (SARE) program. SAN and SARE are working on two fronts to evaluate available information in sustainable agriculture and, subsequently, to identify gaps in the research and information base. Staff has been hired by the national SARE office to read and evaluate SARE project reports. In addition, SAN has contracted with Appropriate Technology Transfer for Rural Areas (ATTRA) to survey ATTRA's 15 information specialists and search the sustainable-agriculture literature to assess gaps in the area of farmer-ready publications. SAN and SARE staff will consult regularly on these projects over the coming months.

Educational and Training Opportunities in Sustainable Agriculture—a directory of farms, institutions, and organizations offering internships, academic programs, or outreach activities that promote ideas and techniques for sustainable agriculture—has been compiled and published annually by AFSIC for the past 11 years. This year AFSIC is cooperating with ATTRA to avoid duplication of effort and to make more effective use of resources. ATTRA has assumed responsibility for all internship or apprenticeship listings while AFSIC will continue to survey and list academic institutions and organizations involved in sustainable agriculture.

National Library of Medicine

8600 Rockville Pike, Bethesda, MD 20894
301-496-6308, 888-346-3656, fax 301-496-4450
E-mail publicinfo@nlm.nih.gov
World Wide Web http://www.nlm.nih.gov

Robert Mehnert

Public Information Officer

The National Library of Medicine (NLM), a part of the Department of Health and Human Services' National Institutes of Health in Bethesda, Maryland, is the world's largest library of the health sciences. NLM has two buildings with 420,000 total square feet. The older building (1962) houses the collection, public reading rooms, exhibition hall, and library staff and administrative offices. The adjacent 10-story Lister Hill Center Building (1980) contains the main computer room, auditorium, audiovisual facility, offices, and research/demonstration laboratories.

Services for the Public

Breaking with more than a century of tradition and practice, the NLM Board of Regents, at its May 1999 meeting, formally affirmed that NLM should seek to serve the general public as well as the health professions. Although NLM has never restricted access to its collections and databases, such factors as search fees, limited access to computers and telecommunications, and the technical nature of much of the information in NLM databases have combined to discourage their use by the general public and the libraries that serve them.

That situation has recently changed as a result of the spectacular growth of the Internet and the World Wide Web and the widespread acceptance of NLM's free MEDLINE service with its two access systems, Internet Grateful Med and PubMed. MEDLINE, which covers the literature from 1966 to the present, logged its 10 millionth journal citation on July 10, 1999. The references and abstracts are taken from almost 4,300 biomedical journals published around the world. Usage of MEDLINE has skyrocketed: from 7 million searches in the last pre-Web year (1997) to a rate of 220 million searches annually by the end of 1999. NLM estimates that about 30 percent of this searching is by consumers.

Most of NLM's databases were designed for use by librarians, researchers, and health professionals, and not with the general public in mind. A consumer who enters MEDLINE and types in "breast cancer," for example, is overwhelmed with an enormous number of hits—more than 100,000—many of them on research-related aspects of the disease outside the interest of the average person. Thus, because millions of ordinary Web users were searching MEDLINE for personal health information, NLM introduced a new, more user-friendly service, MEDLINE*plus*, at the end of 1998. MEDLINE*plus* has evolved rapidly and now has extensive information on 400 health topics. The source of most of the information is the National Institutes of Health (NIH), other federal agencies, universities, professional associations, and other organizations that make high-quality consumer health information freely available on the World Wide Web. With help from members of the National Network of Libraries of Medicine (NN/LM) across the country, NLM information specialists have selected and organized this information and extensively cross-linked it.

In addition to providing full-text information on diseases and wellness issues, MEDLINE*plus* also connects the Web user to dictionaries, individual health practitioners, hospitals, clearinghouses, newsletters, databases, and libraries that provide consumer health information. One popular feature of MEDLINE*plus* is the "prepackaged" MEDLINE searches on health topics. These searches have been formulated to find recent articles (in journals that are likely to be available) that will be of interest to the general public. For example, a search might retrieve review articles and practice guidelines about diagnosing and treating a particular disease. Early in 2000 NLM plans to add MEDLINE*plus* links to a medical encyclopedia and to extensive drug information written for the general public.

In August 1999 NLM introduced a radically redesigned home page for its Web services (http://www.nlm.nih.gov). It is only the second major redesign in the six-year history of the library's Web site. The change was prompted in part by the realization that many users expected to be steered to full-text medical information that would help them with their health questions. The new home page does that by placing a Health Information heading first among five major elements and also presenting a separate, prominent link to MEDLINE*plus*. The other four headings are Library Services (catalogs, publications), Research Programs (medical informatics, computational molecular biology), New and Noteworthy (announcements), and General Information (staff listing, help for visitors).

New Information Services

A new Web-based public catalog was installed by NLM in 1999. Known as LOCATOR*plus*, it allows anyone with Internet access to find out what books, journals, audiovisuals, manuscripts, and other items are cataloged in the library's collections. In many cases, NLM is the only library in the United States to own some of the materials. LOCATOR*plus*, updated daily, is searchable by author, medical subject heading (MeSH), title, conference name, keyword, and other fields. Even information about materials on order but not yet received is available. Many of the records also include hot links to online journals. LOCATOR*plus* brings to the public much information formerly available only to NLM staff.

With the success of Web-based MEDLINE searching and the introduction of LOCATOR*plus*, NLM announced the cessation of command-language access to its services as of September 30, 1999. On that date, all DOS, Windows, and Macintosh versions of Grateful Med, used for more than a decade to search MEDLINE, stopped working. ELHILL, the library's legacy computer retrieval system workhorse, has been put to pasture after 35 years.

Another new Web-based service, ClinicalTrials.Gov, was developed by the library in 1999 and will be released early in 2000. The Food and Drug Administration Modernization Act of 1997 required the government to establish a registry for both federally and privately funded clinical trials of experimental treatments for serious or life-threatening diseases or conditions. The goal of the program is to develop an information system that provides patients, families, and members of the public easy access to information about clinical research studies. Working with NIH, NLM developed ClinicalTrials.Gov, which includes a statement of purpose for each clinical research study, together with the recruiting status, the criteria for patient participation in the trial, the location of the trial, and specific contact information. Later versions will include clinical trials data from other federal agencies and private industry.

Communications Research and Collaboration

The two very large datasets of anatomical data represented by the Visible Human Male and Visible Human Female are being used (without charge) by 1,240 licensees in 41 countries, and at four mirror sites in Asia and Europe. Current uses of these datasets include the following: "surgical simulators" that let doctors rehearse delicate medical procedures; "recyclable cadavers" to help medical students learn about anatomy; and "virtual prototyping," which creates perfectly fitted hip and knee replacements. The Visible Human Project is now entering a new phase of its evolution as it seeks to create a public segmentation and registration software tool kit as a foundation for future medical research. The intent is to amplify the investment being made through the Visible Human Project and future programs for medical image analysis by reducing the reinvention of basic algorithms. Another aspect of this evolution is the collaborative project with other NIH institutes to develop a super-detailed atlas of the head and neck. The application of cutting-edge technologies will allow "fly-through" anatomic relationships (for example, traveling down the optic nerve and viewing the ophthalmic artery and its tributaries).

Biomedical science was profoundly affected by the introduction of desktop computing in the mid-1980s and, more recently, by the Internet and World Wide Web, which effectively tie together millions of computers around the world. To ensure that the Internet will continue to support the health sciences, NLM is a strong supporter of the Next Generation Internet (NGI), a partnership among industry, academia, and government agencies that seeks to provide affordable, secure information delivery at rates thousands of times faster than today. Advanced medical imaging (as exemplified by the Visible Human Project) requires more bandwidth than is currently available. For some health applications, the quality of Internet service is the limiting factor. Other applications require a guaranteed level of service (for example no data loss, or assured privacy protection) that today's Internet cannot provide. NLM is funding a series of projects in three phases to encourage the development of innovative medical test-bed projects that demonstrate the capabilities of NGI. Twenty-four Phase I awards were made in 1998. Eight Phase II awards were issued in 1999 in such areas as advanced medical imaging, patient-controlled personal medical records systems, and televideo applications in a nursing home (summaries are on NLM's Web site). A future Phase III will raise the successful Phase II test-bed projects to the regional or national level.

NLM has in place a number of collaborative programs that in recent years have been directed toward remedying the disparity in health opportunities experienced by certain segments of the American population. One of these programs deals with toxic waste sites and other environmental and occupational hazards that are much more likely to occur near homes in poor neighborhoods. The library has a program to train health professionals, community leaders, and others in minority neighborhoods to use databases of information about hazardous waste. NLM provides minority schools with state-of-the-art equipment, software, and free online access to computerized information sources, including NLM's own toxicology and environmental health information databases. Other federal agencies have joined with NLM, and the project has grown from nine participating minority institutions to more than 60. Similarly, the library has been working closely with institutions that serve minority populations to encourage the use of NLM information services relating to HIV/AIDS, including the databases AIDSLINE (references and abstracts), AIDSTRIALS (clinical trials), AIDSDRUGS (drugs being tested), and DIRLINE (a list of organizations that provide health information to the public).

Another collaborative program in which the library participates is the Multilateral Initiative on Malaria Research. Scientists in many developing countries are unable to communicate in a timely manner, access biomedical information resources and databases, or collaborate on proposal preparation and research implementation with colleagues in industrialized countries. The result is poor coordination and monitoring of research, redundancy of effort, and a growing disparity in research productivity. In the Multilateral Initiative on Malaria Research project, the library is supporting remote malaria research sites in Mali, Kenya, Cameroon, Ghana, and Tanzania. Since Internet connections can effectively carry voice, data, and video image transmissions, the library is helping to transmit such information to scientists in those countries.

Genetic Medicine

Genetic information encompasses DNA and protein sequence data, genome mapping data, three-dimensional macromolecular structure data, and the extensive interplay among this fundamental information to discover the function of genes in humans and the tens of thousands of other organisms that are being studied at a molecular level. NLM's National Center for Biotechnology Information (NCBI) has major programs to collect, analyze, and distribute a wide range of molecular biology data related to genomic analysis. NCBI manages the GenBank database, which, on November 17, 1999, received its billionth "base pair" of human genetic information. The center also develops integrated approaches to data access, visualization, and analysis, and conducts basic research in bioinformatics and computational molecular biology. The steady increase in data generated by the molecular biology research community necessitates an expansion in databases, computational resources, development of analytical tools, and research.

NCBI is the focus of activity related to the creation of PubMed Central, a Web-based repository that is being established to provide barrier-free access to primary reports in the life sciences. It is viewed as the initial site in an international system. The core concept of the proposal is to remove the barriers of access to the scientific literature and to make it available worldwide to the scholarly community at the least cost. PubMed Central is so named because of its integration with the existing PubMed retrieval system that was developed by NCBI for biomedical literature databases. The new system, to be introduced early in 2000, will archive, organize, and distribute peer-reviewed reports from journals, as well as reports that have been screened but not formally peer reviewed.

Basic Library Services

Within the walls of NLM is the world's largest collection of published knowledge in the biomedical sciences. More than 22,000 serial publications are received regularly, and hundreds of pieces of health information materials in many formats arrive daily. Increasingly, this information is in digital form, and NLM, as a national library responsible for preserving the scholarly record of biomedicine, is working with the Library of Congress and the National Agricultural Library to develop a strategy for selecting, organizing, and ensuring permanent access to digital information. Regardless of the format in which the materials are received, ensuring their availability for future generations remains the library's highest priority.

One of the most important factors in the widespread acceptance and use of NLM's information services is the role played by the National Network of Libraries of Medicine (NN/LM). NLM funds the network through eight Regional Medical Libraries, each responsible for a geographic area of the country. Those institutions, together with 140 large academic health science libraries and more than 4,000 hospital libraries and other libraries in the network, provide crucial information services to scientists, health professionals, and, increasingly, the public. More than 3 million requests for journal articles flow through the network each year.

To encourage the widest possible use of the library's information products and services, NLM engages in a variety of outreach activities that involve NN/LM. One of these activities, just completed, is a pilot project to see if public libraries, with assistance, could provide quality health information to their patrons. This project, which involved 40 community library systems, was supported with training and expert advice provided by network members. MEDLINE and MEDLINE*plus* naturally figured prominently in this project. Drawing on the lessons learned in working with the public libraries, early in 2000 NLM will make several dozen "outreach awards" to support NN/LM institutions that form partnerships with public libraries, health professional associations, public health departments, and community-based organizations.

In fiscal year 1999 NLM received and processed 138,000 modern books, serial issues, audiovisuals, and computer-based materials. Preservation microfilming was done for 5,568 volumes (2.8 million pages). The number of journals indexed for MEDLINE is 4,261.

The director of the library is Donald A. B. Lindberg, M.D. NLM is guided in matters of policy by a Board of Regents consisting of 10 appointed and 11 ex officio members. Appointed in 1999 were Alison Bunting, Associate University Librarian for Science at UCLA, and Joseph Newhouse, Director of the Harvard University Division of Health Policy Research and Education. At the board's meeting in September 1999, former Chair Tenley Albright presented to NLM the Hammer Award. The award, given by the vice president of the United States, recognizes systems innovation and improvements made to the library's information services under the Clinton administration's Systems Reinvention Initiative.

Table 1 / Selected NLM Statistics*

Library Operation	Volume
Collection (book and nonbook)	5,785,000
Items cataloged	14,400
Serial titles received	22,400
Articles indexed for MEDLINE	435,000
Circulation requests processed	752,000
For interlibrary loanx	397,000
For on-site users	355,000
Computerized searches (all databases)	191,000,000
Budget authority	$181,400,000
Full-time staff	601

*For the year ending September 30, 1999

Educational Resources Information Center

ERIC Processing and Reference Facility
Computer Sciences Corporation
4483-A Forbes Blvd.
Lanham, MD 20706
301-552-4200, 800-799-3742, fax 301-552-4700
E-mail ericfac@inet.ed.gov
World Wide Web http://ericfac.piccard.csc.com

Ted Brandhorst

Director

ERIC Program Office

Budget

The ERIC Program Office was level-funded for fiscal year 2000 at $10,000,000. This funding must be allocated to support 16 subject-oriented Clearinghouses, three Support Contractors, and ERIC's GPO printing budget, which collectively do the work of ERIC. The competing demands of this family of 20 contractors for limited funds—coupled with the lack of targeted funding for R&D efforts, major system improvement initiatives, or independent third-party evaluation of the system—continues to take its toll on an otherwise remarkably resilient information system.

Clearinghouses

The 16 regular ERIC Clearinghouses completed their first year in 1999 under their new performance-based type of contracts. Because of the interactive nature of the ERIC system, evaluation of one component's performance can be complex if that performance is materially affected by the performance of another component. This can lead to the occasional need for exceptions or dispensations in the evaluation process (which happened during 1999).

At the end of 1999, in addition to the 16 regular Clearinghouses, there were a total of 12 "Adjunct Clearinghouses" and one "Affiliate Clearinghouse." In an adjunct arrangement, an organization having a special subject interest assists ERIC in covering the literature of that subject by contributing documents, books, and articles to the ERIC Clearinghouse with which they are associated at no cost to ERIC. An affiliate is an organization that has an independent existence as an information center in a particular area, that performs many of the same functions as ERIC, and that follows ERIC policies and procedures in performing these functions.

This decentralized nature of the ERIC system can be a source of diversity and strength at the same time that it poses operational problems of coordination and duplication. Of some concern, however, is the fact that it can also be a source of potential confusion for the user community, which may have difficulty distinguishing ERIC Clearinghouses, ERIC Adjunct Clearinghouses, ERIC Affiliate Clearinghouses, ERIC Support Contractors, the ERIC Program Office, and ERIC special projects (like "AskERIC") from one another.

Two new Adjunct Clearinghouses joined the ERIC system during 1999:

- Adjunct ERIC Clearinghouse on School Counseling Services (sponsored by the University of North Texas, College of Education, Department of Counseling, Development, and Higher Education; adjunct to the ERIC Clearinghouse on Counseling and Student Services)
- Adjunct ERIC Clearinghouse for Postsecondary Education and the Internet (sponsored by the University of Virginia, Curry School of Education; adjunct to the ERIC Clearinghouse on Higher Education)

Year 2000 Problem

Most of ERIC's Y2K remedial actions actually took place during 1998. Throughout 1999, however, there were increased requests from the Department of Education for reports, evaluations, tests, and assurances that the various fixes were in place and operational. All ERIC components experienced these requests. By the end of the year, all components were reporting themselves as compliant, and no problems were experienced at the 1999–2000 cross-over.

ERIC Database Size and Growth

The ERIC database consists of two files, one corresponding to the monthly abstract journal *Resources in Education* (*RIE*) and one corresponding to the monthly *Current Index to Journals in Education* (*CIJE*). *RIE* announces education-related documents and books, each with an accession number beginning ED (for educational document). *CIJE* announces education-related journal articles, each with an accession number beginning EJ (for educational journal).

Document records include a full abstract and are approximately 1,800 characters long on average. Journal article records include a brief annotation and are approximately 650 characters long on average.

Through the December 1999 issue of *RIE*, the ERIC database includes 425,608 records for documents. Through the December 1999 issue of *CIJE*, ERIC includes 587,046 records for journal articles. The grand total was 1,012,654 bibliographic records.

Approximately 12,000 document records and 20,000 article records are added annually, for a total of 32,000 records per year. Overall, the ERIC database through 1999 is approximately 1,350 million bytes (1.35 gigabytes) in size and is growing at a rate of around 35 million bytes per year.

(In September 1999, after approximately 35 years of operation, ERIC processed its millionth database record—a document entitled "Excellence in English in Middle and High School: How Teachers' Professional Lives Support Student Achievement" by Judith A. Langer—under a grant from the U.S. Department of Education. The document is identified in ERIC as ED 429 295.)

Number of Records

File	1966–1998	1999	Total
Resources in Education (RIE)	414,563	11,045	425,608
Current Index to Journals in Education (CIJE)	565,911	21,135	587,046
ERIC Database Total	980,474	32,180	1,012,654

ERIC Annual Report, 1999

The *ERIC Annual Report* dated 1999 and covering 1998–1999 was published in August 1999 by ACCESS ERIC and was announced in the January 2000 issue of *RIE* as IR 019 822. (The following summary, with minor changes, has been extracted from ACCESS ERIC's *Interchange* newsletter for Fall 1999):

According to Blane Dessy, Executive Director of the National Library of Education, which oversees ERIC, "ERIC is well on the way to becoming a 'national union catalog' of education resources—the main venue for organizing, linking, describing, and making accessible all key education resources in all formats. Projects such as the Gateway to Educational Materials and the National Parent Information Network help us to serve teachers and parents better than ever by providing access to innovative lesson plans and parenting information."

ERIC has utilized the Internet as a means of increasing access to information and has made rapid progress in providing content-rich Web sites, virtual libraries, full-text access to many resources, and "smart" search engines to support productive database searching. Keith Stubbs, Director of ERIC [succeeded by Luna Levinson in late December 1999], reports that ERIC's new challenges include processing information faster and making it available sooner. "ERIC users have high expectations, and we're working hard to live up to them," he said. "We continually seek customer feedback to let us know how we're doing." ERIC plans to commission a systemwide evaluation of its products and services in the near future.

The annual report includes highlights, an overview of products and services, customer survey results, an ERIC system directory, a budget overview, and future directions. For a free copy, call ACCESS ERIC at 800-LET-ERIC (538-3742), e-mail accesseric@accesseric.org, or go to http://www.accesseric.org/resources/annual99/ on the Web.

ERIC Annual Report Highlights

ERIC is pleased to report on progress toward meeting the ambitious goals we set for ourselves five years ago. These goals are:

1 Easy, affordable access to ERIC bibliographic and full-text resources from every school, library, household, and point of educational decision making.

- Anyone can reach ERIC through a toll-free phone call or via the Internet and will receive free, high-quality information from subject experts.
- The ERIC Document Reproduction Service (EDRS) offers E*Subscribe, which gives library patrons access to electronic copies of ERIC documents through their library's subscription.
- Users who want unlimited access to the ERIC database can search it on the Internet or get an affordable CD-ROM from the ERIC Processing and Reference Facility.
- Free subscriptions to the *ERIC Review* are available, and nearly 1,000 new subscribers signed up in the past year.

2 Expansion of ERIC's database and services to make useful information available to all categories of users.

- ERIC has successfully broadened its audience to include teachers and students. In 1998 fully 25 percent of the people who contacted ERIC Clearinghouses were elementary and secondary faculty and students; another 25 percent were postsecondary faculty and students.

- ERIC welcomed two new Adjunct Clearinghouses, extending its databases coverage and dissemination of materials in the targeted subject areas of school counseling and post-secondary education.
- To support the diverse audience they serve, ERIC Clearinghouses maintain more than 80 electronic discussion groups serving more than 37,000 education policymakers, administrators, teachers, parents, and library/media specialists.
- Users interested in the construction, renovation, and maintenance of schools can now find more information on these topics in the ERIC database and on the Web through ERIC's Affiliate Clearinghouse the National Clearinghouse for Educational Facilities.

3 Expansion of the ERIC information-synthesizing function to include more and a greater variety of publications and to utilize a greater variety of dissemination methods.

- Clearinghouses have expanded their print and electronic publication formats to include newsletters, journal columns and articles, trends and issues alerts, frequently asked questions (FAQs), and practice application briefs.
- The ERIC Clearinghouse on Elementary and Early Childhood Education has recently introduced a refereed electronic journal.
- The Gateway to Educational Materials (GEM) special project now offers teachers full text of more than 6,000 lesson plans and other materials for classroom use from 90 organizations.
- ERIC's 650 "partner" organizations provide links to ERIC from their Web sites and disseminate ERIC products to their constituents and members.

4 Delivery of documents in a variety of full-text electronic formats, as well as in microfiche and paper forms.

- Customers can now get electronic full-text copies of approximately 80 percent of the ERIC documents from 1995 to the present. Three commercial ERIC database search engines offer access to EDRS's store of electronic copies.
- Two Clearinghouses are providing full-text copies of their publications on CD-ROMs.
- To meet the need of users with limited access to technology, ERIC continues to provide free access to ERIC documents on microfiche at more than 1,000 institutions in 26 countries.
- In addition to its more than 1,000 microfiche subscribers, EDRS also filled individual on-demand orders for 35,877 copies of documents in 1998.

5 Further development of ERIC access on the Internet and in other formats, including the development of virtual libraries and World Wide Web sites.

- All ERIC Clearinghouses maintain Web sites with content-rich, full-text resources in their subject areas. Many also offer virtual libraries—full-text collections of online resources from sources within and outside of ERIC grouped around subtopics within their scope areas.
- Users who visit the ERIC systemwide Web site can now search a topic across all ERIC Web sites in one easy step, and more than 600 other Web sites provide links to the main ERIC site.
- To help users navigate the Web, the ERIC Clearinghouse on Higher Education and several other Clearinghouses redesigned and expanded their Web sites to provide tutorials that help lead users to valuable resources beyond ERIC.

ERIC by the Numbers

- ERIC users will find that the database provides coverage of approximately 1,000 education-related journals in addition to documents produced by more than 2,100 leading education organizations (universities, research centers, professional organizations, and federal and state agencies) with which ERIC has standing acquisitions arrangements.

- The ERIC database is made available through several Internet search engines; five commercial online vendors; five CD-ROM vendors; many locally mounted systems, such as online public access catalogs at universities; and the print indexes *Resources in Education (RIE)* and *Current Index to Journals in Education (CIJE)*. More than 1,000 institutions in 26 countries provide on-site access to the ERIC database and the microfiche collection of full-text ERIC documents.

- The National Parent Information Network (NPIN) Web site was visited 651,016 times in 1998.

- The ERIC Clearinghouses produced more than 660 information products in 1998, including newsletters, journal columns, journal articles, ERIC Digests, books, bibliographies, and other formats.

- ERIC components engaged in collaborative outreach, training, publication, and user service efforts with 650 "partner" organizations.

- ERIC components hosted more than 80 listservs having a total of more than 37,000 subscribers.

- In 1998 ERIC staff members responded to 180,978 user requests (19,000 more than in 1997), including 50,729 toll-free calls, 89,036 e-mail requests (including 44,460 received through AskERIC, the ERIC system's question-answering service), 34,733 letters, and 6,480 visitors.

- ERIC personnel went on the road to meet current and potential users by participating in more than 470 education-related meetings, conferences, and workshops; giving more than 230 presentations; and staffing exhibits at more than 80 major conferences.

ERIC Processing and Reference Facility

The ERIC Facility is the centralized database manager for the ERIC system. The main ERIC bibliographic database is maintained by the Facility and is distributed by the Facility to online and CD-ROM vendors and interested academic institutions around the world.

The ERIC Facility contract was competed during the last quarter of 1999 and in January 2000 was awarded to Computer Sciences Corporation (CSC). The principal new system required by the new contract is an online, interactive data entry system centered at the Facility and to be used by the dispersed ERIC Clearinghouses for the expeditious creation of ERIC database records. The system will use a full complement of ERIC authority files and will be designed to provide prompts, many computerized editorial data checks, pull-down menus, and online help in the form of access to the relevant text of the *ERIC Processing Manual*.

ERIC Document Reproduction Service

The ERIC Document Reproduction Service (EDRS) is the document-delivery arm of ERIC and handles all subscriptions for ERIC microfiche and on-demand requests for reproduced paper copy or microfiche. The ERIC microfiche collection (about 10,000 titles annually on 15,000 fiche cards) is available for approximately $2,600 annually. The table below presents prices in effect for the period January 1–December 31, 2000.

Product	Year 2000 Prices
Microfiche	
Monthly subscription (price/fiche)	$ 0.1507 (Silver)
	$ 0.3084 (Diazo)
Back collections (1966–previous month) (price/fiche)	$ 0.1774
Clearinghouse collections (price/fiche)	$ 0.3246
On-demand Documents, per title	
Microfiche (MF) up to 5 fiche (5 fiche = 480 pages)	$ 1.51
Each additional fiche (up to 96 pages)	$ 0.25
Reproduced Paper Copies (PC)	
First 1–25 pages	$ 4.46
Each additional 25–page increment (or part thereof)	$ 4.46
Electronic Page Images	
Base price per electronic document	$ 3.60
Price per page	$ 0.16
Example: A 15-page document costs $6.00 ($3.60 + $2.40)	
1999 Cumulative Indexes (on Microfiche)	
Subject, Author, Title, Institution, Descriptor, and Identifier Indexes	$ 75.00

In response to the growing need for more immediate access to ERIC materials, EDRS began developing a new digital document subscription service for libraries (called E*Subscribe) in 1998. Libraries and other institutions can now subscribe to the ERIC collection of education-related documents in electronic format. The subscription service offers access to the ERIC document database and electronic document images from 1995 forward. Features of the new service include:

- Unrestricted database searching (1966 through the current *Resources in Education* issue)
- Electronic document delivery in Adobe PDF
- Ordering capability for documents not available electronically
- Choices of access mode including user name and password and/or IP address
- A variety of collection options to suit all information needs and budgets
- Access to the subscription service through SilverPlatter's WebSPIRS 4.0 and Ovid Online (E*Subscribe customers only)

E*Subscribe customers may download copyright-cleared ERIC documents from 1996 forward (added charges apply for access to documents released prior to 1996). Visit the EDRS Web site for more information (http://edrs.com).

ACCESS ERIC

ACCESS ERIC is responsible for systemwide outreach, marketing, publicity, and promotion for the ERIC system.

Special outreach activities for 1999 included the distribution of approximately 3,000 copies of *Rising Expectations: A Framework for ERIC's Future in the National Library of Education* to libraries and other education-related organizations with a request for feedback on future priorities for ERIC. ACCESS ERIC also produced an ERIC slide show that includes tips on searching the ERIC database and an overview of ERIC products and services. The slide show, designed both for individual use and in training situations, can be viewed on the ERIC Web site (http://www.accesseric.org/resources/eric_slides.html) or downloaded as a PowerPoint presentation.

One major outreach activity is staffing exhibits and giving presentations on ERIC at education and library conferences. In 1999 ACCESS ERIC exhibited at conferences of the American Library Association, Association for Supervision and Curriculum Development, and the National School Boards Association. A presentation was given (with copresenters from the ERIC Facility and EDRS) at the Government Printing Office for 50 new Federal Depository Library librarians.

ACCESS ERIC works closely with the ERIC Clearinghouses to produce the *ERIC Review*, a free journal on current education issues. One recent issue was produced in collaboration with the ERIC Clearinghouse on Science, Mathematics, and Environmental Education and focused on K–8 science and mathematics instruction. The Clearinghouses also provide material for a series of Parent Brochures, which included the following titles in 1999: *Getting Online: A Friendly Guide for Parents, Students, and Teachers; Which Is the Right College Path for Me?; What Are Charter Schools?; How Can We Prevent Violence in Our Schools?; How Can We Help Transform Our Schools Into Community Learning Centers?* (in process); and *What Do Parents Need to Know About Information Literacy?* (in process).

ACCESS ERIC maintains the ERIC systemwide Web site (http://www. accesseric.org), which provides links to all ERIC-sponsored sites as well as full-text copies of Parent Brochures, the *ERIC Review, All About ERIC*, and other systemwide materials. In 1999 the ERICNews listserv provided bimonthly updates of new ERIC publications and services to more than 1,600 subscribers.

ACCESS ERIC continues to produce a number of information and referral databases and publications including the *Catalog of ERIC Clearinghouse Publications 1999*, the *ERIC Directory of Education-Related Information Centers 1998*, the *Directory of ERIC Resource Collections 1999*, and the 1999 *ERIC Calendar of Education-Related Conferences*. In 1999 an online Conference Calendar Data Collection Form was created to enable organizations to submit their conference information electronically.

ACCESS ERIC is also maintaining the database for the *Education Resource Organizations Directory (EROD)*, available on the Department of Education's Web site (http://www.ed.gov/Programs/EROD/). This directory includes information on more than 2,400 national, regional, and state organizations and is constantly being updated and expanded. Education libraries and curriculum materials centers were added to EROD in 1999.

Selected ERIC Special Projects

AskERIC

AskERIC (http://www.askeric.org) began in September 1992. AskERIC is a personalized, Internet-based service providing education information to teachers, librarians, counselors, administrators, parents, and others interested in education information. AskERIC consists of an Internet/e-mail question-answering service and an Internet Web site portal containing a "virtual library" of education information resources.

Gateway to Educational Materials

The Gateway to Educational Materials (GEM) (http://www.thegateway.org) began in September 1996. GEM is a searchable Web gateway to thousands of lesson plans, curriculum units, and other educational materials distributed on Web sites across the Internet. Educators can search through lists of uniquely GEM-cataloged materials organized by subject, keyword, or grade/education level and then go to the full text of the resource's catalog record.

Virtual Reference Desk

The Virtual Reference Desk (VRD) (http://www.vrd.org), began in June 1997. VRD seeks to identify and provide the resources necessary to link educators, parents, students, and others to evaluated and appropriate human-mediated, Internet-based information systems in order to satisfy information needs. VRD includes the AskA+ Locator, a searchable database of high-quality K–12 digital reference and AskA (ask an expert) Internet services.

The contact for AskERIC, Gateway to Educational Materials, and Virtual Reference Desk is ERIC Clearinghouse on Information & Technology, Syracuse University, 621 Skytop Rd., Suite 160, Syracuse, NY 13244-5290; telephone 315-443-3640 or 1-800-464-9107, fax 315-443-5448.

National Parent Information Network

Since late 1993 the National Parent Information Network (NPIN), funded through the ERIC system as a special project of the ERIC Clearinghouses on Elementary and Early Childhood Education and on Urban Education, has worked to meet its goal of providing national leadership in the delivery of information services related to parenting and parenting education. A key component of this year's activities included distribution of two editions of a new publication, *Parent News Offline*. A smaller, print version of the award-winning bimonthly

Internet news magazine *Parent News*, the new *Parent News Offline* features summaries of frequently requested articles and resources from *Parent News*.

NPIN also played a principal role in collaborating with national parenting and family-support organizations such as the Family Resource Coalition of America, the National Parenting Education Network, Cooperative Extension, and the National Parenting Association. NPIN staff members served on the planning committee and as facilitators for the July 1999 Wingspread Conference—Parent Leadership/Advocacy and a National Voice for Parents. This pivotal meeting brought together more than 50 national agencies and leaders from the field of parenting education and support to develop a strategic direction for parent participation and leadership for the next decade.

NPIN staff continue to provide timely responses to an increasing number of requests for information from parents, educators, and the media (in 1999 staff responded to 2,401 requests from parents).

Another key accomplishment for 1999 was the redesign of the NPIN Web site (http://npin.org) and the NPIN Virtual Library. More than 450 documents from the existing Web site were proofed, cataloged, and entered into a database in preparation for the launch of the redesigned site. The site was made public on December 31 and will provide easier access to the growing number of full-text resources that are available on NPIN.

Miscellaneous

Dictionary of Education

Oryx Press is sponsoring a project to create a new and up-to-date dictionary for the field of education to replace Carter Good's 1973 classic *Dictionary of Education*. The project will be headed by John Collins, Librarian of the Harvard Graduate School of Education, and Nancy O'Brien, Librarian of the Education and Social Sciences Library at the University of Illinois at Urbana/Champaign, serving as co-editors-in-chief.

Twenty-five to 30 contributing editors will be identified and recruited, each of whom will be responsible for a broad topical area of coverage. Each contributing editor, in turn, will identify and recruit contributors to write definitions within specified guidelines. The estimated total project length is 2.5 to 3 years.

The *Oryx Dictionary of Education* will contain 7,000 to 10,000 entries each of 50 to 100 words' length. The entire dictionary will be approximately 400 pages long and will focus on terminology specific to the field of education, broadly interpreted.

ERIC has been asked to cooperate with this project via the ERIC Facility's electronic Thesaurus files and the terminological records of the Facility's more than 30 years of experience in building and maintaining the *Thesaurus of ERIC Descriptors*. The Facility's lexicographer will serve on the project's advisory board. For more information about this project, contact Oryx Press at 800-279-ORYX (6799).

The Most Popular ERIC Documents Ordered From EDRS in 1999

Title	ED Number	Clearinghouse
1 Sexual Harassment: It's Not Academic	ED 423609	Educational Management
2 Doing our Homework: How Schools Can Engage Hispanic Communities	ED 372905	Rural Education and Small Schools
3 Parents Guide to the Internet	ED 410952	Information and Technology
4 Effective Practices in Indian Education	ED 266002	Rural Education and Small Schools
5 An American Imperative: Higher Expectations for Higher Education...Report of the Wingspread Group	ED 364144	Higher Education
6 Charter Schools and Special Education	ED 0407806	Disabilities and Gifted Education
7 Transition from School to Work: Career Training and Development for Youth with Disabilities in Taiwan	ED 417552	Disabilities and Gifted Education
8 Parent-Teacher Interaction for Student Success	ED 415216	Teaching and Teacher Education
9 Art Education and Human Development	ED 336315	Social Studies/Social Science Education
10 Stories of Excellence: Ten Case Studies from a Study of Exemplary Mathematics Programs	ED 348220	Science, Mathematics, and Environmental Education
11 Serving More than Students: A Critical Need for College Student Personnel Services	ED 267678	Higher Education
12 The Era of the New Social Studies	ED 141191	Social Studies/Social Science Education
13 A. Full-Day Kindergarten: A Summary of the Research	ED 345868	Elementary and Early Childhood Education
B. Full-Day Versus Half-Day Kindergarten	ED 369540	Elementary and Early Childhood Education
C. The Effects of Full-Day Kindergarten on Student Achievement and Affect	ED 395691	Elementary and Early Childhood Education
D. Full-Day Kindergarten vs. Half-Day Kindergarten: The Outgoing of First Grade Pending Achievement	ED 417380	Reading, English, and Communication
E. The Impact of Half-Day Versus Full-Day Kindergarten Programs on Student Outcomes	ED 396857	Elementary and Early Childhood Education
14 What Works. Research About Teaching and Learning. Second Edition	ED 280940	Educational Management
15 Executive Leadership Concepts for Higher Education	ED 405928	Community Colleges
16 A Nation at Risk: The Imperative for Educational Reform	ED 2226006	Teaching and Teacher Education
17 Implementing Schoolwide Programs	ED 423615	Educational Management
18 Empowerment for Later Life	ED 321224	Counseling and Student Services
19 Violence Prevention for Young Adults	ED 356442	Counseling and Student Services
20 Accelerated Reader Impact on Feelings about Reading and Library Use	ED 399508	Reading, English, and Communication
21 Preparing to Serve the Student of the Future	ED 395606	Community Colleges
22 101 Ways to Help Children with ADD Learn	ED 389109	Disabilities and Gifted Education
23 Barriers to Learning in Distance Education	ED 416377	Adult, Career, and Adult Education
24 Doing What Matters Most: Investing in Quality Teaching	ED 415183	Teaching and Teacher Education
25 The Interdependence of Reading, Writing, and Spelling	ED 425419	Reading, English, and Communication

ERIC Web Sites

ERIC Program Office: http://www.ed.gov

Support Contractors

ACCESS ERIC: http://www.aspensys.com/eric/
ERIC Facility: http://ericfac.piccard.csc.com
EDRS: http://edrs.com
Oryx Press: http://www.oryxpress.com

ERIC Clearinghouses

Adult, Career, and Vocational Education: http://ericacve.org
Counseling and Student Services: http://www.uncg.edu/~ericcas2
Reading, English, and Communication: http://www.indiana.edu/~eric_rec
Educational Management: http://eric.uoregon.edu
Disabilities and Gifted Education: http://ericec.org
Languages and Linguistics: http://www.cal.org/ericcll
Higher Education: http://www.gwu.edu/~eriche
Information & Technology: http://ericir.syr.edu/ithome
Community Colleges: http://www.gse.ucla.edu/ERIC/eric.html
Elementary and Early Childhood Education: http://ericeece.org/
Rural Education and Small Schools: http://www.ael.org/eric/
Science, Mathematics, and Environmental Education: http://www.ericse.org
Social Studies/Social Science Education: http://www.indiana.edu/~ssdc/
    eric-chess.html
Teaching and Teacher Education: http://www.ericsp.org
Assessment and Evaluation: http://ericae.net
Urban Education: http://eric-web.tc.columbia.edu

Adjuncts and Affiliates

Child Care: http://nc.ams.org
Clinical Schools: http://www.aacte.org/menu2.html
Consumer Education: http://www.nice.emich.edu
International Civic Education: —
Entrepreneurship Education: http://www.celcee.edu
United States-Japan Studies: http://www.indiana.edu/~japan
ESL Literacy Education: http://www.cal.org/ncle
Law-Related Education: http://www.indiana.edu/~ssdc/lre.html
Service-Learning: http://www.nicsl.coled.umn.edu
Test Collection: http://ericze.net/tesxtcol.htm
Educational Facilities: http://www.edfacilities.org
National TRIO Clearinghouse: http://www.trioprograms.org
AskERIC: http://www.askeric.org
NPIN: http://npin.org
Ready Web: http://readyweb.crc.uiuc.edu/

United States Government Printing Office

North Capitol & H Sts. N.W., Washington, DC 20401
202-512-1991, e-mail asherman@gpo.gov
World Wide Web http://www.access.gpo.gov

Andrew M. Sherman
Director, Office of Congressional, Legislative, and Public Affairs

The Government Printing Office (GPO) is part of the legislative branch of the federal government and operates under the authority of the public printing and documents chapters of Title 44 of the U.S. Code. Created primarily to satisfy the printing needs of Congress, today GPO is the focal point for printing, binding, and information dissemination for the entire federal community. In addition to Congress, approximately 130 federal departments and agencies, representing more than 6,000 government units, rely on GPO's services. Congressional documents, Supreme Court decisions, federal regulations and reports, IRS tax forms, and U.S. passports are all produced by or through GPO. Traditionally, GPO's mission was accomplished through production and procurement of ink-on-paper printing. Today, after more than a generation of experience with electronic printing systems, GPO is at the forefront in providing government information through a wide range of formats, including printing, microfiche, CD-ROM, and online technology through GPO Access (http://www.access.gpo.gov).

GPO's central office is located in Washington, D.C. Nationwide, GPO maintains 14 regional printing procurement offices, six satellite procurement facilities, one field printing office, a major distribution facility in Pueblo, Colorado, 23 bookstores, and a retail sales outlet at its publications warehouse in Laurel, Maryland.

This report focuses on GPO's role as the disseminator of government information in print and electronic formats.

Superintendent of Documents

GPO's documents programs, overseen by the Superintendent of Documents, disseminate one of the world's largest volumes of informational literature, distributing more than 65 million government publications every year in print, microform, and electronic formats.

Library Programs

Online U.S. government information became the most prevalent dissemination medium in the Federal Depository Library Program (FDLP) in fiscal year (FY) 1999. This continues the trends of the previous five years and affects both program content and administrative functions. Since the beginning of the electronic transition in 1994, the Library Programs Service (LPS) has concentrated on increasing the electronic content in the program and on building the support mechanisms enabling depository libraries and the public to locate these electronic resources and ensuring that they remain permanently accessible.

In FY 1999 LPS distributed 17.1 million copies of 41,000 titles in tangible formats to depository libraries. In addition, 32,000 titles were provided online, 18,000 of them on GPO Access, GPO's Web site for federal government information, and the remainder on federal agency Web sites.

Most products produced by or through GPO are available to the American public for reference through nearly 1,350 depository libraries located in the United States and its possessions. Depository libraries are public, academic, or other types of libraries designated by members of Congress or by law as official depositories. The Library Programs Service administers the Federal Depository Library Program under the Superintendent of Documents. The mission of the FDLP is to provide equitable, efficient, timely, and dependable no-fee public access to print, microfiche, and electronic government information products within the scope of the program.

Depository libraries assist users in locating government information in tangible formats, such as paper, microfiche, CD-ROM, and floppy disks, as well as providing access to government information available online.

LPS's 1999 highlights include the following:

- Online electronic content became the most prevalent medium in the FDLP
- *Electronic Collection Plan* was published and recognized as a "notable document"
- Electronic Collection Team was established
- Initial implementation and testing of the electronic archive
- GPO/NCLIS *Assessment of Electronic Government Information Products* was published
- Biennial Survey of Depository Libraries was revised and enhanced for 1999; 1997 report was published
- *Internet Service Guidelines* was issued
- Y2K remediation, testing, and compliance were completed

Electronic Collection

LPS staff is concentrating on implementing the plans for the FDLP Electronic Collection, increasing outreach to federal agencies and libraries, and developing the infrastructure and relationships that will provide permanent public access to FDLP electronic information.

Permanent public access will only be possible through partnerships that share the tasks of building, storing, disseminating, and preserving the FDLP Electronic Collection. Partnerships between government agencies, GPO, libraries, and other institutions within the FDLP are being formed to test and expand the available knowledge for providing permanent access.

Online electronic information is the fastest-growing component of the FDLP, and a significant portion of the FDLP Electronic Collection consists of titles at agency sites to which the GPO Access locator tools point. It is GPO's goal to ensure permanent public access to the electronic products to which it links. Meeting the permanent public-access commitment for the FDLP Electronic Collection requires bringing agency-disseminated Internet resources under GPO control, either by establishing a partnership or by incorporating the resources into a digital archive.

A new server and a backup initially configured with two years' projected storage capacity were procured for the pilot digital-archiving project. The first of the new servers was configured for use as the prototype digital archive. Users will be able to search cataloging or Pathway locator services' record descriptions and to be linked to the archive as a backup if the agency file is no longer available. The FDLP Electronic Collection archive became functional late in 1999.

NCLIS Assessment

In March the National Commission on Libraries and Information Science (NCLIS) released the GPO-commissioned *Assessment of Government Electronic Information Products*. The report was distributed to all depository libraries; more than 75 individuals from congressional committees, including the chairman and vice-chairman of the Joint Committee on Printing; government agencies; and library and information-related associations. The study evaluated agency plans for publishing government electronic information products. The final report makes 16 key findings and will be a useful tool as the FDLP continues its transition to a more electronic program.

Web Applications and Tools

GPO staff has been focusing on different audiences and events for GPO Access exhibits and demonstrations, particularly teachers, media specialists, and the K–12 sector. New features on GPO Access are targeted specifically toward students, with the goal of making GPO Access content more understandable for young people. The development of "kids' pages" was announced at the American Association of School Librarians Conference in November 1999. "Ben's Guide to U.S. Government for Kids" is available at http://bensguide.gpo.gov/.

Browse Titles is the central point for all new electronic publications being added to the FDLP Electronic Collection, updated weekly (http://www.access. gpo.gov/su_docs/dpos/btitles.html).

The Browse Topics site provides links from topics to relevant government information sites. Volunteers from depository and information communities maintain more than 150 topics (http://www.access.gpo.gov/su_docs/dpos/pathbrws.html).

Pathway Services, which assists users in locating government information products on the Internet, will continue to expand during 2000.

Nuclear Regulatory Commission Collection

When the Nuclear Regulatory Commission (NRC) ended its Local Public Documents Room (LPDR) program in September 1999, NRC staff and GPO wanted to ensure continued public access to NRC information available in microfiche. LPDR collections in libraries that chose not to retain the collection were redistributed to 18 regional federal depository libraries. This redistribution meets the goal of the GPO and NRC to maintain at least one microfiche collection in a depository library in each state formerly served by a Local Public Documents Room.

Cataloging Services

LPS provides cataloging and locator services to identify, describe, locate, and provide access to government publications and to electronic works available at agency Web sites and archives.

In FY 1999 the Cataloging Branch processed 32,000 pieces, including paper, microfiche, and electronic products. Most FDLP products in paper and CD-ROM and those available via the Internet are cataloged within one or two weeks of receipt. Approximately 50 percent of the titles listed in Browse Electronic Titles (BET) have been cataloged as of the day they appear on the BET list.

GPO's cataloging records are publicly available through various media: print, CD-ROM, and online. The *Monthly Catalog of United States Government Publications* has listed more than 2 million bibliographic records for government information products from 1895 to the present. The current catalog, with abbreviated records, is available on a subscription basis for $38 a year. The CD-ROM edition cumulates complete records on a monthly basis and is for sale at $199. More than 133,000 full cataloging records are also available online at http://www.gpo.gov/catalog. Each of these Web site records is linked with the names and locations of depository libraries that have selected that title, enabling users to identify the nearest depository library where that title is held. Approximately 10,000 records contain links to the actual electronic texts. Records for electronic titles, including records for government agency Web sites, can be found on GPO's Web site through various locator tools.

Users of the Web edition of the *Monthly Catalog* now have a user-friendly display option that includes selected data elements that are clearly labeled as to content. The full-record, numeric MARC-tagged display remains available as an option. The search screen and associated documentation have been enhanced.

The full cataloging records are also available online through the more than 34,000 libraries worldwide that are members of the OCLC (Online Computer Library Center) network. Records are also made available to commercial vendors.

Outreach

GPO held spring and fall meetings of the Depository Library Council to the Public Printer, which advises GPO on depository library issues, in Washington, D.C., in April and in Kansas City, Missouri, in October. A Depository Library Conference was held in conjunction with the fall meeting. The council meetings and conference are free and open to the public.

Each spring LPS sponsors an annual Interagency Depository Seminar, designed as basic training for depository library staff. Participants learn to use significant government information resources produced by a variety of agencies, including the Bureau of the Census and the Patent and Trademark Office.

LPS provided speakers at a number of library conferences and workshops during the year. Approximately 250 depository libraries completed self-study evaluations for compliance with the regulations of the Federal Depository Library Program, with approximately 100 follow-up inspections by LPS librarians.

GPO Access

GPO Access is an online service that provides free public access to electronic government information products. The information retrieved from GPO Access may be used without restriction unless specifically noted. This service was established by the Government Printing Office Electronic Information Access Enhancement Act of 1993 (P.L. 103-40). GPO Access can be reached through GPO's home page or directly at http://www.access.gpo.gov/su_docs. There are more than 104,000 titles available on GPO Access servers, while GPO Access links to more than 62,000 additional titles on other official federal Web sites.

Improvements to GPO Access Web Pages

In April 1999 a new GPO Access home page and related second-level pages were released to provide users with better access to GPO's online resources. The new home page is at http://www.access.gpo.gov/su_docs. Features of the new Web pages include an enhanced design, a new GPO Access logo, and a restructuring of pages and links to make accessing the Web site's information easier and more intuitive for both new and experienced users. Improvements are being made to the site constantly in response to feedback GPO receives from focus group sessions, user surveys, and comments provided to the GPO Access User Support Team on a daily basis.

Responding to numerous requests from its user community for a site search capability, GPO added a service to its Web site that searches HTML documents in selected directories on GPO Access. The macrolevel search function may be used to find specialized database search pages, Web pages for GPO's other online services, and documents on GPO Access that exist as HTML files. However, it does not search for ASCII text or PDF files within databases, such as the Code of Federal Regulations or the Sales Product Catalog. Like the other finding aids on GPO Access, the site search complements traditional database searches and browse features, offering an alternate method of locating and retrieving documents.

As an extension of GPO's mission to disseminate government information to the public, a special section of GPO Access for younger users was created. "Ben's Guide to U.S. Government for Kids" at http://bensguide.gpo.gov enlarges GPO's audience for electronic information in line with President Clinton's April 1997 memorandum to the heads of executive departments and agencies on the subject of "expanding access to Internet-based educational resources." With Benjamin Franklin as a guide, the section's pages cover such topics as the U.S. Constitution, how laws are made, the branches of the federal government, and what it means to be a U.S. citizen. They provide links to other databases on GPO Access and to U.S. government Web sites for children.

A privacy and security notice was posted on GPO Access to explain the policies and practices to which GPO adheres in its efforts to ensure user privacy while providing the best service through GPO Access. Briefly, GPO uses any information it obtains strictly for the purpose of official business. Statistical information is gathered only to improve service on the Web site. Personal information—such as name, address, and telephone number—is acquired only when it is supplied by a user or customer and is used to answer requests for information and to fulfill orders. Web site encryption ensures that online sales transactions are secure, and GPO further guarantees that only authorized personnel view credit card information submitted through the Online Bookstore. In addition, the notice informs users that they are subject to the privacy policies of other Web sites once they leave GPO Access and that the information on GPO Access is considered to be in the public domain, unless otherwise noted.

Government Information Applications

GPO Access currently provides access to more than 1,300 databases through more than 80 different applications. Several additions and enhancements were made to GPO Access applications in 1999, including *Public Papers of the Presidents of the United States* and the *House Journal*. A catalog of congressional bills from the 103rd through the 106th Congress was introduced to give users the option of browsing all versions of all bills for each session of Congress or of browsing one type of legislation (e.g., bills, resolutions, joint resolutions) for a given session of Congress. A feature similar to the one described above allows users to browse a current catalog of public laws.

The majority of the applications available via GPO Access offer results in ASCII text and PDF, and in many cases specialized search pages are available for databases that contain fields, multiple years, or some other feature that makes the database unique to search. These specialized search pages allow users to build very specific searches that result in more-precise lists of search results, and the addition of browse options in several databases gives users the ability to download documents without performing a search.

Federal Bulletin Board

Individual federal agency files are available from the Federal Bulletin Board (FBB), a free electronic bulletin board service maintained by GPO. The FBB enables federal agencies to provide immediate self-service public access to federal information in electronic form, in a variety of file formats. The FBB contains more than 5,000 files in nearly 150 file libraries from more than 20 agencies and organizations representing all three branches of the federal government. Included in these files was the addition of the compressed text files of the *Sales Products Catalog* and the *Monthly Catalog* in USMARC format. The former is updated daily, while the latter is updated on a monthly basis. The FBB can be accessed through a link from GPO Access or directly at http://fedbbs.access.gpo.gov.

Locator Tools and Access to Collections of Government Information

GPO Access provides a number of useful tools for locating government information products available not only on GPO Access but also on other agency Internet sites. These include the following:

- *Monthly Catalog of U.S. Government Publications*
- *Sales Product Catalog*, which provides information on product availability and how to purchase government products through GPO
- Government Information Locator Service (GILS), with GPO Access currently hosting GILS records for 33 agencies
- A variety of other tools that allow users to find government information by title, topic, or keyword search

Additionally, there are 15 federal Web sites that are now hosted by GPO Access. Web sites for the Federal Mine Safety and Health Review Commission and the U.S. Trade Deficit Review Commission were added in 1999.

GPO Access also assists users in finding collections of government information available at federal depository libraries. GPO Access search applications help users find a local depository library in their area that can provide them with tangible government information products.

Methods of Access

GPO recognizes the various needs and technological capabilities of the public. A wide range of information dissemination technologies are supported by GPO Access, from the latest Internet client/server applications to dial-up modem access. Methods compatible with technologies to assist users affected by the Americans with Disabilities Act are also available. Even people without computers can use GPO Access through public-access terminals located at federal depository libraries throughout the country. All depositories are expected to have workstations with a graphical user interface, CD-ROM capability, an Internet connection, and the ability to access government information via the World Wide Web.

GPO Access Usage Statistics

GPO recorded more than 228 million document retrievals in FY 1999 with an average of 19 million retrievals per month. This figure reflects more than a 66 percent increase over the total number of document retrievals in FY 1998. Since January 1996, when GPO Access was made available free to all users, retrieval rates have increased at an average of 392,000 per month.

Document retrievals continue to increase at a steady pace; recent statistics indicate that GPO Access fulfills approximately 21 million document retrievals per month. With the size of each retrieved document averaging 44,000 bytes, approximately 924 terabytes of information are downloaded from GPO Access every month.

Consistent with FY 1998, the Code of Federal Regulations, Federal Register, Commerce Business Daily (CBDNet), United States Code, and Congressional Record were the databases with the highest number of retrievals.

GPO Access Training and Demonstrations

GPO continues to receive many requests for training classes and demonstrations. During FY 1999 staff from the Office of Electronic Information Dissemination Services (EIDS) conducted approximately 30 hands-on training classes and demonstrations of GPO Access for federal depository librarians, members of Congress, professional organizations, various other groups, and the public in Washington, D.C., and across the country. Recent training sessions and demonstrations were conducted in San Diego, Pittsburgh, Philadelphia, Chicago, Detroit, Seattle, Portland, Minneapolis, and New Orleans.

Recognition

In FY 1999 GPO Access continued to be recognized, formally and informally, for its quality of service. In June GPO was named the recipient of the American Association of Law Libraries' first annual Public Access to Government Information Award, which was established to "honor the achievements of those who have championed public access."

The prestigious Hammer Award was presented to GPO and the Department of Energy's Office of Scientific and Technical Information in February 1999 on behalf of Vice President Al Gore and the National Partnership for Reinventing Government. The award recognizes the role of GPO in providing access to the DOE Information Bridge and contributing to a government that works better and costs less.

In August 1999 GPO Access was featured on a "list of five of the most impressive federal World Wide Web sites" that "provide models and examples of the innovative methods the Internet offers to promote public access to information."

User Support

The GPO Access User Support Team averages 6,500 pieces of correspondence—phone calls, e-mails, faxes, and letters—per month. Questions or comments regarding the GPO Access service can be directed to the GPO Access User Support Team by e-mail at gpoaccess@gpo.gov; by toll-free telephone at 888-293-6498; by phone locally in the Washington, D.C, area at 202-512-1530; or via fax at 202-512-1262.

Sales

The Superintendent of Documents' Sales Program currently offers for sale approximately 12,000 government publications on a wide array of subjects. These are sold principally via mail, telephone, fax, electronic, and e-mail orders and through GPO bookstores across the country. The program operates on a cost recovery basis, without the use of tax dollars.

Publications for sale include books, forms, posters, pamphlets, maps, CD-ROMs, computer diskettes, and magnetic tapes. Subscription services for both dated periodicals and basic-and-supplement services (involving an initial volume and supplemental issues) are also offered. U.S. Fax Watch offers customers in the United States and Canada free access to information on a variety of sales products, electronic products and services, and depository library locations. U.S. Fax Watch is available 24 hours a day, seven days a week, at 202-512-1716.

Express service, which includes priority handling and Federal Express delivery, is available for orders placed by telephone for domestic delivery. Orders placed before noon Eastern time for in-stock publications and single-copy subscriptions will be delivered within two working days. Some quantity restrictions apply. Call the order desk at 202-512-1800 for more information.

Consumer-oriented publications are also either sold or distributed free through the Consumer Information Center in Pueblo, Colorado, which GPO operates on behalf of the General Services Administration.

Sales Program Continues Modernization

After an extended period of modification, testing, debugging, and training, GPO's Sales Program expects to have its state-of-the-art, customer-oriented automated system in place midway through 2000. The Integrated Processing System (IPS) is a computer system that will replace 18 different legacy mainframe systems that were developed over the last 20 years to perform a variety of functions. IPS will integrate all these functions using one database.

IPS is being brought in to modernize document sales and to improve customer service. The goal is to process all orders, inquiries, and complaints within 24 hours of receipt in the Customer Service Center. Sales hopes to accomplish this with the following:

- One central database: All transactions go into one database, eliminating duplication and giving faster order processing and real-time access to all customer, inventory, warehouse, and financial information. This will streamline the order-processing and order-tracking capabilities. Scanning and imaging technology will speed work from desk to desk, eliminating the paper trail.
- State-of-the-art warehouse management technology: The IPS system will automatically assign put-away locations and even prioritize the picking locations to maximize warehouse efficiency and space utilization. In addition, hand-held radio frequency bar code scanners will be used to pick the stock, further reducing paperwork and order-processing times.

IPS will bring significant improvements to GPO's Sales Program. Soon after implementation, evaluations will begin on the feasibility of extending IPS to FDLP and other GPO systems.

Online Marketing

A U.S. Government Online Bookstore has been added to GPO's Web site, available at http://www.access.gpo.gov/su_docs/sale.html. This page presents links to sales applications, including the *Sales Product Catalog*, new product announcements, the *U.S. Government Subscriptions* catalog, a list of CD-ROMs for sale, and a list of sales products by topic. It also provides locations of U.S. Government Bookstores; a link to the Consumer Information Center's Web site, which sells GPO's products; and information about the U.S. Fax Watch service.

Further improvement to sales applications on GPO's Web site was achieved through the incorporation of encryption technology into GPO Access. Encryption ensures private, secure transactions for customers who submit electronic orders by credit card or Superintendent of Documents deposit account number through the Online Bookstore.

Another change to the Online Bookstore was to provide an opportunity for each U.S. Government Bookstore to customize its own Web pages on GPO Access. Many bookstores have already tailored their pages to local clientele by describing their stores' product specialization, providing detailed maps to their stores' locations, and including pictures of their storefronts or area attractions.

The Sales Program has begun listing its titles on Barnesandnoble.com, Amazon.com, and other online commercial book-selling sites.

New Sales Program Products

The Sales Program has expanded its efforts to conclude cooperative ventures to obtain, promote, and sell products. Sales has received permission from the Joint Committee on Printing to sell government publications not printed or procured by GPO, as well as government publications produced by federal agencies in cooperation with other parties. Ongoing special projects with the Department of Commerce's Bureau of Export Administration and the National Technical Information Service, the Central Intelligence Agency, the Defense Acquisition Agency, the Department of State, and the Department of Justice's Antitrust Division are continuing. Ventures under development include new partnerships with the Library of Congress, the Federal Aviation Administration, and the Bureau of the Census.

GPO Bookstores

Publications of particular public interest are made available in GPO bookstores. In addition, to meet the information needs of all customers, bookstores can order any government information product currently offered for sale and have it sent directly to the customer. Customers can order by phone, mail, or fax from any GPO bookstore.

GPO bookstores are located in major cities throughout the United States. Their addresses, hours, and a map are available on the GPO Web site.

Catalogs

GPO publishes a variety of free catalogs covering hundreds of information products on a vast array of subjects. The free catalogs include

- *U.S. Government Information*: new and popular information products of interest to the general public
- *New Information*: bimonthly listing of new titles, distributed to librarians and other information professionals
- *U.S. Government Subscriptions*: periodicals and other subscription services

- *Subject Bibliographies* (*SBs*): nearly 200 lists, each containing titles relating to a single subject or field of interest
- *Subject Bibliography Index*: lists all *SB* subject areas
- *Catalog of Information Products for Business*: GPO's largest catalog for business audiences

U.S. Government Subscriptions and *Subject Bibliographies* are also available from U.S. Fax Watch at 202-512-1716 and via the Internet at http://www.access.gpo.gov/su_docs.

Sales Product Catalog

The Superintendent of Documents issues the GPO *Sales Product Catalog* (*SPC*), a guide to current government information products offered for sale through the Superintendent of Documents. The fully searchable SPC database, which is updated every working day, is available online via GPO's Web site.

The SPC is also available online through DIALOG (File Code 166). DIALOG service offers online ordering, retrieval, and research capabilities.

National Library of Education

400 Maryland Ave. S.W., Washington, DC 20202
202-205-5015, e-mail library@inet.ed.gov
World Wide Web http://www.ed.gov/NLE

Background

The National Library of Education (NLE) is the largest federally funded library in the world devoted solely to education. It is the hub of a national network of libraries, archives, and other information providers in the field of education. NLE serves the U.S. Department of Education's staff and other federal employees, the executive office of the president, and the U.S. Congress, as well as the general public.

Mission

The mission of NLE is to ensure the improvement of educational achievement at all levels by serving as a principal center for the collection, preservation, and effective use of research and other information related to education. NLE promotes widespread access to its materials and expands access to the coverage of all education issues and subjects. The library participates with other major libraries, schools, and educational centers across the United States in providing a network of national education resources.

Developments of 1999

The year 1999 saw the continued development of the National Education Network (NEN), which took on responsibility for the Gateway to Educational Materials (GEM) project. GEM, which was initiated in 1998, is developing and implementing a comprehensive metadata tagging structure designed to enable standard coding of education information on the Internet. This structure will, in turn, permit easier and more accurate searching across Web sites by educators and other users. NEN's nationwide network of publishers, education libraries, information services, and organizations is the ideal forum for promoting GEM.

NLE also began revision and upgrading of its own online resources, including the NLE Web site (http://www.ed.gov/NLE) and the Web site of the U.S. Network for Education Information (http://www.ed.gov/NLE/USNEI), the official international information resource. NLE's new online catalog was launched internally and will shortly be available to external users. Consumer demand for the product distribution service ED Pubs, launched in 1998, has continued to grow, and a Spanish-language service was added in 1999. NLE also began the process of reorganizing its rare book collection and making it available online, and entered into arrangements with several Department of Education staff libraries to catalog their collections.

Note: Blane Dessy and Stephen Hunt contributed to this article.

Major Goals and Functions

A major goal of NLE is to establish and maintain a one-stop, central information and referral service, responding to telephone, mail, electronic, and other inquiries from the public on

- Programs and activities of the U.S. Department of Education
- ERIC (Educational Resources Information Center) resources and services of the 16 clearinghouses and ERIC support components (including the ERIC database of more than 980,000 bibliographic records of journal articles, research reports, curriculum and teaching guides, conference papers, and books)
- U.S. Department of Education publications
- Research in the Office of Educational Research and Improvement (OERI) Institutes
- Statistics from the National Center for Education Statistics

Referrals are made to such additional sources of information about educational issues as educational associations and foundations, the private sector, colleges and universities, libraries, and bibliographic databases.

In addition, NLE aims to provide for the delivery of a full range of reference services (including specialized subject searches, search and retrieval in electronic databases, document delivery by mail and fax, interlibrary loan, selective information dissemination, and research counseling, bibliographic instruction, and other training on subjects related to education). The library also aims to promote greater cooperation and resource sharing among libraries and archives with significant collections in education by establishing networks. The quarterly newsletter *The Open Window* and other information on NLE are available on request.

Organizational Structure

NLE reports to the Office of the Assistant Secretary for OERI. Nine staff members work in the Office of the Director of NLE. This office is responsible for the overall management of the library, including supervising three division directors; long-range strategic planning; budgeting; assessing customer service; marketing and outreach, including writing, editing, and producing publications; and initiating and implementing special projects. NLE publications include a quarterly newsletter, a series on advances in education research, an annual report, fact sheets, monographs, brochures, posters, bookmarks, and videos.

The three divisions of NLE are Reference and Information Services (RISD), Collection Development and Technical Services (CTSD), and Resource Sharing and Cooperation (RSCD). RISD and CTSD operate the ED Reference Center, NLE's physical and electronic reference service for department staff and public patrons. Together with the ERIC contractors administered via RSCD, these form the "one-stop information and referral" center mandated by law. The ED Reference Center provides general and legislative reference and statistical and publication information services in response to inquiries received by phone, mail, and the Internet. In addition, RISD is responsible for interlibrary loan of NLE materials. CTSD identifies, selects, acquires, and provides bibliographic and subject access to education publications. RSCD is responsible for the development and maintenance of a national network of education and education-related technologies through the ERIC program. In this capacity, RSCD promotes greater cooperation and resource sharing among education and library professionals, policy makers, the public, and other providers and repositories of education information in the United States; develops new information resources, such as databases, network services, user-friendly interfaces, and knowledge syntheses; and provides leadership in the effective use of technology in all aspects of NLE planning and operation.

History

The federal role in education dates to 1785, prior to the Constitution of the United States, when the Great Northern Act was passed by the Continental Congress under the authority of the Articles of Confederation. This act set aside territorial lands on the Ohio Territory frontier to be used to finance public schools for each territorial township.

In 1867 the U.S. Department of Education was established by an act of Congress for the purpose of

> collecting such statistics and facts as shall show the condition and progress of education in the several states and territories, and of diffusing information as shall aid in the establishment and maintenance of efficient school systems and otherwise promote the cause of education throughout the country."(14 Stat 434 [1867])

The prominent educator Henry Barnard was named as the first U.S. commissioner of education. After one year of independent operation, the Department of Education was placed under the Department of the Interior, where it was renamed the Bureau of Education. When Barnard, who was interested in establishing an education library, resigned as commissioner in 1870, he left his own extensive private collection of books on education with the bureau. During the 70 years of its operation in the Department of the Interior, the Bureau of Education administered an independent library serving the specialized needs of its employees.

In 1939 the Bureau of Education became one of the five constituent agencies of the new Federal Security Agency, forerunner of the Department of Health, Education, and Welfare (HEW). The Bureau of Education library then became part of the Federal Security Agency library, which eventually became the HEW library.

As a result of a 1973 management study that recommended decentralization of the HEW library, the education collection was transferred to the newly established (1972) National Institute of Education (NIE). NIE agreed to maintain an educational research library in an effort to fulfill its mandate to "provide leadership in the conduct and support of scientific inquiry in the education process" (Education Amendments of 1972, U.S. Code, vol. 20, sec. 1221 a [1972]). From 1973 to 1985 the NIE Educational Research Library was the recipient of several fine education collections, including the education and library and information science collections of the HEW library, the library of the Center for Urban Education (formerly in New York City), the National Education Association library, the Community Services Administration library, and the former Central Midwest Regional Education Laboratory (CEMREL) library.

A major reorganization of OERI, which had included NIE as a component, occurred in October 1985. The name of the library was changed to the U.S. Department of Education Research Library. It operated first as part of OERI's Information Services Office, and then under OERI's Library Programs.

In March 1994 Congress authorized the establishment of the National Library of Education, with specific charges. By law, two other units in OERI—the former Education Information Branch and the former Education Information Resources Division—joined forces with the library staff to form NLE, expanding services to department employees and other clients.

Collections

NLE's primary collections include its circulating, reference, serials, and micro-forms collections. The circulating collection largely includes books in the field of education published since 1965, but also includes such related areas as law, public policy, economics, urban affairs, sociology, history, philosophy, psychology, and library and information science. Current periodical holdings number more than 750 English-language journals and newsletters. The collection includes nearly all of the primary journals indexed by the *Current Index to Journals in Education* (*CIJE*) and *Education Index*. The library subscribes to eight major national newspapers and maintains back issues in microform of four national newspapers.

The microforms collection consists of more than 450,000 items, including newspapers, the *Federal Register*, the *Congressional Record*, Newsbank, the William S. Gray Collection on Reading, the Kraus Curriculum Collection, and various education and related journals. It also includes the complete microfiche collection of ERIC documents, a program funded by the U.S. Department of Education. NLE's ERIC collection also includes complete sets of the ERIC indexes and ERIC clearinghouse publications and products (bibliographies, state-of-the-art papers, reviews, and information analyses in the 16 areas of education presently covered by the ERIC system). [See the article on the Educational Resources Information Center earlier in Part I—*Ed.*] The earliest volumes of NLE's rare books collection date to the 15th century. The collection also includes early American textbooks and books about education. This collection began with Henry Barnard's private collection of American schoolbooks, was nurtured by Commissioner John Eaton during his tenure (1870–1886), and was further enriched by several private donors. Other special collections maintained by the library are documents and archives of the former National Institute of Education and the former U.S. Office of Education (including reports, studies, manuals, and statistical publications, speeches, and policy papers).

Online Access

NLE maintains an electronic repository of education information and provides public access through its Web sites, operated in conjunction with the Department of Education's INet, the agency's Internet service program. INet makes information available through World Wide Web and ftp servers in an effort to make all ED services accessible to the public.

World Wide Web

NLE's World Wide Web server can be accessed at http://www.ed.gov/NLE. NLE also maintains the U.S. Network for Education Information's Web server at http://www.ed.gov/NLE/USNEI.

Ftp

Ftp users can access the information at ftp.ed.gov (log on as "anonymous").

Key NLE Telephone Numbers

Library Administration	202-401-3745
Reference/Research/Statistics/Interlibrary Loan	202-205-5015
Outside Washington, D.C., area	800-424-1616
Fax	202-205-6688
Circulation	202-205-4945
Collection Development/Technical Services	202-401-6563
ACCESS ERIC	800-LET-ERIC

National Commission on Libraries and Information Science

1110 Vermont Ave. N.W., Suite 820, Washington, DC 20005-3522
World Wide Web http://www.nclis.gov

Rosalie B. Vlach

Director, Legislative and Public Affairs

Highlights of the Year

Jeanne Hurley Simon continued as chairperson of the National Commission on Libraries and Information Science (NCLIS) in 1999 with Martha B. Gould as vice-chair. Sadly, on February 20, 2000, Mrs. Simon succumbed to cancer. President Clinton designated Gould chairperson on March 3, 2000.

Jack E. Hightower of Austin, Texas, was named to the commission with a term ending in 2003. Hightower formerly served on the Texas Supreme Court and is a former member of the U.S. House of Representatives. President Clinton nominated Bobby L. Roberts and Joan Challinor to second five-year terms. Roberts is director of the Central Arkansas Library System in Little Rock and an author in the field of U.S. history, librarianship, and archival management. Challinor is chairperson of the Advisory Committee of the Schlesinger Library at the Radcliffe Institute for Advanced Study, Harvard University, and a director of Knight Ridder.

Continuing commissioners, in addition to Roberts and Challinor, are Abe Abramson, Walter Anderson, LeVar Burton, Mary Furlong, José-Marie Griffiths, Frank Lucchino, and Joel Valdez. The extension terms for commissioners Lucchino, Roberts, and Valdez expired on July 19, 1998, but they remained in office for an additional year, until July 19, 1999. Winston Tabb continues to represent James H. Billington, the Librarian of Congress, a permanent NCLIS member. Diane Frankel served part of the year, as director of the Institute of Museum and Library Services (IMLS), before leaving IMLS to take a position with the James Irvine Foundation. She was succeeded by Beverly Sheppard, acting IMLS director.

Robert S. Willard, a former commissioner, is NCLIS executive director, and Judith Russell, whose library career included a period as director of the Federal Depository Library Program, is the deputy director. Denise Davis, an academic and public librarian, joined the staff in June as director of statistics and surveys.

The theme for the commission's 1999 programs remained the importance of library and information services in an electronic networked environment. The NCLIS action plan, "Addressing the Library and Information Service Needs of the Nation," continued to serve as a tool to focus the commission's energies and establish its priorities through the year 2000. During 1999 efforts began to develop a new, more comprehensive strategic plan.

NCLIS completed the Assessment of Standards for the Creation, Dissemination, and Permanent Accessibility of Electronic Government Information Products at the request of the Government Printing Office. The report, *Assessment of Electronic Government Information Products,* was issued on March 30, 1999.

The Superintendent of Documents will use the results of this work to plan and implement the transition to a more-electronic Federal Depository Library Program. The commission also intends to continue its examination of information policy as it relates to creation, dissemination, and permanent accessibility of electronic government information.

One of NCLIS's responsibilities is to advise the IMLS director on policies and financial assistance for library services, and to ensure that IMLS policies and activities are coordinated with other activities of the federal government. To that end, NCLIS and the National Museum Services Board held their third meeting in November 1999. NCLIS established a committee to assist IMLS with development of the National Award for Library Service. This award will complement an award currently made in the museum community. The award will recognize extraordinary achievement in serving the public and was scheduled to be presented during National Library Week in April 2000. The commission continues its participation in the cycles of drafts, guidelines, plans, feedback, reports, evaluation, and revision for the federal grants program for libraries and information services administered by IMLS.

Support for Executive and Legislative Branches

Data collection for the Assessment of Electronic Government Information Products was undertaken for the Government Printing Office. Data collection began in 1998 and the results of the study were published in March 1999.

The commission also provided information related to a variety of legislative proposals that would mandate use of filtering software by schools and libraries that offer children access to the Internet. After holding a hearing on the "Perils and Promise of the Internet" in late 1998, the commission published and distributed a brochure titled *Kids and the Internet: The Promise and the Perils,* offering practical guidelines for librarians and library trustees.

Following the announcement by the Department of Commerce of its intention to close the National Technical Information Service (NTIS) and transfer some NTIS functions to other agencies, the commission began discussions with various stakeholders. The discussions will continue well into 2000.

NCLIS continues to work closely with officials of a variety of federal agencies to obtain information and provide timely input on national and international policies affecting library and information services. During 1999 commissioners and staff met with officials of the departments of Education, Labor, Commerce, and State as well as the Federal Communications Commission, Government Printing Office, Library of Congress, National Agricultural Library, National Institute for Literacy, Office of Information and Regulatory Affairs at the Office of Management and Budget, Small Agency Council, and White House Millennium Council, among others. NCLIS also met with representatives of such bodies as the Association for Federal Information Resources Management, Federal Depository Library Council, Federal Publishers Committee, Federal Library and Information Center Committee, and the Interagency Council for Printing and Publication Services.

National Information Activities

The unprecedented NCLIS study on the Assessment of Electronic Government Information Products found that there is an overall lack of government information policy guiding electronic publishing, dissemination, permanent public access, and information-cycle management. This lack is found especially in information policy as it relates to agency missions, and in a lack of overall coordination of these initiatives at the governmental, branch, and even agency level. The survey found that some government agencies have established, or are moving to establish, guidelines or best practices for presenting and organizing government information products on the Web, although full compliance with guidelines is a goal that has not yet been achieved. NCLIS is planning a third phase of the study to identify concrete actions the government could and should pursue, taking into account the results of the study along with an earlier review, undertaken by the Computer Sciences and Technology Board of the National Academy of Sciences in 1997.

The commission recognized that recent advances in information technology have improved conditions for some people with disabilities while presenting new challenges to others. It conducted a hearing on Library and Information Services for Individuals with Disabilities at the Kellogg Conference Center of Gallaudet University in Washington, D.C., in July 1999 that served as a first step in the examination of this complex matter. The information gained from this hearing, in addition to continuing research and study, will ultimately guide action in determining the need for policy recommendations to government agencies and other organizations.

Library and Information Services in a Networked Environment

The commission published a special report titled *Moving Toward More Effective Public Internet Access: The 1998 National Survey of Public Library Outlet Internet Connectivity*, based on research conducted by John Carlo Bertot and Charles R. McClure. The report follows up on *The 1997 National Survey of U.S. Public Libraries and the Internet* (Bertot, McClure, and Fletcher) cosponsored by NCLIS and the American Library Association. NCLIS is planning a sixth study of public libraries and the Internet to be conducted in 2000.

NCLIS/NCES Library Statistics Program

Fiscal Year (FY) 1999 marked the 12th consecutive year of cooperation between the commission and the U.S. Department of Education's National Center for Education Statistics (NCES). The commission serves as a liaison to the library community, organizes meetings and professional development workshops, supports in-state training and technical assistance, monitors trends, and advises NCES on policy matters.

NCLIS is committed to providing access to the work of all steering committees and task groups associated with the NCES Library Statistics Program (LSP). NCES and NCLIS continue planning for an expanded library statistics cooperative. The goal is to facilitate work on crosscutting issues without interfering with the ability of existing constituent groups to continue their work on individual surveys. NCLIS/NCES collaborative activities during 1999 included:

- An enhanced Web site for six library surveys
- A Web-based tool for comparison of definitions across surveys
- Peer search tools for online use of data
- A Digest of Library Statistics

Public library data are collected annually and electronically via the Federal-State Cooperative System administered by NCES in cooperation with NCLIS. Thirty-three annual awards were presented during 1999. The 1998 Keppel Award was given to 32 states and one territory, acknowledging their submission of prompt, complete, and high-quality public library data to the survey. A new award to honor John G. Lorenz, the former NCLIS Library Statistics Coordinator, was created in FY 1999.

The School Library Media Center Survey (SLMCS) is conducted every five years. NCLIS has conducted two meetings of stakeholders in this community to inform NCES of the need to improve timeliness of the survey and consider opportunities for including SLMC questions in other school assessments conducted by NCES. The survey remains unchanged for its current collection cycle.

International Activities

NCLIS and Sister Cities International have embarked on a major initiative, "Sister Libraries: A White House Millennium Council Project." President Clinton and First Lady Hillary Rodham Clinton established the White House Millennium Council to use the widespread interest in the millennium as a force for positive change and to celebrate the accomplishments of this "American century." Sister Libraries is the official White House Millennium Council Project of NCLIS. The initial goal was for public and school libraries in the United States to pair with others worldwide, focusing on programs specifically planned for children and teenagers. In the fall of 1999 the project expanded to include other types of libraries and a wider variety of programs. One hundred libraries were selected as participants during 1999.

The commission completed its 14th year of cooperation with the Department of State to coordinate and monitor proposals for International Contributions for Scientific, Educational and Cultural Activities (ICSECA) funds and to disburse the funds.

During its meeting on April 7, 1999, in Ann Arbor, Michigan, the commission passed a resolution adopting Principles for Public Library Service based on the UNESCO Public Library Manifesto. The principles put forth 12 key missions considered to be the core of public library services. They specifically address issues of funding, legislation, and networks, as well as operation and management issues. Then Vice-Chairperson Martha Gould observed, "We believe that by adopting and implementing these Principles for Public Library Service our libraries will set new and higher standards of service and continue to serve as models for lifelong learning throughout the world."

The commission continues to be an active participant in the International Federation of Library Associations and Institutions (IFLA). Commissioner Challinor and Executive Director Willard represented NCLIS at the August 1999 IFLA General Conference in Bangkok. NCLIS also will be an "International Distinguished Partner" with a special role in the preparations for the IFLA General Conference to be held in Boston in 2001. Preliminary plans include a joint meeting with British library counterparts in conjunction with the IFLA conference.

Publications

Annual Report 1997–1998.

Moving Toward More Effective Public Internet Access: The 1998 National Survey of Public Library Outlet Internet Connectivity, March 1999.

Assessment of Electronic Government Information Products, March 30, 1999 (prepared under contract by Westat for NCLIS and commissioned by the U.S. Government Printing Office).

Kids and the Internet: The Promise and the Perils, April 1999.

Library Statistics Cooperative Program, 1999.

Project Summaries from Designated Sister Libraries, September 1999.

United States Participants in Sister Libraries: A White House Millennium Council Project, September 1999.

Copies of NCLIS print publications are available free in limited quantities from NCLIS until supplies are exhausted. Electronic versions are available on the commission's Web site (http://www.nclis.gov). In addition, selected reports, hearing testimony, comments on various matters before Congress and the Clinton administration, news releases, and other items are also on the Web site.

National Association
and Organization Reports

American Library Association

50 E. Huron St., Chicago, IL 60611
312-944-6780, 800-545-2433
World Wide Web http://www.ala.org

Sarah Ann Long
President

The mission of the American Library Association (ALA) is to provide leadership for the development, promotion, and improvement of library and information services and the profession of librarianship. Major activities in 1999 included upholding First Amendment rights on the Internet, holding the first Congress on Professional Education, and fighting to maintain the "E-rate" education discounts on telecommunications services.

ALA is the voice of America's libraries and the millions of people who depend on them. Its 58,777 members are primarily librarians, but also library trustees, publishers, and other library supporters. All types of libraries are represented—public, school, college, and university—as well as special libraries serving the military, business, prisons, and other institutions.

Founded in 1876, ALA is the world's oldest, largest, and most influential library association. Key action areas are diversity, education and continuous learning, equity of access, intellectual freedom, and 21st-century literacy.

The association encompasses 11 membership divisions focused on areas of special interest: the American Association of School Librarians (AASL), the Association for Library Trustees and Advocates (ALTA), the Association for Library Collections and Technical Services (ALCTS), the Association for Library Service to Children (ALSC), the Association of College and Research Libraries (ACRL), the Association of Specialized and Cooperative Library Agencies (ASCLA), the Library Administration and Management Association (LAMA), the Library and Information Technology Association (LITA), the Public Library Association (PLA), the Reference and User Services Association (RUSA), and the Young Adult Library Services Association (YALSA).

In addition to its Chicago headquarters, the association maintains a legislative office and Office for Information Technology Policy in Washington, D.C., and a Middletown, Connecticut, editorial office for *Choice*, a review journal for academic libraries.

ALA, Libraries, and the Internet

Educating the public about the Internet, especially parents and children, continued to be a major focus of the association's work in 1999.

The number of public libraries offering public access to the Internet at one or more branches grew from 60 percent in 1997 to 73 percent in 1998, according to a survey sponsored by the ALA Office for Information Technology Policy and the U.S. National Commission on Libraries and Information Science (NCLIS). Another 10 percent are connected but do not offer public access.

AASL launched its "Learning Through the Library" Web site (http://www.ala.org/aasl/learning), identifying and disseminating information about successful K–12 teaching-learning practices involving school library media centers; giving summaries of research studies and papers related to improving information literacy and general literacy instruction through school library media centers; and linking to Web sites focusing on programs, standards issues, and studies dealing with instructional improvement in schools.

Some 2,000 parents, grandparents, and other extended-family members signed up for AASL's FamiliesConnect Internet initiative, a free online course offered during National Library Week, April 11–17. The five-lesson course, "FamiliesConnect: An Introduction to the Internet," was designed to help parents learn about the Internet and how to use it to help children with their information needs.

Ongoing Internet resources from ALA include:

- "700+ Great Sites: Amazing, Spectacular, Mysterious, Wonderful Web Sites for Kids and the Adults Who Care About Them" (http://www.ala.org/parentspage/greatsites/), a "cybercollection" of Web sites reviewed and recommended by ALSC
- 2000 Notable Children's Web Sites (http://www.ala.org/alsc/nweb00.html), selected by ALSC
- TEENHoopla: An Internet Guide for Teens, a Web page with links to sites of special interest to teenagers, developed by YALSA (http://www.ala.org/teenhoopla/)
- FamiliesConnect (http://www.ala.org/ICONN/familiesconnect.html), a compilation of Web resources to help families guide their children's Internet use, developed as part of AASL's ICONnect technology initiative
- KidsConnect (http://www.ala.org/ICONN/kidsconn.htm), an online question-and-answer service for K–12 students operated by AASL in partnership with the Information Institute of Syracuse at Syracuse University, with funding from Microsoft Corporation

Washington Report

Ensuring public access to information in cyberspace continued to be a major focus of ALA's work in Washington, D.C. These efforts included opposition to several bills introduced in the 105th Congress that would require schools and libraries to use Internet filters to block material deemed harmful for minors as a condition for receiving E-rate discounts on telecommunications services.

"The E-rate was intended to promote Internet access, not be a barrier," said 1998–1999 ALA President Ann K. Symons. "The American Library Association believes that it's important to protect children. We also believe decisions about local school and library Internet use policies are best made at the community level."

ALA filed comments with the Federal Communications Commission stating that decisions on how best to achieve safe, responsible, and appropriate Internet use by children are most appropriately made at the local level, not by federal mandate, and should not be part of the E-rate application process.

In a July 30 ruling, the U.S. Court of Appeals for the Fifth Circuit upheld the E-rate program, which had been challenged by telecommunication companies and states as an unconstitutional tax. ALA 1999–2000 President Sarah Ann Long hailed the decision as a victory for the E-rate and its supporters. "The Fifth Court's decision upholds what we have said all along: The E-rate is constitutional and good public policy," Long said. "We're thrilled the discounts can continue."

The E-rate discounts, established by a bipartisan act of Congress in the Tele-communications Act of 1996, are intended to promote universal access to electronic information at schools and libraries by making these connections more affordable. The first wave of E-rate commitment letters was sent in late 1998, committing $73 million to schools and libraries. In March 1999 it was announced that a total of $1.66 billion in 1998 funding went to 25,785 applicants, including $65 million to 4,657 library and library consortium applicants.

The Education and Libraries Networks Coalition (EdLiNC), of which ALA is a member, developed an online Action Kit (available at http://www.edlinc.org) containing strategies and sample materials to help spread the word about the discounts, the importance of the E-rate, and how it is improving school and library services in local communities.

ALA also fought to maintain fair-use principles in cyberspace. James Neal, dean of university libraries at Johns Hopkins University and a member of the ALA Executive Board, testified March 18 before a congressional subcommittee on the Collections of Information Antipiracy Act (H.R. 354), revised legislation to provide additional protection for commercial databases. Neal testified on behalf of ALA and four other library associations.

Caroline Long of the George Washington University Library testified before a House subcommittee on behalf of ALA in opposition to the Commerce Department's proposal to close the National Technical Information Service.

The ALA Washington Office and the District of Columbia Library Association celebrated the 25th annual National Library Legislative Day May 5, which brought 600 library advocates from around the country to the nation's capital to visit congressional offices, tell their library stories, and encourage legislators to support the nation's libraries.

ALA joined with Project Vote Smart to help libraries provide their patrons with congressional voting records, campaign donations records, and other information about some 13,000 candidates for president, Congress, and state gubernatorial and legislative offices across the country.

Symons was among those testifying at an open hearing held in November by NCLIS on "Kids and the Internet: The Promise and the Perils."

Bills introduced in the Senate and House endorsed by ALA would authorize support for school library media resources as part of reauthorization of the Elementary and Secondary School Library Media Resources, Training and Advanced Technology Act.

Intellectual Freedom

A meeting of librarians and vendors of Internet filtering systems at the association's headquarters in March 1999 was attended by representatives of a dozen companies including Security Software Systems, Smartstuff Software, Net Nanny, and Log-on Data Corp.

Then-President Symons called the meeting to provide a forum for librarians to share their concerns directly with software vendors, to learn more about state-of-the-art Web management technologies, and to help shape the development of future technology in a way that protects both children and free speech. She expressed hope that the gathering would lead to development of Web management software that protects both children and free speech.

"The American Library Association continues to support full public access to constitutionally protected material in libraries," said Symons. "We encourage and respect the right of local libraries to adopt Internet access policies for their communities."

The 17th annual Banned Books Week, September 25–October 2, highlighted the importance of the First Amendment right to choose to read all books, including banned and challenged ones and other literature considered "objectionable."

Some 478 challenges to library materials in public libraries, schools, and school libraries were reported to ALA in 1999. The "most challenged" fiction book was Robert Cormier's 1974 young adult novel *The Chocolate War*; the nonfiction list was topped by *It's Perfectly Normal*, a sex education book by Robie Harris.

ALA's Office for Intellectual Freedom (OIF) and the Freedom to Read Foundation celebrated their 30th anniversaries at a gala dinner in Philadelphia during the association's January 1999 Midwinter Meeting. Four First Amendment champions received special presidential awards: Judith Krug, OIF director since the office was founded; SIRS Mandarin owners Eleanor and Elliot Goldstein, sponsors of more than 30 intellectual-freedom awards; and, posthumously, Forrest Spaulding, author of the Library Bill of Rights.

Freedom of Information Day was celebrated March 16 (the birthday of James Madison, author of the introduction to the Bill of Rights) at an invitational conference in Arlington, Virginia, sponsored by the Freedom Forum in cooperation with ALA. The 1999 James Madison Award for protecting and promoting access to government information was presented to members of the President John F. Kennedy Assassination Records Review Board and the members of Congress who authorized it.

Public Awareness

Public libraries today serve as cultural centers for their communities, offering a wide range of cultural activities for adults, according to a survey conducted by ALA with funding from the Lila Wallace-Reader's Digest Fund. "The survey reflects that the demand for adult cultural programming at public libraries is greater than ever," said ALA President Long. "The public library enables people of all ages to keep learning and growing throughout their lives, connecting us to the whole world of ideas and information."

National Library Week 1999 was celebrated April 11–17 with the theme "Read! Learn! Connect! @ the Library." The national observance is sponsored by ALA and libraries across the country each April. Events in 1999 included a photo contest organized by ALA and the Library of Congress, "Beyond Words: Celebrating America's Libraries." National Library Week 2000 was set for April 9–15.

The producers of "Arthur," the Emmy Award-winning public television series syndicated by WGBH-TV in Boston, worked with the Association for Library Service to Children to present the show in a library setting in the fall 1999 season.

At the urging of ALA, NBC Television produced a 30-second public service announcement in which "Suddenly Susan" star Brooke Shields urged parents to make sure their children have library cards.

World champion figure skater Michelle Kwan, WNBA basketball player Rebecca Lobo, and NFL football player Tim Dwight served as spokespeople on the "Read Team" for ALA's second annual Teen Read Week, October 17–23. With the theme "Reading Rocks! Read for the Fun of It!" the campaign reminded teens that reading is fun as well as important to their future success. NBC Television developed a "TNBC Reads" theme day for October 23, with characters on TNBC shows reading and talking about books.

Lobo and Kwan appeared on ALA celebrity "READ" posters, as did actress Christina Ricci and singer Monica.

ALA joined the National Education Association and other groups in the Read Across America event, calling for every child in every community across the country to be reading with a caring adult on March 2, the 95th anniversary of children's author Dr. Seuss's birth.

Actress Whoopi Goldberg narrated *America's Libraries Change Lives*, a new video featuring the stories of immigrants and the impact of libraries on their lives. The video is available through ALA with support from Library Champions.

Special Projects

ALA sponsors a variety of projects that promote learning, literacy, and cultural education at libraries, as well as professional-development opportunities for librarians. Many initiatives are grant-supported and provide program models and materials, training, and technical assistance, as well as evaluation and dissemination of results.

Traveling exhibits developed by ALA's Public Programs Office included "The Frontier in American Culture," "The Jazz Age in Paris," and "The Many Realms of King Arthur." The office also offered "From Rosie to Roosevelt: A Film History of Americans in World War II," a national viewing and discussion series about America's experience in World War II, and "StoryLines America," a series of book discussions on public radio.

"LIVE at the Library," an umbrella initiative of the Public Programs Office, focuses on helping libraries become active centers for live cultural programming in their communities. The initiative holds training workshops and offers ongoing resources.

The National Endowment for the Arts gave ALA a $22,000 planning grant for "LIVE at the Library 2000," a Millennium Project to aid libraries in hosting performance and discussion events.

ALA's popular Let's Talk About It reading and discussion series was relaunched with a $235,550 grant from the National Endowment for the Humanities. Themes included issues raised by the approaching millennium, incorporating utopian, dystopian, and post-apocalyptic literature, fantasy and science fiction, and cultural history; the "migration" experience of African Americans; the diversity within Latino literature; and a return of "Not for Children Only," one of the most popular and enduring segments of the original Let's Talk About It series.

Helping parents raise children with healthy bodies and minds is the goal of "Born to Read: How to Nurture a Baby's Love of Learning." A project of ALSC, Born to Read builds partnerships between librarians and health care providers to reach out to new and expectant "at-risk" parents and help them raise children who are "born to read."

Other Highlights

In its second year, ALA's Spectrum Initiative, a scholarship program to increase the number of minority library students, continued to receive funding from library schools, organizations, and individuals. In 1999 the program offered another 50 scholarships to graduate students of color to pursue master's degrees in library and information science.

ASCLA's Library Service to Special Populations Section and the Library Services to People with Visual or Physical Disabilities Forum announced the establishment of the Century Scholarship to recruit people with disabilities into the library profession. The funds for the scholarship were made available by an anonymous donor.

Conferences and Institutes

National conferences and regional institutes sponsored by ALA and its units provided opportunities for professional growth and renewal throughout the year.

"Celebrating the Freedom to Read! Learn! Connect!" was the theme selected by 1998–1999 ALA President Symons for the 118th Annual Conference, held June 24–30, 1999, in New Orleans. Some 22,598 librarians, exhibitors, and guests attended. Gen. Colin Powell, former chairman of the Joint Chiefs of Staff, was keynote speaker. The 1999 Midwinter Meeting, held in Philadelphia January 29–February 2, drew 12,655.

"Racing Toward Tomorrow" was the theme of ACRL's ninth national conference. More than 3,000 attended the event, held April 8–11 in Detroit.

The Black Caucus of the American Library Association (BCALA) held its fourth national conference in Las Vegas July 19–22. The meeting, with the theme "Challenges and Opportunities in a New Millennium," attracted 1,039 registrants.

The ninth national conference of AASL, with the theme "Unleash the Power," was held November 10–14 in Birmingham, Alabama. Some 4,000 people attended.

LITA held a national forum offering educational programming on 21st-century technologies November 5–7 in Raleigh, North Carolina.

ACRL offered a four-and-a-half-day intensive immersion program for instruction librarians at its Institute for Information Literacy, held July 23–28 in Plattsburgh, New York.

Publishing

ALA Editions, the imprint of ALA's book publishing operation, published some 35 books for the library and information services community in 1999. Addressing the theme of intellectual freedom were *Libraries, Access and Intellectual Freedom: Developing Policies for Public and Academic Libraries* by Barbara M. Jones, *Libraries, the First Amendment, and Cyberspace: What You Need to Know*, by Robert S. Peck, and *Speaking Out! Voices in Celebration of Intellectual Freedom*, edited by Ann K. Symons and Sally Gardner Reed. *Stop Talking, Start Doing! Attracting People of Color to the Library Profession* supported the association's diversity goals. Two key revisions were *Concise AACR2: The 1998 Revision* by Michael Gorman and *Planning Academic and Research Library Buildings*, third edition, by Philip D. Leighton and David C. Weber.

ALA's membership journal *American Libraries* began offering weekly news reports via e-mail. The service, available at no charge to ALA members, enables librarians and library supporters to read current news about censorship challenges, legislation, funding initiatives, technological developments, and international concerns shortly before it is posted on the American Libraries Web site.

Choice, the review journal for academic libraries published by ACRL, began offering a subscription-based service, ChoiceReviews.online. The service provides a searchable database of all reviews published by *Choice* since 1988, as well as a customized notification service and list-management functions.

The *Journal of Youth Services in Libraries* (*JOYS*), published by ALSC and YALSA, introduced a four-color, eye-catching design in fall 1999 intended to reflect the "joyful" and "open" attitudes of youth librarians.

Awards

Each year ALA presents more than 100 awards and scholarships to recognize and promote excellence in areas such as children's literature, library service to the elderly, and defense of intellectual freedom.

Louis Sachar, author of *Holes* (Farrar, Straus & Giroux), was awarded the 1999 Newbery Medal for the most distinguished contribution to American literature for children. The Caldecott Medal for the most distinguished American picture book went to Mary Azarian for her illustrations for *Snowflake Bentley* (Houghton Mifflin). ALA President Symons appeared with Sachar and Azarian on a February 2 "Today Show" segment spotlighting the awards. The awards are presented annually by ALSC.

The 1999 Coretta Scott King Awards for the best children's books by African American authors and illustrators went to Angela Johnson for *Heaven* (Simon & Schuster) and Michele Wood, illustrator of *I See the Rhythm* (Children's Book Press).

The Andrew Carnegie Medal for Excellence in Children's Video went to producer Frank Moynihan for *The First Christmas* (Billy Budd Films).

Dial Books for Young Readers, publisher of *Thanks to My Mother*, was named winner of the 1998 Mildred L. Batchelder Award for the most outstanding children's book published first in another language and then in English in the United States.

Anne McCaffrey, author of the Dragonriders of Pern fantasy series, received the Margaret A. Edwards Award for lifetime contribution to literature for young adults. The award is sponsored by *School Library Journal* and administered by YALSA.

Hazel Rochman, assistant editor, books for youth, for *Booklist*, ALA's review magazine, was selected to deliver the May Hill Arbuthnot Lecture in spring 2000. The award is administered by ALSC.

The Healing by Gayl Jones (Beacon Press) and *Spirits of the Cloth: Contemporary African American Quilts* by Carolyn Mazloomi (Clarkson Potter/Publishers) won the 1999 Black Caucus of the American Library Association (BCALA) Literary Awards. *The History of Black Business in America: Capitalism, Race, Entrepreneurship* by Juliet E. K. Walker (Macmillan) was cited as the Outstanding Contribution to Publishing. The literary awards recognize excellence in adult fiction and nonfiction by African American authors.

ALA Associate Executive Director of Communications Peggy Barber received the Joseph W. Lippincott Award for distinguished service to the profession.

Mainstream Loudoun, a Virginia-based grassroots organization, won the 1999 John Phillip Immroth Memorial Award for Intellectual Freedom, presented by ALA's Intellectual Freedom Round Table. The group was selected for its role in *Mainstream Loudoun* v. *Board of Trustees of Loudoun County Library*, in which Judge Leonie M. Brinkema of the U.S. District Court for the Eastern District of Virginia ruled that the highly restrictive Internet-use policy imposed by the trustees on Loudoun County libraries was invalid under the free speech provisions of the First Amendment.

Newspaper editor and First Amendment advocate Charles L. Levendosky received the 1999 Freedom to Read Foundation Roll of Honor Award, which recognizes the unwavering support of intellectual freedom, the freedom to read, and opposition to censorship.

Leadership

Sarah Ann Long, director of the North Suburban Library Systems in Wheeling, Illinois, assumed the ALA presidency in July 1999. She selected the theme "Libraries Build Community." Nancy Kranich, associate dean of libraries at New York University, was elected president for the 2000–2001 term. She will assume office in July 2000.

Emily Sheketoff, a former deputy assistant secretary of labor for the Occupational Safety and Health Administration, was named executive director of ALA's Washington Office. She succeeded Carol Henderson, who retired in August 1999 after nearly 24 years of service.

Elizabeth Dreazen was named director of ALA's new Governance Office, formed to support the programs and initiatives of the ALA president, president-elect, and past president, and to direct activities of the secretariats for the Council and ALA Executive Board.

Association of American Publishers

71 Fifth Ave., New York, NY 10010
212-255-0200, fax 212-255-7007
50 F St. N.W., Washington, DC 20001
202-347-3375, fax 202-347-3690
World Wide Web http://www.publishers.org

Judith Platt
Director of Communications and Public Affairs

The Association of American Publishers is the national trade association of the U.S. book publishing industry. Through its intensive efforts to defend the rights of creators and promote respect for copyright, to advocate freedom of expression at home and abroad, to support education and broaden literacy efforts, and to harness new information technologies in the service of American publishers, AAP is a significant force for social change, promoting values essential to a just, open, and literate society.

The association was created in 1970 through the merger of the American Book Publishers Council, a trade publishing group, and the American Educational Publishers Institute, an organization of textbook publishers. AAP's approximately 230 corporate members include most of the major commercial book publishers in the United States as well as smaller and medium-sized houses, nonprofit publishers, university presses, and scholarly societies.

AAP members publish hardcover and paperback books in every field including general fiction and nonfiction; poetry; children's books; textbooks; Bibles and other religious works; reference works; scientific, medical, technical, professional, and scholarly books and journals; computer software; and a range of such electronic products and services as online databases and CD-ROMs.

AAP also works closely with some 2,000 smaller regional publishers through formal affiliations with the Rocky Mountain Book Publishers Association, the Publishers Association of the South, the Florida Publishers Association, the Small Publishers Association of North America, and the Evangelical Christian Publishers Association.

AAP policy is set by a Board of Directors, elected by the membership for four-year terms, under a chair who serves for two years. There is an Executive Committee composed of the chair, vice-chair, secretary, and treasurer and a minimum of two at-large members. Management of the association, within the guidelines set by the board, is the responsibility of AAP President and CEO Pat Schroeder.

AAP maintains offices in New York and Washington, D.C.

Highlights of 1999

- The Get Caught Reading campaign, launched at BookExpo America, exceeded all expectations in terms of effectiveness and popularity, boosting trade book sales. AAP President Schroeder went on the "Today Show" in April to announce the campaign.

- Schroeder testified on Capitol Hill on distance learning.
- First Lady Hillary Rodham Clinton, Amazon.com founder Jeff Bezos, and Secretary of the Treasury Robert Rubin led a list of speakers at the 1999 Annual Meeting.
- AAP's Washington Office moved to Capitol Hill.
- The association held its first Annual Meeting for Small and Independent Publishers.
- Book sales totaled $23 billion, according to figures released by AAP in February.
- AAP's School Division got a new director, Stephen Driesler, and a new home, moving from New York to the Washington office.
- AAP sponsored a study assessing e-book system security.
- The association played a key role in successfully opposing federal legislation to criminalize the provision of constitutionally protected materials having sexual or violent content (including books and audio books) to anyone under 17.
- The 1999 AAP Honors went to National Public Radio for its work promoting American books and authors.
- The first new survey of the library market in a decade was published.
- An International Freedom to Publish delegation visited the Tehran Book Fair and met with Iranian authors and publishers.
- Publishers filed a landmark piracy suit in Thailand as the AAP board voted increased funding for antipiracy efforts.
- Publishers supported a court challenge to "CDA II," a renewed attempt to censor Internet content.
- AAP initiated a project to develop guidelines for exchanging online information about books.
- There was another court victory in an Internet censorship case in which AAP was a plaintiff, this time in New Mexico.
- The Professional and Scholarly Publishing Division's R. R. Hawkins Award went to Oxford University Press for its *Encyclopedia of Dance*.
- Publisher Martin Levin won the Curtis Benjamin Award for Creative Publishing.
- Long-time AAP Executive Vice-President Tom McKee retired at the end of 1999.

Government Affairs

AAP's Washington office is the industry's front line on matters of federal legislation and government policy. The office keeps AAP members informed about developments on Capitol Hill and in the executive branch to enable the membership to develop consensus positions on national policy issues. AAP's government affairs professionals serve as the industry's voice in advocating the views and concerns of American publishers on questions of national policy.

The AAP Government Affairs Council strengthens communications between the Washington Office and the AAP leadership. The council is composed of individuals designated by AAP board members to speak on behalf of their houses in formulating positions on legislative issues requiring a rapid response. [See the article "Legislation and Regulations Affecting Publishing in 1999" in Part 2—*Ed.*]

Communications and Public Affairs

The Communications and Public Affairs program is AAP's voice, informing the trade press and other media, the AAP membership, and the general public, about AAP's work to promote American publishing. Through the program's regular publications, press releases and advisories, op-ed pieces, and other means, AAP expresses the industry's views and provides up-to-the-minute information on subjects of concern to its members.

AAP's public affairs activities include outreach and cooperative programs with such organizations as the Center for the Book in the Library of Congress, the Arts Advocacy Alliance (supporting the National Endowment for the Arts and other federal arts programs), PEN American Center and its International Freedom to Write Program, a host of literacy and reading promotion efforts including the early childhood literacy initiative Reach Out and Read, and President Clinton's America Reads Challenge.

The association's World Wide Web site can be found at http://www. publishers.org. The AAP newsletter, *AAP Monthly Report*, is available at that site in addition to its traditional print distribution.

BookExpo America

AAP is a cosponsor of BookExpo America, the largest book event of the English-speaking world.

In 1998 presentation of the prestigious Curtis Benjamin Award for Creative Publishing was moved from the AAP Annual Meeting to BookExpo. The 1999 Curtis Benjamin Award was given to publishing "elder statesman" Martin Levin.

Get Caught Reading

In 1999 AAP developed and launched a major new reading promotion campaign called Get Caught Reading. Targeting the elusive 18- to 34-year-old market, the basic aim of the campaign is to recapture "lapsed" readers. The message of the campaign is that "Reading is so much fun it ought to be illegal!" The celebrity-based promotion kicked off at BookExpo America '99 in Los Angeles with posters featuring Whoopi Goldberg and Rosie O'Donnell "caught reading" their favorite books and designation of May 1999 as "Get Caught Reading Month." The entire campaign has been conducted pro bono, including the celebrity appearances, creative work, and media placement in approximately 40 major magazines and newspapers, with almost $2 million in donated print ad space. Among the national magazines that ran full-page Get Caught Reading ads were the *New Yorker, People, Business Week, Disney Magazine, Esquire, Good Housekeeping, National Geographic, TV Guide,* and *Vanity Fair.* Full-page color ads also ran in *USA Today.* The *New York Times Book Review* ran the ad three times in 1999. A celebrity poster featuring Jake Lloyd of *Star Wars: Episode I— The Phantom Menace* was unveiled at the New York Is Book Country street fair in September.

Consumer book purchases at independent and chain book stores rose dramatically in the months following the May launch of the campaign, according to figures released by the Book Industry Study Group (BISG). While consumer purchases of all types of books rose consistently by about 4 percent in early 1999 (including March and April, the months just preceding the campaign), the rate of increase more than doubled—to over 8 percent—in July, two months into the campaign. BISG's conclusion: "Get Caught Reading may, in fact, have increased book purchasing."

Copyright

The AAP Copyright Committee coordinates efforts to protect and strengthen intellectual property rights and to enhance public awareness of the importance of copyright as an incentive to creativity. The committee monitors intellectual property legislation in the United States and abroad and serves as an advisory body to the Board of Directors in formulating AAP policy on legislation and compliance activities including litigation. The committee coordinates AAP's efforts to promote understanding and compliance with U.S. copyright law on America's college and university campuses. Charles Ellis (John Wiley & Sons) chaired the committee in 1999.

AAP conducts a vigorous international program designed to combat the worldwide problem of copyright piracy, to increase fair access to foreign markets, and to strengthen foreign copyright law regimes.

Through its involvement in the International Intellectual Property Alliance (IIPA), AAP works with other U.S. copyright industries to mobilize U.S. government support for intellectual property protection among the nation's trading partners. Rampant piracy, particularly in Southeast Asia, seriously affects publishers' business. This problem was underscored in February 1999 by a Special 301 filing by IIPA to the U.S. Trade Representative that estimated that the U.S. copyright industries lost more than $12.4 billion in 1998 as a result of piracy in 62 countries.

AAP also carries on its own antipiracy enforcement program, bringing court actions against foreign pirates in their own countries. In 1999 AAP coordinated a suit by three member publishers against two photocopy shops in Thailand, which was seen as a test of Thailand's commitment to meet its intellectual property protection obligations as a member of the World Trade Organization. At its November meeting the AAP Board of Directors adopted a copyright committee resolution reaffirming the high priority of the fight against international copyright piracy and committing substantial funding resources to carry on the fight.

Another aspect of AAP's international program is the effort to get 30 countries to ratify and implement the World Intellectual Property Organization (WIPO) Copyright Treaty and Performance and Phonograms Treaty. On September 14, 1999, the United States became the first major industrialized nation to deposit its instrument of ratification for the two treaties.

On December 16 AAP President Schroeder joined the secretary of commerce, the deputy U.S. trade representative, and CEOs from allied copyright-industry organizations at the National Press Club in Washington, D.C., to release a report showing that U.S. copyright industries continue to drive the nation's economic growth, contributing more than any single manufacturing sector.

The copyright committee's Rights & Permissions Advisory Committee (RPAC) serves as a resource for the industry on rights and permissions issues and works to facilitate the permissions process. RPAC sponsored a number of seminars and educational programs during the year. A seminar in February looked at the implications of the Digital Millennium Copyright Act (the WIPO legislation). At the group's annual meeting in May, a symposium covered distance learning, campus copyright education, print-on-demand, and e-books; and in the fall RPAC hosted a tour of the U.S. Copyright Office. RPAC was also responsible for developing materials to help facilitate permission requests to use copyrighted materials.

Education Program

AAP's education program is designed to provide educational opportunities for publishing personnel. Seminars and courses have included an intensive "Introduction to Publishing" course designed to give entry-level employees an overview of the industry; a seminar on human resources and legal issues related to work-for-hire, contracted services, and free-lance work; financial issues for editors; and a tax seminar covering recent state, local, and federal developments affecting the publishing industry and tax issues relating to the Internet and new media.

Enabling Technologies

The Enabling Technologies Committee focuses on publishing in the electronic networked environment and serves as a steering committee, directing AAP's efforts to promote the development of workable systems for managing copyright in the digital environment and for promoting and marketing in cyberspace. John Connors (Harcourt Brace) chaired the committee in 1999.

In 1999 the committee commissioned a study to assess the security provided by three popular electronic books systems, Rocket e-book, Softbook, and Peanut Press. The study was undertaken to help AAP members understand the capabilities of the growing array of e-book systems. The report included a comprehensive checklist of security measures and system vulnerabilities that could be used to help publishers evaluate new systems as they are developed.

In the summer of 1999 AAP announced the launch of MICI (Metadata Information Clearinghouse—Interactive), a clearinghouse of information about metadata projects, standards, and initiatives worldwide. With the rise of electronic commerce, and the production and distribution of digital products, it has become increasingly important for publishers to be able to identify, use, and link different pieces of content within their existing systems as well as with outside vendors. Responding to this need, a number of initiatives are under way that focus on metadata (information that describes content). MICI is a database resource that provides information on these initiatives.

Also in the summer of 1999 the Enabling Technologies Committee hosted a roundtable that brought together more than 70 publishers, online booksellers, and catalog and distribution companies to discuss challenges in providing bibliographic and descriptive content to promote online book sales. That meeting identified an overarching need to standardize the way this information is exchanged. As a result, AAP hired consultant Chris Burns to look at current practices and standards initiatives and to make recommendations for an efficient means of exchanging information that can be understood and used by all of the players involved in the online sale of books. The results of that study were slated for release early in 2000.

Freedom to Read

Protecting intellectual freedom is a fundamental concern for AAP members and for the industry as a whole, and is the mandate of the Freedom to Read Committee. The committee performs three basic functions: early warning, intervention, and education, serving as the association's watchdog in such areas as libel, privacy, school censorship, attacks on public libraries, reporters' privilege (confidentiality of source materials), the Internet and filtering technology, sexually explicit materials, third-party liability, and efforts to punish speech that "causes harm." The Freedom to Read Committee coordinates AAP's participation (as plaintiff or friend-of-the-court) in important First Amendment court cases and provides guidance in developing AAP's posture on legislative issues with free-speech ramifications. Through its publications and educational programs, the committee gets the word out that publishers, and indeed all citizens, need to remain vigilant in defending rights guaranteed by the First Amendment. Jane Isay (Harcourt Brace) chaired the committee in 1999.

The Freedom to Read Committee works closely with allied organizations, especially the American Library Association's Office for Intellectual Freedom and the American Booksellers Foundation for Free Expression (ABFFE), and coordinates AAP participation as a member of the Media Coalition, a group of trade associations formed to fight censorship. The committee had a full agenda over the past year. Among the highlights:

- *Keimer* v. *Buena Vista Books*: AAP is providing amicus support in this California case, which has deeply troubling implications for publishers. A state appellate court has ruled that book jacket copy and other promotional materials are commercial speech and thus not entitled to the same level of constitutional protection as the contents of the book, even when the copy merely reflects those contents. If affirmed by California's Supreme Court, the ruling will allow publishers to be sued under the state's unfair business practices and false advertising statutes when statements taken from books and used as jacket copy are later proven to be false.

- California Right of Publicity Statute: AAP played an important role in mobilizing opposition to legislation to expand the publicity rights of heirs of "deceased personalities," severely undermining the First Amendment protection afforded books and other creative works. The final version of the bill was an acceptable compromise that effectively retained protection for creative works.

- *Huggins* v. *The Daily News*: AAP provided amicus support in this case, which involved the question of when—if ever—a report published by a news organization can be deemed "not arguably within the sphere of legitimate public concern," and thus entitled to a lower standard of legal protection. In a defamation suit brought by a party in a celebrity divorce case, a New York State appellate court ruled in the spring of 1999 that the subject matter of articles published by a New York *Daily News* columnist involved "quintessentially private matters" that were not "arguably within the sphere of legitimate public concern," thus reducing plaintiff's burden under New York law to a showing of simple negligence on the part of the paper instead of the more press-protective standard of "gross irresponsibility." Fortunately, in a ruling issued in December the New York Court of Appeals, the state's highest appellate court, disagreed and repudiated the finding of the lower court, holding that "[a]bsent clear abuse, the courts will not second-guess editorial decisions as to what constitutes matters of genuine public concern."

- Hyde Censorship Bill: AAP played a leadership role in a successful bipartisan effort to defeat federal legislation that would have imposed severe criminal penalties for providing anyone under the age of 17 with constitutionally protected materials having sexual or violent content, including books and audio books.

- COPA Challenge: Continuing to oppose government attempts to censor the Internet, AAP took the lead in amicus briefs filed in federal district court and in the U.S. Court of Appeals for the Third Circuit, supporting the American Civil Liberties Union's legal challenge to the Child Online Protection Act (COPA). COPA imposes criminal and civil penalties for any communication "for commercial purposes" via the World Wide Web that is available to minors and contains material that is "harmful to minors." Its challengers held that COPA suffers the same constitutional infirmities as the Communications Decency Act (CDA), which was struck down by the U.S. Supreme Court. The federal district court struck down COPA, ruling that it is over-broad, unconstitutionally vague, impermissibly restricts information published and received by adults on the Web, and violates the right to publish or receive information anonymously.

- New Mexico "Little CDA": There was a satisfying victory in the ongoing effort to discourage states from passing their own Internet censorship statutes. AAP was a plaintiff in a suit challenging New Mexico's "Little CDA." In November the U.S. Court of Appeals for the 10th Circuit struck down the statute as a violation of both the First Amendment and the Commerce Clause of the U.S. Constitution.

- Brooklyn Museum of Art: AAP joined a broad group of First Amendment and arts organizations in an amicus brief to the Second Circuit Court of Appeals supporting the Brooklyn Museum of Art in its ongoing battle with the City of New York and Mayor Rudolph Giuliani over funding issues and eviction proceedings brought as a result of a controversial art exhibit that included images the mayor and others felt were sacrilegious. AAP held that while the government is not obliged to fund the arts, once the decision to do so has been made, it cannot pick and choose what art is "offensive."

- California "Son of Sam" Statute: AAP filed an amicus brief to the California Supreme Court supporting a challenge to that state's "Son of Sam" law, which requires convicted felons to surrender proceeds from the sale of their stories for books or movies. The California statute suffers the same constitutional infirmities as New York's original "Son of Sam" law—which was struck down by the U.S. Supreme Court—in that it singles out speech-generated assets and discriminates on the basis of the content of that speech. This is the first time since the Supreme Court decision that the highest court of any state will consider the constitutionality of such a statute.

- In carrying out its educational function, the committee joined with ABFFE in presenting a First Amendment program at BookExpo America. With the Office for Intellectual Freedom of the American Library Association (ALA), the committee sponsored a highly praised panel discussion at the ALA Annual Conference in New Orleans on the question of third-party liability in speech cases.

Higher Education

AAP's Higher Education Committee continues to serve the needs and interests of AAP members who publish for the postsecondary educational market. The committee was chaired by June Smith (Houghton Mifflin) in 1999.

The committee again coordinated AAP's participation in the National Association of College Stores Annual Meeting and Campus Exposition held in Salt Lake City in April. The committee continues to refine and improve collection of higher education publishing statistics.

The committee published its annual *AAP College Textbook Publishers Greenbook*, a resource for college store buyers that provides a wealth of information on the college publishing industry.

International

The International Committee represents a broad cross-section of the AAP membership. Deborah Wiley (John Wiley & Sons) chairs the committee. The committee sponsored a successful seminar at BookExpo America '99 in Los Angeles on "The Global Digital Book Market in the 21st Century." The International Committee also cohosted, with the British Publishers Association, a joint briefing at the Frankfurt Book Fair for publishers' regional representatives and sales managers to discuss global antipiracy developments.

International Freedom to Publish

AAP's International Freedom to Publish (IFTP) Committee defends and promotes freedom of written communication worldwide. The committee monitors human rights issues and provides moral support and practical assistance to publishers and authors outside the United States who are denied basic freedoms. The committee carries on its work in close cooperation with other human rights groups, including Human Rights Watch and PEN American Center. William Schwalbe (Hyperion) chaired the committee in 1999.

The committee continued to provide Judith Krug of ALA with information on book censorship around the world. This listing of books that are banned in their own country but available in the United States forms the new international section of the Banned Books Week Resource Guide published by ALA.

A new brochure describing the work and mission of the International Freedom to Publish Committee was published early in 1999 and is available on request from AAP's New York office.

Since the 1970s, the IFTP Committee has worked to secure the freedom of Indonesian writer Pramoedya Ananta Toer, who spent much of his life in prison. On April 22 Pramoedya and his publisher Joesoef Isak were guests of honor at an IFTP luncheon at AAP's New York office. The IFTP Committee and Fordham University sponsored Pramoedya's first visit to the United States, during which he traveled extensively and participated in a two-day symposium at Fordham devoted to his works, which are still banned in Indonesia.

The committee sent an exploratory mission to Iran in late May to meet with publishers and look into the possibility of an exhibit at next year's Tehran Book Fair. The group met with some 25 individuals, including publishers, writers, members of the Writers Association and the Publishers Union, political opposition figures, newspaper editors, and a liberal cleric. The mission visited the Tehran Book Fair, found it well attended, and recommended that the IFTP Committee mount an exhibit there, focusing on books about women, children, or the family.

The committee continued to voice protests on behalf of writers, journalists, and publishers who are denied basic rights of free expression. In 1999 letters were sent to President Hosni Mubarak of Egypt regarding the large number of books banned in that country, and to President Aleksandr Lukashenka of Belarus regarding the disappearance of publisher Anatoly Krasovksy and others.

Literacy

AAP is concerned with the promotion of reading and literacy in the United States. Over the years it has lent its support to a wide variety of reading promotion and literacy programs, working with such partners as the International Reading Association, Reading Is Fundamental, the Barbara Bush Foundation for Family Literacy, and the Center for the Book.

Several years ago AAP became involved in supporting an innovative program, Reach Out and Read, which uses pediatric clinics and medical personnel to promote early childhood literacy. The program is now operating 600 sites at clinics and hospitals nationwide.

AAP is involved in promoting President Clinton's America Reads Challenge, and was among the organizations represented at the White House conference at which First Lady Hillary Rodham Clinton launched the Prescription for Reading partnership.

Speaking at the AAP Annual Meeting in Washington, D.C., in March, the First Lady announced a major reading initiative to be launched by McDonald's Corporation in cooperation with the U.S. Department of Education. Mrs. Clinton said McDonald's would distribute 13 million booklets giving parents practical help on how to nourish their children's brains through reading. The program was launched in October, attaching to every Happy Meal purchase a copy of *A Parent's Guide to Raising Great Readers*. AAP worked with McDonald's in developing the campaign.

Postal

AAP's Postal Committee coordinates activity in the area of postal rates and regulations, monitors developments at the U.S. Postal Service and the independent Postal Rate Commission, and intervenes on the industry's behalf in formal proceedings before the commission. The committee also directs AAP lobbying activities on postal issues. Lisa Pavlock (McGraw-Hill Companies) chairs the committee. [For a detailed summary of postal issues, see the article "Legislation and Regulations Affecting Publishing in 1999" in Part 2—*Ed.*]

Professional and Scholarly Publishing

The Professional and Scholarly Publishing (PSP) Division comprises AAP members who publish technical, scientific, medical, and scholarly materials, including books, journals, computer software, databases, and CD-ROM products. Professional societies and university presses play an important role in the division. Janice Kuta (Groves Dictionaries) chaired the division in 1999.

The 1999 PSP annual meeting was held in Washington, D.C., in February. The division sponsors a prestigious awards program, open only to AAP/PSP members, to acknowledge outstanding achievements in professional, scholarly, and reference publishing. At the 23rd annual PSP awards banquet, the R. R. Hawkins Award for the outstanding professional/scholarly work of the year went to Oxford University Press for the *International Encyclopedia of Dance*. In addition, book awards were presented in 32 subject categories, in design and production, and in journal and electronic publishing.

For the first time in more than a decade, publishers and librarians joined forces to conduct a survey of the library market, exploring the ways in which publishers and vendors market and sell products and services to the library community and assessing the effectiveness of their marketing practices. Survey results were released at a full-day program in June at the ALA Annual Conference in New Orleans. The survey was underwritten by the Professional and Scholarly Publishing Division, ALA, and others.

Among the division's educational activities in 1999 were the following:

- PSP's Marketing Committee sponsored a workshop at BookExpo America '99, exploring the impact of online bookselling and publishing on traditional STM (scientific, technical, and medical) booksellers.
- The PSP Journals Committee held another of its intensive journals publishing "boot camps" in September in Richmond, Virginia.
- A Journals Committee seminar in October focused on "Authors, Editors, Librarians and Readers: What They Want in a Publisher."
- The PSP Electronic Information Committee sponsored a seminar in October on Web site management.

School Division

The School Division is concerned with publishing for the elementary and secondary school (K–12) market. The division works to enhance the role of instructional materials in the education process, to maintain categorical funding for instructional materials and increase the funds available for the purchase of these materials, and to simplify and rationalize the process of state adoptions for instructional materials. It serves as a bridge between the publishing industry and the educational community, promoting the cause of education at the national and state level, and working closely with an effective lobbying network in key adoption states. Julie McGee (Houghton Mifflin) chaired the division in 1999.

The year was one of transition for the School Division. Stephen Driesler, an attorney and experienced trade association executive and lobbyist, replaced Richard Blake as division head, and the division's operations were moved from New York to the AAP Washington, D.C., office. In addition, John Mockler, AAP's longtime legislative advocate in California, left the private sector to become executive director of the California State Board of Education.

Throughout this period of change, the division maintained its high level of service to the members, protecting K–12 publishers from a number of potentially adverse government actions and in several instances inaugurating changes that improved the environment in which educational publishers do business.

AAP was successful in getting legislation enacted in California permitting the $250 million in supplemental funding for instructional materials to be used to purchase standards-based material in any of four core subject areas: mathematics, reading/language arts, science, and history/social studies. An error in the original legislation (SB 264) had restricted use of these funds to math materials for grades K–8 only. AAP also led successful efforts to defeat a proposal that would have allowed instructional materials funds to be used by local school districts for other purposes.

In Florida, AAP lobbied hard for passage of a $9.7 million (5.3 percent) increase in categorical funding for instructional materials. AAP also lobbied successfully to defeat legislation that would have altered the state's adoption process and eliminated spending flexibility that allows school districts to spend up to 50 percent of state instructional materials funds for off-listed materials. In addition, AAP was instrumental in getting the commissioner of education to recommend full funding for instructional materials in the proposed 2000–2001 state budget.

AAP worked with policymakers in several states and at the federal level to ensure that efforts to provide instructional materials to blind and other reading-disabled students would not impose unreasonable financial or administrative burdens on publishers nor jeopardize the security of their intellectual property.

In June AAP filed comments with the Federal Trade Commission in response to proposed regulations implementing the Children's Online Privacy Protection Act.

In North Carolina, AAP persuaded educational officials to extend the deadline for publisher-provided errata sheets for all materials under state contract.

In Texas, AAP worked successfully during the 1999 legislative session to ensure full funding for instructional materials for Proclamations 1996 and 1997, for a new record total amount of funding of $470 million.

In response to an 11th-hour move by the Texas Board of Education that changed the phonics requirements for first-grade reading books, the School Division launched a major public information campaign focusing on two issues: (1) the high quality of the reading materials submitted for adoption, which were developed utilizing the best available research on how to teach children to read, and (2) the basic unfairness (indeed the questionable legality) of the board's action. Although the campaign failed to persuade a majority of the board to reject the proposal, the effort was highly successful in raising public awareness and appears to have had a positive effect in California. In an effort to avoid the kind of controversy and bad press generated in Texas, the California Board of Education adopted very clear and specific criteria on decodability, giving publishers ample time to make any necessary changes in their material.

Trade Publishing

AAP's Trade Publishing group comprises publishers of fiction, general nonfiction, poetry, children's literature, religious, and reference publications, in hardcover, paperback, and electronic formats. Michael Jacobs (Scholastic Inc.) chaired the committee in 1999.

Much of the committee's attention in 1999 focused on the development and launch of the Get Caught Reading campaign, which is discussed in detail earlier in this report.

Annual Meeting

The 280 people who gathered in Washington for AAP's Annual Meeting were rewarded with a program that had both style and substance. The event was the best attended Annual Meeting in recent memory.

The opening dinner March 17 honored a host of distinguished Irish and Irish-American authors including National Book Award winner Alice McDermott and featured writer Malachy McCourt reciting Yeats.

Among highlights before adjournment the following afternoon were the following:

- A luncheon address by First Lady Hillary Rodham Clinton praising AAP and the industry for efforts to bring the joy of reading to all children. Noting that the White House theme for the Millennium was "Honor the Past, Imagine the Future," Mrs. Clinton said she couldn't imagine doing either of these without books.
- A tribute to National Public Radio gave publishers a chance to put faces to some familiar NPR voices—Susan Stamberg, Nina Totenberg, Diane Rehm, Bob Edwards, Laura Knoy, Scott Simon, and hosts from local stations around the country. In a talk that revealed her own love of books, "All Things Considered" host Linda Wertheimer demonstrated why she and her NPR colleagues are so effective at getting listeners across the country to buy books.
- Investment entrepreneur Michael Milken presented an impressive program on the importance of human capital and the publishing industry's role in developing it.
- Jeff Bezos spoke on the retailing revolution he set in motion when he founded Amazon.com.
- Treasury Secretary Robert Rubin led a broad-ranging discussion of current economic issues. Asserting that "the right choices are the difficult choices," the secretary expressed the hope that the nation will have the courage to make those difficult choices, supporting a policy of fiscal discipline and open markets.
- The 80 or so representatives of small presses and publishing organizations who attended AAP's first Annual Meeting for Small and Independent Publishers on March 17 gave the event two thumbs up. The meeting, a direct outgrowth of AAP's efforts to reach and attract smaller and independent publisher members, provided smaller publishers with "how to" guidance on such practical topics as maximizing title visibility with online booksellers, managing foreign rights sales, and dealing with book clubs. Luncheon speaker Morgan Entrekin, president and publisher of Grove/ Atlantic, cheered and encouraged the audience with the story of his own success as an independent publisher. At the business session that closed the meeting, Lynne Rienner (Lynne Rienner Publishers) was elected to fill a newly created seat on the AAP Board of Directors representing small and independent publishers.
- The membership approved an operating budget of $5,491,580 for fiscal year 1999–2000, with $3,826,330 allocated to core programs (including the three committees serving the Trade, Higher Education, and International constituencies) and $1,665,250 allocated to the two divisions ($1,147,500 for the School Division and $517,750 for PSP).
- Peter Jovanovich (Pearson Education) began his second year as AAP board chairman and one new member of the board was elected, Richard Robinson (Scholastic Inc.).

American Booksellers Association

828 S. Broadway, Tarrytown, NY 10591
914-591-2665, fax 914-591-2724
World Wide Web: http://www.bookweb.org
E-mail: info@bookweb.org

Michael F. Hoynes
Senior Marketing Officer

Highlights of 1999

New Strategic Plan

In 1999 the American Booksellers Association (ABA) implemented the first stages of the new ABA Strategic Plan with a prime focus on a complete review and revision of the ABA bylaws to meet the needs of the 21st century.

The ABA Board approved the new set of bylaws, which included a new board structure that reduced the number of board members from 20 to nine. The proposed new bylaws were presented to the full membership for review and discussion at a series of ABA forums across the country prior to the ABA annual meeting at the 1999 BookExpo America in Los Angeles. At the annual meeting, the ABA membership approved the new bylaws without dissent and congratulated board members for their leadership in preparing ABA for the future.

These changes were accompanied by the creation of two new advisory panels, which will serve as strategic "think tanks" and provide ABA with a wide spectrum of views and insights on critical issues facing the industry and the association.

The panels are

- The National Booksellers Leadership Council (NBLC), composed of independent booksellers from all regions of the United States

- The National Book Industry Advisory Forum (NBIAF), which includes representatives of wholesalers, publishers, authors, and others in the book industry

Both panels met for the first time in summer 1999.

Antitrust Lawsuit

On March 18, 1998, ABA, on behalf of itself and more than 20 independent bookstores, filed an antitrust lawsuit in the Northern District Court of California against Barnes & Noble and Borders. The suit alleges that these large national chain stores are using their clout with publishers to obtain secret and illegal deals and preferential treatment. The suit is currently in the deposition phase and is scheduled for trial in May 2000.

Sales Tax Action

On another front, ABA joined efforts in 1999 to ensure that sales tax collections by retailers be equitable, and advocated that state and local governments should enforce existing laws with regard to the collection of sales taxes from all retailers.

Book Sense

The fall of 1998 also witnessed ABA's initial development activities for a national branding and marketing program for independent bookstores. In addition to formally establishing a marketing department, consumer research was conducted to confirm a basic set of assumptions on the unique attributes of independent booksellers. ABA approved a plan for developing the branding program Book Sense—Independent Bookstores for Independent Minds.™

The pilot concept for Book Sense was developed by the Northern California Independent Booksellers Association (NCIBA) with the assistance of the Addison Group, a professional branding and identity company. NCIBA introduced the program in Northern California in November 1998.

Launched nationally on May 1, 1999, at ABA's annual convention and BookExpo America in Los Angeles, the Book Sense program aims to build consumer awareness and interest in independent bookstores. The campaign promotes bookselling attributes including a unique store personality, a knowledge of books, a passion for books, community involvement, and the character of the independent store. The program, an integrated marketing effort, includes such in-store materials as Book Sense decals, shopping bags, and similar items as well as national and regional advertising, direct marketing, special promotions, and public relations.

The national Book Sense program was designed to serve two purposes: to clearly differentiate the independent bookstores from their competition and to enhance the individual bookstore identity. Rather than be a one-size-fits-all model, Book Sense provides participating stores with a variety of options to suit their individual, unique needs.

A major focus of ABA's marketing efforts at BookExpo America 1999 was promoting and highlighting Book Sense. In addition, a major segment of the educational programming at BookExpo America showcased the benefits of becoming a Book Sense bookstore and how members can use the program to maximum advantage.

Book Sense currently has 1,170 members and is growing. A national Book Sense gift certificate program was instituted in September 1999, in time for the holiday season. An independent bestseller list, the Book Sense Independent Bestseller List, was developed in December 1999 with about 200 independent bookstores providing sales data.

Book Sense 76

In fall 1999 the Book Sense 76 list was introduced. Book Sense 76 is a diverse selection of new, recent, and backlist books chosen by independent booksellers every other month. Books receiving the most "votes" make the 76 list, with each book described by a quote from one of the booksellers. About 300,000 flyers are then printed up and distributed to stores, which display the books in the 76 they like best, display the flyer, and take special orders. ABA research shows that 76 status has created several local and national bestsellers and that many other titles have been reordered and sold better than their publishers expected. The program is acknowledged to be extremely successful by both booksellers and publishers and it has received substantial media coverage.

The Book Sense branding program also includes an e-commerce service that will be available to independent bookstores with Book Sense. BookSense.com, which is under development, will allow stores to create their own co-branded Book Sense Web sites. Stores will have the ability to create their own look and feel, upload their own content, take advantage of Book Sense-generated content, and use the BookSense.com e-commerce and fulfillment engine. The program is designed to give stores top-quality e-commerce services at a low price. Customers using BookSense.com Web sites will be able to search, browse, and purchase from a database of more than 1 million titles, and will have the option of picking books up at the store or having them shipped.

Research

A primary source of statistics for the book industry, specifically on trends in market share, has been the Consumer Research Study on Book Purchasing, based on research sponsored jointly by ABA and the Book Industry Group (BISG) and published by BISG. The 1998 study revealed the market share for independent bookstores for the year stood at 17 percent, down from 17.2 percent in 1997, the lowest market share decline in several years. Other findings highlighted by the study included the steady but not surprising hold popular fiction retained on the adult (51 percent) and juvenile (46 percent) markets.

Membership

Although there was a decline in total membership, more than half of this decrease came from the "associate member" category. This category includes representatives of wholesalers, publishers, authors, and others in the book industry. In addition, the decline in the association's core membership was the lowest drop witnessed in several years. Total membership at the end of 1999 stood at about 4,700.

Publications

Throughout 1998 and 1999, ABA's weekly newsletter *Bookselling This Week* (*BTW*) focused on providing useful and timely information to ABA member booksellers and other industry professionals. A new addition to *BTW* is the special section "Book Sense This Week," which includes specific information about the national branding program as well as spotlighting participating bookstores. The Book Sense Bestsellers List is the highlight of this special section.

Affinity Programs

LIBRIS, the casualty and property insurance company formed and owned by ABA, continued to provide member booksellers with broad insurance coverage at competitive cost. For the second consecutive year, participating bookstores realized a 10 percent dividend on their premium.

The joint credit card processing program with Bank of America also continued to serve member bookstores well, and ABA's partnership with Roadways Packaging Service (RPS) continues to provide its members with a money-saving small package freight program.

These affinity programs reduce ABA members' operating costs.

American Booksellers Foundation for Free Expression

Activities of the American Booksellers Foundation for Free Expression (ABFFE) in the last two years have included its well-publicized battle in support of Washington, D.C., bookstore Kramerbooks in successfully resisting a subpoena from Special Prosecutor Kenneth Starr who was trying to get records of Monica Lewinsky's purchases at the store (Lewinsky later turned over the records herself as part of a deal for immunity). ABFFE also published a pamphlet *Protecting Customer Privacy in Bookstores*, to help booksellers protect their customers' right to purchase books without fear that the government will be able to discover their choices. Later in the year ABFFE, Powell's Books, and A Different Light Bookstores became plaintiffs in a case challenging the Child Online Protection Act, an attempt by Congress to censor Internet content. A federal district court has since ruled that the act violates the First Amendment. A decision by the U.S. Court of Appeals was expected early in 2000.

Association of Research Libraries

21 Dupont Circle N.W., Washington, DC 20036
202-296-2296, e-mail arlhq@arl.org, World Wide Web http://www.arl.org

Duane E. Webster

Executive Director

The Association of Research Libraries (ARL) represents the 121 principal research libraries that serve major research institutions in the United States and Canada. ARL's mission is to shape and influence forces affecting the future of research libraries in the process of scholarly communication. ARL programs and services promote equitable access to and effective use of recorded knowledge in support of teaching, research, scholarship, and community service. The association articulates the concerns of research libraries and their institutions, forges coalitions, influences information policy development, and supports innovation and improvement in research library operations. ARL operates as a forum for the exchange of ideas and as an agent for collective action.

ARL fulfills its mission and builds its programs through a set of strategic objectives. To meet these objectives, ARL resources are organized into a framework of programs and capabilities. Annually, the ARL Board of Directors identifies priorities for the year. ARL program staff and the association's standing committees address these priorities in the coming year. The priority activities as outlined in the ARL Program Plan are to

- Intensify copyright awareness efforts within the research and educational communities and continue copyright advocacy activities
- Create and implement cost-effective models and strategies for managing global scholarly communication in partnership with other organizations
- Help research libraries and their constituencies move into a transformed and increasingly diverse environment through the development of human resources, programs, and services
- Ensure that research and learning will flourish through the development of advanced networking applications and Internet2

Scholarly Communication

The Office of Scholarly Communication (OSC) undertakes activities to understand and influence the forces affecting the production, dissemination, and use of scholarly and scientific information. The office seeks to promote innovative, creative, and affordable ways of sharing scholarly findings, particularly through championing evolving electronic techniques for recording and disseminating academic and research scholarship. The office collaborates with others in the scholarly community to build common understanding of the challenges presented by electronic scholarly communication and to generate strategies for transforming the system.

A priority of OSC is to help build community consensus on strategies for transforming the system of scholarly communication from one dominated by commercial interests to one driven by the needs and interests of scholars. To advance this goal, the "New Challenges for Scholarly Communication in the Digital Era" conference was held March 26–27, 1999, in Washington, D.C. The conference—which was sponsored by the American Association of University Professors, the Association of American University Presses (AAUP), American Council of Learned Societies (ACLS), ARL, and the Coalition for Networked Information (CNI)—was attended by more than 200 people. ARL continues to work through the National Humanities Alliance (NHA) Committee on Libraries and Intellectual Property to develop a better understanding of scholarly communication issues as they relate to nonprofit scholarly publishers in the humanities and social sciences. The committee is planning a Higher Education Roundtable discussion on library-nonprofit publisher relations.

Proceedings from the "Specialized Scholarly Monograph in Crisis" conference (sponsored by ARL, ACLS, and AAUP) were published in spring 1999. This conference brought together faculty, administrators, publishers, and librarians to focus attention on the endangered monograph and to explore the potential of emerging technologies that provide both new means of dissemination and new formats for conducting research and communicating the results. The papers by 19 speakers examine the costs of publishing monographs and look into other emerging frameworks for scholarly research and communication.

OSC works to build a better community understanding of intellectual property and copyright issues. A major project is the development of an educational program that can be used on campuses to support efforts to transform the scholarly communication system. A series of brochures that addresses scholarly communication, intellectual-property ownership policies, and copyright awareness are being created for distribution to the campus community. *Embracing Ambiguity: An ARL Copyright Briefing Notebook* was published in 1999 to help explain the impact of the Digital Millennium Copyright Act on libraries. In addition, the teleconference "Copyright in the New Millennium: The Impact of Recent Changes to U.S. Copyright Law" was cosponsored by ARL and its partners in the Shared Legal Capability. The conference was hosted by the George Washington University Library. The panelists for the program included Laura Gasaway (University of North Carolina at Chapel Hill), Georgia Harper (University of Texas), Sharon Hogan (University of Illinois at Chicago), Peter Jaszi (Washington College of Law, American University), and Rick Weingarten (American Library Association). OSC continued to offer licensing workshops for librarians and cosponsored with SLA a videoconference on licensing called "De-mystifying the Licensing of Electronic Resources." The event was broadcast to more than 100 sites in the United States, Canada, and the United Kingdom. Panelists included Molly Sherden of Peabody & Arnold, Pamela Clark of the American International Group, and Trisha Davis of Ohio State University Libraries.

The first edition of the revised *Directory of Scholarly E-Journals and Academic Discussion Lists (DSEJ)* will be available in early 2000. The specialized emphasis on peer-reviewed e-journals will assist acquisitions and collection development staff by including only scholarly material of interest to the research community. *DSEJ* will first be published online using a Web interface and will be followed by a print publication. The e-journal section of the directory will include more than 3,400 peer-reviewed scholarly journals that are available in electronic format and the academic list section will contain more than 4,500 electronic conference entries.

Scholarly Publishing and Academic Resources Coalition

The Scholarly Publishing and Academic Resources Coalition (SPARC) is an alliance of research libraries and institutions that facilitates increased competition in scientific communications. This objective is pursued via publisher partnerships that support innovative models of scholarly publishing and lower-cost, high-quality alternatives to high-priced journals. In return for offering library-friendly pricing and policies, partners receive endorsement and marketing support from SPARC. Public communications activities also are an important component of SPARC's action agenda. Membership currently numbers more than 175 institutions and library consortia in North America, the United Kingdom, Hong Kong, Germany, and Belgium. SPARC is also affiliated with major library organizations in Canada, the United Kingdom, Ireland, Australia, Denmark, and the United States.

The SPARC Alternatives program supports the development of lower-priced alternatives to high-priced scientific, technical, and medical (STM) journals. To date, four Alternatives partnerships have been established. The first of three journals to be created via the SPARC-American Chemical Society (ACS) collaboration is *Organic Letters*, launched in June 1999. *Organic Letters* made an outstanding start in terms of quality and quantity of article submissions as well as subscription placements. In August 1999 ACS and SPARC announced their second collaboration, *Crystal Growth and Design*, to be launched in summer 2000. *Evolutionary Ecology Research,* a partnership with the former editor of a competing commercially published title, has been phenomenally successful, garnering substantial press attention, attracting a strong flow of articles, and winning sufficient subscriptions to break even in its first year. As with ACS, SPARC entered into a three-journal publishing agreement with the Royal Society of Chemistry (RSC). The first of these, *PhysChemComm*, was launched in fall 1998. The key challenge facing *PhysChemComm*, an electronic-only journal, is obtaining a sufficient number of article submissions to establish its prestige among subscribers and authors. RSC will begin charging for the journal in 2000. Discussions are currently under way concerning the suitability of *Geochemical Transactions* as a second RSC-SPARC project. Various other Alternatives partnerships are currently under development, including *Geochemistry: Exploration, Environment and Analysis* (with the Association of Exploration Geochemists and the Geological Society) and *Geometry and Topology* (an independent electronic-only title developed by a group of mathematicians).

SPARC also continues to support next-generation publishing projects that allow its collaborators to offer attractive new models of scientific communications that respond to the needs of libraries and scientists. *BioOne* is a major SPARC initiative undertaken in cooperation with the American Institute of Biological Sciences (AIBS), the University of Kansas, Allen Press, and the Big 12

Plus Libraries Consortium. It will provide Internet access for the first time to a common database of leading journals in the biological, ecological, and environmental sciences at prices and under usage terms sensitive to the interests of both society publishers and institutional subscribers. The project will be launched with a broad selection of the journals self-published by nearly 50 AIBS member societies. Despite their significance, few of the AIBS-affiliated journals are currently available electronically because the societies are undercapitalized to finance their conversion from print. *BioOne* is being created as a nonprofit venture that will ensure that participating journals have broad and cost-effective dissemination.

The SPARC Leading Edge program supports electronic publications that represent a paradigm shift in technology use, introduce an innovative business model, and/or meet the scholarly and research information needs of an emerging or fast-growing STM field. The first Leading Edge partnership is with *Internet Journal of Chemistry*, an initiative of a group of chemists that aims to promote and utilize network resources that enable chemists to communicate better. The journal publishes chemical research that includes materials that are difficult, if not impossible, to include in a traditional journal, especially those articles where the nontraditional presentation is essential for understanding the work. The *New Journal of Physics* is a peer-reviewed, all-electronic journal available at no charge to readers via the Internet. It publishes articles of outstanding scientific quality in all areas of physics. *New Journal of Physics* is produced by the London-based Institute of Physics (IOP) and the Deutsche Physikalische Gesellschaft (DPG) (Germany Physical Society), based in Bad Honnef, Germany. Both are learned, not-for-profit societies that operate as professional organizations serving physicists. Associate members of *New Journal of Physics* include the Australian, Dutch, and Polish physical societies.

The Scientific Communities program includes electronic journals, journal aggregations, and electronic projects formulated around a community of researchers. Scientific Communities program partnerships include BioOne, Columbia Earthscape, the California Digital Library's eScholarship, and MIT CogNet. Columbia Earthscape, eLibrary, and MIT CogNet received grants from SPARC's one-time Scientific Communities Initiative, which awarded $500,000 to projects that help transform scholarly communications.

SPARC also encourages broad-scale change in scientific communication via its support for the Open Archives initiative, a standards development effort supporting the emergence of a fundamental and free layer of scholarly information collected by academic and governmental institutions, above which both free and commercial services could flourish. Steps toward the establishment of such a universal service can be taken by identifying or creating interoperable technologies and frameworks for the dissemination of author self-archived documents (e-prints).

SPARC's first membership meeting, held October 14–15, 1999, in Washington, D.C., attracted more than 220 SPARC members, affiliates, and guests from North America, the United Kingdom, Europe, Asia, and Australia. The meeting was launched with a publisher-librarian forum that allowed attendees to discuss policy, trends, and the needs of libraries with SPARC partners. It led into an afternoon-long advocacy training session that demonstrated to members how to communicate SPARC's message on campus. The second day began with three concurrent panel sessions exploring scholarly-communications issues and concluded with a keynote speech by Jonathan Bagger, professor of physics at Johns Hopkins University. Throughout the meeting, members had an opportunity to meet in small groups and brainstorm about ways that SPARC could help them achieve their goals on campus.

Federal Relations and Information Policy

The Federal Relations and Information Policy program is designed to monitor activities resulting from legislative, regulatory, or operating practices of international and domestic government agencies and other relevant bodies on matters of concern to research libraries. The program analyzes and responds to federal information policies and influences federal action on issues related to research libraries. It examines issues of importance to the development of research libraries and develops ARL positions on issues that reflect the needs and interests of members. Copyright and intellectual-property issues continue to be a major focus for this and other ARL programs.

In 1999 ARL worked to influence legislation in the U.S. Congress on networking and information technology research grants, Internet filtering, Internet gambling, and domain name management.

ARL worked closely with members of the higher-education community, in particular the Consortium of Social Science Associations, to respond to draft revisions of Circular A-110. The Office of Management and Budget (OMB) issued the revisions in response to an amendment that would require federal awarding agencies to ensure that data produced under a federal award be made publicly available via the Freedom of Information Act.

The Department of Commerce proposed that the National Technical Information Service (NTIS) be closed and selected functions moved to other agencies. ARL worked closely with key players to evaluate the administration's proposal and worked with Congress and the agencies to determine how best to rethink the various NTIS activities.

Efforts to revamp U.S. federal information dissemination policies continue. ARL staff participated in numerous discussions with members of the executive and legislative branches, including the Inter-Association Working Group on Government Information (IAWG), regarding changes to Title 44 (printing and procurement). IAWG drafted new legislation on how best to update Title 44 and the Federal Depository Library Program.

ARL continues to participate in a panel sponsored by the secretary of the interior to examine issues relating to the National Land Remote Sensing Archive, specifically focusing on long-term access and preservation issues. ARL collaborated with members of CENDI, a science and technology information (STI) federal agency working group on issues relating to STI government information dissemination and access and in particular on next steps vis-a-vis NTIS. ARL continues to collaborate with others in the public-interest community and with agencies in implementing the Government Information Locator Service (GILS) proposal and, most recently, evaluating Access America, a one-stop shop for federal information. GILS and Access America would provide a framework and common approach for federal agencies to make their information resources publicly available.

ARL worked with the Institute for Museum and Library Services (IMLS), the White House Office of Science and Technology Policy (OSTP), and several federal agencies to provide greater definition to the proposal for a National Digital Library for Education (NDLE). NDLE would be a collaborative online project of the National Science Foundation (NSF), the IMLS, the National Park Service, the Smithsonian Institution, and the Library of Congress. NDLE would provide enhanced access to the wealth of federal agency resources. NSF received approximately $15 million in fiscal year (FY) 2000 for one component of the NDLE: an undergraduate national science, mathematics, engineering, and technology education digital library.

ARL worked in support of FY 2000 appropriations for the NSF, the National Agricultural Library, the National Endowment for the Humanities, the Library of Congress, and the Government Printing Office Superintendent of Documents.

The ARL Geographic Information Systems (GIS) Literacy Project continues to expand and evolve. The project seeks to educate librarians and users about GIS as well as to develop GIS capabilities in research libraries. ARL participated in numerous discussions and conferences related to the development of a national spatial-data standard and issues relating to access to GIS resources, such as the recent National Geodata Forum. The increased reliance upon GIS by multiple communities, including government agencies and members of the academic and research communities, indicates the need for research librarians to be well situated to provide access to the growing array of digital cartographic and spatial information.

Internet2 has been characterized as an initiative to facilitate and coordinate the development, deployment, operation, and technology transfer of advanced network-based applications and network services to further U.S. leadership in research and higher education and to accelerate the availability of new services and applications on the Internet. The ARL Internet2 Working Group continued its work on identifying key issues and priorities of the association regarding Internet2 and delineating strategies for ARL and member library participation in it. The working group met several times in 1999, attended the Internet2 Membership Meeting, and sent a questionnaire to ARL member leaders. The working group also continued to review and evaluate current library activities in Internet2, identify options for ARL and member library participation in Internet2 applications, and collaborate with Internet2 staff and members to determine the best strategies for research library participation.

Intellectual Property and Copyright Issues

The ARL Board of Directors has identified intellectual property and copyright as a defining set of issues for the future of scholarly communications. While these issues have been a priority for several years, activity was accelerated in 1999 due to U.S. legislative developments. As part of the association's interest in raising library and scholarly community awareness of issues associated with copyright and intellectual-property management, ARL participated in a number of collaborative efforts to advance the agenda in these critical areas.

The Shared Legal Capability (SLC)—a collaborative alliance among ARL, the American Association of Law Libraries, the American Library Association, the Medical Library Association, and the Special Libraries Association—seeks to ensure a unified voice and common strategy for the library community in responding to and developing proposals to amend copyright and intellectual-property law and policy for the digital environment. SLC met with members of the Clinton administration and congressional staff to discuss database legislation, submitted statements to several House committees and subcommittees regarding database legislation, drafted and actively supported alternative legislative proposals with others in the Database Coalition, and participated in congressional hearings on distance education.

The Digital Future Coalition (DFC) is composed of a diverse constituency of library, education, legal, scholarly, consumer, and public-interest associations; hardware and software manufacturers; and telecommunications providers. DFC members share common concerns with copyright and intellectual-property legislation and the belief that any legislation must strike a balance between owners, users, and creators of copyrighted works. ARL continues to be a strong voice in the DFC.

The Database Coalition is composed of members of the public and private sectors, including portals such as Yahoo!, financial services companies such as Bloomberg, Inc. and Charles Schwab, telecommunications companies such as MCIWorldcom and AT&T, the leading library associations, and the higher-education community. ARL collaborated with a number of these constituencies to address issues relating to database proposals.

Six major associations (the American Association of Community Colleges, American Association of State Colleges and Universities, American Association of Universities, American Council on Education, National Association of Independent Colleges and Universities, and National Association of State Universities and Land-Grant Colleges) are working collaboratively to identify key issues of importance for higher education in the national policy governing digital networks, intellectual property, and information technology to benefit the teaching, research, and service missions of colleges and universities. ARL and EDUCOM serve as advisers to the efforts of the Higher Education Alliance for Information Technology.

Despite repeated attempts to improve the draft Uniform Commercial Code Article 2B, a seriously flawed Uniform Computer Information Transactions Act (UCITA) proposal emerged and was approved by the National Conference of Commissioners on Uniform State Laws (NCCUSL) on July 29, 1999. UCITA is a proposed "uniform law" designed to harmonize the law regarding computer information transactions from state to state. Notwithstanding opposition from library associations, consumer groups, the Federal Trade Commission, and others, state commissioners are sending UCITA to the states to be approved as a model state law. The negative effects resulting from a state law such as UCITA include greater control by vendors over licensing terms in contracts for software and information products, nonnegotiable contract terms that could be embedded within "shrink-wrap" or "click-on" mass-market licenses, and possible constraints on the downstream use of information, which would affect cultural exchange and scientific research. The principles of copyright laws under which the library community currently operates—such as fair use, preservation, and the unhindered use of works in the public domain—would be threatened by the increased use of mass-market licenses. ARL, along with the Shared Legal Capability, is working to organize opposition to UCITA at the state level.

Access and Technology

The Access capability undertakes activities to support resources sharing among research libraries in the electronic environment and to improve access to research information resources while minimizing costs for libraries. This capability works to strengthen interlibrary loan and document delivery performance, interoperability among library systems, cooperative cataloging programs, and policies that increase user access to information both on site and remotely.

Established in 1993, the ARL North American Interlibrary Loan and Document Delivery (NAILDD) Project promotes developments that maximize access to research resources while minimizing the costs associated with such activities. An ongoing priority of the NAILDD Project is to support the development and vendor use of the international standard for interlibrary loan (ILL) communication: the ISO ILL Protocol, 10160/61. The most active of the several groups convened by the NAILDD Project is the ILL Protocol Implementors Group (IPIG). Established in 1995, IPIG is composed of nearly 40 institutions, organizations, and service providers in eight countries that have committed to work toward interoperability of interlibrary loan messaging systems. IPIG continues to meet regularly, with one meeting held outside the United States each year. In August 1999 the Royal Library of Sweden hosted the meeting in Stockholm. Also in August, IPIG reached a significant milestone: formal approval of the IPIG Profile. The profile outlines the common set of decisions, options, and values included in the ILL Protocol agreed upon by IPIG members. Approval of the IPIG Profile marked an ending and a beginning—the end of nearly four years of active discussions, lively debates, and growing understandings of a very complex standard and the beginning of real intersystem interoperability.

Funded by the Andrew W. Mellon Foundation, the ILL/DD Performance Measures Study was completed in 1998 with the May publication of *Measuring the Performance of Interlibrary Loan Operations in North American Research and College Libraries*. The study's findings provided the framework for follow-up activities to enable librarians to make significant improvements in their ILL operations. This was undertaken through a set of related activities.

The first set of activities was a series of workshops to assist attendees in evaluating and adapting the performance-enhancing procedures and tools for improving ILL/DD services. The "From Data to Action" workshops provide specific techniques for library managers to compare their local operations against the high-performing operations and to develop a work plan for improving their local operations. Three workshops were held in 1999 and at least two are scheduled for 2000. The second set of activities involved working with individual libraries and consortia to help incorporate the "best practices" identified in the study. The program provided consultations and/or training for the Missouri-based MIRACL Consortium, to implement best practices in ILL; the Tri-Institutional Group (Guelph, Waterloo, and Wilfrid Laurier), to improve ILL within their consortium; and the Southeastern New York Library Resources Council (SENYL-RC), to advise on selection and implementation of a standards-based ILL solution.

During 1999 the Access capability and the NAILDD Project collaborated more closely with the AAU/ARL Global Resources Program by advising on several interlibrary loan and document delivery pilots. In February Mary Jackson represented ARL and the AAU/ARL Japan Journal Access Project at a roundtable held in Tokyo on the "Improvement of Document Delivery Services between Japanese and U.S. Academic Libraries." Participants reached agreement on the details of a nine-month pilot project to share copies of journal articles and book chapters. The project will test the effectiveness of using Japanese library resources for materials not held in North American libraries. A second document delivery project with Waseda University Library permits project members to order and pay for book loans and copies of articles from Waseda via OCLC.

The German Resources Project is made up of four areas of activity, one of which is a document delivery project. North American libraries will search and order documents via the GBVdirekt/North America online union catalog and ILL system. Participants receive documents via Ariel or as e-mail attachments. The Access capability serves as the financial officer for the project until a long-term payment scheme is developed. The Access capability also serves as a resource on ILL/DD issues as they emerge in other Global Resources Program projects.

Collection Services

The Collection Services capability pursues initiatives to assist in developing the collections of ARL member libraries and ensuring availability of scholarly resources, regardless of their location. The scope covers both local and collaborative collections management strategies, including efforts to improve the structures and processes for effective cooperative collection development, along with access to digital resources; collaboration with other organizations in collections-related projects, both in North America and internationally; attention to general issues of collections policies and budget management; and the promotion of government and foundation support for collections of national prominence in the United States and Canada.

The first ARL survey of special collections since 1979 was carried out during 1999. The survey focused on the nature and needs of special collections in research libraries. The results of the survey, which had a response rate of over 90 percent, will provide information for future discussion and activity. The May 1999 ARL Membership Meeting on the theme "Special Collections in the Digital Age" featured a report on the survey. The complete findings will be published during 2000.

The AAU/ARL Global Resources Program was established in early 1997 with funding from the Mellon Foundation. The program was the culmination of a series of earlier activities that were focused on the state of foreign acquisitions. The principal goal of the Global Resources Program, to improve access to international research materials through cooperative means and the use of technology, is being addressed in a number of ways. The program currently sponsors six projects, each addressing a particular regional need while sharing a focus on utilizing technology to provide access to materials that previously have been difficult to access.

The AAU/ARL Global Resources Program has granted $25,700 to the Center for Research Libraries, under the sponsorship of the Cooperative Africana Microforms Project (CAMP), for support of the first year of the Cooperative African Newspapers Project. This project is a joint endeavor of CAMP and the Africana Librarians Council of the African Studies Association. Its goal is to create a database of sub-Saharan African newspaper holdings in all languages and all formats that will be Web accessible and will eventually consolidate collections information from North America, Africa, and Europe.

The German Resources Project focuses on improving the acquisition, use, and sharing of German-language materials among North American libraries, as well as fostering collaboration with German research libraries, particularly in resource sharing and the development of digital collections. This project received special funding from the Mellon Foundation to support a series of meetings of German and North American librarians to discuss and design digital collection development agreements. Project priorities include document delivery, bibliographic control, digital libraries, and collection development.

The University of Hawaii is the 34th ARL institution to participate in the Japan Journal Access Project. The project, which initially focused on journal literature and newspapers, seeks to improve access to research materials published in Japan. Coordinated jointly by ARL and the National Coordinating Committee on Japanese Library Resources, the project supports a union list of serials and enables participants to order materials from Waseda University using the OCLC ILL system and its fee management service. A new electronic current-awareness service is available for current Japanese journals and magazines covered by the Union List of Japanese Serials and Newspapers. These resources are part of the Japanese Journal Information Web. The current-awareness service covers approximately 5,000 titles held by 20 libraries. The Web site was developed by the Ohio State University Libraries Japanese Collection for the Japanese Journal Access Project with supplemental funding from the Japan-United States Friendship Commission and Honda R&D Americas.

The goals of the Latin Americanist Research Resources Project are to expand the range of materials available to Latin Americanist students and scholars; restructure access to these materials through distributed, cooperative collection development facilitated by technology; and assist libraries in containing costs through the reallocation of acquisitions funds. Initial funding for the project came from the Mellon Foundation and has been matched by contributions from the 43 participating institutions. A major project component is a searchable Web database of the tables of contents of 400 journals from Argentina, Brazil, and Mexico, through which users can request delivery of articles. Responsibility for collecting these journals and supplying articles to users is distributed among the project members. The project's distributed resources component encourages libraries to reallocate funds to deepen collections in established areas of local emphasis. Individual participants—who each agree to devote at least 7 percent of their Latin American studies monographic budget toward acquiring more specialized research materials—select the fields. As of May 1999 the participants had collectively reallocated approximately $170,000. Six working groups and an advisory committee, chaired by Eudora Loh, coordinate project activities. A recent grant from the U.S. Department of Education's Title VI, Section 606 program, "Technological Innovation and Cooperation for Foreign Information Access," will allow the project to expand to the Andean countries.

Also under a recent grant from the U.S. Department of Education's Title VI, Section 606 program, the Digital South Asia Library (DSAL) will expand to provide full-text access to documents and images over the Internet. This two-year project is developing an Internet-based infrastructure for intercontinental electronic document delivery to and from selected South Asia libraries. The project also includes the indexing of journals and the creation of full-text electronic reference resources and finding aids to improve access to scholarly sources in English, Tamil, and Urdu. Direct delivery of scanned pages of articles will allow scholars to consult these rare publications without travel to India. Indexing records will be created for 38,000 articles in Tamil journals, 38,000 articles in Urdu journals, and 4,750 English journal articles, all published during the 19th and 20th centuries. DSAL also includes the creation of full-text electronic versions of five titles selected from the *Official Publications of India*, one of which will be a statistical source structured as an electronic database. The project's lead institutions are Columbia University Libraries, the University of Chicago Libraries, and CRL, in partnership with the Roja Muthiah Research Library in Madras and the Sundarayya Vignana Kendram in Hyderabad as well as the Urdu Research Library Consortium and the South Asia Microform Project.

The latest project launched under the auspices of the AAU/ARL Global Resources Program is the Southeast Asian Journals Project, a cooperative proposal of the libraries of the Committee on Research Materials on Southeast Asia (CORMOSEA). The project will receive $40,100 over two years to create a Thai-language searchable image database as a prototype for accessing nonroman scripts and to index colonial-era journals for the period predating the *Bibliography of Asian Studies*. Lead institutions on the CORMOSEA project are the University of Washington, the University of Wisconsin, Cornell University, and the Technical Information Access Center in Bangkok. Other institutions represented on the committee that developed the proposal are the University of Michigan and Ohio University.

A more detailed report on Global Resources Program activities in research libraries is provided in the October 1999 special issue of *ARL: A Bimonthly Report on Research Library Issues and Actions from ARL, CNI, and SPARC.*

Preservation

Strategies to accomplish ARL's preservation objective include encouraging and strengthening broad-based participation in national preservation efforts in the United States and Canada, supporting development of preservation programs within member libraries, advocating copyright legislation that supports preservation activities in the electronic environment, supporting effective bibliographic control of preservation-related processes, encouraging development of preservation information resources, and monitoring technological developments that may have an impact on preservation goals.

The ARL Digital Initiatives Database (DID), a collaboration between the University of Illinois at Chicago and ARL, is a Web-based registry for descriptions of digital initiatives in or involving libraries. DID currently contains more than 100 library projects and includes technical features, policy choices, subject matter of the content, and contact information. Preservation data, if applicable, is included in the project descriptions. The database was designed for libraries to enter their own data about all projects, both large and small in scope. In addition to links to each of the projects in the database, DID offers a list of online resources for libraries involved in digital initiatives.

ARL member leaders and staff contributed to a series of meetings with representatives of the Modern Language Association, American Historical Association, Society of American Archivists, Council on Library and Information Resources (CLIR), and others to consider issues involved in the preservation of the artifact and primary records. The group decided to commission a work that would describe, for a general campus readership, the evolution of research libraries in the United States, the strategies libraries have employed in addressing preservation issues, and perspectives on preservation concerns from different segments of the scholarly community.

ARL worked with the National Humanities Alliance and CLIR on a statement in support of preservation and access activities included in the budget request for the National Endowment for the Humanities within the FY 2000 Interior and Related Agencies appropriations bill.

Diversity

The purpose of the Diversity capability is to support and extend efforts within member institutions to promote and develop library staff and library leaders who are representative of a diverse population. These efforts include the recruitment and retention of library personnel from a variety of backgrounds—particularly those from groups traditionally underrepresented in the academic library work force—and through professional-development opportunities that create networks and promote diverse leadership.

In 1997–1998 ARL launched the first Leadership and Career Development (LCD) Program to enhance the leadership skills and visibility of promising librarians of color. The first class consisted of 21 participants representing a diverse combination of professional experiences, cultural backgrounds, library settings, research interest areas, and academic backgrounds. Since the closing of that inaugural program in June 1998, 13 of the participants have advanced within their institutions or accepted new positions with increased leadership responsibility in the academic and research library community. Furthermore, program members are assuming visible leadership roles in the local and national library communities. The success of the pilot program led members to support the continuation of the LCD Program.

The 1999–2000 class of participants was chosen by a selection committee and invited to participate in the program in May 1999. Seventeen librarians of color with diverse areas of specialization, ranging from distance learning to reference and cataloging, make up the current class. Based on experience with and feedback from the inaugural program, several enhancements have been incorporated into the 1999–2000 LCD Program. The most significant programmatic improvement is the development of a distance-learning component to facilitate the ongoing sharing of information and resources before, during, and after institutes. The distance education development is being created and updated by the Office of Leadership and Management Services (OLMS) program officer for distance learning. Other enhancements include working with three new facilitators to build on and go beyond the pilot program design, encouraging more frequent communications between participants and their mentors and home library directors, and expanding the LCD Program Web site for participant, mentor, and faculty interaction.

During the October 1998 Business Meeting, the membership was challenged to develop an ARL scholarship to more aggressively target and recruit minority librarians to ARL libraries. That suggestion led to the formation of ARL's Initiative to Recruit a Diverse Work Force in February 1999. The initiative creates a mechanism for disseminating stipends, at $5,000 each, to MLS students from minority backgrounds. Each stipend recipient agrees to work in an ARL library for a minimum of two years upon graduation.

The diversity program and OLMS have worked closely to create the Research Library Residency and Internship Program Database. The database lists residency and internship information available on a broad range of career opportunities for future and new professionals. This tool was created to attract new and transitioning professionals who are interested in academic and research library careers.

The ARL Career Resources Online Service was established in 1996 to provide job hunters with an easy-to-use tool for finding positions in ARL libraries and to assist institutions in attracting a qualified, talented, and diverse applicant pool. This service was reconfigured in 1999 to allow for faster and easier searching for current vacancy announcements. This new capability allows users to search a database of current announcements by service category, region, state or province, or institution. Since its inception, the service has hosted over 2,300 announcements from members and nonmembers alike.

Office of Leadership and Management Services

The mission of the Office of Leadership and Management Services (OLMS) is to assist large research-oriented libraries to develop leaders who are creative and resourceful and to create workplaces that are effective, productive, and user-oriented. Over the last 25 years OLMS has successfully designed and facilitated some of the most effective and well-attended library staff development programs. OLMS presents a suite of services and products that help leaders to determine their futures through envisioning and assessing that future, as well as through developing staff to better pursue the desired future. OLMS products and services help libraries and information service organizations to best serve their clientele through the intelligent and powerful deployment of engaged and proactive individuals.

To assist libraries in making the transition from traditional roles to increasingly transformational roles within their institutions and globally, the OLMS Organizational Development and Consulting program provides a wide range of consulting services, incorporating new research on effective organizational models and management and leadership practices. In 1999 the program provided academic and research libraries with opportunities to develop workable plans for improvement in such areas as public and technical services, planning, team building, and organizational review and design. OLMS provided on-site and telephone consultation, staff training, written reports, and other materials to aid client libraries in reaching their goals and visions.

The OLMS Information Services program maintains an active publications program composed of SPEC (Systems and Procedures Exchange Center) Kits and Occasional Papers. Publications are produced by ARL/OLMS staff, consultants, and guest authors from member institutions. The highest priority for 1999 was to remedy the backlog in SPEC Kit production. With the publication of SPEC Kit 249, this goal was achieved. A related goal was to evaluate the content and design of the SPEC Kit/Transforming Libraries series. Following the publication of SPEC Kit 250/TL 10, *Transforming Libraries* will cease to be a subseries of SPEC Kits; it will become a stand-alone, unnumbered, irregular publication that reports on transformative operations and services in libraries. The SPEC Kit series will focus on evaluating successful practices in library management and will produce six issues a year. The *SPEC Flyer* will no longer be a separate publication. Instead, its content will become the executive summary for the SPEC Kit.

The OLMS Training and Leadership Development Program provides support for libraries by delivering unique and dynamic learning events that actively and positively assist academic and research libraries to recognize, develop, optimize, and refine staff talents and skills. This OLMS program stays abreast of innovations in library services, library technologies, and library methods while maintaining currency with innovations and the latest research findings in the areas of organizational structure, productivity, learning, and development. The OLMS Training and Leadership Development program staff, consultants, and adjunct faculty design and deliver timely, up-to-date, and focused learning events. In 1999 OLMS provided more than 100 workshops and institutes, public and on site in libraries around the United States and Canada.

ARL and OCLC collaborated on the first in a series of annual events titled "ARL/OCLC Strategic Issues Forum." The forum brought together the executive leaders of academic libraries to engage issues of strategic importance to the future of academic libraries. The inaugural forum focused on the theme "Future Roles and Contributions of Academic Libraries" and was held September 23–25, 1999, at the Keystone Conference Center in Colorado. A set of three guiding principles for academic libraries emerged from the forum's discussions.

In August 1998 OLMS charged Visiting Program Officer Trish Rosseel to discover how OLMS might engage in the arena of distance learning. In 1999 this work developed into a capability that will serve member institutions through a variety of means. The first product of the Distance Learning Initiatives program is the Online Lyceum, a collaborative partnership between ARL/OLMS and Southern Illinois University–Carbondale, Library Affairs, Instructional Support Services. The goal of the Online Lyceum is to provide innovative professional-development opportunities for library professionals and staff and facilitate life-long learning via the integration of ARL and OLMS program content and distance education technologies. The Online Lyceum strives to break down barriers of time, geography, and cost. Its inaugural course offering, "Training Skills Online: Facilitating Effective Learning," was delivered to more than 40 participants across North America. The program also offered "Coaching for Performance" and collaborated with the Diversity and Statistics and Measurement programs to design "The Role of Assessment in Advancing Diversity for Libraries." OLMS collaborates with other ARL program capabilities on projects related to distance-education policy, legislation, and program delivery.

Statistics and Measurement

The Statistics and Measurement Program seeks to describe the characteristics of research libraries today as well as to develop and measure these libraries' contributions to teaching, research, scholarship, and community service. Strategies to accomplish the objectives of the program include collecting, analyzing, and publishing quantifiable information about library collections, personnel, and expenditures, as well as expenditures and indicators of the nature of research institutions; developing new ways to describe and measure traditional and networked information resources and services; developing mechanisms to assess the relationship between campus information resources and high-quality research and the teaching and learning experience of students; providing customized, confidential analysis for peer comparisons; preparing workshops regarding statistics and measurement issues in research libraries; sustaining a leadership role in the testing and application of academic research library statistics for North American institutions of higher education; and collaborating with other national and international library statistics programs and accreditation agencies.

In January 1999 several members of the Statistics and Measurement Committee, the Leadership and Management Committee, and other interested ARL member leaders gathered to discuss what ARL can do to assist members in developing new measures that better describe research libraries and their services. Those attending the retreat addressed a set of questions regarding the data needed to describe research libraries in today's environment, the need for new measures, and the means by which useful data and measurement tools could be developed. Program staff are supporting the development of the new-measures agenda by managing an electronic list of interested member leaders, developing and maintaining a Web site that includes white papers addressing issues related to new measures, investigating current national and international activities on performance measures, providing data when requested, and assisting in the production of reports.

Statistical compilations produced or distributed in 1999 include *Developing Indicators for Academic Library Performance: Ratios from the ARL Statistics 1995–96 and 1996–97; ARL Annual Salary Survey 1998–99; ARL Statistics 1997–98; ARL Academic Law and Medical Libraries Statistics 1997–98;* and

Report on the 1997–98 ARL Supplementary Statistics. The "Library Expenditures as a Percent of E&G Expenditures in ARL University Libraries" survey was not distributed for FY 1997–1998 and 1998–1999 as changes to the accounting standards are being implemented gradually in private and public universities.

Apart from these printed publishing efforts, the program continues its strong presence in electronic publishing activities. Of special interest is the interactive electronic publication of the ARL Statistics on the World Wide Web, which was completely revised by staff of the Geospatial and Statistical Data Center at the University of Virginia. The program's Web site was also revised and is updated regularly with information and data from new editions of ARL statistical publications. Plans call for the design of a revised Web interface for data collection that will offer live data-editing capabilities.

Two workshops on "Electronic Publishing of Data Sets on the WWW" were held in 1999. These workshops provided attendees with the skills to develop Web services in support of data file management.

Office of Research and Development

The ARL Office of Research and Development consolidates the administration of grants and grant-supported projects administered by ARL. The major goal within this capability is to identify and match ARL projects that support the research library community's mission with sources of external funding. Among the projects under way in 1999 were the following:

- The Global Resources Program flourished in its third year of funding from the Andrew W. Mellon Foundation. The program has grown to include six regional projects involving Africa, Germany, Japan, Latin America, South Asia, and Southeast Asia and a set of core activities. The primary goal of the program is to improve access to international research resources, regardless of format or location.

- ARL organized and continues to manage the Shared Legal Capability (SLC), a fund for legal expertise on intellectual property and the networked environment. In addition to ARL, the American Library Association, American Association of Law Libraries, Medical Library Association, and Special Libraries Association each contributed or pledged toward this fund in 1999. In May 1999 SLC sponsored a highly successful teleconference that discussed the impact of the Digital Millennium Copyright Act on libraries.

- With funding from the ALA Government Documents Round Table and the Environmental Systems Research Institute, ARL launched a new phase of the GIS Project. In collaboration with libraries and geographers from the University of Texas–Austin, ESRI, Dalhousie University Library, and the University of Maryland, ARL will help develop a Web-based introduction to GIS for library and information science schools throughout North America. Also in development is a Web-based GIS literacy course for information professionals in collaboration with the OLMS Distance Learning Initiative.

- The Initiative to Recruit a Diverse Work Force was developed in 1999 to create a mechanism for disseminating $5,000 stipends to MLS students from minority or traditionally underrepresented backgrounds. Forty-eight ARL member libraries have contributed or pledged funds to advance this initiative.

- Another initiative of the Office of Research and Development is the ARL Visiting Program Officer (VPO) program. This program provides an opportunity for a staff member in an ARL member library to assume responsibility for carrying out part or all of a project for ARL. It provides a very visible staff development opportunity for an outstanding staff member and serves the membership as a whole by extending the capacity of ARL to undertake additional activities. Typically, the member library supports the salary of the staff person and ARL supports or seeks grant funding for travel or other project-related expenses. Depending on the nature of the project and the circumstances of the individual, a VPO may spend extended periods of time in Washington, D.C., or may conduct most of his or her project from his or her home library. In 1999 VPOs investigated how best to use electronic means to deliver the OLMS training content to libraries and developed a Web resource on digital library activities in ARL libraries. The ARL Web site, http://www.arl.org, reflects the scope of ARL's current agenda and suggests the range of issues where a VPO project could make a contribution.

Communication and External Relations

The mission of the communications and external relations capability is to acquaint ARL members with current, important developments of interest to research libraries; inform the library profession of ARL's position on these issues; influence policy makers and decision makers within higher education and other areas related to research and scholarship; educate academic communities about issues related to research libraries; and provide the library community with information about activities with which research libraries are engaged.

Through print and electronic publications, as well as direct outreach, members of the library, higher-education, and scholarly communication communities are informed of important developments and ARL positions on issues that affect the research library community. External relations with relevant constituencies are also carried on through all ARL programs. This capability provides production and marketing support to all ARL and OLMS programs for their publications and communications.

The ARL publications program offers a full range of timely, accurate, and informative resources to assist library and higher-education communities in their efforts to improve information delivery through technology and education. Print and electronic publications are issued from ARL programs on a regular basis. ARL makes many of its titles available electronically via the World Wide Web; some are available in excerpted form for preview before purchase, and others are available in their entirety. The electronic-publications catalog can be accessed at http://www.arl.org/pubscat/index.html. The ARL-Announce service provides timely information about ARL and news items about ARL member library activities. ARL sponsors more than 75 electronic discussion groups, including both private and public lists. Archives for the lists are updated monthly and made available on the ARL server.

Six issues of *ARL: A Bimonthly Report on Research Library Issues and Actions from ARL, CNI, and SPARC* were published in 1999. With issue 203 (April 1999), the publication title was revised to reflect its broader content. The issues published in 1999 featured the topics of copyright and journal pricing. A special issue on the Global Resources Program was published in October. Current issues of ARL are available on the ARL Web site at http://www.arl.org/newsltr.

Print proceedings from the 1996 and May 1997 Membership Meetings were distributed to members and subscribers. The board approved and membership supported a move to a completely electronic publication effective with the May 1999 meeting. Meeting content will be posted on the proceedings Web site at http://www.arl.org/arl/proceedings/ as appropriate and available.

Association Governance and Membership Activities

The 134th Membership Meeting of ARL, held May 12–14, 1999, in Kansas City, Missouri, and Lawrence, Kansas, was hosted by the Linda Hall Library and the University of Kansas Library. A total of 108 ARL member libraries were represented at the meeting. ARL President Betty Bengtson (University of Washington) convened the meeting, which focused on the array of challenges and opportunities special collections present to library leadership today. The program—planned in collaboration with the ARL Research Collections Committee—brought together directors of libraries, representative directors of special-collections departments, and faculty to discuss and debate the most salient topics in the field.

The fall ARL Membership Meeting took place October 13–14, 1999, in Washington, D.C., and was followed by a SPARC Membership Meeting, October 14–15. The ARL meeting focused on committee and working-group activities and the business meeting.

On October 14, 1999, Ken Frazier (University of Wisconsin) began his term as ARL president. The board elected Shirley Baker (Washington University, St. Louis) as president-elect. Two board members, Jim Neal and William Potter, concluded their terms. Fred Heath, Paul Mosher, and Sarah Thomas were elected to three-year terms on the ARL Board of Directors.

The site of the May 2000 Membership Meeting is Baltimore. Hosted by Johns Hopkins University, the program theme developed by ARL President Frazier will focus on building scholarly communities. Stanley S. Gryskiewicz, author of *Positive Turbulence: Developing Climates for Creativity, Innovation, and Renewal,* is to be the keynote speaker. Gryskiewicz is the vice president of global initiatives and a senior fellow for creativity and innovation at the Center for Creative Leadership in Greensboro, North Carolina.

The fall Membership Meeting is scheduled for October 18–20 in Washington, D.C.

Council on Library and Information Resources

1755 Massachusetts Ave. N.W., Suite 500, Washington, DC 20036-2124
202-939-4750, fax 202-939-4765
World Wide Web http://www.clir.org

Kathlin Smith
Director of Communications

The Council on Library and Information Resources (CLIR) is an independent organization dedicated to improving the management of information for research and for teaching and learning. CLIR identifies critical problems that are amenable to solution at a particular time, engages the best minds in analyzing and solving the problems, and disseminates the results to decision-makers at universities and other research institutions. All of CLIR's projects, while useful to practitioners in their everyday work, are also designed to set the problems in context and to explain what is at risk.

Although CLIR's primary audience has been the research library community, recent technological advances argue for working on projects without restriction by type of institution. All cultural institutions are struggling with the technical questions related to infrastructure and interoperability, standards, and metadata, as well as with questions about economics and leadership. CLIR is convinced that cooperation with like-minded institutions, regardless of institutional focus, is essential.

In 1999 CLIR's staff and board reviewed the existing programs of preservation and access, digital libraries, economics of information, and leadership. Acknowledging that the issues CLIR addresses transcend rigid program boundaries, the staff and board decided to recast CLIR's agenda in terms of six themes, each representing an aspect of the broader problems that CLIR will attempt to solve. The six themes are resources for scholarship, economics of information, preservation awareness, digital libraries, leadership, and international developments. Each theme will be the collective assignment of the staff.

Resources for Scholarship

By defining access to research collections as a primary focus of CLIR's activities, the critical functions of acquisition, description, and preservation can be addressed in an integrated way—that is, as a service to scholarship. CLIR is developing projects to address several important questions:

- How do we ensure scholars' access to resources in the formats that they require?
- How do we describe items and build access systems that can be navigated with ease?
- How do we define texts and other sources in the digital environment?
- How should libraries reposition themselves to best serve the scholar as creator, researcher, and teacher?

Role of the Artifact in Library Collections

In 1999 CLIR formed an international task force on the role of the artifact in library collections. The task force, made up of scholars, librarians, and archivists, is engaging scholars in a structured discussion of the intrinsic value of different types of research materials, how they can best be preserved and made accessible, and how to ensure access to originals when their research demands it. CLIR's work with the American Council of Learned Societies in 1997–1998, convening five task forces that considered the changes libraries must anticipate in providing scholars with the electronic resources they will need, strongly underscored scholars' abiding interest in consulting the original. The task force on the role of the artifact will develop strategies for research libraries and the communities they serve to address the preservation and access needs of nondigital formats.

Collections, Content, and the Web

With special funding from the Institute of Museum and Library Services, CLIR and the Chicago Historical Society sponsored a conference in October 1999 that investigated issues confronting libraries and museums that are digitizing their collections of artifacts for dissemination over the Internet. By convening leaders of public and academic libraries together with leaders of art and historical museums, CLIR provided an opportunity for these institutions to cultivate closer relationships and find common solutions to the problems they all face when putting collections online. A forthcoming report, based on the conference, examines how cultural organizations represent their artifactual collections to virtual visitors and how they engage new audiences in the networked environment.

Authenticity in the Digital Environment

CLIR is organizing a project to examine authenticity in the digital environment. The project aims to answer the question, "What is an authentic digital object?" The concept of authenticity in recorded information connotes precise yet disparate things in different contexts and communities. In each context, however, the concept of authenticity has profound implications for the task of cataloging and describing an item. It has equally profound ramifications for preservation by setting the parameters of what is preserved and, consequently, by what techniques or series of techniques. CLIR is seeking the expertise of groups that have a significant stake in these issues: librarians, archivists, document historians, technologists, humanists, social scientists, and researchers in the physical and biological sciences.

Building Greek Collections

With the Library of Congress, CLIR cosponsored a two-day meeting of American and Greek scholars. Participants shared information about holdings in important collections in the United States and Greece and explored possibilities for cooperation in the preservation and exchange of materials. The conference resulted in a set of recommendations and a plan for their implementation.

Economics of Information

Strategies for providing resources for scholarship cannot be considered apart from the wide range of economic issues that confront university administrators. For example, most libraries and archives belong to a variety of consortia, largely for purposes of resource sharing and interlibrary lending. As physical volumes are displaced by digital surrogates that can be readily copied and widely distributed with entirely new economic and organization models, it is time to reexamine the roles and benefits of consortia. Under what conditions should libraries and archives act independently? Under what conditions are they better off working through consortia? For what purposes are consortia most effective in the digital age? This is but one of several issues that CLIR is planning to address in collaboration with diverse constituents.

CLIR is also organizing projects that address the following questions:

- How can we measure the productivity of those scholars and students using information resources?
- How can we assess the value of library and archival collections as heritage assets?
- How can CLIR help provosts and other university administrators measure the costs of information?
- How can CLIR develop business models for new services that grow out of its activities?

Risk Assessment Model

In 1999 CLIR engaged the accounting firm KPMG Peat Marwick to develop a model for assessing risks to library assets. The project builds on Peat Marwick's considerable experience with the Library of Congress's Heritage Assets Risk Assessment project, and it will result in a model that can be offered to other libraries and archives. The model will help cultural institutions analyze the risks to their collections and determine the ways to mitigate those risks. This management tool will help cultural institutions to view their collections as heritage assets and to describe in business terms to university officers the necessity of preserving them and providing security for the collections.

Licensing of Electronic Resources

The Association of American Publishers and CLIR began a series of informal meetings of publishers and librarians early in 1999 to discuss the licensing of electronic resources and to determine whether there are issues on which the two groups can agree. Librarians and publishers could save significant amounts of money if they could agree on language that could be used in most of their licensing arrangements. Librarians have developed draft language and have presented it to the publishers for their review.

Digital Library Service Models

CLIR is studying what is required to establish digital library service models. As individual institutions move ahead with their digital library programs, they recognize the need for certain services that benefit all of the institutions. Archival repositories, for example, will be necessary, and studies are under way to determine the appropriate business models for establishing them.

Preservation Awareness

According to Association of Research Libraries statistics, libraries are investing less in traditional preservation. Increasingly, funds for preservation compete with funds for digital projects, whether those funds come from institutional budgets or from external sources.

Funding agencies are pushing libraries to find solutions to the problem of preserving digital information, and CLIR, along with many other library organizations, continues to seek answers to the challenge of long-term access. Meanwhile, however, millions of print volumes continue to decay on our libraries' shelves. And there is an urgent need to find solutions to the problem of preserving films, videos, and recorded sound, recording media whose life spans are already known to be far shorter than acidic paper.

While continuing to seek solutions to the challenge of digital preservation, CLIR is framing the following questions related to the preservation of analog media:

- What extraordinary means will be necessary to preserve the deteriorating collections in research libraries?
- Will new models of organization be needed, such as establishing preservation centers to assume the responsibility for preservation on behalf of all?
- What can we learn by reconsidering the full range of preservation methods in collection management, acknowledging that microfilming is but one of the techniques that can be employed?
- Is there merit in establishing emergency procedures for the most important endangered titles—such as working with scholars to identify those titles that are most important to preserve?
- Is it time to revisit the conclusions of the original study of brittle books done in 1986, according to the new understanding and assumptions that inform our current approaches to sound collection management?

Strategies for Digital Archiving

In the area of digital preservation, CLIR has supported several studies, including the development of a tool for risk analysis prepared by Cornell University Library and Cornell's computing science department. The tool will help assess the long-term risk of migrating selected textual and numeric file formats over time. A report on this work and a workbook will be published in 2000. CLIR also commissioned David Bearman to develop his view that migration is the best and most practical approach for ensuring the longevity of library information resources and archival records. Both of these forthcoming reports provide a counterpoint to Jeff Rothenberg's report on the merits of emulation as a preservation strategy, *Avoiding Technological Quicksand*, published in early 1999. CLIR has also commissioned a forthcoming report from an expert on electronic records that advocates the selective use of archival skills by librarians to manage certain types of digital library collections.

Preserving Multimedia Collections

Regarding the preservation of audiovisual collections, CLIR has begun working with the Dance Heritage Coalition, a group of seven leading libraries and dance collections, to address the preservation and access problems of dance collections. CLIR published *Securing Our Dance Heritage: Issues in the Documentation and Preservation of Dance*. The report not only makes a strong case for the intellectual value of these largely ephemeral forms of cultural heritage, but also underscores the need to define best practices for basic preservation treatments for magnetic media.

Best Practices in Hybrid Conversion

Working with the National Endowment for the Humanities and the Research Libraries Group, CLIR began a project in 1999 to codify best practices in hybrid conversion from microform to digital images. On its Web site, CLIR presents a draft report that summarizes the current state of knowledge, identifies areas that need further research and development, and recommends a course of action to meet those needs. Foundations are currently reluctant to fund the dual costs of digitizing and creating computer output of microfilm. It may be necessary, as a practical matter, to accelerate the pace of specifying the requirements for digital images that improve the odds for preservation.

Building Preservation Capacity Abroad

CLIR continued its efforts to cooperate with institutions abroad to raise preservation awareness and build capacity. It initiated a three-year project with the National Book Centre of Greece to translate important preservation literature into Greek and to plan three workshops on preservation management at different locations. Workshop participants will be expected to lead additional training workshops after they return to their home institutions.

CLIR also supported the translation and distribution of a Russian-language version of the *IFLA Principles for the Care and Handling of Library Material*.

CLIR expanded its work in South Africa in 1999, sponsoring preservation workshops in Durban and Cape Town, led by staff of the Northeast Document Conservation Center, and a one-day meeting for librarians, archivists, and museum staff in Cape Town to discuss regional cooperation. Plans were also approved to proceed with a training program in early 2000 that will build on previous training, draw wider participation, engage South African faculty in conducting the workshop, and emphasize techniques for preservation assessments, which will be carried out during the workshop. An explicit objective of the workshop is to train participants who will then train others throughout the country.

Digital Libraries

CLIR is committed to fostering the development of digital libraries as a resource for research and learning today and into the future. CLIR remains deeply interested in the integration of traditional and electronic resources in support of scholarship, teaching, and learning. The construction of digital library services is at the core of CLIR's agenda.

The Digital Library Federation (DLF), sponsored by CLIR, is CLIR's major effort in digital libraries. DLF is a leadership organization that is committed to creating a virtual library of the digital materials held in repositories at many different institutions. To date, 25 research libraries have contributed substantial funds to support dedicated staff and to provide seed money for collaborative projects.

The DLF agenda focuses on three areas:

- Addressing the needs of specific scholarly disciplines
- Fostering the development of an integrated array of digital library services
- Engaging in activities designed to provide a framework for individual institutions to develop digital resources independently but in ways that can be readily integrated into a common networked environment

The problem of preserving digital information remains a primary concern of both CLIR and the members of DLF. More research is needed on possible organizational approaches to ensuring persistent access to digital information. Collaborations among publishers, scholarly societies, and libraries may prove to be the answer, but more work is needed to determine feasible structures for the fail-safe mechanisms called for in the 1996 report of the Task Force on Archiving of Digital Information.

Academic Image Cooperative

The Academic Image Cooperative (AIC) will enable scholars to share images of works, to which they own the rights, referenced in major art history textbooks. It will offer students, teachers, and the broader public curriculum-based sets of monitor-sized images for their free and unrestricted educational use. AIC will offer images that are proximate to traditional course selections. An online concordance will link images to standard art history survey books, and the concordance index will serve as one of the entry points to the image database.

The concordance index for the prototype has been completed, and business models have been developed. The Andrew W. Mellon Foundation approved a grant to fund the AIC prototype. This has spawned database design work, creation of an application list, and work on a contributor's contract. Demonstration of the prototype is planned for spring 2000.

Digital Certificate Prototype

In cooperation with the Corporation for Research and Education Networking (CREN), DLF is working on digital certificates that will allow universities to provide access to a range of campus systems and resources. Under DLF auspices, a group of member institutions and information providers has developed a protocol that enables an information provider to verify that a user bearing a digital certificate has authority from a home institution to use a requested resource. The prototype system combines the use of X.509 digital certificates for authentication with a directory service that authorizes licensed resources based on user attributes. CREN and DLF produced *Digital Certificate Infrastructure: Frequently Asked Questions* in August 1999.

Guides to Quality in Visual Resource Imaging

As libraries obtain more funding to convert analog materials into digital form, there is an urgent need to agree on best practices for image capture. CLIR and DLF have funded a series of five guides to digital image capture, written by experts in the field. The guides will be published on the Research Libraries Group (RLG) and CLIR Web sites in spring 2000.

Workshop on Technical Metadata Elements for Image Files

The National Information Standards Organization (NISO), CLIR, and RLG sponsored a workshop in April 1999 to discuss what technical information is needed to manage and use digital still images that reproduce pictures, documents, and artifacts. Several staff from DLF partner and allied institutions participated, along with other representatives from libraries, universities, museums, archives, the government, and the digital-imaging vendor community. The workshop revealed diverse interests and perspectives on the problem of metadata information. Participants reached agreement on a variety of issues, including a preliminary list of technical metadata elements, the use of industry standard metrics for assessing images, the need to develop methods of pointing at external test charts, and a requirement for mechanisms enabling the metadata associated with an image to persist through various transformations.

Long-term Maintenance of Digital Materials

DLF and RLG have formed a task force to advance the understanding of digital preservation policy and practice. Although few institutions have formal policies in place, many have made commitments to preserve digital materials and are adopting practices to support the handling and long-term maintenance of such materials. The goal of the task force is to identify and document these practices so that DLF and RLG can identify the technical, economic, and organizational barriers that institutions are facing, and what actions are needed to reduce those barriers.

The task force will gather and analyze existing digital preservation policies and practice descriptions for three classes of electronic materials: institutional records in digital form, locally digitized materials, and electronic publications.

In a separate activity, CLIR and DLF convened a small group of library directors and publishers and asked them to consider what is necessary to ensure continuing access to electronic journals for 100 years. Libraries have done little collectively to define their expectations of publishers. Several publishers made the point that they see their role as providing publications that libraries can preserve and distribute. Libraries now need to consider how they will provide continuing access to these publications.

Reference Linking

The Reference Linking Working Group is concerned with linking citations to the electronic journal literature. It is seeking to define the nature and scope of research and user consultation and to identify other work needed to foster the development of general systems of reference linking for marketplace testing. To this end, several meetings on reference linking were held in 1999, and plans have been made to engage computer scientists in additional research on solutions.

Technical Architecture Committee

The Technical Architecture Committee is addressing the challenge of how to deliver location or selection information to users when a library holds more than one copy of an article. Committee members wrote papers outlining solutions to the problem, which served as the basis of a session at the Coalition for Networked Information meeting in December 1999. Librarians and representatives of publishers, abstract and indexing providers, and information aggregators were invited to join in discussing the proposed approaches.

Forum on Digital Library Practices

In July 63 digital library practitioners from DLF institutions attended the first semiannual Forum on Digital Library Practices. The event included presentations on authentication and authorization systems, digital repositories, finding aids, page image navigation systems, and naming systems. Emory University was to host the next forum, scheduled for March 31–April 2, 2000.

Leadership

Rapid developments in information technology will force cultural and educational institutions to change profoundly. How well they adapt to a new environment with new expectations will depend on the strength of their leaders. How will these new leaders be prepared for the challenges ahead? CLIR continues to give high priority to the development of leadership for cultural and educational institutions. The largest project in this area is the establishment of the Frye Leadership Institute, which is being supported by the Robert W. Woodruff Foundation and by contributions from EDUCAUSE and Emory University.

Frye Leadership Institute

The Frye Leadership Institute will bring together in a summer program at Emory University potential leaders from libraries, computing centers, university presses, and faculty ranks in the United States and abroad—those who will manage the information resources of the campus in the future. The two-week residential program will be followed by a year-long practicum to define new leadership models for the networked environment.

Evaluation of Library Curricula

CLIR is also planning a comprehensive study of the requirements for and preparation of those who will work in research libraries in the future. With the changes that are occurring in schools of information studies, including a greater emphasis on technology and information-retrieval skills, it is uncertain whether the research library as an intellectual center holds any place in the new curricula.

Innovation in College Libraries

Leadership development will not be confined to the research library community. Liberal arts colleges, as models for teaching and learning, must reinvent the college library in the digital environment. A volume of case studies and the proceedings of a conference on innovation on the college campus, published this year, form the backdrop for a renewed focus on the digital future of college libraries.

International Developments

Recognizing that all of the foregoing issues have international dimensions, CLIR is focused on identifying relevant work being done in other countries and bringing appropriate groups together with groups in the United States to work on significant problems in common.

International Evaluation of Archival Descriptors

CLIR and the German Research Association are forming an international task force that will examine the problems related to archival descriptions of digital material. The task force will evaluate whether encoded archival descriptors (EAD) can meet the needs of archivists internationally.

International Database of Reformatted Masters

In 1999 CLIR continued its efforts to support the expansion of an international database of microfilm and digital masters. CLIR has worked with the European Register of Microform Masters, which now lists more than 2.3 million bibliographic descriptions of microfilm and digital masters.

Publications

CLIR published the following in 1999:

Reports

Arms, Caroline, with Judith Klavans and Donald J. Waters, eds. *Enabling Access in Digital Libraries: A Report on a Workshop on Access Management* (March 1999).

Beck, Ingrid. *Building Preservation Knowledge in Brazil* (November 1999).

Bouché, Nicole. *Digitization for Scholarly Use: The Boswell Papers Project at the Beinecke Rare Book and Manuscript Library* (March 1999).

Council on Library and Information Resources. *Annual Report 1998–1999* (October 1999).

Council on Library and Information Resources. *Innovative Use of Information Technology by Colleges* (August 1999).

Council on Library and Information Resources. *Scholarship, Instruction, and Libraries at the Turn of the Century: Results from Five Task Forces Appointed by the American Council of Learned Societies and the Council on Library and Information Resources* (January 1999).

Digital Library Federation. *Annual Report 1998–1999* (October 1999).

Fuller Snyder, Allegra, and Catherine Johnson. *Securing Our Dance Heritage: Issues in the Documentation and Preservation of Dance* (July 1999).

Green, Ann, JoAnn Dionne, and Martin Dennis. *Preserving the Whole: A Two-Track Approach to Rescuing Social Science Data and Metadata* (June 1999)

Hurley, Bernard J., et al. *The Making of America II Testbed Project: A Digital Library Service Model* (December 1999).

Rothenberg, Jeff. *Avoiding Technological Quicksand: Finding a Viable Technical Foundation for Digital Preservation* (January 1999).

Smith, Abby. *The Future of the Past: Preservation in American Research Libraries (April 1999).*

Smith, Abby. *Why Digitize?* (February 1999).

Newsletters

CLIR Issues, nos. 7–12.

Preservation and Access International Newsletter, nos. 5–8.

Scholarships and Awards

CLIR administers the A. R. Zipf Fellowship in Information Management, which is awarded each year to a student enrolled in graduate school, in the early stages of study, who shows exceptional promise for leadership and technical achievement in information management. Applicants must be U.S. citizens or permanent residents. See CLIR's Web site for additional information.

In 1999 CLIR awarded the Zipf Fellowship to Debra Ruffner Weiss, a Ph.D. candidate in the School of Information and Library Science at the University of North Carolina at Chapel Hill.

Special Reports

Electronic Journals: A Snapshot

Edward J. Valauskas

As the chief editor of a successful electronic journal, I must admit a great deal of bias about this medium for scholarship and communication.[1] Electronic journals are a relatively recent invention in terms of academic discourse[2] and have had a spectacular impact on the ways in which researchers, students, and the general public interact and discuss new ideas and findings. As a result, there have been some territorial disputes over the use of this new medium from scholars and others.[3] These disputes generally boil down to comparisons of electronic journals with traditional journals, and their methodologies. Do "referee" and "refereed" mean exactly the same in both environments? What are the roles of editors? Who are the publishers? Does digital mean speed at the cost of scientific care and exactitude? This article attempts to address some of these issues, by answering four fundamental questions:

1 What are electronic journals?
2 Who creates electronic journals?
3 How are electronic journals used?
4 Where are electronic journals going?

What Are Electronic Journals?

Electronic journals have been defined in several ways. George Machovec describes electronic serials "as any journal, magazine, e'zine, webzine, newsletter or type of electronic serial publication which is available over the Internet."[4] Contrast this definition with a more traditional description of a serial as a "publication in any medium issued in successive parts bearing numeric or chronological designations intended to be continued indefinitely."[5]

A combination of this traditional definition with Machovec's description would mean that electronic journals

- Must appear with some sort of non-random frequency over time
- Occur with a unique title, date, and sequential numbering system so that the content of any given issue or number does not vary after publication

Edward J. Valauskas is chief editor of *First Monday* at http://firstmonday.org.

- Take a digital form, usually in terms of the most widespread medium available (such as the World Wide Web)
- Continue without end (or at least make the end invisible to readers and contributors alike)

As Steven Shadle points out, many electronic journals fail to meet these primary characteristics. Electronic journals often alter their contents over time; in addition, each title may be completely different in functionality.[6]

Much recent debate about digital journals[7] has focused on those that purport to be peer-reviewed and refereed. If we modify the previous definition, a peer-reviewed electronic journal can then be described as a regularly numbered and dated publication appearing on a regular and continuous basis on the Internet, with its contents passing through an editorial review in advance of public release. Traditional paper-based peer-reviewed academic publications appear on frequency cycles varying from weekly, biweekly, monthly, bimonthly, quarterly, annually, to the ever-infamous "irregular." Electronic academic journals tend to appear with similar frequencies, but generally promise faster delivery (global Internet vs. global postal services[8]) and quicker editorial review and analysis.

Of the thousands of electronic journals and magazines listed in any of the well-known digital directories,[9] only a small percentage would fit this definition exactly. Yet these journals are causing an enormous debate over the future of scholarship and academic communication. Why?

In large part, traditional, paper-based, peer-reviewed journals have been available for literally centuries in their current state. They have been well integrated into academic routines, where they have found a place as determinants of status, stature, and stability. The idiosyncrasies of traditional journals are known, discussed, and accepted, even if they are found at times to be disagreeable and dysfunctional. Like an odd member of the family, traditional journals are tolerated and talked about, when in their odd ways they dispense fame and glory to some and harsh criticism to others. Into this scene came digital journals, promising to correct all of the problems of their older relations, with faster review, global access and readership, minimal academic politics, and enhanced appearances, making many of the troublesome aspects of paper journals vanish as a distant memory. The differences between these types of publications have been aggravated by the questionable—to some—origins of electronic journals. Which leads to a second fundamental question: Who creates electronic journals?

Who Creates Electronic Journals?

Many electronic journals had their origins as individual solutions—by educated, dedicated individuals and clusters of scholars—to collective frustrations with traditional publishers and associated bodies, such as professional, nonprofit organizations. They were an attempt to devise new ways to communicate, independent of traditional and well-worn paths of scholarship, taking advantage of computer networks and the increasing abundance of multimedia-capable computers globally. For example, *Theoretical Anthropology*, produced by Thomas Fillitz, Ralph Fichtner, and Manfred Kremser at the Institute of Social Anthropology at the

University of Vienna, is described as a "forum in which the diversity of scholars becomes apparent and is wished, in order to convey the opportunity of following scientific debates of all kinds. . . . We feel that electronic text can foster discussion [and] communication . . . and reach the scientific community world wide. The journal should not be seen in challenge with the print media. *Theoretical Anthropology* should be understood as a forum for discussion."[10]

Over time, but especially in the past year, electronic journals have become increasingly popular with traditional publishers and professional associations. Traditional scholarship has also been pushed to accept this new model of publication by scholars, who are all too ready to abandon traditional formats with their problems and political issues. Academic institutions are increasingly accepting publication in peer-reviewed digital journals as legitimate and worthy of credit and even praise.[11] No longer is the tenured professor the only one ready to take the risk of publishing noteworthy scholarship in a "new" medium.

Internet-based peer-reviewed journals have proven to be no different from their paper counterparts, except for the accelerated review, rapid publication, global distribution, and professional acceptance. Some disciplines have been slower than others to develop, nurture, accept, and reward electronic journals, but nearly all researchers in nearly all disciplines are demanding new ways to reach larger audiences with ideas and research results.[12] Electronic journals offer a relatively inexpensive path to diverse and large audiences, thanks to the absence of printing and mailing costs.[13] Electronic journals will not replace paper journals, but digital journals without paper parallels will be sites where experimentation will occur, which leads to the next question.

How Are Electronic Journals Used?

Like traditional paper journals, the contents of electronic journals are refereed, edited, published, commented, cited, and ignored. Given the level of discussion about peer review, some digital journals go into great detail about the analysis of content in advance of publication. For example, the electronic journal *Research on Contemplative Life* provides extensive information on the duties of editors, following "the canons of quality scholarship, optimal flexibility, functional standardization, and minimal hyperstandardization."[14] Some journals make it very clear that the medium makes review a much more timely process; *Electronic Geosciences* from Springer, for instance, states, "The use of the Internet, at every step of the reviewing and publication process, leads to exceedingly short publication times of only a few weeks from submission to appearance. Thus, this journal is particularly suitable for publication of results/ideas in rapidly evolving fields."[15]

Unlike traditional paper journals, electronic journals are hyperlinked; include online chats, discussions, debates, and flame wars; feature original as well as republished and recycled materials; contain content copyrighted by authors, not publishers; are often free or available at little cost; and are multimediated (any paper may include graphics, animation, data sets, programs, and other tools not possible with paper-based publications). For example, *G-Cubed (Geochemistry, Geophysics, Geosystems): An Electronic Journal of the Earth Sciences*, sponsored by the American Geophysical Union and the Geochemistry Society, makes it clear in its instructions to authors that the HTML version of the journal "may include ancillary information such as animations, movies, virtual-reality images, downloadable tables of data, computer code, etc., that take advantage of the electronic medium . . . viewed using a standard World Wide Web browser."[16]

Electronic journals are also demonstrating that back issues have some real value in attracting readers. In examining the use of all issues of *First Monday* in 1999, it was found that the most popular article (in terms of readers) was not even published in 1999. As Table 1 demonstrates, accessibility of all papers and all issues on the Internet means that a peer-reviewed electronic journal will be used differently than a paper equivalent. Readers essentially will customize an electronic journal for their own purposes, reading a paper from a current issue or pulling a cited paper from a back file. This phenomenon means that publishers of traditional journals migrating to an Internet state will have to seriously consider the best ways to make archival volumes available in electronic form.

Table 1 / Most Frequently Read Papers in *First Monday*, 1999

1. Kerry Coffman and Andrew M. Odlyzko, 1998. "The Size and Growth Rate of the Internet," *First Monday*, vol. 3, no. 10 (October), at http://firstmonday.org/issues/issue3_10/coffman/.
2. Nikolai Bezroukov, 1999. "Open Source Software Development as a Special Type of Academic Research (Critique of Vulgar Raymondism)," *First Monday*, vol. 4, no. 10 (October), at http://firstmonday.org/issues/issue4_10/bezroukov/.
3. David F. Noble, 1998, "Digital Diploma Mills: The Automation of Higher Education," *First Monday*, vol. 3, no. 1 (January), at http://firstmonday.org/issues/issue3_1/noble/.
4. Gisle Hannemyr, 1999. "Technology and Pleasure: Considering Hacking Constructive," *First Monday*, vol. 4, no. 2 (February), at http://firstmonday.org/issues/issue4_2/gisle/.
5. John Kelsey and Bruce Schneier, 1999. "The Street Performer Protocol and Digital Copyrights," *First Monday*, vol. 4, no. 6 (June), at http://firstmonday.org/issues/issue4_6/kelsey/.
6. Eben Moglen, 1999. "Anarchism Triumphant: Free Software and the Death of Copyright," *First Monday*, vol. 4, no. 8 (August), at http://firstmonday.org/issues/issue4_8/moglen/.
7. Jeannette Allis Bastian, 1997. "Filtering the Internet in American Public Libraries: Sliding Down the Slippery Slope," *First Monday*, vol. 2, no. 10 (October), at http://firstmonday.org/issues/issue2_10/bastian/.
8. Mary Minow, 1997. "Filters and the Public Library: A Legal and Policy Analysis," *First Monday*, vol. 2, no. 12 (December), at http://firstmonday.org/issues/issue2_12/minow/.
9. Michael H. Goldhaber, 1997. "The Attention Economy and the Net," *First Monday*, vol. 2, no. 4 (April), at http://firstmonday.org/issues/issue2_4/goldhaber/.
10. Hal R. Varian, 1996. "Differential Pricing and Efficiency," *First Monday*, vol. 1, no. 2 (August), at http://firstmonday.org/issues/issue2/different/.

Electronic journals will continue to change the ways in which we think about scholarly communication. If these journals function as appropriate filters, they will alter the ways in which scholars examine and accept new ideas and research results. Perhaps more researchers will adopt a "model" devised by Charles Perrow, sociologist at Yale, who wrote, "I try not to read anything until I have three times been pressed to do so by reputable sources. There are countless articles that people have pressed upon me as vital or brilliant or decisive that I have not read. I have not read them because my network does not turn up two other people who, in person or in print, share that judgment."[17]

Perrow's comments point to perhaps the ultimate value of peer-reviewed journals in this time of terabytes of information on the World Wide Web—as filters, verifiers, condensers, editors, and agents. Without these journals, it would indeed be difficult to isolate the virtual gold from the electronic dross.

Where Are Electronic Journals Going?

The vast amount of information on the Internet certainly demands new kinds of finding tools and organizers. As Steve Lawrence and C. Lee Giles of the NEC Research Institute have demonstrated, search engines are not able to keep pace with the growth of information on the Web and are not able to keep abreast of sites as they move, die, or otherwise transmogrify.[18] Into this frustrating equation, electronic journals are emerging as the only true sources of verifiable, exact, accurate, and objective information on the Web. With their rapid growth as a medium, electronic journals may soon put out of business search engines and directories that show more interest in banner ads than accuracy, profitability over accurate reporting, and bandwidth waste over efficiency. Instead of search engines providing faulty responses, we may see electronic journals providing information along an entire "prepublication continuum" where comments and review work in combination to create ideas and research results heretofore unattainable with traditional media.[19]

In the meantime, electronic journals will not replace their paper equivalents, where they exist. Digital journals will provide acceptable alternatives for the quick publication of interesting new ideas and exciting results. With experimentation, electronic journals offer a bright future for scholarship, working in ways unimaginable just a few years ago, overcoming barriers of time and space in linking researchers together with minimal cost.

Notes

1. By "successful," I am referring specifically to the journal's use, not its profitability. An analysis of *First Monday*'s logs for 1999 revealed that 1,055,678 papers were read and downloaded from the current issues and back files of the journal. That measure indicates that the journal was widely examined over the course of the year. As *First Monday* is free and completely accessible, the journal did not earn any revenues in 1999. From a financial perspective, the journal is not "successful" as it generates no income or profit. By my standards, I would prefer millions of readers to millions of dollars.

2. The first scientific journals appeared in 1665 as the *Philosophical Transactions of the Royal Society of London* and the *Journal des Sçavans*, released in Paris. See Ann C. Schaffner, "The Future of Scientific Journals: Lessons from the Past," at http://www.uni-koeln.de/themen/text/schaf94a.htm.

3. On territorial disputes, Declan Butler noted that the recent move in Europe to develop a European digital repository for electronic journals was motivated by the American creation of PubMedCentral. " . . . a European archives was essential to avoid a U.S. monopoly on a global scientific archive." See Declan Butler, 2000. "All Parties Keen to Press On with Europe-Based Science Website," *Nature*, vol. 403 (27 January), pp. 347–348.

4. http://www.coalliance.org/ejournal/.

5. This definition appears in the *Anglo-American Cataloging Rules*, 2nd edition. Chicago: American Library Association, 1988, as cited in Steven C. Shadle, 1998. "A Square Peg in a Round Hole: Applying AACR2 to Electronic Journals," In: Wayne Jones, editor. *E-Serials: Publishers, Libraries, Users, and Standards*. Binghampton, N.Y.: Haworth Press, p. 149.

6. Shadle, p. 152.

7. I will use the terms "electronic journal" and "digital journal" throughout this paper. I consider these terms to be synonymous. There is an overabundance of descriptors for these publications, including ejournals, ezines, webzines, Internet journals, and other assorted monikers.

8. The Internet is well known for its lack of a central governing authority (although there are a number of organizations providing fundamental services such as domain-name resolution and routing). Postal services were organized in 1874 with the Treaty of Berne; they now function according to specifications described by the Universal Postal Union for 184 members. See http://www.upu.int/.

9. John Labovitz's e-zine list, in operation since 1993, counted 4,392 zines as of March 8, 2000; see http://www.meer.net/~johnl/e-zine-list/index.html. A much smaller subset of journals is available at the Committee on International Cooperation (CIC) Electronic Journals Collection (EJC) at http://ejournals.cic.net/. The University of British Columbia Library has a compendium called *Ejournal SiteGuide: A MetaSource* at http://www.library.ubc.ca/ejour/. The Association of Research Libraries maintains the *Directory of Electronic Journals, Newsletters, and Academic Discussion Lists* with thousands of entries; archival volumes of the directory are available at http://www.arl.org/scomm/edir/archive.html.

10. http://www.univie.ac.at/voelkerkunde/theoretical-anthropology/edit.html. *Theoretical Anthropology* was first published in June 1994; the last issue appeared in May 1997.

11. Teresa Y. Neely, 1999. "The Impact of Electronic Publications on Promotion and Tenure Decisions," *Leading Ideas: Issues and Trends in Diversity, Leadership and Career Development*, Issue 10 (October), at http://www.arl.org/diversity/leading/issue10/tneely.html.

12. Ken Eason, Chris Carter, Susan Harker, Sue Pomfrett, Kathy Phillips, and John Richardson, 1997. "A Comparative Analysis of the Role of Multi-Media Electronic Journals in Scholarly Disciplines," at http://www.ukoln.ac.uk/services/elib/papers/tavistock.eason/eason.html.

13. On the economics of electronic journals, see Andrew M. Odlyzko, 1997. "The Economics of Electronic Journals," *First Monday*, vol. 2, no. 8 (August), at http://firstmonday.org/issues/issue2_8/odlyzko/, and Marjolein Bot, Johan Burgemeester, and Hans Roes, 1998. "The Cost of Publishing an Electronic Journal," *D-Lib Magazine* (November), at http://www.dlib.org/dlib/november98/11roes.html.

14. http://www.mnsmc.edu/merton/peer.html. Interestingly, only two issues of this journal seem to have appeared; see http://www.mnsmc.edu/merton/contents1.html.

15. *Electronic Geosciences* at http://link.springer-ny.com/link/service/journals/10069/about.htm.

16. http://gcubed.magnet.fsu.edu/index.asp?ContentPage=authors/authors.html

17. Charles Perrow, 1989. "On Not Using Libraries," In: Humanists at Work: Disciplinary Perspectives and Personal Reflections, symposium sponsored by the Institute of the Humanities and the University Library at the University of Illinois at Chicago, 27–28 April 1989, p. 32.

18. http://meta.rrzn.uni-hannover.de/eusidic/nec-aktu.htm.

19. Andrew M. Odlyzko, "Tragic Loss or Good Riddance? The Impending Demise of Traditional Scholarly Journals," http://www.research.att.com/~amo/doc/tragic.loss.txt.

The Database Protection Debate in the United States

Jonathan Band

Partner, Morrison and Foerster, Washington, D.C.

Makoto Kono

Liaison Representative, Fujitsu Ltd., Washington, D.C.

Two database protection bills are pending before the U.S. House of Representatives: H.R. 354, introduced by Howard Coble (R-N.C.), and H.R. 1858, introduced by Tom Bliley, Jr. (R-Va.). These bills differ significantly in approach and scope. This paper summarizes the background to the debate, compares the two bills, and discusses the possible global ramifications of legislation in this area.

Background

The Status Quo

Historically, America's basic information policy has been that facts reside in the public domain. This allows a second-generation publisher to extract facts from an existing compilation for reuse in its own compilation. Facts are viewed as the building blocks of knowledge that everyone is free to use and reuse.

Nonetheless, a database publisher has several ways of protecting its investment in collecting facts. First, the publisher can rely on copyright. Copyright protects the original selection, coordination, and arrangement of the facts in a compilation, but not the facts themselves. Thus, copyright usually prevents the wholesale copying of a database—which typically contains at least a minimal amount of original expression—but not the extraction and reuse of individual facts.

Second, the publisher can rely on contracts. Many databases, particularly online databases, are distributed subject to license agreements under which the licensee—the user—agrees not to re-disseminate the information.

Third, the publisher can rely on state common law misappropriation. Under this doctrine, the collector can prevent competitors from copying "hot news" or other time-sensitive information. See *NBA* v. *Motorola*, 105 F.3d 841 (2d Cir. 1997).

Fourth, the publisher can rely on technological measures. These measures are particularly effective with respect to online databases, where the publisher can limit the user's access to relatively small amounts of information at any one time. These limitations impede the copying of the database as a whole. Technological measures now receive legal protection under the recently enacted Digital Millennium Copyright Act (DMCA). The DMCA created a new Chapter 12 to the Copyright Act, which prohibits the manufacture and sale of devices that are designed to circumvent technological protection measures.

Feist Decision

Until 1991 the collector could rely on yet another legal doctrine: "sweat of the brow." In a few circuits, courts interpreted the Copyright Act as preventing the copying of facts in a compilation in which there were no original elements in selection or arrangement. Courts in these jurisdictions thought it was unfair and unwise to afford no protection to the efforts of people who assembled "plain vanilla" directories. It is important to note that "sweat of the brow" was largely a stop-gap measure; courts typically applied it to compilations that lacked any expression and that were copied in their entirety.

In 1991, however, the Supreme Court in *Feist* v. *Rural Telephone,* 499 U.S. 340 (1991), found the sweat-of-the-brow doctrine unconstitutional. A unanimous court held that under the copyright clause of the Constitution, copyright protection could extend only to expressive elements in compilations and that effort without creativity could not convert facts into expression. Notwithstanding the loss of the sweat-of-the-brow doctrine, the database industry in the United States has continued to grow, largely because of the protection afforded by copyright, contract, state common law, and technology, as discussed above. Nonetheless, some database publishers have sought to restore the protection afforded by the sweat-of-the-brow doctrine.

EU Database Directive

This effort gained significant momentum in 1996, when the European Union adopted its Database Directive. Under this regime, a second-generation publisher could not extract or reuse a qualitatively or quantitatively substantial part of a first-generation database, even if the second publisher did not extract or reuse any protectable expression. The Database Directive's *sui generis* protection is available only on a reciprocity basis. This means that a non-EU publisher can receive the heightened level of protection only if the publisher's country of origin afforded an equivalent level of protection. In other words, if the United States does not enact database legislation on a par with the Database Directive, then U.S. publishers cannot receive this added protection in Europe.

There is, however, a loophole in this reciprocity requirement. If a non-EU publisher has a subsidiary operating in the EU, then databases distributed by the subsidiary would be able to receive the heightened protection.

In response to the EU Directive, Congressman Carlos Moorhead (R-Calif.) introduced H.R. 3531 in the 104th Congress. H.R. 3531 would have established a *sui generis* database protection regime even more stringent than that of the EU Directive; H.R. 3531 had a 25-year term of protection, while the EU Directive established a 15-year term of protection. H.R. 3531 died with the end of the 104th Congress without further discussion.

Additionally, the EU and the U.S. Patent and Trademark Office suggested that a database treaty modeled on the EU Database Directive be placed on the agenda of the 1996 World Intellectual Property Organization (WIPO) Diplomatic Conference. At the beginning of the conference, however, discussion of a database treaty was deferred because too many other items relating to the Copyright Treaty and the Performances and Phonograms Treaty needed to be resolved. Moreover, representatives from other regions contended that discussion of a database treaty was premature.

H.R. 2652

In the 105th Congress, database protection reappeared in the form of H.R. 2652, introduced by Rep. Coble, chairman of the House Subcommittee on Courts and

Intellectual Property. Although the legislation was styled as a misappropriation bill based on a tort theory, rather than as an intellectual-property right theory, the substantive tests were almost identical to those of H.R. 3531. H.R. 2652 received support only from a small number of large database publishers, such as Reed Elsevier (the Anglo-Dutch owner of LEXIS-NEXIS) and Thomson (the Canadian owner of West).

Value-added publishers and the science, education, and library communities argued that H.R. 2652 was unnecessary—that copyright, contract, common law misappropriation, and technology provided databases with adequate protection. Moreover, these opponents contended that the database industry was healthy and that there was no market failure that required legislative correction.

Nonetheless, H.R. 2652 passed the House twice—once as a stand-alone bill and the second time as part of the House's version of the Digital Millennium Copyright Act. At this point the Department of Commerce, the Department of Justice, and the Federal Trade Commission all registered serious concerns with the bill. In the House-Senate conference on the DMCA in the closing days of the 105th Congress in October 1998, the database portion was dropped.

Database Bills Pending in the 106th Congress

H.R. 354: Collections of Information Antipiracy Act

On January 19, 1999, Chairman Coble introduced H.R. 354, which is very similar to H.R. 2652. Under H.R. 354, a person cannot (1) make available to others (2) a substantial part (3) of a collection of information gathered or maintained by another person through the investment of substantial resources (4) so as to cause material harm to the primary or related market for a product or service containing that collection of information. Additionally, one cannot extract a substantial part of a collection of information so as to cause material harm to the primary market for the collection of information. The goal of the legislation is to protect the investment in databases by restoring the sweat-of-the-brow doctrine and ensuring protection for U.S. publishers under the EU Database Directive through the establishment of a comparable regime here.

Many of the specific problems identified by the critics of H.R. 2652 exist in H.R. 354 as well. According to these critics, H.R. 354 goes far beyond preventing database piracy and prevents legitimate reuse of information for socially valuable purposes. Specifically, given the ambiguity of the term "substantial part," the second-generation publisher is at risk whenever it extracts any information from an existing database; it has no way of knowing what the first publisher, or a court, will consider "substantial."

Further, most, if not all, value-added databases will harm a "related market" for a product containing the first collection of information. Indeed, the market for a value-added database almost by definition is a related market for a product containing the collection of information. H.R. 354 contains a "reasonable use" provision not found in H.R. 2652, but its terms are so vague as to provide little comfort to most value-added publishers.

Another concern identified by opponents of H.R. 354 is sole-source databases. For many database markets, there is no feasible way for another person to collect the information independently. This may be because the information is historical and thus can be found only in an existing database or because the publisher has a special relationship with the producer of the information. The protection afforded by H.R. 354 guarantees these publishers monopoly prices.

A final major concern is that notwithstanding the 15-year term limit, H.R. 354 as a practical matter confers perpetual protection for databases. This is particularly the case with dynamic online databases, where the second publisher has no way of knowing for which portions of the database protection has expired.

For these reasons, the opponents of H.R. 354 believe it will inflict serious harm on many sectors of the economy that rely heavily on access to information. Financial publishers, such as Bloomberg and Dun & Bradstreet, have concluded that it will increase the cost of the information they incorporate in their products. Similarly, many scientists believe that H.R. 354 will destroy the culture of sharing information that is so integral to scientific progress and that has maintained U.S. scientific competitiveness for many decades.

In March 1999 the Intellectual Property Subcommittee held a hearing on H.R. 354. The subcommittee "marked-up" the bill in May 1999; a few days later the full Judiciary Committee adopted it with no substantive debate.

H.R. 1858: Consumer and Investor Access to Information Act

On May 19, 1999, Rep. Bliley, chairman of the House Commerce Committee, ranking member John Dingell (D-Mich.), and the chairmen and ranking members of the Telecommunications and Finance Subcommittees jointly introduced H.R. 1858, the Consumer and Investor Access to Information Act. H.R. 1858 targets the parasitical copying of databases, without prohibiting reuse of information to create new kinds of databases. Specifically, this bill prohibits a person from distributing a duplicate of someone else's database in head-to-head competition with the first database.

By establishing a narrower prohibition than H.R. 354, H.R. 1858 does not prevent reuse of information in innovative databases. It deals with the sole-source database problem by prohibiting misuse of the new protection. It eliminates the chilling effect of frivolous litigation by vesting enforcement authority in the Federal Trade Commission rather than private parties. H.R. 1858 also has a more comprehensive exemption for online service providers than H.R. 354.

This narrow approach has widespread support among financial publishers; the science, education, and research communities; Internet companies; and large corporate users of information. They believe that this bill successfully balances concerns about database piracy with the need to use previously gathered information as a foundation for new products.

The Telecommunications and Finance Subcommittees held hearings on H.R. 1858 during June 1999. Those hearings highlighted the difference between the two bills and emphasized that the Judiciary and the Commerce Committees view the issue of database protection from different perspectives. The Judiciary Committee is more concerned with protecting the publishers' investment, while the Commerce Committee is more concerned with ensuring the availability of information necessary for commercial activity.

H.R. 1858 was marked up in the Telecommunications and Finance Subcommittees in July 1999. It was considered and passed by the full Commerce Committee in early August 1999. It is now up to the Rules Committee and the House Republican leadership to decide how to proceed with these two competing bills.

Senate Action

On January 19, 1999, Senator Orrin Hatch (R-Utah), chairman of the Senate Judiciary Committee, placed a statement concerning database protection in the *Congressional Record*. He attached to his statement, for discussion purposes, three alternative bills: an early draft of H.R. 354, an early draft of H.R. 1858, and a draft his staff had produced during the 105th Congress based on H.R. 2652. As of January, none of these bills had been formally introduced in the Senate.

Further, Senator John McCain (R-Ariz.), chairman of the Senate Commerce Committee, introduced S. 95, also on January 19, 1999. While the other bills discussed above increase protection for databases, the McCain bill heads in the other direction: It prohibits any limitation on "the dissemination by any medium of mass communication" of stock-trading information.

The stock exchanges, particularly the New York Stock Exchange and NASDAQ, have signaled support for H.R. 354. Financial publishers such as Bloomberg, as well as such stock brokerages as Charles Schwab & Co., fear that the exchanges will use broad database protection like H.R. 354 to increase the price of the live feeds of stock quotes and otherwise restrict the downstream use of this information. S. 95 resolves this dispute by making stock information even more available than it is currently. (Although S. 95 targets only stock-trading information, McCain has indicated that he is interested in the broader database issue.)

Administration Position

The Clinton administration has concluded that there is a gap in existing protection for databases that needs to be filled. It has raised specific concerns with the language of both H.R. 354 and H.R. 1858. With respect to H.R. 354, the administration believes that its scope is too broad. It believes that only acts of commercial distribution should be prohibited, not acts of extraction without further dissemination to the public. It has continuing concerns regarding perpetual protection and sole-source databases. It also believes the definitions of terms such as "related markets" need to be tightened. The administration stressed that these concerns need to be addressed in part to ensure that the legislation does not run afoul of the First Amendment of the Constitution. The Department of Justice in particular fears that restrictions on the use of information could violate the fundamental right of free speech.

The Clinton administration also voiced concerns with respect to H.R. 1858. It felt that some terms were too broadly defined, and could result in overprotection. At the same time, it felt that the absence of a private cause of action would result in underprotection. It strongly applauded H.R. 1858's focus on commercial misappropriation.

As of January, the Clinton administration had not signaled its preference of one bill over the other. This is not surprising given that the debate between the two bills has evolved in some measure into a political battle between two very powerful Congressional committees.

Federal Trade Commission Position

On July 1, 1999, the Federal Trade Commission (FTC) issued testimony concerning H.R. 1858. The testimony stated that H.R. 1858 successfully addressed many of the concerns the FTC had raised in 1998 with respect to H.R. 2652, the predecessor to H.R. 354. The FTC testimony identified a few areas where the language of H.R. 1858 was ambiguous, particularly in the misuse section. The FTC also questioned whether it had sufficient resources to enforce H.R. 1858's prohibitions.

International Dimensions

Reciprocity Under the EU Database Directive

Proponents of H.R. 354 argue that H.R. 1858 does not offer comparable protection to the EU Database Directive and therefore will not lead to reciprocal protection under the directive. The administration publicly has stated that the United States should decide for itself what level of protection is appropriate for databases and not worry about comparability with the directive. Underlying this position is the realization that reciprocal protection is the outcome of a political process involving negotiations between the United States and the EU. In other words, the substantive merits of comparability are a minor, if not insignificant, factor in this political process.

WIPO Deliberations

As noted above, the World Intellectual Property Organization (WIPO) in 1996 decided not to consider a database treaty at the Diplomatic Conference. Since 1998 WIPO has held two sessions of the Standing Committee on Copyright and Related Rights to study the subject, and database protection was on the agenda of regional meetings cosponsored by WIPO during the summer of 1999. While currently there seems to be no significant momentum to deliberate the database protection issue in WIPO, it is likely that WIPO will pursue a database treaty after the United States enacts the legislation. This is because the United States at that time probably will join with the EU and place great pressure on WIPO to consider a database treaty very seriously. A database treaty will prove controversial because the developing world will view it as yet another stratagem by the developed world to impede the developing world's progress.

Conclusion

The database bills pending in Congress will head the database industry, and arguably the economy as a whole, in dramatically different directions. While H.R. 354 will grant to first-generation publishers a new weapon against piracy, it will also provide them with unprecedented control over downstream competition. At the other end of the spectrum, S. 95 indicates that the database debate imposes risk on first-generation publishers. Congress may very well decide to deprive them of some of the protections they now have. As noted above, many database publishers are de facto monopolists, and Congress is appropriately suspicious of monopolies in the Information Age. Between these two extremes, H.R. 1858 provides an incremental increase of protection to first-generation publishers against pirates, without constraining legitimate activities by second-generation publishers.

Balance in this area is critical. Information is the oxygen of the new economy; drastic changes to information policy will hinder the expansion of the Internet, impede research, and stifle entrepreneurship and innovation. As Senator Hatch has stated, the U.S. Congress will consider the database issue within the context of the "national Internet policy."

The EU adopted the Database Directive with relatively little public participation. The database debate in the United States, by contrast, involves all stakeholders, including database publishers, Internet companies, commercial users, libraries, universities, science organizations, and a range of financial institutions. Accordingly, the discussion of this issue is far more robust in the United States and far more likely to produce a balanced result. U.S. developments should be closely monitored in countries where there is no such discussion.

As the debate proceeds in the United States and abroad, certain threshold questions must be kept in mind:

- Is additional protection truly needed?
- If so, what is the harm that needs to be addressed?
- Is the legislation that is designed to cure this harm drafted narrowly enough so as not to have unintended negative consequences?

Furthermore, discussion of the database protection issue should reflect other fundamental domestic policies such as future development of the economy and technology.

Change—The Only Certainty in Copyright

Laura N. Gasaway

Introduction

Copyright law has expanded over the years to provide protection for newly developed types of works. Motion pictures were added to the list of protectable works in 1912, audiovisual works were inserted into the motion picture category in the 1976 Copyright Act,[1] and multimedia works and Web pages are protected today as audiovisual works. Along with this growing list of types of works that are eligible for copyright protection, the technology for reproducing these works in libraries has expanded. In the 1960s photocopy technology revolutionized note-taking in libraries, and only 25 years ago video recording was still new. The range of reproduction technologies available today is overwhelming, from fax machines to scanners that can create digital copies from printed works to MP3 recorders for downloading music recordings. The ability to digitize existing copyrighted works in order to facilitate use, manipulation, storage, and access is an attraction for many libraries, librarians, and library patrons. Further, these works may be loaded onto a server and be made available over the World Wide Web to users anywhere in the world. From a work preserved in digital form, perfect copies can be reproduced.

The spread of distance education has also affected the demand for reproduction of copyrighted works. From a few courses only a decade ago, most of them offered through video technology, online courses are rapidly increasing today. Teachers want to use copyrighted works in teaching distance learning courses just as they use them in the classroom. Moreover, libraries in the institutions that originate the courses are being asked to provide services to distant users who are registered for these online courses. Digital technology permits the delivery of copies of articles, chapters from books, and so forth, requested by distant education students—requests that would have been satisfied in the past with photocopies.

These powerful technological developments have not gone unnoticed by the copyright-holder community. Not only have copyright entrepreneurs sought to ensure the same protection and control that they have over their works in the analog world; they have sought increased protections for works in digital format. Control over access to the work is viewed as more significant in the digital environment than in the analog world. Many have indicated a desire to replace traditional copyright-law protection with licensing agreements that will not only control access to the work, but will be more restrictive on users than the current copyright statute. In fact, some publishers and producers have even talked about

Laura N. "Lolly" Gasaway has been director of the Kathrine R. Everett Law Library and professor of law at the University of North Carolina since 1985. She teaches courses in intellectual property and cyberspace law in the Law School and law librarianship and legal resources in the School of Information and Library Science. She is the author of numerous books and articles on copyright, including *Growing Pains: Adapting Copyright for Libraries, Education and Society* (Rothman, 1997).

"pay-per-view" licensing. Libraries report that publishers seem to be assuming a "take-it-or-leave-it" approach to licensing.[2]

Copyrighted works increasingly are being viewed as articles of commerce, and international treaties and international organizations such as the World Intellectual Property Organization (WIPO) are dealing with copyright issues in a global fashion, which requires the U.S. Congress to amend our statute to satisfy U.S. treaty obligations.

Against this backdrop there have been several changes to the copyright statute that impact libraries and educational institutions. Statutory amendments, proposed legislation, and some court decisions address these issues.

Statutory Amendments

Term Extension

The Sonny Bono Copyright Term Extension Act (CTEA)[3] was signed into law on October 27, 1998. It became effective immediately, including its retroactivity provisions.[4] The basic provision of the amendment extends the term of copyright from life of the author plus 50 years to life of the author plus 70 years. For anonymous and pseudonymous works as well as works of corporate authorship, the term is now 95 years after publication or 120 after creation, whichever comes first. Copyright holders argued that term extension was necessary to harmonize U.S. law with that of the European Union. Indeed, the Copyright Act of 1976 adopted the European scheme of copyright protection in a number of significant ways. Among them was the expansion of the term of protection from 28 years after date of first publication (which could be renewed for a second 28 years) to life of the author plus 50 years; in 1995 the European Union extended the term by 20 years to life plus 70.

Those who opposed increasing the term by an additional 20 years argued that the public domain was critical for researchers and scholars and that the extension did nothing to encourage the production of additional works. In fact, it is the heirs of the authors who will benefit from term extension, as well as corporations such as Disney that own the copyrights in works of corporate authorship. Unfortunately for scholars and researchers, the CTEA was retroactive; thus, it will be 2019 before anything else will enter the public domain.

The impact on libraries is significant, especially because the term even for unpublished works was extended. Works that existed but were unpublished on January 1, 1978, and that remain unpublished through the end of 2002, will pass into the public domain at the end of 2002, or at life of the author plus 70 years, whichever is later. Congress did not extend the 2002 date, but left it intact. This provision has considerable import for archival collections around the country. When a library owns an unpublished photograph but does not own the copyright in that photograph, it technically cannot give permission for someone to reproduce the photograph in a publication, on the Web, etc. For years, libraries and archives have charged users a fee for a copy of the photograph, but have required the user to handle the permissions with the copyright owner. For many of these unpublished works, the copyright holder is unknown. These unpublished works, plus works of unknown authorship, will pass into the public domain at the end of

2002, and beginning in 2003 anyone may reproduce the photograph without even asking the library or archives. Of course, if the library holds the only copy of the photograph, it still may sell access to it; but once someone has purchased access and reproduced the photo in a publication, any second user may simply scan the photograph from the publication. Once the work is in the public domain, the library or archives may control access but not reproduction and distribution of copies of the work if it grants access to someone who then publishes or otherwise distributes the work.

For unpublished works that existed as of the effective date of the Copyright Act, January 1, 1978, and which are published between that date and the end of 2002, the term is now life of the author plus 70 years or the end of 2047, whichever is later. It will therefore be 47 years before these works begin to enter the public domain.[5]

The CTEA also contained a provision relating to the preservation of older works by libraries and nonprofit educational institutions.[6] It is discussed below under the heading "library preservation."

A constitutional challenge to the Copyright Term Extension Act is currently progressing through the courts. After the CTEA was enacted, Eric Eldred, Eldritch Press, and others filed a declaratory judgment suit against the government challenging the constitutionality of the 20-year extension of the copyright term. In October 1999 the U.S. District Court for the District of Columbia held that the term extension does not violate the Constitution's copyright clause authority to grant exclusive rights for "limited times."[7] Eldritch Press and the other plaintiffs anticipated using works from 1923 that were to pass into the public domain at the end of 1998, but the retroactive nature of the CTEA prevented that. Claiming that they use, copy, reprint, perform, or restore works of film art and literature in the public domain, the plaintiffs believed that they were damaged by the extension of the copyright term. The court found that the CTEA's extension was within the discretion of Congress.[8] The plaintiffs have appealed the decision.[9]

Digital Millennium Copyright Act

The most comprehensive amendment to the Copyright Act since its passage in 1976 is the Digital Millennium Copyright Act (DMCA),[10] signed into law October 28, 1999, and codified into various sections of the Copyright Act. It made a number of changes in the existing statute relating to libraries, and specifically to notice of copyright on copies reproduced and on library preservation. In addition, the DMCA added two important provisions: online service provider (OSP) liability and anti-circumvention and copyright management.

Notice of copyright—Notice of copyright traditionally has been important not only to copyright owners but also to users of copyrighted works. Copyright notice is a term of art: it means three elements: (1) the word "copyright," abbreviation "copr," or the "C" in a circle; (2) the year of first publication; and (3) the name of the copyright holder.[11] Under the 1909 act, an owner lost his or her rights if he or she published a work and failed to include such notice on copies of the work and did not give actual notice of copyright.[12] The author-friendly 1976 Copyright Act softened the automatic loss provision. An author did not lose his or her copyright for any accidental omissions of notice if, during the first five years after publication, he or she went back and tried to correct this mistake,[13] for example by putting notice on unsold copies. Today, the notice requirement has disappeared altogether.

Under Section 108(a) libraries that reproduce works under the library exemption are required to include a notice of copyright on the copies they make. The whole idea is to inform users that the fact that the library was able to make a copy of a work for them does not mean the work is free of copyright restraints.

There are three requirements that libraries and archives must meet in order to qualify for the library exemption to reproduce a work as detailed in Section 108: (1) there may be no direct or indirect commercial advantage to the library; (2) the library must either be open to the public or to researchers doing research in the same or a similar field; and (3) the reproduction must contain a notice of copyright. There continued to be debate over the meaning of "a notice of copyright." Most copyright lawyers believe that it meant the library should include the three traditional elements that comprise notice of copyright under Section 401(b) as described above (the word "copyright," the abbreviation "copr.," or the symbol, ©; the name of the copyright holder; and the year of first publication). Some librarians argued that a library should be permitted to stamp photocopies and other reproductions with the statement "Notice: This work may be protected by copyright," as recommended by the American Library Association (ALA). Despite this debate, the matter was never litigated. Many libraries religiously used a stamp containing the ALA-recommended wording, while others had a stamp made with ©, _____ (a blank for the year of first publication). Then library staff members would fill in the name of the owner and the year of publication on reproduced copies.

In 1988 the United States joined the Berne Convention, and notice of copyright became optional on the part of the copyright holder. Section 108 was not amended at that time, however, and libraries still were required to place a notice of copyright on copies they reproduced under the exemption. This seemed fundamentally unfair. If the copyright owner did not have to bother alerting the world to its claim of copyright by including a notice on the work, why should libraries have the burden?

The change made in the statute by the DMCA may be due to the above or may be related to the copyright management information provision the DMCA added, which is discussed below. Section 108(a)(3) now reads: "The reproduction and distribution of the work contains a notice of copyright that appears on the copy that is reproduced, or includes a legend stating that the work may be protected by copyright if no such notice appears on the work." Thus, there is no longer any option. The library *must* include the notice that appears on the work. This can be done by reproducing the page that contains this notice or by creating a rubber stamp with ©, _____(for copyright owner), _____(for year published) and filling in the notice information as appears on the work. The only instance in which the stamp or legend "Notice: This work may be protected by copyright" may be used now is when the copyright holder does not place a notice on the work.

Libraries that have an annual license with the Copyright Clearance Center (CCC) may be excused from having to place any notice of copyright on works they reproduce under that license, depending on the terms of the license. This would apply only to works covered by the CCC, however; for others, inclusion of the notice is still required.

The new amendment also has implications for the World Wide Web and for reproducing pages from the Web. While Web pages are copyrighted, often the developer does not include a notice of copyright. Contrary to popular opinion, publishing a Web page without notice does not place the page in the public domain. When printing or reproducing Web pages for users, according to the newly revised statute, librarians must either print the page containing the notice of copyright or stamp the reproduction with "Notice: This work may be protected by copyright" if there is no notice on the Web page.

Library preservation—The 1976 Copyright Act always permitted libraries to reproduce works for preservation or replacement purposes if certain conditions were met. The DMCA amended these provisions to provide for meeting national microfilm standards and to make it clear that digital means might be used for preservation, but it added an additional restriction for works preserved digitally.

Under the original statute, Section 108(b) permitted a library to reproduce one copy of an *unpublished* work for preservation, security, or deposit for research in another library. Section 108(c) allowed a library to reproduce a *published* lost, damaged, stolen, or deteriorating work after the library makes a reasonable effort to obtain an unused copy at a fair price. The statute does not define "fair price," but the legislative history does detail what a reasonable investigation might entail: It would require recourse to commonly known U.S. trade sources, such as retail bookstores, jobbers, and wholesalers; contacting the copyright holder or author, if known; or using an authorized document delivery service.[14] Both sections further required that the work either be currently in the collection of the library or have been there but now be lost. Both sections stated that a library could make a "facsimile copy" when the conditions had been met.[15] There was some disagreement over whether a digital copy could qualify as a facsimile. Many librarians maintained that digital copies that scanned the page and looked exactly like the page were a facsimile; publishers steadfastly claimed that digital copies were not facsimile copies.

The DMCA really terminates the disagreement. It expands the preservation and replacement exemptions in several ways. First, no longer is the library limited to making only one preservation copy of a work. Now it may make three copies, which complies with national microform standards. Second, the word "facsimile" was omitted, and third, the statute specifically permits the copy to be in digital format.[16] While these three changes broaden the preservation exemptions for libraries, each section also contains a new limitation. If the copy that is reproduced is in digital format, the digital copy may not be "made available to the public in that format outside the premises of the library."[17]

Prior to the amendment, a library that reproduced a work under these sections could treat the reproduction just as it did the original work. It could lend it to users, lend the copy through interlibrary loan, and so forth. This new restriction means that if the work is preserved in digital format, it cannot be used outside the library buildings, which is much more restrictive. Surely what Congress meant was that if the reproduction was digital and was available on the library's network, then it could be used only within the premises and not on a campus network or the World Wide Web.

In using the language "digital copy," Congress may actually have narrowed the exemption for works that were originally in digital format. For example, if the original work was a CD-ROM, which now is lost and is not available at a fair price, a library may create another CD that is a digital copy. But the language of the statute says that digital copies cannot be used outside the premises even if the original was a digital copy that could have been outside the library. This is more restrictive and likely is not what Congress meant to accomplish by the amendment.

The DMCA amended Section 108(c) in an important way. In addition to applying to lost, damaged, stolen, or deteriorating works, the amendment added "or if the format in which the work is stored has become obsolete." The library still must make a reasonable effort to determine whether an unused replacement can be found at a fair price. The amendment then explains when a format may be considered obsolete, " . . . if the machine or device necessary to render percepti- ble a work stored in that format is no longer manufactured or is no longer reason- ably available in the commercial marketplace."[18] This is a great help to libraries that currently are dealing with deteriorating 78 rpm recordings, Beta format tapes, and the like. Thus, if the equipment is still produced but is extremely expensive, a library might determine that it is no longer *reasonably* available in the commercial marketplace and may reproduce the work under this amendment. But this is only after the library makes a reasonable effort to purchase a copy of the work in the new format.

The Term Extension Act added another subsection to the act, a new Section 108(h).[19] This section permits a library or a nonprofit educational institution, dur- ing the last 20 years of a published work's term, to reproduce, distribute, display, or perform, in either facsimile or digital form, a copy of a work for purposes of preservation, scholarship, or research. In order to do this, however, the library must by reasonable investigation determine that none of these factors exist: (1) The work is subject to normal commercial expectation; (2) A copy can be obtained at a reasonable price; (3) The copyright owner provides notice pursuant to the Register of Copyright Regulation that neither of the above conditions apply. Further, the exemption provided by this subsection does not apply to any subsequent use by users other than that library. When a digital copy is made as the preservation copy, there is no restriction that it be used only within the premises of the library.[20]

Because of both the age of the material and the scope of the conditions that must be satisfied, this subsection is of limited value to many libraries. It is likely that the only libraries that will take advantage of this subsection are large acade- mic research libraries. At this point, the work is already at least 50 years old and probably much older, depending on how long the author lives after producing the work. The purpose of this amendment was to ameliorate the effect of term exten- sion on libraries and library preservation.

Online Service Provider Liability—After several years of debate, the DMCA added to the Copyright Act a provision exempting online service providers (OSPs) from liability for copyright infringement by the users of their systems. Institutions that provide Internet services such as e-mail and Web server space to staff, students, faculty, and/or members of the public qualify as OSPs and many libraries themselves are OSPs. If it meets the requirements of the statute, an OSP may choose to take advantage of the limitation on liability. In order to qualify for the liability exemption, the OSP must first register an agent to receive complaints about copyright infringement.[21] Libraries and universities have listed a variety of persons as the OSP for their institutions. For some, it is an attorney, for others someone in computer security, and for others it is a member of the library staff. The name of the agent will be listed on the Copyright Office home page,[22] and the institution must also post the name on its home page. This latter requirement is problematic; the intention was that any copyright holder would easily be able to ascertain the name and address of the agent, but many institutional OSPs list the name of the agent on an internal Web page, and it may be difficult to locate that information. Naming an agent is only the first requirement, however.

Only an OSP that acts as a passive conduit for materials that pass through its system qualifies, and the OSP must neither select the material that is transmitted nor alter the material transmitted. It may not select the recipients or know that the materials are infringing. Further, the OSP may not receive any financial benefit from the transmission of such works. The statute recognizes that system caching is a necessity, but it states that materials should not be copied or retained longer than is necessary.[23] When an agent receives a complaint, the institution must investigate the complaint and act expeditiously to remove the material or disable access if it is found to infringe copyright.[24] Thus, the OSP has a heavy burden to conduct investigations. There are penalties if copyright holders make unfounded complaints in order to protect institutions.[25] There is considerable concern that the sheer number of complaints might force institutions to forgo investigations and thus be forced to remove material from the online service in order to avoid liability, even material that might have proven to be non-infringing.

There is a special exemption for nonprofit educational institutions intended to excuse them from liability for some of the actions of their faculty and graduate assistants who are teaching and researching, if three conditions are met. First, the activities do not involve online access to instructional materials that are required or recommended within the past three years. Second, the institution has not received more than two complaints within a three-year period about infringing materials concerning these individuals. And third, the institution provides to all users of the system information that accurately describes and promotes compliance with copyright.[26]

It is unlikely that a library OSP is a passive conduit for the library's own home pages that infringe copyright, so the institution may not even claim the liability exemption for those pages. In this instance the library is an official arm of the OSP, which means that through the library employees who create and maintain the library's Web site the OSP is selecting the material that is transmitted. Therefore, it may not claim the OSP liability exemption for official library Web pages. Thus, the real application to libraries may be for library staff members' own home pages that it hosts or those of members of the public it permits on its servers. A university OSP might avoid liability for faculty home pages under the Section 512(e) conditions detailed above.

Anti-circumvention—Anti-circumvention is designed to prevent users of copyrighted works from defeating technological measures implemented by the copyright holder to prevent unauthorized access to such works.[27] This is the one provision of the DMCA that is not effective until October 28, 2000. Anti-circumvention is an extremely complicated section, and there is little experience with it to date. There has been only one case brought under it, and that in a lower federal court.[28]

The statute recognizes that there are some legitimate reasons for anti-circumvention such as decryption for serious encryption research, for law enforcement, and to determine interoperability of programs.[29] The Librarian of Congress is mandated to conduct a study to determine if there are non-infringing uses of certain classes of works by persons who are likely to be adversely affected by the enactment of this section.[30] The statute then directs the Librarian of Congress to publish the classes of works determined to be adversely affected, and for users of such classes of works there will be no enforcement of the anti-circumvention provision for three years.[31]

There is also a peculiar exemption for nonprofit libraries, archives, and educational institutions. Those organizations will not be liable for anti-circumvention if the purpose of such is to gain access to a work for the sole purpose of determining whether to purchase the work. Further, any copy of the work thus accessed may not be retained longer than is necessary, used for any other purpose, or used for commercial advantage or financial gain.[32]

Copyright management systems—The DMCA also recognized copyright management systems that were being developed by copyright entrepreneurs and made it an infringement for anyone to remove such a system.[33] A copyright management system can be something like watermarking, or something as simple as the copyright notice. The statute contains a list of what constitutes copyright management information: title or other identifying information, name of the author, terms and conditions for the use of a work, plus identifying numbers or symbols (such as the recently implemented Digital Object Identifier).[34] At the same time, providing false copyright management information is prohibited.[35]

Similar to the online service provider provision, law enforcement, intelligence, and other government activities are not prohibited from lawful investigative, protective, or security activities. Neither are information security activities prohibited, i.e., those activities that a government might carry out to identify and address vulnerabilities of government computer systems, networks, and the like.[36]

Damages Provisions

The damages provisions of the Copyright Act were amended not only by the DMCA but also by a 1999 statutory amendment. The anti-circumvention and copyright management information provisions contain separate damages sections applying specifically to these provisions.[37] The damages are somewhat similar to the normal damages provisions in the act, but there are also differences. Section 1203(c) details the civil remedies that are available to anyone who is injured by anti-circumvention or the removal of copyright management information. It provides for both actual damages and profits plus statutory damages as are available for copyright infringement generally; however, the statutory damages in this provision are different from the ones amended above. Statutory damages range from $200 to $2,500 per act of circumvention and from $2,500 to $25,000 for removal of copyright management information.[38] For persons who repeat their infringing activities within a three-year period, the court may award up to triple the amount of damages it would have ordinarily awarded.[39] Damages may also be reduced or even remitted if the infringer can prove he or she is an innocent infringer. Additionally, courts are directed to remit damages when the infringer is a nonprofit library, archives, or educational institution that is not aware nor had reason to believe that its acts violate the Copyright Act.[40]

There are also criminal provisions in the Copyright Act, and the DMCA adds a new one for anti-circumvention and removal of copyright information. If a person violates these provisions of the act willfully for commercial advantage or private financial gain, a first offense may be punished with a fine of not more than $500,000, or not more than five years in federal prison, or both. For subsequent offenses, the fine may be doubled to $1 million and the prison term can be up to 10 years.[41] The criminal penalties do not apply to a nonprofit library, archives, or educational institutions.[42] It is interesting that this provision does not apply to institutions but is silent as to whether it applies to employees of those institutions, such as librarians.

Another amendment to the Copyright Act came from the Digital Theft Deterrence and Copyright Damages Improvement Act of 1999, signed into law on December 9, 1999. The amendment increases the statutory damages for copyright infringement from the current $500 to $20,000 per act of infringement to $750 to $30,000. In cases of willful infringement, the cap is raised from $100,000 to $150,000.[43] While this appears to be a large increase, it has been more than a decade since the damages have been raised.

Distance Learning

The Problem

Several of the exemptions in the Copyright Act recognize the unique position that education plays in American society and the importance of nonprofit education as a public good. This is done through limitations on the exclusive rights of copyright holders. Section 106 of the Copyright Act gives copyright holders a bundle of six rights: reproduction, distribution, adaptation, performance, and display, and—in the case of sound recordings—the right of public performance by digital audio recording.

Fair use is the most important general exemption; it is a privilege that permits someone other than the copyright owner to reproduce, distribute, adapt, perform, or display a work; in other words, activities that otherwise would be within the exclusive rights of the copyright holder.[44] The act states that despite the grant of exclusive rights under Section 106, ". . . [T]he fair use of a copyrighted work, including such use by reproduction in copies or phonorecords or any other means specified by that section for purposes such as criticism, comment, news reporting, teaching (including multiple copying for classroom use), scholarship or research, is not an infringement of copyright." Thus, teaching is mentioned directly in the text of Section 107. The section then lists four factors that a court will consider in determining whether a use is a fair use. The factors are: (1) purpose and character of the use; (2) nature of the copyrighted work; (3) amount and substantiality of the use; and (4) nature of the copyrighted work.

In order to consider distance learning and copyright, it is necessary to contrast it with face-to-face teaching under the act. Section 110(1), referred to as the "classroom exemption," is one of the best exemptions provided in U.S. copyright law. It provides an absolute exemption to the exclusive rights of the copyright holder for performances and displays in the classroom if certain conditions are met. The performance or display must be in the course of face-to-face teaching, in a classroom, and, if the work performed is a motion picture or other audiovisual work, the copy must have been lawfully made.[45] There is no restriction on the types of works that are included, no portion limitations or time limits imposed. Although "classroom" is broadly defined to include any place where instruction is occurring (such as laboratories, gymnasiums, and libraries when the class comes to the library), the face-to-face restriction excludes distance learning from this particular exemption. It requires the simultaneous presence in the same place of students and teachers.[46]

Section 110(2) covers transmissions in the course of instruction, i.e., distance learning, but it is much more restrictive than 110(1). When the act was passed in 1976, the only type of distance learning that Congress envisioned involved television technology and likely an open broadcast. Today, distance education often involves online transmissions rather than just instructional broadcasting, including asynchronous transmissions. While Section 110(1) is very broad, Section 110(2) in contrast is quite narrow. First, only certain types of works may be performed; specifically, nondramatic literary and musical works may be transmitted for distance learning, although any work may be displayed. Second, the transmission of the performance or display must be part of the systematic instructional activities of the institution. Third, reception must be in a classroom or other place similarly devoted to instruction, although disabled persons may receive the transmission anywhere if their condition prevents attendance at a regular classroom. Fourth, the performance must be directly related and of material assistance to the teaching content of the transmission. Each of these four conditions causes difficulty for modern distance learning.

The restriction on the types of works that may be performed is particularly difficult. It is counter-intuitive to teachers that they can use a videotape in face-to-face teaching without seeking permission from the copyright holder, but if that same course is offered to distance learners, use of the tape requires that permission be sought and royalties be paid if the copyright owner requests payment. Teachers find this particularly problematic if the course is offered to students face-to-face in a classroom and is simultaneously transmitted to distance learners. Yet, the act states that a transmission changes the nature of what works may be used in instruction without permission. Certainly, many schools currently seek permission and pay fees to use works such as videotapes for distance learning. Other schools simply black out the time for distance learners when a tape is being shown to students in the classroom. Still others probably ignore the law.

Although the increase in the number of online courses may be changing this, still today most distance learning courses are probably received in a classroom that meets the requirements of the statute. But classrooms are not likely to remain the dominant place for reception of such programs—it will be the home or dormitory room, especially as online courses continue to increase. Even under the current statute, reception of courses in the home by disabled learners and others whose condition prevents attendance at a regular classroom is permitted.[47]

The requirement that the performances and displays be directly related to an act of material assistance to the teaching content presents little problem. The cost of educational transmissions likely prohibits performances of works for entertainment or for any purpose other than instruction.

In addition to the Section 110(2) exemption, fair use certainly applies to performances and displays in the course of instruction. Instead of being an absolute exemption, however, fair use requires the application of four factors to determine whether a use is fair. In fact, even portions of the works excluded under the Section 110(2) exemption may be performed for a distance education course if it is a fair use.

Both educators and librarians sought a solution to these problems in the DMCA, but this was not to be. Instead, Congress mandated that the Register of Copyrights conduct a study on distance learning and report to Congress within six months. The DMCA contained a list of issues that the register was to address in the report. The purpose of the study was to be an examination of how to facilitate distance education without disturbing the current balance in the act between users and owners of copyrighted works.[48] The Copyright Office conducted a series of hearings around the country and produced an excellent report that made several recommendations, which, if enacted, would go a long way to correcting the problems for education. The report was published in May 1999.[49]

The register's report contains a number of important recommendations. Of greatest benefit to the education community is the recommendation that the categories of works included in the exemption be expanded to include dramatic literary and musical works and audiovisual works. The second important recommendation is that the restriction on the place of instruction be removed. The register also suggests retention of the exemption's current limitation to nonprofit educational institutions and governmental bodies rather than expanding the exemption to include for-profit distance learning providers.

The report further recommends that the coverage of rights be expanded to meet technological necessities so that digital copies made incidental to a transmission are not viewed as infringing copies. It also recommends that when the performance of a work is an integral part of the instruction or when the instructor is illustrating a point, the performance be exempted. However, if the work is one that is produced solely for the education market, the report suggests that perhaps only a portion of that work should be performed without seeking permission and paying royalties.[50] Educational institutions would also have some responsibilities if the report's recommendations are adopted: (1) to apply measures to protect against unauthorized access, (2) to provide protection against unauthorized dissemination after access has been acquired, (3) to use only lawfully acquired copies of copyrighted works that are performed or displayed, and (4) to educate the campus community about copyright.[51]

On June 24, 1999, the House Subcommittee on Intellectual Property held hearings on whether an amendment was needed to the Copyright Act for distance education. In addition to the Register of Copyrights, five individuals were invited to testify. Two from the content provider community[52] were opposed to any amendment. They stated that the current licensing system was working fine. The representative from iCopyright, the instant copyright and reprint clearinghouse, talked about licensing generally. Two represented higher education and libraries, and they stated that an amendment was necessary to expand the classroom exemption found in Section 110(1) to distance learning.[53] The major concern articulated by content providers was the necessity to prevent downstream copying and the fact that there are no technological measures yet developed to ensure that such copying does not take place. Libraries and educational representatives agreed, but stated that all institutions should be expected to do is to apply industry standards for technological measures that eliminate downstream copying. As of early 2000, no legislation had been introduced in either the House or the Senate, but there continued to be considerable interest on the part of some legislators as well as educators. It is anticipated that there will be additional bills introduced during the next session of Congress to enact the Register of Copyright's recommendations.

Conclusion

These are but a few of the changes and other important debates that are being held on copyright today. There are some who believe that copyright law will not last in the digital environment, but instead will be replaced by licensing. Others feel that there is no need for copyright law in this environment because all information and copyrighted works should be free. Neither of these positions is likely to comport with reality.

There are important and crucial issues still to be addressed, such as database protection (which is likely to be raised in Congress again during this next year). Additionally, a new report from the National Research Council has even challenged one of the basic assumptions in copyright law and called for a reexamination of this issue. The issue is whether in the digital environment "copying" should be the activity that determines if infringement occurs. Computers, by their very nature, make copies, but these copies are really not relevant as they are merely incidental copies. The whole basis of copyright law today is that reproductions violate the exclusive rights of the copyright holder. The NRC report suggests that this issue should be reexamined to determine if there is a way to focus infringement determinations on the use made of the copy reproduced by a computer rather than the act of reproduction.[54] This is a powerful call to reconsider copyright law and its bases.

Notes

1. 17 U.S.C. § 102(a)(6) (1976).
2. National Research Council, Computer Science and Telecommunications Board, The Digital Dilemma: Intellectual Property in the Information Age 202-04 (2000) [hereinafter Digital Dilemma].
3. Pub. L. 105-298 (1998).
4. Id. §§ 301-304 (1998 Supp.).
5. For an explanation of when works enter the public domain, consult the chart created and maintained by the author at http://www.unc.edu/~unclng/public-d.htm.

6. This provision is now codified at 17 U.S.C. § 108(h) (1998 Supp.).

7. *Eldred* v. *Reno*, 74 F. Supp.2d 1 (D.C.D.C. 1999).

8. Id. at 2-4.

9. See http://cyber.law.harvard.edu/eldredvreno/legaldocs.html.

10. Pub. L. 105-304 (1998).

11. 17 U.S.C. § 401(b) (1994).

12. 17 U.S.C. § 21 (1970).

13. 17 U.S.C. § 405 (1988).

14. H. Rep. 94-1476 (1976) at 75-76.

15. 17 U.S.C. §§ 108(b)-(c) (1994).

16. Id. (1998 Supp.).

17. Id.

18. Id. § 108(c)(3) (1998 Supp.).

19. The amendment also renumbered the old § 108(h) to (i).

20. Id.

21. 17 U.S.C. § 512(c)(2) (1998 Supp.).

22. http://www.loc.gov/copyright/onlinesp/list/index.html.

23. 17 U.S.C. § 512(a)-(b) (1998 Supp.).

24. Id. §§ 512(b)(2)(E) and 512(c)(1)(C).

25. Id. § 512(b)(2) 512(f).

26. Id. § 512(e) (1998 Supp.).

27. Id. § 1201 (1998 Supp.).

28. See *Universal Studios, Inc.* v. *Reimerdes,* 2000 U.S. Dist. LEXIS 906 (Feb 2, 2000).

29. 17 U.S. C. 1201(e)-(g) (1998 Supp.).

30. Id. § 1201(a)(1)(B)-(C). The Librarian of Congress has begun this study and called for comments on November 4, 1999, see 64 Fed. Reg. 66139 (November 24, 1999).

31. 17 U.S.C. § 1201(a)(1)(D) (1998 Supp.).

32. Id. § 1201(d)(1).

33. Id. § 1202.

34. Id. § 1202(c).

35. Id. § 1202(a).

36. Id. § 1202(d).

37. Id. §§ 1203–1204.

38. Id. § 1203(c)(3).

39. Id. § 1203 (c)(4).

40. Id. § 1203(c)(5).

41. Id. § 1204(a).

42. Id. § 1204(b).

43. Pub. L. 106-160 (1999).

44. 17 U.S.C. § 107 (1994).

45. Id. § 110(1).

46. H. Rep. 94-1476 (1976) at 81–82.

47. 17 U.S.C. § 110(2)(C)(ii).

48. Pub. L. 105-304 § 403 (1998).

49. U.S. Copyright Office. *Report on Copyright and Digital Distance Education* (May 1999). See http://www.loc.gov/copyright/disted/.

50. Id. at 140-159.

51. Id. at 150-152.

52. One of the representatives of the content providers was Pat Schroeder, who testified for the Association of American Publishers, of which she is president and CEO.

53. Professor Laura N. Gasaway, representing the major higher education and library associations, and John T. Cross, a law professor at the University of Louisville.

54. Digital Dilemma, supra note 2, at 140–145.

KALIPER Study Identifies Trends in Library and Information Science Education

Karen E. Pettigrew

Assistant Professor, School of Library and Information Science, University of Washington
Principal Investigator, KALIPER

Joan C. Durrance

Professor, School of Information, University of Michigan
Chair, KALIPER Advisory Committee

Introduction

The Kellogg-ALISE Information Professions and Education Reform Project (KALIPER), a groundbreaking two-year project of the Association for Library and Information Science Education (ALISE), was made possible by a grant from the W. K. Kellogg Foundation. Conducted between 1998 and 2000 by a team of 20 scholars from 13 library and information science (LIS) programs in the United States, Canada, and England, it sought to determine the nature and extent of major curricular change in LIS education.

KALIPER was perhaps the most extensive examination of the LIS curriculum since the Williamson Report, the field's first examination of education for librarianship, which was published in 1923. The Williamson Report, credited with major changes in education of librarians including the development of the first standards for library education, was quite negative about the state of library education at the beginning of the 20th century. At the end of the century, the KALIPER scholars found a vibrant, dynamic, changing field in the process of undertaking an array of initiatives.

LIS programs were highly cooperative with the scholars in this study. Eighty-four percent of LIS programs responded to the 1998 survey of LIS deans. Twenty-six schools participated as case-study schools, resulting in the opportunity to look in depth at change in selected schools. An additional seven schools were asked to examine the trends identified among the data collected from the deans and the case-study schools. These served as "confirming schools." In short, the trends and special reports presented by the KALIPER scholars are highly representative of the current state of the field.

All schools at the ALISE 2000 conference were asked to contribute to the LIS education "Defining Moments Timeline," which was displayed throughout the conference. The timeline provided schools with an opportunity to record significant moments in their history and program development, such as launching a new curriculum or program, first use of distance education, changes associated with the arrival of a new dean or director, a merger with another department, and school name changes.

Note: The final results of the KALIPER project were presented in January 2000 at the Annual Meeting of the Association for Library and Information Science Education (ALISE) in San Antonio. The project was initially described in the 1999 edition of the *Bowker Annual*.

Methodology

The purpose of the KALIPER Project was to analyze the nature and extent of major curricular change in LIS education. This work comprised several stages, including:

- A survey of deans and directors about factors affecting curriculum change
- Case studies of 26 schools regarding changes in curriculum
- Curriculum analysis and faculty interviews at seven additional schools to determine whether the project's preliminary findings reflect their experience
- In-depth analysis of curriculum change within such specific areas as archives and records management, school media, distance education, and undergraduate programs
- Analysis of LIS academic job announcements from 1990 to 1998 on the ASIS Jobline and in *American Libraries*
- Analysis of faculty specialization descriptors from ALISE directories

This article shares some of the project's broader findings. The in-depth findings will be made available in future reports.

Deans and Directors Survey

For Stage One a short questionnaire was drafted by the project's advisory committee and sent in summer 1998 to the deans and directors of 56 schools. The response rate was 84 percent. The survey's purpose was to gather baseline data regarding the extent of curricular change within individual schools and the respondents' perceptions of the degree to which this change was affected by particular factors. The preliminary results were used to derive an initial framework for use by the KALIPER scholars.

Thirteen questions were posed. In brief, deans were asked to describe the extent of curricular change within their schools according to ten factors:

1 Vision or mission change
2 New relationships with other campus departments
3 Major funding changes and shifts
4 Market positioning
5 Faculty changes (such as growth, new hires, retirements)
6 New degrees
7 New course content
8 Core requirements
9 Pre-admission requirements
10 Modes of delivery

Respondents were asked to rank the degree of change for each factor with regard to the past three years and what they anticipated would happen in the next three. Respondents were also asked to comment on these changes.

The Case Studies

For the case studies, four teams of scholars studied patterns of curricular change across 26 schools: California–Berkeley, Catholic, Drexel, Florida State, Iowa, Kentucky, Louisiana, Maryland, Michigan, Missouri, North Carolina–Greensboro, North Carolina–Central, North Texas, Pittsburgh, Puerto Rico, Queens, Rhode Island, Rutgers, San Jose, Simmons, South Carolina, South Florida, Syracuse, Tennessee, Texas–Austin, and Wisconsin–Madison. Each team studied a subset of schools and used multiple methods to collect data. Their approaches included questionnaires or interviews with faculty and deans; site visits; analyses of school calendars, course syllabi and descriptions; and analyses of annual reports, COA reports and other self-study studies, and ALISE statistics.

While the extent of methods used varied across the four teams, a common framework was derived for examining the data. Starting with themes that were initially identified from the survey of deans and directors, the teams examined their schools' past and current curriculum and curriculum-review processes, identified factors that influenced change in particular programs, determined the rationale for current structures and the positioning of the school within the university, and so forth. During an all-day meeting in November 1999 the teams discussed their reports and synthesized their findings. A project theme statement was derived that was then tested with seven additional schools: UCLA, Dominican, Illinois, North Carolina–Chapel Hill, Toronto, Washington, and Western Ontario. For these last schools, KALIPER members interviewed faculty about the extent to which the theme statement reflected changes at these schools and examined curricular data on the schools' Web sites.

Limitations

The KALIPER Project represents an unprecedented attempt to document and understand the recent past, current status, and future directions of a field that many believe has finally and truly come into its own. But to yield any worthwhile results, this ambitious undertaking required the participation of many individuals and a majority of schools. With severe limitations on time, distance, and resources, it is a major feat that so much work was accomplished. For this reason all the participants in the KALIPER Project—the scholars, advisory committee, and faculty and deans who participated in the varied surveys and case studies— are to be widely commended. This project is truly a sum of its parts.

But these same limitations and the unprecedented nature of the undertaking prompted logistical difficulties with standardizing data collection techniques and instruments, and methods of analyses. For example, data were not always available for the same time periods across all schools, nor were the same data formats or types always available. So in this sense generalizing is difficult. Moreover, not all the themes reflect the experience at every school examined. So the results suggest trends, trend-setters, early adopters, and field consensus, giving snapshots of life in LIS education that describe the past and core values and may help illuminate the current path.

Aggregate Findings

The aggregate findings suggest that a majority of schools are undergoing significant change, and that while some are in periods of greater flux than others, the areas targeted for change vary from school to school. Six trends regarding curricular change are identified.

Trend 1

In addition to libraries as institutions and library-specific operations, the LIS curriculum is addressing broad-based information environments and information problems.

Although training students for future roles in library settings remains the heart of many programs, there is little doubt that many schools are focusing on broad-based information environments that go beyond traditional library settings. The inherent transferability of library skills to other situations and information problems was evident from the creation and redesigning of curricula to cover concepts and skills with broad implications and relevance. At Catholic, for example, the descriptions of all four core courses emphasize a broad spectrum of information environments.

New courses are being offered that focus on information problems—such as licensing and legal issues, ethics, and the creation and marketing of information products—as well as on the organization and management of digital information (in both private and public sectors) that are relevant beyond library settings. In some instances, traditional LIS courses such as cataloging, classification, and reference are being renamed and retooled or redesignated as electives instead of core requirements.

At Toronto, for example, the cataloging course was transformed into a new core course titled "Representing, Organizing and Storing Information." At UCLA core courses in cataloging and reference were redesignated as electives and the number of courses offered in these areas were reduced from two to one. According to a faculty member at another school, "Professionals must be prepared for the 'big picture,' which includes an awareness of new issues and the institutional view; nonprofessionals are now doing tasks formerly considered 'professional,' such as cataloging." Examples of innovative new courses that go beyond traditional settings include Western Ontario's course in "Information Entrepreneurship," Illinois's course in "Information Consulting," UCLA's new core course on information systems design, Toronto's "Information and Its Social Contexts," and Chapel Hill's "Web Databases" and "Information Security."

Other indicators of the broadening of school focuses were reflected in school name changes (e.g., dropping the "L" word, adding the "I" word), and in the words that schools used to describe their programs to potential students and graduate employers. At Washington, note the use of the plural form in saying that the school "is committed to excellence in preparing new leaders for careers in the information *professions*." But this theme of broadening was also suggested by schools that changed their market positioning, sometimes by employing public relations firms, to capture nascent opportunities for graduates in nontraditional settings and to meet new employers' needs. As one dean explained, "Salaries in new areas are much higher than library jobs, and word is getting around about what our students can do and therefore new employers are asking for them."

Schools reported that employers have a great influence on their program development. While some schools (among them Greensboro, South Carolina, and Puerto Rico) have a continuing strong emphasis on serving a regional library market, others described setting their sights on exploiting the national business, industry, and government-employment market. Other indicators of broadening under Trend 1 include:

- Schools' use of a dean's advisory council made up of individuals from non-library settings
- Schools' engagement in strategic partnerships or mergers with other units that might open new doors
- Schools' hiring of faculty who conduct research on information problems in non-library settings, and adjuncts and other part-time faculty from the private sector who do not work in traditional library settings
- Schools' active recruitment of students with diverse academic backgrounds and work experience who are interested in varied information environments. As one dean explained, "We have students coming from areas outside librarianship who are interested in Web-based stuff, corporate intelligence, etc., and getting jobs in areas one could never imagine ten years ago"
- Schools' offering special workshops and courses that are designed for non-library professionals who work in information-related settings

The significance of moving toward broad-based information environments was reflected in several interviews. According to one dean, "It's our graduates' broad-based problem-solving ability that makes employers from non-traditional areas value our grads so much." Schools located near Silicon Valley and other hi-tech centers said they were being heavily influenced by the demands of employers for technology-capable professionals in information management.

Trend 2

While LIS curriculum continues to incorporate perspectives from other disciplines, a unique core has taken shape that is predominantly user-centered.

The infusion of multidisciplinary perspectives into LIS curricula results naturally as LIS faculty conduct research with or hire faculty from cognate fields, and offer joint programs/courses or team-teach with faculty from other departments. In short, one needs only to take a quick glance across school curricula to identify a plentitude of perspectives from different fields. Whether it's due to a shortage of LIS faculty or a perceived need to hire from outside, the faculty at several schools are growing increasingly multidisciplinary, especially through joint appointments, and this trend is having a strong impact on curriculum development. While Berkeley has been a forerunner in multidisciplinary hires, Pittsburgh lists faculty with joint or visiting appointments from a wide range of fields including computer science, medicine, engineering, psychology, business, and women's studies. At Puerto Rico, joint appointments are anticipated with business, planning, and communications. Michigan recently increased its faculty through joint faculty appointments with public policy, art and design, electrical engineering and computer science, business, psychology, and economics.

However, individuals we interviewed also talked about the importance of consolidating the LIS core and clearly delineating what makes LIS distinct, as a knowledge domain, from other disciplines. But what is this core? Based on our examination of mission statements, course titles, descriptions, and syllabi, LIS schools proclaim their domain as covering cognitive and social aspects of how information and information systems are created, organized, managed, disseminated, filtered, routed, retrieved, accessed, used, and evaluated.

But whether we're talking about individuals, groups, or societies, at the heart of these activities and questions is the user. While employing a user-centered perspective has been a hallmark of some schools' curricula for a long time, there is little doubt that "user-centeredness" has infused or pervaded most of the research and teaching in LIS, and that even "non-user" courses, so to speak, such as cataloging and data management now tend to be based on the user paradigm. And there is no shortage of core courses or course elements that address information seeking. In core revisions, the incorporation of instruction in information seeking was seen in varying degrees of granularity ranging from the cognitive issues of personal information seeking and use to the broad-based role of information in practice and discourse communities. This emphasis on users was also included in school mission and vision statements. At Florida State the primary focus of the LIS program is on "user behavior and its interaction with information products, services and organizations." Florida's programs share the mission of "preparing students for careers in information services, with an emphasis on user needs as well as on management and physical and intellectual access to information." According to Catholic's mission statement, it "prepare(s) graduates to provide user-centered information services." Washington lists students' mastery of knowledge regarding "information needs and information-seeking behavior" as a primary instructional objective. In short, it may well be that the predominant focus on the user is one aspect of what makes library and information science distinct from the others that are interested in information problems.

Trend 3

LIS schools are increasing their investment and infusion of information technology into their curricula.

The increase of schools' investment in information technology infrastructures and the infusion of information technology into the curricula should not be simply dismissed as a sign of the times. Something more meaningful is occurring that is having long-reaching effects. The intense focus on almost anything digital is undoubtedly redefining LIS education as we add more core courses and electives to the curriculum, infuse existing courses with digital elements, and seek out more faculty who can teach in these areas. This is inevitable: Information technology is attractive, it's fast becoming the glue of our daily existence, and market forces and funders of education and research are eager to support IT development and use.

For the same reasons, the parent institutions of LIS schools also are eager to have flagship schools that lead in teaching and research on the electronic frontier. North Carolina Central is an example of a school that has placed strong emphasis on formally incorporating technology; each semester its faculty must provide a written report to the dean on how they integrated electronic technologies in their courses with the expectation that 80 percent of the students completing each course will demonstrate technological understanding or competence.

Generally speaking, information technology is becoming less expensive to purchase, but faculty from several schools remarked that staffing or support costs for maintaining information technology are increasing.

Trend 4

LIS schools are offering students greater flexibility in tailoring their programs around specific areas of interest.

Some say specialization is on the increase; others say not. Perhaps more accurately—to borrow from Leigh Estabrook, dean of the Graduate School of Library and Information Science at the University of Illinois—we're "rethinking specializations" and offering more generic curricula, such as at Berkeley, UCLA, and Texas–Austin where fewer electives and concentrations are planned.

Indeed, interviews revealed a concern among some LIS faculty that there are too many areas of specialization within the curricula, since they lead to logistical problems with sequencing course offerings and can create a sense of fragmentation. A desire to return to simpler programs was expressed.

However, many schools do offer students formal certificates and specializations in school media, health librarianship, law librarianship, and so forth. Kentucky, for example, is considering offering a specialization in health informatics at the master's and doctoral level; Rhode Island has been considering adding a master's degree in information resource management. Schools also are providing multiple courses within specific subject areas or offering flexible programming so that students have choice within the core or can custom-tailor their programs according to their own specific interests. Schools that offer a flexible core include Louisiana, Maryland, Wisconsin–Madison, and South Florida.

Creating areas or tracks of specialization, and hiring faculty with specializations are other key indicators of this trend toward flexible programming. Toronto combined its master's of library science and master's of information science in 1997 into a master's of information studies program so that students can specialize in one of three streams: library and information studies, archival studies, or information systems. At Michigan, students can specialize in one of four areas: library and information services; archives and records management; information economics, management, and policy; or human-computer interaction.

As part of preparing students for specialization, some schools impose program entry requirements such as work experience in industry, or require students to complete practical engagements or compile graduation portfolios that describe their field experiences during their programs. Other exit requirements, such as those at Syracuse, include successfully completing internships, co-ops, or independent studies. Some full two-year programs, such as at Chapel Hill, have comprehensive exams and master's paper requirements in addition to course work.

Trend 5

LIS schools are offering instruction in different formats to provide students with more flexibility.

Flexibility in curricula is perhaps nowhere as evident as in instructional formats. Today's students have more choice than ever regarding course length, day and time of course offering, and on-campus or off-campus meetings. North Texas, for example, offers courses at various locations throughout the state. Providing distance education using the Internet, which is sometimes linked with brief on-site residency requirements, is growing increasingly common. At Illinois, two programs—LEEP (Library Education Experimental Program, a Web-based distance learning program) and Fridays Only—have served as excellent alternative delivery models for several years. In fact, Illinois on-campus students are opting to take LEEP3 courses when room is available. While Drexel offers a complete Internet-based master's degree program, San Jose employs a mixed model in which all students take some campus-based courses and some other courses are delivered remotely. Missouri expects that it will continue to experience great change in delivery modes. Other emerging forms of instruction include inter-university partnerships, in which students from one institution take courses for credit from another LIS school, as well as collaborations with universities in other countries.

Trend 6

LIS schools are expanding their programs by offering related degrees at the undergraduate, master's, and doctoral levels.

Many instances were gathered in which schools are offering or are planning to offer new degrees, or certificate programs at the undergraduate, master's, or doctoral level. Some of these new programs are interdisciplinary or joint programs. At Syracuse and Michigan, combined degree programs were developed with law. Pittsburgh offers a dual degree with the Center for Biomedical Informatics and a Ph.D. in partnership with computer science, electrical engineering, communication, and business. UCLA offers joint master's degrees with history, Latin American studies, and management, and is starting a new program with theater and television. Along more traditional lines, South Carolina offers two joint master's programs with English and applied history. Chapel Hill created a dual master's degree for archivists that includes library science from Chapel Hill and public history from neighboring North Carolina State University at Raleigh.

Also evident was the creation of new majors and minors at the undergraduate level. Illinois offers an undergraduate minor in information studies, and Chapel Hill is planning to expand its minor to a full undergraduate degree in information science. Washington is launching both a bachelor of science in informatics and a Ph.D. program in information science in fall 2000. South Carolina plans to lead campus discussion of an interdisciplinary undergraduate minor in information studies. Undergraduate programs at Drexel and Syracuse have been flourishing for several years. At Syracuse, a series of dual BS degrees was developed with the schools of management and public communications, and they share a certificate in project software management with engineering and computer science.

At the master's level, several schools—including Pittsburgh, Rutgers, and Drexel—offer multiple degrees. Others—including Washington and Western Ontario—soon plan to offer new master's. In short, schools are expanding in many directions. New continuing education programs, workshops, and other alternative programs have enabled schools to tap into expanded markets and provide another potential source of revenue. Since its merger with the College of Education, Missouri has implemented a certificate program in new media at the undergraduate and graduate levels. South Carolina offers two post-master's programs—certificate of graduate study in library and information science, and specialist in library and information science—while Syracuse offers a summer college for high school students in information management and technology. Syracuse also increased its number of graduate certificates to include telecommunications management and software project management with a possible addition of interactive multimedia.

Several schools reported an increase in the number of cross-listed or "service" courses. The alliances forged with other departments include traditional partners (for example education, with which many LIS schools cooperate to capture the school library certification market). However, the number of cross-listed courses with new disciplines is also increasing. South Carolina regularly teaches courses on information retrieval for journalism, children's literature, and information technology for education students, and plans to develop a sequence of integrated information-technology courses for students throughout the university. Greensboro provides a service course on research methods for its department of education. It also notes increasing interest from other departments in cooperation on technology and Internet material.

Factors Affecting Change

While these six trends address types of curricular change, we must further ask: "What prompts such change?" The KALIPER study sought to identify the forces that motivate change and affect its direction. However, it soon became clear that factors that promote change can, in some situations, also be ones that inhibit it. The most common instigators (and sometimes inhibitors) of change, in no particular order, are:

- The demands of students, employers, graduates, and professional associations for graduate competencies
- Growth of and expense of supporting emerging technology
- Internal campus relationships and positioning
- Availability and/or presence of faculty with new subject expertise
- Competition from other LIS programs
- Availability of financial support for innovation

The impetus for the trends identified is both internal and external. Increased enrollments and the need to cater to market niches, along with the interests of parent institutions and external funders, have prompted change. The financial rewards that can be reaped from expanding programs to different levels, such as the bachelor's, and by offering distance learning also promote curricular change.

The Future

As the new century begins, it appears that change in LIS curriculum is spanning a broad spectrum. Some schools are going through a carefully planned evolution in which they're broadening their focus to include other information environments but retaining a solid focus on librarianship. Other schools have implemented a more sudden and significant shift away from their past focus on the institution of the library, changes that reflect total revision as opposed to steady evolution. Perhaps what is most important at the heart of this stability-versus-change nexus is that students and employers do exist at both ends of the spectrum.

But regardless of the nature of LIS curricular change, several faculty expressed concern about a growing shortage of new LIS Ph.D.s that they believe will only worsen. A need for more doctoral students and doctoral programs was emphasized. Others remarked on the need for sharing expertise among LIS schools, and for consolidating, building, and promoting LIS core knowledge lest it be lost in a continued rush to embrace concepts from other disciplines or be taken over by other disciplines that are entering the information field. Still other faculty raised questions about the relationship between information and technology, wondered whether LIS is a profession or a discipline, and questioned if there is a formula for easily spanning both.

In essence, it appears that despite the differences in how schools are changing, common concerns about the future exist and continuing conversation about the nature of LIS and its curriculum is still needed.

Findings of the KALIPER study will be widely disseminated, including those regarding special areas such as archives and school media, and will be published in several formats. Updates will be available on the ALISE Web site (http://www.alise.org/) and the JESSE listserv (http://www.alise.org/nondiscuss/jesse.html).

The KALIPER Team

KALIPER was guided by an outstanding group of well-known faculty who shaped the project, designed the competition for scholars, selected the scholars, and developed the research design with principal investigator Karen Pettigrew, an assistant professor at the University of Washington School of Library and Information Science. The project's advisory committee was chaired by Joan C. Durrance, professor, University of Michigan School of Information. Other members were Leigh Estabrook, dean, Graduate School of Library and Information Science, University of Illinois; Ray von Dran, dean, School of Information Studies, Syracuse University; Joanne Marshall, dean, School of Information and Library Science, University of North Carolina at Chapel Hill; Tom Childers, professor, College of Information Science and Technology, Drexel University; Toni Carbo, dean, School of Information Sciences, University of Pittsburgh; Shirley

Fitzgibbons, associate professor, School of Library Information Science, University of Indiana (ex officio as ALISE president), and Sharon Rogers, executive director, ALISE.

The competitively chosen teams of KALIPER Scholars who conducted the study included:

Scholar Team 1: John Richardson, professor, Department of Library and Information Science, University of California, Los Angeles (UCLA); Matthew Saxton, Ph.D. student, UCLA; Stuart Sutton, associate professor, School of Information Studies, Syracuse University; and Bill Gibbons, Ph.D. student, Syracuse University.

Scholar Team 2: Jane Robbins, dean and professor, School of Library and Information Studies, Florida State University; Beth Logan, associate professor, Florida State University; Prudence Dalrymple, dean, Graduate School of Library and Information Science, Dominican University; and Heidi Julien, assistant professor, School of Library and Information Studies, Dalhousie University.

Scholar Team 3: Richard Cox, associate professor, School of Information Sciences, University of Pittsburgh; Beth Yakel, assistant professor, Pittsburgh; Jeanette Bastian, Ph.D. student, Pittsburgh; and David Wallace, assistant professor, School of Information, University of Michigan.

Scholar Team 4: Daniel Callison, associate professor, School of Library Information Science, University of Indiana; Carol Tilley, Ph.D. student, Indiana; Louise Robbins, director and associate professor, School of Library and Information Studies, University of Wisconsin–Madison; and Pat Lawton, Ph.D. student, University of Wisconsin–Madison.

Scholar Team 5: Thomas Wilson, professor, Department of Information Studies, University of Sheffield, England; Roma Harris, vice-provost, University of Western Ontario, and professor, Graduate School of Library and Information Science, Western Ontario; Joanne Marshall, dean, School of Information and Library Science, University of North Carolina at Chapel Hill; and Victoria Marshall, Ph.D. student, Western Ontario.

KALIPER scholars come from the broad spectrum of scholarship in this field and included junior and senior faculty and doctoral students. Younger scholars are the key to continuation of the KALIPER approach to broad examination of LIS curricula and programs. They are the scholars who will institutionalize this approach. KALIPER scholars volunteered countless hours to bring you these findings. They devised many creative ways to collect data and work together across great distances, to share their data, and to analyze and synthesize their findings. Thanks to the W. K. Kellogg Foundation, the scholars were able to gather for two working meetings over the course of this project.

The authors deeply appreciate the confidence and generosity of Kellogg in this project.

Consortia, Networks, and Publishing in 1999

Angee Baker

Director, Electronic Information Services
SOLINET (Southeastern Library Network)

Tom Sanville

Executive Director, OhioLINK

Expanding consortia and consortia-related activities had a significant impact on the library field in 1999. Partnerships among networks, consortia, and publishers—alliances that had emerged as a force in 1998—expanded and strengthened, with Internet-based services a key factor.

The relationship among consortia, networks, and publishers is evolving, with a mix of beneficial partnerships and diverse goals. Consortia and networks are employing more businesslike methods and long-term strategies to increase their added value to libraries. Through these approaches, consortia and networks are better able to leverage publisher partnerships to deliver increased benefits and value to libraries. The licensing of electronic products and services has demonstrated these benefits very clearly; yet consortia and networks continue to struggle with such issues as price, cost allocation, implementation, training, and support.

Looking at these developments more specifically, this article discusses five key trends that have evolved for consortia, networks, and publishers:

- Consortia are raising the stakes for publishers
- Consortia are moving horizontally while publishers have been moving vertically
- Costs are rising for consortia and network licensing
- Consortia are increasing their role in the development of new products from publishers
- Publishers are using consortia to launch new products

This report will focus on the short- and long-term effects of these key trends.

Consortia Raising the Stakes for Publishers

The risks, rewards, and complexities of a group sale are far greater for a publisher than those of an individual library sale.

Seven significant factors are raising the stakes for publishers who work with consortia today. A consortium-based sale impacts the publisher's sales process, must account for multiple budget cycles across the consortium's members, requires flexible contracts, establishes a need for shared marketing responsibilities, requires more clear-cut cost-benefit analyses, makes necessary a mutual understanding of market share goals and needs, and shatters pricing confidentiality expectations. These factors have played a dramatic role in the database licensing successes of consortia and publisher activities during the past year.

Traditionally, publishers have been in control of the sales process with individual libraries. Consortia remove the publisher one step from the direct subscriber and compound the sales process with an additional layer of group-based product evaluation and price consideration. As stated in a *Library Journal* article in February 1999, "The sanctity and independence of individual library autonomy and budgets are obstacles. Changes in budgets are rarely coordinated across a group; once a commitment of local funds is made to a group license, a change in that commitment now has an impact on every other participating school."[1] Each consortium establishes its own balance between the membership-wide objective of best price and value, the need for individual library budget independence, and buying-cycle limitations.

Consortia provide the publisher with a cost-effective and accelerated opportunity to reach smaller libraries that often represent new customers or new market share. However, the larger libraries in a consortium must typically anchor the license for the price to be affordable for the smaller libraries. This can create a conflict for the vendor, who is concerned about margins the larger libraries may already be delivering as customers at a higher cost than the consortium-based license. In the end all libraries must receive a better price and the publisher must see increased aggregate revenues. A chicken-and-egg dilemma can result. Which commitment comes first—the publisher's price or the consortium's aggregate library commitment? One solution is to create a narrow range of probable prices so that a library can commit to the highest price it is willing to pay for that particular subscription or product. Multi-consortia participation based on a cumulative full-time equivalent (FTE) model is an important component that can drive the probable price range to a level that is usually more affordable for smaller and larger libraries alike. National offers supported by the International Coalition of Library Consortia (ICOLC) have demonstrated the success of this approach over the past two years.

Since the renewal of the CIS/LEXIS-NEXIS agreement for Academic Universe in July 1999 (more than 900 participating libraries and 28 consortia), an average of 20 libraries a month have continued to join the agreement as funds have become available. Differences in funding flexibility and budget cycles may mean that a library waits a year or more to be able to subscribe. Consortium offers that provide an opportunity for libraries to join the agreement during the term of the consortium subscription constitute an evolving trend that benefits the library and the publisher. The stakes are raised when the consortium and the publisher adjust their business systems to accommodate continual monthly add-on libraries to an existing subscription.

The publisher becomes dependent on the consortium or network for new and renewal revenue that could impact the publisher's perspective on its sales personnel investment. The stakes are raised for the publisher because marketing efforts must be coordinated between the publisher and the consortium to reach and accurately inform as many libraries as possible about the offer. National product offers increase the need for coordination among the players in the sale process (the publisher, the networks or consortium, and the institution). Successful national offers have included close marketing coordination between the publishers and consortia.

Another element that is raising the stakes for publishers is demonstrated when publishers compare the value of a consortium or network license to the value of their existing sales with individual participants or sub-cooperatives of that consortium or network. If the net result—the consortium-negotiated price point—is a loss of revenue for the publisher, the program cannot go forward. Publishers must protect existing revenue, while libraries expect significant value (often in the form of savings) from their consortium or network. Further, if there is an additional fee for the consortium (membership fee) or network (cost recovery fee), this additional cost factor—even when coupled with an attractive consortium price point—may make the offer, taken as a whole, unattractive when compared with the library's individually licensed price. These comparisons complicate the cost-benefit analyses for all parties and require a clearer understanding on both sides of the risks involved in achieving a satisfactory solution for the publisher, consortium, and libraries.

Market share concerns also raise the stakes for publishers. A consortium subscription can significantly impact market share. In the past year, especially, statewide virtual-library initiatives have demonstrated that publishers can experience notable revenue gain or loss almost overnight. This type of quick, massive change can dramatically affect the library market's perception of the publisher. Major publisher decisions are often reported quickly via the e-mail grapevine and then the library press. There are more significant downside risks for the publisher in losing a consortium license than in losing an individual library. The cost occurs both in real economic terms and in the perceived viability of the publisher's products. Libraries are a small community to begin with, and groups like ICOLC make the e-mail grapevine among consortium decision-makers very effective.

Changing or adding publishers also creates problems for publishers, consortia, and libraries. They all must battle simultaneous training or retraining and other implementation issues such as setting up Internet authorizations for a larger number of campuses. Nonetheless, we can expect to see more publisher changes as library funding remains tight and administrators demand accountability. Publishers need to be able to partner with consortia to create measurement systems that will meet these new accountabilities.

A small but notable point that is raising the stakes for publishers is that pricing confidentiality has decreased to the point that pricing information can be found almost daily on listservs around the world. Many publishers have declared their desire to be consistent when providing consortia pricing; yet contradictions can be found on a regular basis. The argument can be made that consortium-based pricing should not be consistent given the differences among consortia in library composition, levels of pre-existing business, and levels of participation in the consortium's license. Combine the confidentiality issue with the rise of international organizations like ICOLC and the stakes for publishers have moved beyond small pockets of consortia to worldwide influence on pricing, product development, product content, and performance demands and guidelines.

Consortia Move Horizontally, Publishers Move Vertically

Tension has developed between the needs of consortia and the product development efforts of publishers. Consortia with diverse member libraries want to offer more depth and breadth of content. Vendors are linking products to related Web sites for additional content depth. This does not necessarily provide the desired content depth and breadth required for academic research—nor does it effectively link to competitors' services necessary to meet broad library needs. The year 1999 marked a continuing focus by consortia and networks on licensing commercial services at the most advantageous prices. But if the prices and the ways in which publishers offer their services are not compatible with libraries' long-term needs, will the focus of consortia and networks shift to developing more fundamentally suitable approaches to information access?

Commercial industry has traditionally preferred to avoid long-term risks and relied on government, universities, and nonprofit concerns to bear this cost.[2] We see this trend clearly in the development of the second-generation Internet. Universities are bearing the primary development costs while private industry waits to commercialize the benefits of Internet II.

It has been suggested that academic and public libraries develop primary source material that will provide the required product depth for research content. Digital library initiatives by individual institutions provide us with illustrations of this possibility. Institutions such as the University of Michigan Digital Library Program and the members of the Digital Library Federation have shown the value of consortia pooling resources for a shared common goal while also moving individual institution initiatives forward.

In the December 1999 Council on Library and Information Resources (CLIR) Digital Library Federation program publication, a new generation of the consortium model was proposed. The publication stated that "The library community has a distinguished history of developing standards to enhance the discovery and sharing of print materials. . . . This leadership continues today, as libraries create new best practices and standards that address digital collections and content issues."[3]

The CLIR report proposes a digital library services model that includes services, tools, and digital library objects (content, metadata, and methods). Services will be "provided through tools that discover, display, navigate, and manipulate digital objects from distributed repositories."[4] If this type of effort takes the form of a library and/or consortium partnership with publishers, libraries and consortia will experience pressure from publishers who will likely require commercial relevance.

While funding at the individual institution level is limited, a consortium of libraries could possibly provide enough leverage and volume to develop commercially relevant content. However, Burton Clark, professor emeritus at the University of California, cautions that the pressure to become entrepreneurial and to develop new sources of revenue has many inherent dangers, and libraries must reassert academic values and not become a business.[5]

Recently, a number of European universities have joined to explore alternatives to dependence on the state for funding.[6] As universities define their strengths, identify partners that complement those strengths, and higher education becomes more global, libraries will become a part of the overall strategy for survival.

Consortia play a vital role in gathering individual libraries and increasing the power of those libraries by the strength of group. However, consortia have recognized that to keep library partners, to recruit new library partners, and to move forward, consortia must clarify the benefits for libraries, publishers, or consortia and show how quickly they will come into play.

The Hidden Cost of Consortia Licensing

No doubt we all expect consortia pricing to be lower than individual library licensing. But a number of factors contribute to consortia licensing being less efficient and cost effective than might ideally be achieved. One major factor is overlapping consortia. As consortia have become more active in licensing, duplication of effort and confusion have developed.

Several consortia may be working with the same publisher at the same time and are likely to negotiate different pricing and terms and conditions. Meanwhile, a multi-consortium licensing program may be developed. This creates a dilemma for libraries: Which offer best meets their needs? If a consortium loses a library participant to another consortium, the negotiated offer may need to be reconstructed because of the change in number of participants. This duplication and confusion can also influence the length of time before the contract and implementation are completed—frustrating the library, the publisher, and the consortium. All of these issues and factors influence the true administrative cost of consortia licensing and may also affect the final price to the library.

As the trend in consortia-based licensing continues, the issue of overlapping consortia will be a key topic within states, at the regional level, nationally, and internationally. The regional networks and ICOLC are encouraging discussions and seeking solutions for this growing concern.

In a recent *Library Journal* article about consortia, Barbara Allen of the Committee on Institutional Cooperation (CIC) said: "Because CIC members also belong to statewide or regional consortia that buy databases, the CIC can only buy more expensive, esoteric ones. But there are other roles for such large consortia, such as identifying and agreeing on a tool kit for development of local digital collections."[7]

David Ferriero, Duke University's vice provost for library affairs, envisions the Triangle Research Libraries Network (TLRN) as a future cooperative storage facility to reduce title duplication. "Once we get to the point of a cooperative facility, then we have a locus for document delivery, preservation, cooperative acquisitions, cooperative cataloging, perhaps digitization projects."[8]

Both these comments suggest that for overlapping consortia to coexist, each will have to consider and carefully select its role, allowing other consortia that can be more effective to fulfill other roles.

Pricing models impact the cost of consortium licensing. While the FTE model has been demonstrated as a reasonable approach for consortia—especially across consortia at a regional or national level—an aggregate model requires significant participation before small and medium-size libraries realize significant savings. It also requires equivalency tables when dealing in the multi-type arena of academic, school, and public libraries. The Carnegie Classification has also been used. It is understandable, but with such broad categories it can be a poor tool. The simultaneous-user model is familiar, and when applied school-by-school over time is felt by many to be an effective way to control costs. This model becomes problematic in a consortium setting where each library's price per user is determined by the aggregate. Also, if managed school-by-school it loses the advantage of a consortium-wide pool of simultaneous users, protecting all from variations in demand.

At this point, as pricing models evolve, all approaches can be used and the most suitable may depend on the nature of use of services being offered and the composition of libraries and consortia licensing the service.

Cost recovery has become essential for some consortia. While some state- or member-supported consortia do not have to recover administrative costs, many others do—particularly those that are independent and self-sustaining, which are more often than not referred to as "networks." It is difficult to include this kind of cost in a general membership fee because not all libraries will take advantage of every offer. So a service fee must be attached to the price of the product. The service fee can be minimized if the publisher is willing to recognize that the consortium is functioning in a cost-saving role for the publisher. In the end, this latter approach is just another way of dealing with a cost that must ultimately be reflected in the price. More and more consortia are beginning to recognize the need for cost recovery as offers become complex and the demand for more offers grows.

A recent article in *University Business* talked about changes resulting from the advent of Web-based, online information. "What's really different is the way the library does business. At universities across the country, librarians have been forced to master new skills. Where they once devoted themselves primarily to acquiring resources for specific fields, they must now be adept at negotiating with publishers, setting policy for using online material, and building consortia to increase their economic clout."[9]

As consortia and their licensing activity increase, new business models will emerge to benefit the consortium, its participants, and the publishers. Libraries recognize the need for new business models in an evolving environment and sometimes use consortia as a shield or a weapon. An openness has developed in the past year to exploration of new models and methods as well as a willingness to take a few more risks for longer-term goals.

Consortia Influence Product Development

Consortia have developed more clout in areas other than the ability to negotiate contracts; they have become a means for libraries to impact publishers' products more directly. In the past, publishers relied on advisory boards and focus groups composed of individual library representatives for product development. Today it is becoming increasingly common to have boards populated by consortia administrators and leaders.

Publishers depend on consortia as a source of revenue. They are as interested in securing the renewal subscription as the initial sale. As big, collective licensees, consortia have a voice that can influence product enhancements and new products. Although publishers do not want consortia to dictate product, they must respond to their interests as a reflection of the needs of the libraries they serve.

The CIS/LEXIS-NEXIS Academic Universe contract is an example. The Content Advisory Board (a part of the contract) has established (with CIS) product guidelines for the addition of future content. The Advertising Advisory Board contributes to guidelines for acceptable advertisers for college campuses. A third advisory board has worked closely with CIS on product redesign. Finally, CIS was open to developing a community college model that recognizes the composition of university parallel programs and certificate programs in the community college environment.

There were other examples in 1999 of publishers working with consortium advisory boards in the development of new product. NetLibrary, for example, has focused on collection development concerns while McGraw-Hill has sought advice from multiple communities including universities, public libraries, schools, and international libraries. Bell and Howell Information and Learning formed a consortia advisory board in 1999 and discusses with it its plans for products and pricing. Consortia have been the primary reason why publishers are recognizing the value of ongoing feedback from groups of libraries that represent large revenue sources in a very competitive environment.

Publishers Use Consortia to Launch New Product

During the past year, more and more publishers have recognized the value of consortia for launching new product. The CIS/LEXIS-NEXIS national offer demonstrated that within a very short timeframe publishers could launch an entire product line with almost overnight success around the world.

There has been much discussion about what elements need to be present for such an offer to be successful. The following seven elements are paramount for success:

- All components should be in place before the offer is announced.
- The pricing model must be simple and easy to administer by all consortia, have clear advantages for subscribing libraries, and be appropriate for the product and the libraries of interest.
- Cost-recovery must be insured for the participating consortia that need it.
- A co-marketing plan should be developed with the publisher that defines the roles clearly.
- The offer should be initiated when libraries can take advantage of both year-end dollars and new fiscal-year budgets.
- There must be a means by which libraries can be added periodically as funds become available.
- Clear and realistic expectations of market demand should be established.

A review of the Paratext Poole's Plus program that was offered to consortia in 1999 showed that it did not entirely meet these elements, and the results were limited. It is clear that the Carnegie pricing model that does not aggregate libraries was not very appealing. Further, this 19th century literature index product is esoteric and does not have broad aggregating appeal. That being said, more than 60 libraries signed on in a period of about two months. On the other hand, the CIS national offer received overwhelming response and has been an unqualified success.

Members of ICOLC have conducted a number of discussions with large publishers that currently provide periodical and reference products to the library market. After much analysis with the publishers, it is now clear that a product with a large installed client base does not lend itself to this type of consortia offering. The publisher risk to existing revenue levels is too significant, and the complexities of repackaging or bundling the product(s) into a commonly desired package is not very appealing and lacks significant value.

Conclusions

Consortia are a major force in the future of licensing, dominating the licensing landscape at a local, state, regional, national, and international level. Consortia collaborations are on the rise and will include more licensing activities, digital library initiatives, resource sharing, catalog sharing, and remote storage. Increased communication among consortia, particularly those that overlap, will improve coordination and accelerate the common use of and evolution of the most beneficial cooperative activities.

But there is no road map for either the consortia or publishers. Consortia and publishers are attempting to rapidly change business models in a world that is changing at an even faster rate. This combination raises the stakes, the risks, and the rewards for all that play the licensing game.

Notes

1. Tom Sanville, "A License to Deal," *Library Journal*, February 15, 1999, p. 124.
2. Timothy C. Kuhfus, "The Next-Generation Internet," Vital Speeches of the Day, Next Generation Internet Forum, December 16, 1998, p. 281.
3. Bernard Hurley, John Price-Wilkin, Merrilee Proffitt, Howard Besser, "The Making of America II Testbed Project: A Digital Library Service Model," Digital Library Federation, Council on Library and Information Resources, December 1999, p. 1.
4. Id. p. 5.
5. Burton Bollag, "Some European Universities Are Moving Beyond Reliance on State Support," *Chronicle of Higher Education*, March 19, 1999, p. A51.
6. Id. p. A50.
7. Norman Oder, "Consortia Hit Critical Mass," *Library Journal*, February 1, 2000, p. 49.
8. Id. p. 49.
9. Ron Feemster, "When Libraries Faced the Future," *University Business,* February 2000, p. 25.

International Reports

International Federation of Library Associations and Institutions

Box 95312, 2509 CH The Hague, Netherlands
31-70-3140884, fax 31-70-3834827
E-mail IFLA@ifla.org
World Wide Web http://www.ifla.org

Winston Tabb

Associate Librarian for Library Services, Library of Congress
Vice Chair, IFLA Professional Board

The International Federation of Library Associations and Institutions (IFLA) is the preeminent international organization representing librarians and other information professionals. During 1999 IFLA built on the previous year's work in advancing cataloging standards and service to special groups, expanded its work with libraries in developing regions, and strengthened its emphasis on new technologies in library services.

65th Council and General Conference

The 65th IFLA General Conference, hosted by the Thai Library Association in Bangkok August 20–28, 1999, attracted 2,237 registered participants from 117 countries with its theme "On the Threshold of the 21st Century: Libraries as Gateways to an Enlightened World." Her Royal Highness Princess Maha Chakri Sirindhorn, patron of the Thai Library Association, delivered the keynote address and aptly described IFLA as "the world pillar of the library and information profession and a dynamic catalyst for building up 'an enlightened world' to come in the very near future."

In addition to myriad working meetings, workshops, and seminars, IFLA approved a conceptual outline of a streamlined organizational structure. The conference also featured an international trade exhibition. At the close of the conference, the Conference Planning Committee announced that the 2004 conference would be held in Buenos Aires—the first time IFLA will hold its General Conference in Latin America. The 2006 conference will be in Seoul, and the Conference Planning Committee is accepting expressions of interest in hosting the 2005 Council and General Conference. Other forthcoming conference sites include Jerusalem (2000), Boston (2001), Glasgow (2002), and Berlin (2003).

IFLA also offered several important satellite conferences before the Council and General Conference. A major four-day conference on "Collecting and Safeguarding Oral Traditions" took place in connection with the "Memory of the World" Program sponsored by the United Nations Educational, Scientific and Cultural Organization (UNESCO). "Library Buildings in a Changing Environment," Shanghai Library, Shanghai, showed that breakthroughs in library architecture have not been limited to the widely heralded new national library buildings in Denmark, France, Germany, and Britain; new buildings are also planned or under way from Latvia to Poland and Sarawak to Korea. The Section on Management and Marketing organized a satellite meeting on "Marketing Your Library" in Bangkok. "Bridging the Gap in the Provision of Library Services and Literacy Support for the Blind in Realizing the Information Age," held in Penang, Malaysia, covered day-to-day library service to print-handicapped patrons as well as developments with the digital talking book and computerized production of braille texts.

Library Service to the Visually Handicapped

The IFLA Section of Libraries for the Blind, in the Division of Libraries Serving the General Public, continued to encourage research and development in service to print-handicapped people. In February 1999 the section arranged a training seminar in Grahamstown, South Africa, in cooperation with the South African Library for the Blind, to further the establishment of library service to the print-handicapped in countries where it does not exist or is inadequate. The section was vigilant throughout the year in warning of possible negative impacts of two political and legal trends:

- Privatization of postal services in many nations, which threatens the free or discounted delivery of braille materials and talking books
- Changes in copyright laws intended to safeguard intellectual property rights in a digital age, but which can hamper creation and distribution of braille materials and talking books

The section also promoted DAISY, the Digital Audio-based Information System—an open standard for the production, exchange, and use of digital talking books—and took steps to facilitate international interlibrary loan of materials for print-handicapped readers.

IFLA Moves into the Digital Age

The impact of new digital technologies now permeates IFLA's activities worldwide. In Bangkok, the Section on Bibliography's standing committee expanded its action plan for 2000–2001 to focus on implementing the recommendations from the International Conference on National Bibliographic Services (ICNBS) held in Copenhagen November 25–27, 1998, sponsored by the IFLA UBCIM (Universal Bibliographic Control and International MARC) Core Programme.

The recommendations basically updated the guidelines for national bibliographies (last issued by IFLA and UNESCO after the previous such conference in 1977) to recognize the impact of new electronic technologies. Planning began for a workshop at the IFLA 2001 General Conference to promote national bibliographies in developing countries and multinational bibliographies in areas where it is not feasible to publish national bibliographies.

The section plans to

- Develop a strategy for enlisting publisher cooperation in providing metadata for electronic resources they produce for use of national services
- Investigate "subject gateways" as an emerging technique for producing bibliographies of Internet resources
- Offer selection criteria to assist national bibliographic agencies in deciding which electronic resources to include in their bibliographies—particularly important since many national libraries, including those of Australia, Germany, and Japan, must acquire electronic publications through purchase or voluntary deposit because their nations' legal deposit laws do not cover electronic materials

Also at Bangkok, the Section on National Libraries and the Section on Bibliography sponsored a workshop, "Electronic Publications in National Bibliographies," which suggested that the real question for bibliographic services is not whether to deal with these publications as part of the national bibliography, but how to provide access and control given their challenges, and envisioned closer collaboration between producers of electronic materials and these bibliographic agencies as one approach. The Core Programmes for Preservation and Conservation (PAC) and Universal Availability of Publications (UAP) announced that they would undertake, on behalf of UNESCO, a survey of digitization programs in major cultural institutions in order to establish a "virtual library" of digitized collections worldwide. The Core Programme on Universal Dataflow and Telecommunications organized a one-day workshop on "Uniform Resource Identifiers and the Library Community."

Another conference emphasizing digital technologies, "Networking for Effective Libraries and Information Services," took place October 17–23, 1999, in Colombo, Sri Lanka, sponsored by IFLA's Regional Standing Committee for Asia & Oceania, funded by the Core Programme for Advancement of Librarianship, and organized by the Sri Lanka Library Association. In addition, UBCIM organized a conference with support from the Open Society (Soros) Institute, "International and National Cataloguing Rules: Current Situation and Future Trends," in Moscow, April 20–24, 1999, which featured recent developments in the cataloging rules to account for cataloguing electronic resources.

Membership

IFLA has more than 1,600 members in about 150 countries. It is headquartered in The Hague, Netherlands, reflecting the European and North American focus of its initial establishment in 1927. Although IFLA did not hold a General Conference outside Europe and North America until 1980, there has since been steadily increasing participation from Asia, Africa, South America, and Australia. IFLA, which has a formal affiliation with UNESCO, now maintains regional offices for Africa (in Dakar, Senegal), Asia and Oceania (in Bangkok), and Latin America (in Rio de Janeiro). The organization has five working languages—English, French, German, Russian, and Spanish—and offers four membership categories: international library associations, national library associations, institutions, and personal affiliates.

Personnel, Structure, and Governance

Ross Shimmon became secretary general of IFLA in May 1999. Since 1992 he had been chief executive of the (UK) Library Association. In the British prime minister's 2000 New Year's Honours List, he was named an Officer of the British Empire (OBE) for services to librarianship and information provision.

Sjoerd M. J. Koopman continues as coordinator of professional activities, an IFLA headquarters position.

IFLA's Executive Board is responsible for IFLA's general policy, management and finance, and external communications. The Executive Board consists of an elected president, seven elected members—elected every two years by the General Council of Members (the association and institution members)—and one ex officio member, the chair of the Professional Board. The current president is Christine Deschamps, Directeur, Bibliothèque de l'Université Paris V—René Descartes; the chair of the Professional Board is Ralph W. Manning, National Library of Canada.

IFLA's Professional Board monitors the planning and programming of professional activities carried out by IFLA's two types of bodies: professional groups and core programs. The Professional Board is composed of one elected officer from each division plus a chair elected from the Professional Board by the incoming members. Each division has a coordinating board made up of the chairs and secretaries of the sections. The eight divisions are I: General Research Libraries; II: Special Libraries; III: Libraries Serving the General Public; IV: Bibliographic Control; V: Collections and Services; VI: Management and Technology; VII: Education and Research; and VIII: Regional Activities. The 35 sections include such interest sections as National Libraries, Geography and Maps Libraries, Libraries Serving Children and Young Adults, Statistics, and Library Services to Multicultural Populations. The five Core Programmes are Advancement of Librarianship (ALP), Universal Bibliographic Control and International MARC (UBCIM), Universal Dataflow and Telecommunications (UDT), Universal Availability of Publications (UAP), and Preservation and Conservation (PAC).

Revision of the IFLA Statutes

In Bangkok the council approved a conceptual outline of a major revision of the Statutes and Rules of Procedure, which had not been substantially revised since the 1970s. The outline included the following main changes: president's term shortened to two years; two-year president-elect position introduced; IFLA's

Executive and Professional Boards combined and terms altered; and annual rather than biennial council meetings. The council also formally agreed to permit postal (paper and electronic) voting by council members, enabling more members, including those from developing countries, to participate in the governance of the association. Two other areas that will be explored are the specific programs for developing countries and the traditional core programs, which have experienced funding uncertainties under the present structure.

The next steps for IFLA will be drafting the detailed statutes and rules revisions. A mail ballot before the next conference is the target so that elections at the 2001 conference in Boston will be under the new statutes. The new statutes will enable IFLA to build a stronger, better-organized governance structure that can be more inclusive and more responsive to rapid change.

Special Libraries Association

1700 Eighteenth St. N.W., Washington, DC 20009-2514
202-234-4700, fax 202-265-9317, e-mail sla@sla.org
World Wide Web http://www.sla.org

David R. Bender
Executive Director

Headquartered in Washington, D.C., the Special Libraries Association (SLA) is an international association representing the interests of nearly 15,000 information professionals in 60 countries. Special librarians are information resource experts who collect, analyze, evaluate, package, and disseminate information to facilitate accurate decision-making in corporate, academic, and government settings.

As of June 1999 the association had 56 regional chapters in the United States, Canada, Europe, and the Middle East; 25 divisions representing a variety of industries; and 13 special-interest caucuses.

SLA offers myriad programs and services designed to help its members serve their customers more effectively and succeed in an increasingly challenging environment of information management and technology. Association activities are developed with specific direction toward achieving SLA's strategic priorities: to ensure that SLA members have opportunities to develop professional competencies and skills; to narrow the gap between the value of the information professional and the perceived value of special librarians and information professionals among decision-makers; and to ensure the ongoing relevance of SLA to its members in the next century by managing the transition to SLA's vision of a "virtual association," whereby all members will be able to access SLA services globally, equitably, and continuously.

Computer Services and Technology

Merging and blending new and existing technologies with the association's information infrastructure in order to support strategic goals of the association is the main objective of the Computer Services and Technology department.

During the year, Computer Services added a new association management system, replacing the core computing stations with Pentium II computers. In addition, Windows 3.1 was replaced with Windows 98, 16-bit applications were replaced with 32-two bit versions, workstation memory was increased to 64 MB of RAM, and hubs were replaced with switches to handle the new volume of information.

A new members-only Web site was created, providing members with the ability to update their membership information, view *Who's Who in Special Libraries* online, and search monthly issues of *Information Outlook*.

The virtual association was expanded to incorporate new products and services, including searchable online preliminary and final conference programs that enable members to add program events to their personal itineraries. The association's remote-access server was upgraded to enable staff to access the association's new 32-bit applications at any time or place.

The benefits and utilization of the virtual association were promoted to members and association community. Demonstrations on using the products and services located in the new members-only section were presented during SLA's Annual Conference.

The association's virtual bookstore was enhanced to support Web advertising, customer profiling, and one-to-one personalization of Web pages for customers.

A video server was added to support the association's video broadcasting needs. It will provide live and taped video broadcasts and ultimately pay-per-viewing.

With the implementation of these new services and technologies, in line with the association's strategic plan, the Computer Services and Technologies program will continue to enhance the association's information infrastructure to support SLA's expanding business and information requirements.

Conferences and Meetings

More than 5,500 information professionals from around the world gathered in Minneapolis June 5–10, 1999, to participate in SLA's 90th Annual Conference, "Knowledge Leaders for the New Millennium: Creators of the Information Future."

The conference program was available via the SLA Web site, giving conference attendees the opportunity to plan their conference schedules in advance.

An electronic message center allowed attendees to locate colleagues and leave messages, and a cyber cafe provided the opportunity to check e-mail and tap into the Internet.

The conference featured the largest exhibit hall in SLA history with more than 375 companies mounting 540 booths displaying the latest technology and products available to the profession.

The annual President's Reception raised close to $5,000 for the SLA scholarship fund.

Financial and Administrative Services

The philosophy of the Financial Services program is to ensure the integrity of financial data and to establish and enforce internal controls while maintaining a high level of quality service, both internally and externally. Financial Services staff operates according to a series of detailed planning schedules and written guidelines, policies, and procedures. These policies and procedures are routinely reviewed by staff, management, leadership, and independent counsel for effectiveness and efficiency. The Financial Services staff is committed to providing the most accurate information in the most timely manner possible in order to facilitate the efficient fiscal management of all SLA programs and activities. The program staff is also committed to the cross-training of staff to increase internal controls and to accommodate periods of peak production and staff absences.

The Administrative Services program encompasses human resources, office services, and building management; it essentially serves to support the staff members who, in turn, support the membership. The program is governed by various board-approved policies and procedures, and is reviewed semiannually by the Association Office Operations Committee.

During the year, Financial and Administrative Services

- Added new and improved banking software that allows many services to be done in-house that previously required the aid of bank personnel or a trip to the bank
- Enhanced and expanded online financial management screens for program managers that allow staff to view financial information pertinent to their goals and objectives
- Implemented improvements in the collection of accounts receivable by requiring prepayment for all products and services
- Enhanced the recruitment process for new employees to include assessment of individual technological advancements
- Negotiated with two employment agencies for temporary-to-permanent placement without placement fees, maximizing the association's hiring flexibility and minimizing employment liabilities
- Implemented a customer-service pledge that requires staff to respond to all inquiries within 24 hours
- Initiated a fax-on-demand system, which enables members to access association documents 24 hours a day, 7 days a week
- Developed training schedules for new equipment and office services employed by the association

Fund Development

Association year 1998–1999 saw some notable successes in the Fund Development program.

During the year the program increased corporate support for the annual campaign by 32 percent, increased individual member contributions to the annual campaign by 143 percent, and increased total conference sponsorship income by 138 percent.

In addition, Fund Development significantly increased corporate support for the Annual Conference by adding West Group as the first major conference partner and LEXIS-NEXIS as SLA's Cutting Edge Partner.

Three new special partnerships were established: the Innovations in Technology Award by FIS, Distance Learning Program and Real-Time Desktop courses by West Group, and Information Outlook Online by Standard & Poors.

Information Resources Center

SLA's Information Resources Center (IRC) continues to respond to a high number of requests for information from staff, members, and nonmembers on a variety of aspects of special librarianship and association management. The majority of requests are on education and professional development, careers, salaries, and general library management.

During 1998–1999 the IRC Web pages exceeded 10,000 hits per month, compared with an average of just over 5,000 the previous year.

The electronic information packets (EIPs) accessible via the IRC Web site have been updated monthly, and an average of 40 resources added each month. All EIPs include hypertext links to Web sites of interest or full-text articles where applicable.

CONSULT Online, the database of SLA member consultants, was enhanced to include more than 80 new areas of expertise.

IRC's ongoing goal is to create a "virtual IRC" and a more proactive service for members and staff. The center provides staff Internet training, new-staff orientation, and a monthly IRC Update of information and resources transferred to the IRC. By subscribing to all the SLA division listservs, IRC staff remains environmentally aware of the concerns of SLA members and developments in the information industry.

Leadership Development

The Division and Chapter Officers Leadership Training (DACOLT) program was renamed the Leadership Development Institute (LDI). LDI will enhance the efforts of gaining institutional support for volunteer leaders and allow for an expanded program in the future.

The institute conducted LDI and former DACOLT programs as well as workshops during the Annual Conference for archivists, advocacy, public relations chairs, list hosting, membership chairs, professional development chairs, treasurers, bulletin editors, and Webmasters.

The monthly newsletter *Leadership Update* was added to the SLA Web site, providing unit leaders the ability to direct announcements and information to appropriate unit officers and committee chairs.

A discussion list for unit leadership was created, allowing quick broadcast information from headquarters, cross-training, and issue discussion among unit leaders.

Membership Development

The Membership Development program works in partnership with all other program areas to pursue membership growth through the recruitment and retention of SLA's members. In addition, the Membership Development department works closely with SLA's volunteer leaders to support the activities of the association's chapters, divisions, caucuses, and student groups. Together with SLA's data entry team, the staff maintains the membership database, including adding new and prospective members, processing renewals and address changes, and updating officer information. Further, the Membership Development program promotes and administers the SLA Scholarship program, monitors Student Group activities, works with the Affirmative Action Committee to administer SLA's Diversity Leadership Development program, and supports the activities of the Endowment Fund Grant Committee.

In the past year, the section

- Assisted the implementation and effective utilization of a new association management system, which included the debut of a new members-only area of SLA's Web site and the creation and dissemination of new membership cards permitting access to it
- Refined the telemarketing program to encourage former association members to reinstate membership
- Provided assistance to association leaders through monthly mailings, leadership training sessions, and electronic communications
- Enhanced the *Student Union*, the student group newsletter, to include the utilization of student authors and the inclusion of more photographs
- Continued to work with the Student and Academic Relations Committee (SARC) to build a partnership with SLA leaders and student members to increase membership retention
- Disbursed close to $30,000 in financial aid through the scholarship program. The SARC-sponsored certificate of merit program was continued to honor student groups, chapters, and divisions that demonstrate outstanding activity and/or continued commitment to promoting professional development for students within their organizations

Nonserial Publications

The Nonserial Publications program (NSP) produces products that will prepare and empower the information professional in a rapidly evolving industry. In addition, the program endeavors to make a significant contribution to the literature of the information profession and to increase the influence of the professional and of the field itself. NSP endeavors to anticipate market demands by staying abreast of developments within the industry and producing quality titles that meet those needs.

In 1999 SLA released new titles on change management, the virtual office, measuring the value of information services, content management, and the results of two Goldspiel grant studies ("Providing Information to the Virtual Office" and "Users' Choice of Filtering Methods for Electronic Text").

Nonserial Publications also published new editions of the cornerstone publication *Special Libraries and Information Centers: An Introductory Text,* which is commonly used by graduate library and information science programs, and the *SLA Annual Salary Survey.*

Professional Development

The Professional Development program encompasses cutting-edge continuous-education activities and career services for SLA members. The program strives to help information professionals meet their potential by providing educational opportunities based on the professional and personal competencies outlined in SLA's report *Competencies for Special Librarians of the 21st Century.*

During 1998–1999, a wide variety of continuous-education programs were offered in the areas of technology, library management, strategic planning, budgeting, marketing and public relations, and general management.

The Professional Development department, in cooperation with Pace University, presented four multimedia courses, "Writing Java Applets," "Advanced HTML," "Creating Your Own Home Pages Using HTML," and "The Seven Keys to Highly Effective Web Sites." These asynchronous courses utilized a variety of delivery platforms including online instruction, a videotape, textbook readings, Web assignments, and an online discussion group.

The department also produced its seventh video conference, "Harnessing Intranet Potential," which explained how intranets can enhance the sharing of knowledge and information within their organizations, and the 1998 State-of-the-Art Institute "Content Management: Putting Knowledge to Work." The program explored the issues, challenges, competencies, and opportunities involved in managing both internally and externally produced content along with the new concepts, tools, and strategies needed to master content management.

The 1999 Winter Education Conference, "Crossing the Bridge to the 21st Century," focused on the latest developments in information technology. The Technology and Applications unit of the Middle Management Competencies Institute was also offered during the conference.

The department sponsored a conference, "Management of the Library in the Electronic Era," in Barcelona, Spain, that featured library directors from several countries.

The department also presented the 1999 video conference "De-Mystifying the Licensing of Electronic Resources"; featured 26 continuing-education courses at the basic, intermediate, and advanced levels during the Annual Conference; and operated the Employment Clearinghouse and a Career Advisory Service.

Government Relations

SLA's Government Relations program implemented proactive efforts to reform copyright laws of many nations around the world. In addition, working with other library organizations, educational groups, and corporations, SLA worked to convince the U.S. Congress to amend its proposed digital copyright legislation and reexamine the issue of database protection legislation.

SLA also worked with the European Bureau of Library, Information and Documentation Associations (EBLIDA) to lobby the European Parliament on behalf of the European library community, and coordinated with Canadian chapters of SLA to comment on the Canadian government's efforts to comply with international treaty obligations.

Public Communications

The primary goal of the Public Communications program is to increase awareness and appreciation of the important role special librarians play in their organizations and society. Another goal is to aid the association unit in creating ways in which the association and the profession can be represented positively in the public eye.

During the year, Public Communications

- Coordinated with the Strategic Communications Group to build a sound media relations strategy that touches on the major themes of the day and reveals the positive aspects of the membership and the association
- Expanded the focus on getting coverage of special librarians in metropolitan newspapers worldwide, major trade press, and association business publications
- Recognized 13 SLA members for outstanding service to the association and the profession through the SLA Awards and Honors program; in addition, four SLA student members received scholarships

The 1999 International Special Librarian's Day was a major international success with the theme "Exercise Your Resources." All segments of the membership took advantage of the day to create new celebrations or to reinvigorate long-standing events.

Research

SLA's Research goals are to provide methodologies, data, and analyses that address significant elements of the profession. SLA supports research through a variety of activities. The association independently conducts research, works in collaboration with other organizations in conducting and sponsoring research, and funds research through the Steven I. Goldspiel Memorial Research Grant.

At its June 1999 meeting the SLA Board of Directors approved the Research Committee's nomination of James M. Turner and Michèle Hudon as the recipients of the 1999 Goldspiel Grant for their proposal "Organizing Moving Image Collections for the Digital Era."

The technical report of the 1995 Goldspiel Grant, *Users Choice of Filtering Methods for Electronic Text,* was made available, and the 1997 Goldspiel Grant report by Claire R. McInerney, *Providing Data, Information, and Knowledge to the Virtual Office,* was published by SLA as a monograph.

Research coordinated with Membership, Professional Development, and Nonserial Publications to hold focus groups with SLA members at the Annual Conference. It also revised the 1999 *Annual Salary Survey* to reflect current changes in the profession and the diversity of the membership.

In addition, it conducted the Library and Information Studies Programs Survey to provide a benchmark of information studies curricula and to identify competency areas better served by continuing-education programs offered through professional associations with SLA's Professional Development department, the Medical Library Association, and the Association for Library and Information Science Education.

The Value of Special Libraries was made available as a nonserial publication.

Serial Publications

In January 1997 *Special Libraries* and *SpeciaList* were officially retired, making way for a new four-color monthly magazine, *Information Outlook*. Now in its third year of publication, *Information Outlook* continues to provide members and subscribers with timely and in-depth coverage of issues pertinent to information professionals working in a global environment.

Association news expanded in volume three of *Information Outlook*. Program updates are highlighted each month in recurring columns such as Executive Outlook, Professional Development Outlook, Communications Outlook, Money Matters, Conference Countdown, and Research Briefs. The May and June issues were expanded to 64 pages to accommodate advertising and increased editorial content.

Information Outlook received trademark recognition by the U.S. Patent & Trademark Office and the Canadian Intellectual Property Office. The publication continues to be posted online at http://www.informationoutlook.com for association members. The site offers full text of feature articles as well as regular columns with links to SLA's Coming Events page and the Online Job Search.

Who's Who in Special Libraries, the association's annual membership directory, now contains 400 pages and continues to serve as a valuable networking tool and information resource for the membership. The publication includes chapter and division leadership and member information; member statistics; historical highlights; SLA's Bylaws, Strategic Plan, and Vision Statement; awards and honors winners; past presidents; and a schedule of future meetings and conferences. The online version of the *Who's Who* (at http://www.slawhoswho.com) contains up-to-date information regarding SLA members, board of directors information, and headquarters contacts. Also on the site are the SLA Buyer's Guide and Directory of Manufacturers and Suppliers.

Trends in Library and Information Services in Canada, 1994–1999

Ken Haycock

Helen Moore

School of Library, Archival and Information Studies
University of British Columbia, Vancouver

Since 1994 trends and issues in library and information services in Canada have been identified in an annual report in the *Bowker Annual*. The reports included specific indicators of individual trends, developments in each province and the territories, and examples by environment and type of library.

The reports were developed in collaborative efforts with Doug Brigham, David Chow, Frances Dodd, and Mary Oh (See Haycock, 1995; Haycock & Brigham, 1996; Haycock & Chow, 1997; Haycock & Dodd, 1998; Haycock & Oh, 1999) through interviews with library and association leaders across Canada and analysis of newsletters, magazines, journals, and news reports.

After five years of reporting, and at the dawn of a new century, it seems appropriate to stop and reflect on these activities and developments and to identify the major trends across the sector. Helen Moore analyzed the previous reports and background material. Karen McGrath, corporate development officer at the National Library of Canada, provided themes emerging from the national tour of Canadian libraries and meetings with librarians by Roch Carrier, the new National Librarian of Canada, in the fall of 1999 shortly after his appointment (McGrath, K., personal communication, February 28, 2000). These analyses were combined to form this article.

Several themes and trends emerge. These are identified here with examples; readers are invited to review the previous reports for further detail. As with many aspects of library and information studies, the trends are neither discrete nor exclusive.

Equitable Access to Information

Newer challenges center around electronic resources, funding for acquisition and access, adequate Canadian content, and equitable access—all in the context of decreasing government and institutional funding for library and information services. The library community developed more-current policies and practices that support equitable and universal access to information and ideas, and adherence to the principles of intellectual freedom, through the Canadian Library Association.

Equitable access includes several elements. Provincial networks are enabling integrated, automated library systems accessible to all. Public libraries continue to promote access to the Internet, and Internet training is ubiquitous in public libraries across Canada, leading to greater emphasis on teaching as a necessary skill for librarians. Information literacy, linking most specifically to academic and school libraries, is increasingly important as students need more than ever to be able to analyze and evaluate the information retrieved through the Internet.

Intellectual access to information—ensuring that customers can derive meaning from text as well as simply accessing it—integrates these teaching and literacy programs into the mainstream of library operations.

Some provinces have developed "access for all" strategic plans to institutionalize resource sharing and "one library" province-wide for all residents. Fees, however—whether labeled membership fees, registration fees, or "non-core" service fees—continue to be controversial as an impediment to equitable access for all. Some systems, such as the Calgary and Vancouver public libraries, have instituted business information services, providing specialized services on a fee basis, while "basic" services are still free. The Regina (Saskatchewan) Public Library and Thunder Bay (Ontario) Public Library each launched fee-based research services.

The growing demand for Internet resources, CD-ROMs, and online databases, combined with the pressures of funding cuts and changes to the national telecommunications system, are making it difficult for many public libraries to balance strong traditional services, well supported by the public, with the need to provide more electronic access. There is growing recognition that the public library is a vital community resource and an integral element of the total education process, but this is not translating into dollars for service. Similarly, academic libraries are challenged by the dramatic increase in cost for serials, particularly with the weak purchasing power of the Canadian dollar internationally. In addition, Internet filtering and censorship of school library materials continue as impediments to access.

Integration of Newer Technologies

It was only five years ago that the main issues facing the federal government's Information Highway Advisory Council were how to use the "Information Highway" (when was the last time you heard that term?) to improve the growth and competitiveness of Canadian business, to assure that Canadians have universal access to essential services at reasonable cost, to achieve an appropriate balance between competition and regulation, and to promote the development and distribution of Canadian culture and content. Emphasis continues on the relationship between libraries and electronic access to information on the Internet.

There also continues to be much interest in Z39.50, a standard that allows users to perform searches in many catalogs simultaneously, and its implementation. (The use of Z39.50 could eliminate the need to produce local or regional union catalogs and facilitate resource sharing across the country.) The National Library's Virtual Canadian Union Catalogue project identified and addressed technical issues in the use of Z39.50. Vendors, as partners to the virtual catalog, will promote Z39.50 and run interoperability tests between servers. The National Library's directory of Z39.50 targets also provides online direction for Canadian library cooperation.

Libraries continue to take advantage of technological developments to improve services, with a trend to introducing more client-centered innovations; examples include the use of "smart cards" (a single card that functions as student, library, and debit cards), self-check-out service, and automated security gates. Many systems also launched virtual reference libraries.

The National Library formed the Canadian Initiative on Digital Libraries to ensure both access and quality. A survey to assess digital collections identified several issues:

- Selection criteria
- Long-term access
- Duplication of effort
- Standards
- Copyright and licensing
- Equitable network access
- Funding
- Technology and management
- Staff and user training

The project mandate is to develop the hardware, software, and telecommunications infrastructure to support digital library applications, as well as to manage electronic publications. Standards for publishing government documents in electronic form would be useful in this venture.

There are, of course, difficulties in acquiring new electronic resources and trying to keep print resources current as well when funding levels remain flat. Similarly, there is great concern for the preservation of electronic documents— who will fund preservation and who will do the work?

The National Library passed the 1,000 mark in cataloging remote-access electronic publications. This project seeks to acquire, preserve, and make available a wide range of Canadian electronic products, as well as to create standard bibliographic records for electronic information.

The National Library also launched *Canadiana*, the national bibliography, on CD-ROM. *Canadiana* holds more than 1.4 million records from the database of monographs, serials, government publications, music scores, sound recordings, video recordings, and electronic publications. *Canadiana* also contains the National Library's name authority records and the National Archive's Carto-Canadian records.

Partnerships

Each year of the past decade witnessed more examples of partnerships between libraries and both the public and corporate sectors as a pattern of development. Many of these partnerships were designed to support specific library initiatives and projects. The Toronto Public Library, for example, in partnership with Atomic Energy of Canada, launched ScienceNet, a Web site whose goal is to provide students, educators, and the general public with access to reputable and accurate Internet information in the pure and applied sciences, in English and French.

Literacy programs are another area of partnership. The Toronto Public Library, for instance, accepted Disney sponsorship for its summer reading program.

Continuing decreases in funding meant that new sources of revenue had to be found. In a controversial move, the Vancouver Public Library accepted a corporate donation of $500,000 for displaying a developer's logo on library cards for five years. Some thought this was unacceptable and antithetical to accepted values of library service; others thought that the library should have demanded more money for the honor. Similarly, the Edmonton Public Library renamed its main branch after a major donor.

Consortia with other information and cultural service providers are also growing. In Nova Scotia, for example, EdNet, the Department of Education and Culture's wide area network, was launched linking 135 schools, museums, and regional libraries; and the public electronic information system, NcompasS, provides direct access to library databases throughout the province via EdNet.

The Richmond (British Columbia) Public Library benefited from donation of almost 6,000 Chinese-language books for its large Chinese-Canadian population. Another Chinese-Canadian donated $10,000 after reading about the book donations.

Most public libraries have Internet access, many through the federal government's Community Access Project. Many libraries have also benefited from computer equipment supplied through the Gates Library Foundation and Industry Canada; issues center around the resources and expertise required to maintain the equipment and the need to keep upgrades synchronous with the state of electronic publications.

Resource Sharing

Across the country, there is increased effort to share resources and to address the high cost of purchasing and licensing electronic products. Each province and territory continues to work on ways to improve local and regional resource sharing as more and more catalogs go up on the Internet, leading to much more intra-province/territory borrowing. Provincewide database licensing projects have been initiated with buying determined by consortia that include various combinations of academic, public, school, and special libraries. Resource sharing also includes the sharing of human expertise and greater collaboration in delivering continuing education.

A plan for a Grande Bibliothèque Québécoise, which will house the separate collections of the Bibliothèque Nationale du Québec and the Bibliothèque Centrale de Montréal, continues. The appointment of a journalist, rather than a librarian, to head up the new library was another development. While not ubiquitous, or even widespread, new urban library facilities are being constructed and some urban library boards are engaging nonlibrarians as directors.

Resource sharing has moved internationally as well. For example, the Canadian Institute for Science and Technical Information (CISTI) and the Science and Technology Information Center in Taipei, Taiwan, entered into an agreement to share resources, technologies, and expertise. This agreement gives Canadians access to more than 1,200 Chinese-language journals, published in Taiwan, China, and Southeast Asia.

Taking partnerships and sharing to the extreme, amalgamation of local governments is increasing, with the most visible example in the Toronto area where six public library boards and the Metro Toronto Reference Library were joined to create one of the largest library systems in North America, the new Toronto Public Library with 98 branches. The government of New Brunswick also created a single Public Libraries Board to replace five former regional library boards.

School Libraries

The term "broken front" has been used to describe the current state of school libraries in Canada. School board amalgamations, budget cuts, reassignments, and retirements have been common themes. Overall, school libraries have faced particularly tough times.

Nowhere is the "interface" of Internet hype and library services more evident than in schools. The result is an infusion of information technology, often divorced from the school's library resource center and teacher-librarian, and lack of understanding of the role of the teacher-librarian by decision makers. On the other hand, some schools are now linking all classrooms to the school library in one large local area network so that students can access information from servers and CD-ROM towers without leaving the classroom; some are also connected to wide area networks that cover entire school districts. Teacher-librarians in these schools and districts were able to exhibit strong teaching and partnership skills as well as the integration of both physical and intellectual access to (especially electronic) information in the curriculum.

Teacher-librarians, typically not protected by teacher union contracts, are being replaced by library technicians in some jurisdictions. In British Columbia, however, teacher-librarians were placed in the provincial collective agreement guaranteeing a teacher-librarian in every school, and in the Yukon Territory, the government advanced the state of school libraries with increased support staff and teacher-librarian time and stable acquisition budgets. Every student and teacher now has online access to the full range of the Yukon's educational resources.

The impact of school library funding cuts has also had an effect on public library services. The National Library initiated a "School Library Manifesto" that gained the support of both the International Association of School Librarianship and the International Federation of Library Associations and Institutions (IFLA); it was approved at UNESCO's General Conference in 1999. Canada has always led the world in policy guidelines and best practice for school libraries; the challenge will now be to translate these international guidelines into practice through the restoration of reduced personnel and services.

Education for teacher-librarianship is a national issue as more and more education of certified teacher-librarians is devolving to the library profession. University positions in school librarianship in faculties of education are being eliminated through retirements and attrition.

Marketing and Advocacy

Libraries are also becoming more like other businesses in the sense that they have to market and increasingly fund themselves. Public libraries are giving more attention to planning for the future and focusing on the customer through marketing studies and focus groups. More "friends" groups are being established, fundraising activities organized, and improved marketing programs implemented.

Libraries and librarians are unanimous on the need to get the word out that libraries should exist hand in hand with the Internet—this is a constant battle as decision makers seem to believe that the entire sum of the world's knowledge is on the Internet.

Public-sector restraint and the need for strong advocacy for libraries, and increased emphasis on fund raising, led to a national strategy, Library Advocacy Now!, a project of the Canadian Library Association. Several provincial associations also launched targeted advocacy programs.

The need for libraries to promote their role and important place in the Canadian economy and society is critical. There is also a need to promote the profession, to attract "the best and the brightest" to librarianship.

One might point to the positive example of Prince Edward Island where, after years of effective advocacy by teacher-librarians, renewed support and leadership for school libraries are being demonstrated. Based on local research studies, teacher-librarians have been able to demonstrate their value and the important role of the school library.

Advocacy is also a major issue in the corporate environment, where the value of corporate libraries needs to be marketed in order to promote how they contribute to economic development and growth.

As leaders on the international stage, the British Columbia and Canadian library associations developed policies and advocacy strategies for ensuring that the library voice was heard during the most recent round of negotiations in the World Trade Organization, where the service sectors, including education and culture, were to be discussed. Although subject to different interpretations, there is concern that proposed new international protocols could lead to private-sector companies, no matter where located, competing with local publicly supported institutions for access to public funds and the delivery of public services.

Education and Training

Schools of library and information studies report greater flexibility in the programs being offered. Part-time access and distance education, especially continuing education, are growing trends. Early in 2000 the seven Canadian graduate programs accredited by the American Library Association committed to a national collaborative strategy for distance education. All schools report that graduates are finding an increasing number of professional positions outside traditional librarianship. Other trends are increasing numbers of temporary or contract positions and positions outside the country.

The National Alliance of Libraries, Archives and Records Management (ALARM) was created in 1994 to address personnel issues in the information resources sector. These issues included the impact of technological change, the need to attract more extroverted and politically proactive professionals, credibility within the parent organization, and the need for a better reflection of the cultural and ethnic diversity of communities in the information work force. The summary report "Human Resources Development in the Information Resources Management Sector" confirmed initial findings that soft skills (skills that are not centered on subject-matter expertise but relate to communications and management) are the most important area of training currently needed. Parallel findings included a general concern with the worth of available training, and ongoing preoccupations with the evolution of technology and its impact across all aspects of the sector's work.

Training is an urgent issue in Canadian librarianship. This relates as well to the concern about the "graying" of the profession. According to leaders across the country the majority of professionals currently in managerial and senior positions will be within retirement age within the next five years and there is no one to replace them. There is a large gap between these leaders and more junior professionals who are not considered ready at this point to take on senior management positions.

Conclusion

The 1994 report (Haycock, 1995) concluded with:

> Partnership is the new pattern of development: partnerships with other institutions to share resources; partnerships with business and industry to support and exploit those resources; partnerships with government to make libraries the primary information access point for citizens; partnerships with colleagues and citizens to advocate for libraries and librarians through their associations. Training continues to be the most urgent issue in Canadian librarianship—more training in newer technologies and more training in advocating the importance of the work of information professionals. The newer challenges include acquiring, organizing, preserving, storing, and accessing electronic publications, balancing the increased commercialization of information, government (at all levels) cost-recovery initiatives, providing Canadian content for the information highway and the need for equitable access to information.

In 1998 (Haycock & Oh, 1999) we concluded:

> The trend toward the formation of consortia for the purchase and licensing of electronic resources continues, as well as partnering with the public and private sectors to provide services. Public-sector restraint and the need for strong advocacy for libraries, as well as increased emphasis on fund raising, also continue to be important concerns. As more Canadians become connected to the Internet through libraries, the library community is developing policies and practices that ensure equitable and universal access to information and the principles of intellectual freedom.

Clearly, trends and issues are neither short-term nor easily solved. However, it is reassuring that the articulation of these trends from year to year, validated by other sources including library leaders across the country and the National Librarian's dialogue with the profession, provides a foundation for problem-solving and strategic planning for the future.

References

Haycock, K. "Trends and Issues in Library and Information Services in Canada, 1994." In C. Barr (Ed.), *Bowker Annual Library and Book Trade Almanac* (pp. 92–98). 40th edition. New Providence, N.J.: R. R. Bowker, 1995.

Haycock, K., & Brigham, D. "Trends and Issues in Library and Information Services in Canada, 1995." In D. Bogart (Ed.), *Bowker Annual Library and Book Trade Almanac* (pp. 205–212). 41st edition. New Providence, N.J.: R. R. Bowker, 1996.

Haycock, K., & Chow, D. "Trends and issues in Library and Information Services in Canada, 1996." In D. Bogart (Ed.), *Bowker Annual Library and Book Trade Almanac* (pp. 220–228). 42nd edition. New Providence, N.J.: R. R. Bowker, 1997.

Haycock, K., & Dodd, F. "Trends and Issues in Library and Information Services in Canada, 1997." In Bogart, D. (Ed.), *Bowker Annual Library and Book Trade Almanac* (pp. 231–240). 43rd edition. New Providence, N.J.: R. R. Bowker, 1998.

Haycock, K., & Oh, M. "Trends and Issues in Library and Information Services in Canada, 1998." In Bogart, D. (Ed.), *Bowker Annual Library and Book Trade Almanac* (pp. 223–233). 44th edition. New Providence, N.J.: R. R. Bowker, 1999.

Part 2
Legislation, Funding,
and Grants

Legislation

Legislation and Regulations
Affecting Libraries in 1999

Emily Sheketoff
Executive Director, Washington Office, American Library Association

Mary Rae Costabile
Associate Director, Washington Office, American Library Association

The first session of the 106th Congress ended with various departments of government scrambling to create a cut of 0.38 percent in their fiscal year (FY) 2000 appropriations, which was part of the final omnibus appropriations agreement (P.L. 106-113). Many other pieces of legislation were left pending for the second session of this Congress, which began in late January 2000. Some of these bills may continue to languish while others may move forward during the final months of the 106th Congress amid a presidential election year.

It appeared that Congress would have less than 100 working days scheduled for the next session and a complex appropriations debate brewing. The Budget Committees will try to agree on a budget outline for all FY 2001 spending, with some $17 billion forward-funded already into FY 2001 from FY 2000. If Congress and the administration hold to the spending caps established in the Budget Enforcement Act of 1997, it is projected that $15 billion of cuts in discretionary programs will be needed.

Digital Millennium Copyright Act

Among other new provisions of the Digital Millennium Copyright Act of 1998, Section 1201(a) prohibits circumventing a technological measure that controls access to a copyrighted work. Violators of the prohibition are subject to civil and criminal penalties. Examples of a "technological measure" might include limiting the number of users, blocking the ability to print, employing a "pay-per-search" scheme, or even just requiring a password.

Circumventing a technological measure means descrambling a scrambled work; decrypting an encrypted work; or otherwise avoiding, bypassing, removing, deactivating, or impairing a technological measure without the authority of the copyright owner.

Section 1201(a) also allows, however, for the creation of an exemption to the prohibition so that users of certain types of works can make noninfringing uses of the copyrighted works. The Copyright Office must issue rules (to be effective October 2000) to implement this exemption. In its rulemaking proceeding, the Copyright Office must determine whether such an exemption is warranted and the classes of information product to which the exemption should apply. The American Library Association will submit comments to the Copyright Office.

Database Protection

Although H.R. 354, the Collections of Information Antipiracy Act, did not come up for a House vote during the first session of the 106th Congress, pressure will build for it to come to a vote early in the second session.

H.R. 354 assumes many uses of databases should be unlawful and then lists a series of exceptions that create questions and uncertainty about what uses would incur criminal penalties under the bill. The legislation is far-reaching and overly broad; it would for the first time protect facts and would allow a producer or publisher unprecedented control over uses of information, including downstream, transformative use of facts and government-produced data contained in the database. The legislation would protect factual information and would provide for perpetual protection of a collection, at least for dynamic compilations in electronic form, despite the addition of language in the bill that seeks to remedy this problem.

H.R. 1858, the Consumer and Investor Access to Information Act of 1999, is more narrowly tailored than H.R. 354 and strikes a balance between the interests of selected database producers while ensuring that legitimate and appropriate access to factual information continues.

Funding

The Clinton administration's FY 2000 budget request included major increases for some education programs and a variety of new education initiatives. Congress resisted most of these initiatives during the regular appropriations process. However, November end-of-session negotiations among a few congressional leaders and administration officials produced an agreement that included increases in the administration's priorities. The final agreement allowed government agencies to choose which programs to cut by 0.38 percent. As a result, library program areas suffered alterations to their final total.

The Library Services and Technology Act (LSTA) was reduced from $166,885,000 to $165,809,000. Most LSTA funds go as grants to the states for technological innovation and outreach services in libraries; this portion of LSTA was set at $138,118,000, an increase of $3 million over FY 1999. Again this year, Congress put the largest increase in National Leadership Grants, which received $25 million, of which $12.3 million was earmarked for 20 specific projects, leaving an additional $10.6 million for competition. The Native American Library Service received 1.75 percent of the total as the law provides: $2.6 million.

For ESEA VI, the innovative education strategies block grant to the states that many school libraries depend upon for materials, the administration had requested zero funding in the budget. A letter was again circulated by Reps. Rod Blagojevich (D-Ill.) and Michael Castle (R-Del.), and the House Labor-HHS-Education Appropriations Subcommittee recommended an increase in ESEA VI funding to $385 million, but with only $97 million to pay out in FY 2000, the rest in 2001. The Senate Subcommittee shaved this down to $95 million for FY 2000 and $285 million in 2001. After the final agreement, the Department of Education cut ESEA Title VI the full 15 percent allowed, bringing the total for FY 2000 down to $80.7 million. The $285 million forward-funded to FY 2001 was not affected.

ESEA III—Educational technology also suffered cuts in the Technology Innovation Challenge Grants of $2.4 million, reducing the total for FY 2000 from $148.6 million to $146.255 million.

The Library of Congress received $384,353,000, a decrease from FY 1999; however, the Legislative Branch Appropriations bill (P.L. 106-57) passed in late September, at a time when Congress was considering cuts of up to 19 percent to try to stay within the budget caps. The Government Printing Office's Superintendent of Documents operation, which includes the Federal Depository Library Program, received $29.9 million, lower than GPO's request for FY 2000 of $31.2 million for the account.

The National Endowment for the Humanities (NEH) and the National Endowment for the Arts (NEA) received $115.3 million and $98 million, respectively—flat funding for NEA, but an increase of $5 million for NEH. The Interior Appropriations bill was included in the omnibus bill. The Institute of Museum and Library Services' Office of Museum Services was provided $24.4 million, the same as reported in the House legislation, but higher than the Senate's $23.9 million.

The Telecommunications and Information Infrastructure Assistance Program, administered by the National Telecommunications and Information Administration (NTIA) in the U.S. Department of Commerce, received $15.5 million, a decrease in funding from FY 1999. In announcing the availability of grant applications for FY 2000, NTIA announced a name change for the program to Technology Opportunities Program.

Elementary and Secondary Education Act Reauthorization

The reauthorization of the Elementary and Secondary Education Act (ESEA) process will continue in the next session of the 106th Congress. Thus far, only two bills have been passed by the House as part of the House Education and the Workforce Committee efforts to divide the large reauthorization bill into parts and pass the parts one at a time.

In the Senate, the Senate Health, Education, Labor and Pensions Committee staff members were working hard on a draft bill, but no final version was completed before the session ended.

In June Senators Jack Reed (D-R.I.) and Thad Cochran (R-Miss.) introduced S. 1262, the Elementary and Secondary School Library Media Resources, Training and Advanced Technology Act. The legislation would provide dedicated funds for purchase of school library materials and training for school library media specialists and would aid school libraries in sharing in statewide library networks. The bill would also provide for after-school and summer use of school library media centers.

H.R. 3008, a companion bill, was introduced by Rep. Major Owens (D-N.Y.) in the House. Both bills would amend the technology title in ESEA, Title III.

Discounted Telecommunications Rate (E-rate)

By the close of 1999 the Discounted Telecommunications Rate for Libraries and Schools (E-rate) enjoyed widespread support among many legislators, telecommunications industry leaders, parents, and the public. However, there were still those who introduced legislation that would eliminate or restructure the program, which provided $3.65 billion in discounts during its first two cycles to schools and libraries for basic telecommunications, Internet access, and internal wiring. All of these bills remained pending by the end of the first session of the 106th Congress.

On February 10, 1999, Rep. Tom Tancredo (R-Colo.) introduced H.R. 692, a bill to terminate the E-rate. Later in the spring he joined Sen. Conrad Burns (R-Mont.) and Rep. W. J. "Billy" Tauzin (R-La.) as they simultaneously introduced the Schools and Libraries Internet Access Act (S. 1004 and H.R. 1746), proposing to use a reduced Federal Excise Tax (FET) to fund a greatly diminished version of the E-rate.

The E-rate was one of the primary targets of the Taxpayers Defense Act (H.R. 2636), a bill introduced to require congressional approval of federal agency fees. The E-rate program would be "grandfathered," but the "Gore Tax" partisan rhetoric did not stop. In hearings on H.R. 2636 as well as other Federal Communications Commission oversight hearings, the E-rate was called an illegal tax. In August the U.S. Fifth Circuit Court of Appeals said that the limited connection between internal connections, Internet access, and telecommunications services "does not raise serious doubts as to whether the FCC's interpretation makes the assessment an improperly delegated tax."

Internet Filtering Requirements

At the end of 1999 several bills were left pending that sought to impose overly burdensome or unconstitutional Internet-filtering requirements on schools and public libraries by withholding E-rate discounts or federal program funding. One such bill focusing on the E-rate, the Children's Internet Protection Act (S. 97), sponsored by presidential candidate Sen. John McCain (R-Ariz.), drew the attention of Republicans who announced late in the year that it would be one of their top high-tech priorities for passage during the second session of 106th Congress.

Additionally, Rep. Bob Franks (R-N.J.) was successful in attaching one of his bills, which would require use of filtering or blocking software as a condition of receiving the E-rate, as an amendment to the House juvenile justice legislation (H.R. 1501). That bill was lodged in conference at the end of the session because

Table 1 / Funding for Federal Library and Related Programs, FY 2000
(figures in thousands)

	FY 1999 Appropriation	FY 2000 Appropriation
Library Programs		
GPO Superintendent of Documents	$29,264	$29,872
Library of Congress	391,660	384,353
Library Services and Technology Act	166,175	165,809
National Agricultural Library	19,000	19,900
National Commission on Libraries and Information Science	1,000	1,300
National Library of Medicine (includes MLAA)	181,309	214,068
Library-Related Programs		
Adult Education and Literacy	385,000	470,000
ESEA title I: Education for Disadvantaged	8,357,520	8,700,986
Part B, Even Start	135,000	150,000
ESEA title II: Eisenhower professional development		
Part A, Federal activities	23,300	23,300
Part B, State grants	335,000	335,000
ESEA title III: Educational Technology	698,100	765,805
Part A, Technology Literacy Challenge Fund	550,100	425,000
Part B, Star Schools	45,000	50,550
ESEA title VI: Innovative education program strategies (State grants)	375,000	365,700[1]
ESEA title X-I: 21st Century Community Learning Centers	200,000	453,377
Special Education (IDEA): (State grants)	5,124,146	5,754,685
Educational Research	82,567	84,782
Educational Statistics	68,000	68,000
Educational Assessment	40,000	36,000
Goal 2000	491,000	491,000
HEA title III: Institutional Development	239,750	258,500
HEA title IV-C: College Work-Study	870,000	934,000
HEA title VI: International Education	67,536	69,702
HEA title X-A: Postsecondary Education Improvement Fund	50,000	77,658
Inexpensive Book Distribution (RIF)	18,000	20,000
Reading Excellence Act	260,000	260,000[2]
IMLS Museum Grants	23,405	24,400
NTIA Information Infrastructure Grants, Technical Opportunity Program (TOP)	18,000	15,500
National Archives and Records Administration	224,614	222,621[3]
National Endowment for the Arts	98,000	97,628
National Endowment for the Humanities	110,700	115,260
National Historical Publications and Records Commission	10,000	4,250
Next Generation Internet	67,000	80,000[4]

1 $81 million FY 2000 and $285 million in advance appropriations FY 2001

2 $65 million FY 2000 and $195 million in advance appropriations FY 2001

3 Another $22 million was appropriated for the establishment of the Records Center Revolving Fund

4 Funding divided among several federal agencies

Compiled by: American Library Association, Washington Office of irreconcilable differences on gun control and other issues between the House and the Senate. Rep. Earnest Istook (R-Okla.) also attached a broader filtering mandate to the Labor-HHS-Education appropriations bill, but the measure was dropped in last-minute funding negotiations.

Online Child Safety Studies

With an extended deadline established in the omnibus appropriations bill, the Commission on Online Child Protection will be working in 2000 to examine strategies for dealing with children's online safety. The commission, created by the Children's Online Protection Act of 1998, was charged with identifying "technological or other methods that will help reduce access by minors to material that is harmful to minors on the Internet." It is also expected to make recommendations to Congress on legislation by November 30, 2000. James Schmidt, library science professor and former university librarian for San Jose State University, was appointed to the commission in October 1999.

Access to Government Information

When law enforcement officials warned of the potential terrorism risk posed by making public an Environmental Protection Agency (EPA) database, Rep. Tom Bliley (R-Va.) introduced the Chemical Safety Information and Site Security Act of 1999 (H.R. 1790). EPA previously planned that the entire database would be available online in June 1999. The bill would place limits on who could access the part of the database containing worst-case scenarios. Initially the legislation proposed putting depository library staff in a policing role to enforce these limits. That provision was dropped; however, community right-to-know issues are still at stake. The bill was considered by the House Commerce Committee, but it was also referred to several subcommittees under the House Judiciary and Government Reform Committees, which had not yet taken up the issue by the end of the session.

The U.S. Department of Commerce proposed closing the National Technical Information Service (NTIS) in August 1999. NTIS is the sole source of much government scientific and technical information. Closing the agency would require congressional action and funding, but no legislation was introduced in 1999. [See "National Technical Information Service" in Part 1—*Ed.*]

Legislation and Regulations Affecting Publishing in 1999

Allan Adler

Vice President, Legal and Governmental Affairs
Association of American Publishers

Digital Theft Deterrence and Copyright Damages Improvement Act

(H.R. 3456, enacted as Public Law 106-160, Dec. 9, 1999)

In what may prove for the foreseeable future to represent the high water mark of legislators' concern for copyright protection, Congress amended the Copyright Act to increase by 50 percent the amounts of statutory damages that may be awarded in civil cases for copyright infringement. At the same time, Congress sought to facilitate effective criminal prosecutions under the No Electronic Theft (NET) Act of 1997 by requiring expeditious development of related sentencing guidelines for federal judges.

After the tumultuous battle over the Digital Millennium Copyright Act of 1998, it was unlikely that Congress would quickly move to provide further muscle for enforcement of statutory copyright protections. However, the inadequacy of the statutory damages provisions in existing law was acknowledged in light of the fact that current levels of statutory awards had not been raised—even for inflation—since 1988, despite the advent of the Internet and digital technologies capable of greatly increasing the losses that copyright owners might suffer in individual cases of infringement. The increases made under the new legislation—raising the minimum damages from $500 to $750 and the maximum damages from $20,000 to $30,000, while raising damages for willful infringements from $100,000 to $150,000 but not changing current provisions regarding "innocent infringers" and specified nonprofit entities—are intended to deter infringers. A proposed new damages tier for repeat "pattern or practice" infringers appeared in earlier versions of the legislation, but was dropped due to a failure to agree on the addition of a "state-of-mind" requirement to distinguish between willful and merely negligent repeat infringers.

Similarly, although the NET Act (P.L. 105-147) was adopted to close a loophole in the Copyright Act that had precluded criminal prosecutions for willful copyright infringement in the absence of proof of financial gain, Congress grew concerned about the fact that no prosecutions had been brought under the NET Act's provisions in the two years since its enactment. Congressional hearings revealed that a significant part of the problem lay in the absence of related federal sentencing guidelines that had been mandated in the NET Act but had not been issued by the U.S. Sentencing Commission, which lacked a quorum of serving commissioners during the relevant period.

The new legislation requires the Sentencing Commission to act expeditiously (i.e., within 120 days of enactment or after the first date on which it has a voting quorum, whichever is later) to adopt emergency guideline amendments to implement the NET Act's directive that the applicable sentencing range for a defendant convicted of criminal infringement must be "sufficiently stringent to deter such a crime" and must reflect consideration of the retail value and quantity of the infringed items.

Anticybersquatting Consumer Protection Act

(Title III of S. 1948, enacted in Division B, Section 1000(a)(9) of Public Law 106-113 [H.R. 3194], Nov. 29, 1999)

Explosive growth in Internet traffic and its increasing importance to commerce have highlighted the need to ensure protection of trademark rights in connection with the registration and use of Internet domain names—the location identifier for a Web site. Accordingly, Congress enacted this legislation to extend traditional trademark violation remedies to "cybersquatting"—i.e., registering, trafficking in, or using a domain name that is identical or confusingly similar to, or (in the case of a famous mark) dilutive of, the mark of another, including a personal name that is protected as a distinctive or famous mark. In so doing, Congress also tried to balance the property interests of trademark owners with the interests of Internet denizens seeking to make lawful uses of others' marks under the same "fair use" and First Amendment protections that traditionally apply to trademark law. At the same time, Congress emphasized its intention to neither expand nor limit any "right of publicity" recognized under state law.

Through its major provisions, the new act does the following:

- It creates civil liability under the Trademark Act for any person who, with a "bad faith intent" to profit from another person's protected mark (including a personal name), registers, traffics in, or otherwise uses a domain name that is identical or confusingly similar to, or (in the case of a famous mark) dilutive of, the other person's protected mark. The act lists nine factors for a court to consider in determining whether the requisite "bad faith intent" exists, and provides that such intent shall not be found in any case where the registrant believed—and had reasonable grounds to believe—that the use of the domain name was a "fair use" or otherwise lawful.
- It permits the owner of a protected mark to bring an *in rem* civil action against an infringing domain name in the jurisdiction in which the registrar, registry, or other authority that registered or assigned the domain name is located, if the owner is unable to find or obtain personal jurisdiction over a person who would have been the defendant in the case.
- Apart from trademark infringement, the act also creates civil liability for the registrant of a domain name that consists of the name of another living person, or a name substantially and confusingly similar to such a name, without that person's consent and with the specific intent to profit from such name by selling the domain name for financial gain. However, the act exempts the registrant from liability if (1) the domain name is registered in "good faith," (2) the name of the other person is used in, affiliated with, or related to a copyrighted work, (3) the registrant is the copyright owner or licensee of the work, and intends to sell the domain name in conjunction with the lawful exploitation of the work, and (4) the registration

is not prohibited by a contract between the registrant and the named person.

- In actions involving trademark violations, the act empowers courts to award injunctive relief and monetary damages (including, at the election of the plaintiff, statutory damages instead of actual damages and profits), as well as costs and attorney's fees. In other actions involving domain names that consist of the name of another living person, courts are permitted to award injunctive relief (including forfeiture, cancellation, or transfer of the domain name), as well as costs and attorney's fees.

- In order to encourage domain name registrars and registries to work cooperatively with trademark owners to prevent cybersquatting, the act provides an exemption from liability for monetary damages for registrars and registries that suspend, cancel, or transfer domain names pursuant to a court order or in the implementation of a reasonable policy prohibiting cybersquatting. Such registrars and registries would remain subject to injunctive relief in certain circumstances.

- It requires the Commerce Department, in consultation with the Federal Election Commission, to report to Congress by June 2000 on abusive domain name registrations involving personal names, including those of government officials and candidates for government office. The department is also directed to collaborate with the Internet Corporation for Assigned Names and Numbers in developing dispute resolution guidelines and procedures for such cases.

Trademark Amendments Act of 1999
(S. 1259, enacted as Public Law 106-43, Aug. 5, 1999)

While Congress labored mightily over legislation to prevent "cybersquatters" from harming the interests of trademark owners through the registration of Internet domain names, it moved more quickly and easily to amend previously enacted legislation to help trademark owners prevent the dilution of their marks both online and offline.

Trademark "dilution"—a separate legal theory from the "confusing similarity" issue that is at the heart of trademark protection—is recognized under state law, and refers to the weakening of a mark's distinctiveness through use of a similar mark in connection with completely different products from those associated with the original mark. The Federal Trademark Dilution Act of 1995 established a civil cause of action regarding dilution for owners of famous trademarks. However, while the act authorized injunctive relief after dilution from use of a similar mark had occurred, it did nothing to help trademark owners prevent use of the offending mark in the first place, primarily because it provided no means to oppose the application for such a mark or to cancel its registration.

Under the new legislation, the Trademark Trial and Appeals Board can now consider dilution as grounds for opposing or cancelling registration, and trademark owners now have the right to oppose or seek cancellation of marks that would cause dilution to their existing famous marks when used. This should effectively help trademark owners to prevent dilution before it occurs. In addition, the new act makes damages, as well as injunctive relief, available to trademark owners in cases of "willful" violation of the statute, and also provides for the destruction of articles containing the diluting mark in such cases.

These amendments, which should prevent needless harm to the good will and distinctiveness of famous trademarks and make enforcement of the anti-dilution statute less costly and time-consuming for all involved, became effective on the date of enactment, but do not apply to any civil actions pending on that date.

The new legislation also enacted a waiver of sovereign immunity by the United States for violations of the statutory prohibitions against trademark infringement and dilution, thus permitting private citizens and corporations to bring suits against the United States in federal or state courts (as appropriate) for trademark violations.

Satellite Home Viewer Improvement Act

(Title I of S. 1948; enacted in Division B, Sec. 1000(a)(9) of Public Law 106-113 [H.R. 3194], Nov. 29, 1999)

The most politically popular "copyright" legislation enacted by Congress in 1999 does not directly affect book and journal publishing, but it does offer some sharp lessons regarding the risks inherent in the legislative process when the rights of copyright owners run up against widespread consumer demands and inter-industry competition that are both fueled by exciting technological developments that implicate the ability to control the use of copyrighted works.

At its core, the Satellite Home Viewer Improvement Act uses copyright regulation to promote marketplace competition so consumers can choose multichannel video programming providers other than their local cable television franchises to obtain a wide variety of viewing options at reasonable cost and with exceptional picture quality. In addition to reauthorizing the existing statutory compulsory license that permits satellite television services to retransmit "distant" broadcast signals from network television stations and so-called superstations, the act achieves its purpose primarily through establishment of a new compulsory license that for the first time authorizes satellite carriers to provide their subscribers with the signals of local broadcast television stations.

Although Congress had previously established similar statutory licenses for the cable TV industry, key participants in the legislative process acknowledged that any compulsory license represents an extraordinary departure from basic principles of copyright that generally entitle those who create works of authorship to enjoy certain exclusive rights in them and to bargain freely in the marketplace with others who want to exercise those rights. Consequently, even as the legislation advanced, supporters cautioned that compulsory licenses should be utilized only when necessary, crafted to the most limited possible degree, and construed as narrowly as possible.

Nevertheless, with consumer groups and advocates for the cable, satellite, broadcast, and motion picture industries all vigorously lobbying for their respective interests, discordant notes accompanied final enactment of the legislation and demonstrated how difficult it can be to achieve fairness to all parties in attempting to craft a compulsory license according to such precepts.

For one thing, it was bitterly noted by advocates of the copyright-owning programming communities that, in a reversal of the "marketplace" approach Congress had adopted in reauthorizing the original Satellite Home Viewers Act (SHVA) in 1994, Congress this time put its thumb on the scale and mandated substantial discounts in the royalty fees to be paid by satellite services for distant signals obtained under the compulsory license—despite the fact that the rates it was discounting had only recently been set at "fair market value" by the statutorily created Copyright Arbitration Royalty Panel and upheld by a federal appellate court. This turnabout, while perhaps understandable in the context of Congress's determination to make satellite services competitive with cable franchises, will do little to counter the copyright community's general wariness regarding compulsory licenses.

But a far greater controversy, which will almost certainly bear additional fruit in the next Congress (if not in the upcoming Second Session of the 106th Congress), grew out of the efforts of certain parties to ensure that another potential group of competitive multichannel video programming distributors—Internet service providers—would not be able to avail themselves of the compulsory licenses for retransmission of television broadcast programming that Congress had granted to the satellite and cable television industries.

Although no federal agency or court had ever suggested that these compulsory licenses authorize such retransmission via the Internet or other online services (and the Copyright Office, in an exhaustive 1997 study, had explicitly rejected such an interpretation of the statutory licenses), the little-noticed inclusion of a provision to exclude "digital on-line communications services" from the statutory definition of "satellite carrier" precipitated an 11th-hour battle royal over the legislation as the statutory reauthorization deadline for SHVA—and a planned congressional adjournment—loomed. While supporters of the provision argued that it did nothing more than express the state of current law (which would remain unchanged even without the provision), the Internet community denounced it as an effort to permanently exclude online service providers from eligibility for the license and, consequently, an opportunity to compete in the video programming distribution market.

The lateness of the legislative hour, along with the fact that the issue had not been the subject of hearings or any other substantial consideration by legislators, ultimately led to removal of the controversial provision before final passage of the act. But the issue, once raised, is certain to be rejoined soon.

National Intellectual Property Law Enforcement Coordination Council

(Section 653 of H.R. 2490, enacted as Public Law 106-58, Sept. 29, 1999)

The interest of a single member of Congress can sometimes make all the difference as to whether a specific issue is addressed in legislation and survives the process to enactment. This was clearly the case with a provision in the appropriations legislation for the Treasury Department, the Postal Service, the Executive

Office of the President, and certain other independent government agencies, which established a new interagency working group called the National Intellectual Property Law Enforcement Coordination Council.

The concept for the council grew out of a provision in the Senate version of the legislation, which would have authorized the president to establish and fund an interagency National Intellectual Property Coordination Center within the Executive Office of the President. The provision was added to the legislation by Senator Ted Stevens (R-Alaska), chairman of the Senate Appropriations Committee, in recognition of "the dramatic impact crimes involving the infringement of intellectual property rights have upon the U.S. economy," and the committee's belief that "coordination among local, state and foreign law enforcement entities is essential" to combat this burgeoning criminal enterprise.

Prior to enactment, however, the concept was revised to statutorily establish a free-standing interagency council "to coordinate domestic and international intellectual property law enforcement among federal and foreign entities." The council, which will be composed of the agency officials specified in the statute, is required to report annually to the president and to the Appropriations and Judiciary Committees in the House and Senate on its coordination activities. Although only executive branch officials will actually serve on the council, the legislation requires the council to consult with the Register of Copyrights on copyright law enforcement matters, and preserves the respective authorities of the Secretary of State, the U.S. Trade Representative, and the Register under relevant law.

Animal Cruelty Depiction Punishment Act

(H.R. 1887, enacted as Public Law 106-152, Dec. 9, 1999)

Efforts to outlaw even the most repugnant kinds of speech-related activities tend to have serious First Amendment implications, and Congress found this to be true as it passed legislation to ban the commercial distribution of "crush" videos— films that typically depict women in high-heeled shoes slowly and sadistically crushing hamsters or other small animals, apparently to satisfy a sexual fetish of the film's viewers.

Although all 50 states have animal cruelty laws that permit state prosecution of persons who perpetrate the acts depicted in "crush" videos, such prosecutions are difficult in light of the inability to identify the women involved (only their legs are shown), statute-of-limitations uncertainties, and the fact that such laws generally do not prohibit the production, sale, or possession of such videos. Provided with evidence that more than 3,000 such videos are sold in interstate and international commerce for as much as $100 a copy, Congress determined to eliminate the financial incentive for making them by prohibiting the creation, sale, or possession of a depiction of animal cruelty with the intention of placing the depiction in interstate or foreign commerce.

Not surprisingly, some members of Congress, despite their personal revulsion at the conduct depicted and exploited in this manner, raised First Amendment concerns relating to the potential application of such legislation, which, after all, did not prohibit the actual physical cruelty to the animals but only the creation and communication of depictions of such conduct. For example, with "depiction of animal cruelty" defined as "any visual or auditory depiction . . . in which a living animal is intentionally maimed, mutilated, tortured, wounded or killed," some legislators worried that the legislation could criminalize films of bullfighting in Spain, jockeys whipping their horses in the Kentucky Derby, or a variety of hunting, fishing, and other legal activities in which animals are routinely injured or killed by deliberate human conduct. They raised the possibility that it could criminalize depictions of animal cruelty in news accounts or educational documentaries intended to inform the public about such activities. They also argued that the legislation violated Supreme Court precedents that struck down statutory prohibitions on religious practices involving the killing of animals, as well as "Son-of-Sam" laws that barred criminals from obtaining payment for creative accounts of their criminal activities.

In response to these concerns, the legislation was amended to include an exception for otherwise covered depictions that have serious religious, political, scientific, educational, journalistic, historic, or artistic value. Moreover, the legislation does not criminalize mere possession of such a depiction but only possession with intent to place the depiction in interstate or foreign commerce for commercial gain.

For those who argued against the legislation based on "federalism" concerns, the legislation was narrowed to apply only where the conduct depicted is illegal under federal law or the law of the state in which the creation, sale, or possession of the depiction takes place. Sponsors also emphasized that the legislation does not create a new federal offense of animal cruelty, which is a matter for state law, but only addresses conduct that state law does not reach—namely, the interstate and international sale of depictions of animal cruelty.

Ironically, faced with difficult issues regarding whether animal rights protection could outweigh constitutional precepts of federalism and freedom of expression, legislators emphasized the documented links between animal cruelty and domestic violence, child abuse, and other forms of violent behavior. By invoking prior histories of animal abuse that were evidently shared by such infamous killers as Ted Bundy, Jeffrey Dahmer, David Berkowitz, and Ted Kaczynski, sponsors of the legislation spun a provocative argument that criminal pursuit of the "crush" video purveyors would deter the underlying conduct of animal cruelty and, perhaps, its subsequent evolution into more deadly violence.

Deceptive Mail Prevention and Enforcement Act
(Title I of S. 335, enacted as Public Law 106-168, Dec. 9, 1999)

After extensive House and Senate hearings, Congress determined to enact legislation in response to evidence demonstrating that a number of companies and organizations have been using a variety of deceptive mailings—including sweepstakes, skill contests, facsimile checks, and mailings made to look like government documents—to entice senior citizens and other consumers into making unwanted purchases under the false impression that this would enhance their chances of winning a prize or help them to avoid losing certain government benefits.

The resulting new legislation does the following:

- It prohibits such mailings from misleading use of any terms, symbols, or references "which reasonably could be interpreted or construed as implying any Federal Government connection, approval or endorsement. . . ."
- It requires that all sweepstakes entry mailings must disclose, "clearly and conspicuously," all terms and conditions of the promotion, including rules and entry procedures; odds of winning; the nature, value, and quantity of each offered prize; schedules of payment; and the name and contact information for the sponsor or mailer. Similarly, relevant disclosure requirements are mandated for all "skill contest" entry mailings.
- It also requires that all sweepstakes entry mailings must include, even "more conspicuously" than the other specified matters for disclosure, statements in the mailing, in the rules, and on the order or entry form, that (1) no purchase is necessary to enter, and (2) a purchase will not improve an individual's chances of winning. In addition, it prohibits them from representing that an individual is a winner of a prize unless that individual has actually won the prize, or that non-purchasing individuals may be disqualified from receiving future sweepstakes mailings.
- It requires promoters of sweepstakes or skill contest mailings to establish and maintain a "notification system" that allows individuals to elect to have their names and addresses excluded from all lists used for such mailings; in addition, such promoters must in each such mailing provide a statement that clearly and conspicuously notifies individuals about the system and how they may use it to prohibit other such mailings. Mailings in violation of "opt-out" elections are subject to private suits in state court and federal penalties.
- It provides the Postal Service with additional authority to investigate and stop noncompliant mailings, which (depending on the number of pieces in each mailing) may be subject to civil penalties of up to $2 million. The new act also preserves the ability of states to impose and enforce more strict requirements on such mailings than those imposed by the act itself.

Y2K Act
(H.R. 775, enacted as Public Law 106-37, July 20, 1999)

At the end of the 105th Congress, little more than a year away from the anticipated final deadline for the much-discussed "Year 2000 problem" (i.e., whether the internal clocks in millions of computer systems, software programs and semiconductors would turn from year "99" to year "00" and properly read the latter as representing the year 2000 rather than the year 1900), Congress decided that businesses and other organizations needed to communicate more openly with the public and each other regarding "Y2K" testing processes, proposed remedial solutions, and product readiness efforts. Because fear of litigation arising from such disclosures was having a chilling effect on open communications, Congress enacted the Y2K Information and Readiness Disclosure Act to help mitigate this fear through preemption of state and local liability laws regarding the requisite standard of care for the making of such disclosures.

Last year, as the countdown to the Y2K deadline continued, Congress took on the anticipated explosion of Y2K litigation directly by enacting a liability limitation law that establishes uniform legal standards and procedures for civil litigation arising from actual or potential Y2K failures. In order to encourage non-adversarial remediation of Y2K problems, limit frivolous litigation, and promote the use of alternative dispute resolution processes, Congress made litigation a less attractive route for aggrieved parties by imposing significant restrictions on Y2K civil actions.

The main features of the new legislation can be summarized as follows:

- The act preempts inconsistent state law and applies to any civil action in federal or state court concerning an actual or potential failure of any device or system to perform certain functions concerning year 2000-related data, provided that such action (including any related proceeding) was brought after January 1, 1999, for an actual or potential Y2K failure occurring or allegedly causing harm before January 1, 2003. The act, however, does not apply to personal injury or wrongful death claims, or to securities litigation.

- The act establishes specific pleading requirements; imposes principles of proportionate liability for damages in non-contract actions; places caps on punitive damages where injuries are non-intentional; creates a "duty to mitigate" damages for plaintiffs, except in cases of fraud; permits recovery of lost profits or sales for tort claims; limits class actions relating to defective products or services; and generally permits strict enforcement of written contractual terms (including warranties).

- The act provides special protections for small businesses against the imposition of civil fines for first-time violations of federal rules or regulations (other than those relating to banking or securities) caused by Y2K failures. It also establishes a "Y2K upset" defense that provides a grace period before the government can impose penalties for temporary non-compliance with federally enforceable measurement, monitoring, or reporting requirements caused by Y2K failures. Both of these provisions expire before the end of 2000.

Education Flexibility Partnership Act of 1999

(H.R. 800, enacted as Public Law 106-25, April 29, 1999)

The extent to which state and local educational authorities must comply with federal education policies in order to qualify for federal funding for K–12 education programs is a particularly sore point of disagreement between the Democrats and Republicans in Congress. Nevertheless, after an often bitter debate about the degree of flexibility that should be afforded to the recipients of such funding in determining how it may best be used, Congress managed to enact compromise legislation by building on a 12-state pilot program that gives states limited authority to approve waivers of federal regulations at the local educational agency level.

Basically, the "Ed-Flex" Act establishes a program through which the secretary of education may authorize a state educational agency to waive certain statutory or regulatory requirements applicable to specified programs carried out under the Elementary and Secondary Education Act (ESEA). The act, however, lists certain statutory or regulatory requirements that cannot be waived under its authority, including requirements regarding the distribution of funds to states or to local educational agencies and the use of federal funds to supplement, not supplant, nonfederal funds.

In order to qualify for such waivers, the local agencies must show that they have or are developing an education plan to aid disadvantaged children under Title I of ESEA.

Department of Education Appropriations Act

(Title III of H.R. 3424, enacted in Division B, Section 1000(a)(4) of Public Law 106-113 [H.R. 3194], Nov. 29, 1999)

Once again, the Labor-Health and Human Services-Education appropriations bill was the subject of bitter partisan feuding between Congress and the White House. And once again, the legislation—which was vetoed in its initial version as a stand-alone bill—became law only after enactment as part of an end-of-the-year omnibus appropriations package.

In the end, the legislation embodied a curious deal in which total education funding for the Department of Education would increase by nearly 6.6 percent, or $2.2 billion, to bring the total to $35.7 billion, subject to a subsequent across-the-board cut of 0.38 percent, or nearly $112 million, but without cutting any single program by more than 15 percent.

As in the previous year, school technology projects received special generosity from Congress. Among the line items of possible interest to publishers, as significantly affecting literacy, multimedia curricula, distance education programs, and purchases of instructional materials are the following:

- $7.9 billion for Title I programs under the Elementary and Secondary Education Act (ESEA), including $6.8 billion in basic grants, representing a $209 million increase over the 1999 budget
- $859.4 million for federally connected children under the Impact Aid program, representing more than a $25 million increase over 1999
- $470 million for adult education programs that focus on basic literacy and language skills under the Adult Education and Family Literacy Act, representing an $85 million increase, and including $6 million for the National Institute for Literacy
- $425 million for the Technology Literacy Challenge Fund, which is used to help integrate software and online learning resources (including Internet access and multimedia computers) into classroom curricula
- $260 million to carry out reading and literacy training grants under the Reading Excellence Act

- $166.8 million for libraries, but without $5 million sought by the president for National Leadership Grants for the National Digital Library initiative
- $156.2 million for Technology Innovation Challenge Grants, which support the development of curriculum uses of technology, including the development of quality course content
- $150 million for Even Start child literacy programs
- $75 million for the Teacher Training in Technology Program, which provides grants for focused training of incoming teachers on how to use new technologies to enhance student learning
- $51 million for the Star Schools program, reflecting a $6 million increase in annual funding for demonstration projects that use telecommunications technology to provide instructional programs for students (and professional development activities for teachers) who would not otherwise have access to them
- $23.9 million for the new "Learning Anytime Anywhere Partnership," which more than doubled last year's funding for the largest of a number of initiatives specifically intended to promote distance education programs using interactive digital networks; separate funding of $2.4 million was appropriated for the Western Governors University distance learning initiative

Tax Relief Extension Act of 1999

(Title V of H.R. 1180, enacted as Public Law 106-170, Dec. 17, 1999)

Tax relief was a high-visibility item in the first session of the 106th Congress, with Republican leaders in the House and Senate pushing through a $792 billion "wish list" bill of across-the-brackets personal income tax cuts, a phase-out of the marriage tax penalty, and capital gains tax reductions—only to acquiesce in President Clinton's expected veto of the legislation without even attempting an override vote in either body.

In the end, the only tax legislation able to gain bipartisan congressional support and the president's signature was a relatively modest bill that extended some of the more popular tax breaks that expire annually without explicit reauthorization. This legislation, which was enacted as part of separate legislation intended to allow individuals with disabilities to keep their health insurance benefits while working, was calculated as having a $21 billion cost over a 10-year period that was offset with $2.9 billion in tax code revisions.

The main item of interest for Association of American Publishers (AAP) members in the "extenders" legislation extended the research and development tax credit for five years (from July 1, 1999 through June 30, 2004). This credit applies to research undertaken for the purpose of discovering new information that is technological in nature and new to the taxpayer, not freely available to the general public, and intended to be applied in the development of a new or improved business component of the taxpayer. No startling discoveries are required to qualify for the tax credit; in general, a business that employs existing technologies in a particular field or relies on existing principles of engineering or science is considered to be engaging in "qualified research" for purposes of claiming the tax credit.

Eligible expenses for applying the R&D tax credit consist of (1) in-house expenses of the taxpayer for wages and supplies attributable to qualified research; (2) certain time-sharing costs for computer use in qualified research; and (3) 65 percent of any amounts paid by the taxpayer for qualified research conducted on the taxpayer's behalf ("contract research expenses").

Non-Enacted Legislation Relevant to AAP Policy Priorities

Database Protection Legislation

After failing to win enactment in the 105th Congress, despite passing the House twice, database protection legislation was the subject of significant House committee action in 1999, with rival bills being approved by the House Judiciary and Commerce Committees.

The House Judiciary Committee, which had originated the "misappropriation" approach to database protection in the previous Congress, approved H.R. 354, the proposed Collections of Information Antipiracy Act, in May 1999. Although similar to the earlier House-passed legislation, H.R. 354 was reported with substantial changes designed to mollify the Clinton administration, as well as opponents in the library, education, and scientific communities, who share concerns that "misappropriation" legislation might give database producers too much proprietary control over non-copyrightable factual information. AAP, which favors balancing effective database protection with a liberal "fair use"-like exception, supports H.R. 354 as approved by the committee.

But, in the same spirit of jurisdictional rivalry that complicated enactment of the Digital Millennium Copyright Act in 1998, the House Commerce Committee then approved its own version of database protection legislation in August. H.R. 1858, the proposed Consumer and Investor Access to Information Act, was carefully crafted to the committee's jurisdictional needs and takes a much narrower, less effective and—from AAP's perspective—more problematic approach to database protection than H.R. 354 by limiting its prohibition to selling or distributing a "duplicate" of another person's database. Although the bill has "Permitted Acts" and "Exclusions" provisions similar to those in H.R. 354, it also contains a "Misuse" exception that could undermine enforcement of contracts or the use of technological protection measures by database producers. Moreover, the bill lacks both a civil cause of action and criminal penalties, leaving redress of violations exclusively to the enforcement discretion of the Federal Trade Commission under that agency's statutory authority regarding unfair or deceptive acts or practices.

Other issues, such as whether the legislation should include online service provider liability limitations like those in the Digital Millennium Copyright Act, may further complicate efforts to combine the two bills for consideration by the House. Since the Senate, while awaiting House action, has neither had hearings nor a bill introduced on the subject, the prospects for enactment of database protection legislation in the election-year session remain difficult and uncertain.

Juvenile Crime Legislation

In the wake of the tragic shootings at Columbine High School, the nation's capital erupted in one of its periodic politically charged screaming matches over the appropriate limits of gun control and the causes of juvenile violence. Not surprisingly, Democrats disputed with Republicans, the House disagreed with the Senate, and the White House could not find common ground with Congress, so no legislation was enacted.

But bills were passed in the House and Senate, and they remained on the legislative calendar pending further action in 2000. Based on 1999's action, they warrant continued AAP attention to First Amendment interests.

When the House version (H.R. 1501) of so-called juvenile crime legislation came to the floor in June 1999, the chairman of the House Judiciary Committee offered an extraordinary amendment to address the causes of juvenile violence under the heading "protecting children from the culture of violence." Based on a long-disputed "life imitates art" theory of causation, the amendment would have made it a federal crime to knowingly sell, exhibit, send, or lend to a child under the age of 17 any "picture, photograph, drawing, sculpture, video game, motion picture film, or similar visual representation or image, book, pamphlet, magazine, printed matter, or sound recording, or other matter of any kind containing explicit sexual material or explicit violent material" as the latter terms were defined in related provisions.

Targeting the motion picture and recording industries for proposed regulation of their content is a frequent hue and cry in national political circles, and a fairly predictable one when politicians grope for cultural explanations to social tragedies. But the explicit inclusion of "books" and other "printed matter" in this effort was something of a wake-up call to the "print" community, which had not found itself the target of proposed statutory censorship by Congress in quite some time. Moreover, it was a reminder that, while the First Amendment can be invoked to save books from the application of legislation that unconstitutionally restricts freedom of expression, it is in the interest of publishers (as well as of authors and their readers) to try to ensure that such legislation is not enacted in the first place.

Fortunately, with swift action from AAP and others, the amendment was decisively defeated after an impassioned floor debate. However, as Congress enters an election year with the "juvenile crime" legislation and the issues that haunted its consideration last year still unresolved, book publishers must not allow the First Amendment and their faith in the common sense or accountability of elected officials to make them complacent about the legislative process.

Reauthorization of the Elementary and Secondary Education Act (ESEA)

In 1999 the Senate took a back seat while the House worked in piecemeal fashion on ESEA reauthorization and passed three separate bills that embodied competing proposals of the Republican leadership and the Clinton administration to revise and extend key elements of the landmark 1965 Act, which was last revised by Congress in 1994.

H.R. 1995, the proposed Teacher Empowerment Act, was passed by the House in July. It would revise and reauthorize ESEA Title II regarding "teacher quality," combining a five-year reauthorization that melds separate teacher training programs into annual block grants to local educational authorities, with the president's plan to hire 100,000 new teachers over a seven-year period and reduce average class size to 18 students in grades 1–3. In addition, the bill would reauthorize the Reading Excellence Act for five years; prohibit the use of federal funds to plan, develop, implement, or administer any national teacher test or certification; and clarify that, while nothing in Title II bars any private, religious, or home school from participating in Title II programs, nothing in Title II authorizes federal control over any aspect of any private, religious, or home schooling.

H.R. 2300, the proposed Academic Achievement for All (Straight A's) Act, was passed by the House in July, and represents a scaled-back compromise of a major plan by Republican legislators to permit states to convert ESEA Title I and a variety of other federal education programs into block grants. After much debate over whether this would dilute the effectiveness of federal aid, the House adopted a more modest pilot program that would allow ten states some flexibility in combining and using funding from specified federal programs during a five-year period in exchange for meeting strict accountability standards in the form of performance goals.

H.R. 2, a multi-titled bill that was passed by the House on the same day as H.R. 2300, would provide the third leg to the House reauthorization of ESEA. The proposed Student Results Act, which would provide a five-year reauthorization for ESEA's main Title I programs (including those that fund purchases of instructional materials for disadvantaged children), would comprehensively revise many of them to impose stricter academic standards for participating students and to require participating schools to issue report cards on their students' performance. Among other things, H.R. 2 would also reauthorize programs to eliminate gender-based discrimination in schools, provide bilingual education based on parental consent, and permit states greater flexibility in the use of federal funds for English-only instruction.

ESEA reauthorization will be a top priority for Congress in 2000, but a difficult task in light of election-year pressures, the fragmented House approach, and the Senate's late start.

Electronic Signature/Records Validation Legislation

Shortly before adjournment in November 1999, the House and Senate each passed legislation to ensure the legal standing of electronic transactions consummated with electronic signatures, but ultimately produced different versions that must be reconciled in 2000 if enactment is to occur during the 106th Congress.

With more than 40 states already having some form of law dealing with the validity of electronic signatures, the differences and conflicts among these laws are a source of uncertainty for parties engaging in online transactions, which could create serious impediments to the growth of electronic commerce. Although substantial uniformity among the states is expected to develop as state legislatures amend their laws or enact new ones based on the recently adopted Uniform Electronic Transactions Act (UETA), proponents of electronic commerce remain concerned about the validity of online transactions that take place before the states have acted on UETA.

Thus, rather than enacting permanent federal legislation, the House and Senate both focused on the need for interim federal legislation that could provide uniform standards for recognizing the validity of electronic signatures until UETA (or a substantially similar variation of it) has been incorporated into the laws of the individual states. Agreement on this basic objective, however, did not prevent the proposed legislation from generating heated controversies in both bodies, and from taking divergent paths when passed by the House and Senate.

As passed by the House, H.R. 1714, the proposed Electronic Signatures in Global and National Commerce Act, remained a matter of contention between supporters and critics on issues such as the bill's scope (i.e., validating the use of electronic records, as well as electronic signatures), its treatment of consumer choice (i.e., regarding whether to receive certain materials in electronic or paper form), and its preemption of state laws and regulations that protect consumers in certain types of transactions through requirements that consumers must receive written copies of mandated notices, disclosures, or warranties.

In contrast, S. 761, the proposed Millennium Digital Commerce Act, as passed by the Senate, resembles a proposed substitute for H.R. 1714, which had a more narrow scope and would have provided greater flexibility on matters of consumer choice and federal preemption but was soundly defeated on the House floor.

Some version of this legislation, which could prove quite beneficial to AAP members who are engaging in online transactions, is likely to be enacted by Congress in 2000.

Encryption Legislation

Encryption—i.e., the use of complex numerical sequences to "scramble" electronic transmissions in order to preserve the confidentiality, integrity, or authenticity of communications—is a key tool for guaranteeing the privacy, security, and intellectual property protection necessary for the Internet to grow as a thriving medium for commerce, education, and entertainment. However, the federal government's fear that availability of unbreakable encryption will assist terrorist or other criminal enterprises has caused it to place export restrictions on the most advanced and secure forms of encryption, despite objections from U.S. industry that such restrictions hamper its ability to compete in a global marketplace where strong encryption remains available to and from foreign competitors.

Although five House committees (H.R. 850) and the Senate Commerce Committee (S. 798) approved different measures addressing export controls and restrictions on the domestic use, sale, or import of encryption technologies (including the use of mandatory key escrow systems), no consensus developed for floor consideration in either legislative body.

But, in an effort to broker a compromise acceptable to both sides in the debate, the Clinton administration announced the issuance of new regulations that eliminate restrictions based on "key length" and license requirements in favor of export subject to a "one-time review" by the government. Under the new regulations, retail products can be exported to any user, including foreign governments, unless the government deems the user to be a supporter of terrorism. So far, positive reactions from industry indicate that the new regulations may make encryption legislation a moot issue; however, only time will tell.

AAP did not take a public position or actively lobby on any of the versions of legislation that were pending before Congress in 1999. However, in light of the importance of encryption for online copyright protection and electronic commerce, AAP will continue to monitor the progress of the effort to resolve the debate.

Postal Reform Legislation

Time ran out on efforts to enact comprehensive postal reform legislation in the 105th Congress, after the proposed Postal Reform Act (H.R. 22) advanced through the House Subcommittee on the Postal Service, but made no further progress toward enactment. Reintroduced in 1999 with the same bill number, the proposed postal reform legislation appears unlikely to meet with a kinder fate in the 106th Congress.

In written submissions to the subcommittee, AAP has generally been supportive of the legislation. Its comments have focused on proposed changes to the rate-making process, praising those that would provide for negotiated rate agreements, market tests for experimental new products, the institution of price caps, and a five-year cycle for rate adjustments. However, AAP has expressed concerns about proposals to downgrade the significance of "content" as a rate-making criterion; distinguish between competitive and noncompetitive product categories; and provide an "exigent circumstances" exception to the five-year rate-making cycle for noncompetitive products.

With a newly filed postal rate case pending before the Postal Rate Commission, it is doubtful that Congress will seriously consider changing the statutory rules in the middle of the rate-setting game. Although AAP will continue to monitor the legislative arena for signs of life in the legislation, it will focus its efforts and resources for postal issues on the rate case, where the largest rate increase proposed by the U.S. Postal Service for any single subclass has targeted Bound Printed Matter—a category predominantly used for the delivery of books—and a substantial increase and restructuring has been proposed for Periodicals (a category that includes journals).

Funding Programs and Grant-Making Agencies

National Endowment for the Humanities

1100 Pennsylvania Ave. N.W., Washington, DC 20506
202-606-8400, 800-634-1121
E-mail info@neh.fed.us
World Wide Web http://www.neh.fed.us

Thomas C. Phelps

> Democracy demands wisdom and vision in its citizens.
> —National Foundation on the Arts and Humanities Act of 1965

The Humanities

The humanities are the many voices that shape our lives. They are the voices of our parents and grandparents heard over dinner. They are also the historic voices from the fields of literature, history, and philosophy, voices of Plato and Shakespeare, of Abraham Lincoln and Martin Luther King, of Mark Twain and Frederick Douglass.

A strong nation requires an educated citizenry, a people who understand their roots and who can envision their future. For more than three decades the National Endowment for the Humanities (NEH) has protected both the United States' past and its future. Each of the NEH core programs has given critical support to the nation's educational and cultural life. The Research and Education Divisions support summer seminars and research for teachers that enrich the classroom experience for hundreds of thousands of students each year. Public Programs supports high quality television and radio programs and museum exhibits; the Challenge Grants Division helps build endowment for educational programs; Preservation and Access has saved hundreds of thousands of brittle books and newspapers; and state councils help enrich grass roots humanities programs throughout the nation.

The National Endowment for the Humanities

An act to provide for the establishment of the National Foundation on the Arts and the Humanities to promote progress and scholarship in the humanities and the arts in the United States was adopted by Congress in 1965. The act declared the findings and purposes of the endowments as follows:

The arts and the humanities belong to all the people of the United States.

The encouragement and support of national progress and scholarship in the humanities and the arts, while primarily a matter for private and local initiative, are also appropriate matters of concern to the Federal Government.

An advanced civilization must not limit its efforts to science and technology alone, but must give full value and support to the other great branches of scholarly and cultural activity in order to achieve a better understanding of the past, a better analysis of the present, and a better view of the future.

Democracy demands wisdom and vision in its citizens. It must therefore foster and support a form of education, and access to the arts and the humanities, designed to make people of all backgrounds and wherever located masters of their technology and not its unthinking servants.

It is necessary and appropriate for the Federal Government to complement, assist, and add to programs for the advancement of the humanities and the arts by local, State, regional, and private agencies and their organizations. In doing so, the Government must be sensitive to the nature of public sponsorship. Public funding of the arts and humanities is subject to the conditions that traditionally govern the use of public money. Such funding should contribute to public support and confidence in the use of taxpayer funds. Public funds provided by the Federal Government must ultimately serve public purposes the Congress defines.

The arts and the humanities reflect the high place accorded by the American people to the nation's rich cultural heritage and to the fostering of mutual respect for the diverse beliefs and values of all persons and groups.

About NEH

Over the past 34 years, the endowment has reached millions of Americans with projects and programs that preserve and study America's cultural heritage while providing a foundation for the future.

National Public Library Initiative

NEH, the Carnegie Corporation of New York, the Library of America (LOA), and the American Library Association aim to build American literature collections and enhance public discussion programs in the nation's public libraries through the Millennium Project for Public Libraries. Millions of Americans will soon have access to writings by many of the country's greatest authors through a national library initiative called "A Core Collection for America's Libraries— The Millennium Project for Public Libraries." More than 800 libraries will receive the 50 most recently published volumes of LOA's Distinguished American Literature series. (The Library of America is a nonprofit publisher of classic American literature.) NEH has been awarded a $1 million grant by the Carnegie Corporation to help public libraries add high-quality literary editions to their collections and expand opportunities for educational programs within their communities. The libraries that receive the 50 most recent LOA editions will be selected in an open competition administered by NEH.

Interpretive Exhibitions

Interpretive exhibitions provide opportunities for lifelong learning in the humanities for millions of Americans. Since 1967 NEH has made more than 2,300 grants totaling $181 million for interpretive exhibitions, catalogs, and public programs, which are among the most highly visible activities supported by the endowment.

Forty-nine states and the District of Columbia will host more than 130 exhibitions over the next two years. They range from the Huntington Library's exhibition about George Washington to an exhibition about King Arthur that will travel to more than 60 libraries throughout the country.

Renewing Teaching

Over the years more than 20,000 high school teachers and nearly 30,000 college teachers have deepened their knowledge of the humanities through intensive summer study supported by NEH. It is estimated that more than 140,000 students benefit from these programs in the first year alone.

Reading and Discussion Programs

Since 1982 the endowment has supported reading and discussion programs in the nation's libraries, bringing people together to discuss works of literature and history. Groups are facilitated by scholars in the humanities who provide thematic direction for the discussion programs. Using well-selected texts and such themes as Work, Family, Diversity, and Not for Children Only, these programs have attracted more than a million Americans.

Preserving the Nation's Heritage

The United States Newspaper Program is rescuing countless pieces of history by cataloging and microfilming 57 million pages from 133,000 newspapers dating from the early days of the Republic. Another microfilming program has rescued the content of more than 860,000 brittle books.

Stimulating Private Support

More than $1.23 billion in humanities support has been generated by NEH's Challenge Grants program, which requires most recipients to raise $3 or $4 in nonfederal funds for every dollar they receive.

Presidential Papers

Ten presidential papers projects are underwritten by NEH. Two of them, the Washington and Eisenhower papers projects, have each leveraged more than $1.4 million in nonfederal contributions.

Interactive History

Materials for learning are being put on CD-ROM and interactive video, including a digitized version of the Dead Sea Scrolls. Multimedia projects let students trace the first Spanish settlers of California, compare text and film versions of Shakespeare's plays, and hear Supreme Court oral arguments.

New Scholarship

Endowment grants enable scholars to do in-depth study: Jack Rakove explored the making of the Constitution in his *Original Meanings*, while James McPherson chronicled the Civil War in his *Battle Cry of Freedom*. Both won Pulitzer prizes.

History on Screen

Thirty-eight million Americans saw the Ken Burns documentary *The Civil War* and 750,000 people bought the book. Through such other films as *Liberty!*, *The West*, and *Africans in America* and film biographies of such figures as Gen. Douglas MacArthur, Americans learn about the events and people that shaped the nation.

Library of America

Two million books have been sold as part of the Library of America series, a collection of the riches of American literature. Begun with NEH seed money, the 108 published volumes include the writings of such authors as Henry Adams, Edith Wharton, William James, Eudora Welty, and W. E. B. DuBois, as well as 19th- and 20th-century American poets.

Science and the Humanities

The scientific past is being preserved with NEH-supported editions of *The Letters of Charles Darwin*, *The Works of Albert Einstein*, and the 14-volume papers of Thomas A. Edison.

The Sound of Poetry

One million Americans use cassettes from the NEH-supported Voices and Visions series on poets. As a telecourse, Voices reached more than 200 colleges, 2,000 high schools, and 500 public libraries.

Learning Under the Tent

From California to Florida, a 20th-century version of Chautauqua attracts crowds to see scholars portraying such significant figures as Eleanor Roosevelt, Thomas Jefferson, and Mark Twain in the kind of "village university" envisioned by Henry David Thoreau.

Technology and the Classroom

NEH's Web site assembles the best humanities resources on the Web. For example, online lesson plans help teachers use more than 50 Web sites to enhance their teaching, and 34 schools across the country are developing curricula to bring digital resources to the classroom as part of the Schools for a New Millennium project.

NEH Overview

Division of Preservation and Access

Grants are made for projects that will create, preserve, and increase the availability of resources important for research, education, and public programming in the humanities. Projects may encompass books, journals, newspapers, manuscript and archival materials, maps, still and moving images, sound recordings, and objects of material culture held by libraries, archives, museums, historical organizations, and other repositories.

Preservation and Access Projects

Support may be sought to preserve the intellectual content and aid bibliographic control of collections; to compile bibliographies, descriptive catalogs, and guides to cultural holdings; to create dictionaries, encyclopedias, databases, and other types of research tools and reference works; and to stabilize material culture collections through the appropriate housing and storing of objects, improved environmental control, and the installation of security, lighting, and fire-prevention systems. Applications may also be submitted for national and regional education and training projects, regional preservation field service programs, and research and demonstration projects that are intended to enhance institutional practice and the use of technology for preservation and access.

Proposals may combine preservation and access activities within a single project. Historically black colleges and universities (HBCUs) with significant institutional collections of primary materials are encouraged to apply.

Eligible applicants: Individuals, nonprofit institutions and cultural organizations, state agencies, and institutional consortia.

Application deadline: July 1.

Division of Public Programs

The Division of Public Programs fosters public understanding and appreciation of the humanities by supporting projects that bring significant insights about these disciplines to general audiences of all ages through interpretive exhibitions, radio and television programs, lectures, symposia, multimedia projects, printed materials, and reading and discussion groups.

Public Programs

Grants support consultation with scholars and humanities programming experts to shape an interpretive project; the planning and production of television and radio programs in the humanities intended for general audiences; the planning and implementation of exhibitions, the interpretation of historic sites, and the production of related publications, multimedia components, and educational programs; and the planning and implementation of projects through the use of books, new technologies, and other resources in the collections of libraries and archives in formats such as reading and discussion programs, lectures, symposia, and interpretive exhibitions of books, manuscripts, and other library resources.

Eligible applicants: Nonprofit institutions and organizations including public television and radio stations and state humanities councils.

Application deadlines: Planning grants only, November 1; Planning, scripting, implementation, production, February 1; Consultation grants, May 1 and September 11.

Division of Research Programs

Through fellowships to individual scholars and grants to support complex, frequently collaborative, research, the Division of Research Programs contributes to the creation of knowledge in the humanities.

Fellowships and Stipends

Grants provide support for scholars to undertake full-time independent research and writing in the humanities. Grants are available for a maximum of one year and a minimum of two months of summer study.

> *Eligible applicants*:   Individuals.
> *Application deadlines*:   Fellowships, May 1; Summer Stipends, October 1.

Research

Grants provide up to three years of support for collaborative research in the preparation for publication of editions, translations, and other important works in the humanities, and in the conduct of large or complex interpretive studies including archaeology projects and the humanities studies of science and technology. Grants also support research opportunities offered through independent research centers and international research organizations; a list of these opportunities is available.

> *Eligible applicants*:   Individuals, institutions of higher education, nonprofit professional associations, scholarly societies, and other nonprofit organizations.
> *Application deadlines*:   Collaborative Research, September 1; Fellowships at Independent Research Institutions, September 1.

Division of Education

Through grants to educational institutions, fellowships to scholars and teachers, and through the support of significant research, this division is designed to strengthen sustained, thoughtful study of the humanities at all levels of education and promote original research in the humanities.

Education Development and Demonstration

Grants, including "next semester" Humanities Focus Grants, support curriculum and materials development efforts; faculty study programs within and among educational institutions; and conferences and networks of institutions. The endowment is interested in projects that help teachers use the new electronic technologies to enhance students' understanding of humanities subjects.

> *Eligible applicants*:   Public and private elementary and secondary schools, school systems, colleges and universities, nonprofit academic associations, and cultural institutions, such as libraries and museums.
> *Application deadlines*:   National Education Projects, October 15; Humanities Focus Grants, April 15.

Schools for a New Millennium

Grants enable whole schools, in partnership with colleges and communities, to design professional development activities integrating digital technology into the humanities classroom.

Application deadline: Implementation Grants, October 1.

Seminars and Institutes

Grants support summer seminars and national institutes in the humanities for college and school teachers. These faculty development activities are conducted at colleges and universities across the country. Those wishing to participate in seminars submit their seminar applications to the seminar director.

Eligibility:	Individuals, institutions of higher learning.
Application deadlines for seminars:	Participants, March 1, 2000, for summer 2000 seminars; Directors, March 1, 2000, for summer 2001 seminars.
Application deadline for national institutes:	March 1.

Office of Challenge Grants

Nonprofit institutions interested in developing new sources of long-term support for educational, scholarly, preservation, and public programs in the humanities may be assisted in these efforts by an NEH Challenge Grant. Grantees are required to raise $3 or $4 in new or increased donations for every federal dollar offered. Both federal and nonfederal funds may be used to establish or increase institutional endowments and thus guarantee long-term support for a variety of humanities needs. Funds may also be used for limited direct capital expenditures, where such needs are compelling and clearly related to improvements in the humanities.

Eligible applicants:	Nonprofit postsecondary, educational, research, or cultural institutions and organizations working within the humanities.
Application deadline:	May 1.

Institute of Museum and Library Services
Library Programs

1100 Pennsylvania Ave. N.W., Washington, DC 20506
202-606-5527, fax 202-606-1077
World Wide Web http://www.imls.gov

Beverly Sheppard
Acting Director
Institute of Museum and Library Services

The Library Services and Technology Act (LSTA), Subchapter II of the Museum and Library Services Act of 1996, changed the federal administration of library programs by moving programs from the Department of Education (DOE) to the newly formed Institute of Museum and Library Services (IMLS). In 1997 staff moved from DOE to new offices at IMLS. The first LSTA grants were made in 1998. A total of $166,175,000 was available for these programs in fiscal year (FY) 1999.

The purposes of LSTA are

- To consolidate federal library service programs
- To stimulate excellence and promote access to learning and information resources in all types of libraries for individuals of all ages
- To promote library services that provide all users access to information through state, regional, national, and international electronic networks
- To provide linkages between and among libraries
- To promote targeted library service to people of diverse geographic, cultural, and socioeconomic backgrounds, to individuals with disabilities, and to people with limited functional literacy or information skills

Within IMLS, the Office of Library Services is responsible for the administration of LSTA. It is composed of the Division of State Programs, which administers grants to states, and the Division of Discretionary Programs, which administers the National Leadership Grant program, the Native American Library Services program, and the Native Hawaiian Library Services program.

State-Administered Programs

Approximately 90 percent of the annual federal appropriation under LSTA is distributed to the state library administrative agencies according to a population-based formula. The formula consists of a minimum amount set by the law ($340,000 for the states and $40,000 for the Pacific Territories) and supplemented by an additional amount based on population. State agencies may use the appropriation for statewide initiatives and services or distribute the funds through competitive subgrants or cooperative agreements to public, academic, research, school, or special libraries.

Priorities for funding that support the goals of the act are set by the individual states based on needs identified while preparing the five-year plan required before states can receive funding. The act limits the amount of funds available for administration at the state level to 4 percent and also requires a 34 percent match from nonfederal state or local funds.

Grants to the Pacific Territories and Freely Associated States (FAS) are funded under a Special Rule (20 USCA 9131(b)(3)) that authorizes a small competitive grants program in the Pacific. There are only six eligible entities in two groups: the Pacific Territories (Insular areas) consisting of Guam (GU), American Samoa (AS), and the Commonwealth of Northern Mariana Islands (CNMI); and the FAS, which includes the Federated States of Micronesia (FSM), the Republic of the Marshall Islands (RMI), and the Republic of Palau (PU). The funds for this grant program are taken from the allotments for the FAS (FSM, RMI, and PU), but not from the allotments to the territories. The three territories (GU, AS, and CNMI) receive their allotments through the regular program and in addition may apply for funds under this program. Five entities (GU, CNMI, FSM, RMI, and Palau) received a total of $210,959 in FY 1999. This amount included the set-aside of 5 percent because the competition was facilitated by Pacific Resources for Education and Learning (PREL) based in Hawaii, which received the set-aside amount to administer parts of the program.

In FY 2000 the total distributed to the states was $138,118,000.

(text continues on page 283)

Table 1 / Funding for LSTA State Program, 1999
Total Distributed to States: $138,118,000[1]

State	Federal Allocation[2] 66%	State Matching Fund 34%	Total
Alabama	$2,242,894	$1,155,430	$3,398,324
Alaska	608,473	313,456	921,929
Arizona	2,381,340	1,226,751	3,608,091
Arkansas	1,449,863	746,899	2,196,762
California	14,623,319	7,533,225	22,156,544
Colorado	2,076,291	1,069,604	3,145,895
Connecticut	1,771,574	912,629	2,684,203
Delaware	665,137	342,646	1,007,783
Florida	6,861,953	3,534,945	10,396,898
Georgia	3,681,525	1,896,543	5,578,068
Hawaii	861,635	443,873	1,305,508
Idaho	877,237	451,910	1,329,147
Illinois	5,606,771	2,888,337	8,495,108
Indiana	2,919,400	1,503,933	4,423,333
Iowa	1,591,594	819,912	2,411,506
Kansas	1,489,549	767,343	2,256,892
Kentucky	2,061,219	1,061,840	3,123,059
Louisiana	2,250,314	1,159,253	3,409,567
Maine	884,043	455,416	1,339,459
Maryland	2,585,174	1,331,756	3,916,930
Massachusetts	3,027,809	1,559,780	4,587,589
Michigan	4,632,550	2,386,465	7,019,015
Minnesota	2,406,171	1,239,543	3,645,714
Mississippi	1,543,341	795,054	2,338,395
Missouri	2,717,988	1,400,176	4,118,164
Montana	724,975	373,472	1,098,447

Table 1 / Funding for LSTA State Program, 1999 *(cont.)*
Total Distributed to States: $138,118,000[1]

State	Federal Allocation[2] 66%	State Matching Fund 34%	Total
Nebraska	1,067,017	549,675	1,616,692
Nevada	1,103,824	568,637	1,672,461
New Hampshire	858,158	442,081	1,300,239
New Jersey	3,888,256	2,003,041	5,891,297
New Mexico	1,099,466	566,392	1,665,858
New York	8,287,078	4,269,101	12,556,179
North Carolina	3,639,674	1,874,984	5,514,658
North Dakota	619,070	318,915	937,985
Ohio	5,241,306	2,700,067	7,941,373
Oklahoma	1,803,337	928,992	2,732,329
Oregon	1,775,030	914,409	2,689,439
Pennsylvania	5,587,587	2,878,454	8,466,041
Rhode Island	772,209	397,805	1,170,014
South Carolina	2,017,259	1,039,194	3,056,453
South Dakota	662,762	341,423	1,004,185
Tennessee	2,714,518	1,398,388	4,112,906
Texas	8,979,813	4,625,964	13,605,777
Utah	1,258,111	648,118	1,906,229
Vermont	598,361	308,247	906,608
Virginia	3,309,489	1,704,888	5,014,377
Washington	2,827,608	1,456,647	4,284,255
West Virginia	1,131,921	583,111	1,715,032
Wisconsin	2,623,955	1,351,734	3,975,689
Wyoming	550,275	283,475	833,750
District of Columbia	568,734	292,984	861,718
Puerto Rico	2,039,860	1,050,837	3,090,697
American Samoa	67,890	34,974	102,864
Northern Marianas	70,344	36,238	106,582
Guam	106,337	54,780	161,117
Virgin Islands	92,394	47,597	139,991
Pacific Territories[3]	214,218	110,354	324,572
Total	$138,118,000	$71,151,697	$209,269,697

1 The amount available to states is based on the balance remaining after enacted allocations have been subtracted from the total allocation, as follows:

Library allocation, FY 1999	$166,250,837
Native American Grants (1.75%)	$2,616,000
National Leadership Grants (3.75%)	$22,025,837
Administration (up to 3%)	$3,491,000
Total available to states	$138,118,000

2 Calculation is based on minimum set in the law (P.L. 104-208, as amended by P.L. 105-128 111 Stat 2548) and reflects appropriations enacted by P.L. 106-113. Data for the Marshall Islands, Federated States of Micronesia, Puerto Rico, American Samoa, the Northern Marianas, Guam, the Virgin Islands, and Palau are, as of June 15, 1998, from the Bureau of the Census (BOC) International Data Base (at the Web site http://www.census.gov/cgi-bin/ipc/idbrank.pl). Data are also available by phone at 301-457-2422. Data for the District of Columbia and the 50 states are from BOC estimates as of July 1, 1998, which were made available December 31, 1998. For the continental United States, BOC data can be accessed at the Web site http://www.census.gov/population/estimates/state and are by phone at 301-457-2419. It is important to use the most recent data available at the time distributions are made because BOC estimates sometimes change.

3 Total allotment (including administrative costs) for Palau, the Marshall Islands, and Micronesia. Funds are awarded on a competitive basis and administered by Pacific Resources for Education and Learning.

(continued from page 281)

Discretionary Programs

In 1998 IMLS also began administering the discretionary programs of LSTA. In FY 1999 $27,908,000* was allocated for the National Leadership Grant Program, the Native American Library Services Program, and the Native Hawaiian Library Services Grant Program. This includes $15,435,000 for directed grants.

The Native American Library Services program provides opportunities for improved library services for an important part of the nation's community of library users. The IMLS Native American Library Services program offers three types of support to serve the range of needs of Indian tribes and Alaska Native villages. The Native Hawaiian Library Services program provides opportunities for improved library services to Native Hawaiians through a single award. The National Leadership Grant program provides funding for innovative model programs to enhance the quality of library services nationwide. National Leadership Grants are intended to produce results useful for the broader library community.

The FY 2000 congressional appropriation for discretionary programs includes the following:

- National Leadership Program: $10,275,000 for competitive programs
- Native American Library Services Program: $2,242,000
- Native Hawaiian Library Services Program: $374,000

National Leadership Grant Program

In September 1999 IMLS awarded 50 grants totaling $10,565,000 for National Leadership Grants using FY 1999 funding. This figure represents 3.75 percent of the LSTA appropriation for competitive programs, plus $1,000,000 from the IMLS Office of Museum Services to supplement funding for library and museum collaborations, and additional congressional funding over the formula. A total of 187 applications requesting more than $34,000,000 were received. The projects funded were selected as innovative model projects in the field of library and information science in education and training, research and demonstration, preservation and archiving of digital media, and library and museum collaborations (Table 2).

In 1999 IMLS convened two meetings of leaders in library and information science to seek input on two categories of National Leadership Grant funding—education and training, and research and demonstration projects. The reports from these meetings are on the IMLS Web site (http://www.imls.gov). Both groups encouraged IMLS to take a leadership role in identifying changing needs and in supporting innovative solutions to problems.

The FY 2000 priorities for National Leadership Grant funding are

* Includes $1,000,000 from the IMLS Office of Museum Services to supplement LSTA funding for library and museum collaborations.

Education and Training

- Projects to attract individuals from diverse cultural backgrounds to the field of librarianship and information science
- Projects that implement innovative approaches to education and training and enhance the availability of professional librarians with advanced skills and specializations
- Projects that train librarians to enhance people's ability to use information effectively

Research and Demonstration

- Projects that conduct research and/or demonstrations to enhance library services through the effective and efficient use of new and appropriate technologies
- Projects that conduct research and/or demonstrations to enhance the ability of library users to make more effective use of information resources
- Projects that conduct research and/or demonstrations that will assist in the evaluation of library services, including economic implications of services and other contributions to a community

Preservation or Digitization of Library Materials

- Projects that address the challenges of preserving and archiving digital media
- Projects that lead to the development of standards, techniques, or models related to the digitization and management of digital collections
- Projects that preserve and enhance access to unique library resources useful to the broader community

Library and Museum Collaborations

- Projects to help museums and libraries take a leadership role in the education of lifelong learners in the 21st century
- Projects that develop, document, and disseminate model programs of cooperation between libraries and museums, with emphasis on how technology is used, education is enhanced, or the community is served

Native American Library Services Program

In 1999 IMLS distributed $2,492,562 in grants for American Indian tribes and Alaska Native villages.

The Native American Library Services Program provides opportunities for the improvement of library services to Indian tribes and Alaska Native villages, the latter coming under the definition of eligible Indian tribes as recognized by the secretary of the interior. The program offers three types of support:

(text continues on page 291)

Table 2 / National Leadership Grant Awards, FY 1999

Education and Training: Projects that attract individuals from diverse cultural backgrounds to the field of librarianship and information science; train staff currently employed in libraries in new knowledge, skills, and abilities for the effective use of new technologies; or train librarians to enhance people's ability to use information effectively.

San Jose State University, San Jose, California $234,581

A one-year project to train staff development personnel in libraries of all types as well as library educators in the effective use of new technologies and the design of instructional tools for distance continuing education.

Council on Library and Information Resources, Washington, D.C. $109,800

This two-year project will support the recruitment of 20 individuals from diverse cultural backgrounds to attend the Frye Leadership Institute during the first two years of its operation. The purpose of the institute is to develop leaders capable of effecting fundamental change in the way universities manage their information resources in the digital era.

College of Micronesia, Kolonia, Phonpei $150,042

A two-year project to design a staff training/professional development curriculum that will provide all librarians in the Federated States of Micronesia (FSM) with the ability to improve their skills and knowledge in librarianship.

Southeastern Library Network (SOLINET), Atlanta $152,034

This one-year project will design, implement, and evaluate a continuing education institute to develop and enhance leadership among staff of statewide and multi-type library consortia.

Louisiana State University, Baton Rouge $91,291

This two-year project will develop a national model for teaching librarians, especially those in small libraries, how to plan for building and renovation projects in order to accommodate new technologies. The grant will fund an 18-month Institute on Library Redesign for Technology for up to 225 librarians in Arkansas, Louisiana, and Mississippi.

New England Historic Genealogical Society, Boston $223,687

This two-year project will provide training, demonstrations, and one-on-one consultations on genealogy to public librarians, historical society staff, and volunteers through seminars at major meetings of various professional organizations.

University of Minnesota, Minneapolis $66,349

A two-year project to create a training institute for 20 early-career librarians from groups under-represented in the profession. The institute will train participants in new telecommunication and multimedia technologies and their applications to library services and leadership skills.

University of Missouri, Columbia $127,611

This two-year project will provide training to help librarians, particularly those in public libraries, interact with users in electronic settings.

Columbus Public Schools, Columbus, Nebraska $71,960

This two-year project will promote collaboration and provide technology training for Nebraska library professionals, utilizing state distance learning telecommunications networks.

Kent State University/SLIS, Kent, Ohio $123,396

A two-year project to develop the OhioLEARN Public Library Fellowship Program, which will deliver graduate professional education in library and information science to a targeted underserved population group using a digital distance learning network.

University of the Virgin Islands, St. Thomas $73,000

In this one-year project, the University of the Virgin Islands libraries, in partnership with the Virgin Islands Library Association, will develop training workshops for professional librarians and personnel in charge of libraries in the Virgin Islands. The workshops will incorporate hands-on training sessions to create Web sites for each library and instructional modules to help librarians to deliver effective information instruction in their institutions.

Table 2 / National Leadership Grant Awards, FY 1999 *(cont.)*

University of Wisconsin–Milwaukee $103,449

This one-year project will create a national institute that will provide instruction on the implications of new laws, regulations, and technologies for smaller institutions that may not have in-house legal counsel.

Research and Demonstration. Model projects that conduct research and/or demonstrations to enhance library services through the effective and efficient use of new and appropriate technologies, enhance the ability of library users to make more effective use of information resources, or assist in the evaluation of library services, including the economic implications of services and other contributions to a community.

University of California–Berkeley $242,825

This two-year project aims to demonstrate improved access to written material and numerical data on the same topic when searching two very different kinds of databases: text databases (books, articles, and their bibliographic records) and numerical data (socio-economic databases).

Regents of the University of California, Riverside $498,750

A two-year project to develop the next generation of the Internet information system INFOMINE. The project will respond to the national need to develop comprehensive, publicly supported, user-friendly systems for collecting and disseminating the best of electronic information.

Bibliographical Center for Research, Aurora, Colorado $170,885

This two-year project will supplement the Public Library Association's new "Planning for Results" process by creating new tools that will enable libraries to collect more role-specific library output data and standardized user outcome data.

University of Illinois at Urbana/Champaign $218,872

A two-year project that will develop, implement, and assess community-wide participative models for the creation and management of networked community information services, using as a case study the domain of African American women's physical, emotional, spiritual, and intellectual health.

Eastern Iowa Community College District, Davenport $249,951

This two-year project will develop and demonstrate the Advanced Technology Environmental Education Library (ATEEL) as well as a taxonomy of environmental technology descriptive metadata. ATEEL is an innovative, 24-hour, online library to serve the specialized needs of environmental technology students, faculty, and working technologists.

University of Kentucky, Lexington $215,400

The goals of this two-year project are to describe the information-seeking activities of bio-acoustic researchers by studying their database and citation uses; identify problems created by discipline-based databases and indexing practices, and suggest design solutions using demonstration of a search engine interface prototype system suitable for interdisciplinary researchers in bio-acoustics.

Johns Hopkins University, Baltimore $250,000

Using the already-digitized Levy Collection, this two-year project will develop a comprehensive suite of tools that will diminish the manual input necessary to manage the workflow of large-scale digitization projects. The project will also add Web-based music searching and analysis tools to the database so that users can do tune-based searching, and it will extend plans for developing automated means of mining authoritative name information and creating richer name indexes.

Wayne State University, Detroit $123,048

A two-year study to explore the ways in which the urban poor interact with and benefit from free access to information technology in the public library. The research aims to assess the impact that having access to information technology makes in the lives of the urban poor.

Table 2 / National Leadership Grant Awards, FY 1999 *(cont.)*

Gustavus Adolphus College, St. Peter, Minnesota $79,224

In a two-year project, the college will develop and implement a model for embedding developmental research skills into the undergraduate curriculum and evaluate how students learn best in a hybrid print/electronic information environment.

Research Foundation of SUNY Buffalo, Amherst, New York $154,324

This one-year project will investigate the impact of the Internet on public library use via a national telephone survey. The project will document how people are currently using the public library and the Internet and identify the ways in which libraries and the Internet are competing with and complementing one another.

South Central Regional Library Council, Ithaca, New York $54,234

In a one-year project titled Gateway New York, the council will lay the groundwork for a statewide gateway to information. The gateway will be a publicly accessible Web site through which users can simultaneously search multiple library catalogs, citation databases, and full-text databases around the state.

University of South Carolina–Spartanburg $249,993

This two-year project will demonstrate the fostering of information literacy and library research skills throughout the general education curriculum at USCS.

University of Texas–Austin $224,512

A two-year project to provide a set of tools and guidelines that libraries, museums, and other information agencies can use to improve the utility of their Web sites.

Washington State Library, Olympia $128,250

This one-year project will develop solutions to two issues facing national interoperability of government data: (1) incompatibility of metadata indexes, and (2) inconsistency in the use of controlled vocabularies for classification of government World Wide Web documents and files.

Preservation or Digitization. Projects that preserve and enhance access to unique library resources useful to the broader community; address the challenges of preserving and archiving digital media; or that lead to the development of standards, techniques, or models related to the digitization and management of digital resources.

University of Denver $499,999

A two-year project to increase access to digital objects from the scientific, cultural, and historical collections of Colorado museums and libraries. Access to the images will be enhanced through a clickable map of the state as well as through a union catalog of metadata.

University of Miami, Coral Gables, Florida $250,000

A one-year project to preserve unique and rare materials relating to Cuba that will make the materials accessible in digital form.

State Botanical Garden of Georgia, Athens $241,223

In this two-year project, the State Botanical Garden of Georgia and the Duke University Biological and Environmental Sciences Library will create a Web site that will provide a virtual and easily accessible library of plant information to a wide audience in the region and nationwide.

University of Georgia, Athens $178,628

Approximately 1,000 of the most significant documents and visual images from several major collections relating to the Native American population of the Southeastern United States will be digitized and made available through a Web site in this one-year project.

Illinois State Library, Springfield $390,110

This two-year project will establish a model statewide virtual library of significant historic and government documents.

Amistad Research Center, New Orleans $186,003

During this two-year project, the Amistad Research Center in collaboration with the Louisiana State University Digital Library will digitize rare documents and images related to the historic

Table 2 / National Leadership Grant Awards, FY 1999 *(cont.)*

Amistad Incident. Also included will be documents about the committee of defenders in the Amistad case, from which the American Missionary Association developed.

University of Missouri–Columbia $75,000

This one-year project is to host a conference on digital libraries and to produce a report on the provision of access to a wide variety of digital resources.

Syracuse University, Syracuse, New York $158,076

This one-year project will complete the development of a non-destructive playback system for wax cylinder recordings.

University of North Carolina–Chapel Hill $216,622

In a partnering of the North Carolina Botanical Garden, UNC Herbarium, the UNC School of Information and Library Science, the McDougle Middle School, and the Orange County Public Library, this two-year project will develop and test a Web-based center that links digital images of herbarium specimens and associated data.

Free Library of Philadelphia $108,077

This one-year project will provide access through the World Wide Web to more than 1,200 rare silver-albumen photographs and related original materials documenting the 1876 Centennial Exposition in Philadelphia.

Library of the Academy of Natural Sciences, Philadelphia $151,863

A two-year project to digitize printed texts and illustrations, manuscripts, and drawings that illustrate and document the establishment of a distinctly American approach to natural science during the first half of the 19th century.

University of Virginia Health Sciences Library, Charlottesville $248,245

Approximately 30,000 pages of manuscript material and 1,000 photographs from the Philip S. Hench Walter Reed Yellow Fever Collection will be digitized, arranged, described, preserved, and accessed via the World Wide Web in this two-year project. The project will provide a model for the integration of state-of-the-art, standards-compliant information technology and scholarly resources to make unique library resources more widely available.

Library and Museum Collaborations. Projects that develop, document, and disseminate model programs of cooperation between libraries and museums, with emphasis on how the community is served, technology is used, or education is enhanced; or that help museum and libraries take a leadership role in the education of lifelong learners in the 21st century.

Arizona Department of Libraries, Archives, and Public Records, Phoenix $317,897

The department, the lead agency among four partnering state libraries and three museums in a two-year project, will implement the second phase of a collaborative effort to increase library and curatorial services to American Indian tribal communities.

California Digital Library, Oakland $490,991

The California Digital Library will lead the Bancroft Library and a group of eight museums in a two-year project to evaluate the capabilities of Encoded Archival Description (EAD) to integrate their collection descriptions into the greater context of a "virtual archive" of museum, library, and archival collections.

Huntington Library and Art Gallery, San Marino, California $381,048

This two-year project will create a model exhibition of rare books, manuscripts, photographs, works of art, and other objects drawn from approximately 30 special collections libraries in seven partnering institutions within Los Angeles County. The exhibition, to be held at the Hammer Museum in the fall of 2001, will be accompanied by a printed exhibition catalog, outreach and education programs, and a Web site linking several dozen Los Angeles libraries.

Connecticut Historical Society, Hartford $335,101

The Connecticut Historical Society Thomas J. Dodd Research Center at the University of Connecticut and Mystic Seaport Museum will mount an innovative two-year collaboration called Connecticut Classroom. The project has two major components: the establishment of a comprehensive, Web-based virtual collection of graphic images that document the

Table 2 / National Leadership Grant Awards, FY 1999 *(cont.)*

Connecticut community, and a long-term effort to encourage middle and high school teachers to make meaningful use of the database.

Triton College, River Grove, Illinois $107,835

This one-year library-museum initiative involving the Triton College Library/LRC and the Cernan Earth and Space Center Planetarium and Museum will provide opportunities for adults, educators, community leaders, and professionals in many fields to work with schoolchildren in designing a community for the year 2030 on Mars. The overall goal of the project is to demonstrate the interconnection between technology and the educational process through formal and informal educational opportunities.

Children's Museum of Indianapolis $410,931

This two-year partnership between Rex's Lending Center, the Children's Museum of Indianapolis, and the Indianapolis-Marion County Public Library (I-MCPL) will create library and reading programs that target the museum's inner city neighborhood. The project aims to provide information-rich environments in all galleries and exhibits at the museum and to distribute programs, as well as museum and library resources, throughout the I-MCPL library system and to classrooms and other libraries throughout the state.

Kansas State Historical Society, Topeka $224,076

This two-year partnership between the Kansas State Historical Society and the Kansas Collection at the University of Kansas will digitize significant primary resources from the Civil War era. The project will produce two outcomes: a virtual repository of the best Territorial Kansas information and artifacts from the two institutions, and curriculum units based on selected digitized items developed to enhance the teaching of U.S. history at the middle school, high school, and college levels.

Jefferson Patterson Park and Museum, St. Leonard, Maryland $173,441

This two-year research project will explore the experience of African American educators during the years of change from segregated to integrated public schools. The project will result in a process through which African Americans will advise two local museums (the Jefferson Patterson Park and Museum and the Banneker-Douglass Museum) and an academic Library (the Southern Maryland Studies Center at the Charles County Community College Library), on the overall direction of an exhibition.

Rochester Public Library, Rochester, New York $279,346

This two-year project, titled Rochester Images, models a collaboration among a museum (the Rochester Museum & Science Center), a public library (the Rochester Public Library), and an urban public school district (the Rochester City School District) to demonstrate the development of digitized products for educational use.

Carnegie Mellon University, Pittsburgh $343,023

This two-year partnership between the Carnegie Mellon University Libraries, the Carnegie Museum of Natural History, and the School of Computer Science at Carnegie Mellon University will mitigate the common problem of physical-space constraints that exists in both libraries and museums. The project aims to produce more effective educational outreach to the public in the form of "Smart Web Exhibits" designed to deliver information from library, museum, and archival collections to a diverse online user community.

Montshire Museum of Science, Norwich, Vermont $98,474

This two-year collaboration between the Montshire Museum of Science and the Howe Library will create eight traveling interactive tabletop science exhibits along with companion materials and activities. The materials will travel to other participating libraries, providing rural library communities with a year-long sequence of exhibits and programs designed to encourage family learning.

Madison Children's Museum, Madison, Wisconsin $154,741

The Madison Public Library, Dane County Library Service, and Madison Children's Museum will partner with community centers, neighborhood associations, Head Start, EvenStart centers, and others in a two-year project titled Discovery to Go. The program aims to bring flexible outreach programs, library materials, and exhibits to low-income, disadvantaged, and underserved children, youth, and families.

Table 3 / Native American Library Services Program: Enhancement Grants, FY 1999

Chickasaw Nation
Ada, Oklahoma $149,000

This two-year project will enhance access to the collections by developing an automated library system, digitizing archival materials, and establishing an interlibrary-loan consortium.

Crow Indian Tribe
Crow Agency, Montana $87,722

This one-year project will create public access to the Little Big Horn College library materials at different locations on the Crow Reservation, provide training for staff and patrons in the use of electronic resources, and create Web access to Crow information resources.

Eastern Band of Cherokee Indians
Cherokee, North Carolina $150,000

This two-year project will update computers and the library collection, provide Internet access, and establish a tribal archival collection.

Lac Courte Oreilles Tribal Governing Board
Hayward, Wisconsin $127,867

This two-year project will record and preserve the oral history of the tribe, create a rotating photographic and traveling history exhibit, and provide training to the community members on the use of a GIS system.

Lower Brule Sioux Tribe
Lower Brule, South Dakota $94,624

This one-year project will increase staffing, provide staff training, purchase computer and library equipment, and expand the Native American collection.

Lummi Indian Nation
Bellingham, Washington $149,900

This two-year project will create a Lummi Archive/Museum Web site to enhance access to tribal materials, provide educational programs focused on tribal history, and upgrade the library's collections and services.

Oneida Tribe of Indians of Wisconsin
Oneida, Wisconsin $72,315

This one-year project will increase student and teacher access to computers and the Internet by providing a computer lab and networked CD-ROM reference software that supports the elementary and high school curriculum.

Pala Band of Mission Indians
Pala, California $64,126

This one-year project will provide access to a computerized network, ensure staff training, and enhance the collection of materials.

Pilot Station Traditional Village
Pilot Station, Alaska $68,940

This one-year project will develop and strengthen a regional consortium of village libraries located in the Alaska Native villages of the Yukon Kuskokwim Delta.

Table 3 / Native American Library Services Program: Enhancement Grants, FY 1999
(cont.)

Pueblo of Zuni

Zuni, New Mexico $115,830

This one-year project will upgrade the newly renovated community library by automating the circulation system, installing new furniture and computer workstations, and providing staff training in the use of new technologies.

Red Cliff Band of Lake Superior Chippewa

Bayfield, Wisconsin $130,390

This two-year project will develop the Red Cliff Library as a comprehensive community resource center to serve as the foundation of family literacy services.

Sealaska Corporation

Juneau, Alaska $149,671

This two-year project will enhance tribal library services by cataloging and digitizing the Sealaska Curry-Weissbrodt collection and improving accessibility to the collection through resource sharing, technology, and training.

Spirit Lake Nation

Fort Totten, North Dakota $133,677

This two-year project will enhance library services to the community by providing public Internet access and training classes, increasing the electronic media collection of Native American materials, connecting to the state library interlibrary-loan system, and digitizing the tribal archives.

(continued from page 284)

- Basic Library Services Grants, in the amount of $4,500, support core library operations on a noncompetitive basis for all eligible Indian tribes and Alaska Native villages that apply for such support. IMLS awarded basic grants to 205 tribes in 24 states in 1999.

- Technical Assistance Grants, in the amount of $2,000, heighten the level of professional proficiency of Indian tribal library staff. It is a noncompetitive program to support assessments of library service and provide advice for improvement. IMLS awarded technical assistance grants to 38 tribes in 11 states in 1999.

- Enhancement Grants support new levels of library service for activities specifically identified under the LSTA purposes. In 1999 these competitive awards ranged from $64,126 to $150,000 (Table 3).

Of the 44 applications received, IMLS awarded 13 enhancement grants for a total of $1,494,062.

Native Hawaiian Library Services

The Native Hawaiian Library Services Program provides opportunities for improved library services for an important part of the nation's community of library users through a single grant to a Native Hawaiian organization, as defined in section 9212 of the Native Hawaiian Education Act (20 U.S.C. 7912).

In 1999 the Native Hawaiian Library Services Grant was awarded to ALU-LIKE, Inc. of Honolulu, a private, nonprofit organization serving the Native Hawaiian community, in the amount of $415,438.

Evaluation of IMLS Programs

In order to assure that it is meeting current public and professional needs in library services, IMLS routinely seeks advice from diverse representatives of the library community, carries out studies of library practice, and evaluates its programs with the assistance of external consultants. In 1999 IMLS's study of library-museum partnerships concluded that these are rewarding both for partners and the communities they serve. The Library-Museum Collaboration program of the National Leadership Grants responds to this finding. In 2000 IMLS will carry out a broad study to characterize digital activities in libraries.

IMLS has taken a leadership role in evaluating the success of its programs through incorporating outcome-based measurement as a tool to document effectiveness of funded projects. The evaluation component of applications is being strengthened and project reports are increasingly expected to identify the benefits they provide to a service population in concrete, objective terms. IMLS is in the process of developing training and support materials to build grantee skills in outcome evaluation.

IMLS Web Site

IMLS maintains a Web site (http://www.imls.gov) that provides information on the various grant programs, national awards for library and museum service, projects funded, application forms, and staff contacts. The Web site also highlights model projects developed by libraries and museums throughout the country. Whether libraries are developing computer training centers, as they have in New Jersey, or developing "Cybermobiles," as they have in Indiana, the Web site will provide a national perspective of the latest projects in the library field. Through an electronic newsletter, *Primary Source*, IMLS provides timely information on grant deadlines and opportunities. Details on subscribing to the IMLS newsletter are located on the Web site.

National Award for Library Service

The National Award for Library Service is a new IMLS award for FY 2000. It will honor outstanding American libraries that have made a significant and exceptional contribution to their communities, seeking to recognize libraries that demonstrate extraordinary and innovative approaches to public service, reaching beyond the expected levels of community outreach and core programs generally associated with library services. The principal criterion for selection will be evidenced by the library's systematic and ongoing commitment to public service through exemplary and innovative programs and community partnerships.

The award for FY 2000 will be announced during National Library Week. Nominations are sought in the fall. All information and deadlines will appear on the IMLS Web site during the fall nomination period.

Part 3
Library/Information Science Education, Placement, and Salaries

Guide to Employment Sources in the Library and Information Professions

Maxine Moore

Office for Library Personnel Resources, American Library Association

This guide updates the listing in the 1999 *Bowker Annual* with information on new services and changes in contacts and groups listed previously. The sources listed primarily give assistance in obtaining professional positions, although a few indicate assistance with paraprofessionals (see Council on Library/Media Technicians, Inc., under "Specialized Library Associations and Groups" below or visit the Web site of the Library Support Staff Resource Center under Library Employment Resources at http://www.lib.rochester.edu/ssp/jobs.htm). Paraprofessionals, however, tend to be recruited through local sources.

General Sources of Library and Information Jobs

Library Literature

Classified ads of library vacancies and positions wanted are carried in many of the national, regional, and state library journals and newsletters. Members of associations can sometimes list "position wanted" ads free of charge in their membership publications. Listings of positions available are regularly found in *American Libraries, Chronicle of Higher Education, College & Research Libraries News, Library Journal,* and *Library Hotline.* State and regional library association newsletters, state library journals, foreign library periodicals, and other types of periodicals carrying such ads are listed in later sections.

Newspapers

The *New York Times* Sunday "Week in Review" section carries a special section of ads for librarian jobs in addition to the regular classifieds. Local newspapers, particularly the larger city Sunday editions, such as the *Washington Post, Los Angeles Times,* and *Chicago Tribune* often carry job vacancy listings in libraries, both professional and paraprofessional. The online versions of these newspapers also are useful.

Internet

The many library-related electronic listservs on the Internet often post library job vacancies interspersed with other news and discussion items. A growing number of general online job-search bulletin boards exist; these may include information-related job notices along with other types of jobs. This guide includes information on electronic access where available through the individual organizations listed below. Among useful resources are "Making Short Work of the Job Search" by Marilyn Rosenthal, *Library Journal*, September 1, 1997; "Job Opportunities Glitter for Librarians Who Surf the Net" by A. Paula Azar, *American Libraries*, September 1996; "Library Jobs and Employment: A Guide to Internet Resources" compiled by Jeffery C. Lee, Texas Woman's University, under What's New & Featured Resources/Clearinghouse for Subject-oriented Internet Resource Guides (UM/AllGuides/Library Employment, J. Lee, January 29, 1995), at http://www.clearinghouse.net; "Jobs on the Net for Librarians" by Janet B. Foster in *Public Libraries*, January/February 1999, pp. 27–29; and "Riley's Guided Tour: Job Searching on the Net" by Margaret Riley, et al., *Library Journal*, September 15, 1996, pp. 24–27. These offer guidance on databases that might lead to library and information-related position listings.

Some library-related job-search Web links include:

- Ann's Place—Library Job Hunting Around the World
  (http://uic.edu/~aerobin/libjob/libads.html)
- Finding Library Jobs on the WWW
  (http://toltec.lib.utk.edu/~tla/nmrt/libjobs.html)
- Career and Job Information
  (http://www.peachnet.edu/galileo/internet/jobs/jobsmenu.html)
- Job Opportunities—Librarians and Library Science Net Links
  (http://librarians.miningco.com/msubjobs.htm)
- Library and Information Science Jobs
  (http://www.fidnet.com/~map/default4.htm)
- The Librarian's Job Search Source
  (http://www.zoots.com/libjob/libjob.htm)
- Library Jobs Online
  (http://wings.buffalo.edu/scils/alas/usamap.html)
- The Networked Librarian Job Search Guide
  (http://pw2.netcom.com/~feridun/nlintro.htm)

Library Joblines

Library joblines or job "hotlines" give recorded telephone messages of job openings in a specific geographical area. Most tapes are changed once a week, although individual listings may sometimes be carried for several weeks. Although the information is fairly brief and the cost of calling is borne by the individual job seeker, a jobline provides a quick and up-to-date listing of vacancies that is not usually possible with printed listings or journal ads.

Most joblines carry listings for their state or region only, although some will occasionally accept out-of-state positions if there is room on the tape. While a few will list technician and other paraprofessional positions, the majority are for professional jobs only. When calling the joblines, one may occasionally find a time when the telephone keeps ringing without any answer; this will usually mean that the tape is being changed or there are no new jobs for that period. The classified section of *American Libraries* carries jobline numbers periodically as space permits. The following joblines are in operation:

Jobline Sponsor	Job Seekers (To Hear Job Listings)	Employers (To Place Job Listings)
American Association of Law Libraries	312-939-7877	53 W. Jackson Blvd., Suite 940, Chicago, IL 60604. 312-939-4764; fax 312-431-1097
Arizona Department of Library, Archives and Public Records (Arizona libraries only)	602-275-2325	1700 W. Washington, Phoenix, AZ 85007
British Columbia Library Association (B.C. listings only)	604-430-6411	Jobline, 110-6545 Bonsor Ave., Burnaby, BC V51 1H3, Canada. 604-430-9633
California Library Association	916-447-5627	717 K St., Suite 300, Sacramento, CA 95814-3477. 916-447-8541; fax 916-447-8394
California School Library Association	650-697-8832	1499 Old Bayshore Hwy., Suite 142, Burlingame, CA 94010. 650-692-2350
Cleveland (OH) Area Metropolitan Library System Job Listing Service	216-921-4702	CAMLS, 20600 Chagrin Blvd., Suite 500, Shaker Heights, OH 44122.
Colorado State Library[1] (includes paraprofessionals)	303-866-6741	Jobline, 201 E. Colfax, Rm. 309, Denver, CO 80203-1704. 303-866-6900; fax 303-866-6940; also via Libnet/listserv
Delaware Division of Libraries (Del., N.J., and Pa. listings)	800-282-8696 (in-state) 302-739-4748 ext. 165 (out-of-state)	43 S. Dupont Hwy., Dover, DE 19901.
State Library of Florida	904-488-5232 (in-state)	R. A. Gray Bldg., Tallahassee, FL 32399-0250. 904-487-2651
Library Jobline of Illinois[2]	312-409-5986	Illinois Library Assn., 33 W. Grand, Suite 301, Chicago, IL 60610. 312-644-1896 ($80/2 weeks)
State Library of Iowa (professional jobs in Iowa; only during regular business hours)	515-281-7574	East 12 & Grand, Des Moines, IA 50319. 515-281-7574

Jobline Sponsor	Job Seekers (To Hear Job Listings)	Employers (To Place Job Listings)
Kansas State Library Jobline (also includes paraprofessional and out-of-state)	785-296-3296	State Capitol, 300 S.W. Tenth Ave. N., Topeka, KS 66612-1593. Fax 785-296-6650
Kentucky Job Hotline	502-564-3008 (24 hours)	Dept. for Libs. and Archives, Box 537, Frankfort, KY 40602. 502-564-8300
Long Island (NY) Library Resources Council Jobline	516-632-6658	516-632-6650; fax 516-632-6662
Maryland Library Association	410-685-5760 (24 hours)	400 Cathedral St., 3rd flr., Baltimore, MD 21201. 410-727-7422 (Mon.–Fri., 9:00 A.M.–4:30 P.M.)
Medical Library Association Jobline	312-553-4636 (24 hours)	6 N. Michigan Ave., Suite 300, Chicago, IL 60602. 312-419-9094
Metropolitan Washington (D.C.) Council of Governments Library Council	202-962-3712 (24 hours)	777 N. Capitol St. N.E., Suite 300, Washington, DC 20002. 202-962-3254
Michigan Library Association	517-694-7440 (ext. 28)	6810 S. Cedar, #6, Lansing, MI 48911. 517-694-6615; fax 517-694-4330 ($40/week)
Missouri Library Association Jobline	573-442-6590	1306 Business 63 S., Suite B, Columbia, MO 65201-8404. 573-449-4627; fax 573-449-4655
Mountain Plains Library Association[3]	605-677-5757	c/o I. D. Weeks Library, University of South Dakota, Vermillion, SD 57069. 605-677-6082; fax 605-677-5488
Nebraska Job Hotline (in-state and other openings during regular business hours)	402-471-4019 800-307-2665 (in-state)	Nebraska Library Commission, 1200 N St. 120, Lincoln, NE 68508-2023.
New England Library Jobline (New England jobs only)	617-521-2815 (24 hours)	GSLIS, Simmons College, 300 The Fenway, Boston, MA 02115. Fax 617-521-3192
New Jersey Library Association	609-695-2121	Box 1534, Trenton, NJ 08607; 609-394-8032; fax 609-394-8164 (nonmembers $50)
New York Library Association	518-432-6952 800-252-6952 (in-state)	252 Hudson Ave., Albany, NY 12210-1802. 518-432-6952 (members $15/3 months, nonmembers $25/3 months)

Jobline Sponsor	Job Seekers (To Hear Job Listings)	Employers (To Place Job Listings)
Ohio Library Council	614-225-6999 (24 hours)	35 E. Gay St., Suite 305, Columbus, OH 43215. 614-221-9057; fax 614-221-6234
Oklahoma Department of Libraries Jobline (5:00 P.M.–8:00 A.M., 7 days a week)	405-522-4747	200 N.E. 18 St., Oklahoma City, OK 73105.
Pennsylvania Cooperative Job Hotline[4]	717-234-4646	Pennsylvania Library Assn., 1919 N. Front St., Harrisburg, PA 17102. 717-233-3113 (weekly fee for non-members); fax 717-233-3121
Pratt Institute SILS Job Hotline	718-636-3742	SILS, Brooklyn, NY 11205. 718-636-3702; fax 718-636-3733
University of South Carolina College of Library and Information Science (no geographic restrictions)	803-777-8443	University of South Carolina, Columbia, SC 29208. 803-777-3887
Special Libraries Association	202-234-3632	1700 18th St. N.W., Washington, DC 20009. 202-234-4700
Special Libraries Association, New York Chapter	212-439-7290	Fax 512-328-8852
Special Libraries Association, San Andreas-San Francisco Bay Chapter	415-528-7766	415-604-3140
Special Libraries Association, Southern California Chapter	818-795-2145	818-302-8966; fax 818-302-8983
University of Western Ontario Faculty of Communications and Open Learning	519-661-3542	519-661-2111 ext. 8494; fax 519-661-3506

1. Weekly printed listing sent on receipt of stamps and mailing labels.
2. Cosponsored by the Special Libraries Association Illinois Chapter and the Illinois Library Association.
3. Includes listings for the states of Arizona, Colorado, Kansas, Montana, Nebraska, Nevada, North Dakota, Oklahoma, South Dakota, Utah, and Wyoming, and paid listings from out-of-region institutions—$10/week.
4. Sponsored by the Pennsylvania Library Association; also accepts paraprofessional out-of-state listings. Fee for nonmembers.

Specialized Library Associations and Groups

ACCESS, 1001 Connecticut Ave. N.W., Suite 838, Washington, DC 20036, 202-785-4233, fax 202-785-4212, e-mail commjobs@aol.com, World Wide Web http://www.essential.org/access: Comprehensive national resource on employment, voluntary service, and career development in the nonprofit sector.

Promotes involvement in public issues by providing specialized employment publications and services for job seekers and serves as a resource to nonprofit organizations on recruitment, diversity, and staff development.

Advanced Information Management, 444 Castro St., Suite 320, Mountain View, CA 94041, 415-965-7900, fax 650-965-7907, e-mail aimno.aimusa@juno. com, World Wide Web http://www.aimusa.com/hotjobs.html: Placement agency that specializes in library and information personnel. Offers work on a temporary, permanent, and contract basis for both professional librarians and paraprofessionals in the special, public, and academic library marketplace. Supplies consultants who can work with special projects in libraries or manage library development projects. Offices in Southern California (900 Wilshire Blvd., Suite 1424, Los Angeles, CA 90017, 213-489-9800, fax 213-489-9802) as well as in the San Francisco Bay Area. There is no fee to applicants.

American Association of Law Libraries Career Hotline, 53 W. Jackson Blvd., Suite 940, Chicago, IL 60604, 312-939-4764: Full listings of all current placement ads are available by fax from the AALL Fax-on-Demand service (call 732-544-5901 and request document 730) or at the Web site (http://www.aallnet.org). To place an ad, call the membership coordinator at 312-94904764, ext. 10.

American Libraries "Career LEADS," c/o *American Libraries,* 50 E. Huron St., Chicago, IL 60611: Classified job pages in each monthly issue of *American Libraries* magazine list some 100 job openings grouped by type, plus "Late Job Notices" added near press time as space and time permits. Subsections include "Positions Wanted," "Librarians' Classified," joblines, and regional salary scales. Also contains "ConsultantBase" four times annually (see below).

American Libraries ConsultantBase (CBase): An *American Libraries* service that helps match professionals offering library/information expertise with institutions seeking it. Published quarterly, CBase appears in the Career LEADS section of the January, April, June, and October issues of *American Libraries*. Rates: $5.50/line classified, $55/inch display. Inquiries should be made to Jon Kartman, LEADS Editor, *American Libraries*, 50 E. Huron St., Chicago, IL 60611, 312-280-4211, e-mail careerleads@ALA.org.

American Library Association, Association of College and Research Libraries, 50 E. Huron St., Chicago, IL 60611-2795, 312-280-2513: Classified advertising appears each month in *College & Research Libraries News*. Ads appearing in the print *C&RL News* are also posted to C&RL NewsNet, an abridged electronic edition of *C&RL News* accessible on the Web at http://www.ala.org/acrl/c&rlnew2.html.

American Library Association, Office for Human Resource Development and Recruitment (HRDR), 50 E. Huron St., Chicago, IL 60611, 312-280-4279 (World Wide Web http://www.ala.org/hrdr/placemnt.html): A placement service is provided at each Annual Conference (June or July) and Midwinter Meeting (January or February). Request job seeker or employer registration forms prior to each conference. Persons not able to attend can register with the service and can also purchase job and job seeker listings sent directly from the conference site. Information included when requesting registration forms. Handouts on interviewing, preparing a résumé, and other job-search information are available from ALA/HRDR.

In addition to the ALA conference placement center, ALA division national conferences usually include a placement service. See the *American Libraries* Datebook for dates of upcoming divisional conferences, since these are not held every year. ALA provides Web site job postings from *American Libraries*, C&RL NewsNet, LITA Job Site, and its conference placement services on its library education and employment menu page at http://www.ala.org. Also listed is "Library Job Postings on the Internet," compiled by Sarah L. Nesbeitt.

American Society for Information Science, 8720 Georgia Ave., No. 501, Silver Spring, MD 20910-3602, 301-495-0900, fax 301-495-0810, e-mail asis@asis. org: An active placement service is operated at ASIS Annual Meetings (usually October; locales change). All conference attendees (both ASIS members and nonmembers), as well as ASIS members who cannot attend the conference, are eligible to use the service to list or find jobs. Job listings are also accepted from employers who cannot attend the conference. Interviews are arranged. Throughout the year, current job openings are listed in *ASIS JOBLINE*, a monthly publication sent to all members and available to nonmembers on request (send a stamped, self-addressed envelope).

Art Libraries Society/North America (ARLIS/NA), c/o Executive Director, 1550 S. Coast Hwy., Suite 201, Laguna Beach, CA 92651, 800-892-7547, fax 919-376-3456, e-mail membership@arlisna.org: Art information and visual resources curator jobs are listed in *ARLIS/NA UPDATE* (six times a year) and a job registry is maintained at ARLIS/NA headquarters. Any employer may list a job with the registry, but only members may request job information. Listings also available on the ARLIS-L listserv and Web site. Call ARLIS/NA headquarters for registration and/or published information.

Asian/Pacific American Libraries Newsletter, c/o Sandra Yamate, Polychrome Publishing Corp., 4509 N. Francisco, Chicago, IL 60626, 773-478-4455, fax 773-478-0786: This quarterly includes some job ads. Free to members of Asian/ Pacific American Librarians Association.

Association for Library and Information Science Education, Box 7640, Arlington, VA 22207, 703-243-8040, fax 703-243-4551, World Wide Web http:// www.alise.org: Provides placement service at Annual Conference (January or February) for library and information studies faculty and administrative positions.

Association for Educational Communications and Technology, 1800 N. Stonelake Dr., Suite Z, Bloomington, IN 47404, 812-335-7675, fax 812-335-7678, e-mail aect@aect.org: Maintains a placement listing on the AECT Web site (http://www.aect.org) and provides a placement service at the annual convention. Free to all registrants.

Black Caucus Newsletter, c/o George C. Grant, Editor, Rollins College, 1000 Holt Ave. No. 2654, Winter Park, FL 32789, 407-646-2676, fax 407-646-2546, e-mail bcnews@rollins.edu: Lists paid advertisements for vacancies. Free to members, $10/year to others. Published bimonthly by Four-G Publishers, Inc. News accepted continuously. Biographies, essays, books, and reviews of interest to members are invited.

C. Berger Group, Inc. (CBG), 327 E. Gundersen Dr., Carol Stream, IL 60188, 630-653-1115, 800-382-4222, fax 630-653-1691, e-mail cberger@cberger.com, World Wide Web http://www.cberger.com: CBG conducts nationwide executive searches to fill permanent management, supervisory, and director positions in libraries, information centers, and other organizations nationwide. Direct-hire and temp-to-hire services are also available. Other employment services include supplying professional and support-staff-level temporary workers and contract personnel for short- and long-term assignments in special, academic, and public libraries in Illinois, Indiana, Georgia, Texas, Wisconsin, and other states. CBG also provides library and records management consulting services and direction and staff to manage projects for clients both on site and off site.

Canadian Library Association, 200 Elgin St., Suite 602, Ottawa, ON K2P 1L5, 613-232-9625: Publishes career ads in *Feliciter* magazine. CASLIS division offers job bank service in several cities. Operates Jobmart at the annual conference in June.

Carney, Sandoe & Associates, 136 Boylston St., Boston, MA 02116, 800-225-7986, fax 617-542-9400, World Wide Web http://www.CarneySandoe.com: An educational recruitment firm that places teachers and administrative personnel in private, independent schools across the United States and in other countries. Has placed more than 7,000 teachers and administrators in independent schools since 1977 and has thousands of positions available in all primary and secondary subjects each year. All fees paid by the hiring schools; services are free to the candidate. Teacher certification is not necessary.

Catholic Library Association (CLA), 9009 Carter St., Allen Park, MI 48101: Personal and institutional members of the association are given free space (35 words) to advertise for jobs or to list job openings in *Catholic Library World* (four issues a year). Others may advertise. Contact advertising coordinator for rates.

Chinese-American Librarians Association Newsletter, c/o Sha-Li Zhang, Head of Technical Services, Wichita State University Libraries, Wichita, KS 67260: Job listings in newsletter issued in February, June, and October. Free to members.

Council on Library/Media Technicians, Inc. (COLT), c/o Membership Chair Julia Ree, Box 52057, Riverside, CA 92517-3057, World Wide Web http://library.ucr.edu/COLT/: *COLT Newsletter* appears bimonthly in *Library Mosaics*. Personal dues: U.S. $35, foreign $60, students $30; Institutions: U.S. $60, foreign $85.

Gossage Regan Associates, Inc., 25 W. 43rd St., New York, NY 10036, 212-869-3348, fax 212-997-1127: An executive search firm specializing in the recruitment of library directors and other library/information-handling organization top management. About 50 nationwide searches have been conducted since 1983 for public, academic, and large specialized libraries in all regions. Salary limitation: $70,000 up. Library Executive Recruiters: Wayne Gossage, Joan Neumann. **Wontawk Gossage Associates**, 25 W. 43rd St., New York, NY 10036, 212-869-3348, fax 212-997-1127, and 304 Newbury St., No. 314, Boston, MA 02115, 617-867-9209, fax 617-437-9317: Temporary, long-term, and temporary-to-permanent assignments in the New York/New Jersey/Connecticut and Boston metropolitan areas in all types of libraries/information management, professional and support, all levels of responsibility, all skills. The original library temporaries firm, since 1980, as Gossage Regan. Director of Staffing Services: Sarah Warner.

Independent Educational Services (IES), 1101 King St., Suite 305, Alexandria, VA 22314, 800-257-5102, 703-548-9700, fax 703-548-7171, World Wide Web http://www.ies-search.org: IES is a nonprofit faculty and administrative placement agency for independent elementary and secondary schools across the country. Qualified candidates must possess an MLS degree and some experience in a school setting working with students. Jobs range from assistant librarians and interns to head librarians and rebuilding entire libraries/multimedia centers. Regional offices in Boston and San Francisco.

Labat-Anderson, Inc., 8000 Westpark Dr., No. 400, McLean, VA 22102, 703-506-9600, fax 703-506-4646: One of the largest providers of library and records management services to the federal government. Supports various federal agencies in 27 states, with many positions located in the Washington, D.C., Atlanta, and San Francisco areas. Résumés and cover letters will gladly be accepted from librarians with an ALA-accredited MLS and records managers, or from applicants with library and/or records management experience, for full- and part-time employment.

The Library Co-Op, Inc., 3840 Park Ave., Suite 107, Edison, NJ 08820, 732-906-1777 or 800-654-6275, fax 732-906-3562, e-mail librco@compuserve.com: The company is licensed as both a temporary and permanent employment agency and supplies consultants to work in a wide variety of information settings and functions from library moving to database management, catalog maintenance, reference, retrospective conversion, and more. Recent developments include the forming of two new divisions. LAIRD Consulting provides a full range of automation expertise for hardware, software, LANS, and WANS and is a reseller of INMAGIC software for Windows 95/98 and NT. The second new division is ABCD Filing Services. The company also hired two space planning specialists.

Library Management Systems, Corporate Pointe, Suite 755, Culver City, CA 90230, 310-216-6436, 800-567-4669, fax 310-649-6388, e-mail LMS@ix. netcom.com; and 3 Bethesda Metro Center, Suite 700, Bethesda, MD 20814, 301-961-1984, fax 301-652-6240, e-mail LMSDC@ix.netcom.com: LMS has been providing library staffing, recruitment, and consulting to public and special libraries and businesses since 1983. It organizes and manages special libraries; designs and implements major projects (including retrospective conversions, automation studies, and records management); performs high-quality cataloging outsourcing; and furnishes contract staffing to all categories of information centers. LMS has a large database of librarians and library assistants on call for long- and short-term projects and provides permanent placement at all levels.

Library Mosaics, Box 5171, Culver City, CA 90231, 310-645-4998: *Library Mosaics* magazine is published bimonthly and accepts listings for library/media support staff positions. However, correspondence relating to jobs cannot be handled.

Medical Library Association, 65 E. Wacker Pl., Suite 1900, Chicago, IL 60601-7298, 312-419-9094, ext. 29, World Wide Web http://www.mlanet.org: *MLA News* (10 issues a year, June/July and November/December combined issues) lists positions wanted and positions available in its Employment Opportunities column. The position available rate is $2.80 per word. Up to 50 free words for MLA members plus $2.45 per word over 50 words. Members and nonmembers may rerun ads once in the next consecutive issue for $25. All "positions available" advertisements must list a minimum salary; a salary range is preferred.

Positions wanted rates are $1.50 per word for nonmembers, $1.25 per word for members with 100 free words; $1.25 will be charged for each word exceeding 100. MLA also offers a placement service at the annual meeting each spring. Job advertisements received for *MLA News* are posted to the MLANET Jobline.

Music Library Association, c/o Elisabeth H. Rebman, MLA Placement Officer, 1814 Pine Grove Ave., Colorado Springs, CO 80906-2930, 719-475-1960, e-mail erebman@library.berkeley.edu, World Wide Web http://www.musiclibraryassoc. org/se_job.htm: Monthly job list ($20/year individuals, $25 organizations), from: MLA Business Office, Box 487, Canton, MA 02021, 781-828-8450, fax 781-828-8915, e-mail acadsvc@aol.com.

Pro Libra Associates, Inc., 6 Inwood Pl., Maplewood, NJ 07040, 201-762-0070, 800-262-0070, e-mail prolibra-2@mail.idt.net. A multi-service library firm specializing in personnel placement (permanent and temporary), consulting, management, and project support for libraries and information centers. Has for more than 24 years provided personnel services to catalog, inventory, rearrange, and staff libraries and information centers in corporate, academic, and public institutions.

REFORMA, National Association to Promote Library Service to Latinos and the Spanish-Speaking, Box 832, Anaheim, CA 92815-0832: Those wishing to do direct mailings to the REFORMA membership of 900-plus may obtain mailing labels arranged by zip code for $100. Contact Al Milo, 714-738-6383. Job ads are also published quarterly in the *REFORMA Newsletter*. For rate information, contact Alma Garcia, 510-430-2021, e-mail almag@mills.edu.

Society of American Archivists, 527 S. Wells St., 5th fl., Chicago, IL 60607-3922, fax 312-922-1452, e-mail info@archivists.org, World Wide Web http://www.archivists.org: *Archival Outlook* is sent (to members only) six times annually and contains features about the archival profession and other timely pieces on courses in archival administration, meetings, and professional opportunities (job listings). The Online Employment Bulletin is a weekly listing of professional opportunities posted on the SAA Web site. The SAA Employment Bulletin is a bimonthly listing of job opportunities available to members by subscription for $24 a year, and to nonmembers for $10 per issue. Prepayment is required.

Special Libraries Association, 1700 18th St. N.W., Washington, DC 20009-2508, 202-234-4700, fax 202-265-9317, e-mail sla@sla.org, World Wide Web http://www.sla.org: SLA maintains a telephone jobline, SpeciaLine, 202-234-4700, ext. 1, operating 24 hours a day, seven days a week. Most SLA chapters have employment chairs who act as referral persons for employers and job seekers. Several SLA chapters have joblines. The association's monthly magazine, *Information Outlook*, carries classified advertising. SLA offers an employment clearinghouse and career advisory service during its annual conference, held in June. SLA also provides a discount to members using the résumé evaluation service offered through Advanced Information Management. A "Guide to Career Opportunities" is a resource kit for $20 (SLA members, $15); "Getting a Job: Tips and Techniques" is free to unemployed SLA members. The SLA Job Bulletin Board, a computer listserv, is organized by Indiana University staff. Subscribe by sending the message *subscribe SLAJOB (first name, last name)* to listserv@iubvm.ucs.indiana.edu.

TeleSec CORESTAFF, Information Management Division, 11160 Veirs Mill Rd., Suite 414, Wheaton, MD 20902, 301-949-4097, fax 301-949-8729, e-mail library@corestaff.com: Offers a variety of opportunities to start a library career in the Washington, D.C., area, including direct hire, temporary, temp-to-hire, and contract positions. Positions are in the major federal agencies, law firms, corporations, associations, and academic institutions of metropolitan Washington. TeleSec CORESTAFF has been a leader in the staffing industry since its founding in 1948. See the Web site (http://www.corestaff.com/searchlines/) for library openings and to register online.

Tuft & Associates, Inc., 1209 Astor St., Chicago, IL 60610, 312-642-8889, fax 312-642-8883: Specialists in nationwide executive searches for administrative posts in libraries and information centers.

State Library Agencies

In addition to the joblines mentioned previously, some state library agencies issue lists of job openings within their areas. These include: Colorado (weekly, sent on receipt of stamps and mailing labels; also available via listserv and Access Colorado Library and Information Network—ACLIN; send SASE for access); Indiana (monthly on request) 317-232-3697, or 800-451-6028 (Indiana area), e-mail ehubbard@statelib.lib.in.us; Iowa (Joblist, monthly on request), e-mail awettel@mail.lib.state.ia.us; Mississippi (Library Job Opportunities, monthly); and Nebraska.

State libraries in several states have electronic bulletin board services that list job openings. Web addresses are: Colorado http://www.aclin.org (also lists out-of-state jobs); District of Columbia (Metropolitan Washington Council of Government Libraries Council) http://www.mwcog.org/ic/jobline.html; Florida http://www.dos.state.fl.us/dlis/jobs.html; Georgia http://www.public.lib.ga.us/pls/job-bank; Idaho http://www.lili.org/staff/jobs.htm; Indiana http://www.statelib.lib.in.us/www/ldo/posopl6.html; Iowa http://www.silo.lib.ia.us/joblist.html; Kentucky http://www.kdla.state.ky.us/libserv/jobline.htm; Louisiana http://www.smt.state.lib.la.us/publications/jobs.htm; Massachusetts http://www.mlin.lib.ma.us; Montana http://www.jsd.dli.state.mt.us/; Nebraska http://www.nlc.state.ne.us/libjob; North Carolina http://www.statelibrary.dcr.state.nc.us/jobs/jobs.htm (both professional and paraprofessional library positions); Oklahoma (via modem) 405-524-4089; South Carolina http://www.state.sc.us/scs/lion.html (or via telnet at leo.scsl.state.sc.us, log in as "ebbs"); Tennessee http://toltec.lib.utk.edu/~tla/; Texas http://www.tsl.state.tx.us; Virginia http://www.lva.lib.va.us; Washington http://www.statelib.wa.gov.) In Pennsylvania, the listserv is maintained by Commonwealth Libraries. Arizona offers a jobline service at the e-mail address tcorkery@lib.az.us.

On occasion, the following state library newsletters or journals will list vacancy postings: Alabama (*Cottonboll*, quarterly); Alaska (*Newspoke*, bimonthly); Arizona (*Arizona Libraries NewsWeek*); Indiana (*Focus on Indiana Libraries*, 11/year); Iowa (*Joblist*); Kansas (*Kansas Libraries*, monthly); Louisiana (*Library Communique*, monthly); Minnesota (*Minnesota Libraries News*, monthly); Nebraska (*NCompass*, quarterly); New Hampshire (*Granite State Libraries*, bimonthly); New Mexico (*Hitchhiker*, weekly); Tennessee (*TLA Newsletter*, bimonthly); Utah (*Directions for Utah Libraries*, monthly); and Wyoming (*Outrider*, monthly).

Many state library agencies will refer applicants informally when vacancies are known to exist, but do not have formal placement services. The following states primarily make referrals to public libraries only: Alabama, Arizona, Arkansas, California, Louisiana, Pennsylvania, South Carolina (institutional also), Tennessee, Utah, Vermont, and Virginia. Those that refer applicants to all types of libraries are: Alaska, Delaware, Florida, Georgia, Hawaii, Idaho, Kansas, Kentucky, Maine, Maryland, Mississippi, Montana, Nebraska, Nevada (largely public and academic), New Hampshire, New Mexico, North Carolina, North Dakota, Ohio, Pennsylvania, Rhode Island, South Dakota, Vermont, West Virginia (on Pennsylvania Jobline, public, academic, special), and Wyoming.

The following state libraries post library vacancy notices for all types of libraries on a bulletin board: California, Connecticut, Florida, Georgia, Hawaii, Illinois, Indiana, Iowa, Kentucky, Nevada, New Jersey, New York, Ohio, Oklahoma, Pennsylvania, South Carolina, South Dakota, Utah, and Washington. [Addresses of the state agencies are found in Part 6 of the *Bowker Annual* and in *American Library Directory—Ed.*]

State and Regional Library Associations

State and regional library associations will often make referrals, run ads in association newsletters, or operate a placement service at annual conferences, in addition to the joblines sponsored by some groups. Referral of applicants when jobs are known is done by the following associations: Arkansas, Delaware, Hawaii, Louisiana, Michigan, Minnesota, Nevada, Pennsylvania, South Dakota, Tennessee, and Wisconsin. Although listings are infrequent, job vacancies are placed in the following association newsletters or journals when available: Alabama (*Alabama Librarian*, 7/year); Alaska (*Newspoke*, bimonthly); Arizona (*Newsletter*, 10/year); Arkansas (*Arkansas Libraries*, 6/year); Connecticut (*Connecticut Libraries*, 11/year); Delaware (*Delaware Library Association Bulletin*, 3/year); District of Columbia (*Intercom*, 11/year); Florida (*Florida Libraries*, 6/year); Indiana (*Focus on Indiana Libraries*, 11/year); Iowa (*Catalyst*, 6/year); Kansas (*KLA Newsletter*, 6 issues/bimonthly); Minnesota (*MLA Newsletter*, 6 issues/bimonthly); Missouri (bimonthly); Mountain Plains (*MPLA Newsletter*, bimonthly, lists vacancies and position wanted ads for individuals and institutions); Nebraska (*NLAQ*); Nevada (*Highroller*, 4/year); New Hampshire (*NHLA* Newsletter, 6/year); New Jersey (*NJLA Newsletter*, 10/year); New Mexico (shares notices via state library's *Hitchhiker*, weekly); New York (*NYLA Bulletin*, 10/year; free for institutional members; $25/1 week, $40/2 weeks, others); Ohio (*ACCESS*, monthly); Oklahoma (*Oklahoma Librarian*, 6/year); Oregon (*OLA Hotline, 24/year);* Rhode Island (*RILA Bulletin*, 6/year); South Carolina (*News and Views*); South Dakota (*Book Marks*, bimonthly); Tennessee (*TLA Newsletter*); Vermont (*VLA News*, 6/year. Mailing address Box 803, Burlington, VT 05402); Virginia (*Virginia Libraries*, quarterly); and West Virginia (*West Virginia Libraries*, 6/year).

The following associations have indicated some type of placement service, although it may only be held at annual conferences: Alabama, California, Connecticut, Georgia, Idaho, Indiana, Iowa, Kansas, Kentucky, Louisiana, Maryland, Massachusetts, New England, New Jersey, New York, North Carolina, Ohio, Oregon, Pacific Northwest, Pennsylvania, South Dakota, Southeastern, Tennessee, Texas, Vermont, Wisconsin, and Wyoming.

The following have indicated they have an electronic source for job postings in addition to voice joblines: Alabama, allaonline@mindspring.com; California, http://www.cla-net.org/html/jobline.html; Connecticut, http://www.lib. uconn.edu/cla; Illinois, http://www.ila.org; Kansas, http://www.skyways.lib.ks. us/kansas/KLA/helpwanted (no charge to list job openings); Minnesota, http://www.libmankato.musu.edu:2000; Missouri, http://www.mlnc.com/~mla; Nebraska, http://www.nlc.state.ne.us/libjob/libjob.html; New Hampshire, http://www.state.nh.us/nhsl/ljob.htm; New Jersey Library Association, http://www.njla.org; Oklahoma, http://www.state.ok.us/~odl/fyi/jobline.htm (e-mail bpetrie@oltn.odl.state.ok.us); Pacific Northwest Library Association, e-mail listserv@wln.com or listserv@ldbsu.idbsu.edu; Texas, http://www.txla.org/jobline/jobline.txt; Virginia, http://www.vla.org; Wisconsin, http://www.wla.lib. wi.us/wlajob.htm.

The following associations have indicated they have no placement service at this time: Colorado, Middle Atlantic Regional Library Federation, Minnesota, Mississippi, Montana, Nebraska, Nevada, New Mexico, North Dakota, Oklahoma, Utah, and West Virginia. [State and regional association addresses are listed in Part 6 of the *Bowker Annual.—Ed.*]

Library and Information Studies Programs

Library and information studies programs offer some type of service for their current students as well as alumni. Most schools provide job-hunting and résumé-writing seminars. Many have outside speakers representing different types of libraries or recent graduates relating career experiences. Faculty or a designated placement officer offer individual advising services or critiquing of résumés.

Of the ALA-accredited library and information studies programs, the following handle placement activities through the program: Alabama, Albany, Alberta, Buffalo (compiles annual graduate biographical listings), British Columbia, Dalhousie, Dominican, Drexel, Hawaii, Illinois, Kent State, Kentucky, Louisiana, McGill, Missouri (College of Education), Pittsburgh (Department of Library and Information Science only), Pratt, Puerto Rico, Queens, Rhode Island, Rutgers, Saint John's, South Carolina, Syracuse, Tennessee, Texas–Austin, Toronto, UCLA, Western Ontario, Wisconsin–Madison, and Wisconsin–Milwaukee.

The central university placement center handles activities for the following schools: California–Berkeley (alumni) and Emporia. However, in most cases, library school faculty will do informal counseling regarding job seeking.

In some schools, the placement services are handled in a cooperative manner; in most cases the university placement center sends out credentials while the library school posts or compiles the job listings. Schools utilizing one or both sources include: Alabama, Albany, Arizona (School of Information Resources and Library Science maintains an e-mail list: jobops@listserv.arizona.edu), Buffalo, Catholic, Dominican, Florida State, Indiana, Iowa (fee for students and recent alumni is $25 a year and includes job bulletins and a service that mails references and résumés to employers), Kent State, Long Island, Maryland, Michigan, Montreal, North Carolina–Chapel Hill, North Carolina–Greensboro, North Carolina Central, North Texas, Oklahoma, Pittsburgh, Queens, Saint John's, San Jose, Simmons, South Florida, Southern Connecticut, Southern Mississippi, Syracuse, Tennessee, Texas Woman's, Washington, Wayne State, and Wisconsin–Milwaukee. In sending out placement credentials, schools vary as to whether they distribute these free, charge a general registration fee, or request a fee for each file or credential sent out.

Schools that have indicated they post job vacancy notices for review but do not issue printed lists are: Alabama, Alberta, Arizona, British Columbia, Buffalo, Catholic, Clark Atlanta, Dalhousie, Drexel, Florida State, Hawaii, Illinois, Indiana, Kent State, Kentucky, Long Island, Louisiana, McGill, Maryland, Missouri, Montreal, North Carolina–Chapel Hill, North Carolina–Greensboro, North Carolina Central, Oklahoma, Pittsburgh, Puerto Rico, Queens, Rutgers, Saint John's, San Jose, Simmons, South Carolina, South Florida, Southern Mississippi, Syracuse (general postings), Tennessee, Texas Woman's, Toronto, UCLA, Washington, Wayne State, Western Ontario, and Wisconsin–Madison.

In addition to job vacancy postings, some schools issue printed listings, operate joblines, have electronic access, or provide database services:

- Albany: Job Placement Bulletin free to SISP students; listserv@cnsibm. albany.edu to subscribe
- Alberta: http://www.ualberta.ca/~jhd1/jobs/
- Arizona: listserv@listserv.arizona.edu to subscribe
- British Columbia: uses BCLA Jobline, 604-683-5354 or 800-661-1445, and BCLA jobpage at http://bcla.bc.ca./jobpage
- Buffalo: two job postings listservs; for alumni, sils-l@listserv.acsu. buffalo.edu, for students, ubmls-l@listserv.acsu.buffalo.edu.
- California–Berkeley: Career Center 510-642-5207
- Clarion: http://www.clarion.edu/academic/edu-humn/newlibsci/jobs
- Dalhousie: listserv for Atlantic Canada jobs, send message saying sub list-joblist to mailserv@ac.dal.ca
- Dominican: Placement News every two weeks, free for six months following graduation, $15/year for students and alumni; $25/year others
- Drexel: http://www.cis.drexel.edu/placement/placement.html
- Emporia: weekly bulletin for school, university, public jobs; separate bulletin for special; $42/6 months; Emporia graduates, $21/6 months
- Florida State
- Hawaii

- Illinois: In partnership with Indiana and Washington, free online placement JOBSearch database available on campus and via access through telnet alexia.lis.uiuc.edu, login: jobs, password: Urbaign; or http://www.carousel.lis.uiuc.edu/~jobs/
- Indiana: http://www.slis.lib.indiana.edu/cfdocs/slisjobs/
- Iowa: http://www.uiowa/edu/~edplace/OnlineCenter/placement.htm ($15/year for registered students and alumni)
- Kentucky: http://www.uky.edu/CommInfoStudies/SLIS/jobs.htm
- Maryland: send subscribe message to listserv@umdd.umd.edu
- Michigan: http://www.si.umich.edu/jobfinder
- Missouri: http://www.coe.missouri.edu
- North Carolina–Chapel Hill: http://ils.unc.edu/ils/web/listervs.html or send subscribe message to listproc@ils.unc.edu to subscribe.
- Oklahoma
- Pittsburgh: http://www.sis/pitt.edu/~lsdept/libjobs.htm
- Pratt: free to students and alumni for full-time/part-time professional positions only
- Rhode Island: monthly, $7.50/year
- Rutgers: http://www.scils.rutgers.edu or send subscribe message to scils-jobs@scils.rutgers.edu
- Saint John's: subscribe message to libis@stjohns.edu or fax to 718-990-2071 (lists jobs in United States, Canada, and abroad)
- Simmons: http://www.simmons.edu/gslis/jobline.html; Simmons also operates the New England Jobline (617-521-2815), which announces professional vacancies in the region
- South Carolina: http://www.libsci.sc.edu/career/job.htm
- South Florida: in cooperation with ALISE
- Southern Connecticut: http://www.scsu.ctstateu.edu/~jobline; printed listing twice a month, mailed to students and alumni free
- Syracuse: sends lists of job openings by e-mail to students
- Texas–Austin: Weekly Placement Bulletin $16/6 mos., $28/yr. by listserv, $26/6 mos., $48/yr. by mail (free to students and alumni for one year following graduation); Texas Jobs Weekly, $16/6 months or $28/year, or see http://www.gslis.utexas.edu/~careers/
- Texas Woman's: http://www.twu.edu/slis/
- Toronto: http://www.fis.utoronto.ca/resources/jobsite
- Washington: send notices to slis@u.washington.edu
- Western Ontario: http://www.uwo.ca/gslis/information (to list positions, call 519-661-2111, ext. 8495)
- Wisconsin–Madison: sends listings from Wisconsin and Minnesota to Illinois for JOBSearch
- Wisconsin–Milwaukee: send subscription message to listserv@slis.uwm.edu

Employers will often list jobs with schools only in their particular geographical area; some library schools will give information to non-alumni regarding their specific locales, but are not staffed to handle mail requests and advice is usually given in person. Schools that have indicated they will allow librarians in their areas to view listings are: Alabama, Albany, Alberta, Arizona, British Columbia, Buffalo, California–Berkeley, Catholic, Clarion, Clark Atlanta, Dalhousie, Dominican, Drexel, Emporia, Florida State, Hawaii, Illinois, Indiana, Iowa, Kent State, Kentucky, Louisiana, McGill, Maryland, Michigan, Missouri, Montreal, North Carolina–Chapel Hill, North Carolina–Greensboro, North Carolina Central, North Texas, Oklahoma, Pittsburgh, Pratt, Puerto Rico, Queens, Rhode Island, Rutgers, Saint John's, San Jose, Simmons, South Carolina, South Florida, Southern Connecticut, Southern Mississippi, Syracuse, Tennessee, Texas–Austin, Texas Woman's, Toronto, UCLA, Washington, Wayne State, Western Ontario, Wisconsin–Madison, and Wisconsin–Milwaukee.

A list of ALA-accredited programs with addresses and telephone numbers can be requested from ALA or found elsewhere in Part 3 of the *Bowker Annual*. Individuals interested in placement services of other library education programs should contact the schools directly.

Federal Employment Information Sources

Consideration for employment in many federal libraries requires establishing civil service eligibility. Although the actual job search is your responsibility, the Office of Personnel Management (OPM) has developed the "USA Jobs" Web site (http://www.usajobs.opm.gov) to assist you along the way. The Web site also has an Online Résumé Builder feature for job seekers to create online résumés specifically designed for applying for federal jobs.

OPM's Career America Connection at 912-757-3000 or 202-606-2700 (TDD Service at 912-744-2299) is "USA Jobs by Phone." This system provides current worldwide federal job opportunities, salary and employee benefits information, special recruitment messages, and more. You can also record your request to have application packages, forms, and other employment-related literature mailed to you. This service is available 24 hours a day, seven days a week.

USA Jobs Touch Screen Computer is a computer-based system utilizing touch-screen technology. These kiosks, found throughout the nation in OPM offices, Federal Office Buildings, and other locations, allow you to access current worldwide federal job opportunities, online information, and more.

Another federal jobs Web site is http://www.fedworld.gov/jobs/jobsearch.html.

Applicants should attempt to make personal contact directly with federal agencies in which they are interested. This is essential in the Washington, D.C., area where more than half the vacancies occur. Most librarian positions are in three agencies: Army, Navy, and Veterans Administration.

There are some "excepted service" agencies that are not required to hire through the usual OPM channels. While these agencies may require the standard forms, they maintain their own employee-selection policies and procedures. Government establishments with positions outside the competitive civil service include: Board of Governors of the Federal Reserve System, Central Intelligence Agency, Defense Intelligence Agency, Department of Medicine and Surgery, Federal Bureau of Investigation, Foreign Service of the United States, General Accounting Office, Library of Congress, National Science Foundation, National Security Agency, Tennessee Valley Authority, U.S. Nuclear Regulatory Commission, U.S. Postal Service; Judicial Branch of the Government, Legislative Branch of the Government, U.S. Mission to the United Nations, World Bank and IFC, International Monetary Fund, Organization of American States, Pan American Health Organization, and United Nations Secretariat.

The Library of Congress, the world's largest and most comprehensive library, is an excepted service agency in the legislative branch and administers its own independent merit selection system. Job classifications, pay, and benefits are the same as in other federal agencies, and qualifications requirements generally correspond to those used by the U.S. Office of Personnel Management. The library does not use registers, but announces vacancies as they become available. A separate application must be submitted for each vacancy announcement. For most professional positions, announcements are widely distributed and open for a minimum period of 30 days. Qualifications requirements and ranking criteria are stated on the vacancy announcement. The Library of Congress Human Resources Operations Office is located in the James Madison Memorial Building, 101 Independence Ave. S.E., Washington, DC 20540, 202-707-5620.

Additional General and Specialized Job Sources

Affirmative Action Register, 8356 Olive Blvd., St. Louis, MO 63132: The goal is to "provide female, minority, handicapped, and veteran candidates with an opportunity to learn of professional and managerial positions throughout the nation and to assist employers in implementing their Equal Opportunity Employment programs." Free distribution of a monthly bulletin is made to leading businesses, industrial and academic institutions, and over 4,000 agencies that recruit qualified minorities and women, as well as to all known female, minority, and handicapped professional organizations, placement offices, newspapers, magazines, rehabilitation facilities, and over 8,000 federal, state, and local governmental employment units with a total readership in excess of 3.5 million (audited). Individual mail subscriptions are available for $15 per year. Librarian listings are in most issues. Sent free to libraries on request.

The Chronicle of Higher Education (published weekly with breaks in August and December), 1255 23rd St. N.W., Suite 700, Washington, DC 20037, 202-466-1055; fax 202-296-2691: Publishes a variety of library positions each week, including administrative and faculty jobs. Job listings are searchable by specific categories, keywords, or geographic location on the Internet at http://Chronicle.com/jobs.

Academic Resource Network On-Line Database (ARNOLD), 4656 W. Jefferson, Suite 140, Fort Wayne, IN 46804: This World Wide Web interactive database (http://www.arnold.snybuf.edu) helps faculty, staff, and librarians to identify partners for exchange or collaborative research.

School Libraries: School librarians often find that the channels for locating positions in education are of more value than the usual library ones, for instance, contacting county or city school superintendent offices. Other sources include university placement offices that carry listings for a variety of school system jobs. A list of commercial teacher agencies may be obtained from the National Association of Teachers' Agencies, Dr. Eugene Alexander, CPC, CTC, Treas., c/o G. A. Agency, 524 South Ave. E., Cranford, NJ 07016-3209, 908-272-2080, fax 908-272-2080, World Wide Web http://www.jobsforteachers.com.

Overseas

Opportunities for employment in foreign countries are limited and immigration policies of individual countries should be investigated. Employment for Americans is virtually limited to U.S. government libraries, libraries of U.S. firms doing worldwide business, and American schools abroad. Library journals from other countries will sometimes list vacancy notices. Some persons have obtained jobs by contacting foreign publishers or vendors directly. Non-U.S. government jobs usually call for foreign language fluency. Another source is the librarian job vacancy postings at http://bubl.ac.uk/news/jobs, a listing of U.S. and foreign jobs collected by the Bulletin Board for Libraries.

Council for International Exchange of Scholars (CIES), 3007 Tilden St. N.W., Suite 5M, Washington, DC 20008-3009, 202-686-7877, e-mail cies1@ciesnet.cies.org, World Wide Web http://www.cies.org: Administers U.S. government Fulbright awards for university lecturing and advanced research abroad; usually 10–15 awards per year are made to U.S. citizens who are specialists in library or information sciences. In addition, many countries offer awards in any specialization of research or lecturing. Lecturing awards usually require university or college teaching experience. Several opportunities exist for professional librarians as well. Applications and information may be obtained, beginning in March each year, directly from CIES. Worldwide application deadline is August 1.

Department of Defense, Dependents Schools, Recruitment Unit, 4040 N. Fairfax Dr., Arlington, VA 22203, 703-696-3068, fax 703-696-2697, e-mail recruitment@odeddodea.edu: Overall management and operational responsibilities for the education of dependent children of active duty U.S. military personnel and Department of Defense civilians who are stationed in foreign areas. Also responsible for teacher recruitment. For complete application brochure, write to above address. The latest edition of *Overseas Opportunities for Educators* is available and provides information on educator employment opportunities in over 167 schools worldwide. The schools are operated on military installations for the children of U.S. military and civilian personnel stationed overseas.

International Schools Services (ISS), Box 5910, Princeton, NJ 08543, 609-452-0990: Private, not-for-profit organization founded in 1955 to serve American schools overseas other than Department of Defense schools. These are American, international elementary and secondary schools enrolling children of business and diplomatic families living abroad. ISS services to overseas schools include recruitment and recommendation of personnel, curricular and administrative guidance, purchasing, facility planning, and more. ISS also publishes a comprehensive directory of overseas schools and a bimonthly newsletter, *NewsLinks*, for those interested in the intercultural educational community. Information regarding these publications and other services may be obtained by writing to the above address.

Peace Corps, 1111 20th St. N.W., Washington, DC 20526: Volunteer opportunities exist for those holding MA/MS or BA/BS degrees in library science with one year of related work experience. Two-year tour of duty. U.S. citizens only. Living allowance, health care, transportation, and other benefits provided. Write for additional information and application or call 800-424-8580.

Search Associates, Box 922, Jackson, MI 49204-0922, 517-768-9250, fax 517-768-9252, e-mail JimAmbrose@compuserve.com, World Wide Web http://www.search-associates.com: A private organization composed of former overseas school directors who organize about ten recruitment fairs (most occur in February) to place teachers, librarians, and administrators in about 400 independent K–12 American/international schools around the world. These accredited schools, based on the American model, range in size from under 40 to more than 4,000 and serve the children of diplomats and businessmen from dozens of countries. They annually offer highly attractive personal and professional opportunities for experienced librarians.

Overseas Exchange Programs

Most international exchanges are handled by direct negotiation between interested parties. A few libraries have established exchange programs for their own staff. In order to facilitate exchange arrangements, the *IFLA Journal* (issued January, May, August, and October/November) lists persons wishing to exchange positions outside their own country. All listings must include the following information: full name, address, present position, qualifications (with year of obtaining), language, abilities, preferred country/city/library, and type of position. Send to International Federation of Library Associations and Institutions (IFLA) Secretariat, c/o Koninklijkebibliotheek, Pn Willem-Alexanderhof S. 2595 BE, The Hague, Netherlands, fax 31-70-3834827, e-mail ifla@ifla.org, World Wide Web http://www.ifla.org.

LIBEX Bureau for International Staff Exchange, c/o A. J. Clark, Thomas Parry Library, University of Wales, Aberystwyth, Llanbadarn Fawr, Ceredigion SY23 3AS, Wales, 011-44-1970-622417, fax 011-44-1970-622190, e-mail parrylib@aber.ac.uk, World Wide Web http://www.aber.ac.uk/tplwww/parry.html. Assists in two-way exchanges for British librarians wishing to work abroad and for librarians from the United States, Canada, EC countries, and Commonwealth and other countries who wish to undertake exchanges.

Using Information Skills in Nonlibrary Settings

A great deal of interest has been shown in using information skills in a variety of ways in nonlibrary settings. These jobs are not usually found through the regular library placement sources, although many library and information studies programs are trying to generate such listings for their students and alumni. Job listings that do exist may not call specifically for "librarians" by that title so that ingenuity may be needed to search out jobs where information management skills are needed. Some librarians are working on a freelance basis, offering services to businesses, alternative schools, community agencies, legislators, etc.; these opportunities are usually not found in advertisements but created by developing contacts and publicity over a period of time. A number of information-brokering businesses have developed from individual freelance experiences. Small companies or other organizations often need "one-time" service for organizing files or collections, bibliographic research for special projects, indexing or abstracting, compilation of directories, and consulting services. Bibliographic networks and online database companies are using librarians as information managers, trainers, researchers, systems and database analysts, online services managers, etc. Jobs in this area are sometimes found in library network newsletters or data processing journals. Librarians can also be found working in law firms as litigation case supervisors (organizing and analyzing records needed for specific legal cases); with publishers as sales representatives, marketing directors, editors, and computer services experts; with community agencies as adult education coordinators, volunteer administrators, grants writers, etc.

Classifieds in *Publishers Weekly* and the *National Business Employment Weekly* may lead to information-related positions. One might also consider reading the Sunday classified ad sections in metropolitan newspapers in their entirety to locate descriptions calling for information skills but under a variety of job titles.

The *Burwell World Directory of Information Brokers* is an annual publication that lists information brokers, freelance librarians, independent information specialists, and institutions that provide services for a fee. There is a minimal charge for an annual listing. The Burwell Directory Online is searchable free on the Internet at http://www.burwell.com, and a CD-ROM version is available. Burwell can be reached at Burwell Enterprises, 5619 Plumtree Dr., Dallas, TX 75252-4928, 281-537-9051, fax 281-537-8332, e-mail burwellinfo@burwellinc. com. Also published is a bimonthly newsletter, *Information Broker* ($40, foreign postage, $15), that includes articles by, for, and about individuals and companies in the fee-based information field, book reviews, a calendar of upcoming events, and issue-oriented articles. A bibliography and other publications on the field of information brokering are also available.

The Association of Independent Information Professionals (AIIP) was formed in 1987 for individuals who own and operate for-profit information companies. Contact AIIP Headquarters at 212-779-1855.

A growing number of publications are addressing opportunities for librarians in the broader information arena.

Among articles in periodicals is "You Can Take Your MLS Out of the Library," by Wilda W. Williams (*Library Journal*, Nov. 1994, pp. 43–46).

Opening New Doors: Alternative Careers for Librarians, edited by Ellis Mount (Washington, D.C.: Special Libraries Association, 1993) provides profiles of librarians who are working outside libraries. *Extending the Librarian's Domain: A Survey of Emerging Occupation Opportunities for Librarians and Information Professionals* by Forest Woody Horton, Jr. (Washington, D.C.: Special Libraries Association, 1994) explores information job components in a variety of sectors.

Careers in Electronic Information by Wendy Wicks (1997, 184p.) and *Guide to Careers in Abstracting and Indexing* by Wendy Wicks and Ann Marie Cunningham (1992, 126p.), are available for $29 from the National Federation of Abstracting & Information Services, 1518 Walnut St., Philadelphia, PA 19102, 215-893-1561, e-mail nfais@nfais.org, World Wide Web http://www.nfais.org.

The American Society of Indexers, 11250 Roger Bacon Dr., Suite 8, Reston, VA 20190-5202, 703-234-4147, fax 703-435-4390, e-mail info@asindexing.org, World Wide Web http://www.ASIndexing.org, has a number of publications that would be useful for individuals who are interested in indexing careers.

Temporary/Part-Time Positions

Working as a substitute librarian or in temporary positions may be considered to be an alternative career path as well as an interim step while looking for a regular job. This type of work can provide valuable contacts and experience. Organizations that hire library workers for part-time or temporary jobs include Advanced Information Management, 444 Castro St., Suite 320, Mountain View, CA 94041 (650-965-7799), or 900 Wilshire Blvd., Suite 1424, Los Angeles, CA 90017 (213-489-9800); C. Berger and Company, 327 E. Gundersen Dr., Carol Stream, IL 60188 (630-653-1115 or 800-382-4222); Gossage Regan Associates, Inc., 25 W. 43 St., New York, NY 10036 (212-869-3348) and Wontawk Gossage Associates, 304 Newbury St., Suite 304, Boston, MA 02115 (617-867-9209); Information Management Division, 1160 Veirs Mill Rd., Suite 414, Wheaton, MD 20902 (301-949-4097); The Library Co-Op, Inc., 3840 Park Ave., Suite 107, Edison, NJ 08820 (908-906-1777 or 800-654-6275); Library Management Systems, Corporate Pointe, Suite 755, Culver City, CA 90230 (310-216-6436 or 800-567-4669) and Three Bethesda Metro Center, Suite 700, Bethesda, MD 20814 (301-961-1984); and Pro Libra Associates, Inc., 6 Inwood Place, Maplewood, NJ 07040 (201-762-0070).

Part-time jobs are not always advertised, but often found by canvassing local libraries and leaving applications.

Job Hunting in General

Wherever information needs to be organized and presented to patrons in an effective, efficient, and service-oriented fashion, the skills of librarians can be applied, whether or not they are in traditional library settings. However, it will take considerable investment of time, energy, imagination, and money on the part of an individual before a satisfying position is created or obtained, in a conventional library or another type of information service. Usually, no one method or source of job-hunting can be used alone.

Public and school library certification requirements vary from state to state; contact the state library agency for such information in a particular state. Certification requirements are summarized in *Certification of Public Librarians in the United States*, 4th ed., 1991, from the ALA Office for Library Personnel Resources. A summary of school library/media certification requirements by state is found in *Requirements for Certification of Teachers, Counselors, Librarians and Administrators for Elementary and Secondary Schools*, published annually by the University of Chicago Press. "School Library Media Certification Requirements: 1994 Update" by Patsy H. Perritt also provides a compilation in *School Library Journal*, June 1994, pp. 32–49. State supervisors of school library media services may also be contacted for information on specific states.

Civil service requirements on a local, county, or state level often add another layer of procedures to the job search. Some civil service jurisdictions require written and/or oral examinations; others assign a ranking based on a review of credentials. Jobs are usually filled from the top candidates on a qualified list of applicants. Since the exams are held only at certain time periods and a variety of jobs can be filled from a single list of applicants (e.g., all Librarian I positions regardless of type of function), it is important to check whether a library in which one is interested falls under civil service procedures.

If one wishes a position in a specific subject area or in a particular geographical location, remember those reference skills to ferret information from directories and other tools regarding local industries, schools, subject collections, etc. Directories such as the *American Library Directory*, *Subject Collections*, *Directory of Special Libraries and Information Centers*, and *Directory of Federal Libraries*, as well as state directories or directories of other special subject areas can provide a wealth of information for job seekers. Some state employment offices will include library listings as part of their Job Services department.

Some students have pooled resources to hire a clipping service for a specific time period in order to get classified librarian ads for a particular geographical area. Interesting sources in the library literature are "Employment and Job Search" by Charlie Fox (*Library Mosaics*, v. 10-3. May/June 1999, pp. 5–19; "Have I Got a Job for You" by Joni R. Roberts, *Library Mosaics*, v. 10-3, May/June 1999, pp. 14–15, and "We're Honored that You Applied Here" by Terry Ballard, *Information Today*, v. 15-2, Feb. 1998, p. 42. Other Internet sources not mentioned elsewhere include http://www.careerpath.com.

For information on other job-hunting and personnel matters, or a copy of this guide, contact the ALA Office for Library Personnel Resources, 50 E. Huron St., Chicago, IL 60611.

Placements and Salaries 1998: Beating Inflation Now

Vicki L. Gregory

Director and Associate Professor, School of Library and Information Science, University of South Florida, Tampa

Take the growing need for library and information science (LIS) school graduates and add that to a strong economy. The result: a solid 5.4 percent increase in average starting salaries for 1998 graduates, from $30,270 in 1997 to $31,915.

Also, salary gender equity for library professionals may be approaching, as the tighter job market seems to have weakened residual salary prejudice. As the results of *Library Journal* (*LJ*)'s 48th annual Placements and Salaries Survey show, female 1998 LIS graduates in both the Northeast and Southeast regions actually enjoyed higher average starting salaries than males, a survey first.

As has been the tendency for some years, those new professionals working in technologically oriented jobs garnered higher average starting salaries than those working in areas such as youth services, reference, and cataloging. Salaries for minority graduates rose more slowly than in 1997, perhaps because of the types of jobs taken.

Graduation rates again appear steady. In 1996, 44 schools had reported 4,136 graduates, and in 1997, 46 schools reported 4,370 graduates. Figures for 1998 show 50 schools reporting 4,577 graduates, with women (3,642) accounting for approximately 79.6 percent of this year's graduate pool, and men (935) representing approximately 20.4 percent. (Table 3 shows total graduates and placements by school.)

Job Trends

Table 1 shows the job status—both by region and in total—of those 2,286 graduates of the 49 schools whose graduates reported their job status. Out of all graduates reporting employment in any field, 1,952 (93.2 percent) were employed in some library capacity. Of those 1,952 graduates, 1,811 (about 93 percent) are in permanent or temporary professional positions. About 10 percent of total respondents reported placements in temporary professional positions, which includes part-timers—similar to figures reported in the survey for the last several years.

Of those reporting, 1,590 are working in full-time permanent professional positions (81.5 percent of those employed in libraries), as compared to 1,540 (83.3 percent) in 1997 and 1,383 (89.3 percent) in 1996.

Salaries Keep Rising

The 5.4 percent salary increase ($1,645) for 1998 graduates seems even more significant when compared with the 2.7 percent increase experienced in 1997 and the 1.7 percent increase reported for 1996.

Adapted from *Library Journal*, October 15, 1999.

Because several LIS schools in major metropolitan areas had not participated in the 1997 survey, we also calculated 1998 average salaries for only those schools reporting in 1997 to determine if the current results were skewed by those schools' participation. However, the results were similar: a 5.2 percent average increase.

The rise in salaries also outpaced the cost of living. While the CPI Index increased in 1998 by 2.7 (or 1.7 percent), the *LJ* Salary Index rose a healthy 9.33 (or 5.4 percent) (see Table 5).

For women, the average salary rose 6 percent, a dramatic improvement over the 2.3 percent increase for 1997. For men, the rise was more modest, up 3.2 percent in 1998, compared to a 2.5 percent increase in 1997. Men do continue to enjoy higher average starting salaries than women, except, as noted, in both the Northeast and Southeast regions.

For minority graduates, salaries rose only 2.1 percent ($645), a slowdown from the 6.12 percent rise in 1997. However, compared to 1997, a smaller percentage of 1998 graduates took jobs in higher-paying academic libraries, which may have slowed the increase. Also, more than one-third of minority graduates reporting took jobs in public libraries, which still pay the lowest beginning salaries of the various library types (see Table 8), while in 1997, only 20 percent did so.

As in the past, those graduates employed in technology-related jobs in database management, telecommunications, and automated systems, or as information consultants and webmasters generally enjoy better salaries—about 11 percent higher than the average for all jobs (see Table 6).

Placements Get Easier?

Of the schools commenting on available job openings, 15 reported an increase in the number of openings listed by their placement services or otherwise officially made known to students. Eight schools saw a decrease in their listings, and five schools said the number was steady. Five schools indicated that it was easier to place graduates in 1998 than in 1997, while most said the situation was similar— a good sign, since it had gotten easier for several in 1997. No school reported more difficulty in placing students this year, so it seems that 1998 was a bit more of a graduates' market than either 1997 or 1996.

Most new LIS graduates still tend to find jobs in the same state as their library school: 65.9 percent in 1998, as compared to 64 percent in 1997, and 67 percent in 1996. An additional 17.1 percent on average found jobs in other states of the same region as their library school in 1998, up slightly from the 1997 figure of 15 percent.

Table 4 reflects 1998 placements by library school and type of library. The response rate to this question was considerably lower than in 1997 (1,417 compared to 1,601), so year-to-year comparisons may be less valid. However, reported college and university library placements were down substantially, from 464 (29 percent) in 1997 to 267 (19 percent) in 1998, with public library placements up to 435 (31 percent) in 1998 compared with 375 (23 percent) in 1997. Given

(text continues on page 326)

Table 1 / Status of 1998 Graduates*, Spring 1999

| Region | Number of Schools Reporting | Number of Graduates | Graduates in Library Positions | | | | Graduates in Nonlibrary Positions | Unemployed or Status Unreported |
			Permanent Professional	Temporary Professional	Non-professional	Total		
Northeast	16	840	565	86	54	705	50	85
Southeast	11	335	260	20	18	298	18	19
Midwest	11	590	419	49	44	512	40	38
Southwest	5	300	205	28	15	248	14	38
West	4	186	128	28	5	161	15	10
Canada	2	35	13	10	5	28	5	2
Totals	49	2,286	1,590	221	141	1,952	142	192

* Table based on survey responses from both schools and individual graduates. Figures will necessarily not be fully consistent with some of the other data reported in this study that is based only on overall reporting from schools surveyed. Only a few schools were able to provide individual survey responses from all their 1998 graduates. Tables do not always add up, individually or collectively, because both schools and individuals omitted data in some cases.

Table 2 / Placements and Full-Time Salaries of 1998 U.S. Graduates/Summary by Region

| Region | Number of Placements | Number of Reported Salaries | | | Low | | High | | Average | | | Median | | |
		Women	Men	Total	Women	Men	Women	Men	Women	Men	All	Women	Men	All
Northeast	471	371	78	449	$15,000	$22,000	$80,000	$50,000	$33,677	$32,719	$33,511	$32,000	$31,650	$32,000
Southeast	293	220	56	276	13,000	17,000	64,000	45,000	29,793	29,671	29,768	29,000	29,305	29,058
Midwest	324	241	66	307	12,000	19,750	60,000	58,000	30,949	32,558	31,295	30,000	31,599	30,000
Southwest	162	113	23	136	9,200	22,000	46,000	41,000	29,793	30,745	29,954	29,000	30,000	29,000
West	130	95	27	122	20,000	17,000	72,000	65,000	34,238	36,105	34,651	33,000	34,000	33,000
Canada/Intl.*	17	11	4	15	17,500	28,000	37,420	36,000	27,571	32,525	28,392	26,250	33,050	28,000
Combined (U.S.)	1,380	1,040	250	1,290	9,200	17,000	80,000	65,000	31,852	32,178	31,915	30,000	31,000	30,146

* All international salaries converted to U.S. dollars based on conversion rates for May 19, 1999

Table 3 / 1998 Total Graduates and Placements by School

Schools	Graduates			Employed			Unemployed			Students			Status Unknown		
	Women	Men	Total	Women	Men	Total	Women	Men	Total	Women	Men	Total	Women	Men	Total
Alabama	43	14	57	29	10	39	1	0	1	0	0	0	13	4	17
Arizona	98	13	111	35	5	40	4	3	7	1	1	2	58	4	62
British Columbia	29	8	37	7	3	10	2	1	3	0	0	0	20	4	24
California (UCLA)	39	16	55	12	5	17	0	0	0	1	0	1	26	11	37
Catholic	101	18	119	38	6	44	5	0	5	0	0	0	58	12	70
Clarion	35	7	42	18	4	22	2	0	2	2	1	3	13	2	15
Dalhousie	28	6	34	14	4	18	4	1	5	0	0	0	10	1	11
Dominican	121	23	144	48	9	57	5	1	6	0	0	0	68	13	81
Drexel	80	17	97	54	9	63	5	1	6	1	1	2	20	6	26
Emporia	87	19	106	44	9	53	3	0	3	0	0	0	40	10	50
Florida State	139	19	158	15	2	17	3	0	3	1	0	1	120	17	137
Hawaii	35	12	47	15	3	18	10	1	11	0	0	0	10	8	18
Illinois	77	35	112	46	14	60	1	1	2	1	0	1	29	20	49
Indiana	128	48	176	47	12	59	4	0	4	0	0	0	77	36	113
Iowa	37	13	50	28	10	38	7	2	9	0	1	1	2	0	2
Kent State	113	27	140	55	12	67	6	2	8	0	0	0	52	13	65
Kentucky	80	25	105	25	5	30	3	1	4	1	0	1	51	19	70
Long Island	121	14	135	48	0	48	3	0	3	0	0	0	70	14	84
Louisiana State	59	20	79	36	14	50	1	3	4	2	0	2	20	3	23
Maryland	69	24	93	28	12	40	6	0	6	6	0	6	29	12	41
Michigan	52	22	74	28	7	35	2	0	2	1	0	1	21	15	36
Missouri	53	17	70	18	5	23	1	0	1	0	0	0	34	12	46
N.C. Central	69	14	83	22	7	29	1	0	1	0	0	0	46	7	53
N.C. Chapel Hill	45	13	58	13	2	15	1	0	1	1	0	1	30	11	41

North Texas	82	23	105	34	10	44	2	0	2	1	1	2	45	12	57
Oklahoma	38	4	42	19	4	23	4	0	4	1	1	1	14	0	14
Puerto Rico	9	10	19	9	10	19	0	0	0	0	0	0	0	0	0
Pittsburgh	84	30	114	26	10	36	4	0	4	3	1	4	51	19	70
Pratt	65	21	86	26	9	35	4	2	6	1	0	1	34	10	44
Queens	89	30	119	46	11	57	5	1	6	1	0	1	38	18	56
Rhode Island	56	10	66	32	8	40	8	0	8	1	0	1	15	2	17
Rutgers	114	21	135	42	8	50	3	0	3	1	0	1	68	13	81
St. John's	28	5	33	18	2	20	1	0	1	0	0	0	9	3	11
San Jose	105	29	134	49	11	60	2	0	2	0	0	0	54	18	72
Simmons	163	38	201	113	23	136	7	7	14	2	2	2	41	8	49
South Carolina	113	18	131	37	0	37	4	0	4	2	2	2	70	18	88
South Florida	99	21	120	33	5	38	3	1	4	0	0	0	63	15	78
S. Connecticut	47	17	64	19	8	27	4	1	5	0	0	0	24	8	32
S. Mississippi	34	11	45	16	4	20	1	0	1	0	0	1	17	6	23
SUNY-Albany	63	23	86	29	9	38	2	3	5	1	1	0	32	11	43
SUNY-Buffalo	73	19	92	38	5	43	6	2	8	1	0	1	28	12	42
Syracuse	63	14	77	30	3	33	1	1	2	1	0	1	31	10	41
Tennessee	30	14	44	15	4	19	3	2	5	0	0	0	12	8	20
Texas (Austin)	135	44	179	96	33	129	3	3	6	3	0	3	33	8	41
Texas Woman's	64	5	69	30	2	32	5	0	5	0	0	0	29	3	32
Toronto	n/a	n/a	93	n/a	n/a	35	n/a	n/a	14	0	0	0	n/a	n/a	44
Washington	72	17	89	58	9	67	3	2	5	0	2	2	11	4	15
Wayne State	114	23	137	39	8	47	12	3	15	5	2	7	58	10	68
Wisc. (Madison)	52	15	67	26	13	39	7	1	8	0	0	0	19	1	20
Wisc. (Milwaukee)	n/a	n/a	n/a	34	6	40	5	1	6	1	1	2	n/a	n/a	n/a
Totals	3,530	906	4,529	1,637	384	2,056	179	47	240	41	12	53	1,713	471	2,229

n/a - Data not provided by school.

Table 4 / Placements by Type of Organization

Schools	Public			Elementary & Secondary			College & University			Special			Government			Library Co-op./Network			Vendor			Other			Total		
	Women	Men	Total	Women	Men	Total	Women	Men	Total	Women	Men	Total	Women	Men	Total	Women	Men	Total	Women	Men	Total	Women	Men	Total	Women	Men	Total
Alabama	5	2	7	12	2	14	4	5	9	1	0	1	1	0	1	0	0	0	3	0	3	0	0	0	26	9	35
Arizona	3	0	3	2	0	2	2	0	2	1	0	1	0	0	0	0	0	0	0	0	0	0	0	0	8	0	8
British Columbia	2	0	2	0	0	0	0	1	1	0	2	2	1	0	1	0	0	0	0	0	0	0	0	0	3	3	6
California (UCLA)	4	2	6	0	0	0	0	1	1	5	1	6	0	0	0	0	0	0	0	1	1	1	0	1	10	5	15
Catholic	2	0	2	6	1	7	4	3	7	9	1	10	3	0	3	0	0	0	0	0	0	6	0	6	30	5	35
Clarion	7	3	10	2	0	2	1	1	2	0	0	0	0	0	0	0	0	0	0	1	1	0	0	0	10	4	14
Dalhousie	2	0	2	0	0	0	0	0	0	1	0	1	1	0	1	0	1	1	0	0	0	0	0	0	5	0	5
Dominican	15	3	18	7	0	7	6	3	9	4	1	5	1	0	1	1	0	1	0	0	0	3	1	4	37	8	45
Drexel	6	2	8	5	0	5	1	1	2	6	2	8	1	0	1	0	1	1	0	1	1	5	2	7	24	7	31
Emporia	15	2	17	11	2	13	6	4	10	2	0	2	0	0	0	0	0	0	0	1	1	3	0	3	39	8	47
Florida State	4	1	5	4	0	4	1	0	1	0	0	0	0	0	0	0	0	0	0	1	1	0	1	1	10	2	12
Hawaii	1	0	1	3	0	3	1	1	2	2	0	2	0	0	0	0	0	0	1	1	2	0	0	0	7	2	9
Illinois	12	5	17	2	0	2	10	5	15	5	0	5	2	1	3	0	0	0	1	1	2	3	1	4	35	13	48
Indiana	18	4	22	6	0	6	9	5	14	2	1	3	0	0	0	0	0	0	0	1	1	1	0	1	36	11	47
Iowa	2	1	3	3	1	4	7	2	9	3	0	3	2	0	2	0	0	0	0	0	0	1	1	2	18	5	23
Kent State	19	6	25	13	0	13	3	1	4	3	1	4	0	0	0	1	0	1	0	1	1	1	0	1	41	8	49
Kentucky	6	2	8	7	0	7	3	2	5	2	1	3	0	0	0	0	0	0	0	1	1	0	0	0	19	5	24
Long Island	9	0	9	16	0	16	3	0	3	3	0	3	1	0	1	0	0	0	0	0	0	0	0	0	32	0	32
Louisiana State	6	7	13	12	0	12	7	2	9	3	1	4	0	1	1	0	0	0	1	0	1	0	0	0	29	11	40
Maryland	4	0	4	2	0	2	0	2	2	2	2	4	3	2	5	0	0	0	1	0	1	3	0	3	15	6	21
Michigan	3	1	4	2	0	2	9	1	10	1	2	3	0	0	0	0	1	1	0	0	0	7	3	10	23	7	30
Missouri	4	1	5	3	0	3	2	0	2	2	1	3	1	1	2	0	0	0	2	0	2	0	0	0	14	3	17

School																								Total		
N.C. Central	5	4	9	11	0	11	0	1	1	0	0	0	0	0	0	0	0	0	0	1	1	2	0	2	18	6	24
N.C. Chapel Hill	2	0	2	0	0	0	6	1	7	2	0	2	1	0	1	1	0	1	0	0	0	1	0	1	13	1	14
North Texas	4	3	7	10	0	10	4	3	7	4	2	6	0	1	1	0	0	0	0	1	1	0	0	0	22	10	32
Oklahoma	7	1	8	7	0	7	3	2	5	1	0	1	0	0	0	0	0	0	0	0	0	0	0	0	18	3	21
Pittsburgh	1	1	2	6	0	6	7	2	9	2	1	3	0	0	0	0	0	0	0	2	2	3	0	3	19	6	25
Pratt	7	3	10	2	0	2	2	2	4	10	2	12	0	0	0	0	1	1	0	0	0	0	0	0	21	8	29
Queens	15	4	19	11	1	12	1	3	4	8	1	9	0	0	0	0	0	0	0	2	2	0	0	0	35	11	46
Rhode Island	8	1	9	8	0	8	3	1	4	0	0	0	0	0	0	2	0	2	1	0	1	2	3	5	24	5	29
Rutgers	16	0	16	9	1	10	2	2	4	5	2	7	0	0	0	2	0	2	0	0	0	2	1	3	36	6	42
St. John's	5	0	5	6	0	6	1	0	1	0	1	1	0	0	0	0	0	0	1	0	1	1	0	1	14	1	15
San Jose	13	2	15	4	0	4	3	2	5	7	4	11	1	0	1	1	1	2	1	1	2	1	0	1	31	10	41
Simmons	20	2	22	9	0	9	12	1	13	18	2	20	2	0	2	0	0	0	1	1	2	4	3	7	66	9	75
South Carolina	14	0	14	14	0	14	4	0	4	2	0	2	0	0	0	0	0	0	0	0	0	0	0	0	34	0	34
South Florida	13	1	14	8	0	8	1	1	2	2	2	4	0	0	0	0	0	0	1	0	1	2	0	2	27	4	31
S. Connecticut	7	1	8	6	1	7	1	4	5	0	0	0	0	0	0	0	0	0	0	1	1	0	0	0	14	7	21
S. Mississippi	3	1	4	7	0	7	2	1	3	0	0	0	0	0	0	0	0	0	0	0	0	1	0	1	13	2	15
SUNY-Albany	5	0	5	5	0	5	1	3	4	2	1	3	0	0	0	0	0	0	1	1	2	2	0	2	16	5	21
SUNY-Buffalo	4	2	6	9	0	9	2	1	3	1	1	2	0	0	0	0	0	0	1	1	2	4	0	4	21	5	26
Syracuse	5	0	5	7	0	7	9	2	11	1	1	2	0	0	0	0	0	0	0	0	0	3	0	3	25	3	28
Tennessee	2	0	2	3	1	4	3	0	3	1	0	1	0	0	0	0	0	0	0	1	1	2	1	3	11	3	14
Texas (Austin)	21	3	24	14	2	16	13	5	18	12	5	17	3	3	6	1	0	1	1	6	7	10	3	13	75	27	102
Texas Woman's	2	0	2	2	0	2	3	1	4	2	0	2	0	0	0	0	0	0	1	0	1	11	0	11	21	1	22
Washington	10	2	12	5	0	5	4	0	4	14	0	14	0	0	0	0	0	0	6	1	7	0	1	1	39	4	43
Wayne State	9	2	11	9	0	9	1	0	1	4	0	4	0	0	0	0	0	0	0	0	0	0	1	1	23	3	26
Wisc. (Madison)	4	3	7	3	0	3	5	2	7	2	2	4	0	0	0	1	0	1	0	0	0	1	0	1	16	7	23
Wisc. (Milwaukee)	5	1	6	6	2	8	5	1	6	2	1	3	0	0	0	0	0	0	0	1	1	1	0	1	19	6	25
Total	356	79	435	313	17	330	185	82	267	160	44	204	26	10	36	9	2	11	17	9	26	76	32	108	1,142	275	1,417

(continued from page 320)

the reported increases in average starting salaries for 1998, this discrepancy is difficult to explain, but it may simply reflect incomplete data.

The Graduates Speak

Asked about the placement process and the preparation they received in library school, 86 students responded. One graduate wrote, "Training and experience with the Internet was the only area in which all interviewers expressed an interest. The second most common question was my level of comfort with handling computer problems (as in 'my document won't print.')." Nevertheless, many respondents said that most employers wanted candidates who could master information technology while maintaining the values and skills of traditional librarianship.

Even with the general improvement in salaries, a great majority of respondents indicated that proposed salaries were rigid. Those who reported negotiability said graduate assistantships and internships could nudge up the offer. Though technological skills could help graduates get better offers, respondents cited experience as the key factor, and this naturally put them at a disadvantage.

Asked which library or information science courses had proven to be the most useful or necessary, one student cited "the classes on electronic resources and on telecommunications and the Internet. . . . All the classes I took in library school have been very helpful in one way or another—I wish I had a better background in cataloging, not because I am doing that, but because it would allow me more flexibility in the future."

Some graduates cited theoretical courses as the least useful, but others praised them. Said one graduate, "I truly believe that a strong theoretical background in the issues and practices of librarianship were essential to success at my present job."

Table 5 / Average Salary Index
Starting Library Positions, 1990–1998

Year	Library Schools*	Average Beginning Salary	Dollar Increase in Average Salary	Salary Index	BLS-CPI**
1990	38	$25,306	$725	143.03	130.70
1991	46	25,583	277	144.59	136.20
1992	41	26,666	1,083	150.71	140.50
1993	50	27,116	450	153.26	144.40
1994	43	28,086	970	158.74	148.40
1995	41	28,997	911	163.89	152.50
1996	44	29,480	483	166.62	159.10
1997	43	30,270	790	171.05	161.60
1998	47	31,915	1,645	180.38	164.30

* Includes U.S. schools only.

**U.S. Department of Labor, Bureau of Labor Statistics, Consumer Price Index, All Urban Consumers (CPI-U), U.S. city average, all items, 1982–84=100. The average beginning professional salary for that period was $17,693.

While many stated that they felt adequately prepared, one student wrote, "I think more training on computer networks would have been more useful." Another suggested that LIS schools "consider making courses in computer networking mandatory. If management, reference, and cataloging classes are required . . . librarians should also be prepared to do systems work."

But new jobs concern more than new technologies. Most respondents cited the need for people skills. One wrote, "I would have liked more information on dealing with difficult people. The teachers with whom I work do not understand what is involved in my job. Being assertive usually offends them."

Another noted, "I am in an academic library where there is a huge focus on bibliographic instruction and teaching information literacy. No classes in teaching were provided in library school."

While technical competencies are doubtless vital, one respondent concluded, "I was lucky to land in a program that emphasized the teaching of traditional library values and skills alongside the teaching of new skills and theory."

Table 6 / Salaries of Reporting Professionals by Area of Job Assignment*

Assignment	Number	Percent of Total	Low Salary	High Salary	Average Salary	Median Salary
Acquisitions	12	.9	$15,000	$35,700	$27,683	$27,000
Administration	81	6.3	18,359	65,000	31,912	30,000
Archives	27	2.1	24,000	58,000	32,940	30,000
Automation/ Systems	54	4.2	21,000	53,000	33,378	32,250
Cataloging & Classification	55	4.3	22,000	44,000	29,551	29,200
Circulation	20	1.6	22,000	46,000	30,164	29,500
Collection Development	20	1.6	16,000	50,700	32,344	32,500
Database Management	19	1.5	17,500	65,000	36,915	36,500
Government Documents	5	.4	29,877	40,000	33,009	31,500
Indexing/ Abstracting	6	.5	31,000	70,000	38,400	32,000
Info Consultant	10	.8	30,000	48,000	39,060	39,000
Instruction	20	1.6	27,000	48,000	34,445	34,250
Interlibrary Loans	6	.5	19,700	40,000	28,117	27,000
LAN Manager	4	.3	30,000	37,200	34,300	35,000
Media Specialist	267	20.8	12,459	65,000	33,206	32,000
Reference/ Info Services	407	31.7	15,000	80,000	30,653	30,000
Research	15	1.2	23,000	55,000	34,867	33,000
Solo Librarian	100	7.8	12,000	55,000	32,749	32,000
Tech Services/ Serials	19	1.5	22,000	51,000	32,181	31,197
Telecomm.	4	.3	25,000	35,200	30,300	30,500
Youth Services	113	8.8	13,000	42,000	28,920	29,007
Webmaster	22	1.7	24,000	72,000	38,458	36,250
Total	1,286		$12,000	$80,000	$31,845	$30,091

* Does not include those graduates who did not specify a principal job assignment. Tables do not always add up, individually or collectively, due to omitted data on survey forms.

Table 7 / Placements and Full-Time Salaries of Reporting 1998 Graduates

Schools	Number of Placements	Salaries			Low Salary		High Salary		Average Salary			Median Salary		
		Women	Men	Total	Women	Men	Women	Men	Women	Men	All	Women	Men	All
Alabama	35	25	8	33	$24,000	$27,000	$51,000	$45,000	$35,175	$34,475	$35,005	$35,900	$34,500	$35,000
Arizona	12	11	0	11	9,200	—	56,000	—	31,283	—	31,283	31,700	—	31,700
British Columbia*	6	3	3	6	21,000	28,000	26,250	40,000	24,150	32,700	28,425	25,200	30,100	27,125
California (UCLA)	15	10	5	15	30,000	32,000	38,000	45,000	33,566	35,800	34,311	32,900	33,500	33,000
Catholic	35	28	5	33	23,400	22,000	70,000	37,500	36,008	29,400	35,007	34,000	30,250	33,000
Clarion	14	10	4	14	15,000	23,000	30,900	28,500	25,060	24,750	24,971	26,150	23,750	25,500
Dalhousie*	5	5	0	5	20,000	—	35,000	—	25,700	—	25,700	24,500	—	24,500
Dominican	45	35	8	43	18,000	24,000	45,000	44,172	31,714	30,997	31,581	30,500	29,400	30,000
Drexel	31	22	6	28	22,000	30,000	60,000	36,500	32,711	33,317	32,841	30,041	34,010	31,940
Emporia	47	37	8	45	12,000	24,000	40,000	45,000	28,473	31,888	29,080	28,250	30,750	28,250
Florida State	12	9	2	11	16,000	21,000	64,000	25,800	31,617	23,400	30,123	29,000	23,400	27,000
Hawaii	9	6	2	8	20,000	29,868	43,716	48,000	30,259	38,934	32,428	30,393	38,934	30,434
Illinois	48	31	13	44	25,000	25,000	60,000	58,000	35,060	35,420	35,166	33,600	32,740	33,170
Indiana	47	36	11	47	18,359	26,000	50,700	50,000	30,283	34,232	31,207	29,125	31,500	30,000
Iowa	23	14	4	18	22,008	23,450	36,000	32,000	28,331	28,238	28,310	28,000	28,750	28,250
Kent State	49	38	8	46	12,459	19,750	45,000	38,500	29,057	29,906	29,205	28,300	31,500	28,300
Kentucky	25	20	5	25	19,622	28,000	40,000	32,000	28,676	30,100	28,961	28,028	30,000	28,500
Long Island	32	30	0	30	27,000	—	50,000	—	36,051	—	36,051	35,500	—	35,500
Louisiana State	40	29	11	40	21,000	17,000	40,000	37,950	28,472	26,777	28,006	28,000	26,000	28,000
Maryland	21	11	5	16	16,000	29,500	42,500	41,981	31,824	33,389	32,313	32,100	32,150	32,125
Michigan	30	23	7	30	23,000	23,000	48,000	53,000	35,826	37,286	36,167	38,000	33,000	35,500
Missouri	17	14	3	17	22,000	24,500	45,000	32,000	30,522	28,333	30,135	30,000	28,500	30,000

N.C. Central	24	16	5	21	20,350	26,000	40,000	36,008	30,141	30,021	30,113	30,500	27,596	30,000
N.C. Chapel Hill	14	12	1	13	23,500	30,000	38,000	30,000	31,400	30,000	31,292	30,850	30,000	30,500
North Texas	32	20	10	33	24,400	25,000	44,000	65,000	30,492	32,700	31,228	28,598	30,250	28,848
Oklahoma	21	17	3	20	23,495	29,500	38,000	32,000	27,682	30,500	28,105	26,000	30,000	27,250
Pittsburgh	25	18	6	24	24,000	22,500	60,000	35,000	31,933	27,917	30,929	30,000	28,500	30,000
Pratt	30	18	9	27	21,000	27,000	65,000	44,000	34,142	32,643	33,642	30,000	30,000	30,000
Queens	46	35	11	46	21,000	25,000	80,000	40,000	37,042	32,409	35,934	33,000	32,000	32,250
Rhode Island	29	22	5	27	15,000	27,000	46,000	37,000	31,948	32,200	31,995	30,025	31,000	31,000
Rutgers	42	35	6	41	25,000	35,000	53,850	50,000	32,635	42,200	34,049	32,000	42,400	33,000
St. John's	15	13	1	14	24,000	35,000	62,000	35,000	38,492	35,000	32,000	38,242	35,000	33,396
San Jose	41	30	10	40	24,000	17,000	72,000	54,000	36,048	36,140	36,071	33,250	38,700	34,000
Simmons	76	64	7	71	20,000	22,000	48,229	35,000	32,069	29,921	31,857	31,000	30,000	31,000
South Carolina	34	32	0	32	13,000	—	40,200	—	29,648	—	29,648	29,000	—	29,000
South Florida	31	24	4	28	19,000	24,000	40,000	35,000	28,107	28,500	28,163	27,800	27,500	27,800
S. Connecticut	21	13	7	20	23,000	22,000	55,000	38,500	36,515	30,386	34,370	34,500	29,200	33,500
S. Mississippi	15	13	2	15	18,720	30,000	39,000	32,000	25,651	31,000	26,364	24,000	31,000	24,000
SUNY-Albany	21	16	5	21	24,500	24,000	44,000	37,380	33,019	29,776	32,247	31,650	31,000	31,300
SUNY-Buffalo	26	21	5	26	21,600	22,500	45,000	29,007	31,310	27,301	30,539	30,000	28,000	29,004
Syracuse	28	24	2	26	21,000	29,410	42,000	37,000	30,255	33,205	30,454	30,250	33,205	30,250
Tennessee	14	11	3	14	26,265	28,500	39,270	40,000	30,410	33,500	31,072	29,000	32,000	29,500
Texas (Austin)	102	58	17	75	18,475	26,000	50,000	42,000	30,508	33,826	31,260	30,000	33,650	30,000
Texas Woman's	22	20	1	21	22,500	22,000	46,000	22,000	32,287	22,000	31,797	29,000	22,000	29,000
Washington	43	38	4	42	22,944	27,264	55,000	40,000	32,931	32,816	32,920	31,750	32,000	31,750
Wayne State	26	21	3	24	26,000	27,950	42,000	35,000	31,070	30,983	31,060	31,000	30,000	30,500
Wisc. (Madison)	23	15	7	22	19,500	20,000	39,000	47,400	29,207	31,744	30,005	29,400	32,000	29,500
Wisc. (Milwaukee)	25	19	6	25	23,000	25,000	50,000	44,000	33,800	33,667	33,768	31,000	33,500	31,000

* Canadian salaries converted to US dollars based on conversion rate of May 19, 1999.

Table 8 / Comparison of Salaries by Type of Organization

	Total Placements	Salaries		Low Salary		High Salary		Average Salary			Median Salary		
		Women	Men	Women	Men	Women	Men	Women	Men	All	Women	Men	All
Public Libraries													
Northeast	137	118	19	$15,000	$22,500	$48,000	$31,300	$29,455	$27,922	$29,242	$29,877	$29,000	$29,870
Southeast	77	61	16	13,000	21,000	50,669	36,008	27,628	28,044	27,715	27,147	26,798	27,147
Midwest	109	84	25	18,000	19,750	38,138	44,172	27,749	28,762	27,981	28,000	28,000	28,000
Southwest	41	34	7	9,200	25,000	34,000	30,500	27,392	27,921	27,483	28,000	27,950	28,000
West	38	29	9	23,000	24,000	55,000	54,000	31,953	33,718	32,371	31,500	32,000	31,875
All Public	402	326	76	9,200	19,750	55,000	54,000	28,680	28,910	28,724	28,629	28,500	28,529
School Libraries													
Northeast	106	100	6	20,000	30,000	65,000	42,800	36,761	34,633	36,641	35,000	32,500	35,000
Southeast	83	79	4	16,000	22,000	44,000	34,000	29,959	27,875	29,858	30,000	27,750	29,900
Midwest	64	59	5	12,459	30,000	50,000	44,000	32,940	37,200	33,272	32,000	37,000	32,000
Southwest	38	37	1	18,475	35,717	46,000	35,717	30,038	35,717	30,188	28,000	35,717	28,348
West	13	13	0	20,000	—	43,716	—	31,670	—	31,670	30,000	—	30,000
All School	304	288	16	12,459	22,000	65,000	44,000	33,019	33,814	33,061	32,000	34,000	32,000
College/University Libraries													
Northeast	72	51	21	15,000	22,000	46,000	50,000	31,260	33,166	31,816	30,000	32,000	30,250
Southeast	70	47	23	18,720	17,000	51,000	45,000	30,275	31,291	30,309	30,000	31,500	30,000
Midwest	63	47	16	12,000	23,450	60,000	45,000	31,066	31,544	31,190	30,500	32,000	30,500
Southwest	21	15	6	25,000	22,000	43,000	38,976	31,033	30,213	30,799	30,000	29,750	30,000
West	18	10	8	29,500	29,868	48,000	41,000	34,811	34,746	34,782	33,250	33,750	33,250
All Academic	244	170	74	12,000	17,000	60,000	50,000	31,123	32,166	31,440	30,000	32,000	30,500
Special Libraries													
Northeast	76	59	17	23,000	24,000	80,000	45,000	37,793	34,794	37,122	35,000	35,000	35,000
Southeast	20	16	4	16,000	26,500	38,000	32,150	30,238	29,463	30,083	30,000	29,600	30,000
Midwest	30	22	8	19,000	23,000	43,000	48,000	32,405	36,175	33,410	32,650	34,000	33,150
Southwest	16	12	4	26,000	26,000	40,000	31,000	32,525	28,750	31,581	31,500	29,000	30,550

West	37	30	7	22,944	17,000	50,000	45,000	35,816	34,771	35,619	36,000	36,000	36,000
All Special	179	139	40	16,000	17,000	80,000	48,000	35,189	33,929	34,907	34,000	33,500	34,000

Government Libraries

Northeast	13	9	4	28,000	29,500	43,627	35,000	35,292	32,116	34,315	34,000	31,982	33,650
Southeast	4	2	2	29,016	23,400	34,000	27,000	31,508	25,200	28,354	31,508	25,200	28,008
Midwest	9	6	3	22,008	28,500	32,000	58,000	27,273	39,232	31,259	27,530	31,197	30,060
Southwest	2	2	0	20,000	—	26,200	—	23,100	—	23,100	23,100	—	23,100
West	2	2	0	31,000	—	38,000	—	34,500	—	34,500	34,500	—	34,500
All Government	30	21	9	20,000	23,400	43,627	58,000	31,404	32,951	31,868	31,000	30,313	30,784

Library Cooperatives/Networks

Northeast	2	2	0	27,000	—	34,000	—	30,500	—	30,500	30,500	—	30,500
Southeast	2	1	1	30,000	30,000	30,000	30,000	30,000	30,000	30,000	30,000	30,000	30,000
Midwest	5	5	0	28,900	—	43,000	—	34,083	—	34,083	34,113	—	34,113
Southwest	1	0	1	—	32,000	—	32,000	—	32,000	32,000	—	32,000	32,000
West	0	0	0	—	—	—	—	—	—	—	—	—	—
All Co-op./Network	10	8	2	27,000	30,000	43,000	32,000	32,677	31,000	32,341	32,000	31,000	31,000

Vendors

Northeast	6	3	3	26,500	33,400	37,200	50,000	32,567	43,800	38,183	34,000	48,000	35,600
Southeast	6	4	2	30,000	26,000	64,000	32,000	41,500	29,000	37,333	36,000	29,000	32,000
Midwest	8	5	3	30,000	27,000	42,000	42,000	35,400	34,267	34,975	35,000	33,800	34,400
Southwest	2	2	0	33,000	—	40,000	—	36,500	—	36,500	36,500	—	36,500
West	1	1	0	46,500	—	46,500	—	46,500	—	46,500	46,500	—	46,500
All Vendors	23	15	8	26,500	26,000	64,000	50,000	37,347	36,525	37,061	35,000	33,600	34,000

Other Organizations

Northeast	34	27	7	22,000	22,000	70,000	40,000	36,154	32,843	35,473	32,000	34,020	32,000
Southeast	13	9	4	29,000	21,000	41,000	40,000	34,467	31,353	33,508	35,200	32,205	35,000
Midwest	18	12	6	28,000	28,000	48,000	53,000	38,708	38,167	38,528	39,800	36,500	39,000
Southwest	14	10	4	24,000	33,000	36,000	41,000	31,100	36,925	32,764	31,250	36,850	33,000
West	13	10	3	26,000	40,000	72,000	65,000	37,612	50,000	40,471	33,000	45,000	36,000
All Other	92	68	24	22,000	21,000	72,000	65,000	35,853	36,750	36,087	33,500	36,500	34,460

Accredited Master's Programs in Library and Information Studies

This list of graduate programs accredited by the American Library Association was issued in January 2000. The list of accredited programs is issued annually at the start of each calendar year and is available from the ALA Office for Accreditation. More than 200 institutions offering both accredited and non-accredited programs in librarianship are included in the 52nd edition of *American Library Directory* (R. R. Bowker, 1999).

Northeast: Conn., D.C., Md., Mass., N.J., N.Y., Pa., R.I.

Catholic University of America, School of Lib. and Info. Science, Washington, DC 20064. Peter Liebscher, Dean. 202-319-5085, fax 202-219-5574, e-mail cuaslis@cua.edu. World Wide Web http://www.cua.edu/www/lsc. Admissions contact: Kevin Woods.

Clarion University of Pennsylvania, Dept. of Lib. Science, 840 Wood St., Clarion, PA 16214-1232. Bernard F. Vavrek, Chair. 814-226-2271, fax 814-226-2150, e-mail vavrek@clarion.edu. World Wide Web http://www.clarion.edu/libsci.

Drexel University, College of Info. Science and Technology, 3141 Chestnut St., Philadelphia, PA 19104-2875. David E. Fenske, Dean. 215-895-2474, fax 215-895-2494. World Wide Web http://www.cis.drexel.edu. Admissions contact: Anne B. Tanner. 215-895-2485, e-mail info@cis.drexel.edu.

Long Island University, Palmer School of Lib. and Info. Science, C. W. Post Campus, 720 Northern Blvd., Brookville, NY 11548-1300. Michael Koenig, Dean. 516-299-2866, fax 516-299-4168, e-mail palmer@titan.liunet.edu. World Wide Web http://www.liu.edu/palmer. Admissions contact: Rosemary Chu. 516-299-2487, fax 516-299-4168.

Pratt Institute, School of Info. and Lib. Science, Info. Science Center, 200 Willoughby Ave., Brooklyn, NY 11205. Larry Kroah, Acting Dean. 718-636-3702,

fax 718-636-3733, e-mail info@sils.pratt. edu. World Wide Web http://sils.pratt.edu.

Queens College, City University of New York, Grad. School of Lib. and Info. Studies, 65-30 Kissena Blvd., Flushing, NY 11367. Marianne Cooper, Dir. 718-997-3790, fax 718-997-3797, e-mail gslis @qcunixl.qc.edu. Admissions contact: Karen P. Smith. E-mail Karen_Smith@ qc.edu.

Rutgers University, School of Communication, Info., and Lib. Studies, 4 Huntington St., New Brunswick, NJ 08903-1071. Gustav W. Friedrich, Dean. 732-932-7917, fax 732-932-2644, e-mail scilsmls@sclis. rutgers.edu. World Wide Web http://www.scils.rutgers.edu/lis/index.html. Admissions contact: Carol C. Kuhlthau. 732-932-7916, e-mail kuhlthau@scils. rutgers.edu.

Saint John's University, Div. of Lib. and Info. Science, 8000 Utopia Pkwy., Jamaica, NY 11439. James A. Benson, Dir. 718-990-6200, fax 718-990-2071, e-mail libis@stjohns.edu. World Wide Web http://www.stjohns.edu/academics/sjc/ depts/dlis/index.html. Admissions contact: Patricia Armstrong. 718-990-2028, fax 718-990-5827.

Simmons College, Grad. School of Lib. and Info. Science, 300 The Fenway, Boston, MA 02115-5898. James M. Matarazzo, Dean. 617-521-2800, fax 617-521-3192, e-mail gslis@simmons.edu. World Wide Web http://www.simmons.edu/graduate/ gslis. Admissions contact: Judith Beals. 617-521-2801, e-mail jbeals@simmons. edu.

Southern Connecticut State University, School of Communication, Info., and Lib. Science, 501 Crescent St., New Haven, CT 06515. Edward C. Harris, Dean. 203-392-5781, fax 203-392-5780, e-mail libscienceit @scsu.ctstateu.edu. Admissions contact: Nancy Disbrow.

State University of New York at Albany, School of Info. Science and Policy, 135 Western Ave., Albany, NY 12222. Philip B. Eppard, Dean. 518-442-5110, fax 518-442-5367, e-mail infosci@cnsvax.albany. edu. World Wide Web http://www.albany. edu/sisp/. Admissions contact (e-mail): infosci@cnsvax.albany.edu.

State University of New York at Buffalo, School of Lib. and Info. Studies, 534 Baldy Hall, Buffalo, NY 14260. A. Neil Yerkey, Chair, Dept. of Lib. and Info. Studies. 716-645-2412, fax 716-645-3775, e-mail sils@acsu.buffalo.edu. World Wide Web http://www.sils.buffalo.edu. Admissions contact: A. Neil Yerkey. 716-645-6478.

Syracuse University, School of Info. Studies, 4-206 Center for Science and Technology, Syracuse, NY 13244-4100. Raymond F. von Dran, Dean. 315-443-2911, fax 315-443-5806, e-mail vondran@syr.edu. World Wide Web http://istweb.svr.edu.

University of Maryland, College of Lib. and Info. Services, 4105 Hornbake Lib. Bldg., College Park, MD 20742-4345. Ann E. Prentice, Dean. 301-405-2033, fax 301-314-9145, e-mail ap57@umail.umd.edu. Admissions contact: Diane L. Barlow. 301-405-2039, e-mail clisumpc@umdacc. umd.edu.

University of Pittsburgh, School of Info. Sciences, 505 IS Bldg., Pittsburgh, PA 15260. Toni Carbo, Dean. 412-624-5230, fax 412-624-5231. World Wide Web http: //www.sis.pitt.edu. Admissions contact: Ninette Kay. 412-624-5146, e-mail nk@ sis.pitt.edu.

University of Rhode Island, Grad. School of Lib. and Info. Studies, Rodman Hall, Kingston, RI 02881. W. Michael Havener, Dir. 401-874-2947, fax 401-874-4395. Admissions contact: C. Herbert Carson.

401-874-2947, e-mail gslis@uriacc.uri. edu.

Southeast: Ala., Fla., Ga., Ky., La., Miss., N.C., S.C., Tenn., P.R.

Clark Atlanta University, School of Lib. and Info. Studies, 300 Trevor Arnett Hall, 223 James P. Brawley Dr., Atlanta, GA 30314. Arthur C. Gunn, Dean. 404-880-8697, fax 404-880-8977, e-mail agunn@cau.edu. Admissions contact: Doris Callahan.

Florida State University, School of Info. Studies, Tallahassee, FL 32306-2100. Jane B. Robbins, Dean. 850-644-5775, fax 850-644-9763. World Wide Web http://www. fsu.edu/~lis. Admissions contact: Kathleen Burnett. 850-644-8106, e-mail burnett@ lis.fsu.edu.

Louisiana State University, School of Lib. and Info. Science, 267 Coates Hall, Baton Rouge, LA 70803. Bert R. Boyce, Dean. 225-388-3158, fax 225-388-4581, e-mail slis@lsu.edu. World Wide Web http:// adam.slis.lsu.edu. Admissions contact: Nicole Rozas.

North Carolina Central University, School of Lib. and Info. Sciences, Box 19586, Durham, NC 27707. Benjamin F. Speller, Jr., Dean. 919-560-6485, fax 919-560-6402, e-mail speller@ga.unc.edu. World Wide Web http://www.slis.nccu.edu. Admissions contact: Duane Bogenschneider. 919-560-55211, e-mail duaneb@nccu.edu.

University of Alabama, School of Lib. and Info. Studies, Box 870252, Tuscaloosa, AL 35487-0252. Joan L. Atkinson, Director. 205-348-4610, fax 205-348-3746. World Wide Web http://www.slis.ua.edu.

University of Kentucky, College of Communications and Info. Studies, School of Lib. and Info. Science, 502 King Library Building S, Lexington, KY 40506-0039. Timothy W. Sineath, Dir. 606-257-8876, fax 606-257-4205, e-mail tsineath@pop. uky.edu. World Wide Web http://www. uky.edu/CommInfoStudies/SLIS. Admissions contact: Jane Salsman.

University of North Carolina at Chapel Hill, School of Info. and Lib. Science, CB

3360, 100 Manning Hall, Chapel Hill, NC 27599-3360. JoAnne Gard Marshall, Dean. 919-962-8366, fax 919-962-8071, e-mail info@ils.unc.edu. World Wide Web http://www.ils.unc.edu. Admissions contact: Lucia Zonn. E-mail zonn@ils.unc.edu.

University of North Carolina at Greensboro, Dept. of Lib. and Info. Studies, School of Education, Box 26171, Greensboro, NC 27402-6171. Keith Wright, Chair. 336-334-3477, fax 336-334-5060, e-mail teresa _hughes_holland@uncg.edu. World Wide Web http://www.uncg.edu/lis/. Admissions contact: Beatrice Kovacs. 910-334-3479, e-mail bea_kovacs@uncg.edu.

University of Puerto Rico, Graduate School of Lib. and Info. Science (Escuela Graduada de Bibliotecologia y Ciencia de la Información), Box 21906, San Juan, PR 00931-1906. Consuelo Figueras, Dir. 787-763-6199, fax 787-764-2311, e-mail 73253.312@compuserv.com. Admissions contact: Migdalia Dávila. 809-764-0000, ext. 3530, e-mail m_davila@rrpad.upr.clu. edu.

University of South Carolina, College of Lib. and Info. Science, Davis College, Columbia, SC 29208. Fred W. Roper, Dean. 803-777-3858, fax 803-777-7938. World Wide Web http://www.libsci.sc.edu. Admissions contact: Nancy C. Beitz. 803-777-5067, fax 803-777-0457, e-mail nbeitz@sc.edu.

University of South Florida, School of Lib. and Info. Science, 4202 E. Fowler Ave., CIS 1040, Tampa, FL 33620-7800. Vicki L. Gregory, Dir. 813-974-3520, fax 813-974-6840, e-mail pate@luna.cas.usf.edu. Admissions contact: Sonia Ramirez Wohlmuth. E-mail swohlmut@chuma.cas.usf. edu.ml.

University of Southern Mississippi, School of Lib. and Info. Science, Box 5146, Hattiesburg, MS 39406-5146. Thomas D. Walker, Dir. 601-266-4228, fax 601-266-5774, World Wide Web http://www-dept.usm. edu/~slis.

University of Tennessee, School of Info. Sciences, 804 Volunteer Blvd., Knoxville, TN 37996-4330. Elizabeth Aversa, Dir. 423-974-2148, fax 423-974-4967. World Wide Web http://www.sis.utk.edu. Admis-

sions contact: George Hoemann. 423-974-5917, e-mail hoemann@utk.edu.

Midwest: Ill., Ind., Iowa, Kan., Mich., Mo., Ohio, Wis.

Dominican University, Grad. School of Lib. and Info. Science, 7900 W. Division St., River Forest, IL 60305. Prudence W. Dalrymple, Dean. 708-524-6845, fax 708-524-6657, e-mail gslis@email.dom.edu. World Wide Web http://www.dom.edu/academic/gslishome.html. Admissions contacts: Elisa Topper (Dominican Univ.), Mary Wagner (College of St. Catherine).

Emporia State University, School of Lib. and Info. Management, Box 4025, Emporia, KS 66801. Robert Grover, Dean. 316-341-5203, fax 316-341-5233. World Wide Web http://slim.emporia.edu. Admissions contact: Mirah Dow. E-mail Dowmirah@emporia.edu.

Indiana University, School of Lib. and Info. Science, Main Library 012, 1320 E. 10th St., Bloomington, IN 47405-3907. Blaise Cronin, Dean. 812-855-2018, fax 812-855-6166, e-mail iuslis@indiana.edu. World Wide Web http://www.slis.indiana.edu. Admissions contact: Mary Krutulis. E-mail krutulis@indiana.edu.

Kent State University, School of Lib. and Info. Science, Box 5190, Kent, OH 44242-0001. Richard Rubin, Acting Dir. 330-672-2782, fax 330-672-7965, e-mail rubin @slis.kent.edu. World Wide Web http://web.slis.kent.edu. Admissions contact: Marge Hayden. E-mail slis@slis.kent.edu.

University of Illinois at Urbana-Champaign, Grad. School of Lib. and Info. Science, 501 E. Daniel St., Champaign, IL 61820. Leigh S. Estabrook, Dean. 217-333-3280, fax 217-244-3302. World Wide Web http://alexia.lis.uiuc.edu. Admissions contact: Carol DeVoss. 217-333-7197, e-mail devoss@alexia.lis.uiuc.edu.

University of Iowa, School of Lib. and Info. Science, 3087 Library, Iowa City, IA 52242-1420. Padmini Srinivasan, Dir. 319-335-5707, fax 319-335-5374, e-mail padmini-srinivasan@uiowa.edu. World Wide Web http://www.uiowa.edu/~libsci.

Admissions contact: Ethel Bloesch. E-mail ethel-bloesch@uiowa.edu.

University of Michigan, School of Info., 550 E. University Ave., Ann Arbor, MI 48109-1092. Gary M. Olson, Interim Dean. 734-763-2285, fax 734-764-2475, e-mail si.admissions@umich.edu. World Wide Web http://www.si.umich.edu. Admissions contact: Cindy Tweedy.

University of Missouri–Columbia, School of Info. Science and Learning Technologies, 20 Rothwell Gym, Columbia, MO 65211. John Wedman, Dir. 573-882-4546, fax 573-884-4944. World Wide Web http://www.coe/missouri.edu/~sislt. Admissions contact: Paula Schlager. 573-882-4546, e-mail sislt@coe.missouri.edu.

University of Wisconsin–Madison, School of Lib. and Info. Studies, 600 N. Park St., Madison, WI 53706. Louise S. Robbins, Dir. 608-263-2900, fax 608-263-4849, e-mail uw_slis@doit.wisc.edu. World Wide Web http://polyglot.lss.wisc.edu/slis/. Admissions contact: Barbara Arnold. 608-263-2090, e-mail bjarnold@facstaff.wisc.edu.

University of Wisconsin–Milwaukee, School of Lib. and Info. Science, 2400 E. Hartford Ave., Milwaukee, WI 53211. Mohammed M. Aman, Dean. 414-229-4707, fax 414-229-4848, e-mail info@slis.uwm.edu. World Wide Web http://www.slis.uwm.edu. Admissions contact: Judy Senkevitch. 414-229-5421.

Wayne State University, Lib. and Info. Science Program, 106 Kresge Library, Detroit, MI 48202. Dian Walster, Dir. 313-577-1825, fax 313-577-7563. World Wide Web http://www.lisp.wayne.edu. Admissions contact: af7735@wayne.edu.

Southwest: Ariz., Okla., Texas.

Texas Woman's University, School of Lib. and Info. Studies, Box 425438, Denton, TX 76204-5438. Keith Swigger, Dean. 940-898-2602, fax 940-898-2611, e-mail a_swigger@twu.edu. World Wide Web http://www.twu.edu/slis.

University of Arizona, School of Info. Resources and Lib. Science, 1515 E. First St., Tucson, AZ 85719. Carla Stoffle, Acting Dir. 520-621-3565, fax 520-621-3279, e-mail sirls@u.arizona.edu. World Wide Web http://www.sir.arizona.edu.

University of North Texas, School of Lib. and Info. Sciences, Box 311068, NT Station, Denton, TX 76203. Philip M. Turner, Dean. 940-565-2445, fax 940-565-3101, e-mail slis@unt.edu. World Wide Web http://www.unt.edu/slis/. Admissions contact: Herman L. Totten. E-mail totten@lis.unt.edu.

University of Oklahoma, School of Lib. and Info. Studies, 401 W. Brooks, Norman, OK 73019-0528. June Lester, Dir. 405-325-3921, 405-325-7648, e-mail slisinfo@ou.edu. World Wide Web http://www.ou.edu/cas/slis. Admissions contact: Maggie Ryan.

University of Texas at Austin, Grad. School of Lib. and Info. Science, Austin, TX 78712-1276. Roberta I. Shaffer, Dean. 512-471-3821, fax 512-471-3971, e-mail info@gslis.utexas.edu. World Wide Web http://www.gslis.utexas.edu. Admissions contact: Ronald Wyllys. 512-471-3969, e-mail gradadv@glis.utexas.edu.

West: Calif., Hawaii, Wash.

San Jose State University, School of Lib. and Info. Science, 1 Washington Sq., San Jose, CA 95192-0029. Blanche Woolls, Dir. 408-924-2490, fax 408-924-2476, e-mail office@wahoo.sjsu.edu. World Wide Web http://witloof.sjsu.edu.

University of California at Los Angeles, Grad. School of Education and Info. Studies, Mailbox 951521, Los Angeles, CA 90095-1521. Michèle V. Cloonan, Chair. 310-825-8799, fax 310-206-3076, e-mail mcloonan@ucla.edu. World Wide Web http://dlis.gseis.ucla.edu. Admissions contact: Susan Abler. 310-825-5269, fax 310-206-6293, e-mail abler@gseis.ucla.edu.

University of Hawaii, Lib. and Info. Science Program, 2550 The Mall, Honolulu, HI 96822. Violet H. Harada, Program Chair. 808-956-7321, fax 808-956-5835, e-mail vharada@hawaii.edu. World Wide Web http://www.hawaii.edu/slis/.

University of Washington, School of Lib. and Info. Science, Box 352930, Seattle, WA 98195-2930. Michael B. Eisenberg, Dir. 206-543-1794, fax 206-616-3152. World Wide Web http://www.ischool.washington. edu. Admissions contact: Lynnea Erickson. E-mail lerick@u.washington.edu.

Canada

Dalhousie University, School of Lib. and Info. Studies, Halifax, NS B3H 3J5. Bertrum H. MacDonald, Dir. 902-494-3656, fax 902-494-2451, e-mail slis@is.dal.ca. World Wide Web http://www.mgmt.dal. ca/slis. Admissions contact: Shanna Balogh. 902-494-2453, e-mail shanna@is. dal.ca.

McGill University, Grad. School of Lib. and Info. Studies, 3459 McTavish St., Montreal, PQ H3A 1Y1. Jamshid Beheshti, Dir. 514-398-4204, fax 514-398-7193, e-mail ad27@musica.mcgill.ca. World Wide Web http://www.gslis.mcgill.ca. Admissions contact: Dorothy Carruthers.

Université de Montréal, Ecole de Bibliothéconomie et des Sciences de l'Information, C.P. 6128, Succursale Centre-Ville, Montreal, PQ H3C 3J7. Gilles Deschâtelets, Dir. 514-343-6044, fax 514-343-5753, e-mail gilles.deschatelets@umontreal.ca.

World Wide Web http://www.fas. umontreal.ca/EBSI/. Admissions contact: Diane Mayer. E-mail diane.mayer@ umontreal.ca.

University of Alberta, School of Lib. and Info. Studies, 3-20 Rutherford S., Edmonton, AB T6G 2J4. Alvin Schrader, Dir. 403-492-4578, fax 403-492-2430, e-mail office@slis.ualberta.ca.

University of British Columbia, School of Lib., Archival, and Info. Studies, 1956 Main Mall, Vancouver, BC V6T 1Z1. Ken Haycock, Dir. 604-822-2404, fax 604-822-6006, e-mail slais@interchange.ubc.ca. World Wide Web http://www.slais.ubc.ca. Admissions contact: Richard Hopkins. 604-822-2404, e-mail slais.admissions@ ubc.ca.

University of Toronto, Faculty of Info. Studies, 140 George St., Toronto, ON M5S 3G6. Lynne C. Howarth, Dean. 416-978-8589, fax 416-978-5762. World Wide Web http://www.fis.utoronto.ca. Admissions contact: Pamela Hawes. E-mail Hawes@fis.utoronto.ca.

University of Western Ontario, Grad. Programs in Lib. and Info. Science, Middlesex College, London, ON N6A 5B7. Manjunath Pendakur, Dean. 519-661-3542, fax 519-661-3506, e-mail fimsdean @julian.uwo.ca. Admissions contact: 519-661-2111, e-mail mlisinfo@julian.uwo.ca.

Library Scholarship Sources

For a more complete list of scholarships, fellowships, and assistantships offered for library study, see *Financial Assistance for Library and Information Studies*, published annually by the American Library Association.

American Association of Law Libraries. (1) A varying number of scholarships of a minimum of $1,000 for graduates of an accredited law school who are degree candidates in an ALA-accredited library school; (2) a varying number of scholarships of varying amounts for library school graduates working on a law degree, non-law graduates enrolled in an ALA-accredited library school, and law librarians taking a course related to law librarianship; (3) the George A. Strait Minority Stipend of $3,500 for an experienced minority librarian working toward an advanced degree to further a law library career. For information, write to: Scholarship Committee, AALL, 53 W. Jackson Blvd., Suite 940, Chicago, IL 60604.

American Library Association. (1) The Marshall Cavendish Scholarship of $3,000 for a varying number of students who have been admitted to an ALA-accredited library school. For information, write to Staff Liaison, Cavendish Scholarship Jury, ALA, 50 E. Huron St., Chicago, IL 60611; (2) the David H. Clift Scholarship of $3,000 for a varying number of students who have been admitted to an ALA-accredited library school. For information, write to: Staff Liaison, Clift Scholarship Jury, ALA, 50 E. Huron St., Chicago, IL 60611; (3) the Tom and Roberta Drewes Scholarship of $3,000 for a varying number of library support staff. For information, write to: Staff Liaison, Drewes Scholarship Jury, ALA, 50 E. Huron St., Chicago, IL 60611; (4) the Mary V. Gaver Scholarship of $3,000 to a varying number of individuals specializing in youth services. For information, write to: Staff Liaison, Gaver Scholarship Jury, ALA, 50 E. Huron St., Chicago, IL 60611; (5) the Miriam L. Hornback Scholarship of $3,000 for a varying number of ALA or library support staff. For information, write to: Staff Liaison, Hornback Scholarship Jury, ALA, 50 E. Huron St., Chicago, IL 60611; (6) the Christopher J. Hoy/ERT Scholarship of $3,000 for a varying number of students who have been admitted to an ALA-accredited library school. For information, write to: Staff Liaison, Hoy/ERT Scholarship Jury, ALA, 50 E. Huron St., Chicago, IL 60611; (7) the Tony B. Leisner Scholarship of $3,000 for a varying number of library support staff. For information, write to: Staff Liaison, Leisner Scholarship Jury, ALA, 50 E. Huron St., Chicago, IL 60611; (8) Spectrum Initiative Scholarships of $5,000 for 50 minority students admitted to an ALA-accredited library school. For information, write to: Staff Liaison, Spectrum Initiative Scholarship, ALA, 50 E. Huron St., Chicago, IL 60611.

ALA/American Association of School Librarians. The AASL School Librarians Workshop Scholarship of $2,500 for a candidate admitted to a full-time ALA-accredited MLS or school library media program. For information, write to: Scholarship Liaison, School Librarians' Workshop Scholarship, AASL/ALA, 50 E. Huron St., Chicago, IL 60611.

ALA/Association of College and Research Libraries and the Institute for Scientific Information. (1) The ACRL Doctoral Dissertation Fellowship of $1,000 for a student who has completed all coursework and submitted a dissertation proposal that has been accepted, in the area of academic librarianship; (2) the Samuel Lazerow Fellowship of $1,000 for research in acquisitions or technical services in an academic or research library; (3) the ACRL and Martinus Nijhoff International West European Specialist Study Grant, which pays travel expenses, room, and board for a ten-day trip to the Netherlands and two other European countries for an ALA member (selection is based on proposal outlining purpose of trip). For information, write to: Lisa Grube, ACRL/ALA, 50 E. Huron St., Chicago, IL 60611.

ALA/Association for Library Service to Children. (1) The Bound to Stay Bound Books Scholarship of $6,000 each for two students who are U.S. or Canadian citizens, who have been admitted to an ALA-accredited program, and who will work with children in a library for one year after graduation; (2) the Frederic G. Melcher Scholarship of $6,000 each for two U.S. or Canadian citizens admitted to an ALA-accredited library school who will work with children in school or public libraries for one year after graduation. For information, write to: Scholarship Liaison, ALSC/ALA Jury, 50 E. Huron St., Chicago, IL 60611.

ALA/Association of Specialized and Cooperative Library Agencies. Century Scholarship of up to $2,500 for a varying number of disabled U.S. or Canadian citizens admitted to an ALA-accredited library school. For information, write to: Scholarship Liaison, ALA/ASCLA Jury, 50 E. Huron St., Chicago, IL 60611.

ALA/International Relations Committee. The Bogle Pratt International Library Travel Fund grant of $1,000 for a varying number of ALA members to attend a first international conference. For information, write to: Michael Dowling, ALA/IRO, 50 E. Huron St., Chicago, IL 60611.

ALA/Library and Information Technology Association. (1) Three LITA Scholarships in library and information technology of $2,500 each for students (two of whom are minority students) who have been admitted to an ALA-accredited program in library automation and information science; (2) The LITA/Christian Larew Memorial Scholarship of $3,000 for a student who has been admitted to an ALA-accredited program in library automation and information science. For information, write to: Scholarship Liaison, LITA/ALA Jury, 50 E. Huron St., Chicago, IL 60611.

ALA/New Members Round Table. EBSCO/NMRT Scholarship of $1,000 for a U.S. or Canadian citizen who is a member of the ALA New Members Round Table. Based on financial need, professional goals, and admission to an ALA-accredited program. For information, write to: ALA Scholarship Liaison, 50 E. Huron St., Chicago, IL 60611.

ALA/Public Library Association. The New Leaders Travel Grant Study Award of up to $1,500 for a varying number of PLA members with five years or less experience. For information, write to: PLA/ALA, 50 E. Huron St., Chicago, IL 60611.

American-Scandinavian Foundation. Fellowships and grants for 25 to 30 students, in amounts from $3,000 to $18,000, for advanced study in Denmark, Finland, Iceland, Norway, or Sweden. For information, write to: Exchange Division, American-Scandinavian Foundation, 15 E. 65 St., New York, NY 10021.

Association of Jewish Libraries. The May K. Simon Memorial Scholarship Fund offers a varying number of scholarships of at least $500 each for MLS students who plan to work as Judaica librarians. For information, write to: Sharona R. Wachs, Association of Jewish Libraries, 1000 Washington Ave., Albany, NY 12203.

Association for Library and Information Science Education. A varying number of research grants of up to $2,500 each for members of ALISE. For information, write to: Association for Library and Information Science Education, Box 7640, Arlington, VA 22207.

Association of Seventh-Day Adventist Librarians. The D. Glenn Hilts Scholarship of $1,000 to a member of the Seventh-Day Adventist Church in a graduate library program. For information, write to: Ms. Wisel, Association of Seventh-Day Adventist Librarians, Columbia Union College, 7600 Flower Ave., Takoma Park, MD 20912.

Beta Phi Mu. (1) The Sarah Rebecca Reed Scholarship of $1,500 for a person accepted in an ALA-accredited library program; (2) the Frank B. Sessa Scholarship of $750 for a Beta Phi Mu member for continuing education; (3) the Harold Lancour Scholarship of $1,000 for study in a foreign country related to the applicant's work or schooling; (4) the Blanche E. Woolls Scholarship for School Library Media Service of $1,000 for a person accepted in an ALA-accredited library program; (5) the Doctoral Dissertation Scholarship of $1,500 for a person who has completed course work toward a doctorate. For information, write to: F. William Summers, Executive Director, Beta Phi Mu, Florida State University, SLIS, Tallahassee, FL 32306-2100.

Canadian Association of Law Libraries. The Diana M. Priestly Scholarship of $2,500 for a student with previous law library experience or for entry to an approved Canadian law school or accredited Canadian library school. For information, write to: John Eaton, Prof., Law Library, University of Western Ontario, London, ON N6A 3K7, Canada.

Canadian Federation of University Women. (1) The Alice E. Wilson Award of $1,500 for two Canadian citizens or permanent residents with a BA degree or equivalent accepted into a program of graduate study; (2) the Margaret McWilliams Fellowship of $1,000 for a student at the doctoral level; (3) the CFUW Memorial/Professional Fellowship of $5,000 for a student enrolled in a master's program in science and technology; (4) the Beverly Jackson Fellowship of $3,000 for a student over age 35 enrolled in graduate work at an Ontario University; (5) the 1989 Polytechnique Commemorative Award of $1,400 for students enrolled in graduate studies related particularly to women. For information, write to: Canadian Federation of University Women, 251 Bank St., Suite 600, Ottawa, ON K2P 1X3, Canada.

Canadian Health Libraries Association. The Student Paper Prize, a scholarship of $300 to a student or recent MLIS graduate or library technician; topic of paper must be in health or information science. For information, write to: Student Paper Prize, Canadian Health Libraries Association/ ABSC, Box 94038, 3332 Yonge St., Toronto, ON M4N 3R1, Canada.

Canadian Library Association. (1) The World Book Graduate Scholarship in Library Science of $2,500; (2) the CLA Dafoe Scholarship of $1,750; and (3) the H. W. Wilson Scholarship of $2,000. Each scholarship is given to a Canadian citizen or landed immigrant to attend an accredited Canadian library school; the World Book scholarship can also be used for an ALA-accredited U.S. school; (4) the Library Research and Development Grant of $1,000 for a member of the Canadian Library Association, in support of theoretical and applied research in library and information science. For information, write to: CLA Membership Services Department, Scholarships and Awards Committee, 200 Elgin St., Suite 602, Ottawa, ON K2P 1L5, Canada.

Catholic Library Association. The World Book, Inc., Grant of $1,500 is divided among no more than three CLA members for workshops, institutes, etc. For information, write to: Jean R. Bostley, SSJ, Executive Director, Catholic Library Association, 100 North St., Suite 224, Pittsfield, MA 01201-5109.

Chinese American Librarians Association. (1) The Sheila Suen Lai Scholarship; (2) the C. C. Seetoo/CALA Conference Travel Scholarship. Each scholarship offers $500 to a Chinese descendant who has been accepted in an ALA-accredited program. For information, write to: Meng Xiong Liu, Clark Library, San Jose State University, 1 Washington Sq., San Jose, CA 95192-0028.

Church and Synagogue Library Association. The Muriel Fuller Memorial Scholarship of $115 plus cost of texts for a correspondence course offered by the University of Utah Continuing Education Division. Open to CSLA members only. For information, write to: CSLA, Box 19357, Portland, OR 97280-0357.

Council on Library and Information Resources. The A. R. Zipf Fellowship in Information Management of $5,000 is awarded annually to a student enrolled in graduate school who shows exceptional promise for leadership and technical achievement. For information, write to: Council on Library and Information Resources, 1755 Massachusetts Ave. N.W., Suite 500, Washington, DC 20036.

Sandra Garvie Memorial Fund. A scholarship of $1,000 for a student pursuing a course of study in library and information science. For information, write to: Sandra Garvie Memorial Fund, c/o Director, Legal Resources Centre, Faculty of Extension, University of Alberta, 8303 112th St., Edmonton, AB T6G 2T4, Canada.

Manitoba Library Association. (1) John Edwin Bissett Memorial Fund Scholarships. Awards of varying amounts for a varying number of University of Manitoba graduates who are enrolled full-time in a master's program in library and information science; (2) Jean Thorunn Law Scholarship. An award of a varying amount for a student enrolled in a full-time master's program in library and information who has a year of library experience in Manitoba. For information, write to: Manitoba Library Association, CE Committee, 416-100 Arthur St., Winnipeg, MB R3B 1H3.

Massachusetts Black Librarians' Network. Two scholarships of at least $500 and $1,000 for minority students entering an ALA-accredited master's program in library science, with no more than 12 semester hours toward a degree. For information, write to: Pearl Mosley, Chair, Massachusetts Black Librarians' Network, 27 Beech Glen St., Roxbury, MA 02119.

Medical Library Association. (1) A scholarship of $2,000 for a person entering an ALA-accredited library program, with no more than one-half of the program yet to be completed; (2) a scholarship of $2,000 for a minority student for graduate study; (3) a varying number of Research, Development and Demonstration Project Grants of $100 to $1,000 for U.S. or Canadian citizens who are MLA members; (4) Continuing Education Grants of $100 to $500 for U.S. or Canadian citizens who are MLA members. For information, write to: Development Department, Medical Library Association, 65 E. Wacker Pl., Suite 1900, Chicago, IL 60601-7298.

Mountain Plains Library Association. (1) A varying number of grants of up to $600 each and (2) a varying number of grants of up to $150 each for MPLA members with at least two years of membership for continuing education. For information, write to: Joseph R. Edelen, Jr., MPLA Executive Secretary, I. D. Weeks Library, University of South Dakota, Vermillion, SD 57069.

REFORMA, the National Association to Promote Library Services to Latinos and the Spanish-Speaking. A varying number of scholarships of $1,000 to $2,000 each for minority students interested in serving the Spanish-speaking community to attend an ALA-accredited school. For information, write to: Ninta Trejo, Main Library, University of Arizona, 1510 E. University, Tucson, AZ 85721.

Society of American Archivists. The Colonial Dames Awards, two grants of $1,200 each for specific types of repositories and collections. For information, write to: Debra Mills, Society of American Archivists, 521 S. Wells St., 5th flr., Chicago, IL 60607.

Southern Regional Education Board. For residents of Arkansas, Delaware, Georgia, Louisiana, Virginia, and West Virginia, a varying number of grants of varying amounts to cover in-state tuition for graduate or postgraduate study in an ALA-accredited library school. For information, write to: Academic Common Market, c/o Southern Regional Education Board, 592 Tenth St. N.W., Atlanta, GA 30318-5790.

Special Libraries Association. (1) Three $6,000 scholarships for students interested in special-library work; (2) the Plenum Scholarship of $1,000; (3) the ISI Scholarship of $1,000, each also for students interested in special-library work; (4) the Affirmative Action Scholarship of $6,000 for a minority student interested in special-library work; and (5) the Pharmaceutical Division Stipend Award of $1,200 for a student with an undergraduate degree in chemistry, life sciences, or pharmacy entering or enrolled in an ALA-accredited program. For information on the first four scholarships, write to: Scholarship Committee, Special Libraries Association, 1700 18th St. N.W., Washington, DC 20009-2508; for information on the Pharmaceutical Stipend, write to: Susan E. Katz, Awards Chair, Knoll Pharmaceuticals Science Information Center, 30 N. Jefferson St., Whippany, NJ 07981.

Library Scholarship and Award Recipients, 1999

Library awards are listed by organization. An index listing awards alphabetically by title follows this section.

American Association of Law Libraries (AALL)

AALL Scholarships. Offered by: AALL; Matthew Bender & Company; LEXIS-NEXIS; West Group. *Winners:* (Library Degree for Law School Graduates) Seneca J. Gray, Ann E. Hemmens, Jennifer Korpacz, William E. Magee, Adria P. Olmi; (Library School Graduates Attending Law School) Ginger B. Fearey, Stacey L. Gordon, James R. Wirrell; (Library Degree for Non-Law School Graduates) Marie A. Gosselin, Diana C. Jaque, Kristy A. Yarnell, Tisha M. Zelner; (Library School Graduates Seeking a Non-Law Degree) Not awarded in 1999; (George A. Strait Minority Stipend) Annie Leung, Donna L. Nixon.

American Library Association (ALA)

ALA/Information Today Library of the Future Award ($1,500). For a library, consortium, group of librarians, or support organization for innovative planning for, applications of, or development of patron training programs about information technology in a library setting. *Donor:* Information Today, Inc. *Winner:* Queens Borough (New York) Public Library.

Hugh C. Atkinson Memorial Award ($2,000). For outstanding achievement (including risk-taking) by academic librarians that has contributed significantly to improvements in library automation, management, and/or development or research. Offered by: ACRL, ALCTS, LAMA, and LITA divisions. *Winner:* Susan Nutter.

Carroll Preston Baber Research Grant (up to $7,500). For innovative research that could lead to an improvement in library services to any specified group(s) of people. *Donor:*

Eric R. Baber. *Winner:* Not awarded in 1999.

Beta Phi Mu Award ($500). For distinguished service in library education. *Donor:* Beta Phi Mu International Library Science Honorary Society. *Winner:* D. W. Krummel.

Bogle/Pratt International Library Travel Fund Award ($1,000). To ALA member(s) to attend their first international conference. *Donor:* Bogle Memorial Fund. *Winner:* Wendy Miller.

William Young Boyd Military Novel Award ($10,000). To an author for a military novel that honors the service of American veterans. *Donor:* William Young Boyd. *Winner:* Donald McCaig for *Jacob's Ladder: A Story of Virginia During the War.*

Marshall Cavendish Scholarship ($3,000). To a worthy U.S. or Canadian citizen to begin an MLS degree in an ALA-accredited program. *Winner:* Michelle Simmons.

David H. Clift Scholarship ($3,000). To a worthy U.S. or Canadian citizen to begin an MLS degree in an ALA-accredited program. *Winner:* Michael Lambert.

Melvil Dewey Award. To an individual or group for recent creative professional achievement in library management, training, cataloging and classification, and the tools and techniques of librarianship. *Donor:* OCLC/Forest Press. *Winner:* Helen Moeller.

Tom and Roberta Drewes Scholarship ($3,000). To a library support staff person pursuing a master's degree. *Winner:* Ami Chitwood.

EBSCO ALA Conference Sponsorships (up to $1,000). To allow librarians to attend ALA's Annual Conferences. *Donor:* EBSCO Subscription Services. *Winners:* Jennifer Weil Arns, Jenna Freedman, Dorothy Glew, Alice B. Haldeman, Dona J. Helmer, Leslie Lomers, Muzhgan Nazarova, Gay Helen Perkins, Leroy D. Smith, Holly Williams.

Equality Award ($500). To an individual or group for an outstanding contribution that promotes equality of women and men in the library profession. *Donor*: Scarecrow Press. *Winner*: Kansas City (Missouri) Public Library.

Freedom to Read Foundation Roll of Honor Award. *Winner*: Charles L. Levendosky.

Elizabeth Futas Catalyst for Change Award ($1,000). To recognize and honor a librarian who invests time and talent to make positive change in the profession of librarianship. *Donor*: Elizabeth Futas Memorial Fund. *Winner*: Maureen Sullivan.

Loleta D. Fyan Public Library Research Grant (up to $10,000). For projects in public library development. *Winner*: Dean K. Jue and Christie M. Koontz for their project "Library Market Area Determinations through User Address Data and Use of Geographic Information Systems."

Gale Research Financial Development Award ($2,500). To a library organization for a financial development project to secure new funding resources for a public or academic library. *Donor*: Gale Research Company. *Winner*: Deschutes (Oregon) Public Library District.

Mary V. Gaver Scholarship ($3,000). To a library support staff member specializing in youth services. *Winner*: Jennifer Lindsey.

Grolier Foundation Award ($1,000). For stimulation and guidance of reading by children and young people. *Donor*: Grolier Education Corporation, Inc. *Winner*: Elizabeth Huntoon.

Grolier National Library Week Grant ($4,000). To libraries or library associations of all types for a public awareness campaign in connection with National Library Week in the year the grant is awarded. *Donor*: Grolier Educational Corporation. *Winner*: Detroit Public Library.

Mirian L. Hornback Scholarship ($3,000). To an ALA or library support staff person pursuing a master's degree in library science. *Winner*: Deborah Robertson.

Paul Howard Award for Courage ($1,000). To a librarian, library board, library group, or an individual who has exhibited unusual courage for the benefit of library programs or services. *Donor*: Paul Howard. *Winner*: Jane Rustin.

John Ames Humphry/OCLC/Forest Press Award ($1,000). To an individual for significant contributions to international librarianship. *Donor*: OCLC/Forest Press. *Winner*: Ron Chepesiuk.

Tony B. Leisner Scholarship ($3,000). To a library support staff member pursuing a master's degree program. *Winner*: Sharon Bernard.

Joseph W. Lippincott Award ($1,000). To a librarian for distinguished service to the profession. *Donor*: Joseph W. Lippincott, Jr. *Winner*: Peggy Barber.

Spectrum Initiative Scholarships ($5,000). Presented to 50 minority students admitted to an ALA-accredited library school. *Winners*: Bernadette Bailey, Monecia Barry, Gyasi Burks-Abbott, Rita Cacas, Terry Carlson, Maria Casado, June Degan, Brian Doxator, Khristi Dunn, Hector Escobar, Quintel Freeman, June Gaddy, Kim Gallon, Keshia Garnett, Maria Gonzalez, Michael Gutierrez, Cassandra Harper, Avril Haughton, Ellen Holt, Maria Hudson, Dora Jenkins, Connie Lee, Teresa Lee, Carol Levers, Soraya Magalhaes-Wilson, Ida Martinez, Lee McQueen, Carla Morales-Clayton, Rodolfo Narvaez, Phuoc Nguyen, Camille Noel, Beatriz Pascual, Wendy Poolaw, Astoria Ridley, Julio Rodriguez, Linda Ryan, Neena Sachdeva, Veronica Salaam, Michele Saunders, Sandra Scruggs, Wands Shealey, Chameka Simmons, Eric Stanton, Cecie Streitman, Armando Trejo, Barbara Tunstall, Barbara Vanderhorst, Wenjing Wang, Daisy Waters, Vivien Zazzau.

Virginia and Herbert White Award for Promoting Librarianship ($1,000). Honors a significant contribution to the public recognition and appreciation of librarianship through professional performance, teaching, and writing. *Winner*: Marilyn Gell Mason.

H. W. Wilson Library Staff Development Award ($3,500). To a library organization for a program to further its staff development goals and objectives. *Donor*: The H.

W. Wilson Company. *Winner*: Topeka and Shawnee County (Kansas) Public Library.

Women's National Book Award Association/ Ann Heidbreder Eastman Grant ($500–$1,000). To a librarian to take a course or participate in an institute devoted to aspects of publishing as a profession or to provide reimbursement for such study completed within the past year. *Winner*: Carolyn Gutierrez.

World Book–ALA Goal Grant (up to $10,000). To ALA units for the advancement of public, academic, or school library service and librarianship through support of programs that implement the goals and priorities of ALA. *Donor*: World Book, Inc. *Winners*: ALA Chapter Relations Committee and the Florida Library Association for their project "Stop Talking and Start Doing! Recruitment of People of Color to Librarianship"; ALA International Relations Office for its project "ALA Free Pass Program to the Guadalajara Book Fair."

American Association of School Librarians (AASL)

AASL ABC/CLIO Leadership Grant (up to $1,750). For planning and implementing leadership programs at state, regional, or local levels, to be given to school library associations that are affiliates of AASL. *Donor*: ABC/CLIO. *Winner*: Hawaii Association of School Librarians.

AASL Crystal Apple Award. *Winner*: Delaine Eastin.

AASL/Frances Henne Award ($1,250). To a school library media specialist with five or fewer years in the profession to attend an AASL regional conference or ALA Annual Conference for the first time. *Donor*: R. R. Bowker. *Winner*: Marsha Trentham Hunter.

AASL/Highsmith Research Grant (up to $5,000). To conduct innovative research aimed at measuring and evaluating the impact of school library media programs on learning and education. *Donor*: Highsmith, Inc. *Winners*: Violet H. Harada, Claire Sato, Joan Yoshina.

AASL Information Plus Continuing Education Scholarship ($500). To a school library media specialist, supervisor, or educator to attend an ALA or AASL continuing education event. *Donor*: Information Plus. *Winner*: Betty K. Brackin.

AASL School Librarian's Workshop Scholarship ($2,500). To a full-time student preparing to become a school library media specialist at the preschool, elementary, or secondary level. *Donor*: Library Learning Resources. *Winner*: Marie Granthe.

Distinguished School Administrators Award ($2,000). For expanding the role of the library in elementary and/or secondary school education. *Donor*: Social Issues Resources Series, Inc. (SIRS). *Winner*: Eugene J. Sudol.

Distinguished Service Award, AASL/Baker & Taylor ($3,000). For outstanding contributions to librarianship and school library development. *Donor*: Baker & Taylor Books. *Winner*: Jacqueline C. Mancall.

Information Technology Pathfinder Award ($1,000 to the specialist and $500 to the library). To library media specialists for innovative approaches to microcomputer applications in the school library media center. *Donor*: Follett Software Company. *Winners*: Secondary, Betty K. Brackin; Elementary, Sharlene Miller-Ballas.

Intellectual Freedom Award ($2,000, and $1,000 to media center of recipient's choice). To a school library media specialist who has upheld the principles of intellectual freedom. *Donor*: Social Issues Resources Series, Inc. *Winner*: Not awarded in 1999.

National School Library Media Program of the Year Award ($3,000). To school districts and a single school for excellence and innovation in outstanding library media programs. *Donor*: AASL and Encyclopaedia Britannica Companies. *Winners*: Large school district, Lincoln (Nebraska) Public Schools; Single, not awarded in 1999; Small school district, not awarded in 1999.

American Library Trustee Association (ALTA)

ALTA/Gale Outstanding Trustee Conference Grant Award ($750). *Donor*: Gale Research Company. *Winner*: Joseph M. Mueller.

ALTA Literacy Award (citation). To a library trustee or an individual who, in a volunteer capacity, has made a significant contribution to addressing the illiteracy problem in the United States. *Winners*: Rebecca B. Schroeder, Otissey Denton.

ALTA Major Benefactors Honor Award (citation). To individual(s), families, or corporate bodies that have made major benefactions to public libraries. *Winners*: Lynn and Charles Schusterman, Mr. and Mrs. Marv Patmos.

Trustee Citations. To recognize public library trustees for individual service to library development on the local, state, regional, or national level. *Winners*: Sharon A. Saulmon, Patricia Fitchett Turner.

Armed Forces Libraries Round Table

Armed Forces Library Certificate of Merit. To librarians or "friends" who are members of AFLRT who provide an exemplary program to an Armed Forces library. *Winner*: Larry Osborne.

Armed Forces Library Round Table Achievement Citation. For contributions toward development of interest in libraries and reading in armed forces library service and organizations. Candidates must be members of the Armed Forces Libraries Round Table. *Winner*: Deon Grinnell.

Armed Forces Library Round Table News-Bank Scholarship ($1,000 to the school of the recipient's choice). To members of the Armed Forces Libraries Round Table who have given exemplary service in the area of library support for off-duty education programs in the armed forces. *Donor*: NewsBank, Inc. *Winner*: Katherine Gillen.

Association for Library Collections and Technical Services (ALCTS)

Hugh C. Atkinson Memorial Award. *See under* American Library Association.

Best of *LRTS* Award (citation). To the author(s) of the best paper published each year in the division's official journal. *Winners*: Lois Mai Chan and Diane Vizine-Goetz.

Blackwell's Scholarship Award ($2,000 scholarship to the U.S. or Canadian library school of the recipient's choice). To honor the author(s) of the year's outstanding monograph, article, or original paper in the field of acquisitions, collection development, and related areas of resource development in libraries. *Donor*: Blackwell/North America: *Winner*: Ross Atkinson.

Bowker/Ulrich's Serials Librarianship Award ($1,500). For demonstrated leadership in serials-related activities through participation in professional associations and/or library education programs, contributions to the body of serials literature, research in the area of serials, or development of tools or methods to enhance access to or management of serials. *Donor*: R. R. Bowker/Ulrich's. *Winner*: Regina Romano Reynolds.

First Step Award (Wiley Professional Development Grant) ($1,500). For librarians new to the serials field to attend ALA's Annual Conference. *Donor*: John Wiley & Sons. *Winner*: Charity K. Stokes.

Leadership in Library Acquisitions Award ($1,500). For significant contributions by an outstanding leader in the field of library acquisitions. *Donor*: Harrassowitz Company. *Winner*: Carol Pitts Diedrichs.

Margaret Mann Citation. To a cataloger or classifier for achievement in the areas of cataloging or classification. *Winner*: Nancy Olson.

Esther J. Piercy Award ($1,500). To a librarian with fewer than ten years experience for contributions and leadership in the field of library collections and technical services. *Donor*: Yankee Book Peddler. *Winner*: Stephen Chapman.

Association for Library Service to Children (ALSC)

ALSC/Book Wholesalers Summer Reading Program Grant ($3,000). To an ALSC member for implementation of an outstanding public library summer reading program for children. *Donor*: Book Wholesalers, Inc. *Winner*: Karen M. Allen.

ALSC/Econo-Clad Literature Program Award ($1,000). To an ALSC member who has developed and implemented an outstanding library program for children involving reading and the use of literature, to attend an ALA conference. *Donor*: Econo-Clad Books. *Winner*: Martha Simpson.

ALSC/REFORMA Pura Belpré Award. *Winner*: Not awarded in 1999.

May Hill Arbuthnot Honor Lecturer. To invite an individual of distinction to prepare and present a paper that will be a significant contribution to the field of children's literature and that will subsequently be published in *Journal of Youth Services in Libraries*. *Winner*: Hazel Rochman.

Mildred L. Batchelder Award. See *Literary Prizes, 1999* by Gary Ink in Part 5.

Louise Seaman Bechtel Fellowship ($3,750). For librarians with 12 or more years of professional level work in children's library collections, to read and study at the Baldwin Library/George Smathers Libraries, University of Florida (must be an ALSC member with an MLS from an ALA-accredited program). *Donor*: Bechtel Fund. *Winner*: Julia S. Massie.

Bound to Stay Bound Books Scholarship ($6,000). Two awards for study in the field of library service to children toward the MLS or beyond in an ALA-accredited program. *Donor*: Bound to Stay Bound Books. *Winners*: Caitlin B. Augusta, Barbara Vanderhorst.

Caldecott Medal. See *Literary Prizes, 1999* by Gary Ink in Part 5.

Andrew Carnegie Medal. To the U.S. producer of the most distinguished video for children in the previous year. *Donor*: Carnegie Corporation of New York. *Winner*: Frank Moynihan for *The First Christmas*.

Distinguished Service to ALSC Award ($1,000). To recognize significant contributions to, and an impact on, library services to children and/or ALSC. *Winner*: Lillian N. Gerhardt.

Frederic G. Melcher Scholarship ($5,000). To students entering the field of library service to children for graduate work in an ALA-accredited program. *Winners*: Julie E. Palomaki, Caitlin Delia Ream.

John Newbery Medal. See *Literary Prizes, 1999* by Gary Ink in Part 5.

Penguin Putnam Books for Young Readers Awards. To children's librarians in school

or public libraries with ten or fewer years of experience to attend ALA Annual Conference for the first time. Must be a member of ALSC. *Donor*: Penguin Putnam. *Winners*: Deborah J. DeVita, Virginia Hoover, Mary Jo Peltier, Susan Seitner.

Laura Ingalls Wilder Medal. To an author or illustrator whose works have made a lasting contribution to children's literature. *Winner*: Not awarded in 1999.

Association of College and Research Libraries (ACRL)

ACRL Academic or Research Librarian of the Year Award ($3,000). For outstanding contribution to academic and research librarianship and library development. *Donor*: Baker & Taylor. *Winner*: Hannelore B. Rader.

ACRL Doctoral Dissertation Fellowship ($1,500). To a doctoral student in the field of academic librarianship whose research has potential significance in the field. *Donor*: Institute for Scientific Information. *Winner*: Alenka Sauperl.

ACRL EBSS Distinguished Education and Behavioral Sciences Librarian Award (citation). To an academic librarian who has made an outstanding contribution as an education and/or behavioral sciences librarian through accomplishments and service to the profession. *Winner*: Jo Ann Carr.

Hugh C. Atkinson Memorial Award. *See under* American Library Association.

Miriam Dudley Bibliographic Instruction Librarian Award ($1,000). For contribution to the advancement of bibliographic instruction in a college or research institution. *Donor*: JAI Press. *Winner*: Mary Reichel.

EBSCO Community College Leadership Award ($500). *Donor*: EBSCO Subscription Services. *Winner*: Wanda Johnston Bahde.

EBSCO Community College Program Award ($500). *Donor*: EBSCO Subscription Services. *Winner*: Richland College.

Instruction Section Innovation in Instruction Award (citation). Recognizes and honors librarians who have developed and implemented innovative approaches to instruction within their institution in the preceding two years. *Winner*: University of Arizona Education Project Team.

Instruction Section Publication of the Year Award (citation). Recognizes an outstanding publication related to instruction in a library environment published in the preceding two years. *Winner*: Christine S. Bruce.

Marta Lange/CQ Award ($1,000). Recognizes an academic or law librarian for contributions to bibliography and information service in law or political science. *Donor*: *Congressional Quarterly*. *Winner*: Jolande E. Goldberg.

Samuel Lazerow Fellowship for Research in Acquisitions or Technical Services ($1,000). To foster advances in acquisitions or technical services by providing librarians a fellowship for travel or writing in those fields. *Sponsor*: Institute for Scientific Information (ISI). *Winner*: Not awarded in 1999.

Katharine Kyes Leab and Daniel J. Leab American Book Prices Current Exhibition Catalog Awards (citations). For the three best catalogs published by American or Canadian institutions in conjunction with exhibitions of books and/or manuscripts. *Winners*: (Category One) *The Practice of Letters: The Hofer Collection of Writing Manuals 1514–1800*, David P. Becker and Anne Anninger, and *The Dutch in the Americas: 1600–1800*, Wim Klooster and Norman Fiering; (Category Two) *Radicals and Revolutionaries: The History of Canadian Communism from the Robert S. Kenny Collection*, Sean Purdy and Richard Landon; (Category Three) *The Great War 1914–1918: An Exhibition Drawn from the Joseph M. Bruccoli Collection at the University of Virginia Library and Other Collections*, Patrick Scott.

Martinus Nijhoff International West European Specialist Study Grant (travel funding for up to 14 days research in Europe). Supports research pertaining to West European studies, librarianship, or the book trade. *Sponsor*: Martinus Nijhoff International. *Winner*: Richard Hacken.

Oberly Award for Bibliography in the Agricultural Sciences. Biennially, for the best English-language bibliography in the field of agriculture or a related science in the preceding two-year period. *Donor*: Eunice R. Oberly Fund. *Winner*: Eli MacLaren.

Rare Books & Manuscripts Librarianship Award ($1,000). For articles of superior quality published in the ACRL journal *Rare Books & Manuscripts Librarianship*. *Donor*: Christie, Manson & Woods. *Winner*: Robert A. Gross.

K. G. Saur Award for Best *College and Research Libraries* Article ($500). To author(s) to recognize the most outstanding article published in *College and Research Libraries* during the preceding year. *Donor*: K. G. Saur. *Winner*: Bonnie Gratch Lindauer.

Association of Specialized and Cooperative Library Agencies (ASCLA)

ASCLA Exceptional Service Award. *Winner*: Rangashri Kishore.

ASCLA Leadership Achievement Award. To recognize leadership and achievement in the areas of consulting, multitype library cooperation, and state library development. *Winner*: Jan Beck Ison.

ASCLA/National Organization on Disability Award for Library Service to People with Disabilities ($1,000). To institutions or organizations that have made the library's total service more accessible through changing physical and/or additional barriers. *Donor*: National Organization on Disability, funded by J. C. Penney. *Winner*: Disability Resources, Inc.

ASCLA Professional Achievement Award (citation). For professional achievement within the areas of consulting, networking, statewide services, and programs. *Winner*: Bridget L. Lamont.

ASCLA Research Grant ($1,000). To stimulate researchers to look at state library services, interlibrary cooperation, networking, and services to special populations as valid areas of research interest. *Donor*: Auto-Graphics, Inc. *Winner*: Not awarded in 1999.

ASCLA Service Award (citation). For outstanding service and leadership to the division. *Winner*: Barbara T. Mates.

Francis Joseph Campbell Citation. For a contribution of recognized importance to library service for the blind and physically handicapped. *Winner*: Donald John Weber.

Ethnic Material and Information Exchange Round Table

EMIERT/Gale Research Multicultural Award ($1,000): For outstanding achievement and leadership in serving the multicultural/multiethnic community. *Donor*: Gale Research Company. *Winner*: The Schaffer Library of Union College, Schenectady, New York.

Exhibits Round Table

Friendly Booth Award (citation). *Cosponsor*: New Members Round Table. *Winners*: First place, Hooked on Phonics; second place, Pleasant Company; third place, Facts on File News Services.

Christopher J. Hoy/ERT Scholarship ($3,000). To an individual who will work toward an MLS degree in an ALA-accredited program. *Donor*: Family of Christopher Hoy. *Winner*: Holly Wissink.

Kohlstedt Exhibit Award (citation). To companies or organizations for the best single, multiple, and island booth displays at the ALA Annual Conference. *Winners*: Apple Books, Demco, Bell and Howell Information and Learning.

Federal Librarians Round Table (FLRT)

Federal Librarians Achievement Award. *Winner*: Milton McGee.

Adelaide del Frate Conference Sponsor Award. To encourage library school students to become familiar with federal librarianship and ultimately seek work in federal libraries; for attendance at ALA Annual Conference and activities of the Federal Librarians Round Table. *Winner*: C. J. Houtchens.

Distinguished Service Award (citation). To honor a FLRT member for outstanding and sustained contributions to the association and to federal librarianship. *Winner*: Shirley Loo.

Government Documents Round Table (GODORT)

James Bennett Childs Award. To a librarian or other individual for distinguished lifetime contributions to documents librarianship. *Winner*: Virginia F. Saunders.

CIS/GODORT/ALA Documents to the People Award ($2,000). To an individual, library, organization, or noncommercial group that most effectively encourages or enhances the use of government documents in library services. *Donor*: Congressional Information Service, Inc. (CIS). *Winner*: Donna Koepp.

Bernadine Abbott Hoduski Founders Award (plaque). To recognize documents librarians who may not be known at the national level but who have made significant contributions to the field of state, international, local, or federal documents. *Winners*: Barbie Selby, Bette L. Siegel.

Readex/GODORT/ALA Catharine J. Reynolds Award ($2,000). Grants to documents librarians for travel and/or study in the field of documents librarianship or area of study benefitting performance as documents librarians. *Donor*: Readex Corporation. *Winner*: Not awarded in 1999.

David Rozkuszka Scholarship ($3,000). To provide financial assistance to an individual who is currently working with government documents in a library while completing a master's program in library science. *Winner*: Amanda Wakaruk.

Intellectual Freedom Round Table (IFRT)

John Phillip Immroth Memorial Award for Intellectual Freedom ($500). For notable contribution to intellectual freedom fueled by personal courage. *Winner*: Mainstream Loudon (a citizen group in Loudoun County, Virginia, that successfully led a campaign against Internet censorship by the local library board).

Eli M. Oboler Memorial Award ($1,500). Biennially, to an author of a published work in English or in English translation dealing with issues, events, questions, or controversies in the area of intellectual

freedom. *Donor*: Providence Associates, Inc. *Winner*: Not awarded in 1999.
State and Regional Achievement Award ($1,000). To the intellectual freedom committee of a state library, state library media association, or a state/regional coalition for the most successful and creative project during the calendar year. *Donor*: Social Issues Resource Series, Inc. (SIRS). *Winner*: Oregon Coalition for Free Expression.

Library Administration and Management Association (LAMA)

Hugh C. Atkinson Memorial Award. *See under* American Library Association.
Certificate of Achievement. *Winner*: Not awarded in 1999.
John Cotton Dana Library Public Relations Awards. To libraries or library organizations of all types for public relations programs or special projects ended during the preceding year. *Donor*: H. W. Wilson Company. *Winners*: Enoch Pratt Free Library, Baltimore; Milton S. Eisenhower Library, Johns Hopkins University, Baltimore; Chardon Library, Geauga County Public Library System, Chardon, Ohio; Ela Area Public Library, Lake Zurich, Illinois; Northbrook (Illinois) Public Library; Timberland Regional Library System, Olympia, Washington; State Library of North Carolina; Richmond (Virginia) Public Library; San Antonio (Texas) Public Library; North Suburban Library Foundation of Illinois.
LAMA/AIA Library Buildings Award (citation). A biannual award given for excellence in architectural design and planning by an American architect. *Donor*: American Institute of Architects and LAMA. *Winners*: Arthur Cotton Moore Associates, Washington, D.C.; Davis, Brody Bond, LLP, New York (two awards); Thomas Miller & Partners, Brentwood, Tennessee; Jefferson B. Riley and James C. Childress of Centerbrook Architects and Planners, LLC, Centerbrook, Connecticut; M. W. Steele Group, Inc., La Jolla, California; Polshek Partnership, LLP, New York.
LAMA Cultural Diversity Grant (up to $1,000). To support creation and dissemi-

nation of resources that will assist library administrators and managers in developing a vision and commitment to diversity. *Winner*: Fullerton (California) Public Library.
LAMA President's Award. *Winner*: Not awarded in 1999.
LAMA/YBP Student Writing and Development Award: *Winner*: Not awarded in 1999.

Library and Information Technology Association (LITA)

Hugh C. Atkinson Memorial Award. *See under* American Library Association.
LITA/Gaylord Award for Achievement in Library and Information Technology ($1,000). *Donor*: Gaylord Bros., Inc. *Winner*: Sheila Creth.
LITA/GEAC Scholarship in Library and Information Technology ($2,500). For work toward an MLS in an ALA-accredited program with emphasis on library automation. *Donor*: GEAC, Inc. *Winner*: Clinton Chamberlain.
LITA/Christian Larew Memorial Scholarship ($3,000). To encourage the entry of qualified persons into the library and information technology field. *Donor*: Electronic Business and Information Services (EBIS). *Winner*: Avi Janssen.
LITA/Library Hi Tech Award ($1,000). To an individual or institution for a work that shows outstanding communication for continuing education in library and information technology. *Donor*: Pierian Press. *Winner*: Ann Okerson.
LITA/LSSI Minority Scholarship in Library and Information Science ($2,500). To encourage a qualified member of a principal minority group to work toward an MLS degree in an ALA-accredited program with emphasis on library automation. *Donor*: Library Systems & Services, Inc. *Winner*: Ting Yin.
LITA/OCLC Frederick G. Kilgour Award for Research in Library and Information Technology ($2,000 and expense-paid attendance at ALA Annual Conference). To bring attention to research relevant to the development of information technologies. *Winner*: Dean K. Jue.

LITA/OCLC Minority Scholarship in Library and Information Technology ($2,500). To encourage a qualified member of a principal minority group to work toward an MLS degree in an ALA-accredited program with emphasis on library automation. *Donor*: OCLC. *Winner*: Carrie Hurst.

Library History Round Table (LHRT)

Phyllis Dain Library History Dissertation Award ($500). To the author of a dissertation treating the history of books, libraries, librarianship, or information science. *Winner*: P. Toby Graham.

Justin Winsor Prize Essay ($500). To an author of an outstanding essay embodying original historical research on a significant subject of library history. *Winner*: Christine Pawley.

Library Research Round Table (LRRT)

Jesse H. Shera Award for Distinguished Published Research ($500). For a research article on library and information studies published in English during the calendar year. *Winners*: Christine Pawley for "What to Read and How to Read: The Social Infrastructure of Young People's Reading, Osage, Iowa, 1870–1900" and Pamela Spence Richards for "Soviet-American Library Relations in the 1920s and 1930s: A Study in Mutual Fascination and Distrust."

Jesse H. Shera Award for Excellence in Doctoral Research ($500). For completed research on an unpublished paper of 10,000 words or less on library and information studies. *Winner*: Not awarded in 1999.

Map and Geography Round Table (MAGERT)

MAGERT Honors Award (citation and cash award). To recognize outstanding contributions by a MAGERT personal member to map librarianship, MAGERT, and/or a specific MAGERT project. *Winner*: Patrick McGlamery.

New Members Round Table (NMRT)

NMRT/EBSCO Scholarship ($1,000). To a U.S. or Canadian citizen to begin an MLS degree in an ALA-accredited program. Candidates must be members of NMRT. *Donor*: EBSCO Subscription Services. *Winner*: Caitlin B. Augusta.

NMRT/3M Professional Development Grant. To NMRT members to encourage professional development and participation in national ALA and NMRT activities. *Donor*: 3M. *Winners*: Janet Foster, Margaret Hughes, Jenella Zauha.

Shirley Olofson Memorial Award: *Winner*: Not awarded in 1999.

Public Library Association (PLA)

Advancement of Literacy Award (plaque). To a publisher, bookseller, hardware and/or software dealer, foundation, or similar group that has made a significant contribution to the advancement of adult literacy. *Donor*: *Library Journal*. *Winners*: Sheila Murphy, Lila Wallace-Reader's Digest Fund; Tom Davis, Mount Clemens (Michigan) Rotary Club.

Baker & Taylor Entertainment CD-ROM Grant ($2,500 worth of CD-ROMs). To promote the development of a circulating CD-ROM collection in public libraries and increase the exposure of the CD-ROM format. *Donor*: Baker & Taylor Entertainment. *Winner*: Holly Hentz, Hamburg (Michigan) Township Library.

Demco Creative Merchandising Grant ($1,000 and $2,000 worth of display furniture or supplies). To a public library proposing a project for the creative display and merchandising of materials either in the library or in the community. *Donor*: Demco, Inc. *Winner*: Middle Country Public Library, Centereach, New York.

Excellence in Small and/or Rural Public Service Award ($1,000). Honors a library serving a population of 10,000 or less that demonstrates excellence of service to its community as exemplified by an overall service program or a special program of significant accomplishment. *Donor*: EBSCO Subscription Services. *Winner*:

Little Boston Branch, Kitsap Regional Library, Bremerton, Washington.

Highsmith Library Innovation Award ($2,000). To recognize a public library's innovative achievement in planning and implementation of a creative program or service using technology. *Donor*: Highsmith, Inc. *Winner*: Richmond (British Columbia) Public Library.

Allie Beth Martin Award ($3,000). Honors a librarian who, in a public library setting, has demonstrated extraordinary range and depth of knowledge about books or other library materials and has distinguished ability to share that knowledge. *Donor*: Baker & Taylor Books. *Winner*: Grove Koger.

New Leaders Travel Grant (up to $1,500 each). To enhance the professional development and improve the expertise of public librarians by making their attendance at major professional development activities possible. *Donor*: GEAC, Inc. *Winners*: Jeffrey Gifford, Leah Sparks.

NTC Career Materials Resource Grant ($500 and $2,000 worth of materials from NTC Publishing Group). To a library proposing a project for the development of a career resources collection and program for a target audience either in the library or in the community. *Donor*: NTC Publishing Group. *Winner*: Carnegie Library, Homestead, Pennsylvania.

Charlie Robinson Award ($1,000). Honors a public library director who, over a period of seven years, has been a risk-taker, an innovator, and/or a change agent in a public library. *Donor*: Baker & Taylor Books. *Winner*: Ginnie Cooper.

Leonard Wertheimer Award ($1,000). To a person, group, or organization for work that enhances and promotes multilingual public library service. *Donor*: NTC Publishing Group. *Winner*: Toni Bissessar and staff, Multicultural Center, Brooklyn (New York) Public Library.

Publishing Committee

Carnegie Reading List Awards (amount varies). To ALA units for preparation and publication of reading lists, indexes, and other bibliographical and library aids useful in U.S. circulating libraries. *Donor*:

Andrew Carnegie Fund. *Winner*: Not awarded in 1999.

Whitney-Carnegie Awards (up to $5,000). For the publication of bibliographic aids for research. *Donor*: James Lyman Whitney and Andrew Carnegie Funds. *Winner*: Andy O. Alali, Roger G. Johnson, Joanna Sanders Mann.

Reference and User Services Association (RUSA)

Dartmouth Medal. For creating current reference works of outstanding quality and significance. *Donor*: Dartmouth College, Hanover, New Hampshire. *Winners*: John A. Garraty and Mark C. Carnes for *American National Biography* (Oxford University Press).

Denali Press Award ($500). For creating reference works of outstanding quality and significance that provide information specifically about ethnic and minority groups in the United States. *Donor*: Denali Press. *Winners*: Ronald Fernandez, Serfine Mendez Mendez, and Gail Cueto for *Puerto Rico Past and Present: An Encyclopedia* (Greenwood Press).

Disclosure Student Travel Award (BRASS) ($1,000). To enable a student in an ALA-accredited master's program interested in a career as a business librarian to attend an ALA Annual Conference. *Donor*: Disclosure, Inc. *Winner*: Christina Prendiville.

Facts on File Grant ($2,000). To a library for imaginative programming that would make current affairs more meaningful to an adult audience. *Donor*: Facts on File, Inc. *Winner*: New Mexico State University Library, Las Cruces.

Gale Research Award for Excellence in Business Librarianship (BRASS) ($1,000). To an individual for distinguished activities in the field of business librarianship. *Donor*: Gale Research Co. *Winner*: Priscilla Cheng Geahigan.

Gale Research Award for Excellence in Reference and Adult Services. To a library or library system for developing an imaginative and unique library resource to meet patrons' reference needs ($1,000). *Donor*: Gale Research Co. *Winner*: New Orleans Public Library.

Genealogical Publishing Company/History

Section Award ($1,000). To encourage and commend professional achievement in historical reference and research librarianship. *Donor*: The Genealogical Publishing Company. *Winner*: Thomas J. Muth, Jr.

Margaret E. Monroe Library Adult Services Award (citation). To a librarian for impact on library service to adults. *Winner*: Ann Bradshaw.

Isadore Gilbert Mudge–R. R. Bowker Award ($1,500). For distinguished contributions to reference librarianship. *Winner*: Virginia Massey-Burzio.

Reference Service Press Award ($1,000). To the author of the most outstanding article published in *RQ* during the preceding two volume years. *Donor*: Reference Service Press, Inc. *Winner*: Jennifer Mendelsohn.

John Sessions Memorial Award (plaque). To a library or library system in recognition of work with the labor community. *Donor*: AFL/CIO. *Winner*: Libraries for the Future.

Louis Shores–Oryx Press Award ($1,000). To an individual, team, or organization to recognize excellence in reviewing of books and other materials for libraries. *Donor*: Oryx Press. *Winners*: Brian E. Coutts and John B. Richard.

Social Responsibilities Round Table (SRRT)

Jackie Eubanks Memorial Award ($500). To honor outstanding achievement in promoting the acquisition and use of alternative media in libraries. *Donor*: AIP Task Force. *Winners*: Ed Weber and Julie Herrada.

Coretta Scott King Awards. See *Literary Prizes, 1999* by Gary Ink in Part 5.

Coretta Scott King New Talent Awards (formerly the Genesis Award) ($3,000). For an outstanding book designed to bring visibility to a black writer or artist at the beginning of his or her career. *Winners*: Author, Sharon G. Flake for *The Skin I'm In*; Illustrator, Eric Velasquez for *The Piano Man*.

SRRT Gay, Lesbian, and Bisexual Book Awards. To authors of fiction and nonfiction books of exceptional merit relating to the gay/lesbian experience. *Donor*: SRRT Gay Book Award Committee. *Winners*: Michael Cunningham for *The Hours*, Sarah Schulman for *Stage Struck: Theatre, AIDS and the Marketing of Gay America*.

Young Adult Library Services Association (YALSA)

Alex Awards. *Winners*: Carolyn Alexander for *Endurance*, James Finney Boylan for *Getting In*, Andie Dominick for *Needles*, John Gilstrap for *At All Costs*, Steve Kluger for *Last Days of Summer*, Robert Silverberg (ed.) for *Legends: Stories by the Masters of Modern Fantasy*, Kim Stanley Robinson for *Antarctica*, Esmeralda Santiago for *Almost a Woman*, Danzy Senna for *Caucasia*.

Baker & Taylor Conference Grants ($1,000). To young adult librarians in public or school libraries to attend an ALA Annual Conference for the first time. Candidates must be members of YALSA and have one to ten years of library experience. *Donor*: Baker & Taylor Books. *Winners*: Reed Williams, Patricia McHugh.

Book Wholesalers, Inc./YALSA Collection Development Grant ($1,000). To YALSA members who represent a public library and work directly with young adults, for collection development materials for young adults. *Winners*: Elizabeth S. Gallaway, Karen Hultz.

Margaret A. Edwards Award ($1,000). To an author whose book or books have provided young adults with a window through which they can view their world and which will help them to grow and to understand themselves and their role in society. *Donor: School Library Journal*. *Winner*: Anne McCaffrey.

Great Book Giveaway ($1,200 worth of books, videos, CDs and audio cassettes). *Winner*: Willow Springs (Missouri) High School Library.

Frances Henne/YALSA/VOYA Research Grant ($500 minimum). To provide seed money to an individual, institution, or group for a project to encourage research on library service to young adults. *Donor*: *Voice of Youth Advocates*. *Winners*: Sheila B. Anderson and John P. Bradford.

American Society for Information Science (ASIS)

ASIS Award of Merit. For an outstanding contribution to the field of information science. *Winner*: José Marie Griffiths.

ASIS Best Information Science Book. *Winner*: Not awarded in 1999.

ASIS/ISI Outstanding Information Science Teacher Award ($500). *Winner*: Peter Jacso.

ASIS Research Award. For a systematic program of research in a single area at a level beyond the single study, recognizing contributions in the field of information science. *Winners*: Donald Kraft and David C. Blair.

ASIS Special Award. To recognize long-term contributions to the advancement of information science and technology and enhancement of public access to information and discovery of mechanisms for improved transfer and utilization of knowledge. *Winner*: Not awarded in 1999.

James Cretsos Leadership Award. *Winner*: Douglas Kaylor.

Watson Davis Award. *Winner*: Jessica L. Milstead.

ISI Citation Analysis Research Grant. *Winner*: Ian Rowlands.

ISI I.S. Doctoral Dissertation Proposal Scholarship ($1,500). *Winner*: Brian Detlor.

Pratt Severn Best Student Research Paper. *Winner*: Kelly Maglaughlin.

UMI Doctoral Dissertation Award. *Winner*: Jacqueline Algon.

John Wiley Best JASIS Paper Award. *Winners*: Vol. 48, Paul Soloman; Vol. 49, Special Award for a Series, Peiling Wang and Dagobert Soergel.

Art Libraries Society of North America (ARLIS/NA)

John Benjamins Award. To recognize research and publication in the study and analysis of periodicals in the fields of the fine arts, literature, and cross-disciplinary studies. *Winner*: Tara Leigh Tappert.

Andrew Cahan Photography Award ($750). To encourage participation of art information professionals in the field of photography through reference, research, or bibliographic work. *Winner*: Barbara Mathe.

Distinguished Service Award. Toni Petersen.

Melva J. Dwyer Award. To the creators of exceptional reference or research tools relating to Canadian art and architecture. *Winners*: David Milne, Jr., and David P. Silcox for *David B. Milne: Catalogue Raisonné of Paintings*.

Jim and Anna Emmett Travel Award. To assist a handicapped library professional to participate in the ARLIS/NA annual conference. *Winner*: Not awarded in 1999.

Getty Trust Publications/Avery Index Attendance Award ($500). To encourage conference attendance by ARLIS/NA members. *Winner*: Not awarded in 1999.

G. K. Hall Conference Attendance Award ($400). To encourage attendance at the annual conference by ARLIS/NA committee members, chapter officers, and moderators. *Winner*: Susan Wyngaard.

Howard and Beverly Joy Karno Award ($1,000). To provide financial assistance to a professional art librarian in Latin America through interaction with ARLIS/NA members and conference participation. *Cosponsor:* Howard Karno Books. *Winner*: Carlos Acuna Ramos.

David Mirvish Books/Books on Art Travel Award ($500 Canadian). To encourage art librarianship in Canada. *Winner*: Andrea Retfalvi.

Gerd Muehsam Award. To one or more graduate students in library science programs to recognize excellence in a graduate paper or project. *Winner*: Lena Stebley for *Visual Arts Faculty Perspective on Teaching with Digital Images: Results of Focus Groups*.

Puvill Libros Award ($1,000). To encourage professional development of European art librarians through interaction with ARLIS/NA colleagues and conference participation. *Winner*: Anja Lollesgaard.

Research Libraries Group Asia/Oceania Award ($1,000). To encourage professional development of art information professionals who reside in Asia/Oceania through interaction with ARLIS/NA colleagues and conference participation. *Winner*: Not awarded in 1999.

Research Libraries Group Award ($1,000). To promote participation in ARLIS/NA by supporting conference travel for an individual who has not attended an annual conference. *Winner*: Mikel Breitenstein.

H. W. Wilson Foundation Research Award. To support research activities by ARLIS/NA members in the fields of librarianship, visual resources curatorship, and the arts. *Winner*: Clare Hills-Nova.

Association for Library and Information Science Education (ALISE)

ALISE Doctoral Student Dissertation Awards ($400). To promote the exchange of research ideas between doctoral students and established researchers. *Winner*: Hong Xie.

ALISE Methodology Paper Competition ($500). To stimulate the communication of research methodology. *Winner*: Yin Zhang.

ALISE Research Grant Awards (one or more grants totaling $5,000): Karen E. Pettigrew and Lynee McKechnie, and Christopher Brown-Syed.

ALISE Research Paper Competition ($500). For a research paper concerning any aspect of librarianship or information studies by a member of ALISE. *Winner*: Carolyn Haythornthwaite.

Association of Jewish Libraries (AJL)

AJL Bibliography Book Award. *Winner*: Isaac Goldberg, compiler and ed., for *Solomon ibn Gabirol: A Bibliography of His Poems in Translation*.

AJL Reference Book Award. *Winner*: Fruma Mohrer and Marek Web for *Guide to the YIVO Archives*.

Special Body of Work Citation. *Winner*: Not awarded in 1999.

Sydney Taylor Children's Book Award. *Winner*: Maxine Rose Schur for *The Peddler's Gift*.

Sydney Taylor Manuscript Award. *Winner*: June E. Nislick for *Zayda Was a Cowboy*.

Sydney Taylor Older Children's Book Award. *Winner*: Sybil Rosen for *Speed of Light*.

Beta Phi Mu

Beta Phi Mu Award. *See under* American Library Association.

Beta Phi Mu Doctoral Dissertation Scholarship. *Winner*: Elizabeth Gremore Figa.

Eugene Garfield Doctoral Dissertation Fellowships. *Winners*: Youngbok Choi, Anne R. Diekema, Bill Edgar, Anita Komlodi, Shin-jeng Lin, Rong Tang.

Harold Lancour Scholarship for Foreign Study ($1,000). For graduate study in a foreign country related to the applicant's work or schooling. *Winner*: John Richardson, Jr.

Sarah Rebecca Reed Scholarship ($1,500). For study at an ALA-accredited library school. *Winner*: Kathleen B. Warren.

Frank B. Sessa Scholarship for Continuing Professional Education ($750). For continuing education for a Beta Phi Mu member. *Winner*: Jane Kemp.

E. Blanche Woolls Scholarship. For a beginning student in school library media services. *Winner*: Laurie S. Grey.

Bibliographical Society of America (BSA)

BSA Fellowships ($1,000–$2,000). For scholars involved in bibliographical inquiry and research in the history of the book trades and in publishing history. *Winners*: Gregory S. Brown, Konstantin Dierks, Lamia Doumato, Alison K. Frazier, James W. Hankins, John McDonnell Hintermaier, Trish Loughran, Nicholas Andrew Mason, Nerijus Udrenas.

Canadian Library Association (CLA)

Olga B. Bishop Award. *Winner*: Katherine Profit.

CLA Award for Achievement in Technical Services. *Winner*: Advanced Education Media Acquisitions Centre, Langara College, Vancouver.

CLA Award for the Advancement of Intellectual Freedom in Canada. *Winner*: Greater Victoria Public Library Board and Staff.

CLA Dafoe Scholarship. *Winner*: Theresa Yun Yee Lee.

CLA/Faxon Marketing Award. *Winner*: Richmond (British Columbia) Public Library.

CLA/Information Today Award for Innovative Technology. *Donor*: Information Today, Inc. *Winners*: British Columbia College and Institute Library Services at Langara College, Vancouver, and Université Laval Library, Sainte-Foy, Quebec.

CLA Outstanding Service to Librarianship Award. *Donor*: R. R. Bowker. *Winner*: Frances Schwenger.

CLA Research and Development Grant ($1,000). *Winner*: Not awarded in 1999.

CLA Student Article Award. *Winner*: Gayle Bushell.

OCLC/CLA Award. *Winner*: Not awarded in 1999.

William C. Watkinson Award. *Winner*: Keith Sacré.

H. W. Wilson Scholarship. *Winner*: Claire Lauzon.

World Book Graduate Scholarship in Library Science. *Winner*: Paulette Rothbauer.

Canadian Association of College and University Libraries (CACUL)

CACUL Award for Outstanding Academic Librarian. *Winner*: Richard Ellis.

CACUL/CTCL Award of Merit. *Winner*: Frieda Wiebe.

CACUL Innovation Achievement Award ($1,500). *Winners*: Simon Fraser University, Burnaby, British Columbia; COPPUL, Calgary, Alberta; University of Manitoba, Winnipeg.

Canadian Association of Public Libraries (CAPL)

CAPL Outstanding Public Library Service Award. *Winner*: Jocelyn LeBel.

Canadian Association of Special Libraries and Information Services (CASLIS)

CASLIS Award for Special Librarianship in Canada. *Winner*: Maggie Weaver.

Canadian Library Trustees Association (CLTA)

CLTA Achievement in Literacy Award. For an innovative literacy program by a public library board. *Donor*: ABC Canada. *Winner*: High River Centennial Library Board, High River, Alberta.

CLTA Merit Award for Distinguished Service as a Public Library Trustee. For outstanding leadership in the advancement of public library trusteeship and public library service in Canada. *Winner*: Neil Williams.

Canadian School Library Association (CSLA)

National Book Service Teacher-Librarian of the Year Award. *Winner*: Barbara Poustie.

Margaret B. Scott Award of Merit. For the development of school libraries in Canada. *Winner*: Rose Dotten.

Chinese-American Librarians Association (CALA)

CALA Scholarship. *Winner*: Not awarded in 1999.

Sheila Suen Lai Scholarship ($500). To a student of Chinese nationality or descent pursuing full-time graduate studies for a master's degree or Ph.D. degree in an ALA-accredited library school. *Winner*: Jin Zhang.

C. C. Seetoo/CALA Conference Travel Scholarship ($500). For a student to attend the ALA Annual Conference and CALKA program. *Winner*: Janet Tom.

Church and Synagogue Library Association (CSLA)

CSLA Award for Outstanding Congregational Librarian. For distinguished service to the congregation and/or community through devotion to the congregational library. *Winner*: Mary Jane Conger.

CSLA Award for Outstanding Congregational Library. For responding in creative and innovative ways to the library's mission of reaching and serving the congregation and/or the wider community. *Winner*: St. Paul's United Methodist Church, Kerriville, Texas.

CSLA Award for Outstanding Contribution to Congregational Libraries. For providing inspiration, guidance, leadership, or resources to enrich the field of church or synagogue librarianship. *Winner*: Louise Swartz.

Muriel Fuller Scholarship Award. *Winner*: Not awarded in 1999.

Helen Keating Ott Award for Outstanding Contribution to Congregational Libraries. *Winner*: Not awarded in 1999.

Pat Tabler Memorial Scholarship Award. *Winner*: Shirley McCartney.

Council on Library and Information Resources

A. R. Zipf Fellowship in Information Management ($5,000). Awarded annually to a student enrolled in graduate school who shows exceptional promise for leadership and technical achievement. *Winner*: Debra Ruffner Weiss.

Gale Research Company

ALTA/Gale Outstanding Trustee Conference Grant Award. *See under* American Library Association, American Library Trustee Association.

Gale Research Award for Excellence in Business Librarianship; and Gale Research Award for Excellence in Reference and Adult Services. *See under* American Library Association, Reference and User Services Association.

Gale Research Financial Development Award. *See under* American Library Association.

Medical Library Association (MLA)

Estelle Brodman Award for the Academic Medical Librarian of the Year. To honor significant achievement, potential for leadership, and continuing excellence at mid-career in the area of academic health sciences librarianship. *Winner*: E. Diane Johnson.

Lois Ann Colaianni Award for Excellence and Achievement in Hospital Librarianship ($500). To a member of MLA who has made significant contributions to the profession in the area of overall distinction or leadership in hospital librarianship. *Winner*: Jacqueline D. Bastille.

Cunningham Memorial International Fellowship ($3,000). A six-month grant and travel expenses in the United States and Canada for a foreign librarian. *Winner*: Timothy Shola Abolarinwa.

Louise Darling Medal. For distinguished achievement in collection development in the health sciences. *Winner*: Jonathan Eldredge.

Janet Doe Lectureship ($250). *Winner*: Sherrilynee Fuller.

EBSCO/MLA Annual Meeting Grant ($1,000). *Winner*: Shirley Brooke.

Ida and George Eliot Prize ($200). For an essay published in any journal in the preceding calendar year that has been judged most effective in furthering medical librarianship. *Donor*: Login Brothers Books. *Winners*: Barbara Schloman, Judith Burnham, Linda Slater, Eileen M. Wakiji for "Mapping the Literature of Allied Health," *Bulletin of the Medical Library Association*, vol. 85, 1997.

Murray Gottlieb Prize ($100). For the best unpublished essay submitted by a medical librarian on the history of some aspect of health sciences or a detailed description of a library exhibit. *Donor*: Ralph and Jo Grimes. *Winners*: Godfrey S. Belleh and Eric v.d. Luft.

Joseph Leiter NLM/MLA Lectureship. *Winner*: Daniel Callahan.

MLA Award for Distinguished Public Service. *Winner*: Not awarded in 1999.

MLA Doctoral Fellowship ($2,000). *Donor*: Institute for Scientific Information (ISI). *Winner*: Not awarded in 1999.

MLA Scholarship ($2,000). For graduate study in medical librarianship at an ALA-accredited library school. *Winner*: Cynthia Lynn Ammons.

MLA Scholarship for Minority Students ($2,000). *Winner*: Tomeka Oubichon.

John P. McGovern Award Lectureships ($500). *Winner*: Daniel Burrus.

Marcia C. Noyes Award. For an outstanding contribution to medical librarianship. The award is the highest professional distinction of MLA. *Winner*: T. Mark Hodges.

Rittenhouse Award ($500). For the best unpublished paper on medical librarianship submitted by a student enrolled in, or having been enrolled in, a course for credit in an ALA-accredited library school or a trainee in an internship program in medical librarianship. *Donor*: Rittenhouse Medical Bookstore. *Winner*: Not awarded in 1999.

Frank Bradway Rogers Information Advancement Award ($500). For an outstanding contribution to knowledge of health science information delivery. *Donor*: Institute for Scientific Information (ISI). *Winners*: BioSites, Beryl Glitz, Anne Swedenberg Prussing, Brian Warling, Melissa Just, Mary Buttner, Greg Williamson.

K. G. Saur (Munich, Germany)

Hans-Peter Geh Grant. To enable a librarian from the former Soviet Union to attend a conference in Germany or elsewhere. *Winner*: Natalia Zhadko, Director, Rudomino Training School, Library for Foreign Literature, Moscow.

K. G. Saur Award for Best *College and Research Libraries* Article. *See under* American Library Association, Association of College and Research Libraries.

Society of American Archivists (SAA)

C. F. W. Coker Prize for Finding Aids. *Winners*: Francis X. Blouin, Leonard A. Coombs, Claudia Carlen, Elizabeth Yakel, Katherine J. Gill.

Colonial Dames Scholarship. *Winners*: Melissa Salazar, Erika Piola.

Council Exemplary Service Award. *Winner*: Not awarded in 1999.

Distinguished Service Award. Recognizes outstanding service and exemplary contribution to the profession. *Winner*: Not awarded in 1999.

Fellows Posner Prize. For an outstanding essay dealing with a facet of archival administration, history, theory, or methodology, published in the latest volume of the *American Archivist*. *Winner*: Roy Turnbaugh.

Philip M. Hamer–Elizabeth Hamer Kegan Award. For individuals and/or institutions that have increased public awareness of a specific body of documents. *Winner*: Delaware Public Archives.

Oliver Wendell Holmes Award. To enable overseas archivists already in the United States or Canada for training to attend the SAA annual meeting. *Winner*: Ciaran Trace.

J. Franklin Jameson Award. For an institution not directly involved in archival work that promotes greater public awareness, appreciation, and support of archival activities and programs. *Winner*: John B. Harlan.

Sister M. Claude Lane Award. For a significant contribution to the field of religious archives. *Winner*: Not awarded in 1999.

Waldo Gifford Leland Prize. For writing of superior excellence and usefulness in the field of archival history, theory, or practice. *Winner*: Not awarded in 1999.

Minority Student Award. Encourages minority students to consider careers in the archival profession and promotes minority participation in the Society of American Archivists with complimentary registration to the annual meeting. *Winners*: Tywanna Marie Whorley, Teresa Maria Mora.

Theodore Calvin Pease Award. For the best student paper. *Winner*: Kathleen Feeney, University of North Carolina at Chapel Hill, for "Retrieval of Archival Finding Aids Using World Wide Web Search Engines."

Preservation Publication Award. Recognizes an outstanding work published in North America that advances the theory or the practice of preservation in archival institutions. *Winner*: James M. Reilly.

SAA Fellows. Highest individual distinction awarded to a limited number of members for their outstanding contribution to the archival profession. *Honored*: Bruce Bruemmer, Elizabeth Yakel.

Special Libraries Association (SLA)

Mary Adeline Connor Professional Development Scholarship ($6,000). *Winner*: Not awarded in 1999.

John Cotton Dana Award. For exceptional support and encouragement of special librarianship. *Winner*: Fred Roper.

Dow Jones 21st Century Competencies Award. *Winner*: Lucy Lettis.

Steven I. Goldspiel Research Grant. Sponsor: Disclosure, Inc. *Winners*: James M. Turner and Michèle Hudon for "Organizing Moving Image Collections for the Digital Era."

Hall of Fame Award. To a member or members of the association at or near the end of an active professional career for an extended and sustained period of distinguished service to the association. *Winners*: Ellen Mimnaugh, Angela Pollis.

Innovations in Technology Award ($1,000). To a member of the association for innovative use and application of technology in a special library setting. *Winner*: Not awarded in 1999.

International Special Librarians Day Award. *Winner*: Susan Gleckner.

SLA Affirmative Action Scholarship ($6,000). *Winner*: Salvador Covarrubias.

SLA Fellows. *Winners*: Robert Bellanti, Susan Klopper, Barbara Spiegelman, Gloria Zamora.

SLA Information Today Award for Innovations in Technology. *Winner*: Not awarded in 1999.

SLA President's Award. *Winner*: Not awarded in 1999.

SLA Professional Award. *Winner*: Not awarded in 1999.

SLA Public Relations Media Award. *Winner*: Leigh Buchanan.

SLA Public Relations Member Achievement Award. *Winner*: Lisa Guedea Carreño.

SLA Student Scholarships ($6,000). For students with financial need who show potential for special librarianship. *Winners*: Kim Herzig, Selicia Poe, Kenneth Indles.

Rose L. Vormelker Award. *Winner*: G. Lynn Berad.

H. W. Wilson Company Award. For the most outstanding article in the past year's *Information Outlook*. *Donor*: H. W. Wilson Company. *Winners*: Barbara Greenman and Deborah Grealy for "Special Librarians Set New Standard for Academe" (August 1998).

Alphabetical List of Award Names

Individual award names are followed by a colon and the name of the awarding body; e.g., the Bound to Stay Bound Books Scholarship is given by ALA/Association for Library Service to Children. Consult the preceding list of Library Scholarship and Award Recipients, 1999, which is alphabetically arranged by organization, to locate recipients and further information. Awards named for individuals are listed by surname.

AALL Scholarships: American Association of Law Libraries

AASL ABC/CLIO Leadership Grant: ALA/American Association of School Librarians

AASL Crystal Apple Award: ALA/American Association of School Librarians

AASL/Highsmith Research Grant: ALA/American Association of School Librarians

AASL Information Plus Continuing Education Scholarship: ALA/American Association of School Librarians

AASL School Librarians Workshop Scholarship: ALA/American Association of School Librarians

ACRL Academic or Research Librarian of the Year Award: ALA/Association of College and Research Libraries

ACRL Doctoral Dissertation Fellowship: ALA/Association of College and Research Libraries

ACRL/EBSS Distinguished Education and Behavioral Sciences Librarian Award: ALA/Association of College and Research Libraries

AJL Bibliography Book Award: Association of Jewish Libraries

AJL Reference Book Award: Association of Jewish Libraries

ALA/Information Today Library of the Future Award: ALA

ALISE Doctoral Student Dissertation Awards: Association for Library and Information Science Education

ALISE Methodology Paper Competition: Association for Library and Information Science Education

ALISE Research Award: Association for Library and Information Science Education

ALISE Research Grant Award: Association for Library and Information Science Education

ALISE Research Paper Competition: Association for Library and Information Science Education

ALSC/Book Wholesalers Summer Reading Program Grant: ALA/Association for Library Service to Children

ALSC/Econo-Clad Literature Program Award: ALA/Association for Library Service to Children

ALSC/REFORMA Pura Belpré Award: ALA/Association for Library Service to Children

ALTA/Gale Outstanding Trustee Conference Grant Award: ALA/American Library Trustee Association

ALTA Literacy Award: ALA/American Library Trustee Association

ALTA Major Benefactors Honor Awards: ALA/American Library Trustee Association

ASCLA Leadership Achievement Award: ALA/Association of Specialized and Cooperative Library Agencies

ASCLA/National Organization on Disability Award: ALA/Association of Specialized and Cooperative Library Agencies

ASCLA Professional Achievement Award: ALA/Association of Specialized and Cooperative Library Agencies

ASCLA Research Award: ALA/Association of Specialized and Cooperative Library Agencies

ASCLA Service Award: ALA/Association of Specialized and Cooperative Library Agencies

ASIS Award of Merit: American Society for Information Science

ASIS Best Information Science Book: American Society for Information Science

ASIS Doctoral Dissertation Scholarship: American Society for Information Science

ASIS Outstanding Information Science Teacher Award: American Society for Information Science

ASIS Research Award: American Society for Information Science

ASIS Special Award: American Society for Information Science

Advancement of Literacy Award: ALA/Public Library Association

May Hill Arbuthnot Honor Lecturer: ALA/Association for Library Service to Children

Armed Forces Library Certificate of Merit: ALA/Armed Forces Libraries Round Table

Armed Forces Library Newsbank Scholarship Award: ALA/Armed Forces Libraries Round Table

Armed Forces Library Round Table Achievement Citation: ALA/Armed Forces Libraries Round Table

Hugh C. Atkinson Memorial Award: ALA

Award for the Advancement of Intellectual Freedom in Canada: Canadian Library Association

Carroll Preston Baber Research Grant: ALA

Baker & Taylor Conference Grants: ALA/Young Adult Library Services Association

Baker & Taylor Entertainment CD-ROM Grant: ALA/Public Library Association

Mildred L. Batchelder Award: ALA/Association for Library Service to Children

Louise Seaman Bechtel Fellowship: ALA/Association for Library Service to Children

John Benjamins Award: Art Libraries Society of North America

Best of *LRTS* Award: ALA/Association for Library Collections and Technical Services

Beta Phi Mu Award: ALA

Olga B. Bishop Award: Canadian Library Association

Blackwell's Scholarship Award: ALA/Association for Library Collections and Technical Services

Bogle/Pratt International Travel Fund Award: ALA

Book Wholesalers, Inc. Collection Development Grant: ALA/Young Adult Library Services Association

Bound to Stay Bound Books Scholarship: ALA/Association for Library Service to Children

Bowker/Ulrich's Serials Librarianship Award: ALA/Association for Library Collections and Technical Services, Serials Section

William Young Boyd Military Novel Award: ALA

Estelle Brodman Award for the Academic Medical Librarian of the Year: Medical Library Association

BSA Fellowships: Bibliographical Society of America

CACUL Award for Outstanding Academic Librarian: Canadian Association of College and University Libraries

CACUL Innovation Achievement Award: Canadian Association of College and University Libraries

CACUL/CTCL Award of Merit: Canadian Association of College and University Libraries

Andrew Cahan Photography Award: Art Libraries Society of North America

CAPL Outstanding Public Library Service Award: Canadian Association of Public Libraries

CASLIS Award for Special Librarianship in Canada: Canadian Association of Special Libraries and Information Services

CIS/GODORT/ALA Documents to the People Award: ALA/Government Documents Round Table

CLA Award for Achievement in Technical Services: Canadian Library Association

CLA Award for the Advancement of Intellectual Freedom in Canada: Canadian Library Association

CLA Dafoe Scholarship: Canadian Library Association

CLA/Faxon Marketing Award: Canadian Library Association

CLA/Information Today Award for Innovative Technology: Canadian Library Association

CLA Outstanding Service to Librarianship Award: Canadian Library Association

CLA Research and Development Grants: Canadian Library Association

CLA Student Article Award: Canadian Library Association

CLTA Achievement in Literacy Award: Canadian Library Trustees Association

CLTA Merit Award for Distinguished Service as a Public Library Trustee: Canadian Library Trustees Association

CSLA Award for Outstanding Congregational Librarian: Church and Synagogue Library Association

CSLA Award for Outstanding Congregational Library: Church and Synagogue Library Association

CSLA Award for Outstanding Contribution to Congregational Libraries: Church and Synagogue Library Association

Francis Joseph Campbell Citation: ALA/Association of Specialized and Cooperative Library Agencies

Andrew Carnegie Medal: ALA/Association for Library Service to Children

Carnegie Reading List Awards: ALA/Publishing Committee

Marshall Cavendish Scholarship: ALA

Certificate of Achievement: ALA/Library Administration and Management Association

James Bennett Childs Award: ALA/Government Documents Round Table

David H. Clift Scholarship: ALA

C. F. W. Coker Prize: Society of American Archivists

Lois Ann Colaianni Award for Excellence and Achievement in Hospital Librarianship: Medical Library Association.

Mary Adeline Connor Professional Development Scholarship: Special Libraries Association

James Cretsos Leadership Award: American Society for Information Science

Cunningham Memorial International Fellowship: Medical Library Association

Phyllis Dain Library History Dissertation Award: ALA/Library History Round Table

John Cotton Dana Award: Special Libraries Association

John Cotton Dana Library Public Relations Award: ALA/Library Administration and Management Association

Louise Darling Medal: Medical Library Association

Dartmouth Medal: ALA/Reference and User Services Association

Watson Davis Award: American Society for Information Science

Demco Creative Merchandising Grant: ALA/Public Library Association

Denali Press Award: ALA/Reference and User Services Association

Melvil Dewey Award: ALA

Disclosure Student Travel Award (BRASS): ALA/Reference and User Services Association

Distinguished School Administrators Award: ALA/American Association of School Librarians

Distinguished Service Award: ALA/Federal Librarians Round Table

Distinguished Service Award, AASL/Baker & Taylor: ALA/American Association of School Librarians

Distinguished Service Award, ARLIS/NA: Art Libraries Society of North America

Distinguished Service to ALSC Award: ALA/Association for Library Service to Children

Janet Doe Lectureship: Medical Library Association

Dow Jones 21st Century Competencies Award: Special Libraries Association

Tom C. Drewes Scholarship: ALA

Miriam Dudley Bibliographic Instruction Librarian of the Year: ALA/Association of College and Research Libraries

Melva J. Dwyer Award: Art Libraries Society of North America

EBSCO ALA Conference Sponsorships: ALA

EBSCO Community College Leadership Resources Achievement Awards: ALA/Association of College and Research Libraries

EBSCO Community College Program Award: ALA/Association of College and Research Libraries

EBSCO/MLA Annual Meeting Grant: Medical Library Association

Margaret A. Edwards Award: ALA/Young Adult Library Services Association

Education Behavioral Sciences Section Library Award: ALA/Association of College and Research Libraries

Ida and George Eliot Prize: Medical Library Association

EMIERT/Gale Research Multicultural Award: ALA/Ethnic Materials and Information Exchange Round Table

Jim and Anna Emmett Travel Award: Art Libraries Society of North America

Equality Award: ALA

Jackie Eubanks Memorial Award: ALA/Social Responsibilities Round Table

Excellence in Small and/or Rural Public Service Award: ALA/Public Library Association

Facts on File Grant: ALA/Reference and User Services Association

Federal Librarians Achievement Award: ALA/Federal Librarians Round Table

Fellows Posner Prize: Society of American Archivists

First Step Award, Serials Section/Wiley Professional Development Grant: ALA/Association for Library Collections and Technical Services

Adelaide del Frate Conference Sponsor Award: ALA/Federal Librarians Round Table

Freedom to Read Foundation Roll of Honor Awards: ALA

Friendly Booth Award: ALA/Exhibits Round Table

Elizabeth Futas Catalyst for Change Award: ALA

Loleta D. Fyan Award: ALA

Gale Research Award for Excellence in Business Librarianship (BRASS): ALA/Reference and User Services Association

Gale Research Award for Excellence in Reference and Adult Services: ALA/Reference and User Services Association

Gale Research Financial Development Award: ALA

Mary V. Gaver Scholarship: ALA

Hans-Peter Geh Grant: K. G. Saur

Genealogical Publishing Company/History Section Award: ALA/Reference and User Services Association

Getty Trust Publications/Avery Index Attendance Award: Art Libraries Society of North America

Steven I. Goldspiel Research Grant: Special Libraries Association

Murray Gottlieb Prize: Medical Library Association

Great Book Giveaway: ALA/Young Adult Library Services Association

Grolier Foundation Award: ALA

Grolier National Library Week Grant: ALA

G. K. Hall Conference Attendance Award: Art Libraries Society of North America

Hall of Fame Award: Special Libraries Association

Philip M. Hamer–Elizabeth Hamer Kegan Award: Society of American Archivists

Frances Henne Award: ALA/American Association of School Librarians

Frances Henne/YALSA/VOYA Research Grant: ALA/Young Adult Library Services Association

Highsmith Library Innovation Award: ALA/Public Library Association

Bernadine Abbott Hoduski Founders Award: ALA/Government Documents Round Table

Oliver Wendell Holmes Award: Society of American Archivists

Miriam L. Hornback Scholarship: ALA

Paul Howard Award for Courage: ALA

Christopher J. Hoy/ERT Scholarship: ALA/Exhibits Round Table

John Ames Humphry/OCLC/Forest Press Award: ALA

John Phillip Immroth Memorial Award for Intellectual Freedom: ALA/Intellectual Freedom Round Table

Information Technology Pathfinder Award: ALA/American Association of School Librarians

Innovations in Technology Award: Special Libraries Association

Instruction Section Innovation in Instruction Award: ALA/Association of College and Research Libraries

Instruction Section Publication of the Year Award: ALA/Association of College and Research Libraries

International Special Librarians Day Award: Special Libraries Association.

ISI Citation Analysis Research Grant: American Society for Information Science

ISI I.S. Doctoral Dissertation Scholarship: American Society for Information Science

J. Franklin Jameson Award for Archival Advocacy: Society of American Archivists

Howard and Beverly Joy Karno Award: Art Libraries Society of North America

Kohlstedt Exhibit Award: ALA/Exhibits Round Table

Sheila Suen Lai Scholarship: Chinese-American Librarians Association

LAMA Cultural Diversity Grant: ALA/Library Administration and Management Association

LAMA President's Award: ALA/Library Administration and Management Association

LAMA Recognition of Group Achievement Award: ALA/Library Administration and Management Association

LAMA/YBP Student Writing and Development Award: ALA/Library Administration and Management Association

Harold Lancour Scholarship for Foreign Study: Beta Phi Mu

Sister M. Claude Lane Award: Society of American Archivists

Marta Lange/CQ Award: ALA/Association of College and Research Libraries

Samuel Lazerow Fellowship for Research in Acquisitions or Technical Services: ALA/Association of College and Research Libraries

Katharine Kyes Leab and Daniel J. Leab American Book Prices Current Exhibition Catalogue Awards: ALA/Association of College and Research Libraries

Leadership in Library Acquisitions Award: ALA/Association for Library Collections and Technical Services

Tony B. Leisner Scholarship: ALA

Joseph Leiter NLM/MLA Lectureship: Medical Library Association

Waldo Gifford Leland Prize: Society of American Archivists

Library Buildings Award: ALA/Library Administration and Management Association

LITA/GEAC-CLSI Scholarship in Library and Information Technology: ALA/Library and Information Technology Association

LITA/Christian Larew Memorial Scholarship: ALA/Library and Information Technology Association

LITA/Library Hi Tech Award: ALA/Library and Information Technology Association

LITA/LSSI Minority Scholarship in Library and Information Science: ALA/Library and Information Technology Association

LITA/OCLC Frederick G. Kilgour Award for Research in Library and Information Technology: ALA/Library and Information Technology Association

LITA/OCLC Minority Scholarship in Library and Information Technology: ALA/Library and Information Technology Association

Joseph W. Lippincott Award: ALA

John P. McGovern Award Lecturships: Medical Library Association

MAGERT Honors Award: ALA/Map and Geography Round Table

Margaret Mann Citation: ALA/Association for Library Collections and Technical Services

Allie Beth Martin Award: ALA/Public Library Association

Frederic G. Melcher Scholarship: ALA/Association for Library Service to Children

Minority Student Award: Society of American Archivists

David Mirvish Books/Books on Art Travel Award: Art Libraries Society of North America

MLA Award for Distinguished Public Service: Medical Library Association

MLA Doctoral Fellowship: Medical Library Association

MLA Scholarship: Medical Library Association

MLA Scholarship for Minority Students: Medical Library Association

Margaret E. Monroe Library Adult Services Award: ALA/Reference and User Services Association

Isadore Gilbert Mudge–R. R. Bowker Award: ALA/Reference and User Services Association

Gerd Muehsam Award: Art Libraries Society of North America

National Book Service Teacher-Librarian of the Year Award: Canadian School Library Association

National School Library Media Program of the Year Award: ALA/American Association of School Librarians

New Leaders Travel Grant: ALA/Public Library Association

New Talent Award: ALA/Social Responsibilities Round Table

Martinus Nijhoff International West European Specialist Study Grant: ALA Association of College and Research Libraries

NMRT/EBSCO Scholarship: ALA/New Members Round Table

NMRT/3M Professional Development Grant: ALA/New Members Round Table

Marcia C. Noyes Award: Medical Library Association

NTC Career Materials Resource Grant: ALA/Public Library Association

Oberly Award for Bibliography in the Agricultural Sciences: ALA/Association of College and Research Libraries

Eli M. Oboler Memorial Award: ALA/Intellectual Freedom Round Table

OCLC/CLA Award: Canadian Library Association

Shirley Olofson Memorial Award: ALA/New Members Round Table

Helen Keating Ott Award for Outstanding Contribution to Congregational Libraries: Church and Synagogue Library Association

Theodore Calvin Pease Award: Society of American Archivists

Penguin Putnam Awards: ALA/Association for Library Service to Children

Esther J. Piercy Award: ALA/Association for Library Collections and Technical Services

Pratt Severn Best Student Research Paper: American Society for Information Science

Preservation Publication Award: Society of American Archivists

Puvill Libros Award: Art Libraries Society of North America

Rare Books & Manuscripts Librarianship Award: ALA/Association of College and Research Libraries

Rcadex/GODORT/ALA Catharine J. Reynolds Award: ALA/Government Documents Round Table

Sarah Rebecca Reed Scholarship: Beta Phi Mu

Reference Service Press Award: ALA/Reference and User Services Association

Research Libraries Group Asia/Oceania Award: Art Libraries Society of North America

Research Libraries Group Award: Art Libraries Society of North America

Rittenhouse Award: Medical Library Association

Charlie Robinson Award: ALA/Public Library Association

Frank Bradway Rogers Information Advancement Award: Medical Library Association

David Rozkuszka Scholarship: ALA/Government Documents Round Table

SAA Fellows: Society of American Archivists

K. G. Saur Award for Best *College and Research Libraries* Article: ALA/Association of College and Research Libraries

Margaret B. Scott Award of Merit: Canadian School Library Association

C. C. Seetoo/CALA Conference Travel Scholarship: Chinese-American Librarians Association

Frank B. Sessa Scholarship for Continuing Professional Education: Beta Phi Mu

John Sessions Memorial Award: ALA/Reference and User Services Association

Jesse H. Shera Award for Distinguished Published Research: ALA/Library Research Round Table

Jesse H. Shera Award for Excellence in Doctoral Research: ALA/Library Research Round Table

Louis Shores Oryx Press Award: ALA/Reference and User Services Association

SLA Affirmative Action Scholarship: Special Libraries Association
SLA Fellows: Special Libraries Association
SLA Information Today Award for Innovations in Technology: Special Libraries Association
SLA President's Award: Special Libraries Association
SLA Professional Award: Special Libraries Association
SLA Public Relations Media Award: Special Libraries Association
SLA Public Relations Member Achievement Award: Special Libraries Association
SLA Student Scholarships: Special Libraries Association
SRRT/Gay and Lesbian Task Force, Gay, Lesbian, and Bisexual Book Awards: ALA/Social Responsibilities Round Table
Special Body of Work Citation: Association of Jewish Libraries
State and Regional Achievement Award–Freedom to Read Foundation: ALA/Intellectual Freedom Round Table
Pat Tabler Memorial Scholarship: Church and Synagogue Library Association
Sydney Taylor Children's Book Award: Association of Jewish Libraries
Sydney Taylor Manuscript Award: Association of Jewish Libraries
Sydney Taylor Older Children's Book Award: Association of Jewish Libraries
Trustee Citations: ALA/American Library Trustee Association
UMI Doctoral Dissertation Award: American Society for Information Science
Rose L. Vormelker Award: Special Libraries Association
William C. Watkinson Award: Canadian Library Association
Leonard Wertheimer Award: ALA/Public Library Association
Virginia and Herbert White Award for Promoting Librarianship: ALA
Whitney-Carnegie Awards: ALA
Laura Ingalls Wilder Award: ALA/Association for Library Service to Children
John Wiley Best *JASIS* Paper Award: American Society for Information Science
H. W. Wilson Award: Special Libraries Association
H. W. Wilson Foundation Research Award: Art Libraries Society of North America
H. W. Wilson Library Staff Development Award: ALA
H. W. Wilson Scholarship: Canadian Library Association
Justin Winsor Prize Essay: ALA/Library History Round Table
Women's National Book Award Association/Ann Heidbreder Eastman Grant: ALA
World Book ALA Goal Grants: ALA
World Book Graduate Scholarship in Library Science: Canadian Library Association.
A. R. Zipf Fellowship in Information Management: Council on Library and Information Resources

Part 4
Research and Statistics

Library Research and Statistics

Research on Libraries and Librarianship in 1999

Mary Jo Lynch

Director, Office for Research and Statistics, American Library Association

The prospects for research in the new millennium were strengthened by an unexpected development in the last year of the old. In late April 1999 the American Library Association (ALA) sponsored a two-day Congress on Professional Education (COPE) in Washington, D.C. More than 150 persons attended, most of them representing one of the divisions, round tables, or ethnic caucuses of ALA or the members of many other national organizations in the library field.

The meeting was held because many in the field believed that education for the master's degree in library and information science was failing to produce the quantity and quality of graduates needed to deliver library services in the 21st century. The congress produced 36 recommendations, including six under the heading "Position Librarianship as the 21st Century Profession." Three of those six mention research, as follows:

- *Develop a problem-based research agenda for the profession for the next five years.* The association has many mechanisms and fora to enable identification and articulation of the most pressing research needs of the profession.

- *Fund research important to the profession.* Available research funding should be targeted to the critical research areas identified; research grants might be configured as calls for proposals around topical and practice-based questions for investigation.

- *Disseminate (in appropriate ways) the findings and conclusions from research and their implications for professional practice.* More prominent and creative ways need to be found for disseminating research to the field in a way that makes it meaning and useful, and a catalyst to improved practice.

The ALA Committee on Research and Statistics (CORS) volunteered to design plans to implement those three recommendations, and the ALA Executive Board, at its fall meeting, charged CORS to complete that work within a specific time frame.

Digital Libraries

The recommendations on research quoted above were developed at a meeting convened partly because of the increasing pace and amount of change facing traditional libraries. One major source of change is the development of digital libraries, a complex arena with a complex research agenda. Last year, this article mentioned that the Digital Libraries Initiative—Phase 2 (DLI2) had been announced in 1998 with funding from six federal agencies: the National Science Foundation (NSF), the Defense Advanced Research Projects Agency (DARPA), the National Library of Medicine (NLM), the Library of Congress (LC), the National Aeronautics and Space Administration (NASA), and the National Endowment for the Humanities (NEH). More information became available about DLI2 during 1999 and can be viewed at http://www.nsf.gov/cgi-bin/getpub ?nsf9863. One paragraph from that source is particularly useful in indicating the nature of the work to be done:

> Electronic information is being created by many people and data gathering instruments in many forms and formats, stored in many repositories around the world, and becoming increasingly interconnected via electronic networks. Digital libraries research is faced with the challenge of applying increasing computational capacity and network bandwidth to manage and bring coherence, usability, and accessibility to very large amounts of distributed complex data and transform it into information and knowledge. Since digital libraries are meant to provide intellectual access to stores of information, research in this initiative is concerned with developing concepts, technologies and tools to gain use of the fuller knowledge and meaning inherent in digital collections. For example, for users this means intelligent search, retrieval, organization and presentation tools and interfaces; for content and collections providing this means new information types, structures, document encoding and metadata for enhancing context; for system builders this means designing hardware and software systems capable of interpreting and implementing users' requests by locating, federating and querying collections to provide the user with the structured information sought.

Total support for the initiative from federal resources is projected to be $40 million to $50 million over a five-year period that began in 1998. As of this writing (February 2000), 24 projects were funded (see http://www.dlib.org/projects.html), all based in universities.

Only one of these projects received significant notice in the sources usually monitored for this annual article. That project appeared in three of them, perhaps because of the collaboration between the traditional library and the computer services department of a university. In the fall of 1999 Cornell University announced that its computer scientists and librarians had formed a partnership to develop better ways to manage and ensure the integrity of documents and other data in the digital library of the future. The group received a $2.2 million, four-year grant from NSF, NEH, and other agencies to develop a working prototype digital library system with built-in mechanisms to preserve documents, protect intellectual property rights, and permit interconnections with other digital library systems worldwide.

While several studies have been done to determine the future needs of digital library systems, this may be the first effort to build a working system that can enforce a wide range of security and preservation policies to protect valuable resources in a globally distributed digital library environment. The project will build on research done over the past several years by the Digital Library Research Group in the Cornell Department of Computer Science. Cornell's librarians will collaborate on the project. The library will serve as a test bed and a real-life check on what the computer scientists are developing.

The problems are summed up in the acronym coined for the project: PRISM, standing for preservation, reliability, interoperability, security, and metadata. As more and more documents are stored in digital form, concern has grown over their preservation, largely because rapidly changing technology can make today's digital documents unreadable by tomorrow's computers. But there are many additional problems involved in distributing digital data over the Internet and other networks; librarians must deal with dozens of different systems for storing and reading data and also with differing policies of library systems and with the protection of intellectual property rights.

Public Libraries

Two reports were released by ALA in 1999 on a topic that has received little attention from researchers: programming in public libraries. Sponsored by different arms of the Reader's Digest Fund and directed by different offices at ALA, the two surveys used the same sample and were mailed to public libraries at the same time by the Library Research Center of the University of Illinois Graduate School of Library and Information Science.

"Programs for School-Age Youth in Public Libraries" reports on a survey conducted by the ALA Office for Research and Statistics for the DeWitt Wallace-Reader's Digest Fund as an initial step in a long-term investment to increase the availability of high-quality programs for school-age youth in public libraries, especially in low-income communities, and to build the capacity of public libraries to support and sustain these programs.

In early February 1998 questionnaires were mailed to 1,500 public libraries in the United States. All 461 public libraries serving populations of 100,000 or more received the questionnaire. Libraries serving from 5,000 to 100,000 were sampled if they met certain criteria regarding staff, hours, and annual operating expenditures. The questionnaire listed six common types of programs and asked if the library provided them. The programs are listed below in order of popularity in libraries:

- 99.6 percent provided reading programs
- 82.6 percent provided cultural programs
- 42.2 percent provided community service/leadership programs
- 33.2 percent provided computer classes/workshops
- 23.4 percent provided homework assistance
- 19.2 percent provided career development programs

The report summarizes results on questions about different aspects of those programs such as the roles played by school-age youth and the specific groups of youth targeted by the programs. Also covered are various aspects of the infrastructure for programming: collaboration and partners, sources of support, commitment by stakeholders, training and staff development, and publicity. This report is available at http://www.ala.org/plpyd.

The second survey report, "Cultural Programs for Adults in Public Libraries," was conducted by the ALA Public Programs Office for the Lila Wallace-Reader's Digest Fund. Using the same sample and survey contractor as the study just described, this survey focused on four types of literary programs: book discussion groups, creative writing workshops, author presentation/reading, and adult incentive reading programs.

It also gathered information on lecture series, musical performances, dramatic performances, film series, and dance performances.

In addition to measuring the frequency of each type of program, this report summarizes data on funding, collaboration, and the library's role in cultural programming.

Whereas the first survey was done to help the DeWitt Wallace-Reader's Digest Fund begin a new initiative, the second was done to assess the status of public programming in public libraries after a decade of projects managed by ALA's Public Programs Office and to help set direction for the future. The report can be found on the Web at http://www.ala.org/publicprograms/products.html.

The 1999 National Leadership Grants announced in the fall include three that could provide useful results for public libraries.

- The Bibliographic Center for Research was given $170,885 for a two-year project that will supplement the Public Library Association's new Planning for Results process by creating new tools that will enable libraries to collect more role-specific library output data and standardized user outcome data.
- The Research Foundation of SUNY Buffalo was given $154,324 for a one-year project that will investigate the impact of the Internet on public library use via a national telephone survey. The project will document how people are currently using the public library and the Internet and identify the ways in which libraries and the Internet are competing with and complementing one another.
- Wayne State University was given $122,048 for a two-year study to explore the ways in which the urban poor interact with and benefit from free access to information technology in the public library. The research aims to assess the impact that having access to information technology makes in the lives of the urban poor.

An indication of what may be the result of one of last year's National Leadership Grants became clearer when Glen Holt published an article on "Placing a Value on Public Library Service" in the March/April 1999 issue of *Public Libraries*. Holt and his team have been working since 1994 on the St. Louis Public Library Services Valuation Study. With the help of a grant from the Public Library Association, the study used a variety of techniques to develop and test a practical methodology that large urban public libraries can use to estimate the direct return on annual taxpayer investment. The findings from St. Louis show that public library services generate a positive dollar return on that investment: $4 of value for every $1 spent. As described in the article, the methodology is not simple and it is not yet known if it will work in other settings. Holt's 1998 National Leadership Grant is testing and refining the method in four other large urban systems. A report is expected in the summer of 2000.

Academic Libraries

Increased costs for periodical subscriptions have been a major problem for academic libraries in recent years. Two studies released in 1999 shed light on the problem. The University of Wisconsin General Library System posted on the Web a study titled "Measuring the Cost-Effectiveness of Journals: Ten Years After Barschall" (http://www.library.wisc.edu/projects/glsdo/cost.html).

The study began last year on the 10th anniversary of a landmark research report by the late UW–Madison Physics Professor Henry Barschall. Barschall, a member of the University Library Committee at the time of his research and one of the world's preeminent nuclear physicists, created a scale of cost effectiveness by comparing the frequency with which articles were cited against the price of the library subscription per printed character. He found that journals from commercial publishers generally had the lowest cost-impact. One of those publishers sued the nonprofit organizations named in Barschall's work when they publicized his results. He died in February 1997, just months before a federal judge upheld the decision by the nonprofit organizations to publish his cost-benefit analyses.

The Wisconsin study focuses on journal costs in the subject disciplines of economics, neuroscience, and physics. The article focuses on Barschall's methodology for measuring the cost per thousand characters of journal content and the university's ongoing effort to apply cost measures to the management of the journal collections. The new study confirms Barschall's earlier findings. The article was prepared by George Soete, a consultant affiliated with the Association of Research Libraries, and Athena Salaba, a Ph.D. candidate in the UW–Madison School of Library and Information Studies. Soete places the Wisconsin cost-effectiveness efforts in the broader library-community context. Salaba conducted the 1998 update study and is responsible for the section on methodology and the data.

Another important study of the serial pricing situation was reported in the December 1999 issue of the Association of Research Libraries' *ARL: A Bimonthly Report on Research Library Issues and Actions* (www.arl.org). Mark J. McCabe, author of "The Impact of Publisher Mergers on Journal Prices: An Update," is now an assistant professor of economics at the Georgia Institute of Technology. Previously he was at the U.S. Department of Justice, where he was one of a team of attorneys and economists involved in assessing the antitrust dimension of a proposed merger of two companies that publish many scientific, technical, and medical serials. That particular proposed merger failed, but consolidation among publishers has occurred often in recent years. McCabe has studied these events and concluded that "the cumulative evidence indicates that conventional antitrust procedures are inadequate for evaluating mergers in academic journal markets." He suggests reasons why the academic library market for serials is different from other markets, and suggests that the Department of Justice needs to adopt special guidelines for antitrust cases in the area.

The same newsletter that contains McCabe's article also contains a brief report on "SERVQUAL and the Quest for New Measures." SERVQUAL is a tool developed in the private sector for assessing customer satisfaction. The tool has been used and discussed in the academic library community most recently at Texas A&M University, where it was found to be useful for management decision making at the local level. The big question is whether it can be used for cross-institution comparisons.

At its October membership meeting ARL agreed to support a 24-month pilot project to test the efficacy of SERVQUAL as a best-practices tool for research libraries. Pilot libraries will administer the instrument over the Web, have results scored at Texas A&M, evaluate their own results, and seek among the other participants examples of best practices that may assist with correcting local service deficits. Six to eight ARL member institutions will be selected to administer to their patrons a common, modified version of the SERVQUAL instrument. The participants will be drawn from among the 18 member libraries that have expressed an interest in participating in the pilot. In order that the entire ARL membership may assess the applicability of the results to their local context, an effort will be made to construct as diverse a test group as possible. The administration and scoring of future SERVQUAL studies are expected to be conducted on a continuing basis by the ARL Statistics and Measurement Program.

The December issue of the *ARL* newsletter can be found on the Web at http://www.arl.org/newsltr/207/index.html.

Case study research on a set of smaller institutions (i.e., smaller than members of ARL) was published in 1999 and used as the basis for an invitational conference. *Innovative Use of Information Technology by Colleges* reports on a project sponsored by the Council on Library and Information Resources (CLIR). The project began in spring 1998 when the president of CLIR and the chair of the College Libraries Committee wrote letters to heads of libraries of colleges and mid-sized universities in the United States to ask if they had used technology in a way that significantly enhanced teaching and learning on their campuses. Forty-one libraries from all regions of the country applied, and CLIR selected nine campuses that offered an interesting view of how innovation could be applied. These institutions were not necessarily chosen for their state-of-the-art technology. Rather, they were chosen because their accomplishments would generate ideas that would stimulate and inspire other institutions to make changes on their campuses.

The site visits were conducted between September 1998 and January 1999. Draft versions of the case studies were completed in January. A two-day conference was planned for March 2000 at the Belmont Center in Maryland to discuss the environment that is most conducive to organizational change. The case studies, distributed to participants weeks before the conference, were to serve as a point of departure for a broader discussion of change that is transforming colleges and mid-sized universities.

School Libraries

Research was featured in a special way at the ninth national conference of the American Association of School Librarians (AASL) in Birmingham, Alabama, in mid-November. This conference was cosponsored by the International Association of School Librarianship (IASL), and several different pages of the conference program book described a group of speeches as "IASL Research Forum Presentations." A total of 20 individual presentations were involved. A special panel of IASL members reviewed proposals for these forums and chose the presenters. The research papers are included in IASL's proceedings, which were published by LMC Source.

One of the other presentations at the November AASL conference was titled "Proof of Power: A First Look at the Results of the Colorado Study—and More." Researcher Keith Curry Lance of the Library Research Service at the Colorado State Library and Adult Education Office described early results of three studies under way at the Library Research Service. One is a repetition, with enhancements, of a study released in 1993 that established a positive relationship between a strong library media program in a school and the school's level of achievement on a standard test. Two other states, Alaska and Pennsylvania, contracted with Library Research Service for similar studies. At this writing (February 2000) only one of the three studies had been completed. "Information Empowered: The School Librarian as an Agent of Academic Achievement in Alaska Schools" can be viewed and downloaded at http://www.eed.state.ak.us/lam/library/dev/infoemp.html.

All three studies used the following sources of data:

- Responses to a questionnaire about the library media program in a sample of schools
- Test scores for those same schools
- Data on school characteristics (e.g., teacher-pupil ratio)
- Data on community characteristics (e.g., income level)

In all three studies, the researchers use well-known statistical techniques to demonstrate a strong correlation between characteristics of the library media program and high scores on standardized tests. Each study examines different facets of the library media program. All three studies are summarized on the Web at http://www.lrs.org (scroll down to the heading School Media Studies, then click on the Fast Facts link. Available only in pdf format.).

Special Libraries

New data about special libraries and librarians became available in 1999 because of the Information Services Panel Survey (ISP) conducted among members of the

Special Libraries Association (SLA). In June 1997 the SLA Board endorsed an initiative by Phase 5 Consulting Group, Inc. to survey their members using World Wide Web response as the data collection methodology. In total, 1,630 SLA members participated in the survey, which was posted on the Web during the months of June and July 1998. The main purpose of the initiative was to define and track annual benchmark data that can be used to identify key trends among special librarians and libraries. Specific objectives of the survey were to:

- Profile special libraries
- Describe the roles and responsibilities undertaken by special librarians
- Determine the types of information and subjects used
- Identify the key sources by subject category
- Assess the positioning and performance of information providers
- Describe the technology environment and format preferences
- Profile use of the Internet as a resource
- Identify spending patterns and average spending on information products and services

The survey was sponsored by vendors who serve the special libraries market and can use the findings to profile their target audiences, assess their performance on the basis of key dimensions, and identify opportunities or areas for improvement. The results were also expected to be useful to SLA members for management decision making.

At this writing the following information about the 1998 ISP could be found on the SLA Web site (http://www.sla.org/research/isp98.html): Highlights, Technology and Network Environment, Benchmark Statistics, and Methodology.

Also on the SLA Web site is an article based on the ISP by Doug Church, a founding partner of Phase 5 Consulting Group. The same article appears twice with different titles, the most descriptive of which is "From Librarian to Knowledge Manager and Beyond: The Shift to an End-User Domain." The survey was done in 1999 and will be done again in 2000.

Using Online Databases

For several years Carol Tenopir, a professor at the University of Tennessee School of Information Sciences, has been working on a set of studies that examines how/when/why people use databases in academic and public libraries. The studies have two sources: 1) usage data supplied by a large online producer/aggregator that shows how many people are logged on at any time for each database, and 2) questionnaire data that captures, among other things, why librarians think individuals select a database to use. In 1999 Tenopir reported results in several places including two conferences (ACRL in April and ASIS in November) and two articles in *Library Journal*: May (academic libraries) and June (public libraries). The ACRL paper is available at http://www.ala.org/acrl/pdfpapers99.html. The ASIS proceedings are available in print (see http://www.asis.org/Publications/bookstore/am99p.html).

Central to Tenopir's work was usage data provided by a major database producer and aggregator that provides access to approximately 100 database titles including bibliographic, directory, and full-text journal article databases. The library customers for which this company had usage data include more than 1,200 public, academic, school, and special libraries in several countries, but the majority are public and academic libraries in North America. A random sample of 200 public and academic libraries from the total customer list yielded 99 public and 96 academic libraries with usable data. Public libraries in the sample serve a variety of user populations and academic libraries come from different types of parent academic institutions.

Online usage for every library and each database is captured automatically by the database aggregator in five-minute intervals 24 hours a day. For this study, usage data were sampled once an hour (on the half-hour) from the hours of 8 A.M. to midnight from a six-month period (July–December 1997). Forty-seven different databases were accessed by the 195 libraries in the sample. In all, over one-half million datapoints were collected and analyzed. Analysis of those datapoints revealed much, but the basic conclusions are these: that library users in both public and academic libraries tend to use commercial online databases most frequently early in the week, mid-day, and at times that correspond to the academic calendar (November in this six-month sample). The mean number of simultaneous users is correlated with the size of the population served and the number of workstations available, but relatively low numbers of users are simultaneously logged on to the research databases at all sizes of libraries.

In addition to gathering and analyzing usage data from those 195 libraries, Tenopir also sent surveys to librarians at the same libraries asking for their opinion about what factors influence database use. Again the results are rich, but the final paragraph in Tenopir's article in the June 1, 1999 *Library Journal* on "Influencing Database Use in Public Libraries" provides a good summary:

> . . . several common themes emerge from my surveys of 119 public and academic libraries in the United States and Canada. No single factor will make a database the favorite of a large number of library users. Useful content, an easy-to-use interface, and full text are all essential factors. Library staff, as well as patrons, have to be convinced of the quality and usefulness of each database, since recommendations, instruction classes, and placement on a database menu all will influence how much a database is used.

OCLC

The September/October 1999 issue of the *OCLC Newsletter* carried an announcement that OCLC would continue its policy of making the annual report of its Office for Research available only in electronic format. The 1998 annual report is available at http://www.oclc.org/oclc/research/publications/review98/.

The same issue of the newsletter carried a brief story on a project that began in 1997 and is now bearing interesting fruit. The Web Characterization Project describes the structure, size, usage, and content of the Web. It is also concerned with developing data collection methodologies and metrics of Web description. Project staff are working with the Web Characterization Activity of the World Wide Web Consortium (W3C) as part of a cross-industry effort to promote the evolution, interoperability, and robustness of the Web through analysis of its structure, content, and usage.

Because of the Web's importance to libraries around the world, OCLC is providing timely information that will assist librarians in understanding the Web and using its contents. As of June 1999, researchers at OCLC had determined that the World Wide Web had about 3.6 million sites, of which 2.2 million were publicly accessible. They also found that the largest 25,000 sites represented about 50 percent of the Web's content, and that the number of sites and their size were climbing. The mean size of a public Web site was about 129 pages, a 13 percent increase over last year's estimate of 114 pages. The number of public Web sites approximately tripled in the two-year period from June 1997 to June 1999, increasing from 800,000 to 2.2 million. More information about the latest OCLC Office of Research Web statistics and analysis is available at http://www.oclc.org/oclc/research/projects/webstats/. The June 1999 statistics will be updated in June 2000.

Awards that Honor Excellent Research

All active awards are listed along with the amount of the award, the URL for the award (if available), and the 1999 winners. If the award was not given in 1999, that fact is noted. General ALA awards are listed first, followed by units of ALA in alphabetical order, followed by other agencies in alphabetical order.

ALA/Library and Information Technology Association

Frederick G. Kilgour Award (with OCLC) ($2,000 plus expense-paid trip to ALA Annual Conference)
Winner: Dean K. Jue, Florida State University
Rationale: Jue was selected in recognition of his achievements in developing new technology applications to improve public library service, in enhancing the technical literacy skills of public librarians, in research into public library use and services, and in the use of geographic information systems to assemble and map data that has been of great benefit to public libraries in poor and/or minority areas. His many reports, articles, and presentations document practical applications of technology to enhance and improve public library service and constitute a shining example of the application of theoretical and research skills of a high order to produce practical, real-world results.

ALA/Library History Round Table

Phyllis Dain Library History Dissertation Award ($500)
http://www.ala.org/alaorg/ors/dain.html
Winner: P. Toby Graham, University of Southern Mississippi
Project: "Segregation and Civil Rights in Alabama's Public Libraries, 1918–1965."

Justin Winsor Prize ($500)
http://www.ala.org/alaorg/ors/winsor.html
Winner: Christine Pawley, University of Wisconsin–Madison

Project: "Advocate for Access: Lutie Sterns and the Travelling Libraries of the Wisconsin Free Library Commission, 1895–1914."

ALA/Library Research Round Table

Jesse H. Shera Award for Distinguished Published Research ($500)

http://www.ala.org/alaorg/ors/shera1.html
Note: The award is usually given for a single article published in English during the preceding calendar year. This year the jury decided to make two awards because the articles were of equal significance in the use of primary documents as empirical evidence, the clarity of writing, and significance of findings.
Winner: Christine Pawley, University of Wisconsin–Madison
Project: "What to Read and How to Read: The Social Infrastructure of Young People's Reading, Osage, Iowa, 1870–1900." *Library Quarterly*, Vol. 68 (3), July 1998, pp. 276–297.
Winner: Pamela Spence Richards, Rutgers University
Project: "Soviet-American Library Relations in the 1920s and 1930s: A Study in Mutual Fascination and Distrust." *Library Quarterly*, Vol. 68 (4), October 1998, pp. 390–405.

Jesse H. Shera Award for Excellence in Doctoral Research ($500)

http://www.ala.org/alaorg/ors/shera2.html
Not awarded in 1999.

American Society for Information Science

ASIS Research Award (two given in 1999)

Winner: David Blair
Rationale: Blair has conducted one of the most heavily cited series of experiments in the information science literature. This was his work with M. E. Maron on the effectiveness of a STAIRS-type full-text retrieval system applied to large document collections for litigation support. Perhaps even more important, he has been concerned for many years with developing information retrieval theory in light of the philosophy of language. He is currently working on his second book, which promises to be a major statement on the relevance to information science of the philosopher Ludwig Wittgenstein.
Winner: Donald H. Kraft
Rationale: As editor of the *Journal of the American Society for Information Science*, Kraft has both broadened its scope and increased its frequency of appearance. His own published work brings stellar knowledge of mathematics and computer science to bear on information retrieval. His early work applied principles of operations research to problems in library management. His later work has been concerned with fuzzy set theory, probability theory, and genetic algorithms in information retrieval. Another major contribution to the research infrastructure in information science was his involvement in establishing the Association for Computing Machinery's Special Interest Group in Information Retrieval.

Pratt-Severn Student Research Award

Winner: Kelly L. Maglaughlin, University of North Carolina at Chapel Hill

Project: "The Use of Relevance Criteria in Partially Relevant Documents."

UMI Doctoral Dissertation Award
Winner: Jacqueline Algon, Rutgers University
Project: "The Effect of Task on the Information Related Behaviors of Individuals in Work-Group Environment." The study examines the influence of task on information-related behaviors, a topic of debate over the past three decades that few have investigated. Data collection for this study was based on participant observation and a detailed survey of three project teams in a large pharmaceutical company over a period of three years. It included more than 100 team members and 900 task events. The classification of task and information-related behavior focused on the cognitive aspects of the information-gathering process. The longitudinal observation added depth to the results.

Association for Library and Information Science Education

Doctoral Dissertation Competition ($400 for travel expenses plus 1999 conference registration and membership in ALISE for 1998–1999)
Winner: Hong Xie, Rutgers University
Project: "Planned and Situated Aspects in Interactive IR: Patterns of User Interactive Intentions and Information Seeking Strategies." The particular focus of this study is on specifying hierarchical levels of users' goals, and the in-depth examination of one micro-goal level, "interactive intentions," in relation to information-seeking strategies. This study is based on the idea of information retrieval (IR) as interaction. Forty real users with real information-seeking problems from academic, public, and special libraries were studied.

Methodology Paper Competition ($500)
Winner: Zin Zhang, University of Illinois
Project: "Using the Internet for Survey Research: A Case Study." This paper reviews previous studies that have employed Internet-based surveys and presents a case study of Internet use for survey research. It discusses the methodological issues and problems associated with the method and possible solutions to these problems.

Research Paper Competition ($500)
Winner: Caroline Haythornwaite, University of Illinois
Project: "Network Structures among Computer-Supported Distance Learners: Multiple Relations, Multiple Media, and Time." To explore this complex interaction of technical and social factors, social network data on interactions among members of a class of computer-supported distance learners are used to examine the way in which multiple relations and multiple media project teams dominated who communicated with whom over the term.

Grants that Support Research

All active grants are listed along with the amount of the grant, the URL for the grant (if available), and the 1999 winners. If the grant was not given in 1999, that fact is noted. General ALA grants are listed first, followed by units of ALA in alphabetical order, followed by other agencies in alphabetical order.

American Library Association

Carroll Preston Baber Research Grant ($7,500)
http://www.ala.org/alaorg/ors/baber.html
Not awarded in 1999.

Loleta D. Fyan Grant ($10,000). This is not necessarily a grant for research, but a research project was selected in 1999.
http://www.ala.org/alaorg/ors/fyan.html
Winners: Dean K. Jue and Christine M. Koontz, Florida State University
Project: "Library Market Area Determinations Through User Address Data and Use of Geographic Information Systems (GIS)." This project will identify the library market areas derived from user data, for approximately 40 library outlets in four library systems in Colorado and Florida. A thorough analysis of factors determining each library outlet's market area, size, and shape will be conducted using geographic information system software. Through these analyses, a justifiable methodology will be developed for estimating library market area sizes for any public library outlet.

American Association of School Librarians

AASL/Highsmith Research Grant ($5,000)
Winners: Violet H. Harada, Claire Sato, and Joan Yoshina, Library and Information Science Program, University of Hawaii at Manoa (Honolulu)
Project: "Dialogic Journaling with Elementary Grade Students as a Means to Deeper Student Understanding of the Information Process." This qualitative research study focuses on how dialogic journaling, as a pedagogical strategy, influences students' understanding of the information search process. Teams composed of library media specialists, teachers, and university graduate assistants will conduct a naturalistic inquiry with a sampling of upper elementary grade students at two Hawaii public schools. They will use multiple data-gathering modes to implement the investigation as students work through month-long research assignments at the two sites. Students will do their reflective journaling electronically.

Association of College and Research Libraries

ACRL/ISI Doctoral Dissertation Fellowship ($1,500)
http://www.ala.org/acrl/doctoral.pdf
Winner: Alenka Sauperl
Project: "Subject Determination During the Cataloging Process." The purpose of the research is to investigate how catalogers determine the topic of a document and choose the appropriate subject description. This will be done by gathering data on the process catalogers at three different academic libraries use when assigning subject headings.

Samuel Lazerow Fellowship for Research in Acquisitions or Technical Services in an Academic or Research Library ($1,000)
Not awarded in 1999.

Martinus Nijhoff West European Study Grant (10,000 Dutch guilders)
Winner: Richard Hacken, Brigham Young University
Project: "Towards Reconstructing the Fate of Viennese Jewish Libraries in the Nazi Era." This grant will allow him to delve into historic documents and inventories that he hopes will help categorize types of Viennese Jewish libraries and their main areas of collection strength, data that can show the reading habits of a historic populace at the height of their culture.

Young Adult Library Services Association

Francis Henne/YALSA/VOYA Research Grant ($500)
http://www.ala.org/yalsa/awards/hennewinner.html
Winner: Kay Bishop and Patricia Bauer, University of South Florida
Project: "Attracting Young Adults to Public Libraries." The study will focus in depth on components of successful programs using multiple methodologies to go beyond "how I done it good."

American Society for Information Science

ISI/ASIS Citation Analysis Research Grant ($3,000)
http://www.asis.org/awards/citation.isi.htm
Winner: Ian Rowlands, Department of Information Science, City University, London
Project: "Influence Has Width as Well as Depth: Towards a Complementary Journal Impact Factor Based on Diffusion Data." This research seeks to develop and test two indicators to the ISI journal impact factor—journal diffusion and journal concentration. The potential of this research may provide a new source of information on the breadth of a journal's influence and have application for other levels of scientometric studies concerned with understanding the nature of inter-disciplines.

ISI Information Science Doctoral Dissertation Proposal Scholarship ($1,500 plus $500 toward travel or other expenses)
Winner: Brian Detlor, Doctoral Student, Faculty of Information Studies, University of Toronto
Project: "Utilizing Web Information Systems for Organizational Knowledge Work: An Investigation of the Information Ecology and Information Behaviors of Users in a Telecommunications Company."

Association for Library and Information Science Education

Research Grant Awards (one or more grants totaling $5,000)
http://www.alise.org/Research_grant01.html
Winner ($3,000): Karen E. Pettigrew, University of Michigan, and Lynne McKechnie, University of Western Ontario

Project: "The Use of Theory in Library and Information Science Education and Research." These questions will be studied in three stages. First, a survey of LIS school Web sites to gather baseline data regarding courses offered on theory. Second, a content analysis of all articles that appeared from 1993 to 1997 in six LIS journals for authors' use of theory. Finally, the researchers will trace the academic origins of 20 prominent LIS theories (identified in Stage 2) and then conduct citation analyses to gather evidence of how their theories are being used both within and outside the field.

Winner ($2,000): Christopher Brown-Syed, Wayne State University

Project: "Social Constructs: Self-Revelation and Information Provision in Scholarly Web Pages." This project will consist of a content analysis of material posted on the World Wide Web by academics in a variety of fields, including information science. Following upon work done during pilot studies of listservs, usenet newsgroups, and the Web, it will employ content analysis, conducted in the context of an overall soft systems approach, in an attempt to isolate design features of digital artifacts and patterns of Web creation among academics. Its goals are to assist LIS educators and practitioners in categorizing, assessing, and disseminating digital resources.

Council on Library and Information Resources

A. R. Zipf Fellowship

Winner: Deborah Ruffner Weiss, Doctoral Student, School of Information and Library Science, University of North Carolina at Chapel Hill

Project: Weiss's current research focuses on developing network-based middleware services that enable high-performance data sharing among Internet2 universities and other organizations.

Medical Library Association

ISI/MLA Doctoral Fellowship ($2,000)

Not awarded in 1999.

Research, Development, and Demonstration Grant

Winner: Catherine Graber

Project: To be announced.

OCLC Office for Research

OCLC/ALISE Library and Information Science Research Grants (up to $10,000)

Winner: Allyson Carlyle, University of Washington

Project: "Clustering Fiction Works to Improve Online Catalog Displays." Carlyle's study will determine procedures for automatic clustering of records retrieved in online library catalog searches for works of fiction. Automatic clustering will contribute to efforts to ease the problem of information overload for system users.

Winner: Lois Mai Chan, University of Kentucky

Project: "An LCSH-Based Controlled Vocabulary for Dublin Core Metadata Records: A Feasibility Study." Chan's project will investigate the feasibility of devising a controlled vocabulary based on Library of Congress Subject Headings (LCSH), with a simplified syntax, for use in the creation of Dublin Core metadata records.
Winner: John Richardson, University of California, Los Angeles
Project: "An English-Russian Dictionary of LIS Terminology." Richardson's project proposes an up-to-date and comprehensive bilingual dictionary for scholars and library and information science professionals that will increase scholarly access to professional literature.

Special Libraries Association

Steven I. Goldspiel Memorial Research Grant (up to $20,000)
http://www.sla.org/research/goldfund.html
Winner: James M. Turner and Michèle Hudon
Project: "Organizing Moving Image Collections for the Digital Era." The project will attempt to reach an understanding of the organization of existing vocabulary-management tools used in special libraries with moving image collections. Patterns in vocabulary usage will be identified and studied, with the aim of building a uniform vocabulary available for broad use by librarians who manage collections of moving images.

Assessment of the Role of School and Public Libraries in Support of Educational Reform: Final Report on the Study

Christina Dunn

Project Director and Director, Collections and Technical Services
National Library of Education
202-401-6563, e-mail christina_dunn@ed.gov

In fiscal year (FY) 1994 the U.S. Department of Education began an assessment of the role of school and public libraries in educational reform. Westat, Inc., in cooperation with the American Library Association, conducted the $1.3 million study, funded under the Secretary's Fund for Innovation in Education. The following report is taken from *Assessment of the Role of School and Public Libraries in Support of Educational Reform*, a document prepared by Joan Michie and Bradford Chaney of Westat, Inc. for the U.S. Department of Education in 1999. A status report on the study appeared in the 1999 edition of the *Bowker Annual* (44th edition, pp. 440–443).

Purpose of the Assessment

While education has been considered the primary purpose of school libraries, public libraries also have viewed education as an important part of their mission. Therefore, when *A Nation at Risk*, a report by the National Commission on Excellence in Education (1983), warned of problems in the American educational system, the library community wanted to be part of the reform efforts that were a response to the report.

Libraries must operate in the context of changes within educational systems and the greater society. Among the educational reforms that have occurred since *A Nation at Risk* are the development of the National Education Goals and curriculum standards for each of the content areas. Societal changes include advances in technology and the accompanying information explosion. As a result of these changes, school and public libraries find themselves in the position of reexamining their resources, staff skills, programs, and services.

The purpose of the Assessment of the Role of School and Public Libraries in Support of Educational Reform was to find out how school and public libraries were performing as education providers and how well they were responding to the country's urgent demands for school improvement. It was intended to inform researchers, policymakers, and practitioners on six key issues:

- To what extent are school and public libraries contributing to education reform, and to what extent can they contribute?
- What programs and services are school and public libraries providing to meet the needs of preschool and elementary and secondary (K–12) education providers?
- How well do these services and programs meet the needs of preschool and K–12 education providers?

- Do school and public libraries have the capacity—human and information resources, technology, and facilities—to respond adequately to identified needs and to support systemic reform?
- What new technologies are promoting student opportunity to learn by improving services and resources in school and public libraries?
- What can we learn from successful school and public library programs and services designed to support preschool and K–12 education? Can these programs serve as models for the improvement of all school and public libraries? What are the barriers to effective services and programs?

The assessment included a literature review, two national surveys, ten case studies involving both school and public libraries, and four commissioned papers on selected topics—implications of school reform approaches for school library media services, school and public library relationships, preschool education through public libraries, and independent reading and school achievement.

National Surveys

The two national surveys were conducted in 1997; one was sent to public library outlets and the other went to library media centers in both public and private schools. The sample size for each survey was about 1,000 and was representative of the specific library community. The sample of public schools was selected from the U.S. Department of Education's National Center for Education Statistics (NCES) Common Core of Data Public School Universe File, the sample of private schools from the NCES Private School Survey Universe File, and the sample of public libraries from the most recent NCES Public Library Universe System File. Response rates on the surveys were 86.5 percent, private schools; 90.6 percent, public schools; and 93.1 percent, public libraries, with an overall response rate of 90.1 percent. All response rates exceeded the NCES requirement.

The following report highlights the results of the surveys of school and public libraries. Highlights include staffing and patronage, the use of libraries by students and others, the amount and adequacy of materials and resources, programs and services offered by libraries, availability of technology, access to the Internet, education reform, and cooperation between school and public libraries. All specific statements of comparison made in this report have been tested for statistical significance through t-tests and are significant at the 95 percent confidence level or better.

On the public and private school surveys, data were collected from individual school library media centers (LMCs) rather than school systems. Survey findings for school library media centers are shown for all school libraries and by the following characteristics:

Public

- Educational level—Elementary, Secondary
- Size of school—Less than 300, 300 to 499, 500 to 749, 750 or more
- Free lunch—Less than 20 percent, 20 to 49 percent, 50 percent or more
- Region—Northeast, Southeast, Central, West

Private

- Educational level—Elementary, Secondary, Combined
- Size of school—Less than 150, 150 to 299, 300 to 499, 500 or more
- Religious affiliation—Catholic, Other religious, Nonsectarian

On the public library survey, data were collected from individual public library outlets, rather than systems as a whole. Bookmobiles were excluded from the survey. Survey findings are shown for all library outlets and by the following library characteristics:

- Type of outlet—Central/main, Branch, Single location
- Size of population served by the outlet—0 to 24,999, 25,000 to 99,999, 100,000 or more
- Region of the country—Northeast, Southeast, Central, West
- Presence of a children's, young adult, and/or youth services specialist.

School Library Media Centers

In 1996–1997, 98 percent of public schools and 78 percent of private schools had school library media centers. In spring 1997 a total of 44.8 million public school students and 4.3 million private school students attended schools with library media centers. The total number of schools with LMCs was 75,460 public schools and 16,569 private schools.

Student Use

Students made an average of 598 visits to the school library in public schools and 257 visits in private schools during a typical week in 1997. For both public and private schools, the number of visits was proportional to the school enrollment, with an average of one student visit for each student enrolled. However, this statistic does not imply that all students visited the library every week—students who visited the library more than once in a typical week were counted once for each visit.

Almost three-fourths (70 percent) of all public school LMCs reported that they used flexible scheduling, although it was often used in combination with regular scheduling as well. Half of all libraries (50 percent) said that all classes were regularly scheduled, and 21 percent said that some but not all classes were regularly scheduled. Most secondary school LMCs (95 percent) used flexible scheduling, as did 60 percent of elementary school libraries. Regularly scheduling all classes primarily occurred at the elementary level, where it was used by two-thirds (66 percent) of the school libraries, compared with only one-eighth (12 percent) of secondary school libraries.

Staffing

School library media centers had a total 249,338 staff at public schools and 68,991 staff at private schools. Most of the LMC staff worked part time, accounting for about 65 percent (160,901) in public schools and 87 percent (59,772) in private schools. The full-time staff at public schools were most typically state-certified library media specialists (56 percent), while 11 percent were professional staff who were not certified as library media specialists and 33 percent were other paid employees (Figure 1). The part-time staff were most typically volunteers (69 percent), though 12 percent were professional staff (either certified or not) and 18 percent were other paid employees. Private schools typically do not face the type of certification requirements found in public schools. Thus, only 29 percent of full-time library staff at private schools were certified as library media specialists.

Figure 1 / Staffing at School Library Media Centers (LMCs), by School Type and Type of Staff

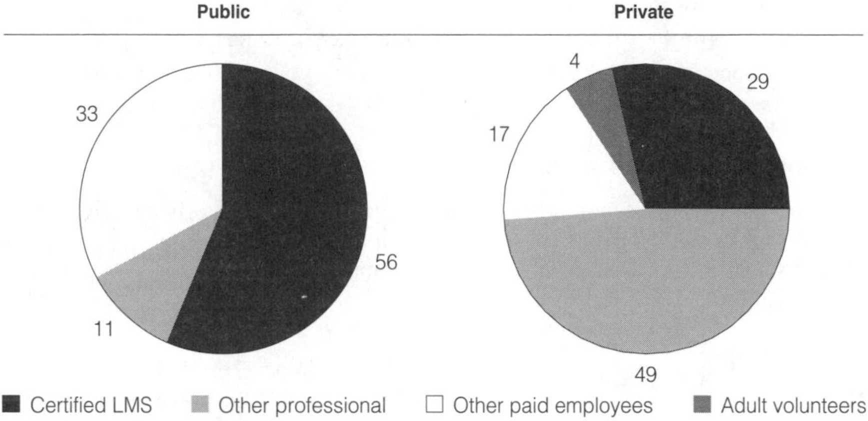

Public

Private

33
56
11

4
29
17
49

■ Certified LMS   ▨ Other professional   □ Other paid employees   ■ Adult volunteers

Note: Percents may not add to 100 due to rounding.

Overall, 78 percent of public schools had a state-certified library media specialist, with an average of 0.7 state-certified librarians per school. If all staff are included, public school libraries had an average of 0.9 professional staff (including noncertified professional staff), 0.6 other paid employees, and 0.7 adult volunteers. On average, there were 648 enrolled students per professional librarian and 397 per paid staff. School enrollments appear to be a good indicator of the workload of school librarians, because the ratios of weekly patronage of the library to the number of staff were roughly the same as the ratios of enrollment to the number of staff (653 in weekly patronage per professional librarian and 400 in weekly patronage per paid staff).

An estimated 11 percent of public schools with LMCs had neither a full-time nor part-time librarian, an absence more frequent at the elementary than at the secondary level (15 percent versus 3 percent). However, such schools typically did have an aide at the library, with only 1 percent of all schools with a library media center having neither a librarian nor an aide. Private schools followed a different pattern. About one-third had no librarian (32 percent), and one-fifth (22 percent) had neither a librarian nor an aide.

Among public schools, 22 percent lacked a full- or part-time library media specialist who was state certified, and 39 percent lacked a full-time state-certified library media specialist.

School LMCs in the Southeast were more fully staffed than were those in other parts of the country. Only 2 percent in the Southeast did not have a librarian compared with 10 to 19 percent for other regions. Only 5 percent of the school libraries in the Southeast did not have a full- or part-time state-certified library media specialist compared with 20 to 35 percent for other regions, and only 9 percent did not have a full-time state-certified specialist compared with 37 to 51 percent for other regions.

Collections

Public school library media centers had a total of 679 million items in their holdings in 1997, primarily consisting of 622 million books. These holdings constituted an average of 15.5 books and 17.7 items per student. The ratio of books and holdings to average weekly patronage was roughly the same (15.4 and 17.5, respectively). Libraries at the larger schools on average had more books per school (13,219 in schools with 750 or more students versus 5,424 in schools with fewer than 300 students), but fewer books per student (11.4 versus 27.6).

The school LMCs were asked about the adequacy of their holdings in supporting seven instructional areas: reading/English, mathematics, science, social studies, foreign languages, arts, and health and safety. For the first four of these areas, they were asked about the overall collection, print materials, video and other audiovisual (AV) materials, and computer software; for the last three, they were asked about the overall collection only.

The results varied greatly by subject area. Reading/English was the best area, with about one-fourth of public school libraries (24 percent) saying the overall collection was excellent, and 57 percent saying it was adequate. For social studies, 19 percent of the public school libraries said the holdings were excellent and an additional 54 percent said they were adequate. Results for science were about the same as social studies. In the other four subject areas (health and safety, arts, mathematics, and foreign languages), no more than 11 percent described the overall collection as excellent, though for health and safety, arts, and mathematics, a majority did describe it as either adequate or excellent. Foreign languages had a somewhat different pattern with 23 percent of public school libraries reporting that materials in foreign languages were neither available nor needed; this primarily occurred at elementary rather than secondary schools (31 percent versus 6 percent).

For those four subject areas where data are available, public school libraries considered their print materials to be at a similar level of adequacy as their overall collection. However, they were frequently dissatisfied with their video/AV materials and computer software. Depending on the subject area, between 49 and 58 percent said their computer software was either inadequate or not available but needed, and between 38 and 52 percent said their video and other audiovisual materials were either inadequate or not available but needed.

School library media centers also were asked about the adequacy of their resources in five other areas. About two-thirds of the LMCs at public schools said that their resources were either adequate or excellent with regard to picture books/easy readers (66 percent), high-interest/low-vocabulary (63 percent), and multicultural education (62 percent). By contrast, only 29 percent described their parenting materials as adequate or excellent, and only 19 percent described English-as-a-second-language as excellent or adequate. Generally, in each area about a third or more felt that their resources were inadequate (30 to 45 percent, except for picture books/easy readers at 15 percent). One exception to the general pattern was resources for English-as-a-second-language, where about half of the library media centers (47 percent) said the category was not applicable.

Except for picture books/easy readers, LMCs at private schools differed from those at public schools by more often saying that the category was not applicable. For example, 82 percent said that English-as-a-second-language was not applicable (compared with 47 percent for public schools) and 44 percent said that parenting materials were not applicable (compared with 27 percent).

Technology

Overall, 78 percent of public school library media centers had a telephone in 1997. Other types of communications equipment were less common; 20 percent had a fax machine and 8 percent a TTY or other equipment for persons with disabilities.

Stand-alone computers in school libraries were more common than telephones, both in public schools (88 percent versus 78 percent) and in private schools (71 percent versus 51 percent). Some of the ways in which computers were set up and used include providing periodical indexes, encyclopedias, or other references on CD-ROMs (77 percent), an automatic circulation system (61 percent), a computer with a shared line (51 percent), a computer with a dedicated line (48 percent), networked automated catalogs (41 percent), stand-alone automated catalogs (23 percent), and online database searching (23 percent).

School LMCs also often had various kinds of television equipment and services. At public schools, 92 percent had one or more VCRs, 72 percent had cable television, and 50 percent had a video laser disk player. Less common were closed circuit television (29 percent), a satellite dish (27 percent), and a television studio (8 percent).

School LMCs often can obtain computer access to the catalogs of other libraries, either through the Internet or through other networks. At public schools, 28 percent of library media centers could access the catalogs of a college or university library, 26 percent could access a public library, 20 percent could access other school library media centers, and 15 percent could access a community college library.

Access and Use of the Internet

As the Internet grows in size and the amount of information provided, it is becoming increasingly important to school LMCs. Among library media centers in public schools, 41,217 (55 percent) had access to the Internet, with 73 percent of those having adopted a policy on student access to the Internet. Most of those public school libraries without Internet access expected to obtain it in a few years: 9,211 LMCs (31 percent) expected to obtain it in 1997, and 11,011 (38 percent) in 1998. Only 14 percent had no plans for establishing Internet access.

Of the 55 percent of public school library media centers with access to the Internet, most (50 percent of all public LMCs) had e-mail accounts available. E-mail accounts were widely allowed for use by teachers (46 percent), but much less so for use by students (20 percent). Altogether, 47 percent of school LMCs had text-based access to the World Wide Web and the same percentage reported having graphical access. Most LMCs that had World Wide Web access reported that the access was used by teachers (45 to 46 percent) and by students (40 to 42 percent).

One application of the Internet for school libraries is to use it to answer reference questions. Almost half of LMCs at public schools used it for answering questions by teachers (49 percent), students (48 percent), and administrators (45 percent). In many cases, LMCs also served as centers for training teachers, students, and administrators how to use the Internet. In public school libraries with access to the Internet, 43 percent arranged Internet training for teachers, 41 percent for students, and 37 percent for administrators.

At public schools, the factors that most often constituted a major or moderate barrier to library media centers' access to the Internet were an insufficient amount of funds allocated for technology (72 percent), staff time (67 percent), telecommunications equipment (57 percent), telephone lines (58 percent), computers (56 percent), and training (49 percent) (Figure 2). Interest in the Internet, however, was generally not even a small barrier. The interest of librarians was not a barrier at 82 percent of public school LMCs, the interest of administrators was not a barrier at 63 percent, the interest of teachers was not a barrier at 56 percent, and the interest of the community was not a barrier at 59 percent.

Programs and Services

The services that library media centers at public schools said they provided frequently were reference assistance to students (93 percent) and reference assistance to teachers (73 percent). No other service was provided frequently by more than 40 percent of the libraries.

Some tasks, by their nature, may be conducted regularly but not frequently. For example, even if working with teachers on textbook selection is an important role, it may be episodic rather than frequent. From this perspective, it is also useful to find which services were sometimes provided as a way of establishing the range of activities in which library media centers are involved. Almost all traditional services were provided by LMCs at least sometimes for most public schools: reference assistance; interlibrary loan; assisting teachers with research projects for students; working on curriculum issues and serving on curriculum development teams; participating in grade-level or department/term meetings; coordinating in-school production of materials; and providing information about technology, including coordinating training about technology integration. The only exceptions where a majority of libraries reported never providing a service were serving on site-based management teams (65 percent), coordinating textbook selection (73 percent), and coordinating distance learning staff (73 percent). In addition, there were three activities where close to half (i.e., 40 percent or more) of LMCs were never involved: coordinating video production (42 percent),

Figure 2 / Percent of Public School Library Media Centers (LMCs)
Facing Various Barriers to Maximizing Internet Access

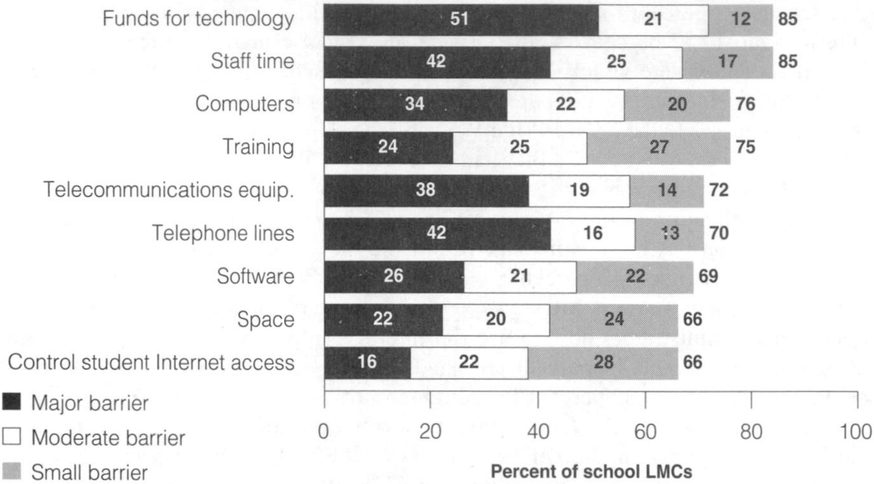

	Major barrier	Moderate barrier	Small barrier	Total
Funds for technology	51	21	12	85
Staff time	42	25	17	85
Computers	34	22	20	76
Training	24	25	27	75
Telecommunications equip.	38	19	14	72
Telephone lines	42	16	13	70
Software	26	21	22	69
Space	22	20	24	66
Control student Internet access	16	22	28	66

■ Major barrier
□ Moderate barrier
▨ Small barrier

0   20   40   60   80   100

Percent of school LMCs

Note: Details may not add to totals due to rounding.

coordinating access to the Internet (47 percent), and providing guidance on evaluating information from the Internet (46 percent).

In general, library media centers at private schools were less likely to provide each service than were public schools. For example, the two most frequently provided services were the same at private schools as at public schools, but the percentage providing those services was lower (78 percent versus 93 percent with regard to reference assistance to students, and 41 percent versus 73 percent with regard to reference assistance to teachers).

The relatively low level of public school libraries' involvement in site-based management teams was due, in part, to the fact that not all schools had site-based management. Among those public schools with site-based management, slightly over half (56 percent) of the LMCs had staff serving on the site-based management teams.

The services provided by school library media centers often varied depending on the subject area involved (Figure 3). In general, public school LMCs were most often involved in working with teachers in reading/English, social studies, and science, while they were least involved in foreign languages and mathematics. For example, about half (54 percent) of the public school library media centers reported working frequently with teachers in selecting and evaluating library media resources in reading/English, 43 percent in social studies, 36 percent in science, and 12 to 22 percent in other subject areas (see Figure 3). Of four listed services, the most commonly provided service was working with teachers in selecting and evaluating library media resources (12 to 54 percent), while it was less common for library media centers to work with teachers in curriculum development (3 to 17 percent), collaboratively teach curriculum units with classroom teachers (2 to 21 percent), or collaboratively evaluate curriculum units with classroom teachers (1 to 8 percent).

Figure 3 / Percent of Public School Library Media Centers That Frequently Provided Various Services to Classroom Teachers in 1996–1997, by Subject Area

Subject	Works with teachers in selecting and evaluating library media resources	Works with teachers on curriculum development	Collaboratively teaches curriculum units with classroom teachers	Collaboratively evaluates curriculum units with classroom teachers
Reading/English	54	17	21	8
Mathematics	15	4	3	2
Science	36	9	9	3
Social studies	43	13	14	5
Foreign language	12	3	2	1
Arts	19	5	4	2
Health and safety	22	6	4	2

Close to two-thirds (63 percent) of public schools with LMCs had an information skills curriculum. Most typically, the way that those schools provided the instruction was by always integrating the instruction into other curriculum areas (61 percent), while 11 percent always provided the instruction through an information skills course and 28 percent used a combination of both means. The curriculum was generally developed by either the district (47 percent) or the school (36 percent) rather than by the state (17 percent). At private schools, the curriculum was primarily developed at the school (87 percent).

School library media centers were asked about eight other types of services, with the focus on how much those services were used. Two services stood out as being available at a majority of public school libraries—services for children with disabilities (80 percent) and extended hours before or after school (59 percent). These services also received the greatest use, with 12 to 14 percent of public school LMCs indicating heavy usage and 28 to 40 percent indicating moderate usage (compared with 4 to 31 percent indicating heavy or moderate usage in the other areas). Additionally, tutoring was offered at about half of the public school libraries (47 percent), with 9 percent indicating heavy usage, and 22 percent indicate moderate usage.

The Needs of School Library Media Centers

School libraries may conduct formal needs assessments or perform other types of evaluations of the materials and services they provide. Overall, 38 percent of public school libraries and 42 percent of private school libraries said they had conducted a needs assessment in the last two years. Some other common ways that public school LMCs evaluated their materials over the last two years were informal evaluations involving only school staff (73 percent), a written survey of school staff (37 percent), an evaluation conducted by a district evaluator (23 percent), and an evaluation involving students or parents (21 percent). Counting these other types of evaluations, 79 percent of public school library media centers conducted at least one type of evaluation in the past two years, and 76 percent of those made changes based on the evaluations.

Of those public schools that had conducted needs assessment, the most common needs were for more computer equipment (92 percent), more materials (90 percent), rewiring the LMC (67 percent), more staff training (60 percent), and more library staff (56 percent). With respect to the first two of these needs, a large majority of schools reported having made changes (71 percent for more materials and 70 percent for more computer equipment). In the remaining areas, fewer than half of the schools had made changes. (However, in four other areas—rewiring the LMC, adding a telephone line, flexible scheduling, and more staff training—more than half of the schools that identified needs in one of those areas also made changes in the same area.)

Between 29 and 87 percent of public school library media centers reported that each of 12 internal factors provided at least a small barrier to providing services and resources to students (Figure 4). The barriers that were most often reported were insufficient time for planning with teachers (87 percent), outdated materials (85 percent), insufficient materials (84 percent), insufficient computer equipment (84 percent), and insufficient library staff (81 percent). In fact, three of these factors were described as *major* barriers by about one-third of the public school LMCs: insufficient library staff (36 percent), insufficient computer equipment (35 percent), and insufficient time for planning with teachers (34 percent).

Figure 4 / Percent of Public School Library Media Centers (LMCs) Reporting That Various Factors Were Barriers to Providing Services and Resources, and the Degree of the Barriers

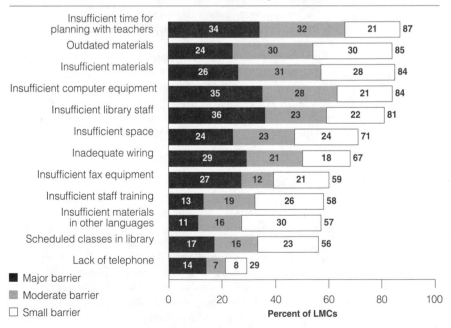

Note: Details may not add to totals due to rounding.

Library Media Centers and Education Reform

Library media centers were asked about their involvement in programs designed to address eight of the National Education Goals. For each of five of the goals, roughly half of the public school LMCs were involved: teacher education and professional development (56 percent); safe, disciplined, and alcohol- and drug-free schools (55 percent); student achievement and citizenship (52 percent); parental participation (51 percent); and mathematics and science (45 percent). The three remaining goals (ready to learn, school completion, and adult literacy and lifelong learning) were each supported by about one-fourth of the libraries.

School library media centers had some involvement in programs or services designed to address new national or state standards in various curriculum areas. As with other library services, the degree of involvement varied by subject area. Public school libraries were most often involved addressing standards in English (45 percent), social studies (44 percent), science (43 percent), and history (40 percent). However, even the areas least often addressed had the involvement of one-fifth or more of the libraries (24 percent for civics and 21 percent for physical education).

Overall, 76 percent of library media centers at public schools had materials to support professional development. Teachers often could obtain such materials though other libraries as well: 77 percent of the public school libraries said the materials were available through a local college or university library, 71 percent through a local public library, 66 percent through another library in the school system, and 44 percent through a library operated on a regional basis for several school districts. (The last category is low in part because 35 percent of school library media centers said there was no such regional library in their area. Only 3 to 16 percent of libraries said one of the other three types of libraries was not in the local area.)

Libraries had a number of other resources for teachers. At public schools, 80 percent had subscriptions to professional journals, with a mean of eight journals per school at those schools with subscriptions. Also, 58 percent had *Information Power: Guidelines for School Library Media Programs*, 56 percent had materials on local school reforms, 51 percent on Goal 2000, and 45 percent on other state reforms. Only 33 percent had the National Council of Teachers of Mathematics (NCTM) standards, which were the earliest set of standards produced under the current wave of reform, but 66 percent of the LMCs had materials on curriculum standards other than NCTM's standards.

Public Library Outlets

In 1996–1997 there were 15,465 public library outlets in the United States. Of these 7,058 represented single locations, 6,718 represented branches, and, 1,689 were central or main libraries.

Public Use

In spring 1997, in a typical week, public library outlets received an average of 1,795 patrons and were open for 40.5 hours, although there were considerable differences across the various outlet characteristics. For example, central or main libraries were open for more hours (55.1) and served almost twice as many patrons (3,502) as the overall average. Outlets serving populations of up to 24,999 received an average of only 748 patrons per week, which was less than half of the average for all outlets, while outlets serving populations of 100,000 or more served an average of 3,196 patrons, which is considerably greater than the overall average.

Public library outlets reported that almost half of their patrons were children (33 percent) or young adults (15 percent) (Figure 5). Since the definitions of "children" and "young adults" vary across the United States, the outlets were asked to provide the age ranges they served under each category. The most common age range for "children" was birth to age 12, a definition used by about one-third (31 percent) of all public library outlets. The most common age ranges for "young adult" were 13 through 18, used by 22 percent of all outlets, and 12 to 18, used by 17 percent.

Figure 5 / Patrons of Public Library Outlets

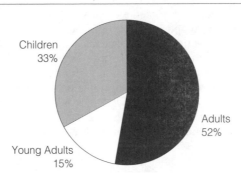

Staffing

In spring 1997 the average number of paid librarians providing services directly to the public was 3.7 librarians for all types of outlets. However, there were differences by type of outlet and size of population served by the outlets. Of the estimated 56,949 paid librarians providing services directly to the public in the United States as a whole, an estimated 8,755 were youth services specialists, 7,054 were children's specialists, and 2,154 were young adult specialists. Therefore, although children and young adults constituted 48 percent of public library patrons, librarians specializing in services to youth made up only 31 percent of the public service librarian population. Even in outlets having a librarian specializing in services to children, young adults, and/or youth, these specialists constituted only 38 percent of all paid librarians who provide service directly to the public, although 49 percent of their patrons were children and young adults.

Public library outlets were asked to identify the staff who were primarily responsible for developing programs for children and young adults in their building. The outlets reported that the development of children's programs was most frequently done by youth services specialists in the building (23 percent), children's specialists in the building (23 percent), or some other building-level librarian (29 percent). Program development for young adults was most frequently done by youth services specialists at the building level (20 percent) or some other building-level librarian. Altogether, 25 percent of all outlets reported that they had no programs for young adults, whereas only 8 percent of all outlets reported that they had no programs for children.

Collections

Public library outlets were asked about the adequacy of their holdings in 13 areas that are especially used by children and young adults. Results varied greatly by area. Picture books/easy readers was the only area in which more than half of the outlets (58 percent) reported that their holdings were excellent. However, most outlets reported that their holdings of picture books/easy readers (96 percent) and children's materials (94 percent) were either adequate or excellent. About four-fifths (79 to 83 percent) of the outlets reported that their young adults' materials, science fair materials, and high-interest/low-vocabulary books were either adequate or excellent, while about three-fifths (64 percent) reported having adequate or excellent multicultural materials. In contrast, only about one-third reported that they had adequate or excellent English-as-a-second-language materials (34 percent) or materials for children and young adults with disabilities (32 percent).

Technology

A wide array of technological equipment is being used by the modern public library. On the survey, outlets were asked about the availability of communications, television, and computer equipment and services. Almost all (99 percent) public library outlets had a telephone and about four-fifths (81 percent) had a fax machine. However, only 19 percent had TTY or other equipment for persons with disabilities. Almost three-fourths (72 percent) had a VCR and about one-fourth (24 percent) had cable. Fewer than 5 percent of all outlets had closed-circuit TV, satellite dish, video laser disk player, or a TV studio.

In 1997 stand-alone computers were available in 76 percent of all outlets, while computers with dedicated lines were found in 59 percent and computer with shared lines in 52 percent. A networked automated catalog was found in 57 percent of all outlets and 22 percent had a stand-alone automated catalog. About three-fifths of the outlets had resources on CD-ROM (62 percent) and about the same percentage had an automated circulation system (61 percent).

The availability and usage of certain technological resources by children and young adults was included on the survey. Technological resources that were *not* available for use by children in 44 to 65 percent of all outlets were computer software for independent use (65 percent), personal computers for independent use (53 percent), CD-ROM services (47 percent), and online computer information services (44 percent). Similar percentages of outlets did not make these resources available to young adults.

Public library outlets were asked about reciprocal borrowing and online access, by the Internet or other networks, to the catalog of other libraries. Most (89 percent) outlets engaged in reciprocal borrowing with another library in their system, while only a little more than half (55 percent) engaged in reciprocal borrowing with a community college library and about one-fourth did reciprocal borrowing with a senior high school library. Online access to the catalogs of other institutions was used less frequently than reciprocal borrowing. Online access to another library in the system was reported by 65 percent of the public library outlets; to a community college library, by 40 percent; and to a senior high school library, by 10 percent. In addition, 40 percent of all outlets reported that their computer could be accessed from remote locations by patrons. This represented about 6,060 outlets.

Access to and Use of the Internet

With the Internet growing as a source of information in today's world, access to it is important to public library outlets. In 1996, 66 percent of all public library outlets (about 10,164 outlets) could access the Internet through a computer in their building (Figure 6). About half of all outlets had a policy on access to the Internet by children and young adults. By the year 2000, 88 percent of all outlets were expecting to have access to the Internet. Of the 34 percent of all outlets that did not have access in 1996, 20 percent, or approximately 860 outlets, had no plans to do so.

Figure 6 / Percent of Public Library Outlets Having or Planning to Have Internet Access, By Year Access Is Expected

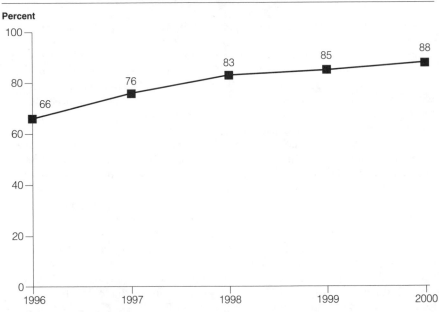

In spring 1997 the average number of computers or terminals connected to the Internet in an outlet was 5.0 terminals, for a total of about 49,965 terminals for the United States as a whole. On average, each outlet had 2.4 terminals connected to the Internet that were available to the public. The availability of terminals connected to the Internet was much greater in central and main libraries, which had an average of 13.4 terminals connected to the Internet and 5.5 terminals connected to the Internet that were available for the public.

Outlets were asked about the availability of five Internet resources—text-based World Wide Web, graphical World Wide Web, electronic indexes, electronic journals, and e-mail accounts—and whether adult patrons and children and young adults were permitted to use them. Each of the resources was available in between 39 and 54 percent of all public library outlets (Figure 7). The percentages of outlets allowing adult patrons to use these resources were about the same as the percentages allowing children and young adults to use them. Generally, the difference between the number of outlets in which the resources were available and the number permitting them to be used by patrons was about 10 percent. One exception was e-mail accounts that were available in 44 percent of the outlets, but only 11 percent permitted adult patrons to use them and 9 percent allowed usage by children and young adults.

Figure 7 / Percent of Public Library Outlets with Various Internet Resources, and the Percent Reporting Those Resources Are Used by Adult Patrons and Children or Young Adults

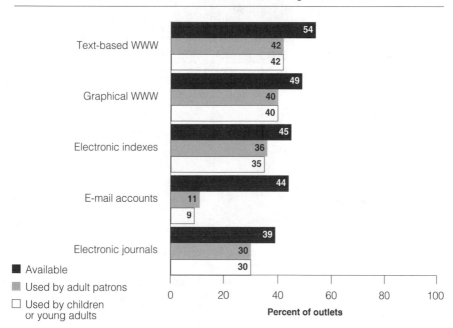

Outlets were asked if two types of Internet services, using the Internet to answer reference questions and providing training on the use of the Internet, were provided to adult patrons and children and young adults. For both services, about the same percentage provide the services to adult patrons as provide them to children and young adults. About 62 percent of all outlets use the Internet to answer reference questions and about 40 percent provide training on the use of the Internet.

Public library outlets were asked about the extent to which the lack of or insufficient amount of 15 factors were barriers to the outlet's ability to gain access or maximize access to Internet services. Factors reported by more than 60 percent of the outlets were the lack of, or insufficient amount of, funds for technology (81 percent), staff time (81 percent), space (74 percent), computers (73 percent), training for librarians (67 percent), telephone lines (64 percent), software (63 percent), and telecommunications equipment such as modems (62 percent) (Figure 8).

Figure 8 / Percent of Public Library Outlets Facing Various Barriers to Maximizing Internet Access, and the Degree of the Barriers

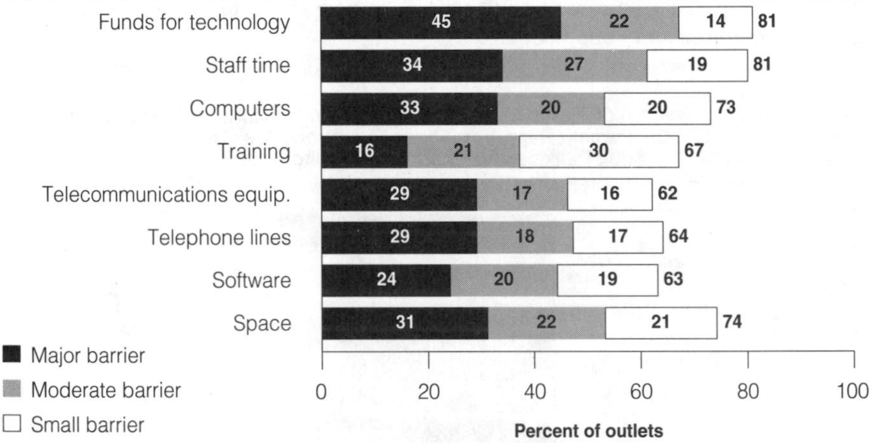

Note: Details may not add to totals due to rounding.

Programs and Services

In the survey, public library outlets were asked if they provided 11 different types of services or programs for parents or caregivers. The most frequently available services, provided by more than three-fifths of all public library outlets, were programs or materials for parents of preschoolers (74 percent) and beginning readers (71 percent) as well as referrals to services from other organizations (64 percent). Services that were least likely to be offered were services to limited-English-proficient (LEP) parents (28 percent), tutoring for low-literate parents or caregivers (16 percent), outreach to new parents (13 percent), and parenting classes (5 percent). For most of the possible comparisons, central or main libraries were more likely to have each of the programs and services for parents and caregivers than were branches or single-location libraries.

In the year prior to the survey, public library outlets provided an average of 58 story hour sessions for preschool children with an average of 15 children per session. Central or main libraries provided an average of 107 preschool story hour sessions in one year, which is significantly higher than the overall outlet average.

Some families choose to educate their children at home. For these families, the public library can be an important resource. About three-fifths (62 percent) of all public library outlets provide services to families involved in home schooling. Thus, approximately 9,521 outlets provide these services. About one-third of all outlets provide a file of information about home schooling in their area (30 percent), special borrowing privileges (33 percent), and use of a meeting room (35 percent).

Public library outlets were asked about the availability and extent of usage of 12 services by children and young adults. Summer reading programs for children were available in most outlets (96 percent), where they were heavily used in 71 percent and moderately used by another 22 percent. In contrast, only about two-thirds (63 percent) of all outlets had summer reading programs for young adults and only 8 percent report heavy usage by young adults with another 31 percent reporting moderate usage. Two services that were available in most library outlets for both children and young adults were study space and interlibrary loans; however, both services received heavier usage by young adults. After-school and weekend programs for children were available in almost half (48 percent) of the outlets, but only 29 percent had these services for young adults. Tutoring was not available in most outlets; only 14 percent provided this service for children and 15 percent for young adults. Fewer than half of all outlets offered homework assistance services to children (42 percent) or young adults (41 percent). About one-third of all outlets provided services to children (33 percent) or young adults (29 percent) with disabilities.

The public library outlets were asked if 13 factors were barriers to the provision of services to children and young adults. For nine of these factors, significantly more public library outlets reported that it was a barrier to providing services to young adults than reported it for children. (Barriers for young adult programming reported by at least half of the public library outlets were insufficient programs (64 percent), lack of outreach programming (60 percent), insufficient space (58 percent), insufficient library staff (54 percent), and insufficient materials (50 percent) (Figure 9).

Needs Assessments and Evaluations

Needs assessments and evaluations are mechanisms for libraries to determine if they are meeting their goals and objectives and if there are unmet needs that they could address. Public library outlets were asked if they or their library system had conducted a needs assessment directed to schools in their service area during the two years prior to the survey, and only 9 percent had done so. However, of the ones that had conducted such a needs assessment, 83 percent had made changes to existing programs or services as a result of the needs assessment, and 74 percent had added new programs or services.

In the two years prior to the survey, 81 percent of all outlets or their library systems had conducted at least one type of evaluation of the materials or services provided by the outlet, and 69 percent of those conducting an evaluation made changes as a result. The most common type of evaluation was an informal one involving library staff only, conducted by 75 percent of all outlets or their systems. An evaluation involving the community was done by 52 percent of the outlets or their systems and a written survey of library staff was done by 38 percent.

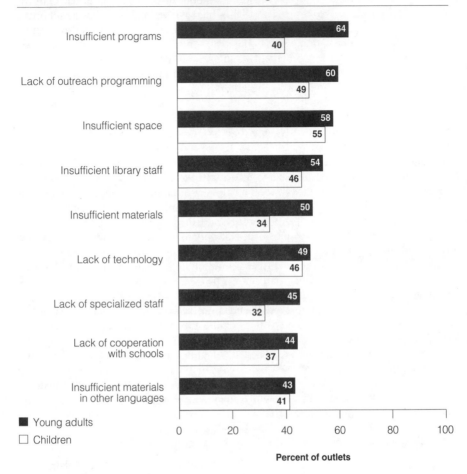

Figure 9 / Public Library Outlets' Most Common Barriers to Providing Services to Children and Young Adults

Outreach Programs

Outreach programs enable public libraries to extend their services to groups or individuals, particularly those who have had little or no experience with libraries. In the survey, public library outlets were asked about outreach programs or services specifically for children, young adults, or their parents that were provided within their service by either the outlets themselves or by their library system. Of the 15 programs listed on the survey, the outreach program provided most frequently by the outlets was outreach to schools, both elementary and secondary, which was done by almost half (46 percent) of the outlets. In addition, 19 percent of the outlets reported that their systems provided outreach to the schools. Other outreach programs provided by at least one-fourth of the outlets were programs for preschools (43 percent), day care centers (31 percent), and Head Start centers (26 percent). The outlets were asked to include bookmobile services in reporting their conduct of outreach programs to various facilities. They were also asked specifically about bookmobile services to schools in their service area. Only 4 percent of the outlets reported that they provided bookmobile services to schools. In addition, 11 percent reported that their library system provided these services.

Cooperation Between Schools and Public Libraries

Both the school and public library surveys contained questions about cooperative activities. Responses are first described from the perspective of the respondents, school library media centers and public library outlets. A comparison of the responses is then provided.

School Library Media Center Perspective

Three-fifths (60 percent) of library media centers at public schools participated in some type of cooperative activity with a local public library during the 12 months preceding the survey. On average, those LMCs that did participate in some type of cooperative activity said they cooperated with 2.3 public libraries. The most likely types of participation were borrowing materials for teachers (48 percent of all library media centers at public schools), borrowing materials for the school library (43 percent), informing the public library of curriculum or homework needs (40 percent), coordinating about student research projects (36 percent), coordinating class visits to the public library (33 percent), and public librarians providing information about using the public library (32 percent). School libraries most typically reported their participation in these activities was either rare or occasional (between 29 and 36 percent) while 2 to 12 percent said their participation was frequent.

At public schools, 21 percent of the library media centers worked with the public library in planning for a summer reading program conducted for school-age children. Such participation was more common at elementary schools than secondary schools (25 percent versus 11 percent).

For some public schools, interaction with the local public library may be facilitated because the school library media center is located in the same building as the local public library. This occurred at 4 percent of the public school library media centers. Only 3 percent of public school library media centers reported not having a local public library in their area. Most public school LMCs had several kinds of libraries in their area, including another library in the school system (89 percent), a local college or university library (84 percent), and a library operated on a regional basis for several school districts (65 percent).

Besides the local public libraries, another potential resource is the library at a local college or university. Among library media centers at public schools, 77 had such a library that provided access to resources for teachers, and 49 percent had one that provided access for students.

Barriers to Interaction with Public Libraries

The library media centers also were asked about the degree to which each of seven different factors was a barrier to the interaction between their school and the public library. The greatest barriers were the schedule of the school LMC staff and an insufficient number of school LMC staff, with 61 percent of library media centers citing each factor as either a major or moderate barrier. The only factor not listed as providing at least a small barrier by a majority of school libraries was distance (52 percent), though even this factor was a major barrier for 10 percent of the school libraries and a moderate barrier for 12 percent.

Figure 10 / Percent of School Library Media Centers (LMCs) Indicating Various Factors Were Barriers to the Interaction Between Their School and the Public Library, and the Degree of the Barriers

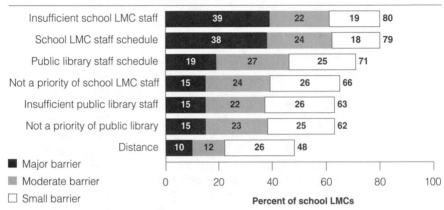

Note: Details may not add to totals due to rounding.

Public Library Perspective

Altogether, 86 percent of all public library outlets participated in some kind of cooperative activity with a local public or private school during the 12 months preceding the survey. For central or main libraries, 97 percent were engaged in such cooperative activities. The most common cooperative activities, in which more than three-fourths of all public library outlets participated, were lending materials to classroom teachers (81 percent), hosting class visits from the schools to the library (80 percent), and introducing the public library summer reading program at schools (76 percent). Cooperative activities in which more than half of the public library outlets had participated were having the schools informing them of curriculum or upcoming homework needs (67 percent), visiting schools to promote or provide general information about using the public library (63 percent), and coordinating with schools regarding student research projects, including science fair projects (60 percent).

About half of the outlets had never been involved in visiting schools to give booktalks (50 percent) or lending materials to the school library (51 percent). Other cooperative activities in which more than half of the outlets had never participated were conducting regular collaborative planning sessions (80 percent); providing information literacy training for teachers or students (76 percent);

sharing equipment (75 percent); participating in automation projects such as shared online resources, searches, or catalogs (75 percent); participating in or providing joint inservice training for school and public librarians (75 percent); and cosponsoring programs regarding parental involvement (68 percent).

For public library outlets involved in cooperative activities with schools, the mean number of public schools in their service area was 6.7, and the mean number with which they cooperated was 4.9. The mean number of private schools located in a public library outlet's service area was 2.1, and the mean number of private schools with which the outlets cooperated was 1.3.

In conducting cooperative activities with schools, public library outlet staff reported that they interacted with teachers or counselors (83 percent of the outlets), school library media specialists (73 percent), and school administrators (67 percent). Staff of central or main libraries were more likely to interact with school staff than were the staff of branches or single location libraries.

In some cases, cooperation may be facilitated by the fact that a public library outlet and a school are located in the same building. Estimates indicated that 3 percent of public library outlets were located in a school building in 1997.

Public library outlets were asked about the adequacy of their resources in various school subject areas. For most of the more traditional subject areas such as history, geography, science, and reading/English, at least two-thirds of the outlets considered their resources to be adequate or excellent. Foreign languages was an area in which only about one-third (37 percent) considered their resources to be adequate or excellent.

One way in which public libraries help school students is by providing various homework assistance programs. More than half of all outlets (58 percent) provide reserve collections for class assignments, and almost half (47 percent) provide telephone assistance for homework assignments. Reference packets in specific subjects are provided by 22 percent of all public library outlets. Less common services are homework centers (17 percent of all outlets) and homework hotlines (2 percent).

Public libraries can assist schools by participating in educational reform efforts. Public library outlets were asked if they had been involved in any programs designed specifically to address the eight of the National Education Goals during the five years prior to the survey. The goal with which the most outlets had been involved was adult literacy and lifelong learning (41 percent). The goal with which the least outlets had been involved was teacher education and professional development (9 percent).

Outlets were asked about the availability of various materials related to school reform. About half of the outlets had the U.S. Department of Education's Read • Write • Now! literacy materials (53 percent). Fewer than 40 percent of the outlets had any of the other reform-related materials such as information on Goal 2000 (38 percent) or local school reform efforts (38 percent).

In spring 1997, 24 percent of all public library outlets reported that they coordinated or supported the U.S. Department of Education's Read • Write • Now! literacy program. Outlets with this program coordinated it with public schools (33 percent), private schools (12 percent), and other community learning partners (33 percent).

Barriers to Interaction with Schools

Public libraries were asked about the barriers to the interaction between public library outlets and schools. Barriers indicated by about two-thirds of the outlets were that interaction was not a priority of the school LMC (67 percent) and insufficient public library staff (67 percent), and almost half of the outlets considered these to be major or moderate barriers (Figure 11). Additional barriers for more than half of the outlets were the schedule of public library staff (61 percent), schedule of the school LMC (59 percent), and insufficient school LMC staff (56 percent), and about one-third of the outlets considered these to be major or moderate barriers.

Figure 11 / Percent of Public Library Outlets Indicating Various Factors Were Barriers to Interaction Between Their Outlet and the Schools, and the Degree of the Barriers

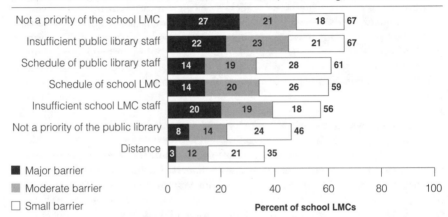

Note: Details may not add to totals due to rounding.

Comparison of the Perspectives

Public library outlets were more likely to participate in cooperative activities than were public school library media centers. In the 12 months preceding the surveys, 86 percent of the public library outlets had engaged in a cooperative activity with a school, whereas only 60 percent of the public school LMCs had participated in a cooperative activity with a public library. The most common cooperative activities were quite similar for the two types of libraries. However, the percentage of public library outlets reporting these activities and the frequency of occurrence was greater for the public library outlets. A possible reason for this difference is that public libraries may be supporting a number of school activities beyond those specifically associated with the school library media center.

Both the school and the public library surveys listed seven factors that might be barriers to cooperation. For five of the factors a greater percentage of public school LMCs considered them to be barriers than did public library outlets. The most common factors identified by public school LMCs were their schedules and insufficient LMC staff. Similarly, insufficient public library staff and staff schedules were among the most common barriers identified by the public library outlets.

Number of Libraries in the United States, Canada, and Mexico

Statistics are from the 52nd edition of the *American Library Directory (ALD)* 1999–2000 (R. R. Bowker, 1999). Data are exclusive of elementary and secondary school libraries.

Libraries in the United States

Public Libraries	16,213	*
Public libraries, excluding branches	9,837	†
Main public libraries that have branches	1,312	
Public library branches	6,376	
Academic Libraries	4,723	*
Junior college	1,274	
Departmental	126	
Medical	6	
Religious	3	
University and college	3,449	
Departmental	1,467	
Law	175	
Medical	214	
Religious	104	
Armed Forces Libraries	352	*
Air Force	100	
Medical	12	
Army	152	
Medical	31	
Navy	100	
Law	1	
Medical	14	
Government Libraries	1,874	*
Law	421	
Medical	219	
Special Libraries (excluding public, academic, armed forces, and government)	9,691	*
Law	1,136	
Medical	1,906	
Religious	1,001	

Note: Numbers followed by an asterisk are added to find "Total libraries counted" for each of the four geographic areas (United States, U.S.-administered regions, Canada, and Mexico). The sum of the four totals is the "Grand total of libraries listed" in *ALD*. For details on the count of libraries, see the preface to the 52nd edition of *ALD—Ed.*

† Federal, state, and other statistical sources use this figure (libraries excluding branches) as the total for public libraries.

Total Special Libraries (including public, academic, armed forces,
and government)   10,808
    Total law   1,741
    Total medical   2,401
    Total religious   1,109
Total Libraries Counted(*)   32,852

Libraries in Regions Administered by the United States

Public Libraries   26 *
  Public libraries, excluding branches   11 †
    Main public libraries that have branches   3
  Public library branches   15
Academic Libraries   57 *
  Junior college   11
    Departmental   3
  University and college   46
    Departmental   20
    Law   2
    Medical   1
Armed Forces Libraries   2 *
  Air Force   1
  Army   1
  Navy   0
Government Libraries   8 *
  Law   1
  Medical   2
Special Libraries (excluding public, academic, armed forces,
and government)   17 *
  Law   4
  Medical   5
  Religious   1
Total Special Libraries (including public, academic, armed forces,
and government)   19
    Total law   7
    Total medical   8
    Total religious   1
Total Libraries Counted(*)   110

Libraries in Canada

Public Libraries   1,673 *
  Public libraries, excluding branches   788 †
    Main public libraries that have branches   134
  Public library branches   855

Academic Libraries	484 *
Junior college	126
Departmental	34
Medical	0
Religious	2
University and college	358
Departmental	162
Law	15
Medical	14
Religious	17
Government Libraries	380 *
Law	23
Medical	5
Special Libraries (excluding public, academic, armed forces, and government)	1,395 *
Law	127
Medical	260
Religious	59
Total Special Libraries (including public, academic, and government)	1,493
Total law	168
Total medical	317
Total religious	104
Total Libraries Counted(*)	3,932

Libraries in Mexico

Public Libraries	22 *
Public libraries, excluding branches	22 †
Main public libraries that have branches	0
Public library branches	0
Academic Libraries	313 *
Junior college	0
Departmental	0
Medical	0
Religious	0
University and college	313
Departmental	246
Law	0
Medical	1
Religious	0
Government Libraries	8 *
Law	0
Medical	1
Special Libraries (excluding public, academic, armed forces, and government)	26 *

Law	0
Medical	10
Religious	0
Total Special Libraries (including public, academic, and government)	32
Total law	0
Total medical	12
Total religious	0
Total Libraries Counted(*)	369

Summary

Total U.S. Libraries	32,852
Total Libraries Administered by the United States	110
Total Canadian Libraries	3,932
Total Mexican Libraries	369
Grand Total of Libraries Listed	37,263

Highlights of NCES Surveys

Academic Libraries

The following are highlights from the *E.D. TABS Academic Libraries: 1996,* released in January 2000.

Services

- In 1996, 3,408 of the 3,792 institutions of higher education in the United States reported that they had their own academic library.
- In fiscal year 1996, general collection circulation transactions in the nation's academic libraries at institutions of higher education totaled 186.5 million. Reserve collection circulation transactions totaled 44.2 million. For general and reference circulation transactions taken together, the median circulation was 15.0 per full-time-equivalent (FTE) student*. The median total circulation ranged from 8.4 per FTE in less than four-year institutions to 28.0 in doctorate-granting institutions.
- In 1996 academic libraries provided a total of about 9.4 million interlibrary loans to other libraries (both higher education and other types of libraries) and received about 7.5 million loans.
- Overall, the largest percentage of academic libraries (44 percent) reported having 60–79 hours of service per typical week. However, 40 percent provided 80 or more public service hours per typical week. The percent of institutions providing 80 or more public service hours ranged from 7 percent in less than four-year institutions to 77 percent in doctorate-granting institutions.
- Taken together, academic libraries reported a gate count of about 16.5 million visitors per typical week (about 1.6 visits per total FTE enrollment).
- About 1.9 million reference transactions were reported in a typical week.
- Over the fiscal year 1996, about 407,000 presentations to groups serving about 7.3 million were reported.

Collections

- Taken together, the nation's 3,408 academic libraries at institutions of higher education held a total of 806.7 million volumes (books, bound serials, and government documents), representing about 449.2 million unduplicated titles at the end of FY 1996.
- The median number of volumes held per FTE student was 58.2 volumes. Median volumes held ranged from 19.0 per FTE in less than four-year institutions to 111.2 in doctorate-granting institutions.
- Of the total volumes held at the end of the year, 44 percent (352.1 million) were held at the 125 institutions categorized under the 1994 Carnegie classification as Research I or Research II institutions. About 55

*FTE enrollment is calculated by adding one-third of part-time enrollment to full-time enrollment. Enrollment data are from the 1995–96 IPEDS Fall Enrollment Survey.

percent of the volumes were at those institutions classified as either Research or Doctoral in the Carnegie classification.

• In FY 1996, the median number of volumes added to collections per FTE student was 1.5. The median number added ranged from 0.6 per FTE in less than four-year institutions to 2.8 in doctorate-granting institutions.

Staff

• There was a total of 95,580 FTE staff working in academic libraries in 1996. Of these about 27,268 (29 percent) were librarians or other professional staff; 40,022 (42 percent) were other paid staff; 291 (less than 0.5 percent) were contributed services staff; and 27,998 (29 percent) were student assistants.

• Excluding student assistants, the institutional median number of academic library FTE staff per 1,000 FTE students was 5.8. The median ranged from 3.6 in less than four-year institutions to 9.5 in doctorate-granting institutions.

Expenditures

• In 1996 total operating expenditures for libraries at the 3,408 institutions of higher education totaled $4.3 billion. The three largest individual expenditure items for all academic libraries were salaries and wages, $2.15 billion (50 percent); current serial subscription expenditures, $780.8 million (18 percent); and books and bound serials, $472.6 million (11.0 percent).

• The libraries of the 538 doctorate-granting institutions (16 percent of the total institutions) accounted for $2.714 billion, or 63 percent of the total operating expenditure dollars at all college and university libraries.

• In 1996 the median total operating expenditure per FTE student was $310.22 and the median for information resource expenditures was $90.07.

• The median percentage of total institutional Education & General (E&G) expenditures for academic libraries was 2.8 percent in 1994. In 1990 the median was 3.0 percent (*Academic Library Survey: 1990*, unpublished tabulation).

Electronic Services

• In FY 1996, 80 percent of institutions with an academic library had access from within the library to an electronic catalog of the library's holdings, 81 percent had Internet access within the library, and 40 percent had library reference service by e-mail.

State Library Agencies

The following are highlights from *E.D. TABS State Library Agencies, Fiscal Year 1998*, released in February 2000.

Governance

- Nearly all state agencies (48 states and the District of Columbia) are located in the executive branch of government. Of these, over 65 percent are part of a larger agency, the most common being the state department of education. In two states, Arizona and Michigan, the agency is located in the legislative branch.

Allied and Other Special Operations

- A total of 15 state library agencies reported having one or more operations. Allied operations most frequently linked with a state library are the state archives (10 states) and the state records management service (10 states).
- Seventeen state agencies contract with libraries in their states to serve as resource or reference/information service centers. Eighteen state agencies operate a State Center for the Book*.

Electronic Services and Information

- All state library agencies plan or monitor electronic network development, 45 states and the District of Columbia operate such networks, and 44 states and the District of Columbia develop network content†.
- Thirty-four state library agencies were applicants to the Universal Service (E-rate discount) Program established by the Federal Communications Commission (FCC) under the Telecommunications Act of 1996 (P.L. 104-104)‡.
- All state library agencies facilitate library access to the Internet in one or more of the following ways: training or consulting library staff in the use of the Internet; providing a subsidy for Internet participation; providing equipment to access the Internet; providing access to directories, databases, or online catalogs; and managing gopher/Web sites, file servers, bulletin boards, or listservs.
- Forty-four state library agencies provide or facilitate library access to online databases through subscription, lease, license, consortial membership, or agreement.
- Almost all state library agencies facilitate or subsidize electronic access to the holdings of other libraries in their state, most frequently through Online Computer Library Center (OCLC) participation (42 states and the District of Columbia). Over half provide access via a Web-based union catalog (30 states) or Telnet gateway (27 states).
- Forty-six state library agencies have Internet terminals available for public use, ranging in number from two to five (15 states), five to nine (13

---

* The State Center for the Book is part of the Center for the Book program sponsored by the Library of Congress which promotes books, reading, and literacy, and is hosted or funded by the state.
† Network content refers to database development. Database development activities may include the creation of new databases or the conversion of existing databases into electronic format. Includes bibliographic databases as well as full text or data files.
‡ Under this program, FCC promotes affordable access to the Internet and the availability of Internet services to the public, with special attention given to schools and libraries.

states), ten to 19 (eight states), 20 to 29 (seven states), and 30 or more (three states). Michigan reported the largest number of public-use Internet terminals (41).

Library Development Service

Services to Public Libraries

- Every state library agency provides the following types of services to public libraries: administration of Library Services and Technology Act (LSTA) grants; collection of library statistics; and library planning, evaluation, and research. Nearly every state library agency provides consulting services and continuing education programs.
- Services to public libraries provided by at least three-quarters of state agencies include administration of state aid, interlibrary loan referral services, library legislation preparation or review, literacy program support, reference referral services, state standards or guidelines, summer reading program support, union list development, and review of technology plans for the Universal Service (E-rate discount) Program.
- Over three-fifths of state agencies provide Online Computer Library Center (OCLC) Group Access Capability (GAC) to public libraries and statewide public relations or library promotion campaigns.
- Less common services to public libraries include accreditation of libraries, certification of librarians, cooperative purchasing of library materials, preservation/conservation services, and retrospective conversion of bibliographic records.

Services to Academic Libraries

- At least two-thirds of state library agencies report the following services to the academic library sector: administration of LSTA grants, continuing education, interlibrary loan referral services, and reference referral services.
- Less common services to academic libraries provided by state agencies include cooperative purchasing of library materials, literacy program support, preservation/conservation, retrospective conversion, and state standards or guidelines. No state library agency accredits academic libraries; only Washington state certifies academic librarians.

Services to School Library Media Centers

- At least two-thirds of state library agencies provide the following services to school library media centers (LMCs): administration of LSTA grants, continuing education, interlibrary loan referral services, and reference referral services. Services to LMCs provided by at least half of all state agencies include consulting services and union list development.
- Less common services to LMCs include administration of state aid, cooperative purchasing of library materials, retrospective conversion, and Universal Service Program review. No state library agency accredits LMCs or certifies LMC librarians.

Services to Special Libraries

- Over two-thirds of state agencies serve special libraries* through administration of LSTA grants, consulting services, continuing education, interlibrary loan referral, reference referral, and union list development.

- Less common services to special libraries include administration of state aid, cooperative purchasing of library materials, and summer reading program support. Only Nebraska accredits special libraries and only Indiana and Washington state certify librarians of special libraries.

Services to Systems

- At least three-fifths of state agencies serve library systems† through administration of LSTA grants, consulting services, continuing education, library legislation preparation or review, and library planning, evaluation, and research.

- Accreditation of systems is provided by only six states and certification of librarians by only five states.

Service Outlets

- State library agencies reported a total of 152 service outlets—72 main or central outlets, 71 other outlets (excluding bookmobiles), and nine bookmobiles.

Collections

- The number of books and serial volumes held by state library agencies totaled 22.0 million, with New York accounting for the largest collection (2.4 million). Five state agencies had book and serial volumes of over one million. In other states, these collections ranged from 500,000 to one million (11 states); 200,000 to 499,999 (12 states); 100,000 to 199,999 (eight states); 50,000 to 99,999 (seven states); and 50,000 or less (six states). The state library agency in Maryland does not maintain a collection, and the District of Columbia does not maintain a collection in its function as a state library agency.

- The number of serial subscriptions held by state library agencies totaled over 82,000, with New York holding the largest number (over 12,100). Ten state agencies reported serial subscriptions of over 2,000. In other states, these collections ranged from 1,000 to 1,999 (seven states), 500 to 999 (16 states), 100 to 499 (13 states), and under 100 (2 states).

---

* A library in a business firm, professional association, government agency, or other organized group; a library that is maintained by a parent organization to serve a specialized clientele; or an independent library that may provide materials or services, or both, to the public, a segment of the public, or to other libraries. Scope of collections and services are limited to the subject interests of the host or parent institution. Includes libraries in state institutions.
† A system is a group of autonomous libraries joined together by formal or informal agreements to perform various services cooperatively such as resource sharing, communications, etc. Includes multitype library systems and public library systems. Excludes multiple outlets under the same administration.

Staff

- The total number of budgeted full-time-equivalent (FTE) positions in state library agencies was 3,766. Librarians with ALA-MLS degrees accounted for 1,206 of these positions, or 32.0 percent of total FTE positions. Rhode Island reported the largest percentage (57.1) of ALA-MLS librarians, and Utah reported the lowest (16.3 percent).

Income

- State library agencies reported a total income of $886.2 million in FY 1998 (81.3 percent came from state sources, 16.7 percent from federal sources, and 2.0 percent from other sources).
- Of state library agency income received from state sources, over $509 million (70.7 percent) was designated for state aid to libraries. In 11 states, over 75 percent of income from state sources was set aside for state aid. Georgia had the largest percentage of state library agency income set aside for state aid (97.3 percent). Six states (Hawaii, Iowa, New Hampshire, South Dakota, Vermont, and Wyoming) and the District of Columbia targeted no state funds for aid to libraries; instead, 95 to 100 percent of their state funds were set aside for state library agency operations.*

Expenditures

- In five states, over 90 percent of total expenditures were from state sources. These states were Georgia (94.0 percent), Massachusetts (93.4 percent), Maryland (90.4 percent), New York (92.3 percent), and West Virginia (90.7 percent). The District of Columbia had the lowest percentage of expenditures from state sources (36.7 percent), followed by Wyoming (52.2 percent).
- Almost 70 percent of total state library expenditures were for aid to libraries, with the largest percentages expended on individual public libraries (55.2 percent) and public library systems (15.9 percent). Most aid-to-libraries expenditures (88 percent) were from state sources, and 11.8 percent were from federal sources.
- Fourteen state library agencies reported expenditures for allied operations. These expenditures totaled over $23.1 million and represented 2.7 percent of total expenditures by state library agencies. Of states reporting allied operations expenditures, Virginia reported the highest expenditure ($3.8 million) and Kansas the lowest ($110,000).†

*The District of Columbia Public Library functions as a state library agency and is eligible for federal LSTA (Library Services and Technology Act) funds in this capacity. The state library agency in Hawaii is associated with the Hawaii State Public Library System and operates all public libraries within its jurisdiction. The state funds for aid to libraries for these two agencies are reported on the NCES Public Libraries Survey, rather than on the STLA survey, because of the unique situation of these two state agencies, and in order to eliminate duplicative reporting of these data.

†Although Alaska reported allied operations, the expenditures are not from the state library agency budget.

Library Acquisition Expenditures, 1998–1999: U.S. Public, Academic, Special, and Government Libraries

The information in these tables is taken from the 52nd edition of the *American Library Directory* (*ALD*) (1999–2000), published by R. R. Bowker. The tables report acquisition expenditures by public, academic, special, and government libraries.

The total number of U.S. libraries listed in the 52nd edition of *ALD* is 32,852, including 16,213 public libraries, 4,723 academic libraries, 9,691 special libraries, and 1,874 government libraries.

Understanding the Tables

Number of libraries includes only those U.S. libraries in *ALD* that reported annual acquisition expenditures (4,214 public libraries, 1,787 academic libraries, 915 special libraries, 279 government libraries). Libraries that reported annual income but not expenditures are not included in the count. Academic libraries include university, college, and junior college libraries. Special academic libraries, such as law and medical libraries, that reported acquisition expenditures separately from the institution's main library are counted as independent libraries.

The amount in the *total acquisition expenditures* column for a given state is generally greater than the sum of the categories of expenditures. This is because the total acquisition expenditures amount also includes the expenditures of libraries that did not itemize by category.

Figures in *categories of expenditure* columns represent only those libraries that itemized expenditures. Libraries that reported a total acquisition expenditure amount but did not itemize are only represented in the total acquisition expenditures column.

Unspecified includes monies reported as not specifically for books, periodicals, audiovisual materials and equipment, microform, preservation, other print materials, manuscripts and archives, machine-readable materials, or database fees (e.g., library materials). This column also includes monies reported for categories in combination—for example, audiovisual *and* microform. When libraries report only total acquisition expenditures without itemizing by category, the total amount is not reflected as unspecified.

Table 1 / Public Library Acquisition Expenditures

State	Number of Libraries	Total Acquisition Expenditures	Books	Other Print Materials	Periodicals	Manuscripts & Archives	AV Materials	AV Equipment	Microform	Machine Readable Materials	Preservation	Database Fees	Unspecified
Alabama	72	7,041,153	3,615,443	396,132	517,132	—	505,412	9,390	344,181	89,890	12,540	111,927	596,901
Alaska	34	2,870,114	936,176	169,542	745,825	—	134,408	3,095	13,500	70,537	1,465	5,606	9,386
Arizona	59	16,024,092	6,643,006	176,381	1,328,170	—	674,622	1,500	120,125	538,836	107,408	1,509,774	296,067
Arkansas	29	4,304,558	2,097,362	8,790	359,754	—	231,747	10,000	55,575	45,124	30,654	49,604	26,748
California	144	81,306,201	44,672,206	797,558	7,936,492	11,229	3,599,075	15,233	1,764,539	1,724,664	590,227	2,365,344	3,861,413
Colorado	58	14,309,998	7,361,254	85,272	778,447	23,100	736,341	29,981	178,527	525,319	42,020	626,208	721,307
Connecticut	120	14,427,231	6,162,667	632,190	868,906	400	684,326	83,779	119,850	223,001	43,552	500,154	274,958
Delaware	14	1,138,308	554,488	600	80,718	—	64,291	—	25,283	26,500	—	18,317	—
District of Columbia	3	12,872,464	1,582	1,539	466	—	683	—	—	—	—	—	—
Florida	101	61,946,825	24,447,226	82,470	3,406,665	39,285	2,788,847	206,966	555,515	893,937	105,966	911,374	275,338
Georgia	40	23,278,114	7,114,534	20,323	326,244	5,829	858,034	20,792	116,663	83,336	14,762	146,215	22,997
Hawaii	2	2,400,529	1,749,579	—	429,154	—	—	—	—	—	—	—	—
Idaho	37	2,226,743	999,428	20,950	128,707	—	85,741	2,000	10,272	13,172	3,213	99,706	5,095
Illinois	304	52,150,057	17,497,452	438,607	2,548,093	19,894	2,672,193	274,083	544,609	1,307,382	123,142	1,027,948	702,446
Indiana	137	29,256,034	14,390,826	77,941	2,014,180	—	3,218,013	59,778	355,710	379,520	121,985	885,366	407,374
Iowa	220	8,588,417	4,573,104	53,063	943,461	—	600,762	36,023	80,604	137,418	7,917	141,174	699,533
Kansas	88	8,049,716	5,268,199	27,110	1,153,447	684	702,165	20,293	34,521	75,425	3,128	102,344	182,159
Kentucky	54	7,956,296	3,023,622	5,210	343,090	1,550	471,241	75,889	45,779	40,339	8,112	331,715	80,400
Louisiana	31	10,322,933	4,912,735	8,440	970,316	—	467,903	14,360	119,795	12,900	22,668	119,286	16,732
Maine	74	2,350,308	1,331,779	2,968	276,266	1,077	118,465	2,537	12,323	12,994	12,524	38,373	7,852
Maryland	24	23,108,197	8,348,763	267,722	524,844	—	1,220,117	54,879	117,563	381,527	1,396	452,811	774,641
Massachusetts	202	24,230,736	9,708,951	33,225	1,317,851	1,000	1,020,763	30,304	332,876	457,185	16,620	330,142	242,603
Michigan	177	27,240,149	12,819,806	66,594	1,448,179	1,500	1,818,198	17,738	193,513	476,599	6,066	395,583	711,448
Minnesota	80	16,322,713	8,162,368	86,110	1,101,810	—	1,233,477	8,741	22,846	525,153	9,586	134,707	8,590
Mississippi	37	4,449,122	2,508,708	14,012	352,629	—	221,115	2,660	52,999	141,838	6,813	28,111	14,328

Categories of Expenditure (Amounts in U.S. Dollars)

Missouri	74	23,280,687	11,180,782	8,306	1,529,399	100	1,683,737	12,076	401,905	718,565	13,693	114,891	630,952
Montana	40	2,406,270	662,870	—	156,269	—	42,965	4,680	2,568	600	7,017	79,155	5,664
Nebraska	66	8,270,340	2,463,295	26,726	275,036	200	640,886	21,411	20,768	72,049	7,355	332,751	27,612
Nevada	15	6,121,238	4,353,356	1,000	618,697	—	263,634	2,194	25,046	246,563	17,246	87,451	102,500
New Hampshire	90	3,006,275	1,329,492	24,385	174,526	—	115,487	9,340	50,054	24,173	10,787	25,879	8,528
New Jersey	160	40,778,746	14,708,945	81,112	2,348,435	14,176	1,321,138	105,212	298,455	801,428	36,542	591,204	877,772
New Mexico	22	4,271,990	852,610	36,931	375,322	—	42,199	7,200	16,885	56,318	7,000	21,821	15,000
New York	284	94,358,434	41,806,905	344,083	7,778,115	409,450	4,660,520	554,719	646,472	1,887,430	181,039	995,669	955,660
North Carolina	86	20,264,881	7,819,877	142,231	875,642	4,127	871,102	47,538	212,017	227,261	17,351	71,283	187,028
North Dakota	20	1,118,118	698,323	8,387	161,571	—	65,781	2,150	26,100	20,500	5,400	20,000	30,932
Ohio	133	69,584,289	34,316,471	981,906	6,719,415	14,498	7,871,936	140,142	1,766,521	1,317,454	931,581	2,874,074	399,135
Oklahoma	38	7,275,561	3,691,473	151,145	888,942	—	500,016	39,122	33,195	48,563	25,030	305,083	894,725
Oregon	63	9,804,095	4,393,417	7,850	884,943	700	761,570	250	35,901	468,105	45,917	54,887	35,583
Pennsylvania	207	34,894,853	8,420,866	67,579	1,753,998	2,400	1,152,155	54,614	693,210	549,157	64,346	450,549	411,392
Rhode Island	26	2,460,105	1,050,800	12,123	187,882	—	126,492	3,450	29,286	79,460	3,800	172,083	7,351
South Carolina	32	11,930,893	6,527,599	168,390	673,307	—	637,000	16,180	216,400	299,821	36,150	84,749	467,559
South Dakota	30	1,591,245	624,143	600	128,350	—	52,171	13,266	19,315	5,511	600	276,845	1,654
Tennessee	66	8,991,817	3,431,439	38,862	515,961	8,000	471,634	45,000	108,542	158,015	80,306	108,271	2,528,423
Texas	204	35,447,637	15,620,727	264,526	2,506,502	5,000	1,808,933	198,616	437,096	674,945	152,056	437,346	439,042
Utah	28	8,745,423	3,489,276	2,372	301,845	—	501,259	1,311	38,454	98,560	6,000	188,900	35,960
Vermont	66	1,041,418	489,121	—	71,623	—	25,057	9,223	4,545	11,160	3,014	6,850	2,000
Virginia	70	26,852,658	14,348,001	22,592	2,644,493	986	766,091	26,091	1,389,288	642,380	37,008	448,534	289,590
Washington	38	14,933,799	7,019,061	150,997	1,208,947	—	946,707	21,900	30,232	220,805	34,297	532,820	181,908
West Virginia	42	3,455,903	2,340,790	2,344	249,252	—	300,837	1,894	14,638	63,372	17,850	6,877	—
Wisconsin	157	15,214,537	6,377,019	27,005	965,468	—	1,013,124	26,926	141,881	322,165	25,903	673,215	887,708
Wyoming	14	926,263	321,340	30,259	33,295	—	52,953	—	14,546	12,162	1,618	31,745	—
Pacific Islands	1	80,950	67,679	—	6,875	—	6,396	—	—	—	—	—	—
Puerto Rico	1	264,188	235,042	—	7,000	—	14,000	—	7,646	—	500	—	—
Total	4,214	915,543,621	397,541,983	6,074,460	63,941,959	565,185	50,843,689	2,344,526	11,898,134	17,209,118	3,061,170	19,324,721	19,361,994
Estimated % of Acquisition Expenditure		67.13		1.03	10.80	0.10	8.59	0.40	2.01	2.91	0.52	3.26	3.27

Table 2 / Academic Library Acquisition Expenditures

Categories of Expenditure (Amounts in U.S. Dollars)

State	Number of Libraries	Total Acquisition Expenditures	Books	Other Print Materials	Periodicals	Manuscripts & Archives	AV Materials	AV Equipment	Microform	Machine Readable Materials	Preservation	Database Fees	Unspecified
Alabama	29	7,236,892	2,622,938	16,200	2,685,310	3,500	105,338	30,879	173,552	137,182	76,099	53,732	549,259
Alaska	3	1,499,993	1,526	—	3,650	—	50	—	—	—	—	—	420
Arizona	14	3,672,846	920,180	26,000	1,524,700	—	124,437	41,850	181,953	244,273	45,287	162,914	319,002
Arkansas	19	9,120,597	1,991,464	77,965	4,202,087	47,000	165,243	24,333	193,363	456,620	131,860	184,794	132,727
California	116	101,737,216	22,358,236	1,055,018	57,837,396	35,000	562,499	218,266	1,175,319	1,877,651	1,618,617	1,650,249	2,285,027
Colorado	24	19,873,010	3,677,263	156,067	6,538,283	—	102,374	8,642	194,244	338,778	143,587	244,749	447,677
Connecticut	24	25,771,839	7,182,302	5,519,000	11,118,396	1,000	191,146	22,520	181,660	525,081	264,507	178,412	44,034
Delaware	6	5,461,383	2,035,564	32,000	3,208,444	—	1,570	7,365	18,354	16,926	1,100	22,855	116,193
District of Columbia	11	16,184,375	2,774,236	38,061	6,419,634	1,613	58,970	5,000	138,880	136,600	138,110	126,596	1,551,416
Florida	61	46,495,517	9,462,612	60,474	13,069,743	2,100	644,306	147,888	1,466,912	1,597,865	548,852	1,084,540	3,434,620
Georgia	42	25,729,515	6,909,969	50,058	13,058,184	31,200	241,818	145,660	1,702,575	681,383	150,189	460,250	1,176,327
Hawaii	10	5,934,975	1,753,904	25,114	872,267	—	50,284	17,095	84,641	41,940	36,031	79,064	2,368,849
Idaho	8	7,268,340	1,595,427	—	4,009,853	500	78,106	183,500	42,426	15,000	174,623	101,414	431,780
Illinois	77	66,062,098	18,195,828	2,980,285	29,308,400	9,995	580,871	736,016	668,691	1,109,733	853,142	688,742	1,701,450
Indiana	41	34,410,911	10,939,580	427,998	16,551,794	9,720	338,614	121,324	242,836	801,461	548,459	726,629	112,600
Iowa	34	22,577,237	5,474,343	171,954	10,301,709	250	155,731	104,497	144,797	185,293	342,851	221,510	450,875
Kansas	30	12,446,264	4,247,284	289,024	6,496,213	2,182	35,024	26,526	95,315	306,235	180,195	61,595	320,903
Kentucky	30	19,614,966	3,932,931	16,745	11,770,626	25,400	180,062	18,106	471,605	818,829	378,865	149,354	603,761
Louisiana	20	14,600,892	2,758,536	28,784	7,088,088	24,690	26,972	34,583	106,885	267,776	165,423	182,183	103,581
Maine	18	7,911,608	1,888,639	2,173	3,934,227	—	52,031	5,325	138,129	115,413	98,697	43,747	49,341
Maryland	31	15,633,097	3,687,792	161,310	6,111,029	—	175,060	119,950	398,052	695,176	352,519	235,346	828,930
Massachusetts	64	68,206,117	12,372,012	769,092	22,957,590	3,191	589,675	318,342	779,319	1,377,936	1,053,180	1,842,541	590,631
Michigan	53	40,520,070	7,474,668	315,806	11,699,695	47,522	236,695	210,510	759,409	857,391	594,313	727,727	422,722
Minnesota	33	21,963,601	3,419,253	738,195	4,982,398	9,517	254,834	80,768	217,348	446,479	186,937	312,095	633,431
Mississippi	24	10,059,586	1,713,762	—	4,523,951	500	225,817	89,949	196,691	196,938	151,603	162,561	409,415

State													
Missouri	47	30,452,345	6,126,530	50,603	12,616,520	3,132	485,561	117,768	667,558	1,384,048	556,508	1,052,038	449,010
Montana	13	936,459	251,682	1,100	383,487		2,575		3,616	5,000	3,521	20,100	
Nebraska	18	4,794,931	1,432,865	137,599	1,742,768		99,454	115,458	81,633	188,898	53,536	117,178	67,325
Nevada	6	7,891,671	2,510,463	1,359	4,328,031	30,000	127,354	44,958	51,770	293,521	222,951	132,933	6,047
New Hampshire	15	4,993,445	1,166,374	45,333	2,861,252		42,034	1,300	57,413	104,969	64,675	77,683	78,864
New Jersey	29	27,863,103	8,103,828	1,187,869	11,071,634	190,815	351,282	80,735	790,138	872,849	145,012	300,237	1,024,807
New Mexico	19	8,909,506	2,879,889	5,000	4,672,876		65,823	119,628	432,447	306,356	231,091	86,329	
New York	123	103,896,366	19,642,995	2,583,137	34,366,508	10,195	1,000,481	217,212	2,121,039	4,045,622	1,777,498	2,409,026	4,368,734
North Carolina	74	43,014,166	14,361,571	48,318	18,333,141	4,350	675,946	550,902	857,793	1,504,270	575,186	717,345	918,838
North Dakota	6	1,606,506	345,424	20,575	1,020,037		23,777	19,507	51,753	4,595	578	85,229	9,200
Ohio	69	37,071,536	10,846,577	243,395	17,976,425	3,800	502,281	324,946	553,536	998,494	679,047	342,253	402,116
Oklahoma	29	14,724,417	2,508,405	159,996	5,187,728	7,100	63,728	125,829	309,236	264,595	208,023	675,202	652,017
Oregon	36	14,486,858	4,001,710	24,701	6,769,803	500	167,975	321,804	585,350	415,192	186,383	354,105	207,914
Pennsylvania	104	72,021,265	14,874,927	1,194,789	26,091,915	25,730	674,001	262,856	927,286	2,487,731	1,659,884	1,246,381	1,494,094
Rhode Island	11	6,462,621	1,455,786	91,000	2,273,529	4,494	72,578	16,902	1,795,013	280,301	82,618	185,801	71,037
South Carolina	35	18,093,045	3,172,279	63,636	6,205,364		103,613	52,037	273,061	515,843	240,671	277,760	163,599
South Dakota	11	6,127,862	2,132,171		2,194,384		29,697	62,535	80,286	394,545	77,335	100,541	258,821
Tennessee	45	25,363,615	5,880,833	587,788	14,464,755	2,550	303,103	68,452	454,482	487,066	299,961	594,194	1,357,893
Texas	97	64,003,695	15,042,275	231,752	23,606,629	35,627	1,038,514	301,202	1,140,735	2,981,790	1,003,968	1,283,310	2,096,044
Utah	8	2,548,435	1,349,349	4,500	672,568	260	130,059	42,181	16,609	20,379	60,916	33,190	149,217
Vermont	15	7,355,462	2,156,525	500	4,015,862	700	102,709	8,000	161,234	124,524	125,443	420,807	21,334
Virginia	41	34,179,674	9,252,734	137,353	14,278,668	43,350	427,684	195,687	583,987	1,562,715	393,531	419,471	305,123
Washington	33	25,879,335	6,208,550	3,109	13,983,424	2,500	238,084	258,290	319,582	555,562	186,663	388,977	221,667
West Virginia	21	5,051,796	1,453,917	64,485	1,994,439	6,174	80,091	59,043	185,035	204,498	103,292	101,271	431,522
Wisconsin	43	14,467,570	4,292,988	25,746	6,868,052	4,300	380,630	59,900	473,191	890,905	160,083	308,098	227,301
Wyoming	4	2,986,283	505,865	17,398	1,975,586		19,607	4,044	2,500		71,919	23,876	309,316
Pacific Islands	4	853,920	253,449		438,121		27,845	21,654	43,210	36,269		25,372	
Puerto Rico	8	3,814,719	1,047,150	1,000	2,470,981	500	65,500	5,000	6,500	3,800	71,700	70,832	
Virgin Islands	1	60,000											
Total	1,787	1,199,903,551	282,647,360	19,889,364	503,138,154	630,957	12,479,613	6,176,724	22,798,949	34,182,296	17,477,039	21,553,138	34,376,811
Estimated % of Acquisition Expenditure		29.59	2.08	52.67	0.07	1.31	0.65	2.39	3.58	1.83	2.26	3.60	

Table 3 / Special Library Acquisition Expenditures

							Categories of Expenditure (Amounts in U.S. Dollars)						
State	Number of Libraries	Total Acquisition Expenditures	Books	Other Print Materials	Periodicals	Manuscripts & Archives	AV Materials	AV Equipment	Microform	Machine Readable Materials	Preservation	Database Fees	Unspecified
Alabama	5	63,893	11,048	—	25,400	945	2,000	500	—	—	1,500	—	—
Alaska	1	15,000	10,000	—	5,000	—	—	—	—	—	—	—	—
Arizona	23	819,472	196,733	12,700	418,743	200	1,825	2,592	900	18,000	9,200	63,240	2,300
Arkansas	2	8,675	6,950	—	1,125	100	—	—	—	—	500	—	—
California	73	6,431,650	943,650	58,203	1,722,318	950	18,805	1,311,738	34,585	69,860	33,324	192,428	62,778
Colorado	19	1,146,239	199,686	3,000	712,588	—	12,797	1,600	—	13,000	9,300	111,900	58,368
Connecticut	17	759,663	153,797	12,000	282,095	750	17,115	500	18,575	35,500	9,350	75,484	3,000
Delaware	3	300,600	10,000	2,000	5,000	—	—	—	—	—	3,600	—	—
District of Columbia	25	4,275,243	604,833	423,150	493,510	—	—	550	7,000	9,600	12,950	184,000	2,300
Florida	35	1,570,733	253,410	4,450	321,480	4,450	6,350	23,359	27,540	44,850	21,628	134,150	6,000
Georgia	16	1,018,203	261,350	2,000	273,453	—	26,707	8,500	—	37,922	220	1,116	10,000
Hawaii	6	262,809	28,053	—	106,229	—	—	—	—	4,200	—	9,627	—
Idaho	5	194,213	4,000	—	42,000	—	—	—	—	—	—	—	—
Illinois	67	6,798,564	1,138,252	16,298	899,007	16,725	30,700	15,900	73,176	40,150	23,157	278,191	102,441
Indiana	23	1,202,542	106,308	—	226,645	—	5,824	2,500	23,125	22,321	1,703	164,662	1,753
Iowa	18	1,114,345	478,300	3,619	283,922	—	5,885	—	1,200	5,650	11,409	14,357	—
Kansas	9	121,525	34,839	100	70,231	150	—	5,650	2,500	—	2,250	5,455	—
Kentucky	8	384,565	33,978	—	89,296	—	—	—	15,000	—	1,200	125	—
Louisiana	7	379,000	19,500	—	168,000	—	3,500	—	—	3,000	—	3,400	—
Maine	10	800,454	72,119	1,100	196,756	100	19,225	380	—	1,100	1,480	140,805	6,480
Maryland	29	2,633,822	554,966	5,350	906,338	6,550	7,892	6,000	72,051	19,055	39,944	558,547	4,365
Massachusetts	37	2,103,260	603,835	7,309	667,124	8,700	20,946	11,027	12,720	20,100	42,968	109,346	122,858
Michigan	24	2,102,659	383,034	10,200	881,814	—	14,848	210	14,406	46,500	125	129,772	100
Minnesota	12	262,830	146,780	6,600	46,250	3,900	7,800	9,000	8,500	15,000	3,250	7,000	—
Mississippi	4	124,068	8,200	—	112,090	—	200	100	238	—	240	3,000	—

Missouri	19	4,112,678	455,061	1,139	2,456,141	300	5,550	—	8,480	39,000	84,152	927,213	14,192
Montana	4	54,000	7,400	—	12,531	—	—	—	—	—	—	2,500	—
Nebraska	12	214,920	36,494	525	102,476	2,000	2,900	—	41,385	—	—	2,390	8,000
Nevada	3	97,600	15,000	—	32,000	—	—	—	—	—	2,600	—	—
New Hampshire	10	1,129,100	239,058	4,000	436,870	5,100	1,500	11,500	2,210	45,000	23,950	26,949	2,000
New Jersey	25	3,589,328	819,623	7,780	433,605	3,000	16,436	9,530	23,067	1,500	7,000	72,665	35,404
New Mexico	14	224,565	75,175	100	98,505	200	3,170	2,200	—	500	3,000	9,290	1,775
New York	84	13,591,784	1,957,531	22,975	1,928,315	53,520	51,178	29,780	15,000	105,543	94,562	4,138,142	259,945
North Carolina	15	594,125	92,600	2,000	112,600	—	300	—	—	500	—	30,000	—
North Dakota	2	64,535	23,694	—	33,696	—	—	—	—	2,500	424	—	3,921
Ohio	36	3,582,431	1,028,539	26,181	1,053,215	—	15,249	3,308	4,149	102,575	24,011	371,046	87,889
Oklahoma	4	374,408	56,437	—	245,471	—	2,500	—	5,000	51,000	500	13,500	—
Oregon	10	205,949	71,585	—	47,258	—	7,279	—	—	300	773	20,000	—
Pennsylvania	52	3,091,506	429,417	338,230	753,829	51,855	20,488	5,790	53,825	69,769	38,518	53,224	23,682
Rhode Island	5	74,967	43,092	165	17,948	—	1,742	—	—	1,748	2,822	5,530	1,915
South Carolina	8	453,435	87,500	—	72,000	20	7,000	5,000	16,000	6,100	8,600	200	1,300
South Dakota	4	164,295	24,544	—	122,971	—	—	—	—	—	—	3,260	—
Tennessee	15	941,446	366,500	50,750	271,800	—	22,600	—	52,600	65,896	700	53,500	—
Texas	34	2,307,165	598,159	13,650	495,972	5,300	28,141	12,407	21,800	110,037	19,064	72,700	8,825
Utah	5	18,200	5,400	50	5,150	—	—	600	500	100	—	—	—
Vermont	5	152,602	8,363	—	77,261	1,874	—	—	280	—	3,263	2,069	1,192
Virginia	31	1,896,996	258,423	9,775	177,981	60,656	7,776	540	18,000	10,000	12,361	41,933	24,356
Washington	17	2,967,591	170,250	2,337	844,270	7,250	1,113	300	10,600	2,400	600	16,201	—
West Virginia	4	397,499	36,664	—	343,735	—	3,200	—	—	—	—	3,500	—
Wisconsin	13	798,336	316,220	17,700	189,119	5,000	—	7,000	138,000	80,000	50	1,700	1,655
Wyoming	1	17,000	—	—	—	—	—	—	—	—	—	—	—
Pacific Islands	1	535,558	140,121	—	—	—	—	—	—	—	—	—	—
Puerto Rico	4	527,352	127,147	4,600	355,455	—	13,150	—	6,150	—	8,500	—	—
Total	915	77,073,398	13,753,618	1,070,036	19,676,588	239,595	413,691	1,488,061	728,562	1,100,276	564,748	8,054,117	858,794
Estimated % of Acquisition Expenditure			28.68	2.23	41.04	0.50	0.86	3.10	1.52	2.29	1.18	16.80	1.79

Table 4 / Government Library Acquisition Expenditures

State	Number of Libraries	Total Acquisition Expenditures	Books	Other Print Materials	Periodicals	Manuscripts & Archives	AV Materials	AV Equipment	Microform	Machine Readable Materials	Preservation	Database Fees	Unspecified
Alabama	4	628,116	250,556	—	152,638	—	11,761	—	14,477	15,032	35,068	128,514	—
Alaska	7	87,850	23,800	5,700	36,750	—	10,700	100	200	1,500	500	4,000	3,000
Arizona	6	545,155	246,567	—	3,450	—	—	—	—	2,228	1,138	2,390	6,038
Arkansas	4	560,545	48,960	—	319,585	—	6,000	—	2,000	39,000	—	145,000	—
California	29	6,535,213	1,388,878	588,620	639,937	—	73,835	—	56,827	88,777	69,958	29,828	18,479
Colorado	7	696,481	61,985	—	153,706	—	10,691	6,000	10,600	89,934	—	23,201	1,720
Connecticut	2	29,000	—	—	—	—	300	—	5,000	—	—	—	—
Delaware	—	—	—	—	—	—	—	—	—	—	—	—	—
District of Columbia	12	2,751,150	169,600	100	581,100	400	28,500	10,500	66,000	51,000	2,750	126,400	79,200
Florida	34	2,352,191	345,209	1,700	328,486	3,000	28,148	—	24,995	12,000	1,500	23,916	126,165
Georgia	—	—	—	—	—	—	—	—	—	—	—	—	—
Hawaii	4	1,392,587	812,048	—	540,382	5,000	—	—	—	—	2,177	2,980	—
Idaho	2	302,000	4,000	—	36,000	—	170	—	—	1,100	—	3,000	—
Illinois	8	5,438,821	130,659	—	379,125	—	200	—	—	61,671	—	32,000	300
Indiana	4	244,000	16,000	—	78,000	—	—	—	—	—	—	—	—
Iowa	2	76,700	13,000	—	43,000	—	400	400	800	6,000	—	4,700	8,400
Kansas	3	930,377	254,903	180,698	163,813	50	3,000	—	—	17,500	7,336	12,443	—
Kentucky	2	465,119	375,169	—	2,950	—	—	—	9,895	—	2,700	7,700	8,863
Louisiana	3	3,069,458	12,000	—	97,458	—	300	—	—	3,000	—	4,700	—
Maine	2	288,143	4,000	—	50,000	—	—	—	—	—	—	—	—
Maryland	7	5,804,354	318,000	—	86,000	—	300	1,500	—	200	4,000	34,500	—
Massachusetts	10	3,299,731	119,658	—	163,373	—	2,000	3,640	8,046	1,000	1,885	5,000	4,000
Michigan	2	86,051	13,750	3,001	56,300	—	1,400	—	100	6,500	—	3,200	—
Minnesota	7	1,379,749	65,262	229,000	825,718	—	1,000	—	38,264	31,769	12,000	149,736	—

State	No.												
Mississippi	4	182,700	3,730	—	—	—	—	—	—	—	—	—	—
Missouri	3	292,500	—	—	—	—	—	—	—	—	—	—	—
Montana	2	287,871	4,935	985	28,851	—	—	—	—	450	—	900	—
Nebraska	4	35,041	6,100	—	2,615	—	—	—	—	—	—	1,600	500
Nevada	4	880,890	524,363	—	108,059	—	—	—	6,181	12,022	7,691	102,235	—
New Hampshire	1	38,000	35,500	—	2,500	—	—	—	—	—	—	—	—
New Jersey	2	17,024	17,000	—	24	—	—	—	—	—	—	—	—
New Mexico	4	470,600	16,800	200,000	62,000	—	—	—	16,000	1,000	15,000	46,300	—
New York	20	2,337,369	1,140,706	2,000	341,653	—	8,139	900	16,000	800	15,000	62,300	3,625
North Carolina	5	828,109	387,955	—	253,330	—	—	—	11,083	7,130	13,300	—	4,546
North Dakota	2	56,000	2,500	27,000	20,000	—	—	800	5,500	—	200	—	—
Ohio	10	560,114	179,319	8,051	39,817	—	2,000	—	7,000	4,000	5,500	2,500	5,761
Oklahoma	2	18,720	1,537	—	15,908	—	—	—	275	—	1,000	—	—
Oregon	3	404,620	49,463	1,500	126,626	—	5,446	—	165,211	500	1,000	1,332	6,142
Pennsylvania	10	1,376,279	943,550	—	5,000	—	—	—	12,000	7,600	—	11,800	—
Rhode Island	1	17,250	6,913	—	7,952	—	453	—	—	—	—	1,932	—
South Carolina	3	99,499	—	—	47	—	500	250	—	—	—	54,355	—
South Dakota	3	109,318	26,931	—	69,408	—	7,837	342	—	3,200	—	800	800
Tennessee	2	230,666	26,472	—	83,502	—	6,731	—	—	—	—	46,746	24,615
Texas	5	307,102	13,483	—	39,044	117	10,200	6,731	25,000	—	20,478	9,522	16,780
Utah	2	188,854	28,610	—	126,858	—	7,422	—	9,401	—	5,842	—	—
Vermont	1	29,597	—	—	—	—	—	—	—	—	—	—	—
Virginia	6	354,952	33,800	500	135,900	—	300	—	8,500	1,000	3,000	4,750	—
Washington	7	1,660,800	14,704	—	31,373	—	11,533	—	5,180	4,603	11,000	—	—
West Virginia	4	198,036	36,661	3,260	67,655	550	7,526	1,500	1,200	10,500	3,500	4,416	10,042
Wisconsin	7	395,400	61,250	—	163,150	—	5,000	—	—	1,000	—	38,000	—
Wyoming	1	224,000	190,000	—	24,000	—	—	—	—	10,000	—	—	—
Total	279	48,564,102	8,426,256	1,252,115	6,493,043	9,117	251,792	25,932	721,583	287,068	230,123	1,132,696	328,976
Estimated % of Acquisition Expenditure			43.98	6.54	33.89	0.05	1.31	0.14	3.77	1.50	1.20	5.91	1.72

LJ Budget Report: Public Libraries
Close Out Millennium on a Fiscal High Note

Evan St. Lifer

Executive Editor, *Library Journal*

> The average well-to-do reader, instead of a five-dollar subscription fee, pays a dollar tax; and for that not only he and his family, but also the families of his neighbors, have access to a superior library. . . . It is almost as important for your neighbor's children to have access to a library as for your own.

So said St. Louis Public Library Director Frederick M. Crunden a century ago, marveling at the value of the public library, with its newly minted status as a tax-supported institution. Perhaps time has dulled our appreciation of the way public libraries are funded to such a degree that we consider it an inevitability. Crunden reminds us that this wasn't always the case, his timeless words reinforcing the significance and wonder of the library as a public good. In a speech entitled "What of the Future?" given at the 1897 American Library Association Annual Meeting in Philadelphia and reported in the October 1897 issue of *Library Journal*, Crunden spoke of "an organized society that leaves ever greater freedom to the individual . . . while at the same time it extends farther and farther its supervision and performance of those things that pertain to the welfare of all."

Crunden might be astounded at the strong fiscal state of public libraries in the United States today, and the degree to which their communities support them. An extended economic prosperity, booming financial markets, and continued low-level inflation have helped dry up some of the nation's depressed pockets, with some exceptions: many inner cities and extreme rural areas with no hint of industry or commerce and sagging property values remain starved for funds.

Still, many big-city libraries are thriving. Chicago and Seattle have been the beneficiaries of millions of dollars in income that will help them transform and update their entire systems. Los Angeles, Queens, and Brooklyn—as well as countless other libraries across the country—have made the most of Gates Learning Foundation grants, which have helped them provide much-needed Internet access for their patrons. States that have reversed flagging financial fortunes include California and Massachusetts, fueled by the technology boom, and Texas, and libraries in those areas are reporting brighter financial outlooks.

Library Journal's indicators reinforce this optimistic outlook. According to the 331 public libraries that participated in *Library Journal*'s tenth annual budget report, total budgets are up an average of 7.5 percent, a marked surge over the previous five-year average increase of 4.7 percent. Materials and salary/personnel budgets received strong support, as evidenced by 8.8 percent and 8.5 percent increases, respectively. Per capita funding, on a national average, continued its steady incremental climb, rising from $26.27 in fiscal year 1999 to $28.04 in fiscal year 2000.

Adapted from *Library Journal*, January 2000

Table 1 / Library Budgets for Fiscal Year (FY) 2000, Percent Change from FY 1999

Population Served	Materials		Salaries		Operating Budgets	
Fewer than 10,000	$21,000	-4.6%	$73,000	NC	$132,000	-2.3%
10,000–24,999	93,000	+6.5	342,000	+6.5%	654,000	+8.0
25,000–49,999	174,000	+6.4	731,000	+7.2	1,190,000	+6.6
50,000–99,999	270,000	+10.4	1,120,000	+7.1	1,848,000	+7.5
100,000–499,999	690,000	+7.0	2,818,000	+6.6	4,612,000	+6.0
500,000 and above	3,729,000	+5.8	14,449,000	+5.9	24,275,000	+5.1
FY 1999 vs. FY 2000	+8.8		+8.5		+7.5	

Source: Library Journal Budget Report 2000
NC: No change

Table 2 / How Libraries Spent Their Internet Dollar in FY 1999

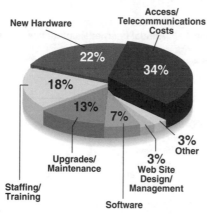

Source: Library Journal Budget Report 2000

Internet's Influence

For those who look back at the end of the last decade/century/millennium, it will be difficult to ignore the emergence of the Internet as the next link in the chain of media and communications innovations to revolutionize the way we receive and send information. Respondents reported a 61 percent increase in online usage from 1998 to 1999. Libraries are therefore adding more terminals with expanded capabilities and have seen Internet costs as a portion of their total budget increase by a full percentage point since last year, from 4.4 percent to 5.4 percent. In fiscal year 1996, by contrast, libraries spent only 2.3 percent of their total budgets on Internet-related goods and services.

The good news for libraries is that two historic initiatives have emerged to help them in their efforts to deliver Internet services to patrons. In addition to the Gates Learning Foundation and its mission to wire the nation's libraries by the end of 2002, Universal Service provisions to provide libraries with discounted telecommunications services via the E-rate have helped enormously. More than eight out of ten libraries reported applying to the Schools and Libraries Corpora-

Table 3 / Looking Ahead: Expected Funds for FY 2000

Population Served	E-Rate	Grant Funding
Fewer Than 10,000	$1,736	$44,300
10,000–24,999	2,305	37,900
25,000–49,999	6,871	37,100
50,000–99,999	19,561	81,400
100,000–499,999	26,903	170,100
500,000 and above	239,672	524,800

Source: Library Journal Budget Report 2000

Table 4 / Annual Internet Maintenance Costs

Population Served	FY 1999
Fewer Than 10,000	$3,300
10,000–24,999	13,900
25,000–49,999	19,800
50,000–99,999	53,500
100,000–499,999	110,100
500,000 and above	347,800

Source: Library Journal Budget Report 2000

tion (SLC) for E-rate discounts (Table 3), with savings ranging from an average of nearly $1,800 for the smallest libraries to more than $240,000 for the largest, and this despite an almost universal appeal by the library community to stream-line the time-consuming application process.

Enhanced Internet access to an increasing number of patrons—including children—raises questions about the type of content they should be allowed to view. Exactly one quarter of all respondents said they employ at least one filter on Internet terminals and that the annual cost for buying and operating such a fil-ter ranged from a few hundred dollars to roughly $4,000.

Public libraries head into the new millennium with a fiscal momentum not seen since the mid-1980s. They continue to redefine themselves, delivering the technology of the moment to patrons—from acid-free paper to copying machines to microfilm to digital books to whatever comes next—while remaining firmly committed to the information-for-all ideal praised by librarian Crunden at the end of the 1800s.

Progress Reports: A Fiscal Snapshot of How Libraries Are Faring

Serving Fewer Than 10,000

Crandon PL, WI
Total FY 2000 budget $28,918

Currently located in a storefront, the library has plans to build a $540,000 facility. The small library has a building fund exceeding $200,000 and a private donor who has pledged $350,000.

Miami Memorial Library, AZ
$136,000

A "good year" in this copper-mining region was capped by a 12 percent increase, although there are fears that job consolidation among mining companies may create "great job loss" and thus hurt the local economy.

Potter County Library, Gettysburg, SD
$41,000

No funding increases in sight, plus a threat to cut the materials budget, or possibly charge fees to use certain materials.

West Bend PL, IA
$65,600

The library must now contend with hardware maintenance costs, since computers are over five years old. With an FY 2000 budget of $65,600, a $10,000 investment in a new server and three new workstations is significant.

Winside PL, NE
$8,612

The library is "well-supported" at present, as evidenced by a 6.2 percent increase in the FY 2000 budget. Costs will "definitely increase" when the building project is completed.

Serving 10,000–24,999

Cromaine District Library, Hartland, MI
$963,000

Located in "one of the fastest-growing areas of the state," the library enjoys a tax base and

income that are growing, with no signs of a slowdown.

Georgetown PL, TX
$780,511

Trying to keep up with "rapid population growth," the library received a 5 percent budget increase for FY 2000 but expects to be funded at "current levels for the next three or four years."

Nyack PL, NY
$1.3 million

Because municipal library budgets in New York are subject to an annual referendum in tandem with school district budgets, the public library's funds cannot be any less than the previous year. Nyack has a positive outlook, receiving a 4.5 percent budget increase in FY 2000.

Randolph Township Free PL, NJ
$608,000

This "well-to-do" and growing community calls its fiscal situation positive; 3 to 4 percent increase is expected this year.

Whitehall Township PL, PA
$528,000

Things are beginning to look up for Whitehall Public Library (4 percent budget increase) and other Pennsylvania libraries, due to much-improved state funding. State incentives to increase local library support should also help.

Serving 25,000–49,999

Eagle Valley Library District, CO
$2.85 million

An "excellent" financial situation is expected to continue in the future, with this resort area experiencing "tremendous growth." Property values continue their upward climb.

Source: Library Journal Budget Report 2000

Galax-Carroll Regional Library, Galax, VA
$406,628

A healthy library is attributed to "new building, good planning" by local government, which has also recognized the library's value to the community. Also cited were good economic times and the general growth of business.

Hopkins County-Madisonville PL, KY
$415,000

The library faces the challenge of serving a growing number of patrons with fewer dollars and is seeking to establish a taxing district. The budget for FY 2000 is unchanged.

Hoboken PL, NJ
$700,000

The fiscal situation "looks positive," while the technological outlook is "strong," amid a growing circulation and user base. This upbeat outlook was helped by $45 million in state matching funds made available to New Jersey public libraries.

Plymouth PL, MA
$1.2 million

The library is "facing lean years" due to the restructuring of the area's major taxpayer, an electric utility.

Serving 50,000–99,999

Calvert County PL, MD
$1.68 million

The library is now experiencing "the best of times," with a 10 percent increase in funding for FY 2000. Still, there is some concern about future funding since the county does not consider raising taxes a viable option.

Denton PL, TX
$1.96 million

A "good" fiscal situation is due to an upswing in population. The library was awaiting the results of a January 15 bond referendum that could yield $6.8 million.

Hammond PL, IN
$3.53 million

Hammond Public Library says it has been "fortunate for the last few years," benefiting from a frozen tax rate. The governor's recent announcement of a statewide Gates Foundation initiative to link all libraries to the Internet should help as well.

Laurens County PL, SC
$807,916

With a substantial 23 percent budget increase, Laurens County Public Libary is not complaining, venturing to predict that things will "remain stable."

San Mateo PL, CA
$3.66 million

The library's fiscal outlook is solid due to a "strong California economy." It is reveling in the recent passage of a $35 million bond issue for a new main library and branch renovations.

Serving 100,000–499,999

Broome County PL, Binghamton, NY
$1.8 million

A new building costing $7.8 million is scheduled to open this year, but the library is strapped for operating funds because of a static budget.

Grand Rapids, MI
$9 million

A strong local economy and population growth add up to prosperity. Voters approved a $6 million bond issue in 1999 to expand the 18-branch system.

Shreve Memorial Library, Shreveport, LA
$9.1 million

Operating at nearly $20 per capita higher than the state average of $16.90, this library characterized its fiscal situation as "excellent." A ten-year, $30 million bond issue in 1996 is paying for an updating and expansion of the system.

Union County PL, Monroe, NC
$1.7 million

The library projects a 12 percent budget increase for FY 2000 and has received $4 million in capital funds "to renovate and expand our libraries."

Warren-Trumbell County PL, OH
$5.88 million

Since the majority of the funding for Ohio's public libraries is from the state, the financial outlook is "excellent" provided Ohio's economy remains strong.

Serving 500,000 and Above

Broward County PL, Fort Lauderdale, FL
$34.3 million

A solid year of fund raising ($2 million) coupled with a $140 million bond issue approved in 1999 will more than offset a static budget.

Detroit PL, MI
$31.8 million

With a 5 percent increase in the budget for FY 2000, the library is planning to appeal to voters for a tax increase.

PL of Nashville & Davidson County, TN
$16.8 million

This system is on a roll, having received more than $1 million in additional operating funds for four new branch libraries. Its net operating budget increases by nearly 22 percent in FY 2000.

San Bernadino County Library, Bakersfield, CA
$10.2 million

The "financial outlook is improving" due to the economy, but the library remains at a "very low level" of financial support. Still, it will see its budget jump by a healthy 10 percent in FY 2000.

Tucson-Pima PL, AZ
$17.7 million

The economy looks good, but the city maintains a conservative approach to budget increases. Contributions from county government, which faces deficits, could become a problem.

Price Indexes for Public and Academic Libraries

Research Associates of Washington,
1200 North Nash St., No. 1112, Arlington, VA 22209
703-243-3399
World Wide Web http://www.rschassoc.com

Kent Halstead

A rise in prices with the gradual loss of the dollar's value has been a continuing phenomenon in the U.S. economy. This article reports price indexes measuring this inflation for public libraries, college and university academic libraries, and school libraries. (Current data for these indexes are published annually by Research Associates of Washington. See *Inflation Measures for Schools, Colleges and Libraries, 1998 Update*.) Price indexes report the year-to-year price level of what is purchased. Dividing past expenditures per user unit by index values determines if purchasing power has been maintained. Future funding requirements to offset expected inflation may be estimated by projecting the indexes.

A price index compares the aggregate price level of a fixed market basket of goods and services in a given year with the price in the base year. To measure price change accurately, the *quality* and *quantity* of the items purchased must remain constant as defined in the base year. Weights attached to the importance of each item in the budget are changed infrequently—only when the relative *amount* of the various items purchased clearly shifts or when new items are introduced.

Public Library Price Index

The Public Library Price Index (PLPI) is designed for a hypothetical *average* public library. The index together with its various subcomponents are reported in Tables 2 through 6. The PLPI reflects the relative year-to-year price level of the goods and services purchased by public libraries for their current operations. The budget mix shown in Table 1 is based on national and state average expenditure patterns. Individual libraries may need to tailor the weighting scheme to match their own budget compositions.

The Public Library Price Index components are described below together with sources of the price series employed.

Personnel Compensation

PL1.0 Salaries and Wages

PL1.1 *Professional libraries*—Average salary of professional librarians at medium and large size libraries. Six positions are reported: director, deputy/associate/assistant director, department head/branch head, reference/information librarian, cataloger and/or classifier and children's and/or young adult services librarian. Source: Mary Jo Lynch, Margaret Myers, and Jeniece Guy, *ALA Survey of Librarian Salaries*, Office for Research and Statistics, American Library Association, Chicago, IL, annual.

(text continues on page 438)

**Table 1 / Taxonomy of Public Library Current Operations Expenditures
by Object Category, 1991–1992 estimate**

Category	Mean	Percent	Distribution
Personnel Compensation			64.7
PL1.0 Salaries and Wages		81.8	
PL1.1 Professional librarians	44		
PL1.2 Other professional and managerial staff	6		
PL1.3 Technical staff (copy cataloging, circulation, binding, etc.)	43		
PL1.4 Support staff (clerical, custodial, guard, etc.)	7		
	100		
PL2.0 Fringe Benefits		18.2	
		100.0	
Acquisitions			15.2
PL3.0 Books and Serials		74.0	
PL3.1 Books printed	82		
PL3.1a Hardcover			
PL3.1b Trade paper			
PL3.1c Mass market paper			
PL3.2 Periodicals (U.S. and foreign titles)	16		
PL3.2a U.S. titles			
PL3.2b Foreign titles			
PL3.3 Other serials (newspapers, annuals, proceedings, etc.)	2		
	100		
PL4.0 Other Printed Materials		2.0	
PL5.0 Non-Print Media		22.0	
PL5.1 Microforms (microfiche and microfilm)	21		
PL5.2 Audio recordings (primarily instructional and children's content)	17		
PL5.2a Tape cassette			
PL5.2b Compact disk			
PL5.3 Video (TV) recordings (primarily books & children's content)	58		
PL5.3a VHS Cassette			
PL5.3b Laser disk			
PL5.4 Graphic image individual item use	2		
PL5.5 Computer files (CD-ROM, floppy disks, and tape)	2		
	100		
PL6.0 Electronic Services		2.0	
		100.0	
Operating Expenses			20.1
PL7.0 Office Operations		27.0	
PL7.1 Office expenses	20		
PL7.2 Supplies and materials	80		
	100		
PL8.0 Contracted Services		38.0	
PL9.0 Non-capital Equipment		1.0	
PL10.0 Utilities		34.0	
		100.0	100.0

Table 2 / Public Library Price Index and Major Component Subindexes, FY 1992 to 1997

1992=100 Fiscal year	Personnel Compensation		Acquisitions				Operating Expenses				Public Library Price Index^ (PLPI)
	Salaries and wages (PL1.0)	Fringe benefits (PL2.0)	Books and serials (PL3.0)	Other printed materials (PL4.0)	Non-print media (PL5.0)	Electronic services (PL6.0)	Office operations (PL7.0)	Contracted services (PL8.0)	Non-capital Equipment (PL9.0)	Utilities (PL10.0)	
1992	100.0	100.0	100.0	100.0	100.0	100.0	100.0	100.0	100.0	100.0	100.0
1993	102.5	104.8	101.7	102.9	75.3	101.9	99.2	102.6	101.8	101.5	101.5
1994	105.8	107.9	103.4	105.5	65.8	104.8	100.8	105.1	103.6	105.8	104.1
1995	110.5	110.6	104.7	107.7	64.8	108.5	102.6	107.7	105.7	103.8	107.2
1996	112.3	113.9	108.8	111.3	67.8	110.3	113.9	113.3	108.5	100.0	109.7
1997	114.6	116.1	115.1	118.5	69.5	110.3	113.3	114.1	110.3	113.7	113.2
1993	2.50%	4.80%	1.70%	2.90%	-24.71%	1.90%	-.80%	2.60%	1.80%	1.50%	1.50%
1994	3.20%	3.00%	1.70%	2.50%	-12.61%	2.80%	1.60%	2.40%	1.70%	4.20%	2.60%
1995	4.40%	2.50%	1.20%	2.10%	-1.41%	3.50%	1.70%	2.50%	2.10%	-1.90%	2.90%
1996	1.60%	3.00%	3.90%	3.30%	4.70%	1.70%	11.10%	3.30%	2.60%	-3.60%	2.40%
1997	2.10%	1.90%	5.90%	6.50%	2.50%	0.00%	-0.50%	2.60%	1.70%	13.70%	3.10%

^ PLPI weightings: See text.

Sources: See text.

Table 3 / Public Library Price Index, Personnel Compensation, FY 1992 to 1997

| 1992=100 Fiscal year | Professional librarians | | | Salaries and wages | | | Salaries & wages index* (PL1.0) | Fringe benefits index (PL2.0) |
	Medium size library~	Large size library~	Index^ (PL1.1)	Other professional & managerial (PL1.2)	Technical staff (PL1.3)	Support staff (PL1.4)		
1992	100.0	100.0	100.0	100.0	100.0	100.0	100.0	100.0
1993	105.0	99.5	102.3	102.8	102.7	102.8	102.5	104.8
1994	109.2	102.7	106.0	105.7	105.7	106.0	105.8	107.9
1995	115.5	106.9	111.2	109.5	110.1	109.1	110.5	110.6
1996	113.7	108.9	111.3	112.9	113.2	112.1	112.3	113.9
1997	119.2	112.0	115.6	115.6	113.6	113.9	114.6	116.1
1993	5.0%	-0.5%	2.3%	2.8%	2.7%	2.8%	2.5%	4.8%
1994	4.0%	3.2%	3.6%	2.8%	2.9%	3.1%	3.2%	3.0%
1995	5.8%	4.1%	5.0%	3.6%	4.2%	2.9%	4.4%	2.5%
1996	-1.6%	1.9%	0.1%	3.1%	2.8%	2.7%	1.6%	3.0%
1997	4.8%	2.8%	3.9%	2.4%	0.4%	1.6%	2.1%	1.9%

~ medium size libraries have service areas from 25,000 to 99,999 population; large libraries, 100,000 or more.

^ Professional librarian salary weights: 50% medium libraries + 50% large libraries.

* Salaries and wages index weights: 44% professional librarians + 6% other professional + 43% technical staff +7% support staff.

Sources: See text.

Table 4 / Public Library Price Index, Books and Serials, FY 1992 to 1997

1992=100	Books printed							Periodicals						Other serials (newspapers)		Books & Serials index** (PL3.0)	Other printed materials index (PL4.0)
	Hardcover		Trade paper		Mass market		Books printed index* (PL3.1)	United States		Foreign		Periodicals index~ (PL3.2)					
Fiscal year	Price^	Index (PL3.1a)	Price^	Index (PL3.1b)	Price^	Index (PL3.1c)		Price^	Index (PL3.2a)	Price^	Index (PL3.2b)		Price^^	Index (PL3.3)		
1992	$12.85	100.0	$7.24	100.0	$2.71	100.0	100.0	$45.17	100.0	$117.71	100.0	100.0	$222.68	100.0	100.0	100.0
1993	12.98	101.0	7.40	102.2	2.79	103.0	101.2	46.97	104.0	123.71	105.1	104.1	229.92	103.3	101.7	102.9
1994	13.16	102.4	7.59	104.8	2.85	105.2	102.7	47.15	104.4	133.48	113.4	105.5	261.91	117.6	103.4	105.5
1995	13.19	102.6	7.75	107.0	2.98	110.0	103.2	49.14	108.8	144.31	122.6	110.5	270.22	121.3	104.7	107.7
1996	13.56	105.5	8.23	113.7	3.32	122.5	106.6	51.58	114.2	158.67	134.8	116.7	300.21	134.8	108.8	111.3
1997	14.43	112.3	8.54	118.0	3.55	131.0	113.2	53.70	118.9	170.09	144.5	122.0	311.77	140.0	115.1	118.5
1993		1.0%		2.2%		3.0%	1.2%		4.0%		5.1%	4.1%		3.3%	1.7%	2.9%
1994		1.4%		2.6%		2.2%	1.5%		0.4%		7.9%	1.3%		13.9%	1.7%	2.5%
1995		0.2%		2.1%		4.6%	0.5%		4.2%		8.1%	4.7%		3.2%	1.2%	2.1%
1996		2.8%		6.2%		11.4%	3.3%		5.0%		10.0%	5.6%		11.1%	3.9%	3.3%
1997		6.4%		3.8%		6.9%	6.2%		4.1%		7.2%	4.5%		3.9%	5.9%	6.5%

^ Book and periodical prices are for calendar year. *Books printed index weights: 89.5% hardcover + 8.2% trade paper + 2.3% mass market.

~ Periodical index weights: 87.9% U.S.titles + 12.1% foreign titles.

^^Other serials prices are for calendar year.

** Books & serials index weights: 82% books + 16% periodicals + 2% other serials.

Sources: See text.

Table 5 / Public Library Price Index, Non-Print Media and Electronic Services, FY 1992 to 1997

| 1992=100 Fiscal year | Microforms (microfilm) Index (PL5.1) | Audio recordings | | | | | Video | | | Graphic image (PL5.4) | Computer files (CD-ROM) | | Non-print media index* (PL5.0) | Electronic services index (PL6.0) |
| | | Tape cassette | | Compact disc | | Audio recordings index* (PL5.2) | VHS cassette | | Video index (PL5.3) | | | | | |
		Price^	Index (PL5.2a)	Price^	Index (PL5.2b)		Price^	Index (PL5.3a)			Price^	Index (PL5.5)		
1992	100.0	$12.18	100.0	n/a	n/a	100.0	$199.67	100.0	100.0	100.0	$1,601	100.0	100.0	100.0
1993	104.3	11.73	96.3	n/a	n/a	96.3	112.92	56.6	56.6	97.3	1,793	112.0	75.3	101.9
1994	107.9	8.20	67.3	$13.36	67.3	67.3	93.22	46.7	46.7	108.4	1,945	121.5	65.8	104.8
1995	110.6	8.82	72.4	14.80	74.6	73.5	84.19	42.2	42.2	111.3	1,913	119.5	64.8	108.5
1996	128.0	7.96	65.4	14.86	74.9	70.1	83.48	41.8	41.8	114.5	1,988	124.2	67.8	110.3
1997	132.9	8.13	66.7	16.43	82.8	74.8	82.10	41.1	41.1	126.5	2,012	125.7	69.5	110.3
1993	4.3%		-3.7%			-3.7%		-43.4%	-43.4%	-2.7%		12.0%	-24.7%	1.9%
1994	3.5%		-30.1%			-30.1%		-17.4%	-17.4%	11.4%		8.5%	-12.6%	2.8%
1995	2.5%		7.6%		10.80%	9.2%		-9.7%	-9.7%	2.7%		-1.6%	-1.5%	3.5%
1996	15.7%		-9.8%		0.04%	-4.6%		-0.8%	-0.8%	2.9%		3.9%	4.7%	1.7%
1997	3.8%		2.1%		10.60%	6.6%		-1.7%	-1.7%	10.5%		1.2%	2.5%	0.0%

^ Prices are for immediate preceding calendar year, e.g., CY 1993 prices are reported for FY 1994.

* Audio recordings index weights: 50% tape cassette + 50% compact disk. Non-print media index weights: 21% microforms + 17% audio recordings +58% video + 2% graphic image + 2% computer files.

Sources: See text

Table 6 / Public Library Price Index, Operating Expenses, FY 1992 to 1997

1992=100 Fiscal year	Office Operations		Office operations index^ (PL7.0)	Contracted services index (PL8.0)	Noncapital equipment index (PL9.0)	Utilities index (PL10.0)
	Office expenses (PL7.1)	Supplies and materials (PL7.2)				
1992	100.0	100.0	100.0	100.0	100.0	100.0
1993	103.1	98.3	99.2	102.6	101.8	101.5
1994	107.3	99.2	100.8	105.1	103.6	105.8
1995	111.1	100.4	102.6	107.7	105.7	103.8
1996	117.8	112.9	113.9	111.3	108.5	100.0
1997	120.0	111.6	113.3	114.1	110.3	113.7
1993	3.10%	-1.70%	-.80%	2.60%	1.80%	1.50%
1994	4.10%	1.00%	1.60%	2.40%	1.70%	4.20%
1995	3.50%	1.20%	1.70%	2.50%	2.10%	-1.90%
1996	6.10%	12.40%	11.10%	3.30%	2.60%	-3.60%
1997	1.80%	-1.20%	-0.50%	2.60%	1.70%	13.70%

^ Office operations index weights: 20% office expenses + 80% supplies and materials.
Sources: See text.

(text continued from page 432)

PL1.2 *Other professional and managerial staff* (systems analyst, business manager, public relations, personnel, etc.)—Employment Cost Index (ECI) for wages and salaries for state and local government workers employed in "Executive, administrative, and managerial" occupations, *Employment Cost Index*, Bureau of Labor Statistics, U.S. Department of Labor, Washington, DC.

PL1.3 *Technical staff* (copy cataloging, circulation, binding, etc.)—ECI as above for government employees in "Service" occupations.

PL1.4 *Support staff* (clerical, custodial, guard, etc.)—ECI as above for government employees in "Administrative support, including clerical" occupations.

PL2.0 Fringe Benefits

ECI as above for state and local government worker "Benefits."

Acquisitions

PL3.0 Books and Serials

PL3.1 *Books printed*—Weighted average of sale prices (including jobber's discount) of hardcover (PL3.1a), trade paper (PL3.1b), and mass market paperback books (PL3.1c) sold to public libraries. Excludes university press publications and reference works. Source: Frank Daly, Baker & Taylor Books, Bridgewater, NJ.

PL3.2 *Periodicals*—Publisher's prices of sales of approximately 2,400 U.S. serial titles (PL3.2a) and 115 foreign serials (PL3.2b) sold to public libraries. Source: *Serials Prices*, EBSCO Subscription Services, Birmingham, AL.

PL3.3 *Other serials* (newspapers, annuals, proceedings, etc.)—Average prices of approximately 170 U.S. daily newspapers. Source: Genevieve S. Owens, University of Missouri, St. Louis, and Wilba Swearingen, Louisiana State University Medical Center. Reported by Adrian W. Alexander, "Prices of U.S. and Foreign Published Materials," in The *Bowker Annual*, R. R. Bowker, New Providence, NJ.

PL4.0 **Other Printed Materials** (manuscripts, documents, pamphlets, sheet music, printed material for the handicapped, etc.)

No direct price series exists for this category. The proxy price series used is the Producer Price Index for publishing pamphlets and catalogs and directories, Bureau of Labor Statistics.

PL5.0 Non-Print Media

PL5.1 *Microforms*—Producer Price Index for micropublishing in microform, including original and republished material, Bureau of Labor Statistics.

PL5.2 *Audio recordings*
    PL5.2a *Tape cassette*—Cost per cassette of sound recording. Source: Dana Alessi, Baker & Taylor Books, Bridgewater, NJ. Reported by Alexander in The *Bowker Annual*, R. R. Bowker, New Providence, NJ.

    PL5.2b *Compact disk*—Cost per compact disk. Source: See Alessi above.

PL5.3 *Video (TV) recordings*
    PL5.3a. *VHS cassette*—Cost per video. Source: See Alessi above.

    PL5.3b. *Laser disk*—No price series currently available.

PL5.4 *Graphic image* (individual use of such items as maps, photos, art work, single slides, etc.). The following proxy is used. Average median weekly earnings for the following two occupational groups: painters, sculptors, craft artists, and artist printmakers; and photographers. Source: *Employment and Earnings Series*, U.S. Bureau of Labor Statistics

PL5.5 *Computer files* (CD-ROM, floppy disks, and tape). Average price of CD-ROM disks. Source: Martha Kellogg and Theodore Kellogg, University of Rhode Island. Reported by Alexander in The *Bowker Annual*, R. R. Bowker, New Providence, NJ.

PL6.0 Electronic Services

Average price for selected digital electronic computer and telecommunications networking available to libraries. Source: This source has requested anonymity.

Operating Expenses

PL7.0 Office Operations

PL7.1 *Office expenses* (telephone, postage and freight, publicity and printing, travel, professional fees, automobile operating cost, etc.)—The price series used for office expenses consists of the subindex for printed materials (PL4.0) described above; Consumer Price Index values for telephone and postage; CPI values for public transportation; the IRS allowance for individual business travel as reported by Runzheimer International; and CPI values for college tuition as a proxy for professional fees.

PL7.2 *Supplies and materials*—Producer Price Index price series for office supplies, writing papers, and pens and pencils. Source: U.S. Bureau of Labor Statistics.

PL8.0 Contracted Services (outside contracts for cleaning, building and grounds maintenance, equipment rental and repair, acquisition processing, binding, auditing, legal, payroll, etc.)

Prices used for contracted services include ECI wages paid material handlers, equipment cleaners, helpers, and laborers; average weekly earnings of production or non-supervisory workers in the printing and publishing industry, and the price of printing paper, as a proxy for binding costs; ECI salaries of attorneys, directors of personnel, and accountant, for contracted consulting fees; and ECI wages of precision production, craft, and repair occupations for the costs of equipment rental and repair.

PL9.0 Non-Capital Equipment

The type of equipment generally purchased as part of current library operations is usually small and easily movable. To be classified as "equipment" rather than as "expendable utensils" or "supplies," an item generally must cost $50 or more and have a useful life of at least three years. Examples may be hand calculators, small TVs, simple cameras, tape recorders, pagers, fans, desk lamps, books, etc. Equipment purchased as an operating expenditure is usually not depreciated. Items priced for this category include PPI commodity price series for machinery and equipment, office and store machines/equipment, hand tools, cutting tools and accessories, scales and balances, electrical measuring instruments, television receivers, musical instruments, photographic equipment, sporting and athletic goods, and books and periodicals.

PL10.0 Utilities

This subindex is a composite of the Producer Price Index series for natural gas, residual fuels, and commercial electric power, and the Consumer Price Index series for water and sewerage services. Source: U.S. Bureau of Labor Statistics.

Academic Library Price Indexes

The two academic library price indexes—the University Library Price Index (ULPI) and the College Library Price Index (CLPI)—together with their various subcomponents are reported in Tables 8–12A. The two indexes report the relative year-to-year price level of the staff salaries, acquisitions, and other goods and services purchased by university and college libraries respectively for their current operations. Universities are the 500 institutions with doctorate programs responding to the National Center for Education Statistics, U.S. Department of Education, *Academic Library Survey*. Colleges are the 1,472 responding institutions with master's and baccalaureate programs.

The composition of the library budgets involved, defined for pricing purposes, and the 1992 estimated national weighting structure are presented in Table 7. The priced components are organized in three major divisions: personnel compensation; acquisitions; and contracted services, supplies, and equipment.

The various components of the University and College Library Price Indexes are described in this section. Different weightings for components are designated in the tables "UL" for university libraries, "CL" for college libraries, and "AL" common for both types. Source citations for the acquisitions price series are listed.

UL1.0 and CL1.0 Salaries and Wages

AL1.1 *Administrators* consists of the chief, deputy associate, and assistant librarian, e.g., important staff members having administrative responsibilities for management of the library. Administrators are priced by the head librarian salary series reported by the College and University Personnel Association (CUPA).

AL1.2 *Librarians* are all other professional library staff. Librarians are priced by the average of the median salaries for circulation/catalog, acquisition, technical service, and public service librarians reported by CUPA.

AL1.3 *Other professionals* are personnel who are not librarians in positions normally requiring at least a bachelor's degree. This group includes curators, archivists, computer specialists, budget officers, information and system specialists, subject bibliographers, and media specialists. Priced by the Higher Education Price Index (HEPI) faculty salary price series (H1.1) as a proxy.

AL1.4 *Nonprofessional staff* includes technical assistants, secretaries, and clerical, shipping, and storage personnel who are specifically assigned to the library and covered by the library budget. This category excludes general custodial and maintenance workers and student employees. This staff category is dominated by office-type workers and is priced by the HEPI clerical workers price series (H2.3) reported by the BLS Employment Cost Index.

AL1.5 *Students* are usually employed part-time for near minimum hourly wages. In some instances these wages are set by work-study program requirements of the institution's student financial aid office. The proxy price series used for student wages is the Employment Cost Index series for non-farm laborers, U.S. Bureau of Labor Statistics.

AL2.0 Fringe Benefits

The fringe benefits price series for faculty used in the HEPI is employed in pricing fringe benefits for library personnel.

UL3.0 and CL3.0 Books and Serials

UL3.1a *Books printed, universities.* Book acquisitions for university libraries are priced by the North American Academic Books price series reporting the average list price of approximately 60,000 titles sold to college and university libraries by four of the largest book vendors. Compiled by Stephen Bosch, University of Arizona.

CL3.1a *Books printed, colleges.* Book acquisitions for college libraries are priced by the price series for U.S. College Books representing approximately 6,300 titles compiled from book reviews appearing in *Choice* during the calendar year. Compiled by Donna Alsbury, Florida Center for Library Automation.

AL3.1b *Foreign Books.* Books with foreign titles *and* published in foreign countries are priced using U.S. book imports data. William S. Lofquist, U.S. Department of Commerce.

AL3.2a *Periodicals, U.S. titles.* U.S. periodicals are priced by the average subscription price of approximately 2,100 U.S. serial titles purchased by college and university libraries reported by EBSCO Subscription Services, Birmingham, AL.

AL3.2b *Periodicals, Foreign.* Foreign periodicals are priced by the average subscription price of approximately 600 foreign serial titles purchased by college and university libraries reported by EBSCO Subscription Services.

AL3.3 *Other Serials* (newspapers, annuals, proceedings, etc.). Average prices of approximately 170 U.S. daily newspapers. Source: Genevieve S. Owens, University of Missouri, St. Louis, and Wilba Swearingen, Louisiana State University Medical Center. Reported by Adrian W. Alexander, "Prices of U.S. and Foreign Published Materials," in The *Bowker Annual*, R. R. Bowker, New Providence, NJ.

Other Printed Materials

These acquisitions include manuscripts, documents, pamphlets, sheet music, printed material for the handicapped, and so forth. No direct price series exists for this category. The proxy price series used is the Producer Price Index (PPI) for publishing pamphlets (PC 2731-9) and catalogs and directories (PCU2741#B), Bureau of Labor Statistics, U.S. Department of Labor.

AL5.0 Non-Print Media

AL5.1 *Microforms.* Producer Price Index for micropublishing in microform, including original and republished material (PC 2741-597), Bureau of Labor Statistics.

AL5.2 *Audio recordings*
    AL5.2a *Tape cassette*—Cost per cassette of sound recording. Source: Dana Alessi, Baker & Taylor Books, Bridgewater, NJ. Reported by Alexander in The *Bowker Annual*, R. R. Bowker, New Providence, NJ.

    AL5.2b *Compact Disc*—Cost per compact disc. Source: See Alessi above.

AL5.3 *Video (TV) recordings*
    PL5.3a *VHS cassette*—cost per video. Source: See Alessi above.

AL5.4 *Graphic image* (individual use of such items as maps, photos, art work, single slides, etc.). No direct price series exists for graphic image materials.

Average median weekly earnings for two related occupational groups (painters, sculptors, craft artists; artist printmakers; and photographers) is used as a proxy. these earnings series are reported in *Employment and Earnings Series*, U.S. Bureau of Labor Statistics.

AL5.5 *Computer files* (CD-ROM floppy disks, and tape). Average price of CD-ROM disks; primarily bibliographic, abstracts, and other databases of interest to academic libraries. Source: Developed from *Faxon Guide to CD-ROM* by Martha Kellogg and Theodore Kellogg, University of Rhode Island. Reported by Alexander in The *Bowker Annual*, R. R. Bowker, New Providence, NJ.

AL6.0 Electronic Services

Average price for selected digital electronic computer and telecommunications networking available to libraries. The source of this price series has requested anonymity.

AL7.0 Binding/Preservation

In-house maintenance of the specialized skills required for binding is increasingly being replaced by contracting out this service at all but the largest libraries. No wage series exists exclusively for binding. As a proxy, the Producer Price Index (PPI) for bookbinding and related work (PC 2789) is used. Source: Bureau of Labor Statistics, U.S. Department of Labor.

AL8.0 Contracted Services

Services contracted by libraries include such generic categories as communications, postal service, data processing, and printing and duplication. The HEPI contracted services subcomponent (H4.0), which reports these items, is used as the price series. (In this instance the data processing component of H4.0 generally represents the library's payment for use of a central campus computer service.) However, libraries may also contract out certain specialized activities such as ongoing public access cataloging (OPAC) that are not distinctively priced in this AL8.0 component.

AL9.0 Supplies and Materials

Office supplies, writing papers, and pens and pencils constitute the bulk of library supplies and materials and are priced by these BLS categories for the Producer Price Index, Bureau of Labor Statistics, U.S. Department of Labor.

AL10.0 Equipment

This category is limited to small, easily movable, relatively inexpensive and short-lived items that are not carried on the books as depreciable capital equipment. Examples can include personal computers, hand calculators, projectors, fans, cameras, tape recorders, small TVs, etc. The HEPI equipment price series (H6.0) has been used for pricing.

Table 7 / Budget Composition of University Library and College Library Current Operations by Object Category, FY 1992 Estimate

Category	University Libraries Percent Distribution	College Libraries Percent Distribution
Personnel Compensation		
1.0 Salaries and wages..................................... 43.4		47.2
1.1 Administrators (head librarian)	10	25
1.2 Librarians	20	15
1.3 Other professionals^	10	5
1.4 Nonprofessional staff	50	40
1.5 Students hourly employed	10	15
	100.0	100.0
2.0 Fringe benefits 10.6		11.5
Acquisitions		
3.0 Books and Serials 28.5		24.8
3.1 Books printed	35	47
3.1a U.S. titles	80	95
3.1b Foreign titles	20	5
3.2 Periodicals	60	48
3.2a U.S. titles	80	95
3.2b Foreign titles	20	5
3.3 Other serials (newspapers, annuals, proceedings, etc.)	5	5
	100.0	100
4.0 Other Printed Materials* 1.2		0.7
5.0 Non-Print Media 1.6		3.3
5.1 Microforms (microfiche and microfilm)	45	45
5.2 Audio recordings	5	5
5.2a Tape cassette		
5.2b Compact disc (CDs)		
5.3 Video (TV) VHS recordings	15	15
5.4 Graphic image individual item use~	5	5
5.5 Computer materials (CD-ROM, floppy disks, and tape)	30	30
	100.0	100.0
6.0. Electronic Services^^ 4.0		3.5
Contracted Services, Supplies, Equipment		
7.0 Binding/preservation 1.3		0.8
8.0 Services** 4.4		3.1
9.0 Supplies and materials 3.1		2.6
10.0 Equipment (non-capital)# 1.9		2.5
	100.0	100

^ Other professional and managerial staff includes systems analyst, business manager, public relations, personnel, etc.
* Other printed materials includes manuscripts, documents, pamphlets, sheet music, printed material for the handicapped, etc.
~ Graphic image individual item use includes maps, photos, art work, single slides, etc.
^^Electronic services includes software license fees, network intra-structure costs, terminal access to the Internet, desktop computer operating budget, and subscription services.
** Contracted services includes outside contracts for communications, postal service, data processing, printing and duplication, equipment rental and repair, acquisition processing, etc.
# Relatively inexpensive items not carried on the books as depreciable capital equipment. Examples include microform and audiovisual equipment, personal computers, hand calculators, projectors, fans, cameras, tape recorders, and small TVs.
Source: Derived, in part, from data published in *Academic Libraries: 1992,* National Center for Education Statistics, USDE.

Table 8 / University Library Price Index and Major Component Subindexes, FY 1992 to 1997

1992=100 Fiscal year	Personnel Compensation		Acquisitions					Operating Expenses			University Library Price Index^ ULPI
	Salaries and wages (UL1.0)	Fringe benefits (AL2.0)	Books and serials (UL3.0)	Other printed materials (AL4.0)	Non-print media (AL5.0)	Electronic services (AL6.0)	Binding/preservation (AL7.0)	Contracted services (AL8.0)	Supplies and material (AL9.0)	Equipment (AL10.0)	
1992	100.0	100.0	100.0	100.0	100.0	100.0	100.0	100.0	100.0	100.0	100.0
1993	103.2	105.4	106.1	102.9	98.7	101.9	100.5	102.6	98.3	101.8	103.9
1994	106.5	110.5	113.1	105.5	100.8	104.8	101.2	106.2	99.2	103.6	108.2
1995	110.0	114.2	121.5	107.7	102.1	108.5	102.9	108.4	100.4	105.7	112.9
1996	113.4	115.8	131.7	111.3	110.3	110.3	107.1	112.4	112.9	108.5	118.4
1997	117.0	117.0	141.6	118.5	113.7	110.3	108.9	114.8	111.6	110.3	123.2
1993	3.2%	5.4%	6.1%	2.9%	-1.3%	1.9%	0.5%	2.6%	-1.7%	1.8%	3.9%
1994	3.1%	4.8%	6.6%	2.5%	2.1%	2.8%	0.7%	3.5%	0.9%	1.8%	4.2%
1995	3.4%	3.4%	7.4%	2.1%	1.3%	3.5%	1.7%	2.1%	1.2%	2.0%	4.4%
1996	3.2%	1.4%	8.4%	3.3%	8.1%	1.7%	4.1%	3.7%	12.5%	2.6%	4.9%
1997	3.1%	1.0%	7.5%	6.5%	3.1%	0.0%	1.7%	2.1%	-1.2%	1.7%	4.0%

^ ULPI weights: See table 3-A.
Sources: See text.

Table 9 / College Library Price Index and Major Component Subindexes, FY 1992 to 1997

1992=100 Fiscal year	Personnel Compensation		Acquisitions					Operating Expenses			College Library Price Index^ CLPI
	Salaries and wages (CL1.0)	Fringe benefits (AL2.0)	Books and serials (CL3.0)	Other printed materials (AL4.0)	Non-print media (AL5.0)	Electronic services (AL6.0)	Binding/ preservation (AL7.0)	Contracted services (AL8.0)	Supplies and material (AL9.0)	Equipment (AL10.0)	
1992	100.0	100.0	100.0	100.0	100.0	100.0	100.0	100.0	100.0	100.0	100.0
1993	103.5	105.4	107.5	102.9	98.7	101.9	100.5	102.6	98.3	101.8	104.2
1994	106.5	110.5	114.4	105.5	100.8	104.8	101.2	106.2	99.2	103.6	108.3
1995	110.0	114.2	119.4	107.7	102.1	108.5	102.9	108.4	100.4	105.7	112.0
1996	113.8	115.8	126.8	111.3	110.3	110.3	107.1	112.4	112.9	108.5	116.8
1997	117.5	117.0	136.0	118.5	113.7	110.3	108.9	114.8	111.6	110.3	121.1
1993	3.5%	5.4%	7.5%	2.9%	-1.3%	1.9%	0.5%	2.6%	-1.7%	1.8%	4.2%
1994	2.9%	4.8%	6.4%	2.5%	2.1%	2.8%	0.7%	3.5%	0.9%	1.8%	3.9%
1995	3.3%	3.4%	4.4%	2.1%	1.3%	3.5%	1.7%	2.1%	1.2%	2.0%	3.4%
1996	3.5%	1.4%	6.2%	3.3%	8.1%	1.7%	4.1%	3.7%	12.5%	2.6%	4.3%
1997	3.2%	1.0%	7.2%	6.5%	3.1%	0.0%	1.7%	2.1%	-1.2%	1.7%	3.7%

^ CLPI weights: See table 3-A
Sources: See text.

Table 10 / Academic Library Price Indexes, Personnel Compensation, FY 1992 to 1997

1992=100 Fiscal year	Administrators (head librarian) (AL1.1)	Librarians (AL1.2)	Other professional (AL1.3)	Non-professional (AL1.4)	Students hourly employed (AL1.5)	Salaries and wages indexes		Fringe benefits index (AL2.0)
						Universities* (UL1.0)	Colleges^ (CL1.0)	
1992	100.0	100.0	100.0	100.0	100.0	100.0	100.0	100.0
1993	105.0	102.6	102.5	103.2	102.7	103.2	103.5	105.4
1994	107.3	106.0	105.6	106.6	105.4	106.3	106.5	110.5
1995	110.6	110.2	109.3	110.1	108.5	110.0	110.0	114.2
1996	116.3	113.6	112.5	113.3	111.8	113.4	113.8	115.8
1997	120.2	116.5	115.8	117.0	115.6	117.0	117.5	117.0
1993	5.0%	2.6%	2.5%	3.2%	2.7%	3.2%	3.5%	5.4%
1994	2.2%	3.3%	3.0%	3.3%	2.6%	3.1%	2.9%	4.8%
1995	3.1%	4.0%	3.5%	3.3%	3.0%	3.4%	3.3%	3.4%
1996	5.2%	3.1%	2.9%	2.9%	3.0%	3.2%	3.5%	1.4%
1997	3.4%	2.6%	3.0%	3.2%	3.4%	3.1%	3.2%	1.0%

* University library salaries and wages index weights: 10 percent administrators, 20 percent librarians, 10 percent other professionals, 50 percent nonprofessional staff, and 10 percent students.
^ College library salaries and wages index weights: 25 percent administrators, 15 percent librarians, 5 percent other professionals, 40 percent nonprofessional staff, and 15 percent students.
Sources: See text.

Table 11 / Academic Library Price Indexes, Books and Serials, FY 1992 to 1997

1992=100	North American		U.S. college		Foreign books		Book indexes	
	Books printed							
Fiscal year	Price~	Index (UL.3.1a)	Price~	Index (CL.3.1a)	Price	Index (AL.3.1b)	University* (UL.3.1)	College^ (CL.3.1)
1992	$45.84	100.0	$44.55	100.0	n/a	100.0	100.0	100.0
1993	45.91	100.2	47.48	106.6		98.9	99.9	106.2
1994	47.17	102.9	48.92	109.8		96.7	101.7	109.2
1995	48.16	105.1	47.93	107.6		105.0	105.0	107.5
1996	48.11	105.0	48.17	108.1		108.3	105.6	108.1
1997	49.86	108.8	50.44	113.2		106.6	108.3	112.9
1993		0.2%		6.6%		-1.1%	-0.1%	6.2%
1994		2.7%		3.0%		-2.2%	1.8%	2.8%
1995		2.1%		-2.0%		8.6%	3.3%	-1.6%
1996		-0.1%		0.5%		3.1%	0.5%	0.6%
1997		3.6%		4.7%		-1.6%	2.6%	4.4%

~ Prices are for previous calendar year, e.g., CY 1993 prices are reported for FY 1994.
* University library books printed index weights: 80 percent U.S. titles, 20 percent foreign titles.
^ College Library books printed index weights: 95 percent U.S. titles, 5 percent foreign titles.
Sources: See text.
n/a Not Available

Table 11A / Academic Library Price Indexes, Books and Serials, FY 1992 to 1997

| 1992=100 | Periodicals | | | | | | Other serials (newspapers) | | Books and serials indexes | | Other printed materials index (AL4.0) |
| | U.S. titles | | Foreign | | Periodical indexes | | | | | | |
Fiscal year	Price~	Index (AL3.2a)	Price~	Index (AL3.2b)	University* (UL3.2)	College^ (CL3.2)	Price~	Index (AL3.3)	University** (UL3.0)	College^^ (CL3.0)	
1992	$146.82	100.0	$370.23	100.0	100.0	100.0	$222.68	100.0	100.0	100.0	100.0
1993	160.03	109.0	421.32	113.8	110.0	109.2	229.92	103.3	106.1	107.5	102.9
1994	174.86	119.1	447.61	120.9	119.5	119.2	261.91	117.6	113.1	114.4	105.5
1995	192.04	130.8	489.64	132.2	131.1	130.9	270.22	121.3	121.5	119.4	107.7
1996	210.83	143.6	586.81	158.5	146.6	144.3	300.21	134.8	131.7	126.8	111.3
1997	230.80	157.2	654.56	176.8	161.1	158.2	311.77	140.0	141.6	136.0	118.5
1993		9.0%		13.8%	10.0%	9.2%		3.3%	6.1%	7.5%	2.9%
1994		9.3%		6.2%	8.6%	9.1%		13.9%	6.6%	6.4%	2.5%
1995		9.8%		9.3%	9.7%	9.8%		3.2%	7.4%	4.4%	2.1%
1996		9.8%		19.9%	11.8%	10.3%		11.1%	8.4%	6.2%	3.3%
1997		9.5%		11.5%	9.9%	9.6%		3.9%	7.5%	7.2%	6.5%

~ Prices are for previous calendar year, e.g., CY 1993 prices are reported for FY 1994.
* University library periodicals index weights: 80 percent U.S. titles, 20 percent foreign titles.
^ College library periodicals index weights: 95 percent U.S. titles, 5 percent foreign titles.
** University library books and serials index weights: 35 percent books, 60 percent periodicals, 5 percent other serials.
^^College library books and serials index weights: 47 percent books, 48 percent periodicals, 5 percent other serials.
Sources: See text.

Table 12 / Academic Library Price Indexes, Non-Print Media and Electronic Services, FY 1992 to 1997

1992=100 Fiscal year	Microforms (microfilm) Index (AL5.1)	Audio recordings					Video		
		Tape cassette		Compact disc		Audio recordings index* (AL5.2)	VHS cassette		Video index (AL5.3)
		Price~	Index (AL5.2a)	Price~	Index (AL5.2b)		Price~	Index (AL5.3a)	
1992	100.0	$12.18	100.0	n/a		100.0	$199.67	100.0	100.0
1993	104.3	11.73	96.3	n/a		96.3	112.92	56.6	56.6
1994	107.9	8.20	67.3	$13.36	67.3	67.3	93.22	46.7	46.7
1995	110.6	8.82	72.4	14.80	74.6	73.5	84.19	42.2	42.2
1996	128.0	7.96	65.4	14.86	74.9	70.1	83.48	41.8	41.8
1997	132.9	8.13	66.7	16.43	82.8	74.8	82.10	41.1	41.1
1993	4.3%		-3.7%			-3.7%		-43.4%	-43.4%
1994	3.5%		-30.1%			-30.1%		-17.4%	-17.4%
1995	2.5%		7.6%		10.8%	9.2%		-9.7%	-9.7%
1996	15.7%		-9.8%		0.4%	-4.6%		-0.8%	-0.8%
1997	3.8%		2.1%		10.6%	6.6%		-1.7%	-1.7%

~ Prices are for previous calendar year, e.g., CY 1993 prices are reported for FY 1994.
* Audio recordings index weights: 50 percent tape cassette, 50 percent compact disc.
Sources: See text.
n/a Not Available

Table 12A / Academic Library Price Indexes, Non-Print Media and Electronic Services, FY 1992 to 1997

1992=100 Fiscal year	Non-print Media Graphic image (AL5.4)	Computer files (CD-ROM) Price~	Index (AL5.5)	Non-print media index# (AL5.0)	Electronic services index (AL6.0)	Total Acquisitions Indexes Univ*	College^	All Institutions**
1992	100.0	$1,601	100.0	100.0	100.0	100.0	100.0	100.0
1993	97.3	1,793	112.0	98.7	101.9	105.2	105.9	105.4
1994	108.4	1,945	121.5	100.8	104.8	111.4	111.8	111.5
1995	111.3	1,961	122.5	102.1	108.5	118.7	116.2	118.0
1996	114.5	1,986	124.0	110.3	110.3	127.6	123.1	126.4
1997	126.5	2,012	125.7	113.7	110.3	136.1	130.6	134.5
1993	-2.7%		12.0%	-1.3%	1.9%	5.2%	5.9%	5.4%
1994	11.4%		8.5%	2.1%	2.8%	5.9%	5.6%	5.8%
1995	2.7%		0.8%	1.3%	3.5%	6.6%	4.0%	5.8%
1996	2.9%		1.3%	8.1%	1.7%	7.5%	5.9%	7.1%
1997	10.5%		1.3%	3.1%	0.0%	6.6%	6.1%	6.5%

~ Prices are for immediate preceding calendar year, e.g., CY 1993 prices are reported for FY 1994.
# Non-print media index weights: 45 percent microforms, 5 percent audio recordings, 15 percent video, 5 percent graphic image, 30 percent computer materials.
* University total acquisitions 1992 weights: 81 percent books, 3 percent other printed material, 5 percent non-print media, and 11 percent electronic services.
^ College total acquisitions 1992 weights: 77 percent books, 2 percent other printed material, 10 percent non-print media, and 11 percent electronic services.
** All institutions total acquisitions weights: 72 percent university acquisitions, 28 percent college acquisitions.
Sources: See text.

State Rankings of Selected Public Library Data, 1997

	Circulation Transactions per capita*		Reference Transactions per capita		Book Volumes per capita		ALA-MLS Librarians per 25,000		Operating Expenditures per capita ($)		Local Income per capita ($)	
	Ranking	No.	Ranking	No.	Ranking	No.	Ranking	No.	Ranking	No.	Ranking	No.
Alabama	48	3.64	45	.60	43	1.98	38	1.95	45	13.40	43	11.31
Alaska	27	6.15	30	.80	20	3.31	18	3.18	5	33.86	3	31.25
Arizona	26	6.18	26	.87	50	1.72	35	2.05	26	20.04	23	18.54
Arkansas	47	4.31	49	.43	37	2.19	50	1.08	48	11.90	45	10.58
California	41	4.92	14	1.12	45	1.95	29	2.23	28	19.07	25	17.55
Colorado	11	8.70	8	1.39	32	2.59	22	2.64	11	26.88	8	27.87
Connecticut	19	7.04	17	1.06	16	3.53	4	4.8	9	27.80	10	24.84
Delaware	38	5.30	41	.67	38	2.17	44	1.75	37	16.53	37	13.61
District of Columbia**	50	2.72	1	2.26	1	5.27	2	5.25	1	40.19	1	38.43
Florida	40	5.00	3	1.73	49	1.80	26	2.37	29	18.66	29	16.44
Georgia	43	4.61	38	.71	48	1.86	33	2.12	41	14.58	46	10.55
Hawaii	25	6.37	16	1.08	31	2.59	16	3.35	34	17.08	n.a.	n.a.
Idaho	14	7.93	27	.86	21	3.22	42	1.86	30	18.28	31	15.87
Illinois	15	7.87	4	1.52	14	3.81	8	4.37	6	33.51	5	30.68
Indiana	2	10.69	9	1.37	11	4.16	10	4.25	4	34.84	4	31.07
Iowa	10	8.80	32	.78	13	3.86	17	3.34	27	19.46	26	17.49
Kansas	5	9.76	7	1.45	8	4.57	19	3.11	15	24.84	11	23.27
Kentucky	36	5.44	51	.41	41	2.05	47	1.63	43	14.17	38	13.40
Louisiana	46	4.34	34	.76	35	2.30	41	1.87	35	16.80	27	16.88
Maine	21	7.00	36	.72	4	4.71	7	4.51	31	18.11	36	13.63
Maryland	7	9.18	6	1.46	27	2.67	1	5.26	10	27.15	20	20.15
Massachusetts	18	7.38	22	.94	2	4.84	6	4.59	12	26.67	14	22.48
Michigan	35	5.44	25	.89	25	2.80	15	3.4	19	22.09	18	20.29
Minnesota	12	8.54	11	1.28	30	2.59	27	2.25	18	23.28	17	20.67
Mississippi	49	3.27	50	.42	46	1.94	49	1.22	50	9.78	48	7.76
Missouri	13	8.39	19	1.01	3	4.77	32	2.16	21	21.74	12	22.87
Montana	29	5.91	43	.63	22	2.96	46	1.65	44	13.42	35	13.91
Nebraska	30	5.89	48	.45	26	2.71	45	1.66	38	15.83	33	14.85
Nevada	39	5.13	15	1.11	36	2.21	36	1.98	17	23.58	16	21.23
New Hampshire	20	7.03	40	.70	9	4.19	5	4.68	23	20.51	24	18.47
New Jersey	32	5.60	23	.91	17	3.52	9	4.34	8	30.08	7	28.06
New Mexico	34	5.45	35	.76	23	2.94	30	2.21	36	16.62	30	15.91
New York	23	6.93	2	1.95	10	4.16	3	5.15	3	36.89	6	30.01
North Carolina	31	5.76	24	.91	44	1.97	40	1.88	39	14.90	41	12.56
North Dakota	22	6.99	37	.72	15	3.72	43	1.81	47	12.69	47	10.42
Ohio	1	12.59	5	1.48	12	4.04	11	4.22	2	39.62	32	15.27
Oklahoma	28	5.97	39	.71	40	2.09	37	1.97	40	14.82	34	13.94
Oregon	4	10.25	33	.77	34	2.47	23	2.63	13	25.64	9	26.77
Pennsylvania	42	4.65	44	.63	39	2.14	24	2.63	32	17.24	44	10.79
Rhode Island	37	5.38	31	.80	19	3.38	13	4.02	24	20.24	28	16.77
South Carolina	44	4.44	13	1.13	47	1.87	28	2.24	42	14.29	39	13.06
South Dakota	6	9.21	46	.57	6	4.65	21	2.68	25	20.09	19	20.17
Tennessee	51	2.60	47	.56	51	.97	51	1.06	51	7.15	50	6.30
Texas	45	4.36	20	1.01	42	1.99	31	2.18	46	12.87	42	12.33
Utah	9	9.01	18	1.02	29	2.64	34	2.07	22	21.38	22	18.88
Vermont	24	6.49	42	.65	7	4.64	12	4.15	33	17.15	40	12.78
Virginia	17	7.56	21	1.00	33	2.53	25	2.62	20	22.00	21	19.02
Washington	3	10.33	10	1.35	24	2.88	20	3.02	7	30.08	2	32.00
West Virginia	33	5.54	28	.85	28	2.65	48	1.44	49	11.39	49	7.41
Wisconsin	8	9.18	12	1.20	18	3.38	14	3.45	14	24.85	13	22.83
Wyoming	16	7.67	29	.81	5	4.68	39	1.93	16	23.80	15	21.91

Source: Rochelle Logan and Marcia J. Rodney, Library Research Service, Colorado State Library, in partnership with the Library and Information Services Department at University College of the University of Denver using statistics from Federal-State Cooperative System (FSCS) for Public Library Data, Public Libraries Survey, Fiscal Year 1997.

* Per capita and per 1,000 population calculations are based on population of legal service area.

** The District of Columbia, while not a state, is included in the state rankings. Special care should be used in making comparisons.

Library Buildings 1999: Structural Ergonomics

Bette-Lee Fox

Managing Editor, *Library Journal*

Libraries continued to grow in 1999 through new buildings and renovation projects. Though technology has shifted patrons' expectations, the need for libraries as information centers and providers remains vital.

The 77 new buildings and 118 renovation/addition projects completed between July 1, 1998, and June 30, 1999, (the fewest reported since 1986) span a range of styles, strategies, and specifications. But community access and service are uppermost.

The 195 projects cost $564.5 million, 71 percent of which came from local funds (including bond issues) and a healthy 14 percent from gifts.

Some larger new projects include the Schaumburg Township District Library in Illinois ($25.5 million, 166,501 square feet); the Carmel Clay Public Library in Indiana ($23 million, 116,385 square feet); and the Tuzzy Consortium Library, Fairbanks, Alaska, part of the Museum Heritage Center ($11 million). Larger addition/renovations include the Cleveland Public Library ($34 million, 261,223 square feet); phase two of the Boston Public Library ($20.6 million, 65,700 square feet); and the renovated Rose Reading Room of the New York Public Library ($13.2 million).

This year's 30 academic projects include the Central Missouri State University Library in Warrensburg ($30.5 million, 196,000 square feet); Homer D. Babbidge Library, University of Connecticut, Storrs ($40 million, 393,085 square feet); and Samford University Library, Birmingham, Alabama ($6 million, 80,000 square feet).

What's especially interesting this year is not the number of construction projects (or lack thereof) but the direction those projects have taken, with the inclusion of computer training rooms and electronic upgrades and capabilities to meet or even surpass the demands of the Internet generation.

Pundits will always predict the demise of the book (and with it, libraries), but as libraries find ways to adapt to the changing environment they will continue to serve patrons in new and different ways.

Adapted from the December 1999 issue of *Library Journal*, which also lists architects' addresses.

Table 1 / New Public Library Buildings, 1999

Community	Pop. ('000)	Code	Project Cost	Const. Cost	Gross Sq. Ft.	Sq. Ft. Cost	Equip. Cost	Site Cost	Other Costs	Volumes	Federal Funds	State Funds	Local Funds	Gift Funds	Architect
Alaska															
Barrow*	8	M	$11,000,000	$1,612,800	6,720	$240.00	$499,895	Owned	$8,887,305	40,000	0	0	$11,000,000	0	LCMF Inc.
Arizona															
Gilbert	230	M	8,651,862	7,159,263	63,814	112.19	988,799	Owned	503,800	250,000	0	0	8,651,862	0	Hofmann/Deitz; Hidell
Sierra Vista	40	M	5,000,000	3,800,000	31,200	121.79	326,282	Owned	873,718	140,000	0	0	5,000,000	0	Burns & Wald-Hopkins
California															
Lamont	14	B	2,308,749	1,728,236	11,426	151.25	197,858	Owned	382,655	43,100	$2,153,341	0	155,408	0	CWA/KSA
Los Angeles	57	B	4,480,862	3,086,779	10,500	293.98	91,800	$979,839	322,444	40,000	0	0	4,480,862	0	Villanueva/Arnoni
Los Angeles	33	B	5,286,643	2,700,200	10,500	257.16	123,542	2,146,739	316,162	40,000	0	0	5,286,643	0	Barton Phelps
Panorama City	110	B	3,330,784	2,103,712	12,500	168.29	127,177	806,387	293,508	45,000	0	0	3,330,784	0	Reibsamen, Nickels...
San Diego	52	M	6,000,000	3,200,000	14,850	215.48	500,000	2,000,000	300,000	80,000	2,750,000	0	250,000	3,000,000	MCM Architects
Soledad	10	M	2,385,000	2,200,000	13,650	161.17	35,000	Owned	150,000	34,000	0	1,384,000	1,001,000	0	Duncan Todd
Colorado															
Lone Tree	10	B	1,520,808	1,346,737	10,000	134.68	91,104	Owned	82,967	53,000	0	0	1,464,601	56,207	Humphries-Poli
Connecticut															
Orange	13	M	4,388,822	3,494,834	23,500	148.72	454,633	120,750	318,605	115,400	100,000	350,000	3,449,189	489,633	Moser, Pilon, & Nelson
Florida															
Alachua	6	B	822,049	546,820	5,665	96.53	63,384	153,000	58,845	36,372	0	313,973	508,076	0	Paul Portal
DeBary	12	B	1,555,003	1,019,441	7,500	135.92	127,500	142,000	266,062	63,000	400,000	0	1,055,003	100,000	Jack Rood
Fort Pierce	173	BS	2,904,481	2,072,412	23,000	90.1	238,000	375,000	219,069	120,000	0	400,000	1,804,481	700,000	Philip S. Steel
New Smyrna Beach	17	B	3,454,984	2,332,585	25,000	93.3	425,000	Owned	697,399	100,000	400,000	0	3,054,984	0	Jack Rood
Pembroke Pines	150	B	3,291,000	2,240,000	24,003	93.32	640,000	Leased	411,000	70,000	0	0	3,291,000	0	Frimet Design
Sarasota	154	M	16,460,000	10,900,000	73,000	149.31	748,000	2,210,000	2,602,000	300,000	0	0	16,275,000	185,000	Gary B. Hoyt
Stuart	132	MS	7,213,017	5,636,713	38,900	144.9	480,000	461,375	634,929	124,000	0	400,000	6,013,017	800,000	Fletcher Harkness...
Tamarac	25	B	n/a	n/a	6,228	n/a	64,000	Leased	n/a	15,000	0	0	64,000	0	Octavio S. Lima
Georgia															
Alpharetta	29	B	8,971,072	5,303,241	25,000	212.13	935,000	149,180	2,583,651	150,000	0	0	8,971,072	0	Cheeks/Hornbein
College Park	20	B	2,750,000	1,679,000	7,500	223.87	297,500	Owned	773,500	40,000	0	0	2,750,000	0	Harris & Partners
Illinois															
Chicago	55	B	5,199,372	3,900,000	15,500	251.61	260,000	355,000	684,372	60,000	0	0	5,199,372	0	Antunovich Assocs.
Chicago	58	B	4,303,299	2,875,000	13,689	210.02	187,000	541,000	700,299	58,000	0	250,000	4,053,299	0	Alphonse G. Guajardo
Chicago	12	B	3,296,160	2,470,000	7,000	352.86	128,000	Owned	698,160	45,000	0	775,371	2,520,789	0	Architects Enterprise
Chicago	7	B	2,881,810	2,215,982	7,000	316.57	127,000	Owned	538,828	40,000	0	250,000	2,631,810	0	Jackson Mehdi, Inc.
Schaumburg	150	M	25,524,911	17,090,862	166,501	102.65	2,411,557	3,130,513	2,891,979	550,000	0	250,000	25,274,911	0	Phillips Swager

*Includes Museum Heritage Center
Symbol Code: B—Branch Library; BS—Branch & System Headquarters; M—Main Library; MS—Main & System Headquarters; S—System Headquarters; n/a—not available

Location															Architect
Indiana															
Carmel	60	M	23,000,000	14,049,371	116,385	120.71	2,773,184	925,132	5,252,313	313,432	0	0	23,000,000	0	0 Meyer... Browning
Columbia City	12	M	4,574,814	3,689,687	24,750	149.07	212,500	30,000	642,627	73,000	0	0	4,105,667	469,147	Morrison Kattman...
Iowa															
Brooklyn	25	M	488,725	347,025	3,400	102.07	107,000	Owned	34,700	13,400	0	0	0	488,725	Brown Healey Stone...
Council Bluffs	80	M	12,500,000	8,000,000	70,951	112.75	1,250,000	2,000,000	1,250,000	210,025	0	6,125	2,400,000	10,093,875	Leo A. Daly Co.
Waverly	n/a	M	3,405,000	2,546,000	24,000	106.08	257,600	311,000	290,400	60,000	0	0	1,305,000	2,100,000	Brown Healey Stone...
Kentucky															
Winchester	30	M	2,961,451	2,143,516	18,200	117.77	293,136	350,080	174,719	85,000	0	350,000	2,575,367	36,084	Sherman-Carter...
Maryland															
Laurel	16	B	4,800,000	2,330,000	15,212	153.17	350,000	500,000	1,620,000	80,000	0	0	4,300,000	500,000	Smith Architects
Massachusetts															
Dunstable	3	M	1,753,050	1,503,456	9,030	166.50	54,394	Owned	195,200	32,500	0	694,000	1,030,000	29,050	Belanger & Foley
Pembroke	16	M	2,948,884	2,473,884	18,300	135.19	235,000	Owned	240,000	83,600	0	1,293,000	1,532,884	123,000	J. Stewart Roberts
Tyngsborough	10	M	1,665,214	1,417,466	11,400	124.34	100,000	Owned	147,748	40,000	0	799,390	814,753	51,071	Belanger & Foley
Michigan															
Central Lake	3	M	734,740	441,381	5,184	85.14	193,726	2,500	97,133	30,000	300,000	0	30,737	404,003	Michael Bensinger
Greenville	15	MS	3,263,010	2,529,785	23,007	109.96	400,925	Owned	332,300	83,949	0	75,000	1,800,000	1,388,010	Fishbeck, Thompson...
Moline	3	M	743,689	527,591	6,000	87.93	71,983	68,000	76,115	48,524	0	0	671,689	72,000	¨AG Architectural
Missouri															
West Plains	9	M	2,570,551	1,773,457	23,500	75.47	321,889	332,205	143,000	100,000	0	0	1,640,000	930,551	Sapp Design
Nebraska															
Ralston	6	M	2,386,017	1,909,000	14,000	136.36	180,144	130,868	166,005	45,000	0	0	1,734,017	652,000	Zenon Berringer...
New Jersey															
New Egypt	7	B	971,286	666,323	6,000	111.05	120,984	102,990	80,989	16,000	0	0	485,643	485,643	James W. Hyres
New York															
Bliss	1	M	118,000	93,000	1,600	58.13	3,000	10,000	12,000	10,000	0	12,000	91,000	15,000	not reported
New Hartford	20	M	1,315,000	1,025,000	10,000	102.5	100,000	100,000	90,000	40,000	75,000	30,000	57,000	1,153,000	Alesia & Crewell
Rotterdam	35	B	1,173,000	863,000	10,000	86.3	130,000	150,000	30,000	55,000	92,442	13,179	917,379	150,000	James Cullen Assocs.
North Carolina															
Charlotte	100	B	6,469,869	3,789,737	33,500	113.13	594,108	1,500,000	586,024	175,000	0	0	4,969,869	1,500,000	Little & Assocs.
Edneyville	5	B	453,003	366,084	3,000	122.03	33,855	Owned	53,064	20,000	0	0	317,003	136,000	Craig, Gaulden, & Davis
Fayetteville	23	B	4,327,265	2,853,609	21,000	135.89	440,000	130,510	903,146	60,500	0	0	4,327,265	0	Shuller, Ferris...
Pembroke	8	B	305,827	269,942	4,400	61.35	15,629	7,000	13,256	7,500	140,125	14,800	104,000	46,902	Elizabeth B. Lee
Spring Lake	31	B	2,436,999	1,613,929	12,000	134.49	267,000	240,000	316,070	41,500	0	0	2,436,999	0	Shuller, Ferris...
Ohio															
Chardon	80	S	2,297,077	1,881,592	21,000	89.6	182,195	Owned	233,290	0	0	0	2,297,077	0	David Holzheimer
Dennison	5	B	377,766	302,363	3,472	87.09	39,858	10,800	24,745	38,380	0	0	255,766	122,000	Gerald L. Cody
Mentor	8	B	626,644	469,825	3,500	134.24	69,754	Owned	87,065	19,000	0	0	545,338	81,306	Meehan Architects

Symbol Code: B—Branch Library; BS—Branch & System Headquarters; M—Main Library; MS—Main & System Headquarters; S—System Headquarters; n/a—not available

Table 1 / New Public Library Buildings, 1999 (cont.)

Community	Pop. ('000)	Code	Project Cost	Const. Cost	Gross Sq. Ft.	Sq. Ft. Cost	Equip. Cost	Site Cost	Other Costs	Volumes	Federal Funds	State Funds	Local Funds	Gift Funds	Architect
New Philadelphia	8	B	345,662	287,231	4,125	69.63	32,911	Owned	25,520	30,000	0	0	146,135	199,527	MKC Assocs.
Solon	19	B	3,966,972	3,372,942	20,800	162.16	320,593	Owned	273,437	120,000	0	0	3,966,972	0	GPD Assocs.
Oklahoma															
Hartshorne	5	B	435,145	357,000	4,312	82.79	30,645	23,500	24,000	20,000	100,000	0	200,000	135,145	Duane Mass
Pennsylvania															
Lititz	26	M	1,575,000	875,000	16,200	54.01	200,000	300,000	200,000	60,500	0	210,000	180,000	1,185,000	Beers & Schillaci
McMurray	14	M	3,433,716	2,663,786	25,200	105.71	473,954	Owned	295,976	110,000	0	326,000	2,759,762	347,954	Ross, Schonder...
South Carolina															
Elgin	5	B	546,181	353,092	3,600	98.08	55,000	90,000	48,089	10,000	100,000	85,000	55,000	306,181	Curt Davis
Hemingway	6	B	560,383	391,000	4,028	97.07	112,754	25,000	31,629	15,500	179,539	266,000	28,191	86,653	W. Daniel Shelley
Kingstree	15	MS	1,111,276	712,000	6,600	107.87	222,625	50,000	126,651	35,000	408,243	459,000	86,000	158,033	W. Daniel Shelley
Ware Shoals	3	B	1,000,000	800,000	9,200	86.96	120,000	Owned	80,000	10,000	0	200,000	40,000	760,000	Craig, Gaulden & Davis
South Dakota															
Waubay	1	M	135,126	116,407	1,500	77.60	8,597	Owned	10,122	15,000	52,000		77,563	5,563	David J. Todd
Tennessee															
Dayton	27	M	587,137	415,506	9,353	44.42	27,110	117,000	27,521	50,000	0	0	487,137	100,000	Upland Design
Henderson	13	M	684,026	434,456	4,995	86.98	43,814	180,000	25,756	n/a	100,000	0	330,026	254,000	Anderson Vaughan
Jamestown	15	M	623,573	553,573	5,516	100.36	50,000	Owned	20,000	20,000	155,000	0	413,573	55,000	Brewer, Ingram...
Memphis	73	B	4,851,012	3,460,000	30,000	115.33	812,600	260,000	318,412	125,000	0	0	4,851,012	0	Hnedak Bobo Group
Texas															
Nederland	18	M	1,273,600	689,008	16,000	43.06	191,539	325,000	68,053	79,000	150,000	0	350,000	773,600	Long Magnuson
Plano	40	B	4,369,014	3,730,683	30,000	124.35	318,724	Owned	319,607	126,000	0	0	4,369,014	0	Phillips Swager
Utah															
Riverton	23	B	2,124,985	1,680,298	13,400	125.4	300,899	54,588	89,200	100,000	0	0	2,124,985	0	M.H.T.N. Architects
Salt Lake City	n/a	SL	7,800,900	6,522,700	90,435	72.13	805,000	Owned	473,200	112,975	0	7,800,900	0	0	Brixton & Christopher
Vermont															
Killington	1	M	1,013,530	765,530	7,540	101.53	104,000	31,500	112,500	18,000	0	0	963,530	50,000	Robinson Green...
Washington															
Kennewick	60	B	4,021,070	2,900,000	32,000	90.63	750,000	Owned	371,070	50,615	0	0	4,021,070	0	Buffalo Design
Redmond	43	B	4,127,480	2,796,781	10,000	279.68	345,000	456,399	529,300	120,000	0	0	4,127,480	0	Johanna Schorr
Wisconsin															
Rothschild	6	B	1,991,267	1,772,362	3,150	69.75	49,000	Owned	169,905	27,348	0	0	1,991,267	0	PMSI—Jeff Musson
Sheboygan	190	S	179,000	118,000	5,000	23.6	61,000	Leased	30,000	30,000	0	115,250	0	63,750	Eppstein Uhen
Sun Prairie	25	M	5,500,000	3,961,197	35,692	110.98	580,654	250,000	708,149	88,658	0	0	3,775,000	1,725,000	Frye Gillan Molinaro

Symbol Code: B—Branch Library; BS—Branch & System Headquarters; M—Main Library; MS—Main & System Headquarters; S—System Headquarters; SL—System Headquarters; n/a—not available

Table 2 / Public Library Buildings, Additions and Renovations, 1999

Community	Pop. ('000)	Code	Project Cost	Const. Cost	Gross Sq. Ft.	Sq. Ft. Cost	Equip. Cost	Site Cost	Other Costs	Volumes	Federal Funds	State Funds	Local Funds	Gift Funds	Architect
Alabama															
Fayette	18	M	$643,911	$528,135	5,655	$93.39	$63,381	Owned	$52,395	65,000	0	0	$50,000	$593,911	Fitts Architects
Geraldine	3	M	75,000	60,000	2,400	25	15,000	Owned	0	n/a	0	0	0	75,000	not reported
Mt. Vernon	1	M	80,200	30,000	2,100	14.29	25,000	$25,000	200	8,000	0	1,200	73,000	6,000	not reported
Pelham	15	M	427,404	322,588	6,000	53.76	72,278	Owned	32,538	60,000	$150,000	0	277,404	8,670	Davis Architects
Arizona															
Phoenix	178	B	2,340,700	1,314,800	19,500	67.42	327,400	100,000	598,500	140,000	0	0	2,199,900	140,000	Richard & Bauer
Arkansas															
Jonesboro	76	M	581,335	525,064	10,016	52.42	16,291	Owned	39,980	7,614	0	0	581,335	C	Brackett Krennerich
Prairie Grove	10	M	389,210	270,210	3,985	67.8	100,000	Owned	19,000	40,000	0	0	374,210	15,000	Cromwell, Truemper....
Warren	12	B	225,102	170,167	2,000	85.08	43,330	Owned	11,605	35,000	88,382	0	98,382	38,338	Connelly, Abbott ...
California															
Alameda	73	M	1,336,000	1,054,900	18,000	58.6	12,000	Leased	269,100	n/a	0	0	1,336,000	0	Muller & Caufield
Daly City	25	B	2,391,959	1,699,456	11,500	147.78	126,541	Owned	565,962	60,000	0	428,500	1,902,459	61,000	Group 4 Architecture
Los Angeles	95	B	1,521,626	1,400,000	11,712	119.53	121,626	Owned	0	55,000	0	0	1,521,626	0	City of Los Angeles...
Los Angeles	97	B	2,758,550	2,410,000	9,273	259.89	133,550	Owned	215,000	35,000	2,542,800	0	215,750	0	City of Los Angeles...
Mill Valley	28	M	5,562,739	3,954,014	27,032	146.27	490,424	Owned	1,118,301	158,000	0	0	5,057,315	505,424	Turnbull Griffin...
Murrieta	40	M	296,200	84,500	4,000	21.13	140,000	21,000	50,700	25,799	0	45,800	257,000	0	Tim Shook Co.
Novato	15	B	214,421	123,665	2,080	59.45	63,247	Leased	27,509	9,400	0	0	214,421	0	BSA Architects
San Francisco	50	B	4,151,807	3,428,268	9,520	360.11	267,438	Owned	456,101	52,500	696,579	0	3,187,790	267,438	Victor Talatala
Santa Paula	28	M	4,598	4,598	20,000	0.46	0	Owned	0	100,000	4,598	0	0	0	Leach Mounce
Sunnyvale	131	M	2,287,173	1,483,833	60,000	24.73	673,176	Owned	130,164	344,205	0	0	2,287,173	0	Oshima & Yee
Connecticut															
Hebron	8	M	2,644,400	1,955,000	16,800	116.37	255,000	50,000	384,400	46,000	250,000	500,000	1,894,400	0	Dale Cutler
Westport	24	M	4,800,833	3,618,499	36,420	99.35	335,881	Owned	846,453	250,000	0	603,833	1,697,000	2,500,000	Herbert S. Newman

Symbol Code: B—Branch Library; BS—Branch & System Headquarters; M—Main Library; MS—Main & System Headquarters; S—System Headquarters; n/a—not available

Table 2 / Public Library Buildings, Additions and Renovations, 1999 *(cont.)*

Community	Pop. ('000)	Code	Project Cost	Const. Cost	Gross Sq. Ft.	Sq. Ft. Cost	Equip. Cost	Site Cost	Other Costs	Volumes	Federal Funds	State Funds	Local Funds	Gift Funds	Architect
Florida															
Tavares	29	M	836,138	570,880	9,100	62.73	135,173	Owned	130,085	38,000	0	400,000	400,000	36,138	Nick Jones
Georgia															
Macon	27	B	417,879	144,907	8,000	18.11	227,372	Leased	45,600	55,000	0	0	417,879	0	Brittain, Thompson...
Illinois															
Cherry Valley	12	M	141,514	107,044	n/a	n/a	0	Owned	34,470	n/a	49,859	0	50,000	91,655	Carow Architects
Cherry Valley	12	M	49,720	14,818	546	27.14	24,736	Owned	10,166	n/a	17,519	0	32,201	0	Carow Architects
Downers Grove	47	M	8,682,000	6,870,050	73,000	94.11	773,463	Owned	1,038,487	300,000	0	250,000	8,432,000	0	Phillips Swager
Eldorado	8	M	14,837	0	7,770	0	1,126	Owned	13,711	n/a	0	14,837	0	0	Walker-Baker
Geneva	21	M	2,849,668	2,014,506	15,300	131.67	412,545	265,000	157,617	160,000	0	250,000	2,260,219	339,449	Durrant Architects
Hazel Crest	30	M	63,968	20,230	6,680	3.03	41,410	Owned	2,328	n/a	0	25,000	38,968	0	Ruck/Pate
Lake Villa	23	M	5,330,449	3,816,297	30,000	127.21	631,114	122,688	760,350	134,550	225,000	0	5,105,449	0	Brown, Healey...
Mt. Vernon	24	M	302,507	270,830	18,860	14.36	0	Owned	31,677	n/a	121,003	0	181,504	0	Kent Piper
Norris City	5	M	215,103	173,442	4,275	40.57	11,610	Owned	30,051	24,540	0	79,432	135,671	0	Tim Raibley
Oak Forest	32	M	438,989	290,850	7,500	38.78	101,114	Owned	47,025	16,000	159,584	0	279,405	0	WCT Architects
Rochelle	12	M	36,521	32,450	2,100	15.45	0	Owned	4,071	n/a	35,000	0	1,521	0	Frye Gillan Molinaro
Wilmette	27	M	1,148,911	1,050,356	14,260	72.66	30,000	Owned	68,555	278,000	0	650,000	498,911	0	Frye Gillan Molinaro
Indiana															
Avon	15	M	3,813,762	3,062,705	42,481	72.1	174,261	115,000	461,796	n/a	0	0	3,813,762	0	K.R. Montgomery
Bloomfield	6	B	139,725	93,164	1,232	75.63	32,061	Owned	14,500	6,150	0	0	139,725	0	Veazey Parrott...
Charlestown	2	B	120,000	102,000	1,200	85	12,000	Owned	6,000	3,000	0	0	49,000	71,000	James Rosenbarger
La Porte	60	MS	623,805	471,799	17,000	27.75	104,174	Owned	47,832	20,323	0	0	623,805	0	K.R. Montgomery
Mishawaka	60	M	7,520,830	5,989,206	81,337	73	608,733	Owned	922,891	196,809	n/a	350,000	7,160,830	10,000	Troyer Group
New Albany	64	M	1,333,403	1,080,686	20,000	54.03	147,900	Owned	104,817	80,000	0	0	1,333,403	0	Applegate Architects
Iowa															
Webster City	8	M	4,300,000	3,400,000	22,300	152.47	330,500	75,800	493,700	54,000	0	0	303,000	3,997,000	Meyer, Sherer...

Symbol Code: B—Branch Library; BS—Branch & System Headquarters; M—Main Library; MS—Main & System Headquarters; S—System Headquarters; n/a—not available

Location	#	Sym														Architect/Firm
Kentucky																
Owingsville	10	M	583,476	469,009	8,563	56.08	42,875	35,400	36,192	34,000	0	255,388	328,088	0		Pearson/Bender
Louisiana																
Gnzles/Donaldson	80	S	762,189	457,500	6,800	67.28	270,148	Owned	34,541	5,000	78,000	23,000	641,189	20,000		Henry Chauvin
Wisner	1	B	59,546	51,396	1,800	28.56	7,050	Leased	1,100	16,000	0	0	34,546	25,000		not reported
Maine																
Bath	17	M	2,900,000	2,000,000	14,030	142.86	449,000	Owned	451,000	55,000	50,000	0	882,755	1,967,245		TFH Architects
Massachusetts																
Acton	19	M	6,383,665	4,892,822	32,000	152.9	342,701	Owned	1,153,142	114,231	0	2,038,733	4,349,481	40,451		Tappé Assocs.
Boston	5,769	M	20,616,876	17,300,000	65,700	263.32	800,000	Owned	2,516,876	n/a	2,760,000	4,895,000	9,226,051	3,735,825		Shepley Bulfinch…
Groton	10	M	3,400,000	2,750,000	17,417	157.89	156,000	30,000	464,000	66,000	0	1,268,536	2,131,464	0		Richard Smith
Haverhill	52	MS	4,911,829	3,833,253	44,000	87,12	33,684	Owned	1,044,892	32,188	0	86,585	1,226,045	3,599,199		Mark B. Mitchell
Ipswich	13	M	2,268,349	1,868,145	17,088	109.32	168,349	Owned	231,855	78,450	0	1,025,135	1,074,865	168,349		Bort Hill/Boston
Southwick	8	M	3,186,000	2,900,000	12,000	241.66	186,000	Owned	100,000	48,000	0	200,000	2,846,000	140,000		Patricia Bairdi
Sudbury	16	M	5,461,974	4,049,475	31,250	129.58	720,637	Owned	691,862	110,000	0	1,811,974	3,000,000	650,000		A. Anthony Tappé
Topsfield	6	M	3,523,871	2,117,561	15,856	133.21	330,737	208,000	867,573	58,907	0	1,331,247	700,000	1,492,624		A. Anthony Tappé
Michigan																
Allegan	15	M	260,000	127,000	6,500	19.54	131,000	Owned	2,000	72,000	0	0	248,000	12,000		Tower, Pinkster…
Beaverton	6	B	253,130	186,273	3,549	52.49	28,567	18,500	19,790	10,080	0	0	234,630	18,500		Wigen, Tincknell…
Berkley	17	M	2,840,000	1,956,000	15,500	126.19	310,000	82,000	492,000	80,000	0	0	2,840,000	0		David W. Osler
Garden City	32	M	364,653	306,453	12,000	25.53	40,000	Owned	18,200	60,000	78,690	0	245,963	40,000		George Hartman
Holland	86	M	11,241,924	8,890,828	72,291	122.99	738,000	Owned	1,613,096	243,389	0	0	9,041,924	2,200,000		Frye Gillan Molinaro
Jackson	3	B	15,320	9,320	1,024	9.1	6,000	Leased	1,530	0	0	0	15,320	0		none
Saginaw	30	B	900,000	495,856	15,000	33.06	219,700	Owned	184,444	105,000	0	0	900,000	0		Wigen, Tincknell…
White Cloud	7	M	392,000	300,000	5,088	58.96	50,000	Owned	42,000	30,000	0	0	10,000	382,000		Otto, Dufty…
Minnesota																
Brooklyn Park	62	B	250,000	n/a	15,117	n/a	20,000	Owned	n/a	n/a	0	0	250,000	0		Bernard Jacob
Dawson	4	M	763,000	592,000	8,500	69.65	50,000	Leased	121,000	49,068	150,000	0	613,000	0		Milton Torrence…
Fairmont	23	MS	273,191	239,107	27,400	8.73	0	Owned	34,084	150,000	0	57,594	215,597	0		Paul R. Johnson
Missouri																
Kansas City	15	B	1,543,550	1,210,283	8,360	144.77	158,120	Owned	175,147	39,000	0	0	1,543,550	0		Mockey Mitchell…

Symbol Code: B—Branch Library; BS—Branch & System Headquarters; M—Main Library; MS—Main & System Headquarters; S—System Headquarters; n/a—not available

459

Table 2 / Public Library Buildings, Additions and Renovations, 1999 (cont.)

Community	Pop. ('000)	Code	Project Cost	Const. Cost	Gross Sq. Ft.	Sq. Ft. Cost	Equip. Cost	Site Cost	Other Costs	Volumes	Federal Funds	State Funds	Local Funds	Gift Funds	Architect
Nebraska															
Omaha	29	B	3,339,582	2,454,080	16,800	146.08	320,735	280,157	284,610	59,600	0	0	3,339,582	0	Alley Poyner
Omaha	93	B	4,188,121	3,246,846	33,850	95.92	482,097	Owned	459,178	136,102	0	0	4,188,121	0	Schemmer; Meyer…
Nevada															
Reno	n/a	B	8,527,701	3,620,366	28,364	127.64	420,502	390,000	586,833	129,700	0	0	8,377,701	150,000	Felden & Partners
New Hampshire															
Franconia	1	M	59,961	50,612	809	62.56	0	Owned	9,349	0	29,943	0	0	30,018	none
Keene	23	M	4,000,000	3,263,000	40,000	81.58	350,000	Owned	387,000	123,400	0	0	4,000,000	0	A. Anthony Tappé
Lancaster	4	M	1,273,562	1,110,360	12,000	92.53	47,269	Owned	115,933	50,000	253,750	0	675,987	343,825	Tennant/Wallace
Newbury	2	M	441,737	357,378	2,850	125.4	33,011	Owned	51,348	9,600	0	0	291,000	150,737	Sherman, Greiner…
Troy	2	M	421,211	385,865	5,274	73.16	9,553	Owned	25,793	21,000	0	0	322,187	99,024	Tennant/Wallace
New Jersey															
Deptford	25	M	930,000	680,000	11,253	60.43	100,000	Owned	150,000	83,000	0	0	900,000	30,000	Tarquini Organization
Fort Lee	33	M	3,267,319	2,729,017	31,000	88.03	125,423	Owned	412,879	130,000	0	0	2,899,319	368,000	Virgona & Virgona
Manalapan	409	M	7,200,000	5,800,000	31,000	187.1	250,000	Owned	1,150,000	185,000	0	0	7,200,000	0	Faridy, Thorne…
Ridgewood	24	M	3,900,000	3,003,000	34,000	88.32	585,000	Owned	312,000	129,000	0	0	1,700,000	2,200,000	Wells Assocs.
New York															
Brooklyn	14	B	2,466,000	1,500,000	13,500	111.11	500,000	Owned	466,000	76,154	78,000	0	2,388,000	0	Stephen Weinstein
Inlet	1	M	6,400	5,400	1,600	3.38	1,000	Leased	0	8,000	0	0	4,400	2,000	none
Massapequa Park	50	M	2,334,463	1,851,964	21,977	84.27	196,564	Owned	275,935	83,237	0	15,380	2,200,000	110,000	Bentel & Bentel
Northport	37	M	3,953,048	3,213,520	36,000	89.26	303,952	Owned	435,576	175,169	37,048	13,500	3,737,500	165,000	Beatty, Harvey
New York	n/a	M	13,212,070	9,000,000	28,750	313.04	2,200,000	Owned	2,012,070	35,000	0	0	0	13,212,070	David Brody Bond
Scarsdale	17	M	913,000	808,000	3,100	260.65	0	Owned	105,000	145,000	0	0	13,000	900,000	Gibbons Heidtmann
Wadhams	1	M	65,000	48,000	1,600	30	10,000	Owned	7,000	8,000	0	26,000	0	39,000	Library committee
North Carolina															
Hayesville	8	B	407,101	352,255	7,500	46.97	26,496	Owned	28,350	43,117	150,000	19,039	132,032	106,030	Moody & Assocs.

Symbol Code: B—Branch Library; BS—Branch & System Headquarters; M—Main Library; MS—Main & System Headquarters; S—System Headquarters; n/a—not available

Location	No.	Code						Tenure								Architect
Ohio																
Beachwood	11	B	1,231,565	746,365	17,940	41.6	310,413	Owned	225,000	174,787	105,000	0	0	1,210,565	21,000	Ziska Architects
Cincinnati	n/a	B	2,080,688	1,320,303	19,950	66.18	190,651	Owned		344,734	6,561	0	2,034,123	46,565	0	Steed-Hammond…
Cincinnati	n/a	B	1,709,086	1,279,097	20,670	61.88	123,366	Owned		306,623	7,443	0	1,668,034	41,052	0	PDT/Architects
Cleveland	500	M	34,220,734	27,134,941	261,223	103.88	1,706,392	Owned		5,379,401	1,480,000	0	0	34,220,734	93,754	Hardy…; Madison
Freeport	5	B	160,754	134,897	864	156.13	1,200	Owned		24,657	7,910	0	0	67,000	0	HRJL Architects
Maple Heights	27	B	1,597,989	1,018,952	35,315	28.85	432,687	Owned		146,350	240,000	0	0	1,597,989	0	David Holzheimer
Parma	88	B	1,737,110	1,238,382	15,602	79.37	239,265	Owned		259,463	90,000	0	0	1,737,110	0	Fogle & Stenzel
Parma	88	S	1,458,807	789,000	29,803	26.48	531,057	Owned		138,750	320,000	0	0	1,458,807	0	Spice Constantino
Springboro	20	S	639,998	448,156	3,800	117.94	75,000	Owned		47,842	20,000	0	0	639,998	0	Pinnace Architects
Wellsville	10	M	1,266,016	973,651	8,334	116.83	103,544	Owned		188,821	28,000	0	0	716,016	550,000	Beck & Tabeling
Oklahoma																
Broken Bow	15	S	1,224,330	883,540	17,000	51.97	95,908	Owned	95,000	149,882	35,000	94,600	0	1,099,430	30,300	Wesley Johnson
Coalgate	6	S	325,000	282,000	6,050	29.92	48,000	Owned	64,000	32,000	15,000	100,000	50,000	0	175,000	Ernie Woodward
Konawa	3	M	352,546	285,300	3,075	92.78	50,000	Owned		17,246	7,500	45,000	0	307,546	0	Locke, Wright, Pruitt
Sapulpa	18	M	1,275,576	1,020,000	18,622	54.77	189,000	Owned		66,576	56,000	0	0	29,376	1,246,200	Olson-Coffey
Tulsa	36	B	720,047	486,656	7,200	67.59	75,504	Owned	120,678	37,209	36,000	0	0	599,369	120,678	Page-Zebrowski
Oregon																
Gresham	n/a	B	714,645	507,000	20,000	25.35	126,525	Owned		81,120	75,000	0	0	714,645	0	Thomas Hacker
Portland	n/a	B	946,240	783,000	5,997	130.57	37,960	Owned		125,280	30,000	0	0	946,240	0	Thomas Hacker
Portland	n/a	B	335,060	269,746	3,500	77.07	22,155	Leased		43,159	25,000	0	0	335,060	0	Hacker R. Brown
Portland	n/a	B	1,100,920	916,000	6,060	151.16	38,360	Owned		146,560	30,000	0	0	1,100,920	0	Thomas Hacker
Pennsylvania																
Conshohocken	9	B	633,121	574,826	6,380	90.1	6,725	Owned		78,570	15,000	65,484	234,000	25,000	335,637	Diseroad Wolff…
Everett	13	M	257,923	241,959	3,600	67.21	8,370	Owned		7,594	60,000	0	126,000	124,002	7,921	Richard C. Kochenour
Rhode Island																
Warwick	85	M	7,142,000	5,973,000	63,000	94.81	412,000	Owned		757,000	300,000	75,000	492,000	4,900,000	1,675,000	Keyes Assocs.
South Dakota																
Rapid City	60	M	207,183	87,809	6,000	14.63	113,954	Owned		5,420	200,000	80,183	0	127,000	0	Lund Assocs.

Symbol Code: B—Branch Library; BS—Branch & System Headquarters; M—Main Library; MS—Main & System Headquarters; S—System Headquarters; n/a—not available

Table 2 / Public Library Buildings, Additions and Renovations, 1999 *(cont.)*

Community	Pop. ('000)	Code	Project Cost	Const. Cost	Gross Sq. Ft.	Sq. Ft. Cost	Equip. Cost	Site Cost	Other Costs	Volumes	Federal Funds	State Funds	Local Funds	Gift Funds	Architect
Vermillion	14	M	290,585	210,326	11,000	19.11	51,314	Owned	28,945	80,000	48,000	0	242,585	0	Chris Schiltz
Viborg	1	M	29,354	20,604	1,440	14.13	8,750	Owned	0	6,870	12,888	0	16,466	0	Viborg PL
Tennessee															
Nashville	21	B	1,188,188	1,013,274	12,210	82.99	71,167	Owned	103,747	10,000	592,188	150,000	446,000	0	McFarlin Huitt...
Texas															
Austin	43	B	2,566,550	166,694	15,120	11.02	52,377	299,243	2,048,236	80,000	0	0	2,566,550	0	T. Michael Rogers
Kingsland	8	B	574,892	433,919	9,200	47.16	55,199	2,000	83,774	27,832	0	0	65,734	509,158	E.R. Biglari
Vermont															
Northfield	6	M	1,344,983	1,045,336	15,324	68.22	20,000	74,350	205,297	n/a	100,000	52,500	400,000	792,483	Black River Design
Washington															
Port Angeles	19	M	5,212,978	3,820,091	36,209	105.5	416,527	571,453	404,907	308,076	0	0	5,212,978	0	M. Lewis...
Wisconsin															
Ripon	11	M	2,100,000	1,536,215	20,000	76.81	140,000	Owned	423,785	25,000	0	0	300,000	1,800,000	Angus Young...
Wyoming															
Lusk	3	M	386,886	339,871	2,016	168.58	12,819	Owned	34,195	30,797	49,085	171,159	143,378	23,263	Ken Tobin
Torrington	12	M	393,621	302,673	6,915	43.77	80,938	Owned	10,010	28,875	0	34,000	278,683	80,938	Daniel P. Swift

Symbol Code: B—Branch Library; BS—Branch & System Headquarters; M—Main Library; MS—Main & System Headquarters; S—System Headquarters; n/a—not available

Table 3 / Public Library Buildings, Six-Year Cost Summary

	Fiscal 1993	Fiscal 1994	Fiscal 1995	Fiscal 1996	Fiscal 1997	Fiscal 1999**
Number of new buildings	113	108	99	100	97	77
Number of ARRs*	105	127	124	145	128	118
Sq. ft. new buildings	1,896,197	1,818,522	2,102,851	2,002,067	2,153,203	1,555,583
Sq. ft. ARRs	1,878,628	2,163,909	2,469,345	2,315,523	2,710,599	2,188,221
New Buildings						
Construction cost	$183,978,065	$176,678,555	$232,050,462	$286,141,319	$227,740,506	$192,319,192
Equipment cost	22 651,001	27,617,314	28,239,712	57,222,035	35,983,384	25,382,314
Site cost	28 353,201	34,696,765	31,406,749	16,391,748	33,630,070	22,634,855
Other cost	32,275,926	30,114,637	42,946,629	49,498,901	40,060,597	43,631,263
Total—Project cost	267,770,932	271,051,271	334,643,552	409,254,003	337,414,557	283,967,624
ARRs—Project cost	160,825,726	345,135,792	281,750,499	314,191,342	324,762,086	280,604,091
New & ARR Project Cost	428,596,658	616,187,063	616,394,051	723,445,345	662,176,643	564,571,715
Fund Sources						
Federal, new buildings	4,320,934	4,483,792	10,532,079	17,719,253	4,572,130	7,655,690
Federal, ARRs	3,646,307	6,188,756	3,292,272	13,771,483	7,698,270	9,268,183
Federal, total	7,967,241	10,672,548	13,824,351	31,490,736	12,270,400	16,923,873
State, new buildings	26,376,138	45,559,588	31,051,654	32,089,611	73,081,134	17,122,988
State, ARRs	10,841,063	10,361,213	28,482,199	21,212,540	62,169,948	21,677,529
State, total	37,217,201	55,920,801	59,533,853	53,302,151	135,251,082	38,800,517
Local, new buildings	208,363,C30	203,676,929	268,609,523	301,996,679	228,793,054	226,616,333
Local, ARRs	141,961,411	302,050,882	227,108,845	182,163,428	233,525,418	201,166,513
Local, total	350,325,341	505,727,811	495,718,368	484,160,107	462,318,472	427,782,846
Gift, new buildings	28,878,559	17,663,214	25,433,205	57,478,470	31,168,178	32,563,613
Gift, ARRs	4,389,236	26,614,547	23,951,472	97,019,403	21,345,010	48,614,252
Gift, total	33,267,795	44,277,761	49,384,677	154,497,873	52,513,188	81,177,865
Total Funds Used	428,777,578	616,598,921	618,461,249	723,450,867	662,353,142	564,685,101

* Additions, remodelings, and renovations.
**Summary statistics were not kept for Fiscal 1998.

Table 4 / New Academic Library Buildings, 1999

Name of Institution	Project Cost	Gross Area (Sq. Ft.)	Sq. Ft. Cost	Construction Cost	Equipment Cost	Book Capacity	Seating Capacity	Architect
Central Missouri State Univ. Lib., Warrensburg	$30,500,000	196,000	$130.10	$25,500,000	$2,750,000	2,300,000	1,400	Shepley, Bulfinch...
East Tennessee State Univ. Lib., Johnson City	28,000,000	191,700	112.91	21,645,000	6,355,000	800,000	1,800	Ken Ross; David Leonard
Eastern Connecticut State Univ., Willimantic	27,647,556	127,000	137.99	17,524,427	2,918,000	519,396	914	Dubose Assocs.
Mesa College Learning Resource Center, San Diego	19,212,776	107,000	153.39	16,412,776	2,800,000	170,000	775,000	M.W. Steele Group
Mather Lib., Geophysical Inst./Intl. Arctic Research Center, Univ. of Alaska, Fairbanks*	18,500,000	14,058	188.00	2,642,900	n/a	48,500	106	Kumin Assocs.
Hollins Univ. Lib., Roanoke, VA	15,199,000	56,400	214.88	12,119,000	1,396,000	300,000	280	Perry, Dean, Rogers
Pendergraft Lib. & Technology Center, Arkansas Tech Univ., Russellville	12,321,000	89,000	100.00	8,900,000	3,421,000	262,000	485	AMR Architects
Stonehill College Lib., N. Easton, MA	n/a	60,000	150.00	9,000,000	287,650	260,000	500	Shepley Bulfinch...
Stetson Univ. College of Law, Gulfport, FL	8,500,000	58,440	116.35	6,800,000	921,980	210,750	487	Canerday & Assocs.
Pikes Peak Community College, LRC, Rampart Range Campus, Colorado Springs	n/a	9,000	100.00	900,000	n/a	15,000	80	Davis Ptnrshp; Christiansen
Center for Creative Studies College of Art & Design, Detroit	145,000	7,500	n/a	n/a	n/a	60,000	80	J. Scott; Ghafari Assocs.

*Library part of larger project.

Table 5 / Academic Library Buildings, Additions and Renovations, 1999

Name of Institution	Status	Project Cost	Gross Area (Sq. Ft.)	Sq. Ft. Cost	Construction Cost	Equipment Cost	Book Capacity	Seating Capacity	Architect
Homer D. Babbidge Library, University of Connecticut, Storrs	Total	$40,150,000	393,085	$82.54	$32,363,696	n/a	2,500,000	2,330	Allan Dehar Assocs.
	New	n/a	17,575	129.07	2,268,439	n/a	n/a	n/a	
	Renovated	n/a	374,510	80.36	30,095,257	n/a	n/a	n/a	
Joyner Library, East Carolina University, Greenville, NC	Total	30,258,396	280,575	81.75	22,938,217	$5,338,683	1,500,000	1,900	Walter Robbs Callahan...
	New	n/a	150,612	n/a	n/a	n/a	n/a	n/a	
	Renovated	n/a	129,963	n/a	n/a	n/a	n/a	n/a	
J. Edgar & Louise S. Monroe Library, Loyola University, New Orleans	Total	18,267,098	148,480	104.17	15,467,098	2,800,000	550,000	700	The Mathes Group
	New	15,124,556	111,392	116.92	13,023,553	2,100,603	430,000	650	
	Renovated	3,142,542	37,088	65.87	2,443,145	699,397	120,000	50	
Dickinson College, Carlisle, PA	Total	12,530,000	113,240	n/a	n/a	n/a	500,000	525	Perry, Dean, Rogers
	New	10,530,000	46,000	n/a	n/a	n/a	n/a	n/a	
	Renovated	2,030,000	67,240	n/a	n/a	n/a	n/a	n/a	
Archbishop Lakoves Library & LRC Hellenic College–Holy Cross School of Theology, Brookline, MA	Total	7,216,000	34,000	164.12	5,580,030	861,000	180,000	168	Tappé/Cunningham...
	New	6,841,000	25,000	214.20	5,355,030	761,000	140,000	96	
	Renovated	375,000	9,000	25.00	225,000	100,000	40,000	72	
Irving S. Gilmore Music Library, Yale University, New Haven, CT	Total	n/a	26,000	n/a	r/a	n/a	125,000	177	Shepley Bulfinch...
	New	n/a	12,700	n/a	r/a	n/a	55,000	158	
	Renovated	n/a	13,300	n/a	r/a	n/a	70,000	19	

Table 6 / Academic Library Buildings, Additions Only, 1999

Name of Institution	Project Cost	Gross Area (Sq. Ft.)	Sq. Ft. Cost	Construction Cost	Equipment Cost	Book Capacity	Seating Capacity	Architect
Fondren Library Center, Southern Methodist University, Dallas	$2,500,000	8,500	$200.00	$1,700,000	$95,000	n/a	125	Leo A. Daly
University of Texas–Pan American Library, Edinburg	n/a	n/a	n/a	n/a	155,000	337,763	91	Tom Ashley

Table 7 / Academic Library Buildings, Renovations Only, 1999

Name of Institution	Project Cost	Gross Area (Sq. Ft.)	Sq. Ft. Cost	Construction Cost	Equipment Cost	Book Capacity	Seating Capacity	Architect
Samford University Library, Birmingham, AL	$6,250,000	80,000	$67.23	$5,378,000	$872,000	621,630	891	Woollen, Molzan...; Richey...
Timken Science Library, College of Wooster (OH)	4,050,000	19,042	161.70	3,079,000	317,000	95,000	144	Perry, Dean, Rogers...
Todd Wehr Memorial Library, Carroll College, Waukesha, WI	2,985,000	44,251	63.28	2,800,000	185,000	190,000	400	Performa
New York School of Interior Design	869,808	3,025	240.00	726,000	115,365	10,000	41	Hardy Holzman Pfeiffer
O.J. Snyder Memorial Library, Philadelphia College of Osteopathic Medicine	787,560	16,176	n/a	n/a	n/a	50,000	126	Granary Design
Payton Philanthropic Studies Library, Indiana Univ., Purdue Univ., Indianapolis (IUPUI)	n/a	18,000	26.17	471,000	$85,000	40,000	120	Gajinder Singh
Tompkins-McCaw Library Training Room, Virginia Commonwealth Univ., Richmond	360,675	1,354	136.12	184,308	176,367	0	20	RGA-SSA Architects
Tompkins-McCaw Library Reading Room, Virginia Commonwealth Univ., Richmond	129,150	3,208	40.26	129,150	0	1,080	50	Kelso & Easter
Purdue University Calumet Library, Hammond, IN	n/a	27,500	4.69	129,000	0	253,388	600	none
Overton Media Center/J. Drake Edens Library, Columbia College, Columbia, SC	83,000	3,000	20.00	60,000	23,000	n/a	58	W. Daniel Shelley
Paul & Philip Gaunt Library, Magnolia Bible College, Kosciusko, MS	n/a	2,793	12.53	35,000	n/a	1,500	6	Gary Kirkendall

Expenditures for Resources in School Library Media Centers, 1997–1998: How Do You Measure Up?

Marilyn L. Miller

Professor Emeritus and Former Chair, Department of Library and Information Studies, University of North Carolina, Greensboro

Marilyn L. Shontz

Associate Professor, Library Education Program, Rowan University, Glassboro, New Jersey

The *School Library Journal* (*SLJ*) survey of school library expenditures for fiscal year 1997–1998 shows that the average school library budget was up $1,000 from two years earlier, and that media specialists were enjoying higher salaries than ever—increases of as much as $4,000 a year for those working at the junior high/middle school level.

The salary boost is a genuine gain, but that rosy budget figure is somewhat misleading. Even with a $1,000 increase there was still a net loss in buying power. That additional grand barely got libraries back to where they were four years earlier, when the average book cost 9 percent less.

In addition to these statistics, here are the other major findings:

- Nine percent of library media specialists (LMSs) are not certified in library media, and 10 percent work only part time.
- Seventy-five percent of library media centers (LMCs) have access to the Web, up from 49 percent two years ago.
- Eighty-one percent of LMCs have acceptable-use policies, and 41 percent use an Internet filter.
- Time for planning with teachers—both formal and informal sessions—has dwindled by an average of 20 percent since 1993–1994.

The purpose of this series, first begun in 1983, is to provide an up-to-date account and longitudinal view of national trends in school library media spending. (For more on how the survey is conducted, see "Behind the Data" on p. 480.) In addition, each biannual survey collects new data that focuses on one or more previously unstudied aspect of our profession. This time we:

- Offer an expanded look at computer-use policies and practices (Table 7)
- Identify access to basic electronic resources (Table 8)
- Examine the preparation and certification of LMC staff (Table 10)
- Look closely at LMS–teacher planning in the elementary school (Table 11)
- Explore communication between LMSs and teachers (Table 13)
- Compare LMC services among grade levels (Table 14)

Adapted from *School Library Journal*, October 1999.

Tables 1–6: Budget Allocation

Thanks to a small increase in local funding, median allocations are back up to $9,500, right where they were in 1993–1994 (Table 1). Though fewer schools report receiving federal funds, the size of the median grant is up $600 since 1994. These two increases bring the average total expenditure up $440 over 1993–1994.

Comparisons of mean and median expenditures from all sources in 1997–1998 show that some schools are on average $7,115 above the median of $12,185. Pursuing this further, we discovered that the range of local expenditures is vast, with one school spending $330 while another spent $632,000. While this latter figure undoubtedly reflects the opening of a new library, significant differences in expenditures between richer and poorer schools are still cause for concern.

Sixty-six percent of the respondents reported receiving funds from gifts and fund raising. Although this number has increased slightly since 1993–1994, their efforts yielded small rewards: an average of $1,000 per school. The means reported in this category indicate some of the respondents are more successful than others, with an average of $3,701. The major sources of gift and fund-raising dollars for school libraries were as follows: 12 percent reported receipts from book fairs; 8 percent received contributions from parent groups; 6 percent reported funds from petty cash, fines, and lost-book revenue; and 6 percent received support from business partnerships.

Table 1 / Mean and Median Expenditures for All Resources, 1997–1998
(all funding sources)

Expenditures	Number Responding	Mean	Median
Local			
Total all local funds	524	$15,918	$9,500
Federal			
Total all federal funds	144	3,669	2,594
Gift Funds			
Total all gift/fund raising	356	3,701	1,200
Total all funds			
Books	504	7,279	6,000
Periodicals	502	1,422	1,000
Microforms	62	1,451	750
AV resources/equipment	430	3,036	1,525
Computer resources/equipment	413	7,697	2,700
Total expenditures	532	$19,300	$12,185

Table 1 presents mean and median expenditures for all resources from most funding sources, including local school budgets, the federal government, gifts, and fund raising. It does not include funds allocated through district media centers, regional consortiums, or other leasing or granting agencies. "Local" defines money allocated by local school boards, states, and/or counties that fund all or part of local school expenses and are administered through a local education agency (LEA).

Tables 2–3 show expenditures for individual schools, while Tables 4–5 reflect per-pupil spending. Local funds for books are $1,000 higher, an increase of 62 cents per pupil over 1995–1996 (Table 5). Table 4 shows that per-pupil expenditures for other resources are not improving. Since 1990 spending for AV materials has actually declined, while expenditures for periodicals, software, and CD-ROMs have been stagnant or shown only small gains (Table 5). Overall, book budgets show promise, but despite an initial influx of technology money earlier in the decade, spending on media and software is now weak, which is ironic given the strong economy and community interest in education and technology.

In Table 6, the mixed-level schools categorized under "Other" had the highest print expenditures and the largest per-pupil Total Materials Expenditures (TME). The median figures also show that compared to schools at other levels, high schools in 1997–1998 added fewer volumes and had fewer books per pupil; on the other hand, high schools purchased more videos per pupil than other schools. Those collection statistics are also mirrored in the spending categories, which indicate that high schools spend less on average for books but more for periodicals, microforms, CD-ROMs, and AV materials than other schools.

(text continues on page 471)

Table 2 / Mean and Median Expenditures per School for LMC Resources, 1997–1998
(local funds only)

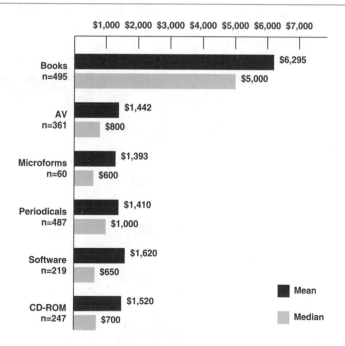

Table 3 / Median Expenditures per School for LMC Resources, 1990–1998
(local funds only)

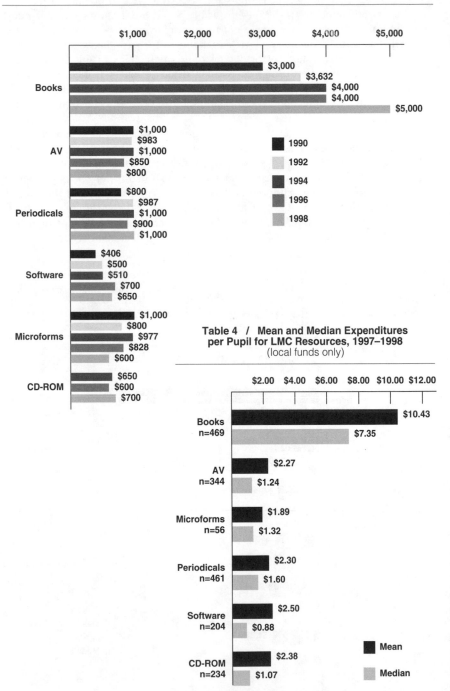

Table 4 / Mean and Median Expenditures
per Pupil for LMC Resources, 1997–1998
(local funds only)

Table 5 / **Median Expenditures per Pupil for LMC Resources, 1990–1998**
(local funds only)

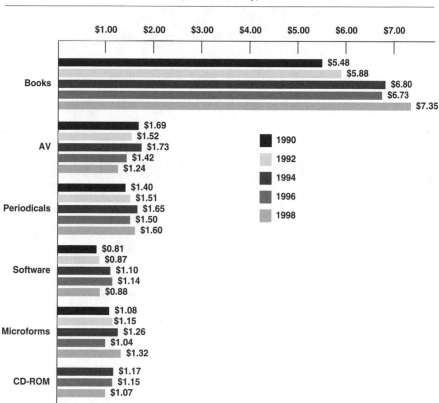

(continued from page 469)

Tables 7–8: Technology

Table 7 reports the growth in acquisition and use of technology. The number of LMCs receiving extra funding—such as gifts, grants, district monies, or federal or special state funds—for technology is up: 46 percent receive extra funding for computer software; 41 percent receive more for telecommunications, which includes e-mail and online services; 30 percent are allocated additional money for resource sharing, such as computer time, postage, and telephone and copying expenses; and 22 percent receive special funding for Web subscriptions and access, a new category for this survey.

In 1995–1996, only half of the schools reported having access to the Internet. In 1997–1998, that number jumped to 74 percent, and of those LMCs that are online, 61 percent reported that the school or LMC has its own home page. We asked media spe-

(text continues on page 474)

Table 6 / LMC Collection Size and Local Expenditures by School Level, 1997–1998

Collections	Elementary n=234		Junior High/Middle n=131		Senior High n=154		Other n=63	
	median	mean	median	mean	median	mean	median	mean
Size of book collection	10,000	10,500	11,000	11,518	12,000	13,888	10,000	12,623
Volumes added, 1997–1998	439	622	400	623	350	505	492	594
Number of books per pupil	17	21	15	17	14	17	23	27
Volumes discarded, 1997–1998	100	262	178	407	100	411	190	271
Size of audio collection	0	9	0	7	0	12	0	7
Number of audio CD items added, 1997–1998	0	3	0	2	0	3	0	2
Audio CD items discarded, 1997–1998	0	0	0	1	0	0	0	0
Size of video collection	151	219	150	221	260	404	160	246
Videos added, 1997–1998	20	38	10	26	25	49	3	60
Videos per pupil	0.31	0.43	0.22	0.31	0.29	0.47	0.36	0.48
Videos discarded	0	5	0	3	0	6	0	4
Size of computer software collection	15	68	10	39	10	29	6	19
Computer software added, 1997–1998	0	5	0	3	0	3	1	3
Computer software per pupil	0.13	0.03	0.01	0.05	0.01	0.04	0.01	0.05
Computer software discarded, 1997–1998	0.00	6.46	0.00	20.08	0.00	5.10	0.00	1.02
Size of CD-ROM collection	30	60	21	40	15	27	20	26
CD-ROMs added, 1997–1998	4	11	3	10	4	6	3	6
CD-ROMs per pupil	0.53	0.12	0.03	0.06	0.02	0.04	0.04	0.06
CD-ROMs discarded, 1997–1998	0.00	0.58	0.00	0.62	0.00	0.90	0.00	0.12

Expenditures

Books	$4,086.00	$5,481.88	$5,150.00	$6,333.71	$6,000.00	$7,861.95	$5,200.00	$5,645.28
Books per pupil	7.46	10.65	7.56	9.43	6.07	11.12	8.34	10.28
Periodicals	650.00	772.41	1,090.00	1,274.76	2,000.00	2,533.80	1,000.00	1,418.20
Periodicals per pupil	1.22	1.54	1.63	2.08	2.44	3.46	2.12	2.90
Microforms	525.00	518.75	700.00	876.21	725.00	1,825.88	650.00	1,349.40
Microforms per pupil	0.75	0.85	1.44	1.43	1.59	2.33	1.98	2.08
Audiovisual materials	675.00	1,329.37	929.00	1,379.00	1,000.00	1,705.00	600.00	1,351.73
Audiovisual materials per pupil	1.22	2.53	1.10	1.82	1.33	2.05	1.72	2.67
Computer software	500.00	1,598.73	700.00	1,108.29	799.50	2,306.15	575.00	873.42
Computer software per pupil	0.91	2.42	1.07	1.75	0.70	3.10	1.53	2.26
CD-ROMs	422.00	654.93	800.00	1,495.89	1,700.00	2,452.56	500.00	1,246.24
CD-ROMs per pupil	0.80	1.35	0.95	2.13	1.88	3.40	0.97	2.61
Total materials expenditures (TME)	$10,970.00	$15,481.86	$11,500.00	$15,437.92	$17,479.00	$29,335.94	$12,606.50	$17,821.84
TME per pupil	$19.00	$28.57	$18.77	$21.97	$18.85	$42.94	$22.59	$34.87

Table 6 describes, quantitatively, the categories of media in LMCs by school level. Expenditures from all sources—local, federal, gifts, and fund raising—are shown as Total Materials Expenditures (TME). TME is reported at the bottom of each column for purposes of comparison. TME excludes salaries, but reflects all expenditures for resources, including AV equipment, computer hardware, online sources, rentals, leasing, supplies, and maintenance.

Table 7 / LMCs & Technology, 1997–1998

	Number Responding "Yes"	Percent
Additional funds provided for (n=543) :		
Computer software	249	46
Telecommunications, Internet access	232	41
CD-ROMs	160	28
Videodiscs	60	11
Technical processing	91	16
Resource sharing	169	30
Online subscriptions	127	22
LMC Uses (n=566):		
Cable TV	385	67
Broadcast TV	200	35
Closed circuit TV	191	33
Distance education, one-way audio-video	47	08
Distance education, two-way audio-video	42	07
LMC Has (n=566):		
Local area network (LAN)	409	71
Wide area network (WAN)	300	52
Computers with modem	327	57
Access to Internet and e-mail	472	83
CD-ROMs	451	80
Access to Web	419	74
Fax machine in LMC	124	22
Access to fax machine in school	385	68
Telephone in LMC	503	90
LMC Is member of resource sharing network (n=566):	318	58
Network is linked electronically	227	41
LMC has online computer catalog	403	71
LMC has online circulation system	472	83
LMC has online catalog and online circulation system	396	70
School or LMC has WWW home page	344	61
School or LMC has acceptable-use policy (AUP)	461	81
School or LMC uses Internet filtering software	236	41

(continued from page 471)

cialists to identify who is responsible for managing their school and LMC home pages, and here's what they reported:

- LMC staff, 14 percent
- School technology staff, 52 percent
- District level staff, 19 percent
- Others (students, parents, teachers, or volunteers), 15 percent

Cable TV remains the most popular television option, with 67 percent of LMCs tuning in. Fifty-eight percent of media specialists continue to participate in resource-

Table 8 / Electronic Resources, 1997–1998

	Available in LMC only	Available school-wide	Total schools with access
Reading tools:			
Accelerated Reader or Reading Counts!*	13%	15%	35%
Reference sources:			
Electric Library	8	7	15
EBSCOhost	17	10	27
InfoTrac	13	5	18
Microsoft Bookshelf	12	5	18
NewsBank	9	3	12
ProQuest	12	8	20
Scholastic Online	4	5	9
SIRS	17	11	30
State Library Database	16	10	27
Tom	4	3	7
WilsonLine RG for Young People	2	1	2
WilsonLine RG Abstracts	3	1	4

*Since this survey was conducted, Electronic Bookshelf was acquired by Scholastic and is now called Scholastic Reading Counts!

sharing networks, of which 41 percent report being linked electronically. An impressive 81 percent of LMSs report having an acceptable-use policy, and 41 percent say their libraries use software to filter the Internet. Table 8 identifies which electronic resources are used in LMCs and elsewhere in schools. In 1998 EBSCO*host*, state library databases, SIRS, and electronic reading programs such as Accelerated Reader and Electronic Bookshelf (which is now called Scholastic Reading Counts!) were available in more than a quarter of the reporting LMCs.

Tables 9–10: Human Resources

Personnel levels in LMCs have remained roughly the same since 1993–1994. On average, LMCs are still staffed by one library media specialist, and the average secondary school still enjoys full-time, paid support staff. Volunteers, including both adult and student assistants, continue to fluctuate in number, and, according to Table 9, are not a major source of assistance. Salaries took a sizable leap and are the most encouraging aspect of the staffing data. Salaries increased across all levels: $2,000 for elementary schools, $4,000 for junior high/middle schools, $3,000 for high schools, and more than $3,500 for those in combined-level schools.

Table 10 reports certification areas of LMSs. Slightly more than half (56 percent) of the respondents are certified both in school library media and a subject area. Thirty-five percent are certified only in school library media, and nine percent have no media certification. This finding raises interesting questions about the readiness of nearly one-half of the LMSs who are without the combination of library and teacher certification: Are they adequately prepared to manage a media center and fully collaborate with teachers?

Table 9 / LMS Experience, Salary, and Supporting Staff, 1997–1998

	Elementary n=234		Junior High/Middle n=131		Senior High n=140		Other n=63		Total All n=573	
	median	mean	median	mean	median	mean	median	mean	median	mean
No. media specialists in school	1.00	0.91	1.00	1.00	1.00	1.21	1.00	1.09	1.00	1.03
Years experience in K–12 schools	18	18	20	20	22	21	15	16	20	19
Years experience in library/media	11	13	13	15	17	15	9	11	12	14
Salary of head media specialist	$40,000	$40,338	$42,000	$43,936	$42,000	$42,700	$31,500	$32,912	$40,000	$41,016
Student assistants	0.00	2.91	0.00	3.85	3.00	5.15	0.00	5.16	0.00	0.00
Support staff/paid clerks	0.50	0.61	1.00	0.72	1.00	0.97	0.50	0.67	0.50	0.74
Adult volunteers	2.00	5.62	0.00	1.59	0.00	0.48	1.00	3.63	0.00	3.18

Table 10 / Certification Areas of Head Library Media Specialist, 1997–1998

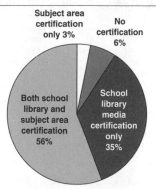

Subject area certification only 3%

No certification 6%

Both school library and subject area certification 56%

School library media certification only 35%

We asked respondents who hold advanced graduate degrees to describe their academic preparation. Respondents reported degrees in:

- School library media only, 47 percent
- Education only, 14 percent
- Subject area only, 2 percent
- School library media and education, 15 percent
- School library media, education, and a subject area, 3 percent
- Education and subject area, 2 percent

Tables 11–14: Programs and Services

An additional focus of the 1997–1998 survey is scheduling and LMS–teacher planning in elementary schools. Those with flexible scheduling report a slightly higher staffing level (Table 11). They also report spending more time planning with teachers and also planning with a higher percentage of teachers. Forty-five percent of the LMSs using flexible scheduling plan with the majority of teachers (more than 71 percent of teachers), compared to 29 percent of those with combined fixed/flexible schedules and only 13 percent of those with fixed schedules. The vision in *Information Power: Building Partnerships for Learning* (ALA, 1998) of the media specialist as teacher depends on LMSs developing and using a variety of strategies to plan instruction alongside classroom teachers. Table 12 indicates that we still have a long way to go before fulfilling that vision. In fact, the figures show a reverse trend. Over the past four years, the number of hours spent in formal and informal planning shows a persistent and disturbing decline at each grade level.

Table 13 describes and compares how LMSs communicate with teachers and principals. (The information on principals comes from the 1995–1996 data of LMC expenditures and resources.) The most consistent opportunity for LMSs to communicate with teachers and principals is the monthly teachers' meeting, where 44.6 percent of LMSs talk to teachers and 72.2 percent talk to principals. When it comes to communication, technology helps, as 43.4 percent report tele-

Table 11 / Comparison of Type of LMC Schedule Used in Elementary LMCs and LMS/Teacher Planning, 1997–1998

	Flexible Schedule n=37	Combined Fixed/Flex n=97	Fixed Schedule n=95
Percent of LMSs who regularly plan with teachers			
Yes	86	72	49
No	14	28	51
Percent of teachers planning with LMS			
0–15%	16	12	31
16–30%	19	25	30
31–70%	19	34	27
More than 71%	45	29	13
Mean no. of hours of teacher/LMS planning per week			
Formal	1.33	0.88	0.35
Informal	2.23	1.83	1.78
Total teacher-LMS planning hours	3.54	2.71	2.13
Mean no. LMS on staff—full and part time	1.00	0.95	0.85
Mean no. support staff—full and part time	0.65	0.64	0.59

phoning and 42.7 percent e-mail their colleagues. One in three LMSs creates an annual report for the principal, but only 12.7 percent share it with teachers.

In past reports, we have identified high-service LMCs as those in which 17 or more of 22 identified services are available to students and teachers. Those reports compared services according to the availability of technology and participation in site-based management. Table 14 compares services among grade levels. Across grade levels, reference assistance and informal library instruction are part of the job for more than 90 percent of LMSs. The same grade-level consistency is revealed for integrating skills instruction into the curriculum, though only 61 percent report doing so. High school LMSs are more likely to provide staff development for teachers than their counterparts at other grade levels, and they are also more likely to help both teachers and students use off-campus resources. On the other hand, high school LMSs are less likely than their counterparts to provide reading, listening, and viewing guidance, and they are also less likely to help parents realize the importance of lifelong learning. Coordinating video production is the responsibility of only one in four LMSs, as is coordinating computer networks. Only a third of all respondents report coordinating in-school production of materials, such as overhead transparencies and posters.

One interesting discrepancy appears in Table 14 with regard to the curriculum-planning role of media specialists. Seventy-nine percent report collaborating with teachers, but only one-half report working with school curriculum committees. And only 58 percent report helping teachers develop and implement learning activities and evaluate outcomes.

Table 15: District-Level Leadership

In 1987–1988, 40 percent of the respondents reported having access to a district-level coordinator of library media services. Ten years later that figure has

Table 12 / LMS/Teacher Instructional Planning Activity by Grade, 1997–1998

	Mean No. Hours Formal Instructional Planning	Mean No. Hours Informal Instructional Planning	Mean No. Hours Total Planning
Elementary	0.75	1.90	2.64
Junior high/middle	0.98	2.78	3.74
High school	1.11	2.43	3.54
Other	0.75	2.08	2.83
Total	0.89	2.25	3.14

Table 13 / Media Specialist Communication with Teachers and Principals, 1997–1998

Ways LMSs Communicate with:	Teachers n=565	Principals n=617
Face-to-face formal meetings daily/weekly	18.9%	27.4%
Face-to-face formal meetings weekly/monthly	18.4	30.3
Face-to-face formal meetings 3–5 times a year	20.2	28.4
Teachers meeting at least once a month	44.6	72.2
Written memo/informational communication daily/weekly	34.2	52.2
Written memo/informational communication monthly	39.8	26.8
Written memo/informational communication 3–5 times a year	24.2	15.2
SLM program newsletter at least twice a year	19.1	16.0
SLM program annual report	12.7	36.3
Phone conversations as needed	43.4	45.9
E-mail as needed	42.7	23.3

dropped to 33 percent. During that same period, the percentage of LMSs report-ing no district coordinator has risen from 46 to 54. The remaining participants report access to half-time district leadership. In comparing services between LMCs with and without that level of leadership, eight characteristics appear at statistically significant levels. Of these eight, six center around technology. Schools with district leadership have more funds available for the repair and maintenance of district computers and AV equipment, use more television, and are more likely to have an online catalog and a wide area network. They are, in other words, more likely to be high-tech schools.

A Look to the Future

A graduate student challenged us following the publication of our last survey. She indicated several places in the text where we had been free in commenting on the data, thus leaving ourselves open to criticism that we are not as objective as we should be. She is right; we aren't always.

We are emotionally as well as intellectually involved with the findings. This series has been a major part of our professional and academic lives. We exult when we find promising results. We lament when we learn how little some professionals have

Table 14 / Comparison of Library Media Program Services by Grade Level

LM Program Service	Elementary (n=234)	Middle/ Junior High (n=131)	Senior High (n=140)	Other (n=63)	Total All (n=565)
1. Offers a program of curriculum-integrated skills instruction	60%	67%	61%	52%	61%
2. Informally instructs students in the use of resources	91	93	96	90	93
3. Conducts workshops for teachers	30	29	43	24	32
4. Assists school curriculum committee with recommendations	53	50	47	40	50
5. Collaborates with teachers	76	83	85	74	79
6. Helps teachers develop, implement, and evaluate learning	55	67	58	55	58
7. Provides teachers with information about new resources	81	85	90	77	84
8. Provides reference assistance to students and teachers	97	95	96	95	96
9. Helps students and teachers use resources outside the school	63	74	79	76	71
10. Provides interlibrary loan service for students and teachers	56	56	63	53	57
11. Provides reading/listening/viewing guidance for students	85	83	78	81	82
12. Helps parents realize the importance of lifelong learning	71	43	21	69	52
13. Coordinates in-school production of materials	28	32	35	32	31
14. Coordinates video production activities	28	26	24	24	26
15. Coordinated cable TV and related activities	41	45	45	40	43
16. Coordinates computer networks	29	27	33	13	27

to work with. And we are cross when we see things slide or take too long to catch on. The rush to wire libraries juxtaposed with the slow emergence of LMS–teacher collaboration is a good example.

To keep a positive perspective, librarians need to be ever mindful of our history. Remember, there were libraries before there were educational institutions. We and our organized resources and programs are the bedrock of learning. Our 90 years of school library development, from Mary Kingsbury and the first high school library in the early years of this century to the hundreds of good programs available as we move into a new century, is a testament to leadership, perseverance, and professionalism. With the new edition of *Information Power*, we are ready to move into 2000. And we hope we will still be asking questions and exulting and exhorting over the findings.

Behind the Data

Survey Population

This data represents the results of a questionnaire mailed in September 1997 to 1,500 LMCs. The respondents were selected by systematic random sampling from *SLJ*'s school-based subscription list covering all 50 states.

Table 15 / LMC and School Characteristics by District-Level Media Director Status, 1997–1998

	With Full-Time n=185		With Part-Time n=73		Without n=295	
	count	percent	count	percent	count	percent
*Use of library media advisory committee	66	36	19	26	45	15
Availability of selection policy	156	84	70	96	220	75
Book collection less than 30% out of date	143	77	59	81	217	74
Materials budget is more than last year	60	33	20	28	103	35
Book budget is more than last year	58	32	15	21	90	30
Additional materials/supplies received from district	137	74	62	85	161	55
*District provided LMC with AV/computer maintenance	79	44	39	54	67	23
Planning with teachers for integrated instruction	136	74	48	66	192	65
Total mean hours LMS/teacher planning more than 2 hours per week	74	40	34	47	111	38
More than 30% of teachers plan with LMS	64	47	36	52	87	44
LM center produces newsletter	43	23	16	22	48	16
LM center produces annual report	31	17	10	14	30	10
LMC member of resource sharing network	107	59	46	63	157	53
Additional funds for resource sharing	46	25	26	37	90	31
Telephone in LMC	170	92	67	92	253	86
*LMC uses cable TV	132	71	60	82	188	64
*LMC uses closed circuit TV	71	39	35	48	83	28
Online library catalog	139	76	59	81	196	66
Automated circulation system	160	87	64	88	239	81
LMC is high tech	136	75	59	81	193	65
LMC has local area network (LAN)	137	74	56	77	209	79
LMC has wide area network (WAN)	119	65	42	57	134	46
LMC has computers with modems	101	55	44	60	169	58
Telecommunications, Internet, e-mail access	156	84	60	64	242	82
CD-ROM searching access	148	80	60	82	277	77
Fax machine in LMC	53	29	14	19	56	19
Access to Web	138	75	57	78	211	72
*Less than 30% of students receive free/reduced lunch	92	49%	47	64%	164	56%

*Statistically significant at $p=.05$

After follow-up mailings to nonrespondents, we received 537 completed questionnaires. Discarding those that were unusable (most often because of incomplete financial data), we were left with a 38.2 percent response rate, the smallest rate yet for this series. (Many of the unusable responses were from those who noted that 1997–1998 was their first year in service.) Of the total number of responses, 57 (or 9.9 percent) were from private schools.

Changes in the geographic and grade-level distribution of respondents were minor. As in previous years, the largest number of responses came from schools in the southern United States and from elementary schools. The "Other" category in Table 16 refers to schools that bridge two or more categories, such as 7–12 and K–12 schools.

Table 16 / Distribution of Respondents by Grade Level, 1997–1998

Table 17 / Distribution of Respondents by Census Region, 1997–1998

Table 18 / Respondents by Enrollment Category, 1997–1998

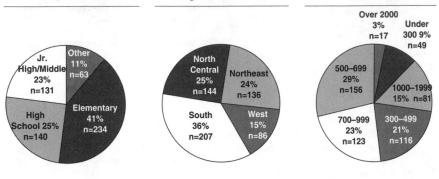

The most notable demographic change is in school size (Table 18). The number of schools serving 300–499 students has dropped from 26 percent in 1995–1996 to 21 percent last year, and the number of schools serving 700–999 increased from 19 to 23 percent.

Methodology

Each response was checked for accuracy, and then coded and entered into a computer data file. Analysis was done using the Statistical Package for the Social Sciences (SPSS). Measures of central tendency (means and medians) were produced for all of the budget collection items listed in the survey. The statistical test Chi-square was used to determine statistical significance for the category variables in Table 18.

Both means and medians are reported wherever appropriate to give a more accurate description of the data. The mean allows for comparisons with other studies that have used this measure; however, the median indicates more accurately the expenditures reported by most LMCs.

Although the mean (or average) is the descriptive statistic most commonly used in studies of this type, analysis showed an upward skew because a few respondents reported spending extremely large amounts in some categories. With data distribution like this, the few large scores inflate the mean and make it a less desirable measure.

To report only the mean instances where data are skewed would be misleading. For example: in 1997–1998, there was a wide range between the minimum of $25 spent by one school on AV materials and the maximum amount of $43,500 spent by another school. In this case the mean would be $2,746 and the median, $1,490. The latter is a more accurate reflection of the average expenditure.

For More Data

For earlier data, see the articles "Expenditures for Resources in School Library Media Centers" in editions of the *Bowker Annual* published in 1992, 1994, 1996, and 1998.

Book Trade Research and Statistics

Prices of U.S. and Foreign Published Materials

Bill Robnett

Chair, ALA ALCTS Library Materials Price Index Committee

The Library Materials Price Index Committee (LMPIC) of the American Library Association's Association for Library Collections and Technical Services continues to monitor library prices for a range of library materials of various origins. Library materials in 1998 generally increased at a rate higher than the U.S. Consumer Price Index (CPI), although hardcover books decreased in price. While 1999 data are very preliminary, the trends appear to be similar. CPI data are obtained from the Bureau of Labor Statistics Web site at http://stats.bls.gov/cpihome.htm.

It should be noted that some indexes have not been updated and are repeated from last year; others update 1998 preliminary data with final pricing. Some vendors are undergoing systems migration, and updated price information was not available at press time.

	Percent Change				
Index	1994	1995	1996	1997/1998*	1999
CPI	2.7	2.9	3.3	1.7	2.7
Periodicals	5.5	10.8	9.9	10.3*	10.4
Serials services	5.0	6.6	3.9	4.5*	n.a.
Hardcover books	22.7	5.6	6.0	-4.4	n.a.
Academic books	2.1	-0.1	3.6	2.1	n.a.
College books	-2.0	4.7	1.8	2.7	-1.3
Mass market paperbacks	-1.4	15.4	12.3	n.a.	n.a.
Trade paperbacks	-2.5	5.4	-1.3	1.1.	n.a.

* Payments made in 1997 for 1998 receipts.
n.a. = not available

U.S. Published Materials

Tables 1 through 10 indicate average prices and price indexes for library materials published primarily in the United States. These are Periodicals (Table 1), Serial Services (Table 2), U.S. Hardcover Books (Table 3), North American

(text continues on page 494)

Table 1 / U.S. Periodicals: Average Prices and Price Indexes, 1998–2000
Index Base: 1984 = 100

Subject Area	1984 Average Price	1998 Average Price	1998 Index	1999 Average Price	1999 Index	2000 Average Price	2000 Index
U.S. periodicals excluding Russian translations*	$54.97	$200.74	365.2	$221.66	403.2	$241.54	439.4
U.S. periodicals including Russian translations	72.47	259.69	358.4	285.04	393.3	311.37	429.7
Agriculture	24.06	79.50	330.4	86.58	359.9	92.72	385.4
Business and economics	38.87	121.77	313.3	131.82	339.1	142.08	365.5
Chemistry and physics	228.90	1,062.49	464.2	1,189.46	519.6	1,302.79	569.2
Children's periodicals	12.21	24.15	197.8	24.69	202.2	25.14	205.9
Education	34.01	103.98	305.7	114.04	335.3	124.23	365.3
Engineering	78.70	306.60	389.6	338.59	430.2	369.23	469.2
Fine and applied arts	26.90	52.08	193.6	54.53	202.7	56.51	210.1
General interest periodicals	27.90	42.26	151.5	43.32	155.3	44.48	159.4
History	23.68	57.31	242.0	59.88	252.9	63.12	266.6
Home economics	37.15	100.39	270.2	108.07	290.9	115.57	311.1
Industrial arts	30.40	99.05	325.8	106.33	349.8	110.83	364.6

Journalism and communications	39.25	104.26	265.6	108.71	277.0	116.17	296.0
Labor and industrial relations	29.87	98.99	331.4	107.74	360.7	114.84	384.5
Law	31.31	89.81	286.8	92.33	294.9	93.44	298.4
Library and information sciences	38.85	86.12	221.7	90.80	233.7	95.78	246.5
Literature and language	23.02	49.98	217.1	53.24	231.3	55.74	242.1
Mathematics, botany, geology general science	106.56	420.36	394.5	466.61	437.9	516.70	484.9
Medicine	125.57	524.65	417.8	597.03	475.5	663.21	528.2
Philosophy and religion	21.94	51.71	235.7	54.42	248.0	58.54	266.8
Physical education and recreation	20.54	48.10	234.2	50.17	244.3	51.87	252.5
Political science	32.43	100.82	310.9	110.45	340.6	121.62	375.0
Psychology	69.74	258.91	371.3	287.91	412.8	319.46	458.1
Russian translations	381.86	1,311.50	343.5	1,421.31	372.2	1,575.51	412.6
Sociology and anthropology	43.87	151.01	344.2	166.48	379.5	182.56	416.1
Zoology	78.35	385.40	491.9	433.79	553.7	470.43	600.4
Total number of periodicals							
Excluding Russian translations	3,731		3,729		3,729		3,729
Including Russian translations	3,942		3,938		3,937		3,935

For further comments, see *American Libraries*, May 1998, May 1999, and May 2000.

Compiled by Barbara Albee, the Faxon Company, and Brenda Dingley, University of Missouri, Kansas City.

*The category Russian translations was added in 1996

Table 2 / U.S. Serial Services: Average Price and Price Indexes 1997–1999
Index Base: 1984 = 100

Subject Area	1984 Average Price	1998 Average Price	1998 Index	1999 Average Price	1999 Percent Increase	1999 Index	2000 Average Price	2000 Percent Increase	2000 Index
U.S. serial services*	$295.13	$604.31	204.8	$638.18	5.60%	216.2	$671.94	5.3%	227.7
Business	437.07	781.33	178.8	798.73	2.20	182.7	820.73	2.8	187.8
General and humanities	196.55	455.78	231.9	492.59	8.10	250.6	503.98	2.3	256.4
Law	275.23	611.71	222.3	668.61	9.30	242.9	703.56	5.2	255.6
Science and technology	295.36	757.33	256.4	804.40	6.20	272.3	866.69	7.7	293.4
Social sciences	283.82	557.34	196.4	577.89	3.70	203.6	600.06	3.8	211.4
U.S. documents	97.37	162.32	166.7	166.57	2.60	171.0	195.16	17.2	200.4
Total number of services	1,537	1,282		1,286			1,294		

Compiled by Nancy J. Chaffin, Arizona State University (West) from data supplied by the Faxon Company, publishers, list prices, and library acquisitions records.

The definition of a serial service has been taken from *American National Standard for Library and Information Services and Related Publishing Practices-Library Materials-Criteria for Price Indexes* (ANSI Z39.20 - 1983).

* Excludes Wilson Index; excludes Russian translations as of 1988.

Table 3 / U.S. Hardcover Books: Average Prices and Price Indexes, 1995–1998

Index Base: 1984 = 100

Subject Area	1984	1995			1996			1997			1998 Final		
	Average Price	Volumes	Average Price	Index	Volumes	Average Price	Index	Volumes	Average Price	Index	Volumes	Average Price	Index
Agriculture	$34.92	392	$49.00	140.3	399	$45.11	129.2	507	$47.54	136.1	539	$42.85	122.7
Art	33.03	1,116	41.23	124.8	1,070	53.40	161.7	870	46.00	139.3	1,072	42.41	128.4
Biography	22.53	1,596	30.01	133.2	1,829	31.67	140.6	1,773	33.50	148.7	1,723	34.34	152.4
Business	26.01	972	46.90	180.3	1,005	52.62	202.3	689	52.89	203.3	800	53.27	204.8
Education	24.47	610	43.00	175.7	652	47.10	192.5	453	45.57	186.2	458	48.48	198.1
Fiction	14.74	2,345	21.47	145.7	2,915	22.89	155.3	2,882	21.41	145.2	3,132	21.92	148.7
General works	35.61	1,209	54.11	152.0	1,181	68.36	192.0	1,200	59.39	166.8	992	59.26	166.4
History	27.53	1,691	42.19	153.3	2,028	45.62	165.7	2,052	43.51	158.0	2,057	42.79	155.4
Home economics	15.70	651	22.53	143.5	655	23.39	149.0	658	23.32	148.5	636	23.29	148.3
Juvenile	10.02	3,649	14.55	145.2	3,730	15.97	159.4	2,013	15.64	156.1	2,010	15.57	155.4
Language	22.97	320	54.89	239.0	399	58.81	256.0	414	57.95	252.3	372	58.57	255.0
Law	43.88	716	73.09	166.6	827	88.51	201.7	740	89.15	203.2	761	82.40	187.8
Literature	23.57	1,302	38.49	163.3	1,575	43.28	183.6	1,299	44.89	190.5	1,248	43.94	186.4
Medicine	40.65	2,035	75.80	186.5	2,480	81.48	200.4	2,088	85.92	211.4	2,001	80.67	198.5
Music	27.79	251	43.27	155.7	253	39.21	141.1	208	43.58	156.8	254	45.14	162.4
Philosophy and psychology	29.70	1,001	45.26	152.4	1,154	48.40	163.0	949	48.06	161.8	983	50.35	169.5
Poetry and drama	26.75	567	34.96	130.7	606	34.15	127.7	568	36.76	137.4	541	36.86	137.8
Religion	17.76	1,364	34.27	193.0	1,544	36.62	206.2	1,385	40.52	228.2	1,384	33.43	188.2
Science	46.57	2,095	93.52	200.8	2,372	90.63	194.6	2,242	78.14	167.8	2,345	74.40	159.8
Sociology and economics	33.35	5,145	55.51	166.4	5,973	53.82	161.4	5,081	55.05	165.1	5,238	58.55	175.6
Sports and recreation	20.16	517	32.14	159.4	591	34.71	172.2	639	32.35	160.5	605	35.21	174.7
Technology	45.80	1,454	88.28	192.8	1,599	91.60	200.0	1,559	89.96	196.4	1,576	86.55	189.0
Travel	21.31	199	38.30	179.7	179	33.92	159.2	236	30.58	143.5	225	34.69	162.8
Total	$29.99	31,197	$47.15	157.2	35,016	$50.00	166.1	30,505	$50.22	167.5	30,952	$48.04	160.2

Compiled by Bill Robnett, California State University Monterey Bay, from data supplied by the R. R. Bowker Company. Price indexes on Tables 3 and 7 are based on books recorded in the R. R. Bowker Company's *Weekly Record* (cumulated in the *American Book Publishing Record*). Final data for each year include items listed between January of that year and June of the following year with an imprint date of the specified year. Please see the following article, "Book Title Output and Average Prices," for restated prices for 1997 and 1998, and preliminary prices for 1999.

Table 4 / North American Academic Books: Average Prices and Price Indexes 1996–1998
(Index Base: 1989 = 100)

Subject Area	LC Class	1989		1996		1997		1998			
		No. of Titles	Average Price	No. of Titles	Average Price	No. of Titles	Average Price	No. of Titles	Average Price	% Change 1997–1998	Index
Agriculture	S	897	$45.13	1,108	$58.84	1,058	$62.40	984	$62.75	0.60	139.0
Anthropology	GN	406	32.81	563	38.73	583	40.14	539	41.74	4.00	127.2
Botany	QK	251	69.02	192	107.06	200	76.99	161	98.81	28.30	143.2
Business and economics	H	5,979	41.67	6,349	53.07	6,396	53.14	6,101	56.60	6.50	135.8
Chemistry	QD	577	110.61	535	175.49	498	147.46	494	149.54	1.40	135.2
Education	L	1,685	29.61	2,248	40.02	2,291	39.43	2,225	39.58	0.40	133.7
Engineering and technology	T	4,569	64.94	5,043	80.73	5,080	84.92	4,777	86.51	1.90	133.2
Fine and applied arts	M-N	3,040	40.72	3,358	44.84	3,403	45.68	3,402	46.98	2.80	115.4
General works	A	333	134.65	129	98.79	145	90.37	98	94.81	4.90	70.4
Geography	G	396	47.34	665	55.21	687	56.53	652	63.29	12.00	133.7
Geology	QE	303	63.49	192	83.22	213	87.03	184	82.31	-5.40	129.6
History	C-D-E-F	5,549	31.34	6,105	37.05	6,106	37.49	6,242	39.38	5.00	125.7
Home economics	TX	535	27.10	773	32.26	691	27.24	638	28.91	6.10	106.7
Industrial arts	TT	175	23.89	218	24.37	203	26.48	173	29.62	11.90	124.0
Law	K	1,252	51.10	1,506	65.06	1,479	66.18	1,573	68.03	2.80	133.1

Subject	LC class										
Library and information science	Z	857	44.51	780	57.60	653	59.06	630	56.66	-4.10	127.3
Literature and language	P	10,812	24.99	11,455	33.58	10,855	35.44	10,649	33.78	-4.70	135.2
Mathematics and computer science	QA	2,707	44.68	3,537	59.37	3,910	61.23	3,550	64.10	4.70	143.5
Medicine	R	5,028	58.38	6,309	69.06	6,446	70.31	5,873	71.48	1.70	122.4
Military and naval science	U-V	715	33.57	537	82.94	458	60.67	417	65.02	7.20	193.7
Physical education and recreation	GV	814	20.38	912	24.19	881	26.48	716	27.88	5.30	136.8
Philosophy and religion	B	3,518	29.06	4,794	42.06	4,755	41.87	4,411	42.70	2.00	146.9
Physics and astronomy	QB	1,219	64.59	1,192	95.83	1,140	92.21	1,118	95.01	3.00	147.1
Political science	J	1,650	36.76	1,858	47.09	1,926	51.75	1,701	50.49	-2.40	137.4
Psychology	BF	890	31.97	1,196	37.62	1,139	39.46	1,057	43.34	9.80	135.6
Science (general)	Q	433	56.10	431	82.64	428	69.55	375	80.76	16.10	135.6
Sociology	HM	2,742	29.36	3,822	38.82	3,749	41.33	3,630	43.00	4.00	146.5
Zoology	QH,L,P,R	1,967	71.28	1,842	83.70	1,736	84.96	1,888	84.95	0.00	119.2
Average for all subjects		59,299	$41.69	67,649	$52.24	67,109	$53.12	64,258	$54.24	2.10	130.1

Compiled by Stephen Bosch, University of Arizona, from electronic data provided by Baker and Taylor, Blackwell North America, and Yankee Book Peddler. The data represent all titles (includes hardcover, trade & paperback books, as well as annuals) treated for all approval plan customers serviced by the three vendors. This table covers titles published or distributed in the United States and Canada during the calendar years listed.

This index does include paperback editions. The overall average price of materials is lower than if the index consisted only of hardbound editions.

Table 5 / U.S. College Books: Average Prices and Price Indexes, 1983, 1997, 1998, 1999
(Index base for all years: 1983=100. 1998 also indexed to 1997; 1999 also indexed to 1998)

Choice Subject Categories	1983		1997			1998				1999			
	No. of Titles	Avg.Price Per Title	No. of Titles	Avg.Price Per Title	Prices Indexed to 1983	No. of Titles	Avg.Price Per Title	Prices Indexed to 1983	Prices Indexed to 1997	No. of Titles	Avg.Price Per Title	Prices Indexed to 1983	Prices Indexed to 1998
General	11	$24.91	22	$46.10	185.1	18	$37.11	149.0	80.5	23	$50.75	203.7	136.7
Humanities	40	$24.53	30	$45.45	185.3	36	$45.41	185.1	99.9	36	$45.73	186.4	100.7
Art and architecture	372	40.31	253	59.34	147.2	304	52.81	131.0	89.0	373	53.21	132.0	100.8
Communication	51	22.22	64	45.92	206.7	68	45.33	204.0	98.7	82	47.38	213.2	104.5
Language and literature	109	23.39	90	44.12	188.6	82	45.11	192.9	102.2	88	45.40	194.1	100.6
African and Middle Eastern [4]	—	—	20	31.27	—	34	35.46	—	113.4	26	37.94	—	107.0
Asian and Oceanian [4]	—	—	25	41.30	—	35	41.27	—	99.9	29	41.02	—	99.4
Classical	19	28.68	36	48.69	169.8	33	46.80	163.2	96.1	25	48.06	167.6	102.7
English and American	579	23.47	543	45.82	195.2	485	46.62	198.6	101.7	512	46.48	198.0	99.7
Germanic	53	20.45	42	48.78	238.5	33	43.17	211.1	88.5	41	42.90	209.8	99.4
Romance	93	20.47	111	45.04	220.0	100	42.72	208.7	94.8	89	42.43	207.3	99.3
Slavic	35	23.09	31	44.93	194.6	24	46.44	201.1	103.4	31	52.81	228.7	113.7
Performing arts	19	24.32	4	43.74	179.9	16	44.66	183.6	102.1	22	42.73	175.7	95.7
Film	67	24.81	82	43.50	175.3	88	46.86	188.9	107.7	79	48.72	196.4	104.0
Music	106	25.09	132	44.15	176.0	116	48.41	192.9	109.6	119	46.56	185.6	96.2
Theater and dance [5]	51	23.18	54	42.73	184.3	53	47.83	206.3	111.9	43	45.01	194.2	94.1
Philosophy	155	26.27	156	46.45	176.8	147	49.61	188.9	106.8	177	47.83	182.1	96.4
Religion	196	19.33	158	42.18	218.2	182	40.44	209.2	95.9	209	38.95	201.5	96.3
Total Humanities [6]	2,038	$26.26	1,831	$46.86	178.4	1,836	$45.64	173.8	97.4	1,981	$46.74	178.0	102.4
Science/Technology	159	$36.11	85	$39.89	110.5	83	$42.83	118.6	107.4	88	$39.94	110.6	93.3
History of science/technology	56	28.45	63	42.06	147.8	54	49.38	173.6	117.4	79	46.32	162.8	93.8
Astronautics/astronomy	18	27.78	53	47.94	172.6	40	50.56	182.0	105.5	34	41.74	150.2	82.6
Biology	145	39.28	104	50.34	128.2	107	49.93	127.1	99.2	103	52.95	134.8	106.0
Botany	23	31.78	81	65.08	204.8	95	68.53	215.6	105.3	86	50.75	159.7	74.1
Zoology	38	44.21	85	65.32	147.7	60	64.40	145.7	98.6	79	47.10	106.5	73.1
Chemistry	30	48.57	62	92.56	190.6	74	74.73	153.9	80.7	64	99.32	204.5	132.9
Earth science	42	35.43	55	68.04	192.0	48	71.45	201.7	105.0	63	58.86	166.1	82.4
Engineering	154	44.88	118	76.26	169.9	113	85.13	189.7	111.6	70	76.12	169.6	89.4
Health sciences	121	24.45	172	46.49	190.2	143	47.30	193.5	101.7	124	41.91	171.4	88.6
Information/computer science	63	29.48	82	48.30	163.8	45	46.70	158.4	96.7	40	43.15	146.4	92.4
Mathematics	44	32.82	103	55.03	167.7	142	53.14	161.9	96.6	70	59.17	180.3	111.3
Physics	38	34.13	59	53.59	157.0	57	62.01	181.7	115.7	38	58.97	172.8	95.1
Sports/physical education	61	18.67	58	37.08	198.6	38	40.85	218.8	110.2	53	35.98	192.7	88.1
Total Science/Technology	992	$34.77	1,180	$55.98	161.0	1,099	$58.27	167.6	104.1	991	$53.22	153.1	91.3

Subject	No.	Avg. price	Index	No.	Avg. price	No.	Avg. price	Index	%	No.	Avg. price	Index	%
Social/Behavioral Sciences	173	$24.24	169.1	44	$40.98	73	$50.15	206.9	122.4	66	$43.50	179.4	86.7
Anthropology	98	26.68	184.4	135	49.20	159	46.75	175.2	95.0	162	51.33	192.4	109.8
Business management/labor	156	25.01	183.1	152	45.78	140	39.80	159.1	86.9	146	41.23	164.8	103.6
Economics	315	27.60	183.9	257	50.76	254	52.18	189.1	102.8	245	48.86	177.0	93.6
Education	120	20.23	219.3	138	44.36	154	44.78	221.3	100.9	204	43.74	216.2	97.7
History, geography/area studies	92	25.58	170.9	49	43.72	43	44.14	172.6	101.0	48	48.43	189.3	109.7
Africa	17	26.94	169.8	46	45.73	43	48.63	180.5	106.3	31	48.75	180.9	100.2
Ancient history	46	31.80	176.4	44	56.09	32	56.21	176.7	100.2	39	53.58	168.5	95.3
Asia and Oceania	58	25.55	186.1	79	47.56	74	52.28	204.6	109.9	61	49.95	195.5	95.5
Central and Eastern Europe [3]	—	—	—	19	46.30	59	45.90	—	99.1	44	50.76	—	110.6
Europe [3]	285	29.55	170.0	186	50.24	—	—	—	—	—	—	—	—
Latin America and Caribbean	25	24.72	188.2	63	46.53	53	52.68	213.1	113.2	47	49.35	199.6	93.7
Middle East and North Africa	33	28.42	194.6	38	55.31	40	55.15	194.1	99.7	34	52.69	185.4	95.5
North America	274	24.42	155.0	388	37.85	406	37.89	155.2	100.1	430	39.76	162.8	104.9
United Kingdom [3]	—	—	—	32	52.05	91	55.01	—	105.7	124	52.90	—	96.1
Western Europe [3]	—	—	—	54	51.14	131	49.75	—	97.3	128	49.73	—	100.0
Political science	439	25.00	189.8	55	47.45	54	50.45	201.8	106.3	24	53.44	213.8	105.9
Comparative politics [2]	—	—	—	175	52.24	224	51.40	—	98.4	202	52.57	—	102.3
International relations [2]	—	—	—	131	50.71	139	43.88	—	96.4	137	50.28	—	102.9
Political theory [2]	—	—	—	92	45.37	64	49.67	—	109.5	59	40.08	—	80.7
U.S. politics [2]	—	—	—	188	44.04	168	48.21	—	109.5	166	42.78	—	88.7
Psychology	162	26.57	169.7	180	45.10	135	49.51	186.3	109.8	141	45.92	172.8	92.8
Sociology	244	24.38	170.4	216	41.54	163	46.92	192.5	113.0	132	47.02	192.9	100.2
Total Social/Behavioral Sciences	2,537	$25.81	178.7	2,761	$46.13	2,699	$47.32	183.4	102.6	2,670	$46.58	180.5	98.4
Total General, Humanities, Science/Technology, Social/Behavioral Sciences (excluding Reference) [6]	5,578	$27.57	175.4	5,794	$48.37	5,652	$48.87	177.3	101.0	5,665	$47.81	173.4	97.8
Reference	506	$44.75	175.0	397	$78.31	—	—	—	—	—	—	—	—
General [1]	—	—	—	47	59.85	120	68.53	—	114.5	64	88.00	—	128.4
Humanities [1]	—	—	—	73	84.74	186	85.92	—	101.4	185	97.60	—	113.6
Science/Technology [1]	—	—	—	16	106.64	75	109.66	—	112.8	73	97.50	—	88.9
Social/Behavioral [1]	—	—	—	77	87.24	206	98.38	—	112.9	236	94.03	—	95.6
Total Reference	506	$44.75	177.7	610	$79.50	587	$89.77	200.6	—	558	$94.98	212.2	105.8
Grand Total (includes Reference) [6]	6,084	$29.00	177.0	6,404	$51.33	6,239	$52.72	181.8	102.7	6,223	$52.04	179.5	98.7

1 Began appearing as separate sections in July 1997.
2 Began appearing as a separate sections in March 1988
3 Began appearing as separate sections, replacing Europe, in July 1997.

4 Began appearing as separate sections in September 1995.
5 Separate sections for Theater and Dance combined in September 1995.
6 1983 totals include Photography (incorporated into Art and Architecture in 1994), Linguistics (incorporated into Language and Literature in 1985), and Non-European/Other (replaced by African and Middle Eastern and Asian and Oceanian in September 1995)

Compiled by Donna Alsbury, Florida Center for Library Automation.

Table 6 / U.S. Mass Market Paperback Books: Average Prices and Price Indexes, 1995–1998
Index Base: 1984 = 100

Subject Area	1984 Average Price	1995 Volumes	1995 Average Price	1995 Index	1996 Volumes	1996 Average Price	1996 Index	1997 Final Volumes	1997 Average Price	1997 Index	1998 Preliminary Volumes	1998 Average Price	1998 Index
Agriculture	$2.85	10	$9.13	320.4	13	$11.59	406.7	1	$18.00	631.6	5	$16.49	578.5
Art	8.28	12	11.24	135.7	8	12.00	144.9	20	16.45	198.6	17	14.26	172.2
Biography	4.45	39	8.08	181.6	38	10.12	227.4	43	13.73	308.5	74	15.97	358.9
Business	4.92	18	10.81	219.7	19	13.25	269.3	22	17.91	364.0	24	16.29	331.1
Education	5.15	29	12.40	240.8	31	10.29	199.8	10	14.04	272.6	19	16.79	326.1
Fiction	3.03	3,680	5.51	181.8	3,569	6.25	206.3	2,950	8.51	280.9	3,150	8.45	278.9
General works	4.58	29	19.37	422.9	34	9.31	203.3	20	13.91	303.7	29	10.42	227.5
History	3.77	24	10.06	266.8	17	10.92	289.7	25	14.71	390.1	30	12.57	333.4
Home economics	4.95	43	8.70	175.8	35	8.67	175.2	72	14.61	295.1	88	14.02	283.2
Juveniles	2.31	396	3.99	172.7	288	4.25	184.0	296	6.29	272.3	295	5.98	258.9
Language	5.56	8	9.60	172.7	8	7.87	141.5	21	8.99	161.7	15	10.59	190.5
Law	5.12	5	9.79	191.2	5	10.39	202.9	12	12.28	239.9	12	12.30	240.2
Literature	3.63	47	8.73	240.5	72	9.42	259.5	68	10.64	293.1	73	10.68	294.2
Medicine	5.01	10	8.38	167.3	20	8.93	178.2	99	11.33	226.1	166	13.84	276.2
Music	5.28	3	24.98	473.1	5	20.57	389.6	7	14.38	283.7	16	14.98	283.7
Philosophy and psychology	4.38	103	4.83	110.3	108	7.58	173.1	133	14.12	322.4	160	12.15	277.4
Poetry and drama	5.11	32	9.70	189.8	28	10.88	212.9	15	10.53	206.0	27	8.61	168.5
Religion	3.87	16	9.39	242.6	16	8.93	230.7	48	13.48	348.3	56	14.77	381.7
Science	3.55	8	11.28	317.7	9	12.16	342.5	25	15.09	425.1	42	14.27	402.0
Sociology and economics	4.42	42	9.60	217.2	34	9.91	224.2	108	16.29	368.6	135	14.14	319.9
Sports and recreation	4.06	82	8.28	203.9	75	8.79	216.5	75	14.67	361.2	99	14.62	360.1
Technology	8.61	22	11.62	135.0	20	11.14	129.4	21	12.08	140.3	27	13.13	152.5
Travel	5.86	3	13.96	238.2	10	9.63	164.3	5	15.57	265.7	4	11.10	189.4
Total	$3.41	4,661	$5.85	171.6	4,462	$6.57	192.7	4,096	$9.31	273.1	4,563	$9.31	273.1

Compiled by Stephen Bosch, University of Arizona, from data supplied by the R. R. Bowker Company. Average prices of mass market paperbacks are based on listings of mass market titles in Bowker's *Paperbound Books in Print*. Please see the following article, "Book Title Output and Average Prices," for restated prices for 1997 and 1998, and preliminary prices for 1999.

Table 7 / U.S. Trade (Higher Priced) Paperback Books: Average Prices and Price Indexes, 1995–1998

Index Base: 1984 = 100

Subject Area	1984 Average Price	1995 Volumes	1995 Average Price	1995 Index	1996 Volumes	1996 Average Price	1996 Index	1997 Volumes	1997 Average Price	1997 Index	1998 Final Volumes	1998 Final Average Price	1998 Final Index
Agriculture	$17.77	218	$26.97	151.8	248	$20.45	115.1	280	$21.34	120.1	338	$21.04	118.4
Art	13.12	874	20.58	156.9	872	21.57	164.4	728	22.10	168.4	841	23.24	177.1
Biography	15.09	813	15.59	109.9	979	17.37	115.1	902	17.56	116.4	953	17.93	118.8
Business	17.10	709	24.24	141.8	687	26.08	152.5	681	26.50	155.0	602	30.24	176.8
Education	12.84	738	22.96	178.8	832	23.76	185.0	608	24.98	194.6	568	25.53	198.8
Fiction	8.95	1,275	12.71	142.0	1,852	12.35	138.0	1,708	13.09	146.2	1,610	13.49	150.7
General works	14.32	1,375	32.99	230.4	1,693	34.65	242.0	1,546	38.50	268.9	1,427	38.62	269.7
History	13.49	1,041	18.48	137.0	1,381	20.09	148.9	1,165	19.69	145.9	1,233	20.74	153.7
Home economics	9.40	629	14.87	158.2	727	15.35	163.3	748	15.30	162.7	641	15.82	168.3
Juveniles	5.94	990	15.75	265.2	1,117	8.30	139.7	954	9.29	156.4	896	8.15	137.2
Language	11.61	304	21.58	185.9	427	21.17	182.3	386	21.94	189.0	399	22.11	190.4
Law	17.61	415	30.26	171.8	434	30.81	175.0	373	31.41	178.4	434	30.58	173.7
Literature	11.70	945	16.54	141.4	1,278	17.69	151.2	984	19.02	162.6	946	19.95	170.5
Medicine	15.78	1,092	27.91	176.9	1,577	27.37	173.4	1,411	27.46	174.0	1,435	26.54	168.2
Music	12.53	174	19.81	158.1	183	20.14	160.7	166	21.54	171.9	144	23.00	183.6
Philosophy and psychology	13.64	800	19.92	146.0	989	18.83	138.0	898	19.12	140.2	801	20.48	150.1
Poetry and drama	8.68	712	15.69	180.8	862	12.92	148.8	789	14.20	163.6	710	14.68	169.1
Religion	9.32	1,723	14.60	156.7	2,100	14.93	160.2	1,951	15.65	167.9	1,758	16.48	176.8
Science	16.22	874	33.42	206.0	1,134	32.95	203.1	936	36.42	224.5	1025	36.32	223.9
Sociology and economics	17.72	3,321	23.69	133.7	3,983	23.47	132.4	3,200	27.29	154.0	3,150	25.31	142.8
Sports and recreation	11.40	900	16.53	145.0	1,028	16.33	143.2	779	17.31	151.9	706	17.95	157.5
Technology	21.11	827	38.75	183.6	890	39.17	185.6	821	37.71	178.6	801	41.45	196.4
Travel	9.88	480	16.38	165.8	537	16.74	169.4	517	16.33	165.2	501	17.16	173.7
Total	$13.86	21,229	$21.71	156.6	25,810	$21.42	154.5	22,531	$22.67	163.5	21,919	$22.90	165.3

Compiled by Bill Robnett, California State University Monterey Bay, from data supplied by the R. R. Bowker Company. Price indexes on Tables 3 and 7 are based on books recorded in the R. R. Bowker Company's *Weekly Record* (cumulated in the *American Book Publishing Record*). Final data for each year include items listed between January of that year and June of the following year with an imprint date of the specified year. Please see the following article, "Book Title Output and Average Prices," for restated prices for 1997 and 1998, and preliminary prices for 1999.

(text continued from page 483)

Academic Books (Table 4), U.S. College Books (Table 5), U.S. Mass Market Paperback Books (Table 6), U.S. Trade Paperback Books (Table 7), U.S. Daily Newspapers and International Newspapers (Tables 8A and 8B), U.S. Nonprint Media (Table 9), and CD-ROMs (Table 10).

Periodical and Serial Prices

The LMPI Committee and Faxon, RoweCom Academic Services, formerly the Faxon Company, jointly produce the U.S. Periodical Price Index (Table 1). The subscription prices shown are publishers' list prices, excluding publisher discount or vendor service charges. This report includes 1998, 1999, and 2000 data indexed to the base year of 1984. More extensive reports on the periodical price index have been published annually in the April 15 issue of *Library Journal* through 1992, and in the May issue of *American Libraries* since 1993.

Compiled by Brenda Dingley and Barbara Albee, this table shows that U.S. periodical prices, excluding Russian translations, increased by 9.0 percent from 1999 to 2000. This figure represents a 1.4 percent decrease from the 10.4 percent figure posted in 1999. Including the Russian translation category, the single-year increase was only slightly higher, at 9.2 percent for 2000. This figure is 0.6 percent lower than the rate of 9.8 percent for the entire sample in 1999. Medicine posted the highest increase of any single subject category this year (at 11.1 percent). After several consecutive years in which Zoology occupied either first or second place in terms of percentage price increase, it dropped to tenth place with an increase of only 8.4 percent for 2000, versus a 12.6 percent increase for 1999. Psychology increased at a rate of 11.0 percent, for the second-highest increase. Other subject categories that posted double-digit increases in 2000 include Russian Translations (at 10.8 percent), Mathematics, etc. (at 10.7 percent), and Political Science (at 10.1 percent). The Sociology and Anthropology, Chemistry and Physics, Engineering, and Business and Economics categories, which all posted a double-digit increase in 1999, showed lesser increases in 2000.

In compiling the U.S. Serial Services Index (Table 2), Nancy Chaffin notes that titles continue to migrate to electronic formats, particularly those that are Web-based. This is particularly true in Business and in U.S. Documents. Compiling the index is further complicated when titles merge, and the compiler continues to identify new replacement titles for the index when other titles cease. As in 1999, average prices for 2000 serial services increased in all subject areas, ranging from 2.3 percent in the General and Humanities category to 17.2 percent for U.S. Documents, with an average increase of 5.3 percent. The Wilson Index listing was dropped from this index in 1998 at the request of the Wilson Co. Readers are referred to the May 2000 *American Libraries* for a more detailed article on serial services pricing.

Book Prices

Due to system conversion at Bowker, 1999 book prices were not available by our deadline. Table 3 (Hardcover Books) indicates 1998 final prices for U.S. hardcover books that replace the preliminary 1998 data from last year's publication.

Overall there is a price decrease of 4.4 percent in U.S. hardcover books in 1998. Business and Language remained constant in pricing that has doubled since 1984, while Religion showed a significant decrease of nearly 18 percent from 1997 to 1998. Science and Technology hardbacks both showed slight decreases. Data in this index is compiled from Bowker's *American Book Publishing Record*. (For 1999 data see the following article, "Book Title Output and Average Prices.")

Stephen Bosch, compiler of the North American Academic Books index, notes that the average price in 1998 (Table 4) increased by a very modest 2.1 percent in contrast to the preceding year, which showed a 5.1 percent increase in pricing. The data used for this index comprises titles treated by Baker and Taylor, Blackwell North America, and Yankee Book Peddler in their approval plans during the calendar years listed. It does include paperback editions as supplied by the vendors, and the recent increase in the number of these editions as part of the approval plans has clearly influenced the prices reflected in the index figures. The inflation variance (hardback versus paperback editions) continues to be

Table 8A / U.S. Daily Newspapers:
Average Prices and Price Indexes, 1990–2000
Index Base: 1990 = 100

Year	No. Titles	Average Price	Percent Increase	Index
1990	165	$189.58	0.0	100.0
1991	166	198.13	4.5	104.5
1992	167	222.68	12.4	117.5
1993	171	229.92	3.3	121.3
1994	171	261.91	13.9	138.2
1995	172	270.22	3.2	142.5
1996	166	300.21	11.1	158.4
1997	165	311.77	3.9	164.5
1998	163	316.60	1.5	167.0
1999	162	318.44	0.6	168.0
2000	162	324.26	1.8	171.0

Table 8B / International Newspapers:
Average Prices and Price Indexes, 1993–2000
Index Base: 1993 = 100

Year	No. Titles	Average Price	Percent Increase	Index
1993	46	$806.91	0.0	100.0
1994	46	842.01	4.3	104.3
1995	49	942.13	11.9	116.3
1996	50	992.78	5.4	123.0
1997	53	1,029.49	3.7	127.6
1998	52	1,046.72	1.7	129.7
1999	50	1,049.13	0.2	130.0
2000	50	1,050.88	0.2	130.2

Compiled by Genevieve S. Owens, Williamsburg Regional Library, and Wilba Swearingen, Louisiana State University Health Sciences Center Library, from data supplied by EBSCO Subscription Services. We thank Kathleen Born from EBSCO for her assistance with this project.

much less clear than it has been in previous years. Price changes vary, as always, among subject areas, with several double-digit increases this year. Price increases in the areas of science, technology, and medicine continue to be larger than other non-STM areas, and the overall prices for STM books remain high. Price decreases in large publishing areas such as literature and political sciences have helped hold down the overall price increase for 1998. Without this moderating influence, the overall price of academic books would have increased by more than 3 percent.

U.S. College Books (Table 5) is compiled by Donna Alsbury from reviews appearing in *Choice* during the calendar year. Hardcover prices were used when available. The table presents price data from 1997, 1998, and 1999 with the indicated base year of 1983. There is a modest 1.3 percent decrease in U.S. college book prices for 1999 after the increase of 2.7 percent from 1997 to 1998. In general, increases occurred in humanities and reference titles, while science and technology and social and behavioral sciences titles decreased in price.

U.S. Mass Market Paperbacks (Table 6) and U.S. Trade Paperbacks (Table 7) are based on data from Bowker's *Paperbound Books in Print*. The former is repeated from last year. The data for U.S. Trade Paperbacks (Table 7) is updated with final 1998 pricing and indicates overall price constancy from 1997 to 1998. The total increase is a slight 1.1 percent. However certain subject areas increased rather sharply, such as technology at nearly 10 percent, business at 14 percent, and music by almost 7 percent. Higher-cost trade paperbacks merit continued observation given these significant increases in some subjects, which may be a result of decreasing sales of hardbound imprints. (For 1999 data for Tables 6 and 7, see the following article, "Book Title Output and Average Prices.")

(text continues on page 503)

Table 9 / U.S. Nonprint Media: Average Prices and Price Indexes, 1997–1998
Index Base: 1980 = 100

Category	1980 Average Price	1997 Average Price	Index	1998 Average Price	Index
Videocassettes					
Rental cost per minute	$1.41*	$1.63	115.6	$1.84	130.5
Purchase cost per minute	7.59	1.72	22.7	1.74	22.9
Cost per video	217.93	72.31	33.2	77.85	35.7
Length per video (min.)		41.84		44.85	
Sound recordings					
Average cost per cassette	9.34	8.31	89.0	8.20	87.8
Average cost per CD**	13.36	14.35	107.4	12.65	94.7

Compiled by Dana Alessi, Baker & Taylor, from data in *Booklist*, *Library Journal*, and *School Library Journal*.

* Rental cost per minute for 16 mm films.
**Base year for compact discs = 1993.

Note: The 16 mm film and filmstrip categories were discontinued due to the small number of reviews of these products.

Table 10 / CD-ROM Price Inventory 1996–1998: Average Costs By Subject Classification

Classification	LC Class	Number of Titles			Average Price per Title			Percent Change	
		1996	1997	1998	1996	1997	1998	1996–1997	1997–1998
General works	A	128	127	125	$1,805	$1,735	$1,499	-4	-14
Philosophy, psychology, and religion	B	22	22	22	1,153	1,059	1,062	-8	0
History: general and Old World	D	7	7	7	786	777	777	-1	0
History: America	E-F	20	20	16	641	645	680	1	5
Geography, anthropology, and recreation	G	35	36	35	1,884	1,876	1,383	0	-26
Social sciences	H	101	108	108	2,196	2,667	2,776	21	4
Business	HB-I-J	118	122	118	3,700	3,298	3,706	-11	12
Political science	J	19	20	19	1,297	1,467	1,558	13	6
Law	K	27	28	28	2,074	2,016	2,169	-3	8
Education	L	30	30	32	921	958	1,026	4	7
Music	M	12	12	10	974	961	1,019	-1	6
Fine arts	N	36	36	36	1,278	1,344	1,295	5	-4
Language and literature	P	44	46	49	2,983	2,860	2,201	-4	-23
Science	Q	172	175	168	2,045	2,173	2,263	6	4
Medicine	R	188	198	180	1,404	1,382	1,445	-2	5
Agriculture	S	32	31	30	4,139	3,754	3,261	-9	-13
Technology	T	72	79	77	2,208	2,119	2,157	-4	2
Military science	U-V	25	28	26	1,094	1,061	1,083	-3	2
Bibliography, library science	Z	72	73	67	1,430	1,525	1,592	7	4
Totals		1,160	1,198	1,153	$1,988	$2,012	$2,007	1	0

Compiled by Martha Kellogg and Theodore Kellogg, University of Rhode Island.

Note: In 1997, 72 titles were added and 34 removed; in 1998, 48 were added and 93 removed.

Table 11 / **British Academic Books: Average Prices and Price Indexes, 1997–1999**
(Index Base: 1985 = 100; prices listed are pounds sterling)

Subject Area	1985		1997			1998			1999		
	No. of Titles	Average Price	No. of Titles	Average Price	Index	No. of Titles	Average Price	Index	No. of Titles	Average Price	Index
General works	29	£30.54	35	£34.62	113.4	29	£68.91	225.6	36	£37.84	123.9
Fine arts	329	21.70	423	32.95	151.8	451	33.32	153.5	387	32.78	151.1
Architecture	97	20.68	150	37.66	182.1	145	29.98	145.0	138	33.82	163.5
Music	136	17.01	136	31.01	182.3	129	36.93	217.1	129	37.00	217.5
Performing arts except music	110	13.30	175	32.38	243.5	164	26.67	200.5	151	34.08	256.2
Archaeology	146	18.80	173	36.98	196.7	183	36.19	192.5	148	42.16	224.3
Geography	60	22.74	57	41.19	181.1	47	41.65	183.2	18	50.80	223.3
History	1,123	16.92	1,373	38.63	228.3	1,322	43.46	256.9	902	33.39	197.3
Philosophy	127	18.41	221	42.70	231.9	264	55.49	301.4	228	42.12	228.8
Religion	328	10.40	421	24.47	235.3	419	30.54	293.7	401	31.11	299.1
Language	135	19.37	193	42.41	218.9	164	50.84	262.5	151	47.13	243.3
Miscellaneous humanities	59	21.71	49	34.98	161.1	42	24.41	112.4	34	37.24	171.5
Literary texts (excluding fiction)	570	9.31	500	15.09	162.1	422	15.27	164.0	325	17.16	184.3
Literary criticism	438	14.82	491	36.01	243.0	527	38.66	260.9	464	37.49	253.0
Law	188	24.64	379	49.10	199.3	342	48.65	197.4	350	52.09	211.4
Library science and book trade	78	18.69	76	42.54	227.6	64	62.20	332.8	64	34.27	183.4
Mass communications	38	14.20	116	34.80	245.1	124	36.09	254.2	92	37.30	262.7
Anthropology and ethnology	42	20.71	62	41.10	198.5	78	45.55	219.9	61	43.48	209.9
Sociology	136	15.24	199	50.89	333.9	218	49.64	325.7	205	43.35	284.4
Psychology	107	19.25	148	39.12	203.2	149	51.03	265.1	182	37.13	192.9
Economics	334	20.48	585	59.99	292.9	535	60.24	294.1	541	54.40	265.6
Political science, international relations	314	15.54	541	40.31	259.4	568	41.60	267.7	569	41.01	263.9
Miscellaneous social sciences	20	26.84	19	38.55	143.6	23	37.23	138.7	30	42.19	157.2
Military science	83	17.69	46	49.14	277.8	40	34.31	194.0	42	31.81	179.8
Sports and recreation	44	11.23	75	20.03	178.4	80	24.33	216.7	58	32.83	292.3
Social service	56	12.17	75	27.20	223.5	114	29.83	245.1	101	34.89	286.7
Education	295	12.22	372	29.42	240.8	337	35.93	294.0	316	39.25	321.2
Management and business administration	427	19.55	599	38.74	198.2	606	42.54	217.6	527	45.06	230.5
Miscellaneous applied social sciences	13	9.58	30	42.20	440.5	23	35.22	367.6	20	33.01	344.6

Criminology	45	11.45	76	34.78	303.8	66	37.62	328.6	65	40.89	357.1
Applied interdisciplinary social sciences	254	14.17	509	35.96	253.8	503	39.87	281.4	559	43.22	305.0
General science	43	13.73	37	40.60	295.7	31	40.67	296.2	28	33.24	242.1
Botany	55	30.54	35	50.64	165.8	31	56.31	184.4	28	58.60	191.9
Zoology	85	25.67	56	53.14	207.0	51	49.91	194.4	39	55.59	216.6
Human biology	35	28.91	19	58.46	202.2	28	43.68	151.1	59	46.68	161.5
Biochemistry	26	33.57	28	86.64	258.1	28	56.01	166.8	34	61.39	182.9
Miscellaneous biological sciences	152	26.64	148	49.69	186.5	145	51.03	191.6	145	53.06	199.2
Chemistry	109	48.84	99	89.07	182.4	97	75.88	155.4	125	80.17	164.1
Earth sciences	87	28.94	95	56.63	195.7	93	62.09	214.5	102	65.44	226.1
Astronomy	43	20.36	50	48.61	238.8	47	39.94	196.2	44	53.61	263.3
Physics	76	26.58	110	60.58	227.9	90	71.76	270.0	207	62.91	236.7
Mathematics	123	20.20	177	39.11	193.6	149	40.40	200.0	178	48.23	238.8
Computer sciences	150	20.14	174	39.51	196.2	174	39.45	195.9	134	39.41	195.7
Interdisciplinary technical fields	38	26.14	49	39.55	151.3	52	54.57	208.8	67	55.43	212.1
Civil engineering	134	28.68	129	61.74	215.3	151	62.89	219.3	117	65.76	229.3
Mechanical engineering	27	31.73	36	77.36	243.8	47	64.30	202.6	21	111.38	351.0
Electrical and electronic engineering	100	33.12	104	58.84	177.7	85	53.63	161.9	74	66.46	200.7
Materials science	54	37.93	87	83.38	219.8	76	82.14	216.6	73	78.51	207.0
Chemical engineering	24	40.48	45	83.95	207.4	32	69.91	172.7	42	82.74	204.4
Miscellaneous technology	217	36.33	215	59.11	162.7	213	66.72	183.6	152	64.25	176.9
Food and domestic science	38	23.75	43	60.03	252.8	29	61.86	260.5	22	73.38	309.0
Non-clinical medicine	97	18.19	159	34.54	189.9	181	34.25	188.3	154	36.93	203.0
General medicine	73	21.03	73	38.85	184.7	76	48.30	229.7	63	53.93	256.4
Internal medicine	163	27.30	171	57.14	209.3	168	51.12	187.3	188	53.45	195.8
Psychiatry and mental disorders	71	17.97	138	31.98	178.0	150	35.51	197.6	142	36.90	205.3
Surgery	50	29.37	63	65.88	224.3	53	70.38	239.6	49	72.74	247.7
Miscellaneous medicine	292	22.08	342	42.34	191.8	303	43.80	198.4	256	45.39	205.6
Dentistry	20	19.39	16	34.89	179.9	20	44.16	227.7	14	29.83	153.8
Nursing	71	8.00	92	20.14	251.8	72	18.93	236.6	74	22.68	283.5
Agriculture and forestry	78	23.69	58	49.72	209.9	62	56.82	239.8	51	50.47	213.0
Animal husbandry and veterinary medicine	34	20.92	47	35.43	169.4	40	41.93	200.4	41	45.72	218.5
Natural resources and conservation	58	22.88	35	38.58	168.6	27	54.42	237.8	41	47.38	207.1
Total, all books	9,049	£19.07	11,710	£39.77	208.5	11,551	£41.96	220.0	10,332	£42.54	223.1

Compiled by Curt Holleman, Southern Methodist University, from data supplied by B. H. Blackwell and the Library and Information Statistics Unit at Loughborough University.

Table 12 / German Academic Books: Average Prices and Price Index, 1996–1998
(Index Base: 1989=100; prices listed are in Deutsche marks)

Subject	LC Class	1989 No. of Titles	1989 Average Price	1996 No. of Titles	1996 Average Price	1996 Percent increase	1996 Index	1997 No. of Titles	1997 Average Price	1997 Percent increase	1997 Index	1998 No. of Titles	1998 Average Price	1998 Percent increase	1998 Index
Agriculture	S	251	DM74.99	335	DM72.62	4.40	96.8	306	DM76.83	5.80	102.5	219	DM85.39	11.10	113.9
Anthropology	GN-GT	129	70.88	187	75.81	11.40	107.0	156	81.54	7.60	115.0	186	90.15	10.60	127.2
Botany	QK	83	109.94	94	115.01	7.60	104.6	74	108.26	-5.90	98.5	48	124.31	14.80	113.1
Business and economics	H-HJ	1,308	86.82	2,560	74.54	6.30	85.9	2,432	78.72	5.60	90.7	2,146	73.81	-6.20	85.0
Chemistry	QD	87	116.50	214	125.86	-7.50	108.0	147	155.73	23.70	133.7	125	168.84	8.40	144.9
Education	L	426	41.64	679	49.83	8.20	119.7	572	50.66	1.70	121.7	562	51.40	1.50	123.5
Engineering and technology	T	906	79.49	994	91.60	1.70	115.2	823	127.14	38.80	160.0	821	109.52	-13.90	137.8
Fine and applied arts	M-N	1,766	55.57	2,515	70.08	-9.10	126.1	1,937	88.18	25.80	158.7	2,337	72.75	-17.50	130.9
General works	A	43	59.63	58	166.11	-44.90	278.5	42	296.50	78.50	497.2	46	120.56	-59.30	202.2
Geography	G-GF	202	48.96	150	76.68	-21.60	156.6	158	93.03	21.30	190.0	141	101.73	9.30	207.8
Geology	QE	46	77.10	76	79.18	-35.00	102.7	60	535.79	576.70	694.9	59	103.86	-80.60	134.7
History	C,D,E,F	1,064	62.93	2,194	67.92	12.10	107.9	1,837	74.99	10.40	119.1	1,994	77.46	3.30	123.1
Law	K	1,006	100.52	1,889	87.72	-3.50	87.3	1,935	106.35	21.20	105.8	1,561	100.94	-5.10	100.4
Library and information science	Z	118	94.71	165	151.38	-54.60	159.8	145	221.55	46.30	233.9	153	319.66	44.30	337.5
Literature and language	P	2,395	52.10	3,689	62.59	11.00	120.1	3,750	67.69	8.10	129.9	3,731	67.17	-0.80	128.9
Mathematics and computer science	QA	367	68.16	779	80.89	-5.30	118.7	689	84.89	5.00	124.5	724	93.42	10.00	137.1
Medicine	R	1,410	82.67	1,849	93.01	-3.50	112.5	1,643	88.02	-5.40	106.5	1,508	98.14	11.50	118.7
Military and naval science	U-V	67	70.43	52	90.15	15.00	128.0	44	63.07	-30.00	89.6	47	57.03	-9.60	81.0
Natural history	QH	78	85.23	185	102.95	5.90	120.8	142	93.77	-8.90	110.0	136	120.25	28.20	141.1
Philosophy and religion	B	918	56.91	1,638	73.46	-0.20	129.1	1,398	90.38	23.00	158.8	1,757	80.43	-11.00	141.3
Physical education and recreation	GV	110	35.65	149	39.82	-8.50	111.7	142	46.68	17.20	131.0	147	42.05	-9.90	118.0
Physics and astronomy	QB-QC	192	85.12	347	91.61	5.50	107.6	239	97.12	6.00	114.1	235	133.03	37.00	156.3
Physiology	QM-QR	163	124.67	168	128.73	13.40	103.3	153	114.28	-11.20	91.7	117	169.11	48.00	135.6
Political science	J	482	50.38	615	59.63	5.60	118.4	571	62.79	5.30	124.6	654	57.44	-8.50	114.0
Psychology	BF	116	54.95	220	58.85	5.30	107.1	204	58.97	0.20	107.3	211	62.81	6.50	114.3
Science (general)	Q	100	115.90	86	80.19	1.00	69.2	90	95.62	19.20	82.5	86	79.96	-16.40	69.0
Sociology	HM-HX	722	41.52	1,034	49.75	9.00	119.8	1,069	47.85	-3.80	115.3	1,196	48.32	1.00	116.4
Zoology	QL	49	82.74	91	100.07	17.70	120.9	100	133.58	33.50	161.4	86	109.55	-18.00	132.4
Total		14,604	DM67.84	23,012	DM74.81	-0.80	110.3	20,858	DM84.65	13.20	124.8	21,033	DM81.08	-4.20	119.5

Compiled by John Haar, Vanderbilt University, from approval plan data supplied by Otto Harrassowitz. Data represent a selection of materials relevant to research and documentation published in Germany (see text for more information regarding the nature of the data). Unclassified material as well as titles in home economics and industrial arts have been excluded. The index is not adjusted for high-priced titles.

Table 13 / German Academic Periodical Price Index, 1998–2000
(Index Base: 1990 = 100; prices in Deutsche marks)

Subject	LC Class	1990 Average Price	1998 No. of Titles	1998 Average Price	1998 Percent Increase	1998 Index	1999 Final No. Titles	1999 Final Average Price	1999 Final Percent Increase	1999 Final Index	2000 Preliminary No. Titles	2000 Preliminary Average Price	2000 Preliminary Percent Increase	2000 Preliminary Index
Agriculture	S	DM235.11	162	DM377.98	-0.3	160.8	166	DM373.87	-1.1	159.0	172	DM380.24	1.7	161.7
Anthropology	GN	112.88	17	156.29	-9.0	138.5	16	185.17	18.5	164.0	17	182.42	-1.5	161.6
Botany	QK	498.79	16	825.07	-2.6	165.4	16	994.49	20.5	199.4	16	1,051.19	5.7	210.7
Business and economics	H-HJ	153.48	259	230.77	2.5	150.4	260	255.01	10.5	166.2	262	263.90	3.5	171.9
Chemistry	QD	553.06	56	2,155.55	7.4	389.7	52	2,737.38	27.0	495.0	52	3,125.98	14.2	565.2
Education	L	70.86	60	91.53	0.3	129.2	57	93.76	2.4	132.3	59	95.70	2.1	135.1
Engineering and technology	T-TT	239.40	354	376.80	9.8	157.4	332	415.79	10.3	173.7	338	435.77	4.8	182.0
Fine and applied arts	M-N	84.15	169	108.70	3.8	129.2	151	112.07	3.1	133.2	152	113.63	1.4	135.0
General	A	349.37	69	435.91	12.7	124.8	68	432.15	-0.9	123.7	70	451.92	4.6	129.4
Geography	G	90.42	22	153.05	1.8	169.3	23	196.95	28.7	217.8	23	197.91	0.5	218.9
Geology	QE	261.30	32	521.27	1.6	199.5	36	637.44	22.3	243.9	36	673.65	5.7	257.8
History	C,D,E,F	66.09	149	97.00	-1.4	146.8	147	103.00	6.2	155.8	149	104.09	1.1	157.5
Law	K	193.88	154	323.26	2.6	166.7	155	350.81	8.5	180.9	156	358.17	2.1	184.7
Library and information science	Z	317.50	44	402.13	8.7	126.7	44	471.68	17.3	148.6	44	379.70	-19.5	119.6
Literature and language	P	102.69	186	142.63	-0.7	138.9	176	155.44	9.0	151.4	176	155.29	-0.1	151.2
Mathematics and computer science	QA	1064.62	53	1,295.38	-7.8	121.7	62	1,370.49	5.8	128.7	62	1,401.04	2.2	131.6
Medicine	R	320.62	347	614.58	3.2	191.7	337	756.80	23.1	236.0	369	755.92	-0.1	235.8
Military and naval science	U-V	86.38	23	99.68	3.7	115.4	21	126.86	27.3	146.9	21	127.59	0.6	147.7
Natural history	QH	728.36	53	1,375.24	-6.8	188.8	47	1,774.61	29.0	243.6	49	1,834.79	3.4	251.9
Philosophy and religion	B	65.00	194	114.34	5.7	175.9	195	112.67	-1.5	173.3	196	113.02	0.3	173.9
Physical education and recreation	GV	81.96	41	103.59	5.1	126.4	41	108.70	4.9	132.6	42	109.43	0.7	133.5
Physics and astronomy	QB-QC	684.40	51	1,899.57	29.2	277.6	50	2,472.22	30.1	361.2	53	2,756.34	11.5	402.7
Physiology	QM-QR	962.83	12	2,649.13	-18.7	275.1	13	3,264.38	23.2	339.0	13	3,434.80	5.2	356.7
Political science	J	80.67	130	105.13	1.4	130.3	117	105.20	0.1	130.4	117	106.05	0.8	131.5
Psychology	BF	94.10	35	158.88	0.8	168.8	33	189.71	19.4	201.6	34	192.81	1.6	204.9
Science (general)	Q	310.54	28	517.91	5.6	166.8	24	602.08	16.3	193.9	24	634.50	5.4	204.3
Sociology	HM-HX	109.61	66	146.30	4.4	133.5	77	147.91	1.1	134.9	77	150.34	1.6	137.2
Zoology	QL	161.02	24	316.23	4.5	196.4	25	406.68	28.6	252.6	27	411.70	1.2	255.7
Totals and Averages		DM228.4	2,806	DM403.69	8.0	176.7	2,741	DM472.68	17.1	207.0	2,806	DM497.45	5.2	217.8

Data, supplied by Otto Harrassowitz, represent periodical and newspaper titles published in Germany; prices listed in marks. Price information for 2000 is preliminary and is 84% complete. Index is compiled by Steven E. Thompson, Brown University Library.

Table 14 / Dutch (English-Language) Periodicals Price Index 1996–1999
(Index Base: 1996=100; currency unit: DFL)

Subject Area	LC Class	1996 No. of Titles	1996 Average Price	1997 No. of Titles	1997 Average Price	1997 Index	1998 No. of Titles	1998 Average Price	1998 Index	1999 No. of Titles	1999 Average Price	1999 Index
Agriculture	S	36	1,215.10	37	1,335.84	109.9	36	1,559.27	128.3	36	1,749.35	144.0
Botany	QK	10	1,654.90	10	1,899.60	114.8	11	1,948.09	117.7	11	2,173.27	131.3
Business and economics	H-HJ	86	721.95	92	766.85	106.2	94	846.98	117.3	99	918.68	127.3
Chemistry	QD	32	4,258.83	32	4,886.74	114.7	39	5,319.49	124.9	40	5,781.60	135.8
Education	L	6	411.67	6	483.83	117.5	8	518.88	126.0	9	563.78	137.0
Engineering and technology	T-TS	77	1,526.30	78	1,725.26	113.0	79	2,084.85	136.6	82	2,292.09	150.2
Fine and applied arts	M-N	3	326.67	2	444.50	136.1	1	539.00	165.0	9	675.00	206.6
Geography	G	8	1,425.88	8	1,563.38	109.6	9	1,668.28	117.0	9	1,889.39	132.5
Geology	QE	25	1,587.60	26	1,764.78	111.2	26	1,956.62	123.2	26	2,215.83	139.6
History	C,D,E,F	9	257.00	9	290.06	112.9	12	312.33	121.5	12	332.75	129.5
Law	K	14	494.21	14	531.50	107.5	29	525.45	106.3	27	574.94	116.3
Library and information science	Z	6	262.67	6	281.83	107.3	6	302.83	115.3	6	313.67	119.4
Literature and language	P	35	348.26	34	380.32	109.2	41	396.34	113.8	42	433.76	124.6
Mathematics and computer science	QA	56	1,473.25	56	1,664.64	113.0	63	1,791.70	121.6	62	2,016.03	136.8
Medicine	R	62	1,357.47	63	1,577.76	116.2	72	1,705.82	125.7	75	1,893.45	139.5
Military and naval science	U-V	1	295.00	1	278.00	94.2	2	181.50	61.5	2	215.00	72.9
Natural history	QH	33	2,226.92	39	2,196.41	98.6	40	2,430.53	109.1	44	2,603.86	116.9
Philosophy and religion	B,BL,BP	33	407.21	34	436.97	107.3	34	487.62	119.8	34	546.38	134.2
Physics and astronomy	QB-QC	43	4,329.47	44	4,694.05	108.4	47	5,007.64	115.7	49	5,487.12	126.7
Physiology	QM-QR	16	3,568.00	16	4,071.56	114.1	17	4,260.00	119.4	18	4,653.89	130.4
Political science	J	4	428.25	4	508.25	118.7	5	474.20	110.7	5	518.40	121.1
Psychology	BF	4	925.50	5	977.00	105.6	9	931.11	100.6	9	1,037.89	112.1
Science (general)	Q	12	1,071.98	12	1,203.92	112.3	10	1,244.70	116.1	10	1,452.80	135.5
Sociology	HM-HX	6	377.33	5	448.60	118.9	3	457.33	121.2	4	409.91	108.6
Zoology	QL	11	776.21	10	992.60	127.9	10	1,100.00	141.7	10	1,252.20	161.3
Total		628	1,560.44	643	1,734.69	111.2	703	1,892.15	121.3	722	2,092.62	134.1

No data exist for Anthropology, General works, Physical education.

Source: Martinus Nijhoff International, compiled by Bas Guijt and Frederick C. Lynden.

(text continued from page 496)

Newspaper Prices

The indexes for U.S. (Table 8A) and International (Table 8B) newspapers were little changed in 2000. Compilers Genevieve Owens and Wilba Swearingen observe that newspaper publishers are grappling with major marketing and technological issues at the start of the 21st century, and they may be holding prices steady in an effort to retain current subscribers. Minimal price increases notwithstanding, the average U.S. newspaper subscription costs libraries nearly $325, and a comparable international title runs about $1,050. These prices make even modest collections of newspapers an expensive proposition for libraries.

Prices of Other Media

Data for the U.S. nonprint media index (Table 9) is repeated from last year due to the unavailability of pricing information at press time. Dana Alessi, index compiler, uses a database of titles reviewed in *Booklist, Library Journal, School Library Journal*, and *Video Librarian* beginning in 1997. The index assumes higher price and longer length when information varies on the same title reviewed in the different source publications.

The CD-ROM price inventory (Table 10) is also repeated from last year, since presently there is no index compiler. Last year's index, compiled by Martha Kellogg and Theodore Kellogg, used data from the *Faxon Guide to CD-ROMs* and *CD-ROMs in Print*, supplemented by selected publishers' catalogs. All prices are for single-user (non-networked) workstations at the most complete level of service, including all archival discs. The title coverage of this particular index can vary from year to year, since it is affected by the conversion of many CD-ROMs to other electronic formats. The small sample in each subject can also cause widely varying prices when a few expensive titles increase in cost.

Foreign Prices

U.S. Purchasing Power Abroad

The financial crises in Asia in 1997 and in Russia in 1998 have played a role in currency exchange rates worldwide. The *Federal Reserve Bulletin* reports that in the fourth quarter of 1999, the dollar depreciated 3.7 percent against the yen and appreciated 6.2 percent against the euro. On an effective trade-weighted basis, this was a dollar appreciation of 0.8 percent. Analyses of prior 1999 quarters are available at http://www.federalreserve.gov/pubs/bulletin/. The adoption of the euro by most European Community member countries may, in the near future, complicate the computation of price fluctuations in international publishing using the LMPIC indexes. The exchange rate table below indicates some of those changes, in that the Federal Reserve Board no longer tracks the U.S. dollar exchange rates against the French franc, German mark, and Netherlands guilder. These three currency exchange rates as of the end of 1999 are taken from the regional Federal Reserve Bank of St. Louis Web site (http://www.stls.frb.org/fred/data/exchange.html). Historical data for Canadian, United Kingdom, Japanese, and other currencies are found at the U.S. Federal Reserve Board site, http://www.bog.frb.fed.us/releases/H10/hist/, with an analysis of historical rate trends at http://www.federalreserve.gov/pubs/bulletin/.

Dates	12/31/94	12/31/95	12/31/96	12/31/97	12/31/98	12/31/99
Canada	1.4088	1.3644	1.3705	1.3567	1.5433	1.5375
France	5.3640	4.9050	5.1900	6.0190	5.5981	6.4882*
U.K.	0.6412	0.6439	0.5839	0.6058	0.5985	0.6014
Germany	1.5525	1.4365	1.5400	1.7991	1.6698	1.9345*
Japan	99.65	103.43	115.85	130.45	129.73	102.16
Netherlands	1.7391	1.6080	1.7410	2.0265	1.8816	2.1797*

* Data from the regional Federal Reserve Bank of Saint Louis. Upon the introduction of the euro on January 1, 1999, the Federal Reserve Board discontinued posting dollar exchange rates against the ECU and the currencies of the 11 countries participating in the European Economic and Monetary Union including the French franc, German mark, and Netherlands guilder.

Price indexes include British Academic Books (Table 11), German Academic Books (Table 12), German Academic Periodicals (Table 13), Dutch English-Language Periodicals (Table 14), and Latin American Periodicals. (Tables 15A and 15B).

British Prices

The price index for British books (Table 11) is compiled by Curt Holleman from information supplied by B. H. Blackwell. Holleman notes that the pound experienced a decrease of 1.4 percent in 1999 in its average daily value compared against the dollar and that the output of British academic books declined by 10.6 percent. When these two factors are combined with the inflation of 1.4 percent in the cost of each British book, the cost for U.S. academic libraries to maintain a proportionate collection of British books declined by 11.4 percent in 1999. In the 14 years that Holleman has compiled the index, this is only the second year of decreased total costs. The average annual increase over 14 years has been just over 10 percent.

German Prices

The price index for German Academic Books (Table 12) is also repeated from last year. Due to system migration, Otto Harrassowitz is unable to provide book prices for 1999 until summer 2000. The published data include all German monographic publications available for U.S. libraries to purchase during calendar year 1998 and do not strictly represent a 1998 imprint year compilation. A small number of German CD-ROMs and other audiovisual materials are included but should not invalidate the price trend data. Readers are referred to the prior year's *Bowker Annual* for the more detailed now-historical price analysis that will not be repeated here.

The index for German Academic Periodicals (Table 13), compiled by Steven E. Thompson, is also based on data provided by Otto Harrassowitz. Final 1999 data indicate that only three subject areas, Anthropology, General, and Philosophy and Religion, decreased in price. When final 1999 prices were tabulated, the overall increase in price was 17.1 percent. In the sciences and medicine most subjects increased in excess of 20 percent in price with a range from 20.5 percent for Botany to 30.1 percent in Physics and Astronomy; others increased in the high teens. In contrast, Engineering and Technology increased 10.3 percent, which, while not an inconsequential increase, is clearly not in lock-step with the related scientific disciplines in the sciences and medicine.

Dutch Prices

The Dutch English-Language Periodicals Index (Table 14) is data published last year and is not updated. Nijhoff, due to conversion to an automated system, has not been able to provide the data to the compiler, Fred Lynden, for inclusion this year. It should be noted that compiling this index has increased in complexity because the publishers no longer distinguish between what is produced in the Netherlands and what is produced in England or the United States. Readers are referred to last year's *Bowker Annual* for a detailed analysis of the data.

Latin American Prices

Scott Van Jacob compiles the Latin American Periodicals indexes (Tables 15A and 15B) from prices provided by Faxon, the Library of Congress's Rio field office, and the University of Texas at Austin. Readers are reminded that the Latin American book index was last published in 1997 and is to be replaced with a new index based on data provided by Latin American book vendors.

Regionally Central America shows the lowest price increase for 1998–1999, while periodicals from Mexico far outpace the other regions in increased costs. The weighted overall mean for Latin American periodicals not including newspapers shows an increase of 20 percent over the index year of 1992. When newspapers are included, the weighted mean decreases slightly to a rise of 18 percent above the index year. As in last year's analysis, Science & Technology and the Social Sciences show the greater increases in periodicals prices.

Using the Price Indexes

Librarians are encouraged to monitor both trends in the publishing industry and changes in economic conditions when preparing budget forecasts and projections. The ALA ALCTS Library Materials Price Index Committee endeavors to make information on publishing trends readily available by sponsoring the annual compilation and publication of price data contained in Tables 1–15. The indexes cover newly published library materials and document prices and rates of price changes at the national/international level. They are useful benchmarks against which local costs may be compared, but because they reflect retail prices in the aggregate, they are not a substitute for cost data that reflect the collecting patterns of individual libraries, and they are not a substitute for specific cost studies.

In part, differences between local prices and those found in national indexes arise because the national indexes exclude discounts, service charges, shipping and handling fees, or other costs that the library might bear. Discrepancies may

Table 15A / Latin American Periodical Price Index, 1998–1999:
Country and Region Index

	Total Titles w/o newspapers	Mean w/o newspapers	Index (1992=100)	Weighted mean w/o newspapers	Index (1992=100)
Country					
Argentina	153	$110.88	127	$83.41	116
Bolivia	6	42.80	98	29.09	84
Brazil	269	71.11	104	63.57	86
Caribbean	32	40.27	95	41.78	106
Chile	89	80.18	160	77.28	164
Colombia	55	45.32	99	52.89	113
Costa Rica	25	34.36	132	47.37	153
Cuba	17	59.41	168	56.06	147
Ecuador	16	86.66	249	84.45	254
El Salvador	7	62.14	327	48.19	312
Guatemala	10	130.61	171	207.73	238
Honduras	n.a.	n.a.	n.a.	n.a.	n.a.
Jamaica	25	42.82	133	36.85	117
Mexico	183	95.50	147	81.40	143
Nicaragua	8	31.81	104	36.31	117
Panama	16	32.62	122	28.66	113
Paraguay	7	27.79	176	10.61	48
Peru	35	82.38	82	98.22	89
Uruguay	17	111.11	334	90.98	278
Venezuela	38	84.15	82	67.67	143
Region					
Caribbean	74	42.76	115	44.52	121
Central America	66	39.46	109	42.31	102
South America	685	76.90	103	71.87	111
Mexico	183	95.50	147	81.40	143
Latin America	1,008	75.44	112	69.43	120

Subscription information was provided by the Faxon Co., Library of Congress, Rio Office, and the University of Texas, Austin. Index based on 1992 LAPPI mean prices. The 1997/1998 subscription prices were included in this year's index if a new subscription price was not given.

Compiled by Scott Van Jacob, University of Notre Dame.

n.a. = fewer than five subscription prices were found.

Table 15B / Latin American Periodical Price Index, 1998–1999: Subject Index

Subjects	Mean	Index (1992=100)	Weighted mean	Index (1992=100)
Social Sciences	$78.36	110	$67.44	125
Humanities	44.45	111	42.17	116
Science/technology	66.63	113	75.24	134
General	104.00	119	93.73	102
Law	117.46	114	92.35	107
Newspapers	544.20	134	394.84	97
Totals w/o newspapers.	$75.44	112	$69.43	120
Total with newspapers	$97.66	112	$75.96	118
Total titles with newspapers = 1,056				
Total titles without newspapers = 1,008				

also be related to subject focus, mix of current and retrospective materials, and the portion of total library acquisitions composed of foreign imprints. Such variables can affect the average price paid by a particular library although the library's rate of price increase may not significantly differ from national price indexes. LMPIC is interested in pursuing studies correlating a particular library's costs with national prices and would appreciate being informed of any planned or ongoing studies. The committee welcomes interested parties to its meetings at the ALA Annual and Midwinter conferences.

In addition to the tables included, the reader may wish to consult a new publication on the costs of law materials: *Price Index for Legal Publications, 1997* prepared by Margaret Axtmann and published by the American Association of Law Libraries. In addition, Yale University Libraries has established a very useful Web page, "Price and Title Output Reports for Collection Management" at http://www.library.yale.edu/colldev.

Current Library Materials Price Index Committee members are Barbara Albee, Margaret Axtmann, Janet Belanger, Pamela Bluh, Martha Brogan, Mae Clark, Doina Farkas, Christian Filstrup, Mary Fugle, Beverly Harris, Harriet Lightman, Bill Robnett (chair), Penny Schroeder, and Sherry Sullivan. Consultants are Dana Alessi, Barbara Albee, Donna Alsbury, Catherine Barr, Dave Bogart, Stephen Bosch, Nancy Chaffin, Brenda Dingley, Wanda Dole, Virginia Gilbert, Curt Holleman, Fred Lynden, Genevieve Owens, Wilba Swearingen, Steven Thompson, and Scott Van Jacob.

Book Title Output and Average Prices:
1998 Final and 1999 Preliminary Figures

Gary Ink
Research Librarian, *Publishers Weekly*

Andrew Grabois
Senior Managing Director, Bibliographies, R. R. Bowker

Experienced users of these title output and price tables will immediately notice that the output figures are dramatically increased for all three years shown—1997 and 1998 final data and preliminary 1999 data. This increase (83 percent, or 54,448 titles between 1997 and 1998) results from the fact that, for the first time, output and price figures were compiled from R. R. Bowker's Books in Print database, a change that results in a more accurate portrayal of the current state of American book publishing.

In years past the basic data used to produce the title output and average price figures have been extracted from Bowker's American Book Publishing Record database, supplemented by data from Paperbound Books in Print and by additional manual calculation. These figures reflected only those books cataloged by the Library of Congress, especially those passing through the Cataloging in Publica-

Table 1 / American Book Title Production, 1997–1999

| Category | All Hard and Paper | | |
	1997 Final	1998 Final	1999 Preliminary
Agriculture	1,303	1,201	892
Art	4,565	4,934	4,272
Biography	2,993	3,206	2,775
Business	4,015	3,844	3,154
Education	3,278	3,391	2,492
Fiction	9,312	11,016	11,570
General works	1,561	1,504	1,238
History	9,704	7,346	6,018
Home economics	2,481	2,518	2,272
Juveniles	8,631	9,195	8,320
Language	3,199	2,862	1,985
Law	2,452	3,007	1,996
Literature	3,467	3,784	3,262
Medicine	7,117	6,718	5,312
Music	1,643	1,398	1,155
Philosophy, psychology	5,622	5,965	4,999
Poetry, drama	2,770	3,018	2,226
Religion	5,748	6,347	4,806
Science	9,304	8,486	6,410
Sociology, economics	14,611	14,645	11,895
Sports, recreation	3,664	3,718	3,208
Technology	9,496	9,103	7,359
Travel	2,326	3,038	2,789
Totals	119,262	120,244	100,405

tion (CIP) program. While CIP is a useful snapshot of general trade publishing from the largest houses, many books published in the United States in a given year do not fall within the scope of CIP. These include inexpensive editions, annuals, and much of the output of small presses and self publishers (each year more than 10,000 new ISBN publisher prefixes are assigned by the U.S. ISBN Agency).

Bowker—along with many in the book industry and in the library community—has recognized that American book title production was being undercounted, particularly in relation to trade paperback and mass market paperback output. (This fact was further reinforced by book title output at the international level, where most of the industrialized nations have appeared to experience more dramatic growth than the United States. For example, the United Kingdom has been reporting title output totals above 100,000 since the mid-1990s.)

In consultation with organizations in the book industry and with the American Library Association, Bowker has worked to extract the basic data from the more sophisticated and comprehensive Books in Print database, providing figures that are up to date and representative of the current reality of the book industry. The Books in Print database is kept current through constant communication with more than 104,000 U.S. publishers, distributors, and wholesalers. In

Table 2 / Hardcover Average Per-Volume Prices, 1997–1999

Category	1997 Prices	1998 Final			1999 Preliminary		
		Vols.	$ Total	Prices	Vols.	$ Total	Prices
Agriculture	$63.70	589	$36,514.51	$61.99	438	$24,391.70	$55.69
Art	55.99	2,406	133,360.97	55.43	2,016	118,645.22	58.85
Biography	54.78	1,649	76,512.89	46.40	1,515	68,713.02	45.36
Business	99.34	1,575	147,159.20	93.43	1,240	158,804.01	128.07
Education	85.74	1,152	69,714.77	60.52	855	52,117.59	60.96
Fiction	24.97	3,719	99,636.28	26.79	3,854	105,826.36	27.46
General works	108.87	759	83,993.64	110.66	630	98,113.37	155.74
History	62.81	3,627	225,862.73	62.27	3,160	169,413.48	53.61
Home economics	36.79	1,103	41,885.18	37.97	1,061	41,798.63	39.40
Juveniles	19.25	5,432	114,602.65	21.10	5,148	115,115.99	22.36
Language	71.90	1,103	83,801.19	75.98	802	43,244.07	53.92
Law	109.95	1,390	130,664.23	94.00	983	90,626.27	92.19
Literature	62.07	2,102	124,014.94	59.00	1,834	128,885.71	70.28
Medicine	111.88	3,122	293,859.43	94.13	2,422	206,472.54	85.25
Music	57.87	531	28,990.61	54.60	452	27,239.03	60.26
Philosophy, psychology	59.87	2,312	129,005.34	55.80	2,075	119,732.08	57.70
Poetry, drama	46.99	1,126	48,494.98	43.07	883	37,518.30	42.49
Religion	54.32	2,624	119,088.74	45.38	1,924	79,479.78	41.31
Science	103.54	4,914	471,523.89	95.96	3,857	363,131.14	94.15
Sociology, economics	79.32	6,876	453,579.16	65.97	5,593	343,055.29	61.34
Sports, recreation	46.97	1,254	55,366.55	44.15	1,189	46,371.55	39.00
Technology	133.58	3,852	430,870.92	111.86	2,823	294,165.15	104.20
Travel	44.87	705	27,176.34	38.55	551	21,892.99	39.73
Totals	$72.67	53,922	$3,425,679.14	$63.53	45,305	$2,754,753.27	$60.80

1999 Bowker editors applied some 3 million additions, changes, and deletions to the more than 3.2 million U.S. records in the database.

In order to provide a basis for year-to-year comparison, data have been extracted for 1997 and 1998, as well as preliminary figures for 1999, restating the final book title output and average price figures for 1997 published in the 1999 *Bowker Annual*. The undercounting that took place when the data depended on CIP information is borne out by the difference between the trade paperback and mass market paperback output totals published in the 1999 *Bowker Annual* and those presented in the restated 1997 totals. As restated, the final figure for 1997 trade paperback output increased by 31,061 titles, and the 1997 mass market paperback total increased by 2,813 titles.

Output by Format and by Category

The final total for American book title output reached 120,244 titles in 1998 (Table 1). This represents an increase of less than 1 percent (982 titles) over the restated final 1997 figure of 119,262 titles. Fiction output, which is generally viewed as an important barometer of the health of the book publishing industry, increased by 18 percent (1,704 titles) between 1997 and 1998. As noted above,

Table 3 / Hardcover Average Per-Volume Prices, Less Than $81, 1997–1999

Category	1997 Prices	1998 Final Vols.	1998 Final $ Total	1998 Final Prices	1999 Preliminary Vols.	1999 Preliminary $ Total	1999 Preliminary Prices
Agriculture	$35.88	471	$15,787.73	$33.52	355	$12,472.76	$35.13
Art	40.29	2,159	84,987.53	39.36	1,788	70,525.05	39.44
Biography	35.09	1,502	50,735.93	33.78	1,389	45,304.85	32.62
Business	43.20	1,208	53,194.29	44.04	962	41,010.55	42.63
Education	41.55	1,016	41,797.23	41.14	762	31,777.44	41.70
Fiction	24.21	3,628	88,293.67	24.34	3,734	92,519.33	24.78
General works	41.69	517	21,557.46	41.70	394	16,010.71	40.64
History	39.78	3,222	131,408.65	40.78	2,833	113,630.79	40.11
Home economics	26.54	1,066	27,311.13	25.62	1,027	25,681.03	25.01
Juveniles	17.18	5,295	95,750.89	18.08	5,057	91,197.57	18.03
Language	42.54	876	39,394.69	44.97	688	28,862.04	41.95
Law	46.58	908	42,987.80	47.34	659	31,125.20	47.23
Literature	40.47	1,730	69,495.55	40.17	1,389	55,202.81	39.74
Medicine	45.23	1,911	82,503.10	43.17	1,547	65,522.54	42.35
Music	40.76	474	19,384.66	40.90	383	15,074.71	39.36
Philosophy, psychology	41.38	2,060	84,949.43	41.24	1,901	73,968.36	38.91
Poetry, drama	35.06	1,034	35,350.58	34.19	768	24,441.32	31.82
Religion	33.38	2,377	78,732.19	33.12	1,758	56,341.74	32.05
Science	44.69	2,966	132,585.51	44.70	2,459	106,486.67	43.30
Sociology, economics	45.41	5,804	261,400.33	45.04	4,832	216,239.35	44.75
Sports, recreation	32.16	1,186	40,255.89	33.94	1,137	37,746.05	33.20
Technology	46.15	2,428	116,160.33	47.84	1,903	84,199.86	44.25
Travel	31.21	667	19,724.38	29.57	520	15,940.71	30.66
Totals	$37.20	44,505	$1,633,748.95	$36.71	38,245	$1,351,281.44	$35.33

major increases for fiction titles have occurred in the mass market and trade paperback formats (Tables 4 and 5).

The preliminary 1999 figure indicates a continuing increase in fiction title output. Other subject categories that appear to have experienced year-to-year growth between 1997 and 1998 include poetry and drama with an increase of 9 percent (248 titles), religion with an increase of 10 percent (599 titles), and travel, which rose 30 percent (712 titles). The important children's category (Juveniles), another barometer of industry health, increased by 6.5 percent (564 titles). These categories have also demonstrated continuing growth in the current dollar sales figures reported by the book industry. The business subject category, which in recent years has been viewed as a growth area by book publishers, registered a decline in overall title output of 4.3 percent (171 titles) between 1997 and 1998.

Average Book Prices

The change in the method for determining average book prices makes it difficult to correlate and compare the 1998 average book prices to those of past years. The best effort that can be made is to make a year-to-year comparison of the 1998 book prices to the restated 1997 prices.

Table 4 / Mass Market Paperbacks Average Per-Volume Prices, 1997–1999

Category	1997 Prices	1998 Final			1999 Preliminary		
		Vols.	$ Total	Prices	Vols.	$ Total	Prices
Agriculture	$7.50	4	$21.43	$5.36	8	$47.31	$5.91
Art	6.54	18	141.44	7.86	25	208.22	8.33
Biography	6.46	55	365.35	6.64	75	482.41	6.43
Business	6.51	5	29.18	5.84	10	83.21	8.32
Education	7.32	17	151.78	8.93	29	209.79	7.23
Fiction	5.40	3,657	19,848.12	5.43	4,045	22,279.44	5.51
General works	7.48	9	62.83	6.98	17	134.65	7.92
History	6.13	34	231.29	6.80	23	153.63	6.68
Home economics	6.89	51	319.31	6.26	54	401.44	7.43
Juveniles	4.69	2,267	11,100.21	4.90	2,066	10,369.31	5.02
Language	5.92	56	374.64	6.69	46	323.06	7.02
Law	6.69	7	54.94	7.85	3	20.97	6.99
Literature	6.72	93	622.35	6.69	119	784.49	6.59
Medicine	6.53	100	601.04	6.01	111	671.64	6.05
Music	7.97	17	121.65	7.16	16	104.78	6.55
Philosophy, psychology	6.52	93	655.19	7.05	220	1,540.33	7.00
Poetry, drama	6.41	37	242.11	6.54	46	301.10	6.55
Religion	6.99	137	1,016.59	7.42	159	1,125.90	7.08
Science	5.17	58	389.49	6.72	64	406.20	6.35
Sociology, economics	6.76	91	583.74	6.41	88	565.50	6.43
Sports, recreation	6.43	67	416.31	6.21	64	386.99	6.05
Technology	6.87	17	113.61	6.68	20	137.59	6.88
Travel	8.75	19	160.84	8.47	15	126.45	8.43
Totals	$5.36	6,909	$37,623.44	$5.45	7,323	$40,864.41	$5.58

The important category of fiction shows an increase of 7.3 percent ($1.82) for hardcover books between restated 1997 and 1998. Trade paperback fiction titles show a 1 percent (19 cents) year-to-year decrease between 1997 and 1998; while mass market paperback fiction titles show a year-to-year increase of less than 1 percent (3 cents) between 1997 and 1998. Children's books (Juveniles) show a year-to-year price increase of 9.5 percent ($1.85) for hardcover titles; while trade paperback titles show a price increase of only 1.8 percent (34 cents), and mass market paperback titles show a year-to-year price decrease of 4.5 percent (21 cents).

The most interesting aspect of the average book prices for 1998 are the popular subject categories that have registered year-to-year price decreases between 1997 and 1998: Travel shows an average price decrease of 14 percent ($6.32) in hardcover, a decrease of 6 percent ($1.19) in trade paperback, and a decrease of 3 percent (28 cents) in mass market paperback; business shows an average price decrease of 6 percent ($5.91) in hardcover, a curiously large price decrease of 65 percent ($83.51) in trade paperback, and a decrease of 10.3 percent (67 cents) in mass market paperback; religion shows an average price decrease of 16.5 percent ($8.94) in hardcover and a decrease of 35 percent (69 cents) in trade paperback, but an increase of 6.2 percent (43 cents) in mass market paperback.

Table 5 / Trade Paperbacks Average Per-Volume Prices, 1997–1999

Category	1997 Prices	1998 Final			1999 Preliminary		
		Vols.	$ Total	Prices	Vols.	$ Total	Prices
Agriculture	$28.50	608	$21,687.92	$35.67	446	$16,983.48	$38.08
Art	27.78	2,510	67,240.68	26.79	2,231	58,201.90	26.09
Biography	19.83	1,502	31,097.11	20.70	1,185	23,085.01	19.48
Business	128.45	2,264	101,743.48	44.94	1,904	88,174.48	46.31
Education	27.41	2,222	60,591.17	27.27	1,608	43,408.35	27.00
Fiction	16.22	3,640	58,361.87	16.03	3,671	59,072.61	16.09
General works	199.57	736	27,420.86	37.26	591	25,429.60	43.03
History	26.24	3,685	99,023.93	26.87	2,835	71,774.35	25.32
Home economics	25.16	1,364	28,346.07	20.78	1,157	21,642.39	18.71
Juveniles	19.26	1,496	29,322.79	19.60	1,106	21,200.45	19.17
Language	28.98	1,703	55,261.32	32.45	1,137	33,658.84	29.60
Law	44.78	1,610	72,003.42	44.72	1,010	50,326.94	49.83
Literature	20.98	1,589	32,508.38	20.46	1,309	25,522.91	19.50
Medicine	47.25	3,496	136,013.21	38.91	2,779	105,288.66	37.89
Music	22.18	850	20,364.00	23.96	687	15,684.36	22.83
Philosophy, psychology	23.72	3,560	78,089.78	21.94	2,704	60,032.56	22.20
Poetry, drama	17.00	1,855	28,971.87	15.62	1,297	20,677.88	15.94
Religion	20.03	3,586	69,366.33	19.34	2,723	50,039.43	18.38
Science	48.57	3,514	143,868.31	40.94	2,489	102,525.34	41.19
Sociology, economics	31.23	7,678	258,651.57	33.69	6,214	235,968.64	37.97
Sports, recreation	23.56	2,397	53,060.89	22.14	1,955	43,092.36	22.04
Technology	69.52	5,234	318,615.24	60.87	4,516	260,775.88	57.74
Travel	20.13	2,314	43,816.37	18.94	2,223	46,550.76	20.94
Totals	$38.45	59,413	$1,835,426.57	$30.89	47,777	$1,479,117.18	$30.96

The average book prices produced using the Books in Print database appear to offer a much closer relationship to the actual book prices to be found in the current consumer marketplace.

As in past years, each of the 23 standard subject groups used here represents one or more specific Dewey Decimal Classification numbers, as follows: Agriculture, 630–699, 712–719; Art, 700–711, 720–779; Biography, 920–929; Business, 650–659; Education, 370–379; Fiction; General Works, 000–099; History, 900–909, 930–999; Home Economics, 640–649; Juveniles; Language, 400–499; Law, 340–349; Literature, 800–810, 813–820, 823–899; Medicine, 610–619; Music, 780–789; Philosophy, Psychology, 100–199; Poetry, Drama, 811, 812, 821, 822; Religion, 200–299; Science, 500–599; Sociology, Economics, 300–339, 350–369, 380–389; Sports, Recreation, 790–799; Technology, 600–609, 620–629, 660–699; Travel, 910–919.

Book Sales Statistics, 1999:
AAP Preliminary Estimates

Association of American Publishers

The industry estimates shown in the following table are based on the U.S. Census of Manufactures. However, book publishing is currently being transferred to the Economic Census, also called the Census of Information. Like the Census of Manufactures, this is a five-year census conducted in years ending in "2" and "7"; 1997 was a transition census with the data being collected and processed by the same government people as in prior years, but the forthcoming output will be under the auspices of the new census. Census data for 1997 had been released and were under review as this publication went to press.

Between censuses, the Association of American Publishers (AAP) estimates are "pushed forward" by the percentage changes that are reported to the AAP statistics program, and by other industry data that are available. Some AAP data are collected in a monthly statistics program, and it is largely this material that is shown in this preliminary estimate table. More detailed data are available from, and additional publishers report to, the AAP annual statistics program, and this additional data will be incorporated into Table S1 that will be published in the AAP 1999 Industry Statistics.

Readers comparing the estimated data with census reports should be aware that the U.S. Census of Manufactures does not include data on many university presses or on other institutionally sponsored and not-for-profit publishing activities, or (under SIC 2731: Book Publishing) for the audiovisual and other media materials that are included in this table. On the other hand, AAP estimates have traditionally excluded "Sunday School" materials and certain pamphlets that are incorporated in the census data. These and other adjustments have been built into AAP's industry estimates.

As in prior reports, the estimates reflect the impact of industry expansion created by new establishments entering the field, as well as nontraditional forms of book publishing, in addition to incorporating the sales increases and decreases of established firms.

It should also be noted that the Other Sales category includes only incidental book sales, such as music, sheet sales (both domestic and export, except those to prebinders), and miscellaneous merchandise sales.

The estimates include domestic sales and export sales of U.S. product, but they do not cover indigenous activities of publishers' foreign subsidiaries.

Non-rack-size Mass Market Publishing is included in Trade—Paperbound. Prior to the 1988 AAP Industry Statistics, this was indicated as Adult Trade Paperbound. It is recognized that part of this is Juvenile (estimate: 20 percent), and adjustments have been made in this respect. AAP also notes that this area includes sales through traditional "mass market paperback channels" by publishers not generally recognized as being "mass market paperback" publishers.

Table 1 / Estimated Book Publishing Industry Sales, 1987, 1992, 1997–1999

	1987	1992	1997	1998	% Change from 1997	1999	% Change from 1998	Compound growth rate 1987–1999	1992–1999
Trade (total)	2,712.8	4,661.6	5,774.1	6,148.9	6.5	6,513.9	5.9	7.6	4.9
Adult hardbound	1,350.6	2,222.5	2,663.6	2,751.5	3.3	2,823.9	2.6	6.3	3.5
Adult paperbound	727.1	1,261.7	1,731.7	1,908.3	10.2	1,969.1	3.2	8.7	6.6
Juvenile hardbound	478.5	850.8	908.5	953.9	5.0	1,060.1	11.1	6.9	3.2
Juvenile paperbound	156.6	326.6	470.3	535.2	13.8	660.8	23.5	12.7	10.6
Religious (total)	638.8	907.1	1,132.7	1,178.0	4.0	1,216.9	3.3	5.5	4.3
Bibles, testaments, hymnals, etc.	177.6	260.1	285.4	296.0	3.7	310.0	4.7	4.8	2.5
Other religious	461.2	647.0	847.3	882.0	4.1	906.9	2.8	5.8	4.9
Professional (total)	2,207.3	3,106.7	4,156.4	4,418.7	6.3	4,717.4	6.8	6.5	6.1
Business	388.8	490.3	768.1	852.0	10.9	n.a.	n.a.	n.a.	n.a.
Law	780.0	1,128.1	1,502.7	1,592.1	5.9	n.a.	n.a.	n.a.	n.a.
Medical	406.5	622.7	856.5	919.0	7.3	n.a.	n.a.	n.a.	n.a.
Technical, scientific, other prof'l	632.0	865.6	1,029.1	1,055.6	2.6	n.a.	n.a.	n.a.	n.a.
Book clubs	678.7	742.3	1,143.1	1,209.4	5.8	1,254.4	3.7	5.3	7.8
Mail order publications	657.6	630.2	521.0	470.5	-9.7	412.8	-12.3	-3.8	-5.9
Mass market paperback, rack-sized	913.7	1,263.8	1,433.8	1,514.1	5.6	1,403.2	-7.3	3.6	1.5
University presses	170.9	280.1	367.8	391.8	6.5	411.7	5.1	7.6	5.7
Elementary and secondary text	1,695.6	2,080.9	3,005.4	3,315.0	10.3	3,415.9	3.0	6.0	7.3
College text	1,549.5	2,084.1	2,669.7	2,888.6	8.2	3,128.8	8.3	6.0	6.0
Standardized tests	104.0	140.4	191.4	204.6	6.9	218.7	6.9	6.4	6.5
Subscription reference	437.6	572.3	736.5	767.4	4.2	788.9	2.8	5.0	4.7
Other sales (incl. AV)	423.8	449.0	510.0	526.3	3.2	541.6	2.9	2.1	2.7
Total	12,190.3	16,918.5	21,641.9	23,033.3	6.4	24,024.2	4.3	5.8	5.1

Source: Association of American Publishers

U.S. Book Exports and Imports: 1999

Albert N. Greco

Associate Professor

Fordham University Graduate School of Business Administration

U.S. Book Exports, 1999

Exports play a pivotal role in the economic structure of the U.S. book-publishing industry, accounting for $1.91 billion (8.2 percent) of total net publisher receipts of $23.26 billion in 1999. This represents a gain of 3.91 percent over 1998's export revenues. Unit export totals reached the 1.05-billion-book level, an increase of 15.1 percent over the previous year.

In 2000 U.S. exports should easily exceed the $2 billion mark because of a number of market drivers. English remains a global language, especially in certain book categories (e.g., technical, scientific, and professional; college textbooks). A sizable number of U.S. authors have an international appeal, notably in the adult trade niche (e.g., John Grisham, Stephen King, and Michael Crichton) (Greco, 1997). Augmenting these drivers is an ever-growing interest in U.S. media and entertainment products, including adult and juvenile fiction, works about the broadcast and film industries, and eclectic religious themes.

In addition, in the last 10 to 15 years U.S.-based publishers have crafted exceptionally effective global business relationships. Sales representatives regularly visit Egypt, Taiwan, Hong Kong, Brazil, and other major markets for American books. A large U.S. presence is always evident at the major international book fairs, and the emergence of effective global communications systems

Table 1 / U.S. Exports of Books: 1999

Category	Value (millions of current $)	Percent change: 1998–1999	Units (millions of copies)	Percent change 1998–1999
Dictionaries and thesauruses	$2.73	-63.36%	0.71	-53.90%
Encyclopedias	16.59	-10.90	3.33	-3.2
Textbooks	325.09	-2.03	51.03	-1.49
Religious books	57.18	13.09	45.62	8.26
Technical, scientific, and professional	522.64	-3.53	81.13	-9.92
Art and pictorial books	9.86	-27.07	5.57	-5.11
Hardcover books, n.e.s.	132.92	-6.18	39.16	-18.94
Mass market paperbacks	234.85	-1.86	122.93	-1.60
Books: flyers/circulars, 1–4 pages	5.76	—	11.52	21.14
Books: pamphlets and brochures 5–48 pages	44.08	29.00	68.04	25.21
Books: more than 49 pages	542.75	23.61	615.22	25.10
Music books	17.92	9.43	3.18	-2.15
Atlases	2.24	-8.20	0.34	-2.86
Total, all books	$1,913.87	3.91	1,047.78	15.10

Note: n.e.s. = Not elsewhere specified. Individual shipments are excluded from the foreign trade data if valued under $2,500.00 Data for individual categories may not add to totals due to statistical rounding.

Source: U.S. Department of Commerce, Bureau of the Census

such as e-mail and fax allows business to be conducted 24 hours a day every day of the year. American publishers have also developed efficient book distribution systems, drawing on fairly rapid sea deliveries and quick (but generally expensive) air deliveries to get books into Asia, the Middle East, Africa, and other important markets.

Yet in 1999 and 1998 book export revenues plateaued because of unsettling international economic events. The Asian economic malaise (1997–1998), the apparent "collapse" of the Russian market, a strengthening of the U.S. dollar, and sharp increases in certain commodities negatively impacted book exports to certain regions. While the overall economic vitality of East Asia increased in 1999, a few markets in the Pacific Rim remained weak because of dollar currency exchange problems. This region has not yet returned to pre-1998 business levels (Mishkin 1999; Truett and Truett 1998).

The end result was unsettling. While total dollar revenues were up overall, book export declines were posted in eight of the 13 major revenue categories, with only religious books, flyers and circulars; pamphlets and brochures; books more than 49 pages, and music titles on the upswing (Table 1). Declines were evi-

Table 2 / U.S. Book Exports to 20 Principal Countries: 1999

Country	Value (millions of current $)	Percent change 1998–1999	Units (millions)	Percent change 1998–1999
Canada	$830.81	2.88%	545.04	14.64%
United Kingdom	260.81	10.02	121.39	29.11
Australia	139.82	-11.41	62.46	-12.57
Japan	84.08	-36.91	25.53	-8.07
Mexico	68.88	17.20	55.15	23.65
Netherlands	68.54	50.97	25.72	32.17
Germany	43.62	7.25	15.83	-2.70
Singapore	41.46	56.72	26.79	67.75
Taiwan	25.57	7.89	11.46	38.91
Belgium	24.52	—	7.16	—
Korea (Republic of)	22.98	42.64	15.35	146.39
New Zealand	22.59	5.96	11.44	40.20
Hong Kong	21.27	-0.09	6.65	-3.03
South Africa	18.18	18.21	7.97	11.00
France	14.99	31.15	5.69	42.61
Brazil	14.46	-20.55	5.64	-14.67
Philippines	14.18	36.87	6.84	29.06
China	12.49	—	2.70	—
Italy	10.32	10.14	3.51	15.84
Argentina	8.29	-12.74	5.26	-20.66
Total, top 20 countries	$1,747.86	6.68%	967.58	15.79%

Note: Individual shipments are excluded from the foreign trade data if valued under $2,500.00

Source: U.S. Department of Commerce, Bureau of the Census

dent in the important mass market, art, and the technical-scientific-professional niches. Unit decline tallies closely followed the dollar revenue pattern.

A shift in export customer patterns also emerged. India and Denmark, long-time U.S. trading partners, dropped from the list of the top 20 U.S. export markets. They were replaced by the People's Republic of China ($12.5 million; 2.7 million units) and Belgium ($24.5 million; 7.2 million units).

Canada remained the primary market for all exports, accounting for $830.8 million and a staggering 545 million units; and the United Kingdom, Australia, Japan, and Mexico rounded out the top five (Table 2). These five trading partners collectively accounted for $1.38 billion and more than 809 million units. Mexico's performance was exceptionally impressive, posting a 17 percent increase in dollar revenues and a 23.7 percent surge in units. Japan and Australia, on the other hand, recorded declines in both of these categories. Other nations on the upswing included Korea, Singapore, and the Philippines. Negative tallies were recorded by Hong Kong, Brazil, and Argentina.

An investigation of specific export categories was revealing. Canada and Australia remain the largest consumers of mass market paperbacks, although Mexico's and South Africa's totals were impressive (Table 3).

Table 3 / U.S. Exports of Mass-Market Paperbacks (Rack-Sized), Top 15 Markets: 1999

Country	Dollars (millions)	Quantity (millions)
Canada	$94.37	55.32
Australia	59.97	27.58
United Kingdom	19.90	10.73
New Zealand	11.53	4.07
South Africa	7.84	2.82
Mexico	6.59	5.05
Netherlands	5.73	3.16
Singapore	4.32	2.16
Philippines	2.96	1.50
Brazil	2.61	1.29
Taiwan	2.18	0.92
Argentina	2.02	1.07
Korea (Republic of)	1.72	1.03
Hong Kong	1.66	0.80
France	1.63	0.46

Source: U.S. Department of Commerce

The somewhat under-performing technical, scientific, and professional niche was dominated by Canada, Japan, the United Kingdom, and the Netherlands. Again, Mexico's showing was sterling, and there were strong sales to China, Brazil, and Israel (Table 4).

Table 4 / U.S. Exports of Technical, Scientific, and Professional Books, Top 15 Markets: 1999

Country	Dollars (millions)	Units (millions)
Canada	$154.91	17.89
Japan	65.18	8.69
United Kingdom	59.78	10.70
Netherlands	47.85	7.77
Australia	31.99	5.56
Germany	19.70	3.02
Belgium	17.19	1.61
Korea (Republic of)	13.86	2.73
Mexico	10.49	6.14
Hong Kong	10.39	1.07
Singapore	9.40	1.69
Taiwan	8.34	1.43
Brazil	6.43	1.06
China	6.27	1.16
Israel	6.23	1.25

Source: U.S. Department of Commerce

Canada barely surpasses Mexico's totals in the encyclopedias and serial installments category, with fairly strong sales to China, the United Arab Emirates, and Trinidad (Table 5).

Table 5 / U.S. Exports of Encyclopedias and Serial Installments, Top 15 Markets: 1999

Country	Dollars (millions)	Units
Canada	$2.92	461,013
Mexico	2.73	579,832
United Kingdom	2.27	473,619
Japan	1.87	373,232
India	1.13	194,178
Philippines	1.11	216,838
South Africa	0.47	75,584
Mauritania	0.44	63,214
Singapore	0.42	84,453
Australia	0.37	44,083
Trinidad	0.27	48,681
China	0.26	205,195
United Arab Emirates	0.25	94,468
Taiwan	0.21	46,482
Spain	0.20	17,312

Source: U.S. Department of Commerce

The United Kingdom remained the leader in the important textbook niche, with Canada and Mexico in the top three markets for U.S. exports (Table 6). China emerged as a major purchaser of texts, along with South Africa and Belgium.

Table 6 / U.S. Exports of Textbooks, Top 15 Markets: 1999

Country	Dollars (millions)	Units
United Kingdom	$105.70	17,171,343
Canada	66.46	6,161,295
Mexico	24.63	4,593,085
Australia	19.53	3,402,648
Japan	17.03	2,802,410
Germany	13.76	2,303,601
Taiwan	9.47	1,337,763
Singapore	8.57	1,729,984
Hong Kong	5.53	1,068,722
South Africa	4.83	1,255,554
New Zealand	3.80	471,705
Korea	3.69	783,637
China	2.87	398,986
Netherlands	2.71	504,666
Belgium	2.37	464,619

Source: U.S. Department of Commerce

All major economic indices indicate that the Pacific Rim will continue its rebound from the 1997–1998 fiscal nightmare, and conditions may improve in other regions (including Russia) in 2000. Yet the slight increase in total export dollar revenues in 1999 indicates that gains (and possibly sharp gains) in export revenues are possible in both 2000 and 2001. These changes can take place if: (1) U.S. publishers increase their global sales and marketing efforts, and (2) the U.S. government strengthens its commitment to the Department of Commerce's international trade division. The market demand for U.S. books remains at a historical high point. Yet competition in the international sales arena from foreign publishers in Europe and Asia is intense and exhibits no signs of abatement—a sign that renewed, not curtailed, efforts are needed to capture a larger share of the export market for American publishing houses.

U.S. Book Imports, 1999

Two important themes were evident in 1999. First, book publishing remains a positive-balance-of-trade industry for the United States. Export book totals reached $1.91 billion and total imports topped $1.41 billion, generating a surplus of more than $500 million. Regrettably, the U.S. Department of Commerce continues to estimate (rather than actually track) all export shipments below the $2,500 level; existing export tallies are therefore quite likely under-reported by

Commerce, indicating that the actual export-import surplus is much larger than $500 million.

The most popular categories of book imports included hardcover books, textbooks, and technical, scientific, and professional books, generating $827 million in revenues (Table 7). Volume declines were evident in the beleaguered dictionaries and thesauruses category (-12.1 percent) because of the move to electronic versions (either initially installed on computers or accessed via CD-ROMs) in the United States, and in the art (-71.71 percent) niche.

Table 7 / U.S. Imports of Books: 1999

Category	Value (millions of current $)	Percent change: 1998–1999	Units (millions)	Percent change: 1998–1999
Dictionaries and thesauruses	$6.99	-12.08%	3.04	44.76
Encyclopedias	5.35	31.77	0.85	-18.27
Textbooks	114.79	-6.93	25.86	2.82
Religious books	72.40	16.91	48.92	26.11
Technical, scientific, and professional	183.32	-2.87	46.81	17.05
Art and pictorial books	10.83	-71.71	6.14	-28.85
Hardcover books, n.e.s.	528.88	20.72	180.80	36.48
Mass market paperbacks	75.81	-7.41	46.29	0.04
Books: flyers/circulars, 1–4 pages	5.14	-16.42	46.33	-39.27
Books: pamphlets and brochures, 5–48 pages	105.52	29.60	262.53	19.21
Books: 49 or more pages	288.68	-13.13	153.88	-14.97
Music books	5.23	17.26	1.17	-47.76
Atlases	8.95	36.85	4.58	54.73
Total, all books	$1,411.89	2.64%	827.20	6.44%

Note: n.e.s. = Not elsewhere specified. Individual shipments are excluded from the foreign trade data if valued under $2,500.00 Data for individual categories may not add to totals due to statistical rounding.

Source: U.S. Department of Commerce, Bureau of the Census

The second remarkable event in 1999 centered on the dramatic performance of China, which represented 10.75 percent of the total value of all imported books and 12.08 percent of all units that entered the United States. China's percentage gains were equally impressive, surging 41.38 percent in revenues and 61.22 percent in units. China's nominal change was the best of the top 20 countries in the survey (Table 8).

Other nations whose book exports generated strong revenues in the United States included Spain and the Republic of Korea; however, the performance of Israel (up 7.09 percent in 1999 in revenues and up 51.13 percent in unit totals), Colombia (revenues up 7.37 percent, units up 6.52 percent), and Mexico (revenues up 32.85 percent, units 63.34 percent) merit recognition.

While the encyclopedias and serial installments category has long been dominated by a small number of countries (primarily Italy, Hong Kong, the United Kingdom, Spain, and Singapore), some emerging nations have carved out a presence in this niche (Table 9). Peru, Malaysia, Mexico, and Colombia all posted strong results. China's performance was also intriguing, accounting for 2.71 per-

Table 8 / U.S. Book Imports from 20 Principal Countries: 1999

Country	Value (millions of current $)	Percent change 1998–1999	Units (millions of copies)	Percent change 1998–1999
United Kingdom	$275.47	-12.23%	54.37	-16.70
Hong Kong	226.19	12.86	157.96	27.51
Canada	214.92	-4.16	248.13	-20.01
China	141.72	41.38	95.70	61.22
Italy	94.49	-7.51	36.50	-5.12
Singapore	88.55	-6.51	38.96	-8.89
Japan	53.58	-8.64	19.71	4.12
Germany	50.79	-19.51	12.22	-1.69
Spain	46.04	23.33	13.48	14.33
Korea (Republic of)	29.26	11.09	13.10	10.55
Mexico	22.69	32.85	63.80	63.34
France	21.83	-7.85	4.91	12.10
Netherlands	19.68	12.07	1.74	-32.56
Belgium	19.57	0.72	6.36	-3.93
Israel	10.58	7.09	3.34	51.13
Australia	9.90	29.07	3.17	-60.52
Taiwan	9.33	-0.74	8.51	-5.86
Colombia	7.37	17.36	6.52	-1.51
Switzerland	5.14	-47.82	1.52	-54.22
New Zealand	2.50	140.38	2.21	190.79
Total: top 20 countries	$1,349.60	0.53%	792.20	1.92%

Source: U.S. Department of Commerce, Bureau of the Census

cent of the revenues and 2.34 percent of the units—larger totals than those achieved by Germany or the Republic of Korea.

A similar pattern was evident in the textbook arena (Table 10). Again, the United Kingdom, Canada, Hong Kong, Italy, and Spain took the lead. Yet Mexico and China (revenues 4.14 percent, units 10.28 percent) made a strong showing. Colombia and Malaysia also made the top 15 nations in this category.

The Republic of Korea, Belgium, and Israel dominated the religious publishing niche (Table 11), with impressive results also registered by Italy, Hong Kong, and the United Kingdom (a preeminent nation in every book category). The emergence of China in this market was a bit unexpected in light of its political and philosophical orientation. It accounted for over 10 percent of total revenues and 12.14 percent of all units (second only to Italy). Colombia also emerged as a strong player in this sector, posting better results than France, Spain, or Germany.

Canada, the United Kingdom, and Germany held exceptionally strong market shares in the technical, scientific, and professional book area (Table 12), although Mexico and China also made the top-15 list.

China made substantial inroads in mass market paperback exports to the United States (Table 13), coming in fourth after Hong Kong, Canada, and the United Kingdom and capturing 10.03 percent of revenues and 10.2 percent of units. Singapore, Spain, and Italy also emerged as major players in this niche.

Table 9 / U.S. Imports of Encyclopedias and Serial Installments, Top 15 Sources: 1999

Country	Dollars	Units
Italy	$1,001,447	109,267
Hong Kong	878,610	178,278
United Kingdom	844,908	101,339
Spain	590,571	38,449
Singapore	480,586	109,630
Peru	275,563	89,760
Malaysia	180,478	47,800
Canada	170,714	11,256
China	145,242	19,866
Korea (Republic of)	130,017	35,200
Israel	113,000	15,148
Indonesia	91,954	13,700
Germany	79,903	10,306
Mexico	69,858	15,589
Colombia	66,866	10,138

Source: U.S. Department of Commerce

Table 10 / U.S. Imports of Textbooks, Top 15 Sources: 1999

Country	Dollars (millions)	Units
United Kingdom	$54.85	7,096,110
Canada	12.02	3,675,080
Hong Kong	9.27	2,873,810
Italy	6.20	2,478,338
Spain	4.88	945,215
Mexico	4.87	1,054,382
China	4.75	2,659,060
Singapore	3.52	843,476
Germany	1.82	121,188
Australia	1.61	293,997
France	1.57	305,406
Japan	1.18	287,507
New Zealand	1.10	1,087,275
Colombia	0.89	302,798
Malaysia	0.68	189,352

Source: U.S. Department of Commerce

Table 11 / U.S. Imports of Bibles, Testaments, Prayer Books,
and Other Religious Books, Top 15 Sources: 1999

Country	Dollars (millions)	Units (millions)
Korea (Republic of)	$11.28	2.99
Belgium	9.48	2.94
Israel	8.62	2.69
China	7.27	5.94
United Kingdom	7.11	1.45
Hong Kong	5.52	4.84
Colombia	3.56	4.52
Singapore	2.57	1.56
France	2.54	1.50
Spain	2.48	0.65
Canada	2.41	2.48
Italy	1.12	9.98
Mexico	0.86	0.59
Australia	0.83	0.73
Germany	0.67	0.34

Source: U.S. Department of Commerce

Table 12 / U.S. Imports of Technical, Scientific,
and Professional Books, Top 15 Sources: 1999

Country	Dollars (millions)	Units (millions)
Canada	$50.56	23.72
United Kingdom	37.42	4.61
Germany	24.12	3.05
Japan	13.33	3.70
Netherlands	12.53	0.88
France	5.59	0.29
Hong Kong	4.78	1.66
Italy	3.57	0.97
Mexico	3.34	1.93
China	3.32	1.35
Belgium	3.00	0.31
Spain	2.36	0.23
Singapore	2.18	0.68
Sweden	2.16	0.43
Switzerland	2.08	0.19

Source: U.S. Department of Commerce

Table 13 / U.S. Imports of Mass Market Paperbacks (Rack Size), Top 15 Sources: 1999

Country	Dollars (millions)	Units
Hong Kong	$21.36	13,858,069
Canada	14.27	13,381,370
United Kingdom	9.36	4,116,649
China	7.60	4,720,160
Singapore	6.06	3,438,335
Spain	4.33	1,559,759
Italy	3.24	1,224,314
Japan	1.83	324,370
Mexico	1.11	314,152
Germany	1.05	389,452
Taiwan	0.92	388,187
France	0.77	159,378
Korea (Republic of)	0.74	559,750
Thailand	0.59	355,660
Belgium	0.57	483,178

Source: U.S. Department of Commerce

International Trade in Books

Despite setbacks sustained at the World Trade Organization's meeting in Seattle in 1999, the United States—and the majority of nations—strongly believe in the ultimate importance of free trade (Treibilcock and Howse, 1998). Yet vexing problems remain. Some nations still maintain numbing trade barriers. Others are recovering from currency devaluations and the debilitating outward flow of capital (Yaghmaian, 1994). Still others seem unable to conquer problems related to liquidity of lending issues and staggering foreign debts (some pegged to the U.S. dollar) (Riveros, 1992).

Fortunately, in 1999 a sizable number of Pacific Rim nations carved out impressive results in the U.S. book import market, providing them with much-needed dollars and some sense of economic stability. They were joined by several nations in the Western Hemisphere, primarily Mexico and Colombia, and Israel (Beenstock, Lavi, and Ribon, 1994).

In reality, assuming that emerging economies would continue to post high growth rates in exports and gross domestic products, along with very high rates of capital accumulation (often in double digits), was an exceptionally flawed strategy in the 1990s. Annual growth rate policies were premised, to a substantial degree, on double-digit export increases. If this scenario worked, hard currencies (primarily dollars) would be generated, allowing these emerging nations to purchase much-needed foreign goods and services. This macroeconomic strategy, as flawed as a Ponzi scheme, worked for a while, generating impressive levels of economic stability in Asia.

Unfortunately, the Asian currency malaise spelled the end of these halcyon dreams. The deep, downward shift in Pacific Rim exports triggered economic

Table 14 / U.S. Trade in Books: 1970–1999
(millions of current dollars)

Year	U.S. Book Exports	U.S. Book Imports	Ratio: U.S. Book Exports/Imports
1970	$174.9	$92.0	1.90
1975	269.3	147.6	1.82
1980	518.9	306.5	1.69
1985	591.2	564.2	1.05
1990	1,415.1	855.1	1.65
1995	1,779.5	1,184.5	1.50
1996	1,775.6	1,240.1	1.43
1997	1,896.6	1,297.5	1.46
1998	1,841.82	1,375.59	1.34
1999	1,913.87	1,411.89	1.36

Source: U.S. Department of Commerce, Bureau of the Census

Due to changes in the classification of U.S. traded products and what constitutes products classified as "books," data prior to 1990 are not strictly comparable to data beginning in 1990.

Table 15 / U.S. Book Industry Shipments Compared with U.S. Book Exports: 1970–1999
(millions of current dollars)

Year	Total Shipments	U.S. Books Exports	Exports as a Percent of Total Shipments
1970	$2,434.2	$174.9	7.2%
1975	3,536.5	269.3	7.6
1980	6,114.4	518.9	8.5
1985	10,165.7	591.2	5.8
1990	14,982.6	1,415.1	9.4
1995	19,471.0	1,779.5	9.1
1996	20,285.7	1,775.6	8.8
1997	21,131.9	1,896.6	9.0
1998	22,507.0	1,841.8	8.2
1999	23,263.9	1,913.87	8.2

Sources: U.S. Department of Commerce, Bureau of the Census; and the Book Industry Study Group, Inc. (BISG). BISG's totals were used for shipments beginning in 1985 through 1999. Commerce totals were used for 1970–1980. Due to changes in the classification of U.S. traded products and what constitutes products classified as "books," data prior to 1990 are not strictly comparable to data beginning in 1990.

instability and ultimately chaos. The end result was damaging to the Asian economy and the market for U.S. books in that region.

The chaos seems to be abating. "Reconfigured" (and far more realistic) economic drivers in the Pacific Rim cooled off key economies that were running the risk of "overheating." Yet a fundamental problem remains. The U.S. book industry closely monitors textbook adoptions in Georgia and Nevada, and in March 2000 it sponsored a well-publicized research study on "electronic book" standards. Ironically, it has not committed the financial resources to evaluate closely macroeconomic and microeconomic conditions in the key foreign markets for U.S. books. Unless this is done, U.S. book publishers dependent on the export market can be whipsawed whenever a nation or a region sustains an economic slowdown, a decline in its gross domestic product (GDP), or a surge in the inflation rate.

The major U.S. book industry trade associations should create a task force to monitor on an ongoing basis foreign economic conditions, paralleling their very successful efforts to track book adoptions on the state level or to find the next generation of authors. Clearly, analyzing foreign economies lacks the glitter of finding the next John Grisham (Hickson and Pugh, 1996; Bernard and Bradford, 1999; Diamantopoulos and Winklhofer, 1999). Yet exports account for 8.2 percent of all U.S. book-publishing revenues. And the pivotal export/import ratio has been declining steadily since 1990, a sign that the rate of export growth has not keep pace with import's performance (Table 14).

Any continued downward shift in the export market places in jeopardy the entire industry, a fact that seems to have escaped the attention of far too many industry leaders, consultants, and pundits (Mas-Colell, 1999).

References

Beenstock, M., Lavi, Y., and Ribon, S. (1994). "The Supply and Demand for Exports in Israel." *Journal of Development Economies,* vol. 44(2), pp. 333–350.

Bernard, A. B., and Bradford, J. J. (1999). "Exceptional Exporter Performance: Cause, Effect, or Both?" *Journal of International Economics*, vol. 47(1), pp. 1–25.

Diamantopoulos, A., and Winklhofer, H. (1999). "The Impact of Firm and Export Characteristics on the Accuracy of Export Sales Forecasts: Evidence from UK Exporters." *International Journal of Forecasting*, vol. 15(1), pp. 67–81.

Greco, A. N. (1997). *The Book Publishing Industry*. Boston: Allyn & Bacon.

Hickson, D. J., and Pugh, D. S. (1996). *Management Worldwide: The Impact of Societal Culture on Organizations Around the Globe*. New York: Penguin.

Mas-Colell, A. (1999). "Should Cultural Goods Be Treated Differently?" *Journal of Cultural Economics*, vol. 23(1/2), pp. 87–93.

Mishkin, F. S. (1999). "Lessons from the Asian Crisis." Working Paper. Cambridge: National Bureau of Economic Research (April), pp. 1–15.

Riveros, L. A. (1992). "Labor Costs and Manufactured Exports in Developing Countries: An Economic Analysis." *World Development*, vol. 20(7), pp. 991–1008.

Treibilcock, M., and Howse, R. (1998). "Trade Liberalization and Regulatory Diversity: Reconciling Competitive Markets with Competitive Politics." *European Journal of Law and Economics*, vol. 6(1), pp. 5–37.

Truett, L. J., and Truett, D. B. (1998). "The Demand for Imports in Korea: A Production Analysis." *Journal of Development Economies*, vol. 56(1), pp. 97–114.

Yaghmaian, B. (1994). "An Empirical Investigation of Exports, Development, and Growth in Developing Countries: Challenging the Neoclassical Theory of Export-Led Growth." *World Development*, vol. 22(12), pp. 1977–1995.

International Book Title Output: 1990–1996

Albert N. Greco

Associate Professor
Fordham University Graduate School of Business Administration

For a number of years, the *Bowker Annual* has relied on UNESCO's data on international title output to prepare this article. In June 1999 UNESCO unexpectedly disbanded its Division of Statistics, which was responsible for preparing the *UNESCO Statistical Yearbook*. The following month, it created the UNESCO Institute for Statistics, which decided to reevaluate the division's data collection policies and procedures. Accordingly, during this transitional year, UNESCO will not release international title output data for 1997.

As a service to our readers, we are reprinting "International Book Title Output: 1990–1996" from our 1999 edition.

Title Output Research

Title output has long been viewed as a significant barometer of intellectual activity in a nation. After all, books educate, inform, and entertain. They spread literacy and provide readers with an inexpensive mechanism to expand their horizons and increase their understanding of distant locations and conflicting theories about a wide variety of topics. Books are a powerful means to transmit ideas—a fact that has concerned tyrants and dictators since the days of Gutenberg.

Researchers seeking to discern changing patterns in fiction and nonfiction, to interpret a nation's "liberal" or "conservative" viewpoint, and to comprehend completely the economic structure and development of a nation's book publishing industry rely extensively on title output statistics. Unfortunately, this type of analysis is an exceedingly difficult task.

While UNESCO's *Statistical Yearbook 1998* (UNESCO Publishing and Bernan Press, 1998) contains rather detailed tables, researchers confront a plethora of problems with these tallies, including:

- Data methodology and collection problems: How detailed are a country's title output surveys? Are both hardcover and paper titles included? Are all book categories (trade, textbook, professional, and so forth) included in the surveys? Are electronic versions of a book included in the totals? Are electronic or paper surveys utilized? What types of follow-up procedures are employed to capture unreported or underreported data?
- Data collection lags: How often are title output surveys conducted? How often do governments report national data to UNESCO?
- Missing data: Why do some nations (especially some of the "advanced" industrial countries—Japan, Belgium, the Netherlands and France, among others) not report data on certain years?
- Discrepancies in the data: Why do some national title output reports differ significantly from UNESCO's tallies? Why do some nations report incredibly large annual increases in title output, followed by sharp declines? Are

these spikes the result of faulty data collecting in certain years rather than just a surge in titles?

• Missing data on certain countries: Some nations are never included in the UNESCO studies. Is this because they are developing nations with fragile publishing infrastructures generating exceptionally small numbers of books each year? Is it because certain nations annually import sizable numbers of titles and are not counted by UNESCO? Are the costs associated with conducting this type of title output beyond the means of certain nations?

Title Output, 1990–1996

In spite of these methodological issues and queries, the UNESCO data provides researchers with the best and most usable framework and overview of book title output. The results for 1990–1996 (the most recent data released by UNESCO) revealed uneven patterns of growth and decline.

While the United Kingdom issued more titles in 1995 (101,764) than any other nation, China's performance in 1996 was stunning, topping 110,283 titles (up 12.41 percent), easily surpassing the United Kingdom (107,263 titles, up 5.4 percent) as the global leader. Other nations that posted sizable increases in title output include Romania (30.49 percent), Poland (18.27 percent), Iran (15.67 percent), the Czech Republic (13.9 percent), the United States (9.89 percent), Argentina (8.09 percent), Russia (7.77 percent), Sweden (6.27 percent), Turkey (4.32 percent), the Ukraine (3.78 percent), Italy (2.3 percent), and India (2.23 percent). These small increases were affected in all likelihood by the global economic malaise triggered by the Asian fiscal "contagion."

On the down side, a large cohort of nations reported declines (in some instances, steep declines) in title output, due in some part to the impact of the Asian fiscal crisis and the resulting economic slowdown. The Republic of Korea's totals were off 14.99 percent, as were Malaysia (down 9.62 percent), Norway (5.02 percent), Spain (4.41 percent), Germany (3.58 percent), Finland (2.89 percent), Hungary (2.35 percent), Austria (2.02 percent), and Denmark (1.01 percent).

Table 1, *International Title Output: 1990–1996*, reveals the patterns of book title growth and reduction for the 47 major nations reporting at least a minimum of 3,000 titles in 1996 (with the exception of the Philippines, which was added to the totals). Nations on this list for the first time include South Africa, Mexico, Sri Lanka, Venezuela, Bulgaria, Yugoslavia, Slovakia, Slovenia, Lithuania, Greece, and Belarus.

International Book Title Outlook

The outlook for title output for 1999 and 2000 remains "cautiously optimistic." While a fairly large number of new countries made the international list for the first time—an indicator of robust growth—the impact of the Asian "contagion" remains cloudy at best. It is likely that it will take several more years before substantive macroeconomic weaknesses (associated with or impacted by the "contagion") are corrected, stimulating positively the book publishing industry in certain nations; and all of these economic factors have a direct bearing on both the intellectual vigor and financial health of book publishing establishments (and, concomitantly, on title output) in many nations.

Table 1 / International Book Title Output: 1990–1996

Country	1990	1991	1992	1993	1994	1995	1996
United Kingdom	n.a.	n.a.	86,573	n.a.	95,015	101,764	107,263
China	73,923	90,156	n.a.	92,972	100,951	98,987	110,283
Germany	61,015	67,890	67,277	67,206	70,643	74,174	71,515
United States	46,743	48,146	49,276	49,757	51,863	62,039	68,175
Spain	36,239	39,082	41,816	40758	44261	48,467	46,330
France	41,720	43,682	45,379	41,234	45,311	34,766	n.a.
Korea, Republic of	39,330	29,432	27,889	30,861	34,204	35,864	30,487
Japan	n.a.	n.a.	35,496	n.a.	n.a.	n.a.	56,221
Italy	25,068	27,751	29,351	30,110	32,673	34,470	35,236
Netherlands	13,691	11,613	15,997	34,067	n.a.	n.a.	n.a.
Russia	n.a.	34,050	28,716	29,017	30,390	33,623	36,237
Brazil	n.a.	n.a.	27,557	20,141	21,574	n.a.	n.a.
Canada*	8,291	8,722	9,192	9,501	10,257	10,620	11,400
India	13,937	14,438	15,778	12,768	11,460	11,643	11,903
Switzerland	13,839	14,886	14,663	14,870	15,378	15,771	15,371
Belgium	12,157	13,913	n.a.	n.a.	n.a.	n.a.	n.a.
Sweden	12,034	11,866	12,812	12,895	13,822	12,700	13,496
Finland	10,153	11,208	11,033	11,785	12,539	13,494	13104
Denmark	11,082	10,198	11,761	11,492	11,973	12,478	12,352
Poland	10,242	10,688	10,727	9,788	10,874	11,925	14,104
Australia	n.a.	n.a.	n.a.	n.a.	10,835	n.a.	n.a.
Iran	n.a.	5,018	6,822	n.a.	10,753	13,031	15,073
Hungary	8,322	8,133	8,536	9,170	10,108	9,314	9,193
Serbia	9,797	4,049	2,618	n.a.	n.a.	n.a.	n.a.
Czech Republic	8,585	9,362	6,743	8,203	9,309	8,994	10,244
Argentina	4,915	6,092	5,628	n.a.	9,065	9,113	9,850
Austria	3,740	6,505	4,986	5,628	7,987	8,222	8,056
Thailand	7,783	7,676	7,626	n.a.	n.a.	n.a.	8,142
Philippines	n.a.	n.a.	n.a.	n.a.	1,233	1,229	927
Norway	3,712	3,884	4,881	4,943	6,946	7,265	6,900
Ukraine	7,046	5,857	4,410	5,002	4,882	6,225	6,460
Portugal	6,150	6,430	6,462	6,089	6,667	n.a.	7,868
Turkey	6,291	6,365	6,549	5,978	4,473	6,275	6,546
Malaysia	n.a.	3,748	n.a.	3,799	4,050	6,465	5,843
Indonesia	1,518	1,774	6,303	n.a.	n.a.	n.a.	4,018

Table 1 / International Book Title Output: 1990–1996 *(cont.)*

Country	1990	1991	1992	1993	1994	1995	1996
Romania	2,178	2,914	3,662	6,130	4,074	5,517	7,158
Mexico	n.a.	n.a.	n.a.	n.a.	n.a.	n.a.	6,183
South Africa	n.a.	n.a.	n.a.	n.a.	n.a.	4,574	5,418
Yugoslavia	n.a.	n.a.	n.a.	n.a.	2,799	3,531	5,367
Bulgaria	n.a.	n.a.	n.a.	n.a.	5,925	5,400	4,840
Greece	n.a.	n.a.	n.a.	n.a.	n.a.	4,134	4,225
Sri Lanka	n.a.	n.a.	n.a.	n.a.	2,929	3,933	4,115
Slovakia	n.a.	n.a.	n.a.	n.a.	3,481	n.a.	3,800
Belarus	n.a.	n.a.	n.a.	n.a.	3,346	3,205	3,809
Lithuania	n.a.	n.a.	n.a.	n.a.	2,885	3,164	3,645
Venezuela	n.a.	n.a.	n.a.	n.a.	3,660	4,225	3,468
Slovenia	n.a.	n.a.	n.a.	n.a.	2,906	3,194	3,441

Note: n.a. = not available

* Source: *UNESCO Statistical Yearbook, 1998*, with the following exception: title output for Canada obtained from *Profile of Book Publishing and Exclusive Agency in Canada*, Canadian Culture, Tourism & the Center for Education Statistics. UNESCO figures for Canada for 1994, 1995, and 1996 were 21,701, 17,931, and 19,900, respectively.

Number of Book Outlets in the United States and Canada

The *American Book Trade Directory* has been published by R. R. Bowker since 1915. Revised annually, it features lists of booksellers, wholesalers, periodicals, reference tools, and other information about the U.S. and Canadian book markets. The data shown in Table 1, the most current available, are from the 1999–2000 edition of the directory.

The 26,769 stores of various types shown are located throughout the United States, Canada, and regions administered by the United States. "General" bookstores stock trade books and children's books in a general variety of subjects. "College" stores carry college-level textbooks. "Educational" outlets handle school textbooks up to and including the high school level. "Mail order" outlets sell general trade books by mail and are not book clubs; all others operating by mail are classified according to the kinds of books carried. "Antiquarian" dealers sell old and rare books. Stores handling secondhand books are classified as "used." "Paperback" stores have more than 80 percent of their stock in paperbound books. Stores with paperback departments are listed under the appropriate major classification ("general," "department store," "stationer," etc.). Bookstores with at least 50 percent of their stock on a particular subject are classified by subject.

Table 1 / Bookstores in the United States and Canada, 1999

Category	United States	Canada
Antiquarian General	1,446	90
Antiquarian Mail Order	570	15
Antiquarian Specialized	260	6
Art Supply Store	64	1
College General	3,259	159
College Specialized	128	11
Comics	243	23
Computer Software	393	0
Cooking	150	7
Department Store	1,821	1
Educational*	319	19
Federal Sites†	253	1
Foreign Language*	127	31
General	5,963	570
Gift Shop	384	13
Juvenile*	319	29
Mail Order General	365	18
Mail Order Specialized	795	42
Metaphysics, New Age, and Occult	282	21
Museum Store and Art Gallery	542	38
Nature and Natural History	143	5
Newsdealer	101	6
Office Supply	49	15
Other§	2,011	162
Paperback‡	295	15
Religious*	3,979	226
Self Help/Development	52	14
Stationer	15	15
Toy Store	115	8
Used*	687	78
Totals	25,130	1,639

* Includes Mail Order Shops for this topic, which are not counted elsewhere in this survey.

† National Historic Sites, National Monuments, and National Parks.

‡ Includes Mail Order. Excludes used paperback bookstores, stationers, drugstores, or wholesalers handling paperbacks.

§ Stores specializing in subjects or services other than those covered in this survey.

Review Media Statistics

Compiled by the staff of the *Bowker Annual*

**Number of Books and Other Media
Reviewed by Major Reviewing Publications, 1998–1999**

	Adult		Juvenile		Young Adult		Total	
	1998	1999	1998	1999	1998	1999	1998	1999
Appraisal[1]	—	22	—	418	—	167	—	607
Booklist[2]	4,206	4,681	2,277	2,484	879	994	7,362	8,159
Bulletin of the Center for Children's Books[3]	—	—	853	738	—	—	853	738
Chicago Sun Times	800	800	125	125	—	—	925	925
Chicago Tribune Sunday Book Section	728	622	53	278	9	12	790	912
Choice[4]	6,252	7,235	—	—	—	—	6,252	7,235
Horn Book Guide[5]	—	—	n.a.	3,235	n.a.	398	n.a.	3,633
Kirkus Reviews[5]	3,261	3,580	1,227	1,211	—	—	4,488	4,791
Library Journal[6]	5,723	6,348	—	—	—	—	5,723	6,348
Los Angeles Times[5]	1,950	n.a.	200	n.a.	—	—	2,150	n.a.
New York Review of Books	473	n.a.	—	—	—	—	473	n.a.
New York Times Sunday Book Review[5]	1,857	1,900	286	300	—	—	2,143	2,200
Publishers Weekly	5,576	5,723	2,076	1,909	—	—	7,652	7,632
Rapport (formerly *West Coast Review of Books*)[7]	624	400	—	—	—	—	624	400
School Library Journal[8]	269	286	1,637	1,895	1,410	1,439	3,615	4,026
Washington Post Book World	1,400	1,400	40	40	25	25	1,465	1,465

n.a.=not available

1 *Appraisal Science Books for Young People* reviews current science books for children and teenagers.

2 All figures are for a 12-month period from September 1, 1998, to August 31, 1999 (vol. 95). YA books are included in the juvenile total. The YA total consists solely of reviews of adult books that are appropriate for young adults.

3 All figures are for 12-month period beginning September and ending July/August.

4 All books reviewed in *Choice* are scholarly publications intended for undergraduate libraries. Total includes 986 internet sites, computer software/CD-ROMs, and databases.

5 Juvenile figures include young adult titles.

6 Total includes 105 reviews in roundups. In addition, *LJ* reviewed 395 audio books, 51 magazines, 389 videos, 773 books in "Prepub Alert," 366 books in "Collection Development," 185 Web sites, and 107 CD-ROMs.

7 Total includes 175 music CDs.

8 Total includes 80 books for professional reading, 61 December holiday books, 51 books in Spanish, 137 reference books, and 4 books in "At-a-Glance."

Part 5
Reference Information

Bibliographies

The Librarian's Bookshelf

Cathleen Bourdon, MLS

Executive Director, Reference and User Services Association, American Library Association

Most of the books in this selective bibliography have been published since 1996; a few earlier titles are retained because of their continuing importance.

General Works

Alternative Library Literature, 1996/1997: A Biennial Anthology. Ed. By Sanford Berman and James P. Danky. McFarland, 1998. Paper $35.

American Library Directory, 2000–2001. 2v. Bowker, 2000. $269.95.

The Bowker Annual Library and Book Trade Almanac, 2000. Bowker, 2000. $185.

Concise Dictionary of Library and Information Science. By Stella Keenan. Bowker Saur, 1995. $45.

Indexing and Abstracting in Theory and Practice. 2nd ed. By F. W. Lancaster. GLIS, Univ. of Illinois, 1998. $47.50.

The Librarian's Companion: A Handbook of Thousands of Facts on Libraries/Librarians, Books/Newspapers, Publishers/Booksellers. 2nd ed. By Vladimir F. Wertsman. Greenwood Press, 1996. $67.95.

Library and Information Science Annual. Vol. 7. Ed. by Bohdan S. Wynar. Libraries Unlimited, 1999. $65.

Library Literature. H. W. Wilson, 1921. Also available online and on CD-ROM, 1984–. Indexes periodicals in librarianship.

Library Reference Center. http://www.epnet.com. Indexes 30 periodicals in librarianship for the past five years.

Library Technology Reports. American Library Association, 1965–. Bi-monthly. $250.

Madame Audrey's Guide to Mostly Cheap But Good Reference Books for Small and Rural Libraries. Ed. by Audrey Lewis. American Library Association, 1999. Paper $45.

Reference Sources for Small and Medium-sized Libraries. 6th ed. Ed. by Scott E. Kennedy. American Library Association, 1999. Paper $60.

The Whole Library Handbook: Current Data, Professional Advice, and Curiosa about Libraries and Library Services. 2nd ed. Comp. by George Eberhart. American Library Association, 1995. Paper $35.

Academic Libraries

ARL Statistics. Association of Research Libraries. Annual. 1964–. $70.

The Academic Library Director: Reflections on a Position in Transition. Ed. by Frank D'Andraia. Haworth, 1997. Paper $39.95.

The Academic Library: Its Context, Its Purposes, and Its Operation. By John M. Budd. Libraries Unlimited, 1998. Paper $35.

Academic Library Trends and Statistics, 1998. Association of College and Research Libraries/American Library Association, 1999. $180.

CLIP (College Library Information Packet) *Notes.* Association of College and Research Libraries/American Library Association, 1980–. Most recent volume is No. 28, 1999. $22.

Constancy and Change in the Worklife of Research University Librarians. By Rebecca Watson-Boone. Association of College and Research Libraries/American Library Association, 1998. Paper $30.

Creating the Agile Library: A Management Guide for Librarians. Ed. by Lorraine J. Haricombe and T. J. Lusher. Greenwood Press, 1998. $49.95.

Librarians as Learners, Librarians as Teachers: The Diffusion of the Internet Experience in the Academic Library. Ed. by Patricia O'Brien Libutti. Association of College and Research Libraries/American Library Association, 1999. Paper $27.

Library and Learning Resources Programs: Evaluation and Self-Study. Ed. by Wanda K. Johnston. Association of College and Research Libraries/American Library Association, 1998. Paper $31.

Measuring Academic Library Performance: A Practical Approach. By Nancy Van House, Beth Weil, and Charles McClure. American Library Association, 1990. Paper $36. Accompanying diskette with data collection and analysis forms $60.

Outsourcing Library Operations in Academic Libraries: An Overview of Issues and Outcomes. By Claire-Lise Benaud and Sever Bordeianu. Libraries Unlimited, 1998. $40.

Preparing for Accreditation: A Handbook for Academic Librarians. By Patricia Ann Sacks and Sara Lou Whildin. American Library Association, 1993. Paper $18.

Recreating the Academic Library: Breaking Virtual Ground. Ed. by Cheryl LaGuardia. Neal-Schuman, 1998. Paper $59.95.

SPEC Kits. Association of Research Libraries. 1973–. 10/yr. $280.

Tenure and Promotion for Academic Librarians: A Guidebook with Advice and Vig- nettes. By Carol W. Cubberly. McFarland, 1996. $32.50.

Administration and Personnel

The ABCs of Collaborative Change: The Manager's Guide to Library Renewal. By Kerry David Carson, Paula Phillips Carson, and Joyce Schouest Phillips. American Library Association, 1997. Paper $37.

Avoiding Liability Risk: An Attorney's Advice to Library Trustees and Others. By Renee Rubin. American Library Association, 1994. Paper $17.

Budgeting for Information Access: Resource Management for Connected Libraries. By Murray Martin and Milton Wolf. American Library Association, 1998. Paper $35.

Charging and Collecting Fees and Fines: A Handbook for Libraries. By Murray S. Martin and Betsy Parks. Neal-Schuman, 1998. Paper $49.95.

Complete Guide to Performance Standards for Library Personnel. By Carole E. Goodson. Neal-Schuman, 1997. Paper $55.

Costing and Pricing in the Digital Age: A Practical Guide for Information Services. By Herbert Snyder and Elisabeth Davenport. Neal-Schuman, 1997. Paper $49.95.

Evaluating Library Staff: A Performance Appraisal System. By Patricia Belcastro. American Library Association, 1998. Paper $35.

Getting Political: An Action Guide for Librarians and Library Supporters. By Anne M. Turner. Neal-Schuman, 1997. Paper $45.

Interpreting and Negotiating Licensing Agreements: A Guidebook for the Library, Research and Teaching Professions. By Arlene Bielefield and Lawrence Cheeseman. Neal-Schuman, 1999. Paper $55.

The Librarian's Community Network Handbook. By Stephen T. Bajjaly. American Library Association, 1999. Paper $32.

Library Public Relations, Promotions and Communications: A How-to-Do-It Manual. By Lisa Wolfe. Neal-Schuman, 1997. Paper $45.

Library Security and Safety Handbook: Prevention, Policies and Procedures. By

Bruce A. Shuman. American Library Association, 1999. Paper $42.

Management of Library and Archival Security: From the Outside Looking In. Ed. by Robert K. O'Neill. Haworth Press, 1998. $29.95.

Managing Overdues: A How-To-Do-It Manual for Librarians. Ed. by Patsy J. Hansel. Neal-Schuman, 1998. Paper $45.

Managing Student Library Employees: A Workshop for Supervisors. By Michael and Jane Kathman. Library Solutions Press, 1995. Paper $45. An accompanying diskette contains presentation slides.

Marketing/Planning Library and Information Services. By Darlene E. Weingand. Libraries Unlimited, 1999. $47.50.

Moving Library Collections: A Management Handbook. By Elizabeth Chamberlain Habich. Greenwood Press, 1998. $79.50

Practical Help for New Supervisors. 3rd ed. Ed. by Joan Giesecke. American Library Association, 1997. Paper $24.

Recruiting Library Staff: A How-To-Do-It Manual for Librarians. By Kathleen Low. Neal-Schuman, 1999. Paper $45.

Safe at Work? Library Security and Safety Issues. By Teri R. Switzer. Scarecrow Press, 1999. $39.50.

Scenario Planning for Libraries. Ed. by Joan Giesecke. American Library Association, 1998. Paper $30.

Strategic Management for Today's Libraries. By Marilyn Gell Mason. American Library Association, 1999. Paper $35.

Stop Talking, Start Doing! Attracting People of Color to the Library Profession. By Gregory L. Reese and Ernestine L. Hawkins. American Library Association, 1999. Paper $30.

Technology and Management in Library and Information Services. By F. W. Lancaster and Beth Sandore. Univ. of Illinois, Urbana-Champaign, 1997. $39.95.

Bibliographic Instruction

Basic Library Skills. 4th ed. By Carolyn Wolf. McFarland, 1999. Paper $24.95.

Designs for Active Learning: A Sourcebook of Classroom Strategies for Information Education. Ed. by Gail Gradowski,

Loanne Snavely, and Paula Dempsey. Association of College and Research Libraries/American Library Association, 1998. Paper with diskette $35.

Library Information Skills and the High School English Program. By Mary H. Hackman. Libraries Unlimited, 1999. Paper $25.

Student Learning in the Information Age. By Patricia Senn Breivik. Oryx Press, 1997. $34.95.

Teaching Electronic Literacy: A Concepts-based Approach for School Library Media Specialists. By Kathleen Craver. Greenwood Press, 1997. $39.95.

Teaching the New Library: A How-to-Do-It Manual. By Michael Blake and others from the Electronic Teaching Center for the Harvard College Libraries. Neal-Schuman, 1996. Paper $49.95.

Working with Faculty to Design Undergraduate Information Literacy Programs: A How-To-Do-It Manual for Librarians. By Rosemary M. Young and Stephena Harmony. Neal-Schuman, 1999. Paper $45.

Cataloging and Classification

ArtMARC Sourcebook: Cataloging Art, Architecture and Their Visual Images. Ed. By Linda McRae and Lynda S. White. American Library Association, 1998. Paper $75.

The Bibliographic Record and Information Technology. 3rd ed. By Ronald Hagler. American Library Association, 1997. Paper $45.

Cataloging Correctly for Kids: An Introduction to the Tools. 3rd ed. Ed. by Sharon Zuiderveld. American Library Association, 1997. Paper $20.

The Concise AACR2: 1998 Revision. By Michael Gorman. American Library Association, 1999. Paper $32.

Dewey Decimal Classification, 21st Edition: A Study Manual and Number Building Guide. By Mona L. Scott. Libraries Unlimited, 1998. $47.50.

Immroth's Guide to the Library of Congress Classification. 5th ed. By Lois Mai Chan. Libraries Unlimited, 1999. $65.

Library of Congress Subject Headings: Principles and Application. 3rd ed. By Lois Mai Chan. Libraries Unlimited, 1995. $46.

Special Libraries: A Cataloging Guide. By Sheila S. Intner and Jean Weihs. Libraries Unlimited, 1998. $55.

Standard Cataloging for School and Public Libraries. 2nd ed. By Sheila S. Intner and Jean Weihs. Libraries Unlimited, 1996. $32.50.

Visualizing Subject Access for 21st Century Information Resources. Ed. by Pauline Atherton Cochrane and Eric H. Johnson. GLIS Publications Office, Univ. of Illinois, 1998. $30.

Children's and Young Adult Services and Materials

Against Borders: Promoting Books for a Multicultural World. By Hazel Rochman. *Booklist*/American Library Association, 1993. Paper $25.

The Center for the Study of Books in Spanish for Children and Adolescents at California State University, San Marcos Web site: http://www.csusm.edu/campus_centers/csb. Recommends books in Spanish for youth.

Connecting Kids and the Internet: A Handbook for Librarians, Teachers, and Parents. By Allen C. Benson and Linda M. Fodemski. Neal-Schuman, 1999. Paper with CD-ROM $49.95.

Connecting Young Adults and Libraries: A How-to-Do-It Manual. 2nd ed. By Patrick Jones. Neal-Schuman, 1998. Paper $45.

Excellence in Library Services to Young Adults: The Nation's Top Programs. 2nd ed. By Mary K. Chelton. American Library Association, 1997. Paper $22.

Family Storytime: 24 Creative Programs for All Ages. Rob Reid. American Library Association, 1999. Paper $28.

Flannelboard Stories for Infants and Toddlers. By Ann Carlson and Mary Carlson. American Library Association, 1999. Paper $25.

The Frugal Youth Cybrarian: Bargain Computing for Kids. By Calvin Ross. American Library Association, 1996. Paper $28.

Inviting Children's Authors and Illustrators: A How-to-Do-It Manual for School and Public Librarians. By Kathy East. Neal-Schuman, 1995. Paper $35.

Learning Environments for Young Children: Rethinking Library Space and Services. By Sandra Feinberg, Joan F. Kuchner, and Sari Feldman. American Library Association, 1998. Paper $35.

Managing Children's Services in the Public Library. 2nd ed. By Adele M. Fasick. Libraries Unlimited, 1998. $34.50.

Medieval Knight: Read Me a Book! By Adrienne Wigdortz Anderson. Scarecrow Press, 1999. Paper $27.50.

Output Measures and More: Planning and Evaluating Public Library Services for Young Adults. By Virginia A. Walter. American Library Association, 1995. Paper $25.

Output Measures for Public Library Service to Children: A Manual of Standardized Procedures. By Virginia A. Walter. American Library Association, 1992. Paper $25.

Programming with Latino Children's Materials: A How-To-Do-It Manual for Librarians. By Tim Wadham. Neal-Schuman, 1999. Paper $39.95.

School Library Journal's Best: A Reader for Children's, Young Adults and School Librarians. Ed. by Lillian N. Gerhardt, Marilyn L. Miller, and Thomas W. Downen. Neal-Schuman, 1997. Paper $45.

Serious About Series: Evaluations and Annotations of Teen Fiction in Paperback Series. By Silk Makowski. Scarecrow Press, 1998. Paper $26.50.

Starting with Assessment: A Developmental Approach to Deaf Children's Literacy. By Martha M. French. Gallaudet Univ., 1999. Paper $39.95

Story: From Fireplace to Cyberspace: Connecting Children and Narrative. Ed. by Betsy Hearne, Janice M. Del Nego, Christine Jenkins, and Deborah Stevenson. GSLIS, Univ. of Illinois, 1998. Paper $21.95.

Storytime Sourcebook: A Compendium of Ideas and Resources for Storytellers. 2nd ed. By Carolyn N. Cullum. Neal-Schuman, 1999. Paper $45.

VOYA Reader Two: Articles from Voices of Youth Advocate. Ed. by Dorothy M. Broderick and Mary K. Chelton. Scarecrow Press, 1998. Paper $24.50.

Collection Development

Building an ESL Collection for Young Adults: A Bibliography of Recommended Fiction and Nonfiction for Schools and Public Libraries. By Laura Hibbets McCaffery. Greenwood, 1998. $39.95.

Collection Evaluation Techniques: A Short, Selective, Practical, Current, Annotated Bibliography, 1990–1998. Ed. by Bonnie Strohl. American Library Association/Reference and User Services Association, 1999. Paper $16.

Collection Management for the 21st Century: A Handbook for Librarians. Ed. by G. E. Gorman and Ruth H. Miller. Greenwood Press, 1997. $75.

Coretta Scott King Award Book, 1970–1999. Ed. by Henritta M. Smith. American Library Association, 1999. Paper $32.

Developing Christian Fiction Collections for Children and Adults: Selection Criteria and a Core Collection. By Barbara J. Walker. Neal-Schuman, 1998. Paper $38.50.

Fiction Acquisition/Fiction Management: Education and Training. Ed. by Georgine N. Olson. Haworth Press, 1998. $29.95

Guide for Training Collection Development Librarians. Ed. by Susan Fales. American Library Association, 1996. Paper $15.

Guide for Written Collection Policy Statements. 2nd ed. Ed. by Joanne S. Anderson. American Library Association, 1996. Paper $15.

Multicultural Resources on the Internet: The United States and Canada. By Vicki L. Gregory, Marilyn H. Karrenbrock Stauffer, and Thomas W. Keene, Jr. Libraries Unlimited, 1999. Paper $28.

Virtually Yours: Models for Managing Electronic Resources and Services. Ed. by Peggy Johnson and Bonnie MacEwan. American Library Association, 1998. Paper $25.

Weeding Library Collections: Library Weeding Methods. 4th ed. By Stanley J. Slote. Libraries Unlimited, 1997. $55.

Copyright

Commonsense Copyright: A Guide for Educators and Librarians. 2nd ed. By R. S. Talab. McFarland Publishers, 1999. Paper $39.95.

Growing Pains: Adapting Copyright for Libraries, Education and Society. By Laura N. Gasaway. Rothman, 1997. $75.

101 Questions About Copyright Law. By Andrew Alpern. Dover Publications, 1999. Paper $2.95.

Plagiarism, Copyright Violation and Other Thefts of Intellectual Property: An Annotated Bibliography with a Lengthy Introduction. By Judy Anderson. McFarland, 1998. Paper $38.

Technology and Copyright Law: A Guidebook for the Library, Research and Teaching Professions. By Arlene Bielefield and Lawrence Cheesemen. Neal-Schuman, 1997. Paper $55.

Customer Service

Assessing Service Quality: Satisfying the Expectations of Library Customers. By Peter Hernon and Ellen Altman. American Library Association, 1998. Paper $40.

Customer Service and Innovation in Libraries. By Glenn Miller. Highsmith Press, 1996. Paper $19.

Customer Service Excellence: A Concise Guide for Librarians. By Darlene E. Weingand. American Library Association, 1997. Paper $30.

Dealing with Difficult People in the Library. By Mark R. Willis. American Library Association, 1999. Paper $28.

Patron Behavior in Libraries: A Handbook of Positive Approaches to Negative Situations. Ed. by Beth McNeil and Denise J. Johnson. American Library Association, 1995. Paper $28.

The Electronic Library

Being Analog: Creating Tomorrow's Libraries. By Walt Crawford. American Library Association, 1999. Paper $28.

Building a Scholarly Communications Center: Modeling the Rutgers Experience. By Boyd Collins, Emily Fabiano, Linda Langscheid, Ryoko Toyama, and Myoung Chung Wilson. American Library Association, 1999. Paper $48.

Creating a Virtual Library: A How-To-Do-It Manual for Librarians. Ed. by Frederick Stielow. Neal-Schuman, 1999. Paper $55.

Digitizing Historical Pictorial Collections for the Internet. By Stephen E. Ostrow. Council on Library and Information Resources, 1998. Paper $20.

Economics of Digital Information: Collection, Storage and Delivery. Ed. by Sul H. Lee. Haworth Press, 1997. $29.95.

Finding Common Ground: Creating the Library of the Future Without Diminishing the Library of the Past. Ed. by Cheryl LaGuardia and Barbara A. Mitchell. Neal-Schuman, 1998. Paper $82.50.

Future Libraries: Dreams, Madness, and Reality. By Walt Crawford and Michael Gorman. American Library Association, 1995. Paper $28. Deflates the overblown "virtual" library concept.

Ink Into Bits: A Web of Converging Media. By Charles T. Meadow. Scarecrow Press, 1998. Paper $24.50.

Innovative Use of Information Technology by Colleges. Council on Library and Information Resources, 1999. Paper $20.

Leading the Wired Organization: The Information Professional's Guide to Managing Technological Change. By Mark Stover. Neal-Schuman, 1999. Paper $49.95.

Technology and Scholarly Communication. Ed. by Richard Ekman and Richard E. Quandt. Univ. of California Press, 1999. Paper $19.95.

Understanding Telecommunications and Public Policy: A Guide for Libraries. Ed. by Karen Adams and William F. Birdsall. Canadian Library Association, 1999. Paper $29.95.

Evaluation of Library Services

Descriptive Statistical Techniques for Librarians. By Arthur W. Hafner. American Library Association, 1997. Paper $55.

The TELL IT! Manual: The Complete Program for Evaluating Library Performance. By Douglas Zweizig, Debra Wilcox Johnson, and Jane Robbins. American Library Association, 1996. Paper $35.

Fund Raising

The Big Book of Library Grant Money 1998–1999: Profiles of Private and Corporate Foundations and Direct Corporate Givers Receptive to Library Grant Proposals. By the Taft Group. American Library Association, 1998. Paper $235.

Friends of Libraries Sourcebook. 3rd ed. Ed. by Sandy Dolnick. American Library Association, 1996. Paper $35.

The Funding Game: Rules for Public Library Advocacy. By Mary Anne Craft. Scarecrow Press, 1999. $35.

Fundraising and Friend-Raising on the Web. By Adam Corson-Finnerty and Laura Blanchard. American Library Association, 1998. Paper $50.

Grantsmanship for Small Libraries and School Library Media Centers. By Sylvia D. Hall-Ellis, Doris Meyer, Frank W. Hoffman, and Ann Jerabek. Libraries Unlimited, 1999. Paper $32.50

The Librarian's Guide to Partnerships. Ed. by Sherry Lynch. Highsmith Press, 1999. Paper $19.

Recognizing Fundraising Opportunities. 11-minute video. Library Video Network, 1998. $99.

Government Documents

Guide to Popular U.S. Government Publications. 4th ed. By Frank W. Hoffman and Richard J. Wood. Libraries Unlimited, 1998. $38.50

International Information: Documents, Publications and Electronic Information of International Governmental Organizations. 2nd ed. Ed. by Peter I. Hajnal. Libraries Unlimited, 1997. $105.

Introduction to United States Government Information Sources. 6th ed. By Joe Morehead. Libraries Unlimited, 1999. Paper $47.50.

Subject Guide to U.S. Government Reference Sources. 2nd ed. By Gayle J. Hardy and Judith Schiek Robinson. Libraries Unlimited, 1996. $45.

Intellectual Freedom

Banned Books Resource Guide. Office for Intellectual Freedom/American Library Association, 2000. Paper $20.

Censorship in America: A Reference Handbook. By Mary E. Hull. ABC-CLIO, 1999. $45.

Intellectual Freedom Manual. 5th ed. ALA Office for Intellectual Freedom. American Library Association, 1996. Paper $38.

Libraries, Access, and Intellectual Freedom: Developing Policies for Public and Academic Libraries. By Barbara M. Jones. American Library Association, 1999. Paper $40.

Speaking Out! Voices in Celebration of Intellectual Freedom. Ed. by Ann K. Symons and Sally Gardner Reed. American Library Association, 1999. Paper $20.

Interlibrary Loan, Document Delivery, and Resource Sharing

The Economics of Access versus Ownership. Ed. by Bruce R. Kingma. Haworth Press, 1996. $29.95.

Interlibrary Loan/Document Delivery and Customer Satisfaction. Ed. by Pat Weaver-Meyers, Wilbur Stolt, and Yem Fong. Haworth, 1997. Paper $19.95.

Interlibrary Loan Policies Directory. 6th ed. Ed. by Leslie R. Morris. Neal-Schuman, 1999. Paper $195.

Interlibrary Loan Practices Handbook. 2nd ed. By Virginia Boucher. American Library Association, 1996. Paper $45.

The Internet

The Amazing Internet Challenge: How Leading Projects Use Library Skills to Organize the Web. By Amy Tracy Wells, Susan Calcari, and Travis Koplow. American Library Association, 1999. Paper $45.

Basic Internet for Busy Librarians: A Quick Course for Catching Up. By Laura K. Murray. American Library Association, 1998. Paper $26.

Children and the Internet: Guidelines for Developing Public Library Policy. American Library Association, 1998. Paper $22.

Civilizing the Internet: Global Concerns and Efforts Toward Regulation. By Joseph Migga Kizza McFarland, 1998. Paper $28.50.

Designing Web Interfaces to Library Services and Resources. By Kristen L. Garlock and Sherry Piontek. American Library Association, 1999. Paper $40.

Internet Access and Use: Metropolitan Public Libraries, Sample Internet Policies. 2v. Urban Libraries Council, 1997. Paper $50.

Internet Issues and Applications, 1997-98. Ed. by Bert J. Dempsey and Paul Jones. Scarecrow Press, 1998. $22.50.

The Internet Public Library Handbook. By Joseph Janes, David Carter, Annette Lagace, Michael McLennen, Sara Ryan, and Schelle Simcox. Neal-Schuman, 1998. Paper $49.95.

The Internet Searcher's Handbook: Locating People, Information and Software. 2nd ed. By Peter Morville, Louis Rosenfeld, Joseph Janes, and GraceAnne A. DeCandido. Neal-Schuman, 1999. Paper $45.

Linking People to the Global Networked Society: Evaluation of the Online at PA Libraries Project: Public Access to the Internet Through Public Libraries. By Charles R. McClure and John Carlo Bertot. ERIC, 1998. Study revealed that having access to the Internet at public libraries contributes to economic development in rural areas.

More Internet Troubleshooter: New Help for the Logged-On and Lost. By Nancy R. John and Edward J. Valauskas. American Library Association, 1998. Paper $36.

Neal-Schuman Authoritative Guide to Evaluating Information on the Internet. By Alison Cooke. Neal-Schuman, 1999. Paper $55.

Neal-Schuman Internet Policy Handbook for Libraries. By Mark Smith. Neal-Schuman, 1999. Paper $49.95.

The 1998 National Survey of U.S. Public Library Outlet Internet Connectivity. By John Carlo Bertot and Charles R. McClure. National Commission on Libraries and Information Science/American Library Association, 1998. http://www.ala.org/oitp/research/survey98.html

A Practical Guide to Internet Filters. By Karen Schneider. Neal-Schuman, 1997. Paper $55.

Searching Smart on the World Wide Web: Tools and Techniques for Getting Quality Results. By Cheryl Gould. Library Solutions, 1998. Paper $40.

Teaching the Internet to Library Staff and Users: 10 Ready-To-Go Workshops that Work. By William D. Hollands. Neal-Schuman, 1999. Paper $9.95.

World Wide Web Troubleshooter: Help for the Ensnared and Entangled. By Nancy R. John and Edward J. Valauskas. American Library Association, 1998. Paper $36.

Librarians and Librarianship

The ALA Survey of Librarian Salaries 1999. Ed. by Mary Jo Lynch. American Library Association, 1999. Paper $55.

ARL Annual Salary Survey, 1998–99. Association of Research Libraries, 1999. Paper $70.

Dewey Decimal System Defeats Truman: Library Cartoons. By Scott McCullar. McFarland, 1998. Paper $22.95.

Ethics, Information and Technology: Readings. Ed. by Richard N. Stichler and Robert Hauptman. McFarland, 1997. $39.95.

Information Brokering: A How-To-Do-It Manual. By Florence Mason and Chris Doson. Neal-Schuman, 1998. Paper $45.

Librarians in Fiction: A Critical Bibliography. By Grant Burns. McFarland, 1998. Paper $25.

Librarianship and the Information Paradigm. By Richard Apostle and Boris Raymond. Scarecrow Press, 1997. $32.

The Manley Art of Librarianship. By Will Manley. McFarland, 1993. $23.95. Other humorous books by Manley include *The Truth About Reference Librarians* and *The Truth About Catalogers.*

Me? A Librarian? 10-minute video. Ohio Library Council, 1997. $20.

Our Singular Strengths: Meditations for Librarians. By Michael Gorman. American Library Association, 1997. Paper $20.

What Else You Can Do With a Library Degree: Career Options for the '90s and Beyond. Ed. by Betty-Carol Sellen. Neal-Schuman, 1997. Paper $32.95.

Women of Color in Librarianship: An Oral History. Ed. by Kathleen de la Peña McCook. American Library Association/OLRP, 1998. Paper $20.

Writing Resumes That Work: A How-To-Do-It Manual for Librarians. By Robert R. Newlen. Neal-Schuman, 1998. Paper and disk $55.

Library Automation

Automating Media Centers and Small Libraries: A Microcomputer-Based Approach. By Dania Meghabghab. Libraries Unlimited, 1997. Paper $32.

Directory of Library Automation Software, Systems, and Services. Ed. by Pamela Cibbarelli. Information Today, 1998. Paper $89. Published biennially.

Improving Online Public Access Catalogs. By Martha M. Lee and Sara Shatford Layne. American Library Association, 1998. Paper $48.

Introduction to Automation for Librarians. 4th ed. By William Saffady. American Library Association, 1999. Paper $60.

Library Systems: Current Developments and Future Directions. By Leigh Watson Healy. Council on Library and Information Resources, 1998. Paper $25.

Securing PCs and Data in Libraries and Schools: A Handbook with Menuing, Antivirus and Other Protective Software. By Allen C. Benson. Neal-Schuman, 1998. Paper with CD-ROM $125.

The Systems Librarian: Designing Roles, Defining Skills. By Thomas C. Wilson. American Library Association, 1998. Paper $38.

Using Microsoft PowerPoint: A How-To-Do-It Manual for Librarians. By Gregory A. Crawford, Huijie J. Chen, Lisa R. Stimatz, and Gary W. White. Neal-Schuman, 1998. Paper, $35.

Wired for the Future: Developing Your Library Technology Plan. By Diane Mayo and Sandra Nelson. American Library Association, 1998. Paper $38.

Library Buildings and Space Planning

Checklist of Building Design Considerations. 3rd ed. By William W. Sannwald. American Library Association, 1996 Paper $30.

The Evolution of the American Academic Library Building. By David Kaser. Scarecrow Press, 1996. $36.

Financing Public Library Buildings. By Richard B. Hall. Neal-Schuman, 1994. Paper $70.

Library Buildings, Equipment, and the ADA: Compliance Issues and Solutions. By Susan E. Cirilolo and Robert E. Danford. American Library Association, 1996. Paper $27.

Planning Academic and Research Library Buildings. 3rd ed. By Philip D. Leighton and David C. Weber. American Library Association, 1999. $155.

Library History

Carnegie Libraries Across America: A Public Legacy. By Theodore Jones. Wiley, 1997. $29.95.

Cuneiform to Computer: A History of Reference Sources. By Bill Katz. Scarecrow Press, 1998. $46.

Enrichment: A History of the Public Library in the United States in the Twentieth Century. By Lowell A. Martin. Scarecrow Press, 1998. $35.

The Evolution of the Book. By Frederick G. Kilgour. Oxford Univ. Press, 1998. $35.

Fiat Lux, Fiat Latebra: A Celebration of Historical Library Functions. By D. W. Krummel. GLIS Publications Office, Univ. of Illinois, 1999. Paper $8.

Irrepressible Reformer: A Biography of Melvil Dewey. By Wayne A. Wiegand. American Library Association, 1996. Paper $38.

Libraries, Immigrants, and the American Experience. By Plummer Alston Jones, Jr. Greenwood, 1999. $59.95.

The Library of Congress: The Art and Architecture of the Thomas Jefferson Building. Ed. by John Y. Cole and Henry Hope Reed. W. W. Norton, 1998. $60.

OCLC 1967–1997: Thirty Years of Furthering Access to the World's Information. Ed. by K. Wayne Smith. Haworth, 1998. Paper $19.95.

The Story of Libraries from the Invention of Writing to the Computer Age. By Fred Lerner. Continuum, 1998. $24.94

Nonprint Materials

Cataloging of Audiovisual Materials and Other Special Materials. 4th ed. By Nancy B. Olson. Media Marketing Group, 1998. Paper $75.

Developing and Managing Video Collections in Libraries: A How-to-Do-It Manual for Public Libraries. By Sally Mason-Robinson. Neal-Schuman, 1996. Paper $45.

Finding and Using Educational Videos: A How-To-Do-It Manual. By Barbara Stein, Gary Treadway, and Lauralee Ingram. Neal-Schuman, 1998. Paper $38.50.

A Library Manager's Guide to the Physical Processing of Nonprint Materials. By Karen C. Driessen and Sheila A. Smyth. Greenwood Press, 1995. $67.95.

Preservation

Avoiding Technological Quicksand: Finding a Viable Technical Foundation for Digital Preservation. By Jeff Rothenberg. Council on Library and Information Resources, 1999. Paper $20.

Disaster Response and Planning for Libraries. By Miriam B. Kahn. American Library Association, 1998. Paper $38.

Preservation Microfilming: A Guide for Librarians and Archivists. 2nd ed. Ed. by Lisa L. Fox. American Library Association, 1996. $80.

Preservation of Library and Archival Materials: A Manual. 3rd ed. Ed. by Sherelyn

Ogden. Northeast Document Conservation Center, 1999. $50.

Preserving Digital Information. By Donald Waters and John Garrett. Commission on Preservation and Access, 1996. Paper $15.

Storage Guide for Color Photographic Materials. By James M. Reilly. New York State Library, 1998. Paper $20.

Public Libraries

Civic Space/Cyberspace: The American Public Library in the Information Age. By R. Kathleen Molz and Phyllis Dain. MIT Press, 1999. $30.

The Library Trustee: A Practical Guidebook. 5th ed. By Virginia G. Young. American Library Association, 1995. $40.

Model Policies for Small and Medium Public Libraries. By Jeanette Larson and Hermon Totten. Neal-Schuman, 1998. Paper $45.

New Measures for the New Library: A Social Audit of Public Libraries. By Rebecca Linley and Bob Usherwood. Univ. of Sheffield, United Kingdom, 1998. Paper $20.

Outsourcing: Metropolitan Public Libraries. By Joey Rodger and Marybeth Schroeder. Urban Libraries Council, 1999. Paper $50.

Planning for Results: A Public Library Transformation Process. By Ethel Himmel and William James Wilson, with the ReVision Committee of the Public Library Association. American Library Association, 1998. Paper $40.

Policy Issues and Strategies Affecting Public Libraries in the National Networked Environment: Moving Beyond Connectivity. By John Carlo Bertot and Charles R. McClure. NCLIS, 1998. Paper free.

Public Librarian's Human Resources Handbook. By David A. Baldwin. Libraries Unlimited, 1998. Paper $30.

Public Library Data Service Statistical Report. Public Library Association/American Library Association, 1998. Paper $75.

The Public Library Effectiveness Study: The Complete Report. By Nancy A. Van House and Thomas A. Childers. American Library Association, 1993. Paper $28.

Sample Evaluations of Public Library Directors. Ed. by Sharon Saulman. American

Library Trustee Association/American Library Association, 1997. Paper $25.

Strategic Management for Public Libraries: A Handbook. By Robert M. Hayes and Virginia A. Walter. Greenwood Press, 1996. $65.

What's Good? Describing Your Public Library's Effectiveness. By Thomas A. Childers and Nancy A. Van House. American Library Association, 1993. Paper $25.

Winning Library Referenda Campaigns: A How-to-Do-It Manual. By Richard B. Hall. Neal-Schuman, 1995. Paper $55.

Reference and Readers' Advisory

ALA's Guide to Best Reading. American Library Association, 1999. Kit $29.95. Camera-ready lists of the year's best books for children, teens, and adults.

Cultural Programs for Adults in Public Libraries: A Survey Report. By Debra Wilcox Johnson. American Library Association, 1999. Paper $25.

Delivering Web Reference Service to Young People. By Walter Minkel and Roxanne Hsu Feldman. American Library Association, 1998. Paper $32.

Developing Reference Collections and Services in an Electronic Age: A How-To-Do-It Manual for Librarians. By Kay Ann Cassell. Neal-Schuman, 1999. Paper $55.

Elements of Bibliography: A Guide to Information Sources and Practical Applications. 3rd ed. By Robert B. Harmon. Scarecrow, 1998. Paper $29.50.

Introduction to Library Public Services. 6th ed. By G. Edward Evans, Anthony J. Amodeo, and Thomas L. Carter. Libraries Unlimited, 1999. Paper $45.

Introduction to Reference Work. 7th ed. 2v. By William A. Katz. McGraw-Hill, 1996. $57.75.

The Making of a Bestseller: From Author to Reader. By Arthur T. Vanderbilt II. McFarland, 1999. Paper $28.50.

Managing the Reference Collection. By Christopher W. Nolan. American Library Association, 1998. Paper $32.

Readers' Advisory Service in the Public Library. 2nd ed. By Joyce G. Saricks and Nancy Brown. American Library Association, 1997. Paper $25.

The Reference Assessment Manual. Comp. by the Evaluation of Reference & Adult Services Committee of RASD/American Library Association. Pierian Press, 1995. Paper $35. A disk with copies of assessment instruments is available for $15.

The Reference Encounter: Interpersonal Communication in the Academic Library. By Marie L. Radford. American Library Association/ACRL, 1998. Paper $30.

The Reference Interview as a Creative Art. By Elaine and Edward Jennerich. Libraries Unlimited, 1997. $26.50

Rethinking Reference: The Reference Librarian's Practical Guide for Surviving Constant Change. By Elizabeth Thomsen. Neal-Schuman, 1999. Paper $45.

Where to Find What: A Handbook to Reference Service. 4th ed. By James M. Hillard. Scarecrow Press, 1999. $45

School Libraries/Media Centers

The Emerging School Library Media Center: Historical Issues and Perspectives. Ed. by Kathy Howard Latrobe. Libraries Unlimited, 1998. $42.

Enhancing Teaching and Learning: A Leadership Guide for School Library Media Specialists. By Jean Donham. Neal-Schuman, 1998. Paper $45.

Foundations for Effective School Library Media Programs. Ed. by Ken Haycock. Libraries Unlimited, 1999. $55.

Information Power: Building Partnerships for Learning. American Library Association, 1998. Paper $35.

Internet for Active Learners: Curriculum-Based Strategies for K–12. By Pam Berger. American Library Association, 1998. Paper $35.

Lessons from Library Power: Enriching Teaching and Learning. By Douglas L. Zweizig and Dianne McAfee Hopkins, with Norman Lott Webb and Gary Wehlage. Libraries Unlimited, 1999. Paper $35.

The Net Effect: School Library Media Centers and the Internet. Ed. by Lyn Hay and James Henri. Scarecrow Press, 1999. Paper $36.

New Steps to Service: Common-Sense Advice for the School Library Media Specialist. By Ann M. Wasman. American Library Association, 1998. Paper $20.

Operating and Evaluating School Library Media Programs: A Handbook for Administrators and Librarians. By Bernice L. Yesner and Hilda L. Jay. Neal-Schuman, 1998. Paper $49.95.

Output Measures for School Library Media Programs. By Frances Bryant Bradburn. Neal-Schuman, 1999. Paper $45.

Shelving: The Ultimate Teaching Tool and Other Timesaving Solutions for Library Media Specialists. By Rhonda Scribner. Brainstorm Press, 1999. 3-ring binder $20.

Special Events Programs in School Library Media Centers. By Marcia Trotta. Greenwood Press, 1997. $35.

Student Assistants in the School Library Media Center. By Therese Bissen Bard. Libraries Unlimited, 1999. Paper $30.

Serials

Gatekeepers of Knowledge: Journal Editors in the Sciences and the Social Sciences. By Stephen McGinty. Bergin & Garvey, Greenwood Publishing Group, 1999. $55.

Guide to Performance Evaluation of Serials Vendors. Association for Library Collections and Technical Services/American Library Association, 1997. Paper $15.

Management of Serials in Libraries. By Thomas E. Nisonger. Libraries Unlimited, 1998. $55.

Serials Cataloging Handbook. By Carol Liheng and Winnie S. Chan. American Library Association, 1998. Paper $75.

Services for Special Groups

Accessible Libraries on Campus: A Practical Guide for the Creation of Disability-Friendly Libraries. Ed. by Tom McNulty. American Library Association, 1999. Paper $22.

Adaptive Technology for the Internet: Making Electronic Resources Accessible to All. By Barbara T. Mates. American Library Association, 1999. Paper $36.

American Indian Library Services in Perspective. By Elizabeth Rockefeller-MacArthur. McFarland, 1998. $29.50.

Choosing and Using Books with Adult New Readers. By Marguerite Crowley Weibel. Neal-Schuman, 1996. Paper $45.

Guidelines for Library Services for People with Mental Retardation. American Library Association/Association of Specialized and Cooperative Library Agencies, 1999. Paper $14.

Including Families of Children with Special Needs: A How-To-Do-It Manual for Librarians. By Sandra Feinberg, Barbara Jordan, Kathleen Deerr, and Michelle Langa. Neal-Schuman, 1998. Paper $39.95.

Information Services for People with Developmental Disabilities: The Library Manager's Handbook. Ed. by Linda Lucas Walling and Marilyn M. Irwin. Greenwood Press, 1995. $75.

The Librarian's Guide to Homeschooling Resources. By Susan G. Scheps. American Library Association, 1998. Paper $25.

Libraries Inside: A Practical Guide for Prison Librarians. Ed. by Rhea Joyce Rubin and Daniel Suvak. McFarland, 1995. $41.50.

Literacy, Access and Libraries Among the Language Minority Population. Ed. by Rebecca Constantino. Scarecrow Press, 1998. $36.

Literacy Is for Everyone: Making Library Activities Accessible for Children with Disabilities. National Lekotek Center, 1998. Paper $49.95.

Poor People and Library Services. Ed. by Karen M. Venturella. McFarland, 1998. Paper $26.50.

Preparing Staff to Serve Patrons with Disabilities: A How-to-Do-It Manual for Librarians. By Courtney Deines-Jones and Connie Van Fleet. Neal-Schuman, 1995. Paper $45.

Serving Print Disabled Library Patrons: A Textbook. Ed. by Bruce Edward Massis. McFarland, 1996. $42.50.

Serving Latino Communities: A How-To-Do-It Manual for Librarians. By Camila Alire and Orlando Archibeque. Neal-Schuman, 1998. Paper $39.95.

Universal Access: Electronic Resources in Libraries. By Sheryl Burgstahler, Dan Comden, and Beth Fraser. American Library Association, 1998. Binder/video $75.

Technical Services

Guide to Managing Approval Plans. Ed. by Susan Flood. American Library Association, 1998. Paper $18.

Library Relocations and Collection Shifts. By Dennis C. Tucker. Information Today, 1999. $35.

Outsourcing Library Technical Services: A How-to-Do-It Manual for Librarians. By Arnold Hirshon and Barbara Winters. Neal-Schuman, 1996. $55. (Sample RFPs are available on diskette for $25 via *Outsourcing Technical Services: Ready-to-Import RFP Specifications Disk.*)

Outsourcing Library Technical Services Operations: Practices in Public, Academic and Special Libraries. Ed. by Karen A. Wilson and Marylou Colver. American Library Association, 1997. Paper $38.

Technical Services Today and Tomorrow. 2nd ed. Ed. by Michael Gorman. Libraries Unlimited, 1998. $38.50

Understanding the Business of Library Acquisitions. 2nd ed. Ed. by Karen A. Schmidt. American Library Association, 1998. Paper $54.

Volunteers

Recruiting and Managing Volunteers in Libraries: A How-to-Do-It Manual for Librarians. By Bonnie F. McCune and Charleszine "Terry" Nelson. Neal-Schuman, 1995. Paper $45.

The Volunteer Library: A Handbook. By Linda S. Fox. McFarland, 1999. Paper $35.

Periodicals and Periodical Indexes

Acquisitions Librarian
Advanced Technology Libraries
Against the Grain
American Libraries
American Society for Information Science Journal
Behavioral and Social Sciences Librarian
Book Links
Book Report: Journal for Junior and Senior High School Librarians
Booklist
The Bottom Line
Cataloging and Classification Quarterly
CHOICE
Collection Management
College and Research Libraries
Community and Junior College Libraries
Computers in Libraries
The Electronic Library
Government Information Quarterly
Information Outlook (formerly *Special Libraries*)
Journal of Academic Librarianship
Journal of Information Ethics
Journal of Interlibrary Loan, Document Delivery and Information Supply
Journal of Library Administration
Journal of Youth Services in Libraries
Knowledge Quest
Law Library Journal
Legal Reference Services Quarterly
Libraries & Culture
Library Administration and Management
Library and Information Science Research (LIBRES)

Library Issues: Briefings for Faculty and Academic Administrators (also available on the Web by subscription at http://www. netpubsintl.com/LI.html)
Library Hi-Tech News
Library Journal
The Library Quarterly
Library Resources and Technical Services
Library Talk: The Magazine for Elementary School Librarians
Library Trends
MLS: Marketing Library Services
Medical Reference Services Quarterly
MultiCultural Review
MultiMedia Schools
Music Library Association Notes
Music Reference Services Quarterly
The One-Person Library
Online & CD-ROM Review
Public and Access Services Quarterly
Public Libraries
Public Library Quarterly
Rare Books and Manuscripts Librarianship
Reference and User Services Quarterly (formerly *RQ*)
Reference Librarian
Reference Services Review
Resource Sharing & Information Networks
Rural Libraries
School Library Journal
Science & Technology Libraries
Serials Librarian
Serials Review
Technical Services Quarterly
Technicalities
Video Librarian
Voice of Youth Advocates (VOYA)

Ready Reference

Publishers' Toll-Free Telephone Numbers

Publishers' toll-free numbers continue to play an important role in ordering, verification, and customer service. This year's list comes from *Literary Market Place* (R. R. Bowker) and includes distributors and regional toll-free numbers, where applicable. The list is not comprehensive, and toll-free numbers are subject to change. Readers may want to call for toll-free directory assistance (800-555-1212).

Publisher/Distributor	Toll-Free No.
A D D Warehouse, Plantation, FL	800-233-9273
A D P Hollander, Plymouth, MN	800-761-9266
A-R Editions Inc., Madison, WI	800-736-0070 (US book orders only)
Abacus, Grand Rapids, MI	800-451-4319
Abbeville Publishing Group, New York, NY	800-ART-BOOK
ABC-CLIO, Santa Barbara, CA	800-422-2546; 800-368-6868
Abdo Publishing, Minneapolis, MN	800-458-8399
ABELexpress, Carnegie, PA	800-542-9001
Aberdeen Group, Addison, IL	800-837-0870
ABI Professional Publications, Arlington, VA	800-551-7776
Abingdon Press, Nashville, TN	800-251-3320
Abrams & Co. Publishers Inc., Waterbury, CT	800-227-9120; fax 800-737-3322
Harry N Abrams Inc., New York, NY	800-345-1359
Academic Press, San Diego, CA	800-321-5068 (cust serv)
Academic Therapy Publications, Novato, CA	800-422-7249
Academy Chicago Publishers, Chicago, IL	800-248-READ
Academy of Producer Insurance Studies Inc., Austin, TX	800-526-2777
Acres USA, Metairie, LA	800-355-5313
Acropolis Books Inc., Lakewood, CO	800-773-9923
ACS Publications, San Diego, CA	800-888-9983 (orders only)
ACTA Publications, Chicago, IL	800-397-2282; fax 800-397-0079
ACU Press, Abilene, TX	800-444-4228
Adams Blake Publishing, Fair Oaks, CA	800-368-ADAM
Adams Media Corp., Holbrook, MA	800-872-5627; fax 800-827-5628
ADDAX Publishing Group, Lenexa, KS	800-598-5550
Addicus Books Inc., Omaha, NE	800-352-2873
Addison Wesley Longman, Don Mills, ON, Canada	800-387-8028

Publisher/Distributor **Toll-Free No.**

Addison Wesley Longman Inc., 800-358-4566 (trade & agency orders);
   Reading, MA 800-552-2259 (sch serv team orders)
800-322-1377 (college serv team orders)
800-552-2499 (college sales orders)
800-822-6339 (corp. & prof. orders)
Adi, Gaia, Esalen Publications Inc., Niagara Falls, NY   800-652-8574; 888-545-0053,
fax 800-458-0025; 800-931-1778
Adirondack Mountain Club, Lake George, NY 800-395-8080
Advantage Publishers Group, San Diego, CA 800-284-3580
Adventure Publications, Cambridge, MN 800-678-7006
Aegean Park Press, Laguna Hills, CA 800-736-3587 (orders only)
Aegis Publishing Group Ltd., Newport, RI 800-828-6961
AEI Press, Washington, DC 800-269-6267
Aerial Photography Services Inc., Charlotte, NC fax 800-204-4910
Africa World Press, Lawrenceville, NJ 800-789-1898
African American Images, Chicago, IL 800-552-1991
Ages Publications, Thornhill, ON, Canada 800-263-1991 (fulfillment)
Agora Inc., Baltimore, MD 800-433-1528
Agreka Books, Sandy, UT 800-360-5284; fax 888-771-7758
Ahsahta Press, Boise, ID 800-992-TEXT
AIMS Education Foundation, Fresno, CA 888-733-2467
Airmont Publishing Co. Inc., New York, NY 800-223-5251
Alba House, Staten Island, NY 800-343-ALBA
Alban Institute Inc., Bethesda, MD 800-486-1318
Alef Design Group, Los Angeles, CA 800-845-0662
Alfred Publishing Co. Inc., Van Nuys, CA 800-292-6122
ALI-ABA Committee on Continuing Professional Education,
   Philadelphia, PA 800-CLE-NEWS
Allied Health Publications, National City, CA 800-221-7374
Allworth Press, New York, NY 800-491-2808
Allyn & Bacon, Needham Heights, MA 800-223-1360
ALPHA Publications of America Inc., Tucson, AZ   800-528-3494; fax 800-770-4329
Alpine Publications Inc., Loveland, CO 800-777-7257 (orders only)
Altair Publications, San Diego, CA 888-853-5937
Altitude Publishing Canada Ltd., Canmore, AB, Canada 800-957-6888
fax 800-957-1477
Alyson Publications, Los Angeles, CA 800-525-9766
AMACOM Books, New York, NY 800-250-5308 (orders)
Frank Amato Publications Inc., Portland, OR 800-541-9498
Ambassador Books, Inc., Worcester, MA 800-577-0909
Amboy Associates, San Diego, CA 800-448-4023
America West Pubs, Carson City, NV 800-729-4130; fax 877-726-2632
American Academy of Orthopaedic Surgeons, Rosemont, IL 800-626-6726
American Academy of Pediatrics, Elk Grove Village, IL 800-433-9016
American Alliance for Health, Physical Education, Recreation
   & Dance, Reston, VA 800-213-7193

Publisher/Distributor	Toll-Free No.
American Association for Vocational Instructional Materials, Winterville, GA	800-228-4689
American Association of Cereal Chemists, St Paul, MN	800-328-7560
American Association of Community Colleges (AACC), Washington, DC	800-250-6557
American Association of Engineering Societies, Washington, DC	888-400-2237
American Association of Petroleum Geologists (AAPG), Tulsa, OK	800-364-AAPG
American Bankers Association, Washington, DC	800-338-0626
American Bible Society, New York, NY	800-322-4253 (orders only)
American Chemical Society, Washington, DC	800-227-9919
American College of Physician Executives, Tampa, FL	800-562-8088
American Correctional Association, Lanham, MD	800-222-5646
American Council on Education, Washington, DC	800-279-6799 ext 642
American Counseling Association, Alexandria, VA	800-422-2648 (book orders only)
	fax 800-473-2329
American Diabetes Association, Alexandria, VA	800-232-6733
American Eagle Publications Inc., Show Low, AZ	800-719-4957
American Federation of Arts, New York, NY	800-AFA-0270
American Federation of Astrologers Inc., Tempe, AZ	888-301-7630
American Foundation for the Blind (AFB Press), New York, NY	800-232-3044
American Geophysical Union, Washington, DC	800-966-2481
American Guidance Service Inc., Circle Pines, MN	800-328-2560
American Health Publishing Co., Dallas, TX	800-736-7323
American Historical Press, Sun Valley, CA	800-550-5750
American Institute of Aeronautics & Astronautics, Reston, VA	800-639-2422
American Institute of Architects, Washington, DC	800-365-ARCH (orders)
American Institute of Certified Public Accountants, Jersey City, NJ	800-862-4272
American Institute of Chemical Engineers (AICHE), New York, NY	800-242-4363
American Law Institute, Philadelphia, PA	800-CLE-NEWS
American Library Association (ALA), Chicago, IL	800-545-2433 (US only)
American Map Corp., Maspeth, NY	800-432-MAPS
American Marketing Association, Chicago, IL	800-262-1150
American Mathematical Society, Providence, RI	800-321-4267
American Medical Association, Chicago, IL	800-621-8335
American Nurses Publishing, Washington, DC	800-637-0323
American Phytopathological Society, St Paul, MN	800-328-7560
American Printing House for the Blind Inc., Louisville, KY	800-223-1839 (cust serv)
	800-572-0844 (sales & mktg)
American Psychiatric Press Inc., Washington, DC	800-368-5777
American Psychological Association, Washington, DC	800-374-2721
American Quilter's Society, Paducah, KY	800-626-5420
American Showcase Inc., New York, NY	800-894-7469
American Society for Nondestructive Testing, Columbus, OH	800-222-2768
American Society of Mechanical Engineers (ASME), New York, NY	800-843-2763 (cust serv)
American Technical Publishers Inc., Homewood, IL	800-323-3471

Publisher/Distributor	Toll-Free No.
Amon Carter Museum, Fort Worth, TX	800-573-1933
Amsco School Publications Inc., New York, NY	800-969-8398
An Awakening Publishing Co., Encino, CA	888-522-9253
Analytic Press, Hillsdale, NJ	800-926-6579 (orders only)
Ancestry Inc., Orem, UT	800-262-3787
Anderson Publishing Co., Cincinnati, OH	800-582-7295
Andrews McMeel Publishing, Kansas City, MO	800-826-4216
Andrews University Press, Berrien Springs, MI	800-467-6369
	(Visa & MC orders only)
Angelus Press, Kansas City, MO	800-966-7337
Ann Arbor Press Inc., Chelsea, MI	800-487-2323
Annabooks, San Diego, CA	800-462-1042
Anness Publishing Inc., New York, NY	800-354-9657
Annual Reviews Inc., Palo Alto, CA	800-523-8635
ANR Publications University of California, Oakland, CA	800-994-8849
Anti-Aging Press, Miami, FL	800-SO-YOUNG
Antique Collectors Club Ltd., Wappingers Falls, NY	800-252-5231
Antique Publications, Marietta, OH	800-533-3433
AOCS Press, Champaign, IL	800-336-AOCS
APDG, Fuquay-Varina, NC	800-227-9681; fax 800-390-5507
Aperture, New York, NY	800-929-2323
Apex Press, New York, NY	800-316-2739
Appalachian Trail Conference, Harpers Ferry, WV	888-287-8673
Applause Theatre Book Publishers, New York, NY	800-798-7787
Aqua Quest Publications Inc., Locust Valley, NY	800-933-8989
Aquila Communications Inc., St Laurent, PQ, Canada	800-667-7071
Ardis Publishers, Dana Pt, CA	800-877-7133 (orders)
ARE Press, Virginia Beach, VA	800-723-1112
Ariel Press, Alpharetta, GA	800-336-7769
Armenian Reference Books Co., Glendale, CA	888-504-2550
Arnold Publishing Ltd., Edmonton, AB, Canada	800-563-2665
Jason Aronson Inc., Northvale, NJ	800-782-0015 (orders)
Arrow Map Inc., Bridgewater, MA	800-343-7500
Arsenal Pulp Press Book Publishers Ltd., Vancouver, BC, Canada	888-600-PULP
Art Image Publications USA Inc., Champlain, NY	800-361-2598; fax 800-559-2598
Art Image Publications USA Inc., Laval, PQ, Canada	800-361-2598; fax 800-559-2598
Artabras Inc., New York, NY	800-ART-BOOK
Arte Publico Press, Houston, TX	800-633-ARTE
Artech House Inc., Norwood, MA	800-225-9977
ASCP Press, Chicago, IL	800-621-4142
Ashgate Publishing Co., Brookfield, VT	800-535-9544
Aslan Publishing, Fairfield, CT	800-786-5427
ASM International, Materials Park, OH	800-336-5152
ASM Press, Washington, DC	800-546-2416
Aspen Publishers Inc., Gaithersburg, MD	800-638-8437 (orders)
Association for Computing Machinery, New York, NY	800-342-6626

Publisher/Distributor	Toll-Free No.
Association for Supervision & Curriculum Development, Alexandria, VA	800-933-2723
Association for the Advancement of Medical Instrumentation, Arlington, VA	800-332-2264
Association of College & Research Libraries, Chicago, IL	800-545-2433
Association of Specialized & Cooperative Library Agencies (ASCLA), Chicago, IL	800-545-2433
Astronomical Society of the Pacific, San Francisco, CA	800-335-2624 (orders only)
ATL Press, Shrewsbury, MA	800-835-7543
Atlantic Publishing Inc., Ocala, FL	800-555-4037
Audio Renaissance Tapes, Los Angeles, CA	800-452-5589 (cust serv)
Augsburg Fortress Publishers, Publishing House of the	800-426-0115
Evangelical Lutheran Church in America, Minneapolis, MN	800-328-4648 (orders)
	800-421-0239 (permissions); fax 800-722-7766 (orders)
August House Publishers Inc., Little Rock, AR	800-284-8784
Augustinian Press, Villanova, PA	800-871-9404
Ave Maria Press, Notre Dame, IN	800-282-1865; fax 800-282-5681
Avery Color Studios, Gwinn, MI	800-722-9925
Avery Publishing Group Inc., Wayne, NJ	800-548-5757
Aviation Heritage Inc., Destin, FL	800-748-9308
Avon Books, New York, NY	800-238-0658; fax 800-223-0239
Avotaynu Inc., Bergenfield, NJ	800-286-8296
Back to the Bible, Lincoln, NE	800-759-2425 (orders)
Baker Books, Grand Rapids, MI	800-877-2665; fax 800-398-3110
Balcony Publishing Inc., Austin, TX	800-777-7949
Ballantine Publishing Group (Ballantine/Del Rey/ Fawcett/House of Collectibles/Ivy/One World), New York, NY	800-638-6460
Bandanna Books, Santa Barbara, CA	800-259-8324
Banner of Truth, Carlisle, PA	800-263-8085 (orders)
Bantam Dell Publishing Group, New York, NY	800-223-6834
Baptist Spanish Publishing House (d/b/a Casa	800-755-5958 (cust serv & orders)
Bautista de Publicaciones), El Paso, TX	800-985-9971 (Casa Bautista Miami)
Barcelona Publishers, Gilsum, NH	800-345-6665
Barefoot Books, New York, NY	888-346-9138
Barnes & Noble Books (Imports & Reprints), Lanham, MD	800-462-6420
Barricade Books Inc., New York, NY	800-592-6657
Barron's Educational Series Inc., Hauppauge, NY	800-645-3476
Basic Books, New York, NY	800-242-7737 (orders)
Battelle Press, Columbus, OH	800-451-3543
Bay Books & Tapes Inc., San Francisco, CA	800-231-4944
Baywood Publishing Co. Inc., Amityville, NY	800-638-7819
Be Puzzled, San Francisco, CA	800-347-4818
Beacham Publishing Corp., Osprey, FL	800-466-9644
Beacon Hill Press of Kansas City, Kansas City, MO	800-877-0700
Bear & Co. Inc., Santa Fe, NM	800-932-3277

Publisher/Distributor	Toll-Free No.
Groupe Beauchemin, Laval, PQ, Canada	800-361-2598 (US & Canada)
	800-361-4504 (Canada only)
Thomas T Beeler Publisher, Hampton Falls, NH	800-251-8726
Beeman Jorgensen Inc., Indianapolis, IN	800-553-5319
Frederic C Beil Publisher Inc., Savannah, GA	800-829-8406
Bell Springs Publishing, Willits, CA	800-515-8050
Bellerophon Books, Santa Barbara, CA	800-253-9943
R Bemis Publishing Ltd., Marietta, GA	800-497-6663
Matthew Bender & Co. Inc., New York, NY	800-227-5158 (outside NY)
	800-722-3288
Benefactory, Fairfield, CT	800-729-7251; fax 800-482-1385
John Benjamins Publishing Co., Erdenheim, PA	800-562-5666
Robert Bentley Publishers, Cambridge, MA	800-423-4595
R J Berg & Co., Publishers, Indianapolis, IN	800-638-3909
Berkeley Hills Books, Berkeley, CA	888-848-7303; fax 888-848-7303
Berkshire House Publishers, Lee, MA	800-321-8526
Bernan, Washington, DC	800-865-3457; fax 800-865-3450
Bernan Associates, Lanham, MD	800-865-3457; fax 800-865-3450
Bess Press, Honolulu, HI	800-910-2377
Best Publishing Co., Flagstaff, AZ	800-468-1055
Betania Editores Caribe, Nashville, TN	800-322-7423; 800-251-4000
Bethany House Publishers, Minneapolis, MN	800-328-6109
Bethlehem Books, Minto, ND	800-757-6831
Betterway Books, Cincinnati, OH	800-289-0963
Between the Lines, Toronto, ON, Canada	800-565-9523
Beverage Marketing Corp., Mingo Junction, OH	800-332-6222
Beyond Words Publishing Inc., Hillsboro, OR	800-284-9673
Bhaktivedanta Book Publishing Inc., Los Angeles, CA	800-927-4152
Biblical Archaeology Society, Washington, DC	800-221-4644
Biblo & Tannen Booksellers & Publishers Inc.,	
Cheshire, CT	800-272-8778 (voice & fax)
Binford & Mort Publishing Inc., Hillsboro, OR	888-221-4514
BioTechniques Books, Natick, MA	800-655-8285
Birkhauser Boston, Cambridge, MA	800-777-4643
George T Bisel Co., Philadelphia, PA	800-247-3526
Bisk Publishing Co., Tampa, FL	800-874-7877; fax 800-345-8273
Black Belt Publishing LLC, Montgomery, AL	800-959-3245; 800-789-7733
Black Diamond Book Publishing, Los Angeles, CA	800-444-2524
Black Rose Books Ltd., Montreal, PQ, Canada	800-565-9523; fax 800-221-9985
Blackbirch Press Inc., Woodbridge, CT	800-831-9183
Blacksmith Corporation, North Hampton, OH	800-531-2665
John F Blair, Publisher, Winston-Salem, NC	800-222-9796
Blizzard Publishing Inc., Winnipeg, MB, Canada	800-694-9256
Bloomberg Press, Princeton, NJ	800-388-2749 ext 4670
Blue Book Publications Inc., Minneapolis, MN	800-877-4867
Blue Dolphin Publishing Inc., Nevada City, CA	800-643-0765

Publisher/Distributor	Toll-Free No.
Blue Dove Press, San Diego, CA	800-691-1008 (orders)
Blue Moon Books Inc., New York, NY	800-535-0007; fax 800-531-0689
Blue Mountain Press Inc., Boulder, CO	800-525-0642; fax 800-545-8573
Blue Note Publications, Cape Canaveral, FL	800-624-0401
Blue Poppy Press Inc., Boulder, CO	800-487-9296
Bluestar Communication Corp., Woodside, CA	800-625-8378
Bluestocking Press, Placerville, CA	800-959-8586
Blushing Rose Publishing, San Anselmo, CA	800-898-2263
BNA Books, Washington, DC	800-960-1220
Bob Jones University Press, Greenville, SC	800-845-5731
Bold Strummer Ltd., Westport, CT	800-375-3786
Bonus Books Inc., Chicago, IL	800-225-3775
Book Peddlers, Minnetonka, MN	800-255-3379
Book Publishing Co., Summertown, TN	888-260-8458
Book Tech Inc., Winchester, MA	800-650-7229
Book World Inc./Blue Star Productions, Sun Lakes, AZ	888-472-2665
BookPartners Inc., Wilsonville, OR	800-895-7323
Books in Motion, Spokane, WA	800-752-3199
Books Nippan, Carson, CA	800-562-1410
Bookwrights Press, Charlottesville, VA	888-823-2977
Botanica Press, Loveland, CO	800-272-2193; 800-645-3675 (orders only)
Thomas Bouregy & Co. Inc., New York, NY	800-223-5251
R. R. Bowker, New Providence, NJ	888-269-5372
Marion Boyars Publishers Inc., New York, NY	800-626-4330 (orders)
	800-243-0138 (orders)
Boyds Mills Press, Honesdale, PA	877-512-8366
Boynton/Cook Publishers Inc., Portsmouth, NH	800-793-2154 (orders)
Boys Town Press, Boys Town, NE	800-282-6657
BradyGAMES, Indianapolis, IN	800-545-5912
Bradygames Publishing, Indianapolis, IN	800-545-5914
Allen D Bragdon Publishers Inc., South Yarmouth, MA	8778-SMARTS
Branden Publishing Co. Inc., Brookline Village, MA	800-537-7335 (MC & Visa only)
Brassey's Inc., Dulles, VA	800-775-2518
Breakaway Books, New York, NY	800-548-4348
Breakthrough Publications, Ossining, NY	800-824-5000
Breakwater Books Ltd., St Johns, NF, Canada	800-563-3333
Brethren Press, Elgin, IL	800-323-8039
Brewers Publications, Boulder, CO	888-822-6273 (Canada & US)
Bridge Learning Systems Inc., American Canyon, CA	800-487-9868
Bridge-Logos Publishers Inc., North Brunswick, NJ	800-631-5802
	fax 800-93-LOGOS
Bridge Publications Inc., Los Angeles, CA	800-722-1733; 800-843-7389 (CA)
Briefings Publishing Group, Alexandria, VA	800-888-2084
Brighton Publications, New Brighton, MN	800-536-2665
Brill Academic Publishers Inc., Boston, MA	800-962-4406
Bristol Publishing Enterprises Inc., San Leandro, CA	800-346-4889

Publisher/Distributor	Toll-Free No.
Britannica Home Library Service, Chicago, IL	800-323-1229
Britannica Publishing Division, Chicago, IL	800-323-1229
Broadway Press, Louisville, KY	800-869-6372
Paul H Brookes Publishing Co., Baltimore, MD	800-638-3775
Brookings Institution Press, Washington, DC	800-275-1447
Brookline Books, Cambridge, MA	800-666-2665
Brookline Books Inc., Cambridge, MA	800-666-2665
Brooks/Cole Publishing Co., Pacific Grove, CA	800-354-9706
Brunner/Mazel Publishing, Levittown, PA	800-821-8312
Buckingham Mint Inc., Lyon, MS	800-443-6753
Building News, Needham, MA	800-873-6397
Bulfinch Press, Boston, MA	800-759-0190
Bull Publishing Co., Palo Alto, CA	800-676-2855
Bureau of Economic Geology, University of Texas at Austin, Austin, TX	888-839-4365 fax 888-839-6277
Burrelle's Information Services, Livingston, NJ	800-876-3342; fax 800-898-6677
Business & Legal Reports Inc., Madison, CT	800-727-5257
Business Research Services Inc., Washington, DC	800-845-8420
Butler Publishing & Farrier Services, LaPorte, CO	800-728-3826
Butte Publications Inc., Hillsboro, OR	800-330-9791
Butterworth-Heinemann, Woburn, MA	800-366-2665 (orders & cust serv) fax 800-446-6520 (orders)
Butterworths Canada Ltd., Markham, ON, Canada	800-668-6481; fax 800-479-2826
C & T Publishing Inc., Concord, CA	800-284-1114
CAAS Publications, Los Angeles, CA	800-206-CAAS
Calendar Islands Publishers LLC, Portland, ME	800-819-7080 (cust serv)
Calyx Books, Corvallis, OR	888-336-2665
Cambridge Educational, Charleston, WV	800-468-4227
Cambridge University Press, New York, NY	800-221-4512
Cameron & Co., San Francisco, CA	800-779-5582
Canada Law Book Inc., Aurora, ON, Canada	800-263-2037
Canada Publishing Corp., Scarborough, ON, Canada	800-667-1115
Canadian Bible Society, Toronto, ON, Canada	800-465-2425
Canadian Institute of Chartered Accountants, Toronto, ON, Canada	800-268-3793 (Canada)
Canadian Museum of Civilization, Hull, PQ, Canada	800-555-5621
Capstone Press Inc., Mankato, MN	800-747-4992; fax 888-262-0705
Career Press Inc., Franklin Lakes, NJ	800-CAREER-1
Career Publishing Inc., Orange, CA	800-854-4014
Editorial Caribe, Nashville, TN	800-322-7423
Carolina Biological Supply Co.-Scientific Multimedia Dept, Burlington, NC	800-334-5551 fax 800-222-7112
Carolrhoda Books Inc., Minneapolis, MN	800-328-4929; fax 800-332-1132
Carroll Press, New York, NY	800-366-7086
Carswell Professional Publishing Canada, Scarborough, ON, Canada	800-387-5164 (Canada & US)

Publisher/Distributor	Toll-Free No.
CarTech Inc., North Branch, MN	800-551-4754
Cascade Pass Inc., Marina Del Ray, CA	888-837-0704
Cason Hall & Co. Publishers, Rockville, MD	800-448-7357
Castle Books Inc., Edison, NJ	800-526-7257 (orders)
CAT Publishing, Redding, CA	800-767-0511
Catbird Press, North Haven, CT	800-360-2391
Catholic News Publishing Co. Inc., New Rochelle, NY	800-433-7771
Cavendish Books Inc., Delta, BC, Canada	800-665-3166; fax 800-665-3167
CCH Canadian Ltd., North York, ON, Canada	800-268-4522 (Canada & US) fax 800-461-4131
CCH Inc., Riverwoods, IL	fax 800-224-8299
Cedar Fort Inc./C F I Distribution, Springville, UT	800-759-2665
Cedco Publishing Co., San Rafael, CA	800-227-6162
CEF Press, Warrenton, MO	800-748-7710
Celebrity Press, Nashville, TN	800-327-5113
Celestial Arts, Berkeley, CA	800-841-BOOK
Center for Futures Education Inc., Grove City, PA	800-966-2554
Center for Healthcare Information, Irvine, CA	800-627-2244
Central Conference of American Rabbis/CCAR Press, New York, NY	800-935-CCAR
Chain Store Guide, Tampa, FL	800-927-9292
Chalice Press, St Louis, MO	800-366-3383
Chandler House Press, Worcester, MA	800-642-6657
Richard Chang Associates Inc., Irvine, CA	800-756-8096
Chaosium Inc., Oakland, CA	800-213-1489
Chariot Victor Publishing, Colorado Springs, CO	800-437-4337
CharismaLife Publishers, Lake Mary, FL	800-451-4598
Douglas Charles Press, North Attleboro, MA	800-752-3769 (New England only)
Charles River Media, Rockland, MA	800-382-8505
Charlesbridge Publishing Inc., Watertown, MA	800-225-3214
Charlton Press, Toronto, ON, Canada	800-442-6042; fax 800-442-1542
Chartwell Books Inc., Edison, NJ	800-526-7257 (orders)
Chatelaine Press, Burke, VA	800-249-9527
Chatsworth Press, Chatsworth, CA	800-262-7367 (US); 800-272-7367 (Canada)
Chelsea Green Publishing Co., White River Junction, VT	800-639-4099
Chelsea House Publishers, Broomall, PA	800-848-BOOK
Chelsea Publishing Co. Inc., Providence, RI	800-821-4267
Chemical Publishing Co. Inc., New York, NY	800-786-3659
Cheng & Tsui Co. Inc., Boston, MA	800-554-1963
Cherokee Publishing Co., Marietta, GA	800-653-3952
Chess Combination Inc., Bridgeport, CT	800-354-4083
Chess Digest Inc., Grand Prairie, TX	800-462-3548
Chicago Review Press, Chicago, IL	800-888-4741
Chicago Spectrum Press, Louisville, KY	800-594-5190
Child's Play, Auburn, ME	800-472-0099; fax 800-854-6989
Chitra Publications, Montrose, PA	800-628-8244
Chivers North America Inc., Hampton, NH	800-621-0182

Publisher/Distributor	Toll-Free No.
Chockstone Press Inc., Helena, MT	800-582-2665
Chosen Books, Grand Rapids, MI	800-877-2665
Christendom Press, Front Royal, VA	800-877-5456
Christian Literature Crusade Inc., Fort Washington, PA	800-659-1240 (orders)
Christian Publications Inc., Camp Hill, PA	800-233-4443
Christian Schools International, Grand Rapids, MI	800-635-8288
Christopher-Gordon Publishers Inc., Norwood, MA	800-934-8322
Chronicle Books, San Francisco, CA	800-722-6657 (orders)
	fax 800-858-7787 (orders)
Chronicle Guidance Publications Inc., Moravia, NY	800-622-7284
Church Growth Institute, Forest, VA	800-553-GROW (orders only)
	fax 800-860-3109 (orders only)
Churchill Livingstone, Philadelphia, PA	800-553-5426
Cinco Puntos Press, El Paso, TX	800-566-9072
Citadel Press, Secaucus, NJ	800-866-1966 (cust serv)
Clarion Books, New York, NY	800-225-3362
Clarity Press Inc., Atlanta, GA	800-533-0301; 877-613-1495
	fax 800-334-3892 (orders)
Clark Publishing Inc., Topeka, KS	800-845-1916
Clear Light Publishers, Santa Fe, NM	800-253-2747
Cleis Press, Inc., San Francisco, CA	800-780-2279
Cleveland State University Poetry Center, Cleveland, OH	888-278-6473
Cliffs Notes, Forster City, CA	800-434-3422
Close Up Publishing, Alexandria, VA	800-765-3131
Clymer Publications, Overland Park, KS	800-262-1954
Coaches Choice, Champaign, IL	800-327-5557
Cold Spring Harbor Laboratory Press, Cold Spring Harbor, NY	800-843-4388
Cole Publishing Group Inc., Glen Ellen, CA	800-959-2717
Collectors Press Inc., Portland, OR	800-423-1848
College Press Publishing Co., Joplin, MO	800-289-3300
Colonial Press, Birmingham, AL	800-264-7541
Colonial Williamsburg Foundation, Williamsburg, VA	800-HISTORY
Colorado Railroad Museum, Golden, CO	800-365-6263
Columba Publishing Co. Inc., Akron, OH	800-999-7491
Columbia Books Inc., Washington, DC	888-265-0600
Columbia University Press, New York, NY	800-944-8648
Combined Publishing, Conshohocken, PA	800-418-6065
Comex Systems Inc., Mendham, NJ	800-543-6959
Common Courage Press, Monroe, ME	800-497-3207
Communication Project, Whitchurch-Stouffville, ON, Canada	800-772-7765
Communication Skill Builders, San Antonio, TX	800-211-8378 (cust serv)
	800-228-0752; fax 800-232-1223
Commuters Library, Falls Church, VA	888-578-5797
Compact Clinicals, Kansas City, MO	800-408-8830
Company's Coming Publishing Ltd., Edmonton, AB, Canada	800-661-5776 (US only)
Competency Press, White Plains, NY	800-603-3779

Publisher/Distributor	Toll-Free No.
Comprehensive Health Education Foundation (CHEF), Seattle, WA	800-323-2433
Conari Press, Berkeley, CA	800-685-9595
Conciliar Press, Ben Lomond, CA	800-967-7377
Concordia Publishing House, St Louis, MO	800-325-3040
Congressional Information Service Inc., Bethesda, MD	800-638-8380
Congressional Quarterly Books, Washington, DC	800-638-1710
Conroca Publishing, Boerne, TX	877-762-2782
Continuing Education Press, Portland, OR	800-547-8887 ext 4891
Continuing Legal Education Society of British Columbia, Vancouver, BC, Canada	800-663-0437
Continuum International Publishing Group, New York, NY	800-561-7704
Conway Greene Publishing Co., South Euclid, OH	800-977-2665
Copley Publishing Group, Acton, MA	800-562-2147
Cornell Maritime Press Inc., Centreville, MD	800-638-7641
Cornerstone Press Chicago, Chicago, IL	888-407-7377
CorpTech (Corporate Technology Information Services Inc.), Woburn, MA	800-333-8036
Cortina Learning International Inc., Wilton, CT	800-245-2145
Corwin Press Inc., Thousand Oaks, CA	fax 800-4-1-SCHOOL
Coteau Books, Regina, SK, Canada	800-440-4471 (Canada only)
Cottonwood Press Inc., Fort Collins, CO	800-864-4297
Council for Exceptional Children, Reston, VA	888-232-7733
Council for Research in Values & Philosophy (RVP), Washington, DC	fax 800-659-9962
Council Oak Books LLC, San Francisco, CA	800-247-8850
Council of State Governments, Lexington, KY	800-800-1910
Countryman Press, Woodstock, VT	800-245-4151
Countrysport Press, Selma, AL	800-367-4114
Course Technology, Cambridge, MA	800-648-7450
Covenant Communications Inc., American Fork, UT	800-662-9545
Covered Bridge Press, N Attleboro, MA	800-752-3769 (New England only)
Cowley Publications, Boston, MA	800-225-1534
Coxton Press, Caldwell, ID	800-657-6465
CQ Press, Alexandria, VA	800-638-1710; fax 800-380-3810
Crabtree Publishing Co. Ltd., Niagara-on-the-Lake, ON, Canada	800-387-7650 fax 800-355-7166
Crabtree Publishing Co., New York, NY	800-387-7650; fax 800-355-7166
Craftsman Book Co., Carlsbad, CA	800-829-8123
Crane Hill Publishers, Birmingham, AL	800-841-2682
CRC Press LLC, Boca Raton, FL	800-272-7737; fax 800-643-9428 (sales) 800-374-3401 (orders)
CRC Publications, Grand Rapids, MI	800-333-8300
Creative Arts Book Co., Berkeley, CA	800-848-7789
Creative Bound Inc., Carp, ON, Canada	800-287-8610 (US & Canada)
Creative Co., Mankato, MN	800-445-6209
Creative Homeowner Press, Upper Saddle River, NJ	800-631-7795

Publisher/Distributor	Toll-Free No.
Creative Publishing International Inc., Minnetonka, MN	800-328-0590
Creative Teaching Press Inc./Youngheart Music,	800-444-4287
Huntington Beach, CA	fax 800-229-9929
Crisp Publications Inc., Menlo Park, CA	800-442-7477
Cross Cultural Publications Inc., South Bend, IN	800-273-6526
Crossing Press, Freedom, CA	800-777-1048
Crossroad Publishing Co. Inc., New York, NY	800-462-6420
Crystal Clarity Publishers, Nevada City, CA	800-424-1055
Crystal Productions, Glenview, IL	800-255-8629
Cumberland House Publishing Inc., Nashville, TN	888-439-2665
Curiosity Canyon Press, Agoura Hills, CA	800-613-1182
Current Clinical Strategies Publishing,	800-331-8227
Laguna Hills, CA	fax 800-965-9420
Current Medicine, Philadelphia, PA	800-427-1796
Da Capo Press Inc., New York, NY	800-242-7737 (orders)
Dandy Lion Publications, San Luis Obispo, CA	800-776-8032
John Daniel & Co., Publishers, Santa Barbara, CA	800-662-8351
Dark Horse Comics, Milwaukie, OR	800-862-0052
Dartnell Corp., Horsham, PA	800-621-5463
DATA Business Publishing, Englewood, CO	800-447-4666
Data Research Inc., Eagan, MN	800-365-4900
Data Trace Publishing Co., Towson, MD	800-342-0454 (orders only)
Database Publishing Co., Anaheim, CA	800-888-8434
Davies-Black Publishing, Palo Alto, CA	800-624-1765
F A Davis Co., Philadelphia, PA	800-523-4049
Davis Publications Inc. (MA), Worcester, MA	800-533-2847
DAW Books Inc., New York, NY	800-526-0275
Dawbert Press, Duxbury, MA	800-93-DAWBERT
Dawn Horse Press, Middletown, CA	800-524-4941
Dawn Publications, Nevada City, CA	800-545-7475
Dawn Sign Press, San Diego, CA	800-549-5350
DBI Books, Iola, WI	888-457-2873
DBS Productions, Charlottesville, VA	800-745-1581
DC Comics, New York, NY	800-759-0190 (distribution)
DDC Publishing, New York, NY	800-528-3897; fax 800-528-3862
De Vorss & Co., Marina Del Rey, CA	800-843-5743
B C Decker Inc., Hamilton, ON, Canada	800-568-7281
Ivan R Dee Publisher, Chicago, IL 800-634-0226 (orders); fax 800-338-4550 (orders)	
Marcel Dekker Inc., New York, NY	800-228-1160 (outside NY)
Delmar Publishers, Albany, NY	800-347-7707 (NY)
Delta Systems Co. Inc., McHenry, IL	800-323-8270; fax 800-909-9901
Demeter Press, San Diego, CA	800-435-2927
Demos Medical Publishing, New York, NY	800-532-8663
Deseret Book Co., Salt Lake City, UT	800-453-3876
Design Image Group, Burr Ridge, IL	800-563-5455
Developmental Studies Center, Oakland, CA	800-666-7270

Publisher/Distributor	Toll-Free No.
DeWitt Books, North Manchester, IN	888-982-6383
Dharma Publishing, Berkeley, CA	800-873-4276
Diablo Press Inc., Emeryville, CA	800-488-2665
Diamond Communications Inc., South Bend, IN	800-480-3717
Diamond Farm Book Publishers, Alexandria Bay, NY	800-481-1353; fax 800-305-5138
DIANE Publishing Co., Upland, PA	800-782-3833
Marcel Didier Inc., Montreal, PQ, Canada	800-361-1664
Dimensions for Living, Nashville, TN	800-281-3320
Discipleship Publications International (DPI), Woburn, MA	888-DPI-Book
Discovery Enterprises Ltd., Carlisle, MA	800-729-1720
Discovery House Publishers, Grand Rapids, MI	800-653-8333
Dissertation.com, Parkland, FL	800-636-8329
Diversity Press, Idabel, OK	800-642-0779; fax 800-642-0779
Dog-Eared Publications, Middleton, WI	888-364-3277
Doheny Publications Inc., Edmonds, WA	888-436-4369
Dominie Press Inc., Carlsbad, CA	800-232-4570; 800-dominie
Donning Co./Publishers, Virginia Beach, VA	800-296-8572
Doral Publishing, Wilsonville, OR	800-633-5385 (orders)
Dorset House Publishing Co. Inc., New York, NY	800-DHBOOKS
Doubleday Broadway Publishing Group, New York, NY	800-223-6834
	800-223-5780 (sales)
Douglas & McIntyre Publishing Group,	800-667-6902 (west-orders only)
Vancouver, BC, Canada	800-565-9523 (east-orders only); fax 800-263-9099 (west)
Dover Publications Inc., Mineola, NY	800-223-3130 (orders)
Down East Enterprise, Camden, ME	800-766-1670 (ME only)
Dramatic Publishing Co., Woodstock, IL	800-448-7469; fax 800-344-5302
Dryden Press, Fort Worth, TX	800-447-9479
Dual Dolphin Publishing Inc., Winter Springs, FL	800-336-5746; fax 888-695-6601
Dufour Editions Inc., Chester Springs, PA	800-869-5677
Duquesne University Press, Pittsburgh, PA	800-666-2211
Dushkin/McGraw-Hill, Guilford, CT	800 338 3987 (cust serv)
Dustbooks, Paradise, CA	800-477-6110
Dynapress, Fern Park, FL	800-826-1049
E M C Corp., St Paul, MN	800-328-1452
E M Press Inc., Manassas, VA	800-727-4630
Eagle's View Publishing, Liberty, UT	800-547-3364 (orders over $100)
Eakin Press, Austin, TX	800-880-8642
East View Publications, Minneapolis, MN	800-477-1005
Eastland Press, Vista, CA	800-453-3278 (US & Canada only); fax 800-241-3329
Eckankar, Minneapolis, MN	800-327-5113 (orders only)
ECS Learning Systems Inc., San Antonio, TX	800-688-3224
ECS Publishing, Boston, MA	800-777-1919
EDC Publishing, Tulsa, OK	800-475-4522; fax 800-747-4509
Nellie Edge Resources Inc., Salem, OR	800-523-4594
EDGE Science Fiction & Fantasy Publishing, Calgary, AB, Canada	877-254-0115
Editions Anne Sigier Inc., Sillery, PQ, Canada	800-463-6846

Publisher/Distributor	Toll-Free No.

Editions du Phare Inc., St-Jerome, PQ, Canada	800-561-2371 (Canada)
Editions du Renouveau Pedagogique Inc., St-Laurent, PQ, Canada	800-263-3678
	fax 800-643-4720
Editions Griffon D'Argile, Sainte-Foy, PQ, Canada	800-268-6898 (Canada only)
Editions Hurtubise, Montreal, PQ, Canada	800-361-1664
Editions La Liberte Inc., Ste Foy, PQ, Canada	800-567-5449 (Canada)
Editions Marie-France, Montreal-Nord, PQ, Canada	800-563-6644
Editions Phidal Inc., Ville Mont-Royal, PQ, Canada	800-738-7349
Editions Yvon Blais Inc., Cowansville, PQ, Canada	800-363-3047
Editorial Bautista Independiente, Sebring, FL	800-398-7187
Editorial Portavoz, Grand Rapids, MI	800-733-2607
Editorial Unilit, Miami, FL	800-767-7726
Educational Impressions Inc., Hawthorne, NJ	800-451-7450
Educational Insights Inc., Carson, CA	800-933-3277
Educational Ministries Inc., Prescott, AZ	800-221-0910
Educational Technology Publications, Englewood Cliffs, NJ	800-952-book
Educators Progress Service Inc., Randolph, WI	888-951-4469
Educators Publishing Service Inc., Cambridge, MA	800-225-5750
Edupress Inc., San Clemente, CA	800-835-7978
Wm B Eerdmans Publishing Co., Grand Rapids, MI	800-253-7521
Elan Press, Toronto, ON, Canada	800-387-0141 (Ontario & Quebec only)
	800-387-0172 (Canada only); 800-805-1083 (US only)
Edward Elgar Publishing Inc., Northampton, MA	800-390-3149 (orders)
Emanuel Publishing Corp., Larchmont, NY	800-362-6835
EMC Paradigm Publishing, St Paul, MN	800-328-1452
Emerald Books, Lynnwood, WA	800-922-2143
EMIS Inc., Durant, OK	800-225-0694
Encore Performance Publishing, Orem, UT	800-927-1605
Encyclopaedia Britannica Educational Corp., Chicago, IL	800-554-9862
Encyclopaedia Britannica Inc., Chicago, IL	800-323-1229
Engineering & Management Press, Norcross, GA	800-494-0460 (orders only)
Engineering Information Inc. (EI), Hoboken, NJ	800-221-1044
Engineering Press, Austin, TX	800-800-1651; fax 800-700-1651
EPM Publications Inc., Delaplane, VA	800-289-2339
ERIC Clearinghouse on Higher Education, Washington, DC	800-773-ERIC ext 13
ERIC Clearinghouse on Reading, English & Communication, Bloomington, IN	800-759-4723
Lawrence Erlbaum Associates Inc., Mahwah, NJ	800-9-BOOKS-9 (orders only)
ETC Publications, Palm Springs, CA	800-382-7869
ETR Associates, Santa Cruz, CA	800-321-4407
Evan-Moor Educational Publishers, Monterey, CA	800-777-4362
Evangel Publishing House, Nappanee, IN	800-253-9315
Evanston Publishing Inc., Louisville, KY	888-BOOKS80
Everyday Learning Corp., Chicago, IL	800-382-7670
Exley Giftbooks, New York, NY	800-423-9539; fax 800-453-5248
Explorers Guide Publishing, Rhinelander, WI	800-487-6029

Publisher/Distributor	Toll-Free No.
F C & A Publishing, Peachtree City, GA	800-226-8024
F J H Music Co. Inc., Ft. Lauderdale, FL	800-262-8744
Faber & Faber Inc., New York, NY	888-330-8477
Factor Press, Mobile, AL	800-304-0077 (orders only)
Facts On File Inc., New York, NY	800-322-8755; fax 800-678-3633
Fairchild Books, New York, NY	800-932-4724
Fairview Press, Minneapolis, MN	800-544-8207
Fairwinds Press, Lions Bay, BC, Canada	877-913-0645
Faith & Fellowship Press, Fergus Falls, MN	800-332-9232
Faith & Life Press, Newton, KS	800-743-2484
Falcon Publishing Inc., Helena, MT	800-582-2665; fax 800-986-3550
Fantagraphics Books, Seattle, WA	800-657-1100
W D Farmer Residence Designer Inc., Tucker, GA	800-225-7526; 800-221-7526 (GA)
Faxon Co., Westwood, MA	800-999-3594
Philipp Feldheim Inc., Nanuet, NY	800-237-7149
Fenn Publishing Co. Ltd., Bolton, ON, Canada	800-267-3366 (Canada only)
	fax 800-465-3422 (Canada only)
Ferguson Publishing Co., Chicago, IL	800-306-9941
Fifth House Publishers, Calgary, AB, Canada	800-387-9776; fax 800-260-9777
Filter Press, Palmer Lake, CO	888-570-2663
Financial Executives Research Foundation Inc., Morristown, NJ	800-680-FERF
Finley-Greene Publications Inc., Island Park, NY	800-431-1131
Fire Engineering Books & Videos, Tulsa, OK	800-752-9768
Firebird Publications Inc., Rockville, MD	800-854-9595
Firefly Books Ltd., Willowdale, ON, Canada	800-387-5085; fax 800-565-6034
Firefly Books Ltd., Buffalo, NY	800-387-5085; fax 800-565-6034
First Avenue Editions, Minneapolis, MN	800-328-4929; fax 800-332-1132
Fisher Books, Tucson, AZ	800-255-1514; fax 800-324-3791
Fisherman Library, Point Pleasant, NJ	800-553-4745
Fitzhenry & Whiteside Limited, Markham, ON, Canada	800-387-9776
Fitzroy Dearborn Publishers, Chicago, IL	800-850-8102
Flower Valley Press Inc., Gaithersburg, MD	800-735-5197
Focus on the Family, Colorado Springs, CO	800-232-6459
Focus Publishing/R Pullins Co. Inc., Newburyport, MA	800-848-7236 (orders)
Fodor's Travel Publications, New York, NY	800-733-3000; 800-533-6478
Foghorn Press, Santa Rosa, CA	800-FOGHORN
Fondo de Cultura Economica USA Inc., San Diego, CA	800-532-3872
Fordham University Press, Bronx, NY	800-247-6553 (orders)
Forest House Publishing Co. Inc. & HTS Books, Lake Forest, IL	800-394-READ
Forest of Peace Publishing Inc., Leavenworth, KS	800-659-3227
Formac Publishing Ltd., Halifax, NS, Canada	800-565-1975
Forward Movement Publications, Cincinnati, OH	800-543-1813
Foundation Center, New York, NY	800-424-9836
Foundation for Economic Education Inc., Irvington-on-Hudson, NY	800-452-3518
Foundation Publications, Anaheim, CA	800-257-6272
Fox Hill Publishing, Ft Worth, TX	877-782-7343; 800-511-4510

Publisher/Distributor	Toll-Free No.
Franciscan University Press, Steubenville, OH	800-783-6357
Franklin Library, Franklin Center, PA	800-843-6468; fax 800-843-6468 (cust serv)
Frederick Fell Publishers Inc., Hollywood, FL	800-771-FELL
Frederick Harris Music Co. Ltd., Mississauga, ON, Canada	800-387-4013 (Canada & US)
Free Spirit Publishing Inc., Minneapolis, MN	800-735-7323
Friends United Press, Richmond, IN	800-537-8839
Frog Ltd., Berkeley, CA	800-337-2665 (book orders only)
Front Row Experience, Byron, CA	800-524-9091; fax 800-524-9091
Fulcrum Publishing Inc., Golden, CO	800-992-2908; fax 800-726-7112
Futech Interactive Products, Waukesha, WI	800-541-2205
Futura Publishing Co. Inc., Armonk, NY	800-877-8761
Future Horizons Inc., Arlington, TX	800-489-0727
G W Medical Publishing Inc., St Louis, MO	800-600-0330
GATF Press, Sewickley, PA	800-910-GATF
Gage Educational Publishing Co., Scarborough, ON, Canada	800-667-1115 (Canada & US)
P Gaines Co., Oak Park, IL	800-578-3853
Gale, Farmington Hills, MI	800-877-GALE; fax 800-414-5043
Gallopade International Inc., Peachtree City, GA	800-536-2GET; fax 800-871-2979
Garamond Press, Aurora, ON, Canada	800-898-9535
Gareth Stevens Inc., Milwaukee, WI	800-341-3569
Garrett Educational Corp., Ada, OK	800-654-9366
Garrett Publishing Inc., Deerfield Beach, FL	800-333-2069 (book orders)
Gateways Books & Tapes, Nevada City, CA	800-869-0658
Gayot/Gault Millau Inc., Los Angeles, CA	800-LE BEST 1
Gefen Books, Hewlett, NY	800-477-5257
GEM Publications, Hudson, WI	800-290-6128
GemStone Press, Woodstock, VT	800-962-4544
Genealogical Publishing Co. Inc., Baltimore, MD	800-296-6687
General Store Publishing House, Burnstown, ON, Canada	800-465-6072
Genesis Press Inc., Columbus, MS	888-463-4461
Geological Society of America (GSA), Boulder, CO	800-472-1988
Georgetown University Press, Washington, DC	800-246-9606
Gessler Publishing Co. Inc., Roanoke, VA	800-456-5825
J Paul Getty Trust Publications, Los Angeles, CA	800-223-3431
GIA Publications, Inc., Chicago, IL	800-442-1358
C R Gibson Co., Norwalk, CT	800-243-6004
Giga Information Group, Norwell, MA	800-874-9980
Glanville Publishers Inc., Dobbs Ferry, NY	800-831-0758
Gleim Publications Inc., Gainesville, FL	800-87-GLEIM; fax 888-375-6940
Glenbridge Publishing Ltd., Lakewood, CO	800-986-4135
Glencoe/McGraw-Hill, Westerville, OH	800-848-1567
Glenlake Publishing Co. Ltd., Chicago, IL	800-537-5920
Peter Glenn Publications, New York, NY	888-332-6700
Global Travel Publishers Inc., Fort Lauderdale, FL	800-882-9453

Publisher/Distributor	Toll-Free No.
Globe Pequot Press, Old Saybrook, CT	800-243-0495
	fax 800-820-2329 (orders & cust serv)
GoalsGuy Learning Systems, Tarpon, FL	800-774-5628; fax 800-731-4625
Gold Horse Publishing Inc., Annapolis, MD	800-966-DOLL
Golden Books Family Entertainment, New York, NY	800-558-5972 (cust serv)
Golden Educational Center, Redding, CA	800-800-1791
Golden West Publishers, Phoenix, AZ	800-658-5830
Goodheart-Willcox Publisher, Tinley Park, IL	800-323-0440; fax 888-409-3900
Goofy Foot Press, W Hollywood, CA	800-310-PLAY
Goosefoot Acres Press, Cleveland Heights, OH	800-697-4858
Gospel Publishing House, Springfield, MO	800-641-4310
Gould Publications Inc., Longwood, FL	800-847-6502
Government Research Service, Topeka, KS	800-346-6898
Grafco Productions Inc., Marietta, GA	888-656-1500
Grail Foundation Press, Gambier, OH	800-427-9217
Donald M Grant Publisher Inc., Hampton Falls, NH	800-476-0510
Grapevine Publications Inc., Corvallis, OR	800-338-4331
Graphic Arts Center Publishing Co., Portland, OR	800-452-3032; fax 800-355-9685
Graphic Arts Publishing Inc., Livonia, NY	800-724-9476
Graphic Learning, Waterbury, CT	800-874-0029; 800-227-9120; fax 800-737-3322
Grayson Bernard Publishers, Bloomington, IN	800-925-7853
Great Quotations Inc., Glendale Heights, IL	800-354-4889
Warren H Green Inc., St Louis, MO	800-537-0655
Greenhaven Press Inc., San Diego, CA	800-231-5163
Greenwillow Books, New York, NY	800-631-1199; fax 888-775-3260 (orders)
Greenwood Publishing Group Inc., Westport, CT	800-225-5800 (orders)
Grey House Publishing Inc., Lakeville, CT	800-562-2139
Grolier Direct Marketing, Danbury, CT	800-955-9877
Grolier Educational, Danbury, CT	800-243-7256
Group Publishing Inc., Loveland, CO	800-447-1070
Grove/Atlantic Inc., New York, NY	800-521-0178
Grove's Dictionaries Inc., New York, NY	800-221-2123
Gryphon Editions, New York, NY	800-633-8911
Gryphon House Inc., Beltsville, MD	800-638-0928
Guernica Editions Inc., Toronto, ON, Canada	800-565-9523; fax 800-221-9985
Guernica Editions Inc., Tonawanda, NY	800-565-9523; fax 800-221-9985
Guild Press of Indiana Inc., Carmel, IN	800-913-9563
Guild.com, Madison, WI	800-969-1556
Guilford Press, New York, NY	800-365-7006 (orders)
Gulf Publishing Co., Book Division, Houston, TX	800-392-4390 (TX)
	800-231-6275 (all other except AK & HI)
H C I A Inc., Baltimore, MD	800-568-3282
H D I Publishers, Houston, TX	800-321-7037
H Squared Co., New Haven, CT	800-243-4545
Hachai Publications Inc., Brooklyn, NY	800-50-HACHAI
Hackett Publishing Co. Inc., Indianapolis, IN	fax 800-783-9213

Publisher/Distributor	Toll-Free No.
Hagstrom Map Co. Inc., Maspeth, NY	800-432-MAPS
Hal Leonard Corp., Milwaukee, WI	800-524-4425
Hambleton Hill Publishing Inc., Nashville, TN	800-327-5113
Alexander Hamilton Institute, Ramsey, NJ	800-879-2441
Hammond World Atlas Corp., Maplewood, NJ	800-526-4953
Hampton-Brown Co. Inc., Carmel, CA	800-933-3510
Hampton Press Inc., Cresskill, NJ	800-894-8955
Hampton Roads Publishing Co. Inc., Charlottesville, VA	800-766-8009 (orders)
	fax 800-766-9042
Hancock House Publishers, Blaine, WA	800-938-1114; fax 800-983-2262
Hancock House Publishers Ltd., Surrey, BC, Canada	800-938-1114; fax 800-983-2262
Hanley & Belfus Inc., Philadelphia, PA	800-962-1892
Hanser-Gardner Publications, Cincinnati, OH	800-950-8977; fax 800-953-8805
Harcourt Brace Legal & Professional Publications, Chicago, IL	800-787-8717 (orders)
	fax 800-433-6303 (orders)
Harcourt Canada Groupe Educalivres Inc., Laval, PQ, Canada	800-567-3671 (info serv)
Harcourt Canada Ltd., Toronto, ON, Canada	800-268-2132 (Canada only)
	800-387-7278 (North America); 800-387-7305 (North America)
	fax 800-665-7307 (North America)
Harcourt Inc., Orlando, FL	800-225-5425 (cust serv)
Harcourt Professional Publishing, San Diego, CA	800-831-7799
Harcourt School Publishers, Orlando, FL	800-225-5425 (cust serv)
Harcourt Trade Division, San Diego Office,	800-543-1918 (cust serv)
San Diego, CA	fax 800-235-0256 (cust serv)
Harmonie Park Press, Warren, MI	800-886-3080
HarperCollins Publishers, New York, NY	800-242-7737; 800-982-4377 (PA)
Harris InfoSource, Twinsburg, OH	800-888-5900; fax 800-643-5997
Harrison House Publishers, Tulsa, OK	800-888-4126; fax 800-830-4126
Hartley & Marks Publishers Inc., Point Roberts, WA	800-277-5887
Hartman Publishing Inc., Albuquerque, NM	800-999-9534; fax 800-474-6106
Harvard Business School Press, Allston, MA	888-500-1016
Harvard Common Press, Boston, MA	888-657-3755
Harvard University Press, Cambridge, MA	fax 800-962-4983 (orders, US & Canada)
Harvest Hill Press, Salisbury Cove, ME	888-288-8900
Harvest House Publishers Inc., Eugene, OR	800-547-8979
Hastings House Book Publishers, Norwalk, CT	800-206-7822
Hatherleigh Press, New York, NY	800-367-2550
Haworth Press Inc., Binghamton, NY	800-342-9678; fax 800-895-0582
Hay House Inc., Carlsbad, CA	800-650-5115 (shipping & receiving)
	800-654-5126 (orders)
Haynes Manuals Inc., Newbury Park, CA	800-442-9637
Hazelden Information & Educational Services, Center City, MN	800-328-9000
Health Communications Inc., Deerfield Beach, FL	800-851-9100 (cust serv)
	800-441-5569 (order entry)

Publisher/Distributor	Toll-Free No.
Health for Life, Marina del Rey, CA	800-874-5339
Health Infonet Inc., San Ramon, CA	800-446-1947
Health Leadership Associates Inc., Potomac, MD	800-435-4775
Health Professions Press, Baltimore, MD	888-337-8808
Health Research, Pomeroy, WA	888-844-2386
Health Science, Santa Barbara, CA	800-446-1990
Heartland Samplers Inc., Minneapolis, MN	800-328-7317
Hearts & Tummies Cookbook Co., Wever, IA	800-571-BOOK
Heartsfire Books, Sante Fe, NM	800-988-5170
William S Hein & Co. Inc., Buffalo, NY	800-828-7571
Heinemann, Westport, CT	800-541-2086
Heinle & Heinle/Thomson Learning, Boston, MA	800-237-0053
Hemingway Western Studies Series, Boise, ID	800-992-TEXT
Hendrickson Publishers Inc., Peabody, MA	800-358-3111
Hensley Publishing, Tulsa, OK	800-288-8520
Herald Press, Waterloo, ON, Canada	800-245-7894 (Canada & US)
Herald Press, Scottdale, PA	800-245-7894
Herald Publishing House, Independence, MO	800-767-8181
Heritage Books Inc., Bowie, MD	800-398-7709; fax 800-276-1760
Heritage Foundation, Washington, DC	800-544-4843
Heritage House, Indianapolis, IN	800-419-0200
Heritage House Publishing Co. Ltd., Surrey, BC, Canada	800-665-3302
Hewitt Homeschooling Resources, Washougal, WA	800-348-1750
Hi Willow Research & Publishing, San Jose, CA	800-873-3043
Hi-Time Pflaum, Dayton, OH	800-543-4383
High-Lonsome Books, Silver City, NM	800-380-7323
High Mountain Press, Santa Fe, NM	800-4-ONWORD; 800-466-9693
High Tide Press, Homewood, IL	888-487-7377; 800-698-3979
Highsmith Press LLC, Fort Atkinson, WI	800-558-2110
Hillsdale College Press, Hillsdale, MI	800-437-2268
Himalyan Institute Press, Honesdale, PA	800-822-4547
Hippocrene Books Inc., New York, NY	fax 800-809-3855 (sales)
W D Hoard & Sons Co., Fort Atkinson, WI	800-236-1013
Hohm Press, Prescott, AZ	800-381-2700
Holly Hall Publications Inc., Elkton, MD	800-211-0719
Hollywood Creative Directory, Santa Monica, CA	800-815-0503 (outside CA)
Holmes & Meier Publishers Inc., New York, NY	800-698-7781 (orders only)
Henry Holt and Co. LLC, New York, NY	888-330-8477 (orders)
Holt, Rinehart and Winston, Austin, TX	800-225-5425 (cust serv)
Home Builder Press, Washington, DC	800-223-2665
Home Planners LLC, Tucson, AZ	800-322-6797
Homestyles Publishing & Marketing Inc., St Paul, MN	888-626-2026
Honor Books, Tulsa, OK	800-678-2126
Hoover Institution Press, Stanford, CA	800-935-2882
Hoover's Inc., Austin, TX	800-486-8666 (orders only)
Hope Publishing Co., Carol Stream, IL	800-323-1049

Publisher/Distributor	Toll-Free No.
Hoppa Productions Inc., Denver, PA	888-445-2824
Horizon Books, Camp Hill, PA	800-233-4443
Horizon Publishers & Distributors Inc., Bountiful, UT	800-453-0812
Houghton Mifflin Co., Boston, MA	800-225-3362 (trade books)
	800-733-2828 (text books); 800-225-1464 (college texts)
House to House Publications, Ephrata, PA	800-848-5892
Howard Publishing, West Monroe, LA	800-858-4109
Howell Press Inc., Charlottesville, VA	800-868-4512; fax 888-971-7204
Human Kinetics Inc., Champaign, IL	800-747-4457
Human Resource Development Press, Amherst, MA	800-822-2801
Humanics Publishing Group, Atlanta, GA	800-874-8844
Hume Publishing Co. Ltd., Toronto, ON, Canada	
	800-733-4863 (Canada & US, orders only)
Hunter House Inc., Publishers, Alameda, CA	800-266-5592
Huntington House Publishers, Lafayette, LA	800-749-4009
Huntington Press Publishing, Las Vegas, NV	800-244-2224
Hyperion, New York, NY	800-343-9204 (orders)
I O P Publishing Inc., Philadelphia, PA	800-632-0880 (book orders only)
IBC Financial Data Inc., Ashland, MA	800-343-5413
Ibex Publishers, Bethesda, MD	888-718-8188
IBFD Publications USA Inc. (International Bureau of Fiscal Documentation), Valatie, NY	800-299-6330
IBTS, Long Island City, NY	800-337-4287
Iconografix Inc., Hudson, WI	800-289-3504 (orders only)
ICS Press, Oakland, CA	800-326-0263
Idaho Center for the Book, Boise, ID	800-992-8398
Ideal Instructional Fair Oublishing Group, Minneapolis, MN	800-328-3831
Ideals Children's Books, Nashville, TN	800-327-5113
IEEE Computer Society Press, Los Alamitos, CA	800-272-6657
Ignatius Press, San Francisco, CA	877-320-9276; fax 800-278-3566
Illumination Arts, Bellevue, WA	888-210-8216
Images from the Past Inc., Bennington, VT	888-442-3204
Imaginart Press, Bisbee, AZ	800-828-1376
Imperius Publishing, Marina Del Rey, CA	800-444-8211
Incentive Publications Inc., Nashville, TN	800-421-2830
Indiana Historical Society, Indianapolis, IN	800-447-1830 (orders only)
Indiana University Press, Bloomington, IN	800-842-6796 (orders only)
Industrial Press Inc., New York, NY	888-528-7852
InfoBooks, Santa Monica, CA	800-669-0409
Information Guides, Hermosa Beach, CA	800-347-3257
Information Plus, Wylie, TX	800-463-6757
Inner Traditions International Ltd., Rochester, VT	800-246-8648
Innisfree Press Inc., Philadelphia, PA	800-367-5872 (nontrade orders)
	800-283-3572 (trade orders)
Institute for International Economics, Washington, DC	800-229-3266
Institute for Language Study, Wilton, CT	800-245-2145

Publisher/Distributor	Toll-Free No.
Institute for Research & Education, Minneapolis, MN	800-372-7775
Institute of Private Investigative Studies Inc., Phoenix, AZ	800-Need-A-PI
Institute of Psychological Research Inc., Montreal, PQ, Canada	800-363-7800
	fax 888-382-3007
Interarts/GeoSys, Mountville, PA	800-626-4655; fax 888-354-1476
Interchange Inc., St Louis Park, MN	800-669-6208; fax 800-729-0395
Intercultural Press Inc., Yarmouth, ME	800-370-2665
Interlink Publishing Group Inc., Northampton, MA	800-238-LINK
International Chess Enterprises (I C E), Seattle, WA	800-26-CHESS
International Conference of Building Officials, Whittier, CA	800-423-6587
International Foundation of Employee Benefit Plans, Brookfield, WI	888-33-IFEBP
International LearningWorks, Durango, CO	800-344-0451
International Linguistics Corp., Kansas City, MO	800-237-1830
International Risk Management Institute Inc., Dallas, TX	800-827-4242
International Scholars Publications, Lanham, MD	800-462-6420
International Society for Technology in Education, Eugene, OR	
	800-336-5191 (orders only)
International Wealth Success Inc., Merrick, NY	800-323-0548
Interpharm Press Inc., Englewood, CO	877-295-9240
Interstate Publishers Inc., Danville, IL	800-843-4774
InterVarsity Press, Westmont, IL	800-843-7225
Interweave Press, Loveland, CO	800-272-2193
Iowa State University Press, Ames, IA	800-862-6657 (orders only)
Irish American Book Co., Niwot, CO	800-452-7115; fax 800-401-9705
Irwin/McGraw-Hill, Burr Ridge, IL	800-338-3987 (cust serv)
Irwin Publishing, Toronto, ON, Canada	800-263-7824 (Canada only)
ISI Books, Wilmington, DE	800-526-7022
Island Press, Washington, DC	800-828-1302
ITP Nelson, Scarborough, ON, Canada	800-268-2222 (cust serv)
	800-668-0671 (sales support)
Richard Ivey School of Business, London, ON, Canada	800-649-6355
Ivy League Press Inc., San Ramon, CA	800-IVY-PRES
J & B Editions Inc., Richmond, VA	800-266-5480
Jalmar Press, Carson, CA	800-662-9662
Jameson Books Inc., Ottawa, IL	800-426-1357
Jane's Information Group, Alexandria, VA	800-243-3852
January Productions Inc., Hawthorne, NJ	800-451-7450
Jester Co. Inc., Palos Verdes Estates, CA	800-9-JESTER; 888-9-JESTER
Jewish Lights Publishing, Woodstock, VT	800-962-4544
Jewish Publication Society, Philadelphia, PA	800-234-3151
JIST Works Inc., Indianapolis, IN	800-648-5478 ext 2130; fax 800-264-3763
John Deere Publishing, Moline, IL	800-522-7448
Johns Hopkins University Press, Baltimore, MD	800-537-5487
Jones & Bartlett Publishers Inc., Sudbury, MA	800-832-0034
Jones McClure Publishing Inc., Houston, TX	800-626-6667 (1-800-OCONNOR)
Jossey-Bass Inc., Publishers, San Francisco, CA	800-956-7739

Publisher/Distributor	Toll-Free No.
Journals Unlimited Inc., Bay City, MI	800-897-8528; fax 800-897-8529
Joy Publishing, Fountain Valley, CA	800-454-8228
Judaica Press Inc., Brooklyn, NY	800-972-6201
Judson Press, Valley Forge, PA	800-458-3766
Kaeden Corp., Rocky River, OH	800-890-7323
Kalimat Press, Los Angeles, CA	800-788-4067
Kalmbach Publishing Co., Waukesha, WI	800-558-1544
Kar-Ben Copies Inc., Rockville, MD	800-4-KARBEN
KC Publications Inc., Las Vegas, NV	800-626-9673
J J Keller & Associates, Inc., Neenah, WI	800-327-6868; fax 800-727-7516
Kendall/Hunt Publishing Co., Dubuque, IA	800-228-0810 (orders only)
	fax 800-772-9165
Kennedy Information, Fitzwilliam, NH	800-531-0007
Kenneth Hagin Ministries Inc., Broken Arrow, OK	888-258-0999 (orders only)
Kensington Publishing Corp., New York, NY	800-221-2647
Kent State University Press, Kent, OH	800-247-6553 (orders)
Key Curriculum Press, Emeryville, CA	800-995-MATH; fax 800-541-2442
Kids Can Press Ltd., Toronto, ON, Canada	800-265-0884
Kids Can Press Ltd., Buffalo, NY	800-265-0884
Kidsbooks Inc., Chicago, IL	800-515-KIDS
Kindred Productions, Winnipeg, MB, Canada	800-545-7322
Kirkbride Bible Co. Inc., Indianapolis, IN	800-428-4385
Neil A Kjos Music Co., San Diego, CA	800-854-1592
Kluwer Law International (KLI), Cambridge, MA	800-577-8118
Allen A Knoll Publishers, Santa Barbara, CA	800-777-7623
Alfred A Knopf, New York, NY	800-638-6460
Konemann, New York, NY	888-317-8855
Kosmic Kurrents, Miami, FL	800-769-6864
Krause Publications, Iola, WI	800-258-0929
Kregel Publications, Grand Rapids, MI	800-733-2607
Krieger Publishing Co., Melbourne, FL	800-724-0025
Kumarian Press Inc., West Hartford, CT	800-289-2664 (orders only)
Ladybug Press, San Carlos, CA	888-892-5000
Lakewood Publications, Minneapolis, MN	800-328-4329
LAMA Books, Hayward, CA	888-452-6244
Landes Bioscience, Georgetown, TX	800-736-9948
Langenscheidt Publishers Inc., Maspeth, NY	800-432-MAPS; fax 888-773-7979
LangMarc Publishing, San Antonio, TX	800-864-1648
Larousse Kingfisher Chambers Inc., New York, NY	800-497-1657; fax 800-874-4027
Larson Publications, Burdett, NY	800-828-2197
Laureate Press, Bangor, ME	800-946-2727
Lawbook Exchange Ltd., Union, NJ	800-422-6686
LDA Publishers, Bayside, NY	888-388-9887
Leadership Publishers Inc., Des Moines, IA	800-814-3757
Leading Edge Reports, Commack, NY	800-866-4648
Learning Connection (TLC), Frostproof, FL	800-338-2282

Publisher/Distributor	Toll-Free No.
Learning Links Inc., New Hyde Park, NY	800-724-2616
Learning Publications Inc., Holmes Beach, FL	800-222-1525 (orders)
Learning Resources Network (LERN), Manhattan, KS	800-678-5376 (orders only)
	fax 888-234-8633
LearningExpress LLC, New York, NY	800-295-9556
Lectorum Publications, New York, NY	800-345-5946 (except NY & NJ)
Legacy Publishing Group, Clinton, MA	800-322-3866
Legal Education Publishing, Madison, WI	800-957-4670
Leisure Arts Inc., Little Rock, AR	800-643-8030
Leisure Books, New York, NY	800-481-9191 (order dept)
Lerner Publishing Group, Minneapolis, MN	800-328-4929; fax 800-332-1132
LernerSports, Minneapolis, MN	800-328-4929; fax 800-332-1132
Letter People, Waterbury, CT	800-227-9120; 800-874-0029
	fax 800-737-3322
Lexis Law Publishing, Charlottesville, VA	800-446-3410
Liberty Fund Inc., Indianapolis, IN	800-955-8335
Libraries Unlimited Inc., Englewood, CO	800-237-6124
Library Research Associates Inc., Monroe, NY	800-914-3379
Lickle Publishing Inc., West Palm Beach, FL	888-454-2553
Lidec Inc., Montreal, PQ, Canada	800-350-5991 (Canada only)
Mary Ann Liebert Inc., Larchmont, NY	800-654-3237
Lifetime Books Inc., Hollywood, FL	800-771-3355 (orders only)
Liguori Publications, Liguori, MO	800-464-2555
LinguiSystems Inc., East Moline, IL	800-PRO-IDEA (800-776-4332)
Linns Stamp News-Ancillary Division, Sidney, OH	fax 800-340-9501
Lippincott-Raven Publishers, Philadelphia, PA	800-638-3030 (MD)
Listen & Live Audio Inc., Roseland, NJ	800-653-9400
Literacy Institute for Education (LIFE) Inc., Pleasantville, NY	877-BKNELSON
Little, Brown and Company, Boston, MA	800-759-0190
Little Tiger Press, Waukesha, WI	800-541-2205
Littlefield, Adams Quality Paperbacks, Lanham, MD	800-462-6420
Liturgical Press, Collegeville, MN	800-858-5450; fax 800-445-5899
Liturgy Training Publications, Chicago, IL	800-933-1800 (US & Canada only)
	fax 800-933-7094 (US & Canada only)
Living Language, New York, NY	800-733-3000 (orders)
Llewellyn Publications, St Paul, MN	800-843-6666
Loizeaux Brothers Inc., Neptune, NJ	800-526-2796
Lone Eagle Publishing Co., Los Angeles, CA	800-345-6257
Lone Pine Publishing, Edmonton, AB, Canada	800-661-9017; fax 800-424-7173
Lonely Planet Publications, Oakland, CA	800-275-8555 (orders)
Longstreet Press, Marietta, GA	800-927-1488
Loompanics Unlimited, Port Townsend, WA	800-380-2230
Looseleaf Law Publications Inc., Flushing, NY	800-647-5547
Lothrop, Lee & Shepard Books, New York, NY	800-843-9389
Lotus Light Publications, Twin Lakes, WI	800-824-6396 (orders only)
Loyola Press, Chicago, IL	800-621-1008

Publisher/Distributor	Toll-Free No.
LRP Publications Inc., Horsham, PA	800-341-7874
LRS, Los Angeles, CA	800-255-5002
Lucent Books Inc., San Diego, CA	800-231-5163
Lyle Stuart, Secaucus, NJ	800-866-1966 (cust serv)
Lyons Press, New York, NY	800-836-0510
Lyrick Publishing, Allen, TX	800-418-2371
Macalester Park Publishing Co., Minneapolis, MN	800-407-9078
McBooks Press, Ithaca, NY	888-266-5711
McClanahan Publishing House Inc., Kuttawa, KY	800-544-6959
McCormack's Guides Inc., Martinez, CA	800-222-3602
McCutchan Publishing Corp., Berkeley, CA	800-227-1540
McDonald & Woodward Publishing Co., Granville, OH	800-233-8787
McDougal Littell Inc., Evanston, IL	fax 800-462-6595
McFarland & Co. Inc. Publishers, Jefferson, NC	800-253-2187 (orders only)
McGraw-Hill College, Boston, MA	800-338-3987 (cust serv)
McGraw-Hill Higher Education, Burr Ridge, IL	800-338-3987 (cust serv)
Macmillan Computer Publishing USA, Indianapolis, IN	800-545-5914
Macmillan Digital Publishing USA, Indianapolis, IN	800-545-5914
Macmillan Publishing USA, New York, NY	800-545-5914
MacMurray & Beck, Denver, CO	800-774-3777
McPherson & Co., Kingston, NY	800-613-8219
Madison Books Inc., Lanham, MD	800-462-6420
Madison House Publishers, Madison, WI	800-604-1776
Mage Publishers Inc., Washington, DC	800-962-0922
Magick Mirror Communications, New York, NY	800-356-6796
Maharishi University of Management Press, Fairfield, IA	800-831-6523
Manhattan Publishing Co., Croton-on-Hudson, NY	888-686-7066
Many Cultures Publishing, San Francisco, CA	800-484-4173 ext 1073
MapEasy Inc., Wainscotte, NY	888-627-3279
MapQuest.com Inc., Mountville, PA	800-626-4655; fax 888-354-1476
MAR CO Products Inc., Warminster, PA	800-448-2197
MARC Publications, Monrovia, CA	800-777-7752 (US only)
March 3rd Books, Columbia, MD	800-536-0454
Market Data Retrieval, Shelton, CT	800-333-8802
Marlor Press Inc., St Paul, MN	800-669-4908
Marquette University Press, Milwaukee, WI	800-247-6553
Marshall & Swift, Los Angeles, CA	800-544-2678
Martingale & Co., Bothell, WA	800-426-3126
Marvin Melnyk Associates Ltd., Queenston, ON, Canada	800-682-0029
Massachusetts Continuing Legal Education, Inc., Boston, MA	800-966-6253
Math Teachers Press Inc., Minneapolis, MN	800-852-2435
Mathematical Association of America, Washington, DC	800-331-1622 (orders)
Maverick Publications Inc., Bend, OR	800-800-4831
Mayfield Publishing Co., Mountain View, CA	800-433-1279
MBI Publishing Co., Osceola, WI	800-458-0454
MCP Software, Indianapolis, IN	800-858-7674

Publisher/Distributor	Toll-Free No.
MDRT Center for Productivity, Park Ridge, IL	800-879-6378
Meadowbrook Press Inc., Minnetonka, MN	800-338-2232
R S Means Co. Inc., Kingston, MA	800-448-8182; fax 800-632-6701
MedBooks, Richardson, TX	800-443-7397
Media & Methods, Philadelphia, PA	800-555-5657
Media Associates, Wilton, CA	800-373-1897 (orders)
Medical Economics, Montvale, NJ	800-442-6657
Medical Physics Publishing Corp., Madison, WI	800-442-5778
Medicode, Salt Lake City, UT	800-999-4600
Russell Meerdink Co. Ltd., Neenah, WI	800-635-6499
Mega Media Press, San Diego, CA	800-803-9416
Mel Bay Publications Inc., Pacific, MO	800-863-5229
Menasha Ridge Press Inc., Birmingham, AL	800-247-9437
Mercer University Press, Macon, GA	800-637-2378, ext 2880 (outside GA)
	800-342-0841, ext 2880 (GA)
Meriwether Publishing Ltd./Contemporary Drama Service, Colorado Springs, CO	800-937-5297
	fax 888-594-4436
Merlyn's Pen: Stories by American Students, East Greenwich, RI	800-247-2027
Merriam-Webster Inc., Springfield, MA	800-828-1880 (orders & cust serv)
Merry Thoughts Inc., Bedford Hills, NY	800-637-7459
Merryant Publishers Inc., Vashon, WA	800-228-8958
Mesorah Publications Ltd., Brooklyn, NY	800-637-6724
Metal Bulletin Inc., New York, NY	800-METAL-25
Metamorphous Press, Portland, OR	800-937-7771
MGI Management Institute Inc., White Plains, NY	800-932-0191
Michelin Travel Publications, Laval, PQ, Canada	800-361-8236 (Canada)
	fax 800-361-6937 (Canada)
Michelin Travel Publications, Greenville, SC	800-423-0485; 800-223-0987
	fax 800-378-7471
MicroMash, Englewood, CO	800-272-7277
Micromedia Limited, Toronto, ON, Canada	800-387-2689
Microsoft Press, Redmond, WA	800-MSPRESS
MidWest Plan Service, Ames, IA	800-562-3618
Midwest Traditions Inc., Shorewood, WI	800-736-9189
Mieklejohn Civil Liberties Institute, Berkeley, CA	888-848-0599
Milady Publishing, Albany, NY	800-998-7498
Miles River Press, Alexandria, VA	800-767-1501
Milkweed Editions, Minneapolis, MN	800-520-6455
Millbrook Press Inc., Brookfield, CT	800-462-4703
Millennium Publishing Group, Monterey, CA	800-524-6826
Miller Freeman Inc., San Francisco, CA	800-848-5594 (orders only)
Milliken Publishing Co., St Louis, MO	800-325-4136; fax 800-538-1319
Minerals, Metals & Materials Society (TMS), Warrendale, PA	800-759-4867
Minnesota Historical Society Press, St Paul, MN	800-647-7827
MIT Press, Cambridge, MA	800-356-0343 (orders only)
Mitchell Lane Publishers Inc., Elkton, MD	800-814-5484

Publisher/Distributor	Toll-Free No.
MMB Music Inc., St Louis, MO	800-543-3771
Modulo Editeur Inc., Mont Royal, PQ, Canada	888-738-9818
Momentum Books Ltd., Troy, MI	800-758-1870
Monday Morning Books Inc., Palo Alto, CA	800-255-6049; fax 800-255-6048
Mondia Editeurs Inc., St-Jerome, PQ, Canada	800-561-2371 (Canada)
Mondo Publishing, Greenvale, NY	800-242-3650
Money Market Directories Inc., Charlottesville, VA	800-446-2810
Monthly Review Press, New York, NY	800-670-9499
Moody Press, Chicago, IL	800-678-8812
Moon Travel Handbooks, Emeryville, CA	800-345-5473
Thomas More, Allen, TX	800-527-5030; 800-264-0368; fax 800-688-8356
Morehouse Publishing Co., Harrisburg, PA	800-877-0012 (orders only)
Morgan Kaufmann Publishers Inc., San Francisco, CA	800-745-7323
Morgan Quitno Corp., Lawrence, KS	800-457-0742
Morgan Reynolds Inc., Greensboro, NC	800-535-1504; fax 800-535-5725
Morningside Bookshop, Dayton, OH	800-648-9710
Morrow Junior Books, New York, NY	800-843-9389; fax 800-237-0657 (cust serv)
Morton Publishing Co., Englewood, CO	800-348-3777
Mosaic Press, Cincinnati, OH	800-932-4044
Mosaic Press, Buffalo, NY	800-387-8992
Mosby, St Louis, MO	800-325-4177
Mount Olive College Press, Mount Olive, NC	800-653-0854
Mountain 'n' Air Books, Tujunga, CA	800-446-9696; fax 800-303-5578
Mountain Press Publishing Co., Missoula, MT	800-234-5308
Mountaineers Books, Seattle, WA	800-553-4453; fax 800-568-7604
Andrew Mowbray Inc. Publishers, Lincoln, RI	800-999-4697
Moyer Bell, Wakefield, RI	888-789-1945
Moznaim Publishing Corp., Brooklyn, NY	800-364-5118
John Muir Publications Inc., Santa Fe, NM	800-285-4078
Mulberry Paperback Books, New York, NY	800-843-9389
Multicultural Publications, Akron, OH	800-238-0297; fax 800-238-0297
Editions Multimondes, Sainte-Foy, PQ, Canada	800-840-3029; fax 888-303-5931
Multnomah Publishers Inc., Sisters, OR	800-929-0910
Municipal Analysis Services Inc., Austin, TX	800-488-3932
Mike Murach & Associates Inc., Fresno, CA	800-221-5528
Museum of New Mexico Press, Santa Fe, NM	800-249-7737 (orders)
Music Sales Corp., New York, NY	800-431-7187
Mustang Publishing Co. Inc., Memphis, TN	800-250-8713
NAFSA: Association of International Educators, Washington, DC	800-836-4994 (book orders only)
Naiad Press Inc., Tallahassee, FL	800-533-1973 (order desk only)
Nancy Renfro Studios Inc., Austin, TX	800-933-5512
Napoleon Publishing/Rendezvous Press, Toronto, ON, Canada	877-730-9052
NAPSAC Reproductions, Marble Hill, MO	800-758-8629
Narwhal Press Inc., Charleston, SC	800-981-1943
National Academy Press, Washington, DC	800-624-6242

Publisher/Distributor	Toll-Free No.

National Archives & Records Administration, Washington, DC 800-234-8861 (orders)
National Association of Broadcasters (NAB), Washington, DC   800-368-5644
National Association of Secondary School Principals, Reston, VA   800-253-7746
National Association of Social Workers (NASW), Washington, DC   800-638-8799
National Braille Press, Boston, MA   800-548-7323
National Council of Teachers of English (NCTE),   800-369-6283
  Urbana, IL   877-369-6283 (cust serv)
National Council of Teachers of   800-235-7566 (orders, registration & membership)
  Mathematics, Reston, VA   fax 800-220-8483 (on demand)
National Council on Radiation Protection & Measurements
  (NCRP), Bethesda, MD   800-229-2652
National Crime Prevention Council, Washington, DC   800-627-2911 (orders only)
National Geographic Society, Washington, DC   800-638-4077
National Golf Foundation, Jupiter, FL   800-733-6006
National Institute for Trial Advocacy, Notre Dame, IN   800-225-6482
National Learning Corp., Syosset, NY   800-645-6337
National Museum of Women in the Arts, Washington, DC   800-222-7270
National Notary Association, Chatsworth, CA   800-876-6827
National Publishing Co., Philadelphia, PA   888-333-1863
National School Services, Wheeling, IL   800-262-4511
National Science Teachers Association (NSTA), Arlington, VA 800-722-NSTA (sales)
National Textbook Co. (NTC), Lincolnwood, IL   800-323-4900 (orders only)
  fax 800-998-3103
National Underwriter Co., Cincinnati, OH   800-543-0874
Natural Heritage/Natural History Inc.,
  Toronto, ON, Canada   800-725-9982 (orders only)
Naturegraph Publishers Inc., Happy Camp, CA   800-390-5353
Naval Institute Press, Annapolis, MD   800-233-8764
NavPress Publishing Group, Colorado Springs, CO   800-947-0550
NBM Publishing Inc., New York, NY   800-886-1223
Neal-Schuman Publishers Inc., New York, NY   fax 800-584-2414
Nebbadoon Press, Etna, NH   800-500-9086
Neibauer Press, Warminster, PA   800-322-6203
Nelson Information, Port Chester, NY   800-333-6357
New City Press, Hyde Park, NY   800-462-5980 (orders only)
New Directions Publishing Corp., New York, NY   800-233-4830 (PA)
New Editions International Ltd., Sedona, AZ   800-777-4751
New Forums Press Inc., Stillwater, OK   800-606-3766
New Harbinger Publications Inc., Oakland, CA   800-748-6273 (orders only)
New Horizon Press, Far Hills, NJ   800-533-7978 (orders only)
New Leaf Press Inc., Green Forest, AR   800-643-9535
New Press, New York, NY   800-233-4830 (orders); fax 800-458-6515
New Readers Press, Syracuse, NY   800-448-8878
New Rivers Press, Minneapolis, MN   800-339-2011
New Victoria Publishers, Norwich, VT   800-326-5297
New World Library, Novato, CA   800-227-3900 ext 902 (retail orders)

Publisher/Distributor	Toll-Free No.
New York Academy of Sciences, New York, NY	800-843-6927
New York State Bar Association, Albany, NY	800-582-2452
New York University Press, New York, NY	800-996-6987 (orders)
NewLife Publications, Orlando, FL	800-235-7255; fax 800-514-7072
Newmarket Press, New York, NY	800-669-3903
Nicholas Brealey Publishing, Naperville, IL	888-BREALEY
Nightingale-Conant, Niles, IL	800-572-2770; fax 800-647-9198
Nightshade Press, Troy, ME	800-497-9258 (book orders only)
Nilgiri Press, Tomales, CA	800-475-2369
Nimbus Publishing Ltd., Halifax, NS, Canada	800-646-2879
No Starch Press, San Francisco, CA	800-420-7240
Nolo Press, Berkeley, CA	800-992-6656
Norman Publishing, San Francisco, CA	800-544-9359
North Atlantic Books, Berkeley, CA	800-337-2665 (book orders)
North Light Books, Cincinnati, OH	800-289-0963
North River Press Publishing Corp., Great Barrington, MA	800-486-2665
	fax 800-BOOK-FAX
Northland Publishing Co., Flagstaff, AZ	800-346-3257; fax 800-257-9082
Northmont Publishing Co., West Bloomfield, MI	800-472-3485
Northstone Publishing, Kelowna, BC, Canada	800-299-2926
Northwestern University Press, Evanston, IL	800-621-2736 (orders only)
Jeffrey Norton Publishers Inc., Guilford, CT	800-243-1234; fax 800-453-4329
W W Norton & Company Inc., New York, NY	800-233-4830 (orders & cust serv)
	fax 800-458-6515
Nova Press, Los Angeles, CA	800-949-6175
Novalis Publishing, Toronto, ON, Canada	800-387-7164; fax 800-204-4140
NTC Contemporary Publishing, New York, NY	800-788-3123
NTC/Contemporary Publishing Group, Lincolnwood, IL	800-323-4900 (orders only)
	fax 800-998-3103
Nystrom, Chicago, IL	800-621-8086
OAG Worldwide, Oak Brook, IL	800-323-3537
Oasis Press/Hellgate Press, Central Point, OR	800-228-2275
Ocean View Books, Denver, CO	800-848-6222
Ohara Publications Inc., Valencia, CA	800-423-2874
Ohio State University Foreign Language Publications, Columbus, OH	800-678-6999
Ohio State University Press, Columbus, OH	800-437-4439; fax 800-678-6416
Ohio University Press, Athens, OH	800-621-2736
Old Books Publishing Co., Earlysville, VA	888-651-8520
Omnibus Press, New York, NY	800-431-7187
Omnigraphics Inc., Detroit, MI	800-234-1340; fax 800-875-1340 (orders)
OneOnOne Computer Training, Addison, IL	800-424-8668
Oneworld Publications Ltd., Boston, MA	800-331-4642
Online Training Solutions Inc., Redmond, WA	800-854-3344
Open Court Publishing Co., Chicago, IL	800-435-6850
Open Horizons Publishing Co., Fairfield, IA	800-796-6130
Opis Directories, Lakewood, NJ	800-275-0950

Publisher/Distributor	Toll-Free No.
Optical Society of America, Washington, DC	800-582-0416
Optima Books, Berkeley, CA	877-710-2196; fax 800-515-8373
Opus Communications, Marblehead, MA	800-650-6787
Orbis Books, Maryknoll, NY	800-258-5838 (orders)
Orca Book Publishers, Custer, WA	800-210-5277
Orchard Books, New York, NY	800-433-3411
Order of the Cross, La Grange, IL	800-611-1361 (voice & fax)
Oregon Catholic Press, Portland, OR	800-548-8749; fax 800-843-8181
Oregon State University Press, Corvallis, OR	800-426-3797 (orders)
O'Reilly & Associates Inc., Sebastopol, CA	800-998-9938
Organization for Economic Cooperation & Development, Washington, DC	800-456-6323
Orion Research Corp., Scottsdale, AZ	800-844-0759
Oryx Press, Phoenix, AZ	800-279-6799; fax 800-279-4663
Osborne/McGraw-Hill, Berkeley, CA	800-227-0900
Other Press LLC, New York, NY	877-THE OTHER (843-6843)
Our Sunday Visitor Publishing, Huntington, IN	800-348-2440 (orders)
Overmountain Press, Johnson City, TN	800-992-2691
Richard C Owen Publishers Inc., Katonah, NY	800-336-5588
Oxbridge Communications Inc., New York, NY	800-955-0231
Oxford University Press Canada, Don Mills, ON, Canada	800-387-8020
	fax 800-665-1771
Oxford University Press, Inc., New York, NY	800-451-7556 (orders)
Oxmoor House Inc., Birmingham, AL	800-633-4910
Ozark Publishing Inc., Prairie Grove, AR	800-321-5671
P & R Publishing Co., Phillipsburg, NJ	800-631-0094
P P I Publishing, Kettering, OH	800-773-6825
P S M J Resources Inc., Newton, MA	800-537-7765
Pacific Heritage Books, Rancho Palos Verdes, CA	888-870-8878
Pacific Press Publishing Association, Nampa, ID	800-447-7377
Paladin Press, Boulder, CO	800-392-2400
Palm Island Press, Key West, FL	800-763-4345
Pangaea Publications, Saint Paul, MN	888-690-3320 (orders only)
Panoptic Enterprises, Burke, VA	800-594-4766
Pantheon Books/Schocken Books, New York, NY	800-638-6460
Papier-Mache Press, Watsonville, CA	800-776-1956
Para Publishing, Santa Barbara, CA	800-PARAPUB
Parabola Books, New York, NY	800-560-6984
Paraclete Press, Orleans, MA	800-451-5006
Paradigm Publications, Brookline, MA	800-873-3946
Paradise Cay Publications, Arcata, CA	800-736-4509
Paragon House, St Paul, MN	800-447-3709; fax 800-494-0997
Parenting Press Inc., Seattle, WA	800-99-BOOKS
Park Place Publications, Pacific Grove, CA	888-702-4500
Parker Publications Division, Carlsbad, CA	800-446-3410
Parkway Publishers Inc., Boone, NC	fax 800-821-9155

Publisher/Distributor	Toll-Free No.
Parlay International, Emeryville, CA	800-457-2752
Parthenon Publishing Group Inc., Pearl River, NY	800-735-4744
Passport Books, Lincolnwood, IL	800-323-4900 (orders only)
Pastoral Press, Portland, OR	800-548-8749; fax 800-462-7329
Path Press Inc., Chicago, IL	800-548-2600
Pathfinder Publishing of California, Oxnard, CA	800-977-2282
Pathways Publishing, Hudson, MA	888-333-7284
Patrice Press, Tucson, AZ	800-367-9242
Patrick's Press Inc., Columbus, GA	800-654-1052
Pauline Books & Media, Boston, MA	800-876-4463 (orders only)
Paulist Press, Mahwah, NJ	fax 800-836-3161 (orders)
PBC International Inc., Glen Cove, NY	800-527-2826
Peachtree Publishers Ltd., Atlanta, GA	800-241-0113; fax 800-875-8909
Peanut Butter & Jelly Press, LLC, Newton, MA	800-408-6226; fax 800-408-6226
Pearce-Evetts Publishing, Greenville, SC	800-842-9571
Pearson Adult Education Division: Invest Learning, San Diego, CA	800-927-9997
Pearson Business & Professional: Appleton & Lange, Stamford, CT	800-423-1359
T H Peek Publisher, Palo Alto, CA	800-962-9245
Peer-to-Peer Communications, Menlo Park, CA	800-420-2677
Peguis Publishers Ltd., Winnipeg, MB, Canada	800-667-9673
Penbrooke Publishing, Tulsa, OK	888-493-2665
Pencil Point Press Inc., Fairfield, NJ	800-356-1299
Penfield Press, Iowa City, IA	800-728-9998
Pennsylvania Historical & Museum Commission, Harrisburg, PA	800-747-7790
Pennsylvania State University Press, University Park, PA	800-326-9180
	fax 877-778-2665
PennWell Books, Tulsa, OK	800-752-9764
Pentrex Pub, Pasadena, CA	800-950-9333 (continental US only)
People's Medical Society, Allentown, PA	800-624-8773
Per Annum Inc., New York, NY	800-548-1108
Peradam Press, Santa Barbara, CA	800-241-8689
Perfection Learning Corp., Des Moines, IA	800-762-2999
Peter Pauper Press Inc., White Plains, NY	800-833-2311
Peterson's, Lawrenceville, NJ	800-338-3282; fax 800-772-2465
Petroleum Extension Service Petex, Austin, TX	800-687-4132; fax 800-687-7839
Peytral Publications Inc., Minnetonka, MN	877-PEYTRAL
Pfeifer-Hamilton Publishers Inc., Duluth, MN	800-247-6789
Phaidon Press Inc., New York, NY	877-742-4366; fax 877-742-4370
Phi Delta Kappa Educational Foundation, Bloomington, IN	800-766-1156
Philosophical Publishing Co., Quakertown, PA	800-300-5168
Philosophy Documentation Center, Bowling Green, OH	800-444-2419
Phoenix Learning Resources, New York, NY	800-221-1274
Phoenix Publishing, Lansing, MI	800-345-0325
Phoenix Society for Burn Survivors, East Grand Rapids, MI	800-888-BURN
Picasso Publications Inc., Edmonton, AB, Canada	fax 877-250-1300
Pictorial Histories Publishing Co., Missoula, MT	888-763-8350

Publisher/Distributor	Toll-Free No.
Picture Me Books, Akron, OH	800-762-6775
Pieces of Learning, Dayton, OH	800-729-5137
Pierian Press, Ann Arbor, MI	800-678-2435
Pilgrim Press/United Church Press, Cleveland, OH	800-537-3394
Pilot Books, Greenport, NY	800-79PILOT
Pineapple Press Inc., Sarasota, FL	800-746-3275 (orders)
Pipeline Press, Chapel Hill, NC	888-822-6657
Pippin Publishing Corp., Toronto, ON, Canada	888-889-0001
Pitspopany Press, New York, NY	800-232-2931
Planetary Publications, Boulder Creek, CA	800-372-3100
Planning/Communications, River Forest, IL	888-366-5200
Plays Inc., Boston, MA	888-273-8214
Plough Publishing House, Farmington, PA	800-521-8011 (sales)
Police Executive Research Forum, Washington, DC	800-202-4563
Polyscience Publications Inc., Champlain, NY	800-840-5870
Pomegranate Communications, Rohnert Park, CA	800-227-1428
Popular Culture Ink, Ann Arbor, MI	800-678-8828
Popular Press, Bowling Green, OH	800-515-5118
Portunus Publishing Co., Carmel, CA	888-450-5021
Possibility Press, Hummelstown, PA	800-566-0534
Clarkson Potter Publishers, New York, NY	800-526-4264
Pottersfield Press, East Lawrencetown, NS, Canada	800-NIMBUS9 (orders only) fax 888-253-3133
Practising Law Institute, New York, NY	800-260-4754; fax 800-321-0093
Prairie View Press, Rosenort, MB, Canada	800-477-7377
Prakken Publications Inc., Ann Arbor, MI	800-530-9673 (orders only)
Precept Press, Chicago, IL	800-225-3775
Prentice Hall Canada, Scarborough, ON, Canada	800-361-6128
PREP Publishing, Fayetteville, NC	800-533-2814
Presbyterian Publishing Corporation, Louisville, KY	800-227-2872 (US only) fax 800-541-5113 (US only)
Primedia Special Interest Publications, Peoria, IL	800-521-2885
Princeton Architectural Press, New York, NY	800-722-6657
Princeton Book Co. Publishers, Hightstown, NJ	800-220-7149
Princeton University Press, Princeton, NJ	800-777-4726; fax 800-999-1958
PRO-ED, Austin, TX	800-897-3202; fax 800-397-7633
Pro Lingua Associates, Brattleboro, VT	800-366-4775
Productivity Inc., Portland, OR	800-394-6868; fax 800-394-6286
Productivity Inc., New York, NY	800-247-8519
Professional Communications Inc., Caddo, OK	800-337-9838
Professional Education Group Inc., Minnetonka, MN	800-229-2531
Professional Publications Inc., Belmont, CA	800-426-1178
Professional Publishing, Burr Ridge, IL	800-2McGraw
Professional Resource Exchange Inc., Sarasota, FL	800-443-3364
Professional Tax & Business Publications, Columbia, SC	800-247-6553
Prometheus Books, Amherst, NY	800-421-0351

Publisher/Distributor	Toll-Free No.
ProStar Publications Inc., Annapolis, MD	800-481-6277; fax 800-487-6277
Providence House Publishers, Franklin, TN	800-321-5692
Pruett Publishing Co., Boulder, CO	800-247-8224; fax 800-527-9727
PST Inc., Redmond, WA	800-284-7043
Psychological Assessment Resources Inc. (PAR), Lutz, FL	800-331-8378
	fax 800-727-9329
Psychological Corp., San Antonio, TX	800-211-8378 (cust serv)
PT Publications, West Palm Beach, FL	800-547-4326
Public Affairs, New York, NY	877-782-1234
Public Utilities Reports Inc., Vienna, VA	800-368-5001
Publications du Quebec, Ste Foy, PQ, Canada	800-463-2100
Publishing Directions Inc., Avon, CT	800-562-4357
Purdue University Press, West Lafayette, IN	800-933-9637
Purple Mountain Press Ltd., Fleischmanns, NY	800-325-2665
QED Press, Fort Bragg, CA	800-773-7782
Quail Ridge Press, Brandon, MS	800-343-1583
Quality Education Data, Denver, CO	800-525-5811
Quality Medical Publishing Inc., St Louis, MO	800-423-6865
Quality Press, Milwaukee, WI	800-248-1946
Quintessence Publishing Co. Inc., Carol Stream, IL	800-621-0387
Quixote Press, Wever, IA	800-571-BOOK
Race Point Press, Provincetown, MA	800-446-5544
Ragged Edge Press, Shippensburg, PA	888-WHT-MANE
Rainbow Books Inc., Highland City, FL	800-356-9315; 888-613-BOOK
Rainbow House Publishing, Bridgeport, CT	800-361-2609
Rainbow Publishers, San Diego, CA	800-323-7337
Rainbow Studies International, El Reno, OK	800-242-5348
Raincoast Book Distribution Ltd., Vancouver, BC, Canada	800-663-5714 (Canada only)
Raintree/Steck-Vaughn Publishers, Austin, TX	888-363-4266; fax 877-578-2638
Rand McNally, Skokie, IL	800-333-0136
Random House Children's Media Group, New York, NY	800-554-1672
Random House Inc., New York, NY	800-726-0600
Random House of Canada Ltd., Mississauga, ON, Canada	800-668-4247
Rayve Productions Inc., Windsor, CA	800-852-4890
RCL Resources for Christian Living, Allen, TX	800-527-5030; fax 800-688-8356
Reader's Chair, Hollister, CA	800-616-1350
Reader's Digest Association Inc., Pleasantville, NY	800-431-1726
Reader's Digest USA, Pleasantville, NY	800-431-1726
Reader's Digest USA Select Editions, Pleasantville, NY	800-431-1726
Record Research Inc., Menomonee Falls, WI	800-827-9810
Red Crane Books Inc., Santa Fe, NM	800-922-3392
Red Sea Press, Lawrenceville, NJ	800-789-1898
Redbird Productions, Hastings, MN	800-950-6898
Redleaf Press, St Paul, MN	800-423-8309; fax 800-641-0115
Thomas Reed Publications Inc., Boston, MA	800-995-4995

Publisher/Distributor	Toll-Free No.
Referee Books, Racine, WI	800-733-6100
Regal Books, Ventura, CA	800-446-7735 (orders)
Regnery Publishing Inc., Washington, DC	800-462-6420
Regular Baptist Press, Schaumburg, IL	800-727-4440 (orders only); 888-588-1600
Rei America Inc., Virginia Gardens, FL	800-726-5337
Reid Publishing Ltd., Oakville, ON, Canada	800-446-4797 (Canada)
Reidmore Books Inc., Edmonton, AB, Canada	800-661-2859
Renaissance Media, Los Angeles, CA	800-266-2834
Research Press, Champaign, IL	800-519-2707
Resort Gifts Unlimited, Tempe, AZ	800-266-5265; fax 800-973-6694
Resurrection Press Ltd., Williston Park, NY	800-892-6657
Fleming H Revell, Grand Rapids, MI	800-877-2665
Review & Herald Publishing Association, Hagerstown, MD	800-234-7630
Rising Sun Publishing, Marietta, GA	800-524-2813
Riverside Publishing Co., Itasca, IL	800-767-8420 (general)
	800-323-9540 (orders)
Rizzoli International Publications Inc., New York, NY	800-522-6657 (orders only)
Roberts Rinehart Publishers, Niwot, CO	800-352-1985; fax 800-401-9705
Rockbridge Publishing, Berryville, VA	800-473-3943
Rocky Mountain Books Ltd., Calgary, AB, Canada	800-566-3336
Rocky River Publishers, Shepherdstown, WV	800-343-0686
Rod & Staff Publishers Inc., Crockett, KY	fax 800-643-1244 (US orders)
Rodale Press Inc., Emmaus, PA	800-848-4735
Ronin Publishing Inc., Berkeley, CA	800-858-2665
Ronsdale Press, Vancouver, BC, Canada	888-879-0919
Rosen Publishing Group Inc., New York, NY	800-237-9932
Ross Books, Berkeley, CA	800-367-0930
Norman Ross Publishing Inc., New York, NY	800-648-8850
Roth Publishing Inc., Great Neck, NY	800-899-ROTH
Rough Notes Co. Inc., Carmel, IN	800-428-4384; fax 800-321-1909
H M Rowe Co., Baltimore, MD	800-638-6026
Rowman & Littlefield Publishers Inc., Lanham, MD	800-462-6420
Royal House Publishing Co. Inc., Beverly Hills, CA	800-277-5535
Rudi Publishing, San Francisco, CA	800-999-6901 (orders only)
Runestone Press, Minneapolis, MN	800-328-4929; 800-332-1132
Running Press Book Publishers, Philadelphia, PA	800-345-5359 (orders)
	fax 800-453-2884
Russell Sage Foundation, New York, NY	800-666-2211
Rutgers University Press, Piscataway, NJ	800-446-9323 (orders only)
Rutledge Hill Press, Nashville, TN	800-234-4234
RV Consumer Group, Quilcene, WA	800-405-3325
William H Sadlier Inc., New York, NY	800-221-5175
Sagamore Publishing Inc., Champaign, IL	800-327-5557 (orders)
St Anthony Messenger Press, Cincinnati, OH	800-488-0488
Saint Anthony Publishing Inc., Reston, VA	800-632-0123
St Augustine's Press Inc., South Bend, IN	888-997-4994

Publisher/Distributor	Toll-Free No.
St Bede's Publications, Petersham, MA	800-507-1000 (orders)
	fax 800-919-5600 (orders)
St James Press, Farmington Hills, MI	800-877-GALE; fax 800-414-5043
St Martin's Press LLC, New York, NY	800-221-7945
Saint Mary's Press, Winona, MN	800-533-8095; fax 800-344-9225
Saint Nectarios Press, Seattle, WA	800-643-4233
Salem Press Inc., Hackensack, NJ	800-221-1592
Howard W Sams & Co., Indianapolis, IN	800-552-3910
J S Sanders & Co. Inc., Nashville, TN	800-350-1101
Sandlapper Publishing Inc., Orangeburg, SC	800-849-7263 (orders only)
Santa Monica Press LLC, Santa Monica, CA	800-784-9553
Santillana USA Publishing Co. Inc., Miami, FL	800-245-8584
Sarpedon Publishers, Rockville Centre, NY	800-207-8045
Sasquatch Books, Seattle, WA	800-775-0817
W B Saunders Company, Philadelphia, PA	800-545-2522 (cust serv)
Savage Press, Superior, WI	800-732-3867
Scarecrow Press Inc., Lanham, MD	800-462-6420
Scepter Publishers, Princeton, NJ	800-322-8773
Schaffer Frank Publications Inc., Torrance, CA	800-421-5565 (cust serv)
Scholarly Resources Inc., Wilmington, DE	800-772-8937
Scholastic Canada Ltd., Markham, ON, Canada	800-268-3860
Schonfeld & Associates Inc., Riverwood, IL	800-205-0030
School Zone Publishing Co., Grand Haven, MI	800-253-0564
Schreiber Publishing Inc., Rockville, MD	800-822-3213 (sales)
Schwann Publications, Woodland, CA	800-845-8444
Science and Behavior Books Inc., Los Altos, CA	800-547-9982
Scott & Daughters Publishing Inc., Los Angeles, CA	800-547-2688
Scott Publications, Livonia, MI	800-458-8237
Scott Publishing Co., Sidney, OH	800-572-6885
Scott's Directories, Don Mills, ON, Canada	800-408-9431
Scurlock Publishing Co. Inc., Texarkana, TX	800-228-6389
Seal Press, Seattle, WA	800-754-0271 (orders)
Seedling Publications Inc., Columbus, OH	877-857-7333
SeedSowers, Sargent, GA	800-228-2665
SelectiveHouse Publishers Inc., Gaithersburg, MD	888-256-6399 (orders only)
Self-Counsel Press Inc., Bellingham, WA	877-877-6490
Self-Counsel Press International Ltd., North Vancouver, BC, Canada	800-663-3007
Severn House Publishers Inc., New York, NY	800-830-3044
M E Sharpe Inc., Armonk, NY	800-541-6563
Harold Shaw Publishers, Wheaton, IL	800-SHAW-PUB
Sheed & Ward, Franklin, WI	800-558-0580; fax 800-369-4448
Sheep Meadow Press, Bronx, NY	800-972-4491
Shelter Publications Inc., Bolinas, CA	800-307-0131
Shen's Books, Auburn, CA	800-456-6660
Sherman Asher Publishing, Santa Fe, NM	888-984-2686 (orders)
Sierra Press, Mariposa, CA	800-745-2631

Publisher/Distributor	Toll-Free No.
Signature Books Inc., Salt Lake City, UT	800-356-5687 (ordering)
Sigo Press, Boston, MA	800-338-0446
SIGS Books & Multimedia, New York, NY	800-871-7447 (orders only)
Silver Moon Press, New York, NY	800-874-3320
Silver Pixel Press, Rochester, NY	fax 800-394-3686
Simon & Pierre Publishing Co. Ltd., Toronto, ON, Canada	800-565-9523 (orders, Canada & US)
Simon & Schuster Inc., New York, NY	800-223-2336; 800-897-7650 (cust serv) fax 800-943-9831 (orders)
Simon & Schuster Trade Division, New York, NY	800-223-2336 (orders) 800-223-2348 (cust serv)
Simpler Gifts Press, San Diego, CA	800-688-1209
Singular Publishing Group Inc., San Diego, CA	800-521-8545; fax 800-774-8398
Six Strings Music Publishing, Torrance, CA	800-784-0203
Skidmore-Roth Publishing Inc., Englewood, CO	800-825-3150
SkillPath Publications, Mission, KS	800-873-7545
Sky Publishing Corp., Cambridge, MA	800-253-0245
Skylight Training & Publishing Inc., Arlington Heights, IL	800-348-4474
Slack Incorporated, Thorofare, NJ	800-257-8290
Smallwood Center for Newfoundland Studies, St Johns, NF, Canada	888-367-6353
Smith & Kraus Inc. Publishers, Hanover, NH	800-895-4331
Gibbs Smith Publisher, Layton, UT	800-748-5439; fax 800-213-3023 (orders only)
M Lee Smith Publishers LLC, Brentwood, TN	800-274-6774
Smithmark Publishers, New York, NY	800-932-0070 (warehouse)
Smithsonian Institution Press, Washington, DC	800-762-4612
Smithsonian Press/Smithsonian Productions, Washington, DC	800-782-4612
Smyth & Helwys Publishing Inc., Macon, GA	800-747-3016; 800-568-1248
Snow Lion Publications Inc., Ithaca, NY	800-950-0313
Society for Industrial & Applied Mathematics, Philadelphia, PA	800-447-SIAM
Society for Mining, Metallurgy & Exploration Inc., Littleton, CO	800-763-3132
Society of Manufacturing Engineers, Dearborn, MI	800-733-4SME
Software Training Resources, Long Beach, CA	800-419-7420 (orders only)
Sogides Ltée, Montreal, PQ, Canada	800-361-4806
Solano Press Books, Point Arena, CA	800-931-9373
Soli Deo Gloria Publications, Morgan, PA	888-266-5734
Sophia Institute Press, Manchester, NH	800-888-9344
Sopris West, Longmont, CO	800-547-6747
Sorin Books, Notre Dame, IN	800-282-1865; fax 800-282-5681
Soundprints, Norwalk, CT	800-228-7839
Sourcebooks Inc., Naperville, IL	800-432-7444
South Carolina Bar, Columbia, SC	800-768-7787 (SC only)
South End Press, Cambridge, MA	800-533-8478
South-Western Educational Publishing, Cincinnati, OH	800-543-0487
Southern Illinois University Press, Carbondale, IL	800-346-2680; fax 800-346-2681
Southern Institute Press, Indian Rocks Beach, FL	800-633-4891
Southwest Parks & Monuments Association, Tucson, AZ	888-569-SPMA

Publisher/Distributor	Toll-Free No.
Spinsters Ink, Duluth, MN	800-301-6860
Spizzirri Publishing Inc., Rapid City, SD	800-325-9819; fax 800-322-9819
Sports Publishing Inc., Champaign, IL	800-327-5557
Springer-Verlag New York Inc., New York, NY	800-SPRINGER
Springhouse Corp., Springhouse, PA	800-346-7844
Squarebooks Inc., Santa Rosa, CA	800-345-6699
ST Publications Book Division, Cincinnati, OH	800-925-1110
STA-Kris Inc., Marshalltown, IA	800-369-5676
Stackpole Books, Mechanicsburg, PA	800-732-3669
Standard Publishing Co., Cincinnati, OH	800-543-1301; fax 877-867-5751
Standard Publishing Corp., Boston, MA	800-682-5759
Starburst Publishers, Lancaster, PA	800-441-1456 (orders only)
Starlite Inc., St Petersburg, FL	800-577-2929
State House Press, Austin, TX	800-421-3378
State University of New York Press, Albany, NY	800-666-2211 (orders)
	fax 800-688-2877 (orders)
Statistics Canada, Ottawa, ON, Canada	800-700-1033 (Canada & US)
	fax 800-889-9734
Steck-Vaughn Co., Austin, TX	800-531-5015; 800-699-9459 (fax orders)
Stemmer House Publishers Inc., Owings Mills, MD	800-676-7511; fax 800-645-6958
Stenhouse Publishers, York, ME	800-988-9812 (sales)
Sterling Publishing Co. Inc., New York, NY	800-367-9692
SterlingHouse Publisher Incorporated, Pittsburgh, PA	800-898-7886
Stillpoint Publishing, Walpole, NH	800-847-4014
Stoddart Publishing Co. Limited,	800-387-0141 (Ontario & Quebec only)
North York, ON, Canada	800-387-0172 (Canada only); 800-805-1083 (US)
Stoeger Publishing Co., Wayne, NJ	800-631-0722
Stone Bridge Press, Berkeley, CA	800-947-7271
Storey Books, Pownal, VT	800-793-9396
Story Press, Cincinnati, OH	800-289-0963
Strang Communications Co./Creation House, Lake Mary, FL	800-283-8494
	800-665-1468 (Canada)
Studio 4 Productions, Northridge, CA	888-PUBLISH
Studio Press, Norfolk, NE	800-228-0629
SubGenius Foundation Inc., Dallas, TX	888-669-2323 (subscriptions)
Sulzburger & Graham Publishing Co. Ltd., New York, NY	800-366-7086
Summers Press Inc., Austin, TX	800-743-6491
Summit Publications, Indianapolis, IN	800-419-0200
Summit University Press, Gardiner, MT	800-245-5445
Summy-Birchard Inc., Miami, FL	800-327-7643
Sunbelt Publications, El Cajon, CA	800-626-6579
Sundance Publishing LLC, Littleton, MA	800-245-3388
Sunset Books, Menlo Park, CA	800-227-7346; 800-321-0372 (CA)
Surrey Books Inc., Chicago, IL	800-326-4430
Swallow Press, Athens, OH	800-621-2736; fax 800-621-8476
Swedenborg Foundation Publishers, West Chester, PA	800-355-3222 (cust serv)

Publisher/Distributor	Toll-Free No.
SYBEX Inc., Alameda, CA	800-227-2346
Synapse Information Resources Inc., Endicott, NY	888-SYN-CHEM
Syracuse University Press, Syracuse, NY	800-365-8929 (orders only)
T J Publishers Inc., Silver Spring, MD	800-999-1168
T L C Genealogy, Miami Beach, FL	800-858-8558
Taft Group, Farmington Hills, MI	800-877-GALE; fax 800-414-5043 (orders)
Tapestry Press Ltd., Acton, MA	800-535-2007
Taschen America, New York, NY	888-TASCHEN
Taunton Press Inc., Newtown, CT	800-283-7252; 800-888-8286 (orders)
Taylor Publishing Co., Dallas, TX	800-677-2800 (voice & fax)
te Neues Publishing Co., New York, NY	800-352-0305
Teach Me Tapes Inc., Minnetonka, MN	800-456-4656
Teacher Created Materials Inc., Westminster, CA	800-662-4321; fax 800-525-1254
Teacher Ideas Press, Englewood, CO	800-237-6124
Teachers & Writers Collaborative, New York, NY	888-BOOKSTW
Teacher's Discovery, Auburn Hills, MI	800-832-2437
Teachers Friend Publications Inc., Riverside, CA	800-343-9680; fax 800-307-8176
Teaching Strategies, Washington, DC	800-637-3652
Technical Association of the Pulp & Paper Industry (TAPPI), Norcross, GA	800-332-8686
Technology Training Systems Inc., Aurora, CO	800-676-8871
Technomic Publishing Co. Inc., Lancaster, PA	800-233-9936
Temple University Press, Philadelphia, PA	800-447-1656; fax 800-207-4442
Templegate Publishers, Springfield, IL	800-367-4844
Ten Speed Press, Berkeley, CA	800-841-BOOK
Tetra Press, Blacksburg, VA	800-526-0650
Texas A&M University Press, College Station, TX	800-826-8911 (orders) fax 888-617-2421 (orders)
Texas Tech University Press, Lubbock, TX	800-832-4042
Texas Western Press, El Paso, TX	800-488-3789 (4UTEP-TWP)
TFH Publications Inc., Neptune City, NJ	800-631-2188
Thames and Hudson, New York, NY	800-233-4830
Theosophical Publishing House, Wheaton, IL	800-669-9425
Theta Reports, Rocky Hill, CT	800-995-1550
Thieme Medical Publishers Inc., New York, NY	800-782-3488
Thinkers' Press/Chessco, Davenport, IA	800-397-7117
Thinking Publications, Eau Claire, WI	800-225-4769; fax 800-828-8885
Charles C Thomas Publisher Ltd., Springfield, IL	800-258-8980
Thomas Geale Publications Inc., Montara, CA	800-554-5457
Thomas Nelson Inc., Nashville, TN	800-251-4000
Thomas Publications, Gettysburg, PA	800-840-6782
Thompson Educational Publishing Inc., Toronto, ON, Canada	800-805-1083 (orders)
Gordon V Thompson Music, Toronto, ON, Canada	800-268-7736 (Canada & US)
Thomson Financial Publishing, Skokie, IL	800-321-3373
Thorndike Press, Thorndike, ME	800-223-6121
Tiare Publications, Lake Geneva, WI	800-420-0579

Publisher/Distributor	Toll-Free No.
Tide-mark Press, East Hartford, CT	800-338-2508
Tidewater Publishers, Centreville, MD	800-638-7641
Timber Press Inc., Portland, OR	800-327-5680
Time Being Books—Poetry in Sight & Sound, St Louis, MO	800-331-6605
	fax 888-301-9121
Time Life Inc., Alexandria, VA	800-621-7026
Timeless Books, Spokane, WA	800-251-9273
Times Books, New York, NY	800-733-3000
Todd Publications, Nyack, NY	800-747-1056
TODTRI Book Publishers, New York, NY	800-241-4477
Tommy Nelson, Nashville, TN	800-251-4000
Tor Books, New York, NY	800-221-7945 (cust serv)
Torah Aura Productions, Los Angeles, CA	800-238-6724
Tower Publishing Co., Standish, ME	800-969-8693
Traders Press Inc., Greenville, SC	800-927-8222
Tradery House, Memphis, TN	800-548-2537; fax 800-794-9806
Trafalgar Square, North Pomfret, VT	800-423-4525
Trails Illustrated/National Geographic Maps, Evergreen, CO	800-962-1643
	fax 800-626-8676
Trakker Maps Inc., Miami, FL	800-432-1730 (FL); 800-327-3108
Tralco Educational Services Inc., Hamilton, ON, Canada	888-487-2526
Transaction Publishers, Piscataway, NJ	888-999-6778
Transnational Publishers Inc., Ardsley, NY	800-914-8186 (orders only)
Transportation Technical Service Inc., Fredericksburg, VA	888-ONLY-TTS
Treasure Publishing, Fort Collins, CO	800-284-0158
Treehaus Communications Inc., Loveland, OH	800-638-4287 (orders)
Triad Publishing Co., Gainesville, FL	800-854-4947
Tricycle Press, Berkeley, CA	800-841-2665
Trinity Press International, Harrisburg, PA	800-877-0012
TripBuilder Inc., New York, NY	800-525-9745
TriQuarterly Books, Evanston, IL	800-621-2736 (orders only)
Triumph Books, Chicago, IL	800-335-5323
Troll Communications LLC, Mahwah, NJ	800-526-5289
TSR Inc., Renton, WA	fax 800-324-6436
Turtle Point Press, Chappaqua, NY	800-453-2992
Charles E Tuttle Co. Inc., Boston, MA	800-526-2778 (cust serv); fax 800-FAX-TUTL
29th Street Press, Loveland, CO	800-621-1544
Twenty-Third Publications Inc., Mystic, CT	800-321-0411
Twin Sisters Productions Inc., Akron, OH	800-248-8946
2 13 61 Publications Inc., Los Angeles, CA	800-992-1361
Two Thousand Three Associates, New Smyrna Beach, FL	800-598-5256
Tyndale House Publishers Inc., Wheaton, IL	800-323-9400
Type & Archetype Press, Gladwyne, PA	800-IHS-TYPE
UAHC Press, New York, NY	888-489-UAHC (8242)
ULI—The Urban Land Institute, Washington, DC	800-462-1254
Ulysses Press, Berkeley, CA	800-377-2542

Publisher/Distributor	Toll-Free No.
University Microfilms International (UMI), Ann Arbor, MI	800-521-0600
Unarius Academy of Science Publications, El Cajon, CA	800-475-7062
Unicor Medical Inc., Montgomery, AL	800-825-7421
UNIPress, Campo, CA	888-463-8654
Unique Publications Books & Videos, Burbank, CA	800-332-3330
United Church Publishing House, Etobicoke, ON, Canada	800-288-7365 (orders, Canada & US)
United Methodist Publishing House, Nashville, TN	800-251-3320
United Nations Publications, New York, NY	800-253-9646
United Seabears Corp., Culver City, CA	800-421-3388
United States Holocaust Memorial Museum, Washington, DC	800-259-9998 (orders)
United States Institute of Peace Press, Washington, DC	800-868-8064 (cust serv)
United States Pharmacopeial, Rockville, MD	800-227-8772
United States Tennis Association, White Plains, NY	800-223-0456
Universal Radio Research, Reynoldsburg, OH	800-431-3939
University Museum of Archaeology & Anthropology, Philadelphia, PA	800-306-1941
University of Akron Press, Akron, OH	877-UAPRESS
University of Alabama Press, Tuscaloosa, AL	800-621-2736 (trade orders only) fax 800-621-8476
University of Alaska Press, Fairbanks, AK	888-252-6657 (US only)
University of Arizona Press, Tucson, AZ	800-426-3797 (orders)
University of Arkansas Press, Fayetteville, AR	800-626-0090
University of British Columbia Press (UBC Press), Vancouver, BC, Canada	877-377-9378 fax 800-668-0821
University of California Press, Berkeley, CA	800-822-6657
University of Chicago Press, Chicago, IL	800-621-2736 (orders)
University of Georgia Press, Athens, GA	800-266-5842 (orders only)
University of Hawaii Press, Honolulu, HI	888-847-7377; fax 800-650-7811
University of Idaho Press, Moscow, ID	800-847-7377
University of Illinois Press, Champaign, IL	800-545-4703 (orders)
University of Iowa Press, Iowa City, IA	800-621-2736 (orders only) fax 800-621-8476
University of Massachusetts Press, Amherst, MA	fax 800-488-1144
University of Michigan Press, Ann Arbor, MI	800-876-1922
University of Missouri Press, Columbia, MO	800-828-1894
University of Nebraska Press, Lincoln, NE	800-755-1105 (orders); fax 800-526-2617
University of Nevada Press, Reno, NV	fax 877-682-6657
University of New Mexico Press, Albuquerque, NM	800-249-7737 (orders only)
University of North Carolina Press, Chapel Hill, NC	800-848-6224 (orders only) fax 800-272-6817 (orders)
University of Notre Dame Press, Notre Dame, IN	800-621-2736 (orders)
University of Oklahoma Press, Norman, OK	800-627-7377 (orders)
University of Oregon ERIC Clearinghouse on Educational Management, Eugene, OR	800-438-8841

Publisher/Distributor	Toll-Free No.
University of Pennsylvania Press, Philadelphia, PA	800-445-9880 (orders & cust serv only)
University of Pittsburgh Press, Pittsburgh, PA	800-666-2211; fax 800-688-2877
University of South Carolina Press, Columbia, SC	fax 800-868-0740 (orders)
University of the South Press, Sewanee, TN	800-367-1179
University of Toronto Press Inc., Toronto, ON, Canada	800-565-9523 (orders, Canada & US)
University of Utah Press, Salt Lake City, UT	800-773-6672
University of Washington Press, Seattle, WA	800-441-4115
University of Wisconsin Press, Madison, WI	800-621-2736 (orders) fax 800-621-8476
University Press of America Inc., Lanham, MD	800-462-6420; fax 800-338-4550
University Press of Colorado, Niwot, CO	800-268-6044
University Press of Florida, Gainesville, FL	800-226-3822 (sales calls only) fax 800-680-1955 (orders)
University Press of Kentucky, Lexington, KY	800-666-2211
University Press of Mississippi, Jackson, MS	800-737-7788
University Press of New England, Hanover, NH	800-421-1561 (orders only)
University Press of Virginia, Charlottesville, VA	800-831-3406; fax 877-288-6400
University Publications of America, Bethesda, MD	800-692-6300
University Publishing Group, Frederick, MD	800-654-8188
Upper Room Books, Nashville, TN	800-972-0433
Urban Institute Press, Washington, DC	877-UIPRESS
US Catholic Conference, Washington, DC	800-235-8722
US Games Systems Inc., Stamford, CT	800-544-2637 (800-54GAMES)
USA Gymnastics, Indianapolis, IN	800-4-USAGYM (memb servs)
Utah Geological Survey, Salt Lake City, UT	888-UTAH-MAP
Utah State University Press, Logan, UT	800-239-9974
VanDam Inc., New York, NY	800-UNFOLDS
Vandamere Press, Arlington, VA	800-551-7776
Vanderbilt University Press, Nashville, TN	800-937-5557 (orders only)
Vanderplas Publications, San Francisco, CA	877-353-1207
Vanwell Publishing Ltd., St Catharines, ON, Canada	800-661-6136
Vault Reports Inc., New York, NY	888-562-8285
VGM Career Horizons, Lincolnwood, IL	800-323-4900 (orders only)
Visible Ink Press, Farmington Hills, MI	800-7666265; fax 800-414-5043
Vista Publishing Inc., Long Branch, NJ	800-634-2498
ViviSphere Publishing, Accord, NY	800-611-1966
Viz Communications Inc., San Francisco, CA	800-394-3042
Vizual Reference Publications, Inc., New York, NY	800-251-4545
Volcano Press Inc., Volcano, CA	800-879-9636
Volt Directory Marketing Ltd., Blue Bell, PA	800-677-3839 (edit) fax 800-897-2491 (orders)
Voyageur Press, Stillwater, MN	800-888-9653
Waite Group Press, Indianapolis, IN	800-858-7674; fax 800-835-3202

Publisher/Distributor	Toll-Free No.
J Weston Walch Publisher, Portland, ME	800-341-6094
Waldman House Press Inc., Minneapolis, MN	888-700-PEEF ext 7333
Walker & Co., New York, NY	800-AT-WALKER; fax 800-218-9367
Wallace Homestead Book Co., Iola, WI	888-457-2873
Walnut Creek CDROM, Concord, CA	800-786-9907
Walter Foster Publishing Inc., Laguna Hills, CA	800-426-0099
Wm K Walthers Inc., Milwaukee, WI	800-877-7171
Warner Bros Publications Inc., Miami, FL	800-468-5010
Warner Press—Church of God Publications, Anderson, IN	800-741-7721
Warren Publishing House, Torrance, CA	800-609-1735; 800-421-5565 (orders) fax 800-837-7260
Washington State University Press, Pullman, WA	800-354-7360
Waterfront Books, Burlington, VT	800-639-6063 (orders)
Waterloo Music Co. Ltd., Waterloo, ON, Canada	800-563-9683 (Canada & US)
Watson-Guptill Publications, New York, NY	800-451-1741
Wayne State University Press, Detroit, MI	800-978-7327
WCB/McGraw-Hill, Burr Ridge, IL	800-338-3987 (cust serv)
Weatherhill Inc., New York, NY	800-788-7323
Weigl Educational Publishers Ltd., Calgary, AB, Canada	800-668-0766
Weil Publishing Co. Inc., Augusta, ME	800-877-WEIL
Samuel Weiser Inc., York Beach, ME	800-423-7087
Wellspring, York, PA	800-533-3561; fax 800-784-0990
Wesley Press, Indianapolis, IN	800-493-7539; fax 800-788-3535
Wesleyan University Press, Middletown, CT	800-421-1561
West Group, Independence, OH	800-362-4500
West Group, Rochester, NY	800-527-0430
Westcliffe Publishers Inc., Englewood, CO	800-523-3692
Westminster John Knox Press, Louisville, KY	800-227-2872
WH&O International, Wellesley, MA	800-553-6678
Wheatherstone Press, Portland, OR	800-980-0077
Whispering Coyote Press, Dallas, TX	800-929-6104
White Cliffs Media Inc., Editorial Dept, Sacramento, CA	800-359-3210
White Cloud Press, Ashland, OR	800-380-8286
White Mane Publishing Co. Inc., Shippensburg, PA	888-WHT-MANE
White Wolf Publishing, Clarkston, GA	800-454-WOLF
Whitehorse Press, North Conway, NH	800-531-1133
Albert Whitman & Co., Morton Grove, IL	800-255-7675
Whittier Publications Inc., Long Beach, NY	800-897-TEXT
Whole Person Associates Inc., Duluth, MN	800-247-6789
W Whorton & Company, Chicago, IL	800-649-7670
Wichita Eagle & Beacon Publishing Co., Wichita, KS	800-492-4043 (orders)
Wide World of Maps Inc., Phoenix, AZ	800-279-7654
Michael Wiese Productions, Studio City, CA	800-379-8808
Wilderness Adventures Press, Belgrade, MT	800-925-3339; fax 800-390-7558
Wilderness Press, Berkeley, CA	800-443-7227

Publisher/Distributor	Toll-Free No.

John Wiley & Sons Canada Ltd., Etobicoke, ON, Canada   800-263-1590 (PRT)
    800-567-4797 (orders only); fax 800-565-6802 (orders)
John Wiley & Sons Inc., New York, NY   800-CALL WILEY
William K Bradford Publishing Co. Inc., Acton, MA   800-421-2009
Williamson Publishing Co., Charlotte, VT   800-234-8791
    fax 800-304-7224
Willow Creek Press, Minocqua, WI   800-850-9453
H W Wilson, Bronx, NY   800-367-6770; fax 800-367-6770
Wimmer Companies/Cookbook Distribution, Memphis, TN   800-727-1034
    fax 800-794-9806
Win Publications!, Tulsa, OK   800-749-4597
Windsor Books, Babylon, NY   800-321-5934
Wine Appreciation Guild Ltd., South San Francisco, CA   800-231-9463
Wintergreen/Orchard House Inc., Itasca, IL   800-323-9540
Winters Publishing, Greensburg, IN   800-457-3230
Wisconsin Dept of Public Instruction, Madison, WI   800-243-8782
Wittenborn Art Books, San Francisco, CA   800-660-6403
WJ Fantasy Inc., Bridgeport, CT   800-ABC-PLAY; fax 800-200-3000
Wood Lake Books Inc., Kelowna, BC, Canada   800-663-2775
Woodbine House, Bethesda, MD   800-843-7323
Woodbridge Press Publishing Co., Santa Barbara, CA   800-237-6053
Woodford Press, San Francisco, CA   800-359-3373
Woodholme House Publishers, Baltimore, MD   800-488-0051
Woodland Books, Pleasant Grove, UT   800-777-2665
Wordware Publishing Inc., Plano, TX   800-229-4949
Workman Publishing Company Inc., New York, NY   800-722-7202
World Bible Publishers Inc., Iowa Falls, IA   800-922-9777
    800-247-5111 (order entry); fax 800-822-4271 (orders)
World Book Educational Products, Chicago, IL   800-967-5325
    fax 800-621-8202 (cust serv)
World Book Inc., Chicago, IL   800-255-1750
World Book Publishing, Chicago, IL   800-255-1750
World Book School and Library, Chicago, IL   800-975-3250 (US)
    800-837-5365 (Canada); fax 800-433-9330
World Citizens, Mill Valley, CA   800-247-6553 (orders only)
World Eagle, Littleton, MA   800-854-8273
World Information Technologies Inc., Northport, NY   800-WORLD-INFO
World Leisure Corp., Boston, MA   800-292-1966
World Leisure Corp., Hampstead, NH   800-292-1966
World Music Press, Danbury, CT   800-810-2040
World Resources Institute, Washington, DC   800-822-0504
World Scientific Publishing Co. Inc., River Edge, NJ   800-227-7562
World Trade Press, Novato, CA   800-833-8586
Worldtariff, San Francisco, CA   800-556-9334
Wright Group, Bothell, WA   800-523-2371 (training dept); 800-345-6073
    fax 800-543-7323 (orders)

Publisher/Distributor	Toll-Free No.
Write Way Publishing, Aurora, CO	800-680-1493
Writer Inc., Boston, MA	888-273-8214
Writer's Digest Books, Cincinnati, OH	800-289-0963
Writings of Mary Baker Eddy/Publisher, Boston, MA	800-288-7090
Wrox Press Inc., Chicago, IL	800-814-4527
Wyndham Hall Press, Bristol, IN	888-947-2665
Wyrick & Co., Charleston, SC	800-227-5898
Yale University Press, New Haven, CT	800-YUP-READ
	fax 800-777-9253
Yardbird Books, Airville, PA	800-622-6044 (sales)
YMAA Publication Center, Roslindale, MA	800-669-8892
York Press Inc., Timonium, MD	800-962-2763
Young People's Press Inc. (YPPI), San Diego, CA	800-231-9774
Yucca Tree Press, Las Cruces, NM	800-383-6183
YWAM Publishing, Seattle, WA	800-922-2143
Zagat Survey, New York, NY	800-333-3421
Zaner-Bloser Inc., Columbus, OH	800-421-3018
Zephyr Press Inc., Tucson, AZ	800-232-2187
Zondervan Publishing House, Grand Rapids, MI	800-727-1309 (cust serv)

How to Obtain an ISBN

Emery Koltay

Director Emeritus
United States ISBN Agency

The International Standard Book Numbering (ISBN) system was introduced into the United Kingdom by J. Whitaker & Sons Ltd., in 1967 and into the United States in 1968 by the R. R. Bowker Company. The Technical Committee on Documentation of the International Organization for Standardization (ISO TC 46) defines the scope of the standard as follows:

> . . . the purpose of this standard is to coordinate and standardize the use of identifying numbers so that each ISBN is unique to a title, edition of a book, or monographic publication published, or produced, by a specific publisher, or producer. Also, the standard specifies the construction of the ISBN and the location of the printing on the publication.
>
> Books and other monographic publications may include printed books and pamphlets (in various bindings), mixed media publications, other similar media including educational films/videos and transparencies, books on cassettes, microcomputer software, electronic publications, microform publications, braille publications and maps. Serial publications and music sound recordings are specifically excluded, as they are covered by other identification systems. [ISO Standard 2108]

The ISBN is used by publishers, distributors, wholesalers, bookstores, and libraries, among others, in 116 countries to expedite such operations as order fulfillment, electronic point-of-sale checkout, inventory control, returns processing, circulation/location control, file maintenance and update, library union lists, and royalty payments.

Construction of an ISBN

An ISBN consists of 10 digits separated into the following parts:

1 Group identifier: national, geographic, language, or other convenient group
2 Publisher or producer identifier
3 Title identifier
4 Check digit

When an ISBN is written or printed, it should be preceded by the letters *ISBN,* and each part should be separated by a space or hyphen. In the United States, the hyphen is used for separation, as in the following example: ISBN 1-879500-01-9. In this example, 1 is the group identifier, 879500 is the publisher identifier, 01 is the title identifier, and 9 is the check digit. The group of English-speaking countries, which includes the United States, Australia, Canada, New Zealand, and the United Kingdom, uses the group identifiers 0 and 1.

The ISBN Organization

The administration of the ISBN system is carried out at three levels—through the International ISBN Agency in Berlin, Germany; the national agencies; and the publishing houses themselves. Responsible for assigning country prefixes and for coordinating the worldwide implementation of the system, the International ISBN Agency in Berlin has an advisory panel that represents the International Organization for Standardization (ISO), publishers, and libraries. The International ISBN Agency publishes the *Publishers International ISBN Directory,* which is distributed in the United States by R. R. Bowker. As the publisher of *Books in Print,* with its extensive and varied database of publishers' addresses, R. R. Bowker was the obvious place to initiate the ISBN system and to provide the service to the U.S. publishing industry. To date, the U.S. ISBN Agency has entered more than 95,630 publishers into the system.

ISBN Assignment Procedure

Assignment of ISBNs is a shared endeavor between the U.S. ISBN Agency and the publisher. The publisher is provided with an application form, an Advance Book Information (ABI) form, and an instruction sheet. After an application is received and verified by the agency, an ISBN publisher prefix is assigned, along with a computer-generated block of ISBNs. The publisher then has the responsibility to assign an ISBN to each title, to keep an accurate record of the numbers assigned by entering each title in the ISBN Log Book, and to report each title to the *Books in Print* database. One of the responsibilities of the ISBN Agency is to validate assigned ISBNs and to retain a record of all ISBNs in circulation.

ISBN implementation is very much market-driven. Wholesalers and distributors, such as Baker & Taylor, Brodart, and Ingram, as well as such large retail chains as Waldenbooks and B. Dalton recognize and enforce the ISBN system by requiring all new publishers to register with the ISBN Agency before accepting their books for sale. Also, the ISBN is a mandatory bibliographic element in the International Standard Bibliographical Description (ISBD). The Library of Congress Cataloging in Publication (CIP) Division directs publishers to the agency to obtain their ISBN prefixes.

Location and Display of the ISBN

On books, pamphlets, and other printed material, the ISBN shall be on the verso of the title leaf or, if this is not possible, at the foot of the title leaf itself. It should also appear at the foot of the outside back cover if practicable and at the foot of the back of the jacket if the book has one (the lower right-hand corner is recommended). If neither of these alternatives is possible, then the number shall be printed in some other prominent position on the outside. The ISBN shall also appear on any accompanying promotional materials following the provisions for location according to the format of the material.

On other monographic publications, the ISBN shall appear on the title or credit frames and any labels permanently affixed to the publication. If the publication is issued in a container that is an integral part of the publication, the ISBN shall be displayed on the label. If it is not possible to place the ISBN on the item or its label, then the number should be displayed on the bottom or the back of the container, box, sleeve, or frame. It should also appear on any accompanying material, including each component of a multitype publication.

Printing of ISBN in Machine-Readable Coding

In the last few years, much work has been done on machine-readable representations of the ISBN, and now all books should carry ISBNs in bar code. The rapid worldwide extension of bar code scanning has brought into prominence the 1980 agreement between the International Article Numbering, formerly the European Article Numbering (EAN), Association and the International ISBN Agency that translates the ISBN into an ISBN Bookland EAN bar code.

All ISBN Bookland EAN bar codes start with a national identifier (00–09 representing the United States), *except* those on books and periodicals. The agreement replaces the usual national identifier with a special "ISBN Bookland" identifier represented by the digits 978 for books (see Figure 1) and 977 for periodicals. The 978 ISBN Bookland/EAN prefix is followed by the first nine digits of the ISBN. The check digit of the ISBN is dropped and replaced by a check digit calculated according to the EAN rules.

Figure 1 / Printing the ISBN in Bookland/EAN Symbology

ISBN 1 - 879500 - 01 - 9

9 781879 500013

The following is an example of the conversion of the ISBN to ISBN Bookland/EAN:

ISBN	1-879500-01-9
ISBN without check digit	1-879500-01
Adding EAN flag	978187950001
EAN with EAN check digit	9781879500013

Five-Digit Add-On Code

In the United States, a five-digit add-on code is used for additional information. In the publishing industry, this code can be used for price information or some other specific coding. The lead digit of the five-digit add-on has been designated a currency identifier, when the add-on is used for price. Number 5 is the code for the U.S. dollar; 6 denotes the Canadian dollar; 1 the British pound; 3 the Australian dollar; and 4 the New Zealand dollar. Publishers that do not want to indicate price in the add-on should print the code 90000 (see Figure 2).

Figure 2 / Printing the ISBN Bookland/EAN Number in Bar Code with the Five-Digit Add-On Code

978 = ISBN Bookland/EAN prefix
5 + Code for U.S. $
0995 = $9.95

90000 means no information
in the add-on code

Reporting the Title and the ISBN

After the publisher reports a title to the ISBN Agency, the number is validated and the title is listed in the many R. R. Bowker hard-copy and electronic publications, including *Books in Print, Forthcoming Books, Paperbound Books in Print, Books in Print Supplement, Books Out of Print, Books in Print Online, Books in Print Plus-CD ROM, Children's Books in Print, Subject Guide to Children's Books in Print, On Cassette: A Comprehensive Bibliography of Spoken Word Audiocassettes, Variety's Complete Home Video Directory, Software Encyclopedia, Software for Schools,* and other specialized publications.

For an ISBN application form and additional information, write to United States ISBN Agency, R. R. Bowker Company, 121 Chanlon Rd., New Providence, NJ 07974, or call 908-665-6770. The e-mail address is ISBN-SAN@bowker.com. The ISBN Web site is at http://www.bowker.com/standards/.

How to Obtain an ISSN

National Serials Data Program
Library of Congress

In the early 1970s the rapid increase in the production and dissemination of information and an intensified desire to exchange information about serials in computerized form among different systems and organizations made it increasingly clear that a means to identify serial publications at an international level was needed. The International Standard Serial Number (ISSN) was developed and has become the internationally accepted code for identifying serial publications. The number itself has no significance other than as a brief, unique, and unambiguous identifier. It is an international standard, ISO 3297, as well as a U.S. standard, ANSI/NISO Z39.9. The ISSN consists of eight digits in arabic numerals 0 to 9, except for the last, or check, digit, which can be an X. The numbers appear as two groups of four digits separated by a hyphen and preceded by the letters ISSN—for example, ISSN 1234-5679.

The ISSN is not self-assigned by publishers. Administration of the ISSN is coordinated through the ISSN Network, an intergovernmental organization within the UNESCO/UNISIST program. The network consists of national and regional centers, coordinated by the ISSN International Centre, located in Paris. Centers have the responsibility to register serials published in their respective countries.

Because serials are generally known and cited by title, assignment of the ISSN is inseparably linked to the key title, a standardized form of the title derived from information in the serial issue. Only one ISSN can be assigned to a title; if the title changes, a new ISSN must be assigned. Centers responsible for assigning ISSNs also construct the key title and create an associated bibliographic record.

The ISSN International Centre handles ISSN assignments for international organizations and for countries that do not have a national center. It also maintains and distributes the collective ISSN database that contains bibliographic records corresponding to each ISSN assignment as reported by the rest of the network. The database contains more than 900,000 ISSNs.

In the United States, the National Serials Data Program at the Library of Congress is responsible for assigning and maintaining the ISSNs for all U.S. serial titles. Publishers wishing to have an ISSN assigned should request an application form from the program, or download one from the program's Web site, and ask for an assignment. Assignment of the ISSN is free, and there is no charge for its use.

The ISSN is used all over the world by serial publishers to distinguish similar titles from each other. It is used by subscription services and libraries to manage files for orders, claims, and back issues. It is used in automated check-in systems by libraries that wish to process receipts more quickly. Copyright centers use the ISSN as a means to collect and disseminate royalties. It is also used as an identification code by postal services and legal deposit services. The ISSN is included as a verification element in interlibrary lending activities and for union catalogs as a collocating device. In recent years, the ISSN has been incorporated into bar codes for optical recognition of serial publications and into the standards for the identification of issues and articles in serial publications.

For further information about the ISSN or the ISSN Network, U.S. libraries and publishers should contact the National Serials Data Program, Library of Congress, Washington, DC 20540-4160; 202-707-6452; fax 202-707-6333; e-mail issn@loc.gov. Non-U.S. parties should contact the ISSN International Centre, 20 rue Bachaumont, 75002 Paris, France; telephone (33 1) 44-88-22-20; fax (33 1) 40-26-32-43; e-mail issnic@issn.org; World Wide Web http://www. ISSN.org.

ISSN application forms and instructions for obtaining an ISSN are also available via the Library of Congress World Wide Web site, http://lcweb.loc. gov/issn.

How to Obtain an SAN

Emery Koltay

Director Emeritus
United States ISBN/SAN Agency

SAN stands for Standard Address Number. It is a unique identification code for addresses of organizations that are involved in or served by the book industry, and that engage in repeated transactions with other members within this group. For purposes of this standard, the book industry includes book publishers, book wholesalers, book distributors, book retailers, college bookstores, libraries, library binders, and serial vendors. Schools, school systems, technical institutes, colleges, and universities are not members of this industry, but are served by it and therefore included in the SAN system.

The purpose of SAN is to facilitate communications among these organizations, of which there are several hundreds of thousands, that engage in a large volume of separate transactions with one another. These transactions include purchases of books by book dealers, wholesalers, schools, colleges, and libraries from publishers and wholesalers; payments for all such purchases; and other communications between participants. The objective of this standard is to establish an identification code system by assigning each address within the industry a discrete code to be used for positive identification for all book and serial buying and selling transactions.

Many organizations have similar names and multiple addresses, making identification of the correct contact point difficult and subject to error. In many cases, the physical movement of materials takes place between addresses that differ from the addresses to be used for the financial transactions. In such instances, there is ample opportunity for confusion and errors. Without identification by SAN, a complex record-keeping system would have to be instituted to avoid introducing errors. In addition, it is expected that problems with the current numbering system such as errors in billing, shipping, payments, and returns, will be significantly reduced by using the SAN system. SAN will also eliminate one step in the order fulfillment process: the "look-up procedure" used to assign account numbers. Previously a store or library dealing with 50 different publishers was assigned a different account number by each of the suppliers. SAN solved this problem. If a publisher indicates its SAN on its stationery and ordering documents, vendors to whom it sends transactions do not have to look up the account number, but can proceed immediately to process orders by SAN.

Libraries are involved in many of the same transactions as book dealers, such as ordering and paying for books and charging and paying for various services to other libraries. Keeping records of transactions, whether these involve buying, selling, lending, or donations, entails similar operations that require an SAN. Having the SAN on all stationery will speed up order fulfillment and eliminate errors in shipping, billing, and crediting; this, in turn, means savings in both time and money.

History

Development of the Standard Address Number began in 1968 when Russell Reynolds, general manager of the National Association of College Stores (NACS), approached the R. R. Bowker Company and suggested that a "Standard Account Number" system be implemented in the book industry. The first draft of a standard was prepared by an American National Standards Institute (ANSI) Committee Z39 subcommittee, which was co-chaired by Russell Reynolds and Emery Koltay. After Z39 members proposed changes, the current version of the standard was approved by NACS on December 17, 1979.

The chairperson of the ANSI Z39 Subcommittee 30, which developed the approved standard, was Herbert W. Bell, former senior vice president of McGraw-Hill Book Company. The subcommittee comprised the following representatives from publishing companies, distributors, wholesalers, libraries, national cooperative online systems, schools, and school systems: Herbert W. Bell (chair), McGraw-Hill Book Company; Richard E. Bates, Holt, Rinehart and Winston; Thomas G. Brady, The Baker & Taylor Companies, Paul J. Fasana, New York Public Library; Emery I. Koltay, R. R. Bowker Company; Joan McGreevey, New York University Book Centers; Pauline F. Micciche, OCLC, Inc.; Sandra K. Paul, SKP Associates; David Gray Remington, Library of Congress; Frank Sanders, Hammond Public School System; and Peter P. Chirimbes (alternate), Stamford Board of Education.

Format

The SAN consists of six digits plus a seventh *Modulus 11* check digit; a hyphen follows the third digit (XXX-XXXX) to facilitate transcription. The hyphen is to be used in print form, but need not be entered or retained in computer systems. Printed on documents, the Standard Address Number should be preceded by the identifier "SAN" to avoid confusion with other numerical codes (SAN XXX-XXXX).

Check Digit Calculation

The check digit is based on *Modulus 11*, and can be derived as follows:

1. Write the digits of the basic number. $\qquad$ 2 3 4 5 6 7
2. Write the constant weighting factors associated with each position by the basic number. $\qquad$ 7 6 5 4 3 2
3. Multiply each digit by its associated weighting factor. $\qquad$ 14 18 20 20 18 14
4. Add the products of the multiplications. $\quad$ $14 + 18 + 20 + 20 + 18 + 14 = 104$
5. Divide the sum by *Modulus 11* to find the remainder. $\qquad$ $104 \div 11 = 9$ plus a remainder of 5

6. Subtract the remainder from the *Modulus 11* to generate the required check digit. If there is no remainder, generate a check digit of zero. If the check digit is 10, generate a check digit of X to represent 10, since the use of 10 would require an extra digit. 11 - 5 = 6

7. Append the check digit to create the standard seven-digit Standard Address Number. SAN 234-5676

SAN Assignment

The R. R. Bowker Company accepted responsibility for being the central administrative agency for SAN, and in that capacity assigns SANs to identify uniquely the addresses of organizations. No SANs can be reassigned; in the event that an organization should cease to exist, for example, its SAN would cease to be in circulation entirely. If an organization using an SAN should move or change its name with no change in ownership, its SAN would remain the same, and only the name or address would be updated to reflect the change.

The SAN should be used in all transactions; it is recommended that the SAN be imprinted on stationery, letterheads, order and invoice forms, checks, and all other documents used in executing various book transactions. The SAN should always be printed on a separate line above the name and address of the organization, preferably in the upper left-hand corner of the stationery to avoid confusion with other numerical codes pertaining to the organization, such as telephone number, zip code, and the like.

SAN Functions and Suffixes

The SAN is strictly a Standard Address Number, becoming functional only in applications determined by the user; these may include activities such as purchasing, billing, shipping, receiving, paying, crediting, and refunding. Every department that has an independent function within an organization could have a SAN for its own identification. Users may choose to assign a suffix (a separate field) to their SAN strictly for internal use. Faculty members ordering books through a library acquisitions department, for example, may not have their own separate SAN, but may be assigned a suffix by the library. There is no standardized provision for placement of suffixes. Existing numbering systems do not have suffixes to take care of the "subset" type addresses. The SAN does not standardize this part of the address. For the implementation of SAN, it is suggested that wherever applicable the four-position suffix be used. This four-position suffix makes available 10,000 numbers, ranging from 0000 to 9999, and will accommodate all existing subset numbering presently in use.

For example, there are various ways to incorporate an SAN in an order fulfillment system. Firms just beginning to assign account numbers to their customers will have no conversion problems and will simply use the SAN as the numbering system. Firms that already have an existing number system can convert either on a step-by-step basis by adopting SANs whenever orders or payments are processed on the account, or by converting the whole file by using the SAN listing provided by the SAN Agency. Using the step-by-step conversion, firms may adopt SANs as customers provide them on their forms, orders, payments, and returns.

For additional information or suggestions, please write to Diana Fumando, SAN Coordinator, ISBN/SAN Agency, R. R. Bowker Company, 121 Chanlon Rd., New Providence, NJ 07974, call 908-771-7755, or fax 908-665-2895. The e-mail address is ISBN-SAN@bowker.com. The SAN Web site is at http://www.bowker.com/standards/.

Distinguished Books

Notable Books of 1999

The Notable Books Council of the Reference and User Services Association, a division of the American Library Association, selected these titles for their significant contribution to the expansion of knowledge or for the pleasure they can provide to readers.

Fiction

Anderson, Scott. *Triage*. Scribner, $23 (0-684-84695-0).

Anthony, Patricia. *Flanders*. Ace, $23.95 (0-441-00528-4).

Barrett, Andrea. *The Voyage of the Narwhal*. W. W. Norton, $24.95 (0-393-04632-X).

Borges, Jorge Luis. *Collected Fictions*. Tr. by Andrew Hurley. Viking, $35 (0-670-84970-7).

Byers, Michael. *The Coast of Good Intentions*. Houghton/Mariner, paper, $12 (0-395-89170-1)

Danticat, Edwidge. *The Farming of Bones*. Soho, $23 (1-56947-126-6).

Hornby, Nick. *About a Boy*. Penguin/Riverhead, $22.95 (1-57322-087-6).

McDermott, Alice. *Charming Billy*. Farrar, $22 (0-374-12080-3).

Moore, Lorrie. *Birds of America*. Knopf, $23 (0-679-44597-8).

Roth, Philip. *I Married a Communist*. Houghton Mifflin, $26 (0-395-93346-3).

Vakil, Ardashir. *Beach Boy*. Scribner, $22 (0-684-85299-3).

Nonfiction

Ackroyd, Peter. *The Life of Thomas More*. Doubleday, $30 (0-385-47709-0).

Berg, A. Scott. *Lindbergh*. Putnam, $30 (0-399-14449-8).

Branch, Taylor. *Pillar of Fire: America in the King Years, 1963–65*. Simon & Schuster, $30 (0-684-80819-6).

Chernow, Ron. *Titan: The Life of John D. Rockefeller, Sr*. Random, $30 (0-679-43808-4).

Clapp, Nicholas. *The Road to Ubar: Finding the Atlantis of the Sands*. Houghton Mifflin, $24 (0-395-87596-X).

Gorney, Cynthia. *Articles of Faith: A Frontline History of the Abortion Wars*. Simon & Schuster, $27.50 (0-684-80904-4).

Hochschild, Adam. *King Leopold's Ghost: A Story of Greed, Terror, and Heroism in Colonial Africa*. Houghton Mifflin, $26 (0-395-75924-2).

Kinder, Gary. *Ship of Gold in the Deep Blue Sea*. Atlantic Monthly, $27.50 (0-87113-464-0).

Nasar, Sylvia. *A Beautiful Mind*. Simon & Schuster, $25 (0-684-81906-6).

Suskind, Ron. *A Hope in the Unseen: An American Odyssey from the Inner City to the Ivy League*. Broadway, $25 (0-7679-0125-8).

Poetry

Doty, Mark. *Sweet Machine*. HarperFlamingo, paper, $12 (0-06-095256-3).

Hall, Donald. *Without*. Houghton Mifflin, $22 (0-395-88408-X).

Hughes, Ted. *Tales from Ovid*. Farrar, $25 (0-374-22841-8).

Matthews, William. *After All: Last Poems*. Houghton Mifflin, $20 (0-395-91340-3).

Best Books for Young Adults

Each January a committee of the Young Adult Library Services Association, a division of the American Library Association, compiles a list of the best fiction and nonfiction appropriate for young adults ages 12 to 18. Selected on the basis of each book's proven or potential appeal and value to young adults, the titles span a variety of subjects as well as a broad range of reading levels.

Fiction

Abelove, Joan. *Saying It Out Loud*. DK Ink/ Richard Jackson, $15.95 (0-7894-2609-9).

Anderson, Laurie Halse. *Speak*. Farrar, $16 (0-374-37152-0).

Atkins, Catherine. *When Jeff Comes Home*. Putnam, $17.99 (0-399-23366-0).

Barrett, Tracy. *Anna of Byzantium*. Delacorte, $14.95 (0-385-32626-2).

Bat-Ami, Miriam. *Two Suns in the Sky*. Front Street/Cricket, $15.95 (0-8126-2900-0).

Calhoun, Dia. *Firegold*. Winslow, $15.95 (1-890817-10-4).

Carbone, Elisa. *Stealing Freedom*. Knopf. $17 (0-679-89307-5); lib. ed. $18.99 (0-679-99307-X).

Card, Orson Scott. *Ender's Shadow*. Tor; dist. by St. Martin's, $24.95 (0-312-86860-X).

Cart, Michael. *Tomorrowland: Ten Stories About the Future*. Scholastic, $15.95 (0-590-37678-0).

Chbosky, Stephen. *The Perks of Being a Wallflower*. Pocket/MTV, $12 (0-671-02734-4).

Cooper, Susan. *King of Shadows*. Simon & Schuster/Margaret K. McElderry, $16 (0-689-82817-9).

Curtis, Christopher Paul. *Bud, Not Buddy*. Delacorte, $15.95 (0-385-32306-9).

Dessen, Sarah. *Keeping the Moon*. Viking, $15.99 (0-670-88549-5).

Ferris, Jean. *Bad*. Farrar, $16 (0-374-30479-3).

Fleischman, Paul. *Mind's Eye*. Holt, $15.95 (0-8050-06314-5).

Friesen, Gayle. *Janey's Girl*. Kids Can, $14.95 (1-55074-461-5).

Gaiman, Neil. *Stardust*. Avon, $22 (0-380-97728-1).

Gilmore, Kate. *The Exchange Student*. Houghton, $15 (0-395-57511-7).

Haddix, Margaret Peterson. *Just Ella*. Simon & Schuster, $17 (0-689-82186-7).

Hewett, Lorri. *Dancer*. Dutton, $15.99 (0-525-45968-5).

Hobbs, Will. *Jason's Gold*. Morrow, $16 (0-688-15093-4).

Hoffman, Alice. *Local Girls*. Putnam, $22.95 (0-399-14507-9).

Holt, Kimberly Willis. *When Zachary Beaver Came to Town*. Holt, $16.95 (0-8050-6116-9).

Holtwijk, Ineke. *Asphalt Angels*. Front Street, $15.95 (1-886910-24-3).

Holubitsky, Katherine. *Alone at Ninety Foot*. Orca, $14.95 (1-55143-129-7).

Hoobler, Dorothy, and Thomas Hoobler. *The Ghost in the Tokaido Inn*. Putnam/Philomel, $17.99 (0-399-23330-X).

Howe, Norma. *The Adventures of Blue Avenger*. Holt, $16.95 (0-8050-6062-6).

Johnson, Scott. *Safe at Second*. Putnam/ Philomel, $17.99 (0-399-23365-2).

Jordan, Sherryl. *The Raging Quiet*. Simon & Schuster, $17 (0-689-82140-9).

King, Stephen. *The Girl Who Loved Tom Gordon*. Scribner, $16.95 (0-684-86762-1).

Lawrence, Iain. *The Smugglers*. Delacorte, $15.95 (0-385-32663-7).

Levine, Gail Carson. *Dave at Night*. Harper-Collins, $15.95 (0-60-028153-7); lib. ed., $15.89 (0-06-028154-5).

Lubar, David. *Hidden Talents*. Tor; dist. by St. Martin's, $16.95 (0-312-86646-1).

McNamee, Graham. *Hate You*. Delacorte, $14.95 (0-385-32593-2).

McNeal, Laura, and Tom McNeal. *Crooked*. Knopf, $16.95 (0-679-89300-8); lib. ed., $18.99 (0-679-99300-2).

Marchetta, Melina. *Looking for Alibrandi.* Orchard, $17.99 (0-531-33142-3); lib. ed. $17.99 (0-531-33142-3).

Meyer, Carolyn. *Mary, Bloody Mary.* Harcourt, $16 (0-15-201906-5).

Morris, Gerald. *The Squire, His Knight, and His Lady.* Houghton, $15 (0-395-91211-3).

Myers, Walter Dean. *Monster.* Illus. HarperCollins, $15.95 (0-06-028077-8); lib. ed., $15.98 (0-06-028078-6).

Namioka, Lensey. *Ties That Bind, Ties That Break.* Delacorte, $15.95 (0-385-32666-1).

Porter, Connie. *Imani All Mine.* Houghton, $23 (0-395-83808-8).

Powell, Randy. *Tribute to Another Dead Rock Star.* Farrar, $17 (0-374-37748-0).

Qualey, Marsha. *Close to a Killer.* Delacorte, $15.95 (0-385-32597-5).

Randle, Kristen D. *Breaking Rank.* Morrow, $16 (0-688-16243-6).

Rottman, S. L. *Head Above Water.* Peachtree/Freestone, $14.95 (1-56145-185-1).

Rowling, J. K. *Harry Potter and the Chamber of Secrets.* Illus. Scholastic/Arthur A. Levine, $17.95 (0-439-06486-4).

Rowling, J. K. *Harry Potter and the Prisoner of Azkaban.* Illus. Scholastic/Arthur A. Levine, $19.95 (0-439-13635-0).

Savage, Deborah. *Summer Hawk.* Houghton, $16 (0-395-91163-X).

Shusterman, Neal. *Downsiders.* Simon & Schuster, $16.95 (0-689-80375-3).

Skurzynski, Gloria. *Spider's Voice.* Simon & Schuster/Atheneum, $16.95 (0-689-82149-2).

Sones, Sonya. *Stop Pretending: What Happened When My Big Sister Went Crazy.* HarperCollins, $14.95 (0-06-028387-4); lib. ed., $14.89 (0-06-028386-6).

Stanley, Diane. *A Time Apart.* Morrow. $16 (0-688-16997-X).

Thesman, Jean. *The Other Ones.* Viking, $15.99 (0-670-88594-0).

Tomey, Ingrid. *Nobody Else Has to Know.* Delacorte, $15.95 (0-385-32624-6).

Vande Velde, Vivian. *Never Trust a Dead Man.* Harcourt, $17 (0-15-201899-9).

Voigt, Cynthia. *Elske.* Simon & Schuster/Anne Schwartz, $18 (0-689-82472-6).

Whitmore, Arvella. *Trapped Between the Lash and the Gun.* Dial, $16.99 (0-803-72384-9).

Wittlinger, Ellen. *Hard Love.* Simon & Schuster, $16.95 (0-689-82134-4).

Young, Karen Romano. *The Beetle and Me: A Love Story.* Greenwillow, $15 (0-688-15922-2).

Nonfiction

Alexander, Caroline. *The Endurance: Shackleton's Legendary Antarctic Expedition.* Illus. Knopf, $29.95 (0-375-40403-1).

Allison, Anthony. *Hear These Voices: Youth at the Edge of the Millennium.* Illus. Dutton, $22.99 (0-525-45353-9).

Armstrong, Jennifer. *Shipwreck at the Bottom of the World: The Extraordinary True Story of Shackleton and the Endurance.* Illus. Crown, $18 (0-517-80013-6); lib. ed. $19.99 (0-517-80014-4).

Calabro, Marian. *The Perilous Journey of the Donner Party.* Illus. Clarion, $20 (0-395-86610-3).

Dominick, Andie. *Needles.* Scribner, $22 (0-684-84232-7).

Freedman, Russell. *Babe Didrikson Zaharias: The Making of a Champion.* Illus. Clarion, $18 (0-395-63367-2).

Garner, Eleanor Ramrath. *Eleanor's Story: An American Girl in Hitler's Germany.* Peachtree/Freestone, $14.95 (1-56145-193-2).

Gaskins, Pearl Fuyo, ed. *What Are You? Voices of Mixed-Race Young People.* Illus. Holt, $18.95 (0-8050-5968-7).

Gourley, Catherine. *Good Girl Work: Factories, Sweatshops, and How Women Changed Their Role in the Workforce.* Illus. Millbrook, $23.40 (0-7613-0951-9).

Hickam, Homer H. *Rocket Boys: A Memoir.* Delacorte, $23.95 (0-385-33320-X); paper, $12.95 (0-385-33321-8).

Jennings, Peter, and Todd Brewster. *The Century for Young People.* Illus. Doubleday. $29.95 (0-385-32708-0).

Kalergis, Mary Motley. *Seen and Heard: Teenagers Talk About Their Lives.* Illus. Stewart, Tabori & Chang, $24.95 (1-5567-0834-3).

Krizmanic, Judy. *Teen's Vegetarian Cookbook.* Viking, $15.99 (0-670-87426-4).

Kuhn, Betsy. *Angels of Mercy: The Army Nurses of World War II*. Illus. Simon & Schuster/Atheneum, $18 (0-689-82044-5).

Mah, Adeline Yen. *Chinese Cinderella: The True Story of an Unwanted Daughter*. Delacorte, $16.95 (0-385-32707-2).

Marrin, Albert. *Terror of the Spanish Main*. Illus. Dutton, $19.99 (0-525-45942-1).

Mattison, Chris. *Snake*. Illus. DK, $29.95 (0-7894-4660-X).

Maurer, Richard. *The Wild Colorado: The True Adventures of Fred Dellenbaugh, Age 17, on the Second Powell Expedition into the Grand Canyon*. Illus. Crown, $19.99 (0-517-70946-5).

Nye, Naomi Shihab. *What Have You Lost?* Illus. Greenwillow, $19 (0-688-16184-7).

Okutoro, Lydia Omolola. *Quiet Storm: Voices of Young Black Poets*. Hyperion/Jump at the Sun, $16.99 (0-786-80461-0).

Opdyke, Irene Gut. *In My Hands: Memories of a Holocaust Rescuer*. Knopf, $18 (0-679-89181-1).

Partridge, Elizabeth. *Restless Spirit: The Life and Work of Dorothea Lange*. Illus. Viking, $21.99 (0-670-87888-X).

Reich, Susanna. *Clara Schumann: Piano Virtuoso*. Illus. Clarion, $18 (0-395-89119-1).

Rubin, Susan Goldman. *Margaret Bourke-White: Her Pictures Were Her Life*. Illus. Abrams, $19.95 (0-8109-4381-6).

Schmidt, Thomas, and Jeremy Schmidt. *The Saga of Lewis & Clark: Into the Uncharted West*. Illus. DK, $35 (0-7894-4638-3).

Schwager, Tina, and Michele Schuerger. *Gutsy Girls: Young Women Who Dare*. Illus. Free Spirit, $14.95 (1-575-42059-7).

Quick Picks for Reluctant Young Adult Readers

The Young Adult Library Services Association, a division of the American Library Association, annually chooses a list of outstanding titles that will stimulate the interest of reluctant teen readers. This list is intended to attract teens who, for whatever reason, choose not to read.

Fiction

Anderson, Laurie. *Speak*. Farrar, $16 (0-374-37152-0).

Applegate, K. A. *EverWorld, Books 1-4*. Scholastic. *Search for Senna*. Book 1, paper, $4.99 (0-590-87743-7); *Land of Loss*. Book 2, paper, $4.99 (0-590-87751-8); *Enter the Enchanted*. Book 3, paper, $4.99 (0-590-87754-2); *Realm of the Reaper*. Book 4, paper, $4.99 (0-590-88760-7).

Atwater-Rhodes, Amelia. *In the Forests of the Night*. Delacorte, $8.95 (0-385-32674-2).

Avi. *Midnight Magic*. Scholastic, $15.95 (0-590-36035-3).

Bennett, Cherie. *The Haunted Heart*. Avon/Flare, paper, $4.50 (0-380-80123-X).

Block, Francesca Lia. *Violet & Claire*. HarperCollins, $14.95 (0-06-027749-1).

Bunting, Eve. *Blackwater*. HarperCollins, $15.95 (0-06-027838-2).

Cadnum, Michael. *Rundown*. Viking, $15.99 (0-670-88377-8).

Cart, Michael, ed. *Tomorrowland: Ten Stories About the Future*. Scholastic, $15.95 (0-590-37678-0).

Chbosky, Stephen. *The Perks of Being a Wallflower*. Pocket/MTV, paper, $12 (0-671-02734-4).

Cooney, Caroline. *Burning Up*. Delacorte, $15.95 (0-385-32318-2).

Cooney, Caroline. *Hush, Little Baby*. Scholastic, paper, $4.99 (0-590-81974-7).

Dressen, Sarah. *Keeping the Moon*. Viking, $15.99 (0-670-88549-5).

Gilmore, Kate. *The Exchange Student*. Houghton, $15 (0-395-57511-7).

Glenn, Mel. *Foreign Exchange: A Mystery in Poems*. Morrow, $16 (0-688-16472-2).

Haddix, Margaret Peterson. *Among the Hidden.* Simon & Schuster, $16 (0-689-81700-2); paper, $4.50 (0-689-82475-0).

Haddix, Margaret Peterson. *Just Ella.* Simon & Schuster, $17 (0-689-82186-7).

Hobbs, Will. *Jason's Gold.* Morrow, $16 (0-688-15093-4).

Johnson, Scott. *Safe at Second.* Putnam/Philomel, $17.99 (0-399-23365-2).

Kehret, Peg. *I'm Not Who You Think I Am.* Dutton, $15.99 (0-525-46153-1).

Kimmel, Eric A. *Sword of the Samurai.* Harcourt/Browndeer, $15 (0-152-01985-5).

Lawrence, Iain. *The Smugglers.* Delacorte, $15.95 (0-385-32663-7).

Lubar, David. *Hidden Talents.* Tor, $16.95 (0-312-86646-1).

McDaniel, Lurlene. *The Girl Death Left Behind.* Dell/Starfire, paper, $4.50 (0-553-57091-9).

McNamee, Graham. *Hate You.* Delacorte, $14.95 (0-385-32593-2).

Myers, Walter Dean. *Monster.* Illus. HarperCollins, $15.95 (0-060-28077-8); lib. ed., $15.89 (0-06-028078-6).

Neufield, John. *Boys Lie.* DK Ink, $16.95 (0-789-42624-2).

Nixon, Joan Lowery. *Who Are You?* Delacorte, $15.95 (0-385-32566-5).

Paulsen, Gary. *Brian's Return.* Delacorte, $15.95 (0-385-32500-2).

Peel, John. *Doomsday.* Scholastic, paper, $4.99 (0-439-06030-3).

Qualey, Marsha. *Close to a Killer.* Delacorte, $15.95 (0-385-32597-5).

Scalora, Suza. *Fairies: The Photographic Evidence of the Existence of Another World.* Illus. HarperCollins, $19.95 (0-06-028234-7).

Sheldon, Dyan. *Confessions of a Teenage Drama Queen.* Candlewick, $16.99 (0-7636-0822-X).

Shusterman, Neal. *Downsiders.* Simon & Schuster, $16 (0-689-80375-3).

Sleator, William. *Boltzmon!* Dutton, $15.99 (0-525-46131-0).

Sleator, William. *Rewind.* Dutton, $14.99 (0-525-46130-2).

Sones, Sonya. *Stop Pretending.* HarperCollins, $14.95 (0-06-028387-4).

Tezuka, Osamu. *Black Jack, Vol. 1.* Viz Comics, paper, $15.95 (1-56931-316-4).

Thompson, Kate. *Midnight's Choice.* Hyperion, $15.99 (0-7868-0381-9); lib. ed., $16.49 (0-7868-2329-1); paper, $5.99 (0-7868-1266-4).

Tomey, Ingrid. *Nobody Else Has to Know.* Delacorte, $15.95 (0-385-32624-6).

Velda, Vivian Vande. *Never Trust a Dead Man.* Harcourt, $17 (0-152-01899-9).

Wittlinger, Ellen. *Hard Love.* Simon & Schuster, $17 (0-689-82134-4).

Zindel, Paul. *Rats.* Hyperion, $15.99 (0-7868-0339-8).

Nonfiction

Bell, Janet Chatham, and Lucille Usher Freeman, eds. *Stretch Your Wings: Famous Black Quotations for Teens.* Little, Brown, paper, $8.95 (0-316-03825-3).

Bell, Karen Magnuson. *Fire in Their Eyes: Wildfires and the People Who Fight Them.* Illus. Harcourt, $18 (0-15-201043-2); paper, $10 (0-15-201042-4).

Best Shots: The Greatest NFL Photography of the Century. Illus. DK, $30 (0-7894-4639-1).

Brewster, Hugh, and Laurie Coulter. *882 1/2 Amazing Answers to Your Questions About the Titanic.* Illus. Scholastic, $16.95 (0-590-18730-9).

Brooke, Michael. *The Concrete Wave: The History of Skateboarding.* Illus. Warwick, paper, $19.95 (1-894020-54-5).

Burgess-Wise, David. *The Ultimate Race Car.* Illus. DK, $29.95 (0-7894-4182-9).

Daldry, Jeremy. *The Teenage Guy's Survival Guide: The Read Deal on Girls, Growing Up, and Other Guy Stuff.* Illus. Little, Brown, paper, $8.95 (0-316-17824-1).

Dee, Catherine, ed. *The Girl's Book of Wisdom.* Illus. Little, Brown, paper, $8.95 (0-316-17956-6).

Fletcher, Ralph. *Relatively Speaking: Poems About Family.* Illus. Orchard, $14.95 (0-531-30141-9); lib. ed., $15.99 (0-531-33141-5).

Holt, David, and Bill Mooney. *Spiders in the Hairdo: Modern Urban Legends.* Illus. August House, paper, $7.95 (0-87483-525-9).

Jenkins, Steve. *Top of the World: Climbing Mount Everest.* Illus. Houghton, $15 (0-395-94218-7).

Jennings, Peter, and Todd Brewster. *The Century for Young People.* Illus. Doubleday, $29.95 (0-385-32708-0).

Jordan, Michael. *For the Love of the Game: My Story.* 1998. Illus. Crown, $50 (0-609-60206-3).

Kalergis, Mary Motley, ed. *Seen and Heard: Teenagers Talk About Their Lives.* Illus. Stewart Tabori & Chang, $24.95 (1-55670-834-3).

Kimmel, Elizabeth Cody. *Ice Story: Shackelton's Lost Expedition.* Illus. Clarion, $18 (0-395-91524-4).

Lord, Trevor. *Big Book of Cars.* Illus. DK, $14.95 (0-7894-4738-X).

Macy, Sue, and Jane Gottesman. *Play Like a Girl: A Celebration of Women in Sports.* Illus. Holt, $15.95 (0-8050-6071-5).

Menzel, Peter, and Faith D'Alusio. *Man Eating Bugs: The Art and Science of Eating Insects.* Illus. Ten Speed, $24.95 (1-58007-051-0); paper, $19.95 (1-58008-022-7).

Meserole, Mike. *Ultimate Sports Lists.* Illus. DK, paper, $17.95 (0-7894-3562-4).

Mitton, Jacqueline. *Informania: Aliens.* Illus. Candlewick, $15.99 (0-7636-0492-5); paper, $7.99 (0-7636-1042-9).

Okutoro, Lydia Omolola, ed. *Quiet Storm: Voices of Young Black Poets.* Hyperion/ Jump at the Sun, $16.99 (0-7868-0461-0).

Oldershaw, Cally. *3-D Rocks and Minerals.* Illus. DK, $16.95 (0-7894-4280-9).

Pierson, Stephanie. *Vegetables Rock! A Complete Guide for Teenage Vegetarians.* Ill-us. Bantam, paper, $12.95 (0-553-37924-0).

Pinsky, Drew, and Adam Carolla. *Dr. Drew and Adam Book: A Survival Guide to Life and Love.* Dell, paper, $14.95 (0-440-50836-3).

Real Teens: Diary of a Junior Year. Scholastic, paper, $4.99 (0-439-08408-3).

Reisfeld, Randi, and Marie Morreale. *Got Issues Much?* Scholastic, paper, $5.99 (0-590-63274-4).

Reynolds, David West. *Star Wars Episode 1: The Visual Dictionary.* Illus. DK, $19.95 (0-7894-4701-0).

Reynolds, David West. *Star Wars Episode I: Incredible Cross-Sections.* Illus. DK, $19.95 (0-7894-3962-X).

Schwager, Tina, and Michele Schuerger. *Gutsy Girls: Young Women Who Dare.* Free Spirit, $14.95 (1-57542-059-7).

Scott, Jerry, and Jim Borgman. *Growth Spurt: Zits Sketchbook 2.* Andrews and McMeel, paper, $9.95 (0-8362-7848-8).

Smith, Charles R. *Rimshots: Basketball Pix, Rolls, and Rhythms.* Dutton, $15.99 (0-525-46099-3).

Stewart, Mark. *Derek Jeter: Substance and Style.* Millbrook/21st Century Books, lib. ed., $22.90 (0-7613-1516-0); paper, $6.95 (0-7613-1039-8).

Tanaka, Shelley. *Secrets of the Mummies: Uncovering the Bodies of Ancient Egyptians.* Illus. Hyperion, $16.99 (0-7868-0473-4).

Vankin, Jonathan. *Big Book of Grimm.* Illus. DC Comics, paper, $14.95 (1-56389-501-3).

Wong, Janet S. *Behind the Wheel: Poems About Driving.* Simon & Schuster/Margaret K. McElderry, $16 (0-689-82531-5).

Notable Children's Books

A list of notable children's books is selected each year by the Notable Children's Books Committee of the Association for Library Service to Children, a division of the American Library Association. Recommended titles are selected by children's librarians and educators based on originality, creativity, and suitability for children. [See "Literary Prizes, 1999" later in Part 5 for Caldecott, Newbery, and other award winners.—*Ed.*]. ISBNs follow the publisher name.

Books for Younger Readers

Andersen, Hans Christian. *Ugly Duckling.* Illustrated by Jerry Pinkney. Morrow (0-688-15932-X).

Bang, Molly. *When Sophie Gets Angry— Really, Really Angry . . .* Scholastic/Blue Sky Press (0-590-18979-4).

Best, Cari. *Three Cheers for Catherine the Great!* Illustrated by Giselle Potter. DK INK (0-7894-2622-6).

Charlip, Remy. *Sleepytime Rhyme.* Greenwillow (0-688-16271-1).

Christelow, Eileen. *What Do Illustrators Do?* Clarion (0-395-90230-4).

Cowley, Joy. *Red-Eyed Tree Frog.* Photographs by Nic Bishop. Scholastic (0-590-87175-7).

Daly, Niki. *Jamela's Dress.* Farrar, Straus & Giroux (0-374-33667-9).

DePaola, Tomie. *26 Fairmount Avenue.* Putnam (0-399-23246-X).

Diakite, Baba Wague. *Hatseller and the Monkeys.* Scholastic (0-590-96069-5).

Feiffer, Jules. *Bark, George.* HarperCollins/ Michael di Capua Books (0-06-205185-7).

George, Kristine O'Connell. *Little Dog Poems.* Illustrated by June Otani. Clarion (0-395-82266-1).

Hush, Little Baby. Illustrated by Marla Frazee. Harcourt Brace/Browndeer Press (0-15-201429-2).

Lester, Helen. *Hooway for Wodney Wat.* Illustrated by Lynn Munsinger. Houghton Mifflin/Walter Lorraine Books (0-395-92392-1).

Lum, Kate. *What! Cried Granny: An Almost Bedtime Story.* Illustrated by Adrian Johnson. Dial (0-803-72382-2).

Marcellino, Fred. *I, Crocodile.* HarperCollins/Michael di Capua Books (0-06-205168-7).

Mollel, Tololwa M. *My Rows and Piles of Coins.* Illustrated by E. B. Lewis. Clarion (0-395-75186-1).

Morimoto, Junko. *Two Bullies.* Crown (0-517-80061-6).

Opie, Iona. *Here Comes Mother Goose.* Illustrated by Rosemary Wells. Candlewick (0-7636-0683-9).

Priceman, Marjorie. *Emeline at the Circus.* Knopf (0-679-87685-5).

Rodowsky, Colby. *Not My Dog.* Farrar, Straus & Giroux (0-374-35531-2).

Sierra, Judy. *Tasty Baby Belly Buttons.* Illustrated by Meilo So. Knopf (0-679-89369-5).

Sis, Peter. *Trucks, Trucks, Trucks.* Greenwillow (0-688-16276-2).

Stanley, Diane. *Raising Sweetness.* Illustrated by G. Brian Karas. Putnam (0-399-23225-7).

Taback, Simms. *Joseph Had a Little Overcoat.* Viking (0-670-87855-3).

Updike, John. *A Child's Calendar.* Illustrated by Trina Schart Hyman. Holiday House (0-8234-1448-0).

Ward, Helen. *Hare and the Tortoise.* Millbrook (0-7613-0988-8).

Wiesner, David. *Sector 7.* Clarion (0-395-74656-6).

Zimmerman, Andrea, and David Clemesha. *Trashy Town.* Illustrated by Dan Yaccarino. HarperCollins (0-06-027139-6).

Books for Middle Readers

Carroll, Lewis. *Alice's Adventures in Wonderland.* Illustrated by Helen Oxenbury. Candlewick (0-7636-0804-1).

Coy, John. *Strong to the Hoop.* Illustrated by Leslie Jean-Bart. Lee & Low (1-880000-80-6).

Curtis, Christopher Paul. *Bud, Not Buddy.* Delacorte (0-385-32306-9).

English, Karen. *Francie*. Farrar, Straus & Giroux (0-374-32456-5).

Erdrich, Louise. *Birchbark House*. Hyperion (0-786-80300-2).

Fleischman, Paul. *Weslandia*. Illustrated by Kevin Hawkes. Candlewick (0-7636-0006-7).

Hamanaka, Sheila, and Ayano Ohmi. *In Search of the Spirit: The Living National Treasures of Japan*. Morrow (0-688-14607-4).

Harris, Robie H. *It's So Amazing: A Book About Eggs, Sperm, Birth, Babies and Families*. Illustrated by Michael Emberley. Candlewick (0-7636-0051-2).

Holm, Jennifer L. *Our Only May Amelia*. HarperCollins (0-06-027822-6).

Hopkinson, Deborah. *Band of Angels*. Illustrated by Raul Colon. Atheneum/An Anne Schwartz Book (0-689-81062-8).

Horvath, Polly. *Trolls*. Farrar, Straus & Giroux (0-374-37787-1).

Jenkins, Steve. *Top of the World: Climbing Mount Everest*. Houghton Mifflin (0-395-94218-7).

Karr, Kathleen. *Man of the Family*. Farrar, Straus & Giroux (0-374-34764-6).

Katzen, Mollie. *Honest Pretzels and 64 Other Amazing Recipes for Cooks Ages 8 & Up*. Tricycle Press (1-883672-88-0).

Lewin, Ted and Betsy. *Gorilla Walk*. Lothrop, Lee & Shepard (0-688-16509-5).

Lisle, Janet Taylor. *Lost Flower Children*. Philomel (0-399-23393-8).

McGill, Alice. *Molly Bannaky*. Illustrated by Chris K. Soentpiet. Houghton Mifflin (0-395-72287-X).

Myers, Christopher. *Black Cat*. Scholastic (0-590-03375-1).

O'Connor, Barbara. *Me and Rupert Goody*. Farrar, Straus & Giroux/Frances Foster (0-374-34904-5).

Rocklin, Joanne. *Strudel Stories*. Delacorte (0-385-32602-5).

Ryan, Pam Munoz. *Amelia and Eleanor Go for a Ride*. Illustrated by Brian Selznick. Scholastic. (0-590-96075-X).

Say, Allen. *Tea with Milk*. Houghton Mifflin/Walter Lorraine Books (0-395-90495-1).

Smith, Charles R., Jr. *Rimshots: Basketball Pix, Rolls and Rhythms*. Dutton (0-525-46099-3).

Stevenson, James. *Candy Corn*. Greenwillow (0-688-15837-4).

Books for Older Readers

Almond, David. *Skellig*. Delacorte (0-385-32653-X).

Billingsley, Franny. *Folk Keeper*. Atheneum/Jean Karl (0-689-82876-4).

Calabro, Marian. *Perilous Journey of the Donner Party*. Clarion (0-395-86610-3).

Carter, David A., and James Diaz. *Elements of Pop-Up*. Simon & Schuster (0-689-82224-3).

Couloumbis, Audrey. *Getting Near to Baby*. Putnam (0-399-23389-X).

Freedman, Russell. *Babe Didrikson Zaharias: The Making of a Champion*. Clarion (0-395-63367-2).

Goldin, Barbara Diamond. *Journeys with Elijah: Eight Tales of the Prophet*. Illustrated by Jerry Pinkney. Harcourt Brace/Gulliver Books (0-15-200445-9).

Holt, Kimberly Willis. *When Zachary Beaver Came to Town*. Henry Holt (0-8050-6116-9).

Levine, Gail Carson. *Dave at Night*. HarperCollins (0-06-028153-7).

Perkins, Lynne Rae. *All Alone in the Universe*. Greenwillow (0-688-16881-7).

Reich, Susanna. *Clara Schumann: Piano Virtuoso*. Clarion (0-395-89119-1).

Books for All Ages

Aliki. *William Shakespeare and the Globe*. HarperCollins (0-06-027820-X).

Bridges, Ruby. *Through My Eyes*. Scholastic (0-590-18923-9).

Dunbar, Paul Laurence. *Jump Back, Honey*. Illustrated by Ashley Bryan, Carole Byard, Jan Spivey Gilchrist, Brian Pinkney, Jerry Pinkney, Faith Ringgold. Hyperion/Jump at the Sun (0-786-80464-5).

Lunge-Larsen, Lise. *Troll with No Heart in His Body and Other Tales of Trolls, from Norway*. Illustrated by Betsy Bowen. Houghton Mifflin (0-395-91371-3).

Rowlings, J. K. *Harry Potter and the Chamber of Secrets*. Scholastic (0-439-06486-4).

Rowlings, J. K. *Harry Potter and the Prisoner of Azkaban*. Scholastic (0-439-13635-0).

Sandburg, Carl. *Huckabuck Family and How They Raised Popcorn in Nebraska and Quit and Came Back*. Illustrated by David Small. Farrar, Straus & Giroux (0-374-33511-7).

Notable Recordings for Children

This list of notable recordings for children was selected by the Association for Library Service to Children, a division of the American Library Association. Recommended titles, many of which are recorded books, are chosen by children's librarians and educators on the basis of their originality, creativity, and suitability.

"The Big Bug Book." Performed by Nelson Runger. 45 min. Book and cassette (40871): $24.20. Recorded Books, Inc.

"Classical Child at the Opera." Performed by various artists. 47 min. Cassette (CC106): $9.95. CD (CC106D): $15.95. Metro Music.

"Colonial Fair." Performed by Dean Shostak & Friends. 56 min. Cassette (014149): $10.00. CD (014125): $15.00. Coastline Music.

"The Dark Is Rising." Performed by Alex Jennings. 8 hours, 40 min. 6 cassettes (YA 990CX): $37.98. Listening Library, an imprint of the Random House Audio Publishing Group.

"The Golden Compass." Performed by full cast production. 10 hours, 40 min. 8 cassettes (YA991CX): $50. Listening Library.

"Harriet the Spy." Performed by Anne Bobby. 7 hours. 4 cassettes (YA993CX): $29.98. Listening Library.

"Harriet Tubman: Conductor on the Underground Railroad." Performed by Peter Francis James. 6 hours, 30 min. 5 cassettes (95753): $46.00. Recorded Books, Inc.

"Harry Potter and the Chamber of Secrets." Performed by Jim Dale. 9 hours. 6 cassettes (YA 137 CXR): $34.00. CD (YA 137CD): $49.95. Listening Library.

"Harry Potter and the Sorcerer's Stone." Performed by Jim Dale. 8 hours, 17 min. 6 cassettes (YA 108): $37.98. Listening Library.

"Holes." Performed by Kerry Beyer. 4 hours, 30 min. 3 cassettes (YA994CX): $23.98. Listening Library.

"Hoot Owl Blues: Tales and Tunes to Conjure Up a Mood." Performed by Jeslyn and Ben Wheeless. 56 min. Cassette: $8.99. CD: $12.99. Jeslyn Wheeless.

"Joey Pigza Swallowed the Key." Performed by Jack Gantos. 2 hours, 58 min. 2 cassettes (YA 120CX): $18. Listening Library.

"Just a Few Words, Mr. Lincoln." Performed by Rex Robbins. 20 min. Book and cassette (MPRA 428): $12.95. Weston Woods Studios, Inc.

"Love From Your Friend, Hannah." Performed by six actors. 4 hours, 25 min. 4 cassettes (YA 996 CX): $29.98. Listening Library.

"Mary Poppins." Performed by Sophie Thompson. 3 hours, 49 min. 3 cassettes (YA997 CX): $23.98. Listening Library.

"The Merman." Performed by June Whitfield. 1 hour, 32 min. 2 cassettes (YA112 CX): $18. Listening Library.

"Meteor!" Performed by Patricia Polacco. 13 min. Book and cassette (6857): $16.95. Spoken Arts.

"My Louisiana Sky." Performed by Judith Ivey. 4 hours. 3 cassettes (BDDAD1015): $24.00. Listening Library.

"On the Good Ship Lollipop." Performed by the Persuasions. 45 min. Cassette (R475794): $9.98. CD (R275794): $15.98. Music for Little People.

"A Pizza the Size of the Sun." Performed by Jack Prelutsky. 54 min. Cassette (FTR205CX): $11. CD (FTR205CD): $14.95. Listening Library.

"Ramona's World." Performed by Stockard Channing. 3 hours. 2 cassettes (YA123CX): $18. Listening Library.

"Rikki-Tikki-Tavi." Performed by Michael York. 30 min. Book and cassette (MHRA385): $24.95. Weston Woods Studios, Inc.

"Sparrows in the Scullery." Performed by Steven Crossley. 5 hours, 30 min. 4 cassettes (95913): $37.00. Recorded Books, Inc.

"Strega Nona." Performed by John McDonough. 15 min. Cassette (95626): $11.00 Recorded Books, Inc.

"Thank You, Mr. Falker." Performed by Patricia Polacco. 18 min. Book and cassette (6854): $27.95. Spoken Arts.

"This Land Is Your Land." Performed by Arlo Guthrie, Nora Guthrie. 12 minutes. Book and cassette (MHRA 388): $24.95. Weston Woods Studios, Inc.

"The Wheel on the School." Performed by Anne T. Flosnik. 6 hours, 20 min. 4 cassettes (YA 104CX): $29.98. Listening Library.

"World Playground: A Musical Adventure for Kids." Performed by various artists. 40 min. Cassette (PUTU154-4): $10.98. CD (PUTU154-2): $15.98. Putumayo World Music.

"Zin! Zin! Zin! A Violin." Performed by Maureen Anderman. 9 min. Cassette (LHBC386): $24.95. Weston Woods Studios, Inc.

Notable Children's Videos

These titles are selected by a committee of the Association for Library Service to Children, a division of the American Library Association. Recommendations are based on originality, creativity, and suitability for young children. The members select materials that respect both children's intelligence and imagination, exhibit venturesome creativity, and encourage the interests of users.

Banjo Frogs. 5 min. Produced by the Australian Broadcasting Corp. Natural History Unit. Distributed by Bullfrog Films. 1998. Clay animation. All ages. $95.

Chato's Kitchen. 11 min. Produced by Weston Woods, distributed by Scholastic. Iconographic. 1999. ISBN 0-78820-710-5. Ages 5–10. $60.

Chato's Kitchen. (Spanish-language version) 11 min. Produced by Weston Woods, distributed by Scholastic. Iconographic. Spanish narration by Jorge Pupo. 1999. ISBN 0-78820-224-3. Ages 5–10. $60.

Chicka Chicka Boom Boom. 6 min. Produced by Weston Woods, distributed by Scholastic. 1999. ISBN 0-78820-722-9. Animation. Ages 3–8. $60.

Dear America: Dreams in the Golden Country. 29 min. Produced by Scholastic. Live action. 1999. Ages 8–14. $12.95.

Degas and the Dancer. 60 min. Produced by Devine Entertainment. ISBN 1-894-449-06-1. Live action. Ages 9 and up. $19.95.

The Face. 22 min. Produced by New Dimension Media, Inc. Live action and computer animation. Ages 7 and up. $159.

Famous Fred. 30 min. Produced by TVC London, manufactured by Sony Wonder. ISBN 0-7389-2547-9. Animated. All ages. $12.98.

Fedora. 28 min. Produced by Alta Films. Live action. Ages 10 and up. ISBN 1-892-442-05-1. $12.95.

Just a Few Words, Mr. Lincoln: The Story of the Gettysburg Address. 18 min. Produced by Weston Woods, distributed by Scholastic. Iconographic. 1999. Ages 6 and up. ISBN 0-78820-744-X. $39.95.

Ludovic: The Snow Gift. 14 min. Produced by National Film Board of Canada. Ages 3–6. Stop action animation. $129.

Magic for Beginners, Vol. 2. Produced by Jobeto, distributed by Brian Richards Entertainment. 1999. Live action. Ages 8 and up. $19.95.

Marie Curie: More Than Meets the Eye. 54 min. Produced by Devine Entertainment. 1998. Live action. Ages 8 and up. $19.95.

Miss Nelson Has a Field Day. 13 min. Produced by Weston Woods, distributed by Scholastic. 1999. Animated. Ages 5–10. ISBN 0-78820-720-2. $60.

Snow Cat. 23 min. Produced by Snow Cat Productions and the National Film Board of Canada. 1999. Finger-paint animation. Ages 5–10.

Notable Software and Web Sites for Children

These lists are chosen by committees of the Association for Library Service to Children, a division of the American Library Association.

Software

Software is selected on the basis of its originality, creativity, and suitability for young children. The members select materials that respect both children's intelligence and imagination, exhibit venturesome creativity, and encourage the interests of users.

Encarta Africana 2000. Microsoft Inc. Windows 95/98. One disk. $69.95.

Encarta Interactive World Atlas 2000. Microsoft Inc. Windows 95/98. One disk and an installation and resources disk. $54.

The Magic School Bus Explores the World of Animals. Microsoft Inc. Windows 95/98. One disk. $19.95. Ages 6–10.

Mind Twister Math. Edmark. Windows 95/98 or PowerPC or better with System 7.1.2 or higher. One disk. Consumer version $29.95; school version (2 CDs) $49.95. Grades 3 and 4.

Music Ace 2. Harmonic Vision. Windows 95/98 or Macintosh 33 Mhz or higher with System 7.5 or higher. One disk. $49.95; school version $79.95. Ages 8–adult.

Virtual Labs: Electricity. Edmark. Windows 95/98 or PowerPC or better with System System 7.0.1 or higher. One disk. $79.95. Grades 6–12.

Web Sites

Notable Web sites for children up to age 14 are those considered outstanding in both content and conception, which reflect and encourage young people's interests in exemplary ways.

Ben's Guide to US Government for Kids
http://bensguide.gpo.gov

Black Voices: Martin Luther King Jr.
http://blackvoices.com/feature/mlk_98/

BookHive: Public Library of Charlotte and Mecklenburg Co.
http://www.bookhive.org

Brooklyn Expedition: Latin America
http://www.brooklynexpedition.org/latin/gateway2.html

Discovering Dinosaurs (Encyclopedia Britannica)
http://dinosaurs.eb.com

Exploratorium
http://www.exploratorium.edu

Figure This! Math Challenges for Families
http://www.figurethis.org

Howard Hughes Medical Institute: Cool Science for Curious Kids
http://www.hhmi.org/science/

Inside the Animal Mind (Nature)
http://wnet.org/nature/animalm

Mineral and Gemstone Kingdom
http://www.minerals.net

Peter Rabbit Homepage (Frederick Warne/PenguinPutnam)
http://www.peterrabbit.co.uk

Savage Earth (PBS)
http://www.pbs.org/wnet/savageearth/

Travel to Oriland
http://library.thinkquest.org/27152/

Underground Railroad (National Geographic)
http://www.nationalgeographic.com/features/99/railroad/

Literary Prizes, 1999

Gary Ink
Research Librarian, *Publishers Weekly*

ABBY Awards. To honor titles that members have most enjoyed handselling in the past year. *Offered by:* American Booksellers Association. *Winners:* (adult) Rebecca Wells for *Divine Secrets of the Ya-Ya Sisterhood* (HarperPerennial); (children's) J. K. Rowling for *Harry Potter and the Sorcerer's Stone* (Scholastic).

J. R. Ackerley Award (United Kingdom). For autobiography. *Offered by:* PEN UK. *Winner:* Margaret Forster for *Precious Lives* (Chatto).

Ambassador Book Awards. To recognize books that have made an exceptional contribution to the interpretation of life and culture in the United States. *Offered by:* English-Speaking Union. *Winners:* Philip Roth for *I Married a Communist* (Houghton Mifflin); Robert Penn Warren for *The Collected Poems of Robert Penn Warren* (Louisiana State Univ.).

American Academy of Arts and Letters Awards in Literature. *Offered by:* American Academy of Arts and Letters. *Winners:* (poetry) Ron Padgett, Sherod Santos, C. K. Williams; (fiction) Edmund Keeley, Susanna Moore, Richard Price, Lee Smith.

Mildred L. Batchelder Award. For an American publisher of a children's book originally published in a foreign language in a foreign country, and subsequently published in English in the United States. *Offered by:* American Library Association, Association for Library Service to Children. *Winner:* Dial Books for Young Readers for *Thanks to My Mother* by Schoschana Rabinovici.

James Beard Awards. For cookbooks. *Offered by:* James Beard Foundation. Winners: (best book by a chef) Jean-Georges Vongerichten with Mark Bittman for *Jean-Georges: Cooking at Home with a Four-Star Chef* (Broadway Books); (best general cookbook) Mark Bittman for *How to Cook Everything* (Macmillan); (cookbook of the year) Joseph E. Dabney for *Smokehouse Ham, Spoonbread and Scuppernong Wine* (Cumberland House); (food photography) Charlie Trotter, with photography by Tim Turner, for *Charlie Trotter's Desserts* (Ten Speed Press); (Americana) Colman Andrews and Dorothy Kalins for *Saveur Cooks* (Chronicle Books); (baking and desserts) Pierre Herme and Dorie Greenspan for *Desserts by Pierre Herme* (Little, Brown); (entertaining) Nathalie Dupree for *Nathalie Dupree's Comfortable Entertaining* (Penguin Putnam); (healthy focus) Steven Raichlen for *Steven Raichlen's Healthy Latin Cooking* (Rodale); (international) Paula Wolfert for *Mediterranean Grains and Greens* (HarperCollins); (reference) Peter Menzel and Faith D'Aluisio for *Man Eating Bugs* (Ten Speed Press); (single subject) Janie Hibler for *Wild About Game* (Broadway Books); (vegetables and vegetarian) James Peterson for *Vegetables* (Morrow); (wine) Dewey Markham, Jr., for *A History of the Bordeaux Classification* (Wiley).

Before Columbus Foundation American Book Awards. For literary achievement by people of various ethnic backgrounds. *Offered by:* Before Columbus Foundation. *Winners:* (fiction) Edwidge Danticat for *The Farming of Bones* (Soho Press); Trey Ellis for *Right Here, Right Now* (Simon & Schuster); James D. Houston for *The Last Paradise* (Univ. of Oklahoma); Anna Linzer for *Ghost Dancing* (Picador USA); Alice McDermott for *Charming Billy* (Farrar, Straus & Giroux); Speer Morgan for *The Freshour Cylinders* (MacMurray & Beck); Gloria Naylor for *The Men of Brewster Place* (Hyperion); Josip Novakovich for *Salvation and Other Disasters* (Graywolf Press); Gioia Timpanelli for *Sometimes the Soul* (Norton); E. Donald Two-Rivers for *Survivor's Medicine* (Univ. of Oklahoma); (creative nonfiction) Luis Alberto Urrea for *Nobody's Son* (Univ. of Arizona); (editor/publisher award) Bobby and Lee Byrd, Robert Hawley; (lifetime achievement) Lawrence Ferlinghetti.

Curtis Benjamin Award for Creative Publishing. *Offered by:* Association of American Publishers. *Winner:* Martin Levin.

Helen B. Bernstein Award for Excellence in Journalism. *Offered by:* New York Public Library. *Winner:* Philip Gourevitch for *We Wish to Inform You that Tomorrow We Will Be Killed with Our Families* (Farrar, Straus & Giroux).

James Tait Black Memorial Prizes (United Kingdom). For the best biography and the best novel of the year. *Offered by:* University of Edinburgh. *Winners:* (biography) Peter Ackroyd for *The Life of Thomas More* (Chatto); (fiction) Beryl Bainbridge for *Master Georgie* (Duckworth).

Bollingen Prize in Poetry. To a living U.S. poet for the best collection published in the previous two years, or for lifetime achievement in poetry. *Offered by:* Yale University. *Winner:* Robert Creeley.

Booker Prize for Fiction (United Kingdom). For the best novel written in English by a Commonwealth author. *Offered by:* Book Trust and Booker PLC. *Winner:* J. M. Coetzee for *Disgrace* (Viking).

Boston Globe-Horn Book Awards. For excellence in children's literature. *Offered by:* *Boston Globe* and *Horn Book Magazine.* *Winners:* (fiction) Louis Sachar for *Holes* (Farrar, Straus & Giroux); (nonfiction) Steve Jenkins for *The Top of the World* (Houghton Mifflin); (picture book) Joy Cowley for *Red-Eyed Tree Frog* illus. by Nic Bishop (Scholastic); (special citation) Peter Sis for *Tibet: Through the Red Box* (Farrar, Straus & Giroux).

Michael Braude Award for Light Verse. *Offered by:* American Academy of Arts and Letters. *Winner:* Thomas M. Disch for *A Child's Garden of Grammar* (Univ. Press of New England).

Witter Bynner Prize for Poetry. To support the work of emerging poets. *Offered by:* American Academy of Arts and Letters. *Winner:* Brigit Pegeen Kelly.

Caldecott Medal. For the artist of the most distinguished picture book. *Offered by:* American Library Association, Association for Library Services to Children. *Winner:* Mary Azarian for *Snowflake Bentley*, text by Jacqueline Briggs Martin (Houghton Mifflin).

John W. Campbell Award for Best New Writer. For science fiction writing. *Offered by:* Center for the Study of Science Fiction. *Winner:* Nalo Hopkinson.

Truman Capote Award for Literary Criticism in Memory of Newton Arvin. To reward and encourage excellence in the field of literary criticism. *Offered by:* University of Iowa Writers' Workshop. *Winner:* Charles Rosen.

Carnegie Medal (United Kingdom). For the outstanding children's book of the year. *Offered by:* The Library Association. *Winner:* David Almond for *Skellig* (Hodder).

Cholmondeley Awards (United Kingdom). For contributions to poetry. *Offered by:* Society of Authors. *Winners:* Vicki Feaver, Geoffrey Hill, Elma Mitchell, Sheenagh Pugh.

Arthur C. Clarke Award (United Kingdom). For the best science fiction novel of the year. *Offered by:* British Science Fiction Association. *Winner:* Patricia Sullivan for *Dreaming in Smoke* (Orion).

David Cohen British Literature Prize (United Kingdom). *Offered by:* The Arts Council. *Winner:* William Trevor.

Commonwealth Writers Prize (United Kingdom). To reward and encourage new Commonwealth fiction and ensure that works of merit reach a wider audience outside their country of origin. *Offered by:* Commonwealth Institute. *Winners:* Murray Bail for *Eucalyptus* (Harvill); (first book) Kerri Sakamoto for *The Electrical Field* (Macmillan).

Thomas Cook/Daily Telegraph Travel Book Award (United Kingdom). *Offered by:* Book Trust. *Winner:* Philip Marsden for *The Spirit Wrestlers* (HarperCollins).

Stephen Crane Award. For first fiction. *Offered by:* Book-of-the-Month Club. *Winner:* Danzy Senna for *Caucasia* (Riverhead).

Sor Juana Ines De La Cruz Prize in Fiction (Mexico). For women writers who have published a novel in Spanish after 1995. *Offered by:* Guadalajara International Book Fair. *Winner:* Silvia Molina for *El Amor que me Juraste* (Fondo de Cultura Economica Press).

Philip K. Dick Award. For a distinguished paperback original published in the United

States. *Offered by:* Norwescon. *Winner:* Geoff Ryman for *253: The Print Remix* (St. Martin's).

John Dos Passos Prize for Literature. To a writer who has a substantial body of significant publication, and whose work demonstrates an intense and original exploration of specifically American themes, an experimental quality, and a whole range of literary forms. *Offered by:* Longwood College. *Winner:* Eric Kraft.

T. S. Eliot Prize (United Kingdom). For poetry. *Offered by:* Poetry Book Society. *Winner:* Ted Hughes for *Birthday Letters* (Faber).

E. M. Forster Award in Literature. To a young writer from England, Ireland, Scotland, or Wales for a stay in the United States. *Offered by:* American Academy of Arts and Letters. *Winner:* Nick Hornby.

Forward Poetry Prizes (United Kingdom). *Offered by:* Forward. *Winners:* (best collection) Jo Shapcott for *My Life Asleep* (Oxford); (best first collection) Nick Drake for *The Man in the White Suit* (Bloodaxe).

Frost Medal for Distinguished Achievement. To recognize achievement in poetry over a lifetime. *Offered by:* Poetry Society of America. *Winner:* Barbara Guest.

Lionel Gelber Prize. For important nonfiction works pertaining to foreign affairs and global issues. *Offered by:* Lionel Gelber Foundation. *Winner:* Adam Hochschild for *King Leopold's Ghost* (Houghton Mifflin).

Kate Greenaway Medal (United Kingdom). For children's book illustration. *Offered by:* The Library Association. *Winner:* Helen Cooper for *Pumpkin Soup* (Transworld).

Eric Gregory Trust Awards (United Kingdom). For poets under the age of 30. *Offered by:* Society of Authors. *Winners:* Matthew Hollis, Ross Cogan, Helen Ivory, Andrew Pidoux, Owen Sheers, Dan Wyke.

Guardian Children's Fiction Prize (United Kingdom). For recognition of a children's novel by a British or Commonwealth writer. *Offered by:* Guardian. *Winner:* Susan Price for *The Sterkarm Handshake* (Scholastic).

Guardian First Book Prize (United Kingdom). For recognition of a first book, either fiction or nonfiction. *Offered by:* Guardian. *Winner:* Philip Gourevitch for *We Wish to Inform You that Tomorrow We Will be Killed with Our Families* (Picador).

Guggenheim Literary Fellowships. For unusually distinguished achievement in the past and exceptional promise for future accomplishment. *Offered by:* Guggenheim Memorial Foundation. *Winners:* (poetry) Robin Behn, David Bottoms, B. H. Fairchild, Jeffrey W. Harrison, Steve Orlen, Ira Sadoff, Susan Wheeler; (fiction) Jonathan Ames, Junot Diaz, Jacqueline Carey, Emmanuel Dongala, Mikhail Iossel, Ha Jin, Josip Novakovich, Carol Shields; (nonfiction) Peter Balakian, Bernard Cooper.

O. B. Hardison, Jr., Poetry Prize. To a U.S. poet who has published at least one book in the past five years, has made important contributions as a teacher, and is committed to furthering the understanding of poetry. *Offered by:* Folger Shakespeare Library. *Winner:* Alan Shapiro.

Heartland Prize. To recognize an outstanding work of fiction about people and places in America's heartland. *Offered by:* Chicago Tribune. *Winner:* Elizabeth Strout for *Amy and Isabelle* (Random House).

Drue Heinz Literature Prize. To recognize and encourage the writing of short fiction. *Offered by:* Drue Heinz Foundation and the University of Pittsburgh. *Winner:* Lucy Honig for *The Truly Needy* (Univ. of Pittsburgh).

Peggy V. Helmerich Distinguished Author Award. To a nationally acclaimed writer for a body of work and contributions to American literature and letters. *Offered by:* Tulsa Library Trust. *Winner:* Margaret Atwood.

Ernest Hemingway Foundation Award. For a distinguished work of first fiction by an American. *Offered by:* PEN New England. *Winner:* Rosina Lippi for *Homestead* (Delphinium).

IMPAC Dublin Literary Award (Ireland). For a book of high literary merit written in English or translated into English. *Offered by:* IMPAC Corp. and the City of Dublin. *Winner:* Andrew Miller for *Ingenious Pain* (Harcourt).

Imus American Book Awards. For fiction and nonfiction books. *Offered by:* Barnes & Noble, barnesandnoble.com, and A&E Network. *Winners:* ($100,000 prize) Richard Price for *Freedomland* (Broadway Books); ($50,000 prizes) Ruth L. Ozeki for *My Year of Meats* (Viking), Taylor Branch for *Pillar of Fire* (Simon & Schuster), David Remnick for *King of the World* (Random House).

Irish Fiction Prize (Ireland). For the best novel by an Irish writer. *Offered by: Irish Times. Winner:* Antonia Logue for *Shadow Box* (Bloomsbury).

Irish Language Prize (Ireland). For the best work written in Gaelic by an Irish writer. *Offered by: Irish Times. Winner:* Mairin Nic Eoin for *B'ait Leo Bean* (An Clochomhar).

Irish Nonfiction Prize (Ireland). For the best nonfiction work by an Irish writer. *Offered by: Irish Times. Winner:* Neil Belton for *The Good Listener* (Phoenix).

Irish Poetry Prize (Ireland). For the best work of poetry by an Irish poet. *Offered by: Irish Times. Winner:* Seamus Heaney for *Opened Ground* (Faber).

Irish Times International Fiction Prize (Ireland). For the best novel by an Irish writer or by a writer of Irish descent living abroad. *Offered by: Irish Times. Winner:* Lorrie Moore for *Birds of America* (Faber).

Rona Jaffe Writer's Awards. To identify and support women writers of exceptional talent in the early stages of their careers. *Offered by:* Rona Jaffe Foundation. *Winners:* Zainab Ali, Stephanie Grant, Kathleen Lee, Ann Claremont Le Zotte, Malena Morling, Michelle Tea, Shao Wei.

Jerusalem Prize (Israel). To a writer whose works best express the theme of freedom of the individual in society. *Offered by:* Jerusalem International Book Fair. *Winner:* Don DeLillo.

Samuel Johnson Prize for Nonfiction (United Kingdom). *Offered by:* an anonymous donor. *Winner:* Antony Beevor for *Stalingrad* (Penguin).

Sue Kaufman Prize for First Fiction. For a first novel or collection of short stories. *Offered by:* American Academy of Arts and Letters. *Winner:* Michael Byers for *The Coast of Good Intentions* (Houghton Mifflin).

Coretta Scott King Awards. For works that promote the cause of peace and brotherhood. *Offered by:* American Library Association, Social Responsibilities Round Table. *Winners:* (author award) Angela Johnson for *Heaven* (Simon & Schuster); (illustrator award) Michelle Wood for *I See the Rhythm* (Children's Book Press).

Kiriyama Pacific Rim Book Prize. For a book of fiction or nonfiction in English that best contributes to a fuller understanding among the nations and peoples of the Pacific Rim. *Offered by:* Center for the Pacific Rim, Univ. of San Francisco. *Winners:* (fiction) Cheng Ch'ing-Wen for *Three-Legged Horse* (Colorado Univ.); (nonfiction) Andrew X. Pham for *Catfish and Madala* (Farrar, Straus & Giroux).

Robert Kirsch Award. To a living author whose residence or focus is the American West and whose contributions to American letters clearly merit body-of-work recognition. *Offered by: Los Angeles Times. Winner:* John Sanford.

Harold Morton Landon Translation Award. For a book of verse translated into English by a single translator. *Offered by:* Academy of American Poets. *Winner:* W. D. Snodgrass for *Selected Translations* (BOA Editions).

Lannan Literary Awards. To recognize both established and emerging writers of poetry, fiction, and nonfiction. *Offered by:* Lannan Foundation. *Winners:* (poetry) Louise Gluck, Dennis O'Driscoll, C. D. Wright; (fiction) Gish Jen, Jamaica Kincaid, Richard Powers, Joanna Scott; (nonfiction) Jared Diamond, Gary Paul Nabhan, Jonathan Schell; (lifetime achievement) Adrienne Rich.

Lannan Prize for Cultural Freedom. To recognize those whose extraordinary and courageous work celebrates the human right to freedom of imagination, inquiry, and expression. *Offered by:* Lannan Foundation. *Winner:* Eduardo Galeano.

James Laughlin Award. To support the publication of a second book of poetry. *Offered by:* Academy of American Poets. *Winner:* Tory Dent for *HIV, Mon Amour* (Sheep Meadow Press).

Ruth Lilly Poetry Fellowships. To help aspiring writers to continue their study and practice of poetry. *Offered by:* Modern Poetry Association. *Winners:* Maudelle Driskell, Kevin Meaux.

Ruth Lilly Poetry Prize. To a United States poet whose accomplishments warrant extraordinary recognition. *Offered by:* Modern Poetry Association. *Winner:* Maxine Kumin.

Locus Awards. For science fiction writing. *Offered by:* Locus Publications. *Winners:* (science fiction novel) Connie Willis for *To Say Nothing of the Dog* (Bantam); (fantasy novel) George R. R. Martin for *A Clash of Kings* (Bantam); (dark fantasy/horror) Stephen King for *Bag of Bones* (Scribner); (first novel) Nalo Hopkinson for *Brown Girl in the Ring* (Warner); (nonfiction) Thomas M. Disch for *The Dreams Our Stuff Is Made Of* (Free Press); (anthology) Robert Silverberg, ed., for *Legends* (Tor); (collection) Grania Davis and Robert Silverberg, eds., for *The Avram Treasury* (Tor); (art book) Arnie and Cathy Fenner, eds., for *Spectrum 5: The Best in Contemporary Fantastic Art* (Underwood).

Los Angeles Times Book Prizes. To honor literary excellence. *Winners:* (fiction) W. G. Sebald for *The Rings of Saturn* (New Directions); (biography) A. Scott Berg for *Lindbergh* (Putnam); (poetry) Alice Notley for *Mysteries of Small Houses* (Penguin); (history) Roy S. Porter for *The Greatest Benefit to Mankind* (Norton); (current interest) Philip Gourevitch for *We Wish to Inform You that Tomorrow We Will Be Killed with Our Families* (Farrar, Straus & Giroux); (science and technology) Douglas Star for *Blood* (Knopf); (young adult fiction) Joan Bauer for *Rules of the Road* (Putnam); (Art Seidenbaum Award for First Fiction) C. S. Godshalk for *Kalimantaan* (Holt).

Amy Lowell Poetry Travelling Scholarship. To a U.S.-born poet to spend one year outside North America in a country the recipient feels will most advance his or her work. *Offered by:* Amy Lowell Poetry Foundation. *Winner:* Phillis Marna Levin.

J. Anthony Lukas Prizes. For nonfiction writing that demonstrates literary grace, serious research, and concern for an important aspect of American social or political life. *Offered by:* Columbia University Graduate School of Journalism and the Nieman Foundation. *Winners:* Kevin Coyne for *The Best Years of Their Lives* (work-in-progress); Henry Mayer for *All on Fire* (St. Martin's); Adam Hochschild for *King Leopold's Ghost* (Houghton Mifflin).

McKitterick Prize (United Kingdom). For a first novel by a writer over the age of 40. *Offered by:* Society of Authors. *Winner:* Magnus Mills for *The Restraint of Beasts* (Flamingo).

Lenore Marshall Poetry Prize. For an outstanding book of poems published in the United States. *Offered by:* Academy of American Poets and the *Nation. Winner:* Wanda Coleman for *Bathwater Wine* (Black Sparrow Press).

Kurt Maschler Award (United Kingdom). For recognition of a children's book in which text and illustration are both excellent and perfectly harmonious. *Offered by:* Book Trust. *Winner:* Helen Oxenbury for *Alice in Wonderland* (Walker).

Somerset Maugham Awards (United Kingdom). For young British writers to gain experience in foreign countries. *Offered by:* Society of Authors. *Winners:* Andrea Ashworth for *Once in a House on Fire* (Picador); Paul Farley for *The Boy from the Chemist Is Here to See You* (Picador); Giles Foden for *The Last King of Scotland* (Faber): Jonathan Freedland for *Bring Home the Revolution* (Fourth Estate).

Addison Metcalf Award. To a young writer of great promise. *Offered by:* American Academy of Arts and Letters. *Winner:* Reginald McKnight.

James A. Michener Memorial Prize. For a first published book by an author age 40 or over. *Offered by:* Random House. *Winner:* Tom McNeal for *Goodnight, Nebraska* (Random House).

National Arts Club Medal of Honor for Literature. *Offered by:* National Arts Club. *Winner:* Toni Morrison.

National Book Awards. *Offered by:* National Book Foundation. *Winners:* (fiction) Ha Jin for *Waiting* (Pantheon); (nonfiction) John W. Dower for *Embracing Defeat*

(Norton); (poetry) Ai for *Vice* (Norton); (children's) Kimberly Willis Holt for *When Zachary Beaver Came to Town* (Holt).

National Book Critics Circle Awards. *Offered by:* National Book Critics Circle. *Winners:* (fiction) Alice Munro for *The Love of a Good Woman* (Knopf); (nonfiction) Philip Gourevitch for *We Wish to Inform You that Tomorrow We Will Be Killed with Our Families* (Farrar, Straus & Giroux); (poetry) Marie Ponsot for *The Bird Catcher* (Knopf); (criticism) Gary Giddins for *Visions of Jazz* (Oxford); (biography/autobiography) Sylvia Nasar for *A Beautiful Mind* (Simon & Schuster); (Nina Balakian Citation for Excellence in Reviewing) Albert Mobilio.

Nebula Awards. For the best science fiction writing. *Offered by:* Science Fiction Writers of America. *Winners:* (best novel) Joe Haldeman for *Forever Peace* (Ace); (Grand Master) Harry C. Stubbs.

John Newbery Medal. For the most distinguished contribution to literature for children. Donor: American Library Association, Association for Library Service to Children. *Medal contributed by:* Daniel Melcher. *Winner:* Louis Sachar for *Holes* (Farrar, Straus & Giroux).

Nobel Prize in Literature. For the total literary output of a distinguished career. *Offered by:* Swedish Academy. *Winner:* Gunter Grass.

Flannery O'Connor Awards for Short Fiction. *Offered by:* PEN American Center. *Winners:* Hester Kaplan for *The Edge of Marriage* (Univ. of Georgia); Darrell Spencer for *Men in Trees* (Univ. of Georgia).

Scott O'Dell Award for Historical Fiction. *Offered by:* Bulletin of the Center for Children's Books, University of Chicago. *Winner:* Harriette Gillem Robinet for *Forty Acres and Maybe a Mule* (Atheneum).

Orange Prize for Fiction (United Kingdom). For the best novel written by a woman and published in the United Kingdom. *Offered by:* Orange PLC. *Winner:* Suzanne Berne for *A Crime in the Neighbourhood* (Viking).

PEN Award for Poetry in Translation. For a book-length translation of poetry from any language into English and published in the United States. *Offered by:* PEN American Center. *Winner:* Richard Zenith for *Fernando Pessoa & Co.* by Fernando Pessoa (Grove).

PEN/Martha Albrand Award for the Art of the Memoir. For a U.S. author's first book-length memoir. *Offered by:* PEN American Center. *Winner:* Ted Solotaroff for *Truth Comes in Blows* (Norton).

PEN Book Awards. For outstanding literary achievement. *Offered by:* PEN American Center. *Winners:* (essay) Marilynne Robinson for *The Death of Adam* (Houghton Mifflin); (memoir) Ted Solotaroff for *Truth Comes in Blows* (Norton); (nonfiction) Philip Gourevitch for *We Wish to Inform You that Tomorrow We Will Be Killed with Our Families* (Farrar, Straus & Giroux).

PEN/Book-of-the-Month Club Translation Prize. For a book-length literary translation from any language into English and published in the United States. *Offered by:* PEN American Center. *Winner:* Michael Hofmann for *The Tale of the 1002nd Night* by Joseph Roth (St. Martin's).

PEN/Faulkner Award for Fiction. To honor the best work of fiction published by an American. *Offered by:* PEN American Center. *Winner:* Michael Cunningham for *The Hours* (Farrar, Straus & Giroux).

PEN/Roger Klein Editorial Award. For distinguished editorial achievement. *Offered by:* PEN American Center. *Winner:* Drenka Willen.

PEN Literary Awards (United Kingdom). For outstanding literary achievement. *Offered by:* PEN UK. *Winners:* (Macmillan Silver Award) Peter Ho Davies for *The Ugliest House in the World* (Granta); (Stern Silver Award) John Bayley for *Iris* (Duckworth); (Gold Award for Lifetime Achievement) Penelope Fitzgerald.

PEN/Malamud Award for Excellence in Short Fiction. To an author who has demonstrated long-term excellence in short fiction. *Offered by:* PEN American Center. *Winner:* John Barth.

PEN/Joyce Osterweil Award for Poetry. To recognize an emerging American poet. *Offered by:* PEN American Center. *Win-*

ner: Nick Flynn for *Some Ether* (Graywolf Press).

Edgar Allan Poe Awards. For outstanding mystery, crime, and suspense writing. *Offered by:* Mystery Writers of America. *Winners:* (novel) Robert Clark for *Mr. White's Confession* (Picador USA); (first novel) Steve Hamilton for *A Cold Day in Paradise* (St. Martin's); (factual crime) Carlton Stowers for *To the Last Breath* (St. Martin's); (paperback original) Rick Riordan for *The Widower's Two-Step* (Bantam); (critical/biographical) Robin Winks and Maureen Corrigan, eds., for *The Literature of Crime, Detection, and Espionage* (Scribner); (young adult) Nancy Werlin for *The Killer's Cousin* (Delacorte); (children's) Wendelin Van Draanen for *Sammy Keyes and the Hotel Thief* (Knopf); (Grand Master) P. D. James.

Poets' Prize. For the best book of poetry published in the United States in the previous year. *Offered by:* Nicholas Roerich Museum. *Winner:* Marilyn Nelson for *Field of Praise* (Louisiana State Univ.).

Premio Aztlan. To a Chicano or Chicana fiction writer who has published no more than two books. *Offered by:* Rudolfo and Patricia Anaya and the University of New Mexico. *Winner:* Ronald L. Ruiz.

Pulitzer Prizes in Letters. To honor distinguished work by American writers, dealing preferably with American themes. *Offered by:* Columbia University, Graduate School of Journalism. *Winners:* (fiction) Michael Cunningham for *The Hours* (Farrar, Straus & Giroux); (history) Edwin G. Burrows and Mike Wallace for *Gotham* (Oxford); (biography) A. Scott Berg for *Lindbergh* (Putnam); (general nonfiction) John McPhee for *Annals of the Former World* (Farrar, Straus & Giroux); (poetry) Mark Strand for *Blizzard of One* (Knopf).

Quality Paperback Book Club New Voices Award. For the most distinct and promising work of fiction by a new writer offered by the club each year. *Offered by:* Quality Paperback Book Club. *Winner:* Carolyn Ferrell for *Don't Erase Me* (Houghton Mifflin).

Raiziss/De Palchi Translation Fellowship. For a translation into English of a significant work of modern Italian poetry. *Offered by:* Academy of American Poets. *Winner:* Geoffrey Brock for *Poesie del disamore* by Cesare Pavese (work-in-progress).

Rea Award for the Short Story. To honor a living writer who has made a significant contribution to the short story as an art form. *Offered by:* Dungannon Foundation. *Winner:* Joy Williams.

Arthur Rense Poetry Prize. To an outstanding American poet for lifetime achievement. *Offered by:* American Academy of Arts and Letters. *Winner:* James McMichael.

Rhone-Poulenc Science Book Award (United Kingdom). *Offered by:* Rhone-Poulenc. *Winner:* Paul Hoffman for *The Man Who Loved Only Numbers* (Fourth Estate).

John Llewellyn Rhys Memorial Award (United Kingdom). *Offered by: Mail on Sunday. Winner:* Peter Ho Davis for *The Ugliest House in the World* (Granta).

Rome Fellowship in Literature. To spend a year in residence at the American Academy in Rome. *Offered by:* American Academy of Arts and Letters. *Winner:* Tom Andrews.

Richard and Hinda Rosenthal Foundation Award. For a work of fiction that is a considerable literary achievement though not necessarily a commercial success. *Offered by:* American Academy of Arts and Letters. *Winner:* Sigrid Nunez for *Mitz: The Marmoset of Bloomsbury* (HarperFlamingo).

Juan Rulfo International Latin American and Caribbean Prize for Literature (Mexico). To a writer of poetry, novels, short stories, drama, or essays who is a native of Latin America or the Caribbean, and who writes in Spanish, Portuguese, or English. *Offered by:* Juan Rulfo Award Committee. *Winner:* Sergio Pitol.

Sagittarius Prize (United Kingdom). For a first novel by a writer over the age of 60. *Offered by:* Society of Authors. *Winner:* Ingrid Mann for *The Danube Testament* (Bellew).

Shelley Memorial Award. To a poet living in the United States who is chosen on the basis of genius and need. *Offered by:* Poetry Society of America. *Winner:* Tom Sleigh.

Smarties Book Prizes (United Kingdom). To encourage high standards and to stimulate interest in books for children. *Offered by:* Book Trust and Nestle Rowntree. *Winners:* (ages 9–11) J. K. Rowling for *Harry Potter and the Prisoner of Azkaban* (Bloomsbury); (ages 6–8) Laurence Anholt and Arthur Robins for *Snow White and the Seven Aliens* (Orchard); (ages 0–5) Julia Donaldson and Alex Scheffler for *The Gruffalo* (Macmillan).

W. H. Smith Literary Award (United Kingdom). For a significant contribution to literature. *Offered by:* W. H. Smith. *Winner:* Beryl Bainbridge for *Master Georgie* (Duckworth).

Tanning Prize. For outstanding and proven mastery in the art of poetry. *Offered by:* Academy of American Poets. *Winner:* A. R. Ammons.

Templeton Prize for Progress in Religion. *Offered by:* Templeton Foundation. *Winner:* Ian G. Barbour.

Betty Trask Awards (United Kingdom). For works of a romantic or traditional nature by writers under the age of 35. *Offered by:* Society of Authors. *Winners:* Elliott Perlman for *Three Dollars* (Faber); Catherine Childgey for *In a Fishbone Church* (Picador); Giles Foden for *The Last King of Scotland* (Faber); Dennis Bock for *Olympia* (Bloomsbury); Rajeev Balasubramanyam for *In Beautiful Disguises* (unpublished); Sarah Waters for *Tipping the Velvet* (Virago).

Kate Frost Tufts Discovery Award. For a first or very early book of poetry by an emerging poet. *Offered by:* Claremont Graduate School. *Winner:* Barbara Ras for *Bite Every Sorrow* (Univ. of Louisiana).

Kingsley Tufts Poetry Award. For a book of poetry by a mid-career poet. *Offered by:* Claremont Graduate School. *Winner:* B. H. Fairchild for *The Art of the Lathe* (Alice James Books).

Lila Wallace-Reader's Digest Fund Writers' Awards. To encourage interactions between talented writers and poets and cultural, educational, and community organizations. *Offered by:* Lila Wallace Foundation. *Winners:* Lucille Clifton, W. S. Di Piero, Jack Gilbert, Mark Halliday, Ed Robertson, Gary Snyder, Ellen Bryant Voight, Rosemarie Waldrop, John Edgar Wideman.

Whitbread Book of the Year (United Kingdom). *Offered by:* Booksellers Association of Great Britain. *Winner:* Ted Hughes for *Birthday Letters* (Faber).

Whitbread Children's Book of the Year (United Kingdom). *Offered by:* Booksellers Association of Great Britain. *Winner:* David Almond for *Skellig* (Hodder).

Whitbread Literary Prizes (United Kingdom). For literature of merit that is readable on a wide scale. *Offered by:* Booksellers Association of Great Britain. *Winners:* (novel) Justin Cartwright for *Leading the Cheers* (Sceptre); (first novel) Giles Foden for *The Last King of Scotland* (Faber); (biography) Amanda Foreman for *Georgiana, Duchess of Devonshire* (HarperCollins); (poetry) Ted Hughes for *Birthday Letters* (Faber).

William Allen White Children's Book Award. *Offered by:* Emporia State University. *Winner:* Andrew Clements for *Frindle* (Simon & Schuster).

Whiting Writers Awards. For outstanding talent and promise. *Offered by:* Mrs. Giles Whiting Foundation. *Winners:* Gordon Grice, Michael Haskell, Ehud Havazelet, Terrance Hayes, Naomi Iizuka, Ben Marcus, Yxta Maya Murray, ZZ Packer, Margaret Talbot, Martha Zweig.

Walt Whitman Award. For poetry. *Offered by:* Academy of American Poets. *Winner:* Judy Jordan for *Carolina Ghost Woods* (Louisiana State Univ.).

Simon Wiesenthal Center-Museum of Tolerance Once Upon a World Children's Book Award. *Offered by:* Simon Wiesenthal Center-Museum of Tolerance. *Winner:* Eve Bunting for *So Far from the Sea.*

Robert H. Winner Memorial Award. For a poem or sequence of poems characterized by a delight in language and the possibilities of ordinary life. *Offered by:* Poetry Society of America. *Winner:* Liz Waldner.

L. L. Winship Award. For a book of fiction, poetry, or nonfiction by a New England author or with a New England topic or setting. *Offered by:* PEN New England. *Winner:* David Hall for *Without* (Houghton Mifflin).

World Fantasy Convention Awards. For outstanding fantasy writing. *Offered by:* World Fantasy Convention. *Winners:* (best novel) Louise Erdrich for *The Antelope Wife* (HarperFlamingo); (anthology) Jack Dann and Janeen Webb, eds., for *Dreaming Down Under* (HarperCollins); (collection) Karen Joy Fowler for *Black Glass* (Holt); (life achievement) Hugh B. Cave.

World Science Fiction Convention Hugo Awards. For outstanding science fiction writing. *Offered by:* World Science Fiction Convention. *Winners:* (best novel) Connie Willis for *To Say Nothing of the Dog* (Bantam); (best related book) Thomas M. Disch for *The Dreams Our Stuff Is Made Of* (Free Press); (best professional editor) Gardner Dozois.

Morton Dauwen Zabel Award in Poetry. To writers of progressive and experimental tendencies. *Offered by:* American Academy of Arts and Letters. *Winner:* Kathryn Davis.

Bestsellers of 1999

Hardcover Bestsellers: So Far, Little Has Changed

Daisy Maryles

Executive Editor, *Publishers Weekly*

Back in 1979 Stephen King made his first appearance on these end-of-the-year lists. King's *The Dead Zone* placed at number six, with sales for that year of about 175,000. The popular author continued to be a fixture for the next 20 years, often garnering one of the top three slots, and missed only in 1988 and 1997—the two years when he chose not to publish any new hardcovers. For 1999, King has two books in the top-10 lineup, a feat he has accomplished many times in the past two decades. All this historical data is worthy of note precisely because the time may come when these annual charts are just history, and our bestsellers may be calculated using distribution channels that are yet to be established.

In fact, less than a month ago King and his publisher Scribner released a 66-page novella, *Riding the Bullet*, exclusively as an e-book. Customer orders for the novella—priced at about $2.50, and even free in many cases—went as high as 500,000 in less than three days—a very hefty figure and one that King certainly never matched in such a brief time with any of his print titles. While King's venture is a clear indication that there is a sizable audience for electronically published works, it is way too early to suspend any traditional book publishing or distribution apparatus. Indeed, we may still be doing these lists 10 or 20 years from now, even though the folks at Microsoft predict that in the year 2020, 90 percent of all books will be sold in electronic form.

And while publishers, authors, agents, and retailers of all types are trying to figure out what the Internet and print-on-demand publishing mean to the future of the book, right now the goal of all of these constituents is, as always, to sell as many books as possible. Success for the predictable present is measured by sales performance, and bestseller charts based on retail sales—through, to a large extent, bricks-and-mortar stores—are still the best barometer.

The Lead Players

So how did the 1999 bestsellers compare to previous years? As usual, the name is still the main part of the game. In fiction, veteran bestseller authors dominate, and for debut novels a nod from Oprah is the only way to real success. The only two first novels in the top 30 are *White Oleander* and *Mother of Pearl*, and both were book club picks on her show. For the sixth year in a row, John Grisham commands the top spot, followed by such familiar names as King, Crichton, Steel, and Cornwell. The only newcomers to the top 15 are two books in the biblical Left Behind series, *Assassins* and *Apollyon*, both by Jerry B. Jenkins and Tim LaHaye. Evangelical Christian publisher Tyndale brilliantly built on the success of these books in the Christian retail marketplace, using carefully coordinat-

Adapted from *Publishers Weekly*, April 10, 2000

Publishers Weekly 1999 Bestsellers

FICTION

1. **The Testament** by John Grisham. Doubleday (2/99) **2,475,000
2. **Hannibal** by Thomas Harris. Delacorte (6/99) **1,550,000
3. **Assassins** by Jerry B. Jenkins & Tim LaHaye. Tyndale (8/99) 1,484,752
4. **Star Wars: Episode 1, The Phantom Menace** by Terry Brooks. Lucas Books/Del Rey (4/99) 1,419,852
5. **Timeline** by Michael Crichton. Knopf (11/99) 1,351,800
6. **Hearts in Atlantis** by Stephen King. Scribner (9/99) **1,325,000
7. **Apollyon** by Jerry B. Jenkins & Tim LaHaye. Tyndale (2/99) 1,172,132
8. **The Girl Who Loved Tom Gordon** by Stephen King. Scribner (4/99) **1,075,000
9. **Irresistible Forces** by Danielle Steel. Delacorte (11/99) **975,000
10. **Tara Road** by Maeve Binchy. Delacorte (3/99). **950,000
11. **White Oleander** by Janet Fitch. Little, Brown (5/99) 903,729
12. **A Walk to Remember** by Nicholas Sparks. Warner (10/99) 860,652
13. **Pop Goes the Weasel** by James Patterson. Little, Brown (10/99) 832,145
14. **Black Notice** by Patricia Cornwell. Putnam (8/99) 800,769
15. **Granny Dan** by Danielle Steel. Delacorte (6/99) **775,000

NONFICTION

1. **Tuesdays with Morrie** by Mitch Albom. Doubleday (8/97) * **2, 500,000
2. **The Greatest Generation** by Tom Brokaw. Random House (11/98) *1,968,597
3. **Guinness World Records 2000 Millennium Edition**. Guinness Publishing (9/99) 1,908,770
4. **'Tis** by Frank McCourt. Scribner (9/99) **1,675,000
5. **Who Moved My Cheese?** by Spencer Johnson. Putnam (9/98) 1,000,000
6. **The Courage to Be Rich** by Suze Orman. Riverhead (3/99) 950,584
7. **The Greatest Generation Speaks** by Tom Brokaw. Random House (11/99) 936,710
8. **Sugar Busters!** by H. Leighton Steward, Morrison C. Bethea, Sam S. Andrews, and Luis A. Balart. Ballantine *762,432
9. **The Art of Happiness** by the Dalai Lama and Howard C. Cutler. Riverhead (11/98) *750,744
10. **The Century** by Peter Jennings & Todd Brewster. Doubleday (11/98) **700,000
11. **Body for Life** by Bill Phillips. HarperCollins (5/99) 698,684
12. **Life Strategies** by Phillip C. McGraw. Hyperion (1/99) 671,954
13. **Have A Nice Day!** by Mick Foley. ReganBooks (10/99) 636,874
14. **Suzanne Somers' Get Skinny on Fabulous Food** by Suzanne Somers. Crown (5/99) 631,952
15. **Don't Sweat the Small Stuff in Love** by Richard and Kristine Carlson. Hyperion (9/99) 631,299

Note: Rankings are determined by sales figures provided by publishers; the numbers generally reflect reports of copies "shipped and billed" in calendar year 1999 and publishers were instructed to adjust sales figures to include returns through February 15, 2000. Publishers did not at that time know what their total returns would be—indeed, the majority of returns occur after that cut-off date—so none of these returns should be regarded as final net sales. (dates in parenthesis indicate month and year of publication.)

*Sales figures reflect books sold only in calendar year 1999.

**Sales figures were submitted to *Publishers Weekly* in confidence, for use in placing titles on the lists. Numbers shown are rounded down to the nearest 25,000 to indicate relationship to sales figures of other titles.

ed marketing and promotion tactics (one-day laydown, massive distribution of point-of-purchase displays and aggressive advertising in print and broadcast media) to get the books into secular stores. Several other authors of religion and inspirational titles enjoyed increased sales in both general and Christian outlets, among them Frank Peretti and Jan Karon.

The top sellers in nonfiction are also by or about recognizable names. Many of the authors have made it onto the charts previously; in fact, four of the best-sellers on the 1998 annual list make a second appearance on the 1999 top 15: *Tuesdays with Morrie, The Greatest Generation, Sugar Busters!* and *The Century.* Self-help, especially in the diet and fitness area, continues to do well. Riverhead is to be congratulated for placing a book by the Dalai Lama on the national charts, something that has not been done before, although His Holiness has written or inspired many books. The only notable new trend among the nonfiction block-busters are two books written by champions of the World Wrestling Federation.

Looking at the Numbers

In 1999 only 92 hardcover novels sold more than 100,000 copies, lower than the record set in 1998 when 101 books reached that level. In nonfiction, the year's tally was 121 books, considerably higher than the 1998 figure of 105 but still lower than the record set in 1997 when 128 new titles hit the six-figure mark. There were more fiction titles at the higher sales units level than in nonfiction. Eight novels went over the one-million mark, versus five in nonfiction. Nine more fiction titles racked up sales of 750,000 copies or more; there were four nonfiction books at this level. Last year, a new sales record was set for the num-ber 15 spot on the fiction annual charts, with Danielle Steel rounding out the list at approximately 775,000 copies for *Granny Dan.* Ten years ago, Martin Cruz Smith was able to take that position with sales of less than 300,000 copies for *Polar Star.* Twenty years ago, Robert Ludlum captured the number one spot with sales of just 250,000 for *The Matarese Circle.*

Nonfiction sales, too, showed major growth. A total of 20 hardcovers were over the 500,000 mark; in 1998 there were only 12 books that could claim those sales. And while a figure of 630,000 plus for the number 15 spot—achieved by *Don't Sweat the Small Stuff in Love*—is impressive, the record at this level was set by *The Bubba Gump Shrimp Co. Cookbook* in 1995, when that title claimed 650,000 plus sales. Both books are the beneficiaries of another trend that flour-ished in the last decade—lots of sales in outlets that are not traditional bookstores.

One interesting trend that continued only in fiction is the number of books with reported sales of more than 100,000 that appeared on *PW*'s weekly charts. Only seven of the 92 novels with sales of more than 100,000 did not show up on a weekly list. That is down considerably from the 22 no-shows in 1998 and the fiction record of 25 books set in 1997. There was a bit of slippage on the nonfic-tion side, where 46 of the 121 books have yet to show up on *PW*'s weekly chart or monthly religion chart. Last year's tally was 39, and the 1997 number was 60. About two-thirds of these no-shows were in the 125,000-copy-or-less level. The fact that more nonfiction titles can attain higher sales levels without book retail benefit is indicative of the many more special sales opportunities or alternative outlets available to them.

Net vs. Gross Issues

Every year we note the same disclaimers: all the calculations for this annual best-seller list are based on shipped-and-billed figures supplied by publishers for new books issued in 1999 and 1998 (a few books published earlier that continued their tenure on this year's bestseller charts are also included). These figures reflect only 1999 domestic trade sales; publishers were specifically instructed not to include book club and overseas transactions. We also asked publishers to take into account returns through February 15. None of the sales figures noted in these pages should be considered final net sales. For many of the books, especially those published in the latter half of last year, returns are still to be calculated.

Also note the tables "Who's on first?" and "What's on Second?" in which we compare *PW*'s top 15 rankings with how those books fared at select groups of independents, chains, and online booksellers. What's missing is how these titles fared at the price clubs, mass merchandisers, and in the gift retail market—figures we tried but were unable to obtain. For many bestsellers—e.g., commercial fiction and titles like *Don't Sweat the Small Stuff in Love*—sales are strongest at some of these outlets. This year we also have figures from Book Corner, reflecting sales at 14 of its stores in transportation locations around the country. While its fiction bestsellers closely matched *PW*'s top-30 bestsellers, that was less true for nonfiction; that list had many business titles not on our list (for example, Hyperion's *How to Become CEO* by Jeffrey Fox was number three on Book Corner's nonfiction chart).

The Fiction Runners-Up

This second tier, too, includes veteran authors whose books have graced these charts for many years. Ten of them have had runs on the weekly charts of 10 weeks or more; three—*Personal Injuries, We'll Meet Again,* and *Mother of Pearl*—were each on the lists for 14 weeks.

16. *Bittersweet* by Danielle Steel (Delacorte)
17. *Atlantis Found* by Clive Cussler (Putnam, 764,769)
18. *Saving Faith* by David Baldacci (Warner, 633,709)
19. *Personal Injuries* by Scott Turow (Farrar, Straus & Giroux, 630,000)
20. *We'll Meet Again* by Mary Higgins Clark (Simon & Schuster, 619,360)
21. *Southern Cross* by Patricia Cornwell (Putnam, 610,564)
22. *Mother of Pearl* by Melinda Haynes (Hyperion, 592,625)
23. *"O" Is for Outlaw* by Sue Grafton (Henry Holt, 560,000)
24. *A New Song* by Jan Karon (Viking, 546,874)
25. *The Visitation* by Frank Peretti (Word, 536,701)
26. *The Looking Glass* by Richard Paul Evans (Simon & Schuster, **450,000)
27. *River's End* by Nora Roberts (Putnam, 425,806)
28. *False Memory* by Dean Koontz (Bantam, 425,000)
29. *The Alibi* by Sandra Brown (Warner, 421,297)
30. *Monster* by Jonathan Kellerman (Random House, 355,460)

Fiction: Who's on First?

How *Publishers Weekly*'s bestsellers compared with the rankings
in major chains, wholesalers, and independents

PW Rankings	Sales Outlets									
	B/N	B	W	S	WS	N	BC	BE	AM.C	BN.C
1. The Testament	1	1	1	1	1	2	2	10	2	2
2. Hannibal	2	2	2	3	2	3	1	5	1	1
3. Assassins	19	29	19	43	13	—	24	—	7	12
4. Star Wars: Episode I	5	7	6	16	3	—	6	—	—	16
5. Timeline	3	4	7	6	10	15	4	15	6	5
6. Hearts in Atlantis	8	10	3	5	—	25	15	—	8	6
7. Apollyon	13	27	21	—	15	—	—	—	12	15
8. The Girl Who Loved Tom Gordon	7	20	4	7	6	20	7	—	14	10
9. Irresistible Forces	23	28	8	30	—	—	—	—	—	26
10. Tara Road	17	6	25	2	22	5	—	14	5	4
11. White Oleander	4	3	9	4	7	7	8	17	3	7
12. A Walk to Remember	6	5	5	13	4	14	12	4	17	14
13. Pop Goes the Weasel	11	11	10	20	16	27	5	3	15	11
14. Black Notice	9	9	13	10	5	12	9	21	14	3
15. Granny Dan	—	—	14	26	—	—	—	—	—	23

Nonfiction: What's on Second?

How *Publishers Weekly*'s bestsellers compared with the rankings
in major chains, wholesalers, and independents

PW Rankings	Sales Outlets									
	B/N	B	W	S	WS	N	BC	BE	AM.C	BN.C
1. Tuesdays with Morrie	1	1	2	1	1	2	1	15	1	1
2. The Greatest Generation	2	2	1	3	3	1	—	16	3	2
3. Guinness World Records 2000	10	15	3	23	—	—	—	—	—	—
4. 'Tis	3	5	6	4	7	4	5	22	5	4
5. Who Moved My Cheese?	12	25	—	14	—	—	—	—	2	3
6. The Courage to Be Rich	—	26	26	35	—	—	22	17	29	—
7. The Greatest Generation Speaks	6	13	4	25	—	—	—	—	17	15
8. Sugar Busters!	4	8	7	20	—	—	15	—	11	12
9. The Art of Happiness	5	6	—	6	2	6	9	—	—	16
10. The Century	7	3	13	8	—	5	—	—	7	7
11. Body for Life	11	12	17	38	—	—	28	—	4	5
12. Life Strategies	8	10	9	—	—	—	27	—	13	11
13. Have A Nice Day!	14	19	11	16	—	—	—	2	10	9
14. Suzanne Somers' Get Skinny . . .	9	11	12	27	—	—	—	—	15	8
15. Don't Sweat the Small Stuff in Love	—	—	—	—	—	—	—	19	—	—

BN   = Barnes & Noble   B   = Borders
W   = Waldenbooks   S   = Harry W. Schwartz
W   = Waterstones   N   = Northshire
BC   = Book Corner   BE   = Bookends
AM.C = Amazon.com   BN.C = BarnesandNoble.com

300,000+ Fiction Didn't Place

Once again, a number of fiction titles with sales of more than 300,000 copies didn't make our top 30 list. This year there are five books, down from a record nine in 1998. All five books had healthy runs on *PW*'s weekly charts, with two marking double-digit runs of 11 weeks apiece; they are *Hunting Badger* by Tony Hillerman (HarperCollins) and *East of the Mountains* by David Guterson (Harcourt). *Certain Prey* by John Sandford (Putnam) and *Vittorio* by Anne Rice (Knopf) each had a nine-week run, and *Ransom* by Julie Garwood (Pocket) was on *PW*'s charts for five weeks.

Fiction's 200,000+ Group

Sixteen books with sales at this impressive level did not make the top-30 fiction list, two more than the 1998 figure. All of the titles did make an appearance on the weekly charts, but four had short runs of less than a month. They are *The Secret of Shambhala* by James Redfield (Warner), *In a Class by Itself* by Sandra Brown (Bantam), *Fortune's Rocks* by Anita Shreve (Little, Brown), and *Void Moon* by Michael Connelly (Little, Brown).

Perhaps the cleanest sale in this group—meaning minimal returns—will be *The Girls' Guide to Hunting and Fishing* by Melissa Bank (Viking), as it was on the list for 18 months. That's twice as long as the next two titles with the highest weekly tally—*Single & Single* by John le Carré (Scribner) and *Ashes to Ashes* by Tami Hoag (Bantam). One book, *In Danger's Path* by W. E. B. Griffin (Putnam), had an eight-week run.

The other bestsellers in the 200,000 plus group are *Vector* by Robin Cook (Putnam), *The Edge* by Catherine Coulter (Putnam), *Dark Lady* by Richard North Patterson (Knopf), *Second Wind* by Dick Francis (Putnam), *The White House Connection* by Jack Higgins (Putnam), *High Tide* by Jude Deveraux (Pocket), *Star Wars: The New Jedi Order, Vector Prime* by R. A. Salvatore (Lucas Books/ Del Rey), and *In Pursuit of the Proper Sinner* by Elizabeth George (Bantam).

At Fiction's 150,000+ Level

There were 16 books with sales of more than 150,000 that did not make the year's top-30 bestsellers, one less than the 17 books in 1998. For the first time, every one of the books in this group appeared on *PW*'s weekly lists. Twelve enjoyed runs of four weeks or more; *Plainsong* by Kent Haruf (Knopf) had the longest tenure at nine weeks. *Dune: House Atreides* by Brian Herbert and Kevin J. Anderson (Bantam) had an eight-week run; *The Best American Short Stories of the Century*, edited by John Updike (Houghton Mifflin), and *A Sudden Change of Heart* by Barbara Taylor Bradford (Doubleday) were on the list for seven weeks each.

Four books in this group had runs of three weeks or less. They are *The Soldier Spies* by W. E. B. Griffin (Putnam), *Beyond the Great Snow Mountains* by Louis L'Amour (Bantam), *Cuba* by Stephen Coonts (St. Martin's), and *Carnal Innocence* by Nora Roberts (Bantam).

The other books with runs of four to six weeks are *Death du Jour* by Kathy Reichs (Scribner), *The Cat Who Saw Stars* by Lilian Jackson Braun (Putnam), *Lake News* by Barbara Delinsky (Simon & Schuster), *Big Trouble* by Dave Barry (Putnam), *Hush Money* by Robert B. Parker (Putnam), *Family Honor* by Robert B. Parker (Putnam), *Soul of the Fire* by Terry Goodkind (Tor), and *Send No Flowers* by Sandra Brown (Bantam).

Looking at the 125,000+ Group

This group includes 15 books that did not make the top-30 list, one more than in 1998. All but three landed on the weekly charts.

Out of the 12 that made the charts, two titles tied for the longest run, seven weeks each—*Abide with Me* by E. Lynn Harris (Doubleday) and *Blue at the Mizzen* by Patrick O'Brian (Norton). *Dangerous Kiss* by Jackie Collins (Simon & Schuster) had a six-week run and *Daughter of Fortune* by Isabel Allende (HarperCollins) was on the charts for four weeks in 1999, but a boost from Oprah put the book back in bestseller play. Other titles with appearances on the charts are *Jupiter's Bones* by Faye Kellerman (Morrow), *Joining* by Johanna Lindsey (Avon), *The Killing Game* by Iris Johansen (Bantam), *A God in Ruins* by Leon Uris (HarperCollins), *All the Queen's Men* by Linda Howard (Pocket), *Hard Time* by Sara Paretsky (Delacorte), *Worst Fears Realized* by Stuart Woods (HarperCollins), and *I Thee Wed* by Amanda Quick (Bantam).

The three that did not make an appearance on *PW*'s weekly lists are *Eye of the Beholder* by Jayne Ann Krentz (Pocket), *Battle Born* by Dale Brown (Bantam), and *Close Range* by Annie Proulx (Scribner).

At the 100,000+ Level

Last year, 10 books with sales of more than 100,000 did not make the top-30 annual list. That was considerably less then the 1998 figure of 23 novels. Five of these 10 books never landed on *PW*'s weekly charts, including authors Belva Plain, John Saul, and Frederick Forsyth, who at one time could count on strong showings on the charts. The other five were on the lists at least four weeks each.

The five that did not make it onto the weekly lists are *The Right Hand of Evil* by John Saul (Ballantine), *Fortune's Hand* by Belva Plain (Dell), *The Phantom of Manhattan* by Frederick Forsyth (St. Martin's), *Gravity* by Tess Gerritsen (Pocket), and *Bagombo Snuff Box* by Kurt Vonnegut (Putnam).

The five that did make the weekly charts are *Ender's Shadow* by Orson Scott Card (Tor), *High Five* by Janet Evanovich (St. Martin's), *Cryptonomicon* by Neal Stephenson (Avon), *Havana Bay* by Martin Cruz Smith (Random House), and *Be Cool* by Elmore Leonard (Delacorte).

The Nonfiction Runners-Up

A motley crew make up the second tier of nonfiction—juicy books about President Clinton, century retrospectives, and inspirational empowerment and food and fitness tomes, to name just a few. According to publishing claims, Monica Lewinsky sold more copies than George Stephanopoulos, even though the former was on the list for only six weeks, with just one week in the top slot, while the latter was on for 13 weeks, including six in the number one spot. John Glenn hit number 21 without a *PW* bestseller appearance. Iyanla Vanzant was the longest-running performer on these charts, with 20 appearances on the weekly lists.

16. *Monica's Story* by Andrew Morton (St. Martin's, 623,704)
17. *All Too Human* by George Stephanopoulos (Little, Brown, 606,279)
18. *The Rock Says . . .* by The Rock (ReganBooks, 542,636)
19. *And the Crowd Goes Wild* by Joe Garner (Sourcebooks, 504,691)
20. *Yesterday, I Cried* by Iyanla Vanzant (Simon & Schuster, **500,000)
21. *John Glenn: A Memoir* by John Glenn with Nick Taylor (Bantam, **450,000)
22. *LIFE: Our Century in Pictures*, edited by Richard Stolley (Little, Brown/Bulfinch, 429,745)
23. *Every Day's a Party* by Emeril Lagasse (Morrow, 416,352)
24. *How to Get What You Want and Want What You Have* by John Gray (HarperCollins, 402,964)
25. *Every Man a Tiger* by Tom Clancy with Gen. Chuck Horner (Ret.) (Putnam, 400,098)
26. *The Carbohydrate Addict's Healthy Heart Program* by Richard and Rachael Heller (Ballantine, 392,558)
27. *Dutch* by Edmund Morris (Random House, 377,175)
28. *Shadow* by Bob Woodward (Simon & Schuster, 350,000)
29. *Business @ the Speed of Thought* by Bill Gates (Warner, 344,816)
30. *When Christ Comes* by Max Lucado (Word, 344,127)

300,000+ NF Didn't Place

Competition in the nonfiction arena was fierce, and for the first time, nine books with sales of 300,000 or more did not make the top-30 chart. Only one of these books—*Sugar Busters Quick & Easy Cookbook* by H. Leighton Steward, Morrison C. Bethea, Sam S. Andrews, and Luis A. Balart (Ballantine)—did not make it onto the weekly charts. And two enjoyed double-digit tenures on the weekly *PW* list. They are *Faith of My Fathers* by John McCain with Mark Salter (Random House) and *When Pride Still Mattered* by David Maraniss (Simon & Schuster).

The other 300,000 plus performers are *Friendship with God* by Neale Donald Walsch (Putnam), *She Said Yes* by Misty Bernall (Plough), *The Other Side and Back* by Sylvia Browne (Dutton), *Reaching to Heaven* by James Van

Praagh (Dutton), *All the Best, George Bush* by George Bush (Scribner), and *A Man Named Dave* by Dave Pelzer (Dutton).

Nonfiction's 200,000+

Fourteen more books with sales of 200,000 and more did not make the top-30 charts. Two of these enjoyed long runs on the weekly charts. *Bella Tuscany* by Francis Mayes (Broadway) was on for 13 weeks and *The Majors* by John Feinstein (Little, Brown) stayed for 14 weeks. Two others in this group had long runs on *PW*'s monthly religion lists: *The Desire of the Everlasting Hills* by Thomas Cahill (Doubleday) and *The Lady, Her Lover, and Her Lord* by Bishop T. D. Jakes (Putnam).

The other titles that made it onto the weekly charts in 1999 are *Children Are from Heaven* by John Gray (HarperCollins), *Real Age* by Michael F. Roizen (HarperCollins/Cliff Street), *The New New Thing* by Michael Lewis (Norton), *Hillary's Choice* by Gail Sheehy (Random House), and *We Interrupt This Broadcast* by Joe Garner (Sourcebooks).

The following eight books with sales of 200,000 plus did not make it onto the weekly *PW* charts: *Martha Stewart's Hors d'Oeuvres* by Martha Stewart (Clarkson Potter), *Julia and Jacques Cooking at Home* by Julia Child and Jacques Pepin (Knopf), *People of the Century* by Dan Rather (Simon & Schuster), *If Love Is a Game These Are the Rules* by Cherie Carter-Scott (Broadway), *Suzanne Somers' 365 Ways to Change Your Life* by Suzanne Somers (Crown), and *A Golfer's Life* by Arnold Palmer and James Dodson (Ballantine).

A New Record for the 150,000+

Last year, 23 books with sales of more than 150,000 copies did not make a top-30 list. This is a new high at this level, breaking the previous record of 21 books set in 1997; the 1998 figure was 17 books. Five of the books with sales of 150,000 plus have yet to make a weekly *PW* chart or the monthly religion chart; that's a big improvement over the 17 of the 21 150,000-plus sellers in 1997 that never landed on a chart in the course of that year.

The five books that did not make the charts are *Aretha* by Aretha Franklin and David Ritz (Villard), *The Tae-Bo Way* by Billy Blanks (Bantam), *How Now Shall We Live?* by Charles Colson and Nancy Pearcey (Tyndale), *The Coming Global Superstorm* by Art Bell and Whitley Strieber (Pocket), and *Living the 7 Habits* by Stephen Covey (Simon & Schuster).

A few books in this group enjoyed more than a month on the weekly charts. *Something More* by Sarah Ban Breathnach (Warner) enjoyed sales of more than 900,000 in 1998 and about 158,000 in 1999 and had a 21-week tenure on the weekly charts. *Blind Man's Bluff* by Sherry Sontag and Christopher Drew (Public Affairs) was on the list for a total of 16 weeks, 13 0f them in 1999. *Encore Provence* by Peter Mayle (Knopf) had an 11-week run in 1999 and *I Ain't Got Time to Bleed* by Jesse Ventura (Villard) had an eight-week run. *Galileo's Daughter* by Dava Sobel was on the list for six weeks in 1999 and two more in

2000. *Are We Living in the End Times?* by Jerry B. Jenkins and Tim LaHaye (Tyndale) was on *PW*'s monthly religion list for three months.

The other bestsellers with runs of six weeks or less are *LaBelle Cuisine* by Patti LaBelle (Broadway), *ESPN SportsCentury*, edited by Michael MacCambridge (Hyperion), *The 30-Day Total Health Makeover* by Marilu Henner (ReganBooks), *The Hungry Ocean* by Linda Greenlaw (Hyperion), *Just Like Jesus* by Max Lucado (Word), *The Lexus and the Olive Tree* by Thomas L. Friedman (Farrar, Straus & Giroux), *River-Horse* by William Least Heat-Moon (Houghton Mifflin), *Ethics for the Next Millennium* by His Holiness the Dalai Lama with Alexander Norman (Riverhead), *Beauty Fades, Dumb Is Forever* by Judy Sheindlin (HarperCollins/Cliff Street), *Perfect Murder, Perfect Town* by Lawrence Schiller (HarperCollins), *The Endurance* by Caroline Alexander (Knopf), and *The Educated Child* by William J. Bennett, Chester E. Finn, Jr., and John T. E. Cribb, Jr. (Free Press).

The 125,000+ Level

This group includes 17 books that did not make our top-30 list, one less than the 1998 group. Only seven books in this group had a presence on last year's weekly charts, and five of them were on the list for more than a month. They are *Isaac's Storm* by Erik Larson (Crown), *Cinderella Story* by Bill Murray with George Peper (Doubleday), *The First World War* by John Keegan with an eight-week tenure (Knopf), *Live Now, Age Later* by Dr. Isadore Rosenfeld (Warner), and *Bill and Hillary: The Marriage* by Christopher Andersen (Morrow). Two others, *Hell to Pay* by Barbara Olson (Regnery) and *The Terrible Hours* by Peter Maas (HarperCollins), had a two-week and a one-week run, respectively.

The 10 that did not make a weekly *PW* slot are *And Never Let Her Go* by Ann Rule (Simon & Schuster), *Dave Pelz's Short Game Bible* by Dave Pelz with James A. Frank (Broadway), *American Thunder* by Jo Sgammato (Ballantine), *A Coach's Life* by Dean Smith with John Kilgo and Sally Jenkins (Random House), *The Secret Language of Destiny* by Gary Goldschneider and Joost Elffers (Viking Studio), *Codes of Love* by Mark Bryan (Pocket), *Cook Right 4 Your Type* by Peter J. D'Adamo (Tarcher), *God Is in the Small Stuff and It All Matters* by Bruce Bickel and Stan Jantz (Barbour), *A Charge to Keep* by George W. Bush with Mickey Herskowitz (Morrow), and *Comfort from a Country Quilt* by Reba McEntire (Bantam).

Nonfiction's 100,000+ List

In 1999, 28 additional hardcovers sold more than 100,000 copies, two more than the same group in 1998. As usual, this is also the group with the largest number of titles that never made *PW*'s weekly lists. Five books did land with runs of three to five weeks. They are *Congratulations! Now What?!?* by Bill Cosby (Hyperion), *Playing for Keeps* by David Halberstam (Random House), *Protecting the Gift* by Gavin de Becker (Dial), *If Life Is a Game, These Are the Rules* by Cherie

Carter-Scott (Broadway), and *Diana in Search of Herself* by Sally Bedell Smith (Times Books).

The 23 that did not show up on the 1999 charts are *Reason for Hope* by Jane Goodall (Warner), *The Bible Jesus Read* by Philip Yancey (Zondervan), *Customers.Com: How to Create a Profitable Business Strategy for the Internet and Beyond* by Patricia B. Seybold with Ronni T. Marshak (Times Books), *Lightposts for Living* by Thomas Kinkade (Warner), *Raising Cain* by Dan Kindlon and Michael Thompson (Ballantine), *The Elegant Universe* by Brian Greene (Norton), *Fresh Faith* by Jim Cymbala with Dean Merrill (Zondervan), *Leadership by the Book* by Ken Blanchard, Bill Hybels and Phil Hodges (Morrow), *Until Now* by Anne Geddes (Cedco), *Shy Boy* by Monty Roberts (HarperCollins), *Women* by Annie Leibovitz with essays by Susan Sontag (Random House), *Witness to Hope* by George Weigel (HarperCollins/Cliff Street), *Blind Eye* by James B. Stewart (Simon & Schuster), *The Way We Lived Then* by Dominick Dunne (Crown), *Another Country* by Mary Pipher (Riverhead), *Letters of the Century* by Lisa Grunwald and Stephen J. Adler (Dial), *Feel This Book* by Ben Stiller and Janeane Garofalo (Ballantine), *First, Break All the Rules* by Marcus Buckingham (Simon & Schuster), *Sincerely, Andy Rooney* by Andy Rooney (Public Affairs), *Hitler's Pope* by John Cornwell (Viking), *How to Get Started in Electronic Day Trading* by David S. Nassar (McGraw-Hill), *All Tomorrow's Parties* by William Gibson (Putnam), and *The New Drawing on the Right Side of the Brain* by Dr. Betty Edwards (Tarcher).

Paperback Bestsellers: The Usual Suspects Prevail

While the 1999 annual paperback bestseller list bears much resemblance to the 1998 list—similar subject categories, author names, and some repeat titles—a few new trends are noteworthy. For the first time, there are more fiction titles among the million-plus trade paperback grouping—six, compared to only one the year before. And while Oprah has had an impact on the sales growth of trade fiction—three of the million-copy performers were her book club picks—the top sellers also include a hardcover favorite, *Memoirs of a Geisha*, and two titles in the Left Behind series based on biblical prophecy from Tyndale. The latter were once top sellers only in the religion marketplace. The trend of more novels selling well in trade paper is also reflected in the increased number of fiction bestsellers on every printing level on this annual list.

In nonfiction, Chicken Soup continues to serve up hot sellers, but sales have slowed. In 1998 there were six books in the one-million group; in 1999 there was only one title there, and all the rest were in the 500,000-plus batch. *Angela's Ashes*, once a fixture on the hardcover lists, gets three mentions in the trade paper listing, as the publisher had various editions, including two movie tie-ins, in the marketplace. The combined total of all three would make Frank McCourt's memoir the bestselling trade paperback in 1999.

Self-help and computer titles remain strong trade paper categories, especially in the 75,000-plus and 50,000-plus groupings. Books with a spiritual theme are also gaining in sales.

Mass Market Favorites

The usual suspects shine in the mass market category, with almost all the top performers remaining the same year after year. The only new name on this year's two-million-plus list is Judy Blume, who writes an adult novel only every 20 years or so. John Grisham once again heads up the paperback list (he does the same in hardcover), and with sales of more than four million he remains the best-selling author no matter what the binding or price point is.

Nora Roberts continues to be the most prolific author in the paperback arena, with six books among the million-plus bestsellers. In 1999 she overtook Danielle Steel in sales. Three of her 1999 bestsellers—*Jewels of the Sun, Homeport,* and *The Reef*—outsold the three Steel books—*Mirror Image, The Long Road Home,* and *The Klone and I*—on this year's list. Steel is still ahead of Roberts in hardcover sales, so it will be interesting to see how the numbers for these two powerhouse female authors play out same time next year.

Reversing a trend noted in the last two years—that nonfiction was making some inroads in mass market bestsellers—the 1999 list includes only two, *The Guinness Book of Records 1999* and *Talking to Heaven.* Two more, *Dr. Atkins' New Diet Revolution* and *Protein Power*, would have been included but both were published in 1997 and this list reflects books published only in 1998 and 1999.

Included in these pages are trade paperback and mass market titles (originals, reprints, or dual editions) published in 1998 and 1999 for which publishers have billed and shipped at least 50,000 copies (for trade paperbacks) or one million copies (for mass market) in 1999. These figures do not always reflect net sales. Titles released in 1998 are marked by an asterisk; two asterisks indicate that the shipped-and-billed number was rounded down to the nearest 25,000 to indicate relationship to sales figures of other titles. The actual figures were given to *PW* in confidence for use in placing titles on the lists.

Trade Paperbacks

1 Million+

The Pilot's Wife. Anita Shreve. Rep. Little, Brown (2,279,134)

Memoirs of a Geisha. Arthur Golden. Rep. Vintage (2,087,739)

*The Reader. Bernhard Schlink. Rep. Vintage (1,528,615)

Angela's Ashes. Frank McCourt. Rep. S&S (1,336,103)

Chicken Soup for the Couple's Soul. Jack Canfield, Mark Victor Hansen, Barbara DeAngelis, and Mark & Chrissy Donnelly. Orig. HCI (1,245,437)

Don't Sweat the Small Stuff at Work. Richard Carlson. Orig. Hyperion (1,164,591)

*Where the Heart Is. Billie Letts. Rep. Warner (1,224,745)

Angela's Ashes. Frank McCourt. Rep. S&S (1,096,103)

Soul Harvest. Jerry B. Jenkins and Tim LaHaye. Reissue. Tyndale House (1,083,333)

Nicolae. Jerry B. Jenkins and Tim LaHaye. Reissue. Tyndale House (1,007,932)

500,000+

Chicken Soup for the Golfer's Soul. Jack Canfield, Mark Victor Hansen, Jeff Aubery, and Mark & Chrissy Donnelly. Orig. HCI (956,941)

*Here on Earth. Alice Hoffman. Rep. Berkley (950,000)

* Indicates the book was published in 1998.
** Indicates the sales figure was rounded down to the nearest 25,000 to show relationship to sales figures of other titles.

Jewel. Brett Lott. Reissue. Pocket (**925,000)

I Know This Much Is True. Wally Lamb. Rep. HarperCollins/Regan (884,316)

Chicken Soup for the Teenage Soul II. Jack Canfield, Mark Victor Hansen, and Kimberly Kirberger. Orig. HCI (856,487)

Windows 98 for Dummies. Andy Rathbone. Orig. IDG (834,000)

Chicken Soup for the College Soul. Jack Canfield, Mark Victor Hansen, Kimberly Kirberger, and Dan Clark. Orig. HCI (814,118)

River, Cross My Heart. Breena Clarke. Rep. Little, Brown (770,889)

Chicken Soup for the Cat & Lover's Soul. Jack Canfield, Mark Victor Hansen, Marty Becker, and Carol Kline. Orig. HCI (767,874)

Caring for Your Baby Birth to 5. American Academy of Pediatrics. Rep. Bantam (**725,000)

The Poisonwood Bible. Barbara Kingsolver. Rep. Perennial (662,842)

Chicken Soup for the Single's Soul. Jack Canfield, Mark Victor Hansen, Marcie Shimoff, and Jennifer Read Hawthorne. Orig. HCI (575,493)

Midnight in the Garden of Good and Evil. John Berendt. Rep. Vintage (575,334)

Chicken Soup for the Unsinkable Soul. Jack Canfield, Mark Victor Hansen, and Heather McNamara. Orig. HCI (568,717)

A 6th Bowl of Chicken Soup for the Soul. Jack Canfield and Mark Victor Hansen. Orig. HCI (564,353)

Charming Billy. Alice McDermott. Rep. Dell (**550,000)

One Day My Soul Just Opened Up. Iyanla Vazant. Orig. S&S (547,099)

250,000+

The Red Tent. Anita Diamant. Rep. Picador (475,494)

A Walk in the Woods. Bill Bryson. Rep. Broadway (462,782)

Bridget Jones's Diary. Helen Fielding. Rep. Penguin (460,790)

Birds of America. Lorrie Moore. Rep. Picador (451,058)

Women's Bodies, Women's Wisdom. Christiane Northup, M.D. Rep. Bantam (**450,000)

Storm of the Century. Stephen King. Orig. Pocket

Midwives. Chris Bohjalian. Rep. Vintage (443,692)

Serpent (A Novel from the Numa Files). Clive Cussler. Orig. Pocket (439,065)

Angela's Ashes. Frank McCourt. Rep./ Movie Tie-in. S&S (430,008)

In the Meantime. Iyanla Vanzant. Rep. S&S (425,900)

Real Boys: Rescuing Our Sons from the Myths of Boyhood. William Pollack. Rep. Holt (420,000)

Don't Give It Away. Iyanla Vanzant. Orig. S&S (417,085)

Suzanne Somers' Eat Great, Lose Weight. Suzanne Somers. Rep. Crown/Three Rivers (411,572)

Chicken Soup for the Kid's Soul. Jack Canfield, Mark Victor Hansen, Patty Hansen, and Irene Dunlap. Orig. HCI (392,539)

Widow for One Year. John Irving. Rep. Ballantine (382,484)

7 Habits of Highly Effective Teens. Stephen R. Covey. Orig. S&S (364,457)

The Millionaire Next Door. Thomas J. Stanley and William D. Danko. Rep. Pocket (**350,000)

Guns, Germs and Steel. Jared Diamond. Rep. Norton

Star Wars: Episode 1, the Making of the Phantom Menace. Laurent Bouzereau. Orig. Lucas/Del Rey (333,210)

Teen Love: On Relationships. Kimberly Kirberger. Orig. HCI (326,116)

Out to Canaan. Jan Karon. Rep. Penguin (324,211)

Tasteberry Tales for Teens. Bettie B. Youngs and Jennifer Leigh Youngs. Orig. HCI (314,458)

Cold Mountain. Charles Frazier. Rep. Vintage (275,839)

Teen Love: A Journal to Relationships. Kimberly Kirberger. Orig. HCI (272,675)

Chicken Soup for the Pet Lover's Soul. Jack Canfield, Mark Victor Hansen, Marty Becker, and Carol Kline. Orig. HCI (260,190)

The Professor and the Madman. Simon Winchester. Rep. Perennial (259,350)

John F. Kennedy Jr.: A Life in the Spotlight. Michael Druitt. Reissue. Andrews McMeel (250,000)

100,000+

Our Dumb Century. Scott Dikkers. Orig. Crown/Three Rivers (248,271)

Rich Dad Poor Dad (What the Rich Teach Their Kids About Money That the Poor and Middle Class Do Not!). Robert T. Kiyosaki with Sharon L. Lechter. Reissue Techpress (237,593)

Don't Sweat The Small Stuff with Your Family. Richard Carlson. Orig. Hyperion (231,189)

Windows 98 Simplified. Ruth Maran. Orig. IDG (229,000)

A Second Chicken Soup for the Woman's Soul. Jack Canfield, Mark Victor Hansen, Marci Shimoff, and Jennifer Read Hawthorne. Orig. HCI (224,763)

Their Eyes Were Watching God. Zora Neale Hurston. Rep. Perennial Classics (211,279)

Don't Step in the Leadership: A Dilbert Book. Scott Adams. Orig. Andrews McMeel (200,000)

The Beach. Alex Garland. Rep. Riverhead (200,000)

* *While Waiting.* George E. Verrilli and Anne Marie Mueser. Rep. St. Martin's (198,116)

Patchwork Planet. Anne Tyler. Rep. Ballantine (196,554)

Vampire Armand. Anne Rice. Rep. Ballantine (196,362)

Weight of Water. Anita Shreve. Rep. Little, Brown (193,057)

Are You Somebody: The Accidental Memoir of a Dublin Woman. Nuala O'Faolain. Rep. Holt (190,000)

Hanna's Daughters. Marianne Fredriksson. Rep. Ballantine (189,700)

Windows 98 for Dummies Quick reference. Andy Rathbone. Orig. IDG (188,000)

The Honk & Holler Opening Soon. Billie Letts. Rep. Warner (183,696)

Lindbergh. A. Scott Berg. Rep. Berkley (175,000)

Carrier. Tom Clancy. Orig. Berkley (175,000)

Falling Leaves. Adeline Yen Mah. Rep. Broadway (172,736)

Teach Yourself Windows 98 Visually. Ruth Maran. Orig. IDG (172,000)

Die Broke. Stephen Pollan. Rep. Harper-Business (170,908)

Endurance. Alfred Lansing. Rep. Carroll & Graf (169,757)

The 7 Worst Things Good Parents Do. John and Linda Friel. Orig. HCI (169,325)

Star Wars: Episode 1, The Phantom Menace: Illustrated Screenplay. George Lucas. Orig. Del Rey (167,503)

Slaves in the Family. Edward Ball. Rep. Ballantine (167,493)

Ophelia Speaks. Sara Shandler. Orig. Perennial (166,834)

Night Without Armor. Jewel. Rep. (166,294)

Last Full Measure. Jeff Shaara. Rep. Ballantine (162,937)

Worst Pills, Best Pills. Sidney M. Wolfe. Rep. Pocket

iMac for Dummies. David Pogue. Orig. IDG (159,000)

Kiss of God. Marshall Stewart Ball. Orig. HCI (157,410)

The Simpsons Forever! Matt Groening. Orig. Perennial (154,898)

The Gifts of the Jews. Thomas Cahill. Rep. Anchor (154,488)

Dilbert Gives You the Business: A Dilbert Book. Scott Adams. Orig. Andrews McMeel (150,000)

Best American Short Stories 1999. Edited by Amy Tan. Orig. Houghton Mifflin (150,000)

Organizing from the Inside Out. Julie Morgenstern. Orig. Holt (150,000)

Amazing Grace. Kathleen Norris. Rep. Riverhead (150,000)

Princess. Lori Wick. Orig. Harvest House (147,200)

The God of Small Things. Arundhati Roy. Rep. Perennial Classics (146,806)

The Illustrated Dream Dictionary. Russell Grant. Sterling (141,000)

Protein Power. Michael R. Eades. Rep. Bantam

The Ten Commandments. Laura Schlessinger. Rep. Cliff Street (136,870)

She's Come Undone. Wally Lamb. Reissue. Pocket

Every Little Thing About You. Lori Wick. Orig. Harvest House

Small Miracles II. Yitta Halberstam and Judith Leventhal. Orig. Adams Media Corporation (125,323)

Adventures of a Psychic. Sylvia Browne. Orig. Hay House (125,023)

Shakespeare. Harold Bloom. Rep. Riverhead (125,000)

The Girlfriend's Guide to Toddlers. Vicki Iovine. Orig. Perigee (125,000)

Ship of Gold in the Deep Blue Sea. Gary Kinder. Rep. Vintage (123,780)

A Monk Swimming. Malachy McCourt. Rep. Hyperion (123,101)

Make the Connection: 10 Steps to a Better Body—And a Better Life. Bob Greene and Oprah Winfrey. Rep. Hyperion (120,748)

Wall Street Journal Guide to Understanding Money and Investing. Kenneth M. Morris. Orig. S&S (120,703)

Small Miracles of Love & Friendship. Yitta Halberstam and Judith Leventhal. Orig. Adams Media Corporation (119,611)

Roaring 2000s. Harry S. Dent Jr. Rep. S&S (116,641)

Complete Idiot's Guide to Windows 98. Paul McFedries. Orig. Que (115,084)

The Girlfriend's Guide to Pregnancy. Vicki Iovine. Orig. Pocket

The Perfect Storm. Sebastian Junger. Rep. Perennial (113,034)

Chocolate for a Mother's Heart. Edited by Kay Allenbaugh. Orig. S&S (110,449)

Tender at the Bone. Ruth Reichl. Rep. Broadway (106,842)

*The Cashglow Quadrant (Rich Dad's Guide to Financial Freedom). Robert T. Kiyosaki with Sharon L. Lechter. Orig. Techpress (103,677)

Confederates in the Attic: Dispatches from the Unfinished Civil War. Tony Horwitz. Rep. Vintage (103,166)

Beauty Secrets. Diane Irons. Orig. Sourcebooks (103,123)

*Experiencing God. Henry T. Blackaby and Claude V. King. Reissue. Broadman & Holman (103,026)

About a Boy. Nick Hornby. Rep. Riverhead (100,000)

*Harley Hahn: Internet and Web Yellow Pages, Millennium Edition. Harley Hahn. Orig. Osborne/McGraw-Hill (100,000)

Quicken 2000: The Official Guide. Maria Langer. Orig. Osborne/McGraw-Hill (100,000)

75,000+

Reading People. Jo-Ellan Dimitrius. Rep. Ballantine (99,097)

Joy of Work. Scott Adams. Rep. HarperBusiness (95,303)

The Sweet Potato Queens' Book of Love. Jill Conner Browne. Orig. Crown/Three Rivers (94,411)

Damascus Gate. Robert Stone. Rep. S&S (93,350)

Cities of the Plain. Cormac McCarthy. Rep. Vintage (93,305)

The Schwarzbein Principle: The Truth About Losing Weight, Being Healthy and Feeling Younger. Diana Schwarzbein, M.D. and Nancy Deville. Orig. HCI (93,243)

Chocolate for a Woman's Spirit. Edited by Kay Allenbaugh. Orig. S&S (93,110)

*Ingenious Lateral Thinking Puzzles. Paul Sloane. Sterling (93,000)

Garfield: Life to the Fullest. Jim Davis. Orig. Ballantine (92,437)

The Innocent. Bertrice Small. Orig. Fawcett (92,097)

*100 Years of Solitude. Gabriel Garcia Marquez. Rep. Perennial Classics (89,533)

Star Wars: Essential Guide to Droids. Daniel Wallace. Orig. Del Rey (89,030)

Y2K. Victor Porlier. Orig. Perennial (88,241)

A Tree Grows in Brooklyn. Betty Smith. Rep. Perennial Classics (87,970)

Bart Simpson's Treehouse of Horror Heebie-Jeebie Hullabaloo. Matt Groening. Orig. Perennial (87,807)

A+ Certification for Dummies. Ron Gilster. Orig. IDG (87,000)

Titan: The Life of John D. Rockefeller, Sr. Ron Chernow. Rep. Vintage (86,629)

Harvey Penick's Little Red Book. Harvey Penick. Rep. S&S (86,515)

Savage Spawn. Jonathan Kellerman. Orig. Ballantine (85,487)

*Road Less Traveled. M. Scott Peck. Reissue. S&S (84,223)

Eat the Rich. P. J. O'Rourke. Rep. Grove/Atlantic (83,848)

Pure Drivel. Steve Martin. Rep. Hyperion (83,379)

The Joy of Work. Scott Adams. Rep. HarperBusiness (82,392)

*Web Design in a Nutshell. Jen Niederst. Orig. O'Reilly (81,812)

Special Edition Using Microsoft Office 2000. E. Bott and W. Leonhard. Orig. Que (81,483)

Making Faces. Kevyn Aucoin. Rep. Little, Brown (81,315)

Inside Microsoft SQL Server 7.0. Ron Soukup and Kalen Delaney. Orig. Microsoft (80,965)

Evening. Susan Minot. Rep. Vintage (80,729)

Strong Women Stay Young. Miriam Nelson. Rep. Bantam

A Brief History of Time. Stephen Hawking. Rep. Bantam

MCSE Core Four Exam Cram Pack. Ed Tittel, Kurt Hudson, and James Michael Stewart. Orig. Coriolis (80,000)

What We Keep. Elizabeth Berg. Rep. Ballantine (79,498)

Victors. Stephen E. Ambrose. Rep. S&S (79,195)

Lord of the Rings. J. R. R. Tolkien. Reissue. Houghton Mifflin (78,000)

Quite a Year for Plums. Bailey White. Rep. Vintage (77,050)

Motley Fool's Investment Workbook. David Gardner. Orig. S&S (76,884)

Bringing Out the Dead. Joe Connelly. Rep. Vintage (76,775)

Microsoft Windows NT Server 4.0 Enterprise Technologies Training. Microsoft. Orig. Microsoft (76,663)

Bosom Buddies: Lessons and Laughter on Breast Health and Cancer. Rosie O'Donnell. Orig. Warner (75,788)

Programming Microsoft Outlook and Microsoft Exchange. Thomas Rizzo. Orig. Microsoft (75,120)

Amsterdam. Ian McEwan. Rep. Anchor (75,043)

Kaaterskill Falls. Allegra Goodman. Rep. Dell (**75,000)

The Lives Behind the Lines: 20 Years of For Better or for Worse. Lynn Johnston. Orig. Andrews McMeel (75,000)

How to Do Everything with iMac. Todd Stauffer. Orig. Osborne/McGraw-Hill (75,000)

Hacking Exposed. Stuart McClure, Joe Scambray, and George Kurtz. Orig. Osborne/McGraw-Hill (75,000)

A+ Certification All in One Exam Guide. Michael J. Meyers. Orig. Osborne/McGraw-Hill (75,000)

Word 2000 for Windows for Dummies. Dan Gookin. Orig. IDG (75,000)

Excel 2000 for Windows for Dummies. Greg Harvey. Orig. IDG (75,000)

50,000+

The Haunting. Shirley Jackson. Rep./ Movie Tie-in. Penguin (73,585)

Easy Windows 98. Shelley O'Hara. Orig. Que (73,270)

Microsoft Age of Empires II: The Age of Kings: Inside Moves. Mark H. Walker. Orig. Microsoft (73,012)

The Celestine Vision. James Redfield. Rep. Warner (72,629)

Blindness. José Saramago. Rep. Harcourt (72,015)

The Hundred Days. Patrick O'Brian. Rep. Norton

Daily Teen Reflections. Stephen R. Covey. Orig. S&S (71,198)

Programming Microsoft Visual Basic. 6.0. Francesco Balena. Orig. Microsoft (70,646)

Our Town. Thornton Wilder. Rep. Perennial Classics (70,288)

Fight Club. Chuck Palahnuik. Rep. Holt (70,000)

Strong Women Stay Slim. Miriam Nelson. Rep. Bantam (70,000)

Master Windows 98 Visually. Ruth Maran, Paul Whitehead, Maarten Heilbron, and Marangraphics Inc. Orig. IDG (70,000)

The Recipe Hall-of-Fame Cookbook. Edited by Gwen McKee and Barbara Moseley. Orig. Quail Ridge (69,825)

All Over but the Shoutin'. Rick Bragg. Rep. Vintage (69,591)

The Only Investment Guild You'll Ever Need. Andrew Tobias. Orig. Harcourt (68,988)

Motley Fools You Have More Than You Think. David Gardner. Rep. S&S (68,731)

Mars and Venus on a Date. John Gray. Rep. Perennial (68,718)

Programming Distributed Applications with COM and Microsoft Visual Basic. Ted Pattison. Orig. Microsoft (68,276)

Microsoft Flight Simulator 2000: Inside Moves. Bart Farkas. Orig. Microsoft (67,733)

The Notebook. Nicholas Sparks. Rep. Warner (67,534)

Citizen Soldiers. Stephen E. Ambrose. Rep. S&S (67,325)

Microsoft Exchange Server Training Kit. Kay Unkroth. Orig. Microsoft (67,307)

Consilience: The Unity of Knowledge. Edmund O. Wilson. Rep. Vintage (67,289)

Lillian Too's Easy-to-Use Feng Shui. Lillian Too. Orig. Sterling (67,000)

Dreamweaver 2 Bible. Joseph W. Lowery. Orig. IDG (67,000)

Where or When. Anita Shreve. Rep. Harcourt (66,651)

Strange Fits of Passion. Anita Shreve. Rep. Harcourt (66,633)

NightWatch: A Practical Guide to Viewing the Universe—3rd Edition. Terence Dickinson. Reviscd. Firefly (66,516)

Desktop Applications with Microsoft Visual Basic 6.0 MCSD Training Kit. Microsoft. Orig. Microsoft (66,469)

Programming Microsoft Visual InterDev 6.0. Nicholas D. Evans, Ken Miller, and Ken Spencer. Orig. Microsoft (65,824)

Programming Microsoft Access 2000. Rick Dobson. Orig. Microsoft (65,505)

Complete Idiot's Guide to Online Investing. Douglas Gerlach. Orig. Que (65,196)

Miracle on the 17th Green. James Patterson. Rep. Little, Brown (65,164)

Best American Mysteries Stories. Edited by Ed McBain. Orig. Houghton Mifflin (65,000)

Questions & Answers on Conversations with God. Neale Donald Walsch. Orig. Hampton Roads (64,479)

Inn at Lake Divine. Elinor Lipman. Rep. Vintage (64,306)

Designing Component-Based Applications. Mary Kirtland. Orig. Microsoft (64,074)

How Computers Work, Millennium Edition. Ron White. Orig. Que (64,062)

Cloudsplitter. Russell Banks. Rep. Perennial (63,895)

Message in a Bottle. Nicholas Sparks. Rep. Warner (63,887)

The Mitford Years Boxed Set. Jan Karon. Rep. Penguin (63,505)

There's a Hair in My Dirt! Gary Larson. Rep. Perennial (63,308)

Microsoft Windows NT Server 4.0 Resource Kit Supplement 4. Origin. Microsoft (63,080)

Clear Your Clutter with Feng Shui. Karen Kingston. Orig. (62,454)

Mythology. Edith Hamilton. Rep. Little, Brown (62,168)

Practical Feng Shui. Simon Brown. Sterling (62,000)

Giving the Love That Heals. Harville Hendrix. Rep. Pocket

Chocolate for a Woman's Heart. Edited by Kay Allenbaugh. Orig. S&S (61,971)

The Short History of a Prince. Jane Hamilton. Rep. Anchor (61,704)

Microsoft BackOffice 4.5 Resource Kit. Microsoft Orig. Microsoft (61,392)

Desktop Applications with Microsoft Visual C++ 6.0 MCSD Training Kit. Microsoft. Orig. Microsoft (60,918)

MTV: The Real World Hawaii. Allison Pollet. Orig. Pocket

Programming Microsoft Visual J++ 6.0. Stephen R. Davis. Orig. Microsoft (60,579)

Dr. Atkins. Vita-Nutrient Solution. Dr. Robert C. Atkins. Rep. S&S (60,331)

Microsoft Office 2000 8-in-1. Joe Habraken. Orig. Que (60,272)

What Your Doctor May Not Tell You About Premenopause. Dr. John R. Lee. Orig. Warner (60,247)

You Know You've Reached Middle Age If . . . Joey Green and Alan Corcoran. Orig. Andrews McMeel (60,000)

A+ Exam Cram. James Jones and Craig Landes. Orig. Coriolis (60,000)

Programming Components with Microsoft Visual Basic 6.0. Guy Eddon and Henry Eddon. Orig. Microsoft (59,764)

98 Degrees: The Official Book. K. M. Squires. Orig. Pocket

Red Hat Linux 6 Unleashed. David Pitts and William Ball. Orig. Sams (59,512)

King of the World. David Remnick. Rep. Vintage (59,352)

The Breast Cancer Prevention Diet. Bob Arnot. Rep. Little, Brown (59,146)

Microsoft SQL Server 7.0 System Administration Online Training Kit. Microsoft. Orig. Microsoft (59,040)

The Perks of Being a Wallflower. Stephen Chbosky. Orig. Pocket

Ideas for Great Kitchens. Sunset Editors. Orig. Sunset (58,883)

Microsoft SQL Server 7.0 Database Implementation Online Training Kit. Microsoft. Orig. Microsoft (58,454)

Native Son. Richard Wright. Rep. Perennial Classics (58,332)

Brain Droppings. George Carlin. Rep. Hyperion (58,056)

The Essential Angel. Buffy the Vampire Slayer. Orig. Pocket

Supporting Microsoft Windows 98 Online Training Kit. Microsoft. Orig. Microsoft (57,489)

Programming Microsoft Windows CE. Douglas Boling. Orig. Microsoft (57,414)

Complete Idiot's Guide to Microsoft Office 2000. Joe Kraynak. Orig. Que (56,384)

Don't Worry, Make Money. Richard Carlson. Rep. Hyperion (56,363)

Death of Outrage. William J. Bennett. Rep. S&S (56,228)

Just Enough Light for the Step I'm On. Stormie Omartian. Orig. Harvest House (55,600)

Inside the Microsoft Windows 98 Registry. Günter Born. Orig. Microsoft (55,232)

Everything Wedding Organizer. Laura Morin. Orig. Adams Media Corporation (55,155)

The Ultimate Decorating Book. Judy Spours. Orig. Sterling (55,000)

Core Java 2, Vol. 1: Fundaments. Gary Cornell and Clay Horstmann. Orig. Prentice Hall (54,538)

In the Year 2000. Conan O'Brien. Orig. Riverhead (54,515)

Deal with It. Esther Drill, Heather McDonald and Rebecca Odes. Orig. Pocket

Newton's Telecom Dictionary 15th Edition. Harry Newton. Reissue. Telecom/ Miller Freeman (54,048)

1001 Ways to Be Romantic: Annotated Edition. Gregory Godek. Orig. Sourcebooks (53,922)

Aphrodite. Isabel Allende. Rep. Perennial (53,836)

How the Mind Works. Steven Pinker. Rep. Norton

The World's Best-Kept Diet Secrets. Diane Irons. Orig. Sourcebooks (53,329)

Cliffs Notes Using Your First PC. Jim McCarter. Orig. IDG (53,000)

Cliffs Notes Getting on the Internet. David Crowder, Rhonda Crowder, and Alan Simpson. Orig. IDG (53,000)

Voyage of the Narwhal. Andrea Barrett. Rep. Norton (52,941)

Ideas for Great Bathrooms. Sunset Editors. Orig. Sunset (52,722)

Potatoes Not Prozac. Kathleen Des Maisons. Rep. S&S (52,475)

Chicken Soup for the Teenage Soul Journal. Jack Canfield, Mark Victor Hansen, and Kimberly Kirberger. Orig. HCI (52,468)

Kid Tips. Tom McMahon. Revised Reissue. Pocket

The Rape of Nanking. Iris Chang. Rep. Penguin (52,444)

The Archivist. Martha Cooley. Rep. Little, Brown (52,211)

The Complete Idiot's Guide to Learning Spanish on Your Own, 2nd Edition. Gail Stein. Reissue. Macmillan USA (52,001)

Access 2000 for Windows for Dummies. John Kaufeld. Orig. IDG (52,000)

Naked. David Sedaris. Rep. Little, Brown (51,622)

Memoirs of Cleopatra. Margaret George. Rep. St. Martin's (51,487)

Animal Miracles. Brad Steiger and Sherry Hansen Steiger. Orig. Adams Media Corporation (51,274)

South. Sir Ernest Shackleton. Rep. Carroll & Graf (51,089)

My Life with Sylvia Browne. Chris Dufresne. Orig. Hay House (51,043)

Die Broke. Stephan Pollan. Rep. HarperBusiness (50,758)

Shagadelically Speaking: The Words and World of Austin Powers. Lance Gould. Orig. Warner (50,731)

The Handmaid's Tale. Margaret Atwood. Rep. Anchor (50,521)

Spending. Mary Gordon. Rep. S&S (50,311)

Y2K Family Survival Guide. Jerry MacGregor. Orig. Harvest House

The Seville Communion. Arturo Pérez-Reverte. Rep. Harcourt (50,283)

Americanos. Edward James Olmos. Duel. Little, Brown (50,218)

Office 2000: The Complete Reference. Stephen L. Nelson. Orig. Osborne/McGraw-Hill (50,000)

Windows 98 for Busy People. Ron Mansfield and Peter Weverka. Orig. Osborne/McGraw-Hill (50,000)

QuickBooks 99: The Official Guide. Kathy Ivens. Orig. Osborne/McGraw-Hill (50,000)

Hewlett-Packard Official Scanner Handbook. David D. Busch, Susan Krzywicki, and Laurel Burden. Orig. IDG (50,000)

MCSE TCP/IP Exam Cram. Gary Novosei, Kurt Hudson, and James Michael Stewart. Orig. Coriolis (50,000)

Almanacs, Atlases & Annuals

The World Almanac and Book of Facts 2000. Robert Famighetti. Orig. World Almanac (1,322,409)

*The World Almanac and Book of Facts 1999. Robert Farmighetti. Orig. World Almanac (317,003)

Old Farmer's Almanac 2000. Edited by Judson Hale. Orig. Villard (298,340)

What Color Is Your Parachute 2000. Richard Nelson Bolles. Orig. Ten Speed (130,198)

2000 ESPN Information Please Sports Almanac. Gerry Brown, Mike Morrison, and the Editors of Information Please. Orig. Hyperion (111,566)

*What Color Is Your Parachute 1999. Richard Nelson Bolles. Orig. Ten Speed (111,457)

The New York Times Almanac 2000. Orig. Penguin (100,035)

Kovels' Antiques and Collectibles Price List 2000 (32nd Edition). Ralph and Terry Kovel. Orig. Crown/Three Rivers (55,915)

Mass Market

2 Million+

The Street Lawyer. John Grisham. Rep. Dell (**4,100,000)

The Testament. John Grisham. Rep. Dell (**3,875,000)

Bag of Bones. Stephen King. Rep. Pocket (**2,200,000)

Point of Origin. Patricia Cornwell. Rep. Berkley (2,200,000)

Rainbow Six. Tom Clancy. Rep. Berkley (2,200,000)

Jewels of the Sun. Nora Roberts. Rep. Jove (2,100,000)

Summer Sister. Judy Blume. Rep. Dell

You Belong to Me. Mary Higgins Clark. Rep. Pocket (2,075,000)

Southern Cross. Patricia Cornwell. Rep. Berkley (2,000,000)

1 Million+

Op Center VI: State of Siege. Tom Clancy and Steve Pieceznik. Rep. Berkley (1,950,000)

Homeport. Nora Roberts. Rep. Jove (1,900,000)

The Reef. Nora Roberts. Rep. Jove (1,900,000)

Power Play: Shadow Watch. Tom Clancy & Martin Greenberg. Orig. Berkley (1,900,000)

Mirror Image. Danielle Steel. Rep. Dell

All Through the Night. Mary Higgins Clark. Rep. Pocket (**1,875,000)

Message in a Bottle. Nicholas Sparks. Rep. Warner Vision (1,817,897)

The Long Road Home. Danielle Steel. Rep. Dell

Net Force #2: Hidden Agenda. Tom Clancy and Steve Pieceznik. Orig. Berkley (1,750,000)

The Klone and I. Danielle Steel. Rep. Dell

Then Came Heaven. Lavyrle Spencer. Rep. Jove (1,600,000)

When the Wind Blows. James Patterson. Rep. Warner Vision (1,596,121)

Seize the Night. Dean Koontz. Rep. Bantam (**1,500,000)

N Is for Noose. Sue Grafton. Rep. Ballantine (1,468,973)

Billy Straight. Jonathan Kellerman. Rep. Ballantine (1,461,912)

Tell Me Your Dreams. Sidney Sheldon. Rep. Warner Vision (1,418,362)

Secret Prey. John Sanford. Rep. Berkley (1,400,000)

The Loop. Nicholas Evans. Rep. Dell

The Simple Truth. David Baldacci. Rep. Warner (1,376, 460)

Rebellion. Nora Roberts. Reissue. Silhouette/Harlequin (1,390,000)

The MacGregors: Daniel & Ian. Nora Roberts. Reissue. Silhouette/Harlequin (1,340,000)

Night Whispers. Judith McNaught. Rep. Pocket (**1,300,000)

No Safe Place. Richard North Patterson. Rep. Ballantine (1,299,219)

Olivia. V. C. Andrews. Orig. Pocket (**1,250,000)

Into the Garden. V. C. Andrews. Orig. Pocket

The MacGregors: Alan & Grant. Nora Roberts. Reissue. Silhouette/Harlequin (1,240,000)

Unspeakable. Sandra Brown. Rep. Warner (1,200,107)

The Target. Catherine Coulter. Rep. Jove (1,200,000)

Hammer of Eden. Ken Follett. Rep. Ballantine (1,101,915)

Critical Mass. Steve Martini. Rep. Jove (1,100,000)

A Man in Full. Tom Wolfe. Rep. Bantam (**1,100,000)

Guinness Book of Records 1999. Mark C. Young, Rep. Bantam (**1,100,000)

Misty. V. C. Andrews. Orig. Pocket (**1,075,000)

The Green Mile. Stephen King. Reissue. Pocket

Ransom. Julie Garwood. Rep. Pocket

Violin. Anne Rice. Rep. Ballantine (1,062,394)

Jewel. Bret Lott. Rep. Pocket

The Present. Johanna Lindsey. Rep. Avon (**1,025,000)

Jade. V. C. Andrews. Orig. Pocket

Star. V. C. Andrews. Orig. Pocket

The Blessing. Jude Deveraux. Rep. Pocket

Coast Road. Barbara Delinsky. Rep. Pocket (**1,000,000)

Talking to Heaven. James Van Praagh. Rep. Signet (1,000,000)

A Sudden Change of Heart. Barbara Taylor Bradford. Rep. Dell (1,000,000)

Black and Blue. Anna Quindlen. Rep. Dell (1,000,000)

Children's Bestsellers: Harry, Pokémon Were the Stars of '99

Diane Roback

Senior Editor, *Publishers Weekly*

For children's publishers, it was a mixed year. There were fewer big hardcover frontlist sellers than in previous years: only 18 books in this category sold more than 200,000 copies last year, compared to 32 titles in 1998 and 39 in 1997. Of course, the total sales figures were greatly helped by a young wizard-in-training; the two Harry Potter frontlist titles, *Chamber of Secrets* and *Prisoner of Azkaban*, sold a total of seven million copies. Tie-ins for *Tarzan, Toy Story 2, Barney,* and *Blue's Clues* also landed in top spots, as did one-offs by such notable names as Maria Shriver, Beverly Cleary, Jan Brett, and Peter Jennings.

The category of hardcover backlist also showed some softening at the top: 18 books sold more than 300,000 copies last year, compared to 23 in 1998. And only 79 titles sold more than 125,000 copies, a sizeable decrease from 1998's figure of 117. Old standbys like *Love You Forever, Goodnight Moon,* and *Green Eggs and Ham* shared top slots with two prominent fiction offerings: *Harry Potter and the Sorcerer's Stone*, first in the series, and *Holes*, the 1998 Newbery and National Book Award winner.

In paperback frontlist, 1998's hot series, Animorphs, faded a bit: 12 Animorphs titles sold more than 300,000 copies each in 1998 (with none at that level in 1999), and 12 (including a few spinoff Megamorphs and Alternamorphs titles) sold above the 200,000 level last year. Their dominance on the list was replaced by Pokémon: seven of the top 10 paperback frontlist titles were Pokémon tie-ins, accounting for more than seven million copies sold for Scholastic and Golden. *Star Wars Episode One* tie-ins from Random and Scholastic also had a strong paperback showing.

Paperback backlist took the biggest hit in 1999. Only 56 titles sold more than 125,000 copies, compared to 91 titles in 1998. Among the more noticeable absentees from the previous year: Leonardo DiCaprio bios, Wishbone books (four in 1998, none in 1999), Rugrats titles (three in 1998, none in 1999), and Winnie the Pooh books (three in 1998, none in 1999). *Chicken Soup for the Kid's Soul*, 1998's bestselling paperback frontlist title with more than 1,300,000 copies sold, took a dip in its sophomore year, though it still sold almost 400,000 copies.

On the plus side, Tyndale House's Left Behind: The Kids fiction series showed some strong numbers in paperback backlist, with the first four books in the series totaling more than 1,300,000 copies, as did such perennial bestsellers as *The Outsiders*, *The Giver*, *Charlotte's Web*, *Where the Wild Things Are*—and everyone's (and now Hollywood's) favorite mouse, *Stuart Little*.

Hardcover Frontlist

300,000+

1. *Harry Potter and the Prisoner of Azkaban.* J. K. Rowling, illus. by Mary GrandPré. Scholastic/Levine (3,600,000)
2. *Harry Potter and the Chamber of Secrets.* J. K. Rowling, illus. by Mary GrandPré. Scholastic/Levine (3,400,000)
3. *Disney's Tarzan Read-Aloud Storybook.* Mouse Works (428,902)
4. *I Spy Treasure Hunt.* Jean Marzollo, illus. by Walter Wick. Scholastic/Cartwheel (384,000)
5. *What's Heaven?* Maria Shriver, illus. by Sandra Speidel. St. Martin's/ Golden (373,628)
6. *Toy Story 2 Read-Aloud Storybook.* Mouse Works (363,695)
7. *Barney's We Wish You a Merry Christmas.* Lyrick (346,176)

200,000+

8. *Why Do You Love Me?* Dr. Laura Schlessinger, illus by Daniel McFeeley. HarperCollins (275,627)
9. *The Cheerios Animal Play Book.* Lee Wade. Little Simon (265,300)
10. *Disney's Tarzan.* Golden (253,795)
11. *Blue's Clues: Figure Out Blue's Clues.* Simon Spotlight (247,178)
12. *Ramona's World.* Beverly Cleary. HarperCollins (241,378)
13. *Gingerbread Baby.* Jan Brett. Putnam (219,800)
14. *Blue's Clues: Crayon World.* Simon Spotlight (217,490)
15. *The Century for Young People.* Peter Jennings and Todd Brewster. Doubleday (217,454)
16. *Baby Bop's Blankey.* Lyrick (210,722)
17. *The Dance.* Richard Paul Evans, illustrated by Jonathan Linton. S&S (207,293)
18. *Barney's ABC, 123 and More!* Lyrick (205,364)

100,000+

19. *Disney's Princess Storybook Collection.* Disney (192,439)

20. *Muppet Babies: I Can Go Potty.* Golden (186,601)
21. *BJ's Rub-a-Dub-Dub.* Lyrick (183,308)
22. *The Very Clumsy Click Beetle.* Illus. by Eric Carle. Philomel, (178,600)
23. *Animorphs: Visser.* K. A. Applegate. Scholastic (178,000)
24. *Eloise at Christmastime.* Kay Thompson, illus. by Hilary Knight. S&S (175,044)
25. *Disney's Tarzan: Jungle Jam.* Mouse Works (173,578)
26. *Barney's Book of Colors.* Lyrick (173,106)
27. *Poky & Friends: The Truth About Kittens and Puppies.* Golden (170,241)
28. *Busy Book: Whose Face? Pooh's Face!* Mouse Works (157,711)
29. *Eloise in Paris.* Kay Thompson, illus. by Hilary Knight. S&S (157,130)
30. *The Sun Maid Raisin Play Book.* B. Alison Weir, illus. by Judith Moffat. Little Simon (155,722)
31. *A Grandmother's Memories to Her Grandchild.* Candy Paull, illus. by Thomas Kinkade. Tommy Nelson (155,474)
32. *Blue's Clues: Blue's Treasure Hunt Notebook.* Simon Spotlight (152,722)
33. *I Spy Little Christmas.* Jean Marzollo, illus. by Walter Wick. Scholastic/ Cartwheel (145,000)
34. *Growing Up with Winnie the Pooh.* Disney (143,740)
35. *Toy Story 2: Friendship Box.* Mouse Works (143,045)
36. *Me and My Dad.* Stuart Hample. Workman (138,883)
37. *What's the Time, Benjamin?* Sterling (138,000)
38. *Star Wars Episode One: Jar Jar Binks.* Random/Lucas (137,427)
39. *Pooh's Sweet Dreams.* Mouse Works (136,817)
40. *Buffy the Vampire Slayer Sunnydale High Yearbook.* Christopher Golden and Nancy Holder. Pocket (136,602)
41. *Legend of the Easter Egg.* Lori Walburg, illus. by James Bernardin. Zonderkidz (135,067)
42. *Toy Story 2: Find the Flag.* Mouse Works (133,888)
43. *Star Wars Episode One: Anakin Skywalker.* Random/Lucas (131,172)
44. *Pooh's Pitter Patter Splash.* Mouse Works (128,914)
45. *Madeline in America.* Ludwig Bemelmans and John Bemelmans Marciano. Scholastic/Levine (128,000)
46. *Disney's Tarzan Me and You.* Mouse Works (126,338)
47. *Winnie the Pooh's Friendly Adventure Read-Aloud Storybook.* Mouse Works (123,225)
48. *Day by Day.* Betty Free, illus. by Eira Reeves. Tyndale (121,998)
49. *Swine Lake.* James Marshall, illus. by Maurice Sendak. HarperCollins/di Capua (120,873)
50. *Barney's Mother Goose Hunt.* Lyrick (119,918)
51. *Auntie Claus.* Elise Primavera. Harcourt/Silver Whistle (119,134)

52. *Dear America: My Heart Is on the Ground: The Diary of Nannie Little Rose, A Sioux Girl.* Ann Rinaldi. Scholastic (119,000)
53. *The Cat in the Hat's Great Big Flap Book.* Dr. Seuss, illus. by Aristides Ruiz. Random (115,397)
54. *Nightmare Hour.* R. L. Stine. HarperCollins (115,370)
55. *Poky & Friends: Lucky Ducks.* Golden (114,756)
56. *Little Miss Spider.* David Kirk. Scholastic/Callaway (113,000)
57. *The Royal Diaries: Elizabeth I: Red Rose of the House of Tudor.* Kathryn Lasky. Scholastic (112,000)
58. *How Are You Peeling?* Saxton Freymann and Joost Elffers. Scholastic/Levine (111,000)
59. *The Magic Show.* Mark Setteducati and Anne Benkovitz, illus. by Steve Ellis. Workman (108,780)
60. *The Pepperidge Farm Goldfish Fun Book.* Barbara Barbieri McGrath, illus. by Frank Mazzola, Jr. HarperFestival (108,463)
61. *The Quiltmaker's Gift.* Jeff Brumbeau, illus. by Gail de Marcken. Pfeifer-Hamilton (107,212)
62. *Rudolph the Red-Nosed Reindeer.* Golden (106,715)
63. *Eloise: The Absolutely Essential Edition.* Kay Thompson, illus. by Hilary Knight. S&S (105,426)
64. *I Spy Little Numbers.* Jean Marzollo, illus. by Walter Wick. Scholastic/Cartwheel (105,000)
65. *Lion King Read-Aloud Storybook.* Mouse Works (104,515)
66. *Dear America: The Great Railroad Race: The Diary of Libby West.* Kristiana Gregory. Scholastic (104,000)
67. *Star Wars Episode One: Great Big Flap Book.* Random/Lucas (103,012)
68. *Toy Story 2: Buzz Book Pal.* Mouse Works (102,870)
69. *Poky & Friends: Scuffy: The Big River Rescue.* Golden (102,812)
70. *Disney's Tarzan: Jungle Adventure.* Mouse Works (101,747)
71. *Pooh Everyday.* Mouse Works (101,194)
72. *Little Bo: The Story of Bonnie Boadicea.* Julie Andrews Edwards, illus. by Henry Cole. Hyperion (101,134)
73. *The Royal Diaries: Cleopatra VII: Daughter of the Nile.* Kristiana Gregory. Scholastic (100,000)

75,000+

74. *Pooh: Opposite.* Mouse Works (99,969)
75. *Rolie Polie Olie.* William Joyce. HarperCollins/Geringer (97,868)
76. *Disney's Tarzan: Family and Friends.* Mouse Works (97,832)
77. *A Grandfather's Memories to His Grandchild.* Candy Paull, illus. by Thomas Kinkade. Tommy Nelson (97,517)
78. *Barney's Peekaboo Halloween.* Lyrick (94,537)

79. *Toy Story 2: Woody Book Pal.* Mouse Works (94,203)
80. *Goodnight, Elmo.* Random/CTW (93,505)
81. *Rub-a-Dub.* Mouse Works (93,228)
82. *Rudolph: Santa from Head to Toe.* Golden (92,587)
83. *Barney's Neighborhood.* Lyrick (92,313)
84. *Disney's Tarzan Flip Book.* Mouse Works (91,266)
85. *Celebrate the Year with Winnie the Pooh.* Disney (91,031)
86. *The Christmas Story.* Golden (89,839)
87. *Seuss-isms for Success.* Dr. Seuss. Random (88,320)
88. *Teletubbies: The Happy Day.* Scholastic (88,000)
89. *Barney Makes Music.* Lyrick (87,852)
90. *The Best Mouse Cookie.* Laura Joffe Numeroff, illus. by Felicia Bond. HarperFestival (87,426)
91. *Here Comes Mother Goose.* Edited by Iona Opie, illus. by Rosemary Wells. Candlewick (87,338)
92. *Rudolph: Helping Holiday Hands.* Golden (86,866)
93. *Bambi Read-Aloud Storybook.* Mouse Works (85,538)
94. *Look-Alikes Jr.* Joan Steiner. Little, Brown (84,121)
95. *Blue's Clues: What Is Blue Feeling?* Simon Spotlight (83,930)
96. *Bear in the Big Blue House: Bear Loves Food!* Simon Spotlight (83,554)
97. *Bear in the Big Blue House: Welcome to the Big Blue House!* Simon Spotlight (83,402)
98. *Bear in the Big Blue House: Bear Loves Water!* Simon Spotlight (83,373)
99. *Dear America: A Light in the Storm: The Civil War Diary of Amelia Martin.* Karen Hesse. Scholastic (83,000)
100. *Barney's Shapes.* Lyrick (82,700)
101. *My Father's Angels.* Gloria Gaither, illus. by Barbara Hranilovich. Zonderkidz (82,331)
102. *Bear in the Big Blue House: Dirt Is Delightful!* Simon Spotlight (81,939)
103. *Arthur's New Baby Book.* Marc Brown. Random (81,749)
104. *Dear America: The Girl Who Chased Away Sorrow: The Diary of Sarah Nita.* Ann Turner. Scholastic (81,000)
105. *My Name Is America: The Journal of Scott Pendleton Collins: A World War II Soldier.* Walter Dean Myers. Scholastic (81,000)
106. *Snappy Little Colors (Pop-Up Fun).* Millbrook (80,000)
107. *Toestomper and the Caterpillars.* Sharleen Collicott. Houghton Mifflin (79,909)
108. *Bear in the Big Blue House: Where Is Bear?* Random (78,178)
109. *Pooh's Pumpkin Surprise.* Mouse Works (77,965)
110. *Jesus Wants All of Me.* Oswald Chambers, adapted and illus. by Phil Smouse. Barbour (77,369)
111. *Muppet Babies: Bye-Bye, Diapers.* Golden (77,028)

112. *A Child's Christmas at St. Nicholas Circle.* Douglas Kaine McKelvey, illus. by Thomas Kinkade. Tommy Nelson (76,987)
113. *The Big Box.* Toni Morrison and Slade Morrison, illus. by Giselle Potter. Hyperion/Jump at the Sun (76,066)
114. *Once Upon a Potty—Boy.* Alona Frankel. HarperFestival (75,486)
115. *The Grouchy Ladybug (board book).* Eric Carle. HarperFestival (75,444)
116. *Snappy Little Numbers (Pop-Up Fun).* Millbrook (75,000)

50,000+

117. *Pooh's Noisy Book.* Mouse Works (74,387)
118. *Pooh Can, Can You?* Mouse Works (74,059)
119. *The Worst Band in the Universe.* Graeme Base. Abrams (73,032)
120. *Once Upon a Potty—Girl.* Alona Frankel. HarperFestival (72,570)
121. *Granddad's Prayers of the Earth.* Douglas Wood, illus. by P. J. Lynch. Candlewick (72,066)
122. *Stuart Little—The Storybook.* Adapted by Amy Jo Cooper. HarperFestival (69,671)
123. *The Crippled Lamb (5th Anniversary Edition).* Max Lucado, illus. by Liz Bonham. Tommy Nelson (68,140)
124. *My Name Is America: The Journal of Joshua Loper: A Black Cowboy.* Walter Dean Myers. Scholastic (67,000)
125. *Tell Me Again About the Night I Was Born (board book).* Jamie Lee Curtis, illus. by Laura Cornell. HarperFestival (66,310)
126. *Toy Story 2: Let's Play.* Mouse Works (66,245)
127. *My Best Friends.* Sterling (66,000)
128. *From Head to Toe (board book).* Eric Carle. HarperFestival (65,903)
129. *The Twelve Dogs of Christmas.* Emma Kragan, illus. by Sharon Collins. Tommy Nelson (65,605)
130. *Tarzan Picture Book.* Disney (64,713)
131. *Oh Say Can You Say Di-no-saur?* Bonnie Worth, illus. by Steve Haefele. Random (64,325)
132. *The 20th Century Children's Poetry Treasury.* Edited by Jack Prelutsky, illus. by Meilo So. Knopf (64,172)
133. *The Star Wars Cookbook: Wookiee Cookies and Other Galactic Recipes.* Robin Davis, photographed by Frankie Frankeny. Chronicle (64,000)
134. *Toy Story 2: Picture Book.* Disney (63,735)
135. *The Kingfisher Children's Encyclopedia.* Kingfisher (63,060)
136. *A Child's Garden of Verses.* Robert Louis Stevenson, illus. by Thomas Kinkade. Tommy Nelson (62,890)
137. *Pooh, Where Are You?* Mouse Works (62,874)
138. *Sector 7.* David Wiesner. Clarion (62,813)
139. *Brian's Return.* Gary Paulsen. Delacorte (62,021)

140. *Pat the Bunny: On the Playground.* Based on the book by Dorothy Kunhardt. Golden (61,552)
141. *Arthur's Chicken Pox (board book).* Marc Brown. Little, Brown (60,660)
142. *10 Button Book.* William Accorsi. Workman (60,580)
143. *Snappy Little Farmyard (Pop-Up Fun).* Millbrook (60,000)
144. *Pat the Bunny: In the Garden.* Based on the book by Dorothy Kunhardt. Golden (59,629)
145. *Snow White & the Seven Dwarfs Read-Aloud Storybook.* Mouse Works (59,581)
146. *Arthur's First Sleepover (board book).* Marc Brown. Little, Brown (59,427)
147. *101 Dalmatians Read-Aloud Storybook.* Mouse Works (59,400)
148. *New Adventures of Curious George.* Margret and H. A. Rey. Houghton Mifflin (58,427)
149. *Barney's Puppet Show.* Lyrick (58,184)
150. *When I Was Little (board book).* Jamie Lee Curtis, illus. by Laura Cornell. HarperFestival (58,144)
151. *Snappy Little Bugs (Pop-Up Fun).* Millbrook. (58,000)
152. *Disney's Winnie the Pooh's Colors.* Mouse Works (57,906)
153. *Winnie the Pooh's Christmas Stories.* Mouse Works (57,432)
154. *Toy Story 2: Flip Book.* Mouse Works (55,352)
155. *Wish for a Fish: All About Sea Creatures.* Bonnie Worth, illus. by Aristides Ruiz. Random (55,333)
156. *My Name Is America: The Journal of Ben Uchida: Citizen #13559, Mirror Lake Internment Camp.* Barry Denenberg. Scholastic (55,000)
157. *Barney's In, Out and All Around.* Lyrick (54,972)
158. *David Goes to School.* David Shannon. Scholastic/Blue Sky (54,000)
159. *Nova's Ark.* David Kirk. Scholastic/Callaway (54,000)
160. *Mickey's Week.* Mouse Works (53,840)
161. *The Story of Easter.* Golden (53,641)
162. *Toy Story Read-Aloud Storybook.* Mouse Works (53,368)
163. *Bob & Larry's ABCs.* Phil Vischer. Tommy Nelson (53,103)
164. *Arthur's Valentine Countdown.* Marc Brown. Random (53,091)
165. *Pooh I Love You Friendly Tale.* Mouse Works (52,829)
166. *Welcome to Samantha's World.* Catherine Gourley. Pleasant Co./American Girls (52,698)
167. *Thomas the Tank Engine's Big Blue Treasury.* Random (52,366)
168. *My Name Is America: The Journal of Sean Sullivan: A Transcontinental Railroad Worker.* William Durbin. Scholastic (52,000)
169. *Barney & Me on Safari.* Lyrick (50,611)
170. *Great Girl Stories.* Compiled by Rosemary Sandberg. Kingfisher (50,489)
171. *Winnie the Pooh Storytime Fun.* Mouse Works (50,292)
172. *Pooh Says Please.* Mouse Works (50,251)
173. *Thomas the Tank Engine's Big Yellow Treasury.* Random (50,014)

Hardcover Backlist

300,000+

1. *Harry Potter and the Sorcerer's Stone.* J. K. Rowling, illus. by Mary GrandPré. Scholastic/Levine, 1998 (3,100,000)
2. *Love You Forever.* Robert Munsch, illus. by Sheila McGraw. Firefly, 1986 (559,865)
3. *Goodnight Moon (board book).* Margaret Wise Brown, illus. by Clement Hurd. HarperFestival, 1991 (515,877)
4. *The Cheerios Play Book.* Lee Wade. Little Simon, 1998 (488,962)
5. *Green Eggs and Ham.* Dr. Seuss. Random, 1966 (452,504)
6. *Scholastic Children's Dictionary.* Scholastic Reference, 1996 (444,000)
7. *Guess How Much I Love You (board book).* Sam McBratney, illus. by Anita Jeram. Candlewick, 1996 (420,936)
8. *Where the Sidewalk Ends.* Shel Silverstein. HarperCollins, 1974 (391,465)
9. *Oh, The Places You'll Go!* Dr. Seuss. Random, 1990 (372,803)
10. *Legend of the Candy Cane.* Lori Walburg, illus. by James Bernadin. Zonderkidz, 1997 (355,753)
11. *Disney's Storybook Collection.* Disney, 1998 (354,914)
12. *The Giving Tree.* Shel Silverstein. HarperCollins, 1964 (352,865)
13. *The Cat in the Hat.* Dr. Seuss. Random, 1966 (338,622)
14. *Holes.* Louis Sachar. Farrar, Straus & Giroux/Foster, 1998 (333,882)
15. *Today I Feel Silly & Other Moods That Make My Day.* Jamie Lee Curtis, illus. by Laura Cornell. HarperCollins/Cotler, 1998 (323,803)
16. *Beginner's Bible.* Karyn Henley, illus. by Dennas Davis. Zonderkidz, 1989 (320,345)
17. *Pooh: King of the Beasties.* Golden, 1998 (304,978)
18. *Falling Up.* Shel Silverstein. HarperCollins, 1996 (304,244)

200,000+

19. *Barney's Twinkle, Twinkle, Little Star.* Lyrick, 1998 (293,642)
20. *A Light in the Attic.* Shel Silverstein. HarperCollins, 1981 (254,081)
21. *If You Give a Pig a Pancake.* Laura Joffe Numeroff, illus. by Felicia Bond. HarperCollins/Geringer, 1998 (237,983)
22. *One Fish Two Fish, Red Fish Blue Fish.* Dr. Seuss. Random, 1966 (237,876)
23. *The Polar Express.* Chris Van Allsburg. Houghton Mifflin, 1985 (237,065)
24. *Pooh's Grand Adventure: The Search for Christopher Robin.* Golden, 1997 (233,042)
25. *Disney's 101 Dalmatians.* Golden, 1997 (230,910)
26. *Dr. Seuss's ABC (board book).* Dr. Seuss. Random, 1996 (229,003)
27. *Thank You, Pooh!* Golden, 1996 (228,798)

28. *The Poky Little Puppy.* Janette Sebring Lowrey, illus. by Gustaf Tenggren. Golden, 1942 (227,111)
29. *Mr. Brown Can Moo! Can You? (board book).* Dr. Seuss. Random, 1966 (224,241)
30. *Disney's Snow White and the Seven Dwarfs.* Golden, 1984 (223,412)
31. *The Very Hungry Caterpillar (board book).* Eric Carle. Philomel, 1984 (215,400)
32. *Disney's Lady and the Tramp.* Golden, 1988 (212,926)
33. *Pooh's 5 Honeypots.* Mouse Works, 1998 (211,422)
34. *Hop on Pop.* Dr. Seuss. Random, 1966 (207,646)
35. *Pooh Red & Blue & Pooh Shaped, Too.* Mouse Works, 1998 (203,395)
36. *Santa Pooh: Friendly Tales.* Mouse Works, 1998 (200,271)

100,000+

37. *Disney's Bambi.* Golden, 1994 (199,983)
38. *Disney's Pinocchio.* Golden, 1990 (199,983)
39. *The Saggy Baggy Elephant.* K. and B. Jackson, illus. by Gustaf Tenggren. Golden, 1947 (198,294)
40. *Pooh: The Grand and Wonderful Day.* Golden, 1997 (195,036)
41. *Disney's The Lion King: Way to Go, Simba!* Golden, 1998 (192,396)
42. *Baby Mickey's Book of Shapes.* Golden, 1986 (189,894)
43. *Disney's Little Mermaid: The Whole Story.* Golden, 1997 (187,899)
44. *Are You My Mother?* P. D. Eastman. Random, 1960 (185,303)
45. *Disney's Mickey & Friends: The Story of Rapunzel.* Golden, 1998 (184,513)
46. *Disney's The Jungle Book.* Golden, 1967 (183,240)
47. *The Tawny Scrawny Lion.* Kathryn Jackson, illus. by Gustaf Tenggren. Golden, 1952 (177,332)
48. *Barney's Storybook Treasury.* Lyrick, 1998 (177,302)
49. *Tootle.* Gertrude Crampton, illus. by Tibor Gergely. Golden, 1945 (176,711)
50. *Disney's The Lion King.* Golden, 1994 (172,090)
51. *The Shy Little Kitten.* Cathleen Schurr, illus. by Gustaf Tenggren. Golden, 1946 (168,100)
52. *Dr. Seuss's ABC.* Dr. Seuss. Random, 1966 (163,509)
53. *Barney's Number Friends.* Lyrick, 1996 (162,053)
54. *Time for Bed (board book).* Mem Fox, illus. by Jane Dyer. Harcourt/Red Wagon, 1997 (159,050)
55. *The Runaway Bunny (board book).* Margaret Wise Brown, illus. by Clement Hurd. HarperFestival, 1991 (158,873)
56. *Guess How Much I Love You.* Sam McBratney, illus. by Anita Jeram. Candlewick, 1995 (157,167)
57. *Go, Dog. Go!* P. D. Eastman. Random, 1966 (157,068)

58. *Barnyard Dance!* Sandra Boynton. Workman, 1993 (155,203)

59. *New Adventure Bible (NIV).* Zonderkidz, 1989 (154,582)

60. *The Little Red Caboose.* Marian Potter, illus. by Tibor Gergeley. Golden, 1953 (153,447)

61. *I Spy Little Animals.* Jean Marzollo, illus. by Walter Wick. Scholastic/Cartwheel, 1998 (147,000)

62. *Barbie: The Special Sleepover.* Golden, 1997 (145,327)

63. *The Going to Bed Book.* Sandra Boynton. Little Simon (143,589)

64. *A Day with Barney.* Lyrick, 1994 (142,352)

65. *Snowflake Bentley.* Jacqueline Briggs Martin, illus. by Mary Azarian. Houghton Mifflin, 1998 (139,882)

66. *The Whispering Rabbit.* Margaret Wise Brown, illus. by Cyndy Szekeres. Golden (139,667)

67. *My First Counting Book.* Lilian Moore, illus. by Garth Williams. Golden (139,198)

68. *The Sailor Dog.* Margaret Wise Brown, illus. by Garth Williams. Golden, 1953 (138,842)

69. *The Little Engine That Could (Classic Edition).* Watty Piper, illus. by George Hauman. Grosset & Dunlap, 1978 (138,400)

70. *Baby Bop Discovers Shapes.* Lyrick, 1993 (136,579)

71. *I Spy Fantasy.* Jean Marzollo, illus. by Walter Wick. Scholastic/Cartwheel, 1994 (136,000)

72. *Butterfly Kisses.* Golden (134,749)

73. *How the Grinch Stole Christmas!* Dr. Seuss. Random, 1966 (134,278)

74. *Fox in Socks.* Dr. Seuss. Random, 1966 (133,223)

75. *If You Give a Mouse a Cookie.* Laura Joffe Numeroff, illus. by Felicia Bond. HarperCollins/Geringer, 1985 (130,032)

76. *Pooh 123.* Mouse Works, 1998 (128,970)

77. *Five Little Monkeys Jumping on the Bed (board book).* Eileen Christelow. Clarion, 1998 (128,757)

78. *Goodnight Gorilla (board book).* Peggy Rathmann. Putnam (128,600)

79. *Olive, the Other Reindeer.* J. Otto Seibold and Vivian Walsh. Chronicle, 1997 (128,000)

80. *Winnie the Pooh and the Honey Tree.* Golden, 1998 (124,574)

81. *Poetry for Young People: Emily Dickinson.* Edited by Frances Schoonmaker Bolin, illus. by Chi Chung. Sterling (123,000)

82. *Bedtime for Baby Bop.* Lyrick, 1996 (121,237)

83. *Poetry for Young People: Robert Frost.* Edited by Gary Schmidt, illus. by Henri Sorenson. Sterling (121,000)

84. *I Spy Christmas.* Jean Marzollo, illus. by Walter Wick. Scholastic/Cartwheel, 1992 (120,000)

85. *Lilly's Purple Plastic Purse.* Kevin Henkes. Greenwillow, 1996 (118,865)

86. *Barney's Colors.* Lyrick, 1998 (117,142)
87. *Disney's Cinderella.* Golden, 1996 (117,125)
88. *Pooh: Friendly Tales.* Mouse Works, 1997 (116,195)
89. *Baby Bop's Purse.* Lyrick, 1998 (116,013)
90. *God Loves Me Bible.* Susan Beck, illus. by Gloria Oostema. Zonderkidz, 1993 (115,871)
91. *Pooh ABC.* Mouse Works, 1998 (114,307)
92. *Barney Says "Night Night."* Lyrick, 1998 (113,853)
93. *Little Critter: Just Say Please.* Gina and Mercer Mayer, illus. by Mercer Mayer. Golden, 1993 (113,844)
94. *My Little Golden Book About God.* Jane Werner Watson, illus. by Eloise Wilkin. Golden, 1956 (107,924)
95. *The Christmas Miracle of Jonathan Toomey.* Susan Wojciechowski, illus. by P. J. Lynch. Candlewick, 1995 (107,450)
96. *The Rainbow Fish.* Marcus Pfister. North-South, 1992 (107,000)
97. *A Bug's Life: Can You Tell the Difference?* Mouse Works, 1998 (106,312)
98. *Love You Forever.* Robert Munsch, illus. by Sheila McGraw. Firefly, 1986 (106,072)
99. *Dear America: Voyage on the Great Titanic: The Diary of Margaret Ann Brady.* Ellen Emerson White. Scholastic (105,000)
100. *I Spy Mystery.* Jean Marzollo, illus. by Walter Wick. Scholastic/Cartwheel, 1993 (104,000)
101. *I Spy School Days.* Jean Marzollo, illus. by Walter Wick. Scholastic/Cartwheel, 1995 (104,000)
102. *My First Little Mother Goose.* Illus. by Lucinda McQueen. Golden, 1996 (103,608)
103. *I Spy Little Book.* Jean Marzollo, illus. by Walter Wick. Scholastic/Cartwheel, 1997 (103,000)
104. *Barney's Alphabet Soup.* Lyrick, 1997 (102,768)
105. *Prayers for Children.* Golden, 1974 (102,573)
106. *The Cat in the Hat Comes Back.* Dr. Seuss. Random, 1966 (102,487)
107. *The Many Adventures of Winnie the Pooh.* Disney, 1997 (102,120)
108. *Barney's Book of Shapes.* Lyrick, 1998 (101,020)
109. *Children's Letters to God.* Workman, 1991 (100,406)

75,000+

110. *Pooh: The Very Best Easter Bunny.* Golden, 1997 (99,833)
111. *Barney's Favorite Mother Goose Rhymes, Vol. 1.* Lyrick, 1993 (99,718)
112. *I Spy Gold Challenger.* Jean Marzollo, illus. by Walter Wick. Scholastic/Cartwheel, 1998 (99,000)
113. *I Spy Spooky Night.* Jean Marzollo, illus. by Walter Wick. Scholastic/Cartwheel, 1996 (99,000)

114. *Where the Wild Things Are (25th anniversary edition).* Maurice Sendak. HarperCollins, 1988 (98,138)

115. *A Bug's Life: Classic Storybook.* Mouse Works, 1998 (96,843)

116. *Noah's Ark.* Golden, 1997 (96,492)

117. *Mama, Do You Love Me?* Barbara M. Joosse, illus. by Barbara Lavallee. Chronicle, 1998 (95,000)

118. *I Spy Super Challenger.* Jean Marzollo, illus. by Walter Wick. Scholastic/Cartwheel, 1997 (93,000)

119. *Pooh and the Dragon.* Golden, 1997 (92,735)

120. *The Very Busy Spider (board book).* Eric Carle. Philomel, 1989 (92,300)

121. *A Walk in the Woods.* Mouse Works, 1997 (92,104)

122. *Miss Spider's Tea Party: The Counting Book (board book).* David Kirk. Scholastic/Callaway, 1997 (92,000)

123. *Goodnight Moon.* Margaret Wise Brown, illus. by Clement Hurd. HarperCollins, 1947 (90,747)

124. *My Little Bible.* Mary Hollingsworth, illus. by Stephanie Britt. Tommy Nelson, 1991 (89,955)

125. *Animal Sounds.* Golden, 1981 (89,380)

126. *The Rainbow Fish (board book).* Marcus Pfister. North-South, 1996 (89,000)

127. *Big Red Barn (board book).* Margaret Wise Brown, illus. by Felicia Bond. HarperFestival, 1995 (88,789)

128. *Seuss-isms.* Dr. Seuss. Random, 1997 (88,238)

129. *Barney Plays Nose to Toes.* Lyrick, 1996 (88,043)

130. *Pooh: Trick or Treat!* Golden, 1997 (86,324)

131. *Pooh: Eeyore, Be Happy!* Golden, 1991 (85,431)

132. *Little Critter: Just a Little Different.* Gina and Mercer Mayer, illus. by Mercer Mayer. Golden, 1998 (84,755)

133. *Tigger: Friendly Tales.* Mouse Works, 1997 (84,225)

134. *Who Hid the Honey?* Mouse Works, 1997 (84,173)

135. *Barney's Animal Homes.* Lyrick, 1998 (83,884)

136. *My Book About Me.* Dr. Seuss. Random, 1969 (83,728)

137. *I Spy Little Wheels.* Jean Marzollo, illus. by Walter Wick. Scholastic/Cartwheel, 1998 (82,000)

138. *NIRV Read with Me Bible.* Illus. by Dennis Jones. Zonderkidz, 1997 (80,248)

139. *Stellaluna.* Janell Cannon. Harcourt, 1993 (79,800)

140. *Mr. Brown Can Moo! Can You?* Dr. Seuss. Random, 1970 (78,282)

141. *Put Me in the Zoo.* Robert Lopshire. Random, 1960 (78,071)

142. *The New Way Things Work.* David Macaulay. Houghton Mifflin/Lorraine, 1998 (77,170)

143. *Nursery Rhymes of Winnie the Pooh.* Disney, 1998 (76,985)

144. *I Can Read with My Eyes Shut!* Dr. Seuss. Random, 1978 (76,901)

145. *Baby 1-2-3.* Golden, 1998 (76,110)

146. *Barney's Toolbox.* Lyrick, 1998 (75,942)
147. *Disney's Mickey and Friends: Let's Go to the Fire Station.* Golden, 1998 (75,938)
148. *Barney's Baby Farm Animals.* Lyrick, 1998 (75,143)

Paperback Frontlist

500,000+

1. *Harry Potter and the Sorcerer's Stone.* J. K. Rowling, illus. by Mary GrandPré. Scholastic/Levine (3,200,000)
2. *The Official Pokémon Deluxe Handbook: Collector's Edition.* Maria Barbo. Scholastic (1,800,000)
3. *Pokémon Chapter Book #1: I Choose You.* Tracey West. Scholastic (980,000)
4. *Pokémon Chapter Book #2: Island of the Giant Pokémon.* Tracey West. Scholastic (960,000)
5. *Pokémon Movie Tie-In Novelization: Mewtwo Strikes Back.* Tracey West. Scholastic (875,000)
6. *Chicken Soup for the Teenage Soul II.* Jack Canfield, Mark Victor Hansen, and Kimberly Kirberger. HCI (856,487)
7. *Pokémon Chapter Book #3: Attack of the Prehistoric Pokémon.* Tracey West. Scholastic (840,000)
8. *Attack of the Prehistoric Pokémon.* Diane Muldrow. Golden (814,215)
9. *Pokémon Chapter Book #4: Night in the Haunted Tower.* Tracey West. Scholastic (813,000)
10. *Bye-Bye Butterfree.* Diane Muldrow. Golden (786,177)
11. *The Official Pokémon Handbook.* Maria Barbo. Scholastic (720,000)
12. *Pokémon: Junior Novelization: Pikachu's Vacation.* Tracey West. Scholastic (574,000)
13. *Star Wars: Episode One: The Phantom Menace.* Patricia Wrede. Scholastic (535,000)

300,000+

14. *Star Wars Episode One: The Phantom Menace Movie Storybook.* Random/Lucas (493,331)
15. *How to Draw Pokémon.* Ron Zalme. Troll (464,799)
16. *Disney's Toy Story 2: Buzz Lightyear, Space Ranger.* Diane Muldrow, illus. by Disney Studios. Golden (448,420)
17. *Pokémon Counting Book.* Golden (445,433)
18. *Star Wars Episode One: The Phantom Menace Movie Scrapbook.* Random/Lucas (381,587)
19. *Blue's Clues: Magenta's Visit.* Simon Spotlight (343,007)

20. *Disney's Toy Story 2.* Golden (330,577)
21. *Teen Love: On Relationships.* Kimberly Kirberger. HCI (326,116)
22. *Tasteberry Tales for Teens.* Bettie B. Youngs and Jennifer Leigh Youngs. HCI (314,458)
23. *Star Wars Storybooks: I Am a Jedi.* Random/Lucas (308,839)

200,000+

24. *Pokémon: Mewto Strikes Back.* Golden (300,084)
25. *Disney's Toy Story 2: Woody's Roundup.* Golden (298,621)
26. *Disney's Tarzan.* Golden (291,885)
27. *Samantha's Winter Party.* Valerie Tripp, illus. by Dan Andreasen. Pleasant Co./American Girls (286,544)
28. *Barney & BJ Go to the Zoo.* Lyrick (284,918)
29. *Left Behind: The Kids #5: Nicolae High.* Jerry B. Jenkins and Tim LaHaye. Tyndale (284,336)
30. *Disney's Tarzan: Terk's Tale.* Golden (281,484)
31. *Left Behind: The Kids #6: The Underground.* Jerry B. Jenkins and Tim LaHaye. Tyndale (280,217)
32. *Kirsten on the Trail.* Janet Shaw, illus. by Renee Graef. Pleasant Co./American Girls (279,307)
33. *Reward for Josefina.* Valerie Tripp, illus. by Jean-Paul Tibbles. Pleasant Co./American Girls (275,288)
34. *Felicity's New Sister.* Valerie Tripp, illus. by Dan Andreasen. Pleasant Co./American Girls (274,670)
35. *Pikachu's Vacation.* Golden (274,585)
36. *Molly Takes Flight.* Valerie Tripp, illus. by Nick Backes. Pleasant Co./American Girls (274,310)
37. *Star Wars Storybooks: Watch Out, Jar Jar!* Random/Lucas (273,599)
38. *Star Wars Jedi Readers: Anakin to the Rescue.* Random/Lucas (271,212)
39. *Animorphs #26: The Attack.* K. A. Applegate. Scholastic (270,000)
40. *Star Wars Storybooks: Anakin's Race for Freedom.* Random/Lucas (269,197)
41. *Star Wars Storybooks: I Am a Droid.* Random/Lucas (268,462)
42. *High Hopes for Addy.* Connie Porter, illus. by John Thompson and Dahl Taylor. Pleasant Co./American Girls (263,801)
43. *Star Wars Jedi Apprentice #1: The Rising Force.* Scholastic (261,000)
44. *Star Wars Jedi Readers: Anakin's Fate.* Random/Lucas (259,631)
45. *Star Wars Jedi Readers: Jar Jar's Mistake.* Random/Lucas (257,765)
46. *Star Wars Jedi Apprentice #2: The Dark Rival.* Scholastic (244,000)
47. *Animorphs #30: The Reunion.* K. A. Applegate. Scholastic (243,000)
48. *Animorphs #29: The Sickness.* K. A. Applegate. Scholastic (238,000)
49. *Star Wars Jedi Readers: Dangers of the Core.* Random/Lucas (235,763)

50. *Animorphs #35: The Proposal.* K. A. Applegate. Scholastic (235,000)
51. *Animorphs #32: The Separation.* K. A. Applegate. Scholastic (235,000)
52. *Animorphs #31: The Conspiracy.* K. A. Applegate. Scholastic (234,000)
53. *Animorphs #36: The Mutation.* K. A. Applegate. Scholastic (233,000)
54. *Animorphs #28: The Experiment.* K. A. Applegate. Scholastic (231,000)
55. *Animorphs: Megamorphs #3: Elfangor's Secret.* K. A. Applegate. Scholastic (231,000)
56. *Rugrats: Thank You, Angelica!* Simon Spotlight (230,607)
57. *Animorphs #33: The Illusion.* K. A. Applegate. Scholastic (228,000)
58. *Animorphs #34: The Prophecy.* K. A. Applegate. Scholastic (227,000)
59. *Alternamorphs: The First Journey.* K. A. Applegate. Scholastic (219,000)
60. *Pooh: Just Be Nice . . . to Your Little Friends.* Golden (210,114)
61. *Star Wars Journals Episode One, #1: Anakin.* Scholastic (204,000)

150,000+

62. *Magic Tree House #17: Tonight on the Titanic.* Mary Pope Osborne, illus. by Sal Murdocca. Random (199,628)
63. *Animorphs #27: The Exposed.* K. A. Applegate. Scholastic (198,000)
64. *Teletubbies: It's Tubby Bedtime.* Scholastic (194,000)
65. *Animorphs: The Hork Bajir Chronicles.* K. A. Applegate. Scholastic (193,000)
66. *Captain Underpants and the Attack of the Talking Toilets.* Dav Pilkey. Scholastic /Blue Sky (185,000)
67. *Road to Reading Mile 2: Little Critter Sleeps Over.* Mercer Mayer. Golden (177,902)
68. *Star Wars Journals Episode One, #2: Amidala.* Scholastic (177,000)
69. *Bear in the Big Blue House: Bear's Friends.* Random (176,357)
70. *Bear in the Big Blue House; Bear's House.* Random (175,207)
71. *Captain Underpants and the Invasion of the Incredibly Naughty Cafeteria Ladies from Outer Space (And the Subsequent Assault of the Equally Evil Lunchroom Zombie Nerds).* Dav Pilkey. Scholastic/Blue Sky (172,000)
72. *Brought to You by the Letter A.* Random/CTW (171,271)
73. *Pooh: Just Be Nice . . . and Not Too Rough!* Golden (170,084)
74. *Junie B. Jones Is (Almost) a Flower Girl.* Barbara Park, illus. by Denise Brunkus. Random (169,436)
75. *Barney & Baby Bop Go to the Library.* Lyrick (168,560)
76. *Are You My Mother? (board book).* P. D. Eastman. Random (168,095)
77. *Bear in the Big Blue House: Bear's Birthday.* Random (167,250)
78. *I Was a Sixth Grade Alien.* Bruce Coville. Minstrel (167,000)
79. *Star Wars Episode One: Writing Letters A to Z.* Random/Lucas (166,876)
80. *Arthur in a Pickle.* Marc Brown. Random (165,388)

81. *Toy Story 2 Junior Novel.* Disney (163,429)
82. *The Adventures of Elmo in Grouchland.* Random/CTW (157,449)
83. *Teletubbies: Dancing with the Skirt.* Scholastic (152,000)
84. *Pooh: The Tigger Movie.* Golden (150,786)
85. *Teletubbies: Po's Magic Watering Can.* Scholastic (150,000)

125,000+

86. *Blue's Clues: Blue's Big Treasure Hunt.* Simon Spotlight (149,227)
87. *Pooh: Hunny, Funny, Sunny Day!* Golden (147,964)
88. *Magic Tree House #18: Buffalo Before Breakfast.* Mary Pope Osborne, illus. by Sal Murdocca. Random (147,667)
89. *The Indian in the Cupboard.* Lynne Reid Banks. Avon/Camelot (145,242)
90. *Brought to You by the Letter B.* Random/CTW (143,378)
91. *Brought to You by the Letter C.* Random/CTW (141,898)
92. *Magic Tree House #19: Tigers at Twilight.* Mary Pope Osborne, illus. by Sal Murdocca. Random (138,743)
93. *Blue's Clues: It's Present Day!* Simon Spotlight (133,133)
94. *Disney: Doug Gets His Wish.* Golden (132,873)
95. *Barney's Night Before Christmas.* Lyrick (127,882)
96. *The World Almanac for Kids 2000.* World Almanac (127,359)

Paperback Backlist

200,000+

1. *Love You Forever.* Robert Munsch, illus. by Sheila McGraw. Firefly, 1986 (559,865)
2. *Left Behind: The Kids #1: The Vanishings.* Jerry B. Jenkins and Tim LaHaye. Tyndale, 1998 (453,168)
3. *Chicken Soup for the Kid's Soul.* Jack Canfield, Mark Victor Hansen, Patty Hansen, and Irene Dunlap. HCI, 1998 (392,539)
4. *The Outsiders.* S. E. Hinton. Puffin, 1997 (382,100)
5. *The Giver.* Lois Lowry. Dell/Laurel-Leaf, 1994 (360,992)
6. *Left Behind: The Kids #2: Second Chance.* Jerry B. Jenkins and Tim LaHaye. Tyndale, 1998 (348,272)
7. *Pat the Bunny.* Dorothy Kunhardt. Golden, 1940 (302,371)
8. *Left Behind: The Kids #3: Through the Flames.* Jerry B. Jenkins and Tim LaHaye. Tyndale, 1998 (294,868)
9. *Left Behind: The Kids #4: Facing the Future.* Jerry B. Jenkins and Tim LaHaye. Tyndale, 1998 (290,176)
10. *Where the Wild Things Are.* Maurice Sendak. HarperTrophy, 1988 (283,038)

11. *Charlotte's Web.* E. B. White, illus. by Garth Williams. HarperTrophy, 1974 (282,072)
12. *The Lion, the Witch and the Wardrobe.* C. S. Lewis, illus. by Pauline Baynes. HarperTrophy, 1994 (278,381)
13. *Little Critter: I Just Forgot.* Mercer Mayer. Golden, 1988 (270,253)
14. *Little Critter: Just Go to Bed.* Mercer Mayer. Golden, 1983 (263,178)
15. *Bridge to Terabithia.* Katherine Paterson. HarperTrophy, 1987 (244,038)
16. *Stuart Little.* E. B. White, illus. by Garth Williams. HarperTrophy, 1974 (241,370)
17. *Hatchet.* Gary Paulsen. Aladdin, 1996 (232,990)
18. *The Care & Keeping of You: The Body Book for Girls.* Valerie Schaefer, illus. by Norm Bendell. Pleasant Co./American Girls, 1998 (231,208)
19. *Little Critter: Just Lost!* Gina and Mercer Mayer, illus. by Mercer Mayer. Golden, 1994 (222,538)
20. *Little House in the Big Woods.* Laura Ingalls Wilder, illus. by Garth Williams. HarperTrophy, 1971 (216,353)
21. *Little House on the Prairie.* Laura Ingalls Wilder, illus. by Garth Williams. HarperTrophy, 1971 (215,923)

150,000+

22. *Disney: Bounce Around, Tigger!* Golden, 1998 (198,761)
23. *Sarah, Plain and Tall.* Patricia MacLachlan. Harper-Trophy, 1987 (197,017)
24. *Little Critter: All By Myself.* Mercer Mayer. Golden, 1983 (196,253)
25. *Number the Stars.* Lois Lowry. Dell/Yearling, 1990 (192,133)
26. *Ella Enchanted.* Gail Carson Levine. HarperTrophy, 1998 (188,245)
27. *Barney's The Chase Is On!* Guy Davis, illus. by Jay Johnson. Lyrick, 1998 (185,715)
28. *Goodnight Moon.* Margaret Wise Brown, illus. by Clement Hurd. Harper-Trophy, 1977 (183,583)
29. *Magic Tree House #1: Dinosaurs Before Dark.* Mary Pope Osborne, illus. by Sal Murdocca. Random, 1992 (182,131)
30. *Little Critter: I Was So Mad!* Mercer Mayer. Golden, 1983 (181, 534)
31. *Stone Fox.* John Reynolds Gardiner, illus. by Bruce Minney. Harper-Trophy, 1983 (172,191)
32. *Shiloh.* Phyllis Reynolds Naylor. Dell/Yearling, 1992 (168,648)
33. *Pocket Flyers Paper Airplane Book.* Workman, 1998 (167,578)
34. *Walk Two Moons.* Sharon Creech. HarperTrophy, 1996 (165,922)
35. *Little Critter: The New Potty.* Gina and Mercer Mayer, illus. by Mercer Mayer. Golden, 1992 (164,172)
36. *Ramona Quimby, Age 8.* Beverly Cleary. Avon/Camelot, 1992 (164,068)

37. *The Magician's Nephew.* C. S. Lewis, illus. by Pauline Baynes. Harper-Trophy, 1994 (160,982)
38. *Tales of a Fourth Grade Nothing.* Judy Blume. Dell/Yearling, 1976 (160,581)
39. *Julie of the Wolves.* Jean Craighead George, illus. by John Schoenherr. HarperTrophy, 1974 (158,934)
40. *Where the Red Fern Grows.* Wilson Rawls. Bantam, 1984 (156,664)
41. *Little Bear.* Else Minarik, illus. by Maurice Sendak. HarperTrophy, 1978 (155,073)

125,000+

42. *Tuck Everlasting.* Natalie Babbitt. Farrar, Straus & Giroux, 1986 (147,363)
43. *Frog & Toad Are Friends.* Arnold Lobel. HarperTrophy, 1979 (147,121)
44. *Barney & BJ Go to the Police Station.* Lyrick, 1998 (146,634)
45. *Amelia Bedelia.* Peggy Parish, illus. by Fritz Siebel. HarperTrophy, 1992 (144,241)
46. *A Wrinkle in Time.* Madeleine L'Engle. Dell/Yearling, 1998 (143,223)
47. *Arthur's Halloween.* Marc Brown. Little, Brown, 1983 (141,959)
48. *The Phantom Tollbooth.* Norton Juster, illus. by Jules Feiffer. Random, 1988 (140,652)
49. *Frindle.* Andrew Clements. Aladdin, 1998 (136,765)
50. *Arthur's Reading Race.* Marc Brown. Random, 1996 (133,972)
51. *Barney & Baby Bop Go to the Restaurant.* Lyrick, 1998 (132,712)
52. *Magic Tree House #2: The Knight at Dawn.* Mary Pope Osborne, illus. by Sal Murdocca. Random, 1993 (132,578)
53. *Magic Tree House #3: Mummies in the Morning.* Mary Pope Osborne, illus. by Sal Murdocca. Random, 1993 (128,358)
54. *The Sign of the Beaver.* Elizabeth George Speare. Dell/Yearling, 1984 (128,335)
55. *Magic Tree House #9: Dolphins at Daybreak.* Mary Pope Osborne, illus. by Sal Murdocca. Random, 1997 (126,816)
56. *Barney's Trick or Treat.* Lyrick, 1997 (125,827)

Part 6
Directory of Organizations

Directory of Library and Related Organizations

Networks, Consortia, and Other Cooperative Library Organizations

This list is taken from the 1999–2000 edition of *American Library Directory* (R. R. Bowker), which includes additional information on member libraries and primary functions of each organization.

United States

Alabama

Alabama Health Libraries Association, Inc. (ALHeLa), Univ. of Southern Alabama Medical Center Lib., 2451 Fillingim St., Mobile 36617. SAN 372-8218. Tel. 334-471-7855, fax 334-471-7857. *Pres.* Jie Li.

American Gas Association–Library Services (AGA–LSC), c/o Alabama Gas Corp., 605 21st St. N., Birmingham 35203-2707. SAN 371-0890. Tel. 205-326-8436, fax 205-326-2619, e-mail cbaker@gol.energen.com. *Chair* Calvin Baker.

Jefferson County Hospital Librarians Association, Brookwood Medical Center, 2010 Brookwood Medical Center Dr., Birmingham 35209. SAN 371-2168. Tel. 205-877-1131, fax 205-877-1189. *Coord.* Lucy Moor.

Library Management Network, Inc., 110 Johnston St. S.E., Decatur 35601. SAN 322-3906. Tel. 256-308-2529, fax 256-308-2533, e-mail charlotte@lmn.lib.al.us. *System Coord.* Charlotte Moncrief.

Marine Environmental Sciences Consortium, Dauphin Island Sea Lab, 101 Bienville Blvd., Dauphin Island 36528. SAN 322-0001. Tel. 334-861-2141, fax 334-861-4646, e-mail cmallon@disl.org. *Dir.* George Crozier.

Network of Alabama Academic Libraries, c/o Alabama Commission on Higher Educ., Box 302000, Montgomery 36130-2000. SAN 322-4570. Tel. 334-242-2211, fax 334-242-0270. *Dir.* Sue O. Medina.

Alaska

Alaska Library Network (ALN), 344 W. Third Ave., Ste. 125, Anchorage 99501. SAN 371-0688. Tel. 907-269-6570, fax 907-269-6580, e-mail aslanc@muskox. alaska.edu. *Contact* Mary Jennings.

Arizona

Maricopa County Community College District, 2411 W. 14th St., Tempe 85281-6942. SAN 322-0060. Tel. 602-731-8774, fax 602-731-8787, e-mail jenkins@dist. maricopa.edu. *Coord. Lib. Technical Services* Vince Jenkins.

Arkansas

Arkansas Area Health Education Center Consortium (AHEC), Sparks Regional Medical Center, 1311 S. I St., Box 17006, Fort Smith 72917-7006. SAN 329-3734. Tel. 501-441-5337, fax 501-441-5339, e-mail grace@sparks.org. *Regional Health Sciences Libn.* Grace Anderson.

Arkansas' Independent Colleges and Universities (formerly Independent College Fund of Arkansas), 1 Riverfront Place, Ste. 610, North Little Rock 72114. SAN 322-0079. Tel. 501-378-0843, fax 501-374-1523, e-mail kdietz@alltel.net. *Pres.* E. Kearney Dietz.

Northeast Arkansas Hospital Library Consortium, 223 E. Jackson, Jonesboro 72401. SAN 329-529X. Tel. 870-972-1290, fax 870-931-0839. *Dir.* Karen Crosser.

South Arkansas Film Coop., 202 E. Third St., Malvern 72104. SAN 321-5938. Tel. 501-332-5442, fax 501-332-6679. *Coord.* Tammy Carter.

California

Area Wide Library Network (AWLNET), 2420 Mariposa St., Fresno 93721. SAN 322-0087. Tel. 559-488-3229. *Dir. Info. Services* Sharon Vandercook.

Bay Area Library and Information Network (BAYNET), 672 Prentiss St., San Francisco 94110-6130. SAN 371-0610. Tel. 415-826-2464, e-mail rosef@exploratorium.edu. *Pres.* Jo Falcon.

Central Association of Libraries (CAL), 605 N. El Dorado St., Stockton 95202-1999. SAN 322-0125. Tel. 209-937-8649, fax 209-937-8292. *System Dir.* Darla Gunning.

Consortium for Distance Learning, 3841 N. Freeway Blvd., Ste. 200, Sacramento 95834-1948. SAN 329-4412. Tel. 916-565-0188, fax 916-565-0189, e-mail cdl@calweb.com. *Exec. Dir.* Jerome Thompson.

Consumer Health Information Program and Services (CHIPS), County of Los Angeles Public Lib., 151 E. Carson St., Carson 90745. SAN 372-8110. Tel. 310-830-0909, fax 310-834-4097. *Libn.* Scott A. Willis.

The Dialog Corporation, PLC (formerly Knight-Ridder Corporation, Inc.), 2440 El Camino Real, Mountain View 94040. SAN 322-0176. Tel. 650-254-7000, fax 650-254-8093. *Pres.* Dan Wagner.

Hewlett-Packard Library Information Network, 1501 Page Mill Rd., Palo Alto 94304. SAN 375-0019. Tel. 650-857-3091, 857-6620, fax 650-852-8187, e-mail eugenie_prime@hp.com. *Chair* Eugenie Prime.

Kaiser Permanente Library System–Southern California Region, Health Sciences Lib., 4647 Zion Ave., San Diego 92120. SAN 372-8153. Tel. 619-528-7323, fax 619-528-3444. *Dir.* Sheila Latus.

Metropolitan Cooperative Library System (MCLS), 3675 E. Huntington Dr., Ste. 100, Pasadena 91107. SAN 371-3865. Tel. 626-683-8244, fax 626-683-8097, e-mail mclshg@mclsys.org. *Exec. Dir.* Barbara Custen.

National Network of Libraries of Medicine–Pacific Southwest Region (PSRML), Louise Darling Biomedical Lib., 12-077 Center for Health Sciences, Box 951798, Los Angeles 90095-1798. SAN 372-8234. Tel. 800-338-7657, fax 310-825-5389. *Dir.* Alison Bunting.

Northern California and Nevada Medical Library Group, 2140 Shattuck Ave., Box 2105, Berkeley 94704. SAN 329-4617. Tel. 916-733-8822, fax 916-733-3879. *Pres.* Andrea Woodruff.

Northern California Association of Law Libraries (NOCALL), 601 Van Ness Ave., No. E3-840, Box 109, San Francisco 94102. SAN 323-5777. Tel. 916-653-8001, fax 916-653-0952. *Pres.* Mary Ann Parker.

Northern California Consortium of Psychology Libraries (NCCPL), California School of Professional Psychology, 1005 Atlantic, Alameda 94501. SAN 371-9006. Tel. 510-523-2300, ext. 185, fax 510-523-5943, e-mail dgaige@mail.cspp.edu; cdassoff@pgsp.edu. *Chair* Deanna Gaige.

OCLC Pacific, 9227 Haven Ave., Ste. 260, Rancho Cucamonga 91730. SAN 370-0747. Tel. 909-941-4220, fax 909-948-9803. *Dir.* Mary Ann Nash.

Peninsula Libraries Automated Network (PLAN), 25 Tower Rd., San Mateo 94402-4000. SAN 371-5035. Tel. 650-358-6704, fax 650-358-6706. *Database Mgr.* Susan Yasar.

Performing Arts Libraries Network of Greater Los Angeles (PALNET), Autry Museum of Western Heritage, 4700 Western Heritageway, Los Angeles 90027. SAN 371-3997. Tel. 323-667-2000, ext. 271, fax 323-660-5721. *Chair, Special Collections Libn. and Archivist* Sharon Johnson.

Research Libraries Group, Inc (RLG), 1200 Villa St., Mountain View 94041-1100. SAN 322-0206. Tel. 800-537-7546, fax 650-964-0943, e-mail bl.ric@rlg.stanford. edu. *Pres.* James Michalko.

San Bernardino, Inyo, Riverside Counties United Library Services (SIRCULS), 3581 Mission Inn Ave., Box 468, Riverside 92502. SAN 322-0222. Tel. 909-369-7995, fax 909-784-1158, e-mail sirculs@ inlandlib.org. *Exec. Dir.* Kathleen F. Aaron.

San Diego and Imperial Counties College Learning Resources Cooperative (SDICC-CL) (formerly Learning Resources Cooperative), Palomar College, 1140 W. Mission Rd., San Marcos 92069. SAN 375-006X. Tel. 760-744-1150, ext. 2848, fax 760-761-3500, e-mail jconte@swc.cc.ca.us. *Pres.* George Mozes.

San Francisco Biomedical Library Network (SFBLN), H. M. Fishbon Memorial Lib., USCF-Mount Zion, UCSF Standard Health Care, 1600 Divisadero St., Rm. A116, San Francisco 94115. SAN 371-2125. Tel. 415-885-7378, fax 415-776-0689. *Coord.* Gail Sorrough.

Santa Clarita Interlibrary Network (SCIL-NET), 24700 McBean Pwky., Santa Clarita 91355. SAN 371-8964. Tel. 805-253-7885, fax 805-254-4561. *Coord.* Frederick B. Gardner.

Serra Cooperative Library System, 5555 Overland Ave., Bldg. 15, San Diego 92123. SAN 372-8129. Tel. 619-694-3600, fax 619-495-5905, e-mail serrahq@electriciti. com. *System Coord.* Susan Swisher.

The Smerc Library, 101 Twin Dolphin Dr., Redwood City 94065-1064. SAN 322-0265. Tel. 650-802-5655, fax 650-802-5665. *Educ. Services Mgr.* Karol Thomas.

Southnet, c/o Silicon Valley Lib. System, 180 W. San Carlos St., San Jose 95113. SAN 322-4260. Tel. 408-294-2345, fax 408-295-7388, e-mail sbcl@netcom.com. *Asst. Systems Dir.* Susan Holmer.

Substance Abuse Librarians and Information Specialists (SALIS), Box 9513, Berkeley 94709-0513. SAN 372-4042. Tel. 510-642-5208, fax 510-642-7175, e-mail salis @arg.org. *Exec. Dir.* Andrea L. Mitchell.

Total Interlibrary Exchange (TIE), 4882 McGrath St., Ste. 230, Ventura 93003-7721. SAN 322-0311. Tel. 805-922-6966, ext. 3475, fax 805-642-9095, e-mail tieweb @rain.org. *Pres.* Marcia Frasier.

Colorado

Arkansas Valley Regional Library Service System (AVRLSS), 635 W. Corona, Ste. 113, Pueblo 81004. SAN 371-5094. Tel. 719-542-2156, fax 719-542-3155, e-mail dmorris@uscolo.edu. *Dir.* Donna Jones Morris.

Bibliographical Center for Research, Rocky Mountain Region, Inc., 14394 E. Evans Ave., Aurora 80014-1478. SAN 322-0338. Tel. 303-751-6277, ext. 117, fax 303-751-9787. *Exec. Dir.* David H. Brunell.

Central Colorado Library System (CCLS), 4350 Wadsworth Blvd., Ste. 340, Wheat Ridge 80033-4638. SAN 371-3970. Tel. 303-422-1150, fax 303-431-9752, e-mail kenomoto@qadas.com. *Dir.* Gordon C. Barhydt.

Colorado Alliance of Research Libraries, 3801 E. Florida Ave., Ste. 515, Denver 80210. SAN 322-3760. Tel. 303-759-3399, fax 303-759-3363. *Exec. Dir.* Alan Charnes.

Colorado Association of Law Libraries, Box 13363, Denver 80201. SAN 322-4325. Tel. 303-492-7312. *Acting Pres.* Georgia Briscoe.

Colorado Council of Medical Librarians (CCML), Box 101058, Denver 80210-1058. SAN 370-0755. Tel. 303-315-6435, fax 303-315-0294, e-mail pat.nelson@ uchsc.edu. *Pres.* Pat Nelson.

Colorado Library Resource Sharing and Information Access Board, c/o Colorado State Lib., 201 E. Colfax, Denver 80203-1799. SAN 322-3868. Tel. 303-866-6900, fax 303-866-6940. *Coord.* Susan Fayed.

High Plains Regional Library Service System, 800 Eighth Ave., Ste. 341, Greeley 80631. SAN 371-0505. Tel. 970-356-4357, fax 970-353-4355, e-mail bhager@ csn.net. *Dir.* Nancy Knepel.

Peaks and Valleys Library Consortium, c/o Arkansas Valley Regional Lib. Service System, 635 W. Corona, Ste. 113, Pueblo 81004. SAN 328-8684. Tel. 719-542-

2156, 546-4197, 546-4677, fax 719-546-4484. *Secy.* Carol Ann Smith.

Southwest Regional Library Service System (SWRLSS), P.O. Drawer B, Durango 81302. SAN 371-0815. Tel. 970-247-4782, fax 970-247-5087. *Dir.* S. Jane Ulrich.

Connecticut

Capitol Area Health Consortium, 270 Farmington Ave., Ste. 352, Farmington 06032-1909. SAN 322-0370. Tel. 860-676-1110, fax 860-676-1303. *Pres.* Robert Boardman.

Capitol Region Library Council, 599 Matianuck Ave., Windsor 06095-3567. SAN 322-0389. Tel. 860-298-5319, fax 860-298-5328, e-mail office@crlc.org. *Exec. Dir.* Dency Sargent.

Council of State Library Agencies in the Northeast (COSLINE), Connecticut State Lib., 231 Capitol Ave., Hartford 06106. SAN 322-0451. Tel. 860-566-4301, 207-287-5600 (Maine), fax 860-566-8940. *Pres.* Kendall Wiggin.

CTW Library Consortium, Olin Memorial Lib., Wesleyan Univ., Middletown 06457-6065. SAN 329-4587. Tel. 860-685-3889, fax 860-685-2661, e-mail ahagyard@ wesleyan. *Dir.* Alan E. Hagyard.

Eastern Connecticut Libraries (ECL), Franklin Commons, 106 Rte. 32, Franklin 06254. SAN 322-0478. Tel. 860-885-2760, fax 860-885-2757, e-mail pholloway@ecl.org. *Dir.* Patricia Holloway.

Hartford Consortium for Higher Education, 260 Girard Ave., Hartford 06105. SAN 322-0443. Tel. 860-236-1203, fax 860-233-9723. *Exec. Dir.* Rosanne Druckman.

LEAP (Library Exchange Aids Patrons), 110 Washington Ave., North Haven 06473. SAN 322-4082. Tel. 203-239-1411, fax 203-239-9458.

Libraries Online, Inc. (LION), 123 Broad St., Middletown 06457. SAN 322-3922. Tel. 860-347-1704, fax 860-346-3707. *Pres.* Edward Murray.

National Network of Libraries of Medicine, New England Region (NN-LM, NE Region), Univ. of Connecticut Health Center, 263 Farmington Ave., Farmington 06030-

5370. SAN 372-5448. Tel. 860-679-4500, fax 860-679-1305. *Dir.* Ralph D. Arcari.

Northwestern Connecticut Health Science Libraries, Charlotte Hungerford Hospital, Torrington 06790. SAN 329-5257. Tel. 860-496-6689, fax 860-496-6631.

Southern Connecticut Library Council, 2911 Dixwell Ave., Ste. 201, Hamden 06518-3130. SAN 322-0486. Tel. 203-288-5757, fax 203-287-0757, e-mail office@sclc.org. *Dir.* Michael Golrick.

Western Connecticut Library Council, Inc., 530 Middlebury Rd., Ste. 210B, Box 1284, Middlebury 06762. SAN 322-0494. Tel. 203-577-4010, fax 203-577-4015, e-mail abarney@wclc.org. *Exec. Dir.* Anita R. Barney.

Delaware

Central Delaware Library Consortium, Dover Public Lib., 45 S. State St., Dover 19901. SAN 329-3696. Tel. 302-736-7030, fax 302-736-5087. *Pres.* Robert S. Wetherall.

Delaware Library Consortium (DLC), Delaware Academy of Medicine, 1925 Lovering Ave., Wilmington 19806. SAN 329-3718. Tel. 302-656-6398, fax 302-656-0470. *Pres.* Gail P. Gill.

Libraries in the New Castle County System (LINCS), Box 128, Odessa 19730. SAN 329-4889. Tel. 302-378-8838, fax 302-378-7803. *Pres.* Lynda Whitehead.

Sussex Help Organization for Resources Exchange (SHORE), Box 589, Georgetown 19947. SAN 322-4333. Tel. 302-855-7890, fax 302-855-7895. *Pres.* Mary Brittingham.

Wilmington Area Biomedical Library Consortium (WABLC), Christiana Care Health System, Box 6001, Newark 19718. SAN 322-0508. Tel. 302-733-1116, fax 302-733-1365, e-mail ccw@christianacare.org. *Pres.* Christine Chastain-Warheit.

District of Columbia

CAPCON Library Network, 1990 M St. N.W., Ste. 200, Washington 20036-3430. SAN 321-5954. Tel. 202-331-5771, fax 202-331-5788, e-mail capcon@capcon.net. *Exec. Dir.* Robert A. Drescher.

Coalition for Christian Colleges and Universities, 329 Eighth St. N.E., Washington 20002. SAN 322-0524. Tel. 202-546-8713, fax 202-546-8913. *Pres.* Robert C. Andringa.

Educational Resources Information Center (ERIC), U.S. Dept. of Educ., Office of Educ. Resources and Improvement, National Lib. of Educ. (NLE), 555 New Jersey Ave. N.W., Washington 20208-5721. SAN 322-0567. Tel. 202-401-6014, fax 202-219-1817, e-mail enic@inet.ed.gov. *Dir.* Keith C. Stubbs.

EDUCAUSE, c/o 1112 16th St. N.W., Ste. 600, Washington 20036. SAN 371-487X. Tel. 202-872-4200, fax 202-872-4318. *Pres.* Brian Hawkins.

FEDLINK (Federal Library and Information Network), c/o Federal Library and Information Center Committee (FLICC), Lib. of Congress, Washington 20540-5110. SAN 322-0761. Tel. 202-707-4800, fax 202-707-4818, e-mail flicc@loc.gov. *Exec. Dir.* Susan M. Tarr.

National Library Service for the Blind and Physically Handicapped, Library of Congress (NLS), 1291 Taylor St. N.W., Washington 20542. SAN 370-5870. Tel. 202-707-5100, fax 202-707-0712, e-mail nls@loc.gov. *Dir.* Frank Kurt Cylke.

Transportation Research Information Services (TRIS), 2101 Constitution Ave. N.W., Washington 20418. SAN 370-582X. Tel. 202-334-3250, fax 202-334-3495. *Dir.* Jerome T. Maddock.

Veterans Affairs Library Network (VAL-NET), Lib. Div. Programs Office, 810 Vermont Ave. N.W., Washington 20420. SAN 322-0834. Tel. 202-273-8694, fax 202-273-9386, e-mail wendy.carter@hq.med.va.gov. *Dir. Lib. Programs* Wendy N. Carter.

Washington Theological Consortium, 487 Michigan Ave. N.E., Washington 20017-1585. SAN 322-0842. Tel. 202-832-2675, fax 202-526-0818, e-mail wtconsort@aol.com. *Exec. Dir.* John Crossin.

Florida

Central Florida Library Cooperative (CFLC), 431 E. Horatio Ave., Ste. 230, Maitland 32751. SAN 371-9014. Tel. 407-644-9050, fax 407-644-7023. *Exec. Dir.* Marta Westall.

Florida Library Information Network, c/o Bureau of Lib. and Network Services, State Lib. of Florida, R. A. Gray Bldg., Tallahassee 32399-0250. SAN 322-0869. Tel. 850-487-2651, fax 850-488-2746, e-mail library@mail.dos.state.fl.us. *Chief, Bureau of Lib. and Network Services* Debra Sears.

Miami Health Sciences Library Consortium (MHSLC), KBI/IDM (142D), 1201 N.W. 16th St., Miami 33125-1673. SAN 371-0734. Tel. 305-324-3187, fax 305-324-3118, e-mail harker.susan@miami.va.gov. *Chief* Susan Harker.

Palm Beach Health Sciences Library Consortium (PBHSLC), c/o Good Samaritan Medical Center Medical Lib., Box 3166, West Palm Beach 33402. SAN 370-0380. Tel. 561-650-6315, fax 561-650-6417. *Chair* Karen Bledsoe.

Panhandle Library Access Network (PLAN), 5 Miracle Strip Loop, Ste. 2, Panama City Beach 32407-3850. SAN 370-047X. Tel. 850-233-9051, fax 850-235-2286, e-mail jaskows@firnvx.firn.edu. *Exec. Dir.* William P. Conniff.

Southeast Florida Library Information Network, Inc. (SEFLIN), 100 S. Andrews Ave., Fort Lauderdale 33301. SAN 370-0666. Tel. 954-357-7345, fax 954-357-6998, e-mail currye@mail.seflin.org. *Exec. Dir.* Elizabeth Curry.

Tampa Bay Library Consortium, Inc., 1202 Tech Blvd., Ste. 202, Tampa 33619. SAN 322-371X. Tel. 813-622-8252, fax 813-628-4425. *Exec. Dir.* Diane Solomon.

Tampa Bay Medical Library Network (TABAMLN), Lakeland Regional Medical Center, 1324 Lakeland Hills Blvd., Lakeland 33805. SAN 322-0885. Tel. 941-687-1176, fax 941-687-1488. *Pres.* Jan Booker.

Georgia

Atlanta Health Science Libraries Consortium, Shepherd Center, 2020 Peachtree Rd., Atlanta 30309. SAN 322-0893. Tel. 404-350-7473, fax 404-350-7736, e-mail pat_herndon@shepherd.org. *Pres.* Pat Herndon.

Biomedical Media, 1440 Clifton Rd. N.E., Rm. 113, Atlanta 30322. SAN 322-0931. Tel. 404-727-9797, fax 404-727-9798. *Dir.* Chuck Bogle.

Consortium of South Eastern Law Libraries (COSELL), Hugh F. MacMillan Law Lib., Emory Univ. School of Law, 1301 Clifton Rd., Atlanta 30322. SAN 372-8277. Tel. 404-627-6720, fax 404-727-5361. *Chair* Rosalie Sanderson.

Georgia Health Sciences Library Association (GHSLA), University Hospital, 1350 Walton Way, Augusta 30901. SAN 372-8307. Tel. 706-774-5078, fax 706-774-8672. *Pres.* Donna Trainor.

Georgia Interactive Network for Medical Information (GaIN), c/o Medical Lib., School of Medicine, Mercer Univ, 1550 College St., Macon 31207. SAN 370-0577. Tel. 912-752-2515, fax 912-752-2051, e-mail rankin.ja@gain.mercer.edu. *Dir.* Jocelyn A. Rankin.

Georgia Online Database (GOLD), c/o Public Lib. Services, 1800 Century Place N.E., Ste. 150, Atlanta 30345-4304. SAN 322-094X. Tel. 404-982-3560, fax 404-982-3563. *Acting Dir.* David Singleton.

Health Science Libraries of Central Georgia (HSLCG), c/o J. Rankin Medical Lib., School of Medicine, Mercer Univ., 1550 College St., Macon 31207. SAN 371-5051. Tel. 912-752-2515, fax 912-752-2051, e-mail rankin.ja@gain.mercer.edu. *In Charge* Michael Shadix.

Metro Atlanta Library Association (MALA), 483 James St., Lilburn 30247. SAN 378-2549. Tel. 770-431-2860, fax 770-431-2862. *Pres.* Michael Seigler.

South Georgia Associated Libraries, 208 Gloucester St., Brunswick 31520-7007. SAN 322-0966. Tel. 912-267-1212, fax 912-267-9597. *Pres.* Tena Roberts.

Southeastern Library Network (SOLINET), 1438 W. Peachtree St. N.W., Ste. 200, Atlanta 30309-2955. SAN 322-0974. Tel. 404-892-0943, fax 404-892-7879, e-mail mrichard@mail.solinet.net. *Exec. Dir.* Kate Nevins.

SWGHSLC, Colquitt Regional Medical Center, Health Sciences Lib., Moultrie 31776. SAN 372-8072. Tel. 912-890-3460, fax 912-891-9345. *Medical Libn.* Susan Statom.

University Center in Georgia, Inc., 50 Hurt Plaza, Ste. 465, Atlanta 30303-2923. SAN 322-0990. Tel. 404-651-2668, fax 404-651-1797. *Pres.* Michael Gerber.

Hawaii

Hawaii-Pacific Chapter of the Medical Library Association (HIPAC-MLA), 1221 Punchbowl St., Honolulu 96813. SAN 371-3946. Tel. 808-536-9302, fax 808-524-6956. *Chair* Carolyn Ching.

Idaho

Boise Valley Health Sciences Library Consortium (BVHSLC), Health Sciences Lib., Saint Alphonsus Regional Medical Center, Boise 83706. SAN 371-0807. Tel. 208-367-3993, fax 208-367-2702. *Contact* Judy Balcerzak.

Canyon Owyhee Library Group, 203 E. Idaho Ave., Homedale 83628. SAN 375-006X. Tel. 208-337-4613, fax 208-337-4933, e-mail stokes@sd370.k12.id.us. *Chair* Ned Stokes.

Catalyst, c/o Boise State Univ., Albertsons Lib., Box 46, Boise 83707-0046. SAN 375-0078. Tel. 208-426-4024, fax 208-426-1394. *Contact* Timothy A. Brown.

Cooperative Information Network (CIN), 8385 N. Government Way, Hayden 83835-9280. SAN 323-7656. Tel. 208-772-5612, fax 208-772-2498, e-mail jhartung@cin.kcl.org. *Contact* John Hartung.

Eastern Idaho Library System, 457 Broadway, Idaho Falls 83402. SAN 323-7699. Tel. 208-529-1450, fax 208-529-1467. *Contact* Paul Holland.

Gooding County Library Consortium, c/o Gooding High School, 1050 Seventh Ave. W., Gooding 83330. SAN 375-0094. Tel. 208-934-4831, fax 208-934-4347, e-mail senators@northrim.com. *Contact* Cora Caldwell.

Grangeville Cooperative Network, c/o Grangeville Centennial Lib., 215 W. North St., Grangeville 83530-1729. SAN 375-0108. Tel. 208-983-0951, fax 208-983-2336, e-mail granglib@lcsc.edu. *Contact* Linda Ruthruff.

Idaho Health Information Association (IHIA), Columbia Eastern Idaho Regional Medical Center, Health Info. Access Center, Box 2077, Idaho Falls 83403. SAN 371-5078. Tel. 208-529-6077, fax 208-529-7014. *Pres.* Kathy Nelson.

Lynx, c/o Boise Public Lib., 715 Capitol Blvd., Boise 83702-7195. SAN 375-0086. Tel. 208-384-4238, fax 208-384-4025, e-mail lmelton@ci.boise.id.us. *Contact* Marilyn Poertner.

Palouse Area Library Information Services (PALIS), c/o Latah County Free Lib. District, 110 S. Jefferson, Moscow 83843-2833. SAN 375-0132. Tel. 208-882-3925, fax 208-882-5098, e-mail lkeenan@norby.latah.lib.id.us. *Contact* Lori Keenan.

Southeast Idaho Document Delivery Network, c/o American Falls District Lib., 308 Roosevelt St., American Falls 83211-1219. SAN 375-0140. Tel. 208-226-2335, fax 208-226-2303. *Contact* Margaret McNamara.

Valnet, Lewis Clark State College Lib., 500 Eighth Ave., Lewiston 83501. SAN 323-7672. Tel. 208-799-2227, fax 208-799-2831. *Contact* Paul Krause.

Illinois

Alliance Library System, 845 Brenkman Dr., Pekin 61554. SAN 371-0637. Tel. 309-353-4110, fax 309-353-8281. *Exec. Dir.* Valerie J. Wilford.

American Theological Library Association (ATLA), 820 Church St., Ste. 400, Evanston 60201-5613. SAN 371-9022. Tel. 847-869-7788, fax 847-869-8513, e-mail atla@atla.com. *Exec. Dir.* Dennis A. Norlin.

Areawide Hospital Library Consortium of Southwestern Illinois (AHLC), c/o Saint Elizabeth Hospital Health Sciences Lib., 211 S. Third St., Belleville 62222. SAN 322-1016. Tel. 618-234-2120, ext. 1181, fax 618-234-0408, e-mail campese@apci. net, campese@exl.com. *Coord.* Michael Campese.

Association of Chicago Theological Schools (ACTS), McCormick Seminary, 5555 S. Woodlawn Ave., Chicago 60637. SAN 370-0658. Tel. 773-947-6300, fax 773-288-2612, e-mail nfisher@nwv.edu. *Pres.* Cynthia Campbell.

Capital Area Consortium, Saint Mary's Hospital Health Sciences Lib., 1800 E. Lakeshore Dr., Decatur 62521-3883. SAN 322-1024. Tel. 217-464-2182, fax 217-429-2925, e-mail smhlibrary@fgi.net. *Coord.* Laura Brosamer.

Center for Research Libraries, 6050 S. Kenwood, Chicago 60637-2804. SAN 322-1032. Tel. 773-955-4545, fax 773-955-4339, e-mail simpson@uhuru.uchicago. edu. *Pres.* Donald B. Simpson.

Chicago and South Consortium, Saint Joseph Medical Center, Health Science Lib., 333 N. Madison Ave., Joliet 60435. SAN 322-1067. Tel. 815-725-7133, ext. 3530, fax 815-725-9459. *Coord.* Virginia Gale.

Chicago Library System (CLS), 224 S. Michigan, Ste. 400, Chicago 60604. SAN 372-8188. Tel. 312-341-8500, fax 312-341-1985, e-mail calabrese@chilibsys.org. *Exec. Dir.* Alice Calabrese.

Consortium of Midwest Community Colleges, Colleges and Universities, 1011 Lake St., Ste. 434, Oak Park 60301. SAN 329-5583. Tel. 708-848-4844, fax 708-848-4888, e-mail jberry@aakton.edu. *Exec. Dir.* John W. Berry.

Consortium of Museum Libraries in the Chicago Area, c/o Morton Arboretum, Sterling Morton Lib., 4100 Illinois Rte. 53, Lisle 60532-1293. SAN 371-392X. Tel. 630-719-2427, fax 630-719-7950. *Chair* Michael T. Stieber.

Council of Directors of State University Libraries of Illinois (CODSULI), Southern Illinois Univ., Medical Lib., Box 19625, Springfield 62795-9625. SAN 322-1083. Tel. 217-782-2658, fax 217-782-0988, e-mail cfakl@eiu.edu. *Dir.* Connie Poole.

East Central Illinois Consortium, Carle Foundation Hospital Lib., 611 W. Park St., Urbana 61801. SAN 322-1040. Tel. 217-383-3011, fax 217-383-3452. *Coord.* Anita Johnson.

Fox Valley Health Science Library Consortium, Central DuPage Hospital Medical Lib., 25 N. Winfield Rd., Winfield 60190. SAN 329-3831. Tel. 630-681-4535, fax 630-682-0028, e-mail gloria_sullivan@cdh.org. *Coord.* Gloria Sullivan.

Heart of Illinois Library Consortium, Carl Sandburg College, Bromenn Healthcare,

Galesburg 61401. SAN 322-1113. Tel. 309-341-5106, fax 309-344-3526, e-mail ttucker@clarkstar.lib.il.us. *Coord.* Mary Evans.

Illinois Health Libraries Consortium, c/o Meat Industry Info. Center, National Cattleman's Beef Assn., 444 N. Michigan Ave., Chicago 60611. SAN 322-113X. Tel. 312-670-9272, fax 312-467-9729. *Coord.* William D. Siarny, Jr.

Illinois Library and Information Network (ILLINET), c/o Illinois State Lib., 300 S. Second St., Springfield 62701-1796. SAN 322-1148. Tel. 217-782-2994, fax 217-785-4326. *Dir.* Bridget L. Lamont.

Illinois Library Computer Systems (ILCSO), Univ. of Illinois, 205 Johnstowne Centre, 502 E. John St., Champaign 61820. SAN 322-3736. Tel. 217-244-7593, fax 217-244-7596, e-mail oncall@listserv.ilcso. uiuc.edu. *Dir.* Kristine Hammerstrand.

Judaica Library Network of Metropolitan Chicago (JLNMC), 618 Washington Ave., Wilmette 60091. SAN 370-0615. Tel. 847-251-0782, e-mail wolfecg@interaccess. com. *Pres.* Margaret Burka.

Libras, Inc., Dominican Univ., River Forest 60305. SAN 322-1172. Tel. 708-524-6875, ext. 6889, fax 708-366-5360, e-mail czange@mail.judson-il.edu. *Pres.* Sonja Terry.

Metropolitan Consortium of Chicago, Webster Lib., Evanston Hospital, 2650 Ridge Ave., Chicago 60201. SAN 322-1180. Tel. 847-570-2664, e-mail libsch@ interaccess.com. *Coord.* Dalia Kleinmuntz.

National Network of Libraries of Medicine, c/o Lib. of the Health Sciences, Univ. of Illinois at Chicago, 1750 W. Polk St., Chicago 60612-7223. SAN 322-1202. Tel. 312-996-2464, fax 312-996-2226. *Assoc. Dir.* Jean Sayre.

Office of Educational Services, K80, Univ. of Illinois at Springfield, Box 19243, Springfield 62794-9423. SAN 371-5108. Fax 217-786-6036, e-mail iscc@uis.edu. *Dir.* Rebecca Woodhull.

Private Academic Libraries of Illinois (PALI), c/o Concordia Univ. Lib., 7400 Augusta St., River Forest 60305-1499. SAN 370-050X. Tel. 708-209-3050, fax 708-209-

3175, e-mail crflatzkehr@curf.edu. *Pres.* Henry R. Latzke.

Quad Cities Libraries in Cooperation (QUAD-LINC), Box 125, Coal Valley 61240. SAN 373-093X. Tel. 309-799-3155, fax 309-799-5103, e-mail mstewart@libb.rbls.lib. il.us. *Mgr. Automation Services* Mary Anne Stewart.

Quad City Area Biomedical Consortium, Perlmutter Lib., 855 Hospital Rd., Silvis 61282. SAN 322-435X. Tel. 309-792-4360, fax 309-792-4362. *Coord.* Barbara Tharp.

River Bend Library System (RBLS), Box 125, Coal Valley 61240. SAN 371-0653. Tel. 309-799-3155, fax 309-799-7916, e-mail jhutchin@libby.rbls.lib.il.us. *Coord.* Judy Hutchinson.

Sangamon Valley Academic Library Consortium, Blackburn College, Lumpkin Lib., 700 College Ave., Carlinville 62626. SAN 322-4406. Tel. 217-854-3231, fax 217-854-8564, e-mail cscha@gorilla.blackburn. edu. *Chair* Carol Schaefer.

Shabbona Consortium, c/o Illinois Valley Community Hospital, 925 West St., Peru 61354. SAN 329-5133. Tel. 815-223-3300, ext. 502, fax 815-223-3394. *Contact* Sheila Brolley.

Upstate Consortium, c/o Menbota Community Hospital, 1315 Memorial Dr., Menbota 61342. SAN 329-3793. Tel. 815-539-7461, ext. 305. *Coord.* Janet Lane.

Indiana

American Zoo and Aquarium Association (AZA-LSIG), Indianapolis Zoo, 1200 W. Washington St., Indianapolis 46222. SAN 373-0891. Tel. 317-630-5110, fax 317-630-5114. *Chair* Suzanne Braun.

Central Indiana Health Science Libraries Consortium, Indiana Univ. School of Medicine Lib., 975 W. Walnut IB100, Indianapolis 46202. SAN 322-1245. Tel. 317-274-2292, fax 317-278-2349, e-mail lshass@stvincent.org, lhass@iquest.net. *Pres.* Peggy Richwine.

Collegiate Consortium Western Indiana, c/o Cunningham Memorial Lib., Indiana State Univ., Terre Haute 47809. SAN 329-4439. Tel. 812-237-3700, fax 812-237-3376.

Assoc. V.P. Info. Services and Dean of Libs. Ellen Watson.

Evansville Area Library Consortium, 3700 Washington Ave., Evansville 47750. SAN 322-1261. Tel. 812-485-4151, fax 812-485-7564. *Coord.* E. Jane Saltzman.

Indiana Cooperative Library Services Authority (INCOLSA), 6202 Morenci Trail, Indianapolis 46268-2536. SAN 322-1296. Tel. 317-298-6570, fax 317-328-2380. *Exec. Dir.* Millard Johnson.

Indiana State Data Center, Indiana State Lib., 140 N. Senate Ave., Indianapolis 46204-2296. SAN 322-1318. Tel. 317-232-3733, fax 317-232-3728, e-mail sandrews@statelib.lib.in.us. *Libns.* Cynthia St. Martin, Ronald Sharpe.

Northeast Indiana Health Science Libraries Consortium (NEIHSL), Lutheran Center for Health Services, Health Sciences Lib., 3024 Fairfield Ave., Fort Wayne 46807. SAN 373-1383. Tel. 219-434-7691, fax 219-434-7695, e-mail avenlc@cris.com. *Coord.* Lauralee Aven.

Northwest Indiana Health Science Library Consortium, c/o N.W. Center for Medical Educ., Indiana Univ. School of Medicine, 3400 Broadway, Gary 46408-1197. SAN 322-1350. Tel. 219-980-6852, fax 219-980-6566, e-mail fyoung@iunhaw1.iun.indiana.edu. *Coord.* Felicia Young.

Society of Indiana Archivists, Univ. Archives, 201 Bryan Hall, Indiana Univ., Bloomington 47405. SAN 329-5508. Tel. 812-855-5897, fax 812-855-8104. *Asst. to Pres.* Philip Bantin.

Wabash Valley Health Science Library Consortium, Indiana State Univ., Cunningham Memorial Lib., Terre Haute 47809. SAN 371-3903. Tel. 812-237-2540, fax 812-237-8028, e-mail libbirk@cml.indstate.edu. *Medical Libn. and Consortium Coord.* Evelyn J. Vail.

Iowa

Bi-State Academic Libraries (BI-SAL), c/o Marycrest International Univ., Davenport 52804. SAN 322-1393. Tel. 319-326-9255.

Consortium of College and University Media Centers, Instructional Technology Center, Iowa State Univ., 121 Pearson Hall, Ames 50011-2203. SAN 322-1091. Tel. 515-294-1811, fax 515-294-8089, e-mail ccumc@ccumc.org. *Exec. Dir.* Don A. Rieck.

Dubuque Area Library Information Consortium, c/o Divine Word College Seminary, 102 Jacoby Dr., Epworth 52045. SAN 322-1407. Tel. 319-876-3353, ext. 207, fax 319-876-3407. *Pres.* Dan Boice.

Iowa Private Academic Library Consortium (IPAL), c/o Buena Vista Univ. Lib., 610 W. Fourth St., Storm Lake 50588. SAN 329-5311. Tel. 712-749-2127, fax 712-749-2059, e-mail proberts@keller.clarke.edu. *Dir.* Jim Kennedy.

Linn County Library Consortium, Stewart Memorial Lib., Coe College, Cedar Rapids 52402. SAN 322-4597. Tel. 319-399-8023, fax 319-399-8019. *Pres.* Richard Doyle.

Polk County Biomedical Consortium, c/o Mercy Hospital Medical Lib., 400 University Ave., Des Moines 50314. SAN 322-1431. Tel. 515-247-4189, fax 515-643-8809, e-mail celtic@netins.net. *Coord.* Pat Styles.

Sioux City Library Cooperative (SCLC), c/o Sioux City Public Lib., 529 Pierce St., Sioux City 51101-1203. SAN 329-4722. Tel. 712-255-2933, ext. 251, fax 712-279-6432. *Agent* Betsy J. Thompson.

State of Iowa Libraries Online Interlibrary Loan (SILO-ILL), State Lib. of Iowa, E. 12th and Grand, Des Moines 50319. SAN 322-1415. Tel. 515-281-4105, fax 515-281-6191. *State Libn.* Sharman B. Smith.

Tri-College Cooperative Effort, Loras College, c/o Wahlert Memorial Lib., 1450 Alta Vista, Dubuque 52004-0178. SAN 322-1466. Tel. 319-588-7164, fax 319-588-7292, e-mail klein@loras.edu. *Dir.* Robert Klein.

Kansas

Associated Colleges of Central Kansas, 210 S. Main St., McPherson 67460. SAN 322-1474. Tel. 316-241-5150, fax 316-241-5153. *Dir.* Donna Zerger.

Dodge City Library Consortium, c/o Dodge City, 1001 Second Ave., Dodge City 67801. SAN 322-4368. Tel. 316-225-0243, fax 316-225-0252. *Pres.* Patty Collins.

Kansas Library Network Board, State Capital, Rm. 343N, 300 S.W. Tenth, Topeka 66612-1593. SAN 329-5621. Tel. 785-296-3875, fax 785-296-6650, e-mail mpiper@ink.org. *Exec. Dir.* Eric Hansen.

Kentucky

Association of Independent Kentucky Colleges and Universities, 484 Chenault Rd., Frankfort 40601. SAN 322-1490. Tel. 502-695-5007, fax 502-695-5057, e-mail gary@mail.aikcu.org. *Pres.* Gary S. Cox.

Eastern Kentucky Health Science Information Network (EKHSIN), c/o Camden-Carroll Lib., Morehead State Univ., Morehead 40351. SAN 370-0631. Tel. 606-783-2610, fax 606-783-5311. *Coord.* William J. DeBord.

Kentuckiana Metroversity, Inc., 3113 Lexington Rd., Louisville 40206. SAN 322-1504. Tel. 502-897-3374, fax 502-895-1647. *Exec. Dir.* Jack Will.

Kentucky Health Science Libraries Consortium, VA Medical Center, Lib. Services 142D, 800 Zorn Ave., Louisville 40206-1499. SAN 370-0623. Tel. 502-894-6240, fax 502-894-6134. *Pres.* Jim Kastner.

Kentucky Library Information Center (KLIC), Kentucky Dept. for Libraries and Archives, 300 Coffee Tree Rd., Box 537, Frankfort 40602-0537. SAN 322-1512. Tel. 502-564-8300, fax 502-564-5773. *Contact* Linda Sherrow.

Kentucky Library Network, Inc., 300 Coffee Tree Rd., Box 537, Frankfort 40602. SAN 371-2184. Tel. 502-564-8300, fax 502-564-5773. *Pres.* William DeBord.

Southern Kentucky AHEC (formerly Bluegrass Medical Librarians), Health Sciences Lib., Southern KYAHEC, 305 Estill St., Berea 40404. SAN 371-3881. Fax 606-986-0534, e-mail skahec@skn.net. *Pres.* Kelly Bickery.

State Assisted Academic Library Council of Kentucky (SAALCK), c/o Steely Lib., Northern Kentucky Univ., Highland Heights 41099. SAN 371-2222. Tel. 606-572-5483, fax 606-572-6181, e-mail winner@nku.edu. *Chair and Pres.* Marian C. Winner.

Team-A Librarians (Theological Education Association of Mid America), Southern Baptist Theological Seminary, 2825 Lexington Rd., Louisville 40280. SAN 377-5038. Tel. 502-897-4807, fax 502-897-4600. *Libn.* Ronald F. Deering.

Louisiana

Baton Rouge Hospital Library Consortium, Earl K. Long Hospital, 5825 Airline Hwy., Baton Rouge 70805. SAN 329-4714. Tel. 504-358-1089, fax 504-358-1240, e-mail estanl@mail.ekl.lsvmc.edu. *Pres.* Eileen H. Stanley.

Health Sciences Library Association of Louisiana, Medical Library, Children's Hospital, 200 Henry Clay Ave., New Orleans 70118. SAN 375-0035. Tel. 504-896-9264, fax 504-896-3932, e-mail estanley@chmcat.cem.lsu.edu. *Chair* Lauren Clement Leboeuf.

Lasernet, State Lib. of Louisiana, Box 131, Baton Rouge 70821. SAN 371-6880. Tel. 225-342-4923, 342-4922, 342-3389, fax 225-219-4804. *Deputy Asst. Libn.* Michael R. McKann.

LOUIS (Louisiana Library Network), Computing Services Center, Tower Dr. at South Stadium, Baton Rouge 70803. Tel. 225-388-3740, fax 225-388-3709, e-mail rjb@lsu.edu. *Dir.* Ralph J. Boe.

Louisiana Government Information Network (LaGIN), c/o State Lib. of Louisiana, Box 131, Baton Rouge 70821. SAN 329-5036. Tel. 225-342-4914, fax 225-342-3547, e-mail jsmith@pelican.state.lib.la.us. *Coord.* Judith D. Smith.

New Orleans Educational Telecommunications Consortium, 2 Canal St., Ste. 2038, New Orleans 70130. SAN 329-5214. Tel. 504-524-0350, fax 504-524-0327. *Chair* Gregory M. St L. O'Brien.

Maine

Health Science Library Information Consortium (HSLIC), USVAM ROC, Box 3395, Togus 04330. SAN 322-1601. Tel. 207-743-5933, ext. 323, fax 207-973-8233, e-mail brunjes@saturn.caps.maine.edu. *Chair* Cindy White.

Maryland

District of Columbia Health Sciences Information Network (DOCHSIN), Shady Grove Adventist Hospital Lib., 9901 Medical Center Dr., Rockville 20850. SAN 323-9918. Tel. 301-279-6101, fax 301-279-6500. *Pres.* Janice Lester.

ERIC Processing and Reference Facility, 1100 West St., 2nd flr., Laurel 20707-3598. SAN 322-161X. Tel. 301-497-4080, fax 301-953-0263, e-mail tbrandho@inet.ed.gov. *Dir.* Ted Brandhorst.

Library Video Network (LVN), 320 York Rd., Towson 21204. SAN 375-5320. Tel. 410-887-2090, fax 410-887-6103, e-mail inlib@mail.bcpl.lib.md.us. *Production Mgr.* Jeff Lifton.

Maryland Association of Health Science Librarians (MAHSL), Saint Agnes Healthcare, 900 Caton Ave., Baltimore 21229. SAN 377-5070. Tel. 410-368-3123. *Pres.* Joanne Sullivan.

Maryland Interlibrary Organization (MILO), c/o Enoch Pratt Free Lib., 400 Cathedral St., Baltimore 21201-4484. SAN 343-8600. Tel. 410-396-5498, fax 410-396-5837, e-mail pwallace@mail.pratt.lib.md.us. *Mgr.* Sharon A. Smith.

Metropolitan Area Collection Development Consortium (MCDAC), c/o Carrol County Public Lib., 15 Airport Dr., Westminster 21157. SAN 323-9748. Tel. 410-876-6008, fax 410-876-3002, e-mail nhaile@ccpl.carr.org. *Coord.* Nancy Haile.

National Library of Medicine, MEDLARS, 8600 Rockville Pike, Bethesda 20894. SAN 322-1652. Tel. 301-402-1076, fax 301-496-0822, e-mail custserv@nlm.nih.gov. *Contact* Carolyn Tilley.

National Network of Libraries of Medicine (NN-LM), National Lib. of Medicine, 8600 Rockville Pike, Rm. B1E03, Bethesda 20894. SAN 373-0905. Tel. 301-496-4777, fax 301-480-1467, e-mail blyon@nlm.nih.gov. *Head* Becky Lyon.

National Network of Libraries of Medicine, Univ. of Maryland Health Sciences and Human Services Lib., 601 W. Lombard St., Baltimore 21201-1583. SAN 322-1644. Tel. 410-706-2855, fax 410-706-0099, e-mail fmeakin@umab.umd.edu. *Exec. Dir.* Janice Kelly.

Regional Alcohol and Drug Abuse Resource Network (RADAR), National Clearinghouse on Alcohol and Drug Info., Box 2345, Rockville 20847-2345. SAN 377-5569. Tel. 301-468-2600. *Dir.* John Noble.

Washington Research Library Consortium (WRLC), 901 Commerce Dr., Upper Marlboro 20774. SAN 373-0883. Tel. 301-390-2031, fax 301-390-2020. *Exec. Dir.* Lizanne Payne.

Massachusetts

Automated Bristol Library Exchange (ABLE, Inc.), 547 W. Grove St., Box 4, Middleboro 02346. SAN 378-0074. Tel. 508-946-8600, fax 508-946-8605. *Exec. Dir.* Deborah K. Conrad.

Boston Area Music Libraries (BAML), Music Lib., Wellesley College, Wellesley 02140. SAN 322-4392. Tel. 781-283-2076, fax 781-283-3687, e-mail dgilbert@wellesley.edu. *Coord.* David Gilbert.

Boston Biomedical Library Consortium (BBLC), c/o Paul E. Woodard Health Sciences Lib., New England Baptist Hospital, 125 Parker Hill Ave., Boston 02120. SAN 322-1725. Tel. 617-754-5155, fax 617-754-6414, e-mail lllnebh@world.std.com. *Chair* Leonard L. Levin.

C W MARS (Central-Western Massachusetts Automated Resource Sharing), 1 Sunset Lane, Paxton 01612-1197. SAN 322-3973. Tel. 508-755-3323, fax 508-755-3721, e-mail jkuklins@cwmars.org. *Exec. Dir.* Joan Kuklinski.

Cape Libraries Automated Materials Sharing (CLAMS), 270 Communication Way, Unit 4E-4F, Hyannis 02601. SAN 370-579X. Tel. 508-790-4399, fax 508-771-4533, e-mail mgrace@clams.lib.ma.us, dtustin@clams.lib.ma.us. *Pres.* Debra DeJonker-Berry.

Catholic Library Association, 100 North St., Ste. 224, Pittsfield 01201-5109. SAN 329-1030. Tel. 413-443-2252, fax 413-442-2252, e-mail cla@vgernet.net. *Exec. Dir.* Jean R. Bostley, SSJ.

Central Massachusetts Consortium of Health Related Libraries (CMCHRL), c/o Medical Lib., Univ. Massachusetts Memorial Healthcare, 119 Belmont St., Worcester 01605. SAN 371-2133. *Pres.* Andy Dzaugis.

Consortium for Information Resources, Emerson Hospital, Old Rd. to Nine Acre Corner, Concord 01742. SAN 322-4503. Tel. 978-287-3090, fax 978-287-3651. *Pres.* Nancy Callander.

Cooperating Libraries of Greater Springfield (CLGS), c/o Hatch Lib., Bay Path College, 588 Longmeadow St., Longmeadow 01106. SAN 322-1768. Tel. 413-565-1284, fax 413-567-8345. *Chair* Jay Schafer.

Corporate Library Group (CLG), 50 Nagog Park, AK02-3/E10, Acton 01720. SAN 370-0534. Tel. 978-264-6500, fax 978-264-7724. *Mgr.,* Mary Lee Kennedy.

Corporate Library Network Group, 50 Nagog Park, Acton 01720. SAN 377-5097. Tel. 978-264-7914. *Dir.* Mary Lee Kennedy.

Fenway Libraries Online (FLO), Wentworth Institute of Technology, 550 Huntington Ave., Boston 02115. SAN 373-9112. Tel. 617-442-2384, fax 617-442-1519. *Network Dir.* Jamie Ingram.

Fenway Library Consortium, Simmons College, 300 The Fenway, Boston 02115. SAN 327-9766. Tel. 617-521-2754, fax 617-521-3093, e-mail ecl_maz@flo.org. *Coord.* Harvey Varnet.

Massachusetts Health Sciences Libraries Network (MAHSLIN), c/o New England Regional Primate Center, Harvard Medical School, Box 9102, Southborough 01772-9102. SAN 372-8293. Tel. 508-624-8028, fax 508-460-1209, e-mail sfingold@warren.med.harvard.edu. *Pres.* Sydney Ann Fingold.

Merrimac Interlibrary Cooperative, c/o J. V. Fletcher Lib., 50 Main St., Westford 01886. SAN 329-4234. Tel. 508-692-5555, fax 508-692-4418, e-mail jefferso@mvlc.lib.ma.us. *Co-Chairs* Sue Jefferson, Nanette Eichell.

Merrimack Valley Library Consortium, 21 Canal St., Lawrence 01840. SAN 322-4384. Tel. 978-687-5300, fax 978-687-5312, e-mail manson@mvlc.lib.ma.us. *Pres.* Sue Ellen Holmes.

Minuteman Library Network, 4 California Ave., 5th flr., Framingham 01701. SAN 322-4252. Tel. 508-879-8575, fax 508-879-5470, e-mail ccaro@mln.lib.ma.us. *Exec. Dir.* Carol B. Caro.

NELINET, Inc., 2 Newton Executive Park, Newton 02162. SAN 322-1822. Tel. 617-969-0400, fax 617-332-9634, e-mail admin@nelinet.org, nelinet@bcvms.bitnet. *Exec. Dir.* Marshall Keys.

New England Law Library Consortium, Inc., Harvard Law School Lib., Langdell Hall, Cambridge 02138. SAN 322-4244. Tel. 617-496-2121, 508-428-5342, fax 617-428-7623, e-mail klaiber@law.harvard.edu. *Exec. Dir.* Diane Klaiber.

North Atlantic Health Sciences Libraries, Inc. (NAHSL), Lamar Soutter Lib., Univ. Massachusetts Medical Center, 55 Lake Ave. N., Worcester 01655. SAN 371-0599. Tel. 508-856-2435, fax 508-856-5899, e-mail bob.sekerak@vtmednet.org. *Chair* Debbie Sibley.

North of Boston Library Exchange, Inc. (NOBLE), 26 Cherry Hill Dr., Danvers 01923. SAN 322-4023. Tel. 978-777-8844, fax 978-750-8472. *Exec. Dir.* Ronald A. Gagnon.

Northeastern Consortium for Health Information (NECHI), Tewksbury State Hospital, 365 E St., Tewksbury 01876. SAN 322-1857. Tel. 978-741-6762, 851-7321, ext. 2255, e-mail glynn@noblenet.org. *Chair* Chris Young.

Northeast Consortium of Colleges and Universities in Massachusetts (NECCUM), c/o Gordon College, 255 Grapevine Rd., Wenham 01984. SAN 371-0602. Tel. 978-927-2300, ext. 4068, fax 978-524-3708, e-mail macleod@hope.gordonc.edu. *Coord.* Stephen MacLeod.

SAILS, Inc., 547 W. Groves St., Box 4, Middleboro 02346. SAN 378-0058. Tel. 508-946-8600, fax 508-946-8605. *Exec. Dir.* Deborah K. Conrad.

Southeastern Automated Libraries, Inc. (SEAL), 547 W. Grove St., Box 4, Middleboro 02346. SAN 371-5000. Tel. 508-946-8600, fax 508-946-8605. *Exec. Dir.* Deborah K. Conrad.

Southeastern Massachusetts Consortium of Health Science Libraries (SEMCO), South

Shore Hospital, 55 Fogg Rd., South Weymouth 02190. SAN 322-1873. Tel. 781-340-8528, fax 781-331-0834, e-mail ubh0341@slh.org. *Chair* Cathy McCarthy.

Southeastern Massachusetts Cooperating Libraries (SMCL), c/o Wheaton College, Madeleine Clark Wallace Lib., Norton 02766-0849. SAN 322-1865. Tel. 508-285-8225, fax 508-286-8275, e-mail pdeekle@wheatonma.edu. *Chair* Peter Deekle.

West of Boston Network (WEBNET), Horn Lib., Babson College, Babson Park 02157. SAN 371-5019. Tel. 781-239-4308, fax 781-239-5226, e-mail benzer@babson.edu. *System Admin.* Susan Benzer.

Western Massachusetts Health Information Consortium, c/o Holyoke Hospital Medical Lib., 575 Beech St., Holyoke 01040. SAN 329-4579. Tel. 413-534-2500, ext. 5282, fax 413-534-2710, e-mail mcaraker@mail.map.com. *Pres.* Mary Caraker.

Worcester Area Cooperating Libraries, c/o Worcester State College Learning Resources Center, Rm. 221, 486 Chandler St., Worcester 01602-2597. SAN 322-1881. Tel. 508-754-3964, 793-8000, ext. 8544, fax 508-929-8198, e-mail gwood@worc.mass.edu. *Coord.* Gladys Wood.

Michigan

Berrien Library Consortium, c/o Lake Michigan College Lib., 2755 E. Napier Ave., Benton Harbor 49022-1899. SAN 322-4678. Tel. 616-927-8605, fax 616-927-6656. *Pres.* Diane Baker.

Capital Area Library Network, Inc. (CAL-NET), 4061 Holt Rd., Holt 48842. SAN 370-5927. Tel. 517-699-1657, fax 517-699-4859, e-mail aholt@isd.ingham.k12.mi.us. *Contact* Ann C. Holt.

Council on Resource Development (CORD), Oakland County Lib., 1200 N. Telegraph Rd., Pontiac 48341. SAN 374-6119. Tel. 248-858-0380, fax 248-452-9145. *Chair* Phyllis Jose.

Detroit Area Consortium of Catholic Colleges, c/o Sacred Heart Seminary, 2701 Chicago Blvd., Detroit 48206. SAN 329-482X. Tel. 313-883-8500, fax 313-868-6440. *Rector and Pres.* Allen H. Vigneron.

Detroit Associated Libraries Region of Cooperation (DALROC), Detroit Public Lib., 5201 Woodward Ave., Detroit 48202. SAN 371-0831. Tel. 313-833-4835, fax 313-832-0877. *Chair* Patrice Merritt.

Kalamazoo Consortium for Higher Education (KCHE), Kalamazoo College, 1200 Academy St., Kalamazoo 49006. SAN 329-4994. Tel. 616-337-7220, fax 616-337-7305. *Pres.* James F. Jones, Jr.

Lakeland Area Library Network (LAKE-NET), 4138 Three Mile N.W., Grand Rapids 49544-1134. SAN 371-0696. Tel. 616-559-5253, fax 616-559-4329.

Library Cooperative of Macomb (LCM), 16480 Hall Rd., Clinton Township 48038. SAN 373-9082. Tel. 810-286-5750, fax 810-286-8951, e-mail turgeont@lcm.macomb.lib.mi.us. *Acting Dir.* Tammy L. Turgeon.

The Library Network, 13331 Reeck Rd., Southgate 48195. SAN 370-596X. Tel. 313-281-3830, fax 313-281-1905, 281-1817, e-mail hrc@tlnlib.mi.us. *Dir.* Harry Courtright.

Michigan Association of Consumer Health Information Specialists (MACHIS), Bronson Methodist Hospital, Health Sciences Lib., 252 E. Lovell St., Box B, Kalamazoo 49007. SAN 375-0043. Tel. 616-341-8627, fax 616-341-8828, e-mail dhummel @bw.brhn.org. *Chair* Marge Kars.

Michigan Health Sciences Libraries Association (MHSLA), c/o Spectrum Health–Downtown Campus, 100 Michigan Ave. N.E., Grand Rapids 49503. SAN 323-987X. Tel. 616-391-1655, fax 616-391-3527, e-mail dianehummel@spectrum-health.org. *Pres.* Diane Hummel.

Michigan Library Consortium (MLC), 6810 S. Cedar St., Ste. 8, Lansing 48911. SAN 322-192X. Tel. 517-694-4242, fax 517-694-9303. *Exec. Dir.* Randy Dykhuis.

Northland Interlibrary System (NILS), 316 E. Chisholm St., Alpena 49707. SAN 329-4773. Tel. 517-356-1622, fax 517-354-3939, e-mail cawleyr@northland.lib.mi.us. *Dir.* Rebecca E. Cawley.

Southeastern Michigan League of Libraries (SEMLOL), c/o Wayne State Univ., Undergraduate Lib., 5150 Anthony Wayne Dr., Detroit 48202. SAN 322-4481. Tel. 313-

577-6630, fax 313-577-5265. *Chair* Lynn Sutton.

Southern Michigan Region of Cooperation (SMROC), 415 S. Superior, Ste. A, Albion 49224-2135. SAN 371-3857. Tel. 517-629-9469, fax 517-629-3812. *Fiscal Agent* James C. Seidl.

Southwest Michigan Library Cooperative (SMLC), 305 Oak St., Paw Paw 49079. SAN 371-5027. Tel. 616-657-4698, fax 616-657-4494. *Dir.* Alida L. Geppert.

UMI Information Store, Inc., 300 N. Zeeb Rd., Box 1346, Ann Arbor 48106-1346. SAN 374-7913. Tel. 734-761-4700, fax 734-761-1032. *Mgr. Customer Service and Product Info.* Cheri Marken.

Upper Peninsula of Michigan Health Science Library Consortium, c/o Marquette General Hospital, 420 W. Magnetic, Marquette 49855. SAN 329-4803. Tel. 906-225-3429, fax 906-225-3524. *Chair* Kenneth Nelson.

Upper Peninsula Region of Library Cooperation, Inc., 1615 Presque Isle Ave., Marquette 49855. SAN 329-5540. Tel. 906-228-7697, fax 906-228-5627. *Pres.* Ken Nelson.

Minnesota

Arrowhead Health Sciences Library Network, Library, Saint Luke's Hospital, Duluth 55805. SAN 322-1954. Tel. 218-726-5320, fax 218-726-5181, e-mail droberts@slhduluth.com. *Coord.* Doreen Roberts.

Capital Area Library Consortium (CALCO), c/o Minnesota Dept. of Transportation, Library MS155, 395 John Ireland Blvd., Saint Paul 55155. SAN 374-6127. Tel. 612-296-1741, fax 612-297-2354. *Pres.* Dennis Skradie.

Central Minnesota Libraries Exchange (CMLE), c/o Learning Resources, Rm. 61, Saint Cloud State Univ., Saint Cloud 56301-4498. SAN 322-3779. Tel. 320-255-2950, fax 320-654-5131, e-mail ppeterson@stcloudstate.edu. *Dir.* Patricia E. Peterson.

Community Health Science Library, c/o Saint Francis Medical Center, 415 Oak St., Breckenridge 56520. SAN 370-0585. Tel.

218-643-7516, fax 218-643-7487. *Dir.* Carla Lobaasen.

Cooperating Libraries in Consortium (CLIC), 1619 Dayton Ave., Ste. 204A, Saint Paul 55104. SAN 322-1970. Tel. 651-644-3878, fax 651-644-6258, e-mail olsonc@macalester.edu. *Exec. Dir.* Chris Olson.

METRONET, 2324 University Ave. W., Ste. 116, Saint Paul 55114. SAN 322-1989. Tel. 651-646-0475, fax 651-646-0657. *Dir.* Mary Treacy.

Metropolitan Library Service Agency (MELSA), 570 Asbury St., Ste. 201, Saint Paul 55104-1849. SAN 371-5124. Tel. 612-645-5731, fax 612-649-3169, e-mail melsa@gopher.melsa.lib.mn.us. *Exec. Dir.* James Wroblewski.

Minitex Library Information Network, c/o S-33 Wilson Lib., Univ. of Minnesota, 309 19th Ave. S., Minneapolis 55455-0414. SAN 322-1997. Tel. 612-624-4002, fax 612-624-4508, e-mail w_dejo@tc.umn.edu. *Dir.* William DeJohn.

Minnesota Department of Human Services Library, DHS Library and Resource Center, 444 Lafayette, Saint Paul 55155-3820. SAN 371-0750. Tel. 612-297-8708, fax 612-282-5340, e-mail kate.o.nelson@state.mn.us. *Dir. and Coord.* Kate Nelson.

Minnesota Theological Library Association (MTLA), c/o Luther Seminary Lib., 2375 Como Ave., Saint Paul 55108. SAN 322-1962. Tel. 612-641-3202, fax 612-641-3280, e-mail twalker@luthersem.edu. *Co-Pres.* Sandy Oslund, Pam Jervis.

North Country Library Cooperative, Olcott Plaza, 820 Ninth St. N., Ste. 110, Virginia 55792-2298. SAN 322-3795. Tel. 218-741-1907, fax 218-741-1907, e-mail nclcmn@northernnet.com. *Dir.* Linda J. Wadman.

Northern Lights Library Network, 318 17th Ave. E., Box 845, Alexandria 56308-0845. SAN 322-2004. Tel. 320-762-1032, fax 320-762-1032. *Dir.* Joan B. Larson.

SMILE (Southcentral Minnesota Inter-Library Exchange), 110 S. Broad, Box 3031, Mankato 56002-3031. SAN 321-3358. Tel. 507-625-7555, fax 507-625-4049, e-mail llowry@tds.lib.mn.us. *Dir.* Lucy Lowry.

Southeast Library System (SELS), 107 W. Frontage Rd., Hwy. 52 N., Rochester

55901. SAN 322-3981. Tel. 507-288-5513, fax 507-288-8697. *Admin.* Ann Hutton.

Southwest Area Multi-County Multi-Type Interlibrary Exchange (SAMMIE), BA 282 Southwest State Univ. Lib., Marshall 56258. SAN 322-2039. Tel. 507-532-9013, fax 507-532-2039, e-mail sammie@starpoint.net. *Coord.* Robin Chaney.

Twin Cities Biomedical Consortium, c/o Health East Saint Joseph's Hospital Lib., 69 W. Exchange St., Saint Paul 55102. SAN 322-2055. Tel. 651-232-3193, fax 651-232-3296. *Chair* Karen Brudvig.

Valley Medical Network, Lake Region Hospital Lib., 712 S. Cascade St., Fergus Falls 56537. SAN 329-4730. Tel. 218-736-8158, fax 218-736-8723. *Pres.* Connie Schulz.

Waseca Interlibrary Resource Exchange (WIRE), c/o Waseca High School, 1717 Second St. N.W., Waseca 56093. SAN 370-0593. Tel. 507-835-5470, ext. 218, fax 507-835-1724, e-mail tlouganl@platec.net. *Dir.* Les Tlougan.

West Group, Box 64526, Saint Paul 55164-0526. SAN 322-4031. Tel. 612-687-7000, fax 612-687-5614. *Dir.* Jennifer Goldbluff.

Mississippi

Central Mississippi Consortium of Medical Libraries (CMCML), Medical Center, U.S. Dept. of Veterans Affairs, 1500 E. Woodrow Wilson Dr., Jackson 39216. SAN 372-8099. Tel. 601-362-4471, 362-5378, 362-1680. *Chair* Rose Anne Tucker.

Central Mississippi Library Council (CMLC), c/o Hinds Community College Lib., Raymond 39154-9799. SAN 372-8250. Tel. 601-857-3255, fax 601-857-3293. *Chair* Tom Henderson.

Mississippi Biomedical Library Consortium, c/o College of Veterinary Medicine, Mississippi State Univ., Box 9825, Mississippi State 39762. SAN 371-070X. Tel. 601-325-1240, fax 601-325-1141, e-mail kinkus@cvm.msstate.edu. *Pres.* Jane Kinkus.

Missouri

Kansas City Library Network, Inc., Univ. of Missouri Dental Lib., 650 E. 25th St., Kansas City 64108. SAN 322-2098. Tel. 816-235-2030, fax 816-235-2157.

Kansas City Metropolitan Library and Information Network, 15624 E. 24th Hwy., Independence 64050. SAN 322-2101. Tel. 816-521-7257, fax 816-461-0966, e-mail sburton@kcmlin.org. *Exec. Dir.* Susan Burton.

Kansas City Regional Council for Higher Education, Park College, 8700 N.W. River Park Dr., No. 40, Parkville 64152-3795. SAN 322-211X. Tel. 816-741-2816, fax 816-741-1296, e-mail kcrche@aol.com, rondoering@aol.com, michmangus@aol.com. *Pres.* Ron Doering.

Missouri Library Network Corporation, 8045 Big Bend Blvd., Ste. 202, Saint Louis 63119-2714. SAN 322-466X. Tel. 314-918-7222, fax 314-918-7727, e-mail sms@mlnc.org. *Dir.* Susan Singleton.

Philsom-Philnet-Bacs Network, c/o Washington Univ., Bernard Becker Medical Lib., 660 S. Euclid Ave., Saint Louis 63110. SAN 322-2187. Tel. 314-362-2778, fax 314-362-0190, e-mail monikar@msnotes.wustl.edu. *Mgr.* Russ Monika.

Saint Louis Medical Librarians Consortia (SLML), c/o Washington Univ., Bernard Becker Medical Lib., 660 S. Euclid Ave., Saint Louis 63110. SAN 375-0027. Tel. 314-362-2778, fax 314-362-0190, e-mail monikar@msnotes.wustl.edu. *Chair* Russ Monika.

Saint Louis Regional Library Network, 9425 Big Bend, Saint Louis 63119. SAN 322-2209. Tel. 314-965-1305, fax 314-965-4443. *Admin.* Bernyce Christiansen.

Nebraska

Eastern Library System (ELS), 11929 Elm St., Ste. 12, Omaha 68144. SAN 371-506X. Tel. 402-330-7884, fax 402-330-1859, e-mail ktooker@neom.nlc.state.ne.us. *Admin.* Kathleen Tooker.

ICON (formerly Information Consortium), 5302 S. 75th St., Ralston 68127. SAN 372-8102. Tel. 402-398-6092, fax 402-398-6923. *Chair* Ken Oyer.

Lincoln Health Sciences Library Group (LHSLG), Univ. of Nebraska, 219 North Love Lib., Lincoln 68588-0410. SAN 329-5001. Tel. 402-472-2554, fax 402-472-5131. *Treas.* Joan Latta Konescky.

Meridian Library System, 3423 Second Ave., Ste. 301, Kearney 68847. SAN 325-3554. Tel. 308-234-2087, fax 308-234-4040, e-mail sosenga@nol.org. *Pres.* Mary Neben.

Mid-America Law School Library Consortium (MALSLC), c/o Klutznick Law Lib., Creighton Univ. School of Law, Omaha 68178-0001. SAN 371-6813. Tel. 402-280-2251, fax 402-280-2244, e-mail andrus@culaw.creighton.edu. *Chair* Kay L. Andrus.

National Network of Libraries of Medicine–Midcontinental Region (NN-LM-MR), c/o 986706 Nebraska Medical Center, Omaha 68198-6706. SAN 322-225X. Tel. 402-559-4326, fax 402-559-5482, e-mail pmullaly@unmcvm.unmc.edu. *Dir.* Nancy N. Woelfl.

Nebase, c/o Nebraska Library Commission, 1200 N St., Ste. 120, Lincoln 68508-2023. SAN 322-2268. Tel. 402-471-4031, fax 402-471-2083. *Dir.* Jo Budler.

Northeast Library System, 2813 13th St., Columbus 68601. SAN 329-5524. Tel. 402-564-1586. *Admin.* Carol Speicher.

Southeast Nebraska Library System, 5730 R St., Ste. C-1, Lincoln 68505. SAN 322-4732. Tel. 402-467-6188, fax 402-467-6196, e-mail bealey@nol.org. *Admin.* Brenda Ealey.

Nevada

Information Nevada, Interlibrary Loan Dept., Nevada State Lib. and Archives, Capitol Complex, Carson City 89710-0001. SAN 322-2276. Tel. 702-687-8325, fax 702-687-8330, e-mail akelley@clan.lib.nv.us. *Dir.* Joan Kerschner.

Nevada Medical Library Group (NMLG), Barton Memorial Hospital Lib., Box 9578, South Lake Tahoe 89520. SAN 370-0445. Tel. 530-542-3000, ext. 2903, fax 530-543-0239, e-mail kanton@oakweb.com. *Chair* Laurie Anton.

Western Council of State Libraries, Inc., Nevada State Lib. and Archives, 100 N.Stewart St., Carson City 89701. SAN 322-2314. Tel. 702-687-8315, fax 702-687-8311. *Pres.* Jim Sheppke.

New Hampshire

Carroll County Library Cooperative, Box 240, Madison 03849. SAN 371-8999. Tel. 603-367-8545. *Pres.* Carolyn Busell.

Hillstown Cooperative, 3 Meetinghouse Rd., Bedford 03110. SAN 371-3873. Tel. 603-472-2300, fax 603-472-2978. *Chair* Frances M. Wiggin.

Librarians of the Upper Valley Cooperative (LUV Coop), Enfield Public Lib., Main St., Box 1030, Enfield 03748-1030. SAN 371-6856. Tel. 603-632-7145. *Secy.* Marjorie Carr.

Merri-Hill-Rock Library Cooperative, c/o Griffin Lib., 22 Hooksett Rd, Box 308, Auburn 03032. SAN 329-5338. Tel. 603-483-5374, e-mail hailstones@juno.com. *Chair* Edith B. Cummings.

New Hampshire College and University Council Libs. Committee, 116 S. River Rd., D4, Bedford 03110. SAN 322-2322. Tel. 603-669-3432, fax 603-623-8182. *Exec. Dir.* Thomas R. Horgan.

North Country Consortium (NCC), Gale Medical Lib., Littleton Regional Hospital, 262 Cottage St., Littleton 03561. SAN 370-0410. Tel. 603-444-7731, ext. 164, fax 603-444-7491. *Coord.* Linda L. Ford.

Nubanusit Library Cooperative, c/o Peterborough Town Lib., 2 Concord, Peterborough 03458. SAN 322-4600. Tel. 603-924-8040, fax 603-924-8041. *Contact* Ann Geisel.

Scrooge and Marley Cooperative, 310 Central St., Franklin 03235. SAN 329-515X. Tel. 603-934-2911. *Chair* Randy Brough.

Seacoast Cooperative Libraries, North Hampton Public Lib., 235 Atlantic Ave., North Hampton 03862. SAN 322-4619. Tel. 603-964-6326, fax 603-964-1107. *Contact* Pam Schwotzer.

New Jersey

Bergen County Cooperative Library System, 810 Main St., Hackensack 07601. SAN 322-4546. Tel. 201-489-1904, fax 201-489-4215. *Exec. Dir.* Robert W. White.

Bergen Passaic Health Sciences Library Consortium, c/o Englewood Hospital and

Medical Center, 350 Engle St., Englewood 07631. SAN 371-0904. Tel. 201-894-3069, fax 201-894-9049, e-mail yoga@csnet.net. *ILL Coord. and Board Rep.* Lia Sabbagh.

Central Jersey Health Science Libraries Association, Saint Francis Medical Center Medical Lib., 601 Hamilton Ave., Trenton 08629. SAN 370-0712. Tel. 609-599-5068, fax 609-599-5773. *Dir.* Donna Barlow.

Central Jersey Regional Library Cooperative–Region V, 4400 Rte. 9 S., Freehold 07728-1383. SAN 370-5102. Tel. 732-409-6484, fax 732-409-6492. *Dir.* Connie S. Paul.

Cosmopolitan Biomedical Library Consortium, Medical Lib., East Orange General Hospital, 300 Central Ave., East Orange 07019. SAN 322-4414. Tel. 973-266-8519. *Pres.* Peggy Dreker.

Dow Jones Interactive, Box 300, Princeton 08543-0300. SAN 322-404X. Tel. 609-520-4679, fax 609-520-4775. *Contact* Pat Rodeawald.

Health Sciences Library Association of New Jersey (HSLANJ), Merck-Medco Managed Care LLC, Medical Resource Center, 101 Paragon Dr., R2-19A, Montvale 07645. SAN 370-0488. Tel. 201-782-3166, 888-447-5265, e-mail skica@umdnj.edu. *Pres.* Doris Eaton.

Highlands Regional Library Cooperative, 31 Fairmount Ave., Box 486, Chester 07930. SAN 329-4609. Tel. 908-879-2442, fax 908-879-8812, e-mail cnersinger@interactive.net or hcarroll@interactive.net. *Exec. Dir.* Carol A. Nersinger.

Infolink Eastern New Jersey Regional Library Cooperative, Inc., 44 Stelton Rd., Ste. 330, Piscataway 08854. SAN 371-5116. Tel. 732-752-7720, 973-673-2343, fax 732-752-7785, 973-673-2710, e-mail glr@infolink.org. *Exec. Dir.* Charles Edwin Dowlin.

LMX Automation Consortium, 1030 Saint George, Ste. 203, Avenel 07001. SAN 329-448X. Tel. 732-750-2525, fax 732-750-9392. *Exec. Dir.* Ellen Parravano.

Lucent Technologies Global Library Network, 600 Mountain Ave., Rm. 3A-426, Murray Hill 07974. SAN 329-5400. Tel. 908-582-4840, fax 908-582-3146, e-mail libnet@library.lucent.com. *Managing Dir.* Nancy J. Miller.

Monmouth-Ocean Biomedical Information Consortium (MOBIC), Community Medical Center, 99 Hwy. 37 W., Toms River 08755. SAN 329-5389. Tel. 732-240-8117, fax 732-240-8354, e-mail rreisler@mail.ckhes.com. *Dir.* Reina Reisler.

Morris Automated Information Network (MAIN), Box 900, Morristown 07963-0900. SAN 322-4058. Tel. 973-989-6112, fax 973-989-6109, e-mail mainhelp@main.morris.org. *Network Admin. and Div. Head* Ellen Sleeter.

Morris-Union Federation, 214 Main St., Chatham 07928. SAN 310-2629. Tel. 973-635-0603, fax 973-635-7827. *Treas.* Diane R. O'Brien.

New Jersey Academic Library Network, c/o The College of New Jersey, Roscoe L. West Lib., 2000 Pennington Rd., Box 7718, Ewing 08628-0718. SAN 329-4927. Tel. 609-771-2332, fax 609-637-5177, e-mail mbiggs@tcnj.edu. *Chair* Mary Biggs.

New Jersey Health Sciences Library Network (NJHSN), Mountainside Hospital, Health Sciences Lib., Montclair 07042. SAN 371-4829. Tel. 973-429-6240, fax 973-680-7850, e-mail pat.regenberg@mtn.ahsys.org. *Chair* Patricia Regenberg.

New Jersey Library Network, Lib. Development Bureau, 185 W. State St., CN-520, Trenton 08625-0520. SAN 372-8161. Tel. 609-984-3293, fax 609-984-7898. *Service Coord.* Marilyn R. Veldof.

Society for Cooperative Healthcare and Related Education (SCHARE), UMDNJ, 1776 Raritan Rd., Scotch Plains 07076. SAN 371-0718. Tel. 908-889-6410, fax 908-889-2487. *Chair* Eden Trinidad.

South Jersey Regional Library Cooperative, Paint Works Corporate Center, 10 Foster Ave., Ste. F-3, Gibbsboro 08026. SAN 329-4625. Tel. 609-346-1222, fax 609-346-2839. *Exec. Dir.* Karen Hyman.

New Mexico

New Mexico Consortium of Academic Libraries, Dean's Office, Univ. of New Mexico, Albuquerque 87131-1466. SAN 371-6872. Fax 505-277-7288, e-mail ctownley@lib.nmsu.edu. *Dean* Bob Migneault.

New Mexico Consortium of Biomedical and Hospital Libraries, c/o Lovelace Medical Lib., 5400 Gibson Blvd. S.E., Albuquerque 87108. SAN 322-449X. Tel. 505-262-7158, fax 505-262-7897. *Contact* Peg Fletcher.

New York

Academic Libraries of Brooklyn, Polytechnic Univ., Bern Dibner Lib., 5 Metrotech Center, Brooklyn 11201. SAN 322-2411. Tel. 718-260-3109, fax 715-260-3756, e-mail jrichman@duke.poly.edu. *Convener* Jana Richman.

American Film and Video Association, Cornell Univ. Resource Center, 8 Business and Techology Park, Ithaca 14850. SAN 377-5860. Tel. 607-255-2090, fax 607-255-9946, e-mail dist_cent@cce.cornell. edu. *AV Libn.* Richard Gray.

Associated Colleges of the Saint Lawrence Valley, 200 Merritt Hall, State Univ. of New York College at Potsdam, Potsdam 13676-2299. SAN 322-242X. Tel. 315-267-3331, fax 315-267-2389, e-mail larranaj@potsdam.edu. *Exec. Dir.* Anneke J. Larrance.

Brooklyn-Queens-Staten Island Health Sciences Librarians (BQSI), Saint John's Episcopal Hospital, South Shore Div. Medical Lib., 327 Beach 19th St., Far Rockaway 11691. SAN 370-0828. Tel. 718-869-7699, fax 718-869-8528, e-mail sjeh2@metgate.metro.org. *Pres.* Kalpana Desai.

Capital District Library Council for Reference and Research Resources, 28 Essex St., Albany 12206. SAN 322-2446. Tel. 518-438-2500, fax 518-438-2872, e-mail cdlc@cdlc.org. *Exec. Dir.* Jean K. Sheviak.

Central New York Library Resources Council (CLRC), 3049 E. Genesee St., Syracuse 13224-1690. SAN 322-2454. Tel. 315-446-5446, fax 315-446-5590, e-mail washburn@clrc.org. *Exec. Dir.* Keith E. Washburn.

Consortium of Foundation Libraries, c/o Carnegie Corporation of New York, 437 Madison Ave., 27th flr., New York 10022. SAN 322-2462. Tel. 212-207-6245, fax 212-754-4073, e-mail rs@carnegie.org. *Chair* Ron Sexton.

Council of Archives and Research Libraries in Jewish Studies (CARLJS), 330 Seventh Ave., 21st flr., New York 10001. SAN 371-053X. Tel. 212-629-0500, ext. 205, fax 212-629-0508, e-mail nsjc@ jewishculture.org. *Pres.* Michael Grunberger.

Educational Film Library Association, c/o AV Resource Center, Cornell Univ., Business and Technology Park, Ithaca 14850. SAN 371-0874. Tel. 607-255-2090, fax 607-255-9946. *AV Sales* Richard Gray.

Health Information Libraries of Westchester (HILOW), New York Medical College, Medical Science Lib., Basic Sciences Bldg., Valhalla 10595. SAN 371-0823. Tel. 914-437-3121, fax 914-437-3002. *Pres.* Mary Jo Russell.

Library Consortium of Health Institutions in Buffalo, 155 Abbott Hall, SUNY at Buffalo, 3435 Main St., Buffalo 14214. SAN 329-367X. Tel. 716-829-2903, fax 716-829-2211. *Exec. Dir.* Martin E. Mutka.

Long Island Library Resources Council, Melville Lib. Bldg., Ste. E5310, Stony Brook 11794-3399. SAN 322-2489. Tel. 516-632-6650, fax 516-632-6662, e-mail director@lilrc.org. *Dir.* Herbert Biblo.

Manhattan-Bronx Health Sciences Libraries Group, c/o KPR Medical Lib., 333 E. 38th St., New York 10016. SAN 322-4465. Tel. 212-856-8721, fax 212-856-8884. *Pres.* Penny Klein.

Medical and Scientific Libraries of Long Island (MEDLI), c/o Palmer School of Lib. and Info. Science, C. W. Post Campus, Long Island Univ., Brookville 11548. SAN 322-4309. Tel. 516-299-2866, fax 516-299-4168, e-mail westerma@titan. liunet.edu. *Pres.* Ludmila Tsytlenok.

Medical Library Center of New York, 5 E. 102nd St., 7th flr., New York 10029. SAN 322-3957. Tel. 212-427-1630, fax 212-860-3496, 876-6697, e-mail mlcny@ metgate.metro.org. *Dir.* Lois Weinstein.

Metropolitan New York Library Council (METRO) (formerly New York Metropolitan Reference and Research Library Agency), 57 E. 11th St., 4th flr., New York 10003-4605. SAN 322-2500. Tel.

212-228-2320, fax 212-228-2598, e-mail hiebing@metgate.metro.org. *Exec. Dir.* Dottie Hiebing.

Middle Atlantic Region National Network of Libraries of Medicine, New York Academy of Medicine, 1216 Fifth Ave., New York 10029-5293. SAN 322-2497. Tel. 212-822-7396, fax 212-534-7042, e-mail rml@nyam.org. *Acting Dir.* Mary Mylenki.

New York State Interlibrary Loan Network (NYSILL), c/o New York State Lib., Albany 12230. SAN 322-2519. Tel. 518-474-5129, fax 518-474-5786, e-mail ill@unixII.nysed.gov. *Dir.* Elizabeth Lane.

North Country Reference and Research Resources Council, 7 Commerce Lane, Canton 13617. SAN 322-2527. Tel. 315-386-4569, fax 315-379-9553, e-mail info@northnet.org. *Exec. Dir.* John J. Hammond.

Northeast Foreign Law Cooperative Group, Fordham Univ., 140 W. 62nd, New York 10023. SAN 375-0000. Tel. 212-636-6913, fax 212-977-2662, e-mail vessien@law.fordham.edu. *Libn.* Victor Essien.

Research Library Association of South Manhattan, New York Univ., Bobst Lib., 70 Washington Sq. S., New York 10012. SAN 372-8080. Tel. 212-998-2566, fax 212-995-4583, e-mail joan.grant@nyu.edu. *Coord.* Joan Grant.

Rochester Regional Library Council (RRLC), 390 Packetts Landing, Box 66160, Fairport 14450. SAN 322-2535. Tel. 716-223-7570, fax 716-223-7712, e-mail rrlc@rrlc.rochestr.lib.ny.us. *Dir.* Kathleen M. Miller.

South Central Regional Library Council, 215 N. Cayuga St., Ithaca 14850. SAN 322-2543. Tel. 607-273-9106, fax 607-272-0740, e-mail scrlc@lakenet.org. *Exec. Dir.* Jean Currie.

Southeastern New York Library Resources Council, 220 Rte. 299, Box 879, Highland 12528. SAN 322-2551. Tel. 914-691-2734, fax 914-691-6987, e-mail shaloiko@senylbc.org or starr@senylrc.org. *Exec. Dir.* John L. Shaloiko.

State University of New York–OCLC Library Network (SUNY–OCLC), System Admin., State Univ. Plaza, Albany 12246. SAN 322-256X. Tel. 518-443-5444, fax 518-432-4346, e-mail sunyoclc@slscva.sysaom.suny.edu. *Dir.* Mary-Alice Lynch.

United Nations System Consortium, c/o Dag Hammarskjold Lib., Rm. L-166A, United Nations, New York 10017. SAN 377-855X. Tel. 212-963-5142, fax 212-963-2608, e-mail cherifm@un.org. *Coord.* Mary F. Cherif.

Western New York Library Resources Council, 4455 Genesee St., Box 400, Buffalo 14225-0400. SAN 322-2578. Tel. 716-633-0705, fax 716-633-1736. *Exec. Dir.* Gail M. Staines.

North Carolina

Cape Fear Health Sciences Information Consortium, Southeastern Regional Medical Center, 300 W. 27th St., Lumberton 28359. SAN 322-3930. Tel. 910-671-5000, fax 910-671-4143. *Dir.* Cathy McGinnis.

Microcomputer Users Group for Libraries in North Carolina (MUGLNC), Rowan Public Lib., Box 4039, Salisbury 28145-4039. SAN 322-4449. Tel. 704-638-3009, fax 704-638-3013, e-mail whites@co.rowan.nc.us. *Pres.* Suzanne White.

Mid-Carolina Academic Library Network (MID-CAL), Methodist College, Davis Memorial Lib., 5400 Ramsey St., Fayetteville 28311. SAN 371-3989. Tel. 910-630-7122, fax 910-630-7119, e-mail gregory@ecsvax.uncecs.edu. *Chair* Susan Pulsipher.

NC Area Health Education Centers, Health Sciences Lib., CB 7585, Univ. of North Carolina, Chapel Hill 27599-7585. SAN 323-9950. Tel. 919-962-0700, fax 919-966-5592. *Network Coord.* Diana C. McDuffee.

North Carolina Community College System, 200 W. Jones St., Raleigh 27603-1379. SAN 322-2594. Tel. 919-733-7051, fax 919-733-0680. *Dir.* Pamela B. Doyle.

North Carolina Library and Information Network, 109 E. Jones St., Raleigh 27601-2807. SAN 329-3092. Tel. 919-733-2570, fax 919-733-8748, e-mail netinfo@ncsl.dcr.state.nc.us. *Dir.* Sandra M. Cooper.

Northwest AHEC Library at Salisbury, c/o Rowan Regional Medical Center, 612 Mocksville Ave., Salisbury 28144. SAN

322-4589. Tel. 704-638-1069, fax 704-636-5050. *Lib. Dir.* Nancy Stine.

Northwest AHEC Library Information Network, Northwest Area Health Education Center, Wake Forest Univ. School of Medicine, Medical Center Blvd., Winston-Salem 27157-1060. SAN 322-4716. Tel. 336-713-7015, fax 336-713-7028, e-mail bladner@bgsm.edu. *Network Coord.* Betty Ladner.

Resources for Health Information Consortium (ReHI), c/o Wake Medical Center Medical Lib., 3024 Newbern Ave., Ste. G01, Raleigh 27610. SAN 329-3777. Tel. 919-250-8529, fax 919-250-8836. *Assoc. Dir.* Beverly Richardson.

Triangle Research Libraries Network, Wilson Lib., CB 3940, Chapel Hill 27514-8890. SAN 329-5362. Tel. 919-962-8022, fax 919-962-4452, e-mail david-carlson@unc.edu.

Unifour Consortium of Health Care and Educational Institutions, c/o Northwest AHEC Library at Hickory, Catawba Memorial Hospital, 810 Fairgrove Church Rd., Hickory 28602. SAN 322-4708. Tel. 828-326-3662, fax 828-326-2464, e-mail klmartin@med.unc.edu. *Dir.* Karen Lee Martinez.

Western North Carolina Library Network (WNCLN), D. Hiden Ramsey Lib., 1 University Heights, Univ. of North Carolina at Asheville, Asheville 28804-3299. SAN 376-7205. Tel. 828-232-5095, fax 828-251-6012, e-mail reichelml@appstate.edu, moulrh@appstate.edu. *Chair* Mary Reichel.

North Dakota

Dakota West Cooperating Libraries (DWCL), 3315 University Dr., Bismarck 58504. SAN 373-1391. Tel. 701-255-3285, fax 701-255-1844. *Chair* Charlene Weis.

Tri-College University Libraries Consortium, 209 Engineering Technology, North Dakota State Univ., Fargo 58105. SAN 322-2047. Tel. 701-231-8170, fax 701-231-7205. *Coord.* Richard Bovard.

Ohio

Central Ohio Hospital Library Consortium, Prior Health Sciences Lib., 376 W. Tenth Ave., Columbus 43210. SAN 371-084X.

Tel. 614-292-4891, fax 614-566-6949, e-mail cohsla@lists.acs.ohio-state.edu. *Contact* Jo Yeoh.

Cleveland Area Metropolitan Library System (CAMLS), 20600 Chagrin Blvd., Ste. 500, Shaker Heights 44122-5334. SAN 322-2632. Tel. 216-921-3900, fax 216-921-7220. *Exec. Dir.* Michael G. Snyder.

Columbus Area Library and Information Council of Ohio (CALICO), c/o Westerville Public Lib., 126 S. State St., Westerville 43081. SAN 371-683X. Tel. 614-882-7277, fax 614-882-5369. *Treas.* Norma Ekleberry.

Consortium of Popular Culture Collections in the Midwest (CPCCM), c/o Popular Culture Lib., Bowling Green State Univ., Bowling Green 43403-0600. SAN 370-5811. Tel. 419-372-2450, fax 419-372-7996, e-mail ascott@bgnet.bgsu.edu. *Chair* Jeanne Somers.

Greater Cincinnati Library Consortium, 3333 Vine St., Ste. 605, Cincinnati 45220-2214. SAN 322-2675. Tel. 513-751-4422, fax 513-751-0463, e-mail gclc@one.net. *Exec. Dir.* Martha J. McDonald.

Health Science Librarians of Northwest Ohio (HSLNO), Raymon H. Mulford Lib., Rm. 0409, Medical College of Ohio, 3045 Arlington Ave., Toledo 43614-5805. SAN 377-5801. Tel. 419-381-4220. *Pres.* Marlene Porter.

MOLO Regional Library System, 1260 Monroe Ave., New Philadelphia 44663-4147. SAN 322-2705. Tel. 330-364-8535, fax 330-364-8537, e-mail molo@tusco.net. *Coord.* Christina Hopkins.

NEOUCOM Council of Associated Hospital Librarians, Ocasek Regional Medical Info. Center, Box 95, Rootstown 44272-0095. SAN 370-0526. Tel. 330-325-6611, fax 330-325-0522, e-mail lsc@neoucom.cdu. *Dir. and Chief Medical Libn.* Larry S. Ellis.

NOLA Regional Library System, 4445 Mahoning Ave. N.W., Warren 44483. SAN 322-2713. Tel. 330-847-7744, fax 330-847-7704. *Dir.* Millie Fry.

Northwest Library District (NORWELD), 181 ½ S. Main St., Bowling Green 43402. SAN 322-273X. Tel. 419-352-2903, fax 419-353-8310. *Dir.* Allan Gray.

OCLC Online Computer Library Center, Inc., 6565 Frantz Rd., Dublin 43017-3395. SAN 322-2748. Tel. 614-764-6000, fax 614-764-6096, e-mail oclc@oclc.org. *Pres.* Robert L. Jordan.

Ohio-Kentucky Coop. Libraries, Box 647, Cedarville 45314. SAN 325-3570. Tel. 937-766-7842, 766-2955, fax 937-766-2337. *Ed.* Janice Bosma.

OhioLINK (Ohio Library and Information Network), 2455 North Star Rd., Columbus 43221. SAN 374-8014. Tel. 614-728-3600, fax 614-728-3610, e-mail info@ohiolink.edu. *Exec. Dir.* Thomas J. Sanville.

OHIONET, 1500 W. Lane Ave., Columbus 43221-3975. SAN 322-2764. Tel. 614-486-2966, fax 614-486-1527. *Exec. Dir.* Michael P. Butler.

Ohio Network of American History Research Centers, Ohio Historical Soc. Archives/Lib., 1982 Velma Ave., Columbus 43211-2497. SAN 323-9624. Tel. 614-297-2501, fax 614-297-2546, e-mail gparkins@winslo.ohio.gov. *Archivist* George Parkinson.

Ohio Valley Area Libraries (OVAL), 252 W. 13th St., Wellston 45692-2299. SAN 322-2756. Tel. 740-384-2103, fax 740-384-2106, e-mail ovalrls@oplin.lib.oh.us, andersen@oplin.lib.oh.us. *Dir.* Eric S. Anderson.

Southwestern Ohio Council for Higher Education, 3171 Research Blvd., Ste. 141, Dayton 45420-4014. SAN 322-2659. Tel. 937-259-1370, fax 937-259-1380, e-mail soche@soche.org. *Exec. Dir.* Tamara Yeager.

Oklahoma

Greater Oklahoma Area Health Sciences Library Consortium (GOAL), 12101 N. MacArthur Blvd., Ste. 251, LRC 6420 S.E. 15th, Oklahoma City 73162-1800. SAN 329-3858. Tel. 405-271-6085, fax 405-271-1926, e-mail sheri-greenwood@ouhsc.edu. *Pres.* Sheri Greenwood.

Metropolitan Libraries Network of Central Oklahoma, Inc. (MetroNetwork), Box 250, Oklahoma City 73101-0250. SAN 372-8137. Tel. 405-231-8602, 733-7323, fax 405-236-5219. *Chair* Sharon Saulmon.

Oklahoma Health Sciences Library Association (OHSLA), Univ. of Oklahoma, HSC Bird Health Science Lib., Box 26901, Oklahoma City 73190. SAN 375-0051. Tel. 271-2672, fax 405-271-3297, e-mail jwilkers@rex.vokhsc.edu. *Pres.* Judy Wilkerson.

Oregon

Chemeketa Cooperative Regional Library Service, c/o Chemeketa Community College, 4000 Lancaster Dr. N.E., Salem 97309-7070. SAN 322-2837. Tel. 503-399-5105, fax 503-399-5214, e-mail cocl@chemek.cc.or.us. *Coord.* Linda Cochrane.

Coos County Library Service District, Extended Service Office, Tioga 104, 1988 Newmark, Coos Bay 97420. SAN 322-4279. Tel. 541-888-7260, fax 541-888-7285. *Extension Services Dir.* Mary Jane Fisher.

Library Information Network of Clackamas County, 16239 S.E. McLoughlin Blvd., Ste. 208, Oak Grove 97267. SAN 322-2845. Tel. 503-655-8550, fax 503-655-8555, e-mail joannar@lincc.lib.or.us. *Network Admin.* Joanna Rood.

Northwest Association of Private Colleges and Universities (NAPCU), c/o Murdock Learning Resource Center, 416 N. Meridian St., Newberg 97132-2698. SAN 375-5312. Tel. 503-554-2411, fax 503-554-3599. *Pres.* Merrill Johnson.

Orbis, 1299 Univ. Oregon, Eugene 97403-1299. SAN 377-8096. Tel. 541-346-3049, fax 541-346-3485, e-mail libsys@oregon.uoregon.edu. *Chair* Victoria Hanawalt.

Oregon Health Sciences Libraries Association (OHSLA), Sacred Heart Medical Center Professional Lib. Services, 1255 Hilyard St., Eugene 97401. SAN 371-2176. Tel. 541-686-6837, fax 541-686-7391. *Pres.* Beverly Schriver.

Portland Area Health Sciences Librarians, c/o Legacy Emanuel Lib., 2801 N. Gantenbein, Portland 97227. SAN 371-0912. Tel. 503-413-2558, fax 503-413-2544, e-mail wittend@ohsu.edu. *Coord.* Cindy Muller.

Southern Oregon Library Federation, c/o Klamath County Lib., 126 S. Third St., Klamath Falls 97601. SAN 322-2861. Tel.

541-882-8894, fax 541-882-6166. *Pres.* Andy Swanson.

Washington County Cooperative Library Services, 17880 S.W. Blanton St., Box 5129, Aloha 97006. SAN 322-287X. Tel. 503-642-1544, fax 503-591-0445. *Mgr.* Eva Calcagno.

Pennsylvania

Associated College Libraries of Central Pennsylvania, c/o Lehman Memorial Lib., Shippensburg Univ., Shippensburg 17257-2299. SAN 322-2888. Tel. 717-532-1473, fax 717-532-1389, e-mail bhl@ship.edu. *Pres.* Berkley Laite.

Association of Vision Science Librarians (AVSL), Medical Lib., Wills Eye Hospital, 900 Walnut St., Philadelphia 19107. SAN 370-0569. Tel. 215-928-3288, fax 215-928-7247, e-mail freeman@indiana. edu. *Chair* Judith Schaeffer Young.

Basic Health Sciences Library Network, Latrobe Area Hospital Health Sciences Lib., 121 W. Second Ave., Latrobe 15650-1096. SAN 371-4888. Tel. 724-537-1275, fax 724-537-1890. *Chair* Marilyn Daniels.

Berks County Public Libraries (BCPLS), Agricultural Center, Box 520, Leesport 19533. SAN 371-8972. Tel. 610-378-5260, fax 610-378-1525, e-mail bcpl@ epix.net. *Admin.* Julie Rinehart.

Central Pennsylvania Consortium, c/o Franklin and Marshall College, Box 3003, Lancaster 17604-3003. SAN 322-2896. Tel. 717-291-3919, fax 717-399-4455, e-mail cpc_dfg@fandm.edu. *Exec. Asst.* Molly Seidel.

Central Pennsylvania Health Science Library Association (CPHSLA), Harrisburg Central Hospital, Pouch A, Harrisburg 17051. SAN 375-5290. Tel. 717-271-8198, fax 717-772-7653, e-mail srobishaw@smpp. geisinger.edu. *Pres.* Martha Ruff.

Consortium for Health Information and Library Services, 1 Medical Center Blvd., Upland 19013-3995. SAN 322-290X. Tel. 610-447-6163, fax 610-447-6164, e-mail ch1@hslc.org. *Exec. Dir.* Barbara R. Devlin.

Cooperating Hospital Libraries of the Lehigh Valley Area, Muhlenberg Hospital Center, 2545 Schoenersville Rd., Bethlehem 18017-

7384. SAN 371-0858. Tel. 610-861-2237, fax 610-861-0711. *Libn.* Nancy Romich.

Delaware Valley Information Consortium, c/o Devereux Foundation Behavioral Healthcare Lib., Box 638, Villanova 19085. SAN 329-3912. Tel. 610-542-3051, fax 610-542-3092, e-mail nlong@wista.wistar. upenn.edu. *Coord.* Rachel Roth.

Eastern Mennonite Associated Libraries and Archives (EMALA), 2215 Millstream Rd., Lancaster 17602. SAN 372-8226. Tel. 717-393-9745, fax 717-393-8751. *Chair* Joel D. Alderfer.

Erie Area Health Information Library Cooperative (EAHILC), Northwest Medical Center Medical Lib., 1 Spruce St., Franklin 16323. SAN 371-0564. Tel. 814-437-7000, fax 814-437-5023, e-mail scott@ hslc.org. *Chair* Ann L. Lucas.

Greater Philadelphia Law Library Association (GPLLA), Box 335, Philadelphia 19105. SAN 373-1375. Tel. 215-898-9013, fax 215-898-6619, e-mail gplla-l@hslc.org. *Pres.* Merle J. Slyhoff.

Health Information Library Network of Northeastern Pennsylvania, c/o Wyoming Valley Health Care System, Inc., Lib. Services, Wilkes-Barre 18764. SAN 322-2934. Tel. 717-552-1175, fax 717-552-1183. *Chair* Rosemarie Taylor.

Health Sciences Libraries Consortium, 3600 Market St., Ste. 550, Philadelphia 19104-2646. SAN 323-9780. Tel. 215-222-1532, fax 215-222-0416, e-mail info@hslc.org. *Exec. Dir.* Joseph C. Scorza.

Interlibrary Delivery Service of Pennsylvania, 471 Park Lane, State College 16803-3208. SAN 322-2942. Tel. 814-238-0254, fax 814-238-9686, e-mail janph2@aol. com. *Admin. Dir.* Janet C. Phillips.

Laurel Highlands Health Sciences Library Consortium, Owen Lib., Rm. 209, Univ. of Pittsburgh, Johnstown 15904. SAN 322-2950. Tel. 814-269-7280, fax 814-266-8230. *Dir.* Heather W. Brice.

Lehigh Valley Association of Independent Colleges, Inc., 119 W. Greenwich St., Bethlehem 18018-2307. SAN 322-2969. Tel. 610-882-5275, fax 610-882-5515. *Exec. Dir.* Galen C. Godbey.

Mid-Atlantic Law Library Cooperative (MALLCO), c/o Allegheny County Law

Lib., 921 City/County Bldg., Pittsburgh 15219. SAN 371-0645. Tel. 412-350-5353, fax 412-350-5889. *Dir.* Joel Fishman.

NEIU Consortium, 1200 Line St., Archbald 18403. SAN 372-817X. Tel. 717-876-9268, fax 717-876-8663. *IMS Dir.* Robert Carpenter.

Northeastern Pennsylvania Bibliographic Center, c/o Marywood Univ. Lib., Scranton 18509-1598. SAN 322-2993. Tel. 717-348-6260, fax 717-961-4769, e-mail chs@ac.marywood.edu. *Dir.* Catherine H. Schappert.

Northwest Interlibrary Cooperative of Pennsylvania (NICOP), Erie County Public Lib., 160 E. Front St., Erie 16507-1554. SAN 370-5862. Tel. 814-451-6920, fax 814-451-6907, e-mail tonyk@gator.ecls.lib.pa.us. *Chair* Tony Keck.

PALINET and Union Library Catalogue of Pennsylvania, 3401 Market St., Ste. 262, Philadelphia 19104. SAN 322-3000. Tel. 215-382-7031, fax 215-382-0022, e-mail palinet@palinet.org. *Exec. Dir.* James E. Rush.

Pennsylvania Citizens for Better Libraries (PCBL), 806 West St., Homestead 15120. SAN 372-8285. Tel. 412-461-1322, fax 412-461-1250. *Chief Exec. Officer* Sharon A. Alberts.

Pennsylvania Community College Library Consortium, c/o Community College of Philadelphia, 1700 Spring Garden St., Philadelphia 19130. SAN 329-3939. Tel. 215-751-8384, fax 215-751-8762, e-mail jjohnson@ccp.cc.pa.us. *Exec. Dir.* Joan E. Johnson.

Pennsylvania Library Association, 1919 N. Front St., Harrisburg 17102. SAN 372-8145. Tel. 717-233-3113, fax 717-233-3121. *Exec. Dir.* Glenn R. Miller.

Philadelphia Area Consortium of Special Collections Libraries (PACSCL), Dept. of Special Collections, Univ. of Pennsylvania Lib., 3420 Walnut, Philadelphia 19104-6206. SAN 370-7504. Tel. 215-898-7552, fax 215-573-9079. *Pres.* Eric Pumory.

Pittsburgh Council on Higher Education (PCHE), Box 954, Pittsburgh 15230-0954. SAN 322-3019. Tel. 412-536-1206, fax 412-536-1199, e-mail hunterb@pitt.edu. *Exec. Dir.* Janet Sherer.

Southeastern Pennsylvania Theological Library Association (SEPTLA), c/o Saint Charles Borromeo Seminary, Ryan Memorial Lib., 100 E. Wynnewood Rd., Wynnewood 19096-3012. SAN 371-0793. Tel. 610-667-3394, fax 610-664-7913, e-mail ebasemlib@ebts.edu or stcthelib@hslc.org. *Pres.* Darren Poley.

State System of Higher Education Libraries Council (SSHELCO), c/o F. H. Green Lib., West Chester Univ. of Pennsylvania, West Chester 19383. SAN 322-2918. Tel. 610-436-2643, fax 610-436-2251. *Chair* Frank Q. Helms.

Susquehanna Library Cooperative, Susquehanna Health System, Learning Resources Center, 777 Rural Ave., Williamsport 17701. SAN 322-3051. Tel. 570-321-2266, fax 570-321-2271, e-mail srobishaw@smpp.geisinger.edu. *Pres.* Michael Heyd.

Tri-County Library Consortium, c/o New Castle Public Lib., 207 E. North St., New Castle 16101. SAN 322-306X. Tel. 724-658-6659, fax 724-658-9012. *Dir.* Susan E. Walls.

Tri-State College Library Cooperative (TCLC), c/o Rosemont College Lib., 1400 Montgomery Ave., Rosemont 19010-1699. SAN 322-3078. Tel. 610-525-0796, fax 610-525-1939, e-mail tclc@hslc.org. *Coord.* Ellen Gasiewski.

Rhode Island

Association of Rhode Island Health Sciences Libraries (ARIHSL), c/o Providence College, River Ave. at Eaton St., Providence 02918. SAN 371-0742. Tel. 401-865-2631, fax 401-865-2823, e-mail jschustr@providence.edu. *Pres.* Janice Schuster.

Consortium of Rhode Island Academic and Research Libraries (CRIARL), Box 40041, Providence 02940-0041. SAN 322-3086. Tel. 401-232-6298, fax 401-232-6126, e-mail mmoroney@bryant.edu. *Pres.* Mary Moroney.

Cooperating Libraries Automated Network (CLAN), c/o Providence Public Lib., 225 Washington St., Providence 02903. SAN 329-4560. Tel. 401-455-8044, 401-455-

8085, 401-732-7687 (Exec. Dir.), fax 401-455-8080, e-mail peterbt@ids.net. *Chair* Tom Channahan.

Rhode Island Library Network (RHILINET), c/o Office of Lib. and Info. Services, 1 Capitol Hill, 4th flr., Providence 02908-5870. SAN 371-6821. Tel. 401-222-2726, fax 401-222-4195. *Chief Info. Officer* Barbara Weaver.

South Carolina

Catawba-Wateree Area Health Education Consortium, 1228 Colonial Commons, Box 2049, Lancaster 29721. SAN 329-3971. Tel. 803-286-4121, fax 803-286-4165. *Libn.* Tonia Harris.

Charleston Academic Libraries Consortium, College of Charleston, Robert Scott Small Lib., Charleston 29424. SAN 371-0769. Tel. 843-953-5530, fax 843-953-8019. *Chair* David Cohen.

Columbia Area Medical Librarians' Association (CAMLA), Professional Lib., 1800 Colonial Dr, Box 202, Columbia 29202. SAN 372-9400. Tel. 803-898-1735, fax 803-898-1712. *Coord.* Neeta N. Shah.

South Carolina AHEC, c/o Medical Univ. of South Carolina, 171 Ashley Ave., Charleston 29425. SAN 329-3998. Tel. 843-792-4431, fax 843-792-4430. *Exec. Dir.* Sabra C. Slaughter.

South Carolina Library Network, South Carolina State Lib., 1500 Senate St., Box 11469, Columbia 29211-1469. SAN 322-4198. Tel. 803-734-8666, fax 803-734-8676, e-mail lea@leo.scsl.state.sc.us. *State Libn.* James B. Johnson, Jr.

Upper Savannah AHEC Medical Library, Self Memorial Hospital, 1325 Spring St., Greenwood 29646. SAN 329-4110. Tel. 864-227-4851, fax 864-227-4838, e-mail libform@ais.ais-gurd.com. *Libn.* Thomas Hill.

South Dakota

South Dakota Library Network (SDLN), University Sta., Box 9672, Spearfish 57799-9672. SAN 371-2117. Tel. 605-642-6835, fax 605-642-6298. *Dir.* Gary Johnson.

Tennessee

Association of Memphis Area Health Science Libraries (AMAHSL), c/o Univ. of Tennessee Health Sciences Lib., 877 Madison Ave., Memphis 38163. SAN 323-9802. Tel. 901-726-8862, fax 901-726-8807, e-mail gjackson@utmem1.utmem.edu. *Pres.* Gwen Jackson.

Association of Southeastern Research Libraries, Univ. of Memphis Libs., Memphis 38152-6500. SAN 322-1555. Tel. 901-678-2201, fax 901-678-8218, e-mail channing@lib.wfu.edu. *Chair* Lester J. Pourciau.

Consortium of Southern Biomedical Libraries (CONBLS), Meharry Medical College, 1005 Dr. D. B. Todd Blvd., Nashville 37208. SAN 370-7717. Tel. 615-327-6728, fax 615-321-2932. *Treas.* Cheryl Hamberg.

Knoxville Area Health Sciences Library Consortium (KAHSLC), c/o Blount Memorial Hospital, Medical Lib., 907 E. Lamar Alexander Pkwy., Maryville 37801-1983. SAN 371-0556. Tel. 423-977-5520, fax 423-981-2473, e-mail njcook@usit.net. *Pres.* Rebecca Marcam.

Mid-Tennessee Health Science Librarians Association, VA Medical Center, Murfreesboro 37129. SAN 329-5028. Tel. 615-867-6142, fax 615-867-5778, e-mail alovvorn@stthomas.org. *Pres.* Pamela Howell.

Tennessee Health Science Library Association (THeSLA), Holston Valley Medical Center Health Sciences Lib., Box 238, Kingsport 37662. SAN 371-0726. Tel. 423-224-6870, fax 423-224-6014, e-mail forbeseh@ctrvax.vanderbilt.edu. *Pres.* Patsy Ellis.

Tri-Cities Area Health Sciences Libraries Consortium, East Tennessee State Univ., James H. Quillen College of Medicine, Medical Lib., Box 70693, Johnson City 37614-0693. SAN 329-4099. Tel. 423-439-6252, fax 423-439-7025, e-mail fisherj@medserv.etsu-tn.edu. *Pres.* Annis Evans.

West Tennessee Academic Library Consortium, Univ. of Tennessee, Paul Mead Lib., Lane Ave., Martin 38301. SAN 322-3175.

Tel. 901-587-7070, fax 901-423-4931. *Chair* Joel Stowers.

Texas

Abilene Library Consortium, 241 Pine St., Ste. 15C, Abilene 79699-9208. SAN 322-4694. Tel. 915-672-7081, fax 915-672-7084, e-mail robert.gillette@alc.org. *Systems Mgr.* Robert Gillette.

Alliance for Higher Education, Ste. 250, LB 107, 17103 Preston Rd., Dallas 75248-1332. SAN 322-3337. Tel. 972-713-8170, fax 972-713-8209. *Pres.* Allan Watson.

AMIGOS Bibliographic Council, Inc., 12200 Park Central Dr., Ste. 500, Dallas 75251. SAN 322-3191. Tel. 972-851-8000, fax 972-991-6061, e-mail amigos@amigos. org. *Exec. Dir.* Bonnie Juergens.

APLIC International Census Network, c/o Population Resources Center (PRC), 1800 Main Bldg., Univ. of Texas, Austin 78712. SAN 370-0690. Tel. 512-471-8335, fax 512-471-4886. *Dir.* Gera Draaijer.

Council of Research and Academic Libraries (CORAL), Box 290236, San Antonio 78280-1636. SAN 322-3213. Tel. 210-536-2651, fax 210-536-2902, e-mail goff @alhr.brooks.af.mil. *Pres.* Marilyn Goff.

Del Norte Biosciences Library Consortium, c/o Reference Dept. Lib., Univ. of Texas at El Paso, 500 W. University, El Paso 79968. SAN 322-3302. Tel. 915-747-6714, fax 915-747-5327, e-mail emoreno @utep.edu. *Pres.* Esperanza A. Moreno.

Forest Trail Library Consortium, Inc. (FTLC), 222 W. Cotton St., Longview 75601. SAN 374-6283. Tel. 903-237-1340, fax 903-237-1327. *Pres.* Jerry McCulley.

Harrington Library Consortium, Box 447, Amarillo 79178. SAN 329-546X. Tel. 806-371-5135, fax 806-345-5678, e-mail roseann@hlc.actx.edu. *Exec. Dir.* Roseann Perez.

Health Library Information Network, John Peter Smith Hospital Lib., 1500 S. Main St., Fort Worth 76104. SAN 322-3299. Tel. 817-921-3431, ext. 5088, fax 817-923-0718. *Chair* Leslie Herman.

Health Oriented Libraries of San Antonio (HOLSA), 59 MDW/MSIL, 2200 Bergquist Dr., Ste. 1, Lakeland AFB 78236-5300. SAN 373-5907. Tel. 210-292-7204, fax 210-292-7030. *Pres.* Rita Smith.

Houston Area Research Library Consortium (HARLiC), c/o Houston Public Lib., 500 McKinney St., Houston 77002. SAN 322-3329. Tel. 713-247-2700, fax 713-247-1266, e-mail dudley-yates@tamu.edu. *Contact* Barbara Gubbins.

National Network of Libraries of Medicine–South Central Region, c/o HAM-TMC Lib., 1133 M. D. Anderson Blvd., Houston 77030-2809. SAN 322-3353. Tel. 713-799-7880, fax 713-790-7030, e-mail ruicham@library.tmc.edu. *Dir.* Naomi Broering.

Northeast Texas Library System (NETLS), 625 Austin, Garland 75040-6365. SAN 370-5943. Tel. 972-205-2566, fax 972-205-2767, e-mail dgf@onramp.net. *Dir.* Claire Bausch.

Piasano Consortium, Victoria College, Univ. of Houston, Victoria Lib., 2602 N. Ben Jordan, Victoria 77901-5699. SAN 329-4943. Tel. 512-573-3291, 576-3151, fax 512-788-6227, e-mail dahlstromj@jadc. vic.uh.edu. *Coord.* Joe F. Dahlstrom.

South Central Academic Medical Libraries Consortium (SCAMeL), c/o Lewis Lib./ UNTHSC, 3500 Camp Bowie Blvd., Fort Worth 76107. SAN 372-8269. Tel. 817-735-2380, fax 817-735-5158. *Chair* Richard C. Wood.

Texas Council of State University Librarians, Univ. of Texas Health Science Center at San Antonio, 7703 Floyd Curl Dr., San Antonio 78284-7940. SAN 322-337X. Tel. 210-567-2400, fax 210-567-2490, e-mail bowden@uthscsa.edu. *Dir.* Virginia M. Bowden.

Texnet, Box 12927, Austin 78711. SAN 322-3396. Tel. 512-463-5406, fax 512-463-8800. *Mgr.* Rebecca Linton.

Utah

Forest Service Library Network (formerly FS-INFO), Rocky Mountain Research Sta., 324 25th St., Ogden 84401. SAN 322-032X. Tel. 801-625-5445, fax 801-625-5129, e-mail library/rmrs_ogden@fs.fed. us. *Coord.* Carol A. Ayer.

Utah Academic Library Consortium (UALC), Marriott Lib., Univ. of Utah, Salt Lake City 84112-0860. SAN 322-3418. Tel. 801-581-8558, fax 801-585-3464. *Chair* Sarah Michalak.

Utah Health Sciences Library Consortium, c/o Eccles Health Science Lib., Univ. of Utah, Salt Lake City 84112. SAN 376-2246. Tel. 801-581-8771, fax 801-581-3632. *Chair* Kathleen McCloskey.

Vermont

Health Science Libraries of New Hampshire and Vermont (HSL-NH-VT), c/o Archivist, Dana Medical Lib., Univ. of Vermont, Burlington 05405. SAN 371-6864. Tel. 802-656-2200, fax 802-656-0762. *Pres.* Norma Phillips.

Vermont Resource Sharing Network, c/o Vermont Dept. of Libs., 109 State St., Montpelier 05609-0601. SAN 322-3426. Tel. 802-828-3261, fax 802-828-2199, e-mail mzunder@dol.state.vt.us. *Dir., Lib. and Info. Services* Marjorie Zunder.

Virgin Islands

VILINET (Virgin Islands Library and Information Network), c/o Div. of Libs., Museums and Archives, 23 Dronningens Gade, Saint Thomas 00802. SAN 322-3639. Tel. 340-774-3407, fax 340-775-1887.

Virginia

American Indian Higher Education Consortium (AIHEC), c/o AIHEC, 121 Oronoco St., Alexandria 22314. SAN 329-4056. Tel. 703-838-0400, fax 703-838-0388, e-mail aihec@aol.com. *Pres.* Janine Pease.

Defense Technical Information Center, 8725 John J. Kingman Rd., Ste. 0944, Fort Belvoir 22060-6218. SAN 322-3442. Tel. 703-767-9100, fax 703-767-9183. *Admin.* Kurt N. Molholm.

Interlibrary Users Association (IUA), c/o Litton PRC, 1500 PRC Dr., McLean 22102. SAN 322-1628. Tel. 703-556-1166, fax 703-556-1174, e-mail kopp_barbara@prc.com. *Pres.* Barbara Kopp.

Lynchburg Area Library Cooperative, Bedford Public Lib., 321 N. Bridge St., Bedford 24523. SAN 322-3450. Tel. 540-586-8911, fax 540-586-7280, e-mail dunn@lynchburg.edu. *Chair* Steve Preston.

Lynchburg Information Online Network, c/o Knight-Capron Lib., Lynchburg College, Lynchburg 24501. SAN 374-6097. Tel. 804-381-6311, fax 804-381-6310. *Project Dir.* John G. Jaffe.

NASA Libraries' Information System - NASA GALAXIE, NASA Langley Research Center, MS 185–Technical Lib., Hampton 23681-0001. SAN 322-0788. Tel. 757-864-2392, fax 757-864-2375, e-mail rridgeway@sti.nasa.gov. *Project Mgr.* Nancy Kaplan.

Richmond Academic Library Consortium (RALC), J. Tyler Community College, 13101 Jefferson Davis Hwy., Chester 23831. SAN 371-3938. Tel. 804-796-4066, fax 804-796-4238, e-mail estephens@vsu.edu. *Pres.* Gary Graham.

Richmond Area Film-Video Cooperative, Richard Bland College Lib., 11301 Johnson Rd., Petersburg 23805. SAN 322-3469. Tel. 804-862-6226, fax 804-862-6125, e-mail nchenaul@vcu.edu. *Chair* Virginia Cherry.

Southside Virginia Library Network (SVLN), Longwood College, 201 High St., Farmville 23909-1897. SAN 372-8242. Tel. 804-395-2633, fax 804-395-2453. *Dir.* Calvin J. Boyer.

Southwestern Virginia Health Information Librarians (SWVAHILI), Danville Regional Medical Center, 142 S. Main St., Danville 24541. SAN 323-9527. Tel. 804-799-4418, fax 804-799-2255. *Chair* Ann Duesing.

United States Army Training and Doctrine Command (TRADOC), ATBO-FL, Bldg. 5A, Rm. 102, Fort Monroe 23651-5000. SAN 322-418X. Tel. 757-727-4096, fax 757-728-5300. *Dir.* Janet Scheitle.

Virginia Independent College and University Library Assn., c/o Mary Helen Cochran Lib., Sweet Briar College, Sweet Briar 24595. SAN 374-6089. Tel. 804-381-6139, fax 804-381-6173. *Chair* John Jankey.

Virginia Library and Information Network (VLIN), c/o Lib. of Virginia, 800 E. Broad St., Richmond 23219-8000. SAN 373-0921. Tel. 804-692-3774, fax 804-692-3771, e-mail nworley@vsla.edu. *State*

Libn. Nolan T. Yelich, *Dir.* Nelson Worley.

Virginia Tidewater Consortium for Higher Education, 5215 Hampton Blvd., William Spong Hall, Rm. 129, Norfolk 23529-0293. SAN 329-5486. Tel. 757-683-3183, fax 757-683-4515, e-mail lgdotolo@aol. com. *Pres.* Lawrence G. Dotolo.

Washington

Consortium for Automated Library Services (CALS), Evergreen State College Lib. L2300, Olympia 98505. SAN 329-4528. Tel. 360-866-6000 ext. 6260, fax 360-866-6790, e-mail metcalfs@elwha.evergreen. edu. *Systems Mgr.* Steven A. Metcalf.

Council on Botanical Horticultural Libraries, 2525 S. 336th St., Box 3798, Federal Way 98063-3798. SAN 371-0521. Tel. 253-927-6960, fax 253-838-4686. *Libn.* Mrs. George Harrison.

Inland Northwest Health Sciences Libraries (INWHSL), Box 10283, Spokane 99209-0283. SAN 370-5099. Tel. 509-324-7344, fax 509-324-7349, e-mail rpringle@wsu. edu. *Chair* Kathy Schwanz.

Inland Northwest Library Automation Network (INLAN), Foley Center, Gonzaga Univ., Spokane 99258. SAN 375-0124. Tel. 509-328-4220, ext. 6110, fax 509-323-5855. *Contact* Robert Burr.

National Network of Libraries of Medicine–Pacific Northwest Region (NN-LM PNR), Univ. of Washington, Box 357155, Seattle 98195-7155. SAN 322-3485. Tel. 206-543-8262, fax 206-543-2469, e-mail nnlm @u.washington.edu. *Dir.* Sherrilynne S. Fuller.

WLN, Box 3888, Lacey 98509-3888. SAN 322-3507. Tel. 360-923-4000, fax 360-923-4009, e-mail info@wln.com. *Pres. and Chief Exec. Officer* Paul McCarthy.

West Virginia

East Central College, Box AJ, Bethany 26032-1434. SAN 322-2667. Tel. 304-829-7812, fax 304-829-7546. *Exec. Dir.* Preston W. Forbes.

Huntington Health Science Library Consortium, Marshall Univ. Health Science Libs., 1600 Medical Center Dr., Ste. 2400, Hunt-

ington 25701-3655. SAN 322-4295. Tel. 304-691-1753, fax 304-691-1766. *Chair* Edward Dzierzak.

Mountain States Consortium, c/o Alderson Broaddus College, Philippi 26416. SAN 329-4765. Tel. 304-457-1700, fax 304-457-6239. *Treas.* Stephen Markwood.

Southern West Virginia Library Automation Corporation, 221 N. Kanawha St., Box 1876, Beckley 25802. SAN 322-421X. Tel. 304-255-0511, fax 304-255-9161, e-mail gunsaulj@raleigh.lib.wv.us. *Pres.* Judy Gunsaulis.

Wisconsin

Council of Wisconsin Libraries, Inc (COWL), 728 State St., Rm. 464, Madison 53706-1494. SAN 322-3523. Tel. 608-263-4962, fax 608-262-6067, e-mail schneid@ doit.wisc.edu. *Dir.* Kathryn Schneider Michaelis.

Fox River Valley Area Library Consortium, Moraine Park Technical College, 235 N. National Ave., Fond Du Lac 54935. SAN 322-3531. Tel. 920-924-3112, fax 920-924-3117, e-mail cpettit@moraine.tecwi. us. *Coord.* Charlene Pettit.

Fox Valley Library Council (FVLC), c/o Owls, Fox Valley Lib. Council, 225 N. Oneida St., Appleton 54911. SAN 323-9640. Tel. 920-832-6190, fax 920-832-6422. *Pres.* Edie Phillips.

Library Council of Metropolitan Milwaukee, Inc., 814 W. Wisconsin Ave., Milwaukee 53233-2309. SAN 322-354X. Tel. 414-271-8470, fax 414-286-2794, e-mail ricec @vms.csd.mu.edu. *Exec. Dir.* Corliss Rice.

North East Wisconsin Intertype Libraries, Inc. (NEWIL), c/o Nicolet Federated Lib. System, 515 Pine St., Green Bay 54301. SAN 322-3574. Tel. 920-448-4412, fax 920-448-4420, e-mail tdhowe@mail.wisc-net.net. *Coord.* Terrie Howe.

Northwestern Wisconsin Health Science Library Consortium, Wausau Hospital, 333 Pine Ridge Blvd., Wausau 54401. SAN 377-5801. Tel. 715-847-2184, fax 715-847-2183. *Coord.* Jan Kraus.

South Central Wisconsin Health Science Library Cooperative, c/o FAMHS Medical Lib., 611 Sherman Ave. E., Fort Atkinson

53538. SAN 322-4686. Tel. 920-568-5194, fax 920-568-5059, e-mail carrie.garity@famhs.org. *Rep.* Carrie Garity.

Southeastern Wisconsin Health Science Library Consortium, Convenant Healthcare Systems Lib., 5000 W. Chambers, Milwaukee 53210. SAN 322-3582. Tel. 414-447-2194, fax 414-447-2128. *Presiding Officer* Sunja Shaikh.

Southeastern Wisconsin Information Technology Exchange, Inc. (SWITCH), 6801 N. Yates Rd., Milwaukee 53217-3985. SAN 371-3962. Tel. 414-351-2423, fax 414-228-4146, e-mail jfri@switchinc.org. *Exec. Dir.* Jack Fritts.

Wisconsin Area Research Center Network ARC Network, State Historical Society of Wisconsin, 816 State St., Madison 53706. SAN 373-0875. Tel. 608-264-6480, fax 608-264-6486, e-mail peter.gottlieb@ccmail.adp.wisc.edu. *State Archivist* Peter Gottlieb.

Wisconsin Interlibrary Services (WILS), 728 State St., Rm. 464, Madison 53706-1494. SAN 322-3612. Tel. 608-263-4962, fax 608-292-6067, e-mail schneid@doit.wisc.edu or cbradley@doit.wisc.edu. *Dir.* Kathryn Schneider Michaelis.

Wisconsin Valley Library Service (WVLS), 300 N. First St., Wausau 54403. SAN 371-3911. Tel. 715-261-7250, fax 715-261-7259, e-mail eldred@wisvalley.lib.wi.us. *Dir.* Heather Ann Eldred.

Wyoming

Health Sciences Information Network (HSIN), Univ. of Wyoming Libs., 104 Coe Lib., Box 3334, Laramie 82071-3334. SAN 371-4861. Tel. 307-766-6537, fax 307-766-3062, e-mail henning@uwyo.edu. *Coord.* Mary M. Henning.

WYLD Network, c/o Wyoming State Lib., Supreme Court and State Lib. Bldg., Cheyenne 82002-0060. SAN 371-0661. Tel. 307-777-7281, fax 307-777-6289. *State Libn.* Lesley Boughton.

Canada

Alberta

Alberta Association of College Librarians (AACL), Alberta Vocational College, 201

Main St. S.E., Lesser Slave Lake, Alberta P0G 2A3. SAN 370-0763. Tel. 403-849-8671, fax 403-849-2570, e-mail lloydp@admin.gmcc.ab.ca. *Chair* Geoff Owens.

Alberta Government Libraries Council (AGLC), c/o Alberta Legislature Lib., 216 Legislature Bldg., 10800 97th Ave., Edmonton T5K 2B6. SAN 370-0372. Tel. 403-422-5085, fax 403-427-5688, e-mail sperry@assembly.ab.ca. *Chair* Christina Andrews.

Northern Alberta Health Libraries Association (NAHLA), 11620 168th St. N.W., Edmonton T5M 4A6. SAN 370-5951. Tel. 403-453-0534, fax 403-482-4459, e-mail lmychaj@nurses.ab.ca. *Pres.* Lorraine Mychajlunon.

British Columbia

British Columbia College and Institute Library Services, Langara College Lib., 100 W. 49th Ave., Vancouver V5Y 2Z6. SAN 329-6970. Tel. 604-323-5237, fax 604-323-5544. *Contact* Atsuko Barbour.

Media Exchange Cooperative (MEC), Vancouver Community College, 250 W. Pender St., Vancouver V6B 1S9. SAN 329-6954. Tel. 604-443-8346, fax 604-443-8329, e-mail pbutler@vcc.bc.ca. *Chair* Phyllis Butler.

Manitoba

Manitoba Government Libraries Council (MGLC), 360-1395 Ellice Ave., Winnipeg R3G 3P2. SAN 371-6848. Tel. 204-239-3162, fax 204-945-8427, e-mail mlavergne@em.gov.mb.ca. *Chair* Linda Petriuk.

Manitoba Library Consortium, Inc. (MLCI), Industrial Technology Centre, 1329 Niakwa Rd. E., Winnipeg R2J 3T4. SAN 372-820X. Tel. 204-945-1413, fax 204-945-1784. *Chair* Betty Dearth.

Nova Scotia

Maritimes Health Libraries Association (MHLA-ABSM), c/o IWK Grace Health Center, 5850-5980 University Ave., Halifax B3H 4N1. SAN 370-0836. Tel. 902-420-6729, fax 902-420-3122. *Pres.* Darlene Chapman.

NOVANET, 6080 Young St., Ste. 601, Halifax B3K 5L2. SAN 372-4050. Tel. 902-

453-2451, ext. 2461, fax 902-453-2369, e-mail novanet@ac.dal.ca. *Mgr. Info. Systems* Scott W. Nickerson.

Ontario

Bibliocentre, 80 Cowdray Ct., Scarborough M1S 4N1. SAN 322-3663. Tel. 416-289-5151, fax 416-299-4841, e-mail falt@cencol.on.ca. *Dir.* Annetta Protain.

Canadian Agriculture Library System, Sir John Carling Bldg., 930 Carling Ave., Ottawa K1A 0C5. SAN 377-5054. Tel. 613-759-7068, fax 613-759-6627, e-mail cal-bca@em.agr.ca. *Dir.* Victor Desroches.

Canadian Association of Research Libraries–Association des Bibliothèques de Recherche du Canada (CARL-ABRC), Univ. of Ottawa Morisset Hall, Rm. 239, 65 University St., Ottawa K1N 9A5. SAN 323-9721. Tel. 613-562-5800, ext. 3652, fax 613-562-5195, e-mail carl@uottawa.ca. *Exec. Dir.* Timothy Mark.

Canadian Health Libraries Association (CHLA-ABSC), Office of Secretariat, 3332 Yonge St., Box 94038, Toronto M4N 3R1. SAN 370-0720. Tel. 416-485-0377, fax 416-485-6877. *Pres.* Marthe Brideau.

Hamilton and District Health Library Network, c/o St. Joseph's Hospital, 50 Charlton Ave. E., Hamilton L8N 4A6. SAN 370-5846. Tel. 905-522-1155, ext. 3410, fax 905-521-6111, e-mail marge@fhs.mcmaster.ca. *Network Coord.* Jean Maragno.

Health Science Information Consortium of Toronto, c/o Gerstein Science Info. Center, Univ. of Toronto, 7 King's College Circle, Toronto M5S 1A5. SAN 370-5080. Tel. 416-978-6359, fax 416-971-2637, e-mail scottl@library.utoronto.ca. *Exec. Dir.* Laurie Scott.

Information Network for Ontario Ministry of Citizenship, Culture and Recreation: Cultural Partnerships Branch, 77 Bloor St. W., 3rd flr., Toronto M7A 2R9. SAN 329-5605. Tel. 416-314-7342, fax 416-314-7635. *Dir.* Michael Langford.

Kingston Area Health Libraries Association (KAHLA), c/o Belleville General Hospital Lib., 265 Dundas St. E., Belleville K8N 1E2. SAN 370-0674. Tel. 613-969-7400, ext. 2540, fax 613-968-8234, e-mail cmartin@bgh.on.ca. *Pres.* Cheryl Martin.

Ontario Council of University Libraries (OCUL), Stauffer Lib., Queen's Univ., 101 Union St., Kingston K7L 5C4. SAN 371-9413. Tel. 705-675-1151, fax 613-545-6362, e-mail jgarnett@library.laurentian.ca. *Chair* Paul Weins.

Ontario Health Libraries Association (OHLA), Library, Sarnia General Hospital, 220 N. Mitton St., Sarnia N7T 6H6. SAN 370-0739. Tel. 519-464-4500, ext. 5251, fax 519-464-4511, e-mail jcampbell@ebtech.net. *Pres.* Jill Campbell.

QL Systems Limited, 1 Gore St., Box 2080, Kingston K7L 5J8. SAN 322-368X. Tel. 613-549-4611, fax 613-548-4260, e-mail hlawford@qlsys.ca. *Pres.* Hugh Lawford.

Shared Library Services (SLS), South Huron Hospital, 24 Huron St. W., Exeter N0M 1S2. SAN 323-9500. Tel. 519-235-2700, ext. 249, fax 519-235-3405, e-mail lwilcox@julian.uwo.ca. *Dir.* Linda Wilcox.

Sheridan Park Association, Library and Information Science Committee (SPA-LISC), 2275 Speakman Dr., Mississauga L5K 1B1. SAN 370-0437. Tel. 905-823-6160, fax 905-823-6160. *Contact* Cindy Smith.

Toronto Health Libraries Association (THLA), Box 94056, Toronto M4N 3R1. SAN 323-9853. Tel. 416-485-0377, fax 416-485-6877. *Pres.* Karen Smith.

Toronto Public Library Systems (formerly Disability Resource Library Network), c/o North York Central Lib., 5120 Yonge St., North York M2N 5N9. SAN 323-9837. Tel. 416-395-5591, fax 416-395-5594. *Contact* Joanne Bar.

Toronto School of Theology, 47 Queen's Park Crescent E., Toronto M5S 2C3. SAN 322-452X. Tel. 416-978-4039, fax 416-978-7821, e-mail fox@library.utoronto.ca. *Chair Lib. Committee* Douglas Fox.

Wellington Waterloo Dufferin (WWD) Health Library Network, c/o Library, Univ. of Guelph, Guelph N1G 2W1. SAN 370-0496. Tel. 519-824-4120, ext. 4214, fax 519-826-7941, e-mail dhull@uoguelph.ca. *Coord.* David Hull.

Quebec

Association des Bibliothèques de la Santé Affiliées a l'Université de Montréal (ABSAUM), c/o Health Lib., Box 6128,

Sta. Downtown, Univ. of Montreal, Montreal H3C 3J7. SAN 370-5838. Tel. 514-343-6826, fax 514-343-2350. *Secy.* Danielle Tardif.

Canadian Heritage Information Network (CHIN), 15 Eddy St., 4th flr., Hull K1A 0M5. SAN 329-3076. Tel. 819-994-1200, fax 819-994-9555, e-mail service@chin. qc.ca. *Dir. Gen.* Lyn Elliot Sherwood.

McGill Medical and Health Libraries Association (MMAHLA), c/o Royal Victoria Hospital, Women's Pavillion Lib., 687 Pine Ave. W., Rm. F4-24, Montreal H3A 1A1. SAN 374-6100. Tel. 514-842-1231, ext. 4738, fax 514-843-1678. *Co-Chairs* Lynda Dickson, Irene Shanefield.

Montreal Health Libraries Association (MHLA), 2365 Côte de Liesse, Montreal H4N 2M7. SAN 323-9608. Tel. 514-333-2057, fax 514-331-6387. *Pres.* Donna Gibson.

Saskatchewan

Saskatchewan Government Libraries Council (SGLC), c/o Saskatchewan Agriculture and Food Lib., 3085 Albert St., Regina S4S 0B1. SAN 323-956X. Tel. 306-787-5151, fax 306-787-0216. *Chair* Helene Stewart.

National Library and Information-Industry Associations, United States and Canada

American Association of Law Libraries

Executive Director, Roger Parent
53 W. Jackson Blvd., Suite 940, Chicago, IL 60604
312-939-4764, fax 312-431-1097
World Wide Web http://www.aallnet.org

Object

The American Association of Law Libraries (AALL) is established for educational and scientific purposes. It shall be conducted as a nonprofit corporation to promote and enhance the value of law libraries to the public, the legal community, and the world; to foster the profession of law librarianship; to provide leadership in the field of legal information; and to foster a spirit of cooperation among the members of the profession. Established 1906.

Membership

Memb. 4,800. Persons officially connected with a law library or with a law section of a state or general library, separately maintained. Associate membership available for others. Dues (Indiv., Indiv. Assoc., and Inst.) $133; (Inst. Assoc.) $256 times the number of members; (Retired) $32.50; (Student) $30; (SIS Memb.) $12 each per year. Year. July 1–June 30.

Officers

Pres. Margaret Maes Axtmann, Univ. of Minnesota Law Lib., 229 19th Ave. S., Minneapolis, MN 55455. Tel. 612-625-4301, fax 612-625-3478, e-mail m-axtm@maroon.tc. umn.edu; *V.P.* Robert L. Oakley, Georgetown Univ. Law Center, Edward Bennett Williams Lib., 111 G St. N.W., Washington, DC 20001-1417. Tel. 202-662-9160, fax 202-662-9168, e-mail Oakley@law.georgetown. edu; *Past Pres.* James S. Heller, College of William & Mary, Marshall-Whythe Law

Lib., S. Henry St., Williamsburg, VA 23187-8795. Tel. 757-221-3252, fax 757-221-3051, e-mail jshell@facstaff.wm.edu; *Secy.* Karl T. Gruben, Vinson & Elkins LLP, 3054 First City Tower, 1101 Fannin St., Houston, TX 77002. Tel. 713-758-2679, fax 713-615-5211, e-mail kgruben@velaw.com; *Treas.* Janis L. Johnston, Univ. of Illinois at Urbana-Champaign, Albert E. Jenner Memorial Law Lib., 142M Law Bldg., 504 E. Pennsylvania Ave., Champaign, IL 61820. Tel. 217-244-3046, fax 217-244-8500, e-mail jljohnst@law.uiuc.edu.

Executive Board

Mark Folmsbee (2000); Ruth A. Fraley (2001); Frank Y. Liu (2001); Heather Braithwaite Simmons (2000); Maryruth Storer (2002), Cossette T. Sun (2002).

Committee Chairpersons

Annual Meeting Program Selection. Anne C. Matthewman.
Awards. Suzanne Thorpe.
Bylaws. William L. Cooper.
Citation Format. Marcia J. Koslov, Paul George.
Copyright. Steven P. Anderson.
Diversity. Yolanda P. Jones.
Executive Board Finance and Budget. Janis L. Johnston.
Executive Board Governance. Karl T. Gruben.
Executive Board Strategic Planning. Ruth A. Fraley.
Government Relations. Keith Ann Stiverson.
Grants. Holly J. Mohler.

Index to Foreign Legal Periodicals (Advisory). Karen S. Beck.
Indexing Periodical Literature (Advisory). Pedro A. Padilla-Rosa.
Mentoring and Retention. Haibin Hu.
Nominations. Donna K. Bausch.
Placement. Patricia Wellinger.
Professional Development. Michael Saint-Onge.
Public Relations. Sue Burch.
Research. Barbara A. Bintliff.
Scholarships. Karen B. Brunner.

Special-Interest Section Chairpersons

Academic Law Libraries. Victoria K. Trotta.

Computing Services. Lyonette Louis-Jacques.
Foreign, Comparative, and International Law. Katherine Topulos.
Government Documents. Pegeen G. Bassett.
Legal History and Rare Books. Daniel Smith.
Legal Information Services to the Public. Angus B. Nesbit.
Micrographics and Audiovisual. Laura Ray.
Online Bibliographic Services. Brian Striman.
Private Law Libraries. Kathie Sullivan.
Research Instruction and Patron Services. Kristin Gerdy.
Social Responsibilities. John H. Davey.
State Court and County Law Libraries. Shirley H. David.
Technical Services. Janet McKinney.

American Library Association

Executive Director, William R. Gordon
50 E. Huron St., Chicago, IL 60611
800-545-2433, 312-280-3215, fax 312-944-3897
World Wide Web http://www.ala.org

Object

The mission of the American Library Association (ALA) is to provide leadership for the development, promotion, and improvement of library and information services and the profession of librarianship in order to enhance learning and ensure access to information for all. Founded 1876.

Membership

Memb. (Indiv.) 54,692; (Inst.) 4,085; (Total) 58,777. Any person, library, or other organization interested in library service and librarians. Dues (Indiv.) 1st year, $50; 2nd year, $75; 3rd year and later, $100; (Trustee and Assoc. Memb.) $45; (Student) $25; (Foreign Indiv.) $60; (Other) $35; (Inst.) $70 and up, depending on operating expenses of institution.

Officers (1999–2000)

Pres. Sarah Ann Long, North Suburban Lib. System, 200 W. Dundee Rd., Wheeling, IL 60090-2799. Tel. 847-459-1300 ext. 125, fax 847-459-0391, e-mail slong@nslsilus.org; *Pres.-Elect* Nancy C. Kranich, New York University Bobst Lib., 70 Washington Sq., New York, NY 10012-1091. Tel. 212-998-2447, fax 212-995-4070, e-mail kranich@elmer4.bobst.nyu.edu; *Immediate Past Pres.* Ann K. Symons, Libn., Juneau-Douglas H.S., 10014 Crazy Horse Dr., Juneau, AK 99801. Tel. 907-463-1947, fax 907-463-1932, e-mail symons@alaska.net; *Treas.* Bruce E. Daniels, 4418 Eagle Village Rd., Manlius, NY 13104. Tel. 315-682-2645, fax 315-682-3583, e-mail bd3ALA@aol.com; *Exec. Dir.* William R. Gordon, ALA Headquarters, 50 E. Huron St., Chicago, IL 60611. Tel. 312-280-3215, fax 312-944-3897, e-mail wgordon@ala.org.

Executive Board

Liz Bishoff (2002); Alice M. Calabrese (2002); Julie Cummins (2002); Martin J. Gomez (2001); Ken Haycock (2003); James G. Neal (2000); Robert R. Newlen (2000); Sally G. Reed (2001).

Endowment Trustees

Bernard A. Margolis; Patricia Glass Schuman, Rick J. Schwieterman; *Exec. Board Liaison* Bruce E. Daniels; *Staff Liaison* Gregory L. Calloway.

Divisions

See the separate entries that follow: American Assn. of School Libns.; Assn. for Lib. Trustees and Advocates; Assn. for Lib. Collections and Technical Services; Assn. for Lib. Service to Children; Assn. of College and Research Libs.; Assn. of Specialized and Cooperative Lib. Agencies; Lib. Admin. and Management Assn.; Lib. and Info. Technology Assn.; Public Lib. Assn.; Reference and User Services Assn.; Young Adult Lib. Services Assn.

Publications

ALA Handbook of Organization (ann.).

American Libraries (11 per year; mcmbs.; organizations $60; foreign $70; single copy $6).

Book Links (6 per year; U.S. $24.95; foreign $29.95; single copy $5).

Booklist (22 per year; U.S. and possessions $69.50; foreign $85; single copy $4.50).

Choice (11 per year; U.S. $185; foreign $210; single copy $24).

Round Table Chairpersons

(ALA staff liaison is given in parentheses.)

Armed Forces Libraries. Carolyn K. Eaton (Patricia May).

Continuing Library Education Network and Exchange. Diane M. Brown (Lorelle R. Swader).

Ethnic Materials and Information Exchange. Clara M. Chu (Satia Orange).

Exhibits. Margaret Sullivan (Deidre Ross).

Federal Librarians. Stephanie Jones (Patricia May).

Gay, Lesbian, Bisexual, Transgendered. Shari C. Clifton and Roland C. Hansen (Satia Orange).

Government Documents. Larry Romans (Patricia May).

Intellectual Freedom. Laurence A. Miller (Don Wood).

International Relations. Lucinda Covert-Vail (Michael Dowling).

Library History. Sibyl E. Moses (Mary Jo Lynch).

Library Instruction. Mitch M. Stepanovich (Mary Jo Lynch).

Library Research. Neal K. Kaske (Mary Jo Lynch).

Map and Geography. Joseph M. Winkler (Danielle M. Alderson).

New Members. Priscilla Shontz (Gerald G. Hodges).

Social Responsibilities. Frederick W. Stoss (Satia Orange).

Staff Organizations. Leon S. Bey (Lorelle R. Swader).

Support Staff Interests. Dolores A. Payne (Lorelle R. Swader).

Video. James C. Scholtz (Irene Wood).

Committee Chairpersons

Accreditation (Standing). Beverly P. Lynch (Ann L. O'Neill).

American Libraries Advisory (Standing). Camila A. Alire (Leonard Kniffel).

Appointments (Standing). Nancy C. Kranich (Elizabeth Dreazen).

Awards (Standing). Bridget Later Lamont (Cheryl Malden).

Budget Analysis and Review (Standing). Mary Elizabeth Wendt (Gregory Calloway).

Chapter Relations (Standing). Kathleen M. Balcom (Gerald G. Hodges).

Committee on Committees (Elected Council Committee). Nancy C. Kranich (Elizabeth Dreazen).

Conference Comittee (Standing). Christine L. Hage (Mary W. Ghikas, Deidre Ross).

Constitution and Bylaws (Standing). Nancy A. Davenport (Linda Mays).

Council Orientation (Standing). James B. Casey (Lois Ann Gregory-Wood).

Education (Standing). Mary Y. Moore (Lorelle R. Swader).

Election (Standing). Judith M. Baker (Ernest Martin).

Human Resource Development and Recruitment (Standing). Harriet C. Ying (Lorelle R. Swader).

Information Technology Policy Advisory. Linda D. Crowe (Frederick Weingarten).

Intellectual Freedom (Standing). Steven L. Herb (Judith F. Krug).

International Relations (Standing). Jordan M. Scepanski (Michael Dowling).

Legislation (Standing). Chadwick T. Raymond (Emily Sheketoff).

Literacy and Outreach (Standing). Judith A. Rake (Satia Orange).

Membership (Standing). Michael A. Golrick (Gerald G. Hodges).

Minority Concerns and Cultural Diversity (Standing). Betty L. Tsai (Sandra Balderrama).

Nominating, 2000 Election (Special). Deborah Miller (Elizabeth Dreazen).

Organization (Standing). Judy Arteaga (Lois Ann Gregory-Wood).

Pay Equity (Standing). Vivian B. Melton (Lorelle R. Swader).

Policy Monitoring (Standing). Donald J. Sager (Lois Ann Gregory-Wood).

Professional Ethics (Standing). Charles Harmon (Judith F. Krug).

Public Awareness Advisory (Standing). Jan Thenell (Linda K. Wallace).

Publishing (Standing). Kay A. Cassell (Donald Chatham).

Research and Statistics (Standing). Peggy D. Rudd (Mary Jo Lynch).

Resolutions. Kenton L. Oliver (Kathryn Osen).

Spectrum Initiative Advisory. Carla Hayden (Sandra Balderrama).

Standards (Standing). Sarah M. Pritchard (Mary Jo Lynch).

Status of Women in Librarianship (Standing). Theresa A. Tobin (Lorelle R. Swader).

Joint Committee Chairpersons

American Association of Law Libraries/American Correctional Association–ASCLA Committee on Institution Libraries (joint). Carl Romalis (ACA); To be appointed (ASCLA).

American Federation of Labor/Congress of Industrial Organizations–ALA, Library Service to Labor Groups, RUSA. John N. Schact (ALA); Anthony Sarmiento (AFL/CIO).

Anglo-American Cataloguing Rules Fund. William R. Gordon (ALA); Vicki L. Whitmell (Canadian Lib. Assn.); Ross Shimmon (Lib. Assn.).

Association of American Publishers–ALA. Sarah Ann Long (ALA); To be appointed (AAP).

Association of American Publishers–ALCTS. Robert P. Holley (ALCTS); Rebecca Seger (AAP).

Children's Book Council–ALA. Lucille C. Thomas (ALA); David Gale (CBC).

Society of American Archivists–ALA (Joint Committee on Library-Archives Relationships). Samuel Boldrick (ALA); William E. Brown, Jr. (SAA).

American Library Association
American Association of School Librarians

Executive Director, Julie A. Walker
50 E. Huron St., Chicago, IL 60611
312-280-4386, 800-545-2433 ext. 4386, fax 312-664-7459
E-mail AASL@ala.org
World Wide Web http://www.ala.org/aasl

Object

The American Association of School Librarians (AASL) is interested in the general improvement and extension of library media services for children and young people. AASL has specific responsibility for planning a program of study and service for the improvement and extension of library media services in elementary and secondary schools as a means of strengthening the educational program; evaluation, selection, interpretation, and utilization of media as they are used in the context of the school program; stimulation of continuous study and research in the library field and establishing criteria of evaluation; synthesis of the activities of all units of the American Library Association in areas of mutual concern; representation and interpretation of the need for the function of school libraries to other educational and lay groups; stimulation of professional growth, improvement of the status of school librarians, and encouragement of participation by members in appropriate type-of-activity divisions; conducting activities and projects for improvement and extension of service in the school library when such projects are beyond the scope of type-of-activity divisions, after specific approval by the ALA Council. Established in 1951 as a separate division of ALA.

Membership

Memb. 8,290. Open to all libraries, school library media specialists, interested individuals, and business firms with requisite membership in ALA.

Officers (1999–2000)

Pres. M. Ellen Jay, Damascus Elementary School, 10201 Bethesda Church Rd., Damascus, MD 20872-1799. Tel. 301-253-7080, fax 301-253-8717, e-mail mejay@umd5.umd. edu; *Pres.-Elect* Harriet S. Selverstone, Norwalk High School, 23 Calvin Murphy Dr., Norwalk, CT 06851-5500. Tel. 203-838-4481 ext. 214, fax 203-866-9418, e-mail Hselve@ aol.com; *Treas./Financial Officer* Carolyn S. Hayes, Warren Central H.S., 9500 E. 16 St., Indianapolis, IN 46229-2008; *Past Pres.* Sharon Coatney, Oak Hill School, 10200 N. 124 St., Overland Park, KS 66213-1873. Tel. 913-681-4335, fax 913-681-4329, e-mail sharonc@unicom.net.

Board of Directors

Officers; Cassandra G. Barnett, Lee D. Gordon, Margaret A. Hallisey, Dennis J. LeLoup, Mary McClintock, A. Jeanie McNamara, Connie Jo Mitchell, Frances R. Roscello, Marilyn L. Shontz, Deborah Roberts Stone, Joie L. Taylor, Sharyn Lynn van Epps, Idella A. Washington, Barbara H. Weathers, Bernice L. Yesner, Julie A. Walker (ex officio).

Publications

Knowledge Quest (5/yr.; memb.; nonmemb. $40). *Eds.* Nancy L. Teger, e-mail tegern @gate.net; Debbie Abilock, e-mail dabilock @pacbell.net.

School Library Media Research (nonsubscription electronic publication available to memb. and nonmemb. at http://www. ala.org/aasl/SLMR). *Ed.* Daniel Callison, School of Lib. and Info. Sciences, 10th and Jordan, Indiana Univ., Bloomington, IN 47405. E-mail callison@indiana.edu.

Committee Chairpersons

AASL/ELMS Executive Committee. Sarah M. Brewer.

AASL/Highsmith Research Grant. Andrea L. Miller.

AASL/ISS Executive Committee. Susan Adland.

AASL/SPVS Executive Committee. Bettie Estes Rickner.

ABC/CLIO Leadership Grant. Mary J. Soucie.

Affiliate Assembly. Terri G. Kirk.

American Univ. Press. Gail A. Richmond.

Annual Conference. Donald C. Adcock.

Awards. Antoinette Negro.

Bylaws and Organization. Jacqueline G. Morris.

Collaborative School Library Media Award. Kenley E. Neufeld.

Competencies for Library Media Specialists in the 21st Century. Ken Haycock.

Continuing Education Task Force. Roxane E. Oakley.

Distinguished Service Award. Jane Bandy Smith.

ICONnect Task Force. Pam Berger.

Implementation of the New National Guidelines/Standards Task Force. Carolyn P. Giambra.

Information Technology Pathfinder Award. Steven M. Baule.

Intellectual Freedom. Carrie Gardner.

Intellectual Freedom Award. Darlene Shiverdecker Basone.

Legislation. Sandy Schuckett.

Nominating, 2000 Election. Elizabeth B. Day.

National School Library Media Program of the Year. James F. Bennett.

Publications. Drucilla Raines.

Research/Statistics. Margie J. Thomas.

School Librarians Workshop Scholarship. Jane E. Robertson

SLMR Electronic Editorial Board. Daniel J. Callison.

Teaching for Learning Task Force. Barbara K. Stripling.

American Library Association
Association for Library Trustees and Advocates

Executive Director, Susan Roman
50 E. Huron St., Chicago, IL 60611-2795
312-280-2161, 800-545-2433 ext. 2161, fax 312-280-3257
World Wide Web http://www.ala.org/alta/

Object

The Association for Library Trustees and Advocates (ALTA) is interested in the development of effective library service for all people in all types of communities and in all types of libraries; it follows that its members are concerned, as policymakers, with organizational patterns of service, with the development of competent personnel, the provision of adequate financing, the passage of suitable legislation, and the encouragement of citizen support for libraries. ALTA recognizes that responsibility for professional action in these fields has been assigned to other divisions of ALA; its specific responsibilities as a division, therefore, are

1. A continuing and comprehensive educational program to enable library trustees to discharge their grave responsibilities in a manner best fitted to benefit the public and the libraries they represent.

2. Continuous study and review of the activities of library trustees.

3. Cooperation with other units within ALA concerning their activities relating to trustees.

4. Encouraging participation of trustees in other appropriate divisions of ALA.

5. Representation and interpretation of the activities of library trustees in contacts outside the library profession, particularly with national organizations and governmental agencies.

6. Promotion of strong state and regional trustee organizations.

7. Efforts to secure and support adequate library funding.

8. Promulgation and dissemination of recommended library policy.

9. Assuring equal access of information to all segments of the population.

10. Encouraging participation of trustees in trustee/library activities, at local, state, regional, and national levels.

Organized 1890. Became an ALA division in 1961.

Membership

Memb. 1,400. Open to all interested persons and organizations. For dues and membership year, see ALA entry.

Officers (1999–2000)

Pres. Patricia Fisher; *1st V.P./Pres.-Elect* G. Victor Johnson; *Past Pres.* Ruth Newell-Minor; *Councilor* Wayne Coco.

Board of Directors

Officers; Council Administrators: Bonnie Bellamy-Watkins, Shirley A. Bruursema, Fabian Lewandowski, Dale H. Ross, Carol K. Vogelman; Regional V.P.s: Judith M. Baker, Sherman Banks, Denise E. Botto, Moises Denis, Gail Dysleski, David H. Goldsmith, James Grayson, Virginia McCurdy, James A. McPherson, Sophie G. Misner, Marguerite E. Ritchey. *Voice Ed.* Sharon Saulmon.

Staff

Exec. Dir. Susan Roman; *Deputy Exec. Dir.* Kerry Ward; *Admin. Secy.* Dollester Thorp-Hawkins.

Publication

The *Voice* (q.; memb.). *Ed.* Sharon Saulmon.

American Library Association
Association for Library Collections and Technical Services

Executive Director, Karen Muller
50 E. Huron St., Chicago, IL 60611
800-545-2433 ext. 5031, fax 312-280-5033
E-mail kmuller@ala.org
World Wide Web http://www.ala.org/alcts/

Object

The Association for Library Collections and Technical Services (ALCTS) is responsible for the following activities: acquisition, identification, cataloging, classification, and preservation of library materials; the development and coordination of the country's library resources; and those areas of selection and evaluation involved in the acquisition of library materials and pertinent to the development of library resources. ALCTS has specific responsibility for:

1. Continuous study and review of the activities assigned to the division
2. Conduct of activities and projects within its area of responsibility
3. Syntheses of activities of all units within ALA that have a bearing on the type of activity represented
4. Representation and interpretation of its type of activity in contacts outside the profession
5. Stimulation of the development of librarians engaged in its type of activity, and stimulation of participation by members in appropriate type-of-library divisions
6. Planning and development of programs of study and research for the type of activity for the total profession

ALCTS will provide its members, other ALA divisions and members, and the library and information community with leadership and a program for action on the access to, and identification, acquisition, description, organization, preservation, and dissemination of information resources in a dynamic collaborative environment. In addition, ALCTS provides forums for discussion, research, and development and opportunities for learning in all of these areas. To achieve this mission, ALCTS has the following organizational goals:

1. To promote the role of the library and information science in an information society
2. To provide its members with opportunities for information exchange
3. To promote innovative and effective library education and training, to foster the recruitment of individuals with diverse qualities to library work, and to provide continuing education for librarians and library practitioners
4. To develop, support, review, and promote standards to meet library and information needs
5. To provide opportunities for members to participate through research and publications and professional growth

6. To manage the association effectively and efficiently

Established 1957; renamed 1988.

Membership

Memb. 4,984. Any member of the American Library Association may elect membership in this division according to the provisions of the bylaws.

Officers (July 1999–July 2000)

Pres. Peggy Johnson, Univ. of Minnesota, 309 19th Ave. S., Minneapolis, MN 55455-0414. Tel. 612-624-2312, fax 612-626-9353, e-mail m-john@tc.umn.edu; *Pres.-Elect* Carlen M. Ruschoff, Georgetown Univ., Lauinger Lib., Box 571174, Washington, DC 20057-1174. Tel. 202-687-7429, fax 202-687-1215, e-mail ruschoff@gusun.georgetown.edu; *Past Pres.* Sheila S. Intner, 11 Hupi Woods Circle, Box 151, Monterey, MA 01245-0151. Tel. 617-521-2790, fax 617-521-3192, e-mail intner@simmons.edu.

Address correspondence to the executive director.

Directors

Officers; exec. dir.; *Div. Councilor* Ross W. Atkinson; *CRG Rep.* Cynthia Watters; *Dirs.* Michele J. Crump, Beverley Geer, Jay H. Lambrecht, Olivia M. A. Madison, D. E. Perushek, Virgilia I. Rawnsley, John J. Riemer, Ann M. Sandberg-Fox, Karen A. Schmidt, Brian E. C. Schottlaender, Dale S. Swensen.

Publications

ALCTS Network News (irreg.; free). *Ed.* Shonda Russell. Subscribe via listproc@ala.org "subscribe an2 [yourname]."
ALCTS Newsletter (6 per year; memb.; nonmemb. $25). *Ed.* Dale S. Swensen, Lee Lib., Brigham Young Univ., Provo, UT 84602.

Library Resources and Technical Services (q.; memb.; nonmemb. $55). *Ed.* Jennifer A. Younger, Univ. of Notre Dame Libs., Notre Dame, IN 46556. Tel. 219-631-7792.

Section Chairpersons

Acquisitions. Michele J. Crump.
Cataloging and Classification. Jay H. Lambrecht.
Collection Management and Development. D. E. Perushek.
Preservation and Reformatting. Virgilia I. Rawnsley.
Serials. Beverley Geer.

Committee Chairpersons

Hugh C. Atkinson Memorial Award. Sherrie Schmidt.
Association of American Publishers/ALCTS Joint Committee. Robert P. Holley, Marsha S. Clark.
Best of *LRTS*. Carol Pitts Diedrichs.
Blackwell's Scholarship Award. Sally W. Somers.
Budget and Finance. Olivia M. A. Madison.
Catalog Form and Function. Patrick F. Callahan.
Commercial Technical Services. Rick J. Block.
Duplicates Exchange Union. Lydia A. Morrow Ruetten.
Education. Lynne C. Howarth.
Electronic Communications. Eleanor I. Cook.
Fund Raising. Karen L. Horny.
International Relations. D. Whitney Coe.
Leadership Development. Edward Shreeves.
Legislation. Lynn F. Sipe.
Library Materials Price Index. Bill Robnett.
LRTS Editorial Board. Jennifer A. Younger.
MARBI. Bruce Johnson.
Media Resources. Diane L. Boehr.
Membership. Martin M. Kurth.

Networked Resources and Metadata. Ann M. Sandberg-Fox.
Nominating. Dorothy H. Hope.
Organization and Bylaws. Caroline L. Early and Sheila S. Intner.
Esther J. Piercy Award Jury. Joan Grant.
Planning. Brian E. C. Schottlaender.
Program. Marilyn G. McSweeney.
Publications. Kerry A. Keck.
Publisher/Vendor Library Relations. Douglas A. Litts.
Research and Statistics. Cynthia M. Coulter.

Discussion Groups

Authority Control in the Online Environment. Rebecca J. Dean.
Automated Acquisitions/In-Process Control Systems. Sue-Ellen J. Johnson and Victoria M. Peters.
Computer Files. Greta G. de Groat and Norma J. Fair.
Creative Ideas in Technical Services. Felicity A. Dykas.
MARC Formats. Robert T. Warwick.
Newspaper. Robert C. Dowd.
Out of Print. Narda Tafuri.
Pre-Order and Pre-Catalog Searching. Valentine K. Muyumba.
Retrospective Conversion. Donna J. Capelle-Cook and Karen Joan Davis.
Role of the Professional in Academic Research Technical Scholarly Communications. Marilyn Mercado.
Serials Automation. Maria Michelle Sitko, Lianhong-Zhou.
Technical Services Administrators of Medium-Sized Research Libraries. Chair to be appointed.
Technical Services Directors of Large Research Libraries. Judith Nadler.
Technical Services in Public Libraries. Ross W. McLachlan.
Technical Services Workstations. Sandra S. Ballasch.

American Library Association
Association for Library Service to Children

Executive Director, Susan Roman
50 E. Huron St., Chicago, IL 60611
312-280-2163, 800-545-2433 ext. 2163
E-mail sroman@ala.org
World Wide Web http://www.ala.org/alsc

Object

Interested in the improvement and extension of library services to children in all types of libraries. Responsible for the evaluation and selection of book and nonbook materials for, and the improvement of techniques of, library services to children from preschool through the eighth grade or junior high school age, when such materials or techniques are intended for use in more than one type of library. Founded 1901.

Membership

Memb. 3,609. Open to anyone interested in library services to children. For information on dues, see ALA entry.

Address correspondence to the executive director.

Officers

Pres. Caroline Ward; *V.P./Pres.-Elect* Virginia Walter; *Past Pres.* Leslie Edmonds Holt.

Directors

Clara Nalli Bohrer, Nell Colburn, Eliza Dresang, Ellen Fader, Sylvia A. Mavrogenes, Sue McCleaf Nespeca, Marie Orlando, Grace Ruth, Kathleen Simonetta.

Publications

Journal of Youth Services in Libraries (*JOYS*) (q.; memb.; nonmemb. $40; foreign $50). *Eds.* Betty Carter, Keith Swigger, School of Lib. and Info. Studies, Texas Woman's Univ., Box 425438, Denton, TX 76204-5438.

Committee Chairpersons

Priority Group I: Child Advocacy

Consultant. Jean B. Gaffney.
Intellectual Freedom.
International Relations.
Legislation.
Library Service to Children with Special Needs.
Preschool Services and Parent Education.
Preschool Services Discussion Group.
Public Library-School Partnership Discussion Group.
School-Age Programs and Service.
Social Issues Discussion Group.

Priority Group II: Evaluation of Media

Consultant. Vacant.
Notable Children's Books.
Notable Children's Recordings.
Notable Children's Videos.
Notable Children's Web Sites.
Notable Computer Software for Children.

Priority Group III: Professional Awards and Scholarships

Consultant. Virginia McKee.
ALSC/Book Wholesalers Summer Reading Program Grant and Reading Program.
ALSC/Econo-Clad Literature Program Award
Arbuthnot Honor Lecture.
Louise Seaman Bechtel Fellowship.
Distinguished Service Award.
Penguin Putnam Books for Young Readers Award.
Scholarships: Melcher and Bound to Stay Bound.

Priority Group IV: Organizational Support

Consultant. Linda Perkins.
Local Arrangements.
Membership.
Nominating.
Organization and Bylaws.
Planning and Budget.
Preconference Planning.

Priority Group V: Projects and Research

Consultant. Kathy Toon.
Collections of Children's Books for Adult Research (Discussion Group).
National Planning of Special Collections.
Oral Record Project.
Publications.
Research and Development.

Priority Group VI: Award Committees

Consultant. Jan Moltzan.
Mildred L. Batchelder Award Selection.
Pura Belpré Award.
Randolph Caldecott Award.

Andrew Carnegie Award.
John Newbery Award.
Laura Ingalls Wilder Award.

Priority Group VII: Partnerships

Consultant Kathy East.
Liaison with National Organizations Serving Children and Youth.
National Children and Youth Membership Organizations Outreach.
Public Library-School Partnerships Discussion Group.
Quicklists Consulting Committee.

Priority Group VIII: Professional Development

Consultant Ellen Fader.
Children and Technology.
Children's Book Discussion Group.
Education.
Managing Children's Services.
Managing Children's Services Discussion Group.
Storytelling Discussion Group.
Teachers of Children's Literature Discussion Group.

American Library Association
Association of College and Research Libraries

Executive Director, Althea H. Jenkins
50 E. Huron St., Chicago, IL 60611-2795
312-280-3248, 800-545-2433 ext. 3248, fax 312-280-2520
E-mail ajenkins@ala.org
World Wide Web http://www.ala.org/acrl/

Object

The Association of College and Research Libraries (ACRL) provides leadership for development, promotion, and improvement of academic and research library resources and services to facilitate learning, research, and the scholarly communication process. ACRL promotes the highest level of professional excellence for librarians and library personnel in order to serve the users of academic and research libraries. Founded 1938.

Membership

Memb. 11,297. For information on dues, see ALA entry.

Officers

Pres. Larry Hardesty, College Libn., Abell Lib., Austin College, 900 N. Grand Ave., Suite 6L, Sherman, TX 75090-4440. Tel. 903-813-2490, fax 903-813-2297, e-mail lhardesty@austinc.edu; *Past Pres.* Maureen

Sullivan, Organizational Development Consultant, 3696 Thomas Point Rd., Annapolis, MD 21403-5026. Tel. 410-268-3539, fax 410-268-3810, e-mail maureen@arl.org; *Pres.-Elect* Betsy Wilson, Assoc. Dir. of Libs., Univ. of Washington, Box 352900, Seattle, WA 98195-2900. Tel. 206-685-1903, fax 206-685-8727, e-mail betsyw@u.washington.edu; *Budget and Finance Chair* John Popko, Univ. Libn., Seattle Univ., 900 Broadway, Seattle, WA 98122-4340. Tel. 206-296-6201, fax 206-296-2572, e-mail jpopko@seattleu.edu; *ACRL Councilor* Helen H. Spalding, Assoc. Dir. of Libs., Univ. of Missouri, 5100 Rockhill Rd., Kansas City, MO 64110-2499. Tel. 816-235-1558, fax 816-333-5584, e-mail spaldinh@umkc.edu.

Board of Directors

Officers; William E. Brown, Jr., Theresa S. Byrd, Lois H. Cherepon, Paul E. Dumont, Barbara Baxter Jenkins, Dana C. Rooks, Robert Rose, Mary Lee Sweat.

Publications

Choice (11 per year; $200; foreign $242.50). Choice Reviews-on-Cards (includes subscription to *Choice* magazine; $460; foreign $505); ChoiceReviews.online (includes archive subscription to *Choice* magazine; $395; foreign $445) *Ed.* Irving Rockwood.

College & Research Libraries (6 per year; memb.; nonmemb. $60). *Ed.* Donald E. Riggs.

College & Research Libraries News (11 per year; memb.; nonmemb. $40). *Ed.* Mary Ellen Kyger Davis.

Publications in Librarianship (formerly *ACRL Monograph Series*) (occasional). *Ed.* John M. Budd.

Rare Books and Manuscripts Librarianship (2 per year; $30). *Eds.* Lisa M. Browar and Marvin J. Taylor.

List of other publications and rates available through the ACRL office, ALA, 50 E. Huron St., Chicago, IL 60611-2795; or call 312-280-2517.

Committee and Task Force Chairpersons

Academic Libraries: Trends & Statistics. William Miller.

Academic Librarian Status. Lara A. Bushallow.

Academic or Research Librarian of the Year Award (Nominations). Maureen Sullivan.

Academic or Research Librarian of the Year Award (Selection). Alma Dawson.

ACRL/Harvard Leadership Institute Advisory. Maureen Sullivan.

ACRL/TLT Group. Jill B. Fatzer.

Appointments. Randy Burke Hensley.

Hugh C. Atkinson Memorial Award. Sherrie Schmidt.

Budget and Finance. John Popko.

Bylaws. Carol Ritzem Kem.

Choice Editorial Board. Richard AmRhein.

Colleagues. William Miller, Mary E. Clack.

College and Research Libraries Editorial Board. Donald E. Riggs.

College and Research Libraries News Editorial Board. Maija M. Lutz.

Conference Program Planning, Chicago (2000). Larry Hardesty.

Copyright. Tammy Nickelson Dearie.

Council of Liaisons. Althea H. Jenkins.

Doctoral Dissertation Fellowship. Beth Sandore.

Equal Access to Software Information Advisory Committee. Tom McNulty.

Excellence in Academic Libraries Award (Nominations). Gloria St. Clair.

Excellence in Academic Libraries Award (Selection). W. Lee Hisle.

Friends of ACRL Advisory. William Miller.

Government Relations. David J. Nutty.

Information Literacy Competency Standards. Patricia Ianuzzi.

Institute for Information Literacy. Cerise Oberman.

Intellectual Freedom. Laurence A. Miller.

International Relations. Connie E. Costantino.

Samuel Lazerow Fellowship. Karen A. Schmidt.

Media Resources. Mary S. Konkel.

Membership. Pamela Moffett Padley.

National Conference Executive Committee, Denver, 2001. W. Lee Hisle.

New Publications Advisory. Susan M. Kroll.

Nominations. Mary J. Petrowski.

Orientation. Maureen Sullivan.

President's Program Planning Committee, Chicago, 2000. Lynn Scott Cochrane.

President's Program Planning Committee, San Francisco, 2001. Jill M. McKinstry.

Professional Development. Lee C. Ketcham Van Orsdel.

Professional Enhancement. Joan Reyes.

Publications. Brian Coutts.

Publications in Librarianship Editorial Board. John M. Budd.

Racial and Ethnic Diversity. Mae Schreiber.

Rare Books and Manuscripts Librarianship Editorial Board. Lisa M. Browar and Marvin J. Taylor.

Recruiting into the Profession. Cindy Swigger.

Research. Rebecca L. Schreiner-Robles.

K. G. Saur Award for Best *College and Research Libraries* Article. Marie A. Kascus.

Standards and Accreditation. Barton Lessin.

Statistics. Jan Kemp.

Discussion Group Chairpersons

Alliances for New Directions in Teaching/Learning. Mark Horan.

Austrian Studies. John D. Blackwell.

Criminal Justice/Criminology. Mary Jane Brustman.

Electronic Reserves. Carmen Blankinship.

Electronic Text Centers. Michael Seadle.

Exhibits and Displays in College Libraries. Michael M. Miller.

Fee-Based Information Service Centers in Academic Libraries. Stephen Coffman.

Heads of Public Services. Pamela Wonsek.

Librarians and Information Science. Cathy Rentschler.

Library Development. Irene Hoffman.

Medium-Sized Libraries. Jeanne G. Sohn, Charlotte Slocum.

MLA International Bibliography. Faye Christenberry.

Personnel Administrators and Staff Development Officers. George Bynon, Kurt Murphy.

Philosophical, Religious, and Theological Studies. Rebecca Lindau.

Popular Cultures. Diane Kachmar.

Research. Darrell L. Jenkins.

Sports and Recreation. Mila C. Su.

Team-Based Organizations. Janet S. Fore.

Undergraduate Librarians. Mark Watson.

Section Chairpersons

Afro-American Studies Librarians. Mary G. Wrighten.

Anthropology and Sociology. Sally Wilson Weimer.

Arts. Floyd M. Zula.

Asian, African and Middle Eastern. William Sheh Wong.

College Libraries. John G. Jaffe.

Community and Junior College Libraries. Kathryn Chilson O'Gorman.

Distance Learning. Harvey R. Gover.

Education and Behavioral Sciences. Ellen D. Gilbert.

English and American Literature. Cathy Larson.

Instruction. Karen Williams.

Law and Political Science. Marifran Bustion.

Rare Books and Manuscripts. Eric Holzenberg.

Science and Technology. Patricia A. Kreitz.

Slavic and East European. Patricia Kincaid Thurston.

University Libraries. James A. Estrada.

Western European Specialists. John M. Cullars.

Woman's Studies. Marlene Manoff.

American Library Association
Association of Specialized and Cooperative Library Agencies

Executive Director, Cathleen Bourdon
50 E. Huron St., Chicago, IL 60611
312-280-4395, 800-545-2433 ext. 4398, fax 312-944-8085
World Wide Web http://www.ala.org/ascla/

Object

To represent state library agencies, specialized library agencies, multitype library cooperatives, and independent librarians. Within the interest of these types of library organizations and individuals, the Association of Specialized and Cooperative Library Agencies (ASCLA) has specific responsibility for

1. Development and evaluation of goals and plans for state library agencies, specialized library agencies, and multitype library cooperatives to facilitate the implementation, improvement, and extension of library activities designed to foster improved user services, coordinating such activities with other appropriate ALA units.

2. Representation and interpretation of the role, functions, and services of state library agencies, specialized library agencies, multitype library cooperatives, and independent librarians within and outside the profession, including contact with national organizations and government agencies.

3. Development of policies, studies, and activities in matters affecting state library agencies, specialized library agencies, multitype library cooperatives, and independent librarians relating to (a) state and local library legislation, (b) state grants-in-aid and appropriations, and (c) relationships among state, federal, regional, and local governments, coordinating such activities with other appropriate ALA units.

4. Establishment, evaluation, and promotion of standards and service guidelines relating to the concerns of this association.

5. Identifying the interests and needs of all persons, encouraging the creation of services to meet these needs within the areas of concern of the association, and promoting the use of these services provided by state library agencies, specialized library agencies, multitype library cooperatives, and independent librarians.

6. Stimulating the professional growth and promoting the specialized training and continuing education of library personnel at all levels of concern of this association and encouraging membership participation in appropriate type-of-activity divisions within ALA.

7. Assisting in the coordination of activities of other units within ALA that have a bearing on the concerns of this association.

8. Granting recognition for outstanding library service within the areas of concern of this association.

9. Acting as a clearinghouse for the exchange of information and encouraging the development of materials, publications, and research within the areas of concern of this association.

Membership

Memb. 971.

Board of Directors (1999–2000)

Pres. Barbara H. Will; *Pres.-Elect* Donna O. Dziedzic; *Past Pres.* John M. Day; *Dirs.-at-Large* Karen Hyman, Amy L. Kellerstrass, Stephen Prine, Rod Wagner; *ex officio* Frederick Duda, Barbara L. Perkis; *Section Reps.*

Leslie B. Burger (ILEX), Carol Ann Desch (SLAS), Martha L. Goddard (LSSPS), Sara G. Laughlin (ICAN).

Executive Staff

Exec. Dir. Cathleen Bourdon; *Deputy Exec. Dir.* Lillian Lewis.

Publications

Interface (q.; memb.; nonmemb. $20). *Ed.* Frederick Duda, Talking Book Service, 4884 Kestral Park Circle, Sarasota, FL 34231-3369. Tel. 941-921-5426.

Committee Chairpersons

ADA Assembly. Rhea J. Rubin.
American Correctional Association/ASCLA Joint Committee on Institution Libraries. Carl Romalis.
Awards. Rhea J. Rubin.
Budget and Finance. John Day and Donna O. Dziedzic.
Conference Program Coordination. Gordon R. Barhydt.
Legislation. Linda D. Crowe.
Library Personnel and Education. Sara Ann Parker.
Membership Promotion. Diane M. Solomon.
Organization and Bylaws. Barbara L. Perkis.
Publications. Patricia L. Owens.
Research. Keith Curry Lance.
Standards Review. Ethel Himmell.

American Library Association
Library Administration and Management Association

Object

The Library Administration and Management Association (LAMA) provides an organizational framework for encouraging the study of administrative theory, for improving the practice of administration in libraries, and for identifying and fostering administrative skill. Toward these ends, the division is responsible for all elements of general administration that are common to more than one type of library. These may include organizational structure, financial administration, personnel management and training, buildings and equipment, and public relations. LAMA meets this responsibility in the following ways:

1. Study and review of activities assigned to the division with due regard for changing developments in these activities.

2. Initiating and overseeing activities and projects appropriate to the division, including activities involving bibliography compilation, publication, study, and review of professional literature within the scope of the division.

3. Synthesizing the activities of other ALA units that have a bearing upon the responsibilities or work of the division.

4. Representing and interpreting library administrative activities in contacts outside the library profession.

5. Aiding the professional development of librarians engaged in administration and encouraging their participation in appropriate type-of-library divisions.

6. Planning and developing programs of study and research in library administrative problems that are most needed by the profession.

Established 1957.

Membership

Memb. 4,996.

Officers (July 1999–July 2000)

Pres. Carol L. Anderson; *Pres.-Elect* Jeanne M. Thorsen; *Past Pres.* Thomas L. Wilding; *Dirs.-at-Large* Camila A. Alire, Deborah J. Leather; *Div. Councilor* Charles E. Beard; *COLA Chair* Diana Graff; *Section Chairs* Emily Batista, Patricia Conor Hodapp, Melissa A. Laning, Claudia J. Morner, Catherine L. Murray-Rust, Phyllis W. Trammell, Desiree Webber; *ex officio* Katharina J. Blackstead, Gail A. Cassagne, Lisabeth A. Chabot, Charles Forrest, Diane J. Graves, Myrna Joy McCallister, Nancy R. Nelson, Virginia Steel, John J. Vasi; *Ed.* Maria Otero-Boisvert; *Assoc. Ed.* Kathryn Hammell Carpenter; *Exec. Dir.* Karen Muller.

Address correspondence to the executive director.

Publications

Library Administration and Management (q.; memb.; nonmemb. $55; foreign $65). *Ed.* Maria Otero-Boisvert; *Assoc. Ed.* Kathryn Hammell Carpenter.

LEADS from LAMA (approx. weekly; free through Internet). *Ed.* Beatrice Calvin. To subscribe, send to listproc@ala.org the message *subscribe lamaleads [first name last name].*

Committee Chairpersons

Budget and Finance. John Vasi.

Certified Public Library Administrator Certification, LAMA/PLA/ASCLA. Anders C. Dahlgren.

Council of LAMA Affiliates. Diana Graff.

Cultural Diversity. Janice D. Simmons-Welburn.

Editorial Advisory Board. Mary Augusta Thomas.

Education. Philip Tramdack.

Governmental Affairs. Janice Feye-Stukas.

Membership. Ann W. Williams.

Nominating, 2000 Elections. John Vasi.

Organization. Virginia Steel.

Leadership Development. Joyce C. Wright.

Partners. Roderick MacNeil.

Program. Anthony M. Dos Santos.

Publications. Joan R. Giesecke.

Recognition of Achievement. Sharon L. Stewart.

Small Libraries Publications Series. Marsha J. Stevenson.

Special Conferences and Programs. Paul M. Anderson.

Section Chairpersons

Buildings and Equipment. Claudia J. Morner.

Fund Raising and Financial Development. Desiree Webber.

Human Resources. Melissa A. Laning.

Library Organization and Management. Phyllis W. Trammell.

Public Relations. Patricia Conor Hodapp.

Statistics. Catherine L. Murray-Rust.

Systems and Services. Emily Batista.

Discussion Groups

Assistants-to-the-Director. Judith M. Panitch.

Diversity Officers. Laura K. Blessing.

Library Storage. Judith A. Scalf.

Middle Management. Christine M. Shupala and Chris A. Watson.

Total Quality Management. To be appointed.

Women Administrators. Cheryl C. Kugler.

American Library Association
Library and Information Technology Association

Executive Director, Jacqueline Mundell
50 E. Huron St., Chicago, IL 60611
312-280-4270, 800-545-2433
World Wide Web http://www.lita.org/

Object

The Library and Information Technology Association (LITA) envisions a world in which the complete spectrum of information technology is available to everyone—in libraries, at work, and at home. To move toward this goal, LITA provides a forum for discussion, an environment for learning, and a program for actions on many aspects of information technology for both practitioners and managers.

LITA is concerned with the planning, development, design, application, and integration of technologies within the library and information environment, with the impact of emerging technologies on library service, and with the effect of automated technologies on people.

LITA's strategic goals include providing opportunities for professional growth and performance in areas of information technology, influencing national and international initiatives relating to information and access, influencing the development of technical standards, and developing services and products needed and valued by its members.

Membership

Memb. 5,000.

Officers (1999–2000)

Pres. Michael Gorman; *V.P./Pres.-Elect* Sara Randall; *Past Pres.* Barbra B. Higginbotham.

Directors

Officers; Pat Ensor, Susan Harrison, Susan Jacobson, Joan L. Kuklinski, George S.

Machovec, Karen J. Starr, Lawrence A. Woods); *Councilor* Tamara Miller; *Bylaws and Organization* Mary Ann E. Van Cura; *Exec. Dir.* Jacqueline Mundell.

Publications

Information Technology and Libraries (q.; memb.; nonmemb. $50; single copy $15). *Ed.* Dan Marmion. For information or to send manuscripts, contact the editor.

LITA Newsletter (q.; electronic only, at http://www.lita.org). *Ed.* Martin Kalfatovic.

Committee Chairpersons

Budget Review. Barbra B. Higginbotham.
Bylaws and Organization. Mary Ann Van Cura.
Education. D. Russell Bailey.
Executive. Michael J. Gorman.
International Relations. John R. James.
ITAL Editorial Board. Dan Marmion.
Leadership Development. Bonnie S. Postlethwaite.
Legislation and Regulation. Nancy K. Roderer.
LITA/Gaylord Award. Mary Ann Tricarico.
LITA/Geac Scholarship. Jennie L. McKee.
LITA/Library Hi Tech Award. Marcia K. Deddens.
LITA/LSSI and OCLC Minority Scholarships. Lynn Kellar.
LITA National Forum 2000. Pat Ensor.
LITA Newsletter. Martin Kalfatovic.
LITA/OCLC Kilgour Award. Judith Wild.
Membership. Patricia Earnest.
Nominating. Linda Miller.
Program Planning. Colby Riggs.
Publications. Thomas C. Wilson.
Regional Institutes. Lynne Lysiak.
Research. Kathleen M. Herick.

Strategic Initiatives Planning. Michael Gorman.
TESLA. Katharina Klemperer.
Technology and Access. Chuck Broadbent.
Top Technology Trends. Pat Ensor.
TER Board. Thomas C. Wilson.
Web-based Education Task Force. D. Russell Bailey.
Web Board. Mary M. Deane

Interest Group Chairpersons

Interest Group Coordinator. Susan Logue.
Authority Control in the Online Environment (LITA/ALCTS).
Customized Applications for Library Microcomputers (CALM).
Distance Learning.
Distributed Systems and Networks.
Electronic Publishing/Electronic Journals.

Emerging Technologies.
Geographic Information Systems (GIS).
Human/Machine Interface.
Imagineering.
Intelligent and Knowledge-Based Systems.
Internet Resources.
Library Consortia/Automated Systems.
MARC Formats (LITA/ALCTS).
Microcomputer Users.
Online Catalogs.
Programmer/Analyst.
Retrospective Conversion (LITA/ALCTS).
Secure Systems and Services.
Serials Automation (LITA/ALCTS).
Technical Issues of Digital Data.
Technical Services Workstations (LITA/ALCTS).
Technology and the Arts.
Telecommunications.
Vendor/User.

American Library Association
Public Library Association

Executive Director, Greta K. Southard
50 E. Huron St., Chicago, IL 60611
312-280-5752, 800-545-2433 ext. 5752, fax 312-280-5029
E-mail pla@ala.org
World Wide Web http://www.pla.org/

Object

The Public Library Association (PLA) has specific responsibility for

1. Conducting and sponsoring research about how the public library can respond to changing social needs and technical developments.

2. Developing and disseminating materials useful to public libraries in interpreting public library services and needs.

3. Conducting continuing education for public librarians by programming at national and regional conferences, by

publications such as the newsletter, and by other delivery means.

4. Establishing, evaluating, and promoting goals, guidelines, and standards for public libraries.

5. Maintaining liaison with relevant national agencies and organizations engaged in public administration and human services, such as the National Association of Counties, the Municipal League, and the Commission on Post-Secondary Education.

6. Maintaining liaison with other divisions and units of ALA and other library organizations, such as the Association of American Library

Schools and the Urban Libraries Council.

7. Defining the role of the public library in service to a wide range of user and potential user groups.

8. Promoting and interpreting the public library to a changing society through legislative programs and other appropriate means.

9. Identifying legislation to improve and to equalize support of public libraries.

PLA enhances the development and effectiveness of public librarians and public library services. This mission positions PLA to

- Focus its efforts on serving the needs of its members

- Address issues that affect public libraries

- Promote and protect the profession

- Commit to quality public library services that benefit the general public

To carry out its mission, PLA will identify and pursue specific goals. These goals will drive PLA's structure, governance, staffing, and budgeting, and will serve as the basis for all evaluations of achievement and performance. The following broad goals and strategies were established for PLA in 1997 for accomplishment by the year 2000:

1. PLA will provide market-driven, mission-focused programs and services delivered in a variety of formats.

2. PLA will have increased its members and diversified its leadership.

3. PLA will have maximized its fiscal resources to enable the full implementation of its goals and to take full advantage of strategic opportunities.

4. PLA will be recognized as a positive, contemporary champion of public librarians and public libraries.

5. PLA will have demonstrated its leadership in developing and promoting

sound public policies affecting public libraries.

6. PLA will have implemented, evaluated, and refined its structure and governance.

7. PLA will have the facilities, technology, staff, and systems required to achieve its mission.

Membership

Memb. 8,500+. Open to all ALA members interested in the improvement and expansion of public library services to all ages in various types of communities.

Officers (1999–2000)

Pres. Harriet Henderson, Montgomery County Dept. of Libs., 99 Maryland Ave., Rockville, MD 20850. Tel. 301-271-3804, fax 301-271-3934, e-mail hendch@co.mo.md.us; *V.P./Pres.-Elect* Kay K. Runge, Davenport Public Lib., 321 Main St., Davenport, IA 52801. Tel. 319-326-7841, fax 319-326-7809, e-mail krunge@lobby.rbls.lib.il.us; *Past Pres.* Christine L. Hage, Clinton-Macomb Public Lib., 43245 Garfield, Clinton Township, MI 48038. Tel. 810-228-7810, fax 810-228-9093, e-mail hagec@metronet.lib.mi.us.

Publication

Public Libraries (bi-m.; memb.; nonmemb. $50; foreign $60; single copy $10). *Managing Ed.* Kathleen Hughes, PLA, 50 E. Huron St., Chicago, IL 60611.

Cluster Chairpersons

Issues and Concerns Steering Committee. Gordon S. Welles.

Library Development Steering Committee. Irene Padilla.

Library Services Steering Committee. Joan L. Clark.

Committee Chairs

Issues and Concerns Cluster

Intellectual Freedom. Bruce S. Farrar.
Legislation. David Macksam.
Library Confidentialty Task Force. Eileen Longsworth.
Recruitment of Public Librarians. Christine Brandau.
Research and Statistics. Diane Mayo.
Workload Measures and Staffing Patterns. Hampton (Skip) Auld.

Library Development Cluster

Branch Libraries. Miriam L. Morris.
Marketing Public Libraries. Tim Grimes.
Metropolitan Libraries. Diane J. Chrisman.
Public Libraries in the Information Superhighway. Andy Peters.
Public Library Systems. Dinah L. Smith-O'Brien.
Rural Library Services. John D. Christenson.
Small and Medium-Sized Libraries. Jo K. Potter.
Technology in Public Libraries. Daniel L. Walters.

Library Services Cluster

Adult Lifelong Learning Services. Jean U. Brinkman.
Audiovisual. Judy A. Napier.
Community Information Services. Donna Reed.
Community Information Technologies. Leland R. Ireland.
Internal Revenue Services. Elizabeth Bingham.
Job and Career Information Services. Frances Roehm.
Publishers Liaison. Penny Pace-Cannon.
Services to Multicultural Populations. Fred Gitner.
Services to Youth and Their Parents. Colleen M. Costello.

Business Committees

2001 Conference Program Coordinating Committee. Mary A. Sherman.
2001 Leadership Development. Jo Ann Pinder.
2001 Nominating Committee. Christine L. Hage.
2001 President's Events. Faye Clow.
2002 National Conference. Christine L. Hage.
2002 National Conference (Local Arrangements). Leslie J. Steffes.
2002 National Conference (Program). Linda Mielke, Jo Ann Pinder.
Awards. La Donna T. Kienitz.
Awards, Advancement of Literacy Award Jury. Jean U. Brinkman.
Awards, Baker & Taylor Entertainment Audio/Music/Video Product Award Jury. Tina M. Theeke.
Awards, Demco Creative Merchandising Grant Jury. Irene M. Paidlla.
Awards, Excellence in Small and/or Rural Public Library Service Award Jury. Catharine Cook.
Awards, Highsmith Library Innovation Award Jury. Jean M. Tabor.
Awards, Allie Beth Martin Award Jury. Malcolm K. Hill.
Awards, New Leaders Travel Grant Jury. Molly E. Fogarty.
Awards, NTC Career Materials Resource Grant Jury. Vera A. Green.
Awards, Charlie Robinson Award Jury. Diane J. Chrisman.
Awards, Leonard Wertheimer Award Jury. Mary Ann Hodel.
Budget and Finance. Kathleen S. Reif.
Bylaws and Organization. Bob Smith.
Certified Public Library Administrator (PLA/LAMA/ASCLA). Anders C. Dahlgren.
Membership. Caryn Katz.
PLA Partners. Samuel F. Morrison.
Publications. Barbara Webb.
Publications, Electronic Communications Advisory. Donald J. Napoli.
Publications, PLA Monographs. Mickey Ann Hinojosa.
Publications, *Public Libraries* Advisory. Susan Cooley.
Publications, *Statistical Report* Advisory. Judith A. Drescher.
Publications, University Press Books for Public Libraries. Angie Stuckey.
State Relations, Deirdre Hanley.

American Library Association
Reference and User Services Association

Executive Director, Cathleen Bourdon
50 E. Huron St., Chicago, IL 60611
312-944-6780, 800-545-2433 ext. 4398, fax 312-944-8085
E-mail rusa@ala.org
World Wide Web http://www.ala.org/rusa

Object

The Reference and User Services Association (RUSA) is responsible for stimulating and supporting in every type of library the delivery of reference/information services to all groups, regardless of age, and of general library services and materials to adults. This involves facilitating the development and conduct of direct service to library users, the development of programs and guidelines for service to meet the needs of these users, and assisting libraries in reaching potential users.

The specific responsibilities of RUSA are

1. Conduct of activities and projects within the division's areas of responsibility.
2. Encouragement of the development of librarians engaged in these activities and stimulation of participation by members of appropriate type-of-library divisions.
3. Synthesis of the activities of all units within the American Library Association that have a bearing on the type of activities represented by the division.
4. Representation and interpretation of the division's activities in contacts outside the profession.
5. Planning and development of programs of study and research in these areas for the total profession.
6. Continuous study and review of the division's activities.

Membership

Memb. 4,766. For information on dues, see ALA entry.

Officers (June 1999–June 2000)

Pres. Peggy A. Seiden; *Pres.-Elect* Catherine R. Friedman; *Secy.* Nancy Huling.

Directors and Other Members

Karen J. Chapman, Elaine Lyon, David Null, A. Craig Hawbaker, Merle L. Jacob, Rebecca Whitaker; *Councilor* Pam Sieving; *Past Pres.* Jo Bell Whitlatch; *Ed., RUSA Update* Beth Woodard; *Ed., RUSQ* Gail Schlachter; *Exec. Dir.* Cathleen Bourdon.

Address correspondence to the executive director.

Publications

RUSA Update (q.; memb.; nonmemb. $20).
RUSQ (q.; memb; nonmemb. $50).

Section Chairpersons

Business Reference and Services. Kelly Janousek.
Collection Development and Evaluation. Diane Zabel.
History. John Haskell, Jr.
Machine-Assisted Reference. Linda Friend.
Management and Operation of User Services. David Null.

Committee Chairpersons

Access to Information. Gregory A. Crawford.
AFL/CIO Joint Committee on Library Services to Labor Groups. John N. Schacht.
Awards Coordinating. Elaine Lyon.
Conference Program. George S. Porter.

Conference Program Coordinating. Susan I. Coburn.
Dartmouth Medal. Danise G. Hoover.
Denali Press Award. Elaina Norlin.
Facts on File Grant. Andrea J. Copeland.
Gale Research Award for Excellence in Reference and Adult Services. Janet Doerge.
Membership. Barbara Pilvin.
Margaret E. Monroe Library Adult Services Award. Ann Coder.
Isadore Gilbert Mudge/R. R. Bowker Award. Louise S. Sherby.

Nominating. Beth S. Woodard.
Organization. Laryne J. Dallas.
Planning and Finance. Jo Bell Whitlatch.
Publications. Donald J. Kenney.
Reference Services Press Award. Marian Shemberg.
John Sessions Memorial Award. Ann C. Sparanese.
Louis Shores/Oryx Press Award. Penelope Papangelis.
Standards and Guidelines. Sarah Sartain Jane.

American Library Association
Young Adult Library Services Association

Executive Director, Julie A. Walker
50 E. Huron St., Chicago, IL 60611
312-280-4390, 800-545-2433 ext. 4390, fax 312-664-7459
E-mail yalsa@ala.org
World Wide Web http://www.ala.org/yalsa/

Object

In every library in the nation, quality library service to young adults is provided by a staff that understands and respects the unique informational, educational, and recreational needs of teenagers. Equal access to information, services, and materials is recognized as a right, not a privilege. Young adults are actively involved in the library decision-making process. The library staff collaborates and cooperates with other youth-serving agencies to provide a holistic, community-wide network of activities and services that support healthy youth development. To ensure that this vision becomes a reality, the Young Adult Library Services Association (YALSA), a division of the American Library Association (ALA),

1. Advocates extensive and developmentally appropriate library and information services for young adults, ages 12 to 18

2. Promotes reading and supports the literacy movement

3. Advocates the use of information and communications technologies to provide effective library service

4. Supports equality of access to the full range of library materials and services, including existing and emerging information and communications technologies, for young adults

5. Provides education and professional development to enable its members to serve as effective advocates for young people

6. Fosters collaboration and partnerships among its individual members with the library community and other groups involved in providing library and information services to young adults

7. Influences public policy by demonstrating the importance of providing library and information services that meet the unique needs and interests of young adults

8. Encourages research and is in the vanguard of new thinking concerning the

provision of library and information services for youth

Membership

Memb. 2,632. Open to anyone interested in library services and materials for young adults. For information on dues, see ALA entry.

Officers (July 1999–July 2000)

Pres. Jana Fine, Clearwater Public Lib., 100 N. Osceola Ave., Clearwater, FL 33755. Tel. 727-462-6800 ext. 252, fax 727-298-0095, e-mail janafine01@sprynet.com; *V.P/Pres.-Elect* Mary Arnold, Cuyahoga County Public Lib., Cleveland, OH. Tel. 216-475-5000, fax 216-587-7281, e-mail mjarnold@hotmail.com; *Past Pres.* Joel Shoemaker, Southeast Junior H.S., Iowa City, IA 52245. Tel. 319-339-6823, fax 319-339-5735, e-mail shoemaker@Iowa-city.k12.ia.us.

Directors

Officers; Betty Acerra (2001), Audra Caplan (2003), Rosemary Chance (2000), David Mowery (2001), Caryn Sipos (2001), Adela Peskorz (2003); *Ex officio Chair, Budget and Finance* Rosemary Chance; *Chair, Organization and Bylaws* Rebecca Loney; *Chair, Strategic Planning* Daphne Daly.

Publications

Journal of Youth Services in Libraries (q.; memb.; nonmemb. $40; foreign $50). *Eds.* Donald J. Kenney, Linda J. Wilson.

Committee Chairpersons

Adult Books for Young Adults Project. Bonnie Kunzel.
ALSC/YALSA JOYS Editorial (Advisory). Betty Carter, Keith Swigger.
Best Books for Young Adults (2000). Suzanne Manczuk.
Best Books for Young Adults (2001). Alice Stern.
Best Young Adult Book Award Feasibility Task Force. Michael Cart.
Budget and Finance. Rosemary Chance.
Directions Revision Task Force. Carole Fiore.
Division Promotion. Amy Alessio.
Education. Hilary Crew.
Margaret A. Edwards Award 2000. Joan Atkinson.
Margaret A. Edwards Award 2001. Jennifer Gallant.
Intellectual Freedom. Charles Harmon.
Legislation. Barbara Balbirer and Elizabeth Reed.
Media Selection and Usage. Stephen Crowley.
Membership. Angelina Benedetti and Jennifer Duffy.
National Organizations Serving the Young Adult. Paula Broehm-Hager.
Nominating (2000). Judy Nelson.
Organization and Bylaws. Rebecca Loney.
Outreach to Young Adults with Special Needs. Jeff Katz.
Oversight. Daphne Daly.
Popular Paperbacks for Young Adults. Bill Stack.
Program Planning Clearinghouse and Evaluation. Brenda Hunter.
Publications. Teri Lesesne.
Publishers Liaison. Lauren Adams.
Quick Picks for Reluctant Young Adult Readers. John Sexton.
Research. Monique King.
Selected Films and Videos for Young Adults. Sheila Anderson.
Serving Young Adults in Large Urban Populations Discussion Group. Susan Raboy.
Strategic Planning. Daphne Daly.
Teaching Young Adult Literature Discussion Group. Mary Cissell.
Technology for Young Adults. Bette Silverman.
Webmaster, YALSA Web site. Linda Braun.
Youth Participation. Sandra Payne.

American Merchant Marine Library Association

(An affiliate of United Seamen's Service)
Executive Director, Roger T. Korner
One World Trade Center, Suite 2161, New York, NY 10048
212-775-1038

Object

Provides ship and shore library service for American-flag merchant vessels, the Military Sealift Command, the U.S. Coast Guard, and other waterborne operations of the U.S. government. Established 1921.

Officers (1999–2000)

Pres. Talmage E. Simpkins; *Chair, Exec. Committee* Edward Morgan; *V.P.s* John M. Bowers, Capt. Timothy Brown, James Capo, David Crockroft, Remo DiFiore, John Halas, René Lioeanjie, Michael R. McKay, George E. Murphy, S. Nakanishi, Capt. Gregorio Oca, Larry O'Toole, Michael Sacco, John J. Sweeney; *Secy.* Donald E. Kadloc; *Treas.* William D. Potts; *Exec. Dir.* Roger T. Korner.

American Society for Information Science

Executive Director, Richard B. Hill
8720 Georgia Ave., Suite 501, Silver Spring, MD 20910
301-495-0900, fax 301-495-0810, e-mail ASIS@asis.org

Object

The American Society for Information Science (ASIS) provides a forum for the discussion, publication, and critical analysis of work dealing with the design, management, and use of information, information systems, and information technology.

Board of Directors

Dirs.-at-Large Raya Fidel, Julie M. Hurd, Ray R. Larson, Kris Liberman, Gary J. Marchionini, Pat Molholt, Victor Rosenberg, Michael Stallings; *Deputy Dirs.* Douglas Kaylor, Gretchen Whitney; *Exec. Dir.* Richard B. Hill.

Membership

Memb. (Indiv.) 3,700; (Student) 600; (Inst.) 200. Dues (Indiv.) $115; (Student) $30; (Inst.) $650 and $800.

Officers

Pres. Eugene Garfield, Institute for Scientific Information; *Pres.-Elect* Joseph Busch, Datafusion; *Treas.* George D. Ryerson, Chemical Abstracts Service; *Past Pres.* Candy Schwartz, Simmons College.

Address correspondence to the executive director.

Publications

Advances in Classification Research, Vols. 1–10. Available from Information Today, 143 Old Marlton Pike, Medford, NJ 08055.

Annual Review of Information Science and Technology. Available from Information Today, 143 Old Marlton Pike, Medford, NJ 08055.

ASIS Thesaurus of Information Science and Librarianship. Available from Information Today, 143 Old Marlton Pike, Medford, NJ 08055.

Bulletin of the American Society for Information Science. Available from ASIS.

Challenges in Indexing Electronic Texts and Images. Eds. Raya Fidel, Trudi Bellardo (Hahn), Edie M. Rasmussen, and Philip J. Smith. Available from Information Today, 143 Old Marlton Pike, Medford, NJ 08055.

Electronic Publishing: Applications and Implications. Eds. Elisabeth Logan and Myke Gluck. Available from Information Today, 143 Old Marlton Pike, Medford, NJ 08055.

Entertainment Technology and the Information Business. Thomas E. Kinney. Available from ASIS.

From Print to Electronic: The Transformation of Scientific Communication. Susan Y. Crawford, Julie M. Hurd, and Ann C. Weller. Available from Information Today, 143 Old Marlton Pike, Medford, NJ 08055.

Historical Studies in Information Science. Eds. Trudi Bellardo Hahn and Michael Buckland. Available from Information Today, 143 Old Marlton Pike, Medford, NJ 08055.

Information Management for the Intelligent Organization: The Art of Environmental Scanning. Chun Wei Choo. Available from ASIS.

Interfaces for Information Retrieval and Online Systems: The State of the Art. Ed. Martin Dillon. Available from Greenwood Press, 88 Post Rd. W., Westport, CT 06881.

Journal of the American Society for Information Science. Available from John Wiley and Sons, 605 Third Ave., New York, NY 10016.

Proceedings of the ASIS Annual Meetings. Available from Information Today, 143 Old Marlton Pike, Medford, NJ 08055.

Scholarly Publishing: The Electronic Frontier. Eds. Robin P. Peek and Gregory B. Newby. Available from MIT Press, Cambridge, Massachusetts.

Studies in Multimedia. Eds. Susan Stone, Michael Buckland. Based on the Proceedings of the 1991 ASIS Mid-Year Meeting. Available from Information Today, 143 Old Marlton Pike, Medford, NJ 08055.

Committee Chairpersons

Awards and Honors. Jay Trolley.
Budget and Finance. George Ryerson.
Constitution and Bylaws. Norman Horrocks.
Education. Trudi Bellardo Hahn.
Membership. Steven Hardin, Dudee Chiang.
Standards. Mark Needleman.

American Theological Library Association

820 Church St., Suite 400, Evanston, IL 60201-5613
888-665-2852, 847-869-7788, fax 847-869-8513
E-mail atla@atla.com; World Wide Web http://www.atla.com

Object

To bring its members into close working relationships with each other, to support theological and religious librarianship, to improve theological libraries, and to interpret the role of such libraries in theological education, developing and implementing standards of library service, promoting research and experimental projects, encouraging cooperative programs that make resources more available, publishing and disseminating literature and research tools and aids, cooperating with organizations having similar aims, and otherwise supporting and aiding theological education. Founded 1946.

Membership

Memb. (Inst.) 240; (Indiv.) 550. Membership is open to persons engaged in professional library or bibliographical work in theological or religious fields and others who are interested in the work of theological librarianship. Dues (Inst.) $75 to $750, based on total library expenditure; (Indiv.) $15 to $150, based on salary scale. Year. Sept. 1–Aug. 31.

Officers

Pres. Milton J. "Joe" Coalter, Ernest Miller White Lib., Louisville Presbyterian Theological Seminary, 1044 Alta Vista Rd., Louisville, KY 40205. Tel. 502-894-3411, ext. 471, e-mail jcoalter@lpts.edu; *V.P.* William Hook, Dir., Vanderbilt Univ. Divinity Lib., 419 21st Ave. S., Nashville, TN 37240-0007. Tel. 615-322-2865, fax 615-343-2918, e-mail hook@library.vanderbilt.edu; *Secy.* Eileen K. Saner, Associated Mennonite Biblical Seminary Lib., 3003 Benham Ave., Elkhart, IN 46517-1999. Tel. 219-296-6233, fax 219-295-0092, e-mail esaner@ambs.edu.

Board of Directors

Officers; Cass Armstrong, Michael P. Boddy, Stephen Crocco, Bruce Eldevik, D. William Faupel, Bill Hook, Alan D. Krieger, Melody Mazuk, Sara Myers, Eileen K. Saner, Sharon Taylor; *Exec. Dir.* Dennis A. Norlin; *Dir. of Finance* Pradeep Gamadia; *Dir. of Member Services* Karen L. Whittlesey.

Publications

ATLA Indexes in MARC Format (semi-ann.).

ATLA Religion database on CD-ROM, 1949–.

Biblical Studies on CD-ROM (ann.).

Catholic Periodical and Literature Index on CD-ROM (ann.).

Index to Book Reviews in Religion (ann.).

Newsletter (q.; memb.; nonmemb. $45). *Ed.* Margaret Tacke.

Old Testament Abstracts on CD-ROM (ann.).

Proceedings (ann.; memb.; nonmemb. $40). *Ed.* Margaret Tacke.

Religion Index One: Periodicals (semi-ann.).

Religion Index Two: Multi-Author Works (ann.).

Religion Indexes: RIO/RIT/IBRR 1975– on CD-ROM.

Research in Ministry: An Index to Doctor of Ministry Project Reports (ann.).

South African Theological Bibliography on CD-ROM (ann.).

Zeitschrifteninhaltsdienst Theologie on CD-ROM (ann.).

Committee Chairpersons and Other Officials

Annual Conference. Mitzi Budde.

Collection Evaluation and Development. Andrew Kadel.

College and University. Elizabeth Leahy, Suzanne Selinger.

Education. Christine Schwarz.

Judaica. David Stewart.

NISO Representative. Myron Chace.

Nominating. Richard Berg.

OCLC Theological User Group. Linda Umoh.

Preservation. Martha Smalley.

Public Services. Roberta Schaafsma.

Publication. Andy Keck.

Special Collections. Andrea Lamb.

Technical Services. Lynn Berg.

Technology. Duane Harbin.

World Christianity. Phillip O'Neill.

Archivists and Librarians in the History of the Health Sciences

President, Elaine M. Challacombe
Curator, Owen H. Wangensteen Historical Library of Biology and Medicine, University of Minnesota
568 Diehl Hall, 505 Essex St. S.E., Minneapolis, MN 55455
612-626-6881

Object

This association is established exclusively for educational purposes to serve the professional interests of librarians, archivists, and other specialists actively engaged in the librarianship of the history of the health sciences by promoting the exchange of information and by improving the standards of service.

Membership

Memb. (Voting) 200. Dues $15, membs.; outside U.S. and Canada, $16.

Officers (May 1998–May 2000)

Pres. Elaine M. Challacombe, Curator, Owen H. Wangensteen Historical Lib. of Biology and Medicine, Univ. of Minnesota, 568 Diehl Hall, 505 Essex St. S.E., Minneapolis, MN 55455. Tel. 612-626-6881, fax 612-626-2454, e-mail e-chal@tc.umn.edu; *Pres.-Elect* Suzanne Porter, Curator, History of Medicine Collections, Duke Univ., Medical Center Lib., Box 3702, Durham, NC 27710. E-mail Porte004@mc.duke.edu; *Secy.-Treas.* Stephen C. Wagner, Dept. of Philosophy, Univ. of Oklahoma, 455 W. Lindsey St., Rm. 605, Norman, OK 73019-2006. E-mail Swagner @ou.edu.

Publication

Watermark (q.; memb.; nonmemb. $16). *Ed.* Lilli Sentz, New York Academy of Medicine, 1216 Fifth Ave., New York, NY 10029-5293. Tel. 212-822-7313, e-mail lsentz@nyam.org.

ARMA International
(Association of Records Managers and Administrators)

Executive Director/CEO, Peter R. Hermann, CAE
4200 Somerset Dr., Suite 215, Prairie Village, KS 66208
913-341-3808, fax 913-341-3742
E-mail phermann@arma.org, World Wide Web http://www.arma.org

Object

To advance the practice of records and information management as a discipline and a profession; to organize and promote programs of research, education, training, and networking within that profession; to support the enhancement of professionalism of the membership; and to promote cooperative endeavors with related professional groups.

Membership

Annual dues $115 for international affiliation. Chapter dues vary. Membership categories are chapter member ($115 plus chapter dues), student member ($15), and unaffiliated member.

Officers (July 2000–June 2001)

Pres.H. Larry Eiring, Senior Records and Info. Mgr., Covington & Burling, 1201 Pennsylvania Ave. N.W., Box 7566, Washington, DC 20044. Tel. 202-662-6563, fax 202-662-6291; *Immediate Past Pres. and Chair of the Board* Tad C. Howington, Lower Colorado River Authority, 3701 Lake Austin Blvd., Austin, TX 78703. Tel. 512-473-4047, fax 512-473-3561, e-mail thowingt@lcra.org; *Pres.-Elect* Terrence J. Coan, Accutrac Software, Inc., 350 S. Figueroa St., Suite 141, Los Angeles, CA 90071. Tel. 213-626-3000, fax 213-229-9095, e-mail tcoan@accutrac. com; *Treas*. Juanita M. Skillman, Fremont Comp., 500 N. Brand Blvd., Suite 1150, Glendale, CA 91203-3392. Tel. 818-552-3860, fax 818-549-4568, e-mail jskillma@fremontcomp.com; *Region Directors* (Mid-Atlantic Region) Donna Ahaladianakis; (Great Lakes Region) Carol E. B. Choksy; (Southeast Region) Susan B. Whitmire; (Midwest/Rocky Mountain Region) Cheryl L. Pederson; (Southwest Region) Susan A. Hubbard; (Pacific Region) Terrence J. Coan; (Northeast Region) Paul J. Singleton; (Great Northwest Region) David P. McDermott; (Canada) Gisele L. Crawford; (International) Hella Jean Bartolo.

Publication

Information Management Journal. Ed. J. Michael Pemberton, Assoc. Professor, School of Info. Sciences, Univ. of Tennessee, 804 Volunteer Blvd., Knoxville, TN 37996-4330, e-mail jpembert@utkux. utcc.utk.edu.

Committee Chairpersons

Awards. Tad C. Howington, Lower Colorado River Authority, 3701 Lake Austin Blvd., Austin, TX 78703. Tel. 512-473-4047, fax 512-473-3561, e-mail thowingt@lcra.org.

Canadian Legislative and Regulatory Affairs (CLARA). Raphael Thierrin, ECOBIO Communications, 223 Armour Rd., 2nd fl., Peterborough, ON K9H 1Y5, Canada. Tel. 705-749-9890.

Education Development. Carol E. B. Choksy, IRAD Strategic Consulting, Inc., 4103 Golden Grove Rd., Greenwood, IN 46143. Tel. 317-535-7117, fax 317-535-7784.

Election Management. Tad C. Howington, Lower Colorado River Authority, 3701 Lake Austin Blvd., Austin, TX 78703. Tel. 512-473-4047, fax 512-473-3561, e-mail thowingt@lcra.org.

Electronic Records Management. Robert Meagher, CONDOR Consulting, Inc., 130 Albert St., Suite 419, Ottawa, ON K1P 5G4, Canada. Tel. 613-233-4962 ext. 23, fax 613-233-4249.

Financial Planning. Juanita M. Skillman, Fremont Comp., 500 N. Brand Blvd., Suite 1150, Glendale, CA 91203-3392. Tel. 818-552-3860, fax 818-549-4568.

Industry Specific Program. Fred A. Pulzello, Merrill Lynch & Co., Records Mgt., 101 Hudson St., Jersey City, NJ 07302-3997. Tel. 201-557-2337, fax 201-557-2465.

International Relations. Hella Jean Bartolo, Sunshine House, 60 Stella Maris St., Silema SLM12, Malta. Tel. 35-624-7480, fax 35-624-3051, e-mail hella@waldonet.net. mt.

Publications Coordination. Jean K. Brown, Univ. Archives, Univ. of Delaware, Pearson Hall, Newark, DE 19716. Tel. 302-831-2750, fax 302-831-6903.

Strategic Planning. Terrence J. Coan, Accutrac Software, Inc., 350 S. Figueroa St., Suite 141, Los Angeles, CA 90071. Tel. 213-626-3000, fax 213-229-9095, e-mail tcoan@accutrac. com.

U.S. Government Relations. Keith C. S. Siu, 5285 Kilauea Ave., Honolulu, HI 96816-5612. Tel. 808-734-7056, fax 808-538-5309.

Art Libraries Society of North America

Executive Director, Howard Adler
1550 S. Coast Hwy., Suite 201
Laguna Beach, CA 92651
800-892-7547, 949-376-3456
E-mail membership@arlisna.org
World Wide Web http://www.arlisna.org

Object

To foster excellence in art librarianship and visual resources curatorship for the advancement of the visual arts. Established 1972.

Membership

Memb. 1,325. Dues (Inst.) $1,000; (Indiv.) $65; (Business Affiliate) $100; (Student) $40; (Retired/Unemployed) $50; (Sustaining) $250; (Sponsor) $500; (Overseas) basic plus $25. Year. Jan. 1–Dec. 31. Membership is open and encouraged for all those interested in visual librarianship, whether they be professional librarians, students, library assistants, art book publishers, art book dealers, art historians, archivists, architects, slide and photograph curators, or retired associates in these fields.

Officers (1999–2000)

Pres. Kathryn M. Wayne, Fine Arts Libn., 308F Doe Lib., Univ. of California, Berkeley, CA 94720. Tel. 510-643-2809, fax 510-643-2155, e-mail kwayne@library.berkeley.edu; *V.P./Pres.-Elect* Karen McKenzie, Chief Libn., Art Gallery of Ontario, E. P. Taylor Research Lib. and Archives, 317 Dundas St. W., Toronto, ON M5T 1G4. Tel. 416-979-6660, ext. 389, fax 416- 979-6602, e-mail Karen_McKenzie@ago.net; *Past Pres.* Mary E. Graham, Arizona State Museum Lib., Univ. of Arizona, Tucson, AZ 85721-0026. Tel. 520-621-4695, fax 520-621-2976, e-mail megraham@u.arizona.edu; *Secy.* Peter B. Blank, Libn., Stanford Univ. Art and Architecture Lib., 102 Cummings Art Bldg., Stanford, CA 94305-2018. Tel. 650-725-1038, fax 650-725-0140, e-mail ppb@leland. stanford.edu; *Treas.* Katharine R. Chibnik, Avery Architectural and Fine Arts Lib., Columbia Univ., 1172 Amsterdam Ave., Mail Code 0301, New York, NY 10027. Tel. 212-854-3506, fax 212-854-8904, e-mail chibnik@columbia.edu.

Address correspondence to the executive director.

Executive Board

Officers; *Regional Reps.* (Northeast) Deborah A. Kempe, (South) Pat M. Lynagh, (Midwest) Louis V. Adrean, (West) Lorna Corbetta-Noyes, (Canada) Marilyn Berger.

Publications

ARLIS/NA Update (bi-m.; memb.).
Art Documentation (s. ann.; memb.).
Handbook and List of Members (ann.; memb.).
Occasional Papers (price varies).
Miscellaneous others (request current list from headquarters).

Committees

Awards.
Cataloging (Advisory).
Collection Development.
Conference.
Development.
Diversity.
Finance.
International Relations.
Membership.
Gerd Muehsam Award.
Nominating.
North American Relations.

Professional Development.
Public Policy.
Publications.
Research.
Standards.
Technology Education.
Technology Relations.
Travel Awards.
George Wittenborn Award.

Chapters

Arizona; Canada (National); Central Plains; D.C.-Maryland-Virginia; Delaware Valley; Michigan; Midstates; Montreal-Ottawa-Quebec; Mountain West; New England; New Jersey; New York; Northern California; Northwest; Ohio Valley; Ontario; Southeast; Southern California; Texas; Twin Cities; Western New York.

Asian/Pacific American Librarians Association

President, Patricia Mei-Yung Wong
Library Program Coordinator of Youth Services
Oakland Public Library
125 14th St., Rm. 6, Oakland, CA 94612
510-238-6706, fax 510-238-6865
E-mail kaiming@ix.netcom.com

Object

To provide a forum for discussing problems and concerns of Asian/Pacific American librarians; to provide a forum for the exchange of ideas by Asian/Pacific American librarians and other librarians; to support and encourage library services to Asian/Pacific American communities; to recruit and support Asian/Pacific American librarians in the library/information science professions; to seek funding for scholarships in library/information science programs for Asian/Pacific Americans; and to provide a vehicle whereby Asian/Pacific American librarians can cooperate with other associations and organizations having similar or allied interests. Founded 1980; incorporated 1981; affiliated with the American Library Association 1982.

Membership

Open to all librarians and information specialists of Asian/Pacific descent working in U.S. libraries and information centers and other related organizations and to others who support the goals and purposes of APALA. Asian/Pacific Americans are defined as those who consider themselves Asian/Pacific Americans. They may be Americans of Asian/Pacific descent, Asian/Pacific people with the status of permanent residency, or Asian/Pacific people living in the United States. Dues (Inst.) $25; (Indiv.) $10; (Students/Unemployed Librarians) $5.

Officers (July 1999–June 2000)

Pres. Patricia Mei-Yung Wong, Lib. Program Coord. of Youth Services, Oakland Public Lib., 125 14th St., Rm. 6, Oakland, CA 94612. Tel. 510-238-6706, fax 510-238-6865, e-mail kaiming@ix.netcom.com; *V.P./Pres.-Elect* Sushila Shah; *Past Pres.* Soon J. Jung; *Secy.* Janet Tom; *Treas.* Rama Vishwanatham, Lib. of the Health Sciences M/C 763, 1750 Polk St., Chicago, IL 60612. Tel. 312-996-8993, fax 312-996-1899, e-mail rama@uic.edu.

Publication

APALA Newsletter (q.). *Ed.* Sandra Yamate, Polychrome Publishing Corp., 4509 N. Francisco Ave., Chicago, IL 60625. Tel. 773-478-4455, fax 773-478-0786.

Committee Chairpersons

Constitution and Bylaws. Lourdes Collantes.
Membership and Recruitment. Katherine Wong.

Newsletter and Publications. Sandra Yamate.

Nominations. Soon Jung.

Program and Local Arrangement. Sushila Shah.

Association for Information and Image Management

President, John F. Mancini
1100 Wayne Ave., Suite 1100, Silver Spring, MD 20910
301-587-8202, fax 301-587-2711
E-mail aiim@aiim.org, World Wide Web http://www.aiim.org
European Office: Chappell House, The Green, Datchet, Berks SL3 9EH, England.
44-1753-592-669, fax 44-1753-592-770.

Object

To provide the global leadership needed to help business and public sector organizations understand the ever-expanding set of document technologies and solutions and how they can be applied to improve critical business processes.

Officers

Chair John A. O'Connell, Staffware PLC, Staffware House, 3 The Switchback, Gardener Rd., Maidenhead, Berks SL6 7RJ, England; *V.-Chair* Jordan M. Libit, JCEB Consulting.

Publication

e-doc Magazine (bi-m.; memb.).

Association for Library and Information Science Education

Executive Director, Sharon J. Rogers
Box 7640, Arlington, VA 22207
703-243-8040, fax 703-243-4551, e-mail sroger7@ibm.net
World Wide Web http://www.alise.org

Object

The Association for Library and Information Science Education (ALISE) is an association devoted to the advancement of knowledge and learning in the interdisciplinary field of information studies. Established 1915.

Membership

Memb. 500. Dues (Inst.) for ALA-accredited programs, sliding scale; (International Affili-

ate Inst.) $125; (Indiv.) $90 or $40. Year. July–June. Any library/information science school with a program accredited by the ALA Committee on Accreditation may become an institutional member. Any school that offers a graduate degree in librarianship or a cognate field but whose program is not accredited by the ALA Committee on Accreditation may become an institutional member at the lower rate. Any school outside the United States and Canada offering a program comparable to that of institutional membership may become an international affiliate institutional member. Any organizational entity wishing to support LIS education may become an associate institutional member. Any faculty member, administrator, librarian, researcher, or other individual employed full time may become a personal member. Any retired or part-time faculty member, student, or other individual employed less than full time may become a personal member at the lower rate. Any student may become a member at a lower rate.

Officers (1999–2000)

Pres. James Matarazzo, Simmons College. E-mail james.matarazzo@simmons.edu; *Past Pres.* Shirley Fitzgibbons, Indiana Univ. E-mail Fitzgibbons@indiana.edu; *Secy.-Treas.* Pat Feehan, Univ. of South Carolina. E-mail proffeehan@yahoo.com.

Directors

Officers; Danny P. Wallace, Kent State Univ. E-mail wallace@slis.kent.edu; Louise S. Robbins, Univ. of Wisconsin–Madison. E-mail LRobbins@macc.wisc.edu; Ann Curry, Univ. of British Columbia. E-mail ann.curry@ubc.ca; *Co-Eds.* Joseph Mika (2001), Wayne State Univ. E-mail jmika@cms.cc.wayne.edu; Ronald W. Powell (2001), Wayne State Univ. E-mail rpowell@cms.cc.wayne.edu; *Exec. Dir.* Sharon J. Rogers. E-mail Sroger7@ibm.net; *Parliamentarian* Norman Horrocks.

Publications

ALISE Library and Information Science Education Statistical Report (ann.; $65).
Journal of Education for Library and Information Science (4 per year; $78; foreign $88).
Membership Directory (ann.; $55).

Committee Chairpersons

Awards and Honors. Norman Horrocks, Dalhousie Univ.
Conference Planning. Joseph Mika, Wayne State Univ.
Editorial Board. Ann Prentice, Univ. of Maryland.
Government Relations. Betty Turock, Rutgers Univ.
International Relations. Ismail Abdullahi, Clark Atlanta Univ.
LIS Education Statistical Report Project. Evelyn Daniel, Jerry Saye, Univ. of North Carolina.
Membership. Lynne Howarth, Univ. of Toronto.
Nominating. Joan Durrance, Univ. of Michigan.
Organization and Bylaws. Heidi Julien, Dalhousie Univ.
Recruitment. Ling Hwey Jen, Univ. of Kentucky.
Research. M. Della Neumann, Univ. of Maryland.
Tellers. Jean Preer, Catholic Univ.

Association of Academic Health Sciences Libraries

2150 N. 107, Suite 205, Seattle, WA 98133
206-367-8704, fax 206-367-8777
E-mail sbinc@halcyon.com

Object

To promote—in cooperation with educational institutions, other educational associations, government agencies, and other nonprofit organizations—the common interests of academic health sciences libraries located in the United States and elsewhere, through publications, research, and discussion of problems of mutual interest and concern, and to advance the efficient and effective operation of academic health sciences libraries for the benefit of faculty, students, administrators, and practitioners.

Membership

Memb. 135. Dues $1,500. Regular membership is available to nonprofit educational institutions operating a school of health sciences that has full or provisional accreditation by the Association of American Medical Colleges. Regular members shall be represented by the chief administrative officer of the member institution's health sciences library. Associate membership (and nonvoting representation) is available at $600 to organizations having an interest in the purposes and activities of the association.

Association of Jewish Libraries

15 E. 26 St., Rm. 1034, New York, NY 10010
212-725-5359, fax 212-678-8998
World Wide Web http://www.jewishlibraries.org

Object

To promote the improvement of library services and professional standards in all Jewish libraries and collections of Judaica; to serve as a center of dissemination of Jewish library information and guidance; to encourage the establishment of Jewish libraries and collections of Judaica; to promote publication of literature that will be of assistance to Jewish librarianship; and to encourage people to enter the field of librarianship. Organized in 1965 from the merger of the Jewish Librarians Association and the Jewish Library Association.

Membership

Memb. 1,100. Dues $35; (Foreign) $60; (Student/Retired) $25; Year. July 1–June 30.

Officers (June 1998–June 2000)

Pres. David Gilner, Hebrew Union College, 3101 Clifton Ave., Cincinnati, OH 45220; *Past Pres.* Esther Nussbaum, Ramaz Upper School Lib., 60 E. 78 St., New York, NY 10021; *V.P./Pres.-Elect* Toby Rossner, Bureau of Jewish Education of Rhode Island, 130 Sessions St., Providence, RI 02906; *V.P., Memb.* Shoshanah Seidman, 9056 Tamaroa Terrace, Skokie, IL 60076; *Treas.* Leah Adler, Yeshiva Univ., 500 W. 185 St., New York, NY 10033; *Recording Secy.* Frances Wolf, Congregation Beth Shalom, 9400 Wornall Rd., Kansas City, MO 64114; *Corresponding Secy.* Elizabeth Stabler, 92nd St. YM-YWHA, 1395 Lexington Ave., New York, NY 10128; *Publications V.P.* Laurel S. Wolfson, Hebrew Union College, 3101 Clifton Ave., Cincinnati, OH 45220.

Address correspondence to the association.

Publications

AJL Newsletter (q.). *General Ed.* Nancy Sack, Northwestern Univ. Lib., 1935 Sheridan Rd., Evanston, IL 60208.

Judaica Librarianship (irreg.). *Ed.* Bella Hass Weinberg, Div. of Lib. and Info. Science, Saint John's Univ., 8000 Utopia Pkwy., Jamaica, NY 11439.

Division Presidents

Research and Special Library. Rick Burke. Synagogue, School, and Center Libraries. Cheryl Banks.

Association of Research Libraries

Executive Director, Duane E. Webster
21 Dupont Circle N.W., Suite 800, Washington, DC 20036
202-296-2296, fax 202-872-0884
E-mail arlhq@arl.org, World Wide Web http://www.arl.org

Object

The mission of the Association of Research Libraries (ARL) is to shape and influence forces affecting the future of research libraries in the process of scholarly communication. ARL's programs and services promote equitable access to and effective use of recorded knowledge in support of teaching, research, scholarship, and community service. The association articulates the concerns of research libraries and their institutions, forges coalitions, influences information policy development, and supports innovation and improvement in research library operations. ARL is a not-for-profit membership organization comprising the libraries of North American research institutions and operates as a forum for the exchange of ideas and as an agent for collective action.

Membership

Memb. 122. Membership is institutional. Dues $16,500.

Officers (Oct. 1999–Oct. 2000)

Pres. Ken Frazier, Dir. of Libs., Univ. of Wisconsin; *Past Pres.* Betty G. Bengtson, Univ. of Washington; *Pres.-Elect* Shirley Baker, Washington Univ., St. Louis.

Board of Directors

Shirley K. Baker, Washington Univ., St. Louis; Betty G. Bengtson, Univ. of Washington; Scott Bennett, Yale Univ.; Meredith Butler, SUNY–Albany; Kenneth Frazier, Univ. of Wisconsin; Joseph A. Hewitt, Univ. of North Carolina; Paula Kaufmann, Univ. of Tennesee; Paul Mosher, Univ. of Pennsylvania; Carolynne Pressar, Univ. of Manitoba; Carla Stoffle, Univ. of Arizona; Sarah Thomas, Cornell.

Publications

ARL: A Bimonthly Newsletter of Research Libraries Issues and Actions (bi-m.).
ARL Academic Law and Medical Library Statistics (ann.).
ARL Annual Salary Survey (ann.).
ARL Preservation Statistics (ann.).
ARL Statistics (ann.).
Developing Indicators for Academic Library Performance: Ratios from the ARL Statistics (ann.).
Systems and Procedures Exchange Center (SPEC) Kits (6 per year).
SPARC (bi-m.).

Committee and Work Group Chairpersons

Access to Information Resources. Shirley Baker, Washington Univ., Saint Louis.

Copyright Issues (Working Group). James G. Neal, Johns Hopkins Univ.

Diversity. Nancy Baker, Washington State Univ.

Information Policies. Fred Heath, Texas A&M Univ.

Leadership and Management of Research Library Resources. Paul Kobulnicky, Univ. of Connecticut.

Preservation of Research Library Materials. Meredith Butler, SUNY–Albany.

Research Collections. Joe A. Hewitt, Univ. of North Carolina at Chapel Hill.

Scholarly Communication. Elaine F. Sloan, Columbia Univ.

SPARC (Working Group). Kenneth Frazier, Univ. of Wisconsin.

Statistics and Measurement. William J. Studer, Ohio State Univ.

ARL Membership

Nonuniversity Libraries

Boston Public Lib., Canada Inst. for Scientific and Technical Info., Center for Research Libs., Linda Hall Lib., Lib. of Congress, National Agricultural Lib., National Lib. of Canada, National Lib. of Medicine, New York Public Lib., New York State Lib., Smithsonian Institution Libs.

University Libraries

Alabama, Alberta, Arizona, Arizona State, Auburn, Boston, Brigham Young, British Columbia, Brown, California–Berkeley, California–Davis, California–Irvine, California–Los Angeles, California–Riverside, California–San Diego, California–Santa Barbara, Case Western Reserve, Chicago, Cincinnati, Colorado, Colorado State, Columbia, Connecticut, Cornell, Dartmouth, Delaware, Duke, Emory, Florida, Florida State, Georgetown, Georgia, Georgia Inst. of Technology, Guelph, Harvard, Hawaii, Houston, Howard, Illinois–Chicago, Illinois–Urbana, Indiana, Iowa, Iowa State, Johns Hopkins, Kansas, Kent State, Kentucky, Laval, Louisiana State, McGill, McMaster, Manitoba, Maryland, Massachusetts, Massachusetts Inst. of Technology, Miami (Florida), Michigan, Michigan State, Minnesota, Missouri, Nebraska–Lincoln, New Mexico, New York, North Carolina, North Carolina State, Northwestern, Notre Dame, Ohio, Ohio State, Oklahoma, Oklahoma State, Oregon, Pennsylvania, Pennsylvania State, Pittsburgh, Princeton, Purdue, Queen's (Kingston, ON, Canada), Rice, Rochester, Rutgers, Saskatchewan, South Carolina, Southern California, Southern Illinois, Stanford, SUNY–Albany, SUNY–Buffalo, SUNY–Stony Brook, Syracuse, Temple, Tennessee, Texas, Texas A&M, Texas Tech, Toronto, Tulane, Utah, Vanderbilt, Virginia, Virginia Polytechnic, George Washington, Washington, Washington (Saint Louis, Mo.), Washington State, Waterloo, Wayne State, Western Ontario, Wisconsin, Yale, York.

Association of Vision Science Librarians

Chair 2000–2001, Bette Anton, Univ. of California Optometry Library, School of Optometry, 490 Minor Hall, Berkeley, CA 94720-2020. 510-642-1020, e-mail banton@library.berkeley.edu

Object

To foster collective and individual acquisition and dissemination of vision science information, to improve services for all persons seeking such information, and to develop standards for libraries to which members are attached. Founded 1968.

Membership

Memb. (U.S.) 60; (Foreign) 15.

Publications

Guidelines for Vision Science Libraries.
Opening Day Book Collection Visual Science.
Ph.D. Theses in Physiological Optics (irreg.).
Standards for Vision Science Libraries.
Union List of Vision-Related Serials (irreg.).

Meetings

Annual meeting held in December in connection with the American Academy of Optometry; midyear mini-meeting with the Medical Library Association.

Beta Phi Mu
(International Library and Information Studies Honor Society)

Executive Director, F. William Summers
School of Information Studies, Florida State University,
Tallahassee, FL 32306-2100
850-644-3907, fax 850-644-6253
E-mail beta_phi_mu@lis.fsu.edu

Object

To recognize high scholarship in the study of librarianship and to sponsor appropriate professional and scholarly projects. Founded at the University of Illinois in 1948.

Membership

Memb. 23,000. Open to graduates of library school programs accredited by the American Library Association who fulfill the following requirements: complete the course requirements leading to a fifth year or other advanced degree in librarianship with a scholastic average of 3.75 where A equals 4 points (this provision shall also apply to planned programs of advanced study beyond the fifth year that do not culminate in a degree but that require full-time study for one or more academic years) and in the top 25 percent of their class; receive a letter of recommendation from their respective library schools attesting to their demonstrated fitness for successful professional careers.

Officers (1999–2001)

Pres. Barbara Immroth, Graduate School of Lib. and Info. Science, Univ. of Texas at Austin, Austin, TX 78712-1276. Tel. 512-471-3875, fax 512-471-3971, e-mail immroth

@uts.cc.utexas.edu; *V.P./Pres.-Elect* Robert S. Martin, School of Lib. and Info. Studies, Texas Woman's Univ., Box 425438, Denton, TX 76204-5438. Tel. 940-898-2617, fax 940-898-2611, e-mail rmartin3@twu.edu; *Past Pres.* Marion T. Reid, Dean of Lib. Services, California State Univ. at San Marcos, 820 Los Vallecitos Blvd., San Marcos, CA 92096-0001. Tel. 760-750-4330, fax 760-750-3287, e-mail mreid@mailhost1.csusm.edu; *Treas.* Sondra Taylor-Furbee, State Lib. of Florida, 500 S. Bronough St., Tallahassee, FL 32399. Tel. 850-487-2651, fax 850-488-2746, e-mail staylor-furbee@mail.dox.state.fl.us; *Exec. Dir.* F. William Summers, School of Info. Studies, Florida State Univ., Tallahassee, FL 32306-2100. Tel. 850-644-8111, fax 850-644-6253, e-mail Beta_Phi_Mu@lis.fsu.edu.

Directors

Susan M. Agent (2002), Donald G. Davis, Jr. (2001), Lois Pausch (2000), Anna Perrault (2000), Louise S. Robbins (2001), Danny P. Wallace (2002).

Publications

Beta Phi Mu Monograph Series. Book-length scholarly works based on original research in subjects of interest to library and information professionals. Available from Greenwood Press, 88 Post Rd. W., Box 5007, Westport, CT 06881-9990.

Chapbook Series. Limited editions on topics of interest to information professionals. Call Beta Phi Mu for availability.

Newsletter. (2 per year). *Ed.* Mary Upshaw Rhodes.

Chapters

Alpha. Univ. of Illinois, Grad. School of Lib. and Info. Science, Urbana, IL 61801; *Beta.* (Inactive). Univ. of Southern California, School of Lib. Science, Univ. Park, Los Angeles, CA 90007; *Gamma.* Florida State Univ., School of Lib. and Info. Studies, Tallahassee, FL 32306; *Delta* (Inactive). Loughborough College of Further Education, School of Libnshp., Loughborough, England; *Epsilon.* Univ. of North Carolina, School of Lib. Science, Chapel Hill, NC 27599; *Zeta.* Atlanta Univ., School of Lib. and Info. Studies, Atlanta, GA 30314; *Theta.* Pratt Inst., Grad. School of Lib. and Info. Science, Brooklyn, NY 11205; *Iota.* Catholic Univ. of America, School of Lib. and Info. Science, Washington, DC 20064; Univ. of Maryland, College of Lib. and Info. Services, College Park, MD 20742; *Kappa.* (Inactive). Western Michigan Univ., School of Libnshp., Kalamazoo, MI 49008; *Lambda.* Univ. of Oklahoma, School of Lib. Science, Norman, OK 73019; *Mu.* Univ. of Michigan, School of Lib. Science, Ann Arbor, MI 48109; *Nu.* (Inactive); *Xi.* Univ. of Hawaii, Grad. School of Lib. Studies, Honolulu, HI 96822; *Omicron.* Rutgers Univ., Grad. School of Lib. and Info. Studies, New Brunswick, NJ 08903; *Pi.* Univ. of Pittsburgh, School of Lib. and Info. Science, Pittsburgh, PA 15260; *Rho.* Kent State Univ., School of Lib. Science, Kent, OH 44242; *Sigma.* Drexel Univ., School of Lib. and Info. Science, Philadelphia, PA 19104; *Tau.* (Inactive). State Univ. of New York at Geneseo, School of Lib. and Info. Science, Geneseo, NY 14454; *Upsilon.* (Inactive). Univ. of Kentucky, College of Lib. Science, Lexington, KY 40506; *Phi.* Univ. of Denver, Grad. School of Libnshp. and Info. Mgt., Denver, CO 80208; *Chi.* Indiana Univ., School of Lib. and Info. Science, Bloomington, IN 47401; *Psi.* Univ. of Missouri at Columbia, School of Lib. and Info. Sciences, Columbia, MO 65211; *Omega.* (Inactive). San Jose State Univ., Div. of Lib. Science, San Jose, CA 95192; *Beta Alpha.* Queens College, City College of New York, Grad. School of Lib. and Info. Studies, Flushing, NY 11367; *Beta Beta.* Simmons College, Grad. School of Lib. and Info. Science, Boston, MA 02115; *Beta Delta.* State Univ. of New York at Buffalo, School of Info. and Lib. Studies, Buffalo, NY 14260; *Beta Epsilon.* Emporia State Univ., School of Lib. Science, Emporia, KS 66801; *Beta Zeta.* Louisiana State Univ., Grad. School of Lib. Science, Baton Rouge, LA 70803; *Beta Eta.* Univ. of Texas at Austin, Grad. School of Lib. and Info. Science, Austin, TX 78712; *Beta Theta.* (Inactive). Brigham Young Univ., School of Lib. and

Info. Science, Provo, UT 84602; *Beta Iota.* Univ. of Rhode Island, Grad. Lib. School, Kingston, RI 02881; *Beta Kappa.* Univ. of Alabama, Grad. School of Lib. Service, University, AL 35486; *Beta Lambda.* North Texas State Univ., School of Lib. and Info. Science, Denton, TX 76203; Texas Woman's Univ., School of Lib. Science, Denton, TX 76204; *Beta Mu.* Long Island Univ., Palmer Grad. Lib. School, C. W. Post Center, Greenvale, NY 11548; *Beta Nu.* Saint John's Univ., Div. of Lib. and Info. Science, Jamaica, NY 11439; *Beta Xi.* North Carolina Central Univ., School of Lib. Science, Durham, NC 27707; *Beta Omicron.* (Inactive). Univ. of Tennessee at Knoxville, Grad. School of Lib. and Info. Science, Knoxville, TN 37916; *Beta Pi.* Univ. of Arizona, Grad. Lib. School, Tucson, AZ 85721; *Beta Rho.* Univ. of Wisconsin at Milwaukee, School of Lib. Science, Milwaukee, WI 53201; *Beta Sigma.* (Inactive). Clarion State College, School of Lib. Science, Clarion, PA 16214; *Beta Tau.* Wayne State Univ., Div. of Lib. Science, Detroit, MI 48202; *Beta Upsilon.* (Inactive).

Alabama A & M Univ., School of Lib. Media, Normal, AL 35762; *Beta Phi.* Univ. of South Florida, Grad. Dept. of Lib., Media, and Info. Studies, Tampa, FL 33647; *Beta Psi.* Univ. of Southern Mississippi, School of Lib. Service, Hattiesburg, MS 39406; *Beta Omega.* Univ. of South Carolina, College of Libnshp., Columbia, SC 29208; *Beta Beta Alpha.* Univ. of California at Los Angeles, Grad. School of Lib. and Info. Science, Los Angeles, CA 90024; *Beta Beta Gamma.* Rosary College, Grad. School of Lib. and Info. Science, River Forest, IL 60305; *Beta Beta Delta.* Univ. of Cologne, Germany; *Beta Beta Epsilon.* Univ. of Wisconsin at Madison, Lib. School, Madison, WI 53706; *Beta Beta Zeta.* Univ. of North Carolina at Greensboro, Dept. of Lib. Science and Educational Technology, Greensboro, NC 27412; *Beta Beta Theta.* Univ. of Iowa, School of Lib. and Info. Science, Iowa City, IA 52242; *Beta Beta Iota.* State Univ. of New York, Univ. at Albany, School of Info. Science and Policy, Albany, NY 12222; *Pi Lambda Sigma.* Syracuse Univ., School of Info. Studies, Syracuse, NY 13210.

Bibliographical Society of America

Executive Secretary, Michèle E. Randall
Box 1537, Lenox Hill Sta., New York, NY 10021
212-452-2500 (tel./fax), e-mail bsa@bibsocamer.org
World Wide Web http://www.bibsocamer.org

Object

To promote bibliographical research and to issue bibliographical publications. Organized 1904.

Membership

Memb. 1,200. Dues $50. Year. Jan.–Dec.

Officers

Pres. Hope Mayo; *V.P.* John Bidwell; *Treas.* R. Dyke Benjamin; *Secy.* Claudia Funke.

Council

Susan Allen (2003), Anne Anninger (2002), T. Anna Lou Ashby (2001), Florence Fearrington (2002), Peter S. Graham (2001), Marie E. Korey (2003), Mark Samuels Lasner (2003), William Reese (2001), William P. Stoneman (2001), Michael Winship (2002), Elizabeth Witherell (2003), David S. Zeidberg (2002).

Publication

Papers (q.; memb.). *Ed.* Trevor Howard-Hill, Thomas Cooper Lib., Univ. of South Carolina, Columbia, SC 29208. Tel./fax 803-

777-7046, e-mail RalphCrane@msn.com.

Committee Chairpersons

Bibliographical Projects. Michael Winship.

Delegate to American Council of Learned Societies. Marcus McCorison.
Fellowship. David Zeidberg.
Finance. Daniel D. Chabris.
Publications. John Bidwell.

Canadian Association for Information Science
(Association Canadienne des Sciences de l'Information)

140 Saint George St., Toronto, ON M5S 3G6, Canada
416-978-8876

Object

To bring together individuals and organizations concerned with the production, manipulation, storage, retrieval, and dissemination of information, with emphasis on the application of modern technologies in these areas. The Canadian Association for Information Science (CAIS) is dedicated to enhancing the activity of the information transfer process; utilizing the vehicles of research, development, application, and education; and serving as a forum for dialogue and exchange of ideas concerned with the theory and practice of all factors involved in the communication of information.

Membership

Institutions and individuals interested in information science and involved in the gathering, organization, and dissemination of information (computer scientists, documentalists, information scientists, librarians, journalists, sociologists, psychologists, linguists, administrators, etc.) can become members of CAIS. Dues (Inst.) $165; (Personal) $75; (Student) $40.

Publication

Canadian Journal of Information and Library Science (q.; $95; outside Canada $110).

Canadian Library Association

Executive Director, Vicki Whitmell
200 Elgin St., Ottawa, ON K2P 1L5, Canada
613-232-9625, ext. 306, fax 613-563-9895
E-mail vwhitmell@istar.ca

Object

To promote, develop, and support library and information services in Canada and to work in cooperation with all who share our values in order to present a unified voice on issues of mutual concern. Offers library school scholarship and book awards; carries on international liaison with other library associations; makes representation to government and official commissions; offers professional development programs; and supports intellectual freedom. Founded in 1946, CLA is a nonprofit voluntary organization governed by an elected executive council.

Membership

Memb. (Indiv.) 2,500; (Inst.) 600. Open to individuals, institutions, and groups interested in librarianship and in library and information services. Dues (Indiv.) $175; (Inst.) $300.

Officers

Pres. Lorraine McQueen, Univ. Libn., Univ. Lib., Acadia Univ., 50 Acadia St., Wolfville, NS B0P 1X0. Tel. 902-585-1510, fax 905-585-1748, e-mail lorraine.mcqueen@acadia. ca; *V.P./Pres.-Elect* Stan Skrzeszewski, ASM Advanced Strategic Mgt. Consultants, 411 Rippleton Pl., London, ON N6G 1L4. Tel. 519-473-7651, fax 519-471-9945, e-mail asmstan@netcom.ca; *Treas.* Kathryn Arbuckle, Law Libn., Univ. of Alberta, John A. Weir Memorial Law Lib., Edmonton, AB T6G 2H5. Tel. 780-492-3717, fax 780-492-7546, e-mail kathryn.arbuckle@ualberta.ca; *Past Pres.* Sydney Jones, Dir., Lib. Operations, Metro Toronto Reference Lib., 789 Yonge St., Toronto, ON M4W 2G8. Tel. 416-393-7214, fax 416-393-7229, e-mail syd@mtrl. toronto.on.ca.

Publication

Feliciter: Linking Canada's Information Professionals (6 per year; newsletter).

Division Representatives

Canadian Association of College and University Libraries (CACUL). Kathleen DeLong, Assoc. Dir., Cameron Lib., Univ. of Alberta, Edmonton, AB T6G 2J8. Tel. 780-492-7675, fax 780-492-8302, e-mail kathleen.delong@ualberta.ca.

Canadian Association of Public Libraries (CAPL). Wendy J. Newman, Brantford Public Lib. 173 Colborne St., Brantford, ON N3T 2G8. Tel. 519-756-2223, fax 519-756-4979, e-mail wnewman@ brantford.library.on.ca.

Canadian Association of Special Libraries and Information Services (CASLIS). Claudette Cloutier, Science Liaison Libn., Univ. of Calgary, MLB 331-C, 2500 University Dr. N.W., Calgary, AB T2N 1N4. E-mail cloutier@ucalgary.ca.

Canadian Library Trustees' Association (CLTA). Gary Archibald, Box 2680, R.R. 2, Yarmouth, NS B5A 4A6.

Canadian School Library Association (CSLA). Ray Doiron, Assoc. Professor, Univ. of Prince Edward Island Faculty of Educ., 550 University Ave., Charlottetown, PEI C1A 4P3. Tel. 902-566-0694, fax 902-566-0416, e-mail raydoiron@upei.ca.

Catholic Library Association

Executive Director, Jean R. Bostley, SSJ
100 North St., Suite 224, Pittsfield, MA 01201-5109
413-443-2252, fax 413-442-2252, e-mail cla@vgernet.net
World Wide Web http://www.cathla.org

Object

The promotion and encouragement of Catholic literature and library work through cooperation, publications, education, and information. Founded 1921.

Membership

Memb. 1,000. Dues $45–$500. Year. July–June.

Officers (1999–2000)

Pres. Rev. Bonaventure Hayes, OFM, Christ the King Seminary, 711 Knox Rd., East Aurora, NY 1452-0607. Tel. 716-652-8940, fax 716-652-8903; *V.P./Pres.-Elect* Sally Anne Thompson, Pope John XXIII Catholic School Community, 16235 N. 60th St., Scottsdale, AZ 85254-7323. Tel. 480-905-0939, fax 4890-905-0955, e-mail desertsat@aol.com; *Past Pres.* Julanne M. Good, St. Louis Public Lib., 5005 Jamieson Ave., St. Louis, MO 63109-3027. Tel. 314-832-2319, e-mail bopeep@inlink.com.

Address correspondence to the executive director.

Executive Board

Officers; Mary Agnes Casey, SSJ, Jersey City Public Lib., Jersey City, NJ 07921; Linda B. Gonzales, 2808-B Madison St., Waukesha, WI 53188; Barbara Anne Kilpatrick, RSM, Saint Vincent de Paul School, Nashville, TN 37212-4202; M. Dorothy Neuhofer, OSB, Saint Leo Univ., Box 6665, MC 2128, Saint Leo, FL 33574-6665; Nancy K. Schmidtmann, 149 Orchard St., Plain-view, NY 11803-4718; Cecil R. White, St. Patrick's Seminary, 320 Middlefield Rd., Menlo Park, CA 94025.

Publications

Catholic Library World (q.; memb.; nonmemb. $60). *Ed.* Allen Gruenke.
Catholic Periodical and Literature Index (q.; $400 calendar year; abridged ed., $100 calendar year; CPL on CD-ROM, inquire). *Ed.* Barry C. Hopkins.

Section Chairpersons

Academic Libraries/Library Education. Helen Fontenot, MSC.
Archives. Mary E. Gallagher, SSJ.
Children's Libraries. Paul E. Pojman.
High School Libraries. Monica Donohoe, CSJP
Parish/Community Libraries. Eileen M. Franke.

Round Table Chairpersons

Bibliographic Instruction. To be appointed.
Cataloging and Classification. To be appointed.
Preservation of American Catholic Materials. To be appointed.

Committee Chairpersons

Catholic Library World Editorial. Mary E. Gallagher, SSJ.
Catholic Periodical and Literature Index. Julanne M. Good.
Constitution and Bylaws. H. Warren Willis.
Elections. To be appointed.

Finance. SallyAnne Thompson.
Grant Development. Jean R. Bostley, SSJ.
Membership Development. To be appointed.
Nominations. Mary E. Gallagher, SSJ.
Publications. Mary E. Gallagher, SSJ.
Scholarship. Kathleen O'Leary.

Special Appointments

American Friends of the Vatican Library
  Board. Jean R. Bostley, SSJ.
Convention Program Coordinator. Jean R.
  Bostley, SSJ.
Parliamentarian. Rev. Jovian Lang, OFM.

Chief Officers of State Library Agencies

167 W. Main Street, Suite 600, Lexington, KY 40507
606-231-1925, fax 606-231-1928

Object

To provide a means of cooperative action among its state and territorial members to strengthen the work of the respective state and territorial agencies, and to provide a continuing mechanism for dealing with the problems faced by the heads of these agencies, which are responsible for state and territorial library development.

Membership

Chief Officers of State Library Agencies (COSLA) is an independent organization of the men and women who head the state and territorial agencies responsible for library development. Its membership consists solely of the top library officers of the 50 states, the District of Columbia, and the territories, variously designated as state librarian, director, commissioner, or executive secretary.

Officers (1999–2001)

Pres. C. Ray Ewick, Dir., State Lib., 140 N. Senate Ave., Indianapolis, IN 46204. Tel. 317-232-3692, fax 317-232-3728, e-mail ewick@statelib.lib.in.us; *V.P./Pres.-Elect* Keith Fiels, Dir., Bd. of Lib. Commissioners, 648 Beacon St., Boston, MA 02215. Tel. 617-267-9400, fax 617-421-9833, e-mail kfiels@state.ma.us; *Secy.* GladysAnn Wells, Dir., Dept. of Libs., Archives and Public Records, State Capital, Rm. 200, 1700 W. Washington, Phoenix, AZ 85007. Tel. 602-542-4035, fax 602-542-4972, e-mail gawells @dlapr.lib.az.us; *Treas.* Duane Johnson, State Libn., State Lib., Capital, 3rd fl., Topeka, KS 66612. Tel. 913-296-3296, fax 913-296-6650, e-mail duanej@ink.org.

Directors

Officers; *Immediate Past Pres.* Sara Parker, State Libn., State Lib., Box 387, 600 W. Main St., Jefferson City, MO 65102-0387. Tel. 573-751-2751, fax 573-751-3612, e-mail sparker@mail.state.mo.us; Michael Lucas, State Libn., State Lib., 65 S. Front St., Columbus, OH 43215-4163. Tel. 614-644-6863, fax 614-466-3584, e-mail mlucas@ mail.slonet.ohio.gov; Jim Scheppke, State Libn., State Lib., 250 Winter St. N.E., Salem, OR 97310-0640. Tel. 503-378-4367, fax 503-588-7119, e-mail jim.b.scheppke@state. or.us.

Chinese American Librarians Association

Executive Director, Sally C. Tseng
949-824-6832, fax 949-824-2059, e-mail sctseng@uci.edu

Object

To enhance communications among Chinese American librarians as well as between Chinese American librarians and other librarians; to serve as a forum for discussion of mutual problems and professional concerns among Chinese American librarians; to promote Sino-American librarianship and library services; and to provide a vehicle whereby Chinese American librarians may cooperate with other associations and organizations having similar or allied interest.

Membership

Memb. 770. Open to everyone who is interested in the association's goals and activities. Dues (Regular) $15; (Student/Nonsalaried) $7.50; (Inst.) $45; (Permanent) $200.

Officers

Pres. Ling Hwey Jeng. E-mail lhjeng00@ukcc.uky.edu; *V.P./Pres.-Elect* Yu-lan Chou. E-mail ychou@library.berkeley.edu; *Treas.* Jian Liu. E-mail jiliu@indiana.edu; *Past Pres.* Linna Yu. E-mail linnay@queenslib.ny.us.

Publications

Journal of Library and Information Science, (2 per year; memb.; nonmemb. $15). *Ed.* Mengxiong Liu. E-mail mliu@email.sjsu.edu.

Membership Directory (memb.).

Newsletter (3 per year; memb.; nonmemb. $10). *Eds.* Sha-li Zhang, e-mail zhang@twsuvm.uc.twsu.edu, and Jian Liu, e-mail jiliu@indiana.edu.

Committee Chairpersons

Awards. Juin-huei Kuo.
Constitution and Bylaws. Tsai-Hong Miller.
Finance. Susan Tsui.
International Relations. Eveline Yang.
Membership. Gregory Gao, Dora Ho.
Public Relations/Fund Raising. Anna McElroy, Joseph McElroy.
Publications. Lan Yang.
Scholarship. Nancy Hershoff.
Long-Range Planning (task force). Clare Fu.

Chapter Presidents

California. Ja-Lih Lee
Florida. Wenxian Zhang.
Greater Mid-Atlantic. Cathy Yang.
Midwest. Vickie Fu Doll.
Northeast. Esther Lee.
Southwest. Kwei-Feng Hsu.

Church and Synagogue Library Association

Box 19357, Portland, OR 97280-0357
503-244-6919, 800-542-2752, fax 503-977-3734
E-mail CSLA@worldaccessnet.com
World Wide Web http://www.worldaccessnet.com/~CSLA

Object

To act as a unifying core for the many existing church and synagogue libraries; to provide the opportunity for a mutual sharing of practices and problems; to inspire and encourage a sense of purpose and mission among church and synagogue librarians; to study and guide the development of church and synagogue librarianship toward recognition as a formal branch of the library profession. Founded 1967.

Membership

Memb. 1,900. Dues (Inst.) $175; (Affiliated) $75; (Church/Synagogue) $45; (Indiv.) $25. Year. July–June.

Officers (July 1999–June 2000)

Pres. Alrene Hall, 10715 Mahaffey Rd., Tomball, TX 77375; *2nd V.P.* Russell Newburn, 12590 Beeson St., Alliance, OH 44601; *Treas.* Marilyn Demeter, 3145 Corydon Rd., Cleveland Heights, OH 44118; *Administrator* Judith Janzen; *Financial Asst.* Thomas Foun-

tain; *Publications Ed.* Karen Bota, 490 N. Fox Hills Dr., No. 1, Bloomfield Hills, MI 48304; *Book Review Ed.* Charles Snyder, 213 Lawn Ave., Sellersville, PA 18960.

Executive Board

Officers; committee chairpersons.

Publications

Bibliographies (1–5; price varies).
Church and Synagogue Libraries (bi-mo.; memb.; nonmemb. $35; Canada $45). *Ed.* Karen Bota.
CSLA Guides (1–17; price varies).

Committee Chairpersons

Awards. Evelyn Pockrass.
Conference. Joyce Burner.
Finance and Fund Raising. Beth Hodgson.
Library Services. Catherine Bishop.
Nominations and Elections. Sheila Liu.
Personnel. Barbra Mall.
Publications. Carol Campbell.

Coalition for Networked Information

Executive Director, Clifford A. Lynch
21 Dupont Circle, Suite 800, Washington, DC 20036
202-296-5098, fax 202-872-0884
E-mail info@cni.org, World Wide Web http://www.cni.org

Mission

The Coalition for Networked Information (CNI) is an organization created to advance the transformative promise of networked information technology for the advancement of scholarly communication and the enrichment of intellectual productivity. The coalition was founded in 1990 by the Association of Research Libraries, CAUSE, and Educom. In 1998 CAUSE and Educom merged to create a new organization, Educause. In establishing CNI, these sponsor organizations recognized the need to broaden the community's thinking beyond issues of network connectivity and bandwidth to encompass networked information content and applications. Reaping the benefits of the Internet for scholarship, research, and education demands new partnerships, new institutional roles, and new technologies and infrastructure. The coalition seeks to further these collaborations, to explore these new roles, and to catalyze the development and deployment of the necessary technology base.

Membership

Memb. 206. Membership is institutional. Dues $5,050. Year. July–June.

Officers (July 1999–June 2000)

Duane Webster, Executive Director, Association of Research Libraries; Brian Hawkins, President, Educause.

Steering Committee

Richard West, California State Univ.; William Graves, COLLEGIS Research Inst.; Marin Runkle, Univ. of Chicago; Miriam Drake, Georgia Inst. of Technology; Shirley Baker, Washington Univ.; Michael Lesk, National Science Foundation; Geoffrey Nunbert, Xerox Parc; Susan L. Perry, Mount Holyoke College; Donald Waters, Andrew Mellon Foundation.

Publications

CNI-Announce (subscribe by e-mail to LISTPROC@CNI.ORG).

Council on Library and Information Resources

1755 Massachusetts Ave. N.W., Suite 500, Washington, DC 20036-2124
202-939-4750, fax 202-939-4765
World Wide Web http://www.clir.org

Object

In 1997 the Council on Library Resources (CLR) and the Commission on Preservation and Access (CPA) merged and became the Council on Library and Information Resources (CLIR). The mission of the council is to identify and define the key emerging issues related to the welfare of libraries and the constituencies they serve, convene the leaders who can influence change, and promote collaboration among the institutions and organizations that can achieve change. The council's interests embrace the entire range of information resources and services from traditional library and archival materials to emerging digital formats. It assumes a particular interest in helping institutions cope with the accelerating pace of change associated with the transition into the digital environment. The council pursues this mission out of the conviction that information is a public good and has great social utility.

The term library is construed to embrace its traditional meanings and purposes and to encompass any and all information agencies and organizations that are involved in gathering, cataloging, storing, preserving, and distributing information and in helping users meet their information requirements.

While maintaining appropriate collaboration and liaison with other institutions and organizations, the council operates independently of any particular institutional or vested interests.

Through the composition of its board, it brings the broadest possible perspective to bear upon defining and establishing the priority of the issues with which it is concerned.

Membership of Board

The council's membership and board of directors are limited to 18 members.

Officers

Chair Stanley Chodorow; *V.-Chair* Marilyn Gell Mason; *Pres.* Deanna B. Marcum. E-mail dmarcum@CLIR.org; *Secy.* David B. Gracy, II; *Treas.* Dan Tonkery.

Address correspondence to headquarters.

Publications

Annual Report.
CLIR Issues.
Preservation and Access International Newsletter.
Various program publications.

Federal Library and Information Center Committee

Executive Director, Susan M. Tarr
Library of Congress, Washington, DC 20540-4930
202-707-4800
World Wide Web http://lcweb.loc.gov/flicc

Object

The committee makes recommendations on federal library and information policies, programs, and procedures to federal agencies and to others concerned with libraries and information centers. The committee coordinates cooperative activities and services among federal libraries and information centers and serves as a forum to consider issues and policies that affect federal libraries and information centers, needs and priorities in providing information services to the government and to the nation at large, and efficient and cost-effective use of federal library and information resources and services. Furthermore, the committee promotes improved access to information, continued development and use of the Federal Library and Information Network (FEDLINK), research and development in the application of new technologies to federal libraries and information centers, improvements in the management of federal libraries and information centers, and relevant education opportunities. Founded 1965.

Membership

Libn. of Congress, Dir. of the National Agricultural Lib., Dir. of the National Lib. of Medicine, Dir. of the National Lib. of Education, representatives from each of the other executive departments, and representatives from each of the following agencies: National Aeronautics and Space Admin., National Science Foundation, Smithsonian Institution, U.S. Supreme Court, U.S. Info. Agency, National Archives and Records Admin., Admin. Offices of the U.S. Courts, Defense Technical Info. Center, Government Printing Office, National Technical Info. Service (Dept. of Commerce), Office of Scientific and Technical Info. (Dept. of Energy), Exec. Office of the President, Dept. of the Army, Dept. of the Navy, Dept. of the Air Force, and chairperson of the FEDLINK Advisory Council. Fifteen additional voting member agencies shall be selected on a rotating basis by the voting members of FEDLINK. These rotating members will serve a three-year term. One representative from each of the following agencies is invited as an observer to committee meetings: General Accounting Office, General Services Admin., Joint Committee on Printing, National Commission on Libs. and Info. Science, Office of Mgt. and Budget, Office of Personnel Mgt., and Lib. of Congress U.S. Copyright Office.

Officers

Chair James H. Billington, Libn. of Congress; *Chair Designate* Winston Tabb, Assoc. Libn. for Lib. Services, Lib. of Congress; *Exec. Dir.* Susan M. Tarr, Federal Lib. and Info. Center Committee, Lib. of Congress, Washington, DC 20540 4930.

Address correspondence to the executive director.

Publications

Annual FLICC Forum on Federal Information Policies (summary and papers).
FEDLINK Technical Notes (m.).
FLICC Newsletter (q.).

Federal Publishers Committee

Chairperson, Glenn W. King
Bureau of the Census, Washington, DC 20233
301-457-1171, fax 301-457-4707
E-mail glenn.w.king.@ccmail.census.gov

Object

To foster and promote effective management of data development and dissemination in the federal government through exchange of information, and to act as a focal point for federal agency publishing.

Membership

Memb. 700. Membership is available to persons involved in publishing and dissemination in federal government departments, agencies, and corporations, as well as independent organizations concerned with federal government publishing and dissemination. Some key federal government organizations represented are the Joint Committee on Printing, Government Printing Office, National Technical Info. Service, National Commission on Libs. and Info. Science, and the Lib. of Congress. Meetings are held monthly during business hours.

Officers

Chair Glenn W. King; *V.-Chair, Programs* Sandra Smith; *V.-Chair, Marketing* June Malina.

Roundtable Leaders

Marketing and Promotion. John Ward.
Subscriptions and Periodicals. Nancy Nicoletti.

Publication

Guide to Federal Publishing (occasional).

Lutheran Church Library Association

Executive Director, Leanna D. Kloempken
122 W. Franklin Ave., No. 604, Minneapolis, MN 55404
612-870-3623, fax 612-870-0170
E-mail lclahq@aol.com

Object

To promote the growth of church libraries by publishing a quarterly journal, *Lutheran Libraries*; furnishing book lists; assisting member libraries with technical problems; and providing workshops and meetings for mutual encouragement, guidance, and exchange of ideas among members. Founded 1958.

Membership

Memb. 1,800 churches, 250 personal. Dues (2000) $28, $40, $55, $70, $75, $100, $500, $1,000. Year. Jan.–Jan.

Officers (1999–2000)

Pres. Willis Erickson; *V.P.* Jeanette Johnson;

Secy. Dorothy Anderson; *Treas.* Diane Erickson.

Address correspondence to the executive director.

Directors

Doris Engstrom, Lila Reinmuth, Betsy Papp, Sue Ellen Golke, Ruth Scholze, Helen Shoup.

Publication

Lutheran Libraries (q.; memb.; nonmemb. $30).

Board Chairpersons

Advisory. Mary Jordan.
Finance. L. Edwin Wang.
Library Services. Marlys Johnson.
Publications. Rod Olson.
Telecommunications. Chuck Mann.

Medical Library Association

Executive Director, Carla Funk
65 E. Wacker Pl., Suite 1900, Chicago, IL 60601
312-419-9094, fax 312-419-8950
E-mail info@mlahq.org; World Wide Web http://mlanet.org

Object

The major purposes of the Medical Library Association (MLA) are to foster medical and allied scientific libraries, to promote the educational and professional growth of health science librarians, and to exchange medical literature among the members. Through its programs and publications, MLA encourages professional development of its membership, whose foremost concern is dissemination of health sciences information for those in research, education, and patient care. Founded 1898; incorporated 1934.

Membership

Memb. (Inst.) 1,100; (Indiv.) 3,800. Institutional members are medical and allied scientific libraries. Individual members are people who are (or were at the time membership was established) engaged in professional library or bibliographic work in medical and allied scientific libraries or people who are interested in medical or allied scientific libraries. Dues (Student) $30; (Emeritus) $50; (Intro.) $90; (Indiv.) $135; (Sustaining) $345; and

(Inst.) $210–$495, based on the number of the library's periodical subscriptions. Members may be affiliated with one or more of MLA's 23 special-interest sections and 14 regional chapters.

Officers

Pres. Frieda O. Weise, Univ. of Maryland–Baltimore Health Sciences and Human Services Lib., 601 W. Lombard St., Balimore, MD 21201; *Pres.-Elect* J. Michael Homan, Mayo Clinic, Mayo Medical Lib., 200 First St. S.W., Rochester, MN 55905; *Past Pres.* Jacqueline Donaldson Doyle, Samaritan Health System, 1111 E. McDowell Rd., Box 2989, Phoenix, AZ 85062-2989.

Directors

Rosalind F. Dudden (2001), Suzanne F. Gertsheim (2001), Nancy L. Henry (2002), Julie McGowan (2002), Jocelyn Rankin (2002), Diane Schwartz (2000), Bernie Todd Smith (2000), Mary Joan Tooey (2001).

Publications

Bulletin of the Medical Library Association (q.; $136).

Directory of the Medical Library Association ($150).

MLA News (10 per year; $48.50).

Miscellaneous (request current list from association headquarters).

Committee Chairpersons

Awards. Dixie Alford Jones.
Books. Anne M. Sleeman.
Bulletin. T. Scott Plutchak.
Bylaws. Barb Lucas.
Continuing Education. Jo Dorsch.
Credentialing. Martha Adamson.
Governmental Relations. Marianne Puckett.
Grants and Scholarships. Ruth Fenske.

Joseph Leiter NLM/MLA Lectureship. Alexa McCray.
Membership. Pat Higginbottom.
National Program (2000). Brett Kirkpatrick.
National Program (2001). Judith Robinson.
National Program (2002). Connie Poole.
Oral History. Susan Bolda Marshall.
Publications. Pamela Schiffer Bradigan.

Ad Hoc Committee and Task Force Charges

Benchmarking. Bernie Todd Smith.
Books Publishing Program (Task Force). Elaine Russo Martin.
Cunningham Fellowship (Task Force). Donna Flake.
Joint MLA/AAHSLD Legislative. Marianne Puckett.
Mentoring Program. Craig Haynes.

Music Library Association

6707 Old Dominion Dr., Suite 315, McLean, VA 22101
703-556-8780, fax 703-556-9301

Object

To promote the establishment, growth, and use of music libraries; to encourage the collection of music and musical literature in libraries; to further studies in musical bibliography; to increase efficiency in music library service and administration; and to promote the profession of music librarianship. Founded 1931.

Membership

Memb. 2,000. Dues (Inst.) $90; (Indiv.) $75; (Retired) $45; (Student) $35. Year. Sept. 1–Aug. 31.

Officers

Pres. Paula D. Matthews, George and Helen Ladd Lib., Bates College, Lewiston, ME 04240. Tel. 207-786-6266, fax 207-786-6055, e-mail pmatthew@abacus.bates.edu; *V.P./Pres.-Elect* James P. Cassaro, Univ. of Pittsburgh, Music Lib., B-30 Music Bldg., Pittsburgh, PA 15260. Tel. 412-624-4130, fax 412-624-4180, e-mail cassaro+@pitt.edu; *Rec. Secy.* Lynn Gullickson, Music Lib., Northwestern Univ., 1935 Sheridan Rd., Evanston, IL 60208-2300. Tel. 847-491-3487, fax 847-491-8306, e-mail l-gullickson@nwu.edu; *Treas.* Laura Gayle Green, Miller Nichols Lib., Univ. of Missouri–Kansas City, 5100 Rockill Rd., Kansas City, MO 64110. Tel. 816-235-1679, fax 816-333-5584, e-mail greenlg@umkc.edu; *Exec. Secy.* Bonna J. Boettcher, Music Lib. and Sound Recording Archives, William T. Jerome Lib., 3rd fl., Bowling Green State Univ., Bowling Green, OH 43403-0179. Tel. 419-372-9929, fax 419-372-7996, e-mail bboettc@bgnet.bgsu.edu.

Members-at-Large

Leslie Bennett, Univ. of Oregon; Jim Farrington, Sibley Music Lib./Eastman School of Music; Allie Goudy, Western Illinois Univ.; Brad Short, Washington Univ.; Leslie Troutman, Univ. of Illinois; Philip Vandermeer, Univ. of Maryland.

Special Officers

Advertising Mgr. Susan Dearborn, 1572 Massachusetts Ave., No. 57, Cambridge, MA 02138. Tel. 617-876-0934; *Business Mgr.*, Kimball & Associates, 6707 Old Dominion Dr., Suite 315, McLean, VA 22101. Tel. 703-556-8780; *Convention Mgr.* Don L. Roberts, Northwestern Univ. Music Lib. 1935 Sheridan Rd., Evanston, IL 60208-2300. Tel. 847-491-3434, fax 847-491-8306, e-mail droberts @nwu.edu; *Asst. Convention Mgr.* Susan H. Hitchens, 1961 School House Lane, Aurora, IL 60504. Tel./fax 630-892-4524, e-mail susadorm@ameritech.net; *Placement* To be appointed; *Publicity* To be appointed.

Publications

MLA Index and Bibliography Series (irreg.; price varies).
MLA Newsletter (q.; memb.).
MLA Technical Reports (irreg.; price varies).
Music Cataloging Bulletin (mo.; $25).
Notes (q.; indiv. $70; inst. $80).

Committee and Roundtable Chairpersons

Administration. Deborah Pierce, Univ. of Washington.
Bibliographic Control. Matthew Wise, New York Univ.
Finance. Brad Short, Washington Univ.
Legislation. Lenore Coral, Cornell Univ.
Membership. H. Stephen Wright, Northern Illinois Univ.
Nominating, November 2000 ballot. Bonnie Jo Dopp, Univ. of Maryland.
Preservation. Marlena Frackowski, Westminster Choir College.
Public Libraries. Anna Seaberg, King County Lib. System.
Publications. Nancy Nuzzo, SUNY Buffalo.
Reference Sharing and Collection Development. William Coscarelli, Univ. of Georgia.

National Association of Government Archives and Records Administrators

Executive Director, Bruce W. Dearstyne
48 Howard St., Albany, NY 12207
518-463-8644, fax 518-463-8656
E-mail nagara@caphill.com
World Wide Web http://www.nagara.org

Object

Founded in 1984, the association is successor to the National Association of State Archives and Records Administrators, which had been established in 1974. NAGARA is a growing nationwide association of local, state, and federal archivists and records administrators, and others interested in improved care and management of government records. NAG-ARA promotes public awareness of government records and archives management programs, encourages interchange of information among government archives and records management agencies, develops and implements professional standards of government records and archival administration, and encourages study and research into records management problems and issues.

Membership

Most NAGARA members are federal, state, and local archival and records management agencies.

Officers

Pres. Roy Turnbaugh, Oregon State Archives; *V.P.* Jeanne Young, Board of Governors of the Federal Reserve System; *Secy.* Gerald G. Newborg, State Historical Society of North Dakota; *Treas.* Jim Berberich, Florida Bureau of Archives and Records Mgt.

Directors

Kent Carter, National Archives and Records Administration, Southwest Region; Diane LeBlanc, National Archives and Records Admin., Northeast Region; L. Elaine Olah, New Mexico Commission on Public Records; David Olson, North Carolina Division of Archives and History; Richard Roberts, City of Hollywood (Florida); Hynda Rudd, City of Los Angeles.

Publications

Clearinghouse (q.; memb.).
Crossroads (q.; memb.).
Government Records Issues (series).
Preservation Needs in State Archives (report).
Program Reporting Guidelines for Government Records Programs.

National Federation of Abstracting and Information Services

Executive Director, Richard T. Kaser
1518 Walnut St., Philadelphia, PA 19102
215-893-1561, fax 215-893-1564
E-mail nfais@nfais.org
World Wide Web http://www.NFAIS.org

Object

NFAIS is an international, not-for-profit membership organization comprising leading information producers, distributors, and corporate users of secondary information. Its purpose is to serve the information community through education, research, and publication. Founded 1958.

Membership

Memb. 50+. Full membership (regular and government) is open to organizations that, as a substantial part of their activity, produce secondary information services for external use. Secondary information products are compilations containing printed or electronic summaries of, or references to, multiple sources of publicly available information. For example, organizations that assemble bibliographic citations, abstracts, indexes, and data are all secondary information services.

Associate membership is available to organizations that operate or manage online information services, in-house information centers, networks, and libraries; conduct research or development work in information science or systems; are otherwise involved in the generation, promotion, or distribution of secondary information products under contract; or publish primary information sources. Members pay dues annually based on the fiscal year of July 1–June 30. Dues are assessed based on the member's revenue derived from information-related activities.

Officers (1999–2000)

Pres. Gladys Cotter; *Past Pres.* James E. Lohr; *Pres.-Elect* Brian Sweet; *Secy.* Timothy Ingoldsby; *Treas.* Marjorie Hlava.

Directors

Brian Earle, Sheldon Kotzin, Jim McGinty, R. Paul Ryan, Michael Tansey, Geoffrey Worton.

Staff

Exec. Dir. Richard T. Kaser; *Asst. Dir.* Marian H. Gloninger; *Office Mgr.* Wendy McMillan; *Customer Service* Margaret Manson.

Publications

Automated Support to Indexing (1992; memb. $50; nonmemb. $75).
Beyond Boolean (1996; memb. $50; nonmemb. $75).
Careers in Electronic Information (1997; memb. $29; nonmemb. $39).
Changing Roles in Information Distribution (1994; memb. $50; nonmemb. $75).
Computer Support to Indexing (1998; memb. $175; nonmemb. $235).
Developing New Markets for Information Products (1993; memb. $50; nonmemb. $75).
Document Delivery in an Electronic Age (1995; memb. $50, nonmemb. $75).
Flexible Workstyles in the Information Industry (1993; memb. $50; nonmemb. $75).
Government Information and Policy: Changing Roles in a New Administration (1994; memb. $50; nonmemb. $75).
Guide to Careers in Abstracting and Indexing (1992; memb. $25; nonmemb. $35).
Guide to Database Distribution, 2nd ed., (1994; memb. $100; nonmemb. $175).
Impacts of Changing Production Technologies (1995; memb. $50, nonmemb. $75).
Metadiversity: The Call for Community (1999; memb./nonmemb. $39).
NFAIS Member Directory and Guide to Leading Information Companies (1996; memb. $25, nonmemb. $35).
NFAIS Newsletter (mo.; North America $120; elsewhere $135).
Partnering in the Information Industry (1996; memb. $50, nonmemb. $75).

National Information Standards Organization

Executive Director, Patricia R. Harris
4733 Bethesda Ave., Suite 300, Bethesda, MD 20814
301-654-2512, fax 301-654-1721
E-mail nisohq@niso.org, World Wide Web http://www.niso.org

Object

To develop technical standards used in libraries, publishing, and information services. Experts from the information field volunteer to lend their expertise in the development and writing of NISO standards. The standards are approved by the consensus of NISO's voting membership, which consists of 70 voting members representing libraries, government, associations, and private businesses and organizations. NISO is supported by its membership and corporate grants. Formerly a committee of the American National Standards Institute (ANSI), NISO, formed in 1939, was incorporated in 1983 as a nonprofit educational organization. NISO is accredited by ANSI and serves as the U.S. Technical Advisory Group to ISO/TC 46.

Membership

Memb. 70. Open to any organization, association, government agency, or company willing to participate in and having substantial concern for the development of NISO standards.

Officers

Chair Donald J. Muccino, Exec. V.P./COO, Online Computer Library Center, 6565 Frantz Rd., Dublin, OH 43017-0702; *Past Chair* Joel H. Baron, Publisher, *New England Journal of Medicine*, 1440 Main St., Waltham, MA 02154; *V.-Chair/Chair-Elect* Beverly P. Lynch, Interim Pres., Center for Research Libs., 6050 S. Kenwood Ave., Chicago, IL 60637-2804; *Exec. Dir./Secy.* Patricia R. Harris, NISO, 4733 Bethesda Ave., Suite 300, Bethesda, MD 20814; *Treas.*

Jan Peterson, V.P., Publisher Relations, RoweCom Inc., 60 Aberdeen Ave., Cambridge, MA 02138.

Publications

Information Standards Quarterly (q.; $80; foreign $120).

NISO published standards are available from NISO Press Fulfillment, Box 451, Annapolis Junction, MD 20701-0451. Tel. 301-362-6904, 877-736-6476 (toll-free), fax 301-206-9789, e-mail nisohq@niso.org.

NISO Press catalogs and the *NISO Annual Report* are available on request.

REFORMA (National Association to Promote Library Services to Latinos and the Spanish-Speaking)

President, Toni Bissessar
Brooklyn Public Library, Multilingual Center,
Grand Army Plaza, Brooklyn, NY 11238
E-mail t.bissessar@brooklynpubliclibrary.org

Object

Promoting library services to the Spanish-speaking for more than 28 years, REFORMA, an ALA affiliate, works in a number of areas: to promote the development of library collections to include Spanish-language and Latino-oriented materials; the recruitment of more bilingual and bicultural professionals and support staff; the development of library services and programs that meet the needs of the Latino community; the establishment of a national network among individuals who share our goals; the education of the U.S. Latino population in regard to the availability and types of library services; and lobbying efforts to preserve existing library resource centers serving the interest of Latinos.

Membership

Memb. 900. Any person who is supportive of the goals and objectives of REFORMA.

Officers

Pres. Toni Bissessar, Brooklyn Public Lib., Grand Army Plaza, Brooklyn, NY 11239. Tel. 718-230-2750, fax 718-230-6798, e-mail tbissessar@brooklynpubliclibrary.org; *V.P./Pres.-Elect* Oralia Garza de Cortéz, 1901 Running Brook Dr., Austin, TX 78723. E-mail odgc@aol.com; *Past Pres.* Jacqueline Ayala, Box 88756, Los Angeles, CA 90009-8756. Tel. 310-282-6279, fax 310-827-9187, e-mail jayala@earthlink.net; *Treas.* Alex Villagran, 2800 Keller Dr., No. 158, Tustin, CA 92680. Tel. 714-838-7834, e-mail alexandervillagran@hotmail.com; *Secy.* Derrie Perez, USF Tampa Campus Lib., 4202 E. Fowler Ave., LIB 122, Tampa, FL 33620-5400. Tel. 813-974-1642, fax 813-974-5153, e-mail dperez@lib.usf.edu; *Newsletter Ed.* Denice Adkins; *Archivist* Sal Guerena; *Membership Coordinator* Al Milo.

Publications

REFORMA Newsletter (q.; memb.). *Ed.* Denice Adkins, Byers Branch Lib., 675 Santa Fe Dr., Denver, CO 80204. Tel. 303-571-1665, e-mail Denice@u.arizona.edu.

Committees

Pura Belpré Award. Yolanda Bonitch.
Children's and Young Adult Service. Pamela Martin-Diaz.
Education. Camila Alire.
Finance. Jacqueline Ayala.
Fund Raising. Toni Bissessar.
Information Technology. Isabel Espinal, Carlos Rodriguez.

Librarian-of-the-Year Award. Verla Peterson.
Nominations. Ben Ocon.
Organizational Development. Paola Ferate.
Public Relations. Brigida A. Campos.
RNC II (National Conference). Susana Hinojosa.
Scholarship. Ninfa Trejo.

Meetings

General membership and board meetings take place at the American Library Association's Midwinter Meeting and Annual Conference. The second REFORMA National Conference will take place Aug. 3–6, 2000, in Tucson, Arizona.

Research Libraries Group

Manager of Corporate Communications, Jennifer Hartzell
1200 Villa St., Mountain View, CA 94041-1100
650-691-2207, fax 650-964-0943
E-mail jlh@notes.rlg.org, World Wide Web http://www.rlg.org

Object

The Research Libraries Group, Inc. (RLG) is a not-for-profit membership corporation of approximately 160 universities, archives, historical societies, national libraries, and other institutions devoted to improving access to information that supports research and learning. RLG exists to support its members in containing costs, improving local services, and contributing to international collective access to scholarly materials. For its members, RLG develops and operates cooperative programs to manage, preserve, and extend access to research library, museum, and archival holdings. For both its members and for nonmember institutions and individuals worldwide, RLG develops and operates databases and software to serve an array of information access and management needs. RLG's main classes of information, available over the Web, are Library Resources (international union catalogs), Citation Resources (article-

and chapter-level data), Archival Resources (full-text finding aids and archival collections cataloging), and Museum/Cultural Resources (exemplified by the AMICO Library of high-quality art images and descriptions from the Art Museum Image Consortium. RLG also provides PC-based document transmission and interlibrary loan software for use over the Web: Ariel and ILL Manager. CitaDel, Eureka, Marcadia, RLIN, and Zephyr are registered trademarks of the Research Libraries Group, Inc. Ariel is a registered trademark of the Ariel Corporation used by RLG under license.

Membership

Memb. c. 160. Membership is open to any nonprofit institution with an educational, cultural, or scientific mission. There are two membership categories: general and special. General members are institutions that serve a clientele of more than 5,000 faculty, academic staff, research staff, professional staff, students, fellows, or members. Special members serve a similar clientele of 5,000 or fewer.

Directors

RLG has a 19-member board of directors, comprising 12 directors elected from and by RLG's member institutions, up to six at-large directors elected by the board itself, and the president. Theirs is the overall responsibility for the organization's governance and for ensuring that it faithfully fulfills its purpose and goals. Annual board elections are held in the spring. In 2000 the board's chair is Reg Carr, director of university library services and Bodley's Librarian at Oxford University. For a current list of directors, see the Web site http://www.rlg.org/boardbio.html.

Staff

Pres. James Michalko; *V.P.* John W. Haeger; *Dir., Integrated Information Services* Susan Yoder; *Dir., Member Programs and Initiatives* Linda West; *Dir., Customer and Operations Support* Jack Grantham; *Dir., Computer Development* David Richards; *Dir., Finance and Administration* John Sundell.

Publications

Research Libraries Group News (2 per year; 20-page news magazine).

RLG DigiNews (bi-m.; Web-based newsletter to help keep pace with preservation uses of digitization).

RLG Focus (bi-m.; eight-page user services newsletter).

For informational, research, and user publications, see the Web site http://www.rlg.org/pub.html, or contact RLG.

Society for Scholarly Publishing

Executive Directors, Francine Butler, Jerry Bowman
10200 W. 44 Ave., Suite 304, Wheat Ridge, CO 80033
303-422-3914, fax 303-422-8894
E-mail ssp@resourcenter.com

Object

To draw together individuals involved in the process of scholarly publishing. This process requires successful interaction of the many functions performed within the scholarly community. The Society for Scholarly Publishing (SSP) provides the leadership for such interaction by creating opportunities for the exchange of information and opinions among scholars, editors, publishers, librarians, printers, booksellers, and all others engaged in scholarly publishing.

Membership

Memb. 900. Open to all with an interest in the scholarly publishing process and dissemination of information. There are four categories of membership: individual ($85), con-

tributing ($500), sustaining ($1,000), and sponsoring ($1,500). Year. Jan. 1–Dec. 31.

Executive Committee (1999–2000)

Pres. Kathleen Case, American College of Physicians, 190 N. Independence Mall W., Philadelphia, PA 19106; *Past Pres.* Frederick Bowes, III, Bowes & Assoc., Box 1637, Buxbury, MA 02331-1637; *Secy.-Treas.* Ray Fastiggi, Rockefeller Univ. Press.

Meetings

An annual meeting is conducted in June. The location changes each year. Additionally, SSP conducts several seminars throughout the year.

Society of American Archivists

Executive Director, Susan E. Fox
527 S. Wells St., Fifth fl., Chicago, IL 60607
312-922-0140, fax 312-347-1452
World Wide Web http://www.archivists.org

Object

To promote sound principles of archival economy and to facilitate cooperation among archivists and archival agencies. Founded 1936.

Membership

Memb. 3,400. Dues (Indiv.) $70–$170, graduated according to salary; (Assoc.) $70, domestic; (Student) $40; (Inst.) $225; (Sustaining) $440.

Officers (1999–2000)

Pres. Thomas Hickerson; *V.P.* Leon Stout; *Treas.* Robert Sink.

Council

Dennis Harrison, Fynnette Eaton, Karen Jefferson, Jan Kenamore, Richard Pearce-Moses, Helen Tibbo, Becky Tousey, Wilda Logan Willis.

Staff

Exec. Dir. Susan E. Fox; *Meetings/Memb. Coord.* Bernice E. Brack; *Publications Dir.* Teresa Brinati; *Publications Asst.* Troy Sturdivant; *Dir. of Finance* Carroll Dendler; *Interim Educ. Dir.* Reneta Webb.

Publications

American Archivist (q.; $85; foreign $90). *Ed.* Philip Eppard; *Managing Ed.* Teresa Brinati. Books for review and related correspondence should be addressed to the managing editor.
Archival Outlook (bi-m.; memb.). *Ed.* Teresa Brinati.

Software and Information Industry Association

1730 M St. N.W., Suite 700, Washington, DC 20036-4510
202-452-1600, fax 202-223-8756
World Wide Web http://www.siia.net

Membership

Memb. 1,200 companies. Formed January 1, 1999, through the merger of the Software Publishers Association (SPA) and the Information Industry Association (IIA). Open to companies involved in the creation, distribution, and use of software information products, services, and technologies. For details on membership and dues, see the SIIA Web site.

Staff

Pres. Kenneth Wasch; *Exec. V.P.* Lauren Looney-Hall.

Board of Directors

Robert E. Aber, NASDAQ; Mauro Ballabeni, MicroBusiness Italiana SRL; Graham Beachum, II, Axtive Software Corp.; Barbara Bellissimo, Privada, Inc.; Herb Brinberg, Parnassus Associates International; Dorothea Coccoli Palsho, Dow Jones & Co.; James E. Coane, N2K, Inc.; Dan Cooperman, Oracle Corp.; Terry Crane, Jostens Learning Corp.; Glenn Goldberg, McGraw-Hill Cos.; Brian Hall, West Group, representing Thomson Corp.; Bob Herbold, Microsoft Corp.; Kathy Hurley, NetSchools Corp.; Gail Littlejohn, LEXIS-NEXIS, representing Reed Elsevier, Inc.; Michael Morris, Sun Microsystems, Inc.; Joel Ronning, Digital River; David W. Turner, Reuters America Holdings, Inc.; Ron Verni, Peachtree Software; Kent Walker, Netscape/AOL; Mark Walsh, VerticalNet, Inc.; Ken Wasch, SIIA.

Special Libraries Association

Executive Director, David R. Bender
1700 18th St. N.W., Washington, DC 20009-2514
202-234-4700, fax 202-265-9317
E-mail sla@sla.org, World Wide Web http://www.sla.org

Object

To advance the leadership role of special librarians in putting knowledge to work in the information and knowledge-based society. The association offers myriad programs and services designed to help its members serve their customers more effectively and succeed in an increasingly challenging environment of information management and technology.

Membership

Memb. 14,500. Dues (Sustaining) $500; (Indiv.) $125; (Student) $35. Year. July–June.

Officers (July 1999–June 2000)

Pres. Susan S. DiMattia; *Pres.-Elect* Donna Scheeder; *Past Pres.* L. Susan Hayes; *Treas.* Richard Wallace; *Chapter Cabinet Chair* Sandy Spurlock; *Chapter Cabinet Chair-Elect* Juanita Richardson; *Div. Cabinet Chair* Joan E. Gervino; *Div. Chapter Chair-Elect* Doris Helfer; *Secy.* Cynthia V. Hill.

Directors

Officers; G. Lynn Berard (2002), Monica M. Ertel (2000), Sandy Moltz (2001), Mary "Dottie" Moon (2002), Wilda B. Newman (2001).

Publications

Information Outlook (mo.) (memb., nonmemb. $65/yr.). *Ed.* Susan Broughton.

Committee Chairpersons

Association Office Operations. Susan DiMattia.
Awards and Honors. Judith J. Field.
Bylaws. Betty Eddison.
Cataloging. Marcia Lei Zeng.
Committees. Jim Tchobanoff.
Conference Plan (2001). Denise Chochrek.
Consultation Service. Barbara Best-Nichols.
Diversity Leadership Development. Andrea Greer.
Finance. Dick Wallace.
Government Affairs/Intellectual Property. David Shumaker.
International Relations. Marydee Ojala.
Networking. Gail Stahl.
Nominating, 2001 Election. Lois Weinstein.
Professional Development. Robert Bellanti.
Public Relations. Ty Webb.
Research. Sharyn Ladner.
SLA Endowment Fund Grants. Karen Holloway.
SLA Scholarship. Larry Walton.
Strategic Planning. Sandy Moltz.
Student and Academic Relations. Barbara Arnold.
Technical Standards. Marje Hlava.

Theatre Library Association

c/o The Shubert Archive, 149 W. 45 St., New York, NY 10036
212-944-3895, fax 212-944-4139
World Wide Web
http://www.brown.edu/Facilities/University_Library/beyond/TLA/TLA.html

Object

To further the interests of collecting, preserving, and using theater, cinema, and performing-arts materials in libraries, museums, and private collections. Founded 1937.

Membership

Memb. 500. Dues (Indiv./Inst.) $30. Year. Jan. 1–Dec. 31.

Officers

Pres. Susan Brady, Yale Univ.; *V.P.* Ken Winkler, New York Lib. for the Performing Arts; *Exec. Secy.* Maryann Chach, Shubert Archive; *Treas.* Paul Newman, private collector.

Executive Board

Pamela Bloom, Nena Couch, Camille Croce Dee, B. Donald Grose, Mary Ann Jensen, Stephen B. Johnson, Brigitte J. Kueppers, Martha S. LoMonaco, Melissa M. Miller, Susan L. Peters, Jason Rubin, Joseph M. Yranski; *Ex officio* Madeleine Nichols, Nancy L. Stokes; *Honorary* Paul Myers; *Historian* Louis A. Rachow.

Publications

Broadside (q.; memb.). *Ed.* Nancy L. Stokes.
Performing Arts Resources (occasional; memb.).

Committee Chairpersons

Awards. Richard Wall.
Membership. Maryann Chach, Paul Newman.
Nominations. To be appointed.
Program and Special Events. Kevin Winkler.

Urban Libraries Council

President, Eleanor Jo Rodger
1603 Orrington Ave., Suite 1080, Evanston, IL 60201
847-866-9999, fax 847-866-9989
E-mail info@urbanlibraries.org, World Wide Web http://www.clpgh.org/ulc/

Object

To identify and make known the problems relating to urban libraries serving cities of 50,000 or more individuals, located in a Standard Metropolitan Statistical Area; to provide information on state and federal legislation affecting urban library programs and systems; to facilitate the exchange of ideas and programs of member libraries and other libraries; to develop programs that enable libraries to act as a focus of community development and to supply the informational needs of the new urban populations; to conduct research and educational programs that will benefit urban libraries and to solicit and accept grants, contributions, and donations essential to their implementation.

ULC currently receives most of its funding from membership dues. Future projects will involve the solicitation of grant funding. ULC is a 501(c)(3) not-for-profit corporation based in the state of Illinois.

Membership

Membership is open to public libraries serving populations of 50,000 or more located in a Standard Metropolitan Statistical Area and to corporations specializing in library-related materials and services. Dues are based on the size of the organization's operating budget, according to the following schedule: under $2 million to $10 million, $3,000; over $10 million, $5,000. In addition, ULC member libraries may choose Sustaining or Contributing status (Sustaining, $12,000; Contributing, $7,000).

Officers (1999–2000)

Chair Susan Kent, Los Angeles Public Lib., 630 W. Fifth St., Los Angeles, CA 90071. Tel. 213-228-7516, fax 213-228-7519, e-mail skent@lapl.org; *V.-Chair/Chair-Elect* Elliot Shelkrot, Free Lib. of Philadelphia, 1901 Vine St., Philadelphia, PA 19103-1189. Tel. 215-686-5300, fax 215-686-5368, e-mail shelkrote@Library.Phila.Gov; *Secy./Treas.* Betty Jane Narver, Inst. for Public Policy Mgt., Univ. of Washington, 324 Parrington Hall, Box 353060, Seattle, WA 98195-3060. Tel. 205-543-0190, fax 205-616-5769, e-mail bjnarver@u.washington.edu; *Past Pres.* Andrew Blau, John and Mary Markle Foundation, 75 Rockefeller Plaza, Suite 1800, New York, NY 10019. Tel. 212-489-6655, fax 212-765-9690, e-mail andrew_blau@markle.org.

Officers serve one-year terms, members of the executive board two-year terms. New officers are elected and take office at the summer annual meeting of the council.

Executive Board

Dan Bradbury. E-mail dan@kcpl.lib.mo.us; Don Estes. E-mail dbestes@aol.com; Jim H. Fish. E-mail jfish@mail.bcpl.net; Diane Frankel. E-mail dfrankel@irvine.org; Toni Garvey. E-mail tgarvey@ci.phoenix.az.us; Frances Hunter. E-mail fran@wolf.csuohio.edu; Marilyn Jackson; Virginia M. "Jenny" McCurdy. E-mail jenny.mccurdy@gbhcs.org; Donna Nicely. E-mail donna_nicely@metro.nashville.org; Eleanor Jo "Joey" Rodger. E-mail ejr@urbanlibraries.org; Dianne L. Sautter. E-mail diannes@chichildresmuseum.org; Pamela J. Seigle. E-mail pseigle@wellesley.edu; Marsha L. Steinhardt. E-mail msteinha@courts.state.ny.us.

Key Staff

Pres. Eleanor Jo Rodger; *V.P., Admin./Memb. Services* Bridget A. Bradley; *Project Dir.* Elaine Meyers.

Publications

Frequent Fast Facts Surveys: *Fees Survey Results* (1993); *Staffing Survey Results* (1993); *Collection Development Survey Results* (1994); *Security Survey Results* (1994); *Public Libraries and Private Fund Raising: Opportunities and Issues* (1994); *Off-Site Survey Results* (1995); *Governance and Funding of Urban Public Libraries Survey Results* (1997); *Outsourcing in Metropolitan Libraries* (1998); *MLS Supply and Demand* (1999).

State, Provincial, and Regional Library Associations

The associations in this section are organized under three headings: United States, Canada, and Regional. Both the United States and Canada are represented under Regional associations.

United States

Alabama

Memb. 1,200. Term of Office. Apr. 1999–Apr. 2000. Publication. *The Alabama Librarian* (q.).

Pres. Janice Franklin, Levi Watkins Learning Center, Alabama State Univ., Montgomery. Tel. 334-229-4106, fax 334-229-4940, e-mail franlin@asunet.alasu.edu; *Pres.-Elect* Rebecca Buckner, Gadsden Public Lib., Gadsden. Tel. 256-549-4791, fax 256-549-4766, e-mail gpl@gadsden.com; *Secy.* Jean Thomason, Samford University Lib., Birmingham. Tel. 205-726-2198, fax 205-726-4009; *Treas.* Dallas Baillio, Mobile Public Lib., Mobile. Tel. 334-434-7100, fax 334-208-5865; *Exec. Dir.* Missy Mathis, 400 S. Union St., Suite 140, Montgomery 36104. Tel. 334-262-5210, fax 334-262-5255, e-mail allaonline@mindspring.com. Organization World Wide Web site http://alala.home.mindspring.com/.

Address correspondence to the executive director.

Alaska

Memb. 403. Publication. *Newspoke* (bi-mo.).

Pres. William H. Smith. E-mail whsakla@yahoo.com; *V.P.* Mary H. "Moe" McGee. E-mail mcgeemh@ci.anchorage.ak.us; *Secy.* Patience Frederiksen. E-mail Patience_Frederiksen@eed.state.ak.us; *Treas.* Debbie Kalvez. E-mail ffdhk@auroura.alaska.edu; *Exec. Secy.* Bob Anderl. E-mail boba@muskox.alaska.edu.

Address correspondence to the secretary, Alaska Library Association, Box 81084, Fairbanks 99708. Fax 907-479-4784, e-mail akla@alaska.net, World Wide Web http://www.alaska.net/~akla/.

Arizona

Memb. 1,200. Term of Office. Nov. 1999–Dec. 2000. Publication. *AzLA Newsletter* (mo.). Articles for the newsletter should be sent to the attention of the newsletter editor.

Pres. Chris Cole, Maricopa County Lib. District, 17811 N. 32 St., Phoenix 85032. Tel. 602-506-2958, fax 602-506-4689, e-mail chriscole@mail.maricopa.gov; *Treas.* Carol Damaso, Mustang Lib., 10101 N. 90 St., Scottsdale 85258. Tel. 480-312-6031, fax 480-312-6094, e-mail cdamaso@ci.scottsdale.az.us; *Exec. Secy.* Jean Johnson, 14449 N. 73 St., Scottsdale 85260-3133. Tel. 480-998-1954, fax 480-998-7838, e-mail meetmore@aol.com.

Address correspondence to the executive secretary.

Arkansas

Memb. 603. Term of Office. Jan.–Dec. 2000. Publication. *Arkansas Libraries* (bi-mo.).

Pres. Carolyn Ashcroft, Arkansas State Lib., 1 Capitol Mall, Little Rock 72201. Tel. 501-682-5288, fax 501-682-1693; *Exec. Dir.* Jennifer Coleman, Arkansas Lib. Assn., 9 Shackleford Plaza, Suite 1, Little Rock 72211. Tel. 501-228-0775, fax 501-228-5535. Organization World Wide Web site http://pw1.netcom.com/~ronruss/arla3.html.

Address correspondence to the executive director.

California

Memb. 2,500. Term of Office. Nov. 1999–Nov. 2000. Publication. *California Libraries* (mo., except July/Aug., Nov./Dec.).

Pres. Linda Crowe; *V.P./Pres.-Elect* Cindy Mediavilla; *Exec. Dir.* Susan E. Negreen, California Lib. Assn., 717 K St., Suite 300,

Sacramento 95814. Tel. 916-447-8541, fax 916-447-8394, e-mail info@cla-net.org. Organization World Wide Web site http://www.cla-net.org.

Address correspondence to the executive director.

Colorado

Memb. 1,100. Term of Office. Oct. 1999–Oct. 2000. Publication. *Colorado Libraries* (q.). *Ed.* Nancy Carter, Univ. of Colorado, Campus Box 184, Boulder 80309.

Pres. Eloise May, Arapahoe Lib. District, 2305 E. Arapahoe Rd., No. 112, Littleton 80122-1583. Tel. 303-798-2444, e-mail emay@ald.lib.co.us; *V.P./Pres.-Elect* Tom Fry, Univ. of Denver Penrose Lib., 2150 E. Evans Ave., Denver 80208. Tel. 303-871-3418, fax 303-871-2290, e-mail tfry@du.edu; *Treas.* George Jaramillo, Univ. of Northern Colorado, Greeley 80634. E-mail gjaramil@unco.edu; *Office Mgr.* Roberta Lindvall-Selinsky.

Address correspondence to the office manager, 4350 Wadsworth Blvd., Suite 340, Wheat Ridge 80033. Tel. 303-463-6400, fax 303-431-9752, e-mail officemanager@cla-web.org, World Wide Web http://www.cla-web.org/.

Connecticut

Memb. 1,100. Term of Office. July 1999–June 2000. Publication *Connecticut Libraries* (11 per year). *Ed.* David Kapp, 4 Llynwood Dr., Bolton 06040. Tel. 203-647-0697.

Pres. Michael Golrick, Southern Connecticut Lib. Council, 2911 Dixwell Ave., Hamden 06518-3130. Tel. 203-288-5757; *V.P./Pres.-Elect* Jay Johnston, Welles Turner Memorial Lib., Glastonbury. Tel. 860-652-7719; *Treas.* Nora Bird, Gateway Community Technical College, North Haven 06473. Tel. 203-789-7064; *Administrator* Karen Zoller, Connecticut Lib. Assn., Box 85, Willimantic 06226. Tel. 860-465-5006, e-mail kzoller@cla.lib.ct.us. Organization World Wide Web site http://www.lib.uconn.edu/cla/.

Address correspondence to the administrator.

Delaware

Memb. 300. Term of Office. Apr. 1999–Apr. 2000. Publication *DLA Bulletin* (3 per year).

Pres. Pat Birchenall, Appoquinimink Community Lib., 118 Silver Lake Rd., Middleton 19709. Tel. 302-378-5290, fax 302-378-5293, e-mail birchenall@tipcat.dtcc.edu; *V.P./Pres.-Elect* Janet Chin, Hockessin Public Lib., 1023 Valley Rd., Hockessin 19707. Tel. 302-239-5106, fax 302-239-1519, e-mail chin@tipcat.lib.de.us.

Address correspondence to the association, Box 816, Dover 19903-0816.

District of Columbia

Memb. 600. Term of Office. Aug. 1999–Aug. 2000. Publication *CAPCON Alert* (mo.).

Pres. Betty Landesman. Tel. 202-434-6224, fax 202-434-6408, e-mail blandesman@aarp.org; *V.P./Pres.-Elect* Judy Solberg. Tel. 202-994-6304, fax 202-994-5154, e-mail judys@gwu.edu; *Secy.* Betty Nibley. Tel. 202-885-3843, fax 202-885-1317, e-mail enibley@american.edu; *Treas.* Cathy Zeljak. Tel. 202-994-0124, fax 202-994-7845, e-mail czeljak@gwu.edu.

Address correspondence to the association, 1990 M St. N.W., Suite 200, Washington 20036. Organization World Wide Web site http://www.dcla.org/.

Florida

Memb. (Indiv.) 1,400; (In-state Inst.) 93. Term of Office. July 1999–June 2000. Publication. *Florida Libraries* (bi-ann.).

Pres. Madison Mosley, Jr., Dana Law Lib., Stetson College of Law, 1401 61st St. S., St. Petersburg 33733. Tel 727-562-7827, fax 727-345-8973, e-mail mosley@law.stetson.edu; *V.P./Pres.-Elect* Mary A. Brown, Lib. Dir., St. Petersburg Public Lib., St. Petersburg 33701. Tel. 727-893-7736, fax 727-822-6828, e-mail brownma@splib.lib.fl.us; *Secy.* Suzanne E. Holler, Lib., Univ. of Central Florida, Box 162430, Orlando 32816-2666. Tel. 407-823-5026, fax 407-823-5865, e-mail s-holler@pegasus.cc.ucf.edu; *Treas.* Ruth O'Donnell, 3509 Trillium Ct., Tallahassee 32312. Tel. 850-668-6911, fax 850-894-

5652, e-mail odonnellr@worldnet.att.net; *Exec. Secy.* Marjorie Stealey, Florida Lib. Assn., 1133 W. Morse Blvd., Winter Park 32789. Tel. 407-647-8839, fax 407-629-2502, e-mail mjs@crowsegal.com. Organization World Wide Web site http://www.flalib.org/.

Address correspondence to the executive secretary.

Georgia

Memb. 950. Term of Office. Oct. 1999–Oct. 2000. Publication *Georgia Library Quarterly*. *Ed.* Susan Cooley, Sara Hightower Regional Lib., 203 Riverside Pkwy., Rome 30161. Tel. 706-236-4621.

Pres. Michael Seigler, Dir., Smyrna Public Lib., 100 Village Green Circle, Smyrna 30080-3478. Tel. 770-431-2860, fax 770-431-2862, e-mail mseigler@bellsouth.net; *1st V.P./Pres.-Elect* Grace McLeod, Technical Services Libn., Chattahoochee Technical Inst., 980 S. Cobb Dr. S.E., Marietta 30060-3398. Tel. 770-528-4536, fax 770-528-4454, e-mail emcleod@chat-tec.com; *2nd V.P.* Deborah Manget, Dir., Conyers-Rockdale Lib. System, 864 Green St., Conyers 30012. Tel. 770-388-5041, fax 770-388-5043, e-mail manget@mail.rockdale.public.lib.ga.us; *Secy.* Gayle Christian, Reference, Documents, and Maps Libn., Georgia State Univ., Pullen Lib., 100 Decatur St. S.E., Atlanta 30303. Tel. 404-651-2185, fax 404-651-2476, e-mail gchristian@gsu.edu; *Treas.* Gordon Baker, Media Center Dir., Eagle's Landing H.S., 301 Tunis Rd., McDonough 30253. Tel. 770-954-9515, fax 770-914-9789, e-mail GordonBaker@mail.clayton.edu; *Past Pres.* Ann Hamilton, Assoc. Univ. Libn., Zach S. Henderson Lib., Georgia Southern Univ., Box 8074, Statesboro 30460-8074. Tel. 912-681-5115, fax 912-681-0093, e-mail ahamilton@gasou.edu; *ALA Councillor* Ralph E. Russell, 8160 Willow Tree Way, Alpharetta 30202. E-mail r1933@mindspring.com.

Address correspondence to the president. Organization World Wide Web site http://wwwlib.gsu.edu/gla/.

Hawaii

Memb. 250. Publications. *HLA Newsletter* (q.); *HLA Membership Directory* (ann.).

Pres. Dave Brier.

Address correspondence to the association, Box 4441, Honolulu 96812-4441. Tel. 808-956-2746, fax 808-956-2750.

Idaho

Memb. 500. Term of Office. Oct. 1999–Oct. 2000. Publication *Idaho Librarian* (q.). *Ed.* Christine DeZelar-Tiedman, Univ. of Idaho Lib., Moscow 83844-2350. Tel. 208-885-2509, e-mail chrisd@belle.lib.uidaho.edu.

Pres. Ron Force, Univ. of Idaho Lib., Moscow 83844. Tel. 208-885-6534, e-mail rforce@uidaho.edu; *1st V.P.* Larry Almeida, 8148 Marabou Dr., Hayden 83835. Tel. 208-772-5612; *Treas.* Sandi Shropshire, F. M. Oboler Lib., Idaho State Univ., Box 8089, Pocatello 83209. Tel. 208-236-2671.

Address correspondence to the president. Organization World Wide Web site http://www.idaholibraries.org/.

Illinois

Memb. 3,000. Term of Office. July 1999–July 2000. Publication *ILA Reporter* (bi-mo.).

Pres. Carolyn Anthony, Skokie Public Lib., 5215 Oakton St., Skokie 60077-3680. Tel. 847-673-7774 ext. 2130, fax 847-673-7797, e-mail anthc@skokie.lib.il.us; *V.P./Pres. Elect* Denise M. Zielinski, Helen M. Plum Memorial Lib., 110 W. Maple St., Lombard 60148-2514. Tel. 630-627-0316, fax 630-627-0336, e-mail dzielins@plum.lib.il.us; *Treas.* Jack Hurwitz, Hinsdale Public Lib., 20 E. Maple St., Hinsdale 60521-3432. Tel. 630-986-1976, fax 630-986-9720, e-mail hurwitzj@sls.lib.il.us or jhurwitz@hinsdale.lib.il.us; *Past Pres.* Pamela Gaitskill, Prairie State College, 202 S. Halsted St., Chicago Heights 60411-8226. Tel. 708-709-3551, fax 708-709-3940, e-mail pgaitskill@prairie.cc.il.us *Exec. Dir.* Robert P. Doyle, 33 W. Grand Ave., Suite 301, Chicago 60610-4306. Tel. 312-644-1896, fax 312-644-1899, e-mail doyle@ila.org. Organization World Wide Web site http://www.ila.org.

Address correspondence to the executive director.

Indiana

Memb. (Indiv.) 4,000; (Inst.) 300. Term of Office. March 2000–April 2001. Publications. *Focus on Indiana Libraries* (11 per year), *Indiana Libraries* (s. ann.). *Ed.* Patricia Tallman.

Pres. Cheryl Blevens, Vigo County Public Lib., Plaza North Branch, 1800 E. Fort Harrison, No. 5, Terre Haute 47804-1492. Tel. 812-232-1113 ext. 302, fax 812-478-9504, e-mail cblevens@vigo.lib.in.us; *1st V.P.* Connie Patsiner, Indiana Visual & Audio Network, 6201 LaPas Trail, No. 280, Indianapolis 46268. Tel./fax 317-329-9163, e-mail iaudio@indy.net; *Secy.* Sara Anne Hook, IUPUI, 355 N. Lansing St., Administration Bldg., Indianapolis 46202. Tel. 317-274-3391, fax 317-278-0695, e-mail sahook @iupui.edu; *Treas.* John M. Robson, Rose-Hulman Inst. of Technology, 5500 Wabash Ave., Terre Haute 47803. Tel. 812-877-8365, fax 812-877-8175, e-mail john.robson@ rose-hulman.edu; *Past Pres.* Patricia Kantner, Purdue Univ. Libs., 1534 Stewart Center, Rm. 372, West Lafayette 47907-1534. Tel. 765-494-2812, fax 765-494-0156, e-mail kantner@purdue.edu.

Address correspondence to the Indiana Lib. Federation, 6408 Carrolton Ave., Indianapolis 46220. Tel. 317-257-2040, fax 317-257-1389, e-mail ilf@indy.net. Organization World Wide Web site http://www.ilfonline. org/.

Iowa

Memb. 1,700. Term of Office. Jan.–Dec. Publication *The Catalyst* (bi-mo.). *Ed.* Naomi Stovall.

Pres. Carol French Johnson, Cedar Falls Public Lib., 524 Main, Cedar Falls 50613. E-mail johnson@iren.net; *V.P.* Robin Martin, Central College Lib., 812 University, Pella 50219. E-mail martinr@central.edu.

Address correspondence to the association, 505 Fifth Ave., Suite 823, Des Moines 50309. Tel. 515-243-2172, fax 515-243-0614, e-mail ialib@mcleoduse.net or ila@ iren.net. Organization World Wide Web site http://www.iren.net/ila/web/.

Kansas

Memb. 1,200. Term of Office. July 1999– June 2000. Publications *KLA Newsletter* (q.); *KLA Membership Directory* (ann.).

Pres. Nancy Soldner, Hutchinson Public Schools, Box 1908, Hutchinson 67504. Tel. 316-665-4434, fax 316-665-4497, e-mail soldner@southwind.net; *1st V.P.* John Stratton, Wallerstedt Lib., Bethany College, 235 E. Swenson, Lindsborg 67456. Tel. 785-227-3380 ext. 8342, fax 785-227-3380, e-mail strattonj@bethany.bethanylb.edu; *Exec. Secy.* Leroy Gattin, South Central Kansas Lib. System, 901 N. Main St., Hutchinson 67501. Tel. 316-663-5441 ext. 110, fax 316-663-9506, e-mail lgatt@hplsck.org; *Secy.* Judith Edelstein, Manhattan Public Lib., 629 Poyntz Ave., Manhattan 66502. Tel. 316-283-2890, fax 316-283-2916; *Treas.* Marcella Kille, Hutchinson Public Lib., 901 N. Main St., Hutchinson 67501. Tel. 316-663-5441. Organization World Wide Web site http:// skyways.lib.ks.us/KLA/.

Address correspondence to the executive secretary.

Kentucky

Memb. 1,900. Term of Office. Oct. 1999– Oct. 2000. Publication *Kentucky Libraries* (q.).

Pres. Carolyn Tassie, Transylvania Univ. Lib., Lexington 40508. Tel. 606-233-8225, fax 606-233-8779, e-mail ctassie@mail. transy.edu; *V.P./Pres.-Elect* Judith Burdine, Pulaski County Public Lib., Somerset 42501. Tel. 606-679-8401, fax 606-679-1779, e-mail jburdine@hyperaction.net; *Secy.* Margarette Morris. Tel. 606-353-7344, e-mail mmorris@ eastky.net; *Exec. Secy.* Tom Underwood, 1501 Twilight Trail, Frankfort 40601. Tel. 502-223-5322, fax 502-223-4937, e-mail kylibasn@mis.net. Organization World Wide Web site http://www.kylibasn.org/.

Address correspondence to the executive secretary.

Louisiana

Memb. (Indiv.) 1,500; (Inst.) 60. Term of Office. July 1999–June 2000. Publication. *LLA Bulletin* (q.). *Ed*. Mary Cosper Le Boeuf, 424 Roussell St., Houma 70360. Tel. 504-876-5861, fax 504-876-5864, e-mail ter @pelican.state.lib.la.us.

Pres. Paige LeBeau. Tel. 318-475-8798, fax 318-475-8806, e-mail paige@grok. calcasieu.lib.la.us; *1st V.P./Pres.-Elect* David Duggar. Tel. 318-675-5472, fax 318-675-5442, e-mail ddugga@lsumc.edu; *2nd V.P*. Sharilynn Aucoin. Tel. 225-342-9714, e-mail Saucoin@pelican.state.lib.la.us; *Secy*. Beverly Laughlin. Tel. 318-261-5793, e-mail maclachlan@aol.com; *Past Pres*. Idella Washington. Tel. 504-896-4028, fax 504-367-8429, e-mail IDEWASH@prodigy.net; *Exec. Secy*. Christy Chandler.

Address correspondence to the association, Box 3058, Baton Rouge 70821. Tel. 225-342 4928, fax 225-342-3547, e-mail lla@ pelican.state.lib.la.us. Organization World Wide Web site http://www.leeric.lsu.edu/lla/.

Maine

Memb. 900. Term of Office. (Pres., V.P.) spring 1998–spring 2000. Publications. *Maine Entry* (q.); *Maine Memo* (mo.).

Pres. Elizabeth Moran, Camden Public Lib., Camden 04843. Tel. 207-236-3440, e-mail emoran@camden.lib.me.us; *V.P*. Jay Scherma, Thomas Memorial Lib., 6 Scott Dyer Rd., Cape Elizabeth. Tel. 207-799-1720, e-mail jscherma@thomas.lib.me.us; *Secy*. Elizabeth Breault, Abbott Memorial Lib., 1 Church St., Dexter 14930. Tel. 207-924-7292; *Treas*. Robert Filgate, McArthur Public Lib., Biddeford 04005. Tel. 207-284-4181.

Address correspondence to the association, 60 Community Dr., Augusta 04330. Tel. 207-623-8428, fax 207-626-5947. Organization World Wide Web site http://mainelibraries. org/.

Maryland

Memb. 1,300. Term of Office. July 1999– July 2000. Publications. *Happenings* (mo.), *The Crab* (q.).

Pres. Mary Baykan, Washington County Free Lib., 100 S. Potomac St., Hagerstown 21740. Tel. 301-739-3250, fax 301-739-5839; *Exec. Dir*. Margaret Carty.

Address correspondence to the association, 400 Cathedral St., Baltimore 21201-4401. Tel. 410-727-7422, fax 410-625-9594, e-mail mla@mdlib.log. Organization World Wide Web site http://mdlib.org/.

Massachusetts

Memb. (Indiv.) 950; (Inst.) 100. Term of Office. July 1999–June 2000. Publication. *Bay State Libraries* (10 per year).

Pres. Molly Fogarty, Springfield City Lib., 220 State St., Springfield 01103-1772. Tel. 413-263-6800, fax 413-263-6825, e-mail lfogarty@spfldlibmus.org; *V.P./Pres.-Elect* Christine Kardokas, Worcester Public Lib., 3 Salem Sq., Worcester 01608-2074. Tel. 508-799-1726, fax 508-799-1652, e-mail ckardoka@cwmarsmail.cwmars.org; *Secy*. Marjorie Oakes, Reuben Hoar Lib., 41 Shattuck St., Littleton 01460. Tel. 978-486-4046, fax 978-952-2323, e-mail oakes@mvlc.lib. ma.us; *Treas*. Patricia T. Cramer, Westfield Athenaeum, 6 Elm St., Westfield 01085-2997. Tel. 413-568-7833, fax 413-568-1558; *Exec. Secy*. Barry Blaisdell, Massachusetts Lib. Assn., Countryside Offices, 707 Turnpike St., North Andover 01845. Tel. 508-686-8543, fax 508-685-9410, e-mail info@ masslib.org. Organization World Wide Web site http://www.masslib.org/.

Address correspondence to the executive secretary.

Michigan

Memb. (Indiv.) 2,200; (Inst.) 375. Term of Office. July 1999–June 2000. Publication. *Michigan Librarian Newsletter* (6 per year).

Pres. Denise Forro. Tel. 517-353-8705, fax 517-432-1445, e-mail forro@msu.edu; *Pres.-Elect* Tom Genson, 1314 Breton Rd. S.E., Grand Rapids Public Lib., Grand Rapids 49506. Tel. 616-456-3621, fax 616-456-3619, e-mail tgenson@grapids.lib.mi.us; *Secy*. Roger Mendel, Mideastern MI Library Co-op., Flint 48502. Tel. 810-232-7119, fax 810-232-6639, e-mail rmendel@gfn.org;

Treas. Faye Backie, MSU Libs., 227 Clarendon, East Lansing 48823. Tel. 517-355-8465, fax 517-432-3693, e-mail backie@msu.edu; *Exec. Dir.* Marianne Hartzell, Michigan Lib. Assn., 6810 S. Cedar St., Suite 6, Lansing 48911. Tel. 517-694-6615. Association World Wide Web site http://www.mla.lib.mi.us/.

Address correspondence to the executive director.

Minnesota

Memb. 1,094. Term of Office. (Pres., Pres.-Elect) Jan.–Dec. 2000; (Treas.) Jan. 2000–Dec. 2001; (Secy.) Jan. 2000–Dec. 2001. Publication. *MLA Newsletter* (6 per year).

Pres. Joan Larson, Northern Lights Lib. Network, Box 845, Alexandria 56308; *Pres.-Elect* Carol Johnson, College of St. Catherine, 2004 Randolph Ave., St. Paul 55105; *ALA Chapter Councillor* Bill Asp, Dakota County Lib., 4137 42nd Ave. S., Minneapolis 55406; *Secy.* Zona Meyer, Hamline Law Lib., 1536 Hewitt, St. Paul 55104; *Treas.* Deborah Burke, Univ. of Minnesota, Twin Cities; *Exec. Dir.* Alison Johnson, 1619 Dayton Ave., Suite 314, Saint Paul 55104. Tel. 651-641-0982, fax 651-641-1035, e-mail mla@mr.net. Organization World Wide Web site http://www.lib.mankato.msus.edu:2000/.

Address correspondence to the executive director.

Mississippi

Memb. 700. Term of Office. Jan.–Dec. 2000. Publication *Mississippi Libraries* (q.).

Pres. Rhonda Tynes, 113 Russell Lane, Pontotoc 38863. Tel. 601-841-8979, fax 601-841-8987, e-mail rtynes50@hotmail.com; *V.P.* Henry Ledet, Box 541, Brookhaven 39601-0541. Tel. 601-833-3369, fax 601-833-3381, e-mail hledet@llf.lib.ms.us; *Secy.* Ruth Ann Gibson, Speed Lib., Mississippi College, Clinton 39056. Tel. 601-925-3433, fax 601-925-3435, e-mail gibson@mc.edu; *Treas.* Shirlene Stogner, Southern Station Box 5053, Hattiesburg 39406. Tel. 601-266-6168, fax 601-266-6033, e-mail shirlene.stogner@usm.edu; *Exec. Secy.* Mary Julia Anderson, Box 2044, Jackson 39289-1448.

Tel. 601-352-3917, fax 601-352-4240, e-mail mla@meta3.net. Organization World Wide Web site http://nt.library.msstate.edu/mla/mla.html.

Address correspondence to the executive secretary.

Missouri

Memb. 1,000. Term of Office. Oct. 1999–Oct. 2000. Publication *MO INFO* (bi-mo.). *Ed.* Jean Ann McCartney.

Pres. Molly Lawson, Central Missouri State Univ., James Kirkpatrick Lib., Warrensburg 64093-5020. Tel. 660-543-8780, 660-543-8001, e-mail mollie@libserv.cmsu.edu; *V.P./Pres.-Elect* Margaret Conroy, Little Dixie Regional Lib., 111 N. 4 St., Moberly 65270-1577. Tel. 660-263-4426, fax 660-263-4024, e-mail mconroy@little-dixie.lib.mo.us; *Exec. Dir.* Jean Ann McCartney, Missouri Lib. Assn., 1306 Business 63 S., Suite B, Columbia 65201. Tel. 573-449-4627, fax 573-449-4655, e-mail jmccartn@mail.more.net.

Address correspondence to the executive director.

Montana

Memb. 600. Term of Office. July 1999–June 2000. Publication *Montana Library Focus* (bi-mo.). *Ed.* Pam Henley, Bozeman Public Lib., 220 E. Lamme, Bozeman 59715-3579.

Pres. Bruce Newell, Montana State Lib., Box 201800, Helena 59620-1800. Tel. 406-444-9810, fax 406-444-5612, e-mail bnewell@state.mt.us; *V.P./Pres.-Elect* Suzanne D. Goodman, Park H.S., 102 View Vista Dr., Livingston 59047. Tel. 406-222-0448, fax 406-222-9404, e-mail sgoodman@livingston.k12.mt.us; *Secy./Treas.* Alice Meister, Bozeman Public Lib., 220 E. Lamme, Bozeman 59715. Tel. 406-582-2401, fax 406-582-2424, e-mail ameister@mtlib.org; *Admin. Asst.* Karen A. Hatcher, 510 Arbor, Missoula 59802-3126. Tel. 406-721-3347, fax 406-243-2060, e-mail hatcher@ism.net.

Address correspondence to the administrative assistant. Organization World Wide Web site http://www.mtlib.org/.

Nebraska

Memb. 925. Term of Office. Oct. 1999–Oct. 2000. Publication *NLA Quarterly* (q.). *Pres*. Mary Nash. E-mail mdnash@ creighton.edu; *V.P.* Kathy Tooker. E-mail ktooker@neon.nlc.state.ne.us; *Secy*. Cindy Bailey. E-mail cbailey@omaha.lib.ne.us; *Treas*. Rose Schinker. E-mail rschinke@ unmc.edu; *Exec. Dir.* Margaret Harding, Box 98, Crete 68333. Tel. 402-826-2636, e-mail gh12521@alltel.net. Organization World Wide Web site http://www.nol.org/home/ NLA/.

Address correspondence to the executive director.

Nevada

Memb. 400. Term of Office. Jan.–Dec. 2000. Publication *Nevada Libraries* (q.). *Pres*. Sara Jones, Elko-Lander-Eureka County Lib. System. Tel. 775-738-3066, e-mail sfjones@clan.lib.nv.us; *V.P./Pres.- Elect* Susan Graf, North Las Vegas Lib. Dist. Tel. 702-633-1070, e-mail susang@ci.north-las-vegas.nv.us; *Treas*. Susan Antipa. Tel. 702-887-2244 ext. 1016, e-mail smantipa@ clan.lib.nv.us; *Exec. Secy*. Salvador Avila, Clark County Lib. Tel. 702-733-7810, e-mail salvadoa@hotmail.com. Organization World Wide Web site http://dmla.clan.lib.nv.us/ docs/nla/organization.htm.

Address correspondence to the executive secretary.

New Hampshire

Memb. 700. Publication. *NHLA News* (bi-mo.). *Pres*. Michael York. E-mail myork@finch. nhsl.lib.nh.us; *V.P.* Terry Pare. E-mail tepare @finch.nhsl.lib.nh.us; *Secy*. Andrea Thorpe. E-mail rfl@sugar-river.net; *Treas*. Greg Sauer. E-mail gsauer@manchester.lib.nh.us.

Address correspondence to the association, Box 2332, Concord, NH 03302. Organization World Wide Web site http://www.state.nh.us/ nhla/.

New Jersey

Memb. 1,700. Term of Office. July 1999–

June 2000. Publication. *New Jersey Libraries Newsletter* (mo.).

Pres. Joseph Keenan, Elizabeth Public Lib., 11 S. Broad St., Elizabeth 07202. Tel. 908-354-6060 ext. 8, fax 908-354-5845, e-mail jkeenan@epl.njpublib.org; *Pres.-Elect* Barbara Thiele, Westfield Public Lib., 550 E. Broad St., Westfield 07090. Tel. 908-789-4090, fax 908-789-0921, e-mail bthiele@ infolink.org; *Secy*. Barbara Jean Sikora, Livingston Public Lib., 10 Robert Harp Dr., Livingston 07039. Tel. 973-992-4600, fax 973-994-2346, e-mail sikora@bccls.org; *Treas*. John Hurley, Woodbridge Public Lib., Geroge Frederick Plaza, Woodbridge 07095; *Exec. Dir.* Patricia Tumulty, New Jersey Lib. Assn., 4 W. Lafayette St., Trenton 08608. Tel. 609-394-8032, fax 609-394-8164, e-mail ptumulty@burlco.lib.nj.us.

Address correspondence to the executive director, Box 1534, Trenton 08607. Organization World Wide Web site http://www.njla. org/.

New Mexico

Memb. 550. Term of Office. Apr. 1999–Apr. 2000. Publication *New Mexico Library Association Newsletter* (6 per year). *Ed.* Jackie Shane. Tel. 505-277-5410, e-mail jshane@ unm.edu.

Pres. Charlene Greenwood, 3540 Haines Ave. N.E., Albuquerque 87106; Tel. 505-256-1379; *V.P.* Laurie Macrae, Taos Public Lib. E-mail laurimac@laplaza.org; *Secy*. Kris Warmoth, Univ. of New Mexico, Valencia Campus. E-mail krisw@unm.edu; *Admin. Svcs.* Linda O'Connell, Box 26074, Albuquerque 87125. Tel. 505-899-3516, e-mail nmla@rt66.com.

Address correspondence to the association, Box 26074, Albuquerque 87125. Organization World Wide Web site http://lib.nmsu. edu/nmla/.

New York

Memb. 3,000. Term of Office. Oct. 1999–Nov. 2000. Publication *NYLA Bulletin* (6 per year). *Ed.* Bruce Robertson.

Pres. Anne Hofmann, New York Public Lib., 20 W. 53 St., New York 10019. Tel.

212-621-0613, e-mail ahofmann@nypl.org; V.P. John Hammond. Tel. 315-386-4569, e-mail john@northnet.org; Treas. Carolyn Giambra. Tel. 716-626-8025, e-mail cgiambra@localnet.com; Exec. Dir. Susan Lehman Keitel, New York Lib. Assn., 252 Hudson Ave., Albany 12210. Tel. 518-432-6952, e-mail nyladirector@pobox.com. Association World Wide Web site http://www.nyla.org/.

Address correspondence to the executive director.

North Carolina

Memb. 2,000. Term of Office. Oct. 1999–Oct. 2001. Publication North Carolina Libraries (q.). Ed. Frances Bradburn, Media and Technology, N.C. Dept. of Public Instruction, 301 N. Wilmington St., Raleigh 27601-2825. Tel. 919-715-1528, fax 919-733-4762, e-mail fbradbur@dpi.state.nc.us.

Pres. Al Jones, Dir. of Lib. Service, Catawba College, 2300 W. Innes St., Salisbury 28144. Tel. 704-637-4449, fax 704-637-4304, e-mail pajones@catawba.edu; V.P./Pres.-Elect Ross Holt, Head of Ref., Randolph County Public Lib., 201 Worth St., Asheboro 27203. Tel. 336-318-6806, fax 336-318-6823, e-mail rholt@ncsl.dcr.state.nc.us; Secy. Sue Ann Cody, Randall Lib., UNC Wilmington, 601 College Rd., Wilmington 28403-3297. Tel. 910-962-7409, fax 910-962-3078, e-mail codys@uncwil.edu; Treas. Diane Kester, Department of Broadcasting, Librarianship & Educational Technology, 102 Joyner E., Greenville 27858-4353. Tel. 252-328-6621, fax 252-328-4368, e-mail kesterd@mail.ecu.edu or Lsddkest@eastnet.ecu.edu; Admin. Asst. Maureen Costello, North Carolina Lib. Assn., 4646 Mail Service Center, Raleigh 27699-4646. Tel./fax 919-839-6252, e-mail ncla@mindspring.com. Organization World Wide Web site http://www.nclaonline.org/.

Address correspondence to the administrative assistant.

North Dakota

Memb. (Indiv.) 400; (Inst.) 18. Term of Office. Oct. 1999–Sept. 2000. Publication. The Good Stuff (q.). Ed. Andrea Collin, 502 Juniper Dr., Bismarck 58501. Tel. 701-222-8714, 701-250-9404.

Pres. Marilyn Johnson, North Dakota Legislative Council, State Capitol, 600 E. Blvd., Bismarck 58501-0360. Tel. 701-328-4900, fax 701-328-3615, e-mail marjohns@state.nd.us; Pres.-Elect Sally Dockter, Chester Fritz Lib., Box 9000, Grand Forks 58202-9000. Tel. 701-777-4640, fax 701-777-3319, e-mail sdockter@plains.nodak.edu; Secy. Marlene Anderson, Bismarck State College Lib., Box 5587, Bismarck 58506-5587. Tel. 701-224-5578, 701-224-5551, e-mail marander @badlands.nodak.edu; Treas. Lila Pedersen, Harley E. French Lib. of the Health Sciences, Box 9002, Grand Forks 58202-9002. Tel. 701-777-3993, fax 701-777-4790, e-mail lpederse@medicine.nodak.edu. Association World Wide Web site http://ndsl.lib.state.nd.us/ndla/.

Address correspondence to the president.

Ohio

Memb. 3,491. Term of Office. Jan.–Dec. Publications. Access (mo.); Ohio Libraries (q.).

Chair James Switzer, 891 Elmore Ave., Akron 44302-1238; Secy. Lenore Koppel, 14450 Summerfield Rd., Cleveland Heights 44118-4637; Exec. Secy. Frances Haley.

Address correspondence to the association, 35 E. Gay St., Suite 305, Columbus 43215. Tel. 614-221-9057, 614-231-6234, e-mail olc@olc.org.

Oklahoma

Memb. (Indiv.) 1,050; (Inst.) 60. Term of Office. July 1999–June 2000. Publication. Oklahoma Librarian (bi-mo.).

Pres. Donna Morris. E-mail morris_donna @mail.mls.lib.ok.us; V.P./Pres.-Elect Sharon Saulmon. E-mail ssaulmon@ms.rose.cc.ok.us; Secy. Rachel C. Butler. E-mail rbutler@okc.cc.ok.us; Treas. Gwen Witherspoon. E-mail gwen@pioneer.lib.ok.us; Exec. Dir. Kay Boies, 300 Hardy Dr., Edmond 73013. Tel./fax 405-348-0506, e-mail kboies@ionet.net. Association World Wide Web site http://www.pioneer.lib.ok.us/ola/.

Address correspondence to the executive director.

Oregon

Memb. (Indiv.) 1,047. Publications. *OLA Hotline* (bi-w.), *OLA Quarterly*.

Pres. Terry Rohe, Portland State Univ. Tel. 503-725-4542, e-mail rohet@pdx.edu; *V.P./Pres.-Elect* Anne Van Sickle, McMinnville Public Lib. Tel. 503-435-5550, e-mail vansica@ci.mcminnville.or.us; *Secy.* Carol Reich, Hillsboro Public Lib., 775 S.E. 10 Ave., Hillsboro 97123. Tel. 503-615-6505, fax 503-615-6501, e-mail carolr@ci.hillsboro.or.us.

Address correspondence to the secretary. Organization World Wide Web site http://www.olaweb.org/.

Pennsylvania

Memb. 1,500. Term of Office. Jan.–Dec. 2000. Publication *PaLA Bulletin* (10 per year).

Pres. David J. Roberts, Wissahickon Valley Public Lib., 713 Stradone Rd., Bala Cynwyd 19004. Tel. 215-643-1320, fax 215-643-6611, e-mail droberts@mciu.org; *1st V.P.* Jack Sulzer, Penn State Univ. Libs., E510 Paterno Lib., University Park 16802. Tel. 814-865-0401, fax 814-865-3665, e-mail jsulzer@psu.edu; *Exec. Dir.* Glenn R. Miller, Pennsylvania Lib. Assn., 1919 N. Front St., Harrisburg 17102. Tel. 717-233-3113, fax 717-233-3121, e-mail gmiller@ezonline.com.

Address correspondence to the executive director.

Rhode Island

Memb. (Indiv.) 341; (Inst.) 59. Term of Office. June 1999–June 2001. Publication. *Rhode Island Library Association Bulletin*. *Ed.* Frank Iacono.

Pres. Helen Rodrigues, Dean of Univ. Libs., Johnson and Wales Univ. Tel. 401-598-1887, fax 401-598-1834, e-mail hrodrigues@jwu.edu; *Secy.* Derryl Johnson, Marian Mohr Memorial Lib., 1 Memorial Drive, Johnston 02919; Tel. 401-231-4980, fax 401-231-4984, e-mail derryljn@lori.state.ri.us.

Address correspondence to the secretary.

South Carolina

Memb. 800. Term of Office. Jan.–Dec. 1999. Publication *News and Views*.

Pres. Norman Belk, Greenville County Lib., 300 College St., Greenville 29601. Tel. 864 242-5000 ext. 238, fax 864 235-8375, e-mail normanbelk@excite.com; *V.P.* Thomas Shepley, South Carolina State Lib., 1500 Senate St., Box 11469, Columbia 29211. Tel. 803-734-8666, fax 803-734-8676, e-mail thomas@leo.scsl.state.sc.us; *2nd V.P.* Patricia Feehan, College of Lib. and Info. Science, Univ. of South Carolina, Columbia 29208. Tel. 803-777-2381, fax 803-777-7938, e-mail patfeehan@sc.edu; *Secy.* Jan W. Cambre, Thomas Cooper Lib., Univ. of South Carolina, Columbia 29208. Tel. 803-777-3151, fax 803-777-4661, e-mail jan@tcl.sc.edu; *Treas.* Michael Giller, Box 3002, Greenville 29602-3002; *Exec. Secy.* Drucie Raines, South Carolina Lib. Assn., Box 219, Goose Creek 29445. Tel. 803-764-3668, fax 803-824-2690, e-mail scla@charleston.net. Association World Wide Web site http://www.scla.org/.

Address correspondence to the executive secretary.

South Dakota

Memb. (Indiv.) 600; (Inst.) 45. Term of Office. Oct. 1999–Oct. 2000. Publication. *Book Marks* (bi-mo.).

Pres. Colleen Kirby, Black Hills State Univ. Lib., Spearfish 57799. Tel. 605-642-6361, e-mail colleenkirby@bhsu.edu; *Secy.* Patricia Andersen, Devereaux Lib., South Dakota School of Mines and Technology, Rapid City 57701; *Treas.* Ann Eichinger, South Dakota State Lib., 800 Governors Dr., Pierre 57501; *ALA Councillor* Ethelle Bean, Karl E. Mundt Lib., Dakota State Univ., Madison 57042; *MPLA Rep.* Deb Hagemeier, Augustana College, Sioux Falls.

Address correspondence to Brenda Standiford, Exec. Secy., SDLA, c/o Black Hills State Univ., 1200 University, Spearfish 57799. Tel. 605-642-6357, fax 605-642-6298, e-mail brendastandiford@bhsu.edu. Organization World Wide Web site http://www.usd.edu/sdla/.

Tennessee

Memb. 875. Term of Office. July 1999–July 2000. Publications. *Tennessee Librarian* (q.), *TLA Newsletter* (bi-mo.).

Pres. Charles A. Sherrill, Tennessee State Lib. and Archives, 403 7th Ave. N., Nashville 37243-0312. Tel. 615-741-2764, fax 615-532-2472, e-mail csherrill@mail.state.tn. us; *V.P./Pres.-Elect* Tena Litherland, Libn., Webb School of Knoxville, Knoxville 37923. Tel. 423-693-0011 ext. 113, e-mail tena_litherland@webbschool.org; *Treas.* Kathy Breeden, Non-Book Services, Univ. of Tennessee, 615 McCallie Ave., Chattanooga 37403. Tel. 423-457-2673, e-mail kathy-breeden @utc.edu; *Past Pres.* Martha Earl, Preston Medical Lib., Univ. of Tennessee, 1924 Alcoa Hwy., Knoxville 37920. Tel. 423-544-6616, e-mail mearl@utk.edu; *Exec. Secy.* Betty Nance, Box 158417, Nashville 37215-8417. Tel. 615-297-8316, fax 615-269-1807, e-mail betty.nance@lipscomb.edu. Organization World Wide Web site http://toltec.lib. utk.edu/~tla/.

Address correspondence to the executive secretary.

Texas

Memb. 7,200. Term of Office. Apr. 1999–Apr. 2000. Publications. *Texas Library Journal* (q.); *TLACast* (9 per year).

Pres. Gleniece Robinson, Fort Worth Public Lib., 500 Third St., Fort Worth 76102. Tel. 817-871-7705, fax 817-871-7734, e-mail RobinsG@ci.fort-worth.tx.us; *Pres.-Elect* Julie B. Todaro, Austin Community College, 1212 Rio Grande St., Austin 78701. Tel. 512-223-3071, fax 512-223-3430, e-mail jtodaro @austin.cc.tx.us; *Treas.* June Koelker, Texas Christian Univ., MCB Lib., Box 298400, Fort Worth 76129. Tel. 817-257-7696, fax 817-481-7282, e-mail j.koelker@.tcu.edu; *Exec. Dir.* Patricia Smith, TLA, 3355 Bee Cave Rd., Suite 401, Austin 78746-6763. Tel. 512-328-1518, fax 512-328-8852, e-mail pats@ txla.org. Organization World Wide Web site http://www.txla.org/.

Address correspondence to the executive director.

Utah

Memb. 650. Term of Office. May 1999–May 2000. Publication *UTAH Libraries News* (bi-mo.).

Pres. Sue Hill, Brigham City Lib., 26 E. Forest, Brigham City 84302. Tel. 435-723-5850, fax 435-723-2813, e-mail sue@peachy. bcpl.lib.ut.us; *V.P./Pres.-Elect* Randy Silverman, 560 Marriott Lib., Univ. of Utah, Salt Lake City 84112. Tel. 801-585-6782, fax 801-585-3464, e-mail rsilverm@library.utah. edu; *Treas./Exec. Secy.* Shannon Reid. Tel. 801-273-8150.

Address correspondence to the executive secretary, Box 711789, Salt Lake City 84171-1789. Tel. 801-378-4433. Organization World Wide Web site http://www.ula. org/.

Vermont

Memb. 450. Publication *VLA News* (10 per year).

Pres. Linda Brew, Bailey/Howe Lib., Univ. of Vermont, Burlington 05405. Tel. 802-656-8133, e-mail lbrew@zoo.uvm.edu; *V.P./Pres.-Elect* Kathy Naftaly, Rutland Free Lib., 10 Court St., Rutland 05701. Tel. 802-773-1860, e-mail RUTLAND_FREE@dol. state.vt.us; *Secy.* Susan Overfield, Essex Free Lib., Box 8093, Essex 05451. Tel. 802-879-0313, e-mail essexlib@together.net; *Treas.* Trina Magi, Bailey/Howe Lib., Univ. of Vermont, Burlington 05405. Tel. 802-656-5723, e-mail tmagi@zoo.uvm.edu. Organization World Wide Web site http://bailey.uvm.edu/ vla/.

Address correspondence to the president.

Virginia

Memb. 1,500+. Term of Office. Jan.–Dec. 2000. Publications. *Virginia Libraries* (q.), *Ed.* Cy Dillon; *VLA Newsletter* (10 per year), *Ed.* Mary Hansbrough, 2505 Gloucester Dr., Blacksburg 24060.

Pres. Carolyn Barkley, Virginia Beach Public Lib., Virginia Beach 23452. Tel. 757-431-3072, fax 757-431-3018; *V.P./Pres.-Elect* Cy Dillon, Stanley Lib., Ferrum

College, Callaway 24067-3002. Tel. 540-365-4428, fax 540-365-4423; *2nd V.P.* Ruth Arnold, Staunton Public Lib., Staunton 24401. Tel. 540-332-3902, fax 540-332-3906; *Secy.* Nancy Newins, McGraw Page Lib., Randolph Macon College, Ashland 23005. Tel. 804-752-4718, fax 804-752-7345; *Treas.* Jeanette Friedman, 403 Carlisle Way, Norfolk 23505. Tel. 757-489-9368; *Past Pres.* Sandra Heinemann, Hampden-Sydney College Lib., Box 122, Hampden-Sydney 23943. Tel. 804-223-6916; *Exec. Dir.* Linda Hahne, Box 8277, Norfolk 23503-0277. Tel. 757-583-0041, fax 757-583-5041, e-mail hahne@bellatlantic.net. Organization World Wide Web site http://www.vla.org.

Address correspondence to the executive director.

Washington

Memb. 1,200. Term of Office. Apr. 1999–Apr. 2001. Publications *ALKI* (3 per year), *WLA Link* (5 per year).

Pres. Cynthia Cunningham. E-mail cindy @amazon.com; *V.P./Pres.-Elect* Carol Gill Schuyler, Kitsap Regional Lib., 1301 Sylvan Way, Bremerton 98310-3498. Tel. 360-405-9127, fax 360-405-9128, e-mail carol@krl. org; *Treas.* Kimberly Hixson, Fort Vancouver Regional Lib., 1007 E. Mill Plain Blvd., Vancouver 98663-3599. Tel. 360-699-8806, fax 360-699-8808, e-mail hixson@fvrl.lib. wa.us; *Secy.* Karen Highum, UW/Suzzallo, Box 352900, Seattle 98195-2900. Tel. 206-685-3981, e-mail highum@u.washington. edu; *Assn. Coord.* Gail E. Willis.

Address correspondence to the association office, 4016 1st Ave. N.E., Seattle 98105-6502. Tel. 206-545-1529, fax 206-545-1543, e-mail wasla@wla.org. Association World Wide Web site http://www.wla.org.

West Virginia

Memb. 700. Term of Office. Dec. 1999–Nov. 2000. Publication *West Virginia Libraries* (6 per year). *Eds.* Denise Ash, Box 149, Spencer 25276. Tel. 304-927-1770; Sue Eichelberger, West Virginia Lib. Commission, 1900 Kana-

wha Blvd. E., Charleston 25305. Tel. 304-558-2531.

Pres. Pam Coyle, South Charleston Public Lib. E-mail coyle@scpl.wvnet.edu; *1st V.P./Pres.-Elect* Dottie Thomas, Ohio County Public Lib. E-mail thomasd@weirton.lib. wv.us; *2nd V.P.* Cheryl Harshman, West Liberty State College Elbin Lib. E-mail harshmac @wlsc.wvnet.edu; *Treas.* Denise Ash, Alpha Regional Lib. E-mail ash_de@wvlc.wvnet. edu; *Secy.* Suzette Lowe, Roane County Lib. E-mail lowesuz@wvlc.wvnet.edu; *Past Pres.* Betty Gunnoe, Martinsburg Public Lib. E-mail gunnoeb@martin.lib.wv.us.

Address correspondence to the president. Organization World Wide Web site http://wvnvaxa.wvnet.edu/~wvla/.

Wisconsin

Memb. 2,100. Term of Office. Jan.–Dec. 2000. Publication *WLA Newsletter* (bi-mo.).

Pres. Barbara J. Kelly, Appleton Public Lib., 225 North Oneida St., Appleton 54911. Tel. 920-832-6168, e-mail bkelly@apl.org; *Pres.-Elect* Michael J. Gelhausen, Hartford Public Lib., 115 North Main St., Hartford 53027-1596. E-mail mikeg@hnet.net; *Secy.* Anita K. Evans, UW-La Crosse Murphy Lib. Tel. 608-785-8805, e-mail evans@mail. uwlax.edu; *Treas.* Joan Airoldi. Tel. 715-682-2365, fax 715-682-2365, e-mail nwls@ win.bright.net; *Exec. Dir.* Lisa Strand. Tel. 608-245-3640, fax 608-245-3646.

Address correspondence to the association, 5250 E. Terrace Dr., Suite A1, Madison 53718-8345. Organization World Wide Web site http://www.wla.lib.wi.us/.

Wyoming

Memb. (Indiv.) 425; (Inst.) 21. Term of Office. Oct. 1999–Oct. 2000.

Pres. Vickie Hoff, Rawlins H.S., Rawlins 82301;; *V.P./Pres.-Elect* Mary Rhoads; *Exec. Secy.* Laura Grott, Box 1387, Cheyenne 82003. Tel. 307-632-7622, fax 307-638-3469, e-mail grottski@aol.com.

Address correspondence to the executive secretary. Organization World Wide Web site http://www.wyla.org/.

Guam

Memb. 75. Publication. *Guam Library Association News* (mo. during school year).

Pres. Nick Goezfritz, RFK Lib., Univ. of Guam, 303 University Dr., UOG Station, Mangilao 96923. Tel. 671-735-2340, fax 671-735-6882, e-mail ngeozfr@uog9.uog.edu; *Pres.-Elect* Christine Scott-Smith, Guam Public Lib., 254 Martyr St., Haganta 96910-5141. Tel. 671-475-3415, fax 671-477-9777, e-mail csctsmith@kuentos.guam.net.

Address correspondence to the association, Box 22515, GMF, Barrigada 96921.

Canada

Alberta

Memb. 500. Term of Office. May 1999–Apr. 2000. Publication *Letter of the LAA* (5 per year). World Wide Web site http://www.laa.ab.ca.

Pres. Alvin Schrader, Dir., SLIS, Rm. 3-20 Rutherford S., Univ. of Alberta, Edmonton T6G 2J4. Tel. 780-492-3932, fax 780-492-2430, e-mail alvin.schrader@ualberta.ca; *Exec. Dir.* Christine Sheppard, 80 Baker Crescent N.W., Calgary T2L 1R4. Tel. 403-284-5832, fax 403-282-6646, e-mail shepparc@cadvision.com.

Address correspondence to the executive director.

British Columbia

Memb. 750. Term of Office. May 2000–April 2001. Publication *BCLA Reporter. Ed.* Ted Benson.

Pres. Sybil Harrison; *V.P./Pres.-Elect* Julie Spurrell; *Exec. Dir.* Michael Burris.

Address correspondence to the association, 150-900 Howe St., Vancouver V6Z 2M4. Tel. 604-683-5354, fax 604-609-0707, e-mail office@bcla.bc.ca.

Manitoba

Memb. 494. Term of Office. May 1999–May 2000. Publication *Newsline* (mo.).

Pres. Jo Ann Brewster, Lib. and Info. Technology Program, Red River Community College, Room F221, 2055 Notre Dame Ave., Winnipeg R3H 0J9. E-mail jbrewste@rrc.mb.ca; *V.P./Pres.-Elect* Sheila Andrich, Elizabeth Dafoe Lib., Univ. of Manitoba, Winnipeg R3T 2N2. E-mail Sheila_Andrich@umanitoba.ca.

Address correspondence to the association, 606-100 Arthur St., Winnipeg R3B 1H3. Tel. 204-943-4567, fax 204-942-1555. Organization World Wide Web site http://www.mla.mb.ca/index.html.

Ontario

Memb. 3,750+. Term of Office. Jan. 2000–Jan. 2001. Publications. *Access* (q.); *Teaching Librarian* (q.); *Accessola.com* (q.).

Pres. Liz Hoffman, Ryerson Polytechnic Univ. Tel. 416-979-5000, fax 416-977-7709, e-mail ehoffman@acs.ryerson.ca; *V.P.* Michael Ridley, University of Guelph; *Treas.* Charlotte Meissner, Oakville Public Lib. Tel. 905-815-2042; *Exec. Dir.* Larry Moore.

Address correspondence to the association, 100 Lombard St., Suite 303, Toronto M5C 1M3. Tel. 416-363-3388, fax 416-941-9581, e-mail info@accessola.com. Organization World Wide Web site http://www.accessola.org.

Quebec

Memb. (Indiv.) 140; (Inst.) 26; (Commercial) 3. Term of Office June 1999–May 2000. Publication. *ABQ/QLA Bulletin* (3 per year).

Pres. Rennie MacLeod; *Exec. Secy.* Pat Fortin, Box 1095, Pointe Claire H95 4H9. Tel. 514-630-4875, e-mail abqla.qc.ca.

Address correspondence to the executive secretary. Organization World Wide Web site http://www.abqla.qc.ca/.

Saskatchewan

Memb. 225. Term of Office. June 1999–May 2000. Publication *Forum* (5 per year).

Pres. Lauraine Armstrong, Health Sciences Lib., Univ. of Saskatchewan Libs., Rm. B205 Health Sciences Bldg., 107 Wiggins Rd., Saskatoon S7N 5E5. E-mail lauraine.armstrong@usask.ca; *V.P.* Julie McKenna, Regina Public Lib., 2311 12th Ave., Box 2311, Regina S4P 3Z5. E-mail julie@rpl.regina.sk.ca; *Exec. Dir.* Judith Silverthorne,

Box 3388, Regina S4P 3H1. Tel. 306-780-9413, fax 306-780-9447, e-mail sla@pleis.lib.sk.ca.

Address correspondence to the executive director. Organization World Wide Web site http://www.lib.sk.ca/sla/.

Regional

Atlantic Provinces: N.B., Nfld., N.S., P.E.I.

Memb. (Indiv.) 196; (Inst.) 20. Term of Office. May 1999–May 2000. Publications. *APLA Bulletin* (bi-mo.), *Membership Directory and Handbook* (ann.).

Pres. Peter Webster, Head of Info. Systems, Patrick Power Lib., Saint Mary's Univ., Halifax, NS B3H 3C3. Tel. 902-420-5507, fax 902-420-5561, e-mail peter.webster @stmarys.ca; *V.P./Pres.-Elect* Pamela Stevens Rosolen, Regional Libn., Saint John Lib. Region, One Market Square, Saint John, NB E2L 4Z6. Tel. 506-643-7247, fax 506-643-7225, e-mail pamela.stevens-Rosolen@ gov.nb.ca; *Secy.* Penny Logan, 74 Avondale Rd., Dartmouth, NS B2V 1H6. Tel. 902-462-8338, fax 902-435-9597, e-mail eastgate@ accesscable.net; *Treas.* Sharon Murphy, Head of Reference and Research, DalTech Lib., Dalhousie Univ., Sexton Campus, Box 1000, Halifax, NS B3J 2X4. Tel. 902-494-3109, fax 902-494-6089, e-mail sharon.murphy@dal. ca.

Address correspondence to Atlantic Provinces Lib. Assn., c/o School of Lib. and Info. Studies, Dalhousie Univ., Halifax, NS B3H 4H8. Organization World Wide Web site http://www.stmarys.ca/partners/apla/.

Mountain Plains: Ariz., Colo., Kan., Mont., Neb., Nev., N.Dak., N.M., Okla., S.Dak., Utah, Wyo.

Memb. 820. Term of Office. One year. Publications. *MPLA Newsletter* (bi-mo.), *Ed. and Adv. Mgr.* Heidi M. Nickisch, I. D. Weeks Lib., Univ. of South Dakota, Vermillion, SD 57069. Tel. 605-677-5121, e-mail nickisch@ usd.edu; *Membership Directory* (ann.).

Pres. Marilyn Hinshaw, Eastern Oklahoma District Lib. System, 814 W. Okmulgee, Muskogee, OK 74401. Tel. 918-683-2846 ext. 234, fax 918-683-0436, e-mail mhinshaw @eok.lib.ok.us; *V.P./Pres.-Elect* Linda M. Rea, Hastings Public Lib., 517 W. 47 St., Box 849, Hastings, NE 68902-0849. Tel. 402-461-2348, fax 402-461-2359, e-mail lrea @hastings.lib.ne.us; *Exec. Secy.* Joe Edelen, I. D. Weeks Lib., Univ. of South Dakota, Vermillion, SD 57069. Tel. 605-677-6082, fax 605-677-5488, e-mail jedelen@usd.edu.

Address correspondence to the executive secretary, Mountain Plains Lib. Assn. Organization World Wide Web site http://www. usd.edu/mpla/.

New England: Conn., Maine, Mass., N.H., R.I., Vt.

Memb. (Indiv.) 1,300; (Inst.) 100. Term of Office. Nov. 1999–Oct. 2000. (Treas., Dirs., and Secy, two years). Publication. *New England Libraries* (bi-mo.). *Ed.* Debra Covell. E-mail sdcovell@empire.net.

Pres. Lucy Gangone, Hartford Public Lib., 500 Main St., Hartford, CT 06103-3075. Tel. 860-543-8563, fax 860-722-6900, e-mail lgangone@hartfordpl.lib.ct.us; *Pres.-Elect* Cheryl McCarth, URI-GSLIS, Rodman Hall, Kingston, RI 02881. Tel. 401-874-4654, fax 401-874-4964, e-mail chermc@uri.edu; *Exec. Secy.* Barry Blaisdell, New England Lib. Assn., 707 Turnpike St., North Andover, MA 01845. Tel. 978-685-5966, e-mail info@ nelib.org

Address correspondence to the executive secretary. Organization World Wide Web site http://www.nelib.org/.

Pacific Northwest: Alaska, Idaho, Mont., Oreg., Wash., Alberta, B.C.

Memb. (Active) 550; (Subscribers) 100. Term of Office. Aug. 1999–Aug. 2000. Publication. *PNLA Quarterly. Ed.* Dona Helmer, Box 220549, Anchorage, AK 99522. E-mail dhelmer@anch.net.

Pres. Karen Labuik, Marigold Lib. System, 710 2nd St., Strathmore, AB T1P 1K4. Tel. 403-934-5334, e-mail klabiuk@ marigold.ab.ca; *1st V.P./Pres.-Elect* Susannah Price, Boise Public Lib., 715 Capitol Blvd., Boise, ID 83702. Tel. 208-384-4026, fax 208-384-4156, e-mail sprice@pobox.ci. boise.id.us; *2nd V.P.* Christine Sheppard,

Lib. Assn. of Alberta, 80 Baker Crescent N.W. Calgary, AB T2L 1R4. Tel. 403-284-5818, e-mail shepparc@cadvision.com; *Secy.* Colleen Bell, Knight Lib., 1299 Univ. of Oregon, Eugene, OR 97403-1299. Tel. 541-346-1817; *Treas.* Robert Hook, Univ. of Idaho Lib., Moscow, ID. E-mail rdhook@uidaho.edu.

Address correspondence to the president, Pacific Northwest Lib. Assn. Organization World Wide Web site http://www.pnla.org/.

Southeastern: Ala., Ark., Fla., Ga., Ky., La., Miss., N.C., S.C., Tenn., Va., W.Va.

Memb. 700. Term of Office. Oct. 1998–Oct. 2000. Publication *The Southeastern Librarian* (q.).

Pres. Frances N. Coleman, 2403 Maple Dr., Starkville, MS 39759. Tel. 601-325-7661, fax 601-325-4263, e-mail fcoleman@library.msstate.edu; *V.P./Pres.-Elect* Barry Baker, Univ. of Central Florida, Box 162666, Orlando, FL 32816-2666. Tel. 407-823-2564, fax (407) 823-2529, e-mail bbaker@mail.ucf.edu; *Secy.* Ellen Johnson, Univ. of Central Arkansas, 31 Forest Ct., Conway, AR 72032. Tel. 501-450-5248, fax 501-450-5208, e-mail ellenj@mail.uca.edu; *Treas.* William McRee, Stow South Carolina Historical Room, Greenville County Lib., 300 College St., Greenville, SC 29601-2086. Tel. 864-242-5000 ext. 241, fax 864-235-8375, wmcree@infoave.net.

Address correspondence to the president or executive secretary, SELA Administrative Services, SOLINET, 1438 W. Peachtree St. N.W., Atlanta, GA 30309-2955. Tel. 404-892-0943. Organization World Wide Web site http://www.seflin.org/sela/.

State and Provincial Library Agencies

The state library administrative agency in each of the U.S. states will have the latest information on its state plan for the use of federal funds under the Library Services and Technology Act (LSTA). The directors and addresses of these state agencies are listed below.

Alabama

Dir., Alabama Public Lib. Service, 6030 Monticello Dr., Montgomery 36130-2001. Tel. 334-213-3900, fax 334-213-3993.

Alaska

Karen R. Crane, Dir., State Lib., Archives, and Museums, Alaska Dept. of Educ., Box 110571, Juneau 99811-0571. Tel. 907-465-2910, fax 907-465-2151, e-mail karen_crane@eed.state.ak.us.

Arizona

GladysAnn Wells, Dir., Dept. of Lib., Archives, and Public Records, State Capitol, Rm. 200, 1700 W. Washington, Phoenix 85007-2896. Tel. 602-542-4035, fax 602-542-4972, e-mail gawells@dlapr.lib.az.us.

Arkansas

John A. (Pat) Murphey, Jr., State Libn., Arkansas State Lib., One Capitol Mall, Little Rock 72201-1081. Tel. 501-682-1526, fax 501-682-1899, e-mail jmurphey@comp.uark.edu.

California

Kevin Starr, State Libn., California State Lib., Box 942837, Sacramento 94237-0001. Tel. 916-654-0174, fax 916-654-0064, e-mail kstarr@library.ca.gov.

Colorado

Nancy Bolt, Dep. State Libn. and Asst. Commissioner, Dept. of Education, 201 E. Colfax Ave., Denver 80203. Tel. 303-866-6733, fax 303-866-6940, e-mail nbolt@csn.net.

Connecticut

Ken Wiggin, State Libn., Connecticut State Lib., 231 Capitol Ave., Hartford 06106. Tel. 806-566-4301, fax 806-566-8940, e-mail kwiggin@cslib.org.

Delaware

Annie Norman, Dir. and State Libn., Div. of Libs., 43 S. DuPont Hwy., Dover 19901. Tel. 302-739-4748, fax 302-739-6787, e-mail anorman@lib.de.us.

District of Columbia

Mary E. (Molly) Raphael, Dir. and State Libn., Dist. of Columbia Public Lib., 901 G St. N.W., Suite 400, Washington 20001. Tel. 202-727-1101, fax 202-727-1129, e-mail mraphael@rapgroup.com.

Florida

Barratt Wilkins, State Libn., Div. of Lib. & Info. Services, R. A. Gray Bldg., Tallahassee 32399-0250. Tel. 904-487-2651, fax 904-488-2746, e-mail bwilkins@mail.dos.state.fl.us.

Georgia

David Singleton, Dir., Public Lib. Services, 1800 Century Pl. N.E., Atlanta 30345-4304. Tel. 404-982-3560, fax 404-982-3563, e-mail dsingleton@dtae.org.

Hawaii

Virginia Lowell, State Libn., Hawaii State Public Lib. System, 465 S. King St., Rm. B1, Honolulu 96813. Tel. 808-586-3704, fax 808-586-3715, e-mail STLIB@lib.state.hi.us.

Idaho

Charles A. Bolles, State Libn., Idaho State Lib., 325 W. State St., Boise 83702-6072. Tel. 208-334-2150, fax 208-334-4016, e-mail cbolles@isl.state.id.us.

Illinois

Jean Wilkins, Dir., Illinois State Lib., 300 S. Second St., Springfield 62701-1796. Tel. 217-782-2994, fax 217-785-4326, e-mail jwilkins@library.sos.state.il.us.

Indiana

C. Ray Ewick, Dir., Indiana State Lib., 140 N. Senate Ave., Indianapolis 46204-2296. Tel. 317-232-3692, fax 317-232-3728, e-mail ewick@statelib.lib.in.us.

Iowa

Sharman B. Smith, State Libn., State Lib. of Iowa, E. 12 and Grand, Des Moines 50319. Tel. 515-281-4105, fax 515-281-6191, e-mail ssmith@mail.lib.state.ia.us.

Kansas

Duane F. Johnson, State Libn., Kansas State Lib., State Capitol, 3rd fl., Topeka 66612. Tel. 785-296-3296, fax 785-296-6650, e-mail duanej@ink.org.

Kentucky

James A. Nelson, State Libn./Commissioner, Kentucky Dept. for Libs. and Archives, 300 Coffee Tree Rd., Box 537, Frankfort 40602-0537. Tel. 502-564-8300, fax 502-564-5773, e-mail jnelson@ctr.kdla.state. ky.us.

Louisiana

Thomas F. Jaques, State Libn., State Lib. of Louisiana, Box 131, Baton Rouge 70821-0131. Tel. 504-342-4923, fax 504-342-3547, e-mail tjaques@pelican.state.lib.la.us.

Maine

J. Gary Nichols, State Libn., Maine State Lib., LMA Bldg., 64 State House Sta., Augusta 04333-0064. Tel. 207-287-5600, fax 207-287-5615, e-mail gary.nichols@ state.me.us.

Maryland

J. Maurice Travillian, Asst. State Superintendent for Libs., Div. of Lib. Development and Services, Maryland State Dept. of Educ., 200 W. Baltimore St., Baltimore 21201-2595. Tel. 410-767-0435, fax 410-333-2507, e-mail mj54@umail.umd.ed.

Massachusetts

Keith Michael Fiels, Dir., Massachusetts Board of Lib. Commissioners, 648 Beacon St., Boston 02215. Tel. 617-267-9400, fax 617-421-9833, e-mail kfiels@state.ma.us.

Michigan

State Libn., Lib. of Michigan, 717 W. Allegan St., Box 30007, Lansing 48909-9945. Tel. 517-373-5504, fax 517-373-4480.

Minnesota

Joyce Swonger, Dir., Office of Lib. Development and Services, Minnesota Dept. of Educ., 440 Capitol Sq. Bldg., 550 Cedar St., Saint Paul 55101. Tel. 612-296-0909, fax 612-296-5418, e-mail joyce.swonger@ state.mn.us.

Mississippi

John A. Pritchard, Exec. Dir., Mississippi Lib. Commission, 1221 Ellis Ave., Box 10700, Jackson 39289-0700. Tel. 601-359-1036, fax 601-354-4181, e-mail japritchard @mlc.lib.ms.us.

Missouri

Sara Parker, State Libn., Missouri State Lib., 600 W. Main, Box 387, Jefferson City 65102-0387. Tel. 573-751-2751, fax 573-751-3612, e-mail sparker@mail.sos.state. mo.us.

Montana

Karen Strege, State Libn., Montana State Lib., 1515 E. Sixth Ave., Box 201800, Helena 59620-1800. Tel. 406-444-3115, fax 406-444-5612, e-mail kstrege@state. mt.gov.

Nebraska

Rod Wagner, Dir., Nebraska Lib. Commission, The Atrium, 1200 N St., Suite 120, Lincoln 68508-2023. Tel. 402-471-4001, fax 402-471-2083, e-mail rwagner@neon.nlc.state.ne.us.

Nevada

Moneteria Hightower, Dir., Dept. of Museums, Libs. and Arts, Capitol Complex, Carson City 89710. Tel. 702-687-8315, fax 702-687-8311, e-mail mhightower@clan.lib.nv.us.

New Hampshire

Michael York, State Libn., New Hampshire State Lib., 20 Park St., Concord 03301-6314. Tel. 603-271-2397, fax 603-271-6826, e-mail myork@finch.nhsl.lib.nh.us.

New Jersey

John H. Livingstone, Jr., State Libn., Div. of State Lib., Dept. of Education, 185 W. State St., CN520, Trenton 08625-0520. Tel. 609-292-6200, fax 609-292-2746, e-mail jaliving@njsl.tesc.edu.

New Mexico

Benjamin Wakashige, State Libn., New Mexico State Lib., Aquisitions Section, 1209 Camino Carlos Rey, Santa Fe 87505. Tel. 505-827-3804, fax 505-827-3888, e-mail ben@stlib.state.nm.us.

New York

Janet M. Welch, State Libn./Asst. Commissioner for Libs., New York State Lib., Cultural Education Center, Albany 12230. Tel. 518-474-5930, fax 518-486-2152, e-mail jwelch2@mail.nysed.gov.

North Carolina

Sandra M. Cooper, State Libn., State Lib. of North Carolina, 4640 Mail Service Center, Raleigh 27601. Tel. 919-733-2570, fax 919-733-8748, e-mail scooper@library.dcr.state.nc.us.

North Dakota

Michael Jaugstetter, State Libn., North Dakota State Lib., Liberty Memorial Bldg., Capitol Grounds, 604 E. Boulevard Ave., Bismarck 58505-0800. Tel. 701-328-2492, fax 701-328-2040, e-mail msmail.mjaugste@ranch.state.nd.us.

Ohio

Michael Lucas, State Libn., State Lib. of Ohio, 65 S. Front St., Columbus 43215-4163. Tel. 614-644-6863, fax 614-466-3584, e-mail mlucas@sloma.state.ohio.us.

Oklahoma

Robert L. Clark, State Libn., Oklahoma Dept. of Libs., 200 N.E. 18 St., Oklahoma City 73105. Tel. 405-521-2502, fax 405-525-7804, e-mail bclark@oltn.odl.state.ok.us.

Oregon

Jim Scheppke, State Libn., Oregon State Lib., State Lib. Bldg., 250 Winter St. N.E., Salem 97310-0640. Tel. 503-378-4367, fax 503-588-7119, e-mail jim.b.scheppke@state.or.us.

Pennsylvania

Gary D. Wolfe, Dep. Secy. and Commissioner of Libs., Pennsylvania Dept. of Educ., Box 1601, Harrisburg 17105. Tel. 717-787-2646, fax 717-772-3265, e-mail gdw@unix1.stlib.state.pa.us.

Rhode Island

Barbara Weaver, Chief Information Officer, Office of Lib. and Info. Services, Rhode Island Dept. of Administration, 1 Capitol Hill, Providence 02908-5870. Tel. 401-222-4444, fax 401-222-4260, e-mail barbarawr@lorl.state.ri.us.

South Carolina

James B. Johnson, Jr., Dir., South Carolina State Lib., 1500 Senate St., Box 11469, Columbia 29211. Tel. 803-734-8666, fax 803-734-8676, e-mail jim@leo.scsl.state.sc.us.

South Dakota

State Libn., South Dakota State Lib., 800 Governors Dr., Pierre 57501-2294. Tel. 605-773-3131, fax 605-773-5502.

Tennessee

Edwin S. Gleaves, State Libn./Archivist, Tennessee State Lib. and Archives, 403 Seventh Ave. N., Nashville 37243-0312. Tel. 615-741-7996, fax 615-741-6471, e-mail egleaves@mail.state.tn.us.

Texas

Robert S. Martin, Dir./State Libn., Texas State Lib. and Archives Commission, Box 12927, Austin 78711-2927. Tel. 512-463-5460, fax 512-463-5436, e-mail robert. martin@tsl.state.tx.us.

Utah

Amy Owen, Dir., Utah State Lib. Div., 250 N. 1950 W., Suite A, Salt Lake City 84115-7901. Tel. 801-715-6770, fax 801-715-6767, e-mail aowen@state.lib.ut.us.

Vermont

Sybil Brigham McShane, State Libn., Vermont Dept. of Libs., 109 State St., Montpelier 05609-0601. Tel. 802-828-3265, fax 802-828-2199, e-mail smcshane@dol. state.vt.us.

Virginia

Nolan T. Yelich, State Libn., Lib. of Virginia, 800 E. Broad St., Richmond 23219-3491. Tel. 804-692-3535, fax 804-692-3594, e-mail nyelich@leo.vsla.edu.

Washington

Nancy L. Zussy, State Libn., Washington State Lib., Box 42460, Olympia 98504-2460. Tel. 360-753-2915, fax 360-586-7575, e-mail nzussy@statelib.wa.gov.

West Virginia

David Price, Exec. Dir., West Virginia Lib. Commission, 1900 Kanawha Blvd. E., Charleston 25305-0620. Tel. 304-558-2041, fax 304-558-2044, e-mail priced@ wvlc.wvnet.edu.

Wisconsin

Calvin Potter, Asst. Superintendent, Div. for Libs. and Community Learning, Dept. of Public Instruction, Box 7841, Madison 53707-7841. Tel. 608-266-2205, fax 608-267-1052, e-mail pottecj@mail.state.wi.us.

Wyoming

Lesley Boughton, State Libn., State Lib. Div., Dept. of Administration and Info., Supreme Court and State Lib. Bldg., Cheyenne 82002-0060. Tel. 307-777-7283, fax 307-777-6289, e-mail lbough@ missc.state.wy.us.

American Samoa

Cheryl Morales, Territorial Libn., Office of Lib. Services, Box 1329, Pago Pago 96799. Tel. 684-633-1181.

Guam

Christine K. Scott-Smith, Dir./Territorial Libn., Nieves M. Flores Memorial Lib., 254 Martyr St., Agana 96910-0254. Tel. 671-475-4751, fax 671-477-9777, e-mail csctsmth@kuentos.guam.net.

Northern Mariana Islands

Commonwealth Libn., Joeten-Kiyu Public Lib., Box 1092, Commonwealth of the Northern Mariana Islands, Saipan 96950. Tel. 670-235-7322, fax 670-235-7550, e-mail psteere@saipan.com; William Matson, Federal Programs Coordinator, Dept. of Educ., Commonwealth of the Northern Mariana Islands, Saipan 96950. Tel. 670-322-6405, fax 670-322-4056.

Palau (Republic of)

Billy G. Kuartei; Minister of Educ., Box 189, Koror 96940. Tel. 680-488-2570, ext. 1003, fax 680-488-2830, e-mail emesiocm @prel.hawaii.edu.; Fermina Salvador, Libn., Palau Public Lib., Box 189, Koror 96940. Tel. 680-488-2973, fax 680-488-3310.

Puerto Rico

Victor Fajardo, Secy., Dept. of Educ., P.I. Box 190759, San Juan 00919-0759. Tel. 809-753-2062, fax 809-250-0275.

Virgin Islands

Jeannette Allis Bastian, Dir. and Territorial Libn., Div. of Libs., Archives and Museums, 23 Dronningens Gade, Saint Thomas 00802. Tel. 809-774-3407, fax 809-775-1887, e-mail jbastia@icarus.lis.pitt.edu.

Canada

Alberta

Punch Jackson, Mgr. Libs. Section, Arts & Libs. Branch, 901 Standard Life Center, 10405 Jasper Ave., Edmonton T5J 4R7. Tel. 403-427-6315, fax 403-422-9132.

British Columbia

Barbara Greeniaus, Dir., Lib. Services Branch, Ministry of Municipal Affairs, Box 9490 Stn. Prov. Govt., Victoria V8W 9N7. Tel. 250-356-1791, fax 250-953-3225, e-mail bgreeniaus@hq.marh.gov.bc.ca.

Manitoba

Sylvia Nicholson, Dir., Manitoba Culture, Heritage, and Tourism, Public Lib. Services, Unit 200, 1525 First St., Brandon R7A 7A1. Tel. 204-726-6864, fax 204-726-6868.

New Brunswick

Jocelyne Thompson, Acting Provincial Libn., New Brunswick Lib. Service, Box 6000, Fredericton E3B 5H1. Tel. 506-453-2354, fax 506-444-4064, e-mail jocelyne.thompson@gov.nb.ca.

Newfoundland

Judy Anderson, Acting Provincial Dir., Provincial Information and Library Resources Board, Arts and Culture Centre, Allandale Rd., St. John's A1B 3A3. Tel. 709-737-3964, fax 709-737-3009, World Wide Web http://www.publib.nf.ca/.

Northwest Territories

Sandy MacDonald, Territorial Libn., Northwest Territories Lib. Services, 75 Woodland Dr., Hay River X0E 1G1. Tel. 867-874-6531, fax 867-874-3321, e-mail sandy_macdonald@gov.nt.ca.

Nova Scotia

Elizabeth Armstrong, Acting Provincial Libn., Nova Scotia Provincial Lib., 3770 Kempt Rd., Halifax B3K 4X8. Tel. 902-424-2455, fax 902-424-0633, e-mail armstreh@gov.ns.ca.

Ontario

Michael Langford, Dir., Cultural Partnerships Branch, Ontario Govt. Ministry of Citizenship, Culture, and Recreation, 77 Bloor St. W., 3rd fl., Toronto M7A 2R9. Tel. 416-314-7342, fax 416-314-7635, e-mail Michael.Langford@mczcr.gov.on.ca.

Prince Edward Island

Harry Holman, Dir., P.E.I. Provincial Lib., Red Head Rd., Box 7500, Morell C0A 1S0. Tel. 902-961-7320, fax 902-961-7322, e-mail plshq@gov.pe.ca.ca.

Quebec

Denis Delangie, Dir., Direction des projets spéciaux et de la coordination, 225 Grande Allée Est, Bloc C, 2e étage, Quebec G1R 5G5. Tel. 418-644-0485, fax 418-643-4080, e-mail patrimoi@mail.mccq.gouv.qc.ca, or Denis_Delangie@MCC.gouv.qc.ca.

Saskatchewan

Joylene Campbell, Acting Provincial Libn., Saskatchewan Provincial Lib., 1352 Winnipeg St., Regina S4P 3V7. Tel. 306-787-2976, fax 306-787-2029, e-mail srp.adm@prov.lib.lib.sk.ca.

Yukon Territory

Linda R. Johnson, Dir., Dept. of Educ., Libs., and Archives, Box 2703, Whitehorse Y1A 2C6. Tel. 867-667-5309, fax 867-393-6253, e-mail Linda.Johnson@gov.yk.ca.

State School Library Media Associations

Alabama

Children's and School Libns. Div., Alabama Lib. Assn. Memb. 650. Publication. *The Alabama Librarian* (q.).

Exec. Dir. Missy Mathis, 400 S. Union St., Suite 140, Montgomery 36104. Tel. 334-262-5210, fax 334-262-5255, e-mail alala@mindspring.com. World Wide Web http://alala.home.mindspring.com/CSLD/csldpage.htm.

Address correspondence to the executive director.

Alaska

Alaska Assn. of School Libns. Memb. 150. Term of office. March 2000–February 2001. Publication. *Puffin* (3 per year).

Pres. Tiki Levinson. E-mail tlevinson@nnk.gcisa.net; *Secy.* Linda Thibodeau. E-mail thibodel@jsd.k12.ak.us; *Treas.* Karen Joynt. E-mail kjoynt@msb.mat-su.k12.ak.us; *School Lib. Coord. for Alaska State Lib.* Lois A. Petersen, 344 W. Third Ave., Suite 125, Anchorage 99501-2337. E-mail lois_petersen@eed.state.ak.us. Organization World Wide Web site http://www.alaska.net/~akla/akasl/home.html.

Arizona

School Lib. Media Div., Arizona Lib. Assn. Memb. 500. Term of Office. Nov. 1998–Dec. 1999. Publication. *AZLA Newsletter.*

Pres. Paul Kreamer, Head Libn., Santa Rita H.S., 3951 S. Pantano, Tucson 85730. Tel./fax 520-733-8027, e-mail kreamep@setmms.tusd.k12.az.us; *Pres.-Elect* Kim Grimes, Libn., Corbett Elementary, 5949 E. 29 St., Tucson 85711. Tel. 520-512-3370, fax 520-617-4323, e-mail kgrimes@tusd.k12.az.us; *Secy.* Linda Sater, Lib. Media Specialist, Deer Valley Middle School, 21100 N. 27 Ave., Phoenix 85027. Tel. 602-581-7900, e-mail lsater@dv.dvusd.k12.az.us.

Address correspondence to the president. Organization World Wide Web site http://www.amphi.com/~bbenedic/AZLASLMD.html.

Arkansas

Arkansas Assn. of School Libns. and Media Educators. Term of Office. Jan.–Dec. 1999.

Chair Loveida Ingram, Jacksonville H.S., 2400 Linda La., Jacksonville 72076. Tel. 501-982-2128, e-mail loveidai@yahoo.com; *V. Chair* Carol Ann Hart, Lee H.S., 523 N. Forrest Ave., Marianna 72360. Tel. 870-295-7130, e-mail hartc@lhs.grsc.k12.ar.us; *Secy.-Treas.* Chanetta Case, Pine Forest Elementary, 400 Pine Forest Dr., Maumelle 72113.

Address correspondence to the chairperson.

California

California School Lib. Assn. Memb. 2,200. Term of Office. Pres, V.P., Secy., Oct. 1998–Nov. 1999; Treas., Oct. 1999–Nov. 2001. Publication. *Journal of the CSLA* (2 per year). *Ed.* Leslie Farmer.

Pres. Marylin Robertson, Los Angeles Unified School Dist., 1320 W. Third St., Los Angeles 90017. Tel. 213-625-5548, e-mail mnrobert@aol.com; *Pres.-Elect* JoEllen Misakian. E-mail jmisakian@fresno.edu; *Secy.* Claudette McLinn, Los Angeles Unified School Dist., 1320 W. Third St., Los Angeles 90017. Tel. 213-625-6481, e-mail cmclinn@lausd.k12.ca.us; *Treas.* Betty Vandivier. E-mail bvandivi@mail.sandi.net; *Business Office Secy.* Nancy D. Kohn, CSLA, 1499 Old Bayshore Hwy., Suite 142, Burlingame 94010. Tel. 650-692-2350, fax 650-692-4956, World Wide Web http://www.schoollibrary.org/.

Address correspondence to the business office secretary.

Colorado

Colorado Educational Media Assn. Memb. 500. Term of Office. Feb. 2000–Feb. 2001. Publication. *The Medium* (5 per year).

Pres. Jody Gehrig, Denver Public Schools, Denver 80204. Tel. 303-405-8101, fax 303-405-8100, e-mail jody_gehrig@dps.cudenver.edu; *Exec. Secy.* Heidi Baker.

Address correspondence to the executive secretary, CEMA, Box 22814, Denver 80222. Tel. 303-292-5434, e-mail cemacolorado@juno.com, World Wide Web http://www.aclin.org/other/education/library/cema/.

Connecticut

Connecticut Educational Media Assn. Memb. 550. Term of Office. May 1999–May 2000. Publications. *CEMA Update* (q.); *CEMA Gram* (mo.).

Pres. Frances Nadeau, 440 Matthews St., Bristol 06010. Tel. 203-589-0813, e-mail nadeau@ccsu.edu; *V.P.* Irene Kwidzinski, 293 Pumpkin Hill Rd., New Milford 06776. Tel. 203-355-0762, e-mail Kwidzinskii. NOR-PO@new-milford.k12.ct.us; *Secy.* Kate Wakefield, 140 Burgundy Hill La., Middletown 06457. E-mail kwakefield@snet.net; *Treas.* Wendell Rector, 4 Woodbury Pl., Woodbury 06798. Tel. 203-263-2707; *Admin. Secy.* Anne Weimann, 25 Elmwood Ave., Trumbull 06611. Tel. 203-372-2260.

Address correspondence to the administrative secretary. Organization World Wide Web site http://www.ctcema.org/.

Delaware

Delaware School Lib. Media Assn., Div. of Delaware Lib. Assn. Memb. 115. Term of Office. Apr. 1999–Apr. 2000. Publications. *DSLMA Newsletter* (irreg.); column in *DLA Bulletin* (3 per year).

Pres. Margaret Prouse, Dover H.S., Dover. E-mail mprouse@den.k12.de.us.

Address correspondence to the president.

District of Columbia

District of Columbia Assn. of School Libns. Memb. 93. Publication. *Newsletter* (4 per year).

Pres. Ellen B. Amey, Hart Junior H.S., Washington. E-mail ebamey@aol.com.

Florida

Florida Assn. for Media in Education. Memb. 1,450. Term of Office. Nov. 1999–Oct. 2000. Publication. *Florida Media Quarterly.* Ed. William H. Taylor, 2991 Foxcroft Dr., Tallahassee 32308. Tel. 850-668-1564.

Pres. Barbara Correll. Tel. 954-765-6154, fax 954-765-6773, e-mail correll_b@popmail.firn.edu; *Pres.-Elect* Jane Terwillegar. Tel. 561-684-5180, fax 561-684-5409, e-mail terwille_j@popmail.firn.edu; *V.P.* Sandra Nelson. Tel. 941-335-1446, fax 941-337-8654, e-mail nelson_s@popmail.firm.edu; *Assn. Exec.* Louise Costello, Box 70577, Fort Lauderdale 33307. Tel./fax 954-566-1312, e-mail lcfame@aol.com. Organization World Wide Web site http://www.firn.edu/fame/.

Address correspondence to the association executive.

Georgia

School Lib. Media Div., Georgia Lib. Assn. Memb. 217. Term of Office. Oct. 1999–Oct. 2000.

Chair Gordon Baker, Media Center Dir., Eagle's Landing H.S., 301 Tunis Rd., McDonough 30253. Tel. 770-954-9515, fax 770 914-9789, e-mail GordonBaker@mail.clayton.edu.

Hawaii

Hawaii Assn. of School Libns. Memb. 250. Term of Office. June 1999–May 2000. Publications. *HASL Newsletter* (4 per year).

Pres. Carolyn Kirio, Waianae H.S. E-mail ckirio@makani.k12.hi.us; *V.P., Programming* Faye Taira, Ilima Intermediate. E-mail faye_taira@notes.k12.hi.us; *V.P., Membership* Irmalee Choo, Lunalilo Elementary. E-mail ichoo@hekili.

Address correspondence to the association, Box 235019, Honolulu 96823. Organization World Wide Web site http://www.k12.hi.us/~hasl.

Idaho

Educational Media Div., Idaho Lib. Assn. Memb. 125. Term of Office. Oct. 1999–Oct. 2000. Publication. Column in *The Idaho Librarian* (q.).

Chair Mary Edmonds, Box 40, Post Falls H.S., Post Falls 83854. E-mail medmonds@sd273.k12.id.us.

Address correspondence to the chairperson.

Illinois

Illinois School Lib. Media Assn. Memb. 1,100. Term of Office. July 1999–June 2000. Publications. *ISLMA News* (5 per year), *ISLMA Membership Directory* (ann.).

Pres. Kenneth Hawley, 135 Dover Dr., Decatur 62521. Tel. 217-424-8857, e-mail khawley@cam.k12.il.us; *Pres.-Elect* Barbara Lund, 2780 Weeping Willow C, Lisle 60532. Tel. 630-305-3141, e-mail blund@lisle.dupage.k12.il.us; *Exec. Secy.* Kay Maynard, Box 598, Canton 61520. Tel. 309-649-0911, fax 309-647-0140, e-mail ISLMA@aol.com.

Address correspondence to the executive secretary. Organization World Wide Web site http://www.islma.org/.

Indiana

Assn. for Indiana Media Educators. Memb. 1,013. Term of Office. May 1999–Apr. 2000. Publications. *Focus* (11 per year).

Pres. Rhonda Hill, Triton Central H.S., Fairfield. E-mail rhill@indy.net; *Pres.-Elect* Marge A. Cox, New Castle. E-mail marge_cox@mail.nobl.k12.in.us; *Exec. Dir., Indiana Lib. Federation* Linda D. Kolb.

Address correspondence to the federation executive office, 6408 Carrolton Ave., Indianapolis 46220. Tel. 317-257-2040, fax 317-257-1393, e-mail ilf@indy.net.

Iowa

Iowa Educational Media Assn. Memb. 500. Term of Office. Mar. 1999–Mar. 2000. Publication. *Iowa Media Message* (4 per year). *Ed.* Karen Lampe, Green Valley AEA, 1405 N. Lincoln, Creston 50801.

Pres. Mary Cameron; *Secy.* Jen Buckingham; *Treas.* Rick Valley; *Exec. Secy.* Paula Behrendt, 2306 6th, Harlan 51537. Tel./fax 712-755-5918, e-mail paulab@harlannet.com.

Address correspondence to the executive secretary.

Kansas

Kansas Assn. of School Libns. Memb. 700. Term of Office. Aug. 1999–July 2000. Publication. *KASL Newsletter* (s. ann.).

Pres. Diane Leupold. Tel. 785-575-6969 ext. 229; *Exec. Secy.* Judith Eller, 8517 W. Northridge, Wichita 67205. Tel. 316-773-6723, e-mail judell@hotmail.com.

Address correspondence to the executive secretary. Organization World Wide Web site http://skyways.lib.ks.us/kasl/.

Kentucky

Kentucky School Media Assn. Memb. 620. Term of Office. Oct. 1999–Oct. 2000. Publication. *KSMA Newsletter* (q.).

Pres. Susan Melcher, Hawthorne Elementary, 2301 Clarendon Ave., Louisville 40205. Tel. 502-485-8263, e-mail smelche1@jefferson.k12.ky.us; *Pres.-Elect* Christine McIntosh, Bernheim Middle School, 700 Audubon Dr., Shepherdsville 40165. Tel. 502-543-7614, e-mail cmcintosh@bullitt.k12.ky.us; *Secy.* Lyn Watson, Fairdale Elementary, 10104 Mitchell Hill Rd., Louisville 40229. Tel. 502-485-8247, fax 502-484-8371, e-mail LLwatson@bellsouth.net; *Treas.* Becky Stephens, Burkhead Elementary, 521 Charlemagne Blvd., Elizabethtown 42701. Tel. 270-769-5983, e-mail bstephen@hardin.k12.ky.us.

Address correspondence to the president. Organization World Wide Web site http://www.uky.edu/OtherOrgs/KSMA/ksma.html.

Louisiana

Louisiana Assn. of School Libns. Memb. 420. Term of Office. July 1999–June 2000.

Pres.; Barbara Burney, Huntington H.S., 6801 Raspberry Lane, Shreveport 71129. Tel. 318-687-6789, e-mail hunths@prysm.net; *1st V.P.* Antonio White, E. A. Martin Middle School, 401 Broadmoor Blvd., Lafayette 70503. Tel. 318-984-9796, e-mail twhite@lft.k12.la.us; *2nd V.P.* Betty Brackins, Baton Rouge Magnet H.S., 2825 Government St., Baton Rouge 70806. E-mail bbrackin@isis.ebrps.subr.edu; *Secy.* Susan Cheshire, Parkview Baptist Elementary, 5750 Parkview Rd., Baton Rouge 70816. Tel. 225-293-2500, e-mail dcheshir@bellsouth.net.

Address correspondence to the association, c/o Louisiana Lib. Assn., Box 3058, Baton Rouge 70821. Organization World Wide Web site http://www.leeric.lsu.edu/lla/lasl/.

Maine

Maine School Lib. Assn. Memb. 350. Term of Office. May 1999–May 2000. Publication.

Maine Entry (with the Maine Lib. Assn.; q.).

Pres. Suzan J. Nelson, Portland H.S., 284 Cumberland Ave., Portland 04101. Tel. 207-874-8250, e-mail sjnelson@saturn.caps.maine.edu; *1st V.P.* Nancy Grant, Penquis Valley H.S. E-mail nbgrant@ctel.net; *Secy.* Margaret McNamee, Lyman Moore Middle School. E-mail margaretmc@lamere.net.

Address correspondence to the president. Organization World Wide Web http://www.maslibraries.org/.

Maryland

Maryland Educational Media Organization. Term of Office. July 1999–June 2000. Publication. *MEMORANDOM.*

Pres. Linda Williams; *Secy.* Jayne Moore, 25943 Fox Grape Rd., Greensboro 21639.

Address correspondence to the association, Box 21127, Baltimore 21228.

Massachusetts

Massachusetts School Lib. Media Assn. Memb. 700. Term of Office. June 1999–May 2000. Publication. *Media Forum* (q.).

Pres. Joan Gallagher. Tel. 781-383-2447, e-mail gallager@massed.net; *Secy.* Betsy Jackson. Tel. 781-659-8810, e-mail bjackson@ssec.nps.org; *Admin. Asst.* Sue Rebello, MSLMA, Box 25, Three Rivers 01080-0025. Tel./fax 413-283-6675.

Address correspondence to the secretary. Organization World Wide Web site http://www.mslma.org/.

Michigan

Michigan Assn. for Media in Education. Memb. 1,400. Term of Office. Jan.–Dec. 2000. Publications. *Media Spectrum* (3 per year); *MAME Newsletter* (4 per year).

Pres. Cyndi Phillip, Grand Haven Public Schools, 1415 S. Beechtree, Grand Haven 49417. Tel. 616-850-5400, e-mail cphillip@remc7.k12.mi.us; *Pres.-Elect* Teri Terry, Pinckney H.S., 10255 Dexter/Pinckney Rd., Box 439, Pinckney 48169. Tel. 810-225-5531, fax 810-225-5535, e-mail t2t_51@yahoo.com; *Secy.* Karen Lemmons, Hutchinson Elementary, 5221 Montclair, Detroit 48213. Tel. 313-852-9912, fax 313-852-9911, e-mail camaraife@aol.com; *Treas.* Susan Thornton, Ezra Eby Elementary Media

Center, 220 West St., Box 308, Napoleon 49261-0308. Tel. 517-536-8667 ext. 463, fax 517-536-8109, e-mail thorntonsl@aol.com; *Exec. Dir.* Burton H. Brooks, 6810 S. Cedar St., Suite 8, Lansing 48911. Tel. 517-699-1717, fax 616-842-9195, e-mail bhbrooks@aol.com.

Address correspondence to the executive director. Organization World Wide Web site http://www.mame.gen.mi.us.

Minnesota

Minnesota Educational Media Organization. Memb. 750. Term of Office. (Pres.) Aug. 1999–Aug. 2000. Publications. *Minnesota Media*; *ImMEDIAte*; *MEMOrandom.*

Co-Pres. Allen Edwards, 2824 The Narrows Dr. S.W., Alexandria 56308. Tel. 612-859-2192, e-mail aedwards@osakis.k12.mn.us; Leslie Erickson, 1396 Summit Ave., Saint Paul 55105-2218. Tel. 651-293-5936, e-mail lerickson@spps.stpaul.k12.mn.us; *Co-Pres.-Elect* Susan Benson Krohn, 325 North Duck Lake Ave., Madison Lake 56063. Tel. 507-387-7698, e-mail skrohn1@mail.isd77.k12.mn.us; Charlie (Linda) Lindberg, R.R. 1, Box 37, Kennedy 56733. Tel. 218-843-2857, e-mail clindberg@kittson.k12.mn.us; *Secy.* Virjean Griensewic, 304 Stoltzman Rd., Mankato 56001. E-mail vgrien1@mail.isd77.k12.mn.us; *Treas.* Kelly Sharkey, 501 E. Main St., New Prague 56071. Tel. 612-401-5531, e-mail kelly.sharkey@minnetonka.k12.mn.us; *Admin. Asst.* Evie Funk, 331 Wedgewood La. N., Plymouth 56467. Tel. 612-546-6214, e-mail evie.funk@worldnet.att.net. Organization World Wide Web site http://memoweb.org/.

Mississippi

School Section, Mississippi Lib. Assn. Memb. 1,300.

Chair Jolee Hussey; *V. Chair* Cindy Harrison; *Secy.* Juanita Owen.

Address correspondence to the association, c/o Mississippi Lib. Assn., Box 2044, Jackson 39289-1448. Tel. 601-352-3917, e-mail mla@meta3.net, World Wide Web http://library.msstate.edu/mla/mla.html.

Missouri

Missouri Assn. of School Libns. Memb.

1,129. Term of Office. June 1999–May 2000. Publication. *Media Horizons* (ann.), *Connections* (q.).

Pres. Brenda Steffens. E-mail hwd000@ mail.connect.more.net; *1st V.P./Pres.-Elect* Dale Guthrie. E-mail Dale_Guthrie@clayton. k12.mo.us; *2nd V.P.* Marianne Fues; *Secy.* Judy Wise; *Treas.* Yvonne Gibbs.

Address correspondence to the association, 1552 Rue Riviera, Bonne Terre 63628-9349. Tel./fax 573-358-1053, e-mail masloffice@ aol.com, World Wide Web http://www.coe. missouri.edu/~masl/.

Montana

Montana School Lib. Media Div., Montana Lib. Assn. Memb. 215. Term of Office. July 1999–June 2000. Publication. *FOCUS* (published by Montana Lib. Assn.) (q.).

Chair Lynn McKinney, Senior H.S., 1001 Babcock Blvd., Billings 59105-2223. Tel. 406-247-2217, fax 406-255-3521, e-mail mckinneyl@billings.k12.mt.us.

Nebraska

Nebraska Educational Media. Assn. Memb. 350. Term of Office. July 1999–June 2000. Publication. *NEMA News* (q.).

Pres. Marilyn Scahill, Dodge Elementary School, 641 South Oak St., Grand Island 68801. Tel. 308-385-5889, fax 402-694-5026, e-mail mscahill@esu10.org; *Pres.-Elect* Sandy White, ESU #14, Box 77, Sidney 69162. Tel. 308-254-4677, fax 308-254-5371, swhite@panesu.esu14.k12.ne.us; *Secy.* Deb Grove, Papillion-LaVista H.S., 402 E. Centennial Rd., Papillion 68046-2078. Tel. 402-339-0405, fax 402-339-6929, e-mail dgrove@esu3.esu3.k12.ne.us; *Treas.* Deborah Larson, Rt. #1, Box 250, St. Edward 68660. Tel. 402-678-2456, fax 402-395-2137, e-mail ldarson@esu7.org; *Exec. Secy.* Joie Taylor, 2301 31st St., Columbus 68601. Tel. 402-564-1781, fax 402-563-7005, e-mail jtaylor@esu7.org.

Address correspondence to the executive secretary. Organization World Wide Web site http://nema.k12.ne.us/.

Nevada

Nevada School and Children's Lib. Section, Nevada Lib. Assn. Memb. 120.

Chair Ida McBride, Nevada Youth Training Center, 100 Youth Center Rd., Elko 89803. Tel. 775-738-5907 ext. 244, fax 775-738-8812, e-mail gdeming@sierra.net; *Co-Chair* Patty Livreri, Bastian H.S., Box 188, Caliente 89008. Tel. 775-726-3140, fax 775-726-3371.

New Hampshire

New Hampshire Educational Media Assn., Box 418, Concord 03302-0418. Memb. 265. Term of Office. June 1999–June 2000. Publications. *On line* (5 per year). *Ed.* Nancy J. Keane, Rundlett Middle School, 144 South St., Concord 03301. Tel. 603-225-0862, fax 603-226-3288.

Pres. Nancy J. Keane, Rundlett Middle School, 144 South St., Concord 03301. E-mail nancy.keane@rundlett.concord.k12. nh.us.

Address correspondence to the president. Organization World Wide Web site http:// www.nhptv.org/kn/nhema/.

New Jersey

Educational Media Assn. of New Jersey. Memb. 1,100. Term of Office. June 1999–June 2000. Publications. *Bookmark* (mo.); *Emanations* (ann.).

Pres. Villy Gandhi, Lakeside Middle School, 316 Lakeside Ave., Pompton Lakes 07442. Tel. 973-835-6221, e-mail villy@ cybertnex.net; *Pres.-Elect* Connie Hitchcock, Clark Mills School, Gordons Corner Rd., Englishtown 07726-3798. Tel. 732-446-8124, e-mail Cahitchco@aol.com; *V.P.* Jackie Gould, Clearview Regional H.S., 625 Breakneck Rd., Box 2000, Mullica Hill 08062. Tel. 609-223-2723, e-mail jegould@ snip.net.

Address correspondence to the president, president-elect, or vice president. Organization World Wide Web site http://www.emanj. org.

New Mexico

[See "New Mexico" under "State, Provincial, and Regional Library Associations" earlier in Part 6—*Ed.*].

New York

School Lib. Media Section, New York Lib.

Assn., 252 Hudson St., Albany 12210. Tel. 518-432-6952, 800-252-6952. Memb. 906. Term of Office. Oct. 1999–Oct. 2000. Publications. *SLMSGram* (q.); participates in *NYLA Bulletin* (mo. except July and Aug.).

Pres. Ellen Rubin, Wallkill Senior H.S., 90 Robinson Dr., Wallkill 12589. Tel. 914-895-2048/8061, fax 914-895-8021, e-mail erubin@int1.mhrcc.org; *V.P./Pres.-Elect* Erin Dinneen, Clinton Middle/H.S., 75 Chenango Ave., Clinton 13323. Tel. 315-853-5574, fax 315-853-8727; *Past Pres.* Christie Frost-Wendlowsky, SCT BOCES, 459 Philo Rd., Bldg. 11, Elmira 14903. Tel. 607-739-3581 ext. 2703; *Secy.* Rosina Alaimo, 540 Ashland Ave., Buffalo 14222. Tel. 716-631-4860, fax 716-631-4867, e-mail Rosella@att.net

Address correspondence to the president or secretary. Organization World Wide Web site http://www.acsu.buffalo.edu/~slms/.

North Carolina

North Carolina Assn. of School Libns. Memb. 800. Term of Office. Oct. 1999–Oct. 2000.

Pres. Karen Gavigan, Rockingham County Schools, Media and Technology Center, 920 Johnson St., Reidsville 27320. Tel. 336-342-1823, fax 336-349-6098, e-mail kgavigan@rock.k12.nc.us; *Secy.* Mary Ashley, Hiwassee Dam School, 7755 Hwy. 294, Murphy 28906. Tel. 828-644-5115, fax 828-644-9463, e-mail ashley@grove.net.

Address correspondence to the president. Organization World Wide Web site http://members.xoom.com/ncasl/.

North Dakota

School Lib. and Youth Services Section, North Dakota Lib. Assn. Memb. 100. Term of Office. Sept. 1999–Sept. 2000. Publication. *The Good Stuff* (q).

Pres. Darlene Fairaizl, 310 12th Ave. N.W., No. 4, Mandan 58554. Tel. 701-663-5796, e-mail fairaizl@sendit.nodak.edu.

Address correspondence to the president.

Ohio

Ohio Educational Lib. Media Assn. Memb. 1,300. Publication. *Ohio Media Spectrum.*

Pres. SarahJane Holzhauer. E-mail orhs_sjh@nwoca.org; *V.P.* Gayle Geitgey. E-mail GayleG1650@aol.com; *Exec. Dir.* Ann Hanning, 1631 N.W. Professional Plaza, Columbus 43220. Tel. 614-326-1460, fax 614-459-2087, e-mail oelma@mecdc.org.

Address correspondence to the executive director. Organization World Wide Web site http://www.mec.ohio.gov/oelma/.

Oklahoma

Oklahoma Assn. of School Lib. Media Specialists. Memb. 3,005. Term of Office. July 1999–June 2000. Publication. *Oklahoma Librarian.*

Chair Janet Coontz, Glenwood Elementary, 824 N. Oakwood, Enid 73703. E-mail glenw@ionet.net; *Chair-Elect* Sandra Austin; *Secy.* Kathleen Lienke; *Treas.* Don Wilson; *AASL Delegate* Bettie Estes Rickner, 12400 S. Mustang Rd., Mustang 73064. E-mail ber@ionet.net.

Address correspondence to the chairperson.

Oregon

Oregon Educational Media Assn. Memb. 600. Term of Office. July 1999–June 2000. Publication. *INTERCHANGE.*

Pres. Sheryl Steinke. E-mail steinke@4j.lane.edu; *Pres.-Elect* Margo Jensen; *Exec. Dir.* Jim Hayden, Box 277, Terrebonne 97760. Tel./fax 541-923-0675.

Address correspondence to the executive director. Organization World Wide Web site http://www.teleport.com/~oema/.

Pennsylvania

Pennsylvania School Libns. Assn. Memb. 1,565. Term of Office. July 1999–June 2000. Publication. *Learning and Media* (q.).

Pres. Linda Carvell, 1419 Hillcrest Rd., Lancaster 17603. Tel. 717-397-9383, fax 717-431-1232, e-mail carvell@redrosc.net; *V.P./Pres.-Elect* Veanna Baxter, 1588 Springville Rd., New Holland 17557. Tel. 717-355-2155, fax 717-355-9703, e-mail vebaxter@epix.net.

Address correspondence to the president. Organization World Wide Web site http://www.psla.org.

Rhode Island

Rhode Island Educational Media Assn.

Memb. 398. Term of Office. June 1998–May 2000. Publication. *RIEMA Newsletter* (q.) and *REIMA Flash* (q.) *Ed.* Barbara Ashby, 22 Winthrope Dr., Barrington 02806. E-mail gjwl@aol.com.

Pres. Marykay W. Schnare, 11 Nelson St., Providence 02908. Tel. 401-331-2059, e-mail ritoy@aol.com; *V.P.* Connie Malinowski, 320 Ives Rd., East Greenwich 02818. Tel. 401-885-0456, e-mail ride0276@ride.ri.net; *Secy.* Susan Peckham, 68 Sefton Dr., Cranston 02905. Tel. 401-785-0987, e-mail ride8096@ride.ri.net; *Treas.* Livia Giroux, 333 Potters Ave., Warwick 02886. Tel. 401-738-5666, e-mail ride7572@ride.ri.net.

Address correspondence to the association, Box 762, Portsmouth 02871.

South Carolina

South Carolina Assn. of School Libns. Memb. 1,100. Term of Office. June 1999–May 2000. Publication. *Media Center Messenger* (5 per year).

Pres. Penny Hayne, Lake Murray Elementary School, 1531 Three Dog Rd., Chapin 29036. Tel. 803-732-8151, e-mail phayne@lex5.k12.sc.us; *Pres.-Elect* Betsy Adams. E-mail badams@richlandone.org; *Secy.* Lynne V. Douglass-Simmons, Walterboro H.S., 588 Hendersonville Hwy., Walterboro 29488. Tel. 843-538-4335; *Treas.* Sue Waddell, Lakeview Middle School, 3801 Old Buncombe Rd., Greenville 29609. Tel. 864-294-4361, fax 864-294-4236, e-mail lakeview@greenville.k12.sc.

Address correspondence to the president. Organization World Wide Web site http://www.libsci.sc.edu/SCASL/scasl.htm.

South Dakota

South Dakota School Lib. Media Assn., Section of the South Dakota Lib. Assn. and South Dakota Education Assn. Memb. 146. Term of Office. Oct. 1999–Oct. 2000.

Pres. Bev Birkeland, Box 55, Faith 57626; *Pres.-Elect* Ray Caffe, 325 W. Fifth St., Miller 57362-1010; *Secy.-Treas.* Linda Demery, Faulkton School, Box 161, Faulkton 57438.

Address correspondence to the secretary-treasurer.

Tennessee

Tennessee Assn. of School Libns. (affiliated with the Tennessee Education Assn.). Memb. 450. Term of Office. Jan.–Dec. 2000. Publication. *Footnotes* (q.).

Pres. Sherry Ball, 7721 Sevilla Rd., Powell 37849. Tel. 865-947-5726, e-mail slball2@aol.com; *V.P./Pres.-Elect* Regina Patterson, 491 W. C. Nursing Home Rd., Dresden 38225. Tel. 901-364-3014; *Secy.* Faye Nelson, 737 Boyds Creek Hwy., Seymour 37865. Tel. 865-573-9320; *Treas.* Bonnie Lockwood, 7995 Gainesborough Rd., Knoxville 37907. Tel. 865-909-9000.

Address correspondence to the president.

Texas

Texas Assn. of School Libns (Div. of Texas Lib. Assn.). Memb. 3,686. Term of Office. Apr. 1999–Apr. 2000. Publication. *Media Matters* (3 per year).

Chair Vicki M. Krebsbach, 21045 Crescent Oaks, San Antonio 78258. Tel. 210-497-6200, fax 210-497-6204; *Chair-Elect* Mary A. Berry, Sam Houston State Univ., Huntsville. Tel. 409-294-1150, fax 409-294-1153, e-mail lis_mab@shsu.edu; *Secy.* Barbara Jinkins, Edna M. Fielder Elementary/Katy ISD, Katy. Tel. 281-396-6450, fax 281-396-6454, e-mail bjinkins@tenet.edu.

Address correspondence to the association, 3355 Bee Cave Rd., Suite 401, Austin 78746. Tel. 512-328-1518, fax 512-328-8852, e-mail tla@txla. org.

Utah

Utah Educational Lib. Media Assn. Memb. 390. Term of Office. Mar. 2000–Feb. 2001. Publication. *UELMA Newsletter* (4 per year).

Pres. Dennis Morgan, Riverview Junior H.S., 751 W. Tripp La., Murray 84123. Tel. 801-264-7406, e-mail dmorgan@rjh.mury. k12.ut.us; *Exec. Dir.* Larry Jeppesen, Cedar Ridge Middle School, 65 N. 200 W., Hyde Park 84318. Tel. 435-563-6229, fax 435-563-3914, e-mail ljeppese@crms.cache.k12.ut.us.

Address correspondence to the executive director. Organization World Wide Web site http://www.uelma.org/.

Vermont

Vermont Educational Media Assn. Memb. 203. Term of Office. May 1999–May 2000. Publication. *VEMA News* (q.).

Pres. Merlyn Miller, Burr and Burton Academy, Seminary Ave., Manchester 05254. Tel. 802-362-1775, fax 802-362-0574, e-mail mmiller@sovern.net; *Pres.-Elect* Melissa Malcolm, Mt. Abraham Union H.S., 4 Airport Dr., Bristol 05443. Tel. 802-453-2333, fax 802-453-4359, e-mail mmalcolm@mtabe.k12.vt.us.

Address correspondence to the president. Organization World Wide Web site http://www.vema.together.com/.

Virginia

Virginia Educational Media Assn. Memb. 1,450. Term of Office. (Pres. and Pres.-Elect) Nov. 1999–Nov. 2000 (other offices 2 years in alternating years). Publication. *Mediagram* (q.).

Pres. Linda Baker Owen, Box 88, Walkerton 23177. Tel. 804-343-6550, e-mail lbowen@henrico.k12.va.us; *Pres.-Elect* Audrey Church, 5900 Cabbage Patch Rd., Keysville 23947. Tel. 804-736-8204, e-mail achurch@pen.k12.va.us; *Exec. Mgr.* Jean Remler. Tel./fax 703-764-0719, e-mail jremler@pen.k12.va.us.

Address correspondence to the association, Box 2744, Fairfax 22031-2744. World Wide Web http://vema.gen.va.us/.

Washington

Washington Lib. Media Assn. Memb. 1,200. Term of Office. Oct. 1999–Oct. 2000. Publications. *The Medium* (3 per year), *The Message* (2 per year). *Ed.* Mary Lou Gregory, 711 Spruce St., Hoquiam 98550. Tel. 206-533-4897.

Pres. Darwin Page. E-mail DAJ421@aol.com; *Pres.-Elect* Jan Weber. E-mail janweb@ix.netcom.com; *V.P.* Anne Shabel. E-mail ashabel@iname.com; *Treas.* Barbara J. Baker. Tel. 425-823-0836, fax 425-821-5254, e-mail denmother@worldnet.att.net; *Secy.*

Nicole Bouvion. E-mail bouvionn@kittitas.wednet.edu.

Address correspondence to the association, Box 1413, Bothell 98041. World Wide Web http://www.wlma.org/default.htm.

West Virginia

West Virginia Technology, Education, and Media Specialists (WVTEAMS). Memb. 200. Term of Office. July 1999–July 2000.

Pres. Sam Snead, Midland Trail H.S., Box 89, Hico 25854. Tel. 304-658-5184, fax 304-658-5185; *Pres.-Elect* Brenda Bleigh, Box 167, Burnsville 26335. Tel. 304-853-2523, fax 304-853-2431, e-mail bbleigh@access.k12.wv.us.

Address correspondence to the president.

Wisconsin

Wisconsin Educational Media Assn. Memb. 1,122. Term of Office. Apr. 1999–Apr. 2000. Publications. *Dispatch* (7 per year).

Pres. Sherry Freiberg, Fond du Lac School Dist., 72 S. Portland St., Fond du Lac 54935. Tel. 920-929-2780, e-mail freibergs@fonddulac.k12.wi.us; *Pres.-Elect* Jim Bowen. Tel. 920-448-2030, fax 920-448-2115; *Secy.* Courtney Rounds, 1300 Industrial Dr., Fennimore 53809. Tel. 608-822-6884 or 608-822-3276, fax 608-822-3828, e-mail crounds@cesa3.k12.wi.us.

Address correspondence to the president or the secretary.

Wyoming

Section of School Library Media Personnel, Wyoming Lib. Assn. Memb. 91. Term of Office. Oct. 1999–Oct. 2000. Publication. *WLA Newsletter*; *SSLMP Newsletter*.

Chair Alice Hild Farris, Central H.S., 5500 Education Dr., Cheyenne 82001. Tel. 307-771-2680, fax 307-771-2699, e-mail afarris@will.state.wy.us *Chair-Elect* Shelly King, Lib. Media Specialist, Greybull Middle School, 636 14th Ave. N., Greybull 82426. Tel. 307-765-4492, e-mail Lking@trib.com.

Address correspondence to the chairperson.

International Library Associations

International Association of Agricultural Information Specialists (IAALD)

c/o J. van der Burg, President
Boeslaan 55, 6703 ER Wageningen, Netherlands
Tel./fax 31-317-422820
E-mail Jvdburg@user.diva.nl

Object

The association facilitates professional development of and communication among members of the agricultural information community worldwide. Its goal is to enhance access to and use of agriculture-related information resources. To further this mission, IAALD will promote the agricultural information profession, support professional development activities, foster collaboration, and provide a platform for information exchange. Founded 1955.

Membership

Memb. 600+. Dues (Inst.) US$90; (Indiv.) $35.

Officers

Pres. J. van der Burg, Boeslaan 55, 6703 ER Wageningen, Netherlands; *Senior V.P.* Pam Andre, National Agricultural Library, USDA, Beltsville, MD 20705, USA; *Secy.-Treas.* Margot Bellamy, c/o CAB International, Wallingford, Oxon, OX10 8DE, United Kingdom. Tel. 44-1491-832111, fax 44-1491-833508.

Publications

Quarterly Bulletin of the IAALD (memb.).
World Directory of Agricultural Information Resource Centres.

International Association of Law Libraries

Box 5709, Washington, DC 20016-1309
804-924-3384, fax 804-924-7239

Object

IALL is a worldwide organization of librarians, libraries, and other persons or institutions concerned with the acquisition and use of legal information emanating from sources other than their jurisdictions, and from multinational and international organizations.

IALL's basic purpose is to facilitate the work of librarians who must acquire, process, organize, and provide access to foreign legal materials. IALL has no local chapters but maintains liaison with national law library associations in many countries and regions of the world.

Membership

More than 500 members in more than 50 countries on five continents.

Officers (1998–2001)

Pres. Larry Wenger (USA); *1st V.P.* Roberta Shaffer (USA); *2nd V.P.* Holger Knudsen (Germany); *Secy.* Marie-Louise H. Bernal (USA); *Treas.* Gloria F. Chao (USA).

Board Members

Joan A. Brathwaite (Barbados); Jacqueline Elliott (Australia); Gabriel Frossard (Switzerland); Britt S. M. Kjölstad (Switzerland); Ann Morrison (Canada); Harald Müller (Germany); Lisbeth Rasmussen (Denmark); Jules Winterton (United Kingdom).

Publications

International Journal of Legal Information (3 per year; US$55 for individuals; $80 for institutions).

Committee Chairpersons

Communications. Richard A. Danner (USA).

International Association of Music Libraries, Archives and Documentation Centres (IAML)

c/o Alison Hall, Secretary-General
Cataloging Dept., Carleton University Library
1125 Colonel By Drive, Ottawa, ON K15 5B6, Canada
Fax 613-520-3583

Object

To promote the activities of music libraries, archives, and documentation centers and to strengthen the cooperation among them; to promote the availability of all publications and documents relating to music and further their bibliographical control; to encourage the development of standards in all areas that concern the association; and to support the protection and preservation of musical documents of the past and the present.

Membership

Memb. 2,000.

Board Members (1998–2001)

Pres. Pamela Thompson, Royal College of Music Lib., Prince Consort Rd., London SW7 2BS, England; *Past Pres.* Veslemoy Heintz, Statens Musikbibliotek, Box 16326, S-103 26 Stockholm, Sweden; *V.P.s* Massimo Gentili-Tedeschi, Ufficio Ricerca Fondi Musicali, Via Conservatorio 12, I-20122 Milan, Italy; Joachim Jaenecke, Staatsbibliothek zu Berlin, Preussischer Kulturbesitz, Tiergarten, Potsdamer Strasse 33, D-10785 Berlin, Germany; John Roberts, Music Lib., 240 Morrison Hall, Univ. of California–Berkeley, Berkeley, CA 94720; Kirsten Voss-Eliasson, Astershaven 149, DK-2765 Smorum, Denmark; *Secy.-Gen.* Alison Hall, Cataloging Dept., Carleton Univ. Lib., 1125 Colonel By Dr., Ottawa, ON K1S 5B6; *Treas.* Martie Severt, Muziekcentrum van de Omroep, Postbus 125, NL-1200 AC Hilversum, Netherlands.

Publication

Fontes Artis Musicae (4 per year; memb.). *Ed.* Susan T. Sommer, New York Public Lib. for the Performing Arts, 111 Amsterdam Ave., New York, NY 10023-7498.

Professional Branches

Archives and Documentation Centres. Inger Enquist, Statens Musikbibliotek, Box 16326, S-10326 Stockholm, Sweden.

Broadcasting and Orchestra Libraries. Kauko Karjalainen, Yleisradio Oy, Box 76, FIN-00024 Yleisradio, Finland.

Libraries in Music Teaching Institutions. Federica Riva, Conservatorio di Musica G.

Verdi, Via del Conservatorio 12, I-20122 Milan, Italy.

Public Libraries. Kirsten Voss-Eliasson, Astershaven 149, DK-2765 Smorum, Denmark.

Research Libraries. Ann Kersting, Music- und Theaterabteilung, Stadt- und Universitätsbibliothek, Bockenheimer Landstr. 134-138, D-60325 Frankfurt, Germany.

International Association of School Librarianship

Ken Haycock, Executive Director
Box 34069, Dept. 300, Seattle, WA 98124-1069
604-925-0266, fax 604-925-0566, e-mail iasl@rockland.com
World Wide Web http://www.hi.is/~anne/iasl.html

Object

The objectives of the International Association of School Librarianship are to advocate the development of school libraries throughout all countries; to encourage the integration of school library programs into the instructional and curriculum development of the school; to promote the professional preparation and continuing education of school library personnel; to foster a sense of community among school librarians in all parts of the world; to foster and extend relationships between school librarians and other professionals connected with children and youth; to foster research in the field of school librarianship and the integration of its conclusions with pertinent knowledge from related fields; to promote the publication and dissemination of information about successful advocacy and program initiatives in school librarianship; to share information about programs and materials for children and youth throughout the international community; and to initiate and coordinate activities, conferences, and other projects in the field of school librarianship and information services. Founded 1971.

Membership

Memb. 850.

Officers and Executive Board

Pres. Blanche Woolls, USA; *V.P.s* Peter Genco, USA; Rebecca Knuth, USA; Ross Todd, Australia; *Financial Officer* Kathy Lemaire, United Kingdom; *Deputy Exec. Dir.* Lynne Lighthall; *Dirs.* Allison Kaplan, North America; Mary Jamil Fasheh, North Africa/ Middle East; Isabel Gomez, Latin America; James Henri, Australia/Pacific Ocean Islands; Mieko Nagakura, East Asia; Monica Milsson, Europe; Sandra Olen, Africa–Sub-Sahara; Cherrell Shelley-Robinson, Caribbean; Diljit Singh, Asia.

Publications

Annual Proceedings of the International Association of School Librarianship: An Author and Subject Index to Contributed Papers, 1972–1984; $10.

Books and Borrowers; $15.

Connections: School Library Associations and Contact People Worldwide; $15.

Indicators of Quality for School Library Media Programs; $15.

School Librarianship: International Perspectives and Issues; $35.

Sustaining the Vision: A Collection of Articles and Papers on Research in School Librarianship; $35.

IASL Worldwide Directory; $15.

U.S. Association Members

American Assn. of School Libns.; American Lib. Assn.; Illinois School Lib. Media Assn.; International Reading Assn.; International School Service; Louisiana Assn. of School Libns.; Michigan Assn. for Media in Education; Washington Lib. Media Assn.

International Association of Technological University Libraries

c/o President, Nancy Fjällbrant, Chalmers University of Technology Library
412 96 Gothenburg, Sweden
46-31-772-37-54, fax 46-31-772-37-39, e-mail nancyf@lib.chalmers.se

Object

To provide a forum where library directors can meet to exchange views on matters of current significance in the libraries of universities of science and technology. Research projects identified as being of sufficient interest may be followed through by working parties or study groups.

Membership

Ordinary, official observer, sustaining, and nonvoting associate. Membership fee is US$117 per year ($307 for three years, $487 for five years). Memb. 207 (in 43 countries).

Officers and Executives

Pres. Nancy Fjällbrant, Chalmers University of Technology Library, 412 96 Gothenburg, Sweden. Tel. 46-31-772-37-54, fax 46-31-772-37-79, e-mail nancyf@lib.chalmers.se; 1st V.P. Michael Breaks, Heriot-Watt Univ. Lib., Edinburgh EH14 4AS, Scotland. Tel. 44-131-439-5111, fax 44-131-451-3164, e-mail m.l.breaks@hw.ac.uk; 2nd V.P. Egbert Gerryts, Univ. of Pretoria, Merensky Lib., Academic Info. Services, Pretoria 0002, South Africa. Tel. 27-12-420-22-41, fax 27-12-342-24-53, e-mail gerrytse@ais.u.ac.za; Secy. Sinikka Koskiala, Helsinki Univ. of Technology Lib., Box 7000, FIN-02015 HUT, Finland. Tel. 358-9-451-4112, fax 358-9-451-4132, e-mail Sinikka.Koskiala@hut.fi; Treas. Leo Waaijers, Delft Univ. of Technology Lib., Postbus 98, 2600 MG Delft, Netherlands. Tel. 3115-785-656, fax 3115-158-759, e-mail Waaijers@library.tudelft.nl; Membs. Gaynor Austen, Australia; Egbert D. Gerryts, South Africa; North American Regional Group Chair Richard P. Widdicombe, USA; Ed. Nancy Fjällbrant, Sweden.

Publications

IATUL News (q.).
IATUL Proceedings (ann.).

International Council on Archives

Joan van Albada, Secretary-General
60 Rue des Francs-Bourgeois, F-75002 Paris, France
33-1-4027-6306, fax 33-1-4272-2065, e-mail 100640.54@compuserve.com
World Wide Web http://www.archives.ca/ica/

Object

To establish, maintain, and strengthen relations among archivists of all lands, and among all professional and other agencies or institutions concerned with the custody, organization, or administration of archives, public or private, wherever located. Established 1948.

Membership

Memb. 1,574 (representing 176 countries and territories). Dues (Indiv.) 67.50 Euros or 105 Euros; (Inst.) 105 Euros; (Archives Assns.) 105 Euros or 231 Euros; (Central Archives Directorates) 231 Euros minimum, computed on the basis of GNP and GNP per capita.

Officers

Secy.-Gen. Joan van Albada; *Deputy Secy.- Gen.* George P. MacKenzie.

Publications

Archivum (ann.; memb. or subscription to K. G. Saur Verlag, Ortlerstr. 8, Postfach 70 16 20, 81-316 Munich, Germany).

Guide to the Sources of the History of Nations (Latin American Series, 12 vols. pub.; African Series, 18 vols. pub.; Asian Series, 28 vols. pub.), North Africa, Asia, and Oceania: 15 vols. pub.; other guides, 3 vols. pub.

ICA Bulletin (s. ann.; memb.).

Janus (s. ann.; memb.)

List of other publications available from the secretariat.

International Federation for Information and Documentation (FID)

J. Stephen Parker, Executive Director
Box 90402, 2509 LK The Hague, Netherlands
31-70-314-0671, fax 314-0667, e-mail fid@fid.nl

Object

To promote, through international cooperation, research in and development of information science, information management, and documentation, which includes inter alia the organization, storage, retrieval, repackaging, dissemination, value adding, and evaluation of information, however recorded, in the fields of science, technology, industry, social sciences, arts, and humanities.

Program

FID devotes much of its attention to corporate information; industrial, business, and finance information; information policy research; the application of information technology; information service management; the marketing of information systems and services; content analysis, for example, in the design of database systems; linking information and human resources; and the repackaging of information for specific user audiences.

The following commissions, committees, and groups have been established to execute FID's program of activities: *Regional Commissions*: Commission for Western, Eastern and Southern Africa (FID/CAF), Commission for Asia and Oceania (FID/CAO), Commission for Latin America (FID/CLA), Commission for the Caribbean and North America (FID/CNA), Commission for Northern Africa and the Near East (FID/NANE), Regional Organization for Europe (FID/ROE); *Committees*: Classification Research for Knowledge Organization, Education and Training, Fundamental Theory of Information, Information for Industry, Information Policies and Programmes, Intellectual Property Issues; *Special Interest Groups*: Banking, Finance, and Insurance Information; Business Intelligence; Environmental Information; Independent Information Profession-als; Information and Communication Technologies; Information Ethics; Information for Development; Freshwater Information; Roles, Careers, and Development of the Modern Information Professional.

Publications

FID *Annual Report* (ann.).
FID *Directory* (bienn.).
FID *Review* (bi.-mo.) with quarterly inserts
Document Delivery Survey and *ET Newsletter*.
FID *Publications List* (irreg.).
International Forum on Information and Documentation (q.).
Proceedings of congresses; directories; bibliographies on information science, documentation, education and training, and classification research.

International Federation of Film Archives (FIAF)

Secretariat, 1 Rue Defacqz, B-1000 Brussels, Belgium
(32-2) 538-3065, fax (32-2) 534-4774, e-mail info@fiafnet.org
World Wide Web http://www.cinema.ucla.edu/fiaf/default.html

Object

Founded in 1938, FIAF brings together institutions dedicated to rescuing films both as cultural heritage and as historical documents. FIAF is a collaborative association of the world's leading film archives whose purpose has always been to ensure the proper preservation and showing of motion pictures. More than 100 archives in more than 60 countries collect, restore, and exhibit films and cinema documentation spanning the entire history of film.

FIAF seeks to promote film culture and facilitate historical research, to help create new archives around the world, to foster training and expertise in film preservation, to encourage the collection and preservation of documents and other cinema-related materials, to develop cooperation between archives, and to ensure the international availability of films and cinema documents.

Officers

Pres. Ivan Trujillo Bolio; *Secy.-Gen.* Roger Smither; *Treas.* Steven Ricci; *Members* Vittorio Boanini, Paolo Cherchi Usai, Peter Konlechner, Robert Daudelin, Vera Gyurey, Vigdis Lian, Mary Lea Bandy, Hong-Teak Chung, Valeria Ciompi, Karl Griep.

Address correspondence to Christian Dimitriu, Senior Administrator, c/o the Secretariat. E-mail c.dimitriu@fiafnet.org.

Publications

Journal of Film Preservation.
International Filmarchive CD-ROM.

For other FIAF publications, see the Web site http://www.cinema.ucla.edu/fiaf/default.html.

International Federation of Library Associations and Institutions (IFLA)

Box 95312, 2509 CH The Hague, Netherlands
31-70-3140884, fax 31-70-3834027
E-mail IFLA@IFLA.org, World Wide Web http://www.IFLA.org

Object

To promote international understanding, cooperation, discussion, research, and development in all fields of library activity, including bibliography, information services, and the education of library personnel, and to provide a body through which librarianship can be represented in matters of international interest. Founded 1927.

Membership

Memb. (Lib. Assns.) 155; (Inst.) 1,092; (Aff.) 322; Sponsors: 35.

Officers and Executive Board

Pres. Christine Deschamps, Bibliothèque de l'Université de Paris, V–René Descartes, Paris, France; *1st V.P.* Nancy John, Univ. of Illinois at Chicago, Chicago, IL; *2nd V.P.* Børge Sørensen, Central Library, Copenhagen, Denmark; *Treas.* Derek Law, Univ. of Strathclyde, Glasgow, Scotland; *Exec. Board* Kay Raseroka, Univ. Lib. of Botswana, Gaborone, Botswana; Ingrid Parent, National Lib. of Canada, Ottawa, Canada; Claudia Lux, Zentral- und Landesbibliothek Berlin, Berlin, Germany; Jeronimo Martines, Biblioteca de Andalucía, Granada, Spain; *Ex officio memb.* Ralph Manning, National Lib. of Canada, Ottawa, Canada; *Secy.-Gen.* Ross Shimmon; *Coord. Professional Activities* Sjoerd M. J. Koopman; *IFLA Office for Universal Bibliographic Control and International MARC Program Dir.* Kurt Nowak; *Program Officer* Marie-France Plassard, c/o Deutsche Bibliothek, Frankfurt am Main, Germany; *IFLA International Program for UAP Program Dir.* Graham Cornish, c/o British Lib. Document Supply Centre, Boston Spa, Wetherby, West Yorkshire, England; *IFLA Office for Preservation and Conservation Program Dir.* M. T. Varlamoff, c/o Bibliothèque Nationale de France, Paris; *IFLA Office for University Dataflow and Telecommunications Program Dir.* Leigh Swain, c/o National Lib. of Canada, Ottawa, Canada; *IFLA Office for the Advancement of Librarianship in the Third World Program Dir.* Birgitta Bergdahl, c/o Uppsala Univ. Lib., Uppsala, Sweden; *IFLA Office for International Lending Dir.* Graham Cornish.

Publications

IFLA Directory (bienn.).
IFLA Council Report (bienn.)
IFLA Journal (6/yr.).
IFLA Professional Reports.
IFLA Publications Series.
International Cataloguing and Bibliographic Control (q.).
PAC Newsletter.
UAP Newsletter (s. ann.).
UDT Digest (electronic).

American Membership

American Assn. of Law Libs.; American Lib. Assn.; Art Libs. Society of North America; Assn. for Lib. and Info. Science Education; Assn. of Research Libs.; International Assn. of Law Libs.; International Assn. of School Libns.; Medical Lib. Assn.; Special Libs. Assn. *Institutional Membs.* There are 141 libraries and related institutions that are institutional members or consultative bodies and sponsors of IFLA in the United States (out of a total of 1,070), and 84 personal affiliates (out of a total of 321).

International Organization for Standardization (ISO)

ISO Central Secretariat, 1 rue de Varembé, Case Postale 56, CH-1211 Geneva 20, Switzerland
41-22-749-0111, fax 41-22-733-3430, e-mail central@iso.ch

Object

Worldwide federation of national standards bodies, founded in 1947, at present comprising some 130 members, one in each country. The object of ISO is to promote the development of standardization and related activities in the world with a view to facilitating international exchange of goods and services, and to developing cooperation in the spheres of intellectual, scientific, technological, and economic activity. The scope of ISO covers international standardization in all fields except electrical and electronic engineering standardization, which is the responsibility of the International Electrotechnical Commission (IEC). The results of ISO technical work are published as International Standards.

Officers

Pres. Giacomo Elias, Italy; *Pres.-Elect* Mario Gilberto Cortopassi, Brazil; *V.P. (Policy)* A. Aoki, Japan; *V.P. (Technical Management)* Ross Wraight, Australia; *Secy.-Gen.* L. D. Eicher.

Technical Work

The technical work of ISO is carried out by some 180 technical committees. These include:

ISO/TC 46–Information and documentation (Secretariat, Deutsches Institut für Normung, 10772 Berlin, Germany). Scope: Standardization of practices relating to libraries, documentation and information centers, indexing and abstracting services, archives, information science, and publishing.

ISO/TC 37–Terminology (principles and coordination) (Secretariat, Österreiches Normungsinstitut, Heinestr. 38, Postfach 130, A-1021 Vienna, Austria). Scope: Standardization of methods for creating, compiling, and coordinating terminologies.

ISO/IEC JTC 1–Information technology (Secretariat, American National Standards Institute, 11 W. 42 St., 13th fl., New York, NY 10036). Scope: Standardization in the field of information technology.

Publications

ISO Annual Report.
ISO Bulletin (mo.).
ISO Catalogue (ann.).
ISO International Standards.
ISO 9000 + ISO 14000 News (bi-mo.).
ISO Memento (ann.).
ISO Online information service on World Wide Web (http://www.iso.ch/).

Foreign Library Associations

The following list of regional and national library associations around the world is a selective one. A more complete list can be found in *International Literary Market Place* (R. R. Bowker).

Regional

Africa

Standing Conference of African Univ. Libs., c/o E. Bejide Bankole, Editor, African Journal of Academic Librarianship, Univ. of Lagos, Akoka, Yaba, Lagos, Nigeria. Tel. 1-524968.

The Americas

Asociación de Bibliotecas Universitarias, de Investigación e Institucionales del Caribe (Assn. of Caribbean Univ., Research and Institutional Libs.), Box 23317, San Juan 00931, Puerto Rico. Tel. 787-764-0000, fax 787-763-5685. *Exec. Secy.* Oneida R. Ortiz.

Seminar on the Acquisition of Latin American Lib. Materials, c/o *Exec. Secy.* Sharon A. Moynahan, General Lib., Univ. of New Mexico, Albuquerque, NM 87131-1466. Tel. 505-277-5102, fax 505-277-0646.

Asia

Congress of Southeast Asian Libns. IV (CONSAL IV), c/o Serafin D. Quiason, National Historic Institute of the Philippines, T. M. Kalaw St., 100 Ermita, Box 2926, Manila, Philippines. Tel./fax 2-590646.

The Commonwealth

Commonwealth Lib. Assn., c/o *Exec. Secy.* Norma Amenu-Kpodo, Box 144, Kingston 7, Jamaica. Tel. 876-927-2123, fax 876-927-1926. *Pres.* Elizabeth Watson; *Exec. Secy.* Norma Amenu-Kpodo.

Standing Conference on Lib. Materials on Africa, Univ. of London, Institute of Commonwealth Studies, Thornhaugh St., Russell Square, London WC1B 30G, England.

Tel. 171-580-5876, ext. 2304, fax 171-636-2834, e-mail rt4@soas.ac.uk. *Chair* J. Pinfold.

Europe

Ligue des Bibliothèques Européennes de Recherche (LIBER) (Assn. of European Research Libs.), c/o H.-A. Koch, Universität Bremen, Postfach 330440, 28334 Bremen, Germany. Tel. 421-218-3361.

National

Argentina

Asociación de Bibliotecarios Graduados de la República Argentina (Assn. of Graduate Libns. of Argentina), Corrientes 1642, 1 piso, Of. 22-2 cuerpo, 1042 Buenos Aires. Tel./fax 1-382-4821, 384-8095, e-mail postmaster@abgra.org.ar. *Pres.* Ana Maria Peruchena Zimmermann; *Exec. Secy.* Rosa Emma Monfasani.

Australia

Australian Lib. and Info. Assn., Box E 441, Kingston, ACT 2600. Tel. 6-285-1877, fax 6-282-2249.

Australian Society of Archivists, Box 83, O'Connor, ACT 2602. Tel. 7-3875-8705, fax 7-3875-8764, e-mail shicks@gil.com. au. *Pres.* Kathryn Dan; *Secy.* Fiona Burn.

Council of Australian State Libs., c/o State Lib. of Queensland, Queensland Cultural Centre, South Brisbane, Qld. Tel. 7-3840-7666, fax 7-3846-2421. *Chair* D. H. Stephens.

Austria

Österreichische Gesellschaft für Dokumentation und Information (Austrian Society for

Documentation and Info.), c/o TermNet, Simmeringer Hauptstr. 24, A-1110 Vienna. Tel. 1-7404-0280, fax 1-7404-0281. *Pres.* Gerhard Richter.

Vereinigung Österreichischer Bibliothekarinnen und Bibliothekare (Assn. of Austrian Libns.), A-1082, Vienna. Tel. 1-4000-84936, 1-4000-7219, e-mail post@m09magwieu.gv.at. *Pres.* Herwig Würtz; *Secy.* Ruth Lotter.

Bangladesh

Lib. Assn. of Bangladesh, c/o Bangladesh Central Public Institute of Library & Information Sciences, Library Bldg., Shahbagh, Ramna, Dacca 1000. Tel. 2-504-269, e-mail msik@bangla.net. *Pres.* M. Shamsul Islam Khan; *Gen. Secy.* Kh Fazlur Rahman.

Barbados

Lib. Assn. of Barbados, Box 827E, Bridgetown. *Pres.* Shirley Yearwood; *Secy.* Hazelyn Devonish.

Belgium

Archives et Bibliothèques de Belgique/Archief-en Bibliotheekwezen in België (Archives and Libs. of Belgium), 4 Blvd. de l'Empereur, B-1000 Brussels. Tel. 2-519-5351, fax 2-519-5533. *Gen. Secy.* Wim De Vos.

Association Belge de Documentation/Belgische Vereniging voor Documentatie (Belgian Assn. for Documentation), Chaussée de Wavre 1683, Waversesteenweg, B-1160 Brussels. Tel. 2-675-5862, fax 2-672-7446, e-mail abd@synec-doc.be. *Pres.* Evelyne Luetkens; *Secy.* Vincent Maes.

Association Professionnelle des Bibliothécaires et Documentalistes, 7 Rue des Marronniers, 5651 Thy-Le Château, Brussels. Tel. 71-614-335, fax 71-611-634. *Pres.* Jean Claude Trefois; *Secy.* Angélique Matlioli.

Vlaamse Vereniging voor Bibliotheek-, Archief-, en Documentatiewezen (Flemish Assn. of Libns., Archivists, and Documentalists), Waterloostraat 11, 2600 Berchem, Antwerp. Tel. 3-281-4457, fax 3-218-

8077, e-mail ms.vvbad@innet.be. *Pres.* Erwin Pairon; *Exec. Dir.* Marc Storms.

Belize

Belize Lib. Assn., c/o Central Lib., Bliss Inst., Box 287, Belize City. Tel. 2-7267. *Pres.* H. W. Young; *Secy.* Robert Hulse.

Bolivia

Asociación Boliviana de Bibliotecarios (Bolivian Lib. Assn.), c/o Biblioteca y Archivo Nacional, Calle Bolivar, Sucre.

Bosnia and Herzegovina

Drustvo bibliotekara Bosne i Hercegovine (Libns. Society of Bosnia and Herzegovina), Obala v Stepe 42, 71000 Sarajevo. Tel. 71-283245. *Pres.* Neda Cukac.

Botswana

Botswana Lib. Assn., Box 1310, Gaborone. Tel. 31-355-2295, fax 31-357291. *Chair* F. M. Lamusse; *Secy.* A. M. Mbangiwa.

Brazil

Associação dos Arquivistas Brasileiros (Assn. of Brazilian Archivists), Rua da Candelária, 9-Sala 1004, Centro, Rio de Janeiro RJ 20091-020. Tel./fax 21-233-7142. *Pres.* Lia Temporal Malcher; *Secy.* Laura Regina Xavier.

Brunei

Persatuan Perpustakaan Kebangsaan Negara Brunei (National Lib. Assn. of Brunei), c/o Language and Literature Bureau Lib., Jalan Elizabeth II, Bandar Seri Begawan. Tel. 2-235501. *Contact* Abu Bakar Bin.

Cameroon

Association des Bibliothécaires, Archivistes, Documentalistes et Muséographes du Cameroon (Assn. of Libns., Archivists, Documentalists and Museum Curators of Cameroon), Université de Yaoundé, Bibliothèque Universitaire, B.P. 337, Yaoundé. Tel. 220744.

Canada

Bibliographical Society of Canada/La Société Bibliographique du Canada, Box 575, Postal Sta. P, Toronto, ON M5S 2T1. World Wide Web: http://www.library. utoronto.ca/~bsc.

Canadian Assn. for Info. Science/Association Canadienne de Sciences de l'Information, c/o CAIS Secretariat, Univ. of Toronto, 140 Saint George St., Toronto, ON M5S 3G6. Tel. 416-978-8876, fax 416-971-1399, e-mail caisasst@fis.utoronto.ca.

Canadian Council of Lib. Schools/Conseil Canadien des Ecoles de Bibliothéconomie, c/o Faculty of Info. Studies, Univ. of Toronto, 140 Saint George St., Toronto M5S 3G6. Tel. 416-978-3202, fax 416-978-5762.

Canadian Lib. Assn., c/o *Exec. Dir.* Vicki Whitmell, 200 Elgin St., Suite 602, Ottawa, ON K2P 1L5. Tel. 613-232-8837, fax 613-563-9895, e-mail whitmell@istar.ca. (For detailed information on the Canadian Lib. Assn. and its divisions, see "National Library and Information-Industry Associations, United States and Canada"; for information on the library associations of the provinces of Canada, see "State, Provincial, and Regional Library Associations.")

Chile

Colegio de Bibliotecarios de Chile AG (Chilean Lib. Assn.), Diagonal Paraguay 383, Depto 122 Torre 11, Santiago 3741. Tel. 2-222-5652, e-mail cdb@interaccesses.cl. *Pres.* Esmerelda Ramos Ramos; *Secy.* Monica Nunez.

China

China Society for Lib. Science, 39 Bai Shi Qiao Rd., Beijing 100081. Tel. 10-684-15566, ext. 5563, fax 10-684-19271. *Secy.-Gen.* Liu Xiangsheng.

Colombia

Asociación Colombiana de Bibliotecarios (Colombian Lib. Assn.), Calle 10, No. 3-16, Apdo. Aéreo 30883, Bogotá.

Costa Rica

Asociación Costarricense de Bibliotecarios (Costa Rican Assn. of Libns.), Apdo. 3308, San José. *Secy.-Gen.* Nelly Kopper.

Croatia

Hrvatsko Bibliotekarsko Drustvo (Croatian Lib. Assn.), Ulica Hrvatske bratske zajednice b b, 10000 Zagreb. Tel. 41-616-4111, fax 41-611-64186. *Pres.* Dubravka Kunstek; *Secy.* Dunja Gabriel.

Cuba

Lib. Assn. of Cuba, Biblioteca Nacional José Marti, Apdo. 6881, Ave. de Independencia e/20 de Mayo y Aranguren, Plaza de la Revolución, Havana. Tel. 7-708-277. *Dir.* Marta Terry González.

Cyprus

Kypriakos Synthesmos Vivliothicarion (Lib. Assn. of Cyprus), Box 1039, Nicosia. *Pres.* Costas D. Stephanov; *Secy.* Paris G. Rossos.

Czech Republic

Svaz Knihovníku Informachních Pracovníku Ceské Republiky (Assn. of Lib. and Info. Professionals of the Czech Republic), Klementinum 190, c/o Národní Knihovna, 110 01 Prague 1. Tel./fax 2-2166-3295, e-mail burget@mondia.cz. *Pres.* Jarmila Burgetová.

Denmark

Arkivforeningen (Archives Society), c/o Landsarkivet for Sjaelland, jagtvej 10, 2200 Copenhagen K K. Tel. 3139-3520, fax 3315-3239. *Pres.* Tyge Krogh; *Secy.* Charlotte Steinmark.

Danmarks Biblioteksforening (Danish Lib. Assn.), Telegrafvej 5, DK-2750 Ballerup. Tel. 4468-1466, fax 4468-1103. *Dir.* Jens Thorhauge.

Danmarks Forskningsbiblioteksforening (Danish Research Lib. Assn.), Campusvej 55, 5230 Odense M. Tel. Tel. 66-15-67-68, fax 66-15-81-62. *Pres.* Mette Stockmarr; *Secy.* D. Skovgaard.

Kommunernes Skolebiblioteksforening (formerly Danmarks Skolebiblioteksforening) (Assn. of Danish School Libs.), Vesterbrogade 20, DK-1620, Copenhagen V. Tel. 3325-3222, fax 3325-3223, e-mail komskolbib@internet.dk, World Wide Web www.ksbk.dk. *Chief Exec.* Paul Erik Sorensen.

Dominican Republic

Asociación Dominicana de Bibliotecarios (Dominican Assn. of Libns.), c/o Biblioteca Nacional, Plaza de la Cultura, Cesar Nicolás Penson 91, Santo Domingo. Tel. 809-688-4086. *Pres.* Prospero J. Mella-Chavier; *Secy.-Gen.* V. Regús.

Ecuador

Asociación Ecuatoriana de Bibliotecarios (Ecuadoran Lib. Assn.), c/o Casa de la Cultura Ecuatoriana Benjamin Carrión, Apdo. 67, Ave. 6 de Diciembre 794, Quito. Tel. 2-528-840, 2-263-474. *Pres.* Eulalia Galarza.

Egypt

Egyptian Assn. for Lib. and Info. Science, c/o Dept. of Archives, Librarianship and Info. Science, Faculty of Arts, Univ. of Cairo, Cairo. Tel. 2-567-6365, fax 2-572-9659. *Pres.* S. Khalifa; *Secy.* Hosam El-Din.

El Salvador

Asociación de Bibliotecarios de El Salvador (El Salvador Lib. Assn.), c/o Biblioteca Nacional, 8A Avda. Norte y Calle Delgado, San Salvador. Tel. 216-312.

Asociación General de Archivistas de El Salvador (Assn. of Archivists of El Salvador), Archivo General de la Nación, Palacio Nacional, San Salvador. Tel. 229-418.

Ethiopia

Ye Ethiopia Betemetshaft Serategnoch Mahber (Ethiopian Lib. Assn.), Box 30530, Addis Ababa. Tel. 1-110-844, fax 1-552-544. *Pres.* Mulugeta Hunde; *Secy.* Girma Makonnen.

Fiji

Fiji Lib. Assn., Govt. Bldgs., Box 2292, Suva. *Secy.* E. Qica.

Finland

Suomen Kirjastoseura (Finnish Lib. Assn.), Kansakouluk 10 A 19, FIN-00100 Helsinki. Tel. 0-694-1844, fax 0-694-1859, e-mail fla@fla.fi. *Pres.* Kaarina Dromberg; *Secy.-Gen.* Tuula Haavisto.

France

Association des Archivistes Français (Assn. of French Archivists), 60 Rue des Francs-Bourgeois, F-75141 Paris cedex 3. Tel. 1-4027-6000. *Pres.* Jean-Luc Eichenlaub; *Secy.* Jean LePottier.

Association des Bibliothécaires Français (Assn. of French Libns.), 7 Rue des Lions-Saint-Paul, F-75004 Paris. Tel. 1-4887-9787, fax 1-4887-9713. *Pres.* Claudine Belayche; *Gen. Secy.* Marie-Martine Tomiteh.

Association des Professionnels de l'Information et de la Documentation (Assn. of Info. and Documentation Professionals)), 25 Rue Claude Tillier, 75012 Paris. Tel. 1-4372-2525, fax 1-4372-3041, e-mail adbs @adbs.fr. *Pres.* Florence Wilhelm.

Germany

Arbeitsgemeinschaft der Spezialbibliotheken (Assn. of Special Libs.), OAR La Eckl, Universitätsbibliothek, Karlsruhe, Postfach 6920, 76049 Karlsruhe. Tel. 721-608-3101, fax 721-608-4886. *Chair* Wolfrudolf Laux; *Secretariat Dir.* Marianne Schwarzer.

Deutsche Gesellschaft für Dokumentation eV (German Society for Documentation), Ostbahnhofstr. 13, 60314 Frankfurt-am-Main 1. Tel. 69-430-313, fax 69-490-9096. *Pres.* Joachim-Felix Leonard.

Deutscher Bibliotheksverband eV (German Lib. Assn.), Alt-Moabit 101A, 10559 Berlin. Tel. 30-3907-7274, fax 30-393-8011, e-mail dbv@dbi-berlin.de. *Pres.* Christof Eichert.

Verein der Bibliothekare an Öffentlichen Bibliotheken (Assn. of Libns. at Public

Libs.), Postfach 1324, 72703 Reutlingen. Tel. 7121-36999, fax 7121-300-433. *Pres.* Konrad Umlauf; *Secy.* Katharina Boulanger.

Verein der Diplom-Bibliothekare an Wissenschaftlichen Bibliotheken (Assn. of Certified Libns. at Academic Libs.), c/o BIOst, Bibliothek, Lindenbornstr. 22, 50823 Cologne. Tel. 221-574-7161, fax 221-574-7110. *Chair* Marianne Saule.

Verein Deutscher Archivare (Assn. of German Archivists), Westphälisches Archivamt, 48133 Münster. Tel. 251-591-3886, fax 251-591-269. *Chair* Norbert Reimann.

Verein Deutscher Bibliothekare (Assn. of German Libns.), Krummer Timpen 3-5, 48143 Münster. Tel. 251-832-4032, fax 251-832-8398. *Pres.* Klaus Hilgemann; *Secy.* Lydia Jungnickel.

Ghana

Ghana Lib. Assn., Box 4105, Accra. Tel. 2-668-731. *Pres.* E. S. Asiedo; *Secy.* A. W. K. Insaidoo.

Great Britain

See United Kingdom.

Greece

Enosis Hellinon Bibliothekarion (Greek Lib. Assn.), Themistocleus 73, 10683 Athens. Tel. 1-322-6625. *Pres.* K. Xatzopoulou; *Gen. Secy.* E. Kalogeraky.

Guyana

Guyana Lib. Assn., c/o National Lib., Church St. & Ave. of the Republic, Georgetown. Tel. 2-62690, 2-62699. *Pres.* Hetty London; *Secy.* Jean Harripersaud.

Honduras

Asociación de Bibliotecarios y Archiveros de Honduras (Assn. of Libns. and Archivists of Honduras), 11a Calle, 1a y 2a Avdas. No. 105, Comayagüela DC, Tegucigalpa. *Pres.* Fransisca de Escoto Espinoza; *Secy.-Gen.* Juan Angel R. Ayes.

Hungary

Magyar Könyvtárosok Egyesülete (Assn. of Hungarian Libns.), Szabó Ervin tér 1, H-1088 Budapest. Tel./fax 1-118-2050. *Pres.* Tibor Horváth; *Secy.* István Papp.

Iceland

Bókavardafélag Islands (Icelandic Lib. Assn.), Box 1497, 121 Reykjavik. Tel. 564-2050, fax 564-3877. *Pres.* H. A. Hardarson; *Secy.* A. Agnarsdottir.

India

Indian Assn. of Special Libs. and Info. Centres, P-291, CIT Scheme 6M, Kankurgachi, Calcutta 700054. Tel. 33-349651.

Indian Lib. Assn., c/o Dr. Mukerjee Nagar, A/40-41, Flat 201, Ansal Bldg., Delhi 110009. Tel. 11-711-7743. *Pres.* P. S. G. Kumar.

Indonesia

Ikatan Pustakawan Indonesia (Indonesian Lib. Assn.), Jalan Merdeka Selatan No. 11, Box 274, Jakarta, Pusat. Tel. 21-375-718, fax 21-310-3554. *Pres.* S. Kartosdono.

Iraq

Iraqi Lib. Assn., c/o National Lib., Bab-el-Muaddum, Baghdad. Tel. 1-416-4190. *Dir.* Abdul Hameed Al-Alawchi.

Ireland

Cumann Leabharlann Na h-Eireann (Lib. Assn. of Ireland), 53 Upper Mount St., Dublin. Tel. 1-661-9000, fax 1-676-1628, e-mail laisec@iol.ie. *Pres.* L. Ronayne; *Hon. Secy.* Brendan Teeling.

Israel

Israel Libns. and Info. Specialists Assn., Box 238, 17 Strauss St., 91001 Jerusalem. Tel. 2-6207-2868, fax 2-625-628. *Pres.* Benjamin Schachter.

Israel Society of Special Libs. and Info. Centers, 31 Habarzel St., Ramat Ha Hayal,

69710 Tel Aviv. Tel. 3-648-0592. *Chair* Liliane Frenkiel.

Italy

Associazione Italiana Biblioteche (Italian Lib. Assn.), C.P. 2461, I-00100 Rome A-D. Tel. 6-446-3532, fax 6-444-1139, e-mail aib.italia@agora.stm.it. *Pres.* Rossella Caffo; *Secy.* Luca Bellingeri.

Jamaica

Jamaica Lib. Assn., Box 58, Kingston 5. *Pres.* P. Kerr; *Secy.* F. Salmon.

Japan

Joho Kagaku Gijutsu Ky kai (Info. Science and Technology Assn.), Sasaki Bldg., 5-7 Koisikawa 2, Bunkyo-ku, Tokyo. *Pres.* T. Gondoh; *Gen. Mgr.* Yukio Ichikawa.

Nihon Toshokan Kyokai (Japan Lib. Assn.), c/o *Secy.-Gen.* Reiko Sakagawa, 1-10 Taishido, 1-chome, Setagaya-ku, Tokyo 154. Tel. 3-3410-6411, fax 3-3421-7588.

Senmon Toshokan Kyogikai (Japan Special Libs. Assn.), c/o National Diet Lib., 10-1 Nagata-cho, 1-chome, Chiyoda-ku, Tokyo 100. Tel. 3-3581-2331, fax 3-3597-9104. *Pres.* Kousaku Inaba; *Exec. Dir.* Fumihisa Nakagawa.

Jordan

Jordan Lib. Assn., Box 6289, Amman. Tel. 6-629-412. *Pres.* Anwar Akroush; *Secy.* Yousra Abu Ajamieh.

Kenya

Kenya Lib. Assn., Box 46031, Nairobi. Tel. 2-214-917, fax 2-336-885, e-mail jwere@ken.healthnet.org. *Chair* Jacinta Were; *Secy.* Alice Bulogosi.

Korea (Republic of)

Korean Lib. Assn., 60-1 Panpo Dong, Seo-cho-ku, Seoul. Tel. 2-535-4868, fax 2-535-5616, e-mail klanet@kol.co.kr. *Pres.* Chal Sakong; *Exec. Dir.* Ho Jo Won.

Laos

Association des Bibliothécaires Laotiens (Assn. of Laotian Libns.), c/o Direction de la Bibliothèque Nationale, Ministry of Education, B.P. 704, Vientiane. *Dir.* Somthong.

Latvia

Lib. Assn. of Latvia, Latvian National Lib., Kr. Barona iela 14, 1423 Riga. Tel. 132-728-98-74, fax 132-728-08-51. *Pres.* Aldis Abele.

Lebanon

Lebanese Lib. Assn., c/o American Univ. of Beirut, Univ. Lib./Gifts and Exchange, Box 113/5367, Beirut. Tel. 1-340740, ext. 2603. *Pres.* Rafi' Ma'rouf; *Exec. Secy.* Linda Sadaka.

Lesotho

Lesotho Lib. Assn., Private Bag A26, Maseru. *Chair* E. M. Nthunya; *Secy.* M. M. Moshoeshoe-Chadzingwa.

Lithuania

Lithuanian Librarians Assn., Didzioji str 10, 2001 Vilnius. Tel. 2-611-875, fax 2-221-1324.

Macedonia

Sojuz na drustvata na bibliotckarite na SR Makedonija (Union of Libns.' Assns. of Macedonia), Box 566, 91000, Skopje. Tel. 91-226846, 91-115177, fax 91-232649. *Pres.* Trajce Pikov; *Secy.* Poliksena Matkovska.

Malawi

Malawi Lib. Assn., Box 429, Zomba. Tel. 50-522-222, fax 50-523-225. *Chair* Joseph J. Uta; *Secy.* Vote D. Somba.

Malaysia

Persatuan Perpustakaan Malaysia (Lib. Assn. of Malaysia), Box 12545, 50782 Kuala

Lumpur. Tel. 3-756-6516. *Pres.* Chew Wing Foong; *Secy.* Leni Abdul Latif.

Mali

Association Malienne des Bibliothécaires, Archivistes et Documentalistes (Mali Assn. of Libns., Archivists, and Documentalists), c/o Bibliothèque Nationale du Mali, Ave. Kasse Keita, B.P. 159, Bamako. Tel. 224963. *Dir.* Mamadou Konoba Keita.

Malta

Ghaqda Bibljotekarji/Lib. Assn. (Malta), c/o Univ. Lib., Msida MSD 06. *Secy.* Marion Borg.

Mauritania

Association Mauritanienne des Bibliothécaires, Archivistes et Documentalistes (Mauritanian Assn. of Libns., Archivists, and Documentalists), c/o Bibliothèque Nationale, B.P. 20, Nouakchott. *Pres.* O. Diouwara; *Secy.* Sid'Ahmed Fall dit Dah.

Mauritius

Mauritius Lib. Assn., c/o The British Council, Royal Rd., Box 11, Rose Hill. Tel. 541-602, fax 549-553. *Pres.* K. Appadoo; *Secy.* S. Rughoo.

Mexico

Asociación Mexicana de Bibliotecarios (Mexican Assn. of Libns.), Apdo. 27-651, Admin. de Correos 27, México D.F. 06760. Tel./fax 5-575-1135, e-mail ambac@solar.sar.net. *Pres.* Elsa M. Ramirez Leyva; *Secy.* Jose L. Almanza Morales.

Myanmar

Myanmar Lib. Assn., c/o National Lib., Strand Rd., Yangon. *Chief Libn.* U Khin Maung Tin.

Nepal

Nepal Lib. Assn., c/o National Lib., Harihar Bhawan, Pulchowk Lib., Box 2773, Kathmandu. Tel. 1-521-132. *Libn.* Shusila Dwivedi.

The Netherlands

Nederlandse Vereniging van Bibliothecarissen, Documentalisten en Literatuur Onderzoekers (Netherlands Libns. Society), NVB-Verenigingsbureau, Plompetorengracht 11, NL-3512 CA Utrecht. Tel. 30-231-1263, fax 30-231-1830, e-mail nvbinfo@worldaccess.nl. *Pres.* H. C. Kooyman-Tibbles; *Secy.* R. Tichelaar.

UKB (Universiteitsbibliotheek Vriji Universiteit) (Assn. of the Univ. Libs., the Royal Lib., and the Lib. of the Royal Netherlands Academy of Arts and Sciences), De Boelelaan 1103, NL-1081 HV Amsterdam. Tel. 44-45140, fax 44-45259. *Pres.* A. C. Klugkist; *Libn.* J. H. de Swart.

New Zealand

New Zealand Lib. and Info. Assn., Level 6, Old Wool House, 139-141 Featherston St., Box 12-212, Wellington. Tel. 4-473-5834, fax 4-499-1480, e-mail nzlia@netlink.co.nz.

Nicaragua

Asociación Nicaraguense de Bibliotecarios y Profesionales a Fines (Nicaraguan Assn. of Libns.), Apdo. Postal 3257, Managua. *Exec. Secy.* Susana Morales Hernández.

Nigeria

Nigerian Lib. Assn., c/o National Lib. of Nigeria, 4 Wesley St., PMB 12626, Lagos. Tel. 1-263-1716, fax 1-616404. *Pres.* A. O. Banjo; *Secy.* D. D. Bwayili.

Norway

Arkivarforeningen (Assn. of Archivists), c/o Riksarkivet, Folke Bernadottes Vei 21, Postboks 10, N-0807 Oslo. Tel. 22-022-600, fax 22-237-489.

Norsk Bibliotekforening (Norwegian Lib. Assn.), Malerhaugveien 20, N-0661 Oslo. Tel. 2-268-8550, fax 2-267-2368. *Dir.* Berit Aaker.

Pakistan

Pakistan Lib. Assn., c/o Pakistan Inst. of Development Economics, University Campus, Box 1091, Islamabad. Tel. 51-921-

4041, fax 51-921-0886, e-mail arshad%pide
@sdnpk.undp.org. *Pres.* Azmat Ullah
Bhatti; *Secy.-Gen.* Hafiz Khubaib Ahmad.

Panama

Asociación Panameña de Bibliotecarios
(Panama Lib. Assn.), c/o Biblioteca Inter-
americana Simón Bolivar, Estafeta Uni-
versitaria, Panama City. *Pres.* Bexie
Rodriguez de León.

Paraguay

Asociación de Bibliotecarios del Paraguay
(Assn. of Paraguayan Libns.), Casilla de
Correo 1505, Asunción. *Secy.* Mafalda
Cabrerar.

Peru

Asociación de Archiveros del Perú (Peruvian
Assn. of Archivists), Archivo Central
Salaverry 2020 Jesús Mario, Universidad
del Pacifico, Lima 11. *Pres.* José Luis
Abanto Arrelucea.
Asociación Peruana de Bibliotecarios
(Peruvian Assn of Libns.), Bellavista 561
Miraflores, Apdo. 995, Lima 18. Tel. 14-
474-869. *Pres.* Martha Fernandez de
Lopez; *Secy.* Luzmila Tello de Medina.

Philippines

Assn. of Special Libs. of the Philippines, Rm.
301, National Lib. Bldg., T. M. Kalaw St.,
Manila. Tel. 2-590177. *Pres.* Zenaida F.
Lucas; *Secy.* Socorro G. Elevera.
Bibliographical Society of the Philippines,
National Lib. of the Philippines, T. M.
Kalaw St., 1000 Ermita, Box 2926, Mani-
la. Tel. 2-583252, fax 2-502329. *Secy.-
Treas.* Leticia R. Maloles.
Philippine Libns. Assn., c/o National Lib. of
the Philippines, Rm. 301, T. M. Kalaw St.,
Manila. Tel. 2-590177. *Pres.* Antonio M.
Sontos; *Secy.* Rosemarie Rosali.

Poland

Stowarzyszenie Bibliotekarzy Polskich (Polish Libns. Assn.), Ul. Konopczynskiego
5/7, 00950 Warsaw. Tel. 22-275296. *Chair*
Stanislaw Czajka; *Secy.-Gen.* Dariusz
Kuzminski.

Portugal

Associação Portuguesa de Bibliotecários,
Arquivistas e Documentalistas (Portuguese
Assn. of Libns., Archivists, and Documentalists), R. Morais Soares, 43C-1 DTD,
1900 Lisbon. Tel. 1-815-4479, fax 1-815-
4508, e-mail badbn@telepac.pt. *Pres.*
António Pina Falcao.

Puerto Rico

Sociedad de Bibliotecarios de Puerto Rico
(Society of Libns. of Puerto Rico), Apdo.
22898, Universidad de Puerto Rico Sta.,
San Juan 00931. Tel. 787-764-0000. *Pres.*
Aura Jiménez de Panepinto; *Secy.* Olga L.
Hernández.

Romania

Asociatüia Bibliotecarilor din Bibliotecile
Publice-România (Assn. of Public Libns.
of Romania), Strada Ion Ghica 4, Sector 3,
79708 Bucharest. Tel. 1-614-2434, fax 1-
312-3381, e-mail bnr@ul.ici.ro. *Pres.*
Gheorghe-Iosif Bercan; *Secy.* Georgeta
Clinca.

Russia

Lib. Council, State V. I. Lenin Lib., Prospect
Kalinina 3, Moscow 101000. Tel. 95-202-
4656. *Exec. Secy.* G. A. Semenova.

Senegal

Association Sénégalaise des Bibliothécaires,
Archivistes et Documentalistes (Sene-
galese Assn. of Libns., Archivists and
Documentalists), BP 3252, Dakar. Tel.
246-981, fax 242-379. *Pres.* Mariétou
Diongue Diop; *Secy.* Emmanuel Kabou.

Sierra Leone

Sierra Leone Assn. of Archivists, Libns., and
Info. Scientists, c/o Sierra Leone Lib.
Board, Box 326, Freetown. *Pres.* Deanna
Thomas.

Singapore

Lib. Assn. of Singapore, c/o Bukit Merah
Central, Box 0693, Singapore 9115. *Hon.
Secy.* Siti Hanifah Mustapha.

Slovenia

Zveza Bibliotekarskih Drustev Slovenije (Lib. Assn. of Slovenia), Turjaska 1, 1000 Ljubljana. Tel. 61-125-50-14, fax 61-125-92-57. *Pres.* Nada Cesnovar; *Secy.* Stanislav Bahor.

South Africa

African Lib. Assn. of South Africa, c/o Lib., Univ. of the North, Private Bag X1106, Sovenga 0727. Tel. 1521-689111. *Secy./Treas.* A. N. Kambule.

Spain

Asociación Española de Archiveros, Bibliotecarios, Museólogos y Documentalistas (Spanish Assn. of Archivists, Libns., Curators and Documentalists), Recoletos 5, 28001 Madrid. Tel. 1-575-1727. *Pres.* Julia M. Rodrigez Barrero.

Sri Lanka

Sri Lanka Lib. Assn., Professional Center, 275/75 Bauddhaloka Mawatha, Colombo 7. Tel. 1-589103, e-mail postmast@slla.ac.lk. *Pres.* Harrison Perera; *Secy.* Wilfred Ranasinghe.

Swaziland

Swaziland Lib. Assn., Box 2309, Mbabane. Tel. 43101, fax 42641. *Chair* L. Dlamini; *Secy.* P. Muswazi.

Sweden

Svenska Arkivsamfundet (Swedish Assn. of Archivists), c/o Riksarkivet, Box 12541, S-10229 Stockholm. Tel. 8-737-6350, fax 8-657-9564, e-mail anna-christina. ulfsparre@riksarkivet.ra.se. *Pres.* Anna Christina Ulfsparre.

Sveriges Allmanna Biblioteksförening (Swedish Lib. Assn.), Box 3127, S-103 62 Stockholm. Tel. 8-241-020, 8-723-0082, fax 8-723-0083, e-mail yvla.mannerheim @bbl.sab.se; World Wide Web: http://www. sab.e/. *Secy.-Gen.* Christina Stenberg.

Switzerland

Association des Bibliothèques et Bibliothécaires Suisses/Vereinigung Schweizerischer Bibliothekare/Associazione dei Bibliotecari Svizzeri (Assn. of Swiss Libns.), Effingerstr. 35, CH-3008 Berne. Tel. 31-382-4240, fax 31-382-4648, e-mail bbs@bbs.ch, World Wide Web: http:// www.bbs.ch. *Secy.* Alain Huber.

Schweizerische Vereinigung für Dokumentation/Association Suisse de Documentation (Swiss Assn. of Documentation), Schmidgasse 4, Postfach 601, CH-6301 Zug. Tel. 41-726-4505, fax 41-726-4509. *Pres.* S. Holláander; *Secy.* H. Schweuk.

Vereinigung Schweizerischer Archivare (Assn. of Swiss Archivists), Archivstr. 24, CH-3003 Berne. Tel. 31-618989. *Secy.* Bernard Truffer.

Taiwan

Lib. Assn. of China, c/o National Central Lib., 20 Chungshan S Rd., Taipei. Tel. 2-331-2475, fax 2-382-0747, e-mail lac@ msg.ncl.edu.tu. *Pres.* James S. C. Hu; *Secy.-Gen.* Teresa Wang Chang.

Tanzania

Tanzania Lib. Assn., Box 2645, Dar es Salaam. Tel. 51-402-6121. *Chair* T. E. Mlaki; *Secy.* A. Ngaiza.

Thailand

Thai Lib. Assn., 273 Vibhavadee Rangsit Rd., Phayathai, Bangkok 10400. Tel. 2-271-2084. *Pres.* K. Chavallt; *Secy.* Karnmanee Suckcharoen.

Trinidad and Tobago

Lib. Assn. of Trinidad and Tobago, Box 1275, Port of Spain. Tel. 868-624-5075, e-mail latt@fm1.wow.net. *Pres.* Esahack Mohammed; *Secy.* Shamin Renwick.

Tunisia

Association Tunisienne des Documentalistes, Bibliothécaires et Archivistes (Tunisian Assn. of Documentalists, Libns., and Archivists), B.P. 380, 1015 Tunis. *Pres.* Ahmed Ksibi.

Turkey

Türk Küüphaneciler Dernegi (Turkish Libns. Assn.), Elgün Sok-8/8, 06440 Yenisehir, Ankara. Tel. 312-230-1325, fax 312-232-0453. *Pres.* A. Berberoglu; *Secy.* A. Kaygusuz.

Uganda

Uganda Lib. Assn., Box 5894, Kampala. Tel. 141-285001, ext. 4. *Chair* P. Birungi; *Secy.* L. M. Ssengero.

Ukraine

Ukrainian Lib. Assn., 14 Chyhorin St., Kyiv 252042, Ukraine. Tel. 380-44-268-2263, fax 380-44-295-8296. *Pres.* Valentyna S. Pashkova.

United Kingdom

ASLIB (The Assn. for Info. Management), Information House, 20-24 Old St., London EC1V 9AP, England. Tel. 171-253-4488, fax 171-430-0514, e-mail aslib@aslib.co.uk. *Dir.* R. B. Bowes.

Bibliographical Society, c/o The Wellcome Institute, Victoria & Albert Museum, 183 Euston Rd., London SW7 2RL, England. Tel. 171-611-7244, fax 171-611-8703, e-mail d.pearson@welcome.ac.uk. *Hon. Secy.* David Pearson.

The Lib. Assn., 7 Ridgmount St., London WC1E 7AE, England. Tel. 171-636-7543, fax 171-436-7218, e-mail info@la-hq.org.uk. *Chief Exec.* Ross Shimmon.

School Lib. Assn., Liden Lib., Barrington Close, Liden, Swindon, Wiltshire SN3 6HF, England. Tel. 1793-537-374, e-mail info@sla.org.uk. *Pres.* Frank N. Hogg; *Exec. Secy.* Kathy Lemaire.

Scottish Lib. Assn., 1 John St., Hamilton ML3 7EU, Scotland. Tel. 1698-458-888, fax 1698-458-899, e-mail sctlb@leapfrog.almac.co.uk. *Dir.* Robert Craig.

Society of Archivists, Information House, 20-24 Old St., London, EC1V 9AP, England. Tel. 171-253-5087, fax 171-253-3942. *Exec. Secy.* P. S. Cleary.

Standing Conference of National and Univ. Libs., 102 Euston St., London NW1 2HA, England. Tel. 171-387-0317, fax 171-383-3197. *Exec. Secy.* A. J. C. Bainton.

Welsh Lib. Assn., c/o Publications Office, College of Wales, Llanbadarn Fawr, Aberystwyth, Dyfed SY23 3AS, Wales. Tel. 1970-622-174, fax 1970-622-190, e-mail a.m.w.green@swansea.ac.uk. *Exec. Officer* Glyn Collins.

Uruguay

Agrupación Bibliotecológica del Uruguay (Uruguayan Lib. and Archive Science Assn.), Cerro Largo 1666, 11200 Montevideo. Tel. 2-405-740. *Pres.* Luis Alberto Musso.

Asociación de Bibliocólogos del Uruguay, Eduardo V Haedo 2255, CC 1315, 11200 Montevideo. Tel. 2-499-989.

Vatican City

Biblioteca Apostolica Vaticana, 00120 Vatican City, Rome. Tel. 6-698-83302, fax 6-698-84795, e-mail Libr@librsbk.vatlib.it. *Prefect* Don Raffaele Farina.

Venezuela

Colegio de Bibliotecólogos y Archivólogos de Venezuela (Assn. of Venezuelan Libns. and Archivists), Apdo. 6283, Caracas. Tel. 2-572-1858. *Pres.* Elsi Jimenez de Diaz.

Vietnam

Hôi Thu-Viên Viet Nam (Vietnamese Lib. Assn.), National Lib. of Viet Nam, 31 Trang Thi, 10000 Hanoi. Tel. 4-52643.

Zambia

Zambia Lib. Assn., Box 32839, Lusaka. *Chair* C. Zulu; *Hon. Secy.* W. C. Mulalami.

Zimbabwe

Zimbabwe Lib. Assn., Box 3133, Harare. *Chair* Driden Kunaka; *Hon. Secy.* Albert Masheka.

Directory of Book Trade and Related Organizations

Book Trade Associations, United States and Canada

For more extensive information on the associations listed in this section, see the annual edition of *Literary Market Place* (R. R. Bowker).

American Booksellers Assn. Inc., 828 S. Broadway, Tarrytown, NY 10591. Tel. 800-637-0037, 914-591-2665, fax 914-591-2720. *Pres.* Richard Howorth, Square Books, Oxford, MS 38665; *V.P.* Neal Coonerty, Bookshop Santa Cruz, Santa Cruz, CA 95060; *Chief Exec. Officer* Avin Mark Domnitz.

American Institute of Graphic Arts, 164 Fifth Ave., New York, NY 10010. Tel. 212-807-1990, fax 212-807-1799, e-mail aiga@aiga.org. *Exec. Dir.* Richard Grefe.

American Literary Translators Association (ALTA), Univ. of Texas–Dallas, Box 830688, Richardson, TX 75083-0688. Tel. 972-883-2093, fax 972-883-6303, e-mail ert@utdallas.edu. *Dir.* Rainer Schulte; *Exec. Dir.* Eileen Tollett.

American Medical Publishers Assn., 14 Fort Hill Rd., Huntington, NY 11743. Tel./fax 516-423-0075, World Wide Web http://www.am-pa.com. *Pres.* Susan Gay; *Exec. Dir.* Jill Rudansky, e-mail jillrudansky-ampa@msn.com.

American Printing History Assn., Box 4922, Grand Central Sta., New York, NY 10163-4922. *Pres.* Anne Anninger; *Exec. Secy.* Stephen Crook.

American Society of Indexers, 11250 Roger Bacon Dr., Suite 8, Reston, VA 20190-5202. Tel. 703-234-4147, fax 703-435-4390, e-mail info@asindexing.org, World Wide Web http://www.asindexing.org. *Exec. Dir.* Maureen Thompson.

American Society of Journalists and Authors, 1501 Broadway, Suite 302, New York, NY 10036. Tel. 212-997-0947, fax 212-768-7414, e-mail ASJA@compuserve.com, World Wide Web http://www.asja.org. *Exec. Dir.* Brett Harvey.

American Society of Media Photographers, 150 N. Second St., Philadelphia, PA 19106. Tel. 215-451-2767, fax 215-451-0880. *Pres.* Les Riess; *Exec. Dir.* Richard Weisgrau.

American Society of Picture Professionals, Inc., 409 S. Washington St., Alexandria, VA 22314. Tel./fax 703-299-0219, e-mail aspp1@idsonline.com, World Wide Web http://www.aspp.com. *Exec. Dir.* Cathy Sachs; *National Pres.* Danita Delimont. Tel. 425-562-1543.

American Translators Assn., 225 Reinekers Lane, Suite 590, Alexandria, VA 22314. Tel. 703-683-6100, fax 703-683-6122, e-mail ata@atanet.org. *Pres.* Ann Macfarlane; *Pres.-Elect* Tom West; *Secy.* Courtney Searls-Ridge; *Treas.* Eric McMillan; *Exec. Dir.* Walter W. Bacak, Jr.

Antiquarian Booksellers Assn. of America, 20 W. 44 St., Fourth fl., New York, NY 10036-6604. Tel. 212-944-8291, fax 212-944-8293, e-mail inquiries@abaa.org, World Wide Web http://www.abaa.org. *Exec. Dir.* Liane T. Wade.

Assn. of American Publishers, 71 Fifth Ave., New York, NY 10003. Tel. 212-255-0200, fax 212-255-7007. *Pres./CEO* Patricia S. Schroeder; *Exec. V.P.* Thomas D. McKee; *Washington Office* 50 F St. N.W., Washington, DC 20001-1564. Tel. 202-347-3375, fax 202-347-3690. *V.P.s* Allan

Adler, Carol Risher; *Dir., Communications and Public Affairs* Judith Platt; *Chair* Peter Jovanovich, Pearson Education; *Treas.* William P. Sisler, Harvard University Press.

Assn. of American Univ. Presses, 71 W. 23 St., Suite 901, New York, NY 10010. Tel. 212-989-1010. *Pres.* Marlie Wasserman; *Exec. Dir.* Peter Givler; *Assoc. Exec. Dir.* Hollis Holmes. Address correspondence to the executive director.

Assn. of Authors' Representatives, Inc., Box 237201, Ansonia Sta., New York, NY 10023. Tel. 212-353-3709, e-mail aarinc@mindspring.com, World Wide Web http://aar-online.org. *Pres.* Vicky Bijur; *Admin. Secy.* Leslie Carroll.

Assn. of Canadian Publishers, 110 Eglinton Ave. W., Suite 401, Toronto, ON M4R 1A3. Tel. 416-487-6116, fax 416-487-8815, World Wide Web http://www.publishers.ca/. *Exec. Dir.* Paul Davidson. Address correspondence to the executive director.

Assn. of Educational Publishers (EdPress), Rowan University, 201 Mullica Hill Rd., Glassboro, NJ 08028-1773. Tel. 609-256-4610, fax 609-256-4926. *Exec. Dir.* Charlene F. Gaynor.

Assn. of Graphic Communications, 330 Seventh Ave., New York, NY 10001. Tel. 212-279-2100, fax 212-279-5381, e-mail bd@agccomm.org, World Wide Web http://www.agcomm.org. *Pres.* William A. Dirzulaitis; *Dir. Ed.* Pam Suett; *Dir. Exhibits* Carl Gessman.

Assn. of Jewish Book Publishers, c/o Jewish Lights Publishing, Box 237, Woodstock, VT 05091. Tel. 802-457-4000, fax 802-457-4004. *Pres.* Stuart M. Matlins. Address correspondence to the president.

Book Industry Study Group, Inc., 160 Fifth Ave., New York, NY 10010. Tel. 212-929-1393, fax 212-989-7542, World Wide Web http://www.bisg.org. *Chair* Richard Hunt; *V. Chair* Robert Severud; *Treas.* Seymour Turk; *Secy.* Deborah Wiley; *Managing Agent* SKP Assocs. Address correspondence to William Raggio.

Book Manufacturers Institute, 65 William St., Suite 300, Wellesley, MA 02481-3800. Tel. 781-239-0103, fax 781-239-0106. *Pres.* Mark Bawden, Von Hoffman Graphics; *Exec. V.P.* Stephen P. Snyder.

Address correspondence to the executive vice president.

Book Publicists of Southern California, 6464 Sunset Blvd., Suite 580, Hollywood, CA 90028. Tel. 323-461-3921, fax 323-461-0917. *Pres.* Barbara Gaughen-Muller; *V.P.* Ernest Weckbaugh; *Secy.* Irwin Zucker; *Treas.* Lynn Walford.

Book Publishers of Texas, Box 831495, Richardson, TX 75083-1495. Tel. 972-671-0002, e-mail Gbivona@wordware.com, World Wide Web http://www.authorlink.com/bpt.html.

Bookbuilders of Boston, Inc., 27 Wellington Dr., Westwood, MA 02090. Tel. 617-266-3335, fax 781-326-2975, World Wide Web http://www.bbboston.org. *Pres.* Andrew Van Sprang, Courier; *1st V.P.* Jennifer Meyer Dare, Houghton Mifflin; *2nd V.P.* Lisa Flanagan, Blackwell Science; *Treas.* John Walsh, Harvard Univ. Press; *Auditor* Doug Buitenhuys, Plymouth Color; *Secy.* Joni McDonald, UUA.

Bookbuilders West, Box 7046, San Francisco, CA 94120-9727. Tel. 415-273-5790, jobs bank 415-643-8600, World Wide Web http://www.bookbuilders.org. *Pres.* Stephen Thomas, Edwards Brothers, Inc.; *V.P.* Mary Lou Goforth, Banta Book Group; *Secy.* Kathryn Collins Duba, R.R. Donnelley & Sons; *Treas.* Paul Butzler, Butzler & Associates.

Canadian Booksellers Assn., 789 Don Mills Rd., Suite 700, Toronto, ON M3C 1T5. Tel. 416-467-7883, fax 416-467-7886, e-mail enquiries@cbabook.org, World Wide Web http://www.cbabook.org. *Exec. Dir.* Sheryl M. McKean.

Canadian ISBN Agency, c/o Acquisitions and Bibliographic Services Branch, National Library of Canada, 395 Wellington St., Ottawa, ON K1A 0N4. Tel. 819-994-6872, fax 819-953-8508.

Canadian Printing Industries Association, 75 Albert St., Suite 906, Ottawa, ON K1P 5E7. Tel. 613-236-7208, fax 613-236-8169, World Wide Web http://www.capitalnet.com/~printing/. *Pres.* Michael Makin.

Catholic Book Publishers Assn. Inc., 2 Park Ave., Manhasset, NY 11030. Tel. 516-869-0122, fax 516-627-1381, e-mail cbpa1@aol.com, World Wide Web http://cbpa.

org. *Pres.* John Wright; *V.P.* Mary Andrews; *Secy.* John G. Powers; *Treas.* Matthew Thibeau; *Exec. Dir.* Charles A. Roth.

Chicago Book Clinic, 825 Green Bay Rd., Suite 270, Wilmett, IL 60091. Tel. 847-256-8448, fax 847-256-8954, e-mail kgboyer@ix.netcom.com, World Wide Web http://www.chicagobookclinic.org. *Pres.* Kim Hawley; *Exec. Dir.* Kevin G. Boyer.

Children's Book Council, Inc., Box 2640, JAF Sta., New York, NY 10116-2640. Tel. 800-999-2160, fax 888-807-9355, e-mail staff@CBCbooks.org, World Wide Web http://www.cbcbooks.org. *Pres.* Paula Quint; *Dir., Marketing and Publicity* JoAnn Sabatino.

Copyright Society of the USA, 1133 Ave. of the Americas, New York, NY 10036. Tel. 212-354-6401, fax 212-354-2847, e-mail info@csusa.org. *Pres.* Michael J. Pollack; *V.P.* Robert J. Bernstein; *Secy.* Phillip M. Cowan; *Treas.* Maria A. Danzilo.

Council of Literary Magazines & Presses, 154 Christopher St., Suite 3C, New York, NY 10014. Tel. 212-741-9110, fax 212-741-9112. *Exec. Dir.* Jim Sitter.

Educational Paperback Assn., *Pres.* Robert J. Laronga; *V.P.* Fred Johnson; *Treas.* Bill Hanlon; *Exec. Secy.* Marilyn Abel, Box 1399, East Hampton, NY 11937. Tel. 212-879-6850.

Evangelical Christian Publishers Assn., 1969 E. Broadway Rd., Suite 2, Tempe, AZ 85282. Tel. 480-966-3998, fax 480-966-1944, e-mail dross@ecpa.org. *Pres.* Doug Ross.

Friendship Press, 475 Riverside Dr., Suite 860, New York, NY 10115. Tel. 212-870-2585, fax 212-870-2550, World Wide Web http://www.nccusa.org.

Graphic Artists Guild Inc., 90 John St., Suite 403, New York, NY 10038. Tel. 212-791-3400, fax 212-792-0333, e-mail execdir@gag.org, World Wide Web http://www.gag.org. *Exec. Dir.* Paul Basista. Address correspondence to the executive director.

Great Lakes Booksellers Assn., c/o *Exec. Dir.* Jim Dana, Box 901, 509 Lafayette, Grand Haven, MI 49417. Tel. 616-847-2460, fax 616-842-0051, e-mail glba@books-glba.org, World Wide Web http://

www.books-glba.org. *Pres.* Rita Williams, Books of Aurora, Aurora, OH 44202.

Guild of Book Workers, 521 Fifth Ave., New York, NY 10175. Tel. 212-292-4444. *Pres.* Karen Crisalli. E-mail karenc5071@aol.com.

International Assn. of Printing House Craftsmen, Inc., 7042 Brooklyn Blvd., Minneapolis, MN 55429. Tel. 612-560-1620, 800-466-4274, fax 612-560-1350, World Wide Web http://www.iaphc.org/. *Chair* Anthony Sarubbi; *V. Chair* Raymond Rafalowski; *Secy.-Treas.* Tom Blanchard; *CEO* Kevin Keane.

International Copyright Information Center, c/o Assn. of American Publishers, 70 F St. N.W., Washington, DC 20001. Tel. 202-232-3335 ext. 228, fax 202-745-0694, e-mail crisher@publishers.org. *Dir.* Carol Risher.

International Standard Book Numbering U.S. Agency, 121 Chanlon Rd., New Providence, NJ 07974. Tel. 908-665-6700, fax 908-665-2895, e-mail ISBN-SAN@bowker.com, World Wide Web http://www.bowker.com/standards/. *Chair* Drew Meyer; *Dir.* Doreen Gravesande; *Industrial Relations Mgr.* Don Riseborough; *SAN Mgr.* Diana Fumando.

Jewish Book Council, 15 E. 26 St., 10th fl., New York, NY 10010. Tel. 212-532-4949 ext. 297, fax 212-481-4174. *Pres.* Moshe Dworkin; *Exec. Dir.* Carolyn Starman Hessel.

Library Binding Institute, 5241 Lincoln Dr., Suite 321, Edina, MN 55436-2703. Tel. 612-939-0165, fax 612-939-0213, e-mail info@lbibinders.org. *Pres.* James M. Larsen; *V.P.* Gary Wert; *Treas.* John Salistean; *Exec. Dir.* J. Wesley Moyer; *Admin. Asst.* Sally M. Moyer.

Magazine Publishers of America, Inc., 919 Third Ave., 22nd fl., New York, NY 10022. Tel. 212-872-3700, fax 212-888-4217, e-mail mpa@magazine.org, World Wide Web http://www.magazine.org.

Midwest Independent Publishers Assn., Box 581432, Minneapolis, MN 55458-1432. Tel. 651-917-0021, e-mail dshidell@aol.com, World Wide Web http://www.mipa.org. *Pres.* Doug Shidell.

Miniature Book Society, Inc., c/o *Pres.* Donn W. Sanford, 210 Swarthmore Ct., Woodstock, IL 60098. Tel. 815-337-2323, fax 815-337-6451, e-mail donn@mc.net. *V.P.* Paul Devenyi, 50 Grange Mill Crescent, Toronto, ON M3B 2J2. Tel. 416-445-2038, fax 416-444-0246; *Secy.* Evron Collins, 2008 Boone Ct., Bowling Green, OH 43402. Tel. 419-352-8735; *Treas.* Mark Palcovic, 620 Clinton Springs Ave., Cincinnati, OH 45229-1325. Tel. 513-861-3554, fax 513-556-2113. *Assn. Web site* http://www.mbs.org.

Minnesota Book Publishers Roundtable. *Pres.* Sid Farrar, Milkweed Press, 430 First Ave. N., No. 668, Minneapolis, MN 55401. Tel. 612-332-3192 ext. 105, fax 612-332-6248, e-mail sidfarrar@milkweed. org; *V.P.* Katherine Werner, Consortium Book Sales and Distribution, 1045 Westgate Drive, St. Paul, MN 55114. Tel. 651-221-9035, fax 651-221-0124, e-mail kwerner@cbsd.com; *Secy.-Treas.* Brad Vogt, Bradley & Assoc., 40214 Wallaby Rd., Rice, MN 56367. Tel. 320-249-9806, fax 320-656-9520, e-mail bvogt@ cloudnet.com. *Assn. Web site* http://www. publishersroundtable.org. Address correspondence to the secretary-treasurer.

Mountains and Plains Booksellers Assn., 19 Old Town Sq., Suite 238, Fort Collins, CO 80524. Tel. 970-484-5856, fax 970-407-1479, e-mail lknudser@mountainsplains. org, World Wide Web http://www. mountainsplains.org. *Exec. Dir.* Lisa Knudsen; *Pres.* Gayle Shanks; *Treas.* Tracey Ballast.

National Assn. for Printing Leadership, 75 W. Century Rd., Paramus, NJ 07652. Tel. 201-634-9600, fax 201-634-0324, e-mail napl@napl.org.

National Assn. of College Stores, 500 E. Lorain St., Oberlin, OH 44074-1294. Tel. 440-775-7777, fax 440-775-4769, e-mail lnakoneczhy@nacs.org, World Wide Web http://www.nacs.org. *Exec. Dir.* Brian Cartier; *Public Relations Dir.* Laura Nakoneczny. Address correspondence to the public relations director.

National Assn. of Independent Publishers, Box 430, Highland City, FL 33846. Tel./ fax 813-648-4420, e-mail NAIP@aol.com.

National Coalition Against Censorship, 275 Seventh Ave., 20th fl., New York, NY 10001. Tel. 212-807-6222, fax 212-807-

6245, e-mail NCAC@NCAC.org.

National Directory Publishing Assn., 4201 Connecticut Ave. N.W., Washington, DC 20008. Tel. 202-342-0250, fax 202-686-9822. *Pres.* Bill Wade. E-mail bwade @asla.org; *Treas.* Tom Johnson. E-mail tojo@worldnet.att.net; *Secy.* Susan Wade. E-mail wadnich@erols.com.

National Ministries Unit, National Council of Churches, 475 Riverside Dr., New York, NY 10115. Tel. 212-870-2227, e-mail news@ncccusa.org. *Dir.* Staccato Powell.

New Atlantic Independent Booksellers Assn., 2667 Hyacinth St.,Westbury, NY 11590. Tel. 516-333-0681, fax 516-333-0689, e-mail info@naiba.com. *Exec. Dir.* Eileen Dengler.

New England Booksellers Assn., 847 Massachusetts Ave., Cambridge, MA 02139. Tel. 617-576-3070, fax 617-576-3091, e-mail neba@neba.org. *Pres.* Fran Keilty; *V.P.* Susan Avery; *Treas.* Sarah Zacks; *Exec. Dir.* Wayne A. Drugan.

New Mexico Book League, 8632 Horacio Place N.E., Albuquerque, NM 87111. Tel. 505-299-8940, fax 505-294-8032. *Ed., Book Talk* Carol A. Myers.

North American Bookdealers Exchange, Box 606, Cottage Grove, OR 97424. Tel. 541-942-7455, fax 541-258-2625, e-mail nabe @bookmarketingprofits.com, World Wide Web http://bookmarketingprofits.com. *Dir.* Al Galasso.

Northern California Independent Booksellers Assn., 5643 Paradise Dr., Suite 12, Corte Madera, CA 94925. Tel. 415-927-3937, fax 415-927-3971, e-mail office@nciba. com, World Wide Web http://www.nciba. com.

Pacific Northwest Booksellers Assn., 317 W. Broadway, Suite 214, Eugene, OR 97401-2890. Tel. 541-683-4363, fax 541-683-3910, e-mail info@pnba.com. *Pres.* Russ Lawrence, Chapter One Bookstore, 252 Main St., Hamilton, MT 59840-2552; *Exec. Dir.* Thom Chambliss.

PEN American Center, Div. of International PEN, 568 Broadway, New York, NY 10012. Tel. 212-334-1660, fax 212-334-2181, e-mail pen@pen.org. *Exec. Dir.* Michael Roberts.

Periodical and Book Assn. of America, Inc., 120 E. 34 St., Suite 7-k, New York, NY

10016. Tel. 212-689-4952, fax 212-545-8328, e-mail PBAA@aol.com. *Exec. Dir.* Richard T. Browne.

Periodical Wholesalers of North American and Periodical Marketers of Canada, 1007-175 Bloor St. E., South Tower, Toronto, ON M4W 3R8. Tel. 416-968-7218, fax 416-968-6182, e-mail pwna@periodical. org, World Wide Web http://www. periodical.org/. *Pres.* Ray Argyle.

Philadelphia Book Clinic, c/o *Secy.* Thomas Colaiezzi, 136 Chester Ave., Yeadon, PA 19050-3831. Tel. 610-259-7022, fax 610-394-9886. *Treas.* Robert Pigeon. Tel. 610-828-2595, fax 610-828-2603.

Publishers Marketing Assn., 627 Aviation Way, Manhattan Beach, CA 90266. Tel. 310-372-2732, fax 310-374-3342, e-mail info@pma-online.org, World Wide Web http://www.pma-online.org. *Exec. Dir.* Jan Nathan.

Research and Engineering Council of the Graphic Arts Industry, Inc., Box 1086, White Stone, VA 22578. Tel. 804-436-9922, fax 804-436-9511, e-mail recouncil @rivnet.net, World Wide Web http://www.recouncil.org. *Pres.* Edmund T. Funk; *Exec. V.P./Secy.* Laura Gale; *Exec. V.P./Treas.* Deborah W. Godfrey; *Managing Dir.* Ronald Mihills.

Rocky Mountain Book Publishers Assn., Box 19013, Boulder, CO 80308. Tel. 303-499-9540, fax 303-499-9584, e-mail info@ rmbpa.com, World Wide Web http://www. rmbpa.com. *Exec. Dir.* Alan Bernhard.

Romance Writers of America, 3707 F.M. 1960 W., Suite 555, Houston, TX 77068. Tel. 281-440-6885, fax 281-440-7510, e-mail info@rwanational.com, World Wide Web http://www.rwanational.com. *Pres.* Jo Ann Ferguson; *V.P.* Debra Dixon; *Secy.* Sunni Jeffers; *Treas.* Betty Rosenthal.

Science Fiction and Fantasy Writers of America, Inc., Box 171, Unity, ME 04988-0171. Tel./fax 207-861-8078, e-mail execdir @sfwa.org. *Pres.* Paul Levinson; *V.P.* A. C. Crispin; *Secy.* Michael A. Burstein; *Treas.* Ian Randal Strock; *Exec. Dir.* Sharon Lee.

Small Press Center, 20 W. 44 St., New York, NY 10036. Tel. 212-764-7021, fax 212-354-5365. *Exec. Dir.* Karin Taylor.

Small Publishers Assn. of North America (SPAN), Box 1306, Buena Vista, CO 81211-1306. Tel. 719-395-4790, fax 719-395-8374, e-mail span@spannet.org, World Wide Web http://www.SPANnet.org. *Exec. Dir.* Marilyn Ross.

Society of Children's Book Writers & Illustrators, 8271 Beverly Blvd., Los Angeles, CA 90048. Tel. 323-782-1010, fax 323-782-1892, e-mail scbwi@juno.com. *Pres.* Stephen Mooser; *Exec. Dir.* Lin Oliver.

Society of Illustrators, 128 E. 63 St., New York, NY 10021. Tel. 212-838-2560, fax 212-838-2561, e-mail SI1901@aol.com, World Wide Web http://www.society illustrators.org/.

Society of National Association Publications, 1595 Spring Hill Rd., Suite 330, Tysons Corner, Vienna, VA 22182. Tel. 703-506-3285, fax 703-506-3266, e-mail snapinfo @snaponline.org, World Wide Web http://www.snaponline.org. *Pres.* Robert Mahaffey; *V.P.* Michael Springer; *Treas.* Howard Hoskins.

Technical Assn. of the Pulp and Paper Industry, Technology Park/Atlanta, Box 105113, Atlanta, GA 30348-5113. Tel. 770-446-1400, fax 770-446-6947. *Exec. Dir.* W. H. Gross.

West Coast Book People Assn., 27 McNear Dr., San Rafael, CA 94901. *Exec. Dir.* Frank G. Goodall. Tel. 415-459-1227, fax 415-459-1227, e-mail goodall27@aol. com.

Western Writers of America, Inc., 1012 Fair St., Franklin, TN 37064. World Wide Web http://www.westernwriters.org. *Pres.* Mike Blakely, Box 1818, Marble Falls, TX 78654. E-mail mike@281.com.

Women's National Book Assn., 160 Fifth Ave., New York, NY 10010. Tel. 212-675-7805, fax 212-989-7542, e-mail skpassoc @internetmci.com, World Wide Web http: //www.wnba-books.org. *Pres.* Diane Ullius; *V.P.* Nancy Stewart; *Secy.* Grace Houghton; *Treas.* Margaret Auer; *Past Pres.* Donna Paz. *Chapters in*: Binghamton, Boston, Dallas, Detroit, Los Angeles, Nashville, New York, San Francisco, Washington, D.C.

International and Foreign Book Trade Associations

For Canadian book trade associations, see the preceding section, "Book Trade Associations, United States and Canada." For a more extensive list of book trade organizations outside the United States and Canada, with more detailed information, consult *International Literary Market Place* (R. R. Bowker), which also provides extensive lists of major bookstores and publishers in each country.

International

Afro-Asian Book Council, 4835/24 Ansari Rd., Daryaganj, New Delhi 110-002, India. Tel. 11-326-1487, fax 11-326-7437. *Chair* Dato Jaji Jumaat; *Secy.-Gen.* Asang Machwe; *Dir.* Abul Hasan.

Centre Régional pour la Promotion du Livre en Afrique (Regional Center for Book Promotion in Africa), Box 1646, Yaoundé, Cameroon. Tel. 22-4782/2936. *Secy.* William Moutchia.

Centro Régional para el Fomento del Libro en América Latina y el Caribe (CERLALC) (Regional Center for Book Promotion in Latin America and the Caribbean), Calle 70, No. 9-52, Apdo. Aéreo 57348, Santafé de Bogotá 2, Colombia. Tel. 1-321-7501, fax 1-321-7503, e-mail cerlalc @impsat.net.co. *Dir.* Carmen Barvo.

Federation of European Publishers, Ave. de Tervueren 204, B-1150 Brussels, Belgium. Tel. 2-736-3616, fax 2-736-1987. *Pres.* Volker Schwarz; *Secy. Gen.* Mechtild Von Alemann.

International Board on Books for Young People (IBBY), Nonnenweg 12, Postfach, CH-4003 Basel, Switzerland. Tel. 61-272-2917, fax 61-272-2757. *Dir.* Leena Maissen.

International Booksellers Federation, Blvd. Lambermont 140 BTE 1, B1030 Brussels, Belgium. Tel./fax 2-242-0957, e-mail eurobooks@skynet.be. *Pres.* Yvonne Steinberger; *Gen. Secy.* Christiane Vuidar.

International Group of Scientific, Technical and Medical Publishers (STM), Keizersgracht 462, 1016 GE Amsterdam, Netherlands. Tel. 20-225214, fax 20-381566. *Secy.* Lex Lefebvre.

International League of Antiquarian Booksellers, 400 Summit Ave., Saint Paul, MN 55102. Tel. 800-441-0076, 612-290-0700, fax 612-290-0646, e-mail rulon@ winternet.com. *Secy. Gen.* Rob Rulon-Miller.

International Publishers Assn. (Union Internationale des Editeurs), Ave. Miremont 3, CH-1206 Geneva, Switzerland. Tel. 22-346-3018, fax 22-347-5717, e-mail secretariat@ipa-uie.org, World Wide Web: http://www.ipa-uie.org. *Pres.* Alain Gründ; *Secy.-Gen.* J. Alexis Koutchoumow.

Seminar on the Acquisition of Latin American Library Materials, Secretariat, General Library, Univ. of New Mexico, Albuquerque, NM 87131-1466. Tel. 505-277-5102, fax 505-277-0646. *Exec. Secy.* Sharon A. Moynahan.

National

Argentina

Cámara Argentina de Publicaciones (Argentine Publications Assn.), Lavalle 437, 6 D-Edif Adriático, 6 piso, 1047 Buenos Aires. Tel./fax 01-394-2892. *Pres.* Bautista Leoncio Tello.

Cámara Argentina del Libro (Argentine Book Assn.), Avda. Belgrano 1580, 6 piso, 1093 Buenos Aires. Tel. 1-381-9277, fax 1-381-9253. *Dir.* Norberto J. Pou.

Fundación El Libro (Book Foundation), Avda. Cordoba 744 PB Dto. 1, 1054 Buenos Aires. Tel. 1-322-2225, fax 1-325-5681, e-mail fund@libro.satlink.net. *Pres.* Jorge Navelro; *Dir.* Marta V. Diaz.

Australia

Australian and New Zealand Assn. of Antiquarian Booksellers, Box 279, Cammeray, NSW 2062. Tel. 3-826-1779, fax 3-521-3412. *Secy.* Nicholas Dawes.

Australian Booksellers Assn., 136 Rundle Mall, Adelaide, SA 5000. Tel. 3-966-37-

888, fax 3-966-37-557. *Pres.* Tim Peach; *Exec. Dir.* Celia Pollock.

Australian Publishers Assn., Suite 59, 89 Jones St., Ultimo, Sydney, NSW 2007. Tel. 2-9281-9788, fax 2-9281-1073, e-mail ape@magna.com.au. *Pres.* Sandy Grant; *Exec. Dir.* Susan Blackwell.

National Book Council, 71 Collins St., Melbourne, Vic. 3000. Tel. 3-663-8043, fax 3-663-8658. *Pres.* Michael G. Zifcak; *Exec. Dir.* Thomas Shapcott.

Austria

Hauptverband des Österreichischen Buchhandels (Austrian Publishers and Booksellers Assn.), Grünangergasse 4, A-1010 Vienna. Tel. 1-512-1535, fax 1-512-8482. *Pres.* Anton C. Hilscher.

Verband der Antiquare Österreichs (Austrian Antiquarian Booksellers Assn.), Grünangergasse 4, A-1010 Vienna. Tel. 1-512-1535, fax 1-512-8482, e-mail hbv-wein@austrobook.co.at. *Pres.* Hansjörg Krug.

Belarus

National Book Chamber of Belarus, 31a Very Khoruzhey St., 220002 Minsk. Tel./fax 172-769-396, e-mail palata@palata. belpak.minsk.by. *Contact* Anatolij Voronko.

Belgium

Vereniging ter Bevordering van het Vlaamse Boekwezen (Assn. for the Promotion of Dutch Language Books/Books from Flanders), Hof ter Schriecklaan 17, 2600 Berchem/Antwerp. Tel. 3-230-8923, fax 3-281-2240. *Pres.* Luc Demeester; *Gen. Secy.* Wim de Mont.

Vlaamse Boekverkopersbond (Flemish Booksellers Assn.), Hof ter Schriecklaan 17, 2600 Berchem/Antwerp. Tel. 3-230-8923, fax 3-281-2240. *Pres.* Luc Vander Velpen; *Gen. Secy.* Carlo Van Baelen.

Bolivia

Cámara Boliviana del Libro (Bolivian Booksellers Assn.), Casilla 682, Avda. 20 de Octubre 2005, Edificio Las Palmas, Planta Baja, La Paz. Tel. 2-327-039, fax 2-391-817. *Pres.* Rolando S. Condori; *Secy.* Teresa G. de Alvarez.

Brazil

Cámara Brasileira do Livro (Brazilian Book Assn.), Av. Ipiranga 1267, 10 andar, 01039-907 Sao Paulo. Tel. 11-220-7855, fax 11-229-7463. *Gen. Mgr.* Aloysio T. Costa.

Sindicato Nacional dos Editores de Livros (Brazilian Publishers Assn.), SDS, Edif. Venancio VI, Loja 9/17, 70000 Brasilia, Brazil. Tel. 21-233-6481, fax 21-253-8502. *Pres.* Sérgio Abreu da Cruz Machado; *Exec. Secy.* Henrique Maltese.

Chile

Cámara Chilena del Libro AG (Chilean Assn. of Publishers, Distributors and Booksellers), Avda. Libertador Bernardo O'Higgins 1370, Of. 501, 13526 Santiago. Tel. 2-698-9519, fax 2-698-9226, e-mail camlibro@reuna.cl. *Exec. Secy.* Carlos Franz.

Colombia

Cámara Colombiana del Libro (Colombian Book Assn.), Carrera 17A, No. 37-27, Apdo. Aéreo 8998, Santafé de Bogotá. Tel. 1-232-7550, 288-6188, fax 1-287-3320.

Cyprus

Cyprus Booksellers Assn., Box 1455, Nicosia 1509. Tel. 2-449500, fax 2-367433. *Secy.* Socrates Heracleous.

Czech Republic

Svaz ceskych knihkupcu a nakladetelu (Czech Publishers and Booksellers Assn.), Jana Masaryka 56, 120 00 Prague 2. Tel./fax 2-2423-9003-0150, e-mail book@login.cz. *Chair* Jan Kanzelsberger.

Denmark

Danske Boghandlerforening (Danish Booksellers Assn.), Siljangade 6, DK-2300 Copenhagen S. Tel. 3154-2255, fax 3157-2422. *Pres.* Hanne Madsen.

Danske Forlaeggerforening (Danish Publishers Assn.), Kobmagergade 11/13, DK-1150 Copenhagen K. Tel. 45-3315-6688, fax 45-3315-6588, e-mail publassn@webpartner.dk. *Dir.* Erik V. Krustrup.

Ecuador

Cámara Ecuatoriana del Libro, Núcleo de Pichincha, Guayaquil 1629, piso 4, Casilla No. 3329, Quito. Tel. 2-212-226, fax 2-566-340, e-mail abyayala@abyayala.org.ec. *Contact* Claudio Mena Villamar.

Egypt

General Egyptian Book Organization, Box 1660, Corniche El-Nile-Boulaq, Cairo. Tel. 2-775-371, 775-649, fax 2-754-213. *Chair* Ezz El Dine Ismail.

Estonia

Estonian Publishers Assn., Box 3366, EE0090 Tallinn. Tel. 2-650-5592, fax 2-650-5590. *Dir.* A. Tarvis.

Finland

Kirja-ja Paperikauppojen Liitto ry (Finnish Booksellers and Stationers Assn.), Eerikinkatu 15-17 D 43-44, 00100 Helsinki. Tel. 694-4866, fax 694-4900, e-mail kpl@kplry.pp.fi. *Chief Exec.* Olli Erakivi.

Suomen Kustannusyhdistys ry (Finnish Book Publishers Assn.), Box 177, FIN-00121 Helsinki. Tel. 9-2287-7250, fax 9-612-1226, e-mail finnpubl@skyry.pp.fi. *Dir.* Veikko Sonninen.

France

Cercle de la Librairie (Circle of Professionals of the Book Trade), 35 Rue Grégoire-de-Tours, F-75006 Paris. Tel. 1-44-41-28-00, fax 1-44-41-28-65. *Pres.* Charles Henri Flammarion.

Fédération Française des Syndicats de Libraires-FFSL (French Booksellers Assn.), 43 Rue de Châteaudun, F-75009 Paris. Tel. 1-42-82-00-03, fax 1-42-82-10-51. *Pres.* Jean-Luc Dewas.

France Edition, 35 Rue Grégoire-de-Tours, F-75006 Paris. Tel. 1-44-41-13-13, fax 1-46-34-63-83. *Chair* Bernard Foulon. *New York Branch* French Publishers Agency, 853 Broadway, New York, NY 10003-4703. Tel. 212-254-4520, fax 212-979-6229.

Syndicat National de la Librairie Ancienne et Moderne (National Assn. of Antiquarians and Modern Booksellers), 4 Rue Git-le-Coeur, F-75006 Paris. Tel. 1-43-29-46-38, fax 1-43-25-41-63. *Pres.* Jean-Etienne Huret.

Syndicat National de l'Edition (National Union of Publishers), 115 Blvd. Saint-Germain, F-75006 Paris. Tel. 1-441-4050, fax 1-441-4077. *Pres.* Serge Eyrolles; *Deputy Gen.* Jean Sarzana.

Union des Libraires de France, 40 Rue Grégoire-de-Tours, F-75006 Paris. Tel. 1-43-29-88-79, fax 1-46-33-65-27. *Pres.* Eric Hardin; *Gen. Delegate* Marie-Dominique Doumenc.

Germany

Börsenverein des Deutschen Buchhandels e.V. (Stock Exchange of German Booksellers), Postfach 100442, 60004 Frankfurt-am-Main. Tel. 69-130-6311, fax 69-130-6300. *Gen. Mgr.* Hans-Karl von Kupsch.

Bundesverband der Deutschen Versandbuchhandler e.V. (National Federation of German Mail-Order Booksellers), An der Ringkirche 6, 65197 Wiesbaden. Tel. 611-44-9091, fax 611-48451. *Mgrs.* Stefan Rutkowsky, Kornelia Wahl.

Verband Deutscher Antiquare e.V. (German Antiquarian Booksellers Assn.), Kreuzgasse 2-4, Postfach 10-10-20, 50450 Cologne. Tel./fax 221-92-54-82-82; *Pres.* Jochen Granier; *V.P.* Inge Utzt.

Ghana

West African University Booksellers Assn., Univ. of Ghana, Box 1, Legon, Accra. Tel. 21-775-301. *Secy.* J. B. Teye-Adi.

Great Britain

See United Kingdom

Greece

Hellenic Federation of Publishers and Booksellers, Themistocleous 73, 10683 Athens. Tel. 1-330-0924, fax 1-330-1617. *Pres.* Georgios Dardanos.

Hungary

Magyar Könyvkiadók és Könyvterjesztök Egyesülése (Assn. of Hungarian Publishers and Booksellers), Vörösmarty tér 1, 1051 Budapest (mail: PB 130, 1367 Budapest). Tel. 1-117-6222. *Pres.* István Bart; *Secy.-Gen.* Péter Zentai.

Iceland

Félag Islenskra Bókaútgefenda (Icelandic Publishers Assn.), Sudurlandsbraut 4A, 108 Reykjavik. Tel. 553-8020, fax 588-8668. *Chair* Olafur Ragnarsson; *Gen. Mgr.* Vilborg Hardardóttir.

India

Federation of Indian Publishers, Federation House, 18/1-C Institutional Area, JNU Rd., Aruna Asaf Ali Marg, New Delhi 110067. Tel. 11-696-4847, 685-2263, fax 11-686-4054. *Pres.* Shri R. C. Govil; *Exec. Secy.* S. K. Ghai.

Indonesia

Ikatan Penerbit Indonesia (Assn. of Indonesian Book Publishers), Jl. Kalipasir 32, Jakarta 10330. Tel. 21-314-1907, fax 21-314-1433. *Pres.* Rozali Usman; *Secy. Gen.* Setia Dharma Majidd.

Ireland

CLE: The Irish Book Publishers Assn., The Writers Centre, 19 Parnell Sq., Dublin 1. Tel. 1-872-9090, fax 1-872-2035. *Contact* Orla Martin.

Israel

Book and Printing Center, Israel Export Institute, 29 Hamered St., Box 50084, Tel Aviv 68125. Tel. 3-514-2910, fax 3-514-2815. *Dir.* Corine Knafo.

Book Publishers Assn. of Israel, Box 20123, Tel Aviv 61201. Tel. 3-561-4121, fax 3-561-1996. *Managing Dir.* Amnon Ben-Shmuel.

Italy

Associazione Italiana Editori (Italian Publishers Assn.), Via delle Erbe 2, 20121 Milan. Tel. 2-86-46-3091, fax 2-89-01-0863.

Associazione Librai Antiquari d'Italia (Antiquarian Booksellers Assn. of Italy), Via Jacopo Nardi 6, I-50132 Florence. Tel./fax 55-24-3253, e-mail alai@dada.it. *Pres.* Vittorio Soave; *Secy.* Francesco Scala.

Jamaica

Booksellers' Assn. of Jamaica, c/o Novelty Trading Co. Ltd., Box 80, Kingston. Tel. 876-922-5883, fax 876-922-4743. *Pres.* Keith Shervington.

Japan

Japan Book Importers Assn., Chiyoda Kaikan 21-4, Nihonbashi 1-chome, Chuo-ku, Tokyo 103. Tel. 3-32-71-6901, fax 3-32-71-6920. *Chair* Nobuo Suzuki.

Japan Book Publishers Assn., 6 Fukuromachi, Shinjuku-ku, Tokyo 162. Tel. 3-32-68-1301, fax 3-32-68-1196. *Pres.* Takao Watanabe; *Exec. Dir.* Toshikazu Gomi.

Kenya

Kenya Publishers Assn., c/o Phoenix Publishers Ltd., Box 18650, Nairobi. Tel. 2-22-2309, 22-3262, fax 2-33-9875. *Secy.* Stanley Irura.

Korea (Republic of)

Korean Publishers Assn., 105-2 Sagan-dong, Jongro-gu, Seoul 110-190. Tel. 2-735-2701, fax 2-738-5414, e-mail kpasibf@soback.kornet.nm.kr. *Pres.* Choon Ho Na; *Secy.-Gen.* Jung Jong-Jin.

Latvia

Latvian Book Publishers Assn., Aspazijas Bulvaris 24, 1050 Riga. Tel. 2-722-5843, fax 2-783-0518.

Lithuania

Lithuanian Publishers Assn., K Sirvydo 6, 62600 Vilnius. Tel. 2-628-945, fax 2-619-696. *Pres.* Vincas Akelis.

Mexico

Cámara Nacional de la Industria Editorial Mexicana (Mexican Publishers' Assn.), Holanda No. 13, CP 04120, Mexico 21. Tel. 5-688-2221, fax 5-604-3147. *Pres.* A. H. Gayosso, J. C. Cramerez.

The Netherlands

Koninklijke Vereeniging ter Bevordering van de Belangen des Boekhandels (Royal Dutch Book Trade Assn.), Postbus 15007, 1001 MA Amsterdam. Tel. 20-624-0212, fax 20-620-8871. *Secy.* M. van Vollen-hoven-Nagel.

Nederlandsche Vereeniging van Antiquaren (Netherlands Assn. of Antiquarian Book-sellers), Postbus 664, 1000 AR Amster-dam. Tel. 20-627-2285, fax 20-625-8970, e-mail a.gerits@inter.nl.net. *Pres.* F. W. Kuyper; *Secy.* A. Gerits.

Nederlandse Boekverkopersbond (Dutch Booksellers Assn.), Postbus 90731, 2509 LS The Hague. Tel. 70-324-4395, fax 70-324-4411. *Pres.* W. Karssen; *Exec. Secy.* A. C. Doeser.

Nederlandse Uitgeversbond (Royal Dutch Publishers Assn.), Postbus 12040, 1100 AA Amsterdam. Tel. 20-430-9150, fax 20-430-9179, e-mail r.vrij@uitgeversverbond. nl. *Pres.* Henk J. L. Vonhoff; *Secy.* R. M. Vrij.

New Zealand

Book Publishers Assn. of New Zealand, North Shore Mail Center, Auckland 1. Tel. 9-309-2561, fax 9-309-7798.

Booksellers New Zealand, Box 11-377, Wellington. Tel. 4-472-8678, fax 4-472-8628. *Chair* Brian Phillips; *Chief Exec.* Jo Breese.

Nigeria

Nigerian Publishers Assn., GPO Box 3541, Dugbe, Ibadan. Tel. 22-411-557. *Pres.* V. Nwankwo.

Norway

Norske Bokhandlerforening (Norwegian Booksellers Assn.), Ovre Vollgate 15, 0158 Oslo 1. Tel. 22-396-800, fax 22-356-810, e-mail bokfor@sn.no. *Dir.* Einar J. Einarsson.

Norske Forleggerforening (Norwegian Pub-lishers Assn.), Ovre Vollgate 15, 0158 Oslo 1. Tel. 22-421-355, fax 22-333-830, e-mail dnf@forleggerforeningen.no. *Dir.* Paul Martens Ríthe.

Pakistan

National Book Council of Pakistan, Block 14D, 1st fl., Al-Markaz F/8, Box 1610, Islamabad. Tel. 51-853-581. *Dir. Gen.* Rafiq Ahmad.

Paraguay

Cámara Paraguaya de Editores, Libreros y Asociados (Paraguayan Publishers Assn.), Ayolas 129, Asunción. Tel./fax 21-497-325. *Dir.* Alejandro Gatti.

Peru

Cámara Peruana del Libro (Peruvian Publish-ers Assn.), Apdo. Postal 10253, Lima 1. Tel. 14-715152. *Pres.* Julio César Flores Rodriguez; *Exec. Dir.* Loyda Moran Bus-tamente.

Philippines

Philippine Educational Publishers Assn., 84 P Florentino St., 3008 Quezon City. Tel. 2-968-316, fax 2-921-3788. *Pres.* D. D. Buhain.

Poland

Polskie Towarzystwo Wydawców Ksiazek (Polish Society of Book Editors), ul. Mazowiecka 2/4, 00-048 Warsaw. Tel./fax 22-826-0735. *Pres.* Janusz Fogler; *Gen. Secy.* Donat Chruscicki.

Stowarzyszenie Ksiegarzy Polskich (Assn. of Polish Booksellers), ul. Mokotowska 4/6, 00-641 Warsaw. Tel. 22-252-874. *Pres.* Tadeusz Hussak.

Portugal

Associação Portuguesa de Editores e Livreiros (Portuguese Assn. of Publishers and Booksellers), Largo de Andaluz, 16-7 Esq., 1000 Lisbon. Tel. 1-556-241, fax 1-315-3553. *Pres.* Francisco Espadinha; *Secy. Gen.* Jorge de Carvalho Sá Borges.

Russia

All-Union Book Chamber, Kremlevskaja nab 1/9, 121019 Moscow. Tel. 95-20271, 95-20272, fax 95-202-3992. *Dir.-Gen.* Yuri Torsuev.

Publishers Assn., 44B Hertsen Str., 121069 Moscow. Tel. 95-202-1174, fax 95-202-3989. *Contact* M. Shishigin.

Singapore

Singapore Book Publishers Assn., 86, Marine Parade Centre, No. 03-213, Singapore 440086. Tel. 344-7801, fax 447-0897. *Pres.* K. P. Sivan; *V.P.* Wu Cheng Tan.

Slovenia

Zdruzenje Zaloznikov in Knjigotrzcev Slovenije Gospodarska Zbornica Slovenije (Assn. of Publishers and Booksellers of Slovenia), c 41, 1504 Ljubljana. Tel./fax 61-342-398. *Contact* Joze Korinsek.

South Africa

Associated Booksellers of Southern Africa, Box 870, Bellville 7530. Tel. 21-951-6611, fax 21-951-4903. *Pres.* M. Hargraves; *Secy.* R. Stoltenkamp.

Publishers Assn. of South Africa, Box 116, 7946 St. James. Tel. 21-788-6470, fax 21-788-6469. *Chair* Basil Van Rooyen.

Spain

Federación de Gremios de Editores de España (Federation of Spanish Publishers Assns.), Juan Ramón Jiménez, 45-9 Izda, 28036 Madrid. Tel. 1-350-9105, fax 1-345-4351. *Pres.* Pere Vincens; *Secy.* Ana Molto.

Sri Lanka

Sri Lanka Assn. of Publishers, 112 S. Mahinda Mawatha, Colombo 10. Tel. 1-695-773, fax 1-696-653. *Pres.* Dayawansa Jayakody.

Sudan

Sudanese Publishers Assn., H. Q. Al Ikhwa Bldg., Flat 7, 7th fl., Box 2771, Khartoum. Tel. 249-11-75051, 79180.

Suriname

Publishers Assn. Suriname, Domineestr. 26, Box 1841, Paramaribo. Tel. 472-545, fax 410-563. *Mgr.* E. Hogenboom.

Sweden

Svenska Förlaggareföreningen (Swedish Publishers Assn.), Drottninggatan 97, S-11360 Stockholm. Tel. 8-736-1940, fax 8-736-1944, e-mail svf@forlagskansli.se. *Dir.* Kristina Ahlinder.

Switzerland

Schweizerischer Buchhandler- und Verleger-Verband (Swiss German-Language Booksellers and Publishers Assn.), Baumackerstr. 42, 8050 Zurich. Tel. 1-312-5343, fax 1-318-6462, e-mail sbvv @dm.krinfo.ch. *Secy.* Egon Raz.

Société des Libraires et Editeurs de la Suisse Romande (Assn. of Swiss French-Language Booksellers and Publishers), 2 Ave. Agassiz, 1001 Lausanne. Tel. 21-319-7111, fax 21-319-7910. *Contact* Philippe Schibli.

Thailand

Publishers and Booksellers Assn. of Thailand, 320 Lat Phrao 94-aphat Pracha-u-thit Rd., Bangkok 10310. Tel. 2-255-93348, fax 2-253-81499.

Uganda

Uganda Publishers and Booksellers Assn., Box 7732, Plot 2C Kampala Rd., Kampala. Tel. 41-259-163, fax 41-251-160. *Contact* Martin Okia.

United Kingdom

Antiquarian Booksellers Assn., 154 Buckingham Palace Rd., London W1V 9PA, England. Tel. 171-730-9273, fax 171-439-3119. *Administrators* Philippa Gibson, Deborah Stratford.

Assn. of Learned and Professional Society Publishers, Sentosa Hill Rd., Fairlight, Hastings, East Sussex TN35 4AE, England. Tel. 1424-812-353, fax 181-663-3583, e-mail donovan@alpsp.demon.co.uk. *Secy.-Gen.* B. T. Donovan.

Book Trust, 45 East Hill, Wandsworth, London SW18 2QZ, England. Tel. 181-516-2977, fax 181-516-2978.

Book Trust Scotland, Scottish Book Centre, 137 Dundee St., Edinburgh EH11 1BG, Scotland. Tel. 131-229-3663, fax 131-228-4293.

Booksellers Assn. of Great Britain and Ireland, Minster House, 272 Vauxhall Bridge Rd., London SW1V 1BA, England. Tel. 171-834-5477, fax 171-834-8812, e-mail 100437.2261@compuserve.com. *Chief Exec.* Tim Godfray.

Educational Publishers Council, 19 Bedford Sq., London WC1B 3HJ, England. Tel. 171-580-6321, fax 171-636-5375. *Dir.* John R. M. Davies.

Publishers Assn., 19 Bedford Sq., London WC1B 3HJ, England. Tel. 171-580-6321, fax 171-636-5375. *Pres.* Trevor Glover; *Chief Exec.* Ronnie Williams; *Secy.* Mandy Knight.

Scottish Publishers Assn., Scottish Book Centre, 137 Dundee St., Edinburgh EH11 1BG, Scotland. Tel. 131-228-6866, fax

131-228-3220. *Dir.* Lorraine Fannin; *Chair* Mike Miller.

Welsh Books Council (Cyngor Llyfrau Cymru), Castell Brychan, Aberystwyth, Ceredigion SY23 2JB, Wales. Tel. 1970-624-151, fax 1970-625-385. *Dir.* Gwerfyl Pierce Jones.

Uruguay

Cámara Uruguaya del Libro (Uruguayan Publishers Assn.), Juan D. Jackson 1118, 11200 Montevideo. Tel. 2-241-5732, fax 2-241-1860.

Venezuela

Cámara Venezolana del Libro (Venezuelan Publishers Assn.), Ave. Andrés Bello, Torre Oeste, 11 piso, Of. 112-0, Apdo. 51858, Caracas 1050-A. Tel. 2-793-1347, fax 2-793-1368. *Secy.* M. P. Vargas.

Zambia

Booksellers and Publishers Assn. of Zambia, Box 31838, Lusaka. Tel. 1-225-195, fax 1-225-282; *Exec. Dir.* Basil Mbewe.

Zimbabwe

Zimbabwe Book Publishers Assn., c/o Longman Zimbabwe, Tourle Rd., Box ST125, Southerton, Harare. Tel 4-750-282, fax 4-751-202.

National Information Standards Organization (NISO) Standards

Information Storage and Retrieval

Z39.2-1994*	Information Interchange Format
Z39.47-1993 (R 1998)	Extended Latin Alphabet Coded Character Set for Bibliograhic Use (ANSEL)
Z39.50-1995	Information Retrieval (Z39.50) Application Service Definition and Protocol Specification
Z39.53-1994*	Codes for the Representation of Languages for Information Interchange
Z39.63-1989*	Interlibrary Loan Data Elements
Z39.64-1989 (R 1995)	East Asian Character Code for Bibliographic Use
Z39.76-1996	Data Elements for Binding Library Materials
Z39.84-2000	Syntax for the Digital Object Identifier

Library Management

Z39.7-1995	Library Statistics
Z39.20-1999	Criteria for Price Indexes for Print Library Materials
Z39.71-1999	Holdings Statements for Bibliographic Items
Z39.73-1994*	Single-Tier Steel Bracket Library Shelving

Preservation and Storage

Z39.32-1996	Information on Microfiche Headers
Z39.48-1992 (R 1997)	Permanence of Paper for Publications and Documents in Libraries and Archives
Z39.62-2000	Eye-Legible Information on Microfilm Leaders and Trailers and on Containers of Processed Microfilm on Open Reels
Z39.66-1992 (R 1998)	Durable Hard-Cover Binding for Books
Z39.74-1996	Guides to Accompany Microform Sets
Z39.77-2000	Guidelines for Information About Preservation Products
Z39.78-2000	Library Binding
Z39.79-2000	Enviromental Conditions for Exhibiting Library and Archival Materials

Publishing

Z39.9-1992*	International Standard Serial Numbering (ISSN)
Z39.14-1997	Guidelines for Abstracts
Z39.18-1995	Scientific and Technical Reports—Elements, Organization, and Design
Z39.19-1993 (R 1998)	Guidelines for the Construction, Format, and Management of Monolingual Thesauri
Z39.22-1989	Proof Corrections
Z39.23-1997	Standard Technical Report Number Format and Creation
Z39.26-1997	Micropublishing Product Information
Z39.41-1997	Printed Information on Spines
Z39.43-1993	Standard Address Number (SAN) for the Publishing Industry
Z39.56-1996	Serial Item and Contribution Identifier (SICI)
Z39.67-1993	Computer Software Description
NISO/ANSI/ISO 12083	Electronic Manuscript Preparation and Markup

In Development

Bibliographic References
Book Item and Contribution Identifier
Circulation Interchange Protocol
Digital Talking Book Features List
Dublin Core Metadata Element Set
Title Pages of Conference Proceedings

NISO Technical Reports

TR-01-1995	Environmental Guidelines for the Storage of Paper Records
TR-02-1997	Guidelines for Indexes and Related Information Retrieval Devices
TR-03-1999	A Guide to Alphanumeric Arrangement and Sorting

*This standard is being reviewed by NISO's Standards Development Committee or is under revision. For further information, please contact NISO, 4733 Bethesda Ave., Suite 300, Bethesda, MD 20814. Tel. 301-654-2512, fax 301-654-1721, e-mail nisohq@niso.org, World Wide Web http://www.niso.org.

Calendar, 2000–2005

The list below contains information on association meetings or promotional events that are, for the most part, national or international in scope. State and regional library association meetings are also included. To confirm the starting or ending date of a meeting, which may change after the *Bowker Annual* has gone to press, contact the association directly. Addresses of library and book trade associations are listed in Part 6 of this volume. For information on additional book trade and promotional events, see the *Exhibits Directory*, published annually by Contemporary Books, 180 N. Michigan Ave., Chicago, IL 60601; *Literary Market Place* and *International Literary Market Place*, published by R. R. Bowker; and the "Calendar" section in each issue of *Library Journal*.

2000

May

1–3	International Publishers Assn.	Buenos Aires, Argentina
2–5	Council on Botanical and Horticultural Libraries	Washington, DC
2–5	Tennessee Library Assn.	Kingsport, TN
4–6	Pennsylvania School Librarians Assn.	Hershey, PA
4–6	Quebec Library Assn.	Montreal, PQ
4–6	School Library Media Section, New York Library Assn.	Syracuse, NY
5–11	Medical Library Assn.	Vancouver, BC
6–11	Jerusalem International Book Fair	Jerusalem, Israel
10–12	Maryland Library Assn.	Towson, MD
10–13	American Society of Indexers	Albuquerque, NM
11–12	Wisconsin Assn. of Public Libraries	Middleton, WI
17	Archivists and Librarians in the History of the Health Sciences	Bethesda, MD
17–19	Washington Library Assn.	Tacoma, WA
18	Long Island Library Conference	Huntington Station, NY
18–20	Warsaw International Book Fair	Warsaw, Poland
19	Academic Libraries Partnering With Our Communities conference	Schenectady, NY
21–23	Maine Library Assn.	Orono, ME
21–6/3	Libraries and Librarianship: Past, Present, and Future	Oxford, England

May 2000 *(cont.)*

24–25	Vermont Library Conference	Burlington, VT
25–27	British Columbia Library Assn.	Kelowna, BC
25–27	Pacific Northwest Library Assn.	Kelowna, BC
27–31	Seminar on the Acquisition of Latin American Materials	Long Beach, CA

June

1–2	Rhode Island Library Assn.	Providence, RI
2–7	Seoul International Book Fair	Seoul, Korea
3–5	BookExpo America	Chicago, IL
5–10	Special Libraries Assn.	Philadelphia, PA
7–9	Assn. of Educational Publishers	Washington, DC
7–10	LOEX-of-the-West	Bozeman, MT
11–13	Copyright Society of the U.S.A.	Botton Landing, NY
12–15	Assn. of Christian Librarians	San Diego, CA
13–17	Western Writers of America	Kerrville, TX
14–16	Australia Book Fair	Sydney, NSW
14–16	New York State Library Assistants Association	Rochester, NY
18–21	Assn. of Jewish Libraries	Washington, DC
21–24	American Theological Library Assn.	Berkeley, CA
21–25	Canadian Library Assn.	Edmonton, AB
22–25	American Assn. of University Presses	Denver, CO
23–24	Museum and Library Archives Institute	Wilbraham, MA

July

3–7	International Assn. of Technological University Libraries (IATUL)	Brisbane, Australia
6–12	American Library Assn. Annual Conference	Chicago, IL
6–12	Beta Phi Mu	Chicago, IL
10–14	Reference Sources for Rare Books	Bloomington, IN
15–20	American Assn. of Law Libraries	Philadelphia, PA
23–25	Church and Synagogue Library Assn.	Kansas City, KS
23–29	Children's Literature New England	Silver Bay, NY
23–8/4	Western Archives Institute	Redlands, CA
28–8/1	Conference in Children's Literature	Los Angeles, CA
28–8/5	Zimbabwe International Book Fair	Harare, Zimbabwe
30–8/5	Assn. of College and Research Libraries/Harvard Leadership Institute	Cambridge, MA

August

3–6	REFORMA National Conference	Tucson, AZ
6–12	International Assn. of Music Libraries, Archives, and Documentation Centres (IAML)	Edinburgh, Scotland

13–18	International Federation of Library Assns. and Institutions (IFLA) General Conference	Jerusalem, Israel
20–24	International Assn. of Law Libraries	Dublin, Ireland
26–27	Sociedad de Bibliotecarios de Puerto Rico	San Juan, PR
28–9/3	Society of American Archivists	Denver, CO
30–9/4	Beijing International Book Fair	Beijing, China

September

2–4	Miniature Book Society	Rutland, VT
6–11	Moscow International Book Fair	Moscow, Russia
14–17	Göteborg International Book Fair	Göteborg, Sweden
14–19	Colorado Library Assn.	Snowmass, CO
15–17	Pacific Northwest Booksellers Assn.	Portland, OR
20–23	American Translators Assn.	Orlando, FL
20–23	North Dakota Library Assn.	Dickinson, ND
21–26	International Conference on Archives	Seville, Spain
24–27	Pennsylvania Library Assn.	Lancaster, PA
25–30	International Federation for Information and Documentation (FID)	Brasilia, Brazil
29–10/1	Great Lakes Booksellers Assn. Trade Show	Toledo, OH

October

1–3	New England Library Assn.	Worcester, MA
2–5	South Dakota Library Assn.	Rapid City, SD
2–6	Michigan Library Assn.	Detroit, MI
3–5	AIIM 2000 Copenhagen	Copenhagen, Denmark
4–5	Chicago Book Clinic Book & Media Show	Oakbank, IL
4–6	Idaho Library Assn.	Lewiston, ID
4–6	South Dakota Library Assn.	Rapid City, SD
4–7	LIBER (Feria Internacional del Libro)	Barcelona, Spain
5–7	Minnesota Educational Media Organization	Duluth, MN
5–7	Nevada Library Assn.	Reno, NV
7–10	Arkansas Library Assn.	Springdale, AR
10–15	Oral History Assn.	Durham, NC
11–13	Georgia Council of Media Organizations	Jekyll Island, GA
11–13	Minnesota Library Assn.	Minneapolis/Saint Paul, MN
12–14	Kaleidoscope 7	Calgary, AB
12–14	Lutheran Church Library Assn.	Englewood, CO
12–14	RUSA National Institute	Baltimore, MD
13–15	Oregon Educational Media Assn.	Portland, OR
14–17	Illinois Library Assn.	Peoria, IL
16–22	Global 2000 (Special Libraries Assn.)	Brighton, England
18–20	Iowa Library Assn.	Ames, IA
18–20	Mississippi Library Assn.	Jackson, MS
18–21	Kentucky Library Assn.	Louisville, KY

October 2000 *(cont.)*

18–22	American Literary Translators Assn.	San Francisco, CA
18–23	Frankfurt Book Fair	Frankfurt, Germany
19–20	Maryland Educational Media Organization	Frederick, MD
19–20	Virginia Library Assn.	Norfolk, VA
19–21	Research & Engineering Council of the Graphic Arts Industry	Atlanta, GA
20–22	Small Publishers Assn. of North America (SPAN)	Torrance, CA
22–24	Educational Media Assn. of New Jersey	Cherry Hill, NJ
22–25	ARMA International	Las Vegas, NV
24–28	Alabama Library Assn.	Mobile, AL
24–28	Southeastern Library Assn.	Mobile, AL
25–27	Mountain Plains Library Assn.	Omaha, NE
25–27	Nebraska Educational Media Assn.	Omaha, NE
25–27	Nebraska Library Assn.	Omaha, NE
25–27	Ohio Educational Library Media Assn.	Columbus, OH
25–28	Michigan Assn. for Media in Education	Lansing, MI
25–28	Nebraska Library Assn. Tri-Conference	Omaha, NE
25–29	Virginia Library Assn.	Williamsburg, VA
31–11/3	Wisconsin Library Assn.	Green Bay, WI

November

1–11	Flanders Book Fair	Antwerp, Belgium
1–4	New York Library Assn.	Saratoga Springs, NY
2–4	Illinois School Library Media Assn.	Lincolnshire, IL
2–5	LITA National Forum 2000	Portland, OR
4–5	Hawaii Library Assn.	Honolulu, HI
4–5	Ontario Library Assn.	Toronto, ON
5–8	Book Manufacturers Institute	Naples, FL
8–10	Ohio Library Council	Columbus, OH
8–11	Illinois School Library Media Assn.	Arlington, IL
9–11	Tennessee Assn. of School Libraries	Gatlinburg, TN
11–14	California Library Assn.	Santa Clara, CA
12–19	Miami Book Fair International	Miami, FL
15–17	Arizona Library Assn.	Phoenix, AZ
15–17	Conference on Bibliographic Control for the New Millennium	Washington, DC
16–21	Salon du Livre de Montreal	Montreal, PQ
30–12/2	LAMA National Institute	Palm Springs, CA
30–12/2	Virginia Educational Media Assn.	Roanoke, VA

2001

January

12–17	American Library Assn. Midwinter Meeting	Washington, DC

March

11–15	World Summit on Media for Children	Thessaloniki, Greece
15–18	Assn. of College and Research Libraries	Denver, CO
26–30	Texas Library Assn.	San Antonio, TX
28–30	Wisconsin Educational Media Assn.	Green Bay, WI
*	Assn. for Indiana Media Educators	Indianapolis, IN

April

4–6	Kansas Library Assn.	Topeka, KS
4–6	Washington Library Assn.	Spokane, WA
16–19	Buenos Aires Feria Internacional del Libro	Buenos Aires, Argentina
17–20	Catholic Library Assn.	Milwaukee, WI
18	Archivists and Librarians in the History of the Health Sciences	Charleston, NC
25–28	Montana Library Assn.	Kalispell, MT
26–28	Pennsylvania School Librarians Assn.	Hershey, PA
28–5/2	Evangelical Christian Publishers Assn.	Hilton Head, SC
*	Alabama Library Assn.	Montgomery, AL

May

1–3	Tennessee Library Assn.	Nashville, TN
1–4	AIIM 2001	New York, NY

June

9–14	Special Libraries Assn.	San Antonio, TX
13–15	National Conference on Asian Pacific American Librarians	San Francisco, CA
14–21	American Library Assn. Annual Conference	San Francisco, CA
16–19	American Assn. of University Presses	Toronto, ON
*	Western Writers of America	Idaho Falls, ID

July

8–14	International Assn. of Music Libraries, Archives, and Documentation Centres (IAML)	Perigueux, France
27–29	National Conference of African American Librarians	Fort Lauderdale, FL

August

26–9/2	Society of American Archivists	Washington, DC

September

30–10/3	ARMA International	Montreal, PQ
*	North Dakota Library Assn.	Williston, ND

October

3–5	South Dakota Library Assn.	Aberdeen, SD
3–7	American Assn. of School Librarians	Pittsburgh, PA
10–12	Iowa Library Assn.	Davenport, IA
12–14	Oregon Educational Media Assn.	Seaside, OR
15–21	Illinois Library Assn.	Springfield, IL
25–27	Illinois School Library Media Assn.	Decatur, IL
31–11/3	American Translators Assn.	Los Angeles, CA

November

6–9	Michigan Library Assn.	Lansing, MI

2002

January

18–23	American Library Assn. Midwinter Meeting	New Orleans, LA

March

5–8	AIIM 2002	San Francisco, CA
*	Assn. for Indiana Media Educators	Indianapolis, IN

April

17–19	Wisconsin Educational Media Assn.	LaCrosse, WI
17–19	Washington Library Assn./	
	Oregon Library Assn.	Jantzen Beach, OR
18–20	Pennsylvania School Librarians Assn.	Hershey, PA
22–26	Texas Library Assn.	Dallas, TX
24–27	Montana Library Assn.	Great Falls, MT

June

8–13	Special Libraries Assn.	Los Angeles, CA
13–19	American Library Assn. Annual Conference	Atlanta, GA

August

4–9	International Assn. of Music Libraries, Archives, and Documentation Centres (IAML)	Los Angeles, CA
19–25	Society of American Archivists	Birmingham, AL

September

26–28	South Dakota, North Dakota, Mountain Plains library assns.	Fargo, ND
29–10/2	ARMA International	New Orleans, LA

October

2–5	Mountain Plains Library Assn.	Fargo, ND
29–11/1	Michigan Library Assn.	Grand Rapids, MI

November

6–9	American Translators Assn.	Atlanta, GA
6–9	Illinois School Library Media Assn.	Arlington, IL

2003

April

7–12	Texas Library Assn.	Houston, TX
8–15	Assn. of College and Research Libraries	Charlotte, NC
9–11	Wisconsin Educational Media Assn.	Milwaukee, WI
10–11	Washington Library Assn.	Yakima, WA
24–26	Pennsylvania School Librarians Assn.	Hershey, PA

October

19–22	ARMA International	Boston, MA
21–26	American Assn. of School Librarians	Kansas City, MO

November

4–8	Mountain Plains Library Assn.	North Lake Tahoe, NV
5–8	American Translators Assn.	Phoenix, AZ
6–8	Illinois School Library Media Assn.	Decatur, IL

2004

February

24–28	Public Libraries Assn.	Seattle, WA

November

3–6	Illinois School Library Media Assn.	Arlington, IL

2005

April

7–10	Assn. of College and Research Libraries	Minneapolis, MN

October

27–29	Illinois School Library Media Assn.	Decatur, IL

* To be determined

Acronyms

A

AALL. American Association of Law
Libraries

AAP. Association of American Publishers

AASL. American Association of School
Librarians

ABA. American Booksellers Association

ABFFE. American Booksellers Foundation
for Free Expression

ACRL. Association of College and Research
Libraries

AgNIC. AgNIC (Agriculture Network
Information Center)

AGRIS. AGRIS (Agricultural Science and
Technology Database)

AIC. Academic Image Cooperative

AJL. Association of Jewish Libraries

ALA. American Library Association

ALARM. National Alliance of Libraries,
Archives and Records Management

ALCTS. Association for Library Collections
and Technical Services

ALIC. Archives Library Information Center

ALISE. Association for Library and
Information Science Education

ALS. Academic Libraries Survey

ALSC. Association for Library Service to
Children

ALTA. Association for Library Trustees and
Advocates

AMMLA. American Merchant Marine
Library Association

APALA. Asian/Pacific American Librarians
Association

ARC. National Archives and Records
Administration, Archival Research
Catalog

ARL. Association of Research Libraries

ARLIS/NA. Art Libraries Society of North
America

ARMA. ARMA International (Association of
Records Managers and Administrators)

ASCLA. Association of Specialized and
Cooperative Library Agencies

ASIS. American Society for Information
Science

ATLA. American Theological Library
Association

ATPA. American Technology Preeminence
Act

B

BCALA. Black Caucus of the American
Library Association

BEA. BookExpo America

BISG. Book Industry Study Group

BSA. Bibliographical Society of America

C

CACUL. Canadian Association of College
and University Libraries

CAIS. Canadian Association for Information
Science

CALA. Chinese-American Librarians
Association

CALS. National Agricultural Library,
Current Awareness Literature Service
(CALS)

CAPL. Canadian Association of Public
Libraries

CASLIS. Canadian Association of Special
Libraries and Information Services

CD-ROM. Compact Disc Read-Only
Memory

CLA. Canadian Library Association;
Catholic Library Association

CLTA. Canadian Library Trustees
Association

COPA. Children's Online Protection Act

CORS. American Library Association, Research and Statistics, Committee on

COSLA. Chief Officers of State Library Agencies

CRCA. Copyright Remedies Clarification Act

CRS. Library of Congress, Congressional Research Service

CSLA. Canadian School Library Association; Church and Synagogue Library Association

CTEA. Copyright Term Extension Act

D

DAISY. DAISY (Digital Audio-based Information System)

DDM. Federal depository libraries, Documents Data Miner

DFC. Digital Future Coalition

DID. Association of Research Libraries, Digital Initiatives Database

DLF. Digital Library Federation

DMCA. Digital Millennium Copyright Act

DOE. Education, U.S. Department of

DSAL. Association of Research Libraries, Digital South Asia Library

DSEJ. Association of Research Libraries, *Directory of Scholarly E-Journals and Academic Discussion Lists*

E

EAR. National Technical Information Service, U.S. Export Administration Regulations

EDB. Energy Science and Technology Database

EDRS. Educational Resources Information Center, ERIC Document Reproduction Service

EMIERT. American Library Association, Ethnic Material and Information Exchange Round Table

ENAL. Egyptial National Agricultural Library

EPA. Environmental Protection Agency

ERIC. Educational Resources Information Center

EROMM. European Register of Microform Masters

F

FBB. GPO Access, Federal Bulletin Board

FBIS. Foreign Broadcast Information Service

FDLP. Government Printing Office, Federal Depository Library Program

FEDRIP. National Technical Information Service, FEDRIP (Federal Research in Progress Database)

FIAF. International Federation of Film Archives

FID. International Federation for Information and Documentation

FLICC. Federal Library and Information Center Committee

FLRT. American Library Association, Federal Librarians Round Table

FNIC. Food and Nutrition Information Center

FPC. Federal Publishers Committee

FSCS. Federal-State Cooperative System for Public Library Data

FTC. Federal Trade Commission

G

GEM. Educational Resources Information Center, Gateway to Educational Materials

GLIN. Global Legal Information Network

GODORT. American Library Association, Government Documents Round Table

GPO. Government Printing Office

GPRA. Government Performance and Results Act

GRC. National Technical Information Service, GOV.Research Center

H

HEA. Higher Education Act

I

IALLD. International Association of Agricultural Information Specialists

IALL. International Association of Law Libraries

IAML. International Association of Music Libraries, Archives and Documentation Centres

IASL. International Association of School Librarianship

IATUL. International Association of Technological University Libraries

ICOLC. International Coalition of Library Consortia

ICSECA. International Contributions for Scientific, Educational and Cultural Activities

IFLA. International Federation of Library Associations and Institutions

IFRT. American Library Association, Intellectual Freedom Round Table

ILL. Interlibrary loan

IMLS. Institute of Museum and Library Services

IPS. Integrated Processing System

IRC. Special Libraries Association, Information Resources Center

ISBN. International Standard Book Number

ISLD. International Special Librarians Day

ISO. International Organization for Standardization

ISP. Special Libraries Association, Information Services Panel Survey

ISSN. International Standard Serial Number

L

LAMA. Library Administration and Management Association

LDI. Special Libraries Association, Leadership Development Institute

LHRT. American Library Association, Library History Round Table

LIS. Library of Congress, Legislative Information System

LIS. Library/information science

LITA. Library and Information Technology Association

LJ. Library Journal

LPS. Government Printing Office (GPO), Library Programs Service

LRRT. American Library Association, Library Research Round Table

LSP. National Center for Education Statistics, Library Statistics Program

LSTA. Library Services and Technology Act

M

MAGERT. American Library Association, Map and Geography Round Table

MICI. Association of American Publishers, MICI (Metadata Information Clearinghouse Interactive)

MLA. Medical Library Association; Music Library Association

N

NAGARA. National Association of Government Archives and Records Administrators

NAILDD. North American Interlibrary Loan and Document Delivery (NAILDD) Project

NAL. National Agricultural Library

NARA. National Archives and Records Administration

NCBI. National Center for Biotechnology Information

NCES. National Center for Education Statistics

NCLIS. National Commission on Libraries and Information Science

NDLE. National Digital Library for Education

NEA. National Endowment for the Arts

NEH. National Endowment for the Humanities

NEN. National Education Network

NET. No Electronic Theft Act

NFAIS. National Federation of Abstracting and Information Services

NGI. Next Generation Internet

NIOSH. National Institute for Occupational Safety and Health

NISO. National Information Standards Organization

NLC. National Library of Canada

NLE. National Library of Education

NLM. National Library of Medicine

NMAM. National Institute for Occupational Safety and Health, Manual of Analytical Methods

NMRT. American Library Association, New Members Round Table

NN/LM. National Network of Libraries of Medicine

NPG. National Institute for Occupational Safety and Health, NIOSH Pocket Guide to Chemical Hazards (NPG)
NPIN. National Parent Information Network
NRC. National Research Council
NRC. Nuclear Regulatory Commission
NTIS. National Technical Information Service
NUS. National Underground Storage, Inc.

O

OCLC. Online Computer Library Center
OSP. Online service provider

P

PLA. Public Library Association
PW. Publishers Weekly

R

RASD. American Library Association, Reference and Adult Services Division. *See new name* Reference and User Services Association
RIC. National Agricultural Library, Rural Information Center
RLG. Research Libraries Group
RTECS. Registry of Toxic Effects of Chemical Substances
RTSD. American Library Association, Resources and Technical Services Division. *See new name* Association for Library Collections and Technical Services
RUSA. Reference and User Services Association

S

SAA. Society of American Archivists
SAN. Standard Address Number

SAN. Sustainable Agriculture Network (SAN)
SASS. Schools and Staffing Survey
SLA. Special Libraries Association
SLC. Shared Legal Capability
SPARC. Scholarly Publishing & Academic Resources Coalition
SRIM. National Technical Information Service, Selected Research in Microfiche
SRRT. American Library Association, Social Responsibilities Round Table
SSP. Society for Scholarly Publishing

T

TIIAP. Telecommunications and Information Infrastructure Assistance Program
TLA. Theatre Library Association

U

UCITA. Uniform Computer Information Transactions Act
ULC. Urban Libraries Council
USDA. United States Department of Agriculture
USPS. Postal Service, U.S.

V

VRD. Educational Resources Information Center, Virtual Reference Desk

W

WIPO. World Intellectual Property Organization Copyright Treaty
WNC. World News Connection
WWW. World Wide Web

Y

YALSA. Young Adult Library Services Association

Index of Organizations

Please note that this index includes cross-references to the Subject Index. Many additional organizations can be found in Part 6 under the following headings: Networks, Consortia, and Cooperative Library Organizations; National Library and Information-Industry Associations, United States and Canada; State, Provincial, and Regional Library Associations; State and Provincial Library Agencies; State School Library Media Associations; International Library Associations; Foreign Library Associations; Book Trade Associations, United States and Canada; International and Foreign Book Trade Associations.

A

Academic Image Cooperative (AIC), 176
AgNIC (Agriculture Network Information Center), 83
AGRICOLA (Agricultural OnLine Access), 12, 78
Agriculture, U.S. Department of (USDA) *see* National Agricultural Library
AGRIS (Agricultural Science and Technology database), 12
American Association of Law Libraries (AALL), 695–696
    awards, 341
American Association of School Librarians (AASL), 375, 699–700
    awards, 343
    FamiliesConnect, 128
    grants, 381
American Booksellers Association (ABA), 149–152
    affinity programs, 152
    antitrust lawsuit, 149
    Consumer Research Study on Book Purchasing, 151
    highlights, 149–150
    independent bookstore program, 150
    membership, 150
    publications, 150–151
    research, 150
    sales tax action, 150
American Booksellers Foundation for Free Expression (ABFFE), 152

American Library Association (ALA), 127–135, 696–717
    academic libraries, 373–374
    Armed Forces Libraries Round Table awards, 344
    awards, 133–134, 341–351, 378–379
    conferences, 132–133, 369
    digital libraries, 370–371
    education reform study, *see* Education reform and school/public libraries
    E-rate, activities related to, 129
    Ethnic Material and Information Exchange Round Table (EMIERT) awards, 347
    Exhibits Round Table awards, 347
    FamiliesConnect, 128
    Federal Librarians Round Table (FLRT) award, 347
    filtering software, position on, 129
    Government Documents Round Table (GODORT) awards, 347
    grants, 381
    Intellectual Freedom Round Table (IFRT), 130, 347–348
    Library History Round Table (LHRT) awards, 349, 378–379
    Library Research Round Table (LRRT) awards, 349, 379
    Map and Geography Round Table (MAGERT) awards, 349
    minority librarians, efforts to increase, 132
    National Library Week, 131
    New Members Round Table (NMRT) awards, 349
    notable books list, 605–615

Subject Index

Please note that many cross-references refer to entries listed in the Index of Organizations.